D0360941

Handwritten notes:
* surfing –
- Rio - stay i[n]
Check with
Brazilian
embassy- Visa
- Pantanal- wild life
Fernando do
Norhona

Brazil

Regis St. Louis, Gary Prado Chandler, Andrew Draffen, Molly Green,
Thomas Kohnstamm, Robert Landon, Ginger Adams Otis

Handwritten note: Airport GIG / GRU   Airlines in Brazil p703

Contents

Destination Brazil

One of the world's most captivating places, Brazil is South America's giant, a dazzling country of pristine beaches, steamy jungles and music-filled metropolises.

The world's fifth-largest country is famed for its Carnaval, but spontaneous celebrations happen almost nightly in the Northeast. Music and dancing are as integral here as eating and sleeping, and you'll find as many regional styles as there are shades of people, from the sensual rhythms of *carimbó*, the music of the Amazon, to the *axé*-charged beats in Bahia.

The coastline – all 7367km of it – contains astounding beauty, with rain forest–covered islands, lush mountain peaks and hundreds of white-sand beaches fronting deep blue sea. In the interior you'll find both the world's largest jungle and the world's largest inland swamp. You can hike through Amazonian wilderness or float across flooded forests, getting an intimate glimpse of Brazil's rich biodiversity.

Brazil is equally famous for its cultural gems. Wander the cobblestone streets in the colonial towns of Minas Gerais or attend a mystical Candomblé ceremony in beautifully preserved Salvador. Catch fast-paced *forró* (the dance style of the Northeast) in tiny towns in Espírito Santo or dance to old-school samba in Rio's many *gafieiras* (dance halls). Brazil also has its share of award-winning architects and filmmakers, and its authors and poets include some of the most colorful stylists in the Americas.

Amid such vast beauty – from stunning landscapes to sensuous rhythms, wild *festas* (parties), gorgeous towns and a lively populace – it's no wonder that so many travelers arrive home already daydreaming of their return.

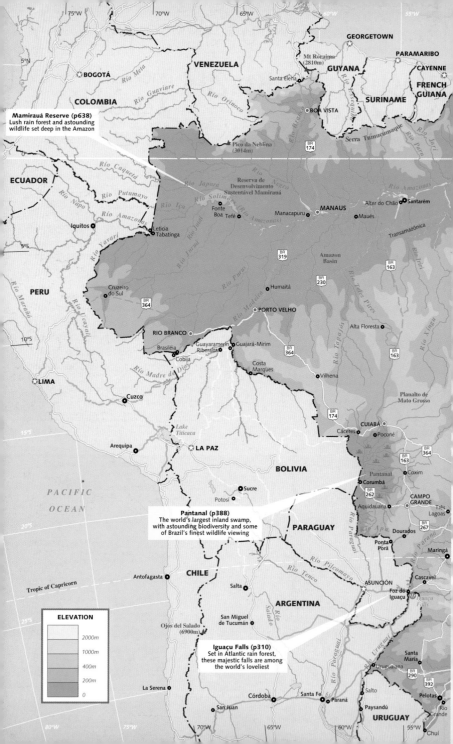

Mamirauá Reserve (p638)
Lush rain forest and astounding
wildlife set deep in the Amazon

Pantanal (p388)
The world's largest inland swamp,
with astounding biodiversity and some
of Brazil's finest wildlife viewing

Iguaçu Falls (p310)
Set in Atlantic rain forest,
these majestic falls are among
the world's loveliest

ELEVATION

2000m
1000m
400m
200m
0

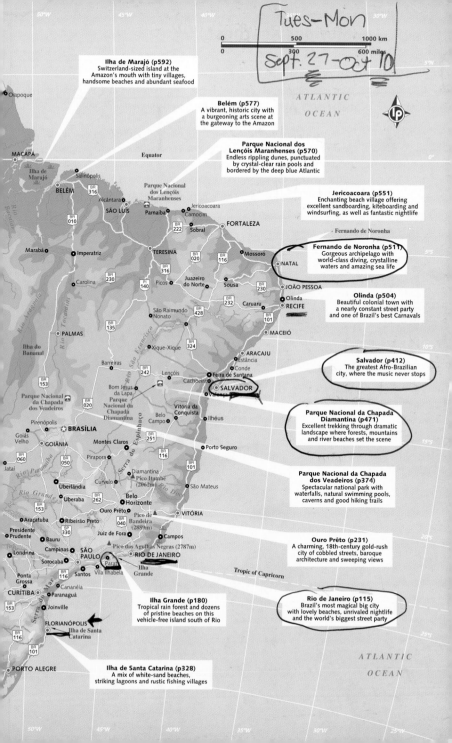

Ilha de Marajó (p592)
Switzerland-sized island at the Amazon's mouth with tiny villages, handsome beaches and abundant seafood

Belém (p577)
A vibrant, historic city with a burgeoning arts scene at the gateway to the Amazon

Parque Nacional dos Lençóis Maranhenses (p570)
Endless rippling dunes, punctuated by crystal-clear rain pools and bordered by the deep blue Atlantic

Jericoacoara (p551)
Enchanting beach village offering excellent sandboarding, kiteboarding and windsurfing, as well as fantastic nightlife

Fernando de Noronha (p511)
Gorgeous archipelago with world-class diving, crystalline waters and amazing sea life

Olinda (p504)
Beautiful colonial town with a nearly constant street party and one of Brazil's best Carnavals

Salvador (p412)
The greatest Afro-Brazilian city, where the music never stops

Parque Nacional da Chapada Diamantina (p471)
Excellent trekking through dramatic landscape where forests, mountains and river beaches set the scene

Parque Nacional da Chapada dos Veadeiros (p374)
Spectacular national park with waterfalls, natural swimming pools, caverns and good hiking trails

Ouro Prêto (p231)
A charming, 18th-century gold-rush city of cobbled streets, baroque architecture and sweeping views

Rio de Janeiro (p115)
Brazil's most magical big city with lovely beaches, unrivaled nightlife and the world's biggest street party

Ilha Grande (p180)
Tropical rain forest and dozens of pristine beaches on this vehicle-free island south of Rio

Ilha de Santa Catarina (p328)
A mix of white-sand beaches, striking lagoons and rustic fishing villages

Tues–Mon
Sept. 27–Oct 10

With over 7000km of coastline, Brazil has hundreds of forest-covered islands, gorgeous beaches and lush mountainous shores fronting cobalt-blue waters that would suit any 'tropical-getaway' photo op. Within a few hours' drive of Rio is the spectacular island setting of **Ilha Grande** (p180), as well as the wild deserted beaches near **Ubatuba** (p283). Those who prefer bathing au naturel should head to **Tambaba** (p526), one of Brazil's favorite nude beaches. Visitors to the Amazon can enjoy the remote beaches of **Ilha de Marajó** (p592), or head 700km inland to the white-sand beaches of **Alter do Chão** (p601).

JOHN PENNOCK

Enjoy the view at Arraial do Cobo (p203)

Get stranded on João Fernandes beach (p206)

JOHN PENNOCK

Hang with the Cariocas on Ipanema Beach (p123)

JOHN MAIER J

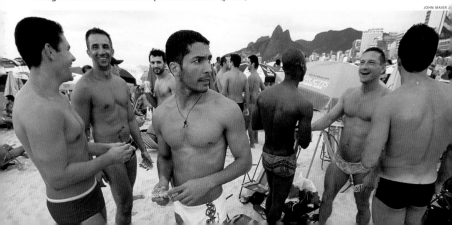

JOHN PENNOCK

Stroll along Ipanema Beach (p123) at sunset

PAUL BIGLAND

Dip into the turquoise waters at Baía dos Porcos (p513)

Plant yourself under an umbrella at Canoa Quebrada (p549)

JANE SWEENEY

HIGHLIGHTS **Natural Wonders & Watching Wildlife**

Steamy jungles, vast wetlands and breathtaking mountains form the backdrop to some spectacular scenery and some amazing wildlife watching. The **Amazon** (p573), not surprisingly, has plenty to offer in that department. You can glide through flooded forests spotting monkeys and river dolphins in the **Mamirauá Reserve** (p638), go on safari in **Alta Floresta** (p386) or soak up the wildlife at a **jungle lodge** (p634) near Manaus. You can trek through high cerrado in **Parque Nacional da Chapada dos Veadeiros** (p374), admire the views from **Parque Nacional da Chapada dos Guimarães** (p384) or go bird-watching in the **Parque Nacional das Emas** (p376).

LEE FOSTER

Spot wildlife in the Pantanal (p388)

Experience Brazil's incredible biodiversity (p69)

ANDREW DRAFFEN

Float down the Rio Amazonas (p619) on a riverboat

GREG CAIRE

JANE SWEENEY

See the largest water lilies in the world at the Parque Ecológico Janauary (p631)

JOHN MAIER JR

Soak up the splendor of Iguaçu Falls (p310)

Make friends with a toco toucan (p78)

MARK NEWMAN

Brazil's colorful landscape is dotted with splendid colonial towns, architectural wonders and national treasures that aren't so easily categorized. **Petrópolis** (p194), once the retreat of the royal court, is full of history and looming mansions. Soak up baroque architecture and sweeping panoramas in the old gold-mining towns of **Ouro Prêto** (p231) and **Diamantina** (p253). For a more urban experience, head to Rio for a football match at **Maracanã** (p140) or a show at the **Teatro Municipal** (p138). Rio's rival **São Paulo** (p267) has some excellent museums and a world-class arts and music scene.

ROBYN JONES

Take in some opera at the Teatro Amazonas (p623) in Manaus

Hop on the *bonde* (p138) to Santa Teresa

RICARDO GOMES

Wander around Aleijadinho's beautiful chapels (p240) in Congonhas

ROBYN JONES

BRUCE YUAN-YUE BI

Visit the nuns at the Convento São Francisco (p505) in Olinda

Wind your way through the cobblestone streets of Tiradentes (p250)

ROBYN JONES

JANE SWEENEY

Explore Cidade Alta (p417), Salvador's historic center

Bask in the colonial ambience of Paraty (p185)

JOHN MAIER JR

The country that gave birth to Carnaval has much more up her sleeve than just a few weeks of pre-Lenten revelry. There are plenty of happening places where you can mingle with locals and foreigners throughout Brazil. **Rio** (p115) and **São Paulo** (p267) take their nightlife seriously, with talented musicians turning up in the oddest places. Some say **Salvador** (p412) is Brazil's music capital, while others prefer the low-key revelry in beach villages such as **Jericoacoara** (p551) and **Canoa Quebrada** (p549). **Belém** (p577) has its share of nightspots, while the music almost never stops in **São Luís** (p562), **Olinda** (p504), **Porto Seguro** (p454) and lately **Arraial d'Ajuda** (p459) and **Trancoso** (p461).

Be dazzled by the costumes of Carnaval (p106)

Boogie to the beat of Olodum (p431) in Bahia

Join in the festivities at Banda de Ipanema (p107)

Getting Started

Before you come to Brazil, find out whether you need a visa. Many nationalities require them, including citizens from the US, Canada and Australia. See p695 for more details.

If you're going to Carnaval in Rio, Salvador or Olinda, secure hotel reservations as far in advance as possible. That also holds true for Rio's Reveillon (New Year's Eve; p152). If you're hitting other major festivals (p685), book your room in advance – often easily done over the Internet. During the busy summer season (December to March), it's also wise to book ahead.

Brazil is a large country, with vast distances between destinations. If you plan to visit a number of regions, consider purchasing a Brazil Airpass (p703), which allows you up to five in-country flights at a set rate. These tickets must be purchased outside the country.

See Climate Charts (p682) for more information.

WHEN TO GO

Brazil's high season runs from December to March. This is when the country fills with both foreign visitors and vacationing Brazilian families (school holidays run from mid-December to Carnaval, usually in February). Prices rise during this time and you'll face more crowds, though this is also the most festive time in Brazil. Brazil's low season corresponds to its winter, running from May to September. With the exception of July, which is also a school-holiday month, this is the cheapest and least-crowded time to visit the country.

Depending on where you go, weather may be a significant factor in your travel plans. In Rio, the humidity can be high in summer, even though temperatures rarely rise above 30°C (86°F); most of the rain falls from October to January. In winter Rio temperatures hover around 23°C (73°F), with a mix of both rainy and superb days.

On the northeast coast, from Bahia to Maranhão, temperatures are a bit warmer year-round than in Rio – rarely far from 28°C (82°F) – but due to a wonderful tropical breeze and less humidity, it's rarely stifling. The rainy season runs from about mid-April to mid-July, though even then you'll encounter gorgeous days.

The Amazon region (the north) is one of the world's rainiest places and rainfall occurs most frequently from January to May, making travel exceedingly difficult then. The rest of the year the region still receives plenty of rain, though showers tend to last only an hour or two.

The Pantanal also has rainy/dry seasons, and if you plan to go, do so during the dry season (mid-April to late September). The rest of the year,

---

DON'T LEAVE HOME WITHOUT...

- Getting your visa, if you need one (p695).
- Learning a few Portuguese words and phrases (p718).
- Insect repellent containing DEET (p715).
- A yellow fever vaccine, if planning a trip to the Amazon. You may want to take medication against malaria as well (p708).
- A waterproof jacket.
- A Brazil Airpass (p703) if you're planning to cover a lot of ground in a short amount of time.

the wetlands receive tremendous rainfall, washing out roads and making traveling a nightmare.

The South has the most extreme temperature changes, and during the coldest winter months (June to August), Rio Grande do Sul, Santa Catarina, Paraná and São Paulo have temperatures between 13°C (55.4°F) and 18°C (64.4°F). In some towns, snow is even possible – but rare. As elsewhere along the coast, summer is quite hot, and you'll have lots of company on the beach.

COSTS & MONEY

The devaluation of the Brazilian real in 1999 made Brazil cheaper for foreign travelers than it had been for a long, long time. Although Brazil is one of South America's most expensive countries, it's still cheaper than North America or Europe, and it should remain so for the foreseeable future.

Many items in Brazil are cheap by European or North American standards: food, clothing, hotel accommodations, bus travel. Car rental and national flights cost about the same as in Europe or the US (although ongoing price wars have made them more economical in recent years), while electronics and film generally cost more.

If you're frugal, you can travel on about US$30 to US$40 a day – paying as little as US$12 for accommodations, US$8 for food and drink, plus bus travel, admission to sights and the occasional entertainment. If you just plan to lie on a beach for a month, eating rice, beans and fish every day, you can probably scrape by on US$20 a day. If you stay in reasonably comfortable hotels, eat in nicer restaurants, go out most nights and book the occasional rental car or guided excursion, you'll probably spend US$100 a day. Those who can swing it can enjoy five-star accommodations, decadent meals and top-notch service (whether in jungle lodges in the Amazon or islands off the coast) with all the extras for US$300 a day and up.

Bear in mind that during the December-to-February holiday season accommodations costs generally increase by around 25% to 30%.

Brazil is not among the kinder destinations for solo travelers. If you share rooms and meals with someone else, you can shave maybe 20% off the above budgets.

TRAVEL LITERATURE

A Death in Brazil by Peter Robb is one of the most fascinating travelogues published in recent years (2004). Robb, who spent 20 years in Brazil, explores four centuries of Brazilian history, while detailing his own modern-day travels, creating a compelling portrait of the country.

Travelers' Tales Brazil, edited by Scott Doggett and Annette Haddad, is a fine anthology of tales of travel and life in Brazil. The excellent 2nd edition (published 2004) includes contributions from writers such as Diane Ackerman, Joe Kane, Petru Popescu and Alma Guillermoprieto.

How to Be a Carioca by Priscilla Ann Goslin is highly recommended for anyone planning to spend time in Rio de Janeiro. Her tongue-in-cheek descriptions of the Carioca (Rio dweller) lifestyle are spot-on. Don't miss the hilarious 'essential vocabulary' section for mastering the local lingo.

Peter Fleming's *Brazilian Adventure* is about the young journalist's expedition into Mato Grosso in the 1930s – a wild region then – in search of vanished explorer Colonel Fawcett. What Fleming found is less important than the telling, written with wry humor.

Although not specifically about Brazil, Redmond O'Hanlon's hilarious *In Trouble Again: a Journey Between the Orinoco and the Amazon* tells of his fretful journey through Latin America.

LONELY PLANET INDEX

Liter of gas (petrol) US$0.65

Liter of bottled water US$0.40

Pint of *chope* (draft beer) US$0.90

Souvenir T-shirt US$6

Freshly squeezed *suco* (juice) US$1

HOW MUCH?

Admission to samba club in Rio US$2 to US$7

Flight from Rio to Salvador (one way) US$145

Double room in a comfy pousada in Jericoacoara US$30

Bus ride from Rio to Ouro Prêto US$13

Three-day jungle excursion from Manaus US$150

TOP TENS

BEST BRAZILIAN ALBUMS

It's no easy task selecting just a mere handful of albums from the scores of talented singers and songwriters who have made Brazil into such an incredible music center. Check out some of the great works below, most of which can be found in Brazil (or you can buy online before you go).

- *Africa Brasil: Coleção Samba Soul*, Jorge Ben
- *Djavan Ao Vivo*, Djavan
- *Elis & Tom*, Elis Reginas and Antonio Carlos Jobim
- *Getz/Gilberto*, Stan Getz and João Gilberto
- *Meus Caros Amigos*, Chico Buarque

- *Os Afros Sambas*, Baden Powell
- *Refazenda*, Gilberto Gil
- *Travessia*, Milton Nascimento
- *Tribalistas*, Arnaldo Atunes, Carlinhos Brown, Marisa Monte
- *Tropicalia – Ou Panis et Circenses*, Caetano Veloso et al

BEST BOOKS

Get inside the Brazilian experience by checking out some of these greats reads, which explore a range of themes – history, anthropology, music, samba schools and the national sport/national identity.

- *Bossa Nova: The Story of the Brazilian Music that Seduced the World*, Ruy Castro (p55)
- *The Brazilian Sound*, Chris McGowan and Ricardo Pessanha (p54)
- *The Brazilians*, Joseph Page
- *Futebol: The Brazilian Way of Life*, Alex Bellos (p50)
- *Gabriela, Clove and Cinnamon*, Jorge Amado (p58)

- *How to Be a Carioca*, Priscilla Ann Goslin (p14)
- *The Posthumous Memoirs of Bras Cubas*, Joaquim Maria Machado de Assis (p58)
- *Samba*, Alma Guillermoprieto (p55)
- *Tristes Tropiques*, Claude Lévi-Strauss (p48)
- *Tropical Truth: a Story of Music and Revolution in Brazil*, Caetano Veloso (p56)

BEST FESTIVALS & EVENTS

Those in search of Brazil's liveliest festivals should definitely base themselves in the Northeast. Throughout the country, you'll find some fantastic, wild and, at times, downright surreal celebrations.

- Boi-Bumbá (p636), late June, Parintins
- Bumba Meu Boi (p566), late June to second week of August, São Luís
- Carnaval, Shrove Tuesday and the fun-filled days preceding it, February or March, Rio de Janeiro (p106), Salvador (p424) or Olinda (p507)
- Cavalhadas (p372), 50 days after Easter, Pirenópolis
- Círio de Nazaré (p583), second Sunday in October, Belém

- Festa da NS de Boa Morte (p439), mid-August, Cachoeira
- Festa de Iemanjá and Reveillon (p152), December 31, Rio de Janeiro
- Folclore Nordestino (p507), late August, Olinda
- Procissão do Senhor Bom Jesus dos Navegantes (p425), January 1, Salvador
- Semana Santa (Holy Week), March or April, Ouro Prêto (p237) or Goiás Velho (p369)

Also not solely about Brazil is Peter Matthiessen's *The Cloud Forest*, an account of a 30,000km journey across the South American wilderness from the Amazon to Tierra del Fuego. It's well worth a read.

Moritz Thomsen's *The Saddest Pleasure: a Journey on Two Rivers* is an engaging book about the author's experiences in South America, including journeys through Brazil and along the Amazon.

Running the Amazon by Joe Kane is the story of the 10 men and one woman who, in 1986, became the first expedition to cover the entire length of the Rio Amazonas (Amazon River), from the Andes to the Atlantic, on foot and in rafts and kayaks.

INTERNET RESOURCES

Brazilian Embassy in London (www.brazil.org.uk) Comprehensive information on many aspects of the country, including practical information for tourists and links to dozens of local tourism sites in Brazil.

Brazzil (www.brazzil.com) In-depth articles on the country's politics, economy, literature, arts and culture.

Hip Gringo's Guide to Brazil (www.brazilmax.com) Excellent guide to Brazilian culture and society; good, selective articles and links but bad title.

Lanic Brazil (http://lanic.utexas.edu/la/brazil) The University of Texas' excellent collection of Brazil links.

Lonely Planet (www.lonelyplanet.com) Summaries on Brazil travel, the popular Thorn Tree bulletin board, travel news and links to other web resources.

Terra Brasil (www.terra.com.br/turismo) Portuguese-language travel site with, among other things, searchable street maps of 128 Brazilian cities and up-to-date information on entertainment, nightlife and dining options in dozens of cities around Brazil.

Itineraries
CLASSIC ROUTES

RIO & THE SOUTHEAST
Three Weeks

Gorgeous beaches, rain forest–covered islands and colonial towns are just some of the things you'll experience on a trip around the Southeast.

Spend a few days discovering **Rio** (p115), the enchanting Cariocas (Rio dwellers) and their beaches, samba and unrivalled nightlife before heading to São Paulo. Along the way, you'll travel the lush Costa Verde, where you can access **Ilha Grande** (p180), an island blanketed by rain forest and ringed by dozens of striking beaches, and **Paraty** (p185), a charming colonial town that hosts lively festivals in a spectacular natural setting. **Ilhabela** (p285) is another gorgeous island of beaches, forests and waterfalls. Stop in **São Paulo** (p267), to experience the restaurants and nightlife of one of the world's most international cities. Then head to the exquisite mountain towns of **Ouro Prêto** (p231), **Diamantina** (p253) and **Tiradentes** (p250), where you can stroll the cobblestone streets of some of Brazil's finest colonial gems.

Connect in **Belo Horizonte** (p224) for the **train ride** (p229) to the coast, or catch a bus to **Parque Nacional de Caparaó** (p262), a thickly forested park with superb views. In **Vitória** (p210), catch a coastal bus south, where you'll pass charming fishing villages and some handsome beaches, particularly around the town of **Guarapari** (p216). Further south are equally stunning beaches, from chic **Búzios** (p206), to **Saquarema** (p201), a surfing favorite.

On the way back to Rio, detour north to **Petrópolis** (p194), a cool mountain retreat. Great hiking is nearby at the **Parque Nacional da Serra dos Órgãos** (p199). You can also get a taste of Switzerland at **Nova Friburgo** (p199).

This 2300km, round-trip takes you west from Rio de Janeiro to São Paulo, and from there north to the mountain towns in Minas Gerais. Belo Horizonte is the transit point for the towns of Minas Gerais and for Vitória on the coast of Espírito Santo. From there, coastal buses connect to Rio de Janeiro.

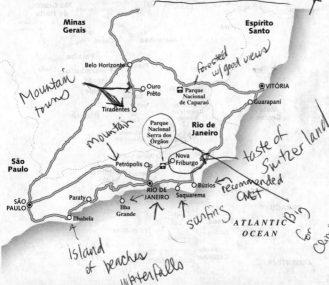

BRAZIL FOR THE COMPLETIST   Three Months

On this epic trip you'll experience the rhythm-infused towns of the North-east, the jungles of the Amazon and the biodiversity of the Pantanal, with beaches, tropical islands and vibrant colonial towns thrown in the mix.

From **São Paulo** (p267), head east to Rio, stopping at glorious beaches such as **Ubatuba** (p283), **Trindade** (p191) and **Paraty-Mirim** (p190) before reaching **Rio** (p115).

From there head north, stopping in the pretty mountain towns of **Ouro Prêto** (p231) and **Diamantina** (p253). The architectural masterpiece that is **Brasília** (p354) is next, and lies near the **Parque Nacional da Chapada dos Veadeiros** (p374), a fantastic wilderness area.

On the way to Bahia, explore the **Parque Nacional da Chapada Diamantina** (p471) before reaching **Salvador** (p412), one of Brazil's liveliest towns. Further up the coast is beautiful **Olinda** (p504), one of Brazil's prettiest towns. From neighboring **Recife** (p497), fly out to the spectacular island of **Fernando de Noronha** (p511).

Back on the mainland, travel the north coast, stopping in **Jericoacoara** (p551) en route to the surreal dunes in the **Parque Nacional dos Lençóis Maranhenses** (p570), a stark contrast to the beauty of nearby **São Luís** (p562).

West lies **Belém** (p577), a culturally rich city near the lush island of **Ilha de Marajó** (p592). Catch a boat up the Amazon to **Manaus** (p621), where you can arrange jungle treks.

From Manaus, head to **Bonito** (p402), and experience the region's water-falls, crystal-clear rivers, lush forests and subterranean caves. Go south to the awe-inspiring **Iguaçu Falls** (p308), with waterfalls straddling three countries. Before completing the circle, explore the secluded beaches and charming Germanic towns around **Florianópolis** (p324).

This 12,500km (!) trip takes you on a loop, hitting the major attractions in Brazil. To really do the country justice, you'll need six months or a year, though with strategically placed flights you'll be able to cover more ground in around three months.

BAHIA & THE NORTHEAST   Six Weeks

Those looking for the soul of Brazil often begin (and end) their search in the Northeast. Historic towns, vibrant festivals and a gorgeous 2700km-long coastline are among the attractions, but it's the people you'll meet that make traveling here so unforgettable.

Start your journey in **Porto Seguro** (p454), a celebratory town near dozens of mesmerizing beaches. Soak up the youthful exuberance of **Arraial d'Ajuda** (p459) and charming **Trancoso** (p461) before continuing to **Itacaré** (p448), a colonial fishing town with great surf. North lies **Salvador** (p412), Bahia's most vibrant and colorful city, where Candomblé, capoeira, and *axé* (Northeastern music with a strong African beat) are just a small part of the city's cultural heritage.

Detour west to the **Parque Nacional da Chapada Diamantina** (p471) for crisp mountain streams, panoramic views and a large network of trails. Back on the coast **Olinda** (p504) is one of Brazil's largest and best-preserved colonial cities and it holds an outstanding Carnaval. From **Recife** (p497), Olinda's sister city, fly out to **Fernando de Noronha** (p511), an exquisite island that boasts amazing marine life and breathtaking beaches.

Back on the mainland, visit the nude beach of **Praia de Tambaba** (p526), or continue on to **Praia da Pipa** (p533), another sun-filled spot. In **Natal** (p528) you can hitch a ride on a dune buggy to explore the nearby **Genipabu dunes** (p533).

In Ceará, **Jericoacoara** (p551) is a gorgeous beach village with fantastic nightlife. West of there, the **Parque Nacional dos Lençóis Maranhenses** (p570) has one of the most striking landscapes in Brazil, with impressive fauna living among the dunes and lagoons. The final stop is **São Luís** (p562), a historic town of rugged beauty, with a burgeoning music scene.

This 4500km trip takes you to gorgeous tropical beaches and colorful, music-filled cities. The journey begins in Porto Seguro and ends in São Luís, both of which have airport connections to major cities. Those with time to spare can easily spend three to six months absorbing the cultural and natural beauty of this fantastic region.

ROADS LESS TRAVELED

THE AMAZON

Six Weeks

This six-week, 3900km trip begins in Belém, and travels mostly by boat along the Rio Amazonas, the world's mightiest river. Several detours include Belém to Ilha de Marajó and Manaus to Santa Elena de Uairén in Venezuela. The trip ends in Tabatinga, where you can catch flights to Manaus and onward.

Few places ignite the imagination like the Amazon. The largest forest on the planet has astounding plant and animal life. Surprising to many visitors, the wetlands also contain historic cities, beautiful river beaches and one of the most important archaeological sites in South America.

Begin in **Belém** (p577), a culturally rich city at the mouth of the great river. From here you can explore the forested-covered island of **Ilha de Marajó** (p592) or head northeast to **Algodoal** (p590), a rustic fishing hamlet in a splendid natural setting.

Get a hammock and travel by boat up the Rio Amazonas. Stop in **Monte Alegre** (p600) to see ancient rock paintings – the oldest-known human creations in the Amazon. Keep heading upstream to **Santarém** (p594), a pleasant city with many nearby attractions. Across the river is **Alenquer** (p601), a town near beautiful and rarely visited countryside. You can also reach the virgin rain forest of the **Floresta Nacional do Tapajós** (p598) and **Alter do Chão** (p601), a picturesque lagoon with white-sand beaches.

Continue upriver to **Manaus** (p621), Amazonia's largest city and its center for arranging jungle treks or visits to the biodiverse **Reserva Xixuaú-Xipariná** (p636). You can also travel to **Santa Elena de Uairén** (p651), across the Venezuelan border, for treks up **Mt Roraima** (p653). Heading into the jungles of **Guyana** (p650) is another option. Northwest of Manaus lies the fairly unexplored **Parque Nacional do Jaú** (p636).

You'll see incredible wildlife at the **Mamirauá Reserve** (p638), outside of **Tefé** (p637). From there, you can continue by river to **Tabatinga** (p639), and into **Leticia** (p641) in Colombia for excursions into **Parque Nacional Natural Amacayacu** (p664) or for stays at **jungle lodges** (p644) along the Rio Javari.

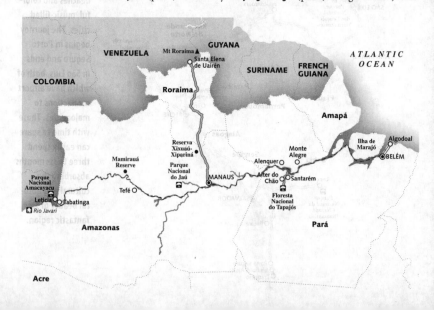

DISCOVERING THE SOUTH
Three Weeks

One of Brazil's most overlooked regions has gorgeous islands and beaches, unexplored national parks and fascinating towns with largely European roots.

Start your journey in **Curitiba** (p297), a clean, cosmopolitan city with a youthful air. From there take the scenic train ride to **Parque Estadual Marumbi** (p302), a wonderful national park with stunning views and excellent trails. Continue by train to **Paranaguá** (p303). This colorful town lies near the charming **Ilha do Mel** (p305), a forest-covered island with fine trails and pretty beaches. From there you can catch a boat to **Ilha do Superaguí** (p308), set in national park with pristine beaches, and much wildlife living among its mangrove forests and salt marshes.

Next go to **Joinville** (p318), a pleasant town straight out of Bavaria. Catch a boat from there to historic **São Francisco do Sul** (p321). **Florianópolis** (p324) is next. There you can soak up the pleasant air of its colonial district before venturing onto **Ilha de Santa Catarina** (p328), an island of beaches, lagoons and tiny fishing villages.

South of Florianópolis is **Praia da Rosa** (p332), one of Brazil's most glorious beaches – and a great spot for sighting whales off-shore. On into Rio Grande do Sul, you'll reach the **Parque Nacional de Aparados da Serra** (p344), one of Brazil's natural wonders, featuring deep canyons, waterfalls and fantastic hiking and climbing.

Head east to **Santo Ângelo** (p349), the gateway to the Jesuit missions. From there you can visit **São Miguel das Missões** (p350), or head across the border to missions in **Paraguay** (p350) or **Argentina** (p350). The last stop is **Foz do Iguaçu** (p308), from where you can visit the Iguaçu Falls, some of the most striking waterfalls on the planet.

This 1600km trip begins in Curitiba, and travels overland to Foz do Iguaçu. Along the way, you'll visit forested islands, mountainous national parks, historic missions and idyllic beaches before reaching the massive waterfalls. From Foz do Iguaçu, catch a bus or plane back to Rio or São Paulo.

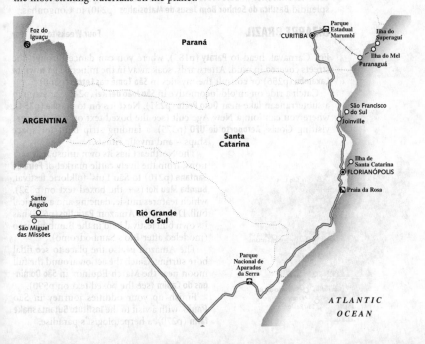

TAILORED TRIPS

WORLD HERITAGE SITES
Five Weeks

Brazil's World Heritage sites offer visitors a glimpse of the astounding natural and cultural diversity of Brazil.

Start your journey in vibrant **Salvador** (p412). Next head to **Olinda** (p504), the seat of Afro-Brazilian culture in the Northeast. The island of **Fernando de Noronha** (p511) is next, with its beautiful reefs and abundant wildlife. On the mainland, go to **Parque Nacional da Serra da Capivara**

(p561), site of prehistoric rock paintings. The historic town of **São Luís** (p562) is next, followed by a flight out to Manaus, from where you can visit the lush forest found in **Parque Nacional do Jaú** (p636).

After the jungle, **Brasília** (p354) will seem startling. From there visit the **Parque Nacional da Chapada dos Veadeiros** (p374), an excellent hiking area. East of the capital is **Goiás Velho** (p368), another colonial gem, and **Parque Nacional das Emas** (p376), home to much wildlife.

Some of the world's best wildlife watching awaits visitors to the **Pantanal** (p388). From there, head south to the **Iguaçu Falls** (p310).

The final stop is in Minas Gerais, among the colonial churches of **Ouro Prêto** (p231) and **Diamantina** (p253), as well as the splendid **Basílica do Senhor Bom Jesus de Matosinhos** (p240) in Congonhas.

BIZARRE BRAZIL
Four Weeks to One Year

For Carnaval, head to **Paraty** (p185), where you can dance through the streets covered in mud. Afterwards, soak away in the mineral spa town of **Caxambu** (p256) or consult the mystics in **São Tomé das Letras** (p260).

Catch a ride on an old locomotive in **São João del Rei** (p245), or swim in a subterranean lake near **Ouro Prêto** (p231). Next it's on to **Brasília** (p354), where you can join a New Age cult (see the boxed text on p357) before visiting Goiás' **Aeroporto de UFO** (p375), a landing strip built for space ships – and mystic rituals.

The Northeast has its own unusual attractions, from the lively cattle market of **Feira de Santana** (p210) to São Luís' folkloric festival, **Bumba Meu Boi** (see the boxed text on p352), which features music, dancing and a magical bull. Deep in the Amazon, **Parintins** (p636) has its own bull festival held in the Bumbódromo (modeled after Rio's Sambódromo).

The Amazon is also the place to see tidal bore surfing. Catch the action around the full moon near the March Equinox in **São Domingos do Capim** (see the boxed text on p590).

Finish up your oddities journey in São Paulo, with a visit to the **Instituto Butantã snake farm** (p270), a herpetologist's paradise.

The Authors

REGIS ST. LOUIS   Coordinating Author, Rio de Janeiro City

Regis' longtime admiration of samba, bossa nova and Brazil's beautiful game *(futebol)* led to his deep involvement with the country – both as a traveler and as a writer. The Cidade Maravilhosa (Marvelous City, aka Rio de Janeiro) is one of his great loves, and he has spent years immersing himself in the vibrant cities and captivating landscapes of Brazil. Regis also updated Lonely Planet's *Rio de Janeiro* city guide, and he researched the Amazon region for *South America on a Shoestring*. When he's not tracking *forró* (popular music of the Northeast) and *maracatu* (Afro-Brazilian music with a slow, heavy beat) in the tropics, Regis makes his living as a freelance writer in New York City.

The Coordinating Author's Favorite Trip

It's hard not to fall under the spell of the Cidade Maravilhosa, especially Ipanema's beach (p123), Lapa's samba clubs (p168) and Santa Teresa's burgeoning art and music scene (p138). Afterwards it's on to the pristine forests and beaches of Ilha Grande (p180) and the colonial splendor of Paraty (p185). A flight up to Belém (p577) reconnects me to the rhythms of the Amazon, while a boat ride away lies Ilha de Marajó (p592), an island of charming villages, fantastic seafood and super-friendly folk. The other direction leads to Algodoal (p590), a remote fishing hamlet of rustic beauty along a lush coastline. The last stop is São Luís (p562), an unpolished colonial gem with one of the country's best music scenes.

Ilha de Marajó
Algodoal
Belém
São Luís
Rio de Janeiro
Paraty
Ollha Grande

GARY PRADO CHANDLER   The Amazon

Gary was already in Brazil – on his honeymoon, in fact – when he got this job. The mother of all rivers proved a real mother to cover: in two months Gary took dozens of boat trips, ten flights, crossed four international borders and three time zones, and caught a grand total of two piranha (but who's counting?). Raised in California, Gary completed a BA in Ethnic Studies at the University of California at Berkeley in 1997 and a Masters in Journalism at Columbia University in New York in 2002. He previously updated the El Salvador and Honduras chapters for Lonely Planet's *Central America on a Shoestring*.

ANDREW DRAFFEN   The Central West

Andrew has been visiting Brazil for over 20 years and has lost count of the number of trips – it's either 15 or 16 – he's made around the country. After catching the travel bug (and a few others) in India, he traveled extensively in Asia, North America and Europe until his first visit to Brazil in 1984. Since then, it's proved extremely difficult to coax him north of the equator. While researching this edition, Andrew almost joined a weird religious sect near Brasília, sampled crocodile paté in the Pantanal, enjoyed thrashing a rental car on the Estrada Parque and waited (in vain) for a flight at the Aeroporto do UFO in Alto Paraíso.

MOLLY GREEN
Bahia, Sergipe & Alagoas

In the same year, both Ilê Ayê and Olodum rocked Molly's home town of Santa Cruz, California, with Afro-Brazilian rhythms, and the victorious Brazilian World Cup team spurred spontaneous street parties, inspiring Molly to learn to samba and embark on a nine-week tour of Brazil. An obsession was born, which led to an intensive study of Brazilian dance, an impressive collection of *axé* music (an Afro-Brazilian pop style), university studies in Brazilian Portuguese and literature, and hours on Brazil's freezing buses and sweaty beaches. While researching this edition, Molly rode a surfboard behind a speed boat driven by a dreadlocked James Bond on the Rio do Inferno and finally submitted to capoeira's call.

THOMAS KOHNSTAMM
Pernambuco, Paraíba & Rio Grande do Norte, Ceará, Piauí & Maranhão

Thomas was studying in Argentina in 1996 when he escaped to Brazil in search of warmer weather and reggae. Between sleeping on the beaches of Ceará and dancing in street parties in Salvador, he fell in love with the country. He returned to live in Rio where he fine-tuned his Portuguese, started playing capoeira and spent an absurd amount of time on the beach. His MA studies at Stanford focused on conservation and development in the Amazon and he is fascinated with ecotourism and other sustainable development programs. Thomas is now a freelance writer based in the East Village in New York City.

ROBERT LANDON
The South

In 2002, Robert went to Brazil for one week, stayed two, returned home only to quit his job and sell all his worldly goods, and – wisely or not – a month later he was living in Copacabana. Now fluent in Portuguese, he has also spent extensive time in both São Paulo and the south of Brazil. A graduate of Stanford University and the University of California at Irvine, Robert has been a travel writer for the last 10 years, including a two-year stint in Paris and one year writing for a fledgling Travelocity.

GINGER ADAMS OTIS
Rio de Janeiro State, Espírito Santo, Minas Gerais, São Paulo State

Ginger has been traveling Latin America for many years as a radio and print journalist. She first went to Brazil in 1997 to cover a story about land struggles between farmers and indigenous people and has returned there frequently, either for work or to relax. Ginger writes for a variety of US publications – the *Village Voice*, the *Nation*, *In These Times*, *MS Magazine*, *JANE* and several others. She does radio work for Pacifica Network, the Associated Press, National Public Radio and the BBC. Ginger's nonfiction travel writing has appeared in anthologies published by Lonely Planet and Seal Press.

CONTRIBUTING AUTHORS

Tom Phillips wrote the History chapter. He was born in London and studied Portuguese at Leeds University. He has lived for two years in Belo Horizonte and Rio de Janeiro, working as a freelance journalist and volunteer in the Rocinha and Morro do Papagaio communities. His idle moments are dedicated to trawling the streets of Cinelândia for Chico Buarque 12-inches and following the increasingly woeful form of the Atlético Mineiro Football Club.

Dr David Goldberg MD wrote the Health chapter. David completed his training in internal medicine and infectious diseases at Columbia-Presbyterian Medical Center in New York City, where he has also served as voluntary faculty. At present, he is an infectious diseases specialist in Scarsdale, New York State, and the editor-in-chief of the website www.MDTravelHealth.com.

Snapshot

For the last 50 years, Brazil hasn't quite been able to shake the gibe of being the 'land of the future – and it always will be'. In spite of its industrial development, and despite being among the world's top 11 economies, it has often had trouble getting off the ground (much like its failed space program).

A historic turning point seemed to arrive in 2003, following the much-watched election that brought President Luíz Inácio (Lula) da Silva into power. For the first time in Brazil's history, its chief of state came from the working class, and Lula entered office promising to address the dire social problems plaguing Brazil; problems with which he had first-hand experience. Following his overwhelming victory, some 200,000 Brazilians showed up at his inauguration in Brasília.

President Lula certainly has his work cut out for him. The problems facing Latin America's giant are staggering. The economic gap between rich and poor is one of the world's largest. A third of the population struggles just to feed itself, while large swaths of the country are populated by landless peasants scratching out a living on drought-stricken land. In the cities, street children are commonplace. All across the country, the *favelas* (shantytowns) are such a visible presence that they can no longer be ignored.

Lula's fiscal restraint surprised his early critics, who worried about a leftist renegade running the country. Lula has also sought to expand Brazil's presence in world markets, shunning George W Bush and the World Trade Organization (WTO) – both of which Lula viewed as having an arrogant attitude to developing countries. Indeed, whenever President Lula speaks at international forums, he always underlines that hunger and poverty are the greatest problems facing the world. In 2003 Lula spearheaded the creation of G-20, a group of (originally 20) nations allied to combat hunger and poverty – a far different agenda than that favored by the WTO. Lula has also helped spur trade between Brazil and China.

Around the world Lula has been hailed as the voice for the downtrodden. Developing countries have praised him for challenging international trade regimes that favor rich countries over poor ones. Yet despite Lula's popularity abroad, domestically many remain disillusioned with his failure to provide meaningful solutions to social problems. His Fome Zero (Zero Hunger) program was a beautiful ad campaign, but has done little for the mass of undernourished men, women and children across the country.

The destruction of the Amazon, the country's greatest ecological catastrophe, is still occurring, and while vowing commitment to the environment, Lula also supports development programs that would speed its demise (p91). Lula's mixed record has left Brazilians resigned that nothing is likely to change for the better. Despite his big heart and desire to improve the lot of the poor, Lula admits that he's no miracle worker and change will only come slowly over the remainder of his term, which ends in 2006.

On other fronts, Brazil has shown itself to be deeply concerned with the welfare of its populace. Despite the high incidence of HIV cases (well over 500,000), Brazil is one of the world leaders among developing countries in treating AIDS victims. Brazilian pharmaceutical companies

FAST FACTS

Population: 184 million

Annual growth: 1.15%

Life expectancy at birth: 67 years (men), 75 years (women)

GDP: US$1.4 trillion (US$7600 per capita)

Number of people living below the poverty line: 40 million

Infant mortality per 1000 live births: 32 (US: 7)

Unemployment: 12%

Adult literacy: 86%

Number of people living with AIDS: 610,000

Sq km of rain forest destroyed annually: 15,000 (roughly the size of US state New Jersey)

were global pioneers in manufacturing cheap generic versions of expensive AIDS drugs; and the government has made sure that all who need the drugs get them. Those who can't afford them receive them for free. Perhaps as many as 100,000 lives have been saved owing to the efforts of Brazil's strong anti-AIDS program.

In this and many other ways, the Brazilian spirit is unbroken. Morale around the country remains high, and nowhere is this more apparent than on the soccer field. A few sociologists, in fact, equate the country's well-being with its success on the football pitch. Games, both local and abroad, are followed intensely, with Brazilian players filling team rosters all over the world. The World Cup victory in 2002 marked the country's fifth. In other areas of sport, Rio is anxiously preparing to host the 2007 Pan American Games.

Meanwhile, civil rights activists are celebrating the 2004 judicial ruling that allows gay couples to marry in the state of Rio Grande do Sul, normally a bastion of conservatism.

Brazil has its admirers, its critics and its cranks, but with the unprecedented election of Lula, more and more are beginning to believe in the Brazilian dream once again. This one doesn't involve dazzling football teams or sensuous samba beats but rather the creation of a just society, something that's long been absent in Brazil's plutocratic history, and one that so many millions desperately need.

History <small>Tom Phillips</small>

Wherever you go in Brazil, you'll hear Brazilians refer to their country as a 'new' one. With just over 500 years of life and 20 of democracy, Brazil is a relative infant. But the description is a touch unfair. By the time the Portuguese rolled up in AD 1500, what is now Brazil had already been populated – albeit under a different name – for as many as 50,000 years.

WHERE IT ALL BEGAN

Little remains of Brazil's prehistoric inhabitants. Unlike the Incas, Brazilian Indians never developed a highly advanced civilization and left few clues for archaeologists to follow. Searching for signs of prehistoric life in the 8.5 million sq km of Brazilian territory is like searching for the tiniest of needles in a very, very large haystack.

The official scientific line is that the region's first inhabitants hailed from Siberia, from where they made the not-so-quick hop to South America over the Bering Strait, long submerged by the ocean. But whether they did this 50,000, 30,000 or just a mere 12,000 years ago remains something of a mystery.

Remnants of these early civilizations are scattered across Brazil; in Piauí's Parque Nacional da Serra da Capivara (p561), on the Ilha de Marajó (p592), in the northern state of Pará and at the Gruta da Lapinha (p230) in Minas Gerais.

A not-so-brief detour on a cruise down the Amazon from Manaus to Belém takes you to the oldest trace of human life in the Amazon region: a series of rock paintings near the town of Monte Alegre (p600).

Prehistoric Brazil is a jungle of uncertainties, conflicting theories, figures that don't add up and dates that don't match. The only certainty is this: it wasn't the Portuguese who discovered *terra brasilis*.

CABRAL & CHUMS

The opening pages of Brazilian history were effectively rewritten in 1500, when a fleet of 13 Portuguese ships carrying 1200 men rolled up near what is today Porto Seguro.

After passing the Cape Verde Islands, off Africa's northeast coast, the fleet headed west. Increasingly it is thought that, far from having been blown off course by strong winds, the Portuguese already had such a giant detour in mind. Whatever the motive, on April 22, 1500 Pedro Álvares Cabral and his gang stepped for the first time onto Brazilian soil. Their indigenous reception committee was ready and waiting.

'There were 18 or 20 men,' marveled scribe Pero Vaz de Caminha in a letter back to the Portuguese king. 'They were brown-skinned, all of them naked, without anything at all to cover their private parts. In their hands they carried bows and arrows.'

The festivities didn't last for long. Having erected a cross and held mass in the land they baptized Terra da Vera Cruz, the Portuguese took to the waves once again. With lucrative spice and diamond markets in Africa

1494	1500
Treaty of Tordesillas divides the New World between Spain and Portugal	Discovery of Brazil by the Portuguese

to exploit, Cabral and chums evidently had bigger fish to fry elsewhere. Over the following decades they neglected their new discovery and only in 1531 did King João III send the first settlers to Brazil.

Brazil's Indians

There were between two and six million indigenous people in the region when Brazil was officially discovered in 1500. But for Brazil's Indians there was little reason for cheer. April 22, 1500 marked the first chapter of their gradual extermination.

Over the following decades a four-front war was waged on the Indian way of life. It was a cultural war, as well as a physical, territorial and biological one. Many *índios* fell victim to the *bandeirantes* – a group of roaming adventurers who spent the 17th and 18th centuries exploring Brazil's interior, pillaging Indian settlements as they went. Those who escaped such a fate were struck down by the illnesses shipped in from Europe, to which they had no natural resistance. Others were worked to death on the sugar plantations.

If the flag-bearing *bandeirantes* were responsible for the physical destruction of the Indians, it was the Jesuits who began their cultural destruction, outlawing their traditions and customs, and replacing them with another culture.

When the Portuguese colonizers arrived in 1500, there were well over 1000 Indian tribes in what is now Brazilian territory. At the start of the 21st century Brazil's indigenous population had been slashed to a mere 300,000 (split into about 200 tribes) – not much larger than Rio's Copacabana neighborhood. Several tribes are now on the verge of extinction, including the Xetá in Paraná, of which just three members remain.

DIVIDING THE LAND

Thirty one years after Brazil's discovery, King João III decided it might actually be worth settling there after all. The first settlement sprung up in São Vicente, when a fleet of five ships carrying some 400 men docked near what is now the modern port of Santos.

DID YOU KNOW?

When the Portuguese arrived in Brazil there were more than 1000 indigenous tribes. Today just 200 remain.

> **BRAZILWOOD**
>
> The Portuguese had little interest in colonization; instead they were after riches like those of India and Africa, where they had established trading stations to obtain spices and ivory.
>
> The only thing to capture Portuguese imaginations was a rock-hard tree known as *pau brazil* (brazilwood). Seeing the value of the red dye it produced, merchants began sending a few ships each year to harvest the trees and take them back to Europe.
>
> For the first half of the 16th century, brazilwood was virtually the only commodity exported from Brazil. As traders filled their pockets with its profits, the colony changed its name from Terra da Vera Cruz to Brazil, in tribute to the tree. Alas, the brazilwood trade, which had never been terribly profitable, was soon in jeopardy. The most accessible trees had been rapidly depleted. French competition for the wood intensified – causing fighting to break out – and the Indians stopped volunteering their labor. When the sugar industry sprung to life in 1532 and *engenhos* (sugar mills) began to spread across the northeast it was, effectively, the finally nail in brazilwood's coffin.

1531	1549
First settlers arrive near what is now the port of Santos	Tomé de Sousa becomes the first governor of Brazil

In an attempt to ward off the ambitions of other European countries, the king divided the Brazilian coast into 15 captaincies, each with about 250km of coastline stretching inland to the west. These territories were awarded to *donatários*, minor gentry favored by the king. It was hoped that through settlement, the long coastline could be secured at minimal cost.

The settlers' lives were made difficult by the climate, hostility from the Indians and competition from the Dutch and French. Four captaincies were never settled and another four destroyed by Indians. Only Pernambuco and São Vicente were profitable.

In 1549 the king sent Tomé de Sousa to be the first governor of Brazil, to centralize authority and save the few remaining captaincies. Sousa was joined by some 1000 settlers; among them Portuguese officials, soldiers, exiled prisoners, new Christians (converted Jews) and the first six Jesuit priests. What is now the state of Bahia was chosen as Sousa's base. The city of Salvador, which remained Brazil's capital until 1763 when Rio de Janeiro took over, was founded.

Updated daily, Brazzil (www.brazzil.com) is an online magazine focused on Brazilian history, politics and culture.

SUGARCANE: SWEETNESS & FIGHTS

The colonists soon worked out that although Brazil didn't boast the spices and ivory of Africa it was a place where sugarcane grew well.

Having lost their grip on the *pau brazil* market (made a state monopoly in 1531), Brazil's early entrepreneurs turned to sugar. Sugar came to Brazil in 1532 and hasn't left since. It was coveted by a hungry European market, which used it for medicinal purposes, to flavor foods and even in wine.

These days sugar is no less popular. You can sip it on the beach in the form of a *caldo de cana* (sugarcane juice). You can neck it in one of Brazil's many *pé-sujo* (dirty-foot) bars as a shot of *cachaça* (white spirit made from sugarcane). You can pour copious amounts of it into your coffee, as do most Brazilians, and you can even run your car on it.

Perhaps envisaging Brazil's sugarcoated future, the colonists turned to this new industry. They lacked just one thing: a workforce.

Slaves

A doorstop of a book about slavery in Pernambuco's sugar plantations, Gilberto Freyre's *The Masters and the Slaves* is considered one of the most important works in Brazilian anthropology. Not for the lighthearted.

Initially the Portuguese seemed to hit it off with Brazil's natives. There was even an exchange of presents between Cabral's men and the Indians on the beach, in which the Portuguese parted company with a sombrero and the Indians, feather headdresses. Relations quickly cooled when the Portuguese started enslaving their neighbors. Yet, for a variety of reasons the Portuguese felt the Indians didn't make great slaves and instead turned to Africa's already existing slave trade.

African slaves started to pour into Brazil's slave markets from about 1550. They were torn from a variety of tribes from Angola, Mozambique and Guiné, as well as the Sudan and Congo.

Though from different regions and cultures, their destinations were identical: slave markets such as Salvador's Pelourinho (p419) or Belém's Mercado Ver-o-Peso. By the time slavery was abolished in 1888, around 3.6 million Africans had been shipped in to Brazil – nearly 40% of the total that came to the New World.

Africans were seen as better workers and less susceptible to the European diseases that had proved the undoing of so many Indians. In short, they were a better investment. Yet the Portuguese didn't go out of their way to protect this investment. Slaves were brought to Brazil in subhuman conditions; taken from their families and packed into squalid ships for the month-long journey to Brazil.

Visitors to the beaches of Porto de Galinhas (p509), near Recife, might not pick up on the area's grim past. Even after abolition, slave traders continued to smuggle in slaves often packed into a ship's hull under crates full of *galinhas* (chickens). The area's name is one of the few remnants of its ties to a past of exploitation and cruelty.

The Masters & the Slaves

For those who survived such ordeals, arrival in Brazil meant only continued suffering. A slave's existence was one of brutality and humiliation, though not all saw it this way.

'Slavery in Brazil is very benign,' opined German writer Joseph Hörmeyer in his 1863 book *What Jorge Has to Say About Brazil*.

'I wouldn't like to say that there aren't cruel owners,' he suggested. 'But, in general, the character of the Brazilian people is far too gentle and indulgent for the slaves to overly suffer.'

Hörmeyer obviously hadn't been put to work in the fields himself. Labor on the plantations was relentless. In temperatures that often exceeded 30°C (86°F), slaves were required to work as many as 17 hours each day, before retiring to the squalid conditions of the *senzala* (slave quarters).

Trapped in such dwellings, into which as many as 200 slaves were packed, the word hygiene was a concept as remote as the distant coasts of Africa. Dysentery, typhus, yellow fever, malaria, tuberculosis and scurvy were rife; malnutrition a fact of life. Syphilis also plagued a slave population often sexually exploited by its masters.

Kind masters were the exception, not the rule. To this day, stomach-churning accounts of their cruel practices remain.

Aside from the *senzala*, the other main institution of the sugar plantation was the *casa grande* ('big house') – the mansion from which the masters would control their slaves. It was here in the luxurious *casa grande* that the overlap between European and African cultures came, something described in microscopic detail by anthropologist Gilberto Freyre in his book *Casa Grande e Senzala* (The Masters and the Slaves).

Freyre's work, often criticized as outdated and even racist, nevertheless underlines the huge African influence on Brazilian society, visible far outside Brazil's Northeast where slavery initially took root. As the Catholic priest Antonio Vieira pointed out at the time: 'Without the blacks, there wouldn't be a Pernambuco.' Nor, indeed, would Brazil be as it is today.

Resistance & the Quilombos

Resistance to slavery took many forms. Documents of the period refer to the desperation of the slaves who starved themselves to death, killed their babies or fled. Sabotage and theft were frequent, as were work slowdowns, stoppages and revolts.

Other slaves sought solace in African religion and culture. The mix of Catholicism (made compulsory by slave masters) and African traditions

Quilombo (directed by Cacá Diegues) is an epic history flick in which the vast Palmares Quilombo – a community of runaway slaves led by the legendary Zumbi – is reconstructed in Rio's Baixada Fluminense. It's blessed with Gilberto Gil's excellent soundtrack.

1624	1695
The Dutch invade Brazil, taking control of the capital for one year	Destruction of the Palmares Quilombo in Brazil's Northeast

spawned a syncretic religion in the sugar plantations, known today as Candomblé. The slaves masked their activities with a facade of Catholic saints and rituals – hardly surprising considering that such customs were illegal in Brazil until the 1940s. The martial art capoeira (see p432) also grew out of the slave communities.

Many slaves escaped from their masters forming *quilombos*, communities of runaway slaves that quickly spread across the countryside. The most famous, the Republic of Palmares, which survived through much of the 17th century, was home to some 20,000 people. Palmares covered a broad tract of lush tropical forest straddling the border of Alagoas and Pernambuco states. Led by Zumbi, who had been a king in Africa, its citizens became pioneers of guerrilla warfare, repeatedly fending off Portuguese attacks between 1670 and 1695. Eventually Palmares fell to a force of *bandeirantes* from São Paulo.

As abolitionist sentiment grew in the 19th century, the *quilombos* received more support and ever-greater numbers of slaves fled the plantations. Only abolition itself, in 1888, stopped the growth of *quilombos*. Over 700 villages that began life as *quilombos* remain today. Some were so isolated that they remained completely out of contact with White Brazilians until the last couple of decades.

InfoBrazil (www.info brazil.com) is a current-affairs magazine, featuring analysis of Brazilian politics and economy.

COLONIAL RIVALS

It's hard to picture what Brazil would have been like under French or Dutch rule. Tom Jobim might have composed a track about the *Meisje* from Ipanema; Brazilians might be tucking into frogs legs and not *feijoada* (bean-and-meat stew) every Sunday. For a time, such an outcome was a distinct possibility.

Technically, the 1494 Treaty of Tordesillas was to have divided the New World between Spain and Portugal. An imaginary line, running from north to south between the mouth of the Amazon and what is now Santa Catarina, was drawn onto the map. Land to the east became Portuguese property; land to the west fell under Spanish control.

But the line was to prove very imaginary indeed. As any traveler brave enough to venture into the further reaches of Mato Grosso will discover, enforcing such a vast border running through thick jungle and swamp was never a particularly viable idea. Brazil's borders remained in a state of constant flux until as late as 1930.

Over the years, Portugal repeatedly ignored the frontier in an attempt to squeeze more land out of its rivals. France and Holland also had their eyes on Brazil's yellow, green and pleasant land.

The French

In 1555 three boatloads of French settlers landed on a small island in Rio's Baía de Guanabara. Obviously liking what they found, the French decided to try to incorporate parts of southern Brazil into their ever-growing empire. Antarctic France would be its name.

Things didn't go to plan – a few years later the *franceses* were expelled by the Portuguese, who landed near Morro da Urca's Praia Vermelha, at the foot of the Sugarloaf Mountain. It was here that Estácio de Sá founded the city of São Sebastião do Rio de Janeiro on March 1, 1565.

1710	1750
The Brazilian gold rush begins	The Treaty of Madrid is signed, with Spain giving six million sq kms of land to Brazil

Further north, the French made another attempt to claw Brazilian soil from the Portuguese, founding the city of São Luís in 1612. The city – which took its name from France's then king, Louis XIII – didn't last long in French hands either. Three years later, the Portuguese arrived and sent the French packing once again.

The Dutch

The challenge from Holland didn't prove so easy to shake off. Although the Dutch West India Company (DWIC), set up in 1621, sounded a harmless enough venture, it was much more than a simple business. Its business, in fact, was war; its goal was to conquer Brazil's Northeast from the Portuguese.

The Dutch bombardment of Salvador began on the morning of May 9, 1624. Twenty six ships, filled with over 3000 men, sprung into action and by the following day, after the customary Calvinist ransacking, they had captured the city.

Salvador's return to Portuguese hands was almost as quick as the invasion; it was just a year before a combined force of 12,000 Spanish and Portuguese troops evicted the Dutch. But the threat didn't end there. Five years later the Dutch were back, storming the city of Recife and setting up the capital of New Holland there – Mauritzstaadt. For the next twenty years the Dutch presided over Pernambuco, while simultaneously extending their lands northwards to the mouth of the Amazon.

Having conquered Pernambuco, the Dutch shipped in their leader, Maurice of Nassau, in 1637. Educated at the University of Basil in, among other things, good manners, Nassau was a definite hit with the locals. His policy of freedom of worship, which left Brazil's Catholics to their own devices despite the Protestant invasion, brought a definite stability to the region.

By 1640 the Dutch controlled much of Brazil's *nordeste* (northeast), from Maranhão in the north to the São Francisco river in Bahia. That Brazilians didn't go on to become Dutch speakers is largely down to the exit of Nassau, who returned to Holland in 1644 after a series of disagreements with the boys from the DWIC. Brazil's settlers had hardly wished their ruler a *boa viagem* (good trip) when violent uprisings broke out, designed to uproot the Dutch invaders. The following decade saw bloody clashes across the Brazilian *sertão* (backlands of the Northeast). Two crucial battles, in which the Portuguese came out victorious even though outnumbered, took place in 1648 and 1649. The Dutch were driven back into Recife and eventually surrendered on January 26, 1654, drawing a line under Holland's role in Brazilian history.

The Bandeirantes

The *bandeirantes*, too, were keen to make inroads into Brazil. Bands of explorers that roamed Brazil's interior in search of Indian slaves, they mapped out undiscovered territory, bumping off the odd indigenous community along the way.

Brazil's *bandeirantes* took their name from the trademark flag-bearer who would front their expeditions. During the 17th and 18th centuries, group after group of *bandeirantes* set out from São Paulo. The majority

DID YOU KNOW?

Portuguese is often described as a minority language – in fact it is the fifth-most-spoken tongue in the world.

The website of the Brazilian embassy in London (www.brazil.org .uk) has lots of interesting tidbits about Brazil, including a breakdown of its often-baffling political system.

1763	1792
Rio de Janeiro takes over from Salvador as the capital of Brazil	Tiradentes, the mastermind behind plots to overthrow the Portuguese, is executed in Rio de Janeiro

were bilingual in Portuguese and Tupi-Guarani, born of Portuguese fathers and Indian mothers. They benefited from Indian survival techniques and European weaponry.

By the mid-1600s they had journeyed as far as the peaks of the Peruvian Andes and the Amazon lowlands. Though Brazil's borders had been defined on paper in 1494, it was the exploits of these discoverers that swelled the country's borders to their current size. In 1750, after four years negotiating with the Spanish, their conquests were secured. The Treaty of Madrid was signed, handing over some six million sq km to the Portuguese and putting Brazil's western borders more or less where they are today.

The *bandeirantes* were known for more than just their colorful flags. Protected from Indian arrows by heavily padded cotton jackets, they waged an all-out war on Brazil's natives, despite the fact that many of them had Indian mothers. Huge numbers of Indians fled inland, searching for shelter in the Jesuit missions. But there was no hiding – it is thought the *bandeirantes* killed or enslaved well in excess of 500,000 Indians.

GOLD RUSH

'As yet we have no way of knowing whether there might be gold, or silver or any kind of metal or iron [here],' reported Pero Vaz de Caminha to his king in 1500.

Though it wasn't discovered until nearly two centuries later, there certainly was gold in Brazil. Unsurprisingly it was the *bandeirantes* who, in between decapitating Indians, discovered it.

For part of the 18th century Brazil became the world's greatest gold 'producer', creating a wealth that helped build many of Minas Gerais' historic cities. The full title of Ouro Prêto, one of the principal beneficiaries of the gold boom, is actually Vila Rica de Ouro Prêto (Rich Town of Black Gold).

Other wild boomtowns such as Sabará, Mariana and São João del Rei sprung up in the mountain valleys. Wealthy merchants built opulent mansions and bankrolled the construction of some stunning baroque churches, many of which remain to this day.

When gold was first discovered, there were no White settlers in the territory of Minas Gerais. By 1710 the population was 30,000, and by the end of the 18th century it was 500,000. An estimated one-third of the two million slaves brought to Brazil in the 18th century were sent to the goldfields, where their lives were often worse than in the sugar fields.

The gold boom didn't last. By 1750 the mining regions were in decline, the migration to the interior was ending and coastal Brazil was returning to center stage.

TIRADENTES

As if the French and Dutch hadn't been enough to deal with, the Portuguese also faced a threat from within. During the 18th century calls for independence grew ever stronger and in 1789 the first organized movement came to life.

'As if the French and Dutch hadn't been enough to deal with, the Portuguese also faced a threat from within'

early 1800s	1807
The first coffee bean arrives in Brazil	The Portuguese royal family hide from Napoleon in Rio de Janeiro

In charge was Joaquim José da Silva Xavier – a dentist known as Tiradentes (Tooth Puller), who lived in Ouro Prêto. Joined by 11 other conspirators – all outraged by attempts to collect taxes – Tiradentes began talks about how best to uproot the Portuguese.

Though the plotters earned themselves a grand name – the Inconfidência Mineira – their plans were quickly foiled. All 12 were arrested and sentenced to death and, although a royal pardon was eventually issued exiling the rebels to Angola and Mozambique, it came too late for Tiradentes.

On April 21, 1792 – 292 years after Brazil's discovery, almost to the day – Tiradentes was publicly hanged in Rio de Janeiro. As a warning to other would-be rebels the authorities sliced up his body and displayed the parts across Minas Gerais. His head was put on show in Ouro Prêto, his house destroyed and, curiously, salt scattered on the ground outside, apparently so that nothing would grow there. According to one version of events, soldiers formally recorded the event on a manuscript – using Tiradentes blood as ink.

Tiradentes became a national martyr – a symbol of resistance – and during the Vargas era, a museum in his honor was mounted in Ouro Prêto's Paço Municipal. Tiradentes' house is now a museum (p236).

DOM JOÃO VI

Brazil became a temporary sanctuary to the Portuguese royal family in 1807. Running scared from Napoleon – whose army was at that moment advancing on Lisbon – some 15,000 court members fled to Rio de Janeiro, led by the prince regent, Dom João.

Like so many *estrangeiros* (foreigners) arriving in Brazil, the regent fell in love with the place and granted himself the privilege of becoming the country's ruler. He opened Rio's Jardim Botânico (Botanical Gardens; p126) to the public in 1822, and they remain there to this day in the upmarket Jardim Botânico neighborhood.

Even after Napoleon's defeat at Waterloo in 1815, Dom João showed no sign of abandoning Brazil. When his mother Dona Maria I died the following year, he became king and declared Rio the capital of the United Kingdom of Portugal. Brazil became the only New World colony ever to have a European monarch ruling on its soil.

INDEPENDENCE

Independence eventually came in 1822, 30 years after the Inconfidência Mineira. Legend has it that, on the banks of São Paulo's Ipiranga river, Brazil's then regent, Pedro, pulled out his sword, bellowing, '*Independência ou morte!*' (Independence or death!). With the same breath he declared himself Emperor Dom Pedro I.

The Portuguese quickly gave in to the idea of a Brazilian empire. Without a single shot being fired, Dom Pedro I became the first emperor of an independent Brazil. The *povo brasileiro* (Brazilian people), however, were not as keen on Pedro as he was about their newly born nation. From all accounts he was a blundering incompetent, whose sexual exploits (and resulting string of love children) horrified even the most permissive of Brazilians. After nine years of womanizing he was forced to abdicate, leaving his five-year-old son, Dom Pedro II, to take over.

DID YOU KNOW?

In April 1993 a referendum was held on whether to bring back Brazil's monarchy. Royalty lost out and Brazil remained a federal republic.

1822	1865
Independence declared from Portugal	War with Paraguay in which nearly 100,000 Brazilians, many of them slaves, are killed

A period of crisis followed: the heir to the throne was, after all, just a child. Between 1831 and 1840 Brazil was governed by so-called *regências* (regencies). The period was characterized by political turmoil and widespread rebellion across Brazil. The only solution was the return of the monarchy and a law was passed, declaring Dom Pedro II an adult, well before his 18th birthday.

Aged just 15, Dom Pedro II received the title of Emperor and Perpetual Defender of Brazil, precipitating one of the most prosperous spells in the country's history, barring the war with Paraguay in 1865. Invaded by its neighbor, Brazil teamed up with Argentina and Uruguay and thrashed the Paraguayans back across the border.

Paraguay was left crippled – its population slashed to just 200,000, of whom around 180,000 were women. Brazil, too, suffered heavily: around 100,000 men died, many of them slaves sent to war in the place of wealthier Brazilians.

ABOLITION & THE REPUBLIC

Since the 16th century, slavery had formed the backbone of a brutally unequal society in Brazil. 'Every dimension of our social existence is contaminated,' lamented abolitionist Joaquim Nabuco in 1880.

To undo something so deeply ingrained into the Brazilian way of life was never likely to be easy. Brazil prevaricated for nearly 60 years before any sort of resolution was reached. The 19th century was punctuated by a series of halfhearted legislative attempts to lay the slave industry to rest. Repeatedly such laws failed.

One law, passed in 1885, freed all slaves over the age of 65. The lawmakers had obviously forgotten that the average life expectancy for a slave at this time was 45. Not until May 13, 1888 – 80 years after Britain had freed its slaves – was slavery in Brazil officially banned.

Not far out of the door behind slavery was the Império Brasileiro. In 1889 a military coup, supported by Brazil's wealthy coffee farmers, decapitated the old Brazilian empire and the republic was born. The emperor went into exile where he died a couple of years later.

A military clique ruled Brazil for the next four years until elections were held, but because of ignorance, corruption and land and literacy requirements, only about 2% of the adult population voted. Little changed, except that the power of the military and the now-influential coffee growers increased, while it diminished for the sugar barons.

FULL OF BEANS

The first coffee bean found its way into Brazil in the early 1800s. The responsible party was, they say, an army officer called Francisco de Mello Palheta who had journeyed to French Guiana in order to settle a border dispute and came back brandishing a handful of coffee beans – a gift from a lover he had left behind. On arrival back in Brazil, the beans were swiftly planted, thus beginning another Brazilian love affair – with *café*.

Whatever the truth, the coffee industry was a huge success. By 1889 coffee accounted for two-thirds of Brazil's exports.

Coffee growers filled the gap left in Brazil's export market by the decline of its sugar industry. Unable to compete with the newly mech-

1888	**1889**
Princesa Isabel signs the Lei Aurea, officially abolishing slavery	Republic declared

anized sugar mills in the West Indies, sugar exports plummeted. Coffee, meanwhile, flourished, and coffee plantations soon took up vast tracts of land in São Paulo and Minas Gerais.

Although coffee was the making of many millionaires in the southern states, it was also the cause of great suffering. The coffee *fazendas* (ranches) in many ways replicated the northeastern sugar plantations; slaves worked inhuman hours in cramped and fetid conditions. In Rio many such estates have now opened their doors to the public, and provide a chilling insight into Brazilian *escravidão* (slavery). After abolition in 1888, the workforce changed, but the conditions did not.

BORDER CROSSING

In the final decade of the 19th century, Brazil opened its borders. Some 800,000 European immigrants – mostly Italians – streamed into Brazil to work on the coffee *fazendas*.

PRINCESA ISABEL – LIBERATOR OF SLAVES

Princesa Isabel's parents didn't leave much space on their daughter's birth certificate. Born at the Palácio de São Cristóvão to Pedro II and Teresina Cristina on July 29, 1846, she found herself the proud owner of no less than 10 names. Isabel Cristina Leopoldina Augusta Micaela Gabriela Rafaela Gonzaga de Bragança e Bourbon. Fortunately for those of us without the lung capacity of an elephant, she became known by a far more memorable title: the liberator of slaves.

For over 300 years Brazilian society had been defined by the slave trade. Keen to cover their tracks, slave traders destroyed many documents relating to their line of work. But it is believed that around 3.6 million slaves were shipped from Africa to Brazil between 1550 and 1888, used as free labor for the sugar (and, later, coffee) plantations.

The first real steps toward abolition came in 1826 when the English, having themselves banned slavery in 1807, forced Brazil to outlaw slave trafficking. Yet over the following decades the numbers of slaves entering Brazil only rose. A series of equally ineffective laws proceeded, of which – as is so often the case in Brazil – not a single one 'pegou' (caught on).

On May 13, 1888, after nearly 80 years of prevarication and crossed words with the pro-abolition English, Isabel put pen to paper on the document that would define her life – the Lei Aurea. The document contained less than 200 words but its implications were huge. 'Slavery,' it pointed out, 'is now extinct in Brazil.'

Increasingly, however, historians look at her actions with cynicism. Abolition eradicated an unquestionable evil from Brazilian society, yet in many ways it posed more questions than it answered. What, for example, would Brazil's 800,000 freed slaves, largely illiterate, unskilled and unemployed, now do to support themselves?

Isabel seems not to have anticipated this particular question. Thousands of ex-slaves were cast out onto the streets without any kind of infrastructure to support them. Many died, while others flooded to Brazil's urban centers, adding to the city's first *favelas*.

Rio's world-famous Mangueira samba school marked the centenary year of the Lei Aurea with a scathing critique of the law, entitled, '100 years of freedom, reality or illusion?' 'Could it be that the Lei Aurea so dreamt about, signed so long ago, was not the end of slavery?' it asked.

A visit to the impoverished Mangueira *favela* in Rio's North Zone, in which many of the inhabitants are paid miserable wages to work as porters and maids for the city's better off, shows the answer is a very definite yes. As the samba points out, Princesa Isabel freed Brazil's Blacks from 'the whips of the *senzala*' but left them stranded 'in the misery of the *favela*.'

1890s	1894
Brazil opens its borders and immigrants come flooding in	Prudente de Morais becomes Brazil's first directly elected civil president

Not long after, millions more immigrants began arriving at the ports in Rio and São Paulo. They hailed from Japan, Germany, Spain and Portugal and added further racial textures to an increasingly mixed Brazil. When you tuck into a pizza in São Paulo's Bela Vista district or sample a *pastel chinês* (Chinese pastry) at one of Rio de Janeiro's many street-corner snack bars, it is more than likely to be this generation of border hoppers you have to thank.

Over the next century, immigrants continued to flood into Brazil. The country became a haven for Jews fleeing persecution at the hands of the Nazis, as well as Nazis looking to avoid being put on trial for war crimes. Arabs, universally known as *turcos* by the Brazilians, also joined the influx of newcomers. Many of the traders you'll meet at Rio de Janeiro's Rua Uruguaiana flea market hail from the Middle East.

DID YOU KNOW?

US secret services cast a suspicious eye on Foz do Iguaçu after the 9/11 terrorists attacks. The area is home to one of Brazil's largest Muslim communities.

RUBBER

Toward the end of the 19th century the Amazon region was the scene of another Brazilian economic boom: that of the *hevea brasiliensis* (rubber tree).

Demand for rubber rocketed in 1890 and its price shot up, bringing huge wealth to the main Amazonian cities of Belém and Manaus. Manaus' spectacular opera house, the Teatro Amazonas (p623), opened in 1896, was one fruit of the rubber boom. Rubber production reached its peak in 1912, when latex exports made up nearly 40% of Brazil's export revenue.

As with all booms, the bust had to come. In football the English might have given Brazil one of its greatest gifts, but the British stole too one of Brazil's greatest assets. In 1876 rubber-tree seeds had been smuggled out of Amazonia to Kew Gardens in London. The seeds quickly found their way to the British colonies in Southeast Asia, where large rubber plantations were established. When the plantations started to yield in 1910, the price of latex plummeted on the world market. The bottom fell out of the Brazilian rubber boom in spectacular fashion.

MILK & COFFEE POLITICS

On November 15, 1894 Prudente de Morais became Brazil's first directly elected civil president. At this time Brazil was dominated by land-owning families from two states: Minas Gerais and São Paulo. These groups controlled national politics and Brazil's presidents came almost without exception from these states of milk and coffee respectively. Each state was dominated by a series of *coronels* (rural landowners who typically controlled the local political, judicial and police systems), and the public cargos were divided between his friends and family.

Such political bias was reflected in the electoral system. The ballot was not secret and those who voted against the ruling powers suffered reprisals. Fraud was common: many people would vote more than once and, from time to time, even the dead found the power to vote.

Disillusioned with the dominance of this wealthy few, a new movement made up of members of the military, known as *tenentismo*, began to form in opposition to the small oligarchies of Minas and São Paulo.

The world-famous Copacabana beach was host for the first rebellion. On July 5, 1922 18 tenants set out from the fort of Copacabana (p127)

1897	1922
First *favela* founded in Rio by soldiers returning from the Battle of Canudos	Members of the *tenentismo* movement rebel against the landowning elite at Copacabana beach

and clashed with government troops. Just two of the tenants – Eduardo Gomes and Siqueira Campos – survived, the latter giving his name to the metro station a few blocks from the beach.

For another eight years Brazil's coffee farmers enjoyed the status of political untouchables. The Wall St bust of 1929 was to change all this. The coffee market all but dried up, prices plummeted and many of Brazil's powerful coffee farmers were left ruined. Such economic and political upheaval would translate into revolution the following year.

THE FATHER OF BRAZIL

On the morning of August 24, 1954 Getúlio Vargas woke up in the bedroom of the Palácio do Catete for the last time. 'I leave this life to enter into history,' he had written the previous night amid calls from the military for his resignation. Shortly after 4:30am Vargas' body was found with a single bullet wound to the heart.

The Vargas era began in 1930 when members of the newly formed Liberal Alliance party decided to contest Vargas' defeat in the presidential elections. The revolution kicked off on October 3 in Rio Grande do Sul and spread rapidly throughout other states. Twenty one days later the president Júlio Prestes was deposed and on November 3 Getúlio Dorneles Vargas became the new 'provisional' president of the Republic.

With the formation of the Estado Novo (New State) in November 1937, Vargas became the first Brazilian president to wield absolute power. Using the notorious Departamento de Imprensa e Propaganda (Department of Press and Publicity, or DIP as it was known), his regime censored artists, imprisoned dissidents and even destroyed the newsroom of one unlucky São Paulo broadsheet.

Despite this, many liked Vargas. The 'father' of Brazil's workers, he created Brazil's minimum wage in 1938. Each year he introduced new labor laws to coincide with Workers' Day on May 1, to sweeten the teeth of Brazil's *operários* (factory workers).

But Vargas didn't earn the title of dictator for nothing. His regime was inspired by the fascist governments of Salazar in Portugal and Mussolini in Italy. He banned political parties, imprisoned political opponents and heavily censored the press.

Like any fascist worth his salt, Vargas began WWII sided with Hitler's Third Reich. Mysteriously, an offer of US investment to the sum of US$20 million in 1942 led Vargas to switch allegiances. The National War Memorial in Flamengo – a huge concrete monument and museum, which represents a pair of hands begging the skies for peace – today pays testament to the 5000 Brazilians who served in Italy.

Vargas, of course, wasn't exactly practicing what he preached. The glaring contradiction of someone fighting for democracy in Europe and maintaining a quasi-fascist state back home soon became impossible. The military forced him to step down.

Yet he remained popular and in 1951 was elected president – this time democratically. Vargas' new administration was plagued by the hallmark of Brazilian politics – corruption. For this, a young journalist called Carlos Lacerda attacked him incessantly. In 1954 Vargas' security chief organized an attempt to assassinate Lacerda. At the crack of dawn on

DID YOU KNOW?

Brazilians are allowed to vote in elections at 16, though voting only becomes compulsory at the age of 18.

DID YOU KNOW?

Vargas' blood-stained pajamas are now on permanent exhibition in the very room where he took his own life at the Museu da República (p134).

1937	1942
Estado Novo (New State) declared by Getúlio Vargas	Brazil switches sides in WWII after an offer of US$20 million US investment

Brazil's definitive road movie, Walter Salles' *Central Station*, examines the issue of north–south immigration through the story of a young orphan searching for his father in the impoverished Northeast.

August 5, two gunmen greeted Lacerda at his home on Rua Toneleros in Copacabana. The troublesome hack was only slightly wounded but an air force major was killed, precipitating a huge scandal. The president responded dramatically, as author Rubem Fonseca recalled in his novel *Agosto* (August; Companhia das Letras, 1990).

> [Vargas] would do what had to be done… A euphoric sense of pride and dignity filled him… He picked up the revolver from the chest of drawers and lay down on the bed. He placed the barrel of the revolver against the left side of his chest and pulled the trigger.

The Vargas era was now very much part of Brazilian history.

HEY BIG SPENDER!

Juscelino Kubitschek de Oliveira, whose tongue twister of a name swiftly earned him the *apelido* (nickname) JK, was elected president in 1956. 'Fifty years in five,' had been his election promise. His critics responded with, 'Forty years' inflation in four.' Sadly for JK, the second assessment came closer to the mark, despite an 80% increase in industrial production during his term.

Kubitschek's lasting legacy was Brasília, Brazil's love-it-or-hate-it capital, located slap bang in the center of the country as a symbol of national unity. Though the construction of such a city was written into the 1891 constitution, it was Kubitschek who, quite literally, made the idea concrete. The windswept, shadeless streets of Brasília were inaugurated with much fanfare on April 21, 1960.

As if Kubitschek hadn't made enough enemies by taking the honor of capital city from the 'Marvelous City' of Rio de Janeiro, his successor, Janio Quadros, went one step further. He tried to outlaw bikinis on the Brazilian beaches, a serious affront to Brazilian popular culture, as a quick visit to any of the country's beaches will tell you.

Bye-Bye Brasil, directed by Cacá Diegues, is a classic in Brazilian cinema. The film follows a traveling circus across Brazil's Northeast, charting the profound changes in Brazilian society that characterized the second half of last century.

Quadros then made the fatal mistake of irritating the military. After six months in office he decorated Che Guevara in a public ceremony in Brasília, triggering plots among the right-wing military. A few days later he resigned, claiming 'occult forces' were at work.

The vice president, a lefty by the name of João Goulart, took power. Though Goulart didn't demonstrate an overt aversion to *fio dental* (dental floss bikinis), the military wasn't keen on him either. In 1964 he was overthrown in a so-called *revolução* (revolution) – really a military coup, believed to have received backing from the US government. Certainly, then-president Lyndon Johnson did nothing to dampen such theories when he cabled the new Brazilian administration, offering it the best of luck.

BYE-BYE BRAZIL

Brazil's military regime was not as brutal as those of Chile or Argentina – a reality that led to the somewhat unkind saying, 'Brazil couldn't even organize a dictatorship properly.'

Yet for the best part of 20 years, freedom of speech became an unknown concept and political parties were banned. The Lei de Segurança

1954	1960
President Getúlio Vargas shoots himself through the heart at his Rio palace	Brazil's new capital, Brasília, is inaugurated

Nacional (national security law) of 1967 tightened the noose on political dissidents, who were often tortured, murdered or – perhaps worse – thrown into Brazilian jail.

The dictatorship coincided with one of the most culturally rich periods in Brazilian history. A generation of composers and academics were exiled for their opposition to the regime – among them musician Gilberto Gil (who later became Lula's culture minister) and Fernando Henrique Cardoso (who would go on to become president).

A draconian censorship law known as the Ato Institutional 5 (AI-5) marked the height of repression in 1968. In response, Brazil's middle-class student movement came to life. In June 1968 the streets of Rio de Janeiro hosted a mass demonstration, known as the Passeata dos cem mil (March of the 100,000), against the dictatorship.

Perversely during a time of such repression, the Brazilian economy flourished. Year after year in the late 1960s and early 1970s, the economy grew by over 10%, as Brazil's rulers borrowed heavily from international banks.

Brazil's obsession with 'mega-projects' was born. Under the quick-spending regime, construction began on numerous colossal (and mostly ill-fated) plans, including the Transamazônica highway, the Rio–Niteroi Bridge and the Ilha do Fundão, which was to house Rio's Federal University.

FOUNDATION OF THE PT (WORKERS' PARTY) – 1980

By the late 1970s, opposition to the regime began to spread from the educated middle classes to the working class.

A series of strikes in the São Paulo car industry signaled the intent of the militant new workers' movement. At the helm was one Luíz Inácio 'Lula' da Silva, who would become Brazil's first working-class president. Lula, who famously lost one *dedo* (finger) in a factory accident, made up in charisma what he lacked in the finger department.

Brazil's Partido dos Trabalhadores (PT; Workers' Party) grew out of these strikes. Its membership was very inclusive; alongside the grass-roots metal workers who formed the *petista* (PT) base were some of Brazil's leading left-wing academics, among them literary critic Antônio Cândido and historian Sérgio Buarque de Hollanda, whose book *Raízes do Brasil* (The Roots of Brasil) remains a defining work in Brazilian scholarship.

In January 1980 the party's first manifesto declared the need to 'build an egalitarian society, where there are neither exploited nor exploiters.' Twenty two years on, with a PT president and 10 other senators installed in Brasília, they discovered how difficult it was to put such ideals into practice.

First came the *abertura* (opening), a period of slow and cautious return to civilian rule that took place between 1979 and 1985. With the economic miracle petering out and popular opposition gathering force, the military announced gradual moves back toward a democratic Brazil. Political prisoners and exiles were granted amnesty. Six new political parties – of which the PT was one – emerged.

The tail end of this *abertura* was marked by the *direitas já* (elections now) movement, which called for immediate and direct presidential elections. The aptly named thinker of Brazilian football, Socrates, showed

DID YOU KNOW?

'Girl from Ipanema' has been covered more than 200 times, including by both Nat King Cole and Louis Armstrong.

Politics Transformed: Lula and the Workers' Party in Brazil by Sue Branford and Bernardo Kucinski, published shortly after Lula's historic election in 2002, is a comprehensive if partisan look at the rise of the Partido dos Trabalhadores.

1962	1964
First public performance of Tom Jobim's much-hummed 'Girl from Ipanema'	An apparently US-backed coup ushers in nearly 20 years of dictatorship

that even Brazil's footballers – known more for their quick feet than political engagement – had something to say. Removing his shirt at the end of a game, it was not one of the usual evangelical elegies printed on his back but a message urging Brazilians to vote in the coming elections.

The haunting story of a street child turned murderer, Hector Babenco's *Pixote* takes us on a grim trawl through 1980s São Paulo. The leading actor, himself from a poor background, was famously killed by police in 1990.

DEMOCRACY RETURNS

In 1985 direct presidential elections were duly held for the first time in over 20 years. When the less-favored Tancredo Neves, opposing the military candidate, came out on top, millions of Brazilians took to the streets to celebrate the end of military rule.

Immediately a spanner was thrown in the works: Neves died from heart failure before he could assume the presidency. His vice-presidential candidate – the whiskered José Sarney, a figure in Brazilian politics to this day – took over.

Sarney – a supporter of the military until 1984 – held office until 1989, a period in which runaway inflation helped Brazil rack up a gargantuan foreign debt. His catchphrase, *'tem que dar certo'* (it has to work out), proved a tragic foresight into his doomed stint as president. Virtually nothing did.

By 1990 the external debt stood at a crippling US$115 billion, a reality that blights Brazil to this day. Though Sarney was unable to harness Brazil's economy, he did implement one crucial law: Brazil's illiterate, previously excluded from the political system, were at last permitted to vote.

Yet economic crisis overshadowed anything else Sarney might have achieved. During his four years in power, Brazil switched currency twice – from the cruzado, to the originally named replacement novo cruzado. Inflation only continued to rise.

THE RED COMMAND

Brazil's most notorious drug faction, the Comando Vermelho (Red Command), was conceived in paradise – more precisely in the Cândido Mendes Penal Institute, an infamous prison on the island retreat of Ilha Grande.

Little is left of Cândido Mendes, save its crumbling perimeter wall and a wealth of stories recounting scenes of torture and failed breakouts. The jail yard is grassed over and the cells, once home to 600 prisoners, have long since been demolished in an attempt to erase the prison's grisly past. A lonely quartet of watchtowers, long abandoned by prison guards, is now overgrown with grass.

The local village, Dois Rios, is a sleepy clutch of dusty streets, flanked by lush rain forest on one side and tropical sands on the other. Its population is almost entirely made up of former prison workers and their families. Many eke out an existence selling cheap lunches to foreign visitors; others have turned to *cachaça* (sugarcane spirit) since Cândido Mendes closed in 1994.

That some of Dois Rios' inhabitants have hit the bottle is hardly surprising given what they have witnessed. It was here, in 1979, that the Comando Vermelho was officially born, at the tail end of a spell of brutal political repression that saw left-wing dissidents thrown into jail with common criminals by Brazil's dictatorship. This mix of political radicals and dangerous criminals – an explosive partnership of brainpower and muscle – laid the foundations of the 'CV'.

Regular prisoners, influenced by revolutionary literature brought into the jail by political prisoners, dreamed up the CV in the late 1970s. Its very name – the Red Command – hints at its communist roots. But the organization was never a political one. Designed to dominate the prison

---

1980	1985
Foundation of Brazil's Workers' Party (PT)	Tancredo Neves becomes president in the first direct elections since 1964; he dies before taking power

In the 1989 elections it was a martial arts champion by the name of Collor who was victorious, beating current president Lula by the smallest of margins.

Lula had looked set to take power, before the *Globo* media empire – owned by the now-late Roberto Marinho (see p44) – intervened. It would be another 13 years before Lula was elected.

I KILLED THE PRESIDENT

The charismatic Fernando Collor de Mello, a former Brazilian karate champion with a penchant for expensive jet-skis, was different from his predecessor in every way. Hailing from the small northern state of Alagoas, where he had been governor, he ended the political dominance of São Paulo and Minas Gerais.

Collor revolutionized consumer laws – when you see a 'best before' date on a tub of Brazilian margarine, it's him you have to thank. 'Sell by' dates, however, couldn't save him from disgrace. Three years into his term, he was accused of heading a gang that had siphoned a reputed US$2 billion from Brazilian savings accounts.

The response was one of outrage. Brazil's student movement, almost invisible since the 1970s, angrily took to the streets. Rapper Gabriel O Pensador – by coincidence the son of one of Collor's media advisors – was among the most vocal critics. His controversial track, 'I'm happy (I killed the President),' went further than most, but in many ways captured the public mood. 'He won the election and forgot the people/and one thing I don't allow is betrayal,' rapped Gabriel, before describing a kick-about at the president's funeral – in which Collor's head is used as the ball.

Alex Bellos' *Futebol: the Brazilian Way of Life*, a fascinating and accessible book, uses football as its starting point to explore many of the political, social and, of course, sporting issues that make Brazil tick.

---

and protect its members, the CV's influence quickly spread through Rio's jails. During the 1980s it expanded dramatically, seizing control of much of the city's cocaine trade and installing itself in the *favelas* for which Rio's urban landscape is known. These days, CV politics go little further than the occasional handout in the communities where it operates.

The CV's birthplace may have been reduced to a heap of rubble in April 1994, but its inheritance lives on in Rio's slums. Twenty five years on from its foundation, the CV, which now divides the city's drug trade with two rival gangs, is thought to have well in excess of 2000 people in its ranks; from the teenage drug lords, who rise to power early and die almost as young, to the preadolescent *aviões* (airplanes), who act as drug runners in and around Rio's 600 *favelas*.

The presence of such gangs makes many such communities, particularly in Rio's Zona Norte, no-go areas to outsiders – in these, state control is virtually nonexistent. Despite occasional police operations, with titles such as 'Maximum Pressure' that drastically overstate their effectiveness, the CV and its rivals grow stronger by the day. Increasingly sophisticated and deadly weapons, such as the stash of land mines uncovered in the Favela de Coréia in 2004, continue to pour into the CV's armory.

A brand name of illicit activity, the CV is tricky to avoid in Rio: celebrated by rappers at many of Rio's funk raves; tattooed onto the bodies or shaved into the heads of its members; splashed across the newspapers on a daily basis. Much of the slang now used in Brazil's *favelas* has roots in the country's prison system, dominated, too, by the Red Command. Its slogan, '*Paz, Justiça e Liberdade*' (Peace, Justice and Freedom), can be seen scribbled on bus seats and concrete walls from Ipanema to Irajá.

1990	1994
Brazil's external debt hits a whopping US$115 billion	President Collor is impeached, accused of robbing US$2 billion from Brazilian bank accounts

Death in Brazil by Peter Robb is a recent novel based loosely around the impeachment of President Collor. The author mixes politics, bloodshed and the obligatory dose of gastronomic journalism in his colorful portrait of today's Brazil.

The kung fu king was eventually impeached. But – as is all too often the case with Brazil's white-collar criminals – 'Fernandinho' managed to wriggle out of a prison sentence, receiving little more than an eight-year ban from politics. Found not guilty of 'passive corruption' by the Supreme Court in 1994, he skedaddled to Miami. Ten years on he is attempting – somewhat improbably – a return to Brazilian politics.

TRAVELING HENRIQUE CARDOSO

Following Collor's impeachment, Vice President Itamar Franco found himself in the hot seat. Despite his reputation as an eccentric, his administration was at least credited with competency and integrity, rare commodities in Brazilian politics.

His greatest achievement was to stabilize Brazil's notoriously erratic economy, introducing yet another new currency, the real. The Plano Real produced a brief economic boom, during which the real was momentarily pegged to the US dollar. The honeymoon didn't last long: a decade on, tourists visiting Brazil enjoy an exchange rate of around three reais to the dollar or five to the pound sterling.

Lula was again a favorite for the 1994 election (the second in which the ex-shoe shine boy had run). Yet the Workers' Party bubble was burst at the last minute as Franco's finance minister – buoyed by the success of his Plano Real – rode in on a landslide victory.

Fernando Henrique Cardoso, known to the media as FHC and the people as Fernando Henrique, was a former left-wing sociologist from

THE BRAZILIAN CITIZEN KANE

Media tycoon Roberto Marinho liked to be known as a journalist. In fact he was one of Latin America's richest and most powerful men – a South American Rupert Murdoch whose influence on 20th-century Brazil eclipsed even his staggering US$2 billion personal fortune.

Born to two Rio hacks in 1904, Marinho almost single-handedly built the *Globo* media empire that now dominates the country. At 26 he became the editor of his late father's *Globo* newspaper and by 1957 he presided over a radio station and TV network.

Marinho died from a heart attack on August 6, 2003, aged 98, drawing the curtain on a lifetime of mammoth political influence and frequent controversy. He was a wily businessman, who went from dictator-cuddler to left-wing Lula supporter, depending on the political and financial gains involved. Marinho's *Globo* empire now boasts a massive 75% share of the advertising market, while *TV Globo* is the world's fourth-largest TV network in terms of viewing figures.

Following Marinho's death, President Lula declared three days' national mourning, lamenting how the country had 'lost a man who spent his life believing in Brazil.'

Marinho didn't always have such faith in Lula. Although *Globo* supported Lula in his 2002 campaign, for years it had rallied against the Workers' Party leader. In 1989 *TV Globo* allegedly sabotaged Lula's presidential campaign by editing a pre-election debate to favor his opponent, Collor.

Marinho's detractors are not hard to come across. A BBC documentary, *Beyond Citizen Kane*, which compared the Brazilian media mogul to Orson Welles' character, has slipped into media folklore and was banned in Brazil in 1993.

Yet his influence on Brazilian popular culture is, for better or worse, irrefutable. The soap operas, for which he was best known, have been known to pull in audiences upwards of 90% of the Brazilian population, and are watched as far afield as Russia and China.

1994	2000
Rio de Janeiro's *favelas* appear on city maps for the first time	Five-hundredth anniversary of Brazil's discovery

the University of São Paulo. His 1969 book *Dependency and Development in Latin America* remains one of the most important works of South American sociology. Although Cardoso spent time in exile during the 1964 dictatorship, as president he was far less radical. 'Forget everything I have said and written,' he said on taking power.

Brazil's economy enjoyed a period of growth during the mid-1990s; the currency remained stable, inflation low and foreign investment hit new heights. Frequent trips abroad to rub shoulders with the likes of Tony Blair and Bill Clinton earned him a third nickname – Viajando (Traveling) Henrique Cardoso.

Cardoso served two terms as president, in which poverty levels began to fall but the day-to-day life of the average *favelado* (slum dweller) improved very little. Attendance levels in Brazil's schools rose – standards did not. When Cardoso left office to enter into a lucrative career as an international statesman, he left behind a critically ill Brazil.

José Padilla's startling documentary *Bus 174* looks at the hijacking of a Rio bus in 2000. Examining the hijacker's past as a survivor of the 1993 massacre of eight street kids in Central Rio, it raises uncomfortable questions about today's Brazil.

LULA & THE LEFT

This was all supposed to change. At the fourth time of asking, Luíz Inácio 'Lula' da Silva was elected by a wave of public support in 2002 – this time with the backing of media giant *Globo*.

But Brazil's enormous problems were never going to be solved in a year – not even by Lula. 'Even Pelé's Santos team got beaten sometimes,' commented one politician in 2004 after an embarrassing defeat for the president in congress over the minimum wage.

The PT's first manifesto talked of bringing a 'new form of democracy' to Brazil, which favored the 'majority of society.' Twenty five years on, Brazilian society – in which the richest 1% earns more than the poorest 50% put together – is still run very much by and for the minority.

2002	2002
Brazil wins its fifth football World Cup to become the world's only *pentacampeão* (five-time champion)	Historic election of Lula, Brazil's first working-class president

The Culture

THE NATIONAL PSYCHE

Sometimes stereotyped as the world's most joyful people, Brazilians are known for lively celebrations (Carnaval is but one manifestation), which generally become more animated the further north you go. This joie de vivre can be seen in football matches, on the beaches, in the samba clubs and on the streets. The flip side of this personality trait is *saudade*, that woeful manifestation of homesickness, longing or deep regret, given much play on old bossa nova records.

In a land of such stark contrasts, the Brazilians themselves exhibit some deep contradictions. A landscape that is universally praised (beaches, mountains and forest) receives incredible destruction (of the Amazon) – and indifference – from its citizens; Brazilian racial harmony is a widely accepted ideal, yet Blacks are egregiously underrepresented in the government and suffer the lion's share of poverty; Carnaval is a time of wild freedom, while sexual repressiveness lurks the rest of the year.

Perhaps owing to the incredible diversity of the population, it's possible to find Brazilians who profess to be Catholics while also attending a Candomblé ceremony (p52) from time to time, who believe in science and market economies while also nurturing beliefs in mystics and fatalism.

Contradictions are most severe in the social-class system, where you can find dirt-poor and filthy-rich living in close proximity, often separated by nothing more than a highway. It's not surprising then that violence is such a prevalent facet of Brazilian society. Nearly every Carioca (Rio resident) and Paulistano (São Paulo city resident) has a horror story of getting mugged. The response is often one of resignation, and 'What can be done?'.

Indeed, there is much resignation in the national character. Some suggest this is a holdover from the government dictatorship that ruled over people's lives for 20 years, creating a docile public. But Brazilians have been a nonconfrontational people since the beginning of the Republic. It was the only country in Latin America to gain its independence without spilling a drop of blood, and slavery ended in 1888 (the last in the Americas) without battles or violent showdowns.

In a country noted for its bureaucracy (the legacy of the military dictatorship of 1964–84), Brazilians have to put up with serious inefficiencies. This has led to some rather creative solutions to one's problems. There's the official way of doing things, and then there's the *jeitinho*, that characteristically Brazilian way around it. A few friends, and a bit of good humor can go a long way.

LIFESTYLE

It's hard to imagine a population living in such polar extremes. At one end are people living in squalid third-world conditions, struggling to get enough to eat. At the other end is the upper class with a lifestyle that few in the US and Western Europe enjoy.

The *favelas* (slums or shantytowns) first appeared during the mass urban immigration in the mid-19th century, and today they surround every major city. Infrastructure varies, but typically *favelados* (slum dwellers) live in shacks tightly crammed together with no access to clean water or health care. The *favelas* are often 'governed' by drug lords and their gangs, who are frequently the communities' only benefactors. They

MEETING CARIOCAS

One kiss on each cheek for ladies (start to the left – her right); a handshake between gents. The same holds true when bidding good-bye.

often try to paint themselves as 'Robin Hood' types, complete with pithy slogans about peace and justice. Dangers to residents come when rival gangs move in. *Bolas perdidas* (stray bullets) pass easily through the thin walls and the body counts grow high during violent confrontations.

In the countryside, conditions for the lower class can be even worse. Unequal land distribution dating back to the colonial era means that thousands of homeless rural families are left to squat on vacant land or

---

RESPONSIBLE TRAVEL *Thomas Kohnstamm*

Most people travel to get away from their normal responsibilities and to take some time to live on their own terms. But anyone who has a clue will realize that they have an impact everywhere they go. Therefore you develop new and different responsibilities while traveling: it is your responsibility to make sure that your impact is a positive one and that you are not contributing to the corruption or degradation of the place that you visit. This phenomenon exists on an environmental level and also on a cultural and economic level – however, all of these issues are intertwined.

Throughout this book we recommend ecotourism operations (businesses that help preserve the environment and support the local community through tourism) and community tourism projects (projects created and controlled – at least partially – by the communities that are visited rather than outside businesses). Community-managed tourism is particularly important when visiting indigenous communities in the Amazon, who are often exploited as tourist attractions by opportunistic agencies that do not return profits into the communities.

Here are some tips on how to be a pro traveler:

- **Don't litter – ever** Obey absolutes in this situation and don't litter just because you see a local do it. It is still wrong.

- **Hire responsible guides** When you hire a guide, try to find a local one. Also find out if they have a good reputation and work in a way that is respectful both to local people and the environment.

- **Don't shell out cash for coral** Never buy products made from endangered plants or animals. In Brazil you will see numerous souvenirs made from coral, turtle shell, rare bird feathers, alligator skin and bits of jaguar skin. Don't be a sucker and fall for the story about how the jaguar was only slain in revenge for killing a baby in the Amazon. Remember that these products are only sold because there is tourist demand for them.

- **Spend at the source** Try to buy arts and crafts directly from the artist or artisan rather than giving most of your money to some guy simply because he has a storefront.

- **Ask before taking photos** This applies to indigenous peoples in the Amazon, who may not feel comfortable being photographed or filmed.

- **Learn the language** OK, that may be a lot to ask, but even basic Portuguese greetings and pleasantries can go a long way to show respect and make sure that you are well received. You would expect the same of people who visit English-speaking countries, no?

- **Support the local community** Try to seek out community-based services that keep dollars local. Ask where your operator is based and where the money ends up.

- **Steer clear of sexual tourism** It is hard not to notice prostitution in Brazil's larger cities. The sexual-tourism boom, fueled by the temptation to earn fast tourist money, is causing deep changes to Brazilian culture and setting a lot of women up for a big fall.

- **Pay your porter, tip your guide** Porters, guides, cooks, hotel staff etc are often horribly underpaid. A direct tip can make a big difference.

- **Respect local traditions** Dress appropriately if visiting places of cultural or religious importance and go easy with your camera. Think about how you would want a visitor to be respectful if visiting an important ceremony in your culture.

work as itinerant laborers. When the harvest time arrives they vie for work spots, which usually pay subsurvival wages for long hours. The families live in shacks or tent camps with few possessions, and every family member pitches in with the work. In addition to the hunger, infant mortality, disease and poverty, they face other dangers: they may be expelled from the land (or in rare cases murdered by gunmen who are hired by landowners in an attempt to rid themselves of the most outspoken squatters on their lands).

Middle- and upper-class Brazilians live in comfortable apartments or houses, with all the trappings of the first world. The wealthiest send their children abroad for university. Maids are common – even among middle-class Brazilians – and some families have chauffeurs, cooks and private bodyguards.

There are a few points where the lives of rich and poor intersect. One is on the beach, which is the social stomping ground of both the *favelado* and the urbanite. The other is Carnaval. In Salvador and in other cities of the Northeast, everyone generally comes together for the lively street parties. In Rio, the action is a bit more segregated, but in general it's one time where the most mixing occurs – particularly since it's the *favelados* putting on the Carnaval.

No matter what the economic class, the family and one's community both play an essential role in Brazilian life.

DID YOU KNOW?

The 1979–83 droughts in the Northeast were among the worst the country ever experienced, leaving between 250,000 and one million people dead.

POPULATION

DID YOU KNOW?

Greater São Paulo had 2.2 million residents in 1950 compared to 17 million today.

Brazil is the world's fifth-most populous country (with 184 million residents), but it also has one of the smallest population densities, with 20 people per square kilometer (the US has 28 people per square kilometer). Most of Brazil's population lives along the coast. The South and the Southeast are the most densely populated areas, home to 75% of the country's inhabitants. Until the mid-20th century, Brazil was largely a rural country – today, it's more than 70% urban. The populations in cities have grown enormously in the last half-century, yet overall, the population is growing less than it did in the past.

In the Northeast is the highest concentration of Afro-Brazilians, with Salvador as its cultural capital. In the Amazon live Caboclos (literally 'copper-colored'), the mixed descendents of indigenous peoples and the Portuguese. In the South is the most European of the Brazilian population, descendents of Italian and German immigrants. Overall the population is 55% White, 6% Black, 38% mixed and 1% other (including Japanese, Arabs and indigenous groups).

MOTELS

Motels are a Brazilian institution and must never be confused with hotels. They have names like Alibi, Ilha do Capri, Sinless, L'Amour and Wet Dreams. Rented by the hour, the motel room is Brazil's solution to the lack of privacy caused by overcrowded living conditions. Used by adults who still live with their parents, kids who want to get away from their parents and parents who want to get away from their kids, they are an integral part of the nation's social fabric, and are treated by Brazilians with what most outsiders consider to be nonchalance.

The quality of motels varies, reflecting their popularity across social classes. Most are away from the city center, with walled-in garages for anonymity. Rooms have circular vibra-beds with mirrors overhead, adult movies and room service with a menu full of foods and sometimes sex toys (with instructions).

If you're having trouble finding accommodations, they're not too expensive.

The indigenous population today is around 350,000, composing 200 tribes – a fraction of the estimated two to six million here at the European arrival. Customs and beliefs vary widely from tribe to tribe – as do the strengths of these traditions in the face of expulsion from traditional lands, declining numbers, missionary activity and other influences. Brazil's largest groups of Indian peoples include the Tikuna on the upper Rio Solimões (numbering 20,000 or more), the Yanomami in northwestern Amazonia (over 11,000), and the 30,000 or so Guarani in the Central West and South.

After centuries of genocidal attacks, slavery, dispossession and death from imported diseases, Brazil's Indian population is now finally growing again, but still faces a host of problems. Most Indians live in the Amazon rain forest and the threats that the rain forest faces – logging, mining, ranching, farming, roads, settlements, dams, hydroelectric schemes – also threaten the Indians whose way of life depends on it.

Tristes Tropiques, by Claude Lévi-Strauss, is both a well-written travelogue and one of the most important anthropological studies of some of Brazil's indigenous peoples.

MULTICULTURALISM

The Brazilian identity has been shaped not only by the Portuguese, who provided its language and main religion, but also by native Indians, Africans and the many immigrants over the years from Europe, the Middle East and Asia.

Indian culture, though often ignored or denigrated by urban Brazilians, has helped shape modern Brazil and its legends, dance and music. Many indigenous foods and beverages, such as tapioca, manioc, potatoes, maté and *guaraná* (a shrub whose berry is a stimulant; also a popular soft drink) have become staples.

The influence of African culture is also very powerful, especially in the Northeast. The slaves imported by the Portuguese brought with them their religion, music and cuisine, all of which have become a part of Brazilian identity.

Brazil had several waves of voluntary immigration. After the end of slavery in 1888, millions of Europeans were recruited to work in the coffee fields. The largest contingent was from Italy (some one million arrived between 1890 and 1920), but there were also many Portuguese and Spaniards, and smaller groups of Germans and Russians. Japanese immigration began in 1908, and today São Paulo has the largest Japanese community outside of Japan.

Survival International (www.survival-international.org) is a good source of information on Brazilian Indians.

Immigration is only part of the picture when considering Brazil's diversity. Brazilians are just as likely to mention regional types, often accompanied by their own colorful stereotypes. Caboclos, who are descendents of the Indians, live along the rivers in the Amazon region and keep alive the traditions and stories of their ancestors. Gauchos populate Rio Grande do Sul, speak a Spanish-inflected Portuguese and can't quite shake the reputation for being rough-edged cowboys. By contrast, Baianos, descendents of the first Africans in Brazil, are stereotyped for being the most extroverted and celebratory of Brazilians. Mineiros (residents of Minas Gerais state) are considered more serious and reserved than Brazil's coastal dwellers, while Sertanejos (residents of the backlands – called *sertão* – of the Northeast) are dubbed tough-skinned individuals with strong folk traditions. Cariocas (residents of Rio city) are superficial beach bums according to Paulistanos (residents of São Paulo), who are often denigrated as being workaholics with no zeal for life – a rivalry that anyone who's lived in LA or New York can understand.

Today there are literally dozens of terms to describe Brazilians' various racial compositions, and it is not uncommon for apparently White

Brazilians to have a mix of European, African and indigenous ancestors. Yet, despite appearances of integration and racial harmony, underneath is a brutal reality. Although Blacks and mulattoes account for 45% of the population, they are sorely underrepresented in government and the business sector, and often see little hope in rising out of poverty. The indigenous are even more openly discriminated against, continuing a cycle that began with the genocidal policies of the first Europeans.

SPORTS
Soccer

An excellent website for results, schedules and league tables is http://cbfnews.uol.com.br (in Portuguese, but not hard to decipher).

Soccer, or football as it's also called (*futebol* to Brazilians), was introduced in the 1890s when a young student from São Paulo, Charles Miller, returned from studies in England with two footballs and a rule book and began to organize the first league. It quickly became the national passion, and Brazil is the only country to have won five World Cups. The rest of world acknowledges that Brazilians are the best footballers, and Brazilians are, to put it mildly, insane about the sport.

No one goes to work on big international game days, a situation that the government – which is prepared to spend whatever it takes to win a World Cup – laments. When Brazil unexpectedly lost to France in the 1998 World Cup final, millions cried on the streets and depression gripped the country for weeks. Since then one of the shady business that goes on behind the soccer scenes has started to come to light, and parliamentary commissions have investigated corruption in football. The fans may criticize the way football is run, but nothing dims their insane passion for the game itself.

Most of the best players leave Brazil for lucrative contracts with European clubs, but that hardly matters when so many gifted kids are waiting

BRAZILIAN FOOTBALL: THE CLUBS

Apart from a couple of short breaks for the Christmas-New Year holiday and Carnaval, professional club competitions go on all year. If you get a chance, don't miss a game in Rio's Maracanã (p140), the world's largest soccer stadium.

Club	Home city	Stadium (capacity)	Jerseys
Bahia	Salvador	Fonte Nova (96,000)	white
Botafogo	Rio de Janeiro	Caio Martins, Niterói (15,000)	black & white stripes
Corinthians	São Paulo	Pacaembu (40,000)	white; black collar
Cruzeiro	Belo Horizonte	Mineirão (90,000)	blue
Flamengo	Rio de Janeiro	Maracanã (100,000)	red; black hoops
Fluminense	Rio de Janeiro	Laranjeiras (10,000)*	red, green & white stripes
Grêmio	Porto Alegre	Olímpico (55,000)	blue, black & white stripes
Internacional	Porto Alegre	Beira-Rio (80,000)	red
Palmeiras	São Paulo	Parque Antarctica (28,000)	green
Santa Cruz	Recife	Arruda (80,000)	white; black & red hoops
Santos	Santos	Vila Belmiro (26,000)	white
São Paulo	São Paulo	Morumbi (65,000)	white; red & black hoops
Sport	Recife	Ilha do Retiro (50,000)	red & black hoops
Vasco da Gama	Rio de Janeiro	São Januário (40,000)	white; black slash

*Fluminense play most of their home games at the Maracanã.

to replace them. You'll see tiny children playing skilled, rough matches in the streets, on the beaches – just about anywhere.

Volleyball

Volleyball is Brazil's second sport. A natural for the beach, it's also a popular spectator sport on TV. A local variation you'll see on Rio's beaches is *futevôlei* (volleyball played without hands), only for the most talented (Brazilian) of players.

Motor Racing

Since the early 1970s Brazilian drivers have won more Formula One world championships than any other nationality. Emerson Fittipaldi was world champion twice in the 1970s, Nelson Piquet won his third world championship in 1987, and the late, great Ayrton Senna took it out three times. The Brazilian Grand Prix at Interlagos, São Paulo, now takes place in October.

Tennis

Tennis is increasingly popular, especially in the Southeast and South. Brazil's tennis hero is the highly popular Gustavo 'Guga' Kuerten from Florianópolis. One of the world's great clay-court players, Guga was the French Open champion in 1997, 2000 and 2001.

For more information on press freedom in Brazil and other countries around the world visit www.rsf.org, the website of the international watchdog association, Reporters without Borders (available in English, Spanish and French).

MEDIA

Until fairly recently, the media and political demagogues worked hand in hand. Shortly after radio arrived in Brazil in the 1930s, President Getúlio Vargas initiated weekday transmissions of the Voice of Brazil as a means of distilling government propaganda to the people. The rise of Brazil's great media mogul, Roberto Marinho, was largely assisted by his decision not to criticize the fascistic regimes of the military government from 1964 to 1985. Other newspapers simply foundered if anything remotely critical of the government was published.

Today the empire created by Marinho extends to TV and Rede Globo is the world's fourth-largest TV network (behind NBC, CBS and ABC). TV is by far the biggest form of media in Brazil, though radio is also popular (with over 2500 radio stations nationwide). The country also publishes 465 daily newspapers and 1600 magazines.

Brazil still has some antiquated press laws dating from the military dictatorship. 'Crimes of opinion' (published articles that besmirch the names of government officials) are criminal offences. Even more alarming is the frequent violence committed against journalists. In the past few years, several reporters have been assassinated for speaking out against local authorities. Journalists covering sensitive subjects also face attacks from police.

RELIGION

Officially, Brazil is a Catholic country and claims the largest Catholic population of any country in the world. But Brazil is also noted for the diversity and syncretism of its many sects and religions, which offer great flexibility to their followers.

Brazil's principal religious roots have been the animism of the indigenous people, Catholicism, and African cults brought by the Blacks during the period of slavery. The colonists prohibited slaves from practicing their religions, just as they forbade music and dance for fear that they would reinforce the group identity of the captives. Religious persecution led to religious syncretism: to avoid persecution the slaves gave Catholic names and identities to all their African gods. This was generally done by finding the similarities between the Catholic images and the *orixás* (deities) of Candomblé. Thus the slaves worshipped their own deities behind representations of Catholic saints.

In the 19th century Brazil wrote freedom of religion into its constitution, but the African cults continued to suffer persecution for many years. Candomblé was seen by White elites as charlatanism that displayed the ignorance of the poorest classes. But the spectrum of religious life was gradually broadened by the addition of Indian animism to Afro-Catholic syncretism, and by the increasing fascination of Whites with the spiritualism of Kardecism.

Today large numbers of converts are being attracted to evangelical Christianity, to the Afro-Brazilian cults, and to spiritualist or mystic sects.

Sacred Leaves of Candomblé, by Robert Voeks, is a nonacademic work on cultural anthropology and ethnobotany. Voeks explores medicinal plants used in Candomblé and the survival of Afro-Brazilian religion in Brazil.

Christianity

Catholicism retains its status as Brazil's official religion, but is declining in popularity. Many people now merely turn up to church for the basics: baptism, marriage and burial. Evangelical Christianity, however, is booming. All over Brazil, especially in poorer communities where people are most desperate, you will come across simple, recently built churches full of worshipers. Sometimes there will be two or three rival evangelical churches on the same street, going by names such as the Assembléia de Deus (Assembly of God), Igreja Pentecostal Deus é Amor (God is Love Pentecostal Church) and even the Igreja do Evangelho Quadrangular (Church of the Quadrangular Gospel). In one, worshipers may be moaning and speaking in tongues, in another they'll simply be listening to the stern words of a preacher.

Note: In this book you will find the abbreviation NS used for 'Nossa Senhora' (Our Lady) or 'Nosso Senhor' (Our Lord), eg NS do Pilar.

Afro-Brazilian Cults
CANDOMBLÉ

Candomblé is the most orthodox of the religions brought from Africa by the Nago, Yoruba and Jeje peoples. Candomblé is an African word denoting a dance in honor of the gods, and is a general term for the religion. Afro-Brazilian rituals are directed by a *pai de santo* or *mãe de santo* (literally saint's father or mother – the Candomblé priests) and practiced in a *casa de santo* (*terreiro*; house of worship). This is where the initiation of novices takes place as well as consultations and rituals. The ceremonies are conducted in the Yoruba language.

The religion centers upon the *orixás* (spirits or deities). Like the gods in Greek mythology, each *orixá* has a unique personality and history. Although *orixás* are divided into male and female types, there are some that can switch from one sex to the other, such as Logunedé, son of two male gods, Ogun and Oxoss, or Oxumaré, who is male for six months of the year and female for the other six months. (Candomblé, not surprisingly, is much more accepting of homosexuality and bisexuality than other religions.)

Candomblé followers believe that every person has a particular deity watching over them – from birth until death. A person's *orixá* can be identified when a *pai* or *mãe de santo* makes successive throws with a handful of *búzios* (shells), in a divination ritual known as Jogo dos Búzios (Casting of Shells). The position of the shells is used to interpret one's luck, one's future and one's past relationship with the gods.

To keep themselves strong and healthy, followers of Candomblé give food or other offerings to their respective *orixá*. The offering depends on the *orixá's* particular preferences. For example, to please Iemanjá, the goddess or queen of the sea, one should give perfumes, white and blue flowers, rice and fried fish. Oxalá, the greatest deity, the god and owner of the sun, eats cooked white corn. Oxúm, god of fresh waters and waterfalls, is famous for his vanity. He should be honored with earrings, necklaces, mirrors, perfumes, champagne and honey. Whichever god is receiving the offering, Exú must first be appeased, as he serves as the messenger between the individual and the god. Exú, incidentally, likes *cachaça* (sugarcane spirit) and other alcoholic drinks, cigarettes and cigars, strong perfumes and meats.

In Bahia and Rio, followers of Afro-Brazilian cults turn out in huge numbers for the festival held during the night of December 31 and on New Year's Day. Millions of Brazilians go to the beach at this time to pay homage to Iemanjá. Flowers, perfumes, fruits and even jewelry are tossed into the sea to please the mother of the waters, or to gain protection and good luck in the new year.

> 'Quimbanda, a form of black magic, is the evil counterpart to Umbanda'

UMBANDA & QUIMBANDA

Umbanda (white magic) is a mixture of Candomblé and spiritualism with Angolan/Bantu roots. The ceremony, conducted in Portuguese, incorporates figures from all the Brazilian ethnicities: *preto velho* (the old Black slave), *o caboclo* (an Indian – in this context) and other Indian deities, *o guerreiro* (the White warrior), and so on. Umbanda is less structured than Candomblé, and rituals vary from region to region. Some sects tend toward practices found in Kardecism (contacting spirits, seances), while others feature more straightforward praying or preaching by the *pai* or *mãe de santo*.

Quimbanda, a form of black magic, is the evil counterpart to Umbanda. Its rituals involve lots of blood, animal sacrifice and nasty deeds, and it's technically illegal.

Kardecism

During the 19th century, Allan Kardec, the French spiritual master, introduced spiritualism to Brazilian Whites in a palatable form.

Kardec's teachings, which incorporated some Eastern religious ideas into a European framework, are now followed by large numbers of Brazilians. Kardecism emphasizes parlor seances, multiple reincarnations and speaking to the dead. Kardec's writings on his teachings include *The Book of Spirits* and *The Book of Mediums*.

Other Cults

A few Indian rites have become popularized among Brazilians without being incorporated into Afro-Brazilian cults. The cults União da Vegetal (in Brasília, São Paulo and the South) and Santo Daime (centered in Acre and Amazonas states) are both based on consumption of the hallucinogenic drink *ayahuasca*, which has been used for centuries by indigenous peoples of South America. *Ayahuasca* aside, these cults are very straight, dictating that moral behavior and dress follow strict codes. The government tolerates the use of *ayahuasca* in these religious ceremonies, and tightly controls its production and supply.

The cult of Santo Daime was founded in 1930 in Rio Branco, Acre, by Raimundo Irineu Serra, a rubber tapper who had been initiated into the use of *ayahuasca* by Indians on the Acre–Peru border. In visions he received instructions to set up a base near Rio Branco to spread the doctrine of *ayahuasca*. The name Santo Daime comes from the wording of the cult's prayers, *'Dai-me força, dai-me luz...'* ('Give me strength, give me light...'). Santo Daime and União da Vegetal together have between 10,000 and 20,000 members. Santo Daime's two major communities are Ceú do Mapiá in Amazonas and Colônia Cinco Mil, near Rio Branco.

The Brasília area, believed by some to be especially propitious for supernatural contact, has syncretic cults that can be visited near the city in Vale do Amanhecer (Valley of the Dawn) and Cidade Eclética (Eclectic City) – see the boxed text on p357.

WOMEN IN BRAZIL

Brazil had one of the earliest feminist movements in Latin America, and women were among the first in the region to gain the right to vote in 1932. Today there is a growing number of feminist Non-Governmental Organizations (NGOs), dedicated to educating women about their legal rights and family planning, while also training police how to handle cases of domestic violence. In Brasília there's even a feminist lobby (Feminist Center for Studies and Advising); they have a Portuguese website www.cfemea.org.br.

In spite of advances, many *machista* (chauvinist) stereotypes persist, and women are still sorely underrepresented in positions of power. Only about 7% of all legislators are women (compared with the 12% to 15% average in the rest of Latin America). Although women represent 44% of the workforce, they tend to be concentrated in low-paying jobs. For equal work, a woman earns about 70% of a man's salary.

Instances of domestic abuse are frighteningly common (one report stated that every 15 seconds a woman is beaten in Brazil). In response, the first women's police station opened in 1990 specifically to handle violence against women. Today, there are more than 250 women's police stations, largely staffed by female police officers.

The birth rate has declined significantly in recent years (from an average of 4.3 births per woman in 1980 to 2.0 in 2004). Many attribute this to the AIDS epidemic and to sterilization. Nearly one in two women of child-bearing age has been sterilized in Brazil. In some regions, women are promised free sterilizations by political candidates in exchange for votes. For the poorest, sterilization means (at least) one less mouth to feed, and better work opportunities: some organizations are reluctant to hire women who may take off for maternity leave. This is such a growing problem that in 1997 the government passed a law allowing sterilization only for women who have at least two children or are over the age of 25.

Although abortions are illegal in Brazil – except in cases of rape and maternal health risks – an estimated 1 million are performed each year (often with substantial health risks).

ARTS
Music & Dance

Brazilians are among the most musical people on the planet, and music is undoubtedly the most highly developed art form here. Perhaps because of its African roots, Brazilian music is a collective community act, a *festa*, a celebration, and is virtually inseparable from dancing. Genres such as *pagode*, samba, *frevo, forró* and lambada all have their corresponding dances.

Shaped by the mixing of varied influences from three continents, Brazilian popular music has always been characterized by great diversity. The *samba canção* (samba song), for example, is a mixture of Spanish bolero with the cadences and rhythms of African music. Bossa nova

Benedita da Silva: An Afro-Brazilian Woman's Story of Politics and Love are the memoirs of Brazil's first Afro-Brazilian female senator, detailing her rise from the *favelas* to becoming one of the most important political voices in Brazil.

DID YOU KNOW?

About one in five Brazilian households is headed by a woman.

The Brazilian Sound, by Chris McGowan and Ricardo Pessanha, is a well-illustrated, readable introduction to Brazilian music, with insight into regional styles and musicians (big-name and obscure). Useful discography included.

was influenced by samba and North American music, particularly jazz. *Tropicalismo* mixed influences ranging from bossa nova and Italian ballads to blues and North American rock. Brazil is still creating new and original musical forms today.

SAMBA & PAGODE

Tudo da samba: everything makes for a samba. The heart and soul of Brazilian music is samba; all other styles that originated in Brazil can be traced back to its vibrant sound. This most popular Brazilian rhythm originated among Black Bahians in Rio de Janeiro and was probably first performed at the Rio Carnaval in 1917, though its roots go back much further. It's intimately linked with African rhythms, notably the Angolan tam-tam, which provided the basis for samba's music and distinctive dance steps. Samba caught on quickly after the advent of radio and records, and has since become a national symbol. It is the music of the masses.

The 1930s are known as the Golden Age of Samba. By then, *samba canção* had also evolved, performed by small groups with European melodies laid over the African percussion – as had *choro*, a romantic, improvised, samba-related music with the small four-stringed *cavaquinho* (a relative of the ukulele) or guitar playing off against a recorder or flute.

Samba was pushed out of favor by other styles in the 1950s, 1960s and early 1970s. Then *pagode* – informal, backyard-party samba, the kind of music that can be made by a four-string *cavaquinho* and a few informal percussion instruments – emerged in Rio. It's relaxed, rhythmic and melodic and enjoys widespread popularity. Pioneers were singers Beth Carvalho (also the queen of *samba canção*), Jorge Aragão and Zeca Pagodinho, and the group Fundo de Quintal, who introduced the banjo and replaced the heavy floor tom-tom with the *repinique*, a tiny tambourine played with plastic drumsticks. Bezerra da Silva invented the *sambandido* (gangsta samba) style, long before American gangsta rap. By the 1990s the name *pagode* was being applied to more commercial, pop and rock-influenced samba. But 'pure *pagode*' pioneers such as Carvalho, Aragão and Pagodinho are still going very strong.

BOSSA NOVA

When bossa nova was invented in the 1950s, the democratic nature of Brazilian music was challenged. Bossa nova was modern and intellectual and became internationally popular. The middle class stopped listening to the old interpretations of samba and other regional music like the *forró* of the Northeast.

Bossa nova initiated a new style of playing and singing. The more operatic, florid style of singing was replaced by a quieter, more relaxed sound. One of bossa nova's most famous recordings is the smooth *The Girl from Ipanema*, composed by the late Antônio Carlos (Tom) Jobim and Vinícius de Moraes. Guitarist João Gilberto, bossa nova's supercool founding father, is still playing, although other leading figures, such as guitarist and composer Baden Powell and singers Nara Leão and Elis Regina, are no longer alive. João Gilberto's daughter, Bebel, has sparked a new wave of popularity for bossa nova rhythms with her crossover lounge/world music albums.

TROPICALISMO

At the end of the 1960s the movement known as *tropicalismo* burst onto the scene. *Tropicalismo* provoked a kind of general amnesty for all the forgotten musical traditions of the past. The leading figures – Gilberto

Samba, by Alma Guillermoprieto, is a colorful portrait of Mangueira, one of Rio's most traditional samba schools and set in the *favela* of the same name. The author, a journalist and trained dancer, spent a year discovering the rhythms and intrigue of *favela* life.

Bossa Nova: The Story of the Brazilian Music that Seduced the World, by Ruy Castro, is an excellent book that captures the vibrant music and its urban backdrop of 1950s Rio.

Tropical Truth: a Story of Music and Revolution in Brazil, by Caetano Veloso, describes the great artistic experiment of *tropicalismo* in 1960s Brazil. Although digressive at times, Veloso vividly captures the music, politics and lifestyles of the era.

Gil, Caetano Veloso, Rita Lee, Maria Betânia and Gal Costa (all of whom are still around) – believed that all musical styles were important and relevant. All the styles and traditions in Brazilian music, plus North American rock and pop, could be freely mixed. This led to innovations like the introduction of the electric guitar and the sound of electric samba. *Tropicalismo* had its political dimension, and Veloso and Gil spent time in jail and exile during the military dictatorship. Gil is now one of Brazil's most famous musical figures, and he's currently performing duties as Lula's Minister of Culture – when he's not recording new albums.

MÚSICA POPULAR BRASILEIRA (MPB)

Paralleling, overlapping with and at times blending the aforementioned musical movements since the 1970s has been the music known as MPB (Brazilian Popular Music). This nebulous term covers a range of styles from innovative jazz- and bossa nova–influenced stuff to some pretty sickly pop.

Early MPB stars were Chico Buarque, mixing traditional samba with a more modern, universal flavor, and Jorge Ben, playing an original pop samba without losing the Black rhythms of the Rio suburbs he came from.

Milton Nascimento, from Minas Gerais, has long been famous in Brazil for his fine voice, stirring anthems and ballads that reflect the spirituality of the Mineiro (someone from Minas). He's also jazz-influenced, and has kept his innovative touch longer than most early MPB names. Roberto Carlos, the composer of many early MPB classics and once a fiery rock 'n' roller, has turned to schmaltzy ballads, sung in Spanish instead of Portuguese, but still somehow manages to occupy more shelf space in Brazilian music shops than anyone else.

More recent stars include Marisa Monte who, in 2002, teamed up with Arnaldo Antunes and Carlinhos Brown to produce the album *Tribalistas*, which has been a hit all over the world. Zeca Baleiro is another talented artist. His *PetShopMundoCão* is among his best albums.

BRAZILIAN ROCK & RAP

Derived more from English than American rock, this is the least Brazilian of all Brazilian music. Pronounced 'hock', big stars are groups such as Kid Abelha, Legião Urbana (who led a wave of punk-driven bands from Brasília), and the reggae-based Skank and Cidade Negra. The versatile and original Ed Motta, from Rio, injects soul, jazz and traditional Brazilian music into rock. Heavy metal band Sepultura, from Minas Gerais, achieved fame among headbangers worldwide in the 1990s. Other big pop-rock bands include Paralamas do Sucesso and Lula Santos. There's even in-your-face Brazilian punk, with artist Charlie Brown Jr poking fun at different styles of Brazilian music.

Racionais MCs, from São Paulo, have led Brazilian rap since the late 1980s with their hard-edged lyrics about life in the *favelas* and jails. Their 1998 album *Sobrevivendo no Inferno* (Surviving in Hell) sold over a million copies – a record for independent releases in Brazil. Another rap star is Gabriel O Pensador, a White middle-class Carioca who directs a biting wit at…White middle-class Cariocas. Members of the Rio rock/rap band Planet Hemp campaign actively for marijuana legalization and get into a lot of legal trouble as a result.

REGIONAL MUSIC

Samba, *tropicalismo* and bossa nova are all national musical forms, but wherever you go in Brazil you'll hear regional specialties.

The Northeast has perhaps the most regional musical and dance styles. The most important is *forró*, a lively, syncopated music centered on the accordion and the *zabumba* (an African drum). Though a few artists such as Luiz Gonzaga and Jackson do Pandeiro have achieved national status, *forró* was long dismissed by urbanites as unsophisticated – as evidenced by the title of one good compilation available internationally, *Forró: Music for Maids and Taxi Drivers*. Lately, however, *forró* has surged in popularity nationwide and at the same time returned from electrification to its roots – accordion, *zabumba*, triangle – with a big helping hand from the film *Eu, Tu, Eles* (Me, You, Them). The movie features lots of *pé-de-serra* (foot of the hills) down-home *forró*, including *tropicalismo* veteran Gilberto Gil singing the hit *Esperando na Janela*. São Paulo forró group Falamansa – with only one Northeasterner in their ranks – sold 800,000 copies of their first album *Deixe Entrar* in the seven months after it was released in 2000.

Another type of distinctive regional music is the wonderful Bumba Meu Boi festival sound from São Luís, Maranhão (p562). There is also *frevo*, a frenetic, samba-related, Carnaval-based music specific to Recife and neighboring Olinda.

The *trio elétrico*, also called *frevo baiano*, began more as a result of a change in technology rather than in music. It started as a joke when, during Carnaval in Salvador in the 1950s, Dodô, Armandinho and Osmar got on top of a truck and played *frevo* with electric guitars. The *trio elétrico* is not necessarily a trio, but it's still the backbone of Salvador's Carnaval, when trucks piled high with speakers – with musicians perched on top – drive through the city surrounded by dancing mobs. It was popularized during the *tropicalismo* era, when Caetano Veloso began writing songs about the *trio elétrico*. Another important element of Carnaval on the streets of Salvador is the *afro bloco* (Afro-Brazilian percussion group). Filhos de Gandhi and Grupo Olodum are the most famous of these – Filhos have deep African roots and are strongly influenced by Candomblé (Afro-Brazilian religion); Olodum invented samba-reggae.

Mangue beat, from Recife, combines folkloric and regional styles with international influences as diverse as hip-hop, neo-psychedelic and *tejano* (instrumental folk music with roots in northern Mexico and Southern Texas). The early leaders of the genre were Chico Science and Nação Zumbi – the title of whose 1996 masterpiece, *Afrociberdelia*, kind of summed up what their music was about. Chico Science died in a 1997 car crash, but Nação Zumbi has gone forward without him, and other bands such as Mestre Ambrósio and Mundo Livre S/A continue to carry the *mangue* torch.

Axé is a label for the profuse samba/pop/rock/reggae/funk/Caribbean fusion music that emerged from Salvador in the 1990s. Taking its cue from Salvador's older Carnaval forms, *axé* was popularized by the powerful, flamboyant Daniela Mercury. Other exponents include the groups Ara Ketu and Chiclete com Banana. At its best it's great, superenergetic music – hear Daniela sing 'Toda Menina Baiana' (Every Bahian Girl) – but some bands overcommercialized it at the end of the 1990s.

The influence of Brazilian Indian music was absorbed and diluted, as was so much that derived from Brazil's indigenous cultures. The *carimbó* music of the Amazon region (where the majority of Indians live today) is influenced primarily by the Blacks of the coastal zones.

> If you want to dig into some Brazilian music before you head off to Brazil (and you surely will when you return), two good places to start are www .allbrazilianmusic.com and www.slipcue.com/music /brazil/brazillist.html.

OTHER STYLES

Lambada, a dance style influenced by *carimbó* and by Caribbean rhythms like rumba, merengue and salsa, became popular in Brazil in the late

1980s and caught on briefly in Europe and the US. The most successful lambada artist was Beto Barbosa with her group Kaoma.

Also hugely popular is *sertanejo,* a kind of Brazilian country and western music, that is a favorite with truck drivers and cowboys. It's characterized by soaring harmonies and lyrics about broken hearts, life on the road etc. Exponents like to pair off in duos, such as Milionário e José Rico, Chitãozinho e Xororó, and Leandro e Leonardo.

Literature

Inferno by Patrícia Mello is a spine-chilling novel about a boy's ascent to the top of Rio's cocaine trade. The author had never set foot in a *favela* before writing it, creating controversy in many quarters.

The best-selling Brazilian author Paulo Coelho, whose dozen titles have sold over 40 million books worldwide, is Latin America's second-most read novelist (after Gabriel García Márquez). Coelho's more recent efforts, such as *Veronika Decides to Die,* about a writer committed to a mental hospital after a suicide attempt, and *The Fifth Mountain,* a fictionalized tale about the prophet Elijah, are more sophisticated than the new-age spiritual fables with which he sprang to fame in the mid-1990s, such as *The Alchemist* and *The Pilgrimage.*

Joaquim Maria Machado de Assis (1839–1908) is widely regarded as Brazil's greatest writer. The son of a freed slave, Assis worked as a typesetter and journalist in late-19th-century Rio. A tremendous stylist with a great sense of humor and irony, Assis had an understanding of human relations that was subtle and deeply cynical. Look for Gregory Rabassa's good late-1990s translations of *Quincas Borba* and *The Posthumous Memoirs of Bras Cubas.* Machado's other major novel was *Dom Casmurro.*

Brazil's most famous writer is Jorge Amado, who died in August 2001. Born near Ilhéus in 1912, and a longtime resident of Salvador, Amado wrote colorful romances about Bahia's people and places. His early work was strongly influenced by Communism. His later books are lighter in subject, but more picturesque and intimate in style. The two most acclaimed are *Gabriela, Clove and Cinnamon,* which is set in Ilhéus, and *Dona Flor and Her Two Husbands,* set in Salvador. *Tent of Miracles* explores race relations in Brazil, and *Pen, Sword and Camisole* laughs its way through the petty worlds of military and academic politics. *The Violent Land* is an early Amado classic.

Without a word wasted, Graciliano Ramos (1892–1953) tells of peasant life in the *sertão* in his best book, *Barren Lives.* The stories are powerful portraits. Read anything you can find by Mário de Andrade (1893–1945), a leader of the country's 1920s artistic renaissance. His comic *Macunaíma,* which pioneered the use of vernacular language in Brazilian literature and was a precursor of magical realism, could only take place in Brazil.

The writings of the existentialist-influenced, Ukrainian-born Clarice Lispector (1925–77) are more subjective, focusing on human isolation, alienation and moral doubt, and conveying a deep understanding of women's feelings. The short-story collections *Family Ties* and *Soulstorm* are among her best works.

Themes of repression and violence gained prominence starting in the late 1960s with the advent of military dictatorship. The bizarre and brutal *Zero,* by Ignácio de Loyola Brandão, was banned by the military government until a national protest lifted the prohibition. *Tower of Glass,* five stories by Ivan Ângelo, is all São Paulo: an absurdist 1970s look at big-city life where nothing that matters, matters. João Ubaldo Ribeiro's *Sergeant Getúlio* is a story of a military man in Brazil's Northeast. No book tells better of the sadism, brutality and patriarchy that run through Brazil's history. Ribeiro's *An Invincible Memory* (which, like *Sergeant*

Getúlio, was translated into English by the author himself) is a hugely popular 400-year saga of two Bahian families from opposite ends of the social spectrum.

Márcio Souza is a modern satirist based in Manaus. His biting humor captures the frightening side of the Amazon, and his imaginative parodies of Brazilian history reveal the stupidity of personal and official endeavors to conquer the rain forest. Do your best to obtain *Mad Maria* (a historical novel about the Madeira–Mamoré Railway) and *Emperor of the Amazon* if you're going to Amazonia.

Dinah Silveira de Queiroz's *The Women of Brazil* is about a Portuguese girl who goes to 17th-century Brazil to meet her betrothed. Another author of interest is Joyce Cavalcante, who emerged in the 1990s as a writer able to express the experience of women in modern Brazil as well as the enduring social problems of the Northeast. Her *Intimate Enemies* is a tale of corruption, violence, polygamy – and humor.

Cinema & TV

The birth of Brazilian cinema began in Rio de Janeiro – from 1942 until 1962 the home of Atlântida Productions, which churned out musicals, comedies and romances. Neorealism was one of the earliest movements affecting Brazil cinema, and *O Cangaceiro* (The Brigand; 1953) by Lima Barreto was one of the first Brazilian films to receive international recognition. The film chronicles the adventures of a roving band of outlaws, and was inspired by the Northeast's most infamous outlaw, Lampião.

Cinema opened the world's ears to bossa nova, by way of Marcel Camus' 1959 film *Orfeu Negro* (Black Orpheus), featuring the stellar Jobim and Bonfá soundtrack. In the 1960s, several directors focused on Brazil's bleak social problems, and the Cinema Novo movement was born. One of the great films from this movement was the 1962 *O Pagador de Promessas* (The Payer of Vows), which garnered much international attention, and even won the Palme D'Or at the Cannes Film Festival. Glauber Rocha was one of the great pioneers in Cinema Novo. In *Deus e o Diabo na Terra do Sol* (Black God, White Devil; 1963), he forged a polemical national style using Afro-Brazilian traditions in conscious resistance to the influences of Hollywood. His work touches on elements of mysticism without steering from political issues.

The military dictatorship stymied much creative expression in the country – and the film industry was naturally affected. As the regime's power waned, the film industry slowly picked up, with *Bye Bye Brasil* (1980) by Carlos Diegues, marking the beginning of a new era. It chronicles the adventures of a theater troupe as they tour the entire country, performing in small villages and towns. Hector Babenco's *Pixote* (1981) came soon after, a powerful film that indicted Brazilian society for its indifference to the poor. It tells the story of a street kid in Rio, who gets swept along from innocent naïveté to murderer by the currents of the underworld. Babenco went on to direct international Hollywood hits like *Kiss of the Spider Woman* (1985) and *Ironweed* (1987).

Bruno Barreto's *O Que É Isso Companheiro* (released as *Four Days in September* in the US; 1998) is based on the 1969 kidnapping of the US ambassador to Brazil by leftist guerrillas. It was nominated for an Oscar in 1998.

Carla Camarut's *Carlota Joaquina – Princesa do Brasil,* a hilarious blend of fairy tale, satire and historical drama, is about a Spanish princess married to the Portuguese prince regent (later Dom João VI) when the entire Portuguese court fled to Brazil to escape Napoleon.

'Cinema opened the world's ears to bossa nova'

Walter Salles is one of Brazil's best-known directors. His first feature film *Terra Estrangeiro* (Foreign Land), shot in 1995, holds an important place in the renaissance of Brazilian cinema. The film won seven international prizes and was shown at over two dozen film festivals. It was named Best Film of the Year in Brazil in 1996, where it screened for over six months. Salles is also a great documentary filmmaker; *Socorro Nobre* (Life Somewhere Else) and *Krajcberg* (The Poet of the Remains), among others, won awards at many international festivals.

Central do Brasil (Central Station; 1998) is one of Salles' most famous films. It won an Oscar in 1998 for best foreign film. The central character is an elderly woman who works in the train station in Rio writing letters for illiterates with families far away. After a chance encounter with a young homeless boy, she accompanies him on a search for his father into the real, unglamorized Brazil. At the time of research, Salles was at Sundance screening his recently completed epic *Diarios de Motocicleta* (The Motorcycle Diaries), which details the historic journey of Che Guevara and Alberto Granada across South America.

Eu, Tu, Eles (Me, You, Them), Andrucha Waddington's comedy about a Northeasterner with three husbands, was also well received when it was released in 2000. It has beautiful cinematography and a score by Gilberto Gil (currently President Lula's Minister of Culture), which contributed to the recent wave of popularity for that funky Northeastern music, *forró*.

Fernando Meirelles is one of Brazil's most talented young directors. His first feature-length film, *Domésticas* (Maids; 2001) gives an insight into the millions of domestic servants who work in Brazil. His latest film, *Cidade de Deus* (City of God), is based on a true story by Paolo Lins. It gives an honest and heart-wrenching portrayal of life in a Rio *favela*. After its release in 2002, it brought much attention to the plight of the urban poor, and director Fernando Meirelles was nominated for an Oscar (Best Director) in 2004. It also spawned many spin-offs, including *Cidade de Homens*, a popular TV series about Rio's *favela* gangs, also directed by Meirelles.

Most recently, Hector Babenco has returned to the mise-en-scène with *Carandiru* (2004), a socially charged drama based on one man's experiences inside one of São Paulo's most horrifying prisons.

City of God, directed by Fernando Mereilles, is an electrifying thriller, based on Paulo Lins' novel, which charts the descent of one of Rio's *favelas* – the notorious Cidade de Deus – into the cocaine-fueled drug wars that characterize many such communities.

Painting & Sculpture

The first colonial painters were the Jesuit and Benedictine missionaries, who painted their churches and sacred objects in a European baroque style. The 17th-century Dutch invasion in the Northeast brought with it some important Flemish artists, such as Frans Post, who painted the flora and fauna in their tropical surroundings.

Brazilian baroque art peaked in the 18th century, when the wealth provided by the gold rush allowed talented artists to realize their full potential. The acknowledged genius of this period was the sculptor and architect Antônio Francisco Lisboa (1738–1814), better known as Aleijadinho (see the boxed text on p231 for information on his life and works).

In the 19th and 20th centuries, Brazilian artists followed international trends such as neoclassicism, romanticism, impressionism, academicism and modernism. Internationally, the best-known Brazilian painter is Cândido Portinari (1903–62). Early in his career he made the decision to paint only Brazil and its people. Strongly influenced by the Mexican muralists like Diego Rivera, he managed to fuse indigenous and expressionist influences into a powerful, socially conscious and sophisticated style.

To immerse yourself in Brazilian art, head for São Paulo (p270), which has the country's best art museums.

Architecture

Salvador (p417), capital of colonial Brazil from 1549 to 1763, has managed to preserve many outstanding Renaissance and Baroque buildings. A special feature of its old town, where more than 600 buildings and monuments have been restored since 1992, are the many brightly colored houses, often decorated with high-quality stucco.

Olinda (p504) is essentially an 18th-century city. Its architectural wealth and unique atmosphere stem from its 20 baroque churches and many convents, chapels and houses with red-tile roofs. In São Luís (p562) the entire street plan of the late-17th-century heart of the city survives, along with many historic buildings, including fine mansions with colorful tiled facades.

The 18th-century mining towns of Minas Gerais harbor further colonial architectural riches. The jewel in the crown is Ouro Prêto (p231), the focal point of the 18th-century gold rush, adorned with the greatest concentration of fine baroque buildings in Brazil, many of them designed or embellished by the genius of Brazilian baroque, Aleijadinho. Lovely Ouro Prêto is joined on the World Heritage list by Diamantina (p253), founded by 18th-century diamond hunters. Other Minas towns, such as Santa Bárbara (p261) and São João del Rei (p245), also enjoy treasures of baroque architecture.

Brazil's architecture in the 19th and early 20th centuries was much influenced by French styles. Neoclassical tastes yielded grandiose, monumental constructions such as Rio de Janeiro's Museu Nacional de Belas Artes (p135) and Amazonian rubber-boom entertainment palaces such as Manaus' Teatro Amazonas (p623) and Belém's Teatro da Paz (p581). Art nouveau style arrived around the turn of the 20th century: an outstanding example in Rio is the interior of the Confeitaria Colombo (p165).

The 1930s was the era of art deco, as exemplified by Rio's central railway station and statue of Christ the Redeemer (p131), and, on a humbler scale, Belém's Hotel Central (p659), a longtime travelers' favorite. The 1930s also saw the emergence of a new generation of Brazilian architects, led by Oscar Niemeyer and influenced by the modernist ideas of Le Corbusier, who would develop the functional style, with its extensive use of steel and glass and its lack of ornamentation. The Catedral Metropolitana (p139) and Museu de Arte Moderna (p131) in Rio de Janeiro, Niemeyer's spaceship-like Museu de Arte Contemporânea (p141) in nearby Niterói, and the Museu de Arte de São Paulo (by Lina Bo Bardi; p270) are all good examples of modern Brazilian architecture.

But the outstanding creation of the 20th century was the city of Brasília (p354), the new national capital created in the 1950s and 1960s from scratch by Niemeyer, urban planner Lúcio Costa and landscape architect Burle Marx. Some love Brasília, some hate it, but none can deny the daring of its very concept: of its aeroplane-shaped street plan, of the crown-shaped cathedral or the Santuário Dom Bosco (with its beautiful stained glass), or of the way arches and water are used in government buildings such as the Palácio do Itamaraty and Palácio da Justiça.

When Brazil Was Modern: a Guide to Architecture: 1928–1960, by Lauro Cavalcanti, is a well-illustrated guide to the 30-odd architects who made important contributions to Brazil's modern landscape.

Curves of Time: Oscar Niemeyer Memoirs is recommended for those interested in the art and life of Brazil's great architect (from exile in Paris to romps with Henry Miller).

Environment

The name Brazil conjures romantic thoughts of sandy beaches and sweaty tropical forests. And the country lives up to the stereotype – boasting an incredible variety of landscapes and an abundance of flora and fauna. Brazil is home to the world's largest rain forest, as well as some of the greatest wetlands and most beautiful beaches. The sleek predatory jaguar dwells here as does the gentle pink river dolphin, and plants range from the mighty mahogany to the delicate orchid.

Brazil has more known species of plants (over 55,000), freshwater fish (around 3000) and mammals (over 520) than any other country in the world. It ranks second for the number of amphibians (517), third for birds (over 1600) and fifth for reptiles (468). Around 10 to 15 million insect species inhabit the country. Some 131 of the mammals, 294 of the amphibians and 172 of the reptiles are unique to Brazil and new species are being discovered all the time, including several previously unknown small primates and amphibians.

Unfortunately, Brazil is also renowned for the destruction of its natural environment. Amazonia, which holds most of the country's biological diversity, has long been in a state of environmental crisis. Less widely known is that all of Brazil's other major ecosystems are also threatened. Even as new species are being discovered, others are becoming extinct. More than 100 Brazilian birds and 70 mammals are considered endangered.

WHY THE RAIN FOREST MATTERS

All sensitivity and emotionalism aside, the two main reasons why the Brazilian rain forests are important to the future of humanity and the planet are their biodiversity and effect on the climate.

Biodiversity

Tropical forests have a far greater concentration of different plant and animal species than most other ecosystems. For example, of the 250,000 species of higher plants known to science, 90,000 can be found in tropical Latin America (and that's triple the number known in tropical Africa). The Amazon rain forest alone contains an estimated one-fifth of all the planet's bird and plant species. This reservoir of genetic diversity is a vital source of food, medicines and chemicals used worldwide. About a quarter of the medicines used in the developed world contain elements extracted from tropical forests. The Amazon rain forest has already given us rubber, manioc (cassava) and cocoa, as well as antimalarial drugs, cancer drugs and hundreds of other medicinal plants. Some 1300 of the Amazon's plants have acknowledged medicinal value, and more are being discovered all the time. Simply put, a cure for AIDS (or breast cancer or the common cold) might be lurking in forest flora or fauna. The destruction of such a storehouse would be an incalculable loss.

Climate

The greenhouse theory, in simple terms, is as follows. Much of the sun's heat that reaches the planet is reflected back into space as infrared radiation. Carbon in the atmosphere, however, in the form of carbon dioxide (CO_2) or methane (CH_4), prevents the radiation from leaving and, in turn, traps heat on the planet like a global greenhouse. The more carbon in the atmosphere, the hotter the Earth gets, with unpredictable and undesirable consequences.

By day, trees absorb carbon dioxide and release oxygen; by night, they absorb oxygen and release carbon dioxide. In a mature forest, the consumption and release of these two gases is in balance. But growing trees absorb more carbon dioxide than they release, and burning or

This relentless human assault on natural Brazil has gone on since Europeans first arrived in 1500. But since the international environmental movement in the 1990s, an awakening of environmental consciousness among Brazilians – and even among some of the country's politicians – means that attitudes are at last slowly starting to change. One aspect of the increased environmental consciousness is an awareness that pristine nature attract tourists (and their dollars). International accessibility to Brazil's natural wonders is increasing quickly. This chapter serves as an introduction to the Brazilian natural environment, including current conservation efforts and the best places to see the country's fascinating wildlife for yourself.

THE LAND

Brazil has five principal ecosystems: Amazonian rain forest, Atlantic rain forest, the caatinga (semiarid land), the central cerrado (savanna) and the wetlands of the Pantanal.

Amazonian Rain Forest

Blanketing nearly all of Brazil's northern region plus parts of Mato Grosso and Maranhão states – a total of 3.6 million sq km, about 42% of Brazil – and a further 2.4 million sq km in neighboring countries, the Amazon rain forest is the largest tropical forest in the world, and the planet's most biologically diverse ecosystem. The Amazon is home to around 20% of the world's bird species, 20% of plant species, 10% of mammal species and some 2000 to 3000 species of fish (in contrast, Europe has about 200). The forest still keeps many of its secrets: to this day, major tributaries of the

dead trees release carbon dioxide without absorbing any at all. So when tree-dense areas are burned or otherwise deforested, levels of carbon in the atmosphere increase and, as a result, the Earth gets hotter.

Another source of carbon in the atmosphere is the burning of fossil fuels by motor vehicles, industrial processes and so on. In 1997 many of the world's rich countries, which emit much more carbon than the poorer countries, signed the Kyoto Protocol, by which they agreed to cut their emissions of greenhouse gases to around 5% of 1990 levels by about 2010.

US President George W Bush, a firm opponent of environmental controls (or anything that stands in the way of US business interests) rejected the treaty upon entering office in 2001. This decision appeared to be the Protocol's death knell. At the time of writing this book, Russia's Vladimir Putin made a somewhat surprising decision to ratify the Protocol, which will allow it to move forward with or without the involvement of the US. Whether the Kyoto Protocol comes to fruition or not, some of the ideas that have spun off are likely to last. And some of these ideas are potential goldmines for countries with rain forests, as the richer countries have come up with schemes to pay other countries to make carbon-emission cuts, instead of making all their cuts themselves.

For example, if an Amazonian state in Brazil undertakes to plant more trees, or even just stall the destruction of trees it had been planning to destroy, it could 'sell' this commitment to a wealthy country that was required to reduce carbon emissions but was reluctant to make the reduction in its own operations. A future global market in such 'carbon credits' is foreseen, and researchers in Brazil and elsewhere have even been trying to figure out ways to measure exactly how much carbon is 'sequestered' (locked away) by different types of trees in different situations.

Another climatic effect of the Amazon rain forest is its release of large quantities of water vapor into the air, which contributes greatly to rainfall both on the rain forest and on nearby areas. As the area that is rain forest shrinks, rainfall is likely to diminish in the northern half of South America, which in turn may have an effect on the rainfall and climates in other regions.

Amazon river are unexplored, thousands of species have not yet been classified and it is possible that some human communities have still avoided contact with the outside world.

Unfortunately, humanity has been destroying the Amazon forests so quickly (see the boxed text on p91 for some figures) that countless animal and plant species are likely to be extinguished before they're even known to us.

Rain forests can occur in areas that receive more than 2000mm of rain falls annually and where this rainfall is spread over the whole year. In the Amazon, half the rain comes from damp trade winds blowing in from the Atlantic Ocean and the rest results from vapor released by Amazonia's own soil and trees – much of which is recycled rain. Humidity is always greater than 80%, and temperatures range fairly constantly between 22°C (72°F) by night and 31°C (88°F) by day.

FLOODPLAIN & DRY LAND
Seasonal rainfall patterns mean that the water levels of the Amazon river and its hundreds of tributaries rise and fall at different points in the year. This produces dramatic alterations in the region's geography. Water levels routinely vary between low and high by 10m to 15m; during high-water periods, areas totaling at least 150,000 sq km (about the size of England and Wales together) are flooded. The high waters link rivers, creeks and lakes that are otherwise unconnected, providing river travelers with numerous shortcuts. The seasons are not the same everywhere in the Amazon Basin: High water on the Amazon itself and its major northern tributary, the Rio Negro, is in June; while high water on the southern tributaries such as the Madeira, Araguaia and Tocantins takes place in March.

The regularly inundated floodplains of the 'white-water' (actually creamy-brown) rivers flowing down from the Andes are known as *várzea* and generally sustain forests no more than 20m tall. Many of the trees have elevated roots. *Igapó*, a name used for a flooded forest, more often refers to areas flooded by the darker waters of the Rio Negro. It's particularly fascinating to boat through a flooded forest because you move along at treetop level and can get closer to the wildlife.

Forests on terra firme (higher land, not subject to flooding) typically grow to 30m in height. Here are found the Brazil nut tree and valuable hardwoods, such as mahogany, all of which prefer a drier environment.

On the waters themselves live aquatic plants, such as the giant *Victoria amazonica* water lilies (named after Britain's Queen Victoria) and even floating islands made of amphibious grasses.

FOREST LAYERS
The rain forest is stratified into layers of plant and animal life. Most of the animal activity takes place in the canopy layer, 20m to 30m above ground, where trees compete for sunshine, and butterflies, sloths and the majority of birds and monkeys live. Here hummingbirds hover for pollen, and macaws and parrots seek out nuts and tender shoots. The dense foliage of the canopy layer blots out the sunlight at lower levels. A few tall trees reaching up to 40m, even 50m, poke above the canopy and dominate the forest skyline. These 'emergent trees' are inhabited by birds such as the harpy eagle and toucan and, unlike most other rain forest plants, disperse their seeds by wind.

Below the canopy is the understory. Epiphytes (air plants) hang at mid-levels and below them are bushes, saplings and shrubs that grow

---

DID YOU KNOW?

The Amazon Basin averages between 130 and 250 rainy days a year, depending on the region.

The National Geographic documentary *Amazon: Land of the Flooded Forest* (1997) explores this unique region, where water and land life intermingle for six months of the year. The film details the fragile interdependency of the wildlife and its habitat.

up to 5m in height. Last is a ground cover of ferns, seedlings and herbs – plants adapted to very little light. Down here live ants and termites, the so-called social insects. The saubas (leaf-cutter ants) use leaves to build underground nests for raising fungus gardens, while army ants swarm through the jungle in huge masses, eating everything that happens to be in their path. Insects, fungi and roots fight for access to nutrients, keeping the forest floor quite tidy. At ground level it's cooler than in the canopy, averaging about 28°C (82°F), but humidity is higher, at about 90%.

The forest's soils are typically shallow. Many trees have buttress roots that spread over wide patches of ground to gather more nutrients.

With Broadax and Firebrand: the Destruction of the Brazilian Atlantic Forest, by Warren Dean, chronicles the history of access to the other rain forest in Brazil, and serves as a warning for the Amazon and other rain forests.

Atlantic Rain Forest

The 'other' tropical rain forest, the Mata Atlântica (Atlantic rain forest) once extended right along the country's southeast-facing coast, from Rio Grande do Norte to Rio Grande do Sul. It formed a band that gradually widened toward the south, where it reached a width of up to 800km. The

THE STATES OF BRAZIL

0 — 1000 km
0 — 600 miles

Atlantic rain forest covered about 1 million sq km in all at its peak when the Portuguese arrived.

If you travel along the coast, you'll have plenty of opportunities to experience the Mata Atlântica, even though no more than 7% of the original forest remains. Today three-quarters of Brazil's population and all its main industrial cities are located in what used to be the Mata Atlântica. Brazilwood extraction, sugarcane and coffee cultivation, farming, ranching, logging, fires and acid rain have also taken their toll of the forest.

Nevertheless, what remains of the Atlantic rain forest – dozens of separate fragments – is incredibly luxuriant, and some areas boast what may be the highest biodiversity levels on earth. The Mata Atlântica is older than the Amazon forest and has evolved independently. Though it shares many animal and plant families with other Brazilian ecosystems, it also contains many unique species – 17 of its 21 primate types are found only here, as are more than 900 of its 2000-plus kinds of butterflies, and many of its more than 600 bird species.

Many species are also endangered, including the four types of lion tamarin (brightly maned small monkeys) and the woolly spider monkey (the largest primate in the Americas).

The Atlantic rain forest's distinctive flora – more than half of its tree species exist nowhere else – includes many large trees such as brazilwood, ironwood, Bahian jacaranda and cedar, as well as a number of rare tree ferns.

The conservation effort received a boost in 1999 when Unesco placed 33 separate areas in Paraná, São Paulo, Espírito Santo and Bahia states, totaling 5820 sq km, on the World Heritage list.

> A superb guide for ecotravelers visiting the Pantanal is *Brazil – Amazon and Pantanal* by David L Pearson and Les Beletsky. Although it is written by a biologist, it's accessible and informative, identifying wildlife, plants, environmental threats and conservation issues.

Caatinga

Caatinga is semiarid land, with hardy vegetation composed mainly of cacti and thorny shrubs adapted to lack of water and extreme heat. Rainfall (300mm to 800mm a year) is irregular, and often torrential when it comes. When it does rain, the trees break into leaf and the ground turns green. Caatinga is the natural environment of much of the interior of the Northeast region plus bits of Minas Gerais state, totaling some 11% of Brazilian territory – although less than one-tenth of this is in its natural state.

Wildlife tends to be nocturnal or subterranean, and much of it – the anteater and armadillo, for example – has been severely depleted by hunting and habitat destruction. The handsome laughing falcon is a typical sight in caatinga skies, but the last known wild Spix's macaw, a beautiful iridescent-blue bird, disappeared from its haunts near Curaçá, Bahia, in 2000. The demise of the last Spix's macaw leaves another caatinga dweller, the Lear's macaw, as the world's rarest macaw, with less than 150 left.

Wood and coal from the caatingas are a primary energy source for many of the region's over 20 million inhabitants. Wood and coal also fuel 30% of the Northeast's industries, generating many jobs and comprising 15% of rural incomes. Centuries of cattle ranching, and more recent ill-advised attempts at irrigated, pesticide-aided agriculture, have devastated large areas of caatinga. Studies have predicted that continued destruction at the present rate will see the caatingas disappear in Paraíba in about 20 years, in Pernambuco in 30 years, in Ceará in 40 years and in Rio Grande do Norte in 55 years.

Cerrado

Typically the cerrado environment is open savanna grasslands dotted with trees, though it can edge into scrub, palm stands or even fairly thick forest. Plant diversity is great – an estimated 10,000 species, of which 44% are found nowhere else in the world – and many are used to produce cork, fibers, oils, handicrafts, medicines and food. Medicinal plants native to cerrado include arnica and golden trumpet. Cerrado covers the central high plains of Brazil – 2 million sq km in a rough triangle from southern Minas Gerais to Mato Grosso to southern Maranhão.

More than half the original cerrado vegetation has already been cleared, and less than 2% is under environmental protection. In the past the major problem was mining, which contaminated rivers with mercury and caused erosion and serious silting of streams. But, since the mid-20th century, intensive farming and cattle ranching, along with an accompanying wave of human settlement, have posed even greater dangers to the natural balance. Intensive farming over large areas, often done with single crops such as soybeans, rice, maize or wheat, has depleted soils and contaminated water and soils with pesticides and fertilizers.

From the cerrado, rivers flow north to Amazonia, south to the Pantanal and east to the coast, meaning that the agricultural toxins from here can have an effect over a very wide range of Brazilian regions. Proposals for *hidrovias* – aquatic freeways, for the export of products such as soybeans, made by dredging and straightening existing rivers so that they can take large river traffic year-round – threaten yet further ecological interference, including disruption to vital seasonal flood and drainage patterns.

None of this bodes well for such rare and mostly endangered cerrado inhabitants as the maned wolf, giant anteater, giant and three-banded armadillo, pampas deer and the largest bird in Brazil, the ground-dwelling rhea.

Conservation International's website, www .conservation.org, covers various aspects of ecotourism and the global conservation movement.

Pantanal

The Pantanal is a vast swampy wetland in the center of South America. It is about half the size of France – 230,000 sq km spread across Brazil, Bolivia and Paraguay. It's the largest inland wetland on earth, and

---

THE PANTANAL UNDER SIEGE

With its abundance of animals in open view, the Pantanal is easy game for poachers. They are doing more damage to the Pantanal than to any other region in Brazil, including Amazonia. Although game hunting has been illegal here since 1967, poaching continues with relative impunity. It's difficult to determine the number of animals killed each year, but estimates start at 500,000.

Animals are smuggled into Bolivia and Paraguay, where poaching is also illegal but the relevant laws are not enforced in even a token manner. The Brazilian government has done little to stem the slaughter, although efforts have improved somewhat and President Lula has made attempts towards enforcing environmental laws. A poorly funded Institute of Environmental Poaching & Control exists in Mato Grosso do Sul, but few prosecutions have been made.

Many of the animals (or their body parts) command high prices in Brazil and especially abroad. The slow and fearless *jacaré* (alligator) is easily shot at short range. An alligator skin is worth up to US$500, but only the supple, small-scaled skin of the *jacaré*'s flanks is used (to make fashionable wallets, belts, purses and shoes). The rest of the carcass is discarded.

Just as poachers supply the fashion industry with skins, they supply American pet shops with rare tropical fish and birds. A hyacinth macaw, for example, will sell in the US for US$6000 to US$12,000, one of its eggs can sell for US$10,000 – though a person involved with the poaching actually receives a fraction of this money.

Tourism, however, for all of its good and bad, is booming – the Pantanal receives over a million visitors per year – and is giving a new value to keeping the fauna alive in its natural habitat.

140,000 sq km of it lies in Brazil, in the states of Mato Grosso and Mato Grosso do Sul.

During the rainy season, from October to March, the waters from the higher surrounding lands run into the Pantanal, inundating as much as two-thirds of it for half the year. The Pantanal, though 2000km upstream from the Atlantic Ocean, is only 100m to 200m above sea level and drains very slowly. Its chief outlet is the Rio Paraguai, which ultimately drains into the Atlantic Ocean via the Rio de la Plata. Waters reach their highest levels, up to 3m above dry-season levels, around March in the northern Pantanal, but not until about June in the south.

This seasonal flooding has made systematic farming impossible and severely limited human incursions into the area. The Pantanal is still one of Brazil's wildest and least explored regions. It's also an enormously rich feeding ground for wildlife, and, if your priority is viewing wildlife, the Pantanal offers greater visible numbers and at least as large a variety of creatures as Amazonia, with which it has many species in common.

The flood waters replenish the soil's nutrients, the waters teem with fish, and the ponds provide ecological niches for many animals and plants. Birds fly in flocks of thousands and six different species may nest on a single tree branch.

'Words can't do justice to the color of a flock of parakeets in flight.'

With cerrado to the east, Amazon rain forest to the north and spots of Atlantic rain forest to the south, Pantanal vegetation – 1700 plant species – is a mishmash of savanna, forest, meadow and even, on some of the highest points, caatinga. In the dry season the lagoons and marshes dry out and fresh grasses emerge on the savanna, while hawks and alligators compete for fish in the shrinking ponds.

The environment supports about 650 bird species – including kites, hawks, herons, woodpeckers, ibis, storks, kingfishers, hummingbirds, parakeets, toucans and macaws. The Pantanal's substantial number of birds of prey reflects its abundance of food sources. Snails, insects and 260 fish species form the basis of their diet.

Words can't do justice to the color of a flock of parakeets in flight or the awkwardness of the jabiru stork, the meter-high, black-hooded, scarlet-collared symbol of the Pantanal, nor can it suggest the beauty of nesting birds settling like snow in the trees, or the swiftness of a sprinting flock of rheas. Listen for the call of the southern lapwing, named *quero-quero* (I want-I want) in Brazil for its distinctive cry. If you're very lucky you'll see the endangered hyacinth macaw.

The Pantanal is also a haven for some 50 reptile and 80 mammal species, including giant anacondas (though snakes on the whole are not common), iguanas, jaguars, ocelots, pumas, maned wolves, pampas and marsh deer, giant and collared anteaters, four species of armadillo, black howler and brown capuchin monkeys, tapirs, opossums, crab-eating raccoons, crab-eating foxes – and somewhere between 10 and 35 million alligators.

The capybara, the world's largest rodent, is the most visible mammal in the Pantanal, with a population of about 600,000. This dog-sized, rabbit-faced animal is often seen in family groups or even large herds.

The giant river otter has been hunted almost out of existence here, although it still exists in some ponds. The marsh deer, down to about 35,000 in number, is also at risk. Both anteater species and the maned wolf are endangered and not easily seen: local people prize anteater meat. The killing of anteaters has led to an increase in ants and termites, and many *fazendas* (ranches) use strong pesticides to destroy the mounds.

With thousands of alligators sunning themselves on the edge of each and every body of water, it's hard to believe that they are endangered by poachers (see the boxed text on p67). Alligators feed mainly on fish, and are the primary check on the growth of the piranha population, which has been growing rapidly as a result of alligator slaughter. The size of an adult alligator is determined by the availability of food: those on the river's edge are often much bigger than those that feed in small ponds.

Cattle live pretty much in harmony with the wildlife, grazing during the dry season and gathering on the little islets that form during the wet. Though some jaguars eat only their natural prey, such as capybaras and tapirs, others will attack sick or injured cattle, and the occasional big cat goes on a rampage, killing healthy cattle. These rogue jaguars (and, unfortunately, sometimes others) are then killed by cattle ranchers. Jaguars are also killed for their valuable skins and are threatened with extinction in the Pantanal.

Other Environmental Zones

The mountainous regions of southern Brazil were once covered by coniferous forests that were dominated by the prehistoric-looking, 30m- to 40m-high araucaria (Paraná pine) tree. The araucaria forests have been decimated by timber cutters and now survive only in scattered areas such as the Aparados da Serra, São Joaquim and Serra da Bocaina national parks and the Parque Estadual Horto Florestal in São Paulo state, generally at altitudes above 500m.

Apart from the cerrado, grasslands occur chiefly in Brazil's far north (northern Roraima) and far south (Rio Grande do Sul). Unlike the cerrado, which has a consistent scattering of medium to tall trees, the Roraima grasslands have only low trees and bushes, while the *campos do sul* (southern fields), on the rolling southern pampas, generally have no trees except where interspersed with patches of woodland.

WILDLIFE

Beyond wild Carnaval and lazy beach vacations, the fabulous natural sights of Brazil are the biggest attractions to the country. Brazil boasts plentiful flora and fauna, making it one of the planet's best destinations for naturelovers and ecotravelers. There are animals here, such as the tiny golden lion tamarin, that are found nowhere else in the world and the foliage of the Amazon, with its giant mahogany trees and dense, verdant canopy, is unrivalled. Although it is not as famous for its marine life, Brazil also has an amazing variety of tropical fish, reefs, sharks and giant sea turtles.

Brazil is a land brimming with life and the richness and diversity of Brazilian fauna are astounding. The following brief portraits cover a selection of the most exciting and most frequently seen species, many of which are widely distributed around the country. Portuguese names and scientific names are included to help identification: the Portuguese names are often the only ones local guides know and sometimes vary depending on the region of the country.

Mammals

EDENTATES

Edentate means 'toothless' and this order covers some of the gentle plantand insect-eating animals, such as anteaters, sloths and armadillos.

The giant anteater (*tamanduá bandeira; Myrmecophaga tridactyla*) can grow well over 2m long. Its Portuguese name, which means 'flag anteater,' refers to its long hairy tail, which waves like a flag as the creature

The giant ground sloth, which grew to the size of an elephant, once inhabited much of Brazil. The slow-moving animal was an easy target for prehistoric hunters and it was presumably hunted to extinction about 10,000 years ago.

The Brazilian version of the Loch Ness monster is the Mapinguari, a nocturnal animal that grows to 2m long, is covered in red hair and can rip apart palm trees. Crytpozoologists believe that it could be a surviving giant ground sloth or unknown species of giant anteater.

forages for ants and termites, tearing open their nests with its sharp claws and lapping up as many as 35,000 a day with its probing sticky tongue. You're most likely to see the giant anteater in cerrado (savanna) habitat. Its meat is prized in some areas of Brazil, and it's a threatened species. The collared or lesser anteater *(tamanduá mirim* or *tamanduá colete; Tamandua tetradactyla)*, growing up to 1.4m long, is yellow and black, mainly nocturnal and often climbs trees.

Sloths *(preguiças)*, true to their name, move very slowly. And they're not, by the look of it, too bright. They hang upside down from branches with their strong arms and legs, feeding on leaves, sleeping up to 18 hours a day and descending to the ground to excrete just once a week. Surprisingly, they're good swimmers. You have a good chance of seeing some if you get a bit off the beaten track in Amazonia: from a moderate distance they look like clumps of vegetation high in trees. The species you're most likely to see is the brown-throated three-toed sloth *(preguiça de três dedos; Bradypus variegatus)*.

Brazil's several species of armadillo *(tatu)* are mainly nocturnal and rarely seen. Two of them are endangered.

The website www
.junglephotos.com has
many photos of Amazonian flora and fauna.

PRIMATES

It's always exciting for people to see monkeys in the wild – to contemplate our similarities with these creatures and observe our obvious differences. About 75 of the world's 250 primate species are found in Brazil and many of these are unique to the country. Some are hunted deep in the forest by settlers and indigenous people for their meat and others live harmoniously in and around beach towns, much like squirrels in North American city parks. Many of the species are rather common and on an Amazon jungle trip you're very likely to see groups of monkeys moving through trees.

The most common primate in Amazonia is the little squirrel monkey *(macaco-de-cheiro* or *mico-de-cheiro; Saimiri sciureus)*, with its pale face, dark nose area, big ears and long tail. It moves in small, noisy groups. The black spider monkey *(macaco prêto* or *macaco aranha; Ateles paniscus)*, growing up to 1.5m long with lengthy thin limbs and a prehensile tail (accounting for 60% of its length), is fairly common in parts of Amazonia where it isn't usually hunted. The woolly spider monkey *(muriqui* or *mono-carvoeiro; Brachyteles arachnoides)* has thicker brown fur and is not a true spider monkey. This endangered species is the largest primate in the Americas: the Parque Nacional da Serra da Bocaina is its main stronghold, where it is easiest to spot.

Howler monkeys *(guariba, bugio* or *barbado* in Portuguese) are much more easily heard than seen: their roar (not really a howl) carries over many kilometers. They're stocky, up to 1.25m long (half tail), and live in groups of up to 20, usually 10m to 20m high in trees, that are led by a single male. In Amazonia you're most likely to encounter the red howler *(Alouatta seniculus)*. Further south, including in the Pantanal, the black howler *(Alouatta caraya)* is the local species. The brown howler monkey *(Alouatta fusca)* inhabits the small remaining areas of the Mata Atlântica. The rumors are true – a howler monkey will try to pelt you with its excrement if it feels threatened, so you may want to consider simply listening to its roar and not trying to get too close for a view.

The lithe capuchin monkey is named for the hair atop their heads, which resembles a monk's cowl. They're widely dispersed – found in Amazonia, the Pantanal, cerrado and Mata Atlântica (even Rio de Janeiro's Parque Nacional & Floresta da Tijuca; p146) – living in groups of up to 20 led by one male. The usual species is the brown capuchin *(macaco-prego; Cebus apella)*, measuring up to 1m (half tail).

The two types of uakari monkey, black-headed and bald, inhabit Amazonian flooded forest. The bald uakari *(uacari* or *bicó; Cacajao calvus)* has a red or pink bald head and thick, shaggy body fur ranging from chestnut-red to white (giving rise to the popular names red uakari and white uakari). The monkey's red complexion and baldness has earned it the nickname *macaco-inglês* (English monkey). Uakaris are endangered, but if you happen to visit the Mamirauá Reserve (Reserva de Desenvolvimento Sustentável Mamirauá; p638) you stand a good chance of seeing the very distinctive white uakari.

Around 20 species of marmoset and tamarin, small – often very small – primates, are found in Brazil. In Portuguese they're generally called *sauim, saguim, sagui* or *soim*. Scientifically the marmosets belong to the genera *Cebuella, Callithrix* and *Callimico*, and the tamarins to *Leontopithecus* and *Saguinus*. Some are fairly common, but the four species of lion tamarin *(mico-leão; genus Leontopithecus)*, inhabitants of the Atlantic rain forests with a resemblance to miniature lions, are all endangered. The golden lion tamarin *(mico-leão-dourado; Leontopithecus rosalia rosalia)* exists only in the Reserva Biológica Poço das Antas in Rio de Janeiro state (within earshot of the interstate Hwy BR-101). A conservationists' campaign to save this species – a squirrel-sized creature with a brilliant orange-gold color – has, amazingly, brought it back from near-extinction. Its population, down to about 100 in the 1970s, passed the 1000 mark in 2001, and the golden lion tamarin has become a symbol of the whole struggle to save the remaining Atlantic rain forest.

The diet of the giant otter includes fish, snakes, birds and even small alligators. They will eat people if they are hungry enough.

CARNIVORES

The greatest of all felines in the Western Hemisphere is the jaguar. Everyone dreams of sighting a wild jaguar *(onça pintada; Panthera onca)*, but few ever have the chance to see this rare and elusive creature. The large cat with yellow with black spots is widely but thinly distributed in Brazil, occurring in Amazonia, the Pantanal, the cerrado and such easterly national parks as Caparaó (p262), Ilha Grande (p180), Monte Pascoal (p464), Chapada Diamantina (p471) and Chapada dos Veadeiros (p374). A male jaguar can grow 2.5m long, including tail, and weigh 120kg (females weigh up to 90kg). The black panther *(onça preta)*, found in Amazonia, is a sleek all-black jaguar.

Jaguars hunt at night, covering large distances. They prey on a wide variety of animals, in trees, water and on the ground, including sloths, monkeys, fish, deer, tapirs, capybaras and agoutis – but rarely people. They're generally solitary and, unusually among cats, good swimmers.

Brazil's five other wild cats are also widely but sparsely distributed, endangered and rarely seen. The puma *(suçuarana* or *onça parda; Felis concolor)*, almost as big as the jaguar, is the same beast as North America's cougar or mountain lion. As well as feeding on deer, it's known to attack herds of domestic animals such as sheep or goats. Three smaller cats have markings similar to the jaguar. The largest of them (up to 1.4m long with tail and weighing 15kg) is the ocelot *(jaguatirica* or *gato-maracajá; Felis pardalis)*; next largest in size is the margay *(jaguatirica* or *gato-maracajá* or *gato-do-mato-grande; Felis wiedii)*; and then the oncilla *(jaguatirica* or *gato-do-mato-pequeno; Felis tigrina)*. Probably more often seen than any other Brazilian feline, because it's active by day, is the jaguarundi *(gato-mourisco; Felis yaguaroundi)*. Also known as the otter-cat, partly due to its swimming ability, it's similar in size to the margay, and has a uniformly colored coat, which may be black or any shade of brown or gray.

The widespread coati (quati; Nasua nasua) is one of the carnivorous animals that you're most likely to come across – possibly as a pet, for it's easily tamed. It's furry and cute, the size of a small- or medium-sized dog, with a long brown-and-yellow-ringed tail, and a long flexible snout that it uses to nose around for food on the ground or up in trees. Scientifically the coati is a procyonid – one of the raccoon family. Its distant relative, the crab-eating raccoon (guaxirim or mão-pelada; Procyon cancrivorus), has a ringed tail and black eye mask, like the North American raccoon. It's found in Amazonia, the Pantanal and in between, always near water, where it finds its diet of crabs, fish, mollusks and small amphibians.

The giant otter (ariranha; Pteronura brasiliensis) can measure 2m from nose to tail tip. It inhabits lakes and calm rivers in forests from Amazonia to the Pantanal, usually in family groups of six to eight. The Alta Floresta district (p386) and Reserva Xixuaú-Xipariná (p636) are two areas where visitors regularly see giant otters. The smaller southern river otter (lontra; Lutra longicaudis) is also widely dispersed.

The maned wolf (lobo guará; Chrysocyon brachyurus) inhabits cerrado and the Pantanal. It is russet colored, fox faced and long legged, grows to about 1m long (plus tail) and has a mane of darker hair on the back of the neck. It's commonly hunted and is another threatened species. Other Brazilian members of the dog family include the crab-eating fox (lobinho or cachorro do mato; Cerdocyon thous) and the bush dog (cachorro do mato vinagre; Speothos venaticus), both present in cerrado and Pantanal. They are pretty rare and you'd be lucky to see any of these three.

Jacques Cousteau's two Amazon movies, *Amazon – River of the Future* (1991) and *Amazon – Journey to a Thousand Rivers* (1991), follow the world's greatest oceanographer as he films the intricacies of this unique ecosystem and makes a persuasive argument for its conservation.

UNGULATES

Though no longer used in formal classification, the term ungulate generally refers to hoofed quadrupeds.

The Brazilian tapir (anta; Tapirus terrestris) can be found in most forested parts of the country but is shy and nocturnal. Related to the horse and about the size of stocky pony (it can weigh 300kg), the tapir has a long snout that helps it forage for leaves, fruit and roots. It rarely strays far from mud, which it uses to keep cool and control parasites.

Peccaries – looking like small wild boars – are fairly widely distributed in forests. They live in groups, are active by day and consume a diet of fruit, roots, carrion and small animals. The collared peccary (cateto or caititu; Pecari tajacu), around 1m long and weighing 20kg, is named for the light-colored semicircle below its neck and is found in groups of 10 to 50. The slightly bigger white-lipped peccary (queixada or porco-do-mato; Tayassu pecari) travels in groups of 50 or more, chewing up and trampling everything in their path.

In the Pantanal, most people see at least a few deer. The biggest, which is active by day, is the marsh deer (cervo-do-pantanal; Blastocerus dichotomus), which has antlers that can grow to 60cm long. Other species – some found as far north as Amazonia – include the pampas deer (veado-campeiro; Ozotoceros bezoarticus), which lives more out in the open than most other deer, and the small (60cm to 70cm long) gray brocket deer (veado-catingueiro; Mazama gouazoubira) and the red brocket deer (veado-mateiro; Mazama americana).

RODENTS

The widespread capybara (capivara; Hydrochaeris hydrochaeris) is the world's largest rodent, 1m long and up to 70kg in weight. It has a guinea pig–like face and a bulky hairy body, but no tail. It's vegetarian and at home on land or in water. Herds of up to 40 may be seen in the Pantanal. Smaller rodents – but still up to 60cm or 70cm long – include the paca *(paca; Agouti paca)* and various species of agouti *(cutia; Dasyprocta)*. You can distinguish the paca by its rows of white spots. Porcupines *(ouriço* or *porco-espinho)* are rodents too: Brazil has several tree-dwelling species.

AQUATIC MAMMALS

On many rivers in the Amazon basin you should catch glimpses of the pink dolphin *(boto* or *boto cor-de-rosa; Inia geoffrensis)*. One of the world's five freshwater cetaceans, it lives only in the Amazon and Orinoco rivers and their tributaries – and it really is pink! It's most often seen where tributaries meet larger rivers, and is most active in the early morning and late afternoon. Sightings are tantalizing – and getting good photos virtually impossible – as the dolphin surfaces unpredictably, for just a second or so at a time, to breathe. Often they don't even lift their heads above the surface. The pink dolphin has a lumpy forehead, a long beak, no dorsal fin (just a ridge) and tiny eyes – it's almost blind but has a highly evolved sonar system. Adults are 1.8m to 2.5m long, weighing 85kg to 160kg.

Amazonian rivers are also home to the gray dolphin *(tucuxi; Sotalia fluviatilis)*, which is a bit smaller than the pink but often found together with it. Unlike the pink dolphin, the gray also inhabits the sea, in coastal waters from Florianópolis to Panama. When it surfaces it usually lifts its head and part of its body out of the water.

Larger than the dolphins is the Amazon manatee *(peixe-boi; Trichechus inunguis)*, a slow-moving vegetarian that is illegally hunted for its meat by riverbank dwellers and consequently is in danger of extinction. Prospects are even poorer for the marine West Indian manatee *(peixe-boi-marinho; Trichechus manatus)*, of which there are just 400 left in coastal waters north of the Amazon's mouth.

Seven whale species occur off the coast of Brazil. The country's first dedicated whale sanctuary, Praia da Rosa (p332), was declared along 130km of the Santa Catarina coast in 2000, to protect the southern right whale *(baleia franca do sul; Eubalaena australis)*, once the abundant raw material of a Brazilian whaling industry but now down to a world population of about 7000. Mothers and calves can be seen from Praia da Rosa beach between June and October.

> 'the pink dolphin... lives only in the Amazon and Orinoco rivers and their tributaries – and it really is pink!'

ANACONDA LOVE

The name 'anaconda' is derived from the Tamil word *anaikolra*, which means 'elephant killer.' These feared snakes can grow to 11m in length and inhabit parts of the Amazon and the Pantanal. Due to their size, these creatures have few predators, except for humans who sometimes hunt them for their skin. Their average life span is approximately 10 years, but they can live to be well over 30.

The male anaconda reaches sexual maturity at 18 months of age or approximately 2m in length. The dominant female does so at three years of age or 3m in length. When they mate, the snakes wind themselves together into a 'breeding ball' that can consist of two to 12 males coiled around a single female. They take their time and can stay like this for two to four weeks. As a sign of endearment, sometimes the postcoital females then cannibalize a couple of males. Experts think that they may eat their breeding partners in order to survive the seven-month fast during pregnancy.

Another rare whale, the humpback *(baleia jubarte; Megaptera novae-angliae)*, breeds in the same months in the Parque Nacional Marinho de Abrolhos (p465), off the coast of southern Bahia. Arraial do Cabo (p203) is another good humpback-watching spot.

The Fernando de Noronha archipelago (p511), off Natal in Northeast Brazil, is a good site for observing large groups of spinner dolphins *(golfinho rotador; Stenella longirostris)*, small marine dolphins less than 1.8m long. They gather by the hundreds in the bays at sunrise and playfully swim around the bows of tour boats.

Reptiles
SNAKES

The general Brazilian word for snake is *cobra*. The infamous anaconda *(sucuri; Eunectes notaeus or Eunectes murinus)* kills its victims by coiling around them to crush and suffocate, then eats them whole. On extremely rare occasions, an anaconda kills a person. It's not poisonous but can bite viciously. Generally an olive-brown color with black patterning, anacondas can live in water or on land and are considered common in the Pantanal.

Other constrictor snakes – using the same cheerful coil-crush-suffocate technique – include the boa constrictor *(jibóia; Boa constrictor)*, which is 3m to 5m long, generally brown patterned and lives off small animals in varied and widespread habitats; and the handsome green-and-white emerald tree boa *(jibóia-verde; Corallus caninus)*. A number of other snakes live in trees, but most are harmless.

Although it is rare to encounter a venomous snake in the wild, Brazil still has quite a few species of them, including rattlesnakes *(cascavel)*, vipers *(vibora, peçonhenta or cobra covinha)* and coral snakes *(cobra coral)*. The most dangerous in the Pantanal is Wied's lancehead *(jararaca-pintada or boca-de-sapo; Bothrops neiwiedi)*, a gray, black and white patterned viper up to 70cm long that sometimes hides in houses and has a bite that can be fatal if not treated quickly. Also to be steered clear of is the Brazilian coral snake *(cobra coral; Micrurus frontalis)*, with its

The official Tamar Project website, www.tamar .org.br, contains plenty of information on the Brazilian turtle.

MAN BITES PIRANHA

Why are people scared of piranhas? The fish should be terrified of us, as humans eat piranhas a billion times more often than piranhas eat people. They're reasonably good tasting too, if a bit small and bony. A standard activity on an Amazon jungle trip is catching your own piranha lunch. You'll be taken by canoe and given a simple fishing rod constructed of cane, line and hook, and a supply of small chunks of meat for bait. Put a piece of bait onto the hook, drop it into the water, and – presto – free lunch. For the piranhas, that is, who will nibble the bait right off your hook without getting caught.

Your more-skilled local companions, however, will catch half a dozen of them without even trying – and *these* will be your lunch.

Not all piranhas are the same, of course. There are about 50 species of the *Serrasalmo* genus. Piranhas are found in the basins of the Amazon, Orinoco, Paraguay and São Francisco rivers and in the rivers of the Guiana watershed. Some live on seeds and fruits, some on other fish and only a handful of species are potentially a risk to larger creatures. These types are at their least amiable when stuck in tributaries, meanders or lakes that get cut off from main rivers in the dry season. When they have eaten all the other fish, the piranhas will attack more or less anything, including wounded mammals entering their waters. The scent of blood or bodily fluids in the water can whip a shoal into a feeding frenzy. Confirmed accounts of human fatalities caused by piranhas are extremely few and far between, but plenty of Amazonian river folk have scars or missing fingers to testify just how sharp and vicious those little triangular teeth can be.

rings of red, black and white. It lurks under rocks or logs and only bites when it feels threatened – but it's very poisonous when it does. The fake coral snakes (*cobra falsa-coral; genus Atractus*) are, lucky for them, nearly impossible to distinguish from the real thing.

ALLIGATORS

Brazil has five species of alligator and caiman (*jacaré*). They eat fish, amphibians, crustaceans and some birds. In the Pantanal, the most common is a subspecies called the Paraguayan caiman (*jacaré-do-Pantanal; Caiman crocodilus yacare*). Amazonia has four species. The biggest is the black caiman (*jacaré açu; Melanosuchus niger*), which reaches up to 6m long and is endangered because it's hunted for its skin and meat.

The most common Amazonian alligator – the one you'll probably get to handle on nighttime alligator expeditions – is the spectacled caiman (*jacaré tingá; Caiman crocodilus*), which can grow up to 2.3m long. Alligators lay eggs in nests of leaves and stalks, and these are vulnerable to predators such as coatis and lizards; the hatched young are prey to herons and storks.

> The pirarucu has gills but they are basically useless. It can survive for up to 24 hours out of the water, but will drown in a couple of minutes if it doesn't surface to breathe.

TURTLES

Brazil's five species of sea turtle (*tartaruga marinha*) are all under effective official protection (see the boxed text on p441), though here and there shells are still sold and eggs eaten. There are Tamar Project sites from São Paulo state to Ceará. There are also several species of river turtle (*quelônio*), which live throughout the country and tend not to be endangered.

Fish

Amazonia is home to at least 2000 freshwater fish species, and the Pantanal to 260 species.

The king of Amazonian fish is the beautiful and enormous pirarucu (*Arapaima gigas*), which can grow to 3m long and weigh well over 100kg – its red and silvery-brown scale patterns are reminiscent of Chinese paintings. The pirarucu is a voracious hunter of other fish, and a rich food source for humans. To try to preserve the shrinking population, it's forbidden to catch the fish if they are less than 1.5m in length or during the October-to-March spawning season.

> **DID YOU KNOW?**
>
> The stingray will only strike if you step on it. To avoid this, don't raise your feet far off the bottom as you walk in shallow, unclear water.

The pirarucu, with gills that are basically useless, quite often comes to the river surface to breathe. It's a member of the primitive Osteoglossidae order, characterized by a bony tongue and rear fins that almost join the tail. The male protects the young for up to the first six months of their lives.

A similar Amazonian fish, which also has edible meat, is the *aruanã* (*Osteoglossum bicirrhosum*). Up to 1m long, it can leap 2m into the air to grab fruit or catch insects. The adult males nurture the young inside their mouths.

The most important food fish of central Amazonia is the little jaraqui (*Semaprochilodus taeniurus*), which swims in shoals of thousands. Two further food fish – the pirapitinga (*Piaractus brachypomus*) and the tambaqui (*Colossoma macropomum*) – are of the same family (*Serrasalmidae*) as piranhas. The rotund tambaqui can reach 1m in length and weigh up to 25kg. Normally it lives on nuts (which it can crack with its jaws) and seeds, but when the waters recede it turns carnivorous and will eat what it can.

Amazonia harbors at least 100 species of catfish, named for the long barbels (bristles) that help them search for food on river bottoms. One catfish, the piraíba (*Brachyplatystoma filamentosum*), is the biggest of all

Amazonian fish, growing up to 3m long and weighing as much as 200kg. It's an aggressive creature and will even attack water birds. The dourado *(Brachyplatystoma flavicans)*, growing up to 1m long with pale gold sides, is common in the Pantanal as well as in Amazonia, and is generally considered the best-tasting catfish, making it a popular dish in restaurants throughout the country. It is a carnivore and its own diet consists mainly of other fish. The piramutuba *(Brachyplatystoma vaillanti)* lays its eggs in the upper Rio Solimões, then descends in big shoals to mature at the mouth of the Amazon River. It can grow to more than 1m long and is heavily fished on the lower Amazonas.

You will probably hear rumors about the infamous candiru in Amazonia. There are many species of these small catfish of the *Trichomycteridae* family, most of them pretty obnoxious. The really infamous type of candiru is one of the *Vandellia* genus, about 5cm long. This little charmer normally lives inside the gills of other fish to suck their blood, but is attracted to urine and reputedly able to wriggle up humans' urinary tracts, where it lodges itself with sharp spines and can only be removed by surgery. The belief that it can actually swim up a stream of urine to get inside you is almost certainly false, but it's probably not a good idea to urinate in Amazonian waters just the same. Locals wear clothing to exclude the candiru in areas where it's known.

Other best-avoided inhabitants of Brazilian freshwaters include the stingray *(arraia; Potamotrygon motoro)* and the electric eel *(poraquê; Electrophorus electricus)*. The stingray lives on river floors and can inflict deep, painful cuts with the barbs in its tail. The electric eel, growing up to 2.75m long, is capable of a 600-volt discharge to stun its prey and could potentially kill a human with a volley of electric pulses.

A fish that, by contrast, is very much sought after in Amazonia – both for its delicious taste and its famous fighting qualities as a sport fish – is the peacock bass *(tucunaré; Cichla monoculus)*. Growing to 50cm or more, it has a peacocklike 'eye' spot on its tail. Also sought – for home aquariums the world over – are the tiny but brightly colored tetra 'fighting' fish *(Hyphassobrycon)*. They come from the murky *igapós* (flooded Amazon forests) of Amazonia, where they would doubtless go unseen if more demurely pigmented.

Birds

There are fantastic birds in almost every region of Brazil, making the country a major destination for birding trips. The biggest Brazilian bird is the flightless rhea *(ema; Rhea americana)*, found in the cerrado and Pantanal. It grows to 1.4m tall and weighs some 30kg. The smallest are the numerous types of hyperactive humming bird *(beija-flor; Trochilidae)*, which are found throughout the country.

WATERFOWL

Widely seen freshwater fishing birds include a couple of types of cormorant *(biguá; genus Phalacrocorax)* and the similar anhinga *(biguatinga or cararâ; Anhinga anhinga)*. You can often see them standing on waterside branches, their wings spread out to dry.

The *Ciconiiformes* order comprises herons *(garça or socó)*, egrets *(garça or garcinha)*, storks *(cegonhas)*, ibises *(curicaca)* and their relatives. They're mostly large, highly visible birds, often seen flapping inelegantly along waterways or standing motionless in shallows or on branches just above the water ready to jab for fish with their long beaks. Many species are found in the Pantanal and Amazonia. The tiger heron *(socó-boi; Tigrisoma*

Jaguar (p71)

Scarlet macaw (p77)

Caimans (p75)

RICARDO GOMES

Heron (p76)

JASON EDWARDS

Puma (p71)

Monkey (p70)

JOHN MAIER

JANE SWEENEY

Thin-spined porcupine (p72)

lineatum), with its brown and black stripes, is particularly distinctive. Hundreds of snowy egrets *(garcinha; Egretta thula)* gather by in waterside rookeries, looking like a sudden blooming of white flowers in the treetops.

Of the storks, the tall (1.40m) black-headed and red-necked jabiru *(tuiuiú* or *jaburu; Jabiru mycteria)* has become a symbol of the Pantanal and is also found in Amazonia. In the Pantanal, also look for the similarly sized maguari stork *(tabuiaiá; Ciconia maguari)*, which is mainly white with a pinkish face, and the smaller wood stork *(cabeça-seca; Mycteria americana)*, with its black head and beak with a curved end. The beautiful pink roseate spoonbill *(colhereiro; Platalea ajaja)* is another Pantanal inhabitant of this order. Brazil's most spectacular ibis is the scarlet ibis *(guará; Eudocimus ruber)*, which is very pink, 50cm long and found living in flocks on the Ilha de Marajó (p502), at the mouth of the Amazon.

Kingfishers *(martim-pescador* or *ariramba)* are among the most visible birds along many of Brazil's waterways, flying across or along rivers as boats approach. There are several species, the biggest being the 42cm-long ringed kingfisher *(martim-pescador-matraca, martim-pescador-grande* or *ariramba-grande; Ceryle torquata)*, which is predominantly bright turquoise with a rust-colored underside.

Hummingbirds beat their wings up to 80 times a second, allowing them to hover while extracting pollen from flowers – making a light humming noise as they do.

BIRDS OF PREY

Much like great cats, birds of prey command respect and are always an object of fascination. Brazil has around 40 species of eagle, hawk, falcon, kite, caracara and kestrel, some quite common, and they're generally not easy to tell apart. The Portuguese word *gavião* is used for almost any of them; *águia* means eagle and *falcão* means falcon.

The crested caracara *(caracará* or *carcará; Polyborus plancus)* is common in many areas – it's 50cm to 60cm long with a 1.2m or 1.3m wingspan. Its broad diet includes fish dying from a lack of oxygen as Pantanal ponds dry up, and animals that have been run over on roads or burnt in forest fires. Also common in Amazonia and the Pantanal is the yellow-headed caracara *(gavião-pinhé* or *carrapateiro; Milvago chimachima)*, which grows to about 40cm long, and the black-collared hawk *(gavião-belo; Busarellus nigricollis)*, a reddish-brown fish-catcher, with a white head and chest, that reaches lengths of about 45cm. The osprey *(aguia pescadora; Pandion haliaetus)*, also known as the fishing eagle, is bigger (55cm to 60cm; wingspan 1.45m to 1.7m), with a darker brown body.

Brazil's most emblematic bird of prey is the ferocious, very large (and rare) harpy eagle *(águia real* or *harpia; Harpia harpyja)*, found chiefly in Amazonia, where it enjoys a diet of monkeys, sloths and other large animals (see the boxed text on p385).

MACAWS & PARROTS

These are the kind of birds that have come to be recognized as the symbol of tropical rain forests and people visit from all over the world to see the dozens of different species. The general Brazilian word for macaw is *arara*; for parrot, it's *papagaio* or *maracanã*; for parakeet, *periquito*. These charismatic colorful birds have strong, curved beaks that they use to break open seeds and nuts and they also eat soft clay to temper the acidity of their other foods. They are aggressive and it is not unheard of for them to eat food off someone's plate at a jungle lodge.

Macaws, the biggest of these birds, grab most of the glamour. You can distinguish them by their dead-straight body shape when flying, and straight-as-an-arrow trajectory. They often go about in pairs and make a lot of raucous noise. They travel up to 25km a day foraging for food.

The name of scarlet macaw *(arara vermelha)* is given to two large, gloriously colored species – *Ara chloroptera*, also called the red-and-green macaw, which grows up to 90cm to 95cm long and has blue-and-green wings and a red-striped face, and *Ara macao*, which is a bit smaller and has blue-and-yellow wings. The latter bird is restricted to Amazonia, but the red-and-green macaw also inhabits other regions, including the Pantanal, cerrado and even the caatinga. The blue-and-yellow macaw *(arara-amarela* or *arara-canindé; Ara ararauna)*, about 85cm long, is also widely distributed. The yellow covers its underside, the blue its upper parts.

Unfortunately, the beautiful plumage of the macaws makes them a major target for poachers. Poaching has contributed greatly to the decline of the hyacinth macaw *(arara-azul; Anodorhynchus hyacinthinus)*, the world's largest parrot (1m long), which is endemic to the Pantanal. This gorgeous bird, deep blue with splashes of bright yellow on the face, is down to a population of about 3000 and conservationists are struggling to bring it back from the verge of extinction.

HUMMINGBIRDS

These beautiful little birds, with their dazzling iridescent colors, may be seen all over Brazil, including in cities. They flit rapidly, almost insect-like, from one spot to the next, and can even fly backwards. The lyrical Brazilian name for them is *beija-flor* (flower-kisser). There are many dozens of species (family *Trochilidae*) and they occupy an important role in Brazilian art and folklore, are often mentioned in famous music and poetry and are the symbol of one of the best-known samba schools in Rio, Beija-Flor.

TROGONS

This family of medium-sized, brightly colored, sometimes iridescent birds with long tails – called *surucuá* or *saracuá* in Portuguese – includes the celebrated quetzals. You may see them perching and flying at medium heights in tropical forests. Amazonia has at least seven species, including the pavonine quetzal *(surucuá açu; Pharomacrus pavoninus)*. The blue-crowned trogon *(surucuá-de-coroa-azul; Trogon curucui)* also inhabits the Pantanal.

TOUCANS

Among the most well-known and colorful groups of Latin American birds, the toucan *(tucano* or *araçari)* has a huge rainbow-colored beak, sometimes as long as its body, which enables it to reach berries at the end of branches. But the beak is light and almost hollow, allowing the bird to fly with a surprising agility. It lives at forest treetop level and is often best seen from boats.

Brazil's biggest is the toco toucan *(tucanuçu* or *tucano; Ramphastos toco)*, with habitats ranging from Amazonia to the cerrado to the Pantanal. The bird is around 55cm long, including its bright orange beak, and its plumage is black except for a white neck area. In Amazonia you may see the white-throated toucan *(tucano-assoviador; Ramphastos tucanus)* or the yellow-ridged toucan *(tucano-rouco* or *tucano pequeno de papo branco; Ramphastos culminatus)*. Both of these birds are fairly large, with black beaks.

Endangered Species

From the cunning jaguar to the serene sea turtle, an alarming number of Brazilian animal species are endangered. There are government and activist programs that attempt to help and protect some of the more charismatic species, such as the monkeys, turtles, great cats and predatory birds. But, numerous lesser-known creatures are disappearing daily and any species, regardless of how insignificant it may seem, plays an irreplaceable role in the ecosystem. Humans may not care about the extinction of the brazilian spiny rice rat or the bushy-tailed opossum, but if nothing else, they both occupy a spot in the food chain and their disappearance will forever affect the other plants and animals around them.

There are three main causes for the extinction of Brazilian wildlife. The most infamous cause is hunting; however, in reality, it is only responsible for about 25% of extinction. The destruction of habitats accounts for around 36% of the loss and the least known, yet most lethal cause is the introduction of competing species, which is responsible for some 39% of the destruction. Dogs, pigs, rats and lizards (not to mention humans) have wreaked havoc on untold thousands of smaller species. Even if no one ever hunted a jaguar again it would still be at risk of extinction as it needs a huge amount of habitat to hunt and a large gene pool for mating. The reduced population and habitat may already mean the jaguar is on its way to existing only in zoos.

Endangered species are much sought after by travelers interested in wildlife; however, most are difficult if not nearly impossible to spot. Some are visible only in small reserves or specific parts of national parks.

Critically endangered mammal species include the black-faced lion tamarin, the Brazilian arboreal mouse, the capuchin (ring-tail) monkey, Coimbra's titi monkey, the golden-rumped lion tamarin, the Northern Bahian blond titi monkey, and the northern woolly spider monkey.

Other endangered species are the Brazilian spiny rice rat, the buffy-headed marmoset, Cleber's arboreal rice rat, the pacarana, the fin whale, the giant armadillo, the golden-headed lion tamarin, the maned three-toed sloth, the pied tamarin, the pygmy short-tailed opossum, the Rio de Janeiro rice rat, the southern woolly spider monkey, the white-whiskered spider monkey and white-eared marmoset.

Plants

Brazil's history and future are inextricably tied to its forests and nature. So close is this association that the country even gets its name from the brazilwood tree (*pau brasil*), which the Portuguese explorers cut and exported as fast as they could for a valuable red dye found in its core.

The last ice age did not make its way to Brazil and the rain forests have never suffered long droughts, so the area has had an unusually

DID YOU KNOW?

The British smuggled a rubber seedling out of Brazil, cultivated it in Kew Gardens and planted competing rubber crops in Sri Lanka, which led to the collapse of the Brazilian rubber industry.

DID YOU KNOW?

A Brazil nut tree takes 10 years to reach maturity and can produce over 450kg of nuts per year.

USING NATURE TO ITS FULLEST

The lives of people in rural Maranhão state and the babaçu palm are deeply intertwined. Locals carefully cultivate the tree and use it to make just about anything and everything. The nuts can be eaten straight out of the fruit or crushed to produce vegetable oil (for margarine) or industrial lubricating oils; the tips of the young palms can be eaten as 'hearts of palm'; and the older trunks are used for the construction of homes, with roofing material supplied by the leaves – which can also be used for the production of cellulose and paper. The residue from the crushed nuts provides excellent fertilizer and cattle feed, and the hulls of the fruit are used in the production of acetates, tar and methyl alcohol. Finally, the hulls are turned to charcoal for use in smelting. While in Maranhão, don't forget to buy some arts and crafts made from various babaçu parts. Match that up against anything growing in your garden.

long period of time to develop plant species that are found nowhere else in the world. Although many of these long-evolved species have been destroyed in the last 30 years through heavy deforestation, there remains an impressive range of flora in Brazil – from over 200 varieties of tiny delicate orchids to 90m-tall hardwood trees.

It would be impossible to determine an exact number of plant species in the Amazon, let alone in the whole of Brazil, as new plants are being discovered all the time and, unfortunately, others are disappearing with a terrifying frequency. The great majority of the plants in the rain forests of Brazil are trees – estimated at some 70% of the total vegetation. On average, trees grow from 30m to 35m in height, with some tall ones reaching 50m to 90m. Because they survive in the same habitat, most rain forest trees look similar even though they are of different species. In some parts, a trained eye can find over 400 species of tree per hectare.

Ron Mader's fantastic www.planeta.com has many ecotourism resources, from photos and practical information to more theoretical online symposiums.

One of the most economically important trees is the rubber tree, which grows in the wild or on sustainable plantations for the large-scale production of latex – yes, condoms too come from the Amazon. Another sustainable forest product is the nut from the Brazil nut tree, a good snack if you are able to get the shell off without having a nervous breakdown. Mahogany is perhaps the most valuable of the Brazilian hardwoods and is used for quality furniture and specialized items. These supposedly protected trees are often illegally cut down and exported to first-world consumers.

The trees compete for sunlight in the dense canopy and have few lower branches, which allows the trees to grow close to each other. This dense vegetation creates a hosts of different environments for plants and animals to live in, sort of like a multistory apartment building. The canopy is the penthouse of the forest and many smaller vines and flowers only reside at this level. The different levels teem with figs, laurels, begonias, orchids and palms.

The International Ecotourism Society (www.ecotourism.org) is the definitive source for ecotourism and sustainable travel information the world over.

Many edible fruits also grow in the rain forest, so many in fact that a number of them only have names in Portuguese. Some of the more popular fruits, including açaí, acerola and cupuaçu can be found at juice bars throughout the country. Guaraná berries, which contain a stimulant similar to caffeine, are also making their way into energy drinks world over.

Outside of the rain forests the plant life is quite different. It is true that in some of the drier and coastal parts of the country it may seem that the only plants that grow are palm trees, shrubs or thorny cacti. Let's hope that the rain forests do not soon look the same.

NATIONAL PARKS & PROTECTED AREAS

Much of Brazil is, officially at least, under environmental protection. Over 350 areas throughout the country, covering more than 300,000 sq km (more than 5% of Brazil), are protected in a confusing variety of conservation units, ranging from national parks and national forests to extractive reserves and sustainable development reserves. Some of these are run by the federal government, some by state governments and some by private individuals or Non-Governmental Organizations (NGOs).

Unfortunately, the degree of protection these areas actually receive is also variable and in some cases practically nonexistent. Private areas and ecotourism projects often have better management and enforcement than the larger national parks. The federal government's environmental agency, Instituto Brasileiro do Meio Ambiente e dos Recursos Naturais Renováveis (IBAMA; Brazilian Institute of the Environment & Renewable Natural Resources), has a relatively small budget and is even unable to protect many of the 40 national parks from illegal logging, ranching, settlement and poaching. Contrary to popular perception, much of the country is inhabited. The Amazon has supported humans for many thousands of years and any conservation projects must take into account the local populations.

Permits, or at least an official guide, are needed to visit many conservation units legally. Wherever possible, regulations of this type are cited in this book. The categories *parque nacional* (Parna; national park), *parque estadual* (PES; state park), *estacão ecológica* (ESEC; ecological station), *reserva biológica* (Rebio; biological reserve), and *reserva ecológica* (Resec; ecological reserve) are classified as *de uso indireto* (indirect use). This means that their ecosystems are supposedly under total government protection.

Flora and fauna may not be consumed, collected, damaged or destroyed. National and state parks and ecological stations are also designated exclusively for scientific research. In national and state parks, recreational uses and ecological tourism are also permitted.

The categories *área de protecão ambiental* (APA; environmental protection area), *área de relevante interesse ecológico* (ARIE; area of ecological interest), *floresta nacional* (Flona; national forest), *floresta estadual* (FES; state forest), and *reserva extrativista* (Resex; extractive reserve) are all *de uso direto* (direct use), meaning their resources can be exploited or managed in ways compatible with nature conservation. National and state forests are areas of predominantly native forest, geared to sustainable exploitation and scientific research. Extractive reserves are areas with human populations dependent on traditional extractive activities – such as rubber tapping, fruit or nut collecting or fishing – in conjunction with subsistence agriculture. Extractive reserves are dedicated to protecting these peoples' ways of life while ensuring the sustainable use of reserve resources.

Any of these conservation units can be run at either the state or federal level (except, of course, for national and state parks, and national and state forests, which are run at federal or state level as their titles indicate).

Three more state-level categories – *reserva de desenvolvimento sustentável* (REDS; sustainable development reserve), *floresta estadual de rendimento sustentável* (FERS; sustainable-yield state forest) and *floresta estadual extrativista* (FEEX; state extractive forest) – aim to combine sustainable exploitation, research into resource management, and improved living standards for local populations.

Private owners can also create nature reserves under the title *reserva particular patrimônio natural* (RPPN; private natural heritage reserve).

Terras indígenas (indigenous lands) occupy about 11% of Brazilian territory. Though these are not explicitly dedicated to nature conservation, their inhabitants tend to use them with considerably less environmental impact.

Where to Go

Brazil is a huge country and its flora and fauna are spread across the vast regions: some in national parks, some in regional and local parks, some in private protected areas and some in open land. It is impossible to see everything in one place, so it is best to plan a trip around specific natural interests and do some pretravel research. Following are listed some of the many national parks and protected areas where visitors can encounter wildlife up close (also see the table of protected areas on p84-5 for a quick reference of parks and other conservation zones).

John Kricher's *A Neotropical Companion*, while not specific to Brazil, is a good introductory text for neotropical ecology and explains many of the forest's intricacies in straightforward terms.

SOUTHEAST

In Rio de Janeiro itself, the Parque Nacional & Floresta da Tijuca (p146) offers magnificent panoramic views and walks in lush Mata Atlântica (Atlantic rain forest), with the possibility of seeing monkeys. The mountainous Parque Nacional de Itatiaia (p193), 150km northwest of the city, is a favorite with walkers and climbers – its big attraction is the Pico das Agulhas Negras (2787m). Some 400 bird and 67 mammal species have been recorded here. Another climbing mecca is the Parque Nacional da Serra dos Órgãos (p199), 86km northeast of Rio. As well as spectacular peaks, it offers some great walks, with plenty of trails. These last two parks both possess a well-developed visitor infrastructure.

The Parque Nacional da Serra da Bocaina is where the coastal escarpment meets the sea, and the Atlantic rain forest quickly changes to araucaria forest as you move up from the coast. The varied and plentiful wildlife includes the endangered woolly spider monkey. The park is not easily accessible but has many walking trails.

The Iporanga area (p289) of São Paulo state is one of the least-disturbed zones of Atlantic rain forest, and it is of international importance for its biodiversity.

The Parque Nacional de Caparaó (p262) contains Brazil's third-highest peak, Pico da Bandeira (2890m), where you can reach the summit in a day hike from campsites in the park or accommodations just outside it.

The Parque Nacional da Serra do Cipó (p262), northeast of Belo Horizonte, is a beautiful area of mountains, waterfalls and cerrado, noted for its many flower species. You can camp in or near the park or stay in a nearby *pousada* (guesthouse). Also in Minas Gerais is the Parque Natural do Caraça (p261), a beautiful transitional area between Mata Atlântica and wild mountain vegetation, with easily accessible hiking trails and creeks that form waterfalls and natural swimming pools.

SOUTH

More than 340 bird and 40 mammal species have been recorded in the forests of the Parque Nacional do Iguaçu (p310), on the Brazilian side of the famous Iguaçu Falls, but for those interested in fauna and flora, the Argentine Parque Nacional del Iguazú on the far side of the falls is actually better.

On the coast of Paraná is the Parque Nacional do Superaguí (p308), which has one of the largest remaining tracts of Mata Atlântica and offers hiking, beaches and pousadas in the village of Vila do Superaguí. The park's abundant wildlife includes the rare black-faced lion tamarin, a small primate discovered in the 1990s (numbering about 400), and the endangered purple-faced parrot. Also notable is the huge number of wild orchids.

Brazil's first whale sanctuary was declared in 2000 along part of the coast of Santa Catarina state. The beautiful bay of Praia da Rosa (p332) is a breeding ground for southern right whales: mothers and calves can be seen from the beach from June to October. In Santa Catarina's Serra do Mar, where it even snows sometimes, the Parque Nacional de São Joaquim (p333) contains rare araucaria forests and dramatic rock formations, but has no infrastructure for visits.

Brazil's southernmost state, Rio Grande do Sul, contains the unforgettable Parque Nacional de Aparados da Serra, with the 700m-deep Cânion do Itaimbezinho. This park has trails for day hikes and a visitors center. The adjoining Parque Nacional da Serra Geral, where there is another stunning fissure in the earth, the Cânion da Fortaleza, has no infrastructure, but camping is allowed.

'The beautiful bay of Praia da Rosa is a breeding ground for southern right whales.'

CENTRAL WEST
Pantanal
If you're looking to see animals in the wild, don't miss the Pantanal, which has the greatest concentration of fauna in the New World. In the Amazon, the animals hide in the dense foliage, but in the open spaces of the Pantanal, wildlife is visible to the most casual observer. There are three main access cities for the Brazilian Pantanal – Cuiabá (p379) to the north, Campo Grande (p302) to the east and Corumbá (p392) to the west.

Basically there are four ways to visit the Pantanal. Firstly, you can make your own way along the Transpantaneira, the rough road leading into the northern Pantanal from Poconé, south of Cuiabá. This requires driving or hitchhiking. Secondly, it is possible to take a safari with a small tour operator from Cuiabá, staying on farms. The third option is to take a cheap three- to four-day tour from Corumbá or Campo Grande, staying in tent or hut camps along Estrada Parque, a 117km dirt road looping through the southern Pantanal. Lastly, you can base yourself at a *hotel-fazenda* (ranch-style hotel) or pousada and take trips out from there. Many have horses and boats for hire. For details on all of these options, see p388.

One River: Explorations and Discoveries in the Amazon Rain Forest, by Wade Davis, reflects on the importance of the Amazon and its contents to the planet as a whole.

Near the southern Pantanal is the small town of Bonito (p402), which has become popular for wet-suit swimming in rivers teeming with fish, and snorkeling and diving in lakes.

If possible, visit the Pantanal during the dry season, which is from April/May to September/October. The best months to watch birds are July to September – but reservations are definitely needed for all accommodations in July.

National Parks
The Parque Nacional da Chapada dos Veadeiros (p374), 200km north of Brasília, contains rare fauna and flora, as well as spectacular waterfalls and canyons in a sublime landscape. You need to enter with a guide but this is easy and not costly to arrange. There are accommodations in the nearby village, São Jorge, and town, Alto Paraíso.

In southwest Goiás is the remote Parque Nacional das Emas (p376), the best-preserved tract of savannalike cerrado in Brazil, with abundant visible wildlife including the *emas* (rheas) for which it's named. Go with a guide from one of the nearby towns. There are no accommodations or camping in the park.

Near Cuiabá is the popular Parque Nacional da Chapada dos Guimarães (p384), with its waterfalls, huge valleys and strange rock formations – best visited in a hire car or on an excursion from nearby Chapada dos Guimarães town, which has accommodations.

NORTHEAST
In Bahia, the Parque Nacional da Chapada Diamantina (p471) has a network of trails offering great hiking to peaks, waterfalls and rivers. It's easily accessible from the attractive and popular old mining town of Lençóis.

On the southern Bahia coast, the Parque Nacional de Monte Pascoal (p464), with ecosystems ranging from Atlantic rain forest to mangroves and reefs, has a visitors center reachable by taxi from the town of Itamaraju. Guides will accompany you along the park's trails, including up Monte Pascoal itself, which was the first piece of Brazil seen by Portuguese eyes. It's also possible to enter the park from the coastal villages of Caraíva and Corumbau, which have accommodations.

Protected area	Features	Activities	Best time to visit	Page
Ecoparque de Una	private Mata Atlântica reserve with rare golden-headed lion tamarin	hiking, wildlife, endangered species	any	p453
Fernando de Noronha archipelago	gorgeous marine park on islands 350km from Natal	marine life, Tamar Project (marine turtle project) branch, swimming, scuba, hiking	any	p511
Floresta Nacional do Tapajós	lush Amazonian rain forest preserve	boat trips, wildlife, rare plants	any	p598
Ilha de Marajó	island in the mouth of the Amazon	wetlands, hiking, wildlife	any	p592
Ilha do Bananal	huge island in the intersection of 2 rivers in Tocantins	cerrado, wetlands, Amazon, wildlife, hiking	any	p615
Ilha Grande	tract of Mata Atlântica, just off the coast of Rio state	swimming, hiking, diving, flora & fauna	any	p180
Jalapão	area of eastern Tocantins	cerrado, rivers, lakes, dunes	Jun-Sep	p614
Mamirauá Reserve (Reserva de Desenvolvimento Sustentável Mamirauá)	floodplain reserve with ecotourism program, near Colombia	rare wildlife & plants	any	p638
Pantanal	these wetlands are the best place to see wildlife in Brazil	wildlife, hiking, safari, horseback riding, boating, snorkeling	Apr-Oct	p388
Parque Estadual de Itaúnas	branch of Tamar Project	tour project	Sep-Mar to see turtles hatching	p215
Parque Nacional da Chapada Diamantina	large preserve in Bahia with gorgeous landscape	waterfalls, hiking, climbing, rivers	any	p471
Parque Nacional da Chapada dos Guimarães	waterfalls, valleys & bizarre rock formations	hiking, safari	any	p384
Parque Nacional da Chapada dos Veadeiros	near Brasília, with waterfalls & rare flora & fauna	hiking, wildlife, swimming	Apr-Oct	p374
Parque Nacional da Serra da Capivara	park in southern Piauí with thousands of prehistoric paintings & amazing rock formations	hiking, archaeology	any, cooler during rainy season Nov-Mar	p561
Parque Nacional da Serra do Cipó	mountains, waterfalls & cerrado, near Belo Horizonte	hiking, camping, climbing	any	p262
Parque Nacional da Serra dos Órgãos	mountains & cliffs, 86km from Rio	climbing, hiking any		p199
Parque Nacional da Serra Geral	adjoining Parque Nacional de Aparados da Serra	hiking, camping	any	p344
Parque Nacional das Emas	fantastic cerrado preserve with rheas	wildlife, hiking	any	p376

Protected area	Features	Activities	Best time to visit	Page
Parque Nacional de Aparados da Serra	contains a 700m-deep canyon, in Rio Grande do Sul	hiking	any	p344
Parque Nacional de Caparaó	contains some of Brazil's highest mountain peaks	hiking, climbing, camping	Jun-Aug	p262
Parque Nacional de Itatiaia	mountain peaks & wildlife, 150km from Rio	hiking, climbing, wildlife	any	p193
Parque Nacional de Monte Pascoal	first point discovered by the Portuguese	mountains, mangroves, reefs, hiking	any	p464
Parque Nacional de Saõ Joaquim	araucaria forests, rock formations & even some snow	hiking	any	p333
Parque Nacional de Sete Cidades	unique rock formations in Piauí	hiking, swimming, archaeology	any	p560
Parque Nacional de Ubajara	small Ceará park with huge caves entered on foot or by cable car	caves, hiking	any	p555
Parque Nacional do Iguaçu	Brazilian side of the international waterfalls park	waterfalls, wildlife	any	p310
Parque Nacional do Jaú	one of the world's largest tracts of protected tropical rain forest; little infrastructure	rare flora & fauna	any	p636
Parque Nacional do Superaguí	large area of Mata Atlântica	wildlife including endangered species, rare flora, hiking, beaches	any	p308
Parque Nacional dos Lençóis Maranhenses	sand-dune preserve along beach with clear rain pools	hiking, swimming, wildlife	any	p570
Parque Nacional & Floresta da Tijuca	Mata Atlântica & mountains right in Rio	jungle views, hiking	any	p146
Parque Nacional Marinho de Abrolhos	marine park, 80km off the coast of Bahia	coral reefs, whale watching, marine & bird life	any	p465
Parque Natural do Caraça	variety of terrain, from Mata Atlântica to wild mountain vegetation	hiking, swimming	any	p261
Pico da Neblina	Brazil's highest peak (3014m), on the Venezuelan border	hiking, climbing	any	p636
Praia da Rosa	whale sanctuary in Santa Catarina	whale watching	Jun-Oct	p332
Praia do Forte	headquarters of Tamar Project	tour project	any	p441
Reserva Xixuaú-Xipariná	remote ecotourism project, 1½-day boat trip from Manaus	rare flora & fauna	any	p636
Rio Guaporé	ecolodge and extractive reserve zone along the river in Rondônia	wildlife, rare flora, hiking	any	p667
Rio Javari	area near Peruvian border with some pristine rain forest	wildlife, jungle, boat trips, hiking	any	p644

The Ecoparque de Una (p453), 45km south of Olivença, is a private Atlantic rain forest reserve where guides will lead you on a two-hour trail to see such rare species as the golden-headed lion tamarin.

Approximately 80km off the southernmost stretch of the Bahia coast is Parque Nacional Marinho de Abrolhos (p465). Its attractions are coral reefs, whale-watching and the marine and bird life of the numerous reefs and islets. Access is by organized boat trips, chiefly from Caravelas.

Tamar Project, a government-backed project to save Brazil's five sea turtle species, has 21 stations on the coasts. The headquarters, which you can visit, is at Praia do Forte (p441) in Bahia. Other stations open to visits are in the Parque Estadual de Itaúnas (p215), in Espírito Santo, and on the Fernando de Noronha archipelago (p511), 350km out into the Atlantic from Natal. The marine and bird life and the diving and snorkeling at Fernando de Noronha are outstanding. Access is by plane from Recife or Natal, and you can go independently or by organized tour from either city. There are plenty of accommodations on the islands.

In Maranhão state, the Parque Nacional dos Lençóis Maranhenses (p570) has spectacular beaches, mangroves, dunes and lagoons and interesting fauna. You can arrange for access by boat from the town of Barreirinhas, or take a tour from Barreirinhas or São Luís. More adventurous travelers can stay near the park in the small town of Atins and access the park on foot.

NORTH

The Amazon region is trying hard to realize its ecotourism potential and offer more visitors a richer experience than is available in the immediate vicinity of Manaus. A government program called Proecotur, with funding from the Inter-American Development Bank, aims to create 10,000 new jungle lodge–type beds by 2006 in environmentally protected areas of Amazonia. It's to be hoped this will be done in a small-scale, low-impact way, with community involvement.

On the large Ilha de Marajó (p592), in the mouth of the Amazon River, you can stay on a *hotel-fazenda* and explore a unique wetland ecosystem with varied wildlife. In Tocantins state, Ilha do Bananal (p615), a 20,000-sq-km island between two branches of the mighty Rio Araguaia, forms a transition zone between cerrado, wetlands and Amazon rain forest. The island and nearby areas are rich in wildlife, and there is lodging available in several nearby spots. In eastern Tocantins, the unique, sparsely populated Jalapão district (p614) combines cerrado, rivers, lakes and desertlike areas with sand dunes, and can be visited on tours from Palmas city.

Upstream on the Amazon, possibilities in the Santarém region include riverboat excursions to take you through the floodplains and creeks from Monte Alegre and Santarém itself, and visits to the Floresta Nacional do Tapajós (p598).

Manaus is the nature-tourism capital of Brazilian Amazonia. Several jungle lodges are within a few hours of the city by road and/or river. In a stay at one of these – typically costing around US$100 per day in total, including transportation from and back to Manaus – you'll do things like jungle walks, piranha fishing and nighttime alligator spotting. An alternative is to take a tour or river cruise with one of the numerous Manaus agencies. Budget operators cater to backpackers for US$45 to US$65 a day, staying a couple of nights in rustic cabins with maybe a night or two camping in the jungle and with many of the same activities included as you'd do at a jungle lodge.

At the other end of the price scale, you could take a customized expedition of two weeks (or even longer) to distant tributaries in search of, say, jaguars or rare macaws, using a reasonably comfortable riverboat. The further you get from sprawling, urban Manaus, the more wildlife you're likely to see. On a trip of less than five days from Manaus you will probably see pink and gray river dolphins, alligators, piranhas, a fair variety of birds and a few monkeys, but it won't be the teeming jungles you might have imagined. See p631 for tour options.

One of the very best places for wildlife-spotting in Amazonia is the Mamirauá Reserve (p638), between the Solimões and Japurá rivers, about halfway from Manaus to the Colombian border. Accessible by a couple of hours' motorboat ride from the town of Tefé (which is reachable by plane or riverboat from Manaus or Tabatinga), this floodplain reserve runs a very professional ecotourism program on which you are sure to see plenty of monkeys, sloths, river dolphins, alligators and birds.

Dedicated nature-lovers could consider a trip to the Reserva Xixuaú-Xipariná (p636), 1½ days' boat trip north from Manaus, which has ecotourism facilities and a great abundance and diversity of wildlife. The Parque Nacional do Jaú (p636), in the Rio Negro basin, northwest of Manaus, is one of the world's biggest pieces of protected tropical rain forest, very rich in biodiversity. If you have a boat at your disposal, you can enter the park with a permit from the Instituto Brasileiro do Meio Ambiente e dos Recursos Naturais Renováveis (IBAMA; Brazilian Institute of the Environment and Renewable Natural Resources) in Manaus, but visitor facilities are nonexistent. Another area the adventurous and well-funded might head for is the upper Rio Negro, where there's a good lodge (p637) in the remote settlement of São Gabriel da Cachoeira. From here it's even possible to mount an expedition up Brazil's highest peak, Pico da Neblina (3014m), on the Venezuelan border. Neblina is in the remote Parque Nacional do Pico da Neblina, which lacks any kind of standard tourist infrastructure.

The contiguous towns of Tabatinga (Brazil; p639) and Leticia (Colombia), in the triple-frontier area where Brazil, Colombia and Peru meet, are jumping-off points for several good ecotourism destinations, including some reasonably priced lodges along the Rio Javari, which forms the Brazil–Peru border. Relatively untouched jungle areas are easier to reach here than from Manaus.

In the state of Rondônia, an interesting-looking ecotourism program is being set up along the Guaporé Valley and there's a very good German-run ecolodge, the Hotel Fazenda Rancho Grande (p667), near Cacaulândia. On the southern edge of the Amazon rain forest in the north of Mato Grosso state, the area around Alta Floresta (p386) offers some of the best wildlife viewing in all of Brazilian Amazonia. Accommodations include the good Cristalino Jungle Lodge.

> 'The Parque Nacional do Jaú is one of the world's biggest pieces of protected tropical rain forest.'

ORGANIZED TOURS

Plenty of companies inside and outside Brazil are eager to organize an entire nature-oriented trip for you. All will doubtless use the buzz-word 'ecotourism' somewhere in their blurb. This term has about as many interpretations as people who utter it, but those who give thought to such matters consider true ecotourism to mean something more specific than just 'nature tourism.' The real thing should incorporate such elements as education, conservation, sustainable development and benefits to (and involvement with) local communities (read more from the International Ecotourism Society at www.ecotourism.org). It's worth keeping these notions in mind and asking around about a company's reputation when selecting a tour.

For your own satisfaction, you should also look into what equipment the company provides to help you observe fauna and flora (such as a telescope and a tape recorder with playback), what reference materials are available (ask for species lists before the trip) and what qualifications and experience their guides have (look for professional naturalists).

Operators specific to single localities are covered in the regional chapters in this book. The following are among the companies offering a wider range of trips.

Focus Tours (☎ 505-466-4688; www.focustours.com; 103 Moya Rd, Santa Fe, NM 87505-8360, USA) is a highly rated birding and nature-tour firm using English-speaking naturalist guides. It uses tape recorders to record and play-back calls, encouraging wildlife to come into view. It's active in conservation too. Destinations include the Pantanal, Chapada dos Guimarães, Alta Floresta, the Emas and Itatiaia national parks, Foz do Iguaçu and the Parque Natural do Caraça. Focus' owner, Doug Trent, has been running ecological tours to Brazil since before the word 'ecotourism' was coined, and what he doesn't know about birds isn't worth knowing.

Brazil Eco Travel Center (☎ 0xx21-2512 8882; www.ecotravelcenter.com.br; 2nd fl, Rua Visconde de Pirajá 572, Ipanema, Rio de Janeiro) is a dedicated and professional firm that offers trips to a complete range of Brazil's best natural destinations, including the Pantanal, national parks in the cerrado and Mata Atlântica. The center offers Amazon lodge and river trips, ascents of the Pico da Neblina and visits to emblematic conservation projects such as Tamar Project in Bahia and the Reserva Biológica Poço das Antas in Rio de Janeiro state.

Field Guides (☎ 800 728 4953; www.fieldguides.com; Suite 150, Bldg 1, 9433 Bee Cave Rd, Austin, TX 78733, USA) is a well-established US-based birding tour operator. It runs six specialized bird-watching tours in Brazil with expert guides.

Victor Emanuel Nature Tours (VENT; ☎ 800 328 8368; www.ventbird.com; PO Box 33008, Austin, TX 78764) is another highly professional US-based birding tour company, VENT has a number of experienced guides.

Discover The World (☎ 01737-218802; www.discover-the-world.co.uk; 29 Nork Way, Banstead, Surrey, SM7 1PB, UK) specializes in wildlife-encounter trips, offering whale-watching stays in Santa Catarina state, with surfing and dolphin-watching thrown in for those who wish.

Ecotour Expeditions (☎ 401-423-3377; www.naturetours.com; PO Box 128, Jamestown, RI 02835-0128, USA) is a US-based ecotourism operator that does Pantanal lodge trips and boat-based Amazonia trips.

Forum International (☎ 800-252-4475; www.foruminternational.com; No 21 91 Gregory Lane, Pleasant Hill, CA 94523, USA) offers a wide range of Brazilian tour options including Amazon river trips, Alta Floresta birding and Pantanal lodge visits.

There are literally dozens of parks and official protected areas in Brazil, plus scores of privately owned preserves, ecotourism projects and extractive reserves. The following chart is a quick reference for the best of these places to see and experience Brazil's flora, fauna and fantastic natural scenery. It does not cover every protected area in the country, but lists the top spots, their features, available activities, the best time to visit and the page in this book where the area is described in greater detail. See Where to Go on p81 for more details on many of these parks.

ENVIRONMENTAL ISSUES

In 2003 over 14,760 sq km of the Amazon forest disappeared – the second-greatest amount on record. To put this figure in perspective, that is an area approximately the same size as the US state of New Hampshire. Some studies argue that the national figure for 2003 was even higher, almost at a whopping 25,000 sq km.

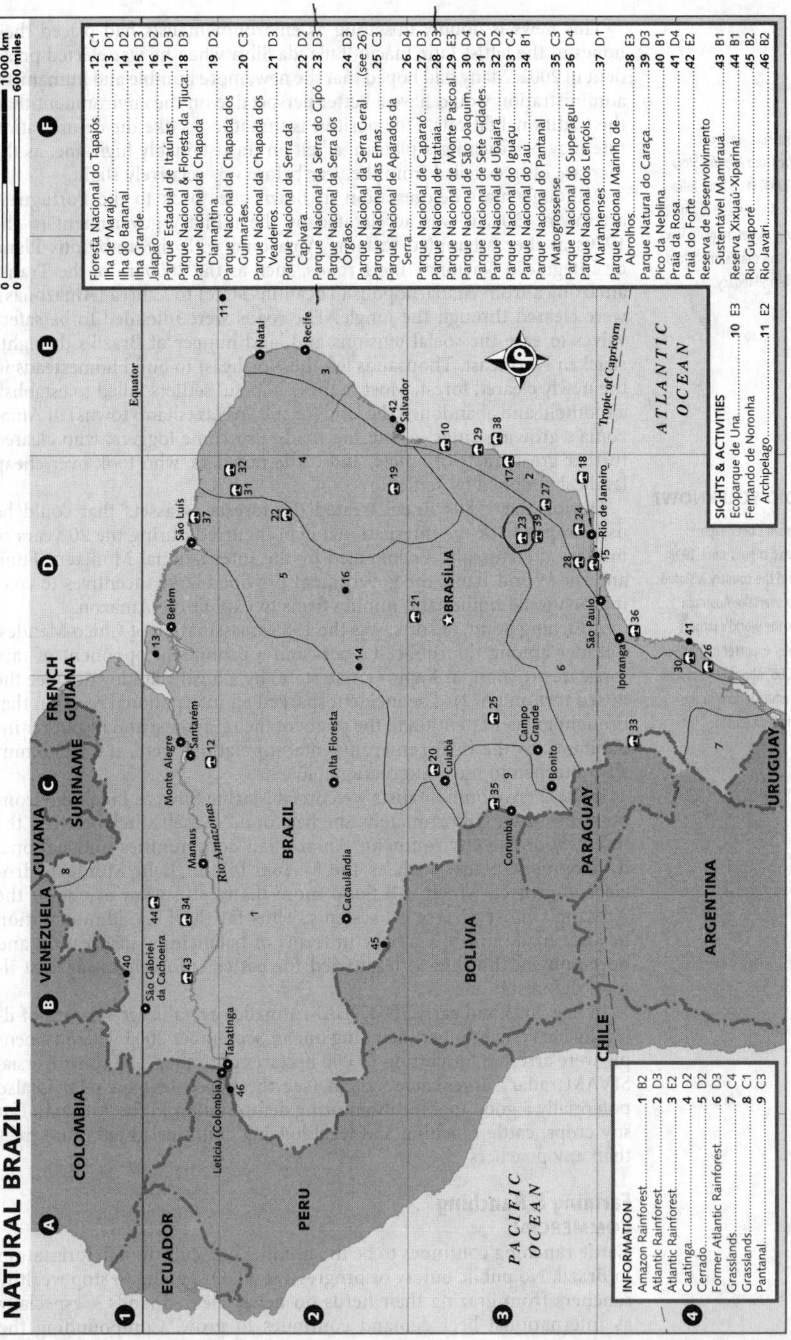

NATURAL BRAZIL
0 1000 km
0 600 miles
A B C D E F
1 2 3 4
COLOMBIA
VENEZUELA
GUYANA
SURINAME
FRENCH GUIANA
ECUADOR
PERU
BOLIVIA
BRAZIL
PARAGUAY
CHILE
ARGENTINA
URUGUAY
PACIFIC OCEAN
ATLANTIC OCEAN
Equator
Tropic of Capricorn
Rio Amazonas
Leticia (Colombia)
Tabatinga
São Gabriel da Cachoeira
Manaus
Monte Alegre
Santarém
Belém
São Luís
Natal
Recife
Salvador
Cacaulândia
Alta Floresta
Cuiabá
Corumbá
Campo Grande
Bonito
BRASÍLIA
São Paulo
Rio de Janeiro
Iporanga
INFORMATION
Amazon Rainforest 1 B2
Atlantic Rainforest 2 D3
Atlantic Rainforest 3 E2
Caatinga 4 D2
Cerrado 5 D2
Former Atlantic Rainforest 6 D3
Grasslands 7 C4
Grasslands 8 C1
Pantanal 9 C3
SIGHTS & ACTIVITIES
Ecoparque de Una 10 E3
Fernando de Noronha Archipelago 11 E2
Floresta Nacional do Tapajós 12 C1
Ilha de Marajó 13 D1
Ilha do Bananal 14 D2
Ilha Grande 15 D3
Jalapão 16 D2
Parque Estadual de Itaúnas 17 D3
Parque Nacional & Floresta da Tijuca 18 D3
Parque Nacional da Chapada Diamantina 19 D2
Parque Nacional da Chapada dos Guimarães 20 C3
Parque Nacional da Chapada dos Veadeiros 21 D3
Parque Nacional da Serra da Capivara 22 D2
Parque Nacional da Serra do Cipó 23 D3
Parque Nacional da Serra dos Órgãos 24 D3
Parque Nacional da Serra Geral (see 26)
Parque Nacional das Emas 25 C3
Parque Nacional de Aparados da Serra 26 D4
Parque Nacional de Caparaó 27 D3
Parque Nacional de Itatiaia 28 D3
Parque Nacional de Monte Pascoal 29 E3
Parque Nacional de São Joaquim 30 D4
Parque Nacional de Sete Cidades 31 D2
Parque Nacional de Ubajara 32 D2
Parque Nacional do Iguaçu 33 C4
Parque Nacional do Jaú 34 B1
Parque Nacional do Pantanal Matogrossense 35 C3
Parque Nacional do Superagüi 36 D4
Parque Nacional dos Lençóis Maranhenses 37 D1
Parque Nacional Marinho de Abrolhos 38 E3
Parque Natural do Caraça 39 D3
Pico da Neblina 40 B1
Praia da Rosa 41 D4
Praia do Forte 42 E2
Reserva de Desenvolvimento Sustentável Mamirauá 43 B1
Reserva Xixuaú-Xipariná 44 B1
Rio Guaporé 45 B2
Rio Javari 46 B2

The Burning Season: the Chico Mendes Story (1994) stars Raul Julia as Mendes and is a quick way to get an overview of this man's important life and legacy.

This news is doubly upsetting as environmentalists had placed their hopes in the leftist Luíz Inácio 'Lula' da Silva when he was elected president in 2002. Many had hoped that the new, more humble and humanistic administration would have a better perspective on the environment than the traditional fat cats. One positive is that it looks like the deforestation rate may be reaching a plateau, albeit an unsustainably high one, as the increase of trees felled from the year before was relatively slight.

Although mass deforestation in Brazil goes back to the Portuguese arrival in 1500, it was accelerated by the military government in the 1970s as they attempted to tame Amazonia with the ambitious Plano de Integração Nacional. Long roads, such as the 2000km of the Transamazônica from Aguiarnópolis (Tocantins state) to Labrea (Amazonas), were cleared through the jungle. The roads were intended to be safety valves to ease the social tensions and land hunger of Brazil's drought-stricken Northeast. Thousands left the Northeast to build homesteads in the newly cleared forest. Most of these hopeful settlers failed to establish a foothold and abandoned the land for the *favelas* (shantytowns) of Amazonia's growing cities. Along the roads also came loggers, who cleared further great tracts of jungle, and cattle ranchers, who took over cheap lands abandoned by settlers.

DID YOU KNOW?

Brazil's beef exports have tripled since 1998 and the country is slated to overtake Australia as the world's largest beef exporter in 2005 or 2006. About 80% of new pasture land is in the Amazon region.

During the 1980s Brazil treated the forests as assets that could be used to pay back the international debt incurred during the 20 years of military dictatorship. Encouraged by the International Monetary Fund and the World Bank, the government provided large incentives to coax multinational timber and mining firms to exploit the Amazon.

A turning point, of sorts, was the 1988 assassination of Chico Mendes, a leader among the rubber tappers and a prominent opponent of rain forest destruction, in Xapuri (Acre state) by a hostile landowner (see the boxed text on p672). The incident sparked an international reaction that brought greater attention to the plight of the rain forest and its poorer inhabitants. By the 1990s, environmental stipulations were, at least nominally, attached to most international loans.

In 2002 environmentalists welcomed Marina Silva as Lula's environment minister. Unfortunately, she has found herself stuck between the interests of the environment, Amazonian communities and national development plans, such as the US$6.6 billion Belo Monte hydroelectric project, which will flood more than 240 sq km of one of the Amazon's most diverse ecosystems. Thus far the Lula administration has not made much headway in terms of balancing conservation and development, but has at least tried for better enforcement against illegal deforestation.

In late 2003 and early 2004, IBAMA made several large seizures of illegally harvested timber including one in September 2003 where 17 people were arrested for cutting 10,000 hectares of timber. The controversial SIVAM radar surveillance system (see the boxed text on p93) is also potentially a good tool for monitoring deforestation in the Amazon. But soy crops, cattle ranching and legal logging continue to fell more trees than any poachers.

Farming & Ranching
COMMERCIAL

Cattle ranching continues to be the number one culprit of deforestation in Brazil. No public outcry or progressive NGO is going to stop wealthy ranchers from grazing their herds on newly cleared lands – especially as international beef demand continues to grow. Compounding the

ADVANCE BRAZIL, BUT AT WHAT COST?

In the 1970s, the human assault on the Amazon gained a lot of momentum. By the year 2000, approximately 14% of the Brazilian Amazon rain forest had been completely destroyed, amounting to a loss of around 550,000 sq km, an area roughly the size of France. In 2003 more trees were lost than any other year on record except for 1995. Over the same decades that the Amazon has been demolished, the Brazilian economy has swelled into one of the largest in the world.

Lula, like the presidents before him, is faced with the choice between development or conservation of the Amazonian region. Rather than attempting to rechart the country's political course (as some had hoped that he would), Lula has made some efforts towards better enforcement of the environmental laws already on the book and decided to continue the Avança Brasil (Advance Brazil) development plan initiated in 1999 under the Cardoso administration. The program is comprised of a bevy of new infrastructure projects for Amazonia, continuing through 2007. The basics of Avança Brasil are as follows:

- Paving or construction of 8000km of roads
- Opening or expansion of more than a dozen river ports and four airports
- Opening of two gas pipelines
- Building three new thermal power stations
- Opening of the second stage of the giant Tucuruí hydroelectric project on the Rio Tocantins, and constructing a new hydroelectric project at Belo Monte on the Rio Xingu
- Opening of *hidrovias* along the Madeira, Araguaia and Tocantins rivers, totaling 3300km in length
- Putting in a new 1400km stretch of the Ferrovia Norte–Sul freight railroad
- Adding thousands of kilometers of new electric power lines

Environmental scientists inside and outside of Brazil predict some very dire consequences from Avança Brasil. They base their forecasts on the effects of past infrastructure projects in Amazonia, especially construction of roads. Roads make it easy for not only loggers but also cattle ranchers, miners and small farmers to move in and clear forest, increasing the risk of fires.

One group, made up of researchers from the Woods Hole Research Center in the US and Instituto de Pesquisa Ambiental da Amazônia (IPAM) and Instituto Socioambiental (ISA) in Brazil, looked back at three roads paved during the 1960s and 1970s. The group reported that in less than two decades of building the roads, 55% of the vegetation had been destroyed within 50km on either side of the Brasília–Belém highway, 40% within 50km of the parallel Hwy PA-150 (the 'timber corridor' of southeast Pará), and 33% within 50km of Hwy BR-364, the Cuiabá–Porto Velho road. The researchers predicted that, with the implementation of Avança Brasil, by about 2030 the total deforested area in Brazilian Amazonia could amount to about 1.3 million sq km – more than a third of the existing rain forest area.

Another group, led by American biologist William Laurance of the Smithsonian Tropical Research Institute, forecast that by the year 2020 somewhere between 1.05 and 1.6 million sq km of rain forest would be completely devastated or heavily degraded. And these figures did not include other areas that would be damaged to a lesser degree. In the worst case, the team calculated, a further 1.2 million sq km would be moderately degraded, 1 million sq km lightly degraded, and less than 200,000 sq km would remain in its pristine state.

On the other side of the argument, the Brazilian government suggests that Avança Brasil is guided by principles of environmental preservation and sustainable development, and that improving the living standards of the generally poor Amazonian population would discourage deforestation. They also state that important factors have changed since the building of the 1960s and 1970s highways: incentives to settle in Amazonia have been removed, and new measures to protect the Amazon forest mean that today's infrastructure projects are less destructive than those of years past.

environmental effects of cattle grazing, ranchers often use fire to clear the land and encourage grass growth. The massive fires release large amounts of carbon dioxide into the atmosphere.

The number two culprit is agribusiness, also known as big-time professional farming. As new machinery, irrigation systems and pesticides allow people to farm ever larger plots of land, new transportation and preservation techniques make it easier to find more and more markets for the product. When there is money to be made, it is hard to convince farmers that the land should be left fallow.

But the lushness of the Amazon is deceptive. Only about 17% of Amazonia is suitable for sustained agriculture or livestock raising. Most of the soil is too thin and too lacking in calcium, phosphorus and potassium to be good for crops. The jungle ecosystem recycles most organic matter before it can even be absorbed into the soil. As a result, ranchers and farmers move on as the land is depleted and remove any new forest in their paths.

DID YOU KNOW?

Bad news for all those who quit eating meat because cattle ranching was killing the rain forest: soybean farming is now one of the biggest causes of deforestation in Brazil.

SUBSISTENCE
Small-scale slash-and-burn agriculture worked well for the traditional indigenous populations, who would fell small areas of trees and burn off remaining material. The resulting ash would support a few years' growth of varied crops: squash, corn, manioc, plantains and beans. After a couple of seasons, the Indians would move on. The clearings were small in size and number and the land was left fallow long enough for the jungle to recover.

By contrast, the agricultural techniques of modern settlers have generally proven disastrous. Fire is used by small farmers to clear virgin forest, to burn off land that is already partly cleared, to clear away secondary forest growth and to burn cattle pastures to encourage grass growth. Many new settlers do not know how to use this technique responsibly and fires often get out of control. The problem becomes particularly acute when the annual rains do not come as expected after the August to September burning season. The crops often fail as settlers find that the soil's fertility is exhausted after a few years. Even as pasture, the land often ceases to be useful after 15 or 20 years of continuous use. With all its nutrients exhausted, such land recovers very slowly, if at all.

Breakfast of Biodiversity:
the Truth about Rainforest
Destruction, by John
Vandermeer, is an
insightful look at tropical
deforestation and the
many social and political
reasons that lead to this
complex and unfortunate
situation.

Hydroelectricity & Mining
Further damage to the Amazonian environment and its indigenous human population has been caused by hydroelectric schemes (which in flat Amazonia flood unusually large areas of forest) and mining.

Garimpeiros (prospecting miners, usually seeking gold) have a hand in deforestation and erosion. They rarely pay attention to park boundaries or environmental regulations and use mercury separation to extract gold from ore. Large quantities of highly poisonous mercury are washed into the rivers, where they become a serious health hazard. At the other end of the mining spectrum is the vast Provincia Mineral de Carajás, in the southeast of Pará state, with its huge workings of iron and other minerals, its own railway to the coast at São Luís and its own purpose-built hydroelectric station at Tucuruí.

Searching for Solutions
Deforestation can be understood as two basic types: commercial deforestation and subsistence deforestation. Deforestation caused by commercial big business is an obvious villain, but deforestation for personal subsist-

JOHN MAIER JR

Christo Redentor (p131), Corcovado, Rio de Janeiro

RICARDO GOMES

Towels for sale, Ipanema Beach (p123),
Rio de Janerio

NS de Nazaré church (p202),
Saquarema, Rio de Janeiro
state

JOHN PENNOCK

JOHN MAIER JR

Hippie Fair (p173), Ipanema, Rio de Janerio

Pão de Açúcar (p130), with views of Copacabana Beach (far left), Praia Vermelha (left) and Botafogo, Rio de Janerio

Copacabana Beach (p127), Rio de Janeiro

The *bonde* (p138) traveling across Arcos do Lapa, Rio de Janeiro

ence is a more complex problem. It's easy for foreigners in first-world countries to rail against destruction of the Amazon forest and forget that some 20 million Brazilians are trying to eke out an existence there. What's more, foreign governments and international institutions have in the past actively encouraged destructive development schemes in Amazonia. Any viable solution to Amazonia's problems has to address the aspirations of its inhabitants, who are mostly poor and lacking in adequate education, medical care and sanitation.

The rancher-landowner-agribusiness lobby is extremely powerful in Brazilian politics and generally opposes attempts to conserve the environment. Even when governments legislate to protect Brazil's forests, enforcement is poor, largely because of a shortage of funds. Illegal logging and animal poaching is rife in Amazonia. Even some Amazonian national parks are encroached upon with near impunity by loggers, *garimpeiros* and settlers. The arrival in Brazil in the 1990s of many Asian logging companies, in search of new timber sources now that they have exhausted their own forests, does not increase Amazonia's conservation prospects. The logging industry is the third-largest employer in Amazonia (after agriculture and fishing) but has in the past been conducted inefficiently, with heavy wastage. It was previously estimated that for every 27 trees felled in the state of Pará only one actually arrived at a timber mill.

The environmental initiatives that seemingly offer the best prospects of success are those that make conservation act in the interests of the local populace – such as extractive reserves and sustainable development reserves (see p80 for an elaboration of these terms), fish-farming,

---

BIG BROTHER IS WATCHING – EVEN IN THE AMAZON

Serviço Integrado de Vigilância da Amazônia (SIVAM; the Integrated Amazonian Vigilance Service) was unveiled at Rio's 1992 Earth Summit as a space-age surveillance tool to monitor and hopefully control deforestation. At the time of writing this book, components of the system were becoming fully operational.

The government and other supporters argue that the system will decrease corruption as aerial observation discourages officials from taking bribes from poachers, illegal loggers and miners. It will also help the military to prevent incursions by Colombian and Peruvian rebels and crack down on drug runners.

Opponents object that SIVAM is a military scheme dressed up like an environmental savior and is simply a veil for greater control over the region. Not only will it be a way to keep tabs on the indigenous population, it will also help plan how to develop and legally deforest with greater efficiency. Moreover it will compromise Brazilian sovereignty as a tool for the United States' War on Drugs.

The US$1.4 billion contract was handled by the good old American defense contractor and missile developer Raytheon. SIVAM is based around eight ground-based radar stations, weather satellites and 50 manned weather stations that are combined with LandSat images to monitor the entire expanse of the Amazon. Air- and ground-based surveillance radars will be able to follow drug traffickers in the air, on the rivers or traveling overland. Remote sensors will check the quality of river water – an increase in mercury could be an indication of illegal gold mining.

Headquartered in Brasília, SIVAM will collect and process all the data and forward it to three regional coordinating centers at Belém, Manaus and Porto Velho (on the border with Bolivia). These branches will be responsible for pinpointing and investigating suspicious activities in their regions, dispatching troops to problem areas and organizing drugs raids. Over 20,000 troops are already involved in SIVAM, although they do not seem to be coming down too hard on illegal deforestation, which continues to grow. Either way, after 500 years of trying, it looks like the Amazon is one step closer to full colonization.

fishing tourism and community ecotourism projects. Unfortunately, most of these are alarmingly small-scale compared with the size of the Amazonian population and the amount of destruction that is being wreaked throughout the region's ecosystem.

Politicians, even when sympathetic to environmental causes, tend to respond more readily to proposals for development and economic growth than plans for conservation. Lula's term as president thus far is case in point. Domestic and international environmental groups have already repeatedly confronted Lula about a wave of planned infrastructure schemes in Amazonia (see the boxed text on p91) including pipelines, highways and new dam projects.

Hopes for more rational logging practices have been raised by international certification schemes. Such schemes seek to certify timber that has been produced by sustainable methods, something that is increasingly demanded by domestic and international consumers of Brazilian timber. This type of consumer demand encourages reduced-impact logging, a practice that began to take off in Brazil in the 1990s, whereby forestry areas are divided into blocks to be exploited on a rotating basis and given sufficient time to regenerate. At the same time, the largest specimens of valuable tree species are left standing in order to reseed the block, and care is taken to minimize damage to trees that are not being felled. Some major Brazilian home-supply stores and a number of international stores carry certified lumber, however, the majority of individual and commercial consumers still shop with their wallet and not with their conscience.

> 'international certification schemes … seek to certify timber that has been produced by sustainable methods.'

Environmental Organizations

The Brazilian conservation movement and the general level of environmental awareness in the country have progressed over the last few years. But there are a great many battles still to fight, not least against the 'megaproject' mentality, which looks to large-scale human interference in nature as the way forward for Brazil's economy. Such interference takes the form of construction of long-distance roads through the rain forest, flooding of large areas for hydroelectricity, the dredging of hundreds of kilometers of river for shipping freeways, and the planting of vast areas of bush with chemically fertilized soybeans. The 'mega' mentality remains prevalent in most circles of Brazilian government and Lula has realized that it is the easiest way to employ desperate people and pump money into the economy.

The following organizations are among those working actively to protect Brazil's environment. Strategies range from campaigns to save a single animal or plant species to lobbying in Brasília and pressuring institutions to stop financing destructive projects. A few groups concentrate primarily on research and some do hands-on activist work – a number of organizations can arrange volunteer work for those interested. Many of their websites are in English as well as Portuguese.

AUSTRALIA
Friends of the Earth (☎ 03-9419 8700; www.foe.org.au; PO Box 222, Fitzroy 3065, Victoria)
Greenpeace (☎ 1800 815 151; www.greenpeace.org.au; Level 4, 35-39 Liverpool St, Sydney 2000, NSW)

BRAZIL
Amazonia Program (☎ 0xx11-3887 9369; www.amazonia.org.br; Rua Bento de Andrade, São Paulo) Amazonia is an Amazon-oriented conservation program and has a good English-language environmental news section. It is associated with Amigos da Terra (Friends of the Earth).

Conservation International (☎ 0xx31-3261 3889; www.conservation.org.br; Av Getúlio Vargas, 1300 - 7° andar - Belo Horizonte) This is the Brazilian branch of a large international field-based organization working for biodiversity and sustainable development. In Brazil it's involved in grassroots conservation projects and national policy initiatives.

Ecológica (☎ 0xx63-215 1279; www.ecologica.org.br; Rua SO 11, Quadra 103 Sul, Conjunto 03, Lote 28, 77100-040 Palmas, Tocantins) This one's a dynamic institute involved in carbon sequestration research, climate-change consultancy, environmental education and ecotourism.

Greenpeace (☎ 0xx11-3035 1155; www.greenpeace.org.br; Rua Alvarenga, 2331, Butantã, São Paulo)

Instituto do Homem e Meio Ambiente da Amazônia (IMAZON; ☎ 0xx91-235 4214; www.imazon.org.br; Caixa Postal 5101, 66613-397 Belém, Pará) This research organization promotes sustainable development with an eye on both human and environmental concerns in the Amazon.

Instituto de Pesquisa Ambiental da Amazônia (IPAM; ☎ 0xx91-241 6700; www.ipam .org.br; Av Nazaré 669, 66035-170 Belém, Pará) An environmental research institute and pressure group, IPAM is dedicated to sustainable development in Amazonia. It receives funding from the Woods Hole Research Center of Massachusetts, a US ecological research institute. The institute organizes courses for environmentalists around Brazil and forms alliances of naturalist/environmentalist professionals.

Instituto Socioambiental (ISA; ☎ 0xx11-3660 7949; www.socioambiental.org; Av Higienópolis 901, 01238-001 São Paulo) ISA campaigns and lobbies for Brazil's environment and indigenous peoples. It publishes a journal, maps and other interesting information.

The Nature Conservancy (☎ 0xx61-468 481; www.nature.org; SHIN Centro de Atividades 05, Conjunto J Bloco B, Salas 301-309, 71503-505 Brasília, Distrito Federal) This is the Brazil office of a US-based organization geared to protecting fragile ecosystems and endangered species; in Brazil it works with local partner organizations to preserve ecosystems and promote sustainable, environmentally friendly development.

Tamar Project (Projeto Tamar; ☎ 0xx71-468 481; www.tamar.com.br; Caixa Postal 2219, 40223-970 Rio Vermelho, Salvador, Bahia) Tamar is the official Brazilian government project to protect sea turtles along its coasts. The Salvador branch is the original office, but it also has stations in such places at Fernando de Noronha.

SOS Mata Atlântica (☎ 0xx11-3055 7888; www.sosmatatlantica.org.br; Rua Manoel da Nóbrega 456, Paraíso, 04001-001 São Paulo) SOS is one of the few Brazilian NGOs with good financial resources; it carries out political pressure work and environmental education, chiefly in defense of the Atlantic rain forest.

WWF Brasil (☎ 0xx61-364 7400; www.wwf.org.br; SHIS EQ QL 6/8, conjunto E 2° andar, 71620-430 Brasília, Distrito Federal) Part of the largest nature protection network in the world, WWF Brazil works to bring into balance human activities, preservation of biodiversity, and sustainable use of natural resources.

CANADA
Greenpeace (☎ 416-597 8408; www.greenpeacecanada.org; 250 Dundas St W, Suite 605, Toronto, Ontario M5T 2Z5)

UK
Friends of the Earth (☎ 020-7490 1555; www.foe.co.uk; 26-28 Underwood St, London N1 7JQ)
Greenpeace (☎ 020-7865 8100; www.greenpeace.org.uk; Canonbury Villas, London N1 2PN)
Rainforest Foundation UK (☎ 020-7251 6345; www.rainforestfoundationuk.org; Suite A5, City Cloisters, 196 Old St, London EC1V 9FR) This organization helps indigenous and traditional rain forest populations protect their environment and at the same time obtain their rights.

USA
Conservation International (☎ 800-406-2306; www.conservation.org; Suite 600, 1919 M St NW, Washington, DC 20036)

You can do your bit to protect Brazil's environment using environmentally friendly tourism services wherever possible.

Environmental Defense (☎ 212-505-2100; www.environmentaldefense.org; 257 Park Ave S, New York, NY 10010) Environmental Defense organizes a number of environmental and human based campaigns.

Greenpeace (☎ 800-326-0959; www.greenpeaceusa.org; 702 H St NW, Washington DC 20001)

The Nature Conservancy (☎ 800-628-6860; www.nature.org; Suite 100, 4245 N Fairfax Dr, Arlington, VA 22203-1606)

Rainforest Action Network (RAN; ☎ 415-398-4404; www.ran.org; Suite 500, 221 Pine St, San Francisco, CA 94104) RAN works to protect rain forests and support inhabitants' rights through education, grassroots organizing and nonviolent direct action.

Rainforest Alliance (☎ 212-677-1900; www.rainforest-alliance.org; Suite 500, 665 Broadway, New York, NY 10012)

Rainforest Foundation USA (☎ 212-431-9098; www.savetherest.org; Suite 1107, 270 Lafayette St, New York, NY 10012)

Food & Drink

In Brazil, eating is, like so many other things, another pretext for pleasure-taking. There is no such thing as Brazilian haute cuisine per se, but the food tastes damned good almost anywhere you go. Even more remarkable is the cultural know-how about what, where, when and how to eat.

This *arte de comer bem* (art of eating well) has nothing to do with either fussiness, *á francesa*, or pseudo-scientific taboos, *á americana*. Brazilians simply understand that the body feels better when it's kept hydrated with fruit and water while at the beach, or that a fattening little snack and a few sips of strong coffee or cold beer make the ride home from work infinitely more pleasant.

The food is as syncretic as the country itself. The most basic 'Brazilian' meal can include Portuguese olive oil, native manioc, Japanese sushi, African okra, Italian pasta, German sausage and Lebanese tabbouleh. Still, the cuisine can be reduced to three delightful principles: generosity, freshness and simplicity.

First, you should plan for some of the largest portions on the planet – a single main course can leave two people stuffed. It's hard to go hungry here, even on the most modest budget. As for freshness, the fertile soil and luxuriant climate ensure that a stunning variety of produce is available at all times. Many of the local fruit and vegetable names have no translation simply because they exist nowhere else. Packaged foods are generally frowned upon, and farm animals are rarely pumped full of hormones, if only because of the prohibitive cost.

Given the richness and variety of fresh ingredients, Brazilians generally eat their food neat. They feel no need for fancy sauces or rarefied cooking processes. Meat is coated in salt and set on the grill, while veggies are steamed and served straight up. Simply add a drizzle of olive oil and a bit of salt to taste. That said, there are complex regional dishes that are well worth their careful preparation.

You can be sure of one thing in Brazil – you're going to eat well.

STAPLES & SPECIALITIES

Just as there's no 'typical' Brazilian face, there's no single Brazilian cuisine. Foodies prefer to say it's a conglomeration of regional cuisines, each itself a hybrid of ethnic cuisines adapted to local conditions. That said, here follows a description of a typical Brazilian meal – available just about anywhere you go.

Certainly, the meal will include *arroz e feijão* (rice and beans), the principle staples of the Brazilian diet. Each is cooked with garlic and onions. To the rice add tomatoes, and to the beans add bay leaves and perhaps some bacon. On top of the beans, sprinkle *farofa* – manioc flour sautéed in butter, perhaps with bits of egg or bacon. Grilled meats, known as *churrasco* or *grelhadas*, are the meal's crowning glory: chicken, beef or pork is dredged in salt, set on a spit and grilled slowly over an open fire. A green salad or sautéed or steamed vegetables (beets, carrots, green beans, yams or kale) round out the main course. A digestive pause is followed by *sobremesa* (dessert), which could include either fresh or preserved fruit, a pudding enlivened with coconut or passion fruit, or the flanlike *quindim*. The meal only comes to an end with the consumption of a strong, sweet shot of – of course – Brazilian coffee.

DID YOU KNOW?
Rock-hard, often bitter, and sometimes poisonous, manioc root – once properly processed – forms the basis for everything from cakes and bread to stews and the ubiquitous *farofa* (manioc flour sautéed with butter).

Eat Smart in Brazil, by Joan and David Peterson, provides an excellent introduction to Brazil's culinary history, some classic recipes and an extensive and very useful glossary.

It should be noted that, even in restaurants, food is generally served family-style – that is, with generous helpings on communal plates. Except in finer restaurants, all the dishes (except dessert) are served at once – there are no formal courses.

CookBrazil.com (www .cookbrazil.com) has easy-to-follow, English-language recipes for classic Brazilian food and drink.

Bahia & the Northeast

Brazilian restaurants outside of Brazil tend to serve, more specifically, Bahian cuisine, perhaps because it's the most obviously exotic. It developed in the kitchens of the region's sugar plantations, and its African origins reveal themselves in the three main ingredients: coconut milk; the spicy *malagueta* pepper; and *dendê* oil, a reddish-orange extraction of west African palm. The delicious seafood stew known as *moqueca* includes all three and is a classic Bahian speciality. On the streets of Bahia, you can't escape the smell of *acarajé* – fritters made with brown beans and shrimp fried in *dendê* oil.

The Amazon

Amazonian cuisine is strongly influenced by the region's native Tupi people, who live largely on manioc, freshwater fish, yams and beans, and exotic fruit. *Caldeirada* is a popular fish stew not unlike bouillabaisse, and *pato no tucupí* is a regional favorite made with duck, garlic, *jambú* herb and the juice of both lemons and manioc roots.

The Central West

Occupying the prairielike cerrado, the Central West is dominated by sprawling *fazendas* (ranches) that produce pork and beef, as well as staples such as corn, rice, kale and manioc. The region's rivers offer up the meaty *dourado* fish, the *pintado* (a type of catfish), and, of course, the infamous piranha. Recipes tend to be simple but delicious, relying on the freshness of local ingredients.

Rio, São Paulo & the Southeast

The mountainous state of Minas Gerais offers the most distinctive regional cuisine of the Southeast. Pork is particularly popular, as is the kalelike *couve*, which is sautéed in oil with garlic and onions. *Frango ao molho pardo* (chicken stewed in its own blood with vegetables) sounds gruesome but tastes delicious. *Queijo minas* is a soft, vaguely sweet white cheese that, when served with *goiabada* (guava paste), makes a refreshing dessert.

TRAVEL YOUR TASTEBUDS

acarajé – Eat these Bahian fritters, made of brown beans and dried shrimp, as soon as they've been fished from a spattering pot of *dendê* (palm) oil.

açaí – This addictive, deep-purple, vitamin-rich berry from the Amazon is a staple of both Tupi Indians and Rio bodybuilders.

caipirinha – The divine national cocktail is made from limes, sugar and *cachaça* (a high-proof sugarcane alcohol).

cafezinho – A small shot of Brazilian coffee that should be strong as the devil, hot as hell and sweet as love.

feijoada completa – Plan for a long, digestive nap after indulging in this stew of black bean and well-larded meat and sausage

jambú – This Amazonian herb makes the tongue tingle, then go slightly numb.

picanha – Not to be confused with piranha, Brazil's favorite cut of beef comes from the cow's rump; eaten pinkish, salty and fresh from the grill.

piranha – Take a bite out of this flesh-eater; the meat is delicious, but beware of sharp bones.

São Paulo is the gastronomic capital of Brazil, thanks to high levels of disposable wealth and a large Italian community that places a high social value on refined eating. Here you'll find temples of fine dining as well as humble ethnic restaurants that reflect the city's dazzling number of immigrant communities, of whom the Japanese deserve special mention. Forming the largest colony outside Japan, they have made sushi popular throughout Brazil. Note that pizza baked in a wood-burning oven is a Sunday-night tradition.

Rio doesn't have its own cuisine per se, but as the adopted home of Brazilians of all stripes, it offers excellent food from every region. As the former colonial capital, the Portuguese influence is less adulterated here than elsewhere, evidenced by the popularity of *bacalhau* (codfish). *Feijoada*, a bean-and-meat stew served with rice, *farofa*, kale and sliced orange, is the city's contribution to the national cuisine. Because it takes a few hours to cook as well as digest, it is traditionally served on Saturday.

The South

Italian and German food rules the day in the South. The country's love affair with pasta and beer began here – both have become Brazilian staples. Expect to see lots of sausage and sauerkraut in the German enclaves of Joinville and Blumenau. Brazilian wine, rarely excellent but often quite good, comes from grapes lovingly imported from Italy and planted in the accommodating soil of Rio Grande do Sul.

As in Argentina, the pampas (grassy plains) of the far south were long dominated by gauchos – Brazilian cowboys who taught the region to love beef above all other meats. *Churrasco* is better here than anywhere else in the country. The region preserves another cowboy tradition – *erva maté* tea (see the boxed text on p347).

DRINKS
Nonalcoholic Drinks
JUICES

Brazilian *sucos* (juices) are divine. Staples include known quantities such as orange, lime, papaya, banana, passion fruit, carrot, beet, pineapple, melon, watermelon and avocado. Then there are the Amazonian fruits that hardly exist outside Brazil. The berrylike *açaí* is prized for its nutritional value and addictive taste, while guaraná (a type of berry) is loaded with caffeinelike stimulants. They defy translation, as do *graviola*, *cupuaçu* and *fruta do conde*.

Caldo de cana is extracted directly from lengths of sugarcane, usually with a machine that's a hand-cranked, multicogged affair. *Agua de côco* (coconut juice) is available anywhere that it's hot and where there are people. With a few strokes of a butcher's knife, vendors open a hole large enough for a straw. It sounds touristy but it's not – the juice is high in electrolytes, and Brazilians value its rehydrating properties.

Juice bars are around in abundance, even in small towns, and a good-sized glass costs US$0.50 to US$1. In Rio, where juice is a way of life, corner bars can offer 30 or 40 different varieties. The juices may be made from fresh fruit and vegetables or from pulp. Request them *sem açúcar e gelo* or *natural*, if you don't want sugar and ice. Juices often have water mixed in; this is almost certain to be purified but if you're worried about it, you can ask for juices mixed with *suco de laranja* (orange juice) instead of water, or for a *vitamina*, which is juice with milk. Orange juice is rarely adulterated.

Joaquim Machado de Assis, Brazil's greatest 19th-century writer, was also a famous gourmand. Cooking and eating are essential ingredients of his eerily postmodern novels.

GlobalGourmet.com (www.globalgourmet.com/destinations/brazil/) provides a good introduction to the history and culture of Brazilian cuisine, with pages highlighting two much-loved staples – guaraná (a type of berry) and manioc.

CAFFEINE

Brazilians like their coffee as strong as the devil, as hot as hell and as sweet as love. In the morning they take it with milk (café com leite). For the rest of the day, it's cafezinhos, regular coffee served either in a drinking glass or an espresso-sized coffee cup and often presweetened. It is sold in stand-up bars and dispensed free in large thermoses in restaurants, at hotel reception desks and in offices to keep the general population perky the whole day through. Espresso is increasingly available in more upscale establishments, and just about everywhere in São Paulo, which boasts a highly evolved coffee culture.

A good cup of tea is harder to come by, but erva maté is a potential alternative. It's available throughout the country and is usually served cold and cloyingly sweet. Only in the state of Rio Grande do Sul is it drunk hot (see the boxed text on p347).

Made from an Amazonian berry, guaraná 'champagne' rivals Coca Cola as Brazil's favorite soft drink. It's served cold, carbonated and sweet, and it's reputed to have all sorts of health-giving properties.

DID YOU KNOW?

The Maué Indians so revere guaraná – an Amazonian fruit whose caffeine-packed seed resembles the human eye – that its plant is said to have given birth to the tribe's founder.

Alcoholic Drinks

BEER

Brazilians enjoy their beer served bem gelada (icy cold). In general, a cerveja refers to a 600ml bottled beer, a 'longneck' is a 300ml bottle, and a cervejinha is a 300ml can. Antártica (ant-okt-chee-kah) and Brahma are the best national brands. Keep your eyes peeled for regional brands, including Bohemia from Petrópolis, Cerpa from Pará, Cerma from Maranhão and the tasty Serramalte from Rio Grande do Sul. For thicker palates, try the stoutlike Caracu or Xingu, sweet black beers from Santa Catarina.

Chope (shop-ee) is a pale blond pilsner draft that's lighter and generally superior to canned or bottled beer. Antárctica and Brahma produce the two most widespread versions. In big cities you may even find chope escuro, a kind of light stout. Key phrase: Moço, mais um chope, por favor! (Waiter, another draft, please!).

DID YOU KNOW?

Capital amassed by São Paulo's coffee barons, plus the creation of infrastructure for the exporting of coffee (including trains and port facilities) fueled the city's startlingly rapid industrialization, beginning in the 1880s.

CACHAÇA

Also called pinga or aguardente, cachaça is a high-proof sugarcane alcohol produced and drunk throughout the country. It can be cheaper than water (literally) or as dear as whisky, and yes, price definitely signals a difference in taste and effect (and after effect!). Velho Barreiro, Ypioca, Pitú, Carangueijo, and São Francisco are some of the better labels.

The caipirinha is the unofficial Brazilian national drink. Ingredients are simple – cachaça with crushed lime, sugar and ice – but the results are sublime when sipped in the cool of an evening. You can replace the cachaça with vodka (to make a caipirosca) and the lime with a variety of fruit, including strawberries, kiwi, the cherrylike pitanga and the haunting limão de Persia (a light-yellow lime).

CELEBRATIONS

Brazilians love to eat (then again who doesn't?), and holidays and celebrations are another excuse for the hearty consumption of both food and alcohol. Any day off from work is an occasion for churrasco – grilled meats. Many of the gastronomic traditions are borrowed wholesale from European and American culture: turkey at Christmas, chocolate at Easter, champagne at the New Year, iced cakes for birthdays and weddings. In addition, pork and lentils augur good luck at the New Year, and during the winter feast days know as Juninas (June saints' days), *cachaça* is spiced with cinnamon, cloves and ginger and served warm. Despite the cultural importance of Carnaval, there is not a specific cuisine – alcohol trumps food.

WHERE TO EAT & DRINK

Eating out in Brazil can mean fried treats at the corner *lanchonete* (snack bar or greasy spoon); a lunchtime *prato feito* (ready-to-eat hot meal including rice, beans, a meat dish and salad) at a *bar* (pub) or *botequim* (working man's restaurant); a gorge session at a sit-down *rodízio* (all-you-can-eat) restaurant; or à la carte dining on white linen.

To eat quickly, cheaply and well, head to a *por-kilo* restaurant, which, as the name suggests, serves food by weight, and usually costs from US$4 to US$6 per kilogram. Offerings generally include fresh veggies, rice and beans, and grilled meat and fish, plus regional specialities. It's a great option for travelers, as you don't have to decipher a menu. Try to get there early (noon for lunch or 7pm or 8pm for dinner) when offerings are freshest and available in abundance.

Churrascarias are generally *rodízio*-style and include a salad bar plus meat that's brought to your table fresh from the grill. *Rodízio* restaurants serving pizza and *massa* (pasta) are also popular and cost between US$3 and US$5.

Lone travelers will be made to feel at home wherever they go. If you want to strike up a conversation, head to the closest corner bar or food stand, where bonhomie is almost certain to abound.

Tipping is not necessary – your bill will include a 10% service charge. In restaurants frequented by tourists, count your change and make sure your check is itemized: *Pode discriminar?* (Can you itemize?). There is no pressure to turn a table – you can linger as long as you like just about anywhere you go.

Quick Eats

In Brazil, you're never far from a *lanchonete*, where you can get *salgadinhos* (savory snacks, usually fried) – also known as *tira-gostos* and *petiscos* – for around US$0.50. Try *kibe*, which is cracked wheat stuffed with spiced meat then deep fried – it's both delectable and rib-sticking. *Pasteis* (dough filled with meat, cheese or seafood then deep-fried) are unbeatable when piping hot. *Pão de queijo* (a concoction of cheese and tapioca dough) is also deliciously ubiquitous.

For a few more centavos, you can get a *sanduiche*, a term that covers a multitude of hot sins from the *X-tudo* (cheeseburger with everything) to the dependable *misto quente* (toasted ham-and-cheese sandwich). Cold sandwiches, usually on crustless white bread, are called *sanduiche natural*.

BRAZIL'S TOP FIVE

- **Antiquarius** (p161) Rio de Janeiro
- **Arante** (p332) Ilha de Santa Catarina
- **Brik a Brak** (p190) Paraty
- **Dona Chika-ka** (p429) Salvador
- **Flor do Ipê** (p370) Goiás Velho

VEGETARIANS & VEGANS

Vegetarianism is very much a minority activity in Brazil. Many Brazilian waiters consider *sem carne* (without meat) to include such 'vegetable' groups as chicken, pork and animal fats, so be very clear when ordering in restaurants. Beware especially the typical black-bean dishes, which are often flavored with meat.

Most cities offer a few all-vegetarian options, but where this is neither convenient nor possible, head to a *por-kilo* restaurant – they usually offer at least half a dozen different salad, vegetable and bean dishes.

WHINING & DINING

Brazilians love children, and yours will be welcome wherever you go, as long as they're reasonably behaved. Note that bratty behavior is little tolerated by Brazilian parents, who consider a quick swat far more constructive than mere 'time-out.'

Familiar food is available for unadventurous palates just about anywhere you go, from burgers and pizza to grilled cheese sandwiches. Prepackaged baby food is generally available from supermarkets, though not from corner stores.

HABITS & CUSTOMS

Looking to reproduce Brazilian dishes you've tried on your travels? Check out *The Art of Brazilian Cookery* by Dolores Botafogo. It's the classic text on Brazilian cuisine, with recipes adapted for North American and European cooks.

Brazilians tend to have a small *café da manha* (breakfast; often shortened to *café*) of coffee with milk and a sweet or savory baked good; a big *almoço* (lunch), anytime from noon to 3pm; a hearty *lanche* (late-afternoon snack) of a *salgadinho* with juice, coffee or beer; and a light *jantar* (dinner) of a soup and/or sandwiches or a smaller recapitulation of lunch, usually sometime around 9pm or later. Extended families religiously gather for Sunday lunch, the most important meal of the week. It can last until 5pm or later and may seamlessly blend *lanche* and *jantar*. Snacking is perfectly acceptable at any time of the day or night, as is a quick shot of ultrasweet coffee.

COOKING COURSES

During week-long courses in baroque Ouro Prêto, the **Brazilian Academy of Cooking** (☎ 1-617 262 8455; yara@cookingnpleasures.com) provides you with first-hand experience in preparing dishes from Minas Gerais, Bahia and the Amazonas region. Informative field trips take in coffee plantations and a sugarcane distillery. The course costs around US$2500 per person per week. The school's main offices are located in the US, in Boston, Massachusetts.

Sandy's Brazilian & Continental Cuisine (☎ 1-203 596 9685; sandyna@juno.com), based in the US, in Waterbury (Connecticut), organizes culinary tours to Rio, São Paulo and other parts of Brazil.

DOS & DON'TS

Brazilians are casual about many things. Table manners are not one of them. Where possible, avoid eating with your hands – middle-class Brazilians often eat sandwiches with a knife and fork. Eat finger food with a napkin. If you dine in someone's home, bring a small gift such as wine or flowers – or win permanent friends with a liter of duty-free whiskey.

Smoking is generally acceptable, sometimes even in designated nonsmoking areas. It's considered polite, however, to ask fellow diners if it's OK to light up, especially in private homes. Brazilians love their cell phones – you can make or receive a quick call on any occasion except the most formal.

EAT YOUR WORDS

Use the following guide to help you order correctly and better understand – and enjoy – the dishes once they arrive. For pronunciation guidelines see p719.

Useful Phrases

The menu (in English), please.   *O cardapio (en inglês), por favor.*
  o kar-*da*-pyo eng eeng-*gles* porr fa-*vorr*
What would you recommend?   *O que você recomenda?*
  o ke vo-*se* he-ko-*meng*-da
I'm a vegetarian.   *Eu sou vegetariano/a.* (m/f)
  e-oo so ve-zhe-ta-ree-*a*-no/a
I'd like ...   *Queria ...*
  ke-*ree*-a ...
I'm full/I've eaten well.   *Estou satisfeito/a.* (m/f)
  es-to sa-tees-*fay*-to/a
Do you have ...?   *Tem ...*
  teng ...
The check, please.   *A conta, por favor.*
  a *kong*-ta porr fa-*vorr*

> The recipes may be hard to follow, but who cares? Christopher Idone's *Brazil: A Cook's Tour* provides a terrific photographic tour of Brazil and its varied cuisine.

Menu Decoder

MENU BASICS

almoço – lunch
arroz – rice
aves – poultry
azeite – olive oil
bebida – drink
café da manha – breakfast
carne – meat (usually beef)
churrasco – barbecue
comida caseira – home-style cooking
comida por kilo – pay-by-weight buffet
dendê – reddish palm oil
entrada – first course, appetizer
farinha de mandioca – manioc flour; the staple food of Brazil's Indians before colonization and the staple for many Brazilians today, especially in the Northeast and Amazon
farofa – garnish of manioc flour sautéed with butter
feijão – bean
frutos do mar – seafood
grelhadas – grilled meat or fish
lanche – hearty, late-afternoon snack
lanchonete – snack bar
molho – sauce
peixe – fish
por-kilo – per kilogram; used for self-serve restaurants
prato – main course
prato feito – literally 'made plate'; plate of the day; typically, an enormous and cheap meal
pratos típicos – local dishes
refeição – meal
refeição comercial – meal/serving of various dishes (normally comes with enough food for two to share)
rodízio – smorgasbord, usually with lots of meat
sobremesa – dessert

MAIN DISHES

barreado – a mixture of meats and spices cooked in a sealed clay pot for 24 hours and served with banana and *farofa*; the state dish of Paraná

bobó de camarão – manioc paste flavored with dried shrimp, coconut milk and cashew nuts

canja – soup made with rice and chicken broth

carne de sol – tasty, salted meat, grilled and served with beans, rice and vegetables

casquinha de siri – stuffed crab

cozido – a meat stew heavy on vegetables

feijoada – bean-and-meat stew served with rice and orange slices, traditionally eaten for Saturday lunch

frango ao molho pardo – chicken pieces stewed with vegetables and the blood of the bird

moqueca – Bahian fish stew cooked in a clay pot with *dendê* oil, coconut milk and spicy peppers

pato no tucupí – roast duck flavored with garlic, juice of the manioc plant and jambú; a favorite in Pará

pirarucu ao forno – a preparation of Brazil's most famous fish from the rivers of Amazonia, in which the fish is oven-cooked with lemon and other seasoning

tutu á mineira – savory black-bean mash typical of Minas Gerais

vatapá – a seafood dish of African origins with a thick sauce of manioc paste, coconut and *dendê* oil

xinxim de galinha – pieces of chicken flavored with garlic, salt and lemon

Maria-Brazil.org (www.maria-brazil.org/brazilian_recipes.htm) has a very good section on Brazilian food, including a guide to shopping in the country's supermarkets and street fairs.

Food Glossary

FRUIT & VEGETABLES

abacate – avocado
abacaxí – pineapple
açaí – gritty, deep-purple forest berry
acerola – acidic, cherry-flavored fruit; a megasource of vitamin C
alface – lettuce
alho – garlic
batata – potato
beterraba – beetroot
caju – fruit of the cashew plant
carambola – starfruit
cenoura – carrot
cupuaçu – acidic, slightly pearlike fruit
fruta do conde – sugar-apple fruit
goiaba – guava
graviola – custard apple
jaca – jackfruit
laranja – orange
limão – lime or lemon
maçã – apple
mamão – papaya
mandioca – cassava (also known as *aipim*)
manga – mango
maracujá – passion fruit
melancia – watermelon
melão – honeydew melon
morango – strawberry
pupunha – a fatty, vitamin-rich Amazonian fruit taken with coffee
uva – grape

SNACKS

acarajé – Bahian fritters made of brown beans and dried shrimp fried in *dendê* oil
empadão – a tasty pie, typical of Goiás, made from meat, vegetables, olives and eggs
kibe – cracked wheat stuffed with spiced meat then deep fried

pão de queijo – balls of cheese-stuffed tapioca bread
pastel – thin square of dough stuffed with meat, cheese or fish, then fried
salgadinhos – savory snacks; also *salgados*
salgados – savory snacks; also *salgadinhos*

MEAT, FISH & DAIRY
camarão – shrimp
carne – meat in general, also beef; also known as *bife* and *carne de vaca*
carneiro – lamb
dourado – meaty freshwater fish
frango – chicken
leite – milk
ovos – eggs
porco – pork
queijo – cheese
requeijão – cream cheese
siri – crab
tainha – a meaty but tender local fish

DESSERT
arroz doce – rice pudding
brigadeiro – *doce de leite* covered with chocolate
bolo – cake
cocada – baked coconut treat
doce de leite – creamy milk-and-sugar concoction
goiabada – sweet guava paste
pavé – creamy cake
quindim – egg-based sweet
sorvete – ice cream

DRINKS
agua – water
aguardente – firewater, rotgut; any strong drink, but usually *cachaça*
batida – blended drink
cachaça – sugarcane spirit
café – coffee
caipirinha – drink made from *cachaça* and crushed citrus fruit, such as lemon, orange or maracujá
cerveja – beer
chope – draft beer
erva maté – popular tea of southern Brazil
guaraná – soft drink made from Amazonian berry
pinga – another name for *cachaça*
refrigerante – soft drink
suco – juice
vitamina – juice with milk

Carnaval in Rio

Colorful, outrageous, hedonistic – words do little justice to the bacchanalian spectacle that lends Rio so much notoriety. Visitors arrive in droves to join Cariocas (residents of Rio) as they drink, dance, celebrate and chalk up a few sins before Ash Wednesday brings it all to a close. Carnaval officially lasts from the Friday to the Tuesday preceding Lent, but revelry begins well in advance. Rehearsals at the *escolas de samba* (samba schools) start around September.

Cariocas celebrate Carnaval in every form and fashion. Nightclubs and bars throw special costumed events, while formal balls draw an elegantly dressed (or costumed) crowd. Parks and plazas (Largo do Machado, Arcos da Lapa, Praça General Osório) often host free live concerts on Carnaval weekend. The common denominators among them all are music, dancing and celebration.

Bandas, also called *blocos*, are another good way to celebrate à la Carioca. These consist of a procession of drummers and vocalists followed by anyone who wants to dance through the streets of Rio. Many encourage people to dress up – drag is popular (among gays and straights alike).

The parade through the Sambódromo is the culmination of Carnaval, on Sunday and Monday nights. It's a spectacle that features thousands of costumed dancers, elaborate floats and exuberant fans cheering on their favorite schools.

Although there's a lot going on around town, don't expect the Carnaval to come to you. Many visitors show up with the expectation that the party will be all around them. Not so; you have to seek it out. See below to get some ideas on how to celebrate King Momo's return.

To get more information on events during Carnaval, check the *Veja* insert, *Veja Rio* (sold on Sunday in newsstands), or visit **Riotur** (Map pp136-7; www.rio.rj.gov.br/riotur; 9th fl, Rua Assembléia 10) near metro stop Carioca. They're the ones in charge of Carnaval, by the way.

'To compensate for the deprivation ahead, they rack up sins in advance with wild parties in honor of King Momo, the king of Carnaval'

HISTORY

Carnaval, like Mardi Gras, originated from various pagan spring festivals. During the Middle Ages, these tended to be wild parties until tamed, in Europe, by both the Reformation and the Counter-Reformation. But not even the heavy hand of the Inquisition could squelch Carnaval in the Portuguese colony, where it came to acquire Indian costumes and African rhythms.

Some speculate that the word *carnaval* derives from the Latin *carne vale,* meaning 'goodbye meat,' owing to the 40 days of abstinence (from meat and other worldly pleasures) that Lent entails. To compensate for the deprivation ahead, they rack up sins in advance with wild parties in honor of King Momo, the king of Carnaval.

SIGHTS & ACTIVITIES
Bandas: Carnaval on the Streets

Attending a *banda* is one of the best ways to celebrate Carnaval. *Bandas*, also called *blocos*, consist of a procession of drummers and singing, followed by anyone who wants to dance through the streets. To join in, all you have to do is show up. Note that some *bandas* ask you to march in one of their colors. Many sell shirts on the spot (US$5) or you can just show up in the right colors. Some *bandas* are featured on the next page; for complete listings, check with Riotur (p122).

Banda Carmen Miranda (Map pp124-5; Praça General Osório, Ipanema; 🕑 4pm Carnaval Sun) A hilarious good time, Banda Miranda features lots of men decked out like the Brazilian bombshell. A lively mix of straights and gays parades through Ipanema's streets.

Banda de Ipanema (Map pp124-5; Praça General Osório, Ipanema; 🕑 4pm 2nd Sat before Carnaval & Carnaval Sat) This longstanding *banda* starts from Ipanema. It's a wild crowd, complete with drag queens and others in costume. Don't miss it.

Banda de Sá Ferreira (Map pp128-9; Cnr Av Atlântica & Rua Sá Ferreira, Copacabana; 🕑 3pm Carnaval Sat & Sun) This popular Copacabana *banda* marches along the ocean from Posto 1 to Posto 6.

Barbas (cnr Rua Assis Bueno & Rua General Polidoro, Botafogo; 🕑 2pm Carnaval Sat) One of the oldest *bandas* of the Zona Sul parades through the streets with a 60-piece percussion band. A water truck follows along to spray the crowd of some 2500. Colors: red and white.

Bloco Cacique de Ramos (Map pp136-7; cnr Presidente Vargas & Rio Branco, Centro; 🕑 6pm Carnaval Sun) Participants in this *bloco* are expected to dress as Indians.

Bloco de Bip Bip (Rua Almirante Gonçalves 50, Copacabana; 🕑 Carnaval Sat & 9:30pm Carnaval Tue) Has perhaps the best music of any *banda*, owing to the professional musicians who drop in from time to time. Leaves from the old samba haunt, Bip Bip (see the boxed text on p169).

Bloco de Segunda (Map pp132-3; Cobal Humaitá, Rua Voluntários de Pátria 446, Botafogo; 🕑 5pm Carnaval Mon) An excellent percussion band joins 2000 or so revelers. T-shirt is obligatory; buy at the dance academy beforehand.

Cordão do Bola Preta (Map pp136-7; cnr Av 13 de Maio & Rua Evaristo da Veiga, Centro; 🕑 10am Carnaval Sat) The oldest *banda* in activity, features lots of men dressed as women (who are often straight), and a chaotic march that leads the group to stop at bars along the way. Costumes always welcome – especially those with black and white spots.

Dois Pra Lá, Dois Pra Cá (Map pp136-7; Carlinho de Jesus Dance School, Rua da Passagem 145, Botafogo; 🕑 2pm Carnaval Sat) This fairly long parade travels from the dance school to the Copacabana Palace hotel. Bring along your swimsuit for a dip in the ocean afterwards.

Empurra Que Pega (Map pp124-5; Cnr Rua Carlos Góis & Rua Ataulfo de Paiva, Leblon; 🕑 6pm Carnaval Sat & Sun) A beautiful Leblon crowd of some 4000 take to the streets.

Simpatia É Quase Amor (Map pp124-5; Praça General Osório, Ipanema; 🕑 3pm 2nd Sat before Carnaval & Carnaval Sun) A big *bloco*, with 10,000 participants and a 50-piece percussion band.

Carnaval Balls

Carnaval balls are surreal and erotic events. The most famous one is held at the Copacabana Palace (p156). It's a formal affair, so you'll need a tux or a ball gown. You'll have

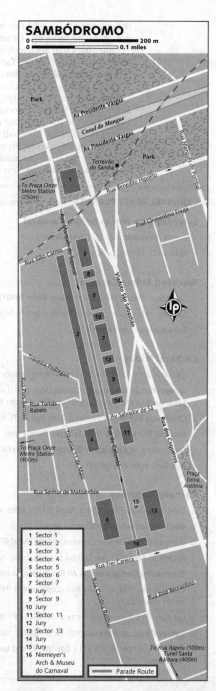

SAMBÓDROMO

0 — 200 m
0 — 0.1 miles

1 Sector 1
2 Sector 2
3 Sector 3
4 Sector 4
5 Sector 5
6 Sector 6
7 Sector 7
8 Jury
9 Sector 9
10 Jury
11 Sector 11
12 Jury
13 Sector 13
14 Jury
15 Jury
16 Niemeyer's Arch & Museu do Carnaval

Parade Route

the opportunity to celebrate with Rio's glitterati as well as the occasional pop star who turns up. Tickets cost around US$200.

Other balls that are decidedly less upper class are held at **Scala** (Map 124-5; Av Afrânio de Melo Franco, Leblon); **Canecão** (Av Venceslau Brás 215, Botafogo); and **Help** (Map p128-9; Av Atlântica 3432, Copacabana). The most extravagant balls for gays are found at Le Boy (p171) in Copacabana. The most popular ball is held in Centro at Praça Floriano (p135), which attracts around 60,000 revelers. Every night of Carnaval weekend (from 9pm onward, Friday to Tuesday), bands take the stage in front of the Câmara Municipal, in the northwest corner of the plaza. This ball is free.

Tickets go on sale roughly two weeks beforehand, and the balls are held nightly for the week preceding and all through Carnaval. Buy a copy of *Veja* magazine with the *Veja Rio* insert. It has details of all the balls.

CARNAVAL PARTY PLANNER *Marcos Silviano do Prado*

Saturday Two Weeks Before Carnaval

■ Banda de Ipanema (p107), from 4pm

■ Rehearsals at Samba Schools

Weekend Before Carnaval

■ Saturday – Banda Simpatia é Quase Amor (p107), in Ipanema at 4pm

■ Sunday – Monobloco at 4pm (Leblon Beach; Map pp124-5)

■ Rehearsals at samba schools

Carnaval Friday

■ Carnaval 2004 King Momo is crowned by mayor at 1pm on Av Rio Branco, Centro

■ Shows start at Terreirão do Samba (Map p107) and Rio Folia (Map pp136-7), near the Arcos do Lapa, next to the Catedral Metropolitana, from 8pm

■ Cinelândia Ball (Praça Floriano; Map pp136-7), from 9pm – free

■ Red and Black Ball at Scala (above), from 11pm

■ Dance Party at **Cine Ideal** (Map pp136-7; Rua da Carioca 62)

■ Gay Balls at Le Boy (p171)

Carnaval Saturday

■ Cordão do Bola Preta Street Band (p107), from 9:30am

■ Banda de Ipanema (p107), from 4pm

■ Competition of deluxe costumes at the Hotel Glória (p158), from 7pm

■ Parade of Access Group Samba Schools, from 7pm at the Sambódromo (Map p107)

■ Street Band Competition at Av Rio Branco, Centro (Map pp136-7), from 8pm – free

■ Copacabana Palace Luxury Ball (Copacabana Palace; p156), from 11pm – costumes or black-tie are mandatory

■ Off-Carnaval: X-Demente Party at Fundição Progresso (p170)

■ Carnaval Balls at Scala (above), Help (above) and other venues, from 11pm

■ Gay Ball in Copacabana at Le Boy (p171) and **Incontrus** (Map pp128-29; Praça Serzedelo Correia 15A, Copacabana)

Samba-School Parades

The main parade takes place in the **Sambódromo** (Map p107; Rua Marques do Sapuçaí), near Praça Onze metro station, and it's nothing short of spectacular. Before an exuberant crowd of some 30,000, each of 14 samba schools has their hour and twenty minutes to dazzle the audience.

The parades begin in moderate mayhem and work themselves up to a higher plane of frenzy. The announcers introduce the school, the group's theme colors and the number of wings. Far away the lone voice of the *puxador* starts the samba. Thousands more voices join him, and then the drummers kick in, approximately 200 to 400 per school. The pounding drums drive the parade. Sambas, including the themes for each group, flood the airwaves for weeks before the beginning of Carnaval.

- Off-Carnaval Parties at Bunker 94 (p171) and other dance clubs
- Shows start at Terreirão do Samba (Map p107) and Rio Folia (Map pp136-7), near the Arcos do Lapa, next to the Catedral Metropolitana, from 8pm

Carnaval Sunday

- Samba Parade at the Sambódromo (Map p107), from 9pm to 6am
- Carnaval Balls at Scala (opposite) and Help (opposite), from 11pm
- Gay Balls at Le Boy (p171) and **Elite** (Map pp142-3; Rua Frei Caneca, Centro)
- Rave Party at theme park Terra Encantada (p150)
- Off-Carnaval Parties at Bunker 94 (p171) and other dance clubs
- Shows start at Terreirão do Samba (Map p107) and Rio Folia (Map pp136-7), near the Arcos do Lapa, next to the Catedral Metropolitana, from 8pm

Carnaval Monday

- Samba Parade at the Sambódromo (Map p107), from 9pm to 6am
- Carnaval Balls at Scala (opposite), Help (opposite) and other venues, from 11pm
- Gay Balls at Le Boy (p171) and Elite (above)
- Off-Carnaval: Parties at Bunker 94 (p171) and other dance clubs
- Shows start at Terreirão do Samba (Map p107) and Rio Folia (Map pp136-7), near the Arcos do Lapa, next to the Catedral Metropolitana, from 8pm

Carnaval Tuesday

- Banda de Ipanema (p107), from 4pm
- Parade of Group B Samba Schools at Sambódromo (Map p107), from 9pm
- Scala Gay Costume Ball in Leblon (Map pp124-5), from 11pm
- Carnaval Balls at Help (opposite) and other venues, from 11pm
- Gay balls at Le Boy (p171) and **Garden Hall** (Barra Garden Shopping Center, Av das Américas 3255, Barra da Tijuca)
- Off-Carnaval: X-Demente Party at Fundição Progresso (p170)
- Off-Carnaval: Parties at Bunker 94 (p171) and other dance clubs
- Shows start at Terreirão do Samba (Map p107) and Rio Folia (Map pp136-7), near the Arcos do Lapa, next to the Catedral Metropolitana, from 8pm

Next come the main wings of the school, the big allegorical floats, the children's wing, the drummers, the celebrities and the bell-shaped *baianas* (women dressed as Bahian 'aunts') twirling in elegant hoopskirts. The *baianas* honor the history of the parade itself, which was brought to Rio from Salvador da Bahia in 1877.

The *mestre-sala* (dance master) and *porta-bandeira* (flag-bearer) waltz and whirl. Celebrities, dancers and tambourine players strut their stuff. The costumes are fabulously lavish: 1.5m feathered headdresses, long flowing capes that sparkle with sequins, and rhinestone-studded G-strings.

More than an hour after the parade begins, the school makes it past the arch and the judges' stand. The whole procession is also an elaborate competition. A hand-picked set of judges chooses the best school on the basis of many components, including percussion, the *samba do enredo* (theme song), harmony between percussion, song and dance, choreography, costumes, story line, floats and decorations. The championship is hotly contested, with the winner becoming the pride of Rio and all of Brazil.

The Sambódromo parades start on Friday night with the *mirins* (young samba-school members) and continue on through Saturday night when the Group A samba schools strut their stuff. Sunday and Monday are the big nights, when the Grupo Especial – the best 14 samba schools in Rio – parade: seven of them on Sunday night and into the morning, and seven more on Monday night. The following Saturday, the eight top schools perform once more in the Parade of Champions. Each event starts at 9pm and runs until 6am. If you go, you're allowed to bring in plastic bottles (two 500ml sizes per person), but no glass. A good option if you plan to drink while you're there.

CARNAVAL BEYOND RIO

Around Carnaval, if you bump into any Salvadorenos (inhabitants of Salvador) en route to Rio, they'll be quick to tell you that the world's best Carnaval happens not in the Cidade Maravilhosa (Marvelous City), but in Bahia. Brazil has plenty of other cities that throw a fantastic party, allowing you to judge for yourself which one hosts the brashest bash:

■ Carnaval in Salvador (p424) happens mostly on the streets, where music and spontaneity rule and *trios elétricos* (electrically amplified bands playing atop trucks) work thousands of revelers into a frenzy.

■ Everyone dons a costume for the 11 days and nights of Olinda's Carnaval (p507). Balls, nights of samba and *afoxé* (the music of Bahia, which has strong African rhythms and close ties to Candomblé), and plenty of street-style merriment characterize the festas.

■ Recife (p501) starts its Carnaval weeks in advance, with *bailes* (dances) in the clubs and *blocos* (drumming and dancing processions) on the streets. The pounding rhythms of *maracatu* (slow, heavy Afro-Brazilian drumbeats) aren't for wallflowers.

■ Porto Seguro (p457) throws an impressive and hedonistic bash, complete with plenty of dancing in the streets, round-the-clock music jams and no-holds-barred partying.

■ In Rio state, Paraty (p187) has its own odd version of the party, more akin to Woodstock than Carnaval, as hundreds of young revelers cover themselves in mud and dance through the cobblestone streets.

■ Two months after Carnaval, Feira de Santana (p466) throws its Carnaval-style party called Micareta. The best bands of Salvador fill the air with song and well over 100,000 party for five days straight.

■ Carnatal is Natal's (p531) out-of-season Carnaval, held the first week of December. The same festive atmosphere and rhythm-charged music prevails.

TICKETS
Getting tickets at legitimate prices can be tough. Many tickets are sold well in advance of the event. **Riotur** (Map pp136-7; www.rio.rj.gov.br/riotur; 9th fl, Rua Assembléia 10) can advise on where to get them, as the official outlet can vary from year to year. People line up for hours, and travel agents and scalpers snap up the best seats. Riotur reserves seats in private boxes for tourists for US$200, but you should be able to pick up regular tickets from a travel agent or from the **Maracanã stadium box office** (Map pp142-3; ☎ 2568-9962) for around US$40. Try to get seats in the center, as this is the liveliest section – and the best views are from here.

By Carnaval weekend, most tickets will have sold out, but there are lots of scalpers. If you buy a ticket from a scalper (no need to worry about looking for them – they'll find you!), make sure you get both the plastic ticket with the magnetic strip and the ticket showing the seat number. The tickets for different days are color-coded, so double-check the date as well.

If you haven't purchased a ticket but still want to go, you can show up at the Sambódromo at around midnight, three or four hours into the show. This is when you can get grandstand tickets for about US$10 from scalpers outside the gate. Make sure you check your sector. Most ticket sellers will try to pawn off their worst seats.

And if you can't make it during Carnaval proper, there's always the cheaper (but less exciting) Parade of Champions the following Saturday.

GETTING TO THE SAMBÓDROMO
Don't take a bus to or from the Sambódromo. It's much safer to take a taxi or the metro, which runs round the clock during Carnaval until 11pm Tuesday. This is also a great opportunity to check out the paraders commuting in costume.

Make sure you indicate to your taxi driver which side of the stadium you're on. If you decide to take the metro, remember the stop you get off

---

SAMBÓDROMO GLOSSARY

alas – literally, the 'wings.' These are groups of samba-school members responsible for a specific part of the central theme *(samba do enredo)*. Special *alas* include the *baianas*, women dressed as Bahian 'aunts' in full skirts and turbans. The *abre ala* of each school is the opening wing or float.

bateria – the drum section. This is the driving beat behind the school's samba and the 'soul' of the school.

carnavalescos – the artistic directors of each school, who are responsible for the overall layout and design of the school's theme.

carros alegóricos – the dazzling floats, usually decorated with near-naked women. The floats are pushed along by the school's maintenance crew.

desfile – the procession. The most important samba schools *desfilar* (parade) on the Sunday and Monday night of Carnaval. Each school's *desfile* is judged on its samba, drum section, master of ceremonies and flag bearer, floats, leading commission, costumes, dance coordination and harmony.

destaques – the richest and most elaborate costumes. The heaviest ones usually get a spot on one of the floats.

diretores de harmonia – the school organizers, who usually wear white or the school colors; they run around yelling and 'pumping up' the wings and making sure there aren't any gaps in the parade.

enredo – the central theme of each school. The *samba do enredo* is the samba that goes with it. Themes vary tremendously.

passistas – a school's best samba dancers. They roam the parade in groups or alone, stopping to show their fancy footwork along the way. The women are usually scantily dressed and the men usually hold tambourines.

puxador – the interpreter of the theme song. He (they're invariably male) works as a guiding voice leading the school's singers at rehearsals and in the parade.

JOINING A SAMBA SCHOOL

There's nothing to stop you from taking part in a Carnaval parade. Most samba schools are happy to have foreigners join one of the wings. Several websites have sprung up recently that make it possible to choose and buy your costume online before you even get to Rio de Janeiro. One good one with an English version is www.geocities.com/alavaisacudir.

Fantasias (costumes) vary in price according to how elaborate they are, but they usually cost between US$200 and US$300.

If you don't want to buy online, it is always possible to get one by phoning the samba schools directly once you're in Rio, even as little as two weeks before Carnaval. (For information on how to contact the samba schools, see p168.)

Those who would like a view of what it's like to join a samba school, long term, should read Alma Guillermoprieto's excellent book, *Samba*.

at depends on where your seats are. For sectors 2, 4 and 6, exit at Praça Onze. Once outside the station, turn to the right, take another right and then walk straight ahead (on Rua Júlio Carmo) to sector 2. For sectors 4 and 6, turn on Rua Carmo Neto and proceed to Av Salvador de Sá. You'll soon see the Sambódromo and hear the roar of the crowd. Look for signs showing the entrance to the sectors. If going to sectors on the other side (1, 3, 5, 7, 9, 11 and 13), exit at Central station. You'll then have to walk about 700m along Av Presidente Vargas until you see the Sambódromo.

Samba Land

The Sambódromo's latest addition is the **Terreirão do Samba** (Map p107; Praça Onze, Av Presidente Vargas), an open-air courtyard next to sector 1. Performances are presented the weekend before Carnaval, then continue from the following Friday all the way through to Tuesday. Samba Land also hosts a party the Saturday after Carnaval, which is the Parade of Champions.

Samba-School Rehearsals

Around August or September, rehearsals start at the *escolas de samba* (samba 'schools' or clubs). Rehearsals usually take place in the *favelas* and are open to visitors. They're fun to watch, but go with a Carioca for safety. Mangueira and Salgueiro are among the easiest to get to, and are popular with a mix of Cariocas and tourists. See p168 for complete listings of samba schools.

DATES

Dates for Carnaval (Friday to Tuesday) in coming years are February 4 to 8, 2005; February 24 to 28, 2006; February 16 to 20, 2007; and February 1 to 5, 2008.

The Southeast

Everyone is attracted to the dynamic and abundant energy of the Southeast. Migrant workers come in droves every year hoping to find work in the industrial triangle of Rio de Janeiro, São Paulo and Belo Horizonte (the country's three richest and largest cities). Surfers and nature-lovers flow back and forth between relaxed beach towns such as Saquarema, Arraial do Cabo and fashionable Búzios (all in Rio state). History buffs marvel at the colonial splendors of Ouro Prêto, São João del Rei, Tiradentes and Diamantina in Minas Gerais, and few can resist the seductive call of Brazil's Cidade Maravilhosa (Marvelous City), Rio

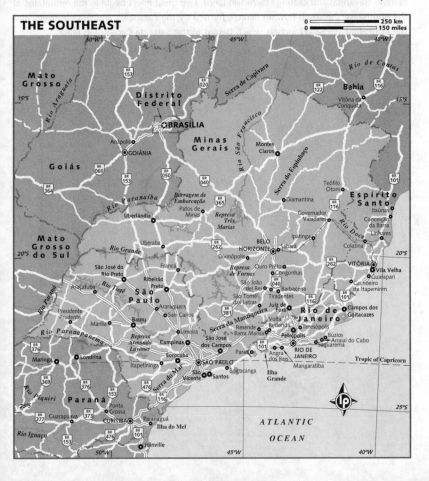

de Janeiro. As if that weren't enough, the Southeast (Sudeste to Brazilians) is jam-packed with gorgeous national parks that dot the landscape, from the northernmost tip of coastal Espírito Santo all the way down to the megalopolis of São Paulo.

Then there are the people – the hard-working Paulistas (from São Paulo state), the fun-loving Cariocas (from Rio), the strong-willed Capixabas (from Espírito Santo) and the spiritual Mineiros (from Minas Gerais). More than 44% of Brazil's population lives in the Southeast, and you'll hear Japanese, German, French, Italian and certain indigenous languages almost as frequently as Portuguese.

Geographically, the Southeast contains the most mountainous areas of the Planalto Brasileiro (Brazilian Plateau): the Serras da Mantiqueira, do Mar and do Espinhaço. Most of the region was once covered by lush Mata Atlântica (Atlantic rain forest), but this has been devastated since the arrival of the Portuguese. Inland Minas Gerais also contains areas of cerrado (savanna) and caatinga (semiarid land). Two great rivers begin in the mountains of the Southeast: the south-flowing Paraná, formed by the Paranaíba and Grande rivers, and the north-flowing São Francisco, which begins in the Serra da Canastra in Minas.

Rio de Janeiro City

HIGHLIGHTS

- Racking up a few sins at **Carnaval** (p106), the world's largest party
- Sun-worshiping on lovely **Ipanema Beach** (p123), one of Brazil's most famous beaches
- Gazing over the Cidade Maravilhosa (Marvelous City) from atop **Pão de Açúcar** (p130), Rio's most famous peak
- Riding the cog train 710m up Corcovado for stunning views beneath **Cristo Redentor** (p131), the city's open-armed savior
- Partying at samba clubs in **Lapa** (p170), one of Rio's most vibrant neighborhoods

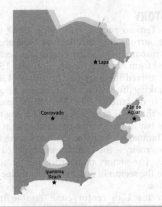

★ Lapa
★ Corcovado
★ Pão de Açúcar
★ Ipanema Beach

■ TELEPHONE CODE: 0xx21   ■ POPULATION: 7 MILLION   ■ AREA: 808 SQ KM

When Brazilians say 'Deus é Brasileiro' (God is Brazilian), some of Rio's citizens probably think, Deus é carioca (God is a Rio-dweller). The city has received more than its fair share of natural and cultural riches. Its setting is spectacular: 37 white-sand beaches fronting blue sea with lush green peaks rising up around them. On the streets, Rio's energy is blazing…

On a typical Friday night in Lapa, samba spills out of old colonial buildings as revelers pack the streets, wandering among the bars and old music halls in search of the soul of samba. Just around the corner, a long stretch of antique shops doubles as a jazz spot, with bossa nova–infused sounds filling warmly lit 19th-century mansions. Further south, in the Zona Sul, the open-air bars and restaurants along the lake fill with music. Just a few blocks further south again, lie the stylish lounges of Leblon and Ipanema, hidden among tree-lined streets.

As the first light of day illuminates Cristo Redentor (Christ the Redeemer) atop Corcovado, another brand of Carioca takes over the streets. Early-morning joggers and cyclists move swiftly along the shoreline to the backdrop of palm trees and crashing waves. Out in the water, surfers and swimmers greet the sun's rays. Other Cariocas have grander schemes – rock-climbing the face of Pão de Açúcar (Sugarloaf Mountain), hang-gliding over São Conrado or hiking through Atlantic rain forest. A little later, sun worshipers, football and volleyball players, and roaming vendors take to the sands of Barra, Copacabana, Ipanema and Leblon.

This portrait of the city would not be complete without considering the city's age (around 500) and its place in history, best observed in Rio's historic downtown. Hillside colonial churches, palaces from the Portuguese reign and splendid neoclassical buildings lie scattered about Centro. Not ones to watch history slowly crumble around them, Cariocas infuse these places with new energy: cultural centers, galleries, concert halls and theaters all inhabit old spaces, setting the stage for Rio's vibrant arts and music scene.

HISTORY

The Tamoio people were living along the land surrounding the Baía de Guanabara (Guanabara Bay) when Gaspar de Lemos sailed from Portugal for Brazil in May 1501 and entered the huge bay in January 1502. Mistaking the bay for a river, Lemos named it Rio de Janeiro. The French, however, were the first Europeans to settle along the great bay in 1555. After a brief alliance with the Tamoio – who hated the Portuguese for their cruelty – the French were expelled in 1567. The victors then drove the Tamoio from the region in another series of bloody battles.

By the 17th century, the Tamoio had been wiped out. Those who weren't taken into slavery died from disease. Other In-

dians were 'pacified' and taken to live in settlements organized by the Jesuits. The Portuguese had set up a fortified town on the Morro Castelo in 1567 and, by the 17th century, Rio became Brazil's third-most important settlement (after Salvador da Bahia and Recife-Olinda). African slaves streamed in and the sugar plantations thrived. Even more slaves arrived to work in the gold mines of Minas Gerais during the 18th century.

In 1807 Napoleon's army marched on Lisbon. Two days before the invasion, 40 ships carrying the Portuguese prince regent (later known as Dom João VI) and his entire court of 15,000 set sail for Brazil. When the prince regent arrived in Rio, his Brazilian subjects celebrated wildly, dancing in the streets. He immediately took over the rule of Brazil from his viceroy.

Dom João fell in love with Brazil. Even after he became king of Portugal, he remained and declared Rio the capital of the United Kingdom of Portugal, Brazil and the Algarve. This made Brazil the only New World colony to ever have a European monarch ruling on its soil.

At the end of the 19th century the city's population exploded because of European immigration and internal migration (mostly ex-slaves from the declining coffee and sugar regions). By 1890 Rio boasted more than a million inhabitants, a quarter of them foreign-born, and the city spread rapidly.

The early 1920s to the late 1950s were Rio's golden age. With the inauguration of the grand hotels (the Glória in 1922 and the Copacabana Palace in 1924), Rio became a romantic, exotic destination for Hollywood celebrities and international high society who came to play and gamble at the casinos and dance or perform in the nightclubs.

Rio continued to change. Three large landfill projects were undertaken to ease the strain on a city restricted by its beautiful surroundings. The first was to become Aeroporto Santos Dumont, near Centro. The second resulted in Flamengo Park, and the third expanded the strand at Copacabana.

Rio remained the political capital of Brazil until 1960, when the government moved to Brasília. During the 1960s, modern skyscrapers rose in the city, and some of Rio's most beautiful buildings were lost. During the same period, the *favelas* (shantytowns) of Rio grew to critical mass with immigrants from poverty-stricken areas of the Northeast and interior, swelling the number of Rio's urban poor. The Cidade Maravilhosa (Marvelous City) began to lose its gloss as crime and violence increased.

The final decade of the military dictatorship that ruled Brazil from 1964 to 1985 was not kind to Rio. There were numerous protests during that period (notably in 1968 when some 100,000 marched upon the Palácio Tiradentes). Even Rio's politicians opposed the military regime, which responded by withholding vital federal funding. The administration was forced to tighten its belt, and infrastructure deteriorated as the city's coffers dried up.

A turning point for Rio came when it was chosen as host city for Eco 92, the United Nations Conference on Environment and Development. In the buildup to the conference, the federal government poured in almost US$1 billion to improve Rio's infrastructure. Approximately US$18 million was spent on satellite communications alone, and Riocentro, a huge convention center, was built.

Today Rio is more full of optimism and hope than it has been in years. The city buzzes with an unstoppable creative energy, and long-awaited projects are finally being financed. The biggest is the controversial Favela-Bairro project, which strives to integrate *favelas* into the rest of the city by providing basic sanitation and by planning leisure areas, health clinics, schools, preschools and community centers (Rio has pledged a total of US$1 billion over the life of the project). At the same time, some of Rio's aging colonial gems are being revitalized, and businesses are springing up all over town. Other projects on the horizon that mayor Cesar Maia has helped bring to Rio include the 2007 Pan American Games and a branch of the Guggenheim Museum, the first ever in Latin America.

ORIENTATION

Rio is a city of unusual urban diversity, with beaches, mountains, skyscrapers and the omnipresent *favelas* all woven into the fabric of the landscape. The city itself can be divided into two zones: the Zona Norte (North Zone), which consists of industrial, working-class neighborhoods, and the Zona Sul (South Zone), full of middle- and upper-class neighborhoods and Rio's well-known beaches. Centro, Rio's business district and the site of its first settlement, marks the boundary between the two, and a number of the important museums and colonial buildings are there.

The parts of Rio you are most likely to explore stretch along the shore of the Baía de Guanabara and the Atlantic Ocean. South from Centro are the neighborhoods of Lapa, Glória, Catete, Flamengo, Botafogo and Urca – where the striking peak of Pão de Açúcar dominates the landscape. Further south lie the neighborhoods of Copacabana, Ipanema and Leblon, the only stops for many travelers to the city.

0 —————————— 8 km
0 —————————— 4 miles

Other areas of interest include the quaint, colonial neighborhood of Santa Teresa, on a hill overlooking Centro, and the looming statue of Cristo Redentor, atop Corcovado in Cosme Velho, from where there are fabulous views of both zones of the city.

Aside from the bus station, Maracanã Football Stadium and the international airport, most travelers have few reasons to visit the Zona Norte.

Rio de Janeiro's international airport, Aeroporto Galeão (GIG; also called Aeroporto António Carlos Jobim) is 15km north of the city center. Santos Dumont airport, used by most domestic flights, is by the bayside in the city center, 1km east of Cinelândia metro station. Rio's central bus station, Rodoviária Novo Rio, lies several kilometers northwest of Centro. For information on getting into town from the bus station or from the airports, see p175.

Maps

Guia Quatro Rodas publishes an excellent city map of Rio de Janeiro (US$3.50), available at most newsstands. Lonely Planet also produces a good city map. Riotur, the city's tourist information center, provides free street maps at its offices. For physical and topographical maps, head to **Editora Geográfica J Paulini** (Map pp136-37; ☎ 2220 0181; Shop K, Rua Senador Dantas 75, Centro).

INFORMATION
Bookstores

Argumento (Map pp124-5; ☎ 2239 5294; Rua Dias Ferreira 417, Leblon) Small but decent selection of foreign-language books and magazines. Café in back.

Bar das Artes (Map pp136-7; ☎ 2215 5795; Praça XV de Novembro 48, Centro) Charming bistro/bookstore/music shop, inside the Paço Imperial.

Boca do Sapo (Map pp124-5; ☎ 2287 5207; Rua Visconde de Pirajá 12D, Ipanema) Used books and records.

Dantes (Map pp124-5; ☎ 2511 3480; Rua Dias Ferreira 45B, Leblon) A handsome bookshop in Leblon with new and used books – in foreign languages as well.

Letras e Expressões Ipanema (Map pp124-5; ☎ 2521 6110; Rua Visconde de Pirajá 276, Ipanema; 🕑 8am-midnight); Leblon (Map pp124-5; ☎ 2511 5085; Av Ataulfo de Paiva 1292, Leblon; 🕑 24hr) A decent selection of foreign-language books, English-language magazines and an Internet café at each of the three branches.

Livraria da Travessa Av Rio Branco (Map pp136-7; No 44, Av Rio Branco, Centro); Rua Visconde de Pirajá (Map pp124-5; ☎ 2249 4977; Rua Visconde de Pirajá 572, Ipanema); Travessa do Ouvidor (Map 136-7; No 17, Travessa do Ouvidor, Centro; 🕑 9am-8pm Mon-Fri, 10am-1pm Sat) Books and periodicals, CDs and an excellent café at the Ipanema branch.

Livraria Prefácio (Map pp132-3; ☎ 2527 5699; Rua Voluntarios da Pátria 39, Botafogo) This charming bookshop occasionally hosts poetry readings or a record-release party in the fine café in the back.

Luzes da Cidade (Map pp132-3; ☎ 2226 4108; Rua Voluntarios da Pátria 35, Botafogo)

RIO IN...

One Day

If you have just one day in Rio, head early to the lovely beach of **Ipanema** (p123). At lunchtime ride the *bonde* (tram) to **Santa Teresa** and devour traditional cuisine at **Bar do Mineiro** (see the boxed text on (p159) or **Sobrenatural** (p166). In the afternoon, take the cable car to **Pão de Açúcar** (p130), to watch the sunset over Rio. At night, dine in stylish **Leblon** (p160) before heading to **Lapa** (p168) for serious samba beats.

Five Days

On your second day, take in an exhibition at a cultural center or at the **Museu de Arte Moderna** (MAM; p131). At lunchtime, dine in one of Centro's excellent restaurants. Walk off those *chopes* (draft beers) by exploring the pedestrian streets surrounding Av Rio Branco. Afterwards, grab dinner at **Porcão Rio's** (p165) or **Marius** (p163), a couple of famed *churrascarias* (restaurants featuring barbecued meat). On day three, watch a football match at **Maracanã Football Stadium** (p172), followed by a trip up Corcovado to **Cristo Redentor** (p131), for outstanding views. Lagoa's lakeside **kiosks** (p162) make a fine setting for the evening's meal. On the fourth day, book a **hang-gliding flight** (p145) over São Conrado. Afterwards, it's on to **Parque Nacional da Tijuca** (see the boxed text on p146) for a hike through tropical rain forest. On your last day, load up on handicrafts and Northeastern cuisine at the action-packed **Feira Nordestina** (p140).

Maria Fumaça (Map pp132-3; ☎ 2225 6711; Rua do Catete 164, Catete) A classic used bookshop.
Nova Livraria Leonardo da Vinci (Map pp136-37; ☎ 2533 2237; Av Rio Branco 185, Centro) One of Rio's best collections of foreign-language books.

Cultural Centers

Arte-Sesc Cultural Center (Map pp132-3; ☎ 3138 1343; Rua Marquês de Abrantes 99, Flamengo; admission free; ☉ noon-6pm Tue-Wed, to 8pm Thu-Sat, 11am-5pm Sun)
Casa França-Brasil (Map pp136-7; ☎ 2253 5366; www.casafrancabrasil.rj.gov.br; Rua Visconde de Itaboraí 78, Centro; admission free; ☉ noon-8pm Tue-Sun) Opened in 1990 for the purpose of advancing cultural relations between France and Brazil.
Centro Cultural Banco do Brasil (Map pp136-7; ☎ 3808 2000; www.cultura-e.com.br; Rua Primeiro de Março 66, Centro; general admission free, exhibitions US$2-4; ☉ noon-8pm Tue-Sun) One of Rio's best cultural centers, with excellent exhibitions, a film series and lunchtime and evening concerts.
Centro Cultural Carioca (Map pp136-7; ☎ 2242 9642; www.centroculturalcarioca.com.br; Rua do Teatro 37, Centro; ☉ noon-8pm Mon-Sat) On Praça Tiradentes, this cultural center hosts superb musical groups along with dance recitals, book releases and ongoing exhibitions.
Centro Cultural Justiça Federal (Map pp136-7; ☎ 2510 8846; Av Rio Branco 241, Centro; admission free; ☉ noon-7pm Tue-Sun)
Centro Cultural Laurinda Santos Lobo (Map pp136-7; ☎ 2224 3331; Rua Monte Alegre 306, Santa Teresa; admission free; ☉ 8am-5pm) The large mansion built in 1907 plays an active role in the neighborhood by hosting exhibitions and open-air concerts.
Fundição Progresso (Map pp136-7; ☎ 2220 5070; Rua dos Arcos 24, Cinelândia; admission free; ☉ 9am-6pm Mon-Fri) This former foundry hosts avant-garde exhibitions, performances and popular samba parties during the summer.
Instituto Moreira Salles (☎ 3284 7400; www.ims .com.br; Rua Marquês de Sao Vicente 476, Gávea; admission free; ☉ 1-8pm Tue-Sun) A beautiful cultural center that hosts impressive exhibitions. Stunning gardens and a café lie next door.

Emergency

Report robberies to the **tourist police** (Map pp124-5; ☎ 3399 7170; Rua Afrânio de Melo Franco 159, Leblon; ☉ 24hr).
Other useful numbers:
Ambulance (☎ 192)
Fire department (☎ 193)
Police (☎ 190)

Internet Access

Most of the Internet places charge US$2 to US$3 per hour.

IPANEMA   **Map pp124-5**
Central Fone – Ipanema (Shop B, Rua Vinícius de Moraes 129, Ipanema; ☉ 9:30am-8pm Mon-Fri, 11am-6pm Sat & Sun)
Letras & Expressões (☎ 2521 6110; Rua Visconde de Pirajá 276, Ipanema; ☉ 8am-midnight)

LEBLON   **Map pp124-5**
Letras & Expressões (☎ 2511 5085; Av Ataulfo de Paiva 1292, Leblon; ☉ 24hr)

COPACABANA   **Map pp128-9**
Fone Rio (Rua Constante Ramos 22, Copacabana; ☉ 9am-midnight)
Locutório (Av NS de Copacabana 1171, Copacabana; ☉ 8-2am)
Tele Rede (Av NS de Copacabana 209A, Copacabana; ☉ 8-2am)

CATETE   **Map pp132-3**
Eurogames (Rua Corrêa Dutra 39B, Catete)
Museu da República (153 Rua do Catete; ☉ 9am-10pm Mon-Fri, to 9pm Sat & Sun) Entrance in back of museum, through the Parque do Catete.

CENTRO & LAPA   **Map pp136-7**
Central Fone (basement level, Av Rio Branco 156, Centro; ☉ 9am-9pm Mon-Fri, 10am-4pm Sat)
Cyber Café (Av Rio Branco 43, Centro; ☉ 9am-7pm Mon-Fri)
Cyber Café Fundição Progresso (Rua dos Arcos 24, Lapa)

Internet Resources

www.ipanema.com Dubbed 'the insider's guide to Rio,' this website provides an excellent introduction to the city.
www.rio.rj.gov.br/riotur Riotur has a more comprehensive website, in Portuguese and English.

Laundry

A convenient drop-off, wash-and-fold service costs around US$0.80 per kilogram.
Laundromat (Map pp132-3; Rua Arturo Bernardes 14, Catete)
Laundromat (Map pp128-9 Rua Barata Ribeiro 181B, Copacabana) Across from the metro station.
Laundromat (Map pp128-9 ; Av NS de Copacabana 1226, Copacabana)

Media

Rio's main daily papers are *Jornal do Brasil* (www.jbonline.com.br) and *O Globo* (www

.globo.com.br). Both have entertainment and event listings, particularly strong on Thursday and Sunday. The national publication *Veja* has a *Veja Rio* insert, which spells out weekly entertainment options (it comes out on Sunday).

Medical Services

There are scores of pharmacies in town, a number of which stay open 24 hours, including two branches of **Drogaria Pacheco** (Av NS de Copacabana 115 (Map pp128-9; Av NS de Copacabana 115, Copacabana; 24hr); Av NS de Copacabana 534 (Map pp128-9; Av NS de Copacabana 534, Copacabana; 24hr); Rua Visconde de Pirajá (Rua Visconde de Pirajá, Ipanema) and **Farmácia do Leme** (Map pp128-9; Av Prado Júnior 231, Copacabana). In Leblon, **Farmácia Piauí** (Map pp124-5; ☎ 2274 8448; Av Ataulfo de Paiva 1283, Leblon) also stays open 24 hours.

For medical emergencies visit one of the following:

Galdino Campos Cárdio Copa (Map pp128-9; ☎ 2255 9966; Av NS de Copacabana 492, Copacabana; 24hr) English- and French-speaking staff.
Hospital Ipanema (Map pp124-5; ☎ 3111 2300; Rua Antônio Parreiras 67, Ipanema)
Miguel Couto Hospital (Map pp124-5; ☎ 2274 2121; Av Bartolomeu Mitre 1108, Gávea)

Money

ATMs can be found throughout the city. Banco do Brasil, Bradesco, Citibank and HSBC are the best banks to try when using a debit or credit card. Even though many ATMs advertise 24-hour service, these 24 hours usually fall between 6am and 10pm. On holidays, the ATM access ends at 3pm. Easier than dealing with banks is going to *casas de câmbio* (exchange offices).

AEROPORTO GALEÃO (INTERNATIONAL AIRPORT)
Banco do Brasil (3rd floor) ATM machines and money exchange.

CENTRO   Map pp136-7
A number of *câmbios* can be found on either side of Av Rio Branco, several blocks north of Av Presidente Vargas. Other options include the following:
Banco 24 Horas (near Ave Rio Branco, Centro) Outside Carioca metro stop, has ATMs.
Banco do Brasil (Rua Senador Dantas 105, Centro) for ATM and (2nd fl, Rua Senador Dantas 105, Centro) to exchange money.

Bank Boston (Av Rio Branco 110, Centro) Amex traveler's checks only.
Banerj (Av Nilo Peçanha 175, Centro) Traveler's checks only.
Casa Aliança (☎ 2224 4617; Rua Miguel Couto 35C, Centro) 9am-5:30pm) A recommended *câmbio.*
Citibank (Rua da Assembléia 100, Centro) Has ATM and money exchange.
HSBC (Av Rio Branco 108, Centro) ATM

COPACABANA   Map pp128-9
Other *câmbios* can be found on Av NS de Copacabana, near the Copacabana Palace hotel.
Banco do Brasil (Av NS de Copacabana 1292) ATM.
Banco do Brasil (Av NS de Copacabana 594) Exchange money.
Casa Universal (Av NS de Copacabana 371) One recommended *câmbio.*

IPANEMA   Map pp124-5
Find other *câmbios* scattered along Rua Visconde de Pirajá, west of Praça NS de Paz.
Citibank (Rua Visconde de Pirajá 459A, Ipanema) ATM and money exchange.

Post

Most *correios* (post offices) are open from 8am to 6pm Monday to Friday, and on Saturday until noon. Any mail addressed to Posta Restante, Rio de Janeiro, Brazil, ends up at the **main post office** (Map pp128-9; Rua Primeiro de Março 64, Centro).

Other branches include the following:
Botafogo post office (Map pp132-3; Praia de Botafogo 324, Botafogo)
Copacabana post office (Map pp128-9; Av NS de Copacabana 540, Copacabana)
Ipanema post office (Map pp124-5; Rua Prudente de Morais 147, Ipanema)

Telephone

For local telephone calls – and calls within Brazil – you will need to buy a *cartão telefônico* (phonecard; US$1 to US$4.50), available from newsstands and street vendors. See p691 for more info. Many Internet cafés offer an international calling service.

CENTRO   Map pp128-9
Central Fone (basement level, Av Rio Branco 156, Centro; 9am-9pm Mon-Fri, 10am-4pm Sat)

COPACABANA   Map pp128-9
Fone Rio (Rua Constante Ramos 22, Copacabana; 9am-midnight)

Locutório (Av NS de Copacabana 1171, Copacabana; ☉ 8–2am)
Tele Rede (Av NS de Copacabana 209A, Copacabana; ☉ 8–2am)

IPANEMA   **Map pp124-5**
Central Fone – Ipanema (Shop, Rua Vinícius de Moraes 129, Ipanema; ☉ 9:30am-8pm Mon-Fri, 11am-6pm Sat & Sun)

Tourist Information

Riotur is Rio's tourism agency. It has a tourist information hot line called **Alô Rio** (☎ 0800-707 1808, 2542 8080; ☉ 9am-6pm). The receptionists speak English and are very helpful. Riotur's useful multilingual website, www.rio.rj.gov.br/riotur, is also a good source of information.

All of the Riotur offices distribute maps and the excellent (and updated) quarterly *Rio Guide*, listing the major events of the season. The **Riotur Centro** (Map pp128-9; 9th fl, Rua Assembléia 10, Centro) is the best office for obtaining information. English-speaking staff are always on hand, and they'll call around for you to find a hotel if you show up without a reservation. There is a second branch in **Copacabana** (Map pp128-9; ☎ 2541 7522; Av Princesa Isabel 183, Copacabana; ☉ 9am-6pm Mon-Fri).

Riotur also has the following information booths with brochures and maps:
Aeroporto Galeão (☉ 6am-11pm)
Maracanã Football Stadium (Map pp142-3; Rua Professor Eurico Rabelo, São Cristóvão; ☉ 9am-6pm)
Rodoviária Novo Rio (Map pp142-3; Av Francisco Bicalho, São Cristóvão; ☉ 8am-8pm)

Another good source of information is the **Rio Convention & Visitors Bureau** (Map pp124-5; ☎ 2511 2592; www.rioconventionbureau.com.br; Rua Visconde de Pirajá 547, Ipanema).

Travel Agencies

American Express (Map pp128-9; ☎ 2548 2148; Av Atlântica 1702, Copacabana CEP 20040; ☉ 9am-5:30pm Mon-Fri)
Andes Sol (Map pp128-9; ☎ 2275 4370; Av NS de Copacabana 209, Copacabana) A good multilingual agency.
Casa Aliança (Map pp128-9; ☎ 2224 4617; casaalianca@casaalianca.com.br; Rua Miguel Couto 35C, Centro; ☉ 9am-5:30pm)
Le Bon Voyage (Map pp124-5; ☎ 2287 4403; lebonvoyage@hotmail.com; Rua Visconde de Pirajá 82, Ipanema)

DANGERS & ANNOYANCES

Rio, like other metropolitan destinations, has its share of crime and violence. But if you travel sensibly when visiting the city, you will likely suffer nothing worse than a few bad hangovers. All the same, theft is not uncommon, and you should do what you can to minimize the risks of getting robbed.

Buses are well-known targets for thieves. Avoid taking them after dark, and keep an eye out while you're on them. Take taxis at night to avoid walking along empty streets and beaches. That holds especially true for Centro, which becomes deserted in the evening and on weekends, and is better explored during the week.

Purse- and bag-snatching is extremely common on the beaches of Copacabana and Ipanema, where thieves work with lightning speed. Always keep an eye on your stuff. Don't take anything of value to the beach, and always stay alert – especially during holidays when the sands get fearfully crowded.

Maracanã Football Stadium is worth a visit, but take only spending money for the day and avoid the crowded sections. Don't wander into the *favelas* unless you're with a guide who really knows the area.

If you have the misfortune of being robbed, hand over the goods. Thieves in the city are only too willing to use their weapons.

Scams

A common beach scam is for one thief to approach you from one side and ask you for a light or the time. While you're distracted, the thief's partner grabs your gear from the other side.

SIGHTS

The Cidade Maravilhosa has much more to offer than simply the lovely beaches of Ipanema and Leblon. Just up from these tree-lined neighborhoods is Lagoa, a charming lakeside setting near the lush Jardim Botânico (Botanical Gardens). Further east you'll encounter the seaside neighborhood of Urca and the striking views atop Pão de Açúcar. The historical gems of Centro and Catete lie north of there, while a short tram ride from Centro leads to Santa Teresa, Rio's most bohemian hood. Visible all

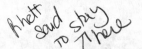
Rhett said stay 7 there

over the city, Cristo Redentor (Christ the Redeemer) stands atop Corcovado, a neighboring hill.

Greater Rio has many attractions, including the Maracanã Football Stadium in São Cristóvão, boat rides across the bay to Niterói and the eastern beaches, and gorgeous beaches to the west.

Ipanema & Leblon   Map pp124–5

Boasting a magnificent beach and tree-lined streets full of boutiques, restaurants and colorful bars and cafés, Ipanema and Leblon are Rio's loveliest destinations, and the favored residence for young, beautiful (and wealthy) Cariocas. With a mix of well-to-do families, models and hipsters of both the gay and straight variety, the twin neighborhoods boast some of the city's highest rents – the result, no doubt, of its appeal.

Ipanema acquired international fame in the early '60s as the home of the bossa nova character 'The Girl from Ipanema.' It became the hangout of artists, intellectuals and wealthy liberals, who frequented the sidewalk cafés and bars. After the 1964 military coup and the resulting crackdown on liberals, many of these bohemians were forced into exile. Today Ipanema continues to be a center of Carioca chic and remains one of the most animated and exciting neighborhoods of Rio.

During the '70s, Leblon became the nightlife center of Rio. The restaurants and bars of Baixo (Lower) Leblon, on Av Ataulfo de Paiva, between Ruas Aristídes Espínola and General Artigas, were the meeting points for a new generation of artists and musicians. Nightlife continues to be very animated here today.

IPANEMA & LEBLON BEACHES

Although the beaches of Ipanema and Leblon are really one long beach, the *postos* (posts) along them subdivide the beach into areas as diverse as the city itself. **Posto 9**, right off Rua Vinícius de Moraes, is **Garota de Ipanema**, which is where Rio's most lithe and tanned bodies tend to migrate. The area is also known as the **Cemetério dos Elefantes** because of the old leftists, hippies and artists who hang out there. The beach in front of Rua Farme de Amoedo, also called **Bolsa de Valores** and **Crystal Palace**, is the gay section, while **Posto 8** is mostly the domain

of *favela* kids. **Arpoador**, between Ipanema and Copacabana, is Rio's most popular surf spot. Leblon attracts a broad mix of single Cariocas, as well as families from the neighborhood.

Whatever spot you choose, you'll enjoy cleaner sands and sea than those found in neighboring Copacabana. Keep in mind that if you go on Saturday or Sunday, it gets very crowded. Incidentally, the word *ipanema* is Indian for 'bad, dangerous waters' – pretty accurate given the strong undertow and often oversized waves crashing on the shore. Be careful, and swim only where the locals do.

A few fishermen, casting out to sea, mingle with couples admiring the view from the lookout known as **Mirante do Leblon**, at the west end of Leblon Beach, stretching down Leblon and Ipanema Beaches.

MUSEU H STERN

The headquarters of H Stern, the famous jeweler, contains an interesting fine-jewelry museum, the **Museu H Stern** (☎ 2259 7442; www .hstern.com.br in Portuguese; Rua Garcia D'Avila 113; admission free; ☉ 8:30am-6pm Mon-Fri, to noon Sat). You can get a free cab ride to and from the shop and anywhere in the Zona Sul by calling ☎ 2274 6171.

If you're in the market for it, the adjoining store has an array of finely crafted jewellery, watches and other accessories for sale.

MUSEU AMSTERDAM SAUER

Next door to Museu H Stern, the **Museu Amsterdam Sauer** (☎ 2512 1132; www.amsterdamsauer .com; Rua Garcia D'Avila 105; admission free; ☉ 9:30am-2:30pm Mon-Fri, 10am-2pm Sat) also houses an impressive collection of precious stones – over 3000 items in all. It also has two life-size replicas of mines.

Like H Stern, the Amsterdam Sauer store is the place to lay down some serious cash if you're looking for precious gems or well-made accessories – watches, pens, wallets and an array of jewelry.

Gávea, Jardim Botânico & Lagoa

Just north of Ipanema, the well-to-do suburbs of Gávea, Jardim Botânico and Lagoa have a mix of eclectic restaurants, stylish bars and attractive parks. Jardim Botânico gets its name from the lush botanical

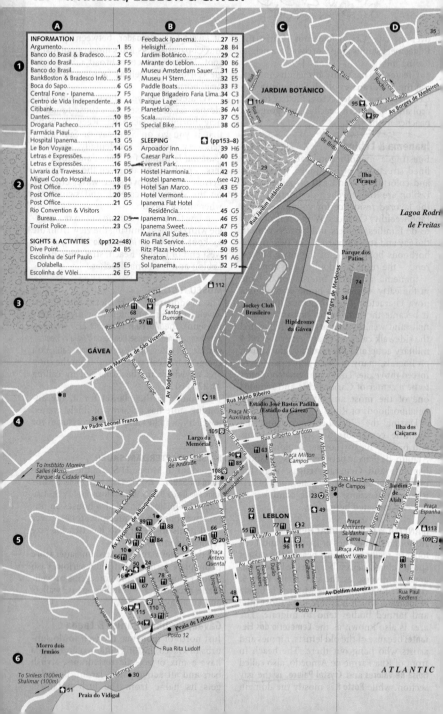

JARDIM BOTÂNICO

Ilha Piraquê

Lagoa Rodri de Freitas

Parque dos Patins

Jockey Club Brasileiro

Hipódromo da Gávea

GÁVEA

Praça Santos Dumont

Rua Major Rubens Vaz

Rua dos Oitis

Rua Marquês de São Vicente

Av Bartolomeu Mitre

Av Rodrigo Otávio

Rua Artur Araripe

Av Padre Leonel Franca

To Instituto Moreira
Salles (4km);
Parque da Cidade (5km)

Rua Itaquira

Rua Coduíba

Rua Mário Ribeiro

Estádio José Bastos Padilha
(Estádio da Gávea)

Praça NS
Auxiliadora

Largo da
Memória

Rua Cap Cesar
de Andrade

Rua Conde de
Bernadotte

Rua Gilberto Cardoso

Praça Milton
Campos

Rua Humberto
de Campos

Jardim de
Alah

Praça
Espanha

Ilha dos
Caiçaras

Av Visconde de Albuquerque

Rua Dias Ferreira

Rua Humberto de Campos

Av Bartolomeu Mitre

LEBLON

Av Ataulfo de Paiva

Praça
Almirante
Saldanha
Cama

Praça Alm
Belfort Vieira

Av General San Martin

Rua Aristides Espínola

Rua Cupertino Durão

Rua João Lira

Rua Carlos Góis

Rua Almirante
Guilhem

Rua Henrique
Dumont

Rua Aperana

Morro dois
Irmãos

To Sinless (100m);
Shalimar (100m)

Praça
Antero
Quental

Rua General Venâncio Flores

Rua Rainha Guilhermina

Rua General Artigas

Rua General Urquiza

Av General San Martin

Rua José
Linhares

Av Delfim Moreira

Rua Paul
Redfern

Posto 11

Praia de Leblon
Posto 12

Rua Rita Ludolf

Av Niemeyer

Praia do Vidigal

ATLANTIC

0 — 500 m
0 — 0.3 miles

E **F** **G** **H**

EATING	(pp158–67)
00	(see 36)
Antiquarius	53 B6
Armazém do Café	54 B5
Ataúlfo	55 C5
Ateliê Culinário	56 B5
BI	(see 17)
Braseiro da Gávea	57 B3
Cafeína	58 F5
Caffé Felice	59 G5
Capricciosa	60 F5
Casa da Feijoada	61 G5
Celeiro	62 B5
Cobal de Leblon	63 C4
Colher de Pau	64 F5
Da Silva	65 E5
Fellini	66 B5
Garcia & Rodrigues	67 B5
Guimas	68 B3
Gula Gula	69 E5

HortiFruti	70 B5
Kurt	71 B5
L'Assiette	72 G5
Lagoa Kiosks	73 F3
Lagoa Kiosks	74 D3
Mil Frutas	75 E5
Mistura Fina	76 E1
Mustafá	77 C5
Nam Thai	78 B5
New Natural	79 F5
Olympe	80 E1
Osteria Dell'Angelo	81 D5
Polis Sucos	82 B5
Satyricon	83 F5
Sushi Leblon	84 B5
Vegetariano Social Club	85 C4
Yemanjá	86 E5
Zazá Bistrô Tropical	87 F5
Zona Sul Supermarket	88 B5
Zuka	89 B5

DRINKING	(pp167–8)
Academia da Cachaça	90 C4
Bar Bofetada	91 F5
Bar Bracarense	92 C5
Bar D'Hotel	(see 48)
Bar Lagoa	93 F4
Caneco 70	94 B6
Caroline Café	95 D1
Clipper	96 C5
Cozumel	97 D1
Devassa	98 B6
Empório	99 E5
Garota de Ipanema	100 F5
Hipódromo Up	101 B3
Irish Pub	102 G5
Lord Jim Pub	103 D5
Shenanigan's	104 G5

ENTERTAINMENT	(pp168–72)
Bar do Tom	105 B4
Casa da Cultura Laura Alvim	106 G5
Cineclube Laura Alvim	(see 106)
Dama de Ferro	107 F4
Espaço Leblon	108 B4
Estação Ipanema	109 D5
Melt	110 B6
Teatro Leblon	111 C5

SHOPPING	(pp172–4)
Babilônia Feira Hype	112 B3
Empório Brasil	113 D5
Hippie Fair	114 G5
No Meio do Caminho	115 B6
O Sol	116 C1
Toca do Vinicius	117 F5

TRANSPORT	(pp174–6)
Varig	118 F5
VASP	119 E5

Parque Tom Jobim

Morro dos Cabritos (385m)

Av Epitácio Pessoa

Parque da Catacumba

Parque do Cantagalo

Rua Bolívar

Rua Xavier da Silveira

Rua Miguel Lemos

Av Henrique Dodsworth

Morro do Cantagalo (202m)

Av Epitácio Pessoa

Rua Alberto de Campos

Rua Saint-Roman

Morro do Pavão

Rua Barão de Jaguaripe

Rua Nascimento da Silva

Rua Redentor

Rua Barão da Torre

Praça Nossa Senhora da Paz

IPANEMA

Rua Garcia D'Ávila

Rua Maria Quitéria

Rua Vinícius de Moraes

Rua Visconde de Pirajá

Rua Farme de Amoedo

Rua Teixeira de Melo

Rua Antônio Parreiras

Rua Barão de Ipanema

Rua Bulhões de Carvalho

Rua Francisco Sá

Rua Júlio de Castilhos

Rua Conselheiro Lafaiete

Rua Raul Pompéia

Rua Joana Angélica

Praça General Osório

Rua Gomes Carneiro

Rua Rainha Elizabeth

Rua Joaquim Nabuco

Prudente de Morais

Av Vieira Souto

Praia de Ipanema

Posto 9

Praia do Arpoador

Posto 8

Rua Francisco Otaviano

ARPOADOR

Parque Garota de Ipanema

Praça do Arpoador

Praia do Arpoador

Praia de Diabo

Posto 7

Ponta do Arpoador

OCEAN

See Copacabana & Leme Map (pp129–9)

Jardim Botânico

Rua Maria Angélica

Av Alexandre Ferreira

gardens at its edge. Lagoa also earns its moniker from one of the Zona Sul's natural attractions, a picturesque saltwater lagoon. With lovely views of Corcovado and the mountains, the lake is one of Rio's gems. By day, joggers and cyclists circle its shores, while at night music-filled restaurants serve diners under the open sky.

LAGOA RODRIGO DE FREITAS

One of the city's most picturesque spots, **Lagoa Rodrigo de Freitas** (Map pp124–5) has a 7.2km cycling/walking path around it. Bikes are available for hire near **Parque Brigadeiro Faria Lima** (Map pp124–5), as are paddle boats (p162). For those who prefer *caipirinhas* (drinks made from sugarcane spirit and crushed citrus) to plastic swan boats, the kiosks on either side of the lake offer alfresco dining, often accompanied by live *forró* (music of the Northeast).

PARQUE DA CATACUMBA

Brazil's first outdoor sculptural garden, **Parque da Catacumba** (Map pp124–5; Av Epitácio Pessoa, Lagoa; 8am-7pm) sits atop the Morro dos Cabritos, which rises from the Lagoa Rodrigo de Freitas. During the summer Catacumba often hosts free Sunday-afternoon concerts in its outdoor amphitheater.

JARDIM BOTÂNICO

The exotic **Jardim Botânico** (Map pp124–5; 22 94 9349; www.jbrj.gov.br; Rua Jardim Botânico 920, Jardim Botânico; admission US$2; 8am-5pm), housing over 5000 varieties of plant, was designed by order of the Prince Regent Dom João in 1808. It's quiet and serene on weekdays and blossoms with families and music on weekends. A pleasant outdoor café overlooks the gardens.

PARQUE LAGE

Beautiful **Parque Lage** (Map pp124–5; 2538 1091; www.eavparquelage.org.br; Rua Jardim Botânico 414, Jardim Botânico; 7am-6pm) has English-style gardens, little lakes and the **Instituto Nacional de Belas Artes**, which often hosts art exhibitions and an occasional performance.

PARQUE DA CIDADE & MUSEU HISTÓRICO DA CIDADE

The 19th-century mansion on the lovely grounds of the **Parque da Cidade** (admission free; 7am-6pm) now houses the **Museu Histórico da Cidade** (City History Museum; Map p118; 2512 2353; www.rio.rj.gov.br/cultura; Estrada de Santa Marinha 505, Gávea; admission US$2; 10am-4pm Tue-Sun), which portrays Rio from its founding in 1565 to the mid-20th century. The museum also has exhibitions of furniture, porcelain, photographs and paintings by well-known artists.

INSTITUTO MOREIRA SALLES

The beautiful **Instituto Moreira Salles** (Map p118; 3284 7400; www.ims.com.br; Rua Marquês de Sao Vicente 476, Gávea; admission free; 1-8pm Tue-Sun), next to the Parque da Cidade, contains an archive of more than 80,000 photographs, many portraying old streets of Rio. It's well worth checking the website to see what's on when you're in town.

PLANETÁRIO

Gávea's stellar attraction, the **Planetário** (Planetarium; Map pp124–5; 2274 0096; www.rio.rj.gov .br/planetario in Portuguese; Av Padre Leonel Franca 240, Gávea; 10am-5pm Tue-Sun) features a museum, a *praça dos telescópios* (square of telescopes) and two state-of-the-art operating domes, each capable of projecting over 6000 stars on its walls. There are free guided observations through the far-reaching telescopes on Monday, Wednesday and Thursday from 6:30pm to 8:30pm. Periodically, the Planetário hosts live concerts. The Planetário's hypermodern **Museu do Universo** (Universe Museum) houses permanent exhibitions.

Copacabana & Leme   Map pp128-9

Fronted by sea and backed by steep hills, the neighborhoods of Copacabana and Leme harbor one of the world's best-known beaches, stretching 4.5km from end to end. Copacabana is also one of the planet's most densely populated areas, with over 25,000 people per square kilometer crammed into the narrow strip of land.

The name Copacabana comes from a small Bolivian village on Lake Titicaca. Historians believe a statue of the Virgin Mary (Our Lady of Copacabana) was brought to Rio and consecrated inside a small chapel near Arpoador. Copacabana remained a small fishing village until Túnel Velho opened in 1891, connecting Copacabana with the rest of the city.

The construction of the neoclassical Copacabana Palace hotel in 1923 heralded a new era for Copacabana as South America's premier destination for the rich and fabulous. Today, the neighborhood is a mix of chaos and beauty – gorgeous beach shore fronted by luxury hotels, with the *favelas* ever present. Copacabana is also the heart of Rio's red-light district. After dark, prostitutes troll the restaurants along Av Atlântica while overstimulated foreigners wander the strip clubs around Av Princesa Isabel.

In spite of its chaotic streets and seedy elements, Copacabana retains its charm. Old-school *botecos* (small, open-air bars), eclectic restaurants and nightclubs, myriad shops selling everything under the tropical sun, and the handsome beach – they still cast a spell on many visitors.

COPACABANA & LEME BEACH

A magnificent confluence of land and sea, the long, scalloped beach of Copacabana and Leme always has a flurry of activity stretching its length: overamped footballers singing their team's anthem, Cariocas and tourists lining up for *caipirinhas* at kiosks, *favela* kids showing off their football skills, and beach vendors picking their way through the mass of bronzed bodies.

As in Ipanema, each group stakes out its stretch of sand. Leme is a mix of older residents and *favela* kids, while the area between the Copacabana Palace and Rua Fernando Mendes is the gay and transvestite section, known as the Stock or Stock Market – easily recognized by the rainbow flag. Young football and *futevôlei* (volleyball played without the hands) players hold court near Rua Santa Clara. Posts 5 and 6 are a mix of *favela* kids and Carioca retirees, while the beach next to the Forte de Copacabana is the unofficial *posto de pescadores* (fishermen's post). In the morning, you can buy the fresh catch of the day.

The beach is lit at night and there are police in the area, but it's still not wise to walk there after dark – stay on the hotel side of Av Atlântica if you take a stroll. Av NS de Copacabana is also dangerous – watch out on weekends, when the shops are closed and few locals are around.

MUSEU HISTÓRICO DO EXÉRCITO E FORTE DE COPACABANA

Built in 1914, on the promontory of the old Our Lady of Copacabana chapel, the Forte de Copacabana (Copacabana Fort) was one of Rio's premier defenses against attack. You can still see its original features, including walls up to 12m thick, defended by Krupp cannons. The several floors of exhibits in the **Museu Histórico do Exército e Forte de Copacabana** (☎ 2521 1032; cnr Av Atlântica & Rua Francisco Otaviano, Copacabana; admission US$2; ⏰ 10am-4pm Tue-Sun), tracing the early days of the Portuguese colony to the mid-19th century, aren't the most tastefully done, but the view alone warrants a visit. There's a lovely café overlooking Copacabana.

Botafogo   Map pp132-3

A largely middle-class residential area, Botafogo lacks the sensuality of Ipanema and the decadence of Copacabana, but it's one of Rio's most traditional neighborhoods. It boasts small museums, excellent theaters, quaint bookstores, neighborhood bars and a welcome shortage of high-rise buildings.

The area attained prominence in the late 1800s when the Portuguese court arrived in Brazil. Dom João VI's wife, Carlota Joaquina, had a country villa built in Botafogo with convenient access to Baía de Guanabara, one of her favorite bathing spots. With royalty established in the area, many mansions were constructed, some of which still stand – as schools, theaters and cultural centers.

MUSEU DO ÍNDIO

Featuring multimedia exhibitions on Brazil's northern tribes, the small **Museu do Índio** (☎ 2286 8899; www.museudoindio.org.br; Rua das Palmeiras 55, Botafogo; admission US$2; ⏰ 9:30am-5:30pm Tue-Fri, 1-5pm Sat & Sun) provides an excellent introduction to the economic, religious and social life of Brazil's indigenous people.

MUSEU VILLA-LOBOS

Housed in a century-old building, the modest **Museu Villa-Lobos** (☎ 2266 3845; Rua Sorocaba 200, Botafogo; admission free; ⏰ 10am-5:30pm Mon-Fri) is dedicated to the memory of Brazil's greatest classical composer, Heitor Villa-Lobos. Here you'll find personal items, scores and musical instruments, including the piano on which Villa-Lobos composed. The gardens were designed by landscape architect Burle Marx.

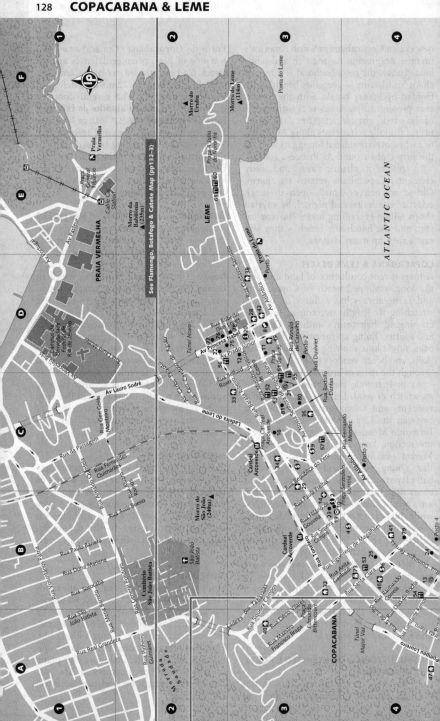

ATLANTIC OCEAN

Ponta do Leme

Morro do Leme (114m)

Praia Azúlio de Suvrita

Morro do Urubu

LEME

PRAIA VERMELHA

Praia Vermelha

Praça General Tibúrcio

Cable Car Station

Morro da Babilônia (235m)

Campus da Universidade Federal do Rio de Janeiro

Morro de São João (240m)

São João Batista

Cemitério São João Batista

COPACABANA

Túnel Novo

Túnel Major Vaz

See Flamengo, Botafogo & Catete Map (pp132–3)

Morro da Saudade

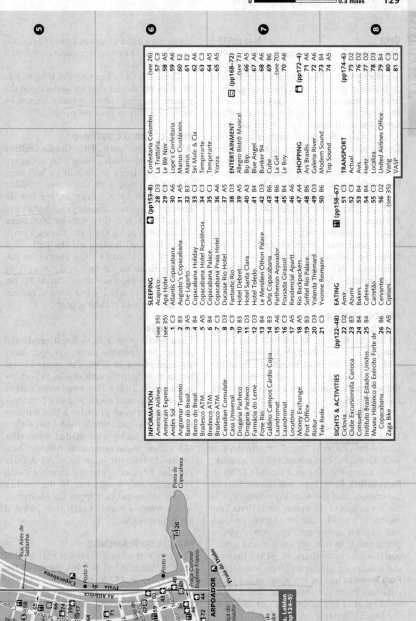

Urca

Map pp132-3

The tranquil, shady streets of Urca offer a pleasant escape from the urban bustle of other parts of the city. An eclectic mix of building styles and manicured gardens lines its streets, with local residents strolling among them. Along the sea wall, which forms the northwestern perimeter of Pão de Açúcar, fishermen cast for dinner as couples lounge beneath palm trees, taking in views of Baía de Guanabara and Cristo Redentor off in the distance. Tiny Praia Vermelha, in the south, has one Rio's finest beach views. A lovely walking trail begins from here.

Although it was the site of one of the first Portuguese garrisons in the region, almost 300 years elapsed before Urca developed into a residential neighborhood. Today it holds the distinction of being one of the safest and – in spite of Pão de Açúcar being in its midst – least discovered by foreign visitors.

PÃO DE AÇÚCAR

Seen from its peak, the dazzling **Pão de Açúcar** (Sugarloaf Mountain; ☎ 2546 8400; Praça General Tibúrcio, Urca; admission US$10; ⏰ 8am-10pm), Rio is undoubtedly the most beautiful city in the world. There are many good times to make the ascent, but sunset on a clear day is the most rewarding.

A visit to Pão de Açúcar is a must, but if you can, avoid it from about 10am to 11am and 2pm to 3pm, which is when most tourist buses arrive. Avoid cloudy days as well. Two cable cars connect to the summit, 396m above Rio. The first ascends 220m to **Morro da Urca**. From here, you can see Baía de Guanabara and the winding coastline. On the ocean side of the mountain is Praia Vermelha, in a small, calm bay. Morro da Urca has its own restaurant, souvenir shops, a playground, an outdoor theater and a helipad (for helicopter tours, see p151). Beneath the shadow of Morro da Urca, the narrow **Praia Vermelha** has superb views of the rocky coastline from the shore. Its coarse sand, unlike that of any other beach in Rio, gives the beach the name *vermelha* (red).

The second cable car goes up to Pão de Açúcar. At the top, the city unfolds beneath you, with Corcovado mountain and Cristo Redentor off to the west, and the long curve of Copacabana Beach to the south. If the breathtaking heights unsteady you, a drink stand is on hand to serve *caipirinhas* or *cerveja* (beer). The two-stage cable cars depart every 30 minutes.

Those who'd rather take the long way to the summit should sign up with one of the granite-hugging climbing tours offered by various outfits in Rio (see p146).

PISTA CLÁUDIO COUTINHO

A paved 2km path, **Pista Cláudio Coutinho** (⏰ 6am-sunset) winds along the southern contour of Morro da Urca. It's a lush area, shaded by trees, with the waves crashing on the rocks below. Keep an eye out for families of *micos* – monkeys with gray fur, striped tails and tiny scrooge-like faces. About 300m along the path, there's a small unmarked trail leading off the path. This leads up to Morro da Urca. From here you can continue on up to Pão de Açúcar by cable car, saving a few reais. Pão de Açúcar can also be climbed – but it's not recommended without climbing gear.

Flamengo

Flamengo was once Rio's finest residential district, but when the tunnel to Copacabana was completed in 1904, the upper classes began moving to the unblemished shoreline in the south. Today, Flamengo maintains its largely residential roots, and like Botafogo, the neighborhood provides a fine window into Rio at its most unadorned – but no less disarming. Along tree-shaded sidewalks, old-school restaurants and historic bars lie beside fragrant juice bars and Música Popular Brasileira–playing Internet cafés. Flamengo also boasts one of the world's largest urban parks, Parque do Flamengo, which fronts a scenic beach (too polluted for swimming).

PARQUE DO FLAMENGO

The result of a landfill project that leveled the São Antônio hill in 1965, **Parque do Flamengo** (Map pp132-3) now spreads all the way from downtown Rio through Glória, Catete and Flamengo, and on around to Botafogo. Cyclists and rollerbladers glide along the paths winding through the park, while the many football fields and sports courts are framed against the sea. On Sunday and holidays, the avenues through the park are closed (from 7am to 6pm), bringing a welcome calm to the verdant park.

Designed by famous Brazilian landscaper Burle Marx (who also landscaped Brasília), the park features some 170,000 trees of 300 different species. In addition there are several museums in the park, including the Museu de Arte Moderna and the Museu Carmen Miranda.

MUSEU DE ARTE MODERNA

At the north end of Parque do Flamengo, the **Museu de Arte Moderna** (MAM; Map pp136-7; ☎ 2240 4944; www.mamrio.org.br in Portuguese; Av Infante Dom Henrique 85, Flamengo; admission US$5; ☒ noon-6pm Tue-Fri, to 7pm Sat & Sun) is immediately recognizable by the striking postmodern edifice designed by Alfonso Eduardo Reidy. The landscaping of Burle Marx is no less impressive. After a devastating fire in 1978 that consumed 90% of its collection, the museum is finally back on its feet, and now houses 11,000 permanent works, including pieces by Brazilian artists Bruno Giorgi, Di Cavalcanti and Maria Martins. You'll find excellent photography and design exhibits, and the cinema hosts regular film festivals throughout the year. Check its website for details.

MUSEU CARMEN MIRANDA

Although Carmen Miranda is largely forgotten in Hollywood, the once-great Brazilian singer still has her fans, and has become a cult icon among Rio's gay community. In addition to photographs and music of her era, the **Museu Carmen Miranda** (Map pp132-3; ☎ 2551 2597; facing Av Rui Barbosa 560, Flamengo; admission US$0.50; ☒ 10am-5pm Tue-Fri, noon-5pm Sat & Sun) showcases the starlet's iconographic costumes and jewelry.

Cosme Velho

Cosme Velho lies east of Laranjeiras and is one of the city's most visited neighborhoods – if only for the statue of Christ the Redeemer soaring above its curvy streets. The district also contains a museum of Arte Naïf and the charming Largo do Boticario, a preserved plaza that gives onlookers a glimpse of 19th-century Rio.

CRISTO REDENTOR

Atop Corcovado (which means 'hunchback'), **Cristo Redentor** (Christ the Redeemer; ☎ 2558 1329; www.corcovado.com.br; Rua Cosme Velho 513-Cog station, Cosme Velho; admission US$10; ☒ 8:30am-

6:30pm) gazes out over Rio, a placid expression on his well-crafted face. The mountain rises straight up from the city to 710m, and at night, the brightly lit, 38m-high statue is visible from nearly every part of the city – all 1145 tons of the open-armed redeemer.

The view from the top of Corcovado provides a spectacular panorama of Rio and its surroundings. Corcovado lies within the Parque Nacional da Tijuca. You can get there by car or taxi (taxi drivers typically charge around US$20 for return trips with waiting time), but the best way is to go up in the cog train (departures every 30 minutes). For the best view, sit on the right-hand side going up. Be sure to choose a clear day to go up.

LARGO DO BOTICÁRIO

The brightly painted houses on the picturesque square of **Largo do Boticário** (Map pp132-3; Rua Cosme Velho 822) date from the early 19th century. Largo do Boticário was named in honor of the Portuguese gentleman – Joaquim Luiz da Silva Souto – who once ran a *boticário* (apothecary) utilized by the royal family.

MUSEU INTERNACIONAL DE ARTE NAÏF DO BRASIL

The collection of arte naïf (primitivist) paintings in the **Museu Internacional de Arte Naïf do Brasil** (Map pp132-3; ☎ 2205 8612; www .museunaif.com.br; Rua Cosme Velho 561, Cosme Velho; admission US$2.50; ☒ 10am-6pm Tue-Fri, noon-6pm Sat & Sun) is extensive: over 8000 pieces, executed by artists from 130 countries, dating from the 15th century to the present. Visitors receive a 20% discount by showing a ticket stub from the Corcovado cog train, which is a block away.

Catete & Glória

Like Flamengo, these twin districts flourished in the mid-19th century, when their location at the outskirts of the city made them among the most desirable places to live.

The **Palácio do Catete** (Catete Palace), which once served as the republic's seat of power, remains the jewel of the neighborhood, and its attached gardens are a peaceful refuge from the often-chaotic streets outside. Another place of historic interest is the baroque Igreja de NS da Glória do Outeiro, atop a small hill overlooking the bay.

A   B   C   D

1

See Centro, Cinelândia & Lapa Map (pp136-7)

Rua Hapirú

Rua Baro de Petrópolis

Rua Falet

Rua Cruzeiro

Rua Falet

Túnel Santa Bárbara

Morro da
Nova Cintra
(267m)

48 🏛 55

Rua Arturo
Bernardes

Morro de
Santos
Rodriguez

Rua Gago Coutinho

Parque
Guinle

Rua Gen Mariante

Rua Gen Mariante

Rua Pereira da Silva

Rua Erbuit

Rua das Laranjeiras

FLAMEN

2

Rua Prof João Teipas

Rua Almirante Alexandrino

Morro So
Judas Tadeu
▲ (246m)

Otoni

Rua Conde de Bacp

Rua Esteves Júnior

Praça Sã
Salvado

Rua Dr Júlio

Rua Alice

59 🏛 Rua Alice

Rua Mário Portela

LARANJEIRAS

Rua Coelho Neto

62 🏛

Rua Passandu

Rua Pinheiro Machado

3

COSME VELHO

Rua das Laranjeiras

Praça David
Ben Gurión

Rua Alice

Rua Cardoso Júnior

● 15

🏛 60

19 🏛 Rua Cosme Velho

Corcovado
Train Station

Rua General Glicério

Rua Prof Luís Cantanhede

Rua Juçana

Morro Mundo
Novo (128m)
▲

Flameng

Rua Baro do Itambi

4

Mirante
Dona Marta
▲ (363m)

Rua Couto
Fernandes

Rua Osvaldo
Seabra

Rua Jaguá

Rua Mundo Novo

Rua Marquês Olinda

Rua Assunção

Rua Bambina

Rua Muniz Barreto

Praia de Botafogo

Av dos Nações Unidas

🏖 Praia do
Botafogo

Parque Nacional
da Tijuca

Túnel André Rebouças

Est. Mirante Dona Marta

Praça
Radial Sul

Rua Bario de
Lucerna

12 🏛

4 🏛

49 🏛

Rua Prof Alfredo
Gomes

5 🏛

5

HUMAITÁ

Rua Alfredo
Chaves

Rua São Clemente

Rua Eduardo
Guinle

Rua 19
Fevereiro

BOTAFOGO

Botafogo
Ⓜ

61

47 🏛

11 🏛

Morro do
Pasmado

Rua David
Clemente
Alvim

Rua Miranda
Valverde

Rua da Matriz

Rua dos Palmeiras

18 🏛

20 🏛

Rua Clarício
Alvim

Rua Conde de Irajá

Rua Voluntários da Pátria

Rua Paulino

Rua Prof Fernandes

Rua Álvaro Rodrigues

Rua Gen Polidoro

Rua Real Grandeza

Rua Dona Mariana

7 🏛

Rua General

6

Rua João Afonso

Rua Vilva
Lacerna

Cobal
🏛 43
6 🏛

Rua Visconde
de Caravelas

58 🏛

Rua Henrique
de Novaes

Rua Mena
Barreto

39 🏛

Rua Elvira
Machado

54 🏛

Rua Arnaldo Quintela

Rua Fernandes
Guimarães

34 🏛
14 ●

Rua Gen
Monte

Rua Humaitá

Rua Macedo
Sobrinho

57 🏛

23 🏛

Rua Capitão Salomão

Rua Pinheiro Guimarães

Rua Visconde da Silva

Rua General Polidoro

Cemitério São
João Batista

Rua Álvaro Ramos

Baía de Guanabara

Enseada de Botafogo

Praia do Flamengo

Parque do Flamengo

Praia da Urca

Praia de Fora

URCA

Pão de Açúcar (395m)

Morro da Urca (220m)

Morro Cara de Cão (72m)

PRAIA VERMELHA

Universidade Federal de Rio de Janeiro

Instituto e Teatro Benjamin Constant

Universidade Rio de Janeiro

Cable-Car Station

Praia Vermelha

Morro da Babilônia (235m)

Pista Cláudio Coutinho

Praça Euzébio Oliveira

Praça General Tibúrcio

See Copacabana &
Leme Map (pp128–9)

IGREJA DE NS DA GLÓRIA DO OUTEIRO

The tiny **Igreja de NS da Glória do Outeiro** (Map pp136-7; ☎ 2557 4600; www.outeirodagloria.org.br; Praça de NS da Glória 135) commands lovely views over Parque do Flamengo and the bay. Considered one of the finest examples of religious colonial architecture in Brazil, the church dates from 1739 and became the favorite of the royal family upon their arrival in 1808.

MUSEU DA REPÚBLICA

Located in the Palácio do Catete, the **Museu da República** (Map pp132-3; ☎ 2558 6350; www .museudarepublica.org.br; Rua do Catete 153, Catete; admission US$2; ⊗ noon-5pm Tue-Fri, 2-6pm Sat & Sun) has a good collection of art and artifacts from the Republican period, and also houses an outdoor café, cinema and bookstore. Built between 1858 and 1866 and easily distinguished by the bronze condors on the eaves, the palace was home to the president of Brazil from 1896 until 1954, when President Getúlio Vargas killed himself. The bedroom in which the suicide occurred is eerily preserved on the 3rd floor.

MUSEU DE FOLCLÓRICO EDSON CARNEIRO

Next door to the Palácio do Catete, the **Museu de Folclórico Edson Carneiro** (Map pp132-3; ☎ 2205 0090; Rua do Catete 181, Catete; admission US$1; ⊗ 11am-6pm Tue-Fri; 3pm-6pm Sat) is an excellent introduction to Brazilian folk art. Its permanent collection includes Candomblé costumes, ceramic figurines and religious costumes used in festivals. The museum also has a folklore library and a small shop selling handicrafts, books and folk music.

PARQUE DO CATETE

The tiny, landscaped **Parque do Catete** (Map pp132-3; ☎ 2205 0090; Rua do Catete 181, Catete; admission US$1; ⊗ 11am-6pm Tue-Fri; 3-6pm Sat & Sun), on the grounds of the Palácio do Catete, provides a quiet refuge from the city. The Bistrô Jardins (p165), overlooking the park, makes a fine spot for afternoon tea.

Centro   Map pp136-7

Rio's bustling commercial district, Centro is a blend of high-rise office buildings and remnants of its grand past: looming baroque churches, wide plazas and cobblestone streets lined with colorful colonial buildings are scattered throughout the district.

Many pedestrian-only areas crisscross Centro. The most famous of these is known as **Saara**, a giant street bazaar crammed with discount stores. In the last century, Saara attracted an influx of immigrants from the Middle East, and if you're in search of authentic Lebanese cuisine, this is the place to go.

BIBLIOTECA NACIONAL

Inaugurated in 1910, the **Biblioteca Nacional** (National Library; ☎ 2262 8255; Av Rio Branco 219/239, Centro; admission free; ⊗ 9am-8pm Mon-Fri, to 3pm Sat, free guided visits 11am, 1pm & 4pm Mon-Fri) is the largest in Latin America, with more than eight million volumes. The 2nd floor contains rare books and manuscripts. Designed by Francisco Marcelino de Souza Aguiar, the building is neoclassical in style and surrounded by Corinthian columns.

CENTRO CULTURAL DO BANCO DO BRASIL

Housed in a beautifully restored building dating from 1906, the **Centro Cultural do Banco do Brasil** (CCBB; ☎ 3808 2000; www.cultura-e.com.br in Portuguese; Rua Primeiro de Março 66; general admission free, exhibitions US$2-4; ⊗ noon-8pm Tue-Sun) is now one of Brazil's best cultural centers, with a cinema, two theaters and excellent exhibitions. There's always something going on at CCBB – visit its website for listings.

CENTRO CULTURAL JUSTIÇA FEDERAL

The stately building overlooking the Praça Floriano was once the headquarters of the Supremo Tribunal Federal (Supreme Court). Today it houses the **Centro Cultural Justiça Federal** (☎ 2510 8846; Av Rio Branco 241, Centro; admission free; ⊗ noon-7pm Tue-Sun), a cultural center with excellent exhibitions. There's a bookstore on the 1st floor.

IGREJA SÃO FRANCISCO DA PENITÊNCIA & CONVENTO SANTO ANTÔNIO

Overlooking the Largo da Carioca is the baroque **Igreja São Francisco da Penitência & Convento Santo Antônio** (☎ 2262 0197; Largo da Carioca 5, Centro; ⊗ 9am-noon & 1-4pm Tue-Fri), dating from 1726. Recently restored to its former glory, the church's sacristy has blue Portuguese tiles and an elaborately carved altar made out of jacaranda wood. It also has a roof panel by José Oliveira Rosa depicting St Francis receiving the stigmata. The church's statue of Santo Antônio is an object of great devotion to many Cariocas in search of a husband or wife.

IGREJA DE NS DE CANDELÁRIA

The construction of the original church to NS de Candelária (dating from the late 16th century), on the present site, was credited to a ship's captain who had almost been shipwrecked at sea. Upon his safe return he vowed to build a church to her. A later design led to its present-day grandeur, which rated **Igreja de NS de Candelária** (☎ 2233 2324; Praça Pio X, Centro; 🕑 8am-4pm Mon-Fri, 9am-1pm Sat & Sun) among the largest and wealthiest churches of imperial Brazil. The interior is a spectacular combination of Baroque and Renaissance styles. The ceiling above the nave features six large panels that depict the romanticized version of the sea captain's journey and the subsequent origin of the church. The cupola, fabricated entirely from limestone shipped from Lisbon, is one of its most striking features. Mass is said at 9am, 10am and 11am on Sunday.

MOSTEIRO DE SÃO BENTO

Another fine colonial gem, the **Mosteiro de São Bento** (☎ 2291 7122; Rua Dom Gerardo 68, Centro; 🕑 8-11am & 2:30-6pm) was built between 1617 and 1641 on Morro de São Bento, one of the four hills that once marked colonial Rio. The simple facade hides a baroque interior richly decorated in gold. Among its historic treasures are wood carvings designed by Frei Domingos da Conceição (executed by Alexandre Machado) and paintings by José de Oliveira Rosa. On Sunday, the High Mass at 10am includes a choir of Benedictine monks singing Gregorian chants. To reach the monastery from Rua Dom Gerardo, go to No 40 and take the elevator to the 5th floor.

MUSEU HISTÓRICO E DIPLOMÁTICO

Housed in the neoclassical Palácio Itamaraty, the **Museu Histórico e Diplomático** (Museum of History & Diplomacy; ☎ 2253 7961; Av Marechal Floriano 196, Centro; admission free; 🕑 guided visit only 2pm, 3pm & 4pm Mon, Wed, Fri) once served as the private presidential home, from 1889 until 1897. The museum has an impressive collection of art, antiques and maps. Visits are by guided 45-minute tours. Call ahead to ensure an English- or French-speaking guide, or just show up for the Portuguese tours.

MUSEU NACIONAL DE BELAS ARTES

Rio's **Museu Nacional de Belas Artes** (Av Rio Branco 199, Centro; admission US$1.50; 🕑 10am-6pm Tue-Fri, 2-6pm Sat & Sun) houses more than 800 original paintings and sculptures ranging from the 17th to the 20th centuries. One of its most important galleries is the Galeria de Arte Brasileira, with 20th-century classics such as Cândido Portinari's *Café*. Other galleries display Brazilian folk art, African art and furniture, as well as contemporary exhibits. Guided tours are available in English (call ahead).

PAÇO IMPERIAL

Built in 1743, the **Paço Imperial** (Imperial Palace; ☎ 2533 4407; Praça XV de Novembro, Centro; 🕑 noon-6:30pm Tue-Sun) was originally a governor's residence. Later it became the home of Dom João and his family when the Portuguese throne transferred the royal seat of power to the colony. In 1888 Princesa Isabel proclaimed the Freedom from Slavery Act from the palace's steps. The building is used for exhibitions and concerts; its cinema frequently screens foreign and art-house films. There's a bookshop and bistro on the 1st floor.

PRAÇA FLORIANO

The heart of modern Rio, the **Praça Floriano** (Av Rio Branco, Centro) comes to life at lunchtime and after work when the outdoor cafés are filled with beer drinkers, samba musicians and political debate. The square is also Rio's political marketplace. There's daily speechmaking, literature sales and street theater. Most city marches and rallies culminate here on the steps of the old Câmara Municipal (Town Hall), in the northwest corner of the plaza.

PRAÇA XV DE NOVEMBRO

The first residents on the historic site of **Praça XV de Novembro**, near Primeiro de Março, were Carmelite fathers who built a convent here in 1590. It later came under the property of the Portuguese crown and became Largo do Paço, which surrounded the Paço Imperial. A number of important historic events took place here: the coronation of Brazil's two emperors (Pedro I and Pedro II), the abolition of slavery in 1888, and the deposition of Emperor Pedro II in 1889.

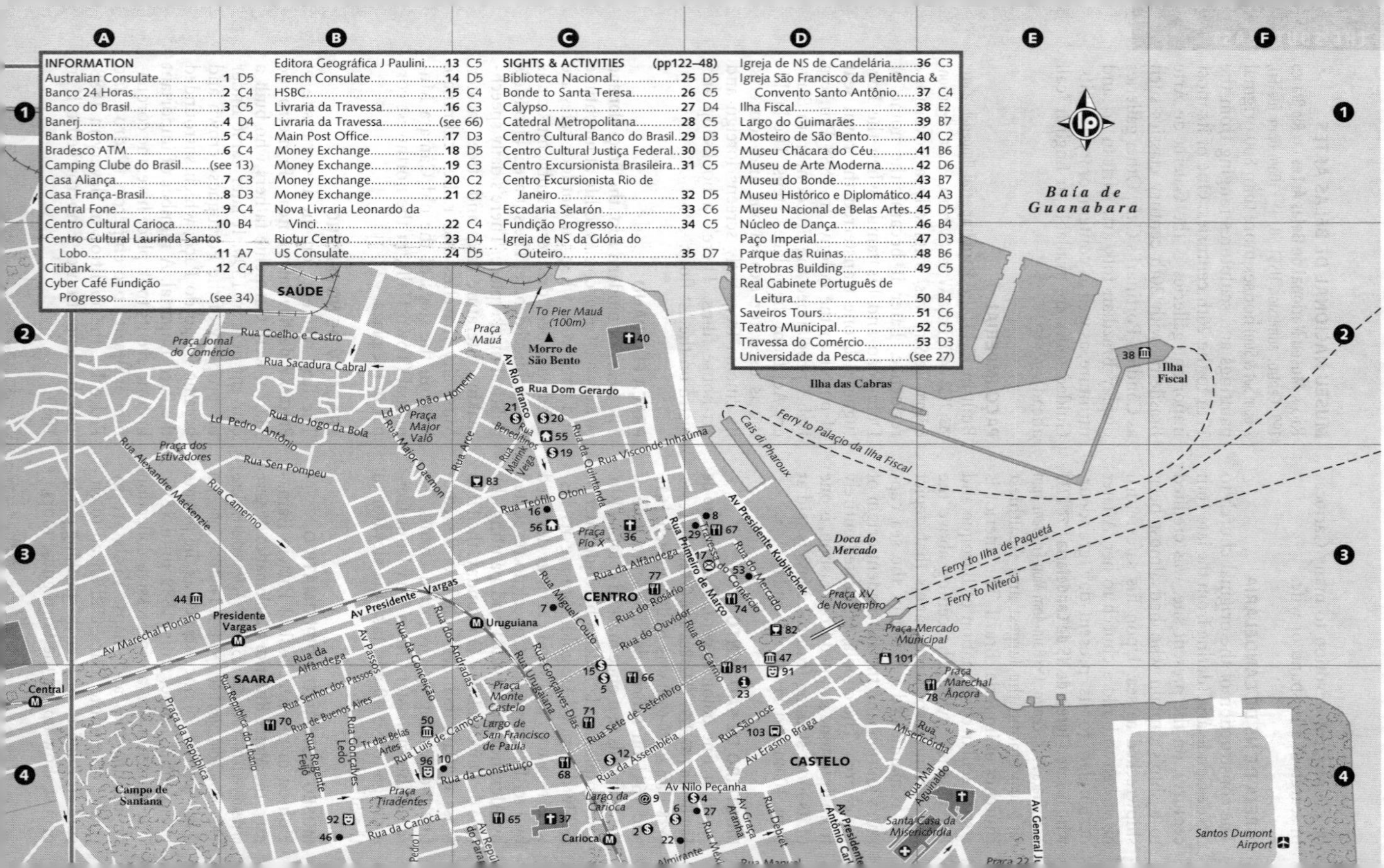

Baía de
Guanabara

Santos Dumont
Airport

Av General Ju

Av Presidente
Antônio Carl

CASTELO

CENTRO

SAÚDE

SAARA

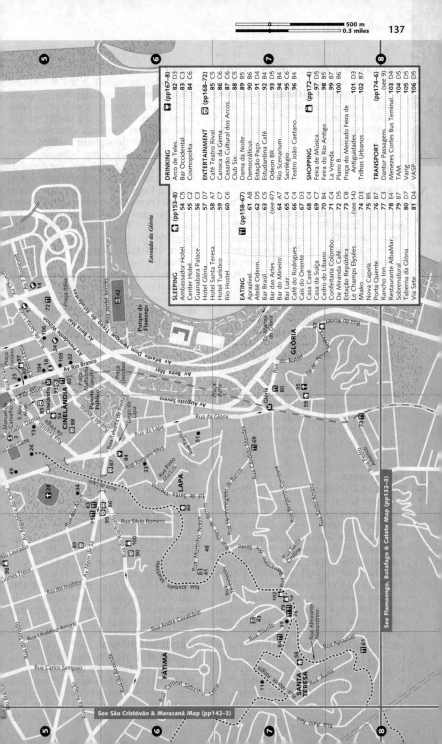

137

0 500 m
0 0.3 miles

SLEEPING (pp153–8)
Ambassador Hotel...54 C5
Center Hotel...55 C2
Guanabara Palace...56 C3
Hotel Glória...57 D7
Hotel Santa Teresa...58 A7
Hotel Turístico...59 C7
Rio Hostel...60 C6

EATING (pp158–67)
Aprazível...61 A8
Ateliê Odeon...62 D5
Bar Brasil...63 C5
Bar das Artes...(see 47)
Bar do Mineiro...64 A7
Bar Luiz...65 C4
Café do Rodrigues...66 C4
Cais do Oriente...67 D3
Casa Cavé...68 C4
Casa da Suíça...69 C7
Cedro do Líbano...70 B4
Confeitaria Colombo...71 C4
De Miranda Café...72 D5
Estação República...73 C8
Le Champs Elysées...(see 14)
Miako...74 D3
Nova Capela...75 B5
Porta Quente...76 B7
Rancho Inn...77 C3
Restaurante AlbaMar...78 E4
Sobrenatural...79 B7
Taberna da Glória...80 D7
Via Sete...81 D4

DRINKING (pp167–8)
Arco de Teles...82 D3
Bar Occidental...83 C3
Cosmopolita...84 C6

ENTERTAINMENT (pp168–72)
Café Teatro Rival...85 C5
Carioca da Gema...86 C6
Casarão Cultural dos Arcos...87 C6
Club Six...88 C5
Dama da Noite...89 B5
Democráticus...90 B6
Estação Paço...91 D4
Estudantina Café...92 B4
Odeon BR...93 D5
Rio Scenarium...94 B4
Sacrilégio...95 C6
Teatro João Caetano...96 B4

SHOPPING (pp172–4)
Feira de Música...97 D5
Feira do Rio Antigo...98 B5
La Vereda...99 B7
Plano B...100 B6
Praça do Mercado Feira de Antiguidades...101 D3
Trilhos Urbanos...102 B7

TRANSPORT (pp174–4)
Dantur Passagens...(see 9)
Menezes Cortes Bus Terminal...103 D4
TAM...104 D5
Varig...105 D5
VASP...106 D5

REAL GABINETE PORTUGUÊS DE LEITURA
Built in the Manuelin Portuguese style in 1837, the gorgeous **Real Gabinete Português de Leitura** (Portuguese Reading Room; ☎ 2221 3138; Rua Luís de Camões 30; admission free; ☼ 9am-6pm) houses over 350,000 works, many dating from the 16th, 17th and 18th centuries. It also has a small collection of paintings, sculptures and ancient coins.

TEATRO MUNICIPAL
Built in 1905 in the style of the Paris Opera, the magnificent **Teatro Municipal** (Municipal Theater; general info ☎ 2299 1716; bookings ☎ 2262 3501; Rua Manuel de Carvalho, Centro; guided tour US$2; ☼ 9am-5pm Mon-Fri) is the home of Rio's opera, orchestra and ballet. Bilingual guided tours are a worthwhile investment (call ☎ 2544 2900 to book one). If you get a chance, go to a performance there.

TRAVESSA DO COMÉRCIO
Beautiful two-story colonial townhouses line the narrow cobblestone street of **Travessa do Comércio** (Near Praça XV de Novembro), leading off of Praça XV de Novembro. The archway known as Arco de Teles leading into the area was once a part of an old viaduct running between two buildings. Today, the street contains half a dozen restaurants and drinking spots that open onto the streets. It's a favorite spot for Cariocas after work.

Santa Teresa

Set on a hill overlooking the city, the cobbled streets and aging mansions of Santa Teresa are a vision of days long past. Named after the Carmelite convent founded here in 1750, Santa Teresa was the uppermost residential neighborhood in the 19th century, when Rio's upper class lived here and rode the *bonde* to work in Centro. During the 1960s and 1970s many artists and bohemians moved into Santa Teresa's mansions, initiating a revitalization process that still continues. Throughout the year, impromptu festivals and street parties fill the air, ranging from Maracatu (Afro-Brazilian music with a slow, heavy beat) drumming along Rua Joaquim Murtinho and live jazz at Parque Ruinas to the annual Portas Abertas event, where dozens of local artists open their studios and cover the streets with living installations.

BONDE
The **bonde** (tram; Map pp136-7; ☎ 2240 5709; station at Rua Lélio Gama 65, Centro; ticket US$0.65; ☼ departures every 30min, 7am-10pm) that travels up to Santa Teresa from Centro is the last of the historic streetcars that once crisscrossed the city. Its clatter through the cobbled streets has made it the icon for bohemian Santa Teresa. The tram travels over the Arcos do Lapa and up Rua Joaquim Murtinho before reaching Largo do Guimarães. From there, one line (Paula Matos) takes a northwestern route, terminating at Largo das Neves. The longer route (Dois Irmãos) continues from Largo do Guimarães uphill and southward before terminating near the water reservoir at Dois Irmãos.

Although a policeman often accompanies the tram, the *favelas* down the hillsides still make this a high-crime area. Go by all means, but don't bring any valuables. Tram tours depart every Saturday highlighting historic points in the neighborhood (see p151 for details).

LARGO DAS NEVES
A slice of small-town life in the city, the tiny square of **Largo das Neves** (Map pp142-3; end of Rua Progresso) is the gathering point of neighborhood children and families, who lounge on the benches by day. On weekend nights, the bars surrounding the square come alive.

MUSEU CHÁCARA DO CÉU
The former mansion of art patron and industrialist Raymundo Ottoni de Castro Maya is now the **Museu Chácara do Céu** (Map pp136-7; ☎ 2507 1932; Rua Murtinho Nobre 93, Santa Teresa; admission US$3; ☼ noon-5pm Wed-Mon), with a small collection of modern art. In addition to works by Portinari, Di Cavalacanti, Picasso, Matisse and Salvador Dali, the museum displays furniture and Brazilian maps dating from the 17th and 18th centuries. Beautiful gardens surround the museum, with fine views of Centro and Baía de Guanabara.

PARQUE DAS RUINAS
Connected to the Chácara do Céu by a walkway, the **Parque das Ruinas** (Map pp136-7; ☎ 2252 1039; Rua Murtinho Nobre 169, Santa Teresa; admission free; ☼ 10am-8pm Tue-Sun) contains the ruins of the mansion that belong to Brazilian heiress Laurinda Santos Lobo. Her

house was a meeting point for Rio's artists and intellectuals for many years until her death in 1946. Today the park often stages open-air concerts and performances. Don't miss the excellent view from the top floor.

Lapa
Map pp136-7

Formerly a residential neighborhood of the wealthy, Lapa had its best days before the 20th century, and its mansions are now sadly neglected. Although Lapa still recalls decades of dereliction in the minds of many Cariocas, the district has recently experienced a cultural renaissance, and its old buildings are slowly being restored. Lapa is the center of a vibrant bohemian scene in Rio, and the setting for many Brazilian novels.

At night, Lapa boasts one of Rio's most vibrant street parties as revelers mingle among samba clubs and music-filled bars. On weekends it gets crowded here as thousands gather for the chaotic street scene. In spite of some restoration, the neighborhood still remains fairly edgy. Take care when walking around here.

Lapa's landmark aqueduct, Arcos do Lapa, is one of the neighborhood's most prominent features. Narrow tracks course over the 64m-high structure, carrying the famous *bonde* to and from Santa Teresa.

CATEDRAL METROPOLITANA

The enormous cone-shaped **Catedral Metropolitana** (☎ 2240 2669; Av República do Chile 245, Lapa; admission free; ⏰ 7am-5:30pm) was inaugurated in 1976 after 12 years of construction. Among

---

ROCINHA: RIO'S LARGEST FAVELA *Tom Phillips*

Rocinha (Map p118) wasn't the first of Rio de Janeiro's *favelas* (that honor falls to the Morro da Providência, founded in 1897 by slaves migrating from the Northeast's sugar plantations after the abolition of slavery), but it is now indisputably the largest, with over 127,000 inhabitants. It is also one of the most developed, elevated to *bairro* (district) status in 1992 by the controversial government project Favela-Bairro. Manhole covers, electricity cables and Internet cafés all pay testament to the fact that Rocinha is no ordinary 'slum.' In fact, to dismiss it as such is to rather miss the point.

From the patio of Rocinha's Casa de Cultura on Rua 1, the vast *comunidade* (community) spreads out before the eye; a mishmash of red-brick housing stretches down towards the affluent beachside district of São Conrado. It's not just an architectural patchwork. Split into various boroughs, the area is a complex web of social groups and people. Many occupants hail originally from the northeastern state of Paraíba, while there is a smattering of foreign students to whom the area is also home. There is a community of transvestites (generally well respected by locals) and even a man who lives in a cave with running water, electricity, 12 dogs and a cell phone. There are evangelists clad in suits, who clasp copies of the Nova Testemunha (New Testament) as they march home from *cultos* (church services). Doctors, lawyers and maids all live here alongside the unemployed and impoverished.

According to a survey carried out by Rocinha's local TV channel last year, 56% of inhabitants use the local shopping mall, 23% have a credit card and 93% have at least one TV at home. It's perhaps not what you would expect from what is so often referred to as 'South America's largest slum.'

In many ways Rocinha is a normal, safe and welcoming place; a reality underlined by the increasing number of tourists making the pilgrimage to the Estrada de Gávea to photograph stunning views of Corcovado, and to glimpse the *other* side of Rio life. Yet it remains one of the more deprived parts of the city, with widespread unemployment.

The *favela* – once one of the most dangerous parts of the city – has mellowed considerably in the last decade. Part of the reason for this is the drug traffickers, whose deadly style of community policing serves as a brutal but effective deterrent. People here live by a strict code. It is forbidden to talk to the few police that can be found here in two tiny stations. Problems are resolved within the community.

'Roça' is a lively, tight-knit and fascinating community, which desperately needs normalizing. The trouble is, it's not normal yet.

its sculptures, murals and other works of art are four breathtaking stained glass windows, which stretch 60m to the ceiling. The small **Museu de Arte Sacra** (Museum of Sacred Art) is in the basement. It contains historical items such as the throne of Dom Pedro II, the baptismal basins used at the christenings of royal princes and the golden roses Princesa Isabel received from Pope Leo XIII after signing the law abolishing slavery in Brazil.

ESCADARIA SELARÓN

An ever-expanding installation, the **Escadaria Selarón** (Selarón Staircase; btwn Rua Joaquim Silva, Lapa & Rua Pinto Martins, Santa Teresa), leading up from Rua Joaquim Silva, became a work of art when Chilean-born artist Selarón decided to cover the steps with colorful mosaics. A dedication to the Brazilian people, the 215 steps are a vivid riot of color.

FUNDIÇÃO PROGRESSO

Once a foundry for safes and ovens, the **Fundição Progresso** (☎ 2220 5070; Rua dos Arcos 24, Lapa; admission free; ☯ 9am-6pm Mon-Fri) today hosts avant-garde exhibitions, performances and popular samba parties during the summer.

Greater Rio

Although visitors tend to stick to the Zona Sul and Centro, Rio's outer regions offer a variety of attractions, from sweeping views on the other side of the bay to football rowdiness at Maracanã.

To the west of Rio, São Cristóvão encompasses the Quinta da Boa Vista, a large park containing the Museu Nacional and the Jardin Zoológico (zoo). It's also the site of the Maracanã Football Stadium and the Feira Nordestina, one of Brazil's wildest weekend markets. In the 19th century the suburb was the home of the nobility, including the monarchs themselves. It has since become one of the most populous suburbs in Rio.

To the east of Centro lies Rio's lovely bay. Unfortunately, it's too polluted for swimming, but it makes a fine setting for a cruise to either Ilha de Paquetá or Niterói.

SÃO CRISTÓVÃO   Map pp142-3
Feira Nordestina

The enormous **Feira Nordestina** (☎ 3860 9976; www.feiradesaocristovao.com.br in Portuguese; Campo de São Cristóvão, São Cristóvão; ☯ Fri-Sun) is not to be missed. The fair (32,000 sq meters with 658 stalls) showcases the culture from the Northeast, with *barracas* (stalls) selling Bahian dishes as well as beer and *cachaça* (sugarcane spirit), which flows in great abundance here. Bands perform *forró*, samba and Música Popular Brasileira (MPB). You'll also be able to watch comedy troupes and *rodas de capoeira* (capoeira circles), where the highly skilled demonstrate their prowess at the Afro-Brazilian martial art/dance. The vibrant scene starts around 8pm on Friday and continues nonstop through to Sunday evening. (Many club kids stop by here just before sunrise.) In addition to the food and drink, you can stock up on second-hand clothes, some well-priced hammocks and a few Northeastern gifts such as leather cowboy hats.

Maracanã Football Stadium

Brazil's temple of soccer, **Maracanã Football Stadium** (☎ 2568 9962; Rua Professor Eurico Rabelo, São Cristóvão; admission US3-10) easily accommodates more than 100,000 people. On certain occasions, such as the World Cup match of 1950 or Pelé's last game, it has squeezed in close to 200,000 crazed fans – although it's now been modified to hold fewer.

For a quasi psychedelic experience, go to a *futebol* (football) match – preferably a championship game or one between local rivals Flamengo, Vasco da Gama, Fluminense or Botafogo. See p172 for details.

A **sports museum** (☯ 9am-5pm Mon-Fri) inside the stadium displays photographs, posters, cups and the uniforms of Brazilian sporting greats, including Pelé's famous No 10 shirt. There's also a store where you can buy football shirts. Enter through gate No 18 on Rua Professor Eurico Rabelo.

Quinta da Boa Vista

The residence of the imperial family until the Republic was proclaimed, today **Quinta da Boa Vista** (☎ 2234 1609; Rua Paula e Silva, São Cristóvão; ☯ 9am-5pm) is a large and busy park with gardens and lakes. On weekends it's crowded with soccer games and families from the Zona Norte. The former imperial mansion houses the **Museu Nacional** (☎ 2568 8262; admission US$1; ☯ 10am-4pm Tue-Sun) and **Museu da Fauna**. In addition to Etruscan ceramics, Egyptian mummies and stuffed prehistoric animals, the Museu Nacional contains a small Brazilian section with relics from the country's early indigenous people. For a chance to see a wide assortment of plants and flowers – both native and imported species – visit the Museu da Fauna.

The **Jardim Zoológico** (☎ 2569 2024; admission US$2; ☼ 9am-4:30pm Tue-Sun), Rio's zoo, is 200m away. It boasts a medium-size collection of Brazilian mammals and endangered species. Highlights include the tropical bird aviary (the gardens are a good place for birdwatchers) and the Nocturnal House, offering visitors a close-up view of sloths, bats and other creatures of the night.

BAÍA DE GUANABARA & NITERÓI
Ilha Fiscal

The lime-green, neo-Gothic palace of **Ilha Fiscal** (Map pp136-7; ☎ 3870 6992; admission US$3; ☼ 1pm, 2:30pm & 4pm Thu-Sun except on the 2nd weekend of each month), sitting in the Baía de Guanabara, looks like something out of a fairy tale. It was designed by engineer Adolfo del Vecchio and was the location of the last Imperial Ball on November 9, 1889. Today it's open for guided tours, which leave from the dock near Praça XV de Novembro.

Ilha de Paquetá

The island of **Ilha de Paquetá** (Map pp118; ferry ☎ 2533 6661, hydrofoil ☎ 2533 7524), in the Baía de Guanabara, was once a popular tourist spot and is now frequented mostly by families from the Zona Norte. There are no cars on the island. Transport is by foot, bicycle (with hundreds for rent) or horse-drawn carts. There's a certain dirty, decadent charm to the colonial buildings, unassuming beaches and businesses catering to local tourism. The place gets crowded on weekends.

Go to Paquetá for the boat ride through the bay and to see Cariocas at play – especially during the Festa de São Roque, which is celebrated over five days in August.

Boats leave from near the Praça XV de Novembro in Centro. The regular ferry takes an hour and costs US$.50. The more comfortable hydrofoil takes only 25 minutes and costs US$5. Ferry services go from 5:30am to 11pm, leaving every two to three hours. During the week, the hydrofoil leaves at 10am, noon, 2pm and 4pm and returns at 7:40am, 11:40am, 12:30pm, 2:30pm and 4:30pm. On weekends, it leaves Rio every

hour on the hour from 8am to 4pm and returns hourly from 8:30am to 5:30pm.

NITERÓI

Niterói's principal attraction is the famous Museu do Arte Contemporânea. The cruise across the bay, however, is perhaps just as valid a reason for leaving Rio. The ferry costs about US$0.75 and leaves from Praça XV de Novembro in Centro; it's usually full of commuters. The faster and more comfortable alternative is the jumbo catamaran, which runs every 15 minutes from 7am to 4pm and costs US$2. Once you reach the dock, there isn't much to see in the immediate area. It's a busy commercial area, full of pedestrians and crisscrossing intersections. From here catch a bus to the MAC or to one of the beaches.

Museu do Arte Contemporânea

Designed by Brazil's most famous architect, Oscar Niemeyer, the **Museu do Arte Contemporânea** (MAC; ☎ 2620 2400; www.macniteroi.com in Portuguese; Mirante da Boa Viagem s/n, Niterói; admission US$1.75; ☼ 11am-7pm Tue-Sun) is a curvilinear building with breathtaking views, but the expositions inside aren't always so hot. To get here from the Niterói ferry terminal,

---

BEACHES EAST OF NITERÓI

A number of beaches lie just east of Niterói. The ones closest to town are too polluted for swimming, but as you continue out, you'll reach some pristine beaches – **Piratininga**, **Camboinhas**, **Itaipu** and finally **Itacoatiara**, the most fabulous of the bunch. Framed by two looming hills on either side and backed by vegetation, the white sands of Itacoatiara seem a world removed from the urban beaches of Rio. *Barracas* (food stalls) sell scrumptious plates of fish, and there are also food stands overlooking the beach (try Sanduiches Onda for a *natural* – a sandwich of tuna, chicken or cottage cheese, with additional ingredients such as carrots, raisins or olives). The surf is strong here – as evidenced by the abundance of surfers – so swim with caution. To get there, you can take bus 38 from the ferry terminal (US$1; 50 minutes) or any bus labeled 'Itacoatiara.' If you're traveling in a group you can negotiate a return fare with a taxi driver.

Baía

To Estádio de São Januário

SÃO CRISTÓVÃO

MARACANÃ

TIJUCA

Canal do Mangue

Praça da Bandeira

São Cristóvão

Afonso Pena

São Francisco Xavier

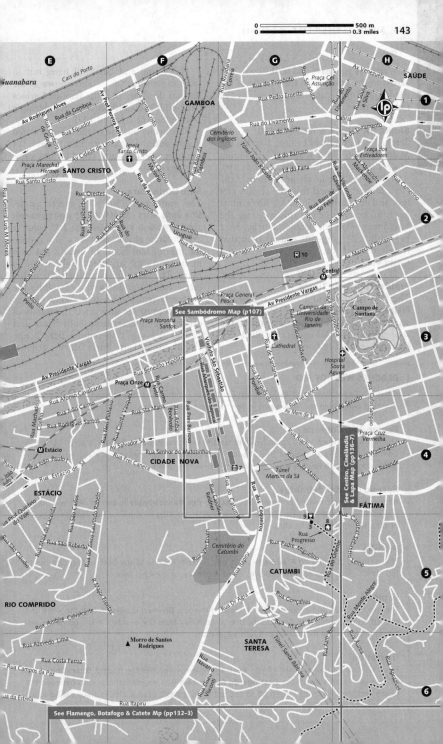

turn right as you leave and walk about 50m across to the bus stop in the middle of the road; a 47B minibus will drop you at the museum door.

BARRA DA TIJUCA & WEST OF RIO
Ten kilometers west of Leblon, Barra is the Miami of Rio, with malls and shopping centers set against the tropical landscape. At 12km long, the lovely beach here is the city's longest. Beyond this, the region gets less and less urban. Some of Rio's most beautiful beaches lie out this way (see the boxed text below for details). Further west begins Brazil's gorgeous coastal road that travels through the region known as the Costa Verde.

Praia da Barra da Tijuca
The best thing about Barra is the beach, **Praia da Barra da Tijuca** (Map p118). It's a long, scenic spot with blue sea lapping at the shore; the first few kilometers are filled with bars and seafood restaurants.

The young and beautiful hang out in front of *barraca* No 1 – also known as the Barraca do Pepê, after the famous Carioca hang-gliding champion who died during a competition in Japan in 1991.

The further out you go the more deserted it gets, and the stalls turn into trailers. It's calm on weekdays and crazy on hot summer weekends.

Sitio Burle Marx
The enormous 350,000-sq-meter estate, **Sitio Burle Marx** (☎ 2410 1412; burlemarx@alternex .com.br; Estrada da Barra de Guaratiba 2019, Guaratiba; ⏰ 7am-4pm, by advance appointment only) was once the magnificent home of Brazil's most famous landscape architect, Roberto Burle Marx. The beautifully lush gardens of the estate easily warrant a visit. Strolling the verdantly landscaped area allows visitors the chance to see and smell thousands of exotic plant species from both Brazil and abroad. A lovely 17th-century Benedictine chapel, along with Burle Marx's original

---

BEACHES WEST OF RIO
Although Copacabana and Ipanema are Rio's most famous stretches of sand, there are many stunning beaches in the area, some in spectacular natural settings.

Pepino/São Conrado
The first major beach you'll reach heading west of Leblon is **Praia do Pepino** (Map p118) in São Conrado. Pepino is a beautiful beach, and is less crowded than Ipanema. It's also where hang-glider riders like to lounge when they're not soaring overhead.

Recreio dos Bandeirantes
Although it gets crowded on weekends, **Recreio dos Bandeirantes** is almost deserted during the week. The large rock acts as a natural breakwater, creating a calm bay. The 2km-long stretch of sand is popular with families.

Prainha
The secluded 700-m-long **Prainha** lies just past Recreio. It's one of the best surfing beaches in Rio, so it's always full of surfers. Waves come highly recommended here.

Grumari
The most isolated and unspoiled beach close to the city, **Grumari** is quiet during the week and packed on weekends with Cariocas looking to get away from city beaches. It is a gorgeous setting, surrounded by mountains and lush vegetation.

Guaratiba
From Grumari, a narrow road climbs over a jungle-covered hillside toward **Guaratiba**. West of here is a good view of the **Restinga de Marambaia** (the vegetation-rich strip between the beach and the mainland), closed off to the public by a naval base. Cariocas enjoy eating lunch at several of the seafood restaurants in the area.

farmhouse and studio, completes the idyllic setting.

ACTIVITIES

Given the mountains, beaches and lush forests at their doorstep, it's not surprising that Cariocas are an active bunch. The coastline brings an array of options: jogging, hiking, walking, cycling, and surfing. The mountains offer their own allure: you can hang-glide off of them or rock-climb up them. Great hiking trails through Atlantic rain forest lie just outside the city.

Cycling

Rio has over 74km of bike paths around the city, making it an excellent way to get some exercise. There are bike paths around Lagoa Rodrigo de Freitas, along Barra da Tijuca, and on the oceanfront from Leblon to Leme. This last path goes all the way to Flamengo and into the center. In the Tijuca forest, a 6km bikeway runs from Cascatinha to Açude. On Sundays the road along the beaches – from Leblon to Leme – is closed as is the road through Parque do Flamengo. Bilingual bike tours are available through **Rio by Bike** (☎ 2247 7269, 9985 7540; Hostel Ipanema, House 14, Rua Barão da Torre 175, Ipanema).

You can rent bikes from a stand along the west side of Lagoa Rodrigo de Freitas for US$6 per hour. A few other places to rent bikes:

Ciclovia (Map pp128-9; ☎ 2275 5299; Av Prado Junior 330, Copacabana) A small selection, but good prices at US$10 per day.

Consuelo (Map pp128-9; ☎ 2513 0159, 8811 5552; Posto 4, Copacabana) In addition to a pickup service on Copacabana Beach, it also delivers to all hotels in the Zona Sul.

Special Bike (Map pp124-5; ☎ 2521 2686; www .specialbike.com.br; Rua Visconde de Pirajá 135B, Ipanema; ◷ 9am-7pm Mon-Fri, to 2pm Sat) Excellent bikes rent for US$5 per hour or US$15 per day.

Zaga Bike (Map pp128-9; ☎ 2235 1859; Rua Barata Ribeiro 834A, Copacabana) Features a good selection of new and used bikes for sale and rent.

Diving

Calypso (Map pp136-7; ☎ 2542 8718, 9939 5997; www .calypsobrasil.com.br; No 502, Rua México 111, Centro) offers diving courses (up to Dive Master) in waters near Rio. It also offers excellent excursions for certified divers to Arraial

do Cabo, Angra dos Reis and Fernando Noronha, the gorgeous archipelago in the Northeast.

Dive Point (Map pp124-5; ☎ 2239 5105; www.dive point.com.br in Portuguese; Shop 4, Av Ataulfo de Paiva 1174, Leblon) features diving courses and tours around Rio's main beaches and the Cagarras Island (in front of Ipanema), as well as trips to Angra dos Reis and Búzios.

Fishing

Universidade da Pesca (Map pp136-7; ☎ 2240 8117, 9949 2363; www.upesca.com.br in Portuguese; No 502, Rua México 111, Centro) offers a wide range of fishing tours – from day trips in Baía de Guanabara and the Cagarras Island to weeklong adventures in the Amazon.

Golf

Green fees at the 18-hole golf course of **Gávea Golf & Country Club** (Map p118; ☎ 3322 4141; Estrada da Gávea 800, São Conrado; ◷ 7am-sunset weekdays) are about US$75 a round, plus club rental of US$25 and caddie hire for US$25. On weekends, you have to be invited by a member to play here.

Near Praia da Barra da Tijuca, opposite Posto 7, **Golden Green Golf Clinic** (☎ 2434 0696; Av Canal de Marapendi 2901, Barra da Tijuca; ◷ 7am-10pm) features six par-three holes. The green fees are US$20 during the week and US$26 on the weekend.

Hang Gliding

If you weigh less than 100kg (about 220lb) and have US$80 to spend, you can do the fantastic hang glide off 510m-high Pedra Bonita – one of the giant granite slabs that tower above Rio – onto Praia do Pepino in São Conrado. No experience is necessary and we're told that the winds are very safe here. Guest riders are secured in a kind of pouch attached to the kite.

Flights naturally depend on weather and wind conditions. You can usually fly on all but three to four days per month, and conditions during winter are even better. If you fly early in the day, you have more flexibility to accommodate weather delays. The cheapest, but probably not the safest, way to arrange a flight is to go to the far end of Praia do Pepino, on Av Prefeito Mendes de Morais, where the flyboys hang out at the Vôo Livre club. During the week, you can probably get a flight for around US$60.

Travel agents can also book tandem flights for you, but they tack on their own fee. To cut out the middlemen, call direct.

Just Fly (☎ 2268 0565, 9985 7540; www.justfly.com .br; Hostel Ipanema, House 14, Rua Barão da Torre 175, Ipanema) Paulo Celani is a highly experienced tandem flyer with over 6000 flights to his credit. His fee includes picking you up and dropping you off at your hotel.

SuperFly (☎ 3322 2286, 9982 5703; Casa 2, Estrada das Canoas 1476; São Conrado) Ruy Marra, founder of SuperFly, has more than 23 years of experience flying and is an excellent tandem glider pilot. Widely regarded as one of the best in Rio, Ruy is also the person to see if you're interested in paragliding (gliding with a special parachute).

Tandem Fly (☎ 2422 6371, 2422 0941; www.riotandem fly.com.br) Three experienced pilots run this tandem flight outfit, and they'll arrange pick up and drop off at your hotel. They also give lessons for those wanting to learn how to fly solo.

Hiking & Climbing

Visitors can hike one of the many trails through the Floresta da Tijuca (see the boxed text below) or head to Rio's nearby national parks, Parque Nacional da Serra dos Órgãos, p199, and Parque Nacional de Itatiaia, p193).

In recent years, there's been a boom in organized hikes around the city, including hikes through wilderness areas around Corcovado, Morro da Urca, Pão de Açúcar and, of course, Tijuca. It's advisable to go with a guide for a number of reasons – to avoid getting lost and getting robbed are top of the list. Group outings can also be a good way to meet Cariocas.

Rio is also the center of rock climbing in Brazil, with around 350 documented climbs within an hour's drive. Rio has several well-

---

PARQUE NACIONAL & FLORESTA DA TIJUCA

The Floresta da Tijuca is all that's left of the Atlantic rain forest that once surrounded Rio de Janeiro. In just 15 minutes you can go from the concrete jungle of Copacabana to the 120-sq-km tropical jungle of the **Parque Nacional da Tijuca** (Map p118). A more rapid and dramatic contrast is hard to imagine. The forest is an exuberant green, with beautiful trees, creeks and waterfalls, mountainous terrain and high peaks. It has an excellent, well-marked trail system. Candomblistas (devotees of the Candomblé religion) leave offerings by the roadside, families have picnics and serious hikers climb the 1012m to the summit of **Pico da Tijuca**.

The heart of the forest is the Alto da Boa Vista area, which has many lovely natural and artificial features. Among the highlights of this beautiful park are several waterfalls (**Cascatinha Taunay**, **Cascata Gabriela** and **Cascata Diamantina**), a 19th-century chapel (**Capela Mayrink**) and numerous caves (**Gruta Luís Fernandes**, **Gruta Belmiro** and **Gruta Paulo e Virgínia**). Also in the park is a pleasant picnic spot (**Bom Retiro**) and several restaurants (Restaurante Os Equilos and Restaurante a Floresta, which is near the **Ruínas do Archer**, the ruins of Major Archer's house). A recommended culinary experience is dining at the open-air brunch at the **Museu do Açude** (☎ 2492 2119; Estrada do Açude 764, Floresta da Tijuca), held on the last Sunday of the month.

The park is home to many different bird and animal species, including iguanas and monkeys, which you might encounter on one of the excellent day hikes you can make here. Maps can be obtained at the small artisan **shop** (◷ 7am-9pm), just inside the park entrance.

The entire park closes at sunset. It's best to go by car, but if you can't, catch a No 221, 233 or 234 bus. Alternatively, take the metro to Saens Pena then catch a bus going to Barra da Tijuca and get off at Alta da Boa Vista. The best route by car is to take Rua Jardim Botânico two blocks past the Jardim Botânico (heading east from Gávea). Turn left on Rua Lopes Quintas and then follow the Tijuca or Corcovado signs for two quick left turns until you reach the back of the Jardim Botânico, where you turn right. Then follow the signs for a quick ascent into the forest and past the **Vista Chinesa** (get out for a good view) and the **Mesa do Imperador**, both of which offer some fantastic views of Rio's mountainous seascape. As soon as you seem to come out of the forest, turn right onto the main road and you'll see the stone columns at the entrance of Alto da Boa Vista on your left after a couple of kilometers. You can also drive up to Alto da Boa Vista by heading out to São Conrado and turning right up the hill at the Parque Nacional da Tijuca signs.

Warning: There have been occasional reports of armed robberies within the park. Most Cariocas recommend going on weekends when there are more people around.

organized climbing clubs, which have regular weekly meetings to discuss upcoming outings. The clubs definitely have a social component, and are a good place to meet locals.

Centro Excursionista Brasileira (CEB; Map pp136-7; ☎ 2252 9844; www.ceb.org.br in Portuguese; 8th fl, Av Almirante Barroso 2, Centro; ☯ meeting 7pm Thu, office 2-6pm Mon-Fri) sponsors day hikes and weekend treks (with camping). It also arranges trips further out – such as two-week hikes across Ushuaia in southern Argentina. Attend a meeting or stop in to say hello and take a look at the bulletin board, which lists upcoming excursions – as does the website.

Centro Excursionista Rio de Janeiro (CERJ; Map pp136-7; ☎ 2220 3548; www.cerj.org.br in Portuguese; Av Rio Branco 277/805, Centro; ☯ meeting 8pm Thu) offers a wide range of outdoor activities, from hikes to technical climbs. Stop by at one of the meetings or check out the website to see what's on.

Clube Excursionista Carioca (Map pp128-9; ☎ 2255 1348; No 206, Rua Hilário de Gouveia 71, Copacabana; ☯ meeting 8:30pm Thu) typically arranges hikes and technical climbs, although from time to time it goes rappelling and rafting. It's also involved in preservation and education efforts and gives five-week courses on basic mountaineering.

Led by Denise Werneck and her son Gabriel, who both speak English, **Rio Hiking** (☎ 2552 9204, 9721 0594; www.riohiking.com.br; Rua Coelho Neto 401, Laranjeiras) tours range from easy to strenuous and cover a variety of terrains in and around Rio. Popular treks include hikes up Pico da Tijuca (the highest point in the national park), Pedra da Gávea, Pão de Açúcar and Corcovado, most of which cost around US$40. Cycling and diving adventures, surfing and rappelling can all be arranged.

Tangara Ecological Hikes (☎ 2252 8202, 9656 1460; www.tangarapasseios.com.br) offers an enormous variety of excursions, from kayaking excursions off Praia Vermelha to climbs up Pedra da Gávea. It has two-day trips: exploring Ilha Grande, rafting excursions in Mont Serrat and climbing treks up Pedra do Baú. Hikes are rated according to level of difficulty (easy, moderate and hard), and the outings are popular with young Brazilians. Guides speak English, Spanish and Portuguese.

Although **Trilharte Ecoturismo** (☎ 2245 5626; www.trilharte.com.br in Portuguese) guides don't speak English, this ecologically minded organization offers exceptional excursions, catering to adventurers 'with a passion for photography.' It offers hiking, rappelling, rafting and horseriding trips, which cost from US$10 to US$50. It also hosts photographic safaris, where participants study under a professional photographer on a weekend- or daylong excursion. Past trips have ranged from the aesthetic (Holy Week in Ouro Prêto) to the far out (nudes in nature). Visit the website to check out upcoming excursions (click on '*cronograma de passeios*'). Most activities are held on weekends.

Paddle Boating

Although most Cariocas laugh at the idea of paddling a big swan boat out across the Lagoa Rodrigo de Freitas, the truth is, many of them have done it. Located on the east shore of the lake near the kiosks, **paddle boats** (Map pp124-5; Parque do Cantaglo, Lagoa; per half-hr US$8) are available for hire throughout the year on the weekends. During the summer, you can hire boats until late in the night on weekends – and it's always an admirable goal to paddle toward the Christmas tree across the way if you're around in December.

Surfing

When the surf is good, it gets crowded. Praia do Arpoador, between Copacabana and Ipanema, draws large flocks of surfers, though there are much better breaks further out in Barra, Grumari, Joá and Prainha – by far the best surf spot in Rio. Across the bay, Itacoatiara also has good breaks.

If you don't have a board, you can hire or buy one in Arpoador at **Galeria River** (Map pp128-9; Rua Francisco Otaviano 67, Arpoador), a commercial center full of surf shops and boutiques.

Escolinha de Surf Paulo Dolabella (Map pp124-5; ☎ 2490 4077, 2259 2320; in front of Rua Maria Quitéria, Ipanema Beach) Although you'll have to ask around to find him, Paulo gives private lessons for around US$7 per hour.

Escolinha de Surf Barra da Tijuca (☎ 3209 0302; 1st kiosk after Post 5, Av Sernambetiba, Praia da Barra da Tijuca) This surfing school is run by a Brazilian ex-champion and former professional surfer. Open daily.

Tennis

Although the humidity in the summer can make games rather unpleasant, if you fancy a hit of tennis, you can book a court at the **InterContinental** (Map pp118; ☎ 3322 2200; Av Preifeito Mendes de Morais, São Conrado) or the **Sheraton** (Map pp124-5; ☎ 2274 1122; Av Niemeyer 121, Vidgal). Courts are available to nonguests for around US$10 an hour during the day, a bit more at night. In Barra, you can play at the **Rio Sport Center** (☎ 3325 6644; Av Ayrton Senna 2541, Barra da Tijuca), opposite the Terra Encantada amusement park.

Volleyball & Other Beach Sports
Volleyball is Brazil's second most popular sport (after football). A natural activity for the beach, it's also a popular spectator sport on TV. A local variation of volleyball you'll see on Rio's beaches is *futevôlei*. It's fun to watch, but frustratingly difficult to play.

Peteca is a cross between volleyball and badminton. It's played with a *peteca*, an object similar to, but a little larger than, a shuttlecock – you'll see them being hawked on the beach. *Peteca* is a favorite with older Cariocas who are getting a bit slow for volleyball.

Usually played on the firm sand at the shoreline, *frescobol* involves two players, each with a wooden racquet, hitting a small rubber ball back and forth as hard as possible.

Those interested in improving their game – or just meeting some Cariocas – should pay a visit to Pelé at **Escolinha de Vôlei** (Map pp124-5; ☎ 9702 5794; www.voleinapraia.com.br in Portuguese; near Rua Garcia D'Avila, on Ipanema Beach). Pelé, who speaks English, has been giving one-hour volleyball lessons for 10 years. Lessons are in the morning (from about 8am to 11am) and in the afternoon (5pm to 7pm). He charges around US$17 for the month and you can come as often as you like. Look for his large Brazilian flag on the beach.

Walking & Jogging
There are some good walking and jogging paths in the Zona Sul. If you're staying in the Catete/Flamengo area, Parque do Flamengo (Map pp132-3) has plenty of space and lots of workout stations. Around Lagoa Rodrigo de Freitas (Map pp124-5) a 7.5km track provides a path for cyclists, joggers and power walkers (and saunterers). At the Parque do Cantalago, you can hire bicycles, tricycles or quadricycles. Along the seaside,

from Leme to Barra da Tijuca, there's a bike path and footpath. On Sunday (7am to 6pm) the road is closed to traffic. The road skirting through Parque do Flamengo is also closed on Sundays.

Closed to bicycles but open to walkers and joggers is the Pista Cláudio Coutinho (Map pp132-3), between the mountains and the sea at Praia Vermelha in Urca. It's open from 7am until 6pm daily and is very secure because of the army post nearby. People in bathing suits aren't allowed in (unless they're running). It's a nice place to be around sunset.

WALKING TOUR
A blend of historic buildings and young skyscrapers, the center of Rio makes an excellent place to discover the city's charm away from its beaches and mountains. Among the hustle and bustle, you'll find museums, charming bars, theaters and open-air bazaars. This tour is best done during the week, when Centro is at its most vibrant (and safest).

Start at the **Praça Floriano** (**1**; p135), which is the heart of modern Rio. Praça Floriano comes to life at lunchtime and after work when the outdoor cafés fill with Cariocas. The neoclassical **Teatro Municipal** (**2**; p138) overlooking the plaza, is one of Rio's finest buildings.

On the east side of Av Rio Branco, facing Praça Floriano, is an open-air music market, **Rua Pedro Lessa (3)**, where you can browse the record and CD stalls. Next to it is the **Centro Cultural Justiça Federal** (**4**; p134), which often hosts decent exhibitions. The solid **Biblioteca Nacional** (**5**; p134) is next door, while north on Av Rio Branco is another historic building, today hosting the **Museu Nacional de Belas Artes** (**6**; p135). Take a peek inside if you interested in seeing some of Rio's best-known 19th-century painters.

Now cross Av Rio Branco and walk in front of the Teatro Municipal, then take a left down Av 13 de Maio. Cross a street and you're in the **Largo da Carioca (7)**, a pedestrian area that gets packed with vendors during the week. Up on the hill is the recently restored **Convento de Santo Antônio** (**8**; p134). The original church here was started in 1608, making it one of Rio's oldest.

Gazing at the skyline from the convent, you'll notice the **Petrobras building (9)**, whose boxlike metal chassis seems to cast an ominous shadow over the area. Behind it is the ultramodern Catedral Metropolitana.

Come back down from the church and take a right on Rua da Carioca and a left on Rua Gonçalves Dias and stop in the **Confeitaria Colombo** (**10**; p165) for a dose of caffeine and art nouveau. Head back to Rua da Carioca. Along this street, you'll find an array of old shops, a slice out of 19th-century Rio. **Bar Luiz** (**11**; p165), at number 39, makes a fine stop for a bite or a *chope* (draft beer).

At the end of the block you'll pass the **Cinema Iris** (**12**), which used to be one of Rio's most elegant theaters, and emerge into the hustle of **Praça Tiradentes** (**13**). Soak up some of the stately ambience here. On opposite sides of the square are the Teatro João Caetano and the Teatro Carlos Gomez, historic buildings that still stage some excellent music, dance and theatre performances. Around the corner is the **Centro Cultural Carioca** (**14**; p120). Stop in here to see what's on musically for the evening. Just across from the theater is the **Real Gabinete Português de Leitura** (**15**; p138), with a lovely collection of books.

Walk up to Rua da Conceição and take a left. When you reach Rua da Alfândega take another left. This will take you into the heart of Saara, a longstanding neighborhood bazaar packed with shops, pedestrians and Lebanese restaurants. Walk, shop and snack as far as Campo de Santana. Make a U-turn there and proceed back along Rua Senhor dos Passos. Take a right on Rua Regente Feijó. When this street ends take a short left and then a right and head down Rua do Lavradio. This street is famous for its antique shops set in the colorful 19th-century buildings. A number of great nightspots, such as **Rio Scenarium** (**16**; see the boxed text on p169) have sprung up on this street, some set in brick-lined colonial relics. The blend of samba-jazz and antiques makes a lively mix.

When you reach Av República do Chile take a left and stop in the **Catedral Metropolitana** (**17**; p139) for a break. There, check out the marvelous stained glass windows. When you leave, head back to Rua do Lavradio for more antique browsing. When you reach Av Mem de Sá, take a left and follow the

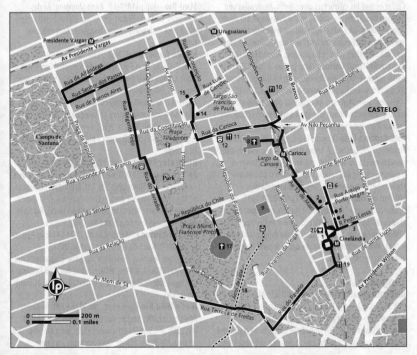

road around the curve as you pass beneath the **Arcos do Lapa (18)**. This is Rio's big samba center at night, with clubs and old-school bars scattered all over the neighborhood. When you reach the Largo da Lapa, a small plaza along which a restaurant and a few samba clubs are scattered, take a left and walk along Rua do Passeio. You'll have great views of the arches from here. In two more blocks you'll be back to where you started. When you reach Praça Floriano, stop in at **Ateliê Odeon (19**; p165) or **Amarelinho (20)** for a *chope* or freshly squeezed *suco* (juice), a fine cap to the walk.

COURSES
Dance
Given the resurgent popularity of samba throughout the city, it's not surprising that there are a number of places where you can learn the moves. A dance class is also a good place to meet other people while getting those two left feet to step in time.

Casa de Dança Carlinhos de Jesus (Map pp132-3; ☎ 2541 6186; www.carlinhosdejesus.com.br; Rua Álvaro Ramos 11, Botafogo) At this respected dance academy, Carlinhos and his instructors give samba, *forró*, salsa and hip-hop classes daily – mostly in the evenings from about 7pm to 10pm. On Friday night the academy often hosts open dance parties for students and guests. One of Botafogo's colorful Bloco parties begins here around Carnaval.

Centro Cultural Carioca (Map pp136-7; ☎ 2252 6468; www.centroculturalcarioca.com.br; Rua do Teatro 37, Centro; 6-week course meeting 2/week US$25-35; ⏰ noon-8pm Mon-Sat) An excellent place to take classes. Its large dance hall hosts live samba parties on Friday. For more information check out the website or stop in.

Estudantina Café (Map pp136-7; ☎ 2242 5062; Praça Tiradentes 79, Centro), A broad mix of skilled and unskilled dancers meets for Tuesday- and Friday-night classes at a cultural center and samba club. Excellent parties are thrown here on weekends. See p168 for details.

Núcleo de Dança (Map pp136-7; ☎ 2221 1011; 2nd fl, Rua da Carioca 14, Centro) On the edge of Lapa; offers classes on *forró*, tango, salsa and samba. Instructor Marcia Pinheiro is flexible, and you can usually drop in and join a class. Most are held during the day – around noon – so stop in to see what's on.

Language
Instituto Brasil-Estados Unidos (IBEU; Map pp128-9; ☎ 2548 8430; www.ibeu.org.br in Portuguese; 5th fl, Av NS de Copacabana 690, Copacabana; 4-week course meeting 3/week US$500) One of the older, more respected language institutions in the city. It has four different levels

of classes from beginner through advanced. Classes typically meet for two hours a day, Monday through Thursday for four weeks.

Feedback Ipanema (Map pp124-5; ☎ 2522 0598; www.cursofeedback.com.br in Portuguese; Rua Farme de Amoedo 35, Ipanema; class per person per hr private/for 2 US$17/11) Offers group and private courses at its schools throughout the city (it also has locations in Copacabana, Botafogo and Centro).

RIO FOR CHILDREN
Brazilians are very family-oriented. Many hotels let children stay free, although the age limit varies. Babysitters are readily available and most restaurants have high chairs.

Lonely Planet's *Travel with Children*, by Cathy Lanigan, gives a lot of good tips and advice on traveling with kids in the tropics.

Good sights for kids are the shows at the **Planetário** (p123) and the **Jardim Zoológico** (p140).

In addition, children may also enjoy:

Fazenda Alegria (Map p118; ☎ 2442 1992; admission US$10; ⏰ 10am-5pm Sat, Sun & holidays) Small children's farm on the Estrada da Boca do Mato in Vargem Pequena.

Mini-Rio (Map p118; 1st fl, Barra Shopping, Av das Américas, Barra da Tijuca; ⏰ 10am-10pm) Small amusement area with bumper cars, boat and plane rides for tiny tots.

Museu Aerospacial (Map p118; ☎ 3357 5212; www.musal.aer.mil.br in Portuguese; Av Marechal Fontenele 2000, Campo dos Afonsos; admission free; ⏰ 9am-3pm Tue-Fri, 9:30am-4pm Sat & Sun) Expositions on Santos Dumont (the Brazilian father of aviation), Air Marshal Eduardo Gomes, the history of Brazilian airmail and the role of Brazil's air force in WWII. Lots of old planes, including replicas of Santos Dumont's planes: the *14 Bis* and the *Demoiselle*.

Rio Water Planet (Map p118; ☎ 2428 9000; Estrada das Bandeirantes 24,000, Recreio dos Bandeirantes; admission US$14; ⏰ 10am-5pm Sat, Sun & holidays) Claims to be the biggest aquatic park in Latin America. Also incorporates Rio Kart Planet (an open-air kart track), Rio Show Planet (an area for shows) and Rio Circus Planet.

Terra Encantada (Map p118; ☎ 2421 9444; Av Ayrton Senna 2800, Barra da Tijuca; adult/child US$12/14; ⏰ 2-9pm Thu-Sun, noon-9pm Sun) The Enchanted Land includes Cabhum, a 64m, 100km/h free fall, and Ressaca, a toboggan ride that goes over a waterfall, as well as many other rides.

Wet'n'Wild Rio (Map p118; ☎ 2428 9300; Av das Américas 22,000, Recreio dos Bandeirantes; adult/child US$13/7; ⏰ Sep-May) Its water slides are a bit more radical than Rio Water Planet. Opening hours vary here.

TOURS
Favela Tours

Marcelo Armstrong (☎ 3322 2727, 9989 0074; www
.favelatour.com.br; per person US$20) The pioneer of *favela*
tourism, Marcelo takes small groups to visit the *favelas* of
Rocinha and Vila Canoas near São Conrado. Tours include
a visit to a school, medical center and private houses, and
English-speaking guides make an effort to explain the social and political context of the *favela* in relation to greater
Rio de Janeiro. Like Paulo, Marcelo donates a portion of his
profits to social projects that benefit the *favela*.

Paulo Amendoim (☎ 3322 8498, 9747 6860;
pauloamendoim@hotmail.com; 2-3hr tour per person
US$20) President of Rocinha's resident association Paulo
leads tours through Rio's biggest *favela* and offers visitors
the chance to see beneath the stereotypes that characterize *favela* life. Paulo, who speaks English, picks up visitors
at their hotel, takes them to the top of Rocinha, then leads
a guided walking tour downhill through the *favela*. Paulo
seems well liked by many *favelados*, perhaps owing to his
involvement in a Rocinha childcare project.

Walking Tours

Cultural Rio (☎ 3322 4872, 9911 3829; www.culturalrio
.com.br; 4hr tour per person US$50) Run by the loquacious
and erudite Carlos Roquette, this tour offers visitors an in-
depth look at social and historical aspects of Rio de Janeiro.
Itineraries include a night at the Teatro Municipal, colonial
Rio, baroque Rio, imperial Rio and a walking tour of Centro.
Professor Roquette has been in business for over 20 years.

Fabio Sombra (☎ 2275 8605; www.fasombra.cjb.net;
tour for 4 people US$70) A multilingual artist still active as
an arte naïf painter, Fabio leads tours around Centro and
Santa Teresa. His most popular tour covers the ruins of the
old port and historical sites around Praça XV de Novembro,
the Mosteiro de São Bento and the Catedral Metropolitana,
passing through Lapa and ending in Santa Teresa.

Luiz Amaral Tours (☎ 2259 5532; www.travelrio.com)
Run by Luiz, a friendly, well-traveled Carioca with a good
command of English, this company offers a wide range of
tours. Luiz' more unique excursions include a combined
hike/climb up Pão de Açúcar (US$30 per person for groups
of two), an exploration of beaches south of Barra (US$27
per person for groups of four) and nightlife tours in Rio
(US$20 per person for two or more).

Private Tours (☎ 2232 9710; www.privatetours.com
.br) Pedro Novak has been leading excursions around the
city and further afield since 1992. He also offers jeep tours
to Tijuca and Praia de Grumari as well as trips to Paraty,
Parque Nacional de Itatiaia and beyond. He speaks English,
French, Spanish, Italian and Portuguese.

Other Tours

Angramar Turismo (Map pp128-9; ☎ 2235 1989;
angramar2000@yahoo.com.b; Av NS de Copacabana 534,

Copacabana; tour incl round-trip transportation & admission around US$15; ☼ Sep-Feb or Mar) Samba-school
tours during Carnaval season offer regular trips to some of
the better-known samba schools, providing visitors with
the opportunity to see a live rehearsal and party with the
school participants. Angramar has regular departures to
Viradouro (8:30pm Tuesday), Salgueiro (7:30pm Wednesday), Beija-Flor (10pm Thursday), Grande Rio (10pm
Friday) and its most popular destination, Mangueira (10pm
Saturday).

Bonde Historico (☎ 2242 2354, 2524 2508; per
person US$3.50; ☼ depart10am Sat) Tram tours run by
the Museu do Bonde (Tram Museum). Guided tours of the
Santa Teresa neighborhood illuminate historic points along
the journey from downtown to Silvestre and back, with a
stop at the Museu do Bonde. Trams depart from the *bonde*
station (Map pp136–7) on Rua Lélio Gama in Centro.

Gray Line Tours (☎ 2512 9919; www.grayline.com.br;
Av Niemeyer 121, Leblon; per person around US$30) City
bus sightseeing tours in and around Rio. The Rio-based
branch of this international chain offers four-hour trips
to Corcovado, historic Centro and Baía de Guanabara. The
down side of these tours is that you may spend more time
on the bus than at the sights.

Helisight (Map pp124-5; ☎ 2511 2141; www
.helisight.com.br; Shop 119, Rua Conde de Bernadotte 26,
Leblon; per person 6min/ 30min US$43/148; ☼ 9am-
6pm) Running helicopter tours since 1991, there are eight
different tours to choose from, lasting from six to 60
minutes. From one of its four helipads, helicopters travel
around Cristo Redentor. Helisight also has flights over the
Parque Nacional da Tijuca and above the mountains and
beaches that are woven into Rio's lush landscape. There are
helipad locations in the Parque Nacional da Tijuca facing
Corcovado; on Morro da Urca, the first cable-car stop up
Pão de Açúcar; on the edge of Lagoa; and at Pier Mauá,
downtown at the docks. Note: there is a three-person
minimum.

Jeep Tour (☎ 2589 0883; www.jeeptour.com.br; 4hr
tour incl hotel pick-up & drop-off per person around
US$40) Jeep Tour offers travel to the lush Parque Nacional
da Tijuca from aback a large, convertible jeep. The tour
consists of a stop at the Vista Chinesa, then on to the forest
for an easy hike and a stop for a swim beneath a waterfall,
before making the return journey.

Rough Trip (☎ 2572 9991; www.roughtrip.com.br)
Motorcycle tours that head off-road on a 200cc motorcycle
around Rio's beaches, forests and mountains. Bikes and
guides are provided (as are helmets and gloves). Rough
Trip also offers excursions to Búzios or you can custom-
design your own tour.

Saveiros Tours (Map pp136-7; ☎ 2224 6990;
saveiros@saveiros.com.br; Rua Conde de Lages 44s 1001,
Glória; ☼ 9:30-11:30am Tue-Sun) These bay tours
involve two-hour cruises out over Baía de Guanabara in

large schooners. The route follows the coastline of Rio and Niterói and you'll get excellent views of Pão de Açúcar, the MAC, Ilha Fiscal and the old fort of Urca. You'll also sail under the Niterói bridge. You can purchase tickets in advance at the **Marina de Glória** (☼ 8am-6pm Mon-Fri).

FESTIVALS & EVENTS

Carnaval is, of course, Rio de Janeiro's biggest and most famous bash (see p106 for details). There are, however, many other exciting events that take place at other times of the year.

Dia de São Sebastião January 20 – The patron saint of the city is commemorated with a procession that carries his image from the Igreja de São Sebastião dos Capuchinos in Tijuca (Rua Haddock Lobo 266) to the Catedral Metropolitana, where it's blessed in a Mass celebrated by the archbishop of Rio de Janeiro.

Dia da Fundação da Cidade March 1 – The founding of the city by Estácio de Sá in 1565 is commemorated with a Mass in the church of its patron saint, São Sebastião.

Sexta-Feira da Paixão March or April – Good Friday is celebrated throughout the city. The most important ceremony is a reenactment of the Stations of the Cross under the Arcos do Lapa, carried out by more than a hundred actors.

Portas Abertas One weekend in May and in November – Santa Teresa's artists open their studios and the neighborhood becomes a living installation in this twice-yearly event. Dates change so stop by at Cama e Café (p154) or Parque das Ruínas (p138) for more information.

Festas Juninas June – The June Festival is one of the most important folkloric festivals in Brazil. In Rio, it's celebrated in various public squares throughout the month, primarily on June 13 (Dia de Santo Antônio), June 24 (Dia de São João) and June 29 (Dia de São Pedro).

Festa da São Pedro do Mar July 13 – The fishing community pays homage to its patron saint in a maritime procession. Decorated boats leave from the fishing district of Caju and sail to the statue of São Pedro in Urca.

Festa de NS da Glória do Outeiro August 15 – A solemn Mass is held in the Igreja de NS da Glória do Outeiro, which is ablaze with decorated lights, with a procession into the streets of Glória to mark the Feast of the Assumption. This festival includes music and colorful stalls set up in the Praça NS da Glória. Festivities start at 8am and continue all day.

Dia de Independência do Brasil September 7 – Independence Day is celebrated with a big military parade down Av Presidente Vargas. It starts at 8am at Candelária and goes just past Praça Onze, north of the Sambódromo.

Rio International Film Festival September and October – The festival is one of the biggest in Latin America. Over 200 films from all over the world are shown at some 35 theaters. The festival usually runs for 15 days from the last week of September through the first week of October. Check the website (www.festivaldorio.com.br in Portuguese) for details.

Rio Jazz Festival October – Features three nights of great music. National and international acts present a wide variety of music – not just jazz. Dates vary from year to year.

Festa da Penha October and November – This is one of the largest religious and popular festivals in the city. It takes place every Sunday in October and the first Sunday in November, at Igreja NS da Penha de França, Largo da Penha 19 in Penha. It's very lively.

GAY & LESBIAN RIO

Rio is the gay capital of Latin America. There is no law against homosexuality in Brazil and during Carnaval, thousands of expatriate Brazilian and gringo gays fly in for the festivities. Transvestites steal the show at all Carnaval balls, especially the gay ones. Outside of Carnaval, the gay scene is active, but markedly less visible than in cities like San Francisco and Sydney.

Ipanema is the most 'out' area of Rio. Rua Teixeira de Melo is a major gathering spot for gays and the beaches of Copacabana and Ipanema have gay sections: near Rua Farme de Amoedo (p123), in Ipanema and near the Copacabana Palace (p127) in Copacabana.

You may hear or read the acronym GLS, particularly in the entertainment sections of newspapers and magazines. It stands for Gays, Lesbians and Sympathizers, and basically indicates that anyone with an open mind is welcome. In general, the scene is much more integrated than elsewhere; and most parties involve a pretty mixed crowd. For information on gay and lesbian nightclubs, see p171.

The excellent Rio gay guide at www.riogayguide.com is full of information for gay and lesbian tourists in Rio, including sections on 'Bars and Cruisy Areas,' 'Rio Gay Carnival' and 'Rio for Beginners.' It's available in German, English and Portuguese versions. Another informative site with lots of good links is www.pridelinks.com/Regional/Brazil.

The gay and lesbian press in Rio and Brazil is represented by *O Grito* and by the glossy *G Magazine* – both available at newsstands.

Reveillon & Festa de Iemanjá December 31 – New Year's Eve (Reveillon) in Rio is celebrated by millions of people. Tons of fireworks explode in the sky over Copacabana. New Year's Eve coincides with the festival of Iemanjá, the sea goddess. Wearing white, the faithful carry a statue of Iemanjá to the beach and launch flowers and other offerings into the sea.

SLEEPING

Rio's continued popularity as the tropical Cidade Maravilhosa means that there is no shortage of accommodations. Until recently, most of these options were limited to boxy high-rises stacked with drearily furnished rooms and basic amenities. With the arrival of more and more visitors, however, hoteliers have begun reinvesting in the city, giving much-needed face-lifts to old haunts, and opening a wave of new hotels.

Reservations are a good idea in Rio, and you can save 30% just by booking ahead. Hotel rates rise during the summer months (December through February), and often triple during New Year's Eve and Carnaval. Most hotels will only book in four-day blocks around these holidays.

Keep in mind that many hotels add in a combined 15% service and tax charge. The cheaper places don't generally bother with this.

Ipanema & Leblon Map pp124-5

Ocean views with access to some of Rio's loveliest beaches, restaurants and bars make Ipanema and Leblon a magnet among travelers seeking the best of Rio. Prices here are higher than elsewhere, though it's still possible to find affordable – if rather modest – lodging.

BUDGET

Hostel Harmonia (☎ 2523 4905; www.hostelharmonia .com; House 18, Rua Barão da Torre 175, Ipanema; dm/d US$14/28; 🖵) Halfway between the beach and the lake, Hostel Harmonia is a converted home in one of Rio's prettiest neighborhoods. It's a friendly place to stay with four well-maintained dorm rooms that sleep two to six, and a private double room for couples. A kitchen is available to guests. English, French, German and Swedish are spoken.

LONG-TERM RENTALS

If you're planning to stay in Rio for longer than a few nights, you may consider renting an apartment. There is a number of agencies dedicated to tracking down long-term rentals for foreigners, and it's a fairly straightforward affair. Usually, you'll pay a small deposit along with the price of the rental up front, sign away your life, and you're all set. Although most of the agencies are in Copacabana, they can help find flats in other areas of town if you want to get off the beaten path. As is the case for hotels, the price of apartment rentals rises considerably during Carnaval and New Year's – though there's usually something available.

Apartur Imóveis (☎ 2287 5757; Rua Visconde de Pirajá 371S/204, Ipanema) This Ipanema-based agency specializes in one- and two-bedroom apartments in the area.

Copacabana Holiday (Map pp128-9; ☎ 2542 1525; www.copacabanaholiday.com.br; Rua Barata Ribeiro 90A, Copacabana) Rents apartments for a minimum of three days starting at US$30 per night. The manager Cláudio speaks English and is very helpful.

Fantastic Rio (Map pp128-9; ☎ 2543 2667; www.fantasticrio.hpg.com.br; Apt 501, Av Atlântica 974, Leme) Multilingual Peter Corr of Fantastic Rio rents a range of apartments, from modest one-bedrooms to spacious four-bedrooms with beach views.

Rio Apartment Services (☎ 2256 7920; www.rioapartmentservices.com) One of the larger agencies in town, it lists dozens of places for hire on its website.

Rio Flat Service (Map pp124-5; ☎ 2512 9922; 332 Rua Almirante Guilherm, Leblon) This Leblon-based agency has a range of local listings.

Vanna Rocha (☎ 2548 5030; www.vannarioflats.com) Vanna maintains a website of competitively priced apartment listings for Leblon, Ipanema and Copacabana. English spoken.

Yolanda Thiémard (Map pp128-9; ☎ 2267 0054; Av Prado Junior 165 C02, Copacabana) Yolanda has a small selection of apartments in Copacabana; her prices are among the best in the area. She speaks French and English.

Yvonne Reimann (Map pp128-9; ☎ 2267 0054; Apt 605, Av Atlântica 4066, Copacabana) Yvonne rents a range of apartments in the area, some with local phone service. She speaks French, German and English.

Hostel Ipanema (☎ 2247 7269; hostelipanema@justfly.com.br; House 14, Rua Barão da Torre 175, Ipanema; dm US$14) Next door to Harmonia, Hostel Ipanema is run by Carioca Paulo Celani, one of Rio's best hang gliders (p146). Accommodations are more basic than Harmonia's, but it's a friendly spot. Kitchen and laundry facilities are available, as well as bike rental.

MID-RANGE

Ipanema Inn (☎ 2523 6092; www.ipanema.com/hotel/ipanema_inn.htm; Rua Maria Quitéria 27, Ipanema; s/d from US$70/80) Simple but attractive, Ipanema Inn's rooms are pleasant with nice touches including woodblock prints on the walls and modern bathrooms with full tubs. Several suites on the top floors can accommodate larger groups. The multilingual staff is friendly.

Ritz Plaza Hotel (☎ 2540 4940; www.ritzhotel.com.br; Av Ataulfo de Paiva 1280, Leblon; d US$75, apt US$110; 🖳) This elegant all-suites hotel is in a sub-

lime part of Leblon. All rooms have kitchen units, balconies – some with partial ocean views – plus art on the walls, good lighting and spotless bedrooms. The one-bedroom apartments have a separate lounge/dining area. Excellent value.

Ipanema Flat Hotel Residência (☎ 2523 1292; fax 2287 9844; Rua Gomes Carneiro 137, Ipanema; s/d US$50/65) The place is suffering from a bad case of style envy: cheaply furnished rooms are seriously short on it and just aching to get some. The simple apartments have kitchens, balconies (no view) and bland but clean bedrooms at prices you're not likely to find elsewhere in this neighborhood.

Arpoador Inn (☎ 2523 0060; www.riodejaneiroguide.com/hotel/arpoador_inn.htm; Rua Francisco Otaviano 177, Ipanema; s/d US$60/70) This six-story hotel is the only one in Ipanema and Copacabana that doesn't have a busy street between it and the beach. The rooms here have decent beds and renovated bathrooms, although the carpets are a bit worn. A friendly staff,

---

THE AUTHOR'S CHOICE

Rio Hostel (Map pp136-7; ☎ 3852 0827; www.riohostel.com.br; Rua Joaquim Murtinho 361, Santa Teresa; dm US$13, d US$32; 🖳) The Rio Hostel provides travelers with a home away from home. The spacious lounge and backyard patio with pool add to the charm of one of Santa Teresa's hidden gems. The rooms are clean and comfortable, and the lovely double room features stunning views when you throw open the shutters – book it if you can. The hostel overlooks downtown Rio and lies along the *bonde* line. It can be a bit tricky to find – if you reach Praça de Curvelo (the first *bonde* stop), you've gone too far. Disembark and walk 200m back down the hill.

Cama e Café (Map pp142-3; ☎ 2221 7635; www.camaecafe.com.br; Rua Progresso 67, Santa Teresa; d from US$30) Cama e Café is a bed-and-breakfast network that links travelers with local residents. It has a pool of some 50 houses to choose from, and guests can select their accommodations by location, by comfort level or by shared interests – art, music, a love of small dogs – with their prospective host(s). All in all, it's a brilliant way of experiencing the charming neighborhood of Santa Teresa. Accommodations range from modest to lavish, with a decent breakfast and sizable rooms with private bathrooms common to all. Check Cama e Café's website to see listings.

Marina All Suites (Map pp124-5; ☎ 2540 5212; www.marinaallsuites.com.br; Av Delfim Moreira 696, Leblon; d from US$235) Marina All Suites offers style and comfort with wonderful ocean views. Elegantly furnished suites have decent sound systems and space enough for you to host your own small parties. That may be one of the reasons why the All Suites is popular with Giselle Bündchen and Arnold Schwarzenegger, among other well-known guests. The rooftop pool, private lounge space for guests and small movie theater are all nice touches. On the 2nd floor, the Bar D'Hotel (p167) attracts a mix of the beautiful crowd and modelizers.

Parthenon Arpoador (Map pp128-8; ☎ 3222 9600; parthenonarpoador@accorhotels.com.br; Rua Francisco Otaviano 61, Copacabana; ste from US$150; 🖳) The all-suites Parthenon Arpoador opened in 2003, which makes it one of Rio's newest hotels. It's also one of its most stylish. Young, good-looking staff lead guests to spotless suites with a cozy yet urbane air about them. Each has sleek white leather sofas that open into beds, modern kitchenettes, TVs with stereo and DVD player, ambient lighting and comfortable bedrooms. All have verandas – though there's no view. In addition to the long swimming pool, there's also a sauna and a workout room.

beach-facing bar-restaurant and excellent location near Ipanema make Arpoador an attractive choice.

Hotel Vermont (☎ 2522 0057; fax 2267 7046; Rua Visconde de Pirajá 254, Ipanema; d from US$62) One of the few nonluxury hotels in Ipanema, the Hotel Vermont offers guests no-frills accommodations in a high-rise a few blocks from the beach. The Vermont's small rooms need renovation. Still, the location can't be beat.

Hotel San Marco (☎ 2540 5032; www.sanmarco hotel.net; Rua Visconde de Pirajá 524, Ipanema; d from US$54) Like the Vermont up the road, it's all about location if you stay at the San Marco. Rooms are a bit cramped, and the green bedspreads aren't winning any style awards. In its defense, the rooms are clean, the staff is friendly and the beach is close.

Ipanema Sweet (☎ Rua Visconde de Pirajá 161, Ipanema; s/d US$80/110; 🖳) The modern, furnished apartments at this amiable spot each have a kitchen, lounge and balcony (no view), and are good value. A mix of Brazilians and international visitors consistently rate the place well.

TOP END

Everest Park (☎ 2525 2200; www.everest.com.br; Rua Maria Quitéria 19, Ipanema; d from US$105) Just a block from the beach in a fantastic neighborhood, Everest Park is a fine hotel. The multilingual staff is very approachable, and the rooms are comfortable and nicely maintained. A woodsy smell in the corridors brings a scent of the country to the place.

Caesar Park (☎ 2525 2525; www.Caesar-park.com; Av Vieira Souto 460, Ipanema; d from US$275; 🖳) One of Ipanema's finest hotels caters largely to business travelers, though the beachside location and excellent amenities attract a few well-heeled vacationers as well. Caesar Park features impeccable service, spectacular views, and modern, spacious rooms with artwork, flat-screen TVs and high-speed Internet connections.

Sol Ipanema (☎ 2525 8484; www.solipanema.com .br; Av Vieira Souto 320, Ipanema; d from US$120; 🖳) The 15-story Sol Ipanema has an enviable position overlooking the beach. The rooms recently received a much-needed renovation and now feature modern furnishings, sleek bathrooms and new carpeting. Ocean-front rooms cost about 20% more and are a worthy splurge if you can swing it.

Copacabana & Leme   Map pp128-9

Copacabana has the highest number of hotels of any neighborhood in the city; Av Atlântica is lined with them. The quality and price varies considerably here. During New Year's Eve, this is the best place to be. If you have a beach-facing view, you'll be able to see the fireworks from your window (which will be adequately reflected in your bill).

BUDGET

Rio Backpackers (☎ 2236 3803; www.riobackpack ers.com.br; Travessa Santa Leocádia 38, Copacabana; dm US$14; 🖳) Young backpackers flock to this popular spot. Guests have access to the pool table, lounge, kitchen and Internet. The welcoming Brazilian owner can advise on how to spend a decadent night out, arrange Portuguese lessons or provide other travel tips.

Che Lagarto (☎ 2256 2776; www.chelagarto.com; Rua Anita Garibaldi 87, Copacabana; dm/d US$14/30) This expat-owned hostel attracts a lively crowd that gathers around the pool table on most evenings for cheap drinks and pickup games. It's a good place to meet young partiers, but the quarters are tight here.

Pousada Girassol (☎ 2256 6951; pousadagirassol@ infolink.com.br; Travessa Angrense 25A, Copacabana; s/d/tr US$26/38/44) On a small lane off busy Av NS de Copacabana, two small pousadas lie side by side. Girassol is the better of the two and has bright, cheerful rooms with ceiling fans, decent beds and OK bathrooms.

MID-RANGE

Acapulco (☎ 2275 0022; www.acapulcopacabanahotel .com.br; Rua Gustavo Sampaio 854, Leme; s/d from US$40/50) Acapulco lies on a quiet street a block from the beach. Its 122 rooms are comfortable and clean, but could use an update. It has a handful of suites for those seeking a bit more room.

Hotel Santa Clara (☎ 2256 2650; www.hotelsanta clara.com.br; Rua Décio Vilares 316, Copacabana; s/d US$35/42) Up the street from a neighborhood park lies the charming Hotel Santa Clara, with its whitewashed exterior and blue shutters. The upstairs rooms are best, with wood floors, a writing desk and a balcony that catches a refreshing breeze in the evenings.

Hotel Debret (☎ 2522 0132; www.debret.com; Av Atlântica 3564, Copacabana; d from US$65) The Hotel Debret is a traditional hotel in a converted apartment building. It has simple colonial-style furnishings and great views from the top-floor restaurant. The ocean-fronting rooms *(luxos)* are good value.

Ducasse Rio Hotel (☎ 2522 1191; www.hotel ducasse.com.br in Portuguese; Rua Sá Ferreira 76, Copacabana; s/d US$45/55; ☒) At this price bracket, Ducasse is ahead of the rest. The medium-sized rooms are simply furnished but bright and cozy. All rooms ending in 1, 2, 3 and 4 have balconies, which are just large enough to step out onto and take a breath of ocean air.

Copacabana Hotel Residência (☎ 2548 7212; www.copahotelresid.com.br; Rua Barata Ribeiro 222, Copacabana; s/d US$70/90; ☒) A few blocks from the beach, the Copacabana Hotel Residência has 70 spacious suites with small kitchen units, living rooms and clean, well-maintained quarters. Although the rooms are all cheaply furnished, it's good value for the money. There are good discounts for long-term guests.

Augusto's Copacabana (☎ 2547 1800; www.aug ustoshotel.com.br; Rua Bolívar 119, Copacabana; s/d from US$65/75; ☒) Two blocks from the beach, Augusto's is a fairly recent addition to Copacabana. Its modern, comfortable rooms attract a mix of Brazilians, foreign visitors and 'businessmen in affairs' (according to the brochure). A rooftop pool, hot tub, sauna and fitness center are all additional features.

Copacabana Praia Hotel (☎ 2522 5646; www.copa cabanapraiahotel.com.br; Rua Francisco Otaviano 30, Copacabana; d US$60; ☒) All rooms in the 11-story hotel have balconies and top-floor digs have partial sea views. Rooms are comfortable but compact and a good deal.

Residencial Apartt (☎ 2522 1722; www.apartt .com.br; Rua Francisco Otaviano 42, Arpoador; s/d US$60/75) Located in Arpoador between Copacabana and Ipanema, this hotel has 25 one-bedroom suites, each with a small kitchen, a lounge room (with cable TV) and a bedroom. Furnishings here are dated – floral patterns, dingy yellows and greens dominate. Still, for all the space you get and the nearby beach location, the price isn't bad.

Atlantis Copacabana (☎ 2521 1142; atlantisres ervas@uol.com.br; Rua Bulhões de Carvalho 61, Copacabana; s/d from US$55/65; ☒) Between Copacabana and Ipanema, Atlantis is in a good location for exploring either neighborhood. The rooms here are short on elegance and inexpensively furnished, but the price isn't

bad and the staff is helpful. Rooms above the 9th floor have views.

Apa Hotel (☎ 2548 8112; www.apahotel.com.br; Rua República do Peru 305, Copacabana; s/d/t US$45/50/62) The Apa is dated but has decent prices, helpful staff and clean rooms.

Hotel Toledo (☎ 2257 1995; hoteltoledo@bol.com .br; Rua Domingos Ferreira 71, Copacabana; s/d US$45/55) A block from the beach, the Toledo has rooms in need of modernizing, but they're tidy and adequately furnished; the hospitable staff here struggles with English.

TOP END

Orla Copacabana (☎ 2525 2425; www.orlahotel.com .br; Av Atlântica 4122, Copacabana; s/d from US$95/120; ☒) The recently opened Orla Copacabana wins the style award – at least on this side of Arpoador. Sleek lounge chairs, artfully lit flower arrangements and giant canvases line the narrow lobby. Upstairs, the design falters a bit in lower-end rooms (standards) but still presents modern furnishings, excellent marble-fixtured bathrooms and decent views. The rooftop pool and patio are gorgeous.

Le Meridien Othon Palace (☎ 3873 8888; www .meridien-br.com; Av Atlântica 1020, Leme; d from US$150) A decadent affair, Le Meridien has all the trappings of luxury: the crisply dressed staff, the elegant lobby, the excellent French restaurant on the 37th floor. It's quite likely that your stay at this hotel will be a success. The rooms are comfortable and spacious but hardly inspiring. The view, however, is, so be sure to book the *de luxo* (luxury room).

Copacabana Palace (☎ 2548 7070; www.copaca banapalace.com.br; Av Atlântica 1702, Copacabana; d from US$300) The city's most famous hotel, the Palace has hosted heads of state, rock stars and prominent personalities. The dazzling white facade dates from the 1920s, when it became a symbol of the city. Inside you'll find spacious rooms with balconies, a wonderful pool, excellent restaurants – the formal Cipriani and the Pergula – and service suitable for royalty (Princess Di stayed here, as did Queen Elizabeth).

Sofitel Rio Palace (☎ 2525 1232; www.accorhotels .com; Av Atlântica 4240, Copacabana; d from US$180) Neck-in-neck with that *other* five-star hotel (the Copacabana Palace), Sofitel does its best to dazzle visitors with its lavishness. The excellent service, large and comfortable rooms, exquisite restaurants, beautiful pools and splendid views have earned the Sofitel many fans.

Botafogo & Urca

Botafogo and Urca are among the neighborhoods least explored by foreign visitors. There aren't many accommodations in the area, but this is where you'll find an authentic slice of Rio – its tree-lined streets, old-school *botecos* and undiscovered restaurants.

BUDGET

Carioca Easy Hostel (Map pp132-3; ☎ 2295 7805; www .cariocahostel.com.br; Rua Marechal Cantuária 168, Urca; dm US$15) This locally owned hostel gets excellent reviews from guests. A mix of Brazilian and international backpackers enjoys the tranquil location near Pão de Açúcar and the hostel's laid-back vibe. The friendly English-speaking owner takes an interest in her guests and helps to arrange nights out to samba clubs, dance parties or whatever they have in mind. It's the only place to stay in Urca.

Albergue da Juventude Chave Rio do Janeiro (Map pp132-3; ☎ 2286 0303; www.riohostel.com.br; Rua General Dionísio 63, Botafogo; dm US$12) The HI hostel in Botafogo was one of Rio's first hostels. It's still a successful endeavor, attracting a mix of Brazilians and international travelers to drink up Rio's nightlife. The dorm accommodates 70 and it often gets crowded here (reservations are wise). Nonmembers pay 50% more, but you can buy an HI card here for US$10.

MID-RANGE

O Veleiro (☎ 3473 3022; www.oveleiro.com; d US$50-80) O Veleiro is a bed-and-breakfast surrounded by remnants of Atlantic rain forest on all sides. It's a 20-minute walk up from Botafogo beach on an old, colonial cobblestone road, with a fine view of Cristo Redentor. There's a pool, backyard and garden on site. The owners only give out the address to those confirming reservations. For more information, visit the website.

Flamengo, Catete & Glória

One of Rio's oldest neighborhoods, Flamengo attracts visitors seeking an authentically Carioca experience – its neighborhood feel and youthful inhabitants add to the charm. Flamengo's other big draw is its

range of decent accommodations at much lower prices than those found in Copacabana or Ipanema. In Catete, budget hotels sprout like weeds from the crumbling buildings on either side of the Catete metro station. If you don't mind roughing it, you'll be able to take advantage of the city's cheapest accommodations.

BUDGET

Hotel Turístico (Map pp136-7; ☎ 2557 7698; fax 2558 9388; Ladeira da Glória 30, Glória; s/d US$25/29) On a quiet street near the Igreja de NS da Glória do Outeiro, the Turístico is a friendly spot with clean, well-maintained rooms – some with balconies.

Hotel Ferreira Viana (Map pp132-3; ☎ 2205 7396; Rua Ferreira Viana 58, Flamengo; s without/d with bathroom US$14/19-24) The best rooms here have good light, bright tiled floors, modern furnishings and plenty of space. Not all the rooms are decent, however, so see a few before committing.

Hotel Regina (Map ppv; ☎ 2556 1647; www .hotelregina.com.br; Rua Ferreira Viana 29, Flamengo; s/d US$27/37) On a quiet street in Flamengo, the Hotel Regina offers decent rooms with recently renovated bathrooms. The carpets are worn, the furnishings are cheap, and the floorboards creak, but overall the Regina isn't bad.

Hotel Riazor (Map pp132-3; ☎ 2225 0121; hotel riazor1@hotmail.com; Rua do Catete 160, Catete; s/d/tr US$15/18/28) The pretty colonial facade of the Riazor hides basic quarters, which are not bad for the price. Sparkling wall paint and round beds are features in some. Others are simple, straightforward affairs: bed, bathroom, TV, air-conditioning, door by which to exit the room and explore the city.

Hotel Rio Claro (Map pp132-3; ☎ 2558 5180; Rua do Catete 233, Catete; s/d/tw US$20/25/30; 🖄) The barebones Rio Claro is the best of the budgets for those looking to sleep on the cheap. Clean, well-maintained rooms have halfdecent beds and bathrooms with whitetiled floors.

Hotel Monterrey (Map pp132-3; ☎ 2265 9899; Rua Arturo Bernardes 39, Catete; s US$12, s/d with bathroom US$16/21) Short of sleeping in the metro station, you can't find much cheaper lodging than the Hotel Monterrey. Rooms here are basic: a small bed, a TV, a fan and maybe a window, but the place is fairly clean, and the owner is a kind-hearted soul.

MID-RANGE

Hotel Flórida (Map pp132-3; ☎ 2556 5242; www
.windsorhoteis.com; Rua Ferreira Viana 81, Flamengo; d from
US$72; 🏊) One of Flamengo's best hotels, the
Flórida has a variety of rooms. At the low
end, the space is small and the furnishings
dated, but the mattresses are still new and
the bathrooms are modern. The *luxos* have
huge beds, ample space and whirlpools in
the bath. The rooftop pool has terrific views
(including of Pão de Açúcar); there's also a
workout center and sauna.

Mengo Palace Hotel (Map pp132-3; ☎ 2556 5343;
mengohotel@infolink.com.br; Rua Corrêa Dutra 31, Flamengo;
ste s/d US$45/55) Offering some of the more af-
fordable suites in Rio, Mengo Palace is a
clean, modern hotel with a forlorn air about
it. The suites are small with pressed wood
floors, carpeting on the walls and whirlpool
bathtubs big enough for two. The beds are
a little stiff.

Imperial Hotel (Map pp132-3; ☎ 2556 5212; www
.imperialhotel.com.br; Rua do Catete 186, Catete; s/d from
US$35/45; 🏊) The Imperial Hotel is a good
choice for Catete. The lovely white building
has only three stories but goes back endlessly to reveal a crop of recently renovated
rooms and suites (the only difference between suites and *luxos* are the whirlpool
tubs. Most of the rooms are bright and well
maintained.

TOP END

Hotel Glória (Map pp136-7; ☎ 2555 7373; www.hotel
gloriario.com.br; Rua do Russel 632, Glória; d from US$90;
🏊) Once a grand 1920s beachfront hotel,
Glória still retains the aura of its past splendor. Red carpets line the hallways, which
are filled with old paintings, antique fixtures and liberal use of brass. Glória lost
its glory when the tunnel to Copacabana
was constructed. It later lost its beach in
1965, when landfill was landscaped into the
Parque do Flamengo. If you plan to stay
here, book your room in the old part of
the hotel, with its antique-filled rooms, fine
verandas and sitting rooms. The new wing
lacks the charm of the rest of the Glória.

Centro   Map pp136-7

Centro caters mostly to Brazilian business
travelers with small expense accounts. Aside
from its proximity to good lunch spots,
shopping areas and a few noteworthy street
carnivals, the area doesn't hold much appeal.

Centro is deserted and unsafe after 10pm
during the week and on weekends.

Ambassador Hotel (☎ 2299 2870; fax 2220 4783;
Rua Senador Dantas 25, Centro; s/d US$24/28) This
high-rise hotel has unintended style: a few
art-deco fixtures and trims are scattered
among rooms full of brown, angry curtains
and clinical-looking beds.

Center Hotel (☎ 2296 6677; www.centerhotel.com
.br; Av Rio Branco 33, Centro; s/d from US$50/60) This
12-story hotel, on busy Av Rio Branco, is
a good option for those wishing to stay in
Centro. Rooms are clean, comfortable and
have some nice touches – carved-wood
headboards, artwork on the walls. Higher
floors have decent views of downtown.

Guanabara Palace (☎ 2216 1313; www.windsor
hoteis.com; Av Presidente Vargas 392; d from US$110; 🏊)
Centro's nicest hotel has clean, modern
rooms with hardwood furnishings and nice
views of Baía de Guanabara. Some of the
rooms feel cramped, although there's abundant space on the rooftop, which has a pool,
bar and spectacular views of the bay.

Santa Teresa

Although accommodations are sparse in
the Montmartre of the tropics, some of the
more unusual accommodations options lie
just a short tram ride from Centro. The area
attracts travelers seeking the artistic heart
of Rio. Vibrant restaurants and bars and
its proximity to the samba clubs in Lapa
add to Santa Teresa's appeal, though you'll
want to take care when walking around,
day or night.

Hotel Santa Teresa (Map pp136-7; ☎ 2508 9355;
Rua Almirante Alexandrino 660, Santa Teresa; s/d without
bathroom US$12/18, s/d/tr with bathroom US$17/27/44)
The worn hotel has seen better days. Its
murky swimming pool and grungy carpets
need some work, and the rooms are spare
with flabby beds. Still, there's something
alluring about the place – perhaps its old
banisters and wooden stairs, tall ceilings
and shutters opening onto the city.

To stay in one of Rio's loveliest hostels or
in one of the locally owned mansions, see
the boxed text on p154.

EATING

Cariocas are known for their samba, their
football and their Carnaval, but most visitors still equate eating out in Rio to masti-
cating on rump roast at a beachside diner.

While the merits of Rio's many fine *churrascarias* (steak houses) should not be underestimated, the Cidade Maravilhosa has much more to offer than just *carne* (meat). In fact, the city is in the full grip of a culinary renaissance – and has been for some time. Every week eclectic new bistros, sushi bars and restaurants open their doors, creating some fierce competition for Rio's many epicureans.

The bounty of the coastline, the lush tropical setting (fresh fruit juices, anyone?) and the diversity of Rio's large immigrant population add up to some fantastic dining opportunities. Regional cuisines from all over Brazil – Minas Gerais, Bahia and even Amazonia – are well represented, and any night of the week you can enjoy traditionally prepared Italian, French, German, Japanese and Syrian cuisine.

In general, Ipanema and Leblon boast the best of Rio's dining scene. Here you'll find excellent chefs, beautifully set dining rooms and the style mavens that fill them. Centro's restaurants garner as many awards as those found throughout the Zona Sul, while Copacabana has both the hidden and the indiscreet, many of which spill along Av Atlântica and overlook the beach. Other areas have their gems, notably Santa Teresa, which has a handful of restaurants serving delightful cuisine amid lovely views, and Botafogo with its fine tucked-away spots.

Rio can be light or hard on the wallet. Juice bars and *botecos* are the cheapest places to get a meal, where you can order a *misto quente* (hot ham-and-cheese sandwich) and juice or a *prato feito* (plate of the day) for around US$3. Another budget option is the pay-by-weight restaurant.

THE AUTHOR'S CHOICE

Yorubá (Map pp132-3; ☎ 2541 9387; Rua Arnaldo Quintela 94, Botafogo; mains US$10-20; ⏰ 7-11pm Wed-Fri, 2-11pm Sat, noon-6pm Sun) Yorubá looks as if it's always ready for the arrival of an *orixá* (deity of Candomblé). Leaves lie scattered across the floor as candles flicker on the walls. Young waiters stand at attention while something mystical transpires in the kitchen. And if the gods Iemanjá or Oxúm were to pay a surprise visit, it's unlikely they'd be disappointed. Plates here are heavenly: plump shrimp and rich coconut milk blend to perfection in *babão de camarão*, and the *moqueca* (Bahian fish stew) is outstanding. As a final offering: don't pass up *queijo quebras* (condensed milk and coconut sweets).

Sushi Leblon (Map pp124-5; ☎ 2512 7830; Rua Dias Ferreira 256, Leblon; dinner for 2 US$25-45; ⏰ noon-4pm & 7pm-1.30am Mon-Fri, 1.30pm until last customer Sat & Sun) Leblon's premier sushi destination, Sushi Leblon boasts creative additions to its award-winning sashimi. Shrimp with foie gras and duck sashimi are all part of the menu. The usual stylish crowd gathers here – and the wait can be exhausting – so steel yourself with a few rounds of sake.

Cais do Oriente (Map pp136-7; ☎ 2203 0178; Rua Visconde de Itaboraí 8, Centro; mains US$8-14; ⏰ noon-4pm Mon, to midnight Tue-Sat) Brick walls lined with tapestries stretch high to the ceiling in this almost cinematic 1870s mansion. Set on a brick-lined street hidden from the masses, Cais do Centro blends West with East in dishes such as filet steak and sesame tuna. On Friday and Saturday night, live bands perform in the restaurant (US$10 cover).

Bar do Mineiro (Map pp136-7; ☎ 2221 9227; Rua Paschoal Carlos Magno 99, Santa Teresa; mains US$6-10; ⏰ 11-2am Tue-Thu, to 4am Fri & Sat, to 8pm Sun) Photographs of old Rio cover the walls of this old-school *boteco* in the heart of Santa Teresa. Lively crowds have been filling this spot for years to enjoy traditional Minas dishes. *Feijoada* (bean and meat stew served with rice and orange slices) is tops on Saturday. Other good-anytime dishes include *carne seca* (dried meat with spices) and *linguiça* (garlicky pork sausages). Strong *caipirinhas* will help get you in the mood.

Zazá Bistrô Tropical (Map pp124-5; ☎ 2247 9101; Rua Joana Angélica 40, Ipanema; mains US$10; ⏰ 7:30pm-midnight) French-colonial décor and delicately spiced cuisine await those venturing inside this charming converted house in Ipanema. Inventive combinations, such as pumpkin and chestnut risotto or sesame-battered tuna with wasabi cream, match the seductive mood inside. Upstairs, diners lounge on throw pillows, with candles glowing along the walls. You can also eat your dinner on the porch out front, enjoying healthy plates alfresco – everything served up here is organic.

Prevalent throughout the city, these eateries vary in price and quality, but average about US$7 per kilogram (a fairly loaded plate will cost US$4).

Mid-range places offer a vast array of dining options, and you can expect to pay between US$6 and US$10 for a main course. *Churrascarias* offer all-you-can-eat dining options (try to fast for at least six hours before going). Most charge around US$10 to US$15, which includes more food than you could possibly imagine (much less *eat*).

Ipanema & Leblon   Map pp124–5

Rio's most decadent dining scene offers a variety of international and Brazilian cuisines in a charming, neighborhood setting. By day its busy cafés and juice bars fill with bronze bodies heading to and from the beach, while at night its tree-lined streets set the stage for open-air dining. Rua Barão da Torre in Ipanema and Rua Dias Ferreira in Leblon are the major restaurant strips in each hood. The newest, hottest spots opening here don't always live up to the hype, but these twin neighborhoods feature plenty of time-tested favorites that do.

BUDGET

L'Assiette (☎ 2227 1477; Rua Visconde de Pirajá, Ipanema; weekday specials US$3.25; ☯ noon-9pm) This charming bistro, just off the beaten path, has a small but lovely menu of French specialities, none of which cost more than US$6. If you're really on a dime, try the weekday specials, featuring the plate of the day (stroganoff, grilled chicken etc) served with salad and a drink.

New Natural (☎ 2287 0301; Rua Barão da Torre 167, Ipanema; lunch specials US$4; ☯ 11am-6pm Tue-Sun) Featuring an excellent vegetarian lunch buffet, New Natural has fresh pots of soup, rice, veggies and beans for less than US$5.

Polis Sucos (☎ 2247 2518; Rua Maria Quitéria 70, Ipanema; juices US$1.50-3; ☯ 7am-midnight) Freshly squeezed fruits feature prominently in the 40 or so juices served at Polis Sucos, and you can pair those tangy beverages with sandwiches (vegetarian, chicken, filet mignon), *pão de queijo* (balls of cheese-stuffed tapioca bread) or a slice of *bolo* (cake).

MID-RANGE

Yemanjá (☎ 2247 7004; Rua Visconde de Pirajá 128A, Ipanema; moquecas for 2 US$12-20; ☯ 6pm-midnight Mon-

Thu, noon-midnight Fri & Sat, noon-10pm Sun) At this traditional spot, *bobó de camarão* (shrimp and coconut stew) and *moqueca* (seafood stew cooked in coconut milk) are an excellent introduction to Bahian cuisine.

Casa da Feijoada (☎ 2247 2776; Rua Prudente de Morais 10B, Ipanema; feijoada for 2 US$15; ☯ noon-11:30pm) At this 15-year-old institution, any day is fine to sample the rich, black bean and salted pork dish. The *feijoada* is served with the requisite orange slices, *farofa* (manioc flour sautéed with butter) and grated kale, all of which pair nicely with a *caipirinha*.

Gula Gula (☎ 2259 3084; Rua Aníbal de Mendonça 132, Ipanema; mains US$6-10; ☯ noon-midnight) Gula Gula is a popular, low-key spot serving quiches and salads, as well as grilled meats and other Brazilian dishes. For dessert, try the rich chocolate mousse. Order it *quente* (hot).

B! (☎ 2249 4977; Rua Visconde de Pirajá 572, Ipanema; salads US$4-6; ☯ 9am-midnight Mon-Sat, 1pm-midnight Sun) On the 2nd floor of the bookstore Livraria da Travessa, this stylish café makes a fine setting for a light lunch after some rainy-day browsing. Salads, quiches and chocolaty brownies are served by attentive waitstaff.

Capricciosa (☎ 2494 2212; Rua Vinícius de Moraes 134, Ipanema; pizzas US$9-13; ☯ 6pm onward) This trendy spot serves lovingly prepared, thin-crust pizzas with daring combinations.

Caffé Felice (☎ 2522 7749; Rua Gomes Carneiro 30, Ipanema; sandwiches US$5-8; ☯ noon-late) Try this indoor-outdoor spot for sandwiches, salads and *sorvete* (ice cream), which make a great combo after a steamy day at the beach.

Fellini (☎ 2511 3600; Rua General Urquiza 104, Leblon; plates US$8-15; ☯ 11:30am-4pm & 7:30pm-midnight Mon-Sat, 11:30am-4pm & 7:30pm-midnight Sun) Fellini's high-quality buffet has something for everyone: salads, pastas, grilled fish and shrimp, sushi and roast meats.

Nam Thai (☎ 2259 2962; Rua Rainha Guilhermina 95B, Leblon; mains US$7-13; ☯ 7pm until last customer Tue-Fri, noon until last customer Sat, to 10pm Sun) The charming, colonial Nam Thai features Thai and fusion dishes, such as spicy shrimp curry with pineapple and squid salad. Don't miss the *caipivodca de lychee* (litchi vodka *caipirinha*).

Vegetariano Social Club (☎ 2540 6499; Rua Conde de Bernadotte 26L, Leblon; mains US$5-8; ☯ noon-5:30pm) On Saturday vegetarians can sample Brazil's signature dish at this zenlike spot when tofu *feijoada* is served. Other offerings include salads, soups, *sucos* and organic wine.

TOP END

Osteria Dell'Angolo (☎ 2259 3148; Rua Paul Redfern 40, Ipanema; mains US$12-17; ⏲ noon-4pm & 6pm until last customer Mon-Fri, 6pm until last customer Sat & Sun) Northern Italian cuisine is served here with consummate skill, and the *risotto nero di sepia* (squid risotto in ink sauce) is one of the best dishes on the menu. President Lula, among other notable visitors, has dined here.

Satyricon (☎ 2521 0955; Rua Barão da Torre 192, Ipanema; mains US$16-25; ⏲ 6pm-2am Mon, noon-2am Tue-Sat, to midnight Sun) Satyricon serves pure decadence from its hallowed kitchen. Lovingly prepared fish, oysters and shrimp as well as delicacies such as live lobster sashimi are enjoyed by a well-dressed crowd – and the occasional international pop star.

Antiquarius (☎ 2294 1049; Rua Aristídes Espínola 19, Leblon; mains US$25-35; ⏲ noon-2am) It's hard to think of a better place to lay down some serious reais than five-star Antiquarius. The menu features items as decadent as wild boar in red wine sauce. Before venturing into the antique-filled dining room, don't forget to dress the part.

Zuka (☎ 3205 7154; Rua Dias Ferreira 233, Leblon; mains US$12-20; ⏲ 7pm-1.30am Mon, noon-4pm & 7pm-1.30am Tue-Fri, 1.30pm-1.30am Sat & Sun) This highly acclaimed restaurant serves excellent fusion cuisine, including morsels of tuna foie gras in thyme and smoked duck with caramelized pineapple.

CAFÉS & DESSERT SHOPS

Armazém do Café (☎ 2259 0170; Rua Rita Ludolf 87B, Leblon; cappuccino US$1.50; ⏲ 9am-midnight) Dark wood furnishings and the scent of freshly ground coffee lend an authenticity to this Leblon coffeehouse. Armazém also serves snacks and desserts.

Cafeína (☎ 2521 2194; Rua Farme de Amoedo 43, Ipanema; desserts US$2-4; ⏲ 9am-8pm Sun & Mon, 8am-11:30pm Tue-Sat) The popular café, in the heart of Ipanema, has outdoor tables for enjoying the waffles, desserts, dark coffees and espressos. There is also a branch in Copacabana.

Ateliê Culinário (☎ 2239 2825; Rua Dias Ferreira 45, Leblon; desserts US$3-4; ⏲ 6pm-1am Mon-Fri, 1pm-1am Sat & Sun) At this small café, specialities include dense cheesecake with guava sauce and moist chocolate cake.

Colher de Pau (☎ 2274 8295; Rua Farme de Amoedo 39, Ipanema; desserts US$2-5; ⏲ 10am-8pm) The cakes and pies here are irresistible. The popular charlotte de chocolate won't disappoint.

Kurt (☎ 2294 0599; Rua General Urquiza 117B, Leblon; pastries US$1.50-3; ⏲ 8am-5pm Mon-Fri) At Kurt, flaky strudels and palm-sized tortes with strawberries and kiwi fruit pair nicely with cappuccinos.

QUICK EATS

Ataúlfo (☎ 2540 0606; Av Ataulfo de Paiva 630, Leblon; sandwiches US$3, mains US$6-10; ⏲ 9am-midnight Mon-Thu & Sun, to 2am Fri & Sat) Grab quiche, a tasty sandwich or a juice at the front counter. In the back there's small but excellent self-serve lunch buffet. At night it's à la carte.

Celeiro (☎ 2274 7843; Rua Dias Ferreira 199, Leblon; salads US$6-10; ⏲ 10am-5.30pm Mon-Sat) This casual spot is famed for its salads, though the small eatery also serves excellent soups, pastries and quiches.

Da Silva (☎ 2521 1289; Rua Barão da Torre 340, Ipanema; plates US$7-15; ⏲ 11:30-2am) Da Silva spreads a fine buffet of excellent Portuguese cuisine, including lamb stew, pork tenderloin and delicate desserts.

Mil Frutas (☎ 2521 1384; Rua Garcia D'Avila 134A, Ipanema; ice cream US$2-4; ⏲ 10:30-1am Mon-Fri, 9:30-1am Sat & Sun) On chichi Rua Garcia D'Avila, Mil Frutas serves tasty ice cream that showcases fruits from the Amazon and abroad. Try the *jaca* (jackfruit), litchi or *açai* (berrylike fruit).

SELF-CATERING

Garcia & Rodrigues (☎ 3206 4100; Av Ataulfo de Paiva 1251, Leblon; ⏲ 8am-midnight Mon-Thu & Sun, to 1am Fri & Sat) This French restaurant has a lovely deli where you'll find breads and cheeses, a good wine selection and desserts.

Zona Sul Supermarket (☎ 2259 4699; Rua Dias Ferreira 290, Leblon; ⏲ 24hr, closed midnight Sun till 7am Mon) The best branch of Rio's supermarket chain stocks plenty of freshly baked breads, imported cheeses, wine, prosciutto and thousands of other products.

HortiFruti (☎ 2512 6820; Rua Dias Ferreira 57, Leblon; ⏲ 8am-8pm Mon-Sat, to 2pm Sun) Leblon's popular indoor fruit and vegetable market.

Mustafá (☎ 2540 7299; Av Ataulfo de Paiva 1174, Leblon; hummus US$2-4; ⏲ noon-7pm) This small take-out counter in Leblon serves fresh pita bread, tabbouleh, hummus and *kibe* (cracked wheat stuffed with spiced meat, then deep-fried).

Cobal de Leblon (☎ 2239 1549; Rua Gilberto Cardoso, Leblon; ☺ closed Sun) This charming market has lots of fruit and veggies for sale. You can also grab a bite at one of the many restaurants and cafés here.

Other *feiras* (produce markets) are on Monday on Rua Henrique Dumont (Ipanema), Tuesday on Praça General Osório (Ipanema), Thursday on Rua General Urquiza (Leblon) and Friday on Praça NS de Paz (Ipanema). On Sunday, the Hippie Fair, in Praça General Osório (Ipanema), has a stall in the southeast corner of the plaza where you can buy tasty Northeastern cuisine. Don't miss it.

Gávea, Jardim Botânico & Lagoa
Map pp124–5

With small outdoor restaurants perched along its shore, Lagoa is the region's centerpiece. During the summer, live music fills the air as diners eat, drink and stroll along the lake. The east side, around Parque do Cantaglo, offers more choices than the west side; a number of restaurants lies scattered in the streets overlooking the lake.

BUDGET
Braseiro da Gávea (☎ 2239 7494; Praça Santos Dumont 116, Gávea; plates US$4–8; ☺ 11–1am Mon-Sat) This open-air spot serves large portions of its popular steak, pot roast and fried chicken.

MID-RANGE
Lagoa Kiosks Parque Brigadeiro Faria Lima (Parque Brigadeiro Faria Lima, Jardim Botânico; mains US$5–12; ☺ 5pm until last customer Mon-Fri, noon until last customer Sat & Sun); Parque do Cantaglo (Parque do Cantaglo, Lagoa; mains US$5–12; ☺ 5pm until last customer Mon-Fri, noon until last customer Sat & Sun) Scattered along the edge of the lake lie a dozen or so restaurants, offering a range of regional and international cuisines. You can dine on sushi, Italian, Lebanese and German foods, or cuisine from Minas Gerais among others. Music happens nightly, making for one of Rio's more seductive open-air scenarios.

Guimas (☎ 2259 7996; Rua José Roberto Macedo Soares 5, Gávea; mains US$10–13; ☺ noon–1am) A classic open-air *boteco* with a creative flair, Guimas has been going strong for almost 20 years. Trout with leeks and roast duck

go well with superfine *caipivodcas* (vodka *caipirinhas*).

Mistura Fina ☎ 2537 2844; www.misturafina.com .br in Portuguese; Av Borges de Medeiros 3207, Lagoa; dishes US$8–14; ☺ noon-late) This popular Lagoa restaurant serves excellent cuisine, such as roast duck, filet mignon and *feijoada* (on Saturday). The nightly music shows upstairs and the views from the veranda downstairs, however, are the big attractions.

TOP END
00 (Zero Zero; ☎ 2540 8041; Planetário, Av Padre Leonel Franca 240, Gávea; ☺ 8pm-late) Inside Gávea's planetarium, 00 is a sleek restaurant-lounge that serves Brazilian cuisine with Asian and Mediterranean overtones. After dinner, have a few cocktails and stick around: some of Rio's best DJs spin at parties here.

Olympe (☎ 2539 4542; Rua Custódio Serrão 62, Lagoa; plates US$13–20; ☺ 7pm-12:30am Mon-Thu & Sat, noon-4pm & 7pm-12:30am Fri) The casual but stylish interior features the brilliant French cuisine of chef Claude Troisgros. Quail, risotto with crayfish and shrimp with Moroccan couscous are among the offerings.

Copacabana & Leme
Map pp128–9

Copacabana has a variety of choices, from venerable five-star institutions atop beachfronting hotels to charming mid-20th-century bistros. Although the open-air restaurants along Av Atlântica have a nice view, the food isn't so hot, and things get seedy here at night, as prostitutes and their dons crowd the outdoor tables.

BUDGET
Cervantes (☎ 2275 6147; Av Prado Júnior 335B, Copacabana; sandwiches US$3–6; ☺ noon-late Tue-Sun) This Copacabana institution gathers a mixed crowd who feast on trademark meat-and-pineapple sandwiches. Fussy waiters are quick to the tap when your *chope* runneth dry. Around the corner, at Rua Barato Ribeiro 7, is Cervantes' stand-up *boteco*, good for a meal in a hurry.

Carretão (☎ 2542 2148; Rua Ronald de Carvalho 55, Copacabana; all-you-can-eat US$8; ☺ 11:30am-midnight) It's all about the meat at this inexpensive *churrascaria*. There is another branch in Ipanema, at Rua Visconde de Pirajá 112.

Lope's Confeiteria (Av NS de Copacabana 1334, Copacabana; lunch plates US$3–4; ☺ 7am-midnight) Lope's is a vision of 1950s Rio: black-and-white photos along the walls, noisy lunch crowds, and food that hasn't changed much over the years – portions are large, grease is plentiful and the dessert shop lies next door.

Temperarte Av NS de Copacabana 1250 (☎ 2267 1149; Av NS de Copacabana 1250, Copacabana; plates US$4-8; ✆ 11am-10:30pm Mon-Sat, 11am-5pm Sun); Av NS de Copacabana 266 (Av NS de Copacabana 266, Copacabana; ✆ 11:30am-3pm) One of Copa's best pay-by-weight restaurants, it has salads, roast meats, vegetables, sushi and desserts.

Yonza (☎ 2521 4248; Rua Miguel Lemos 21B, Copacabana; crepes US$3-5; ✆ 10am-midnight Tue-Fri, 6pm-midnight Sat & Sun) A young crowd flocks to this colorful creperie at night to fill up on hearty, inexpensive plates. Best not to get too experimental: the simple *queijo e tomate* (cheese and tomato) is fine.

MID-RANGE

Siri Mole & Cia (☎ 2267 0894; Rua Francisco Otaviano 50, Copacabana; mains US$10-17; ✆ 7pm until last customer Mon, noon until last customer Tue-Sun) Understated elegance is the key to Siri Mole & Cia's long-standing success – both in ambience and in the perfectly prepared seafood. Among the favorites: *moqueca de siri mole* (spicy, soft-shell crab stew), and *acarajé* (spicy, shrimp-filled croquettes).

Amir (☎ 2275 5596; Rua Ronald de Carvalho 55C, Copacabana; platters for 2 US$7-12; ✆ closed Sun) A cozy air pervades this restaurant near the beach. Handsomely dressed waiters bring consistently good plates – hummus, *kaftas* (savory meat balls), falafel and salads – which are rivaled only by the delectable desserts.

Azumi (☎ 2541 4294; Rua Ministro Viveiros de Castro 127, Copacabana; plates US$7-14; ✆ 7pm-midnight Tue-Thu & Sun, to 1am Fri & Sat) This low-key sushi bar is a favorite among the *nisei* (second-generation Japanese born in Brazil) community. Azumi's *sushiman* (sushi chef) masterfully prepares delectable sushi and sashimi, though tempuras and soups are also excellent.

La Trattoria (☎ 2255 3319; Rua Fernando Mendes 7A, Copacabana; mains US$6-12; ✆ 11-1am) This casual but festive Italian trattoria has been a neighborhood favorite for over 25 years. Seafood pasta dishes come in particular recommended.

Le Blé Noir (☎ 2287 1272; Rua Xavier da Silveira 15A, Copacabana; mains US$8-12; ✆ 7pm-1am Wed, Thu & Sun, to 2am Fri & Sat) Flickering candles, subdued conversation and tasty crepes make this popular restaurant a real date-pleaser.

Marius (☎ 2542 2393; Av Atlântica 290B, Leme; per person US$18; ✆ noon-4pm & 6pm-midnight Mon-Fri, noon-midnight Sat & Sun) In addition to the array of juicy meats carried from table to table, this Leme *churrascaria* features a lavish buffet table full of oysters, sushi, grilled vegetables and much more.

TOP END

Cipriani (☎ 2545 8747; Copacabana Palace, Av Atlântica 1702, Copacabana; mains US$25-35; ✆ 12:30-3pm & 7pm-1am Mon-Sat, 12:30-4pm & 7pm-1am Sun) In a candlelit setting, Cipriani serves fine northern Italian cuisine to a well-dressed and largely non-Brazilian crowd.

Marius Crustáceos (☎ 2543 6393; Av Atlântica 290A, Leme; per person US$30; ✆ noon-4pm & 6pm-midnight Mon-Fri, noon-midnight Sat & Sun) Marius' all-you-can-eat seafood restaurant has many fans. The waiters file through the dining room bearing delectable fruits of the sea – tuna, salmon, lobster, mussels, scallops and other selections.

CAFÉS & DESSERT SHOPS

Bakers (☎ 2256 7000; Rua Santa Clara 86B, Copacabana; Danishes US$1.50; ✆ 9am-8pm Mon-Fri, to 6.30pm Sat, 9am-5pm Sun) Behind shiny countertops lie tasty banana Danishes, apple strudels and flaky croissants. Coffee and cappuccinos go nicely with the baked goods.

Cafeína (☎ 2547 8651; Rua Constante Ramos 44, Copacabana; pastries US$0.75; ✆ 8:30am-11:30pm Tue-Sat, 9am-8:30pm Sun-Mon) A few blocks from the beach, Cafeína is a pleasant indoor-outdoor spot that serves good coffee and a variety of baked goods, including quiches.

SELF-CATERING

Copacabana *feiras* by day fall on Wednesday on Rua Domingos Ferreira, Thursday on Rua Belford Roxo and Rua Ronald de Carvalho, and Sunday on Rua Decio Vilares.

Botafogo & Urca   Map pp132-3

Diners looking for something a little different should look to check out these neighborhoods.

BUDGET

Bar Urca (☎ 2295 8744; Rua Cândido Gaffré 205, Urca; lunch specials US$3-5; ✆ 11am-5pm) This upstairs spot has a nice view of the bay and inexpensive plates of *bobó de camarão*, grilled fish and squid.

Garota da Urca (☎ 2541 8585; Av João Luís Alves 56, Urca; mains US$4-8; ☼ 11am-late) Overlooking the small Praia da Urca, this neighborhood restaurant serves standard Brazilian fare, but the stunning views from the open-air veranda are the real draw.

MID-RANGE

Bom Dia Maria (☎ 2275 6971; Rua Elvira Machado 10, Botafogo; mains US$7-11; ☼ noon-4pm Tue & Wed, to 4pm & 7pm-midnight Thu-Sat, noon-6pm Sun) In an old mansion on a quiet street, Bom Dia Maria serves delights from Amazonia. You'll find wondrously spiced fish and stews – and intoxicating *caipirinhas* to accompany them (infused with Amazonian fruits such as *cupuaçú* and *murici*).

Adega do Valentim (☎ 2541 1166; Rua da Passagem 178, Botafogo; mains US$8-14; ☼ noon-1am) *Bacalhau* (cod) is the speciality at this old-fashioned Portuguese restaurant, which offers over a dozen different ways of preparation. Jocular old waiters also serve up plenty of other favorites.

Livraria Prefácio (☎ 2527 5699; Rua Voluntários da Pátria 39, Botafogo; mains US$4-7; ☼ 2-10pm) In the back of a small bookshop, this café is a charming spot for a light meal or a drink.

Pax (☎ 2550 9713; Praia do Botafogo 400, Botafogo; mains US$7-12; ☼ noon-8:30pm) Located on the 7th floor of the Botafogo Praia Shopping, Pax has an eclectic menu (pastas, seafood, meats) and spectacular views of Pão de Açúcar. It's one of many eateries in the mall.

Pizza Park (☎ 2537 2602; Rua Voluntários da Pátria 446, Botafogo; pizzas US$7-14; ☼ 10-1am) A lively crowd gathers at this popular spot until late into the evening most nights. Pizza Park's thin-crust pizzas and ice-cold *chope* are a beautiful combination on a steamy summer night.

Praia Vermelha (☎ 2275 7245; Praça General Tibúrcio, Urca; mains US$5-10; ☼ noon-midnight) Perched over the beach of the same name, Praia Vermelha has gorgeous views. By night, live *forró* and *chorinho* (an informal, instrumental genre of music that developed in Rio in the late 19th century) musicians play from 6pm onward. The ambience is spectacular, but the food *isn't*: pizzas from the wood-burning oven are the best bet.

SELF-CATERING

Cobal de Humaitá (Rua Voluntários da Pátria 446, Botafogo; ☼ closed Sun) The city's largest farmers market sells plenty of veggies and fruit; there are also numerous cafés and restaurants, which get quite lively on weekend nights.

Flamengo, Catete & Glória

Flamengo has its share of historic restaurants and young upstarts scattered among its tree-lined streets. On weekend nights, the restaurants and bars lining Rua Marquês de Abrantes grow crowded with people eating, drinking and flirting, all of which Cariocas do rather well. As the twin rulers of Rio's budget-hotel kingdom, Glória and Catete offer plenty of inexpensive restaurants to match. The northeast corner of Largo do Machado has a handful of restaurants that are quite popular.

BUDGET

Bonomia (Map pp132-3; Rua Marquês de Abrantes 38, Flamengo; juices US$1-2) The best juice bar in Flamengo serves more than 30 kinds of fruit juices. Try the delicious Amazonian flavors such as the smooth *cupuaçú* or the dark, rich *açaí*.

Abrantes (Map pp132-3; Rua Marquês de Abrantes 56, Flamengo; crepes US$2-4) This low-key restaurant and café prepares tasty dinner and dessert crepes.

Tacacá do Norte (Map pp132-3; Rua Barão do Flamengo 35R, Flamengo; Tacacá US$2.50; ☼ 9am-7pm) This simple lunch counter serves the traditional snack from the Amazonian state of Pará. Tacacá is a fragrant soup consisting of manioc paste, *jambú* leaves (an Amazonian herb) and fresh and dried shrimp. It's not for everyone, but then again, neither is the Amazon.

Catete Grill (Map pp132-3; ☎ 2285 3442; Rua do Catete 239, Catete; mains US$4-8; ☼ 11am-11pm) The Catete Grill has already won over the neighborhood for its excellent buffet – served all day long.

Estação República (Map pp132-3; ☎ 2225 2650; Rua do Catete 104, Catete; plates US$4-8; ☼ 11am-11pm) Estação's buffet table is a neighborhood institution. Featuring an extensive selection of salads, meats, pastas and vegetables, it's easy to indulge without breaking the bank.

MID-RANGE

Belmonte (Map pp132-3; ☎ 2552 3349; Praia do Flamengo 300, Flamengo; mains US$4-8; ☼ 7am-late) One of the most classic *botecos* in Rio, Belmonte is a vision of Rio from the '50s. Beneath globe lights, a few patrons steel their nerves with *cachaça* as unhurried waiters make their way across the tile floors, carrying plates of trout or steak sandwiches.

Churrascaria Majórica (Map pp132-3; ☎ 2285 6789; Rua Senador Vergueiro 11, Flamengo; ☿ noon-midnight Tue-Sat) Meat is very serious business at Majórica, and if you're looking for an authentic *churrascaria* experience, look no further.

Lamas (Map pp132-3; ☎ 2556 0799; Rua Marquês de Abrantes 18A, Flamengo; dishes US$8-14; ☿ 8-2:30am) This classic restaurant opened in 1874, and in spite of the mileage, dishes here hold up well. You can't go wrong with grilled *linguiça* or filet mignon.

Porção Rio's (Map pp132-3; ☎ 2554 8535; Av Infante Dom Henrique, Flamengo; all-you-can-eat US$15; ☿ 11:30am-midnight) Set in the Parque do Flamengo with a stunning view of Pão de Açúcar, this is an excellent *churrascaria*.

Taberna da Glória (Map pp136-7; ☎ 2265 7835; Rua do Russel 32A, Glória; US$5-10; ☿ 11:30am-1am) On a small plaza in the heart of Glória, the large outdoor eatery serves decent Brazilian staples, and its *feijoada* on Saturday still draws crowds.

Amazónia (Map pp132-3; ☎ 2557 4569; upstairs, Rua do Catete 234, Catete; mains US$7-12; ☿ 11am-midnight) Traditional Brazilian cuisine comes in many forms at this simple eatery: try the juicy steak, tasty grilled chicken with creamed-corn sauce or *feijão manteiga* (butter-simmered beans).

TOP END

Casa da Suíça (Map pp136-7; ☎ 2552 5182; Rua Cândido Mendes 157, Glória; mains US$10-20; ☿ noon-3pm & 7pm-midnight Mon-Fri, 7pm-1am Sat, noon-4pm & 7-11pm Sun) Tucked away on a quiet street in Glória, lies a slice of Switzerland in the tropics. Featuring flambés, fondues and an ever-changing menu, the Casa da Suíça creates an almost tangible aura of sensuality.

CAFÉS

Bistrô Jardins (Map pp132-3; ☎ 2558 2673; Parque do Catete, Catete; cappuccino US$1.25; ☿ 9:30am-6pm) Behind the Museu da República, this charming outdoor café overlooks the Parque do Catete and offers a verdant respite from the chaotic streets. Skip the lunch plates in favor of cappuccinos, desserts and quiches.

Centro
Map pp136-7

Catering to Rio's workaday crowds, Centro offers a wide variety of restaurants, from divey diners, haute cuisine, sushi bars and French bistros to juice bars and *churrascarias*. With a few exceptions, most restaurants open only for lunch during the week. An area worth exploring is Travessa do Comércio, just after work when the restaurants and cafés fill with chatter. The cafés and restaurants around Praça Floriano are also popular gathering spots.

BUDGET

Cedro do Líbano (☎ 2224 0163; Rua Senhor dos Passos 231, Saara; mains US$4-8; ☿ 11am-5pm) In the heart of Saara, this 70-year-old institution serves traditional Lebanese cooking: *kibes*, *kaftas*, lamb – tender portions of perfection.

Via Sete (☎ 2221 8020; Rua Sete de Setembro 43, Centro; wraps US$3-4; ☿ 10am-8pm Mon-Fri) A wooden patio fronts Via Sete, making a fine spot to enjoy the tasty wraps and sandwiches while watching Cariocas hurry about their day.

MID-RANGE

Ateliê Odeon (☎ 2240 0746; Praça Floriano, Cinelândia; mains US$6-10; ☿ noon-10pm Mon-Fri) Next to the cinema of the same name, the new Ateliê Odeon serves up decent Brazilian fare to a festive crowd on its open-air terrace. On weekends, Ateliê opens around film screenings next door.

Confeitaria Colombo (☎ 2232 2300; Rua Gonçalves Dias 34, Centro; desserts US$2-4; ☿ 8am-8pm Mon-Fri, 10am-5pm Sat) Stained-glass windows, brocaded mirrors and marble countertops create one of the most lavish settings for coffee or a meal.

Bar das Artes (☎ 2215 5795; Praça XV de Novembro 48, Centro; sandwiches US$3-4; ☿ 9am-8pm Mon-Fri, to 2pm Sat) Inside this book and record store in the Paço Imperial, lunchtime diners enjoy quiches, salads and lighter fare. Several other restaurants lie in this building.

Bar Luiz (☎ 2262 6900; Rua da Carioca 39, Centro; mains US$6-10; ☿ 11am-11:30pm Mon-Sat) A festive air fills this old saloon (opened in 1887), where you can get your fill of traditional German cooking – potato salad and smoked meats – along with ice-cold draughts.

Rancho Inn (☎ 2263 5197; 2nd fl, Rua do Rosário 74, Centro; mains US$5-8; ☿ 11:30am-3:30pm Mon-Fri) Exposed brick and tall windows overlooking the narrow street lend a vaguely Parisian air to this charming lunchtime spot. *Caprese raviolini* (mini ravioli stuffed with mozzarella, tomatoes and basil), grilled snapper, and daily lunch specials are all quite good.

Café do Rodrigues (☎ 3231 8015; Travessa do Ouvidor 17, Centro; lunch US$3-6; ☿ 9am-8pm Mon-Fri) Inside the quaint bookstore Livraria da Travessa, Café do Rodrigues serves lighter fare such as *torta do palmito* (heart of palm quiche), soups and flavorful salads.

De Miranda Café (☎ 2262 3552; Av Beira Mar 406C, Cinelândia; mains US$4-6; ☿ 11:30am-8pm) This charming little restaurant features a simple menu of Brazilian and international dishes, any of which plainly showcase the talents of the young chef. Try chicken with fruit compote and roasted potatoes.

TOP END

Miako (☎ 2222 2397; upstairs, Rua do Ouvidor 45, Centro; sushi for 2 US$12-24; ☿ 11:30am-3:30pm Mon-Thu, to 3:30pm & 6-11pm Fri) A bastion of tradition, Miako prepares sashimi and sushi that's no less exquisite than it was at its founding.

Le Champs Elysées (☎ 2220 4713; 12th fl, Av Presidente Antonio Carlos 58, Centro; mains US$12-20; ☿ 11am-4:30pm Mon-Fri) Gallic chefs reinvent themselves week after week to give diners a royal experience, supported by fine views over the city.

Restaurante AlbaMar (☎ 2240 8378; Praça Marechal Âncora 186; mains US$10-20; ☿ 11:30am-6pm Tue-Sun) Perched over the water, this old favorite offers excellent views of the Baía de Guanabara and Niterói. Favorites include *peixe brasileira* (fish in coconut milk).

CAFÉS

Casa Cavê (☎ 2222 2358; Rua Sete de Setembro 137; mains US$7-12; ☿ 9am-7pm Mon-Fri, to 1pm Sat) This simple but historic coffeehouse has a few stand-up tables and a long counter full of yummy desserts.

Santa Teresa & Lapa

Santa Teresa has a range of attractive dining spots. Great views, historic ambience and live music are a few of the ingredients that make the neighborhood's regional and international restaurants such an attraction.

BUDGET

Porta Quente (Map pp136-7; ☎ 2232 6298; Rua Almirante Alexandrino 470, Santa Teresa; pizzas US$4-8; ☿ noon-midnight Mon-Sat) Porta Quente serves

good, thin-crust pizzas, salads and lighter fare. The small café sometimes hosts live bands on the weekend.

MID-RANGE

Aprazível (Map pp136-7; ☎ 3852 4935; Rua Aprazível 62, Santa Teresa; mains US$10-16; ☿ 8pm-late Thu, noon-midnight Fri & Sat, 1-6pm Sun) Hidden on a windy road high up in Santa Teresa, Aprazível offers beautiful views and a lush garden setting. The menu features Brazilian fare with a twist: succulent quail and salmon with mango chutney. Thursday night is dedicated to live *chorinho* (US$5 cover). Reservations are recommended.

Bar Brasil (Map pp136-7; ☎ 2509 5943; Av Mem de Sá 90, Lapa; mains US$6-12; ☿ 11:30am-11pm Mon-Fri, to 4pm Sat) This restaurant serves traditional German cuisine: sauerkraut, wursts, lentils, and an ever-flowing tap quench the appetites of the sometimes-rowdy Lapa crowd.

Nova Capela (Map pp136-7; ☎ 2252 6228; Av Mem de Sá 96, Lapa; mains US$6-12; ☿ 11am-late) Like Bar Brasil next door, Nova Capela stays open late into the night, and fills with a garrulous mix of artists, musicians and party kids. Legendarily bad-tempered waiters (no surprise given what they have to work with) serve up big plates of traditional Portuguese cuisine. *Cabrito* (goat) is very popular.

Sobrenatural (Map pp136-7; ☎ 2224 1003; Rua Almirante Alexandrino 432, Santa Teresa; mains US$5-10; ☿ 11:30am-midnight Mon-Sat) The exposed brick and old hardwood ceiling set the stage for feasting on the *frutos do mar* (seafood). Lines gather on weekends for grilled fish and *moqueca*. During the week, stop by for US$3 to US$4 lunchtime specials.

QUICK EATS

Nega Teresa (Map pp132-3; Rua Almirante Alexandrino 1458, Santa Teresa; dishes US$2-4; ☿ 5-10pm Thu-Sun) Nega has quite a following in Santa Teresa. She's also won a few fans from more distant neighborhoods. They all come to sample her home-cooked Bahian specialties, such as *acarajé*, which she serves from a stand in front of Favela Hype (p172).

Barra & Greater Rio

Other parts of Rio offer some of the city's more rustic dining experiences. Outside the city limits one can find fresh seafood in open-air spots overlooking the coast.

Bira (☎ 2410 8304; Estrada da Vendinha 68A, Barra de Guaratiba; mains US$13-20; ☼ noon-midnight Mon-Sat) Splendid views of Restinga de Marambaia await diners who make the trek to Bira, about 45 minutes outside of the city. On a breezy, wooden deck, you can feast on *moquecas*, sea bass, shrimp and crabmeat pastries.

Tia Palmira (☎ 2410 8169; Caminho do Souza 18, Barra de Guaratiba; set lunch US$17; ☼ 11:30am-5pm Tue-Sun) A venerable destination for 40 years, Tia Palmira wins fans with its seafood *rodízio* (smorgasbord). Plate after plate of *vatapá* (a seafood dish with a thick sauce of manioc paste, coconut and *dendé* or palm oil), crab-meat, grilled fish, shrimp pastries and other fruits of the sea come to your table until you can eat no more.

DRINKING
Rio's drinking spots vary considerably. Leblon and Ipanema offer flashy nightspots, as well as old-school watering holes. A youthful bar scene draws revelers to Gávea, while a more sedate crowd enjoys Lagoa's scenic spots. Centro's narrow pedestrian streets attract drinkers during weekday cocktail hours, while a mix of old and new clutters the streets of Santa Teresa.

Ipanema & Leblon   Map pp124-5
Academia da Cachaça (☎ 2239 1542; Rua Conde de Bernadotte 26G, Leblon; ☼ noon-2am Mon-Sat, to 1am Sun) Although *cachaça* has a bad reputation in some parts, here the fiery liquor is given the respect it nearly deserves. This pleasant spot serves over 500 varieties.

Bar Bofetada (☎ 2227 1676; Rua Farme de Amoedo 87, Ipanema; ☼ 8am-late) A buff and predominantly gay crowd gathers at this lively Ipanema spot for cold drinks after a day at the beach.

Bar Bracarense (☎ 2294 7494; Rua José Linhares 85B, Leblon; ☼ 7-1am Mon-Fri, 9am-8pm Sat) A classic Carioca watering hole, Bar Bracarense is famous for its simple, unpretentious ambience and its heavenly *salgados* (snacks).

Bar d'Hotel (☎ 2540 4990; 2nd fl, Marina All Suites, Av Delfim Moreira 696, Leblon; ☼ 7-1am Sun-Thu, to 2am Fri & Sat) The waves crashing on the shore are part of the ambience at this bar overlooking Ipanema Beach. The intimate space is a magnet for the style set.

Caneco 70 (☎ 2294 1180; Av Delfim Moreira 1026, Leblon; ☼ 11-4am) Facing the beach, the large, open-air Caneco 70 is one of Leblon's most traditional after-beach hangouts.

Clipper (☎ 2259 0148; Rua Carlos Góis 263A, Leblon; ☼ 8-1am) At night, a celebratory air pervades this neighborhood bar as old bohemians, young professionals, burned-out socialites, and an occasional pro-footballer pack the indoor-outdoor space.

Cobal de Leblon (Rua Gilberto Cardoso, Leblon; ☼ closed Mon) Leblon's popular market features a number of open-air bars and restaurants, and it's a major see-and-be-seen destination in the summer.

Devassa (☎ 2540 6087; Av General San Martin 1241, Leblon; ☼ 5pm-late Mon-Fri, noon-late Sat & Sun) Serving Rio's best beer, Devassa makes its own creamy brews (in Vargem Grande), before offering them up to thirsty, festive crowds at the two-story *chopperia* (beer hall). An occasional Música Popular Brasileira (MPB) band adds to the din upstairs.

Empório (☎ 2267 7992; Rua Maria Quitéria 37, Ipanema; ☼ noon-2am) A young mix of Cariocas and gringos stirs things up over cheap cocktails at this battered favorite in Ipanema.

Garota de Ipanema (☎ 2523 3787; Rua Vinícius de Moraes 49, Ipanema; ☼ 10:30-2:30am) This bar is famed as the spot where Tom Jobim and Vinícius de Moraes wrote 'A Garota de Ipanema' (The Girl from Ipanema). Originally called Bar Veloso, the Garota is now pretty touristy, but the beer is ice-cold and the crowd is lively.

Lord Jim Pub (☎ 2259 3047; Rua Paul Redfern 63, Ipanema; ☼ 6pm-2am Mon-Fri, 2pm-3am Sat, to 2am Sun) Something of a novelty for Cariocas, Lord Jim is one of several English-style pubs scattered about the Zona Sul. Darts, English-speaking waiters and all the requisite expat beers are on hand.

Shenanigan's (☎ 2267 5860; Rua Visconde de Pirajá 112A, Ipanema; ☼ 6pm-3am Mon-Fri, 2pm-3am Sat, to 2am Sun) Overlooking the Praça General Osório, Shenanigan's packs crowds most nights. The exposed brick walls, pool table, and mix of spoken languages all contribute to the dark and pubby ambience.

Irish Pub (☎ 2227 6173; Rua Jangadieiros 14A, Ipanema; ☼ 7pm-late) Less of a pickup scene than Shenanigan's, the Irish Pub is full of visitors who've traveled a long way to get their hands on that pint of Guinness.

Gávea, Jardim Botanico & Lagoa   Map pp124-5
Bar Lagoa (☎ 2523 1135; Av Epitácio Pessoa 1674, Lagoa; ☼ 6pm-2am Mon, noon-2am Tue-Sun) Overlooking

the lake, Bar Lagoa is one of the neighborhood's classic haunts. Excellent beer flows among the ever-crowded tables, and a youthful air pervades the old bar.

Caroline Café (☎ 2540 0705; Rua JJ Seabra 10, Jardim Botânico; ☼ 6pm-3am Sun-Thu, to 4am Fri, 7pm-4am Sat) The usual sexy, young crowd fills the tables at this sceney indoor-outdoor spot.

Cozumel (☎ 2294 2915; Av Lineu de Paula Machado 696, Jardim Botânico; ☼ 8pm-late) Frozen margaritas and *caipirinhas* are consumed by the gallon at this Mexican nightspot in Jardim Botânico. Popular with a young, easily intoxicated crowd.

Hipódromo Up (☎ 2274 9720; Praça Santos Dumont 108, Gávea; ☼ 8-3am) Hipódromo Up is one of several bars in the area responsible for the local residents' chronic lack of sleep. A young college-age crowd celebrates here most nights.

Centro
Map pp136-7

Arco do Teles (☎ 2242 9589; Travessa do Comércio 2, Centro; ☼ noon-10pm Mon-Fri) Hidden in a narrow lane leading off of Praça XV de Novembro, the Arco do Teles is one of several open-air bars on the colonial Travessa do Comércio. The scenic lane is a popular meeting spot and gets crowded with Cariocas at workday's end.

Bar Occidental (Rua Miguel Couto 124, Centro; ☼ 5-10pm Mon-Fri) One of several sidewalk bars in the area, Bar Occidental is the place to go for ice-cold *chope* and fried sardines.

Santa Teresa & Lapa

Café Neves (Map pp142-3; ☎ 2221 4863; Largo das Neves 11, Santa Teresa; ☼ 6pm-late Tue-Sat) Small but charming, Café Neves is one of Santa Teresa's gems. It faces out onto Largo das Neves, and the occasional tram rattles by in the early evening. The open-sided bar draws a vibrant mix on weekends, and there's nearly always live music somewhere on hand. Several other lovely bars lie around the square.

Cosmopolita (Map pp136-7; ☎ 2224 7820; Travessa da Mosqueira 4, Lapa; ☼ 11am-late Mon-Thu, to 5am Fri & Sat) Behind the stained-glass doors of this 1906 saloon, patrons gather about the bar as the street scene unfolds outside.

Mike's Haus (Map p132-3; ☎ 2509 5248; Rua Almirante Alexandrino 1458A, Santa Teresa; ☼ 11:30am-midnight Mon-Sat) This German-style pub attracts a mix of expats and Cariocas on weekend nights. It's a bit off the beaten path, so plan on sticking around a while before moving on.

ENTERTAINMENT
Music & Dancing

Describing Rio's contemporary music scene is quite simple: Rio has one of the best music scenes on the planet. Trying to encapsulate the diversity of its musical offerings, on the other hand, is difficult in a city with so much to offer. Samba, jazz, bossa nova, MPB, rock, hip-hop, reggae, electronic music and the many fusions among them are a big part of the picture. Brazil's many regional styles – *forró*, *chorinho*, *pagode* (popular samba music) – are no less contributors.

JAZZ, CHORINHO & OTHER REGIONAL STYLES

Allegro Bistrô Musical (Map pp128-9; ☎ 2548 5005; www.modernsound.com.br; Modern Sound, Rua Barata Ribeiro 502, Copacabana; admission free; ☼ 9am-9pm Mon-Fri, to 8pm Sat) The small café in Copacabana's excellent music store, Modern Sound, features live music most nights of the week. The majority of groups plays from 5pm to 9pm, though Allegro has lunchtime performances periodically (1pm to 5pm).

Bar do Tom (Map pp124-5; ☎ 2274 4022; Churrascaria Plataforma, Rua Adalberto Ferreira 32, Leblon; admission US$10; ☼ 10:30pm Fri & Sat) A mix of Cariocas and tourists – but mostly tourists – fills this downstairs space at Plataforma in Leblon. The 350-seat bar has excellent acoustics and hosts a range of top musicians.

Café Teatro Rival (Map pp136-7; ☎ 2240 4469; www.rivalbr.com.br; Rua Álvaro Alvim 33, Cinelândia; admission US$5-15; ☼ closed Sun) Near Praça Floriano, this 450-seat hall hosts MPB, *pagode*, samba, *chorinho* and *forró* groups four or five nights a week, from 7:30pm. The schedule varies.

Clan Café (Map pp132-3; ☎ 2558 2322; Rua Cosme Velho 564, Cosme Velho; admission free; ☼ 6pm-1am Tue & Wed, to 1.30am Thu & Fri, 1pm-2am Sat) Set against the hillside of Corcovado, Clan Café has a large open-air patio that makes a great spot for live music. Tuesday belongs to *chorinho*, while MPB rules on Wednesday, and jazz on Saturday. The music starts around 9pm.

SAMBA CLUBS

Gafieiras (dance halls) are experiencing a renaissance in the bombed-out neighborhood of Lapa, and today this is center stage for Rio's nightlife. Inside of worn, colonial buildings, you'll find broad dance floors and long stages often packed with musicians. On weekends, music spills out into the streets on Rua do Lavradio, Rua Joaquim Silva and Rua da Lapa.

Dama da Noite (Map pp136-7; ☎ 2221 2072; www .damadanoite.com.br; Av Gomes Freire 773, Lapa; admission US$4-7; ☒ 9pm-2am Tue-Fri, 11pm-3am Sat) This 1907 mansion hosts excellent samba shows during the week. In addition to the stage and dance floor, an outdoor patio, several bars and a creperie (not to be missed) lie scattered about the old building. Check Dama's website for show listings or to reserve a table (recommended).

Estudantina Café (Map pp136-7; ☎ 2507 8067; Praça Tiradentes 79, Centro; admission US$3-5; ☒ 11pm-3:30am Thu-Sat) Overlooking the Praça Tiradentes, the old dance hall packs in large crowds on the weekend to enjoy excellent samba bands. The open-air veranda provides a nice spot to cool off.

Ballroom (Map pp132-3; ☎ 2537 7600; www.ball room.com.br; Rua Humaitá 110, Botafogo; admission US$5-8; ☒ from 8pm Sun-Wed, from 8:30pm Thu-Sat) Ballroom hosts various parties throughout the week. Orquestra Imperial gets the large dance floor going one night a week – currently Monday nights. The talented musicians play a brand of old-school samba with a modern-infused sound. Catch them if you can.

THE AUTHOR'S CHOICE

Casa Rosa (Pink House; Map pp132-3; ☎ 9363 4645; Rua Alice 550, Laranjeiras; admission US$3-7; ☒ 11pm-5am Fri & Sat, 7pm-2am Sun) In the first decades of the 20th century, Casa Rosa was one of the city's most famous brothels. Today the Pink House is one of Rio's best nightspots. It has a large outdoor patio between several dance floors, where different bands play throughout the night. There's also a thrift shop on the facility – open till about 3am. The rest of the party keeps going until dawn. Saturday is the best night to go, though Casa Rosa's new Sunday *roda de samba* (a traditional form of samba that features women dancing inside a circle to live samba beats) party also draws its fans – a good mix of Cariocas.

Rio Scenarium (Map pp124-5; ☎ 3852 5516; Rua do Lavradio 20, Lapa; admission US$5-6; ☒ 6:30pm-2am Tue-Sat) Perhaps Rio's most beautiful nightspot, Rio Scenarium has three floors, each lavishly decorated with antiques. Balconies overlook the stage on the 1st floor, where dancers keep time to the jazz-infused samba, *choro* (samba-related music) or *pagode*. The endless rooms in Rio Scenarium make for fine exploration if you need to walk off some of those *caipirinhas*. Many other nightspots are scattered along vibrant Rua do Lavradio.

Democráticus (Map pp136-7; ☎ 9864 1603; Rua do Riachuelo 91, Lapa; admission US$3-5; ☒ 9:30pm-2am Wed-Sat) Murals line the foyer walls of this 1867 mansion, and rhythms filter from above. Follow the sound up the marble staircase and out into a large hall filled with tables, an enormous dance floor and a long stage, covered with musicians. In spite of the high ceilings and vast interior, Anjos da Lua, the group that plays here on Wednesday, easily fills the space with music. A wide mix of Cariocas gathers here to dance, revel in the music and soak up the splendor of the samba-infused setting.

Casa da Matriz (Map pp136-7; ☎ 2266 1014; www.casadamatriz.com.br in Portuguese; Rua Henrique de Novaes 107, Botafogo; ☒ 11:30pm-5am Mon, Thu, Fri & Sat) Artwork decorates the walls of this avant-garde space in Botafogo. With numerous little rooms to explore – lounge, screening room, dance floors – this old two-story mansion embodies the most creative side of the Carioca spirit. Check the website for party listings – click *'festas.'*

Bip Bip (Map pp124-5; ☎ 2267 9696; Rua Almirante Gonçalves 50, Copacabana; ☒ 10pm-1am Mon, 9:30pm-midnight Tue, 8-11pm Sun) A storefront with a few battered tables, some yellowing photographs along the walls and a cooler full of unopened beer bottles is about all the ambience that Bip Bip has to offer. As the evening progresses, however, the tree-lined neighborhood becomes the setting as music and revelers spill out onto the sidewalk. For years, Bip Bip has been the underground favorite of musicians passing through town, and you never know who's going to show up at the impromptu jam sessions. Sunday is samba night. Monday and Tuesday nights are devoted to *choro*.

Carioca da Gema (Map pp136-7; ☎ 2221 0043; Av Mem de Sá 79, Lapa; admission US$3-5; ✶ closed Sun & Mon) This small, colorful club, situated on a busy Lapa street, hosts popular parties throughout the week. Friday and Saturday are samba nights. On other nights, the easygoing crowd meets up for rapid-fire *choro* or MPB.

Casarão Cultural dos Arcos (Map p136-7; ☎ 2552 8910; Av Mem de Sá 23, Lapa; admission US$4-6; ✶ 10pm-2am Wed & Thu, 11pm-4am Fri) A creatively decked place, the Casarão gathers young and the seriously dance-prone to its frequent jam sessions.

Centro Cultural Carioca (Map pp136-7; ☎ 2242 9642; www.centroculturalcarioca.com.br; Rua do Teatro 37, Centro; ✶ Tue-Sun) This restored theater, on Praça Tiradentes, books top samba groups throughout the year, and it's a historic setting in which to hear – and dance to – live music. To find out who's playing, check the website.

Sacrilégio (Map pp136-7; ☎ 2222 7345; Av Mem de Sá 81, Lapa; admission US$3-6; ✶ 8:30pm-1am Tue-Sat) Next door to Carioca da Gema, Sacrilégio is another charming spot for catching live bands in an intimate setting. It has a fine outdoor garden for cooling off.

SAMBA SCHOOLS

Starting in September, most big samba schools, in preparation for Carnaval, open their rehearsals to the public. These are large dance parties, and provide a good chance to mingle with Cariocas. Schools typically charge US$2 to US$5 at the door. Many samba schools are in the *favelas*, so use common sense when going.

You can visit the samba schools on a tour (see p151), or you can go by yourself: you can catch a taxi there, and there are always cabs outside the schools waiting to take people home. It's a good idea to confirm that the rehearsals are on before heading out. Following is a listing of some of the more popular samba schools, rehearsal days and contact information. The most popular schools for tourists are Mangueira and Salgueiro.

Beija-Flor (☎ 2791 2866; Praçinha Wallace Paes Leme 1025, Nilópolis; ✶ 9pm Thu)

Caprichosos de Pilares (☎ 2592 5620; Rua Faleiros 1, Pilares; ✶ 11pm Sat)

Grande Rio (☎ 2775 8422; Rua Almirante Barroso 5-6, Duque de Caixas; ✶ 10pm Sat)

Imperatriz Leopoldinense (☎ 2560 8037; Rua Professor Lacê 235, Ramos; ✶ 10pm Fri)

Mangueira (☎ 2567 4637; Rua Visconde de Niterói 1072, Mangueira; ✶ 10pm Sat) This school is popular and gets packed near Carnaval.

Mocidade Independente de Padre Miguel (☎ 3332 5823; Rua Coronel Tamarindo 38, Padre Miguel; ✶ 10pm Sat)

Paraíso do Tuiuti (☎ 3860 6298; Campo de São Cristóvão 33, São Cristóvão; ✶ 10pm Fri)

Porta da Pedra (☎ 2605 2984; Rua João Silva 84, São Gonçalo; ✶ 10pm Fri)

Portela (☎ 2489 6440; Rua Clara Nunes 81, Madureira; ✶ 10pm Fri)

Salgueiro (☎ 2238 5564; Rua Silva Teles 104, Andaraí; ✶ 10pm Sat) This is another good choice for tourists.

Tradição (☎ 3833 4612; Estrada Intendente Magalhães 160, Campinho; ✶ 10pm Fri)

União da Ilha do Governador (☎ 3396 4951; Estrada do Galeão 322, Ilha do Governador; ✶ 10pm Sat)

Unidos da Tijuca (☎ 2516 4053; Clube dos Portuários, Rua Francisco Bicalho 47, Cidade Nova; ✶ 11pm Sat)

Viradouro (☎ 2628 7840; Av do Contorno 16, Barreto, Niterói; ✶ 10pm Sat)

NIGHTCLUBS

Rio's vibrant dance scene features DJs spinning a wide variety of beats – from house and hip-hop to more uniquely Brazilian combinations such as electrosamba and bossa jazz. In addition to Brazilian DJs, Rio attracts a handful of vinyl gurus from New York, Los Angeles and London to spin at bigger affairs. Flyers advertising dance parties and raves (pronounced 'hah-vees') can be found in some of the boutiques in Ipanema and Leblon, and in the surf shops in Galeria River, near Praia de Arpoador. Most clubs give a discount if you've got a flyer.

Fundição Progresso (Map pp136-7; ☎ 2220 5070; Rua dos Arcos 24, Lapa; admission US$5-8; ✶ 11pm-4am Sat) An old factory with a battered facade hides one of Lapa's best Saturday-night parties. A celebratory straight and gay crowd finds its groove at this nonstop *festa*.

Melt (Map pp124-5; ☎ 2512 1662; Rua Rita Ludolf 47A, Leblon; admission US$5-10; ✶ 10pm-3am) The sinewy Melt club is one of those places that couldn't possibly be anywhere but Leblon. Models and their admirers lie draped around the candlelit lounge, while lovely waitstaff glide between the tables delivering peach- or guava-colored elixirs. Upstairs, DJs break beats over the dance floor, occasionally accompanied by a few percussionists.

00 (Zero Zero; Map pp124-5; ☎ 2540 8041; Planetário, Av Padre Leonel Franca 240, Gávea; admission US$5-10; ⏰ 10pm-4am Fri-Sat, 7pm-2am Sun) Housed in Gávea's planetarium, 00 is a restaurant by day, sleek lounge by night. A mix of Cariocas joins the fray here, though they mostly tend to be a fashion-literate, Zona Sul crowd.

Bunker 94 (Map pp128-9; ☎ 2521 0367; www .bunker94.com.br; Rua Raul Pompéia 94, Copacabana; ⏰ 11:30pm-3am Thu-Sat) Featuring big parties on weekends, Bunker 94 is one of Copacabana's big draws. Its three rooms fill with an eclectic mix of Cariocas and tourists as hip-hop, acid jazz, rock, trance or deep house plays overhead. Weekends get very crowded here.

Club Six (Map pp136-7; ☎ 2510 3230; Rua das Marrecas 38, Lapa; male/female US$15/10; ⏰ 11pm-6am Fri & Sat) Near the Arcos do Lapa, the castlelike Club Six has three dance floors, five bars and a number of loungey spots scattered about the building. DJs spin house, hip-hop, trance and MPB till daybreak.

Cube (Map p128-9; ☎ 9802 9020; Rua Francisco Otaviano 20, Arpoador; admission US$5-8; ⏰ 9pm-3am Thu-Sat) On the border between Copacabana and Ipanema, the Cube hosts weekend parties of changing themes. It features a number of relaxed rooms for quick retreats when the drum 'n' bass gets to be a bit much. Some nights feature live music – *chorinho*, samba and bossa nova – followed by DJs, so check listings to see what's on.

Nautillus (Map pp132-3; ☎ 2558 3431; Rua do Catete 124, Catete; admission US$3-5; ⏰ 11pm-4am Fri & Sat) Friday is the night to go to this dance spot in nightlife-starved Catete. Seriously young club kids converge here.

GAY & LESBIAN VENUES

In addition to the nightclubs listed below, Rio has a few prominent gathering spots for gays and lesbians. Check out the boxed text on p152 for more tips.

Dama de Ferro (Map pp124-5; ☎ 2247 2330; Rua Vinícius de Moraes 288, Ipanema; admission US$4-8; ⏰ 11pm-3am Fri-Sun) A mix of buff, Ipanema boys and older neighborhood queens checks each other out in the downstairs lounge before moving it upstairs to the dance floor. DJs spin house most nights.

Le Boy (Map pp128-9; ☎ 2513 4993; Rua Raul Pompéia 102, Copacabana; admission US$3-5; ⏰ 11pm-4am Tue-Sun) Trannies and pretty boys gather at this festive Copacabana dance club for dancing, drinking and perhaps just a bit of debauchery. A house-throbbing dance floor sprinkled with go-go boys and the Dark Room (the destination of choice after 3am) give this party space an air of unbridled celebration.

La Girl (Map pp128-9; ☎ 2247 8342; Rua Raul Pompéia 102, Copacabana; admission US$3-5; ⏰ 11pm-2am Tue-Sun) Rio's first and only girl bar, La Girl attracts a mix of lesbians – stylish and over-it – to this upstairs lounge in Copacabana. Run by the same owner as (and upstairs from) Le Boy, La Girl is a fine place without pretensions.

Blue Angel (Map pp128-9; ☎ 2513 2501; Rua Júlio de Castilhos 15B, Copacabana; admission US$2-4; ⏰ 10pm-2am Wed-Sat) Unmarked by day, at night, the blue light comes on and Rio's freethinkers converge. A mixed crowd arrives during the week, while weekends belong to the boys. It's a cozy bar, and on weekends there's not much room for dancing – although you'll probably want to (DJs spin a good mix).

Cinemas

Rio de Janeiro is one of Latin America's most important film centers. The market here is remarkably open to foreign and independent films, documentaries and avant-garde cinema. On weekends, theaters get crowded, so buy tickets (US$3 to US$5) early. For listings and show times pick up *O Globo*, *Jornal do Brasil* or *Veja Rio*.

Casa França-Brasil (Map pp136-7; ☎ 2253 5366; www.casafrancabrasil.rj.gov.br; Rua Visconde de Itaboraí, Centro) The small 53-seat theater shows French films and an occasional independent classic.

Cineclube Laura Alvim (Map p124-5; ☎ 2267 1647; Av Vieira Souto 176, Ipanema) Facing the beach, the charming Laura Alvim cultural center screens foreign and independent flicks.

Espaço Leblon (Map pp124-5; ☎ 2511 8857; Store 101, Rua Conde de Bernadotte 26, Leblon) This one-screen theater shows foreign and independent films. There is a number of restaurants and cafés nearby.

Espaço Museu da República (Map pp132-3; ☎ 3826 7984; Museu da República, Rua do Catete 153, Catete) In the dramatic Museu da República, film selections focus on world cinema – both contemporary and classic.

Espaço Unibanco de Cinema (Map pp132-3; ☎ 3221 9221; Rua Voluntários da Pátria 35, Botafogo)

This two-screen cinema shows a wide range of films. It has a lovely café inside and a used bookshop.

Estação Ipanema (Map pp124-5; ☎ 2540 6445; Rua Visconde de Pirajá 605, Ipanema) On the 1st floor of a small shopping complex.

Estação Paço (Map pp136-7; ☎ 2529 4829; Paço Imperial, Centro) This small screening room has an excellent selection of foreign and independent films.

Teatro Leblon (Map p124-5; ☎ 3221 9292; Av Ataulfo de Paiva 391, Leblon) Leblon's popular theater shows the latest Hollywood releases.

Odeon BR (Map pp136-7; ☎ 2262 5089; Praça Mahatma Gandhi 5, Cinelândia) Rio's landmark cinema, the Odeon is one of the last remnants of the once-flourishing epic of movie houses that gave the name to this neighborhood – Cinelândia.

São Luiz (Map pp132-3; ☎ 3221 9292; Rua do Catete 307, Catete) Catete's new cinema has three screens playing a mix of contemporary Hollywood and Brazilian releases.

UCI – New York City Center (☎ 2432 4840; New York City Center, Av das Americas 5000, Barra da Tijuca) Rio's largest megaplex features 18 different screening rooms, all with stadium seating.

Spectator Sports
FOOTBALL

Maracanã Football Stadium (Map pp142-3; ☎ 2568 9962; Rua Professor Eurico Rabelo, São Cristóvão; admission US$3-10) Nearly every child in Brazil dreams of playing in Maracanã, Rio's enormous shrine to football. Matches here rate among the most exciting in the world, and the behavior of the fans is no less colorful. The devoted pound huge samba drums as their team takes the field, and if things are going badly – or very well – fans are sometimes driven to sheer madness. Some detonate smoke bombs in team colors, while others launch beer bottles, cups full of urine or dead chickens into the seats below. Enormous flags are spread across large sections of the bleachers, as people dance in the aisles (this has been known to inspire a goal or two).

Games take place year round and can happen any day of the week. Rio's big four clubs are Flamengo, Fluminense, Vasco da Gama and Botafogo. Although many buses run to the stadium, the metro is safer and less crowded on game days. The safest seats are on the lower level *cadeiras* (chairs), where

the overhead covering protects you from descending objects. After the game, avoid the crowded buses, and go by metro or taxi.

To see some of Rio's favorite teams in action, go to their home stadiums:

Botafogo (☎ 2611 2656; Estádio Caio Martins, Rua Presidente Backer, Niterói) Its temporary stadium until 2006.

Flamengo (Map p124-5; ☎ 2529 0100; Estádio José Bastos Padilha, Av Borges de Medeiros 997, Lagoa) The stadium is also known as Estádio da Gávea. Most of Flamengo's home games are, however, played at Maracanã.

Fluminense (Map pp132-3; ☎ 2553 7240; Estádio Laranjeiras, Rua Álvaro Chaves, Laranjeiras)

Vasco da Gama (☎ 2580 7373; Estádio de São Januário, Rua General Almério de Moura 131, São Cristóvão)

HORSE RACING

Jockey Club Brasileiro (Map pp124-5; ☎ 2512 9988; www.jcb.com.br in Portuguese; 1003 Jardim Botânico, Gávea) One of the country's loveliest racetracks, the Jockey Club seats 35,000 and lies on the Gávea side of the Lagoa Rodrigo de Freitas opposite Praça Santos Dumont. It's a beautiful track, with a great view of the mountains and Corcovado, and a nice bar and restaurant overlooking the track. Races are held on Saturday and Sunday afternoons and Monday and Friday nights. The big event of the year is the Brazilian Grand Prix, which falls on the first Sunday in August.

SHOPPING

Rio has much in the way of shopping, from colorful markets straight out of the Northeast to chic Zona Sul boutiques. Some of the major strips in the city for window shopping and browsing include the following:

Av Ataulfo de Paiva, Leblon (Map pp124-5) Boutiques selling haute couture sprinkled among cafés, bookshops and restaurants.

Rua do Lavradio, Lapa (Map pp136-7) Rows of antique stores, mixed with hypermodern furniture shops, along with a few cafés and bars – sometimes inside the stores.

Rua Visconde de Pirajá, Ipanema (Map pp124–5) Ipanema's vibrant shopping strip has boutiques, shopping centers and scores of dining and coffee-sipping options.

Rua Senhor dos Passos, Centro (Map pp136–7) One of the main streets coursing through the Middle Eastern–bazaarlike Saara, with clothing and curio shops spilling onto the street.

Av NS de Copacabana, Copacabana (Map pp128–9) Packed during the week, this strip is lined with shops selling everything from chocolates to soccer balls. There are plenty of street vendors hawking their wares along the sidewalks.

Handicrafts & Artwork

Several of the best places to buy handicrafts are in Santa Teresa; other shops are scattered about town.

La Vereda (Map pp136-7; ☎ 2222 1848; Rua Almirante Alexandrino 428, Santa Teresa) A colorful selection of Brazilian handicrafts as well as work from local artists and artisans is featured here. You can buy pottery, furniture, paintings, handmade dolls and old prints highlighting historic Santa Teresa.

Trilhos Urbanos (Map pp136-7; ☎ 2242 3632; Rua Almirante Alexandrino 402A, Santa Teresa; ☜ closed Mon) Trilhos Urbanos has a small but interesting assortment of handicrafts. Works by local artists and artisans are also for sale – photographs, picture frames, paintings and works in metal.

Empório Brasil (Map pp124-5; ☎ 2512 3365; Rua Visconde de Pirajá 598, Ipanema; ☜ closed Sun) Hidden in the back of a small shopping center, Empório Brasil sells some of Rio's loveliest objets d'art. Works here showcase the talents and fibers of the country – jewelry, vases, instruments, baskets and an ever-changing array of works produced by Brazilian artists and artisans.

Ars Brasilis (Map pp128-9; ☎ 2287 2488; Rua Souza Lima 37, Copacabana) Colorful handicrafts from Minas Gerais and the Northeast are for sale here. The friendly shopkeepers also cook up small, tasty plates of cuisine from Minas Gerais.

O Sol (Map pp124-5; ☎ 2294 5099; Rua Corcovado 213, Jardim Botânico; ☜ closed Sun) Run by a nonprofit organization, this delightful store displays the works of regional artists and sells baskets, woven rugs and Brazilian folk art in clay, wood and porcelain.

No Meio do Caminho (Map pp124-5; ☎ 2294 1330; Av General San Martin 1247, Leblon; ☜ closed Sun) Showcasing the work of talented Brazilian artisans, No Meio do Caminho has two floors full of pottery, vases, ceramics and woodwork. Decorative items here are more akin to art pieces – and priced accordingly. No Meio do Caminho will ship goods anywhere.

Markets

Rio's best market is found at the weekend Feira Nordestina (p140) in São Cristóvão. There are also some other lively markets.

Babilônia Feira Hype (Map pp124-5; www.babiloniahype.com.br; Jockey Club, Rua Jardim Botânico 971, Jardim Botânico; admission US$2; ☜ 2-10pm Sat & Sun)

A younger crowd mills through the many clothing, sunglasses and jewelry stalls here on weekends. Often live bands and dance performances are staged here; you can also get your fortune read by místicos (fortune tellers) or receive a henna tattoo. Plenty of food stalls (mostly of the fried sausages and beer variety) litter the fairgrounds.

Hippie Fair (Feira de Arte de Ipanema; Map pp124-5; Praça General Osório, Ipanema; ☜ 9am-5pm Sun) The Zona Sul's big market, the Hippie Fair has lots of artwork, jewelry, handicrafts, leather goods and even furniture for sale. A stall in the southeast corner of the plaza sells tasty Northeastern cuisine.

Praça do Mercado Feira de Antiguidades (Map pp136-7; Praça Mercado Municipal, Centro; ☜ 9am-5pm Sat) This antique market, next to the Niterói ferry terminal, has a vast array of antiques and not-so-antique finds – silverware, carpets, pocket watches, jewelry, typewriters, records, art-deco and art-nouveau items. You can find nearly anything here, making it a browser's paradise.

Feira do Rio Antigo (Rio Antiques Fair; Map pp136-7; Rua do Lavradio, Centro; ☜ 10am-6pm 1st Sat of month) Although the Rio Antiques Fair happens just once a month, don't miss it if you're in town. The colonial buildings become a living installation as the whole street fills with antiques and music – samba and MPB bands – creating a fine ambience.

Music

Rio has a wide selection of music stores, and most places will let you listen to CDs before you buy.

Modern Sound (Map pp128-9; ☎ 2548 5005; www.modernsound.com.br; Rua Barata Ribeiro 502, Copacabana) One of Brazil's largest music stores stocks an impressive selection, including staff recommendations, top Rio artists and imports. Live music shows are staged here most days, at Allegro Bistrô Musical (p168).

Plano B (Map pp136-7; ☎ 2507 9860; Rua Francisco Muratori 2A, Lapa) An underground favorite among local DJs, Plano B has new and used records and CDs, as well as a tattoo parlor in the back.

Feira de Música (Map pp136-7; Rua Pedro Lessa, Centro; ☜ 9am-5pm Mon-Fri) During the week browse through bins of records and CDs at this open-air market in Centro.

Toca do Vinícius (Map pp124-5; ☎ 2247 5227; www.tocadovinicius.com.br; Rua Vinícius de Moraes 129,

Ipanema) Bossa nova's smooth grooves live on in this shop dedicated to old and new artists of the genre. Upstairs, Vinícius de Moraes fans can get a glimpse of his life's work in the small museum dedicated to him. Bossa nova concerts are staged here several nights a week.

Top Sound (Map pp128-9; ☎ 2267 9607; Av NS de Copacabana 1103C, Copacabana) A small store with a decent selection of new and used CDs.

Shopping Malls

Rio has quite a few large *shoppings* (malls). Most keep hours from 10am to 10pm Monday through Saturday. Some open on Sunday as well (3pm to 10pm, typically). The most centrally located mall is **Rio Sul** (Map pp132-3; Rua Lauro Müller 116, Botafogo) in Botafogo. For name-brand stores at discounted prices, don't miss **Rio-Off Price** (Map pp132-3; Rua General Severiano 97, Botafogo). The **Botafogo Praia Shopping** (Map p132-3; Praia de Botafogo 400, Botafogo) is also quite popular. For the most upscale boutiques, visit the small **São Conrado Fashion Mall** (Map p118; Estrada da Gávea 899, São Conrado). Barra is the kingdom of shopping malls. The largest is **Barra Shopping** (Map p118; Av das Américas 4666, Barra da Tijuca), which has 500 stores, 42 restaurants and five movie screens. A more stylish alternative is **Rio Design Center** (Map p118; Av das Américas 7770, Barra da Tijuca) where you can find elegant home furnishings and beautiful decorative pieces.

Urban Fashion

Favela Hype (Map pp142-3; ☎ 3852 8504; Rua Almirante Alexandrino 1458, Santa Teresa; ☑ 2-10pm Tue-Sun) Favela Hype is a gallery, thrift shop and café all rolled up into one. Browse through fashions from the '50s, '60s and '70s or take a peek at some of the vanguard fashions of local designers. Kitsch furnishings abound, and the gallery in the back hosts ongoing art exhibitions. The café serves tasty sandwiches and *caipirinhas*.

GETTING THERE & AWAY
Air

Most flights depart from Aeroporto Galeão (Map p118; also called Aeroporto António Carlos Jobim), 15km north of the center. Shuttle flights to/from São Paulo, and some flights for other nearby cities, use Aeroporto Santos Dumont (Map p118), in the city center. Many international airlines have

offices on or near Av Rio Branco, Centro. In addition to ticket counters at the airport, Brazil's principal airlines have the following offices in the city:

TAM (☎ 2524 1717; Av Rio Branco 245, Centro)
Varig Centro (Map p136-7; ☎ 2534 0333; Av Rio Branco 277, Centro); Copacabana (Map pp128-9; ☎ 2541 6343; Rua Rodolfo Dantas 16, Copacabana); Ipanema (☎ 2523 0040; Rua Visconde de Pirajá 351, Ipanema)
VASP Centro (Map pp124-5; ☎ 3814 8000; Rua de Santa Luzia 735, Centro); Copacabana (Map pp136-7; ☎ 3814 8094; Av NS de Copacabana 262, Copacabana); Ipanema (Map pp124-5; ☎ 3814 8098; Rua Visconde de Pirajá 444, Ipanema)

The following price information and schedule is subject to change. Prices quoted are one-way and leave from Aeroporto Galeão.

Destination	Airline	Cost	Frequency
Belém	Gol	US$292	daily except Sat
	TAM	US$354	daily
	Varig	US$264	3 daily
	VASP	US$173	daily
Fortaleza	Gol	US$190	2 daily
	TAM	US$242	4 daily
	Varig	US$267	4 daily
	VASP	US$210	3 daily
Foz do Iguaçu	TAM	US$195	daily
	Varig	US$181	2 daily
	VASP	US$189	daily
Manaus	Gol	US$205	daily except Sat
	Varig	US$286	2 daily with extra services Tue, Thu & Sun
	VASP	US$204	2 daily
Recife	Gol	US$194	daily
	Rio Sul	US$165	2 daily
	TAM	US$207	4 daily
	Varig	US$225	4 daily
	VASP	US$146	3 daily
Salvador	Gol	US$100	4 daily Sun-Fri, 3 daily Sat
	Rio Sul	US$125	2 daily
	TAM	US$142	4 daily
	Varig	US$175	3 daily, extra service Tue
	VASP	US$99	2 daily
São Paulo	Gol	US$145	4 daily
	TAM	US$81	8 daily
	Varig	US$88	3 daily, with extra services Tue, Thu & Sun
	VASP	US$80	2 daily

Bus

Buses leave from the **Rodoviária Novo Rio** (Novo Rio Bus Station; Map pp142-3; ☎ 2291 5151; www.novo rio.com.br; Av Francisco Bicalho, São Cristóvão), about 2km northwest of Centro. Several buses depart daily to most major destinations, but it's a good idea to buy tickets in advance. Many travel agencies in the city sell bus tickets. If you're in Centro, try **Dantur Passagens** (Map p136-7; ☎ 2262 3424; downstairs, Store 134, Av Rio Branco 156, Centro; ☑ 10am-5pm Mon-Fri).

If you arrive in Rio by bus, it's a good idea to take a taxi to your hotel, as the bus station is in a very seedy area. To arrange a cab, go to the small booth near the Riotur desk, on the 1st floor of the bus station. Average fares are US$12 to the international airport and US$10 to Copacabana or Ipanema.

In addition to destinations below, buses leave Novo Rio every 15 minutes or so for São Paulo (US$15, six hours).

Destination	Duration	Cost
International		
Asunción, Paraguay	30hr	US$42
Buenos Aires, Argentina	46hr	US$91
Santiago, Chile	60hr	US$106
National		
Angra dos Reis	3hr	US$6
Belém	52hr	US$85
Belo Horizonte	7hr	US$12
Brasília	18hr	US$35
Cabo Frio	3½hr	US$6
Curitiba	11hr	US$22
Florianópolis	18hr	US$34
Foz do Iguaçu	22hr	US$32
Goiâna	18hr	US$33
Ouro Prêto	7hr	US$12
Paraty	4hr	US$9
Petrópolis	1½hr	US$4
Porto Alegre	26hr	US$58
Porto Velho	54hr	US$88
Recife	38hr	US$60
Salvador	26hr	US$50
São João del Rei	5½hr	US$9
Vitória	8hr	US$13

GETTING AROUND
To/From the Airports

Rio's international airport, Aeroporto Galeão (GIG) is 15km north of the city center, on Ilha do Governador. Aeroporto Santos Dumont, used by most domestic flights, is by the bayside in the city center, 1km east of Cinelândia metro station.

Real Auto Bus (☎ 0800 240 850) operates safe, air-conditioned buses from the international airport (outside the arrivals floor of Terminal 1 or the ground floor of Terminal 2) to Rodoviária Novo Rio, Av Rio Branco (Centro), Aeroporto Santos Dumont, southward through Glória, Flamengo and Botafogo and along the beaches of Copacabana, Ipanema and Leblon to Barra da Tijuca (and vice versa). The buses run every 30 minutes, from 5:20am to 12:10am, and will stop wherever you ask. Fares are around US$2. You can also transfer to the metro at Carioca metro station.

Heading to the airports, you can catch the Real Auto bus in front of the major hotels, along the main beaches, but you have to look alive and flag them down.

Taxis from the international airport may try to rip you off. The safest course, a radio taxi for which you pay a set fare at the airport, is also the most expensive. A yellow-and-blue *comúm* (common) taxi should cost around US$25 to Ipanema if the meter is working. A radio taxi costs about US$35.

Boat

Rio has several islands in the bay that you can visit by ferry; another way to see the city is by taking the commuter ferry to Niterói. See p141 for more information.

Ilha de Paquetá (Map p118 ferries ☎ 2533 6661, hydrofoils ☎ 2533 7524) The regular ferry takes an hour and costs US$.50. The more comfortable hydrofoil takes 25 minutes and costs US$5. Ferry services run from 5:30am to 11pm, leaving every two to three hours. During the week, the hydrofoil leaves at 10am, noon, 2pm and 4pm and returns at 7:40am, 11:40am, 12:30pm, 2:30pm and 4:30pm. On weekends, it leaves Rio every hour on the hour from 8am to 4:30pm and returns hourly from 8:30am to 5:30pm.

Niterói (Map p118) The ferry costs US$0.75 and leaves every 20 minutes from Praça XV de Novembro in Centro (Map pp136-7). Faster and more comfortable catamarans run every 15 minutes from 7am to 4pm and cost US$2.

Car & Motorcycle

Driving can be a frustrating experience even if you know your way around. If you do drive in Rio, it's good to know a couple of things: Cariocas don't always stop at red lights at night, because of the small risk of robberies at deserted intersections. Instead they slow at red lights and proceed if no one is around. Another thing to know is that if you park your car on the street, it's common to pay the *flanelinha* (parking attendant) a few reais for looking after it. Some of them work for the city; others are 'freelance,' but regardless, it's a common practice throughout Brazil.

HIRE

Car-hire agencies can be found at either airport or scattered along Av Princesa Isabel in Copacabana. At the international airport, **Hertz** (☎ 3398 4377), **Localiza** (☎ 3398 5445) and **Unidas** (☎ 3398 3452) provide hire cars. In Copacabana the following are worth a try: **Avis** (Map pp128-9; ☎ 2543 8481; Av Princesa Isabel 350, Copacabana), **Localiza** (Map pp128-9; ☎ 2275 3340; Av Princesa Isabel 150, Copacabana), **Actual** (Map pp128-9; ☎ 2541 3444; Av Princesa Isabel 181, Copacabana) and **Hertz** (Map pp128-9; ☎ 2275 7440; Av Princesa Isabel 500, Copacabana).

Although no agencies hire out motorcycles, you can arrange a motorcycle tour with **Rough Trip** (☎ 2572 9991; www.roughtrip.com .br). See p151 for more details.

For more information on renting a car, see p706.

Public Transportation

METRO

Rio's subway system is an excellent, cheap way to get around. It's open from 5am to midnight Monday through Saturday and 7am to 11pm on Sunday and holidays. During Carnaval the metro operates non-stop from Friday morning until Tuesday at midnight.

Both air-conditioned lines are clean, fast and safe. The main line from Siqueira Campos in Copacabana to Saens Peña has 17 stops. The first 14 – from Copacabana to Estácio – are common to both lines. The lines split at Estácio: one line continues

west towards the neighborhood of Andaraí, while the secondary line goes north to São Cristóvão, Maracanã and beyond. More stations are planned in the coming years, and eventually Ipanema (Praça General Osório) will be linked to the system. You can buy one-way, round-trip or 10-ride tickets. A basic single costs US$0.75, and there's no discount for round-trip or multiple-ride tickets. Free subway maps are available at most ticket booths.

BUS & VAN

Rio buses are fast, frequent and cheap, and because Rio is long and narrow it's easy to get the right bus and usually no big deal if you're on the wrong one. Most buses going south from the center will go to Copacabana, and vice versa. The buses are, however, often crowded, stuck in traffic, and driven by raving maniacs. They're also the sites of many of the city's robberies, and it's not wise to ride late at night. On most buses you now board at the front, and pay the fare to the money collector. To avoid pickpockets and muggers, try to sit near the front of the bus. Avoid packed buses.

Minibuses (Cariocas call them vans) provide a faster alternative between Av Rio Branco in Centro and the Zona Sul as far as Barra da Tijuca. The destination is written in the front window. The flat fare costs US$1.50.

Taxi

Rio's taxis are reasonably priced and quite handy for zipping around town. The metered taxis charge around US$1 flat rate, plus US$0.50 per km – slightly more at night and on Sunday. Radio taxis are 30% more expensive, but safer.

A selection of radio taxis includes **Central-táxi** (☎ 2593 2598), **Coopatáxi** (☎ 3899 4343), **JB** (☎ 2501 3026) and **Transcoopass** (☎ 2560 4888).

Rio de Janeiro State

HIGHLIGHTS

- Exploring the pristine beaches and old prison ruins on beautiful **Ilha Grande** (p180)

- Twisting and turning through **Paraty's** (p185) colonial streets after a day of beach hopping.

- Trying to navigate the highly polished hardwood floors of Petrópolis' **Museu Imperial** (p195) while wearing mandatory protective fuzzy slippers

- Hiking through the wonderfully verdant and well-protected forests in **Parque Nacional de Itatiaia** (p193)

- Staying out all night with the locals in charming **Búzios** (p206)

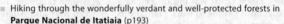

Parque Nacional de Itatiaia ★
Petrópolis ★
Búzios ★
Paraty ★
Ilha Grande

- POPULATION: 15 MILLION
- AREA: 43,919 SQ KM

Rio de Janeiro
State

A massive explosion of beauty permeates the mid-size (by Brazilian standards) state of Rio de Janeiro. Known for the sweeping grandeur of its beaches, backed by inland peaks, ridges and hills at least partially covered by tropical forests, this engaging swath of territory has something for everyone. Along the Costa Verde – which stretches to the west of Rio – and the giant Baía de Guanabara are hundreds of islands, including Ilha Grande and the Restinga de Marambaia, which make for easy swimming and boating. Beaches wait to be explored, particularly as you get farther away from Rio city. The coastal road stays close to the ocean here and the views are spectacular.

To the east, along the Costa do Sol, the littoral is filled with lagoons and swamps. Plains stretch about 30km from the coast to the mountains. Búzios and Cabo Frio, famous for their beauty and luxury, are only two hours from Rio by car. Saquarema, one of Brazil's best surfing beaches, is even closer. Driving due north from Rio city, you pass through the city's industrial section and soon reach a wall of jungle-covered mountains. After the climb, you're in the cool air of the Serra dos Órgãos. The resort cities of Petrópolis and Teresópolis are nearby, and offer Cariocas (residents of Rio de Janeiro) an escape from the tropical summer heat. The fantastic peaks of the Parque Nacional da Serra dos Órgãos, outside Teresópolis, provide superb hiking and climbing opportunities.

The other mountain region where Cariocas play is the Itatiaia area in the inland corner of the state, near the borders of São Paulo and Minas Gerais. Stop in for some Swiss chocolate, a sauna and a night of Finnish folk dancing – not too much has changed since some northern Europeans first set up camp here about a hundred years ago.

History

The first European visitors to Brazil arrived by ship on January 1, 1502. Thinking they were sailing into the mouth of a river (instead of a bay known to indigenous tribes as the Guanabara or arm of the sea), the Portuguese began referring to the area as Rio de Janeiro or January river. For a short while it appeared that the newcomers were going to cohabit peacefully with the indigenous people populating the coastline and interior valleys, but once colonizing started in earnest in the early 16th century, everything changed. The history of the state is associated with the development of roads and settlements along the outposts. Great effort was put into enslaving indigenous people to work plantations and converting them to Christianity. In the 16th century, the first established road linked Paraty with the valley of the Rio Paraíba, continuing into southern Minas Gerais. By the early 19th century, the first coffee plantations were established in the province, expanding throughout the 19th century as far as the state of São Paulo and other parts of Brazil. The crop was taken by mule train to new ports on the Baías de Guanabara, Sepetiba and Ilha Grande and these roads were the main means of communication until the coming of the railways after 1855. Rio state continues to generate significant revenue for the country thanks to a surge in the shipbuilding industry, but of course, tourism remains the primary source of income.

Climate

Climatically speaking, the best time to visit Rio state (and city, for that matter) is between May and August, when balmy trade winds cool the region and the average temperature hovers around the mid-80°F mark (around 30°C). Between December and March, the rainy season, it's hotter, wetter and just a wee bit wilder (think Carnaval).

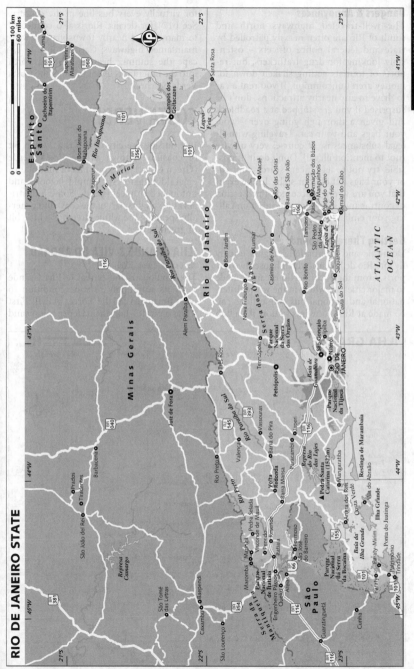

RIO DE JANEIRO STATE

0 ————— 100 km
0 ————— 60 miles

Dangers & Annoyances

The well-traveled highways north and south of Rio are often heavily patrolled by state and federal police officers – ostensibly looking for drug traffickers, but reports of tourists getting shaken down for money aren't uncommon. If you rent a car to drive to any nearby attractions, don't be surprised if you are stopped at a roadblock and given a thorough going over – you, your bags and your car. Traveling with illegal substances is, of course, very unwise (not to mention illegal). Don't do it. If possible, try not to let officers search your car or your bags out of your sight. In the event that you are wrongly accused of possession of contraband, stay calm and insist on calling your embassy.

Getting There & Around

Domestic and international flights usually fly into Rio de Janeiro, which houses two airports. From there, connections can be made to major cities anywhere in the world. International and national bus connections can be made at Rio's local bus station; it's a hub

for virtually every bus line in the country. See p174 for details. Rio is also connected to many of the nearby towns via two well-maintained highways; Cariocas love to escape the summer heat by heading north into the mountains or south along the Costa Verde beaches.

COSTA VERDE

Just outside the city of Rio is a 270km bit of coastline known as the Costa Verde (Green Coast), a unique mix of mountains, emerald rain forests, limpid lagoons and untouched tropical islands. Some industrialization blights part of the coast, but generally speaking the whole stretch is a little bit of green heaven.

ILHA GRANDE & VILA DO ABRAÃO

☎ 0xx24 / pop 3000

The fabulous island retreat of Ilha Grande owes its stunningly pristine condition to what Brazilians call the 'Forces of Evil.' First it was a pirates' lair, then a leper colony and

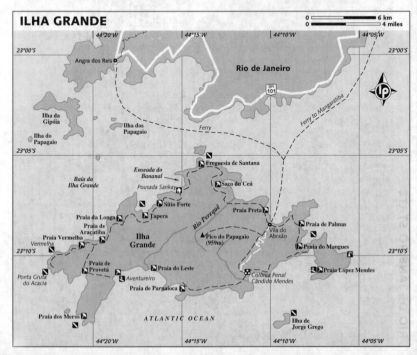

ILHA GRANDE

finally, a prison for some of Brazil's most violent and deranged criminals. All that remains of those days are some half-buried stone foundations (still hair-raising), but the island's history kept developers at bay for a long time. Consequently, beautiful tropical beaches and virgin Atlantic rain forest (now protected from development by the federal government) abound – there are actually only three settlements on the island. Freguesia de Santana is a small hamlet with no regular accommodations. Praia de Parnaioca has a few homes by a lovely strip of beach near the old prison, the Colônial Penal Câmdido Mendes.

Vila do Abraão is the main village on the island. Arriving at this palm-studded beachfront town, dominated by a tidy white church, is like stepping onto a movie set – it's so perfectly quaint. The village is comprised of a few dirt roads and everybody congregates down near the dock and beach at night, although new pousadas (guesthouses) and bars are popping up on the streets behind the main church all the time. On weekends and during high season it can get a bit claustrophobic, because as a base on Ilha Grande you can't go past Abraão – it's the only large settlement around.

Orientation & Information

The ferry from the mainland (Angra dos Reis and Mangaratiba) docks on the far west of Abraão's beach. As you disembark, look for the **Centro de Informaçoes Turística** (☎ 3361-5508; www.ilhagrande.com.br) kiosk on the right side. The hours of operation vary, but generally Marcia tries to be present for the arrival and departure of every ferry; she can make reservations for you, suggest a range of lodging choices, hook you up with local guides, get you on boats going to the other side of the island and generally just help out. The Centro de Informações Turísticas (see p174) in Angra dos Reis is also useful for information on the island.

In front of the tourist office is a small brown shack. National and international phone calls can be made from here, but the hours of operation are unfathomable. When an attendant is there, it's open. Also to the west of the dock are the ferry ticket office, a guesthouse for military police, the road to Praia Preta and the trail to the ruined old prison.

To the east of the dock is the cobbled Rua da Igreja, and at the far end of the beach, a trail leads to Praia de Palmas, Praia do Mangues and Praia Lopes Mendes. The main village of Abraão is easily visible to the east of the dock. The top-end hotels and tourist shops do change money but you'll pay for the convenience. Much better to do it before you arrive. There are no ATMs on the island, although credit cards are accepted at some places.

Activities

The options for things to do in the island are pretty attractive. Unsignposted trails through the lush, steamy forest lead to various beaches around the island. For instance, it is a three-hour trek from Abraão to **Praia Lopes Mendes**, which some claim to be the most beautiful beach in Brazil. It stretches for what seems like forever down the island's coast – not a building in sight. **Praia de Parnaioca** also ranks up there. And these are only two of the island's 102 beaches!

A visit to the old prison ruins makes for a fun, easy jaunt. Along the way you'll find tons of little beaches that locals jump in and out of (especially the kids coming home from school) and you can see and hear all sorts of birds, trees and jungle creatures. Once into the thicker part of the trail and near the ruins, the jungle's palpable weight really starts to oppress – it must have been terribly claustrophobic inside those old, moss-covered walls. To lighten the mood, follow the trail to the old aqueduct and keep a sharp eye out for the large natural river pool next to it. A fabulous spot for a picnic and dip in refreshing river water.

Tramping about the island to the beaches and abandoned penitentiary and through the forests, hills and waterfalls is a marvelous experience, but plan your trips wisely. Let people at your pousada know where you're going and when you'll be back (write it down for them) and stock up on water, bug repellent and bring a flashlight, as darkness comes swiftly under the jungle canopy. Guides are available and it's a good idea to hire one if you're really going to explore the interior – there have been reports of run-ins with poisonous snakes in recent years.

The **Associação de Barqueiros** (☎ 3361 5046) has an information booth near the dock. This outfit organizes day cruises to the northern beaches (from US$15 per person) and from December to March in good weather offers a circumnavigation tour of the island for US$40. A ton of scuba-diving and day-trip tour operators has sprung up recently and in low season rates are very reasonable. Ask about diving around the sunken helicopter – quite a sight!

Sudoeste SW Turismo (☎ 3361 5516; www.sudo estesw.com.br; Rua da Praia 647), next door to the Hotel Pescador, has excellent bilingual guides available for treks around the island. You can also arrange private boat tours with them or rent one of their kayaks.

Sleeping

Some street addresses in this chapter use the term s/n (*sem número*; without number).

BUDGET

The cheapest option is to camp and there is a slew of cute grounds set back from the beach on Rua Getúlio Vargas. Some locals also rent rooms, especially in high season. Just ask around as you stroll the main street.

Portal Abraão Pousada (☎ 9987 3032; Rua da Romana 85; s/d US$20/30) An attractive option not far from the beach, this pousada has a little sauna and offers very good value for your money.

Pousada Beira Mar (☎ 3361 5051; beiramar 2000@uol.com.br; s/d US$25/45) A good choice on the beach, 300m from the dock, is Beira Mar. Lutz, a German who has made

Abraão his home, enjoys meeting fellow travelers and showing them his extensive photo collection.

Pousada Casablanca (☎ 3361 5040; Rua da Praia 34; d from US$30) Just off the main beach path, Casablanca has clean, modern rooms, some with small balconies.

Camping das Palmeiras (☎ 3361 5059; campingd aspalmeiras@backpacker.com.br; Rua Getúlio Vargas 8; per person US$3) A very basic camp ground with reasonable facilities, most Brazilians like to come here and sling their hammocks up between the trees.

Emilia's Eco Camping (☎ 3361 5094; www.eco camping.com.br in Portuguese; Rua Amancio de Souza 18; per person US$5) Check out the table-tennis table at this place! There's lots of fun things to do at Emilia's, and amenities include separate showers (with hot water) for men and women.

MID-RANGE & TOP END

Several high-end hotels have set up shop in remote parts of the island. It's usually another hour of boating to get there once you've touched down in Abraão, but many are worth the extra effort. Most of the pousadas in Abraão cost between US$40 and US$70 for a double in low season (March to November). Prices double in summer (December to February); those quoted here are for low season.

Pousada Sankay (☎ 3365 1090; www.pousada sankay.com.br in Portuguese; s/d US$35/70) If you really, really, really want to get away from it all,

VILA DO ABRAÃO

| | 0 | 100 m |
| | 0 | 0.1 miles |

this is the remotest place you can go and still have protection from the mosquitoes. It's on Enseada do Bananal, on the north-western side of the island. Dinner included in the rate.

Beto's Pousada (☎ 3361 5312; Travessa do Beto 63; s/d US$20/30) You'll find spotless *apartament-os* (rooms with private bathroom) at Beto's and a friendly, helpful staff makes your stay that much more pleasant. Pretty rooms, well-appointed and with a nice breakfast.

Pousada Tropicana (☎ 3361 5047; Rua da Praia 28; s/d US$40/65) The French owner has turned this extremely popular pousada into some-thing of a brand unto itself – it now boasts a delicious (and expensive) restaurant on the grounds (which are very beautiful, by the way) and offers tours around the island. A lively, upbeat place, but expect to hear French or English more than Portuguese.

Hotel Mar da Tranquilidade (☎ 3361 5001; Rua da Igreja; s/d US$15/30) Sitting on top of the restaur-ant Adega do Corsário Negro, this hotel has good *apartamentos* but prices go up on weekends and things can get a little noisy when the crowds start packing in to eat.

Pousada Portal das Borbas (☎ 3361 5085; Rua das Flores 4; d US$40) This pousada is set just a bit back from the beach, a short stroll from the church along Rua Getúlio Vargas. It has rooms with verandas facing a nice garden courtyard and some with views to the hill and forest.

O Pescador (☎ 3361 5114; opescadordailha@uol.com .br; Praia do Abraão; low-/high-season d from US$40/55) Cozily furnished rooms and one of the is-land's best restaurants (don't miss the tasty local fish speciality *casquinha de seri*) make an excellent combination at this charming spot overlooking the beach. The friendly owners speak English.

Pousada Agua Viva (☎ 3361 5166; Rua da Igreja; d from US$30) Right across from the dock, this pousada has ample suites and top-notch amenities.

Ilha Azul (☎ 3361 5091; Rua da Igreja; d from US$25; 🖭) Straight up from the dock is the decent Ilha Azul. Upstairs rooms are best with plenty of light. A pool and hot tub are popular features.

Eating

There's no shortage of delicious places to eat on the island. Strolling along the beach to the left of the dock will bring you to Buganvilla, a small pedestrian walkway lined with cute shops, pizzerias, a self-serve and a couple of top-end restaurants. Dur-ing weekends and the high season you'll see lots of sweets carts being pushed about, and on the roads behind the main church, entrepreneurial islanders set up barbecues and sell delicious, freshly grilled seafood snacks (as well as frothy *caiparinhas*, made from sugarcane spirit and crushed citrus).

Minha Deusa (Rua da Igreja 7; lunch US$6) If you'd like a sit-down meal, this simple eatery next to the church serves excellent *caldo de ca-marão* (shrimp soup) and *moqueca* (deli-cious fish stew that's a regional speciality of Espírito Santo).

Kathe's Coffee House (Rua Santana; 🕓 4-11pm) Cappuccinos, cakes and sweets are served in this pleasant café. If it's raining they sometimes open earlier in the day (chess-board available).

Restaurante AleCrim (Rua da Praia 34; meals US$15; 🕓 6pm-midnight) Next door to the Casablanca, AleCrim is a small, pleasant spot, serving lovely steak and fish dinners with French overtones.

Getting There & Away

A Conerj ferry makes the trek between Ilha Grande and Mangaratiba and Angra dos Reis on the mainland several times a day. Ferries are sometimes added during high season and the schedule can fluctuate, so it's wise to confirm with your hotel when you make a reservation.

The ferry between Mangaratiba and Abraão (US$3, two hours) leaves Manga-ratiba at 8am daily and 10pm Friday; it leaves Abraão at 5:30pm daily. The ferry between Abraão and Angra dos Reis (US$3, two hours) leaves Abraão at 10am daily and Angra dos Reis at 3pm daily (an extra high-season service for US$5 leaves Angra dos Reis at 10am on Saturday and Sunday).

On the mainland, if you miss catching a Conerj ferry, head down to the Angra dos Reis docks and try your luck with the local fishermen. If enough people show up and are willing to pay then someone will usually agree to run you over to Ilha Grande (with a stop at a floating gas pump en route!) for about US$10 to US$15. These boats don't carry dinghies or life jackets and usually op-erate without any kind of headlights. When darkness falls and you're motoring along at a good clip the lack of lights certainly adds a lot of romance (as does the phosphorescence trailing from the sides) but if you can't swim, you might want to wait for the larger, safety-equipped Conerj. Also be aware that you may have to clamber across several other boats and then leap up to the dock at Ilha Grande to disembark – drivers often just pull up to a boat that's already moored rather than try to maneuver in closer.

ANGRA DOS REIS
☎ 0xx24 / pop 114,000

The savage beauty of Angra dos Reis's tropical, fordlike coastline has been badly blemished by industrialization. Supertankers dock in Angra's port, a railway connects Angra to the steel town of Volta Redonda, there's a Petrobras oil refinery and, thanks to the military government and the International Monetary Fund, a controversial nuclear power plant nearby. It's a good place for a stopover while heading to one of the islands or beaches offshore, but there's no real reason to linger.

INDIAN NAMES

Many place names you'll find in Rio state have their origins in Indian words, including the following:

Araruama – place where the macaw eats
Baré – in the middle of many fish
Cunhambebe – women who talk too much
Grataú – ghost's den
Grumari – a kind of tree
Guanabara – arm of the sea
Guaratiba – place with much sun or place of many holes
Ipanema – place that gives bad luck or place of dangerous sea
Itacuruçá – a cross made of stone
Itaipu – stone that the sea hits
Itaipuaçu – little Itaipu
Jabaquara – crack in the earth
Jeribá – a kind of coconut palm
Mangaratiba – banana orchard
Maricá – belly
Paraty – a kind of fish
Piratininga – dry fish
Sapeca – burned
Saquarema – lagoon without shells
Tijuca – putrid-smelling swamp

Information

Banco do Brasil (Rua do Comércio) Changes traveler's checks.
Bradesco Has an ATM diagonally opposite its branch office.
Cambisul Câmbio (Travessa Santa Luzia) Changes cash.
Centro de Informações Turísticas (☎ 3365 1175; Av Júlio Maria 10; ☉ 8am-7pm Mon-Fri & 9am-4pm Sat & Sun) Helpful, English-speaking staff provides information about attractions and places to stay in Angra and Ilha Grande.
Post office (Praça Lopes Trovão)
Telemar (Av Raul Pompéia 97) Long-distance telephone calls.

Sleeping

The nicest pousadas and hotels are to be found set back from the main highway leading from Rio and down to Paraty, or on strips of beach far from the city center. If you must stay in Angra, there are a few good options.

Porto Rico (☎ 3365 0992; Rua Colonel Carvalho 54; s/d US$10/15) If you want a shower in your room, the Porto Rico is your best budget bet. It has small, clean *apartamentos* with fans but no breakfast.

Pousada da Praia (☎ 3365 0605; Estrada do Contorno 2940; s/d US$15/30) Located on Praia Grande, this little pousada has a nice courtyard and classy rooms. To get there take the 'Vila Velha' bus.

Palace Hotel (☎ 3365 0032; Rua Coronel Carvalho 275; d US$45; ❀) A good place to come when you want a clean, three-star room with TV, telephone and hot water.

Eating

Taberna 33 (cnr Rua Coronel Carvalho & Rua Raul Pompéia; dinner US$10; ☉ 11am-4pm & 6pm-11pm) Good seafood and a nice atmosphere make Taberna a local hangout.

Fogão de Minas (Rua Júlio Maria 398; buffet US$6) Fogão de Minas, near the market, has very good and cheap self-serve by the kilo.

Getting There & Around

Angra's **bus station** (☎ 3365 1280; Largo da Lapa) is northeast of the center. Buses leave for Rio (US$9; three hours) every hour from 4am to 10:45pm daily and head to Paraty (US$4, two hours, six local buses) from 6am to 11pm daily.

During high season and on weekends the Costa Verde bus line that runs between

Angra and Rio will have a bus idling at the Angra docks to greet ferries returning from Ilha Grande, reservations not needed. If that bus fills up (very likely) before you can get in line, walk out to the main road from the dock and turn right, heading up the road until you see a plaza. Costa Verde buses to Rio stop here, as do local buses to Paraty. You don't have to double back to the bus station itself.

PARATY
☎ 0xx24 / pop 17,000

Oh! Deus, se na terra houvesse um paraíso, não seria muito longe daqui!
(Oh! God, if there were a paradise on earth, it wouldn't be very far from here!)

Amerigo Vespucci

Set on a shoreline of jutting peninsulas and secluded beaches, Paraty is backed by steep, jungled mountains that seem to leap down towards the hundreds of islands dotting the clear, warm waters. The town grew up and grew wealthy as a stopover between Rio and the Minas Gerais goldfields in the early 18th century, but started to decline when a new Rio–Minas road via the Serra dos Órgãos was opened in the 1720s.

Paraty is both a great colonial relic, well preserved and architecturally unique, and a launchpad to a dazzling section of the Brazilian coastline. The buildings have simple lines that draw the eye to the general rather than the specific, and earthy colors and textures that magnify, through contrast, the natural beauty that envelops the town. So, while the individual buildings in Paraty may well be attractive, the town, when viewed as a whole, is truly a work of art.

The town – a couple of kilometers off the Rio to Santos highway, in the southwest corner of Rio de Janeiro state – is easy to look around. Just stroll on the *pes-de-moleque* (street urchins' feet – the local name for the irregular cobblestone streets) washed clean by the rains and high tides. Dozens of secluded beaches are within a couple of hours of Paraty by boat or bus.

Paraty is crowded and lively throughout the summer holidays, brimming with Brazilian and European vacationers and good music. There are plenty of beaches to ac-commodate all visitors, and the town is renowned for its excellent *cachaça* (sugarcane spirit). It's truly a delight!

History
Paraty was inhabited by the Guianas Indians when Portuguese from São Vicente, 200km southwest, settled here in the 16th century. With the discovery of gold in Minas Gerais at the end of the 17th century, Paraty became an obligatory stopover for those coming from Rio de Janeiro, as it was the only point where the escarpment of the Serra do Mar could be scaled. The precarious road was an old Guianas Indian trail that cut past the Serra do Facão (where the town of Cunha in São Paulo is today) to the valley of the Rio Paraíba, and from there to Pindamonhangaba, Guaratinguetá and then to the mines.

Paraty became a busy, important port as miners and supplies headed for the gold mines disembarked, and gold was shipped to Europe. The small town prospered and, as always, the wealthy built churches to prove it.

Paraty's glory days didn't last long. After the 1720s, a new road from Rio via the Serra dos Órgãos cut 15 days off the journey to Minas Gerais, and Paraty started to decline. In the 19th century, the local economy revived with the coffee boom and now, with the recent construction of the road from Rio, the town's coffers are once again being filled. Until 1954 the only access to Paraty was by sea. In that year a road was built through the steep Serra do Mar, passing the town of Cunha, 47km inland. In 1960 the coastal road from Rio, 253km away, was extended to Paraty and 330km beyond to São Paulo.

Orientation
Paraty is small and easy to navigate, but street names and house numbers can be confusing. Many streets have more than one name (eg Rua Marechal Deodoro da Fonseca is also known as Rua da Cadeia), which is thoroughly perplexing for locals as well as tourists. The numbering system seems to be totally random.

Information
Baia de Paraty (Rua da Lapa 245; ☽ 10am-10pm) Internet access (also available in many other places around town).

Banco do Brasil (Av Roberto Silveira; ⏰ 9am-3pm) Changes cash and traveler's checks. A new Banco do Brasil has opened up near the bus station and has ATMs.

Centro de Informações Turísticas (☎ 3371 1897/ 1222; www.paraty.com.br in Portuguese; Av Roberto Silveira; ⏰ 9am-9pm) Staffed by friendly locals. Jackson speaks excellent English.

Post office (cnr Rua Marechal Deodoro da Fonseca & Rua Domingo Gonçalves de Abreu)

Telemar Office is at the bus station, for telephone calls.

Sights & Activities
CHURCHES

Paraty's 18th-century prosperity is reflected in its beautiful old homes and churches. Three main churches were used to separate the races.

The **Igreja NS do Rosário e São Benedito dos Homens Pretos** (Rua Dr Samuel Costa s/n) was built in 1725 by and for slaves. Renovated in 1857, the church has gilded wooden altars dedicated to Our Lady of the Rosary, St Benedict and St John. The pineapple crystals are for prosperity and good luck.

The **Igreja Santa Rita dos Pardos Libertos** (Rua Santa Rita) was the church for freed mulattos (persons of mixed black and European parentage). Built in 1722, it has a tiny museum of sacred art and some fine woodwork on the doorways and altars.

Capela de NS das Dores (Rua Fresca), the church of the colonial white elite, was built in 1800 and renovated in 1901. The cemetery is fashioned after the catacombs. **Matriz NS dos**

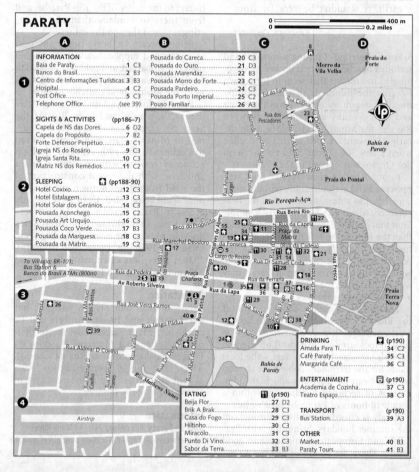

PARATY

| 0 | 400 m |
| 0 | 0.2 miles |

INFORMATION	
Baia de Paraty	1 C3
Banco do Brasil	2 B3
Centro de Informações Turísticas	3 B3
Hospital	4 C2
Post Office	5 C3
Telephone Office	(see 39)

SIGHTS & ACTIVITIES	(pp186-7)
Capela de NS das Dores	6 D2
Capela do Propósito	7 B2
Forte Defensor Perpétuo	8 C1
Igreja NS do Rosário	9 C3
Igreja Santa Rita	10 C3
Matriz NS dos Remédios	11 C2

SLEEPING	(pp188-90)
Hotel Coxixo	12 C3
Hotel Estalagem	13 C3
Hotel Solar dos Gerânios	14 C3
Pousada Aconchego	15 C2
Pousada Art Urquijo	16 C3
Pousada Coco Verde	17 B3
Pousada da Marquesa	18 C3
Pousada da Matriz	19 C2

Pousada do Careca	20 C3
Pousada do Ouro	21 D3
Pousada Marendaz	22 B3
Pousada Morro do Forte	23 C1
Pousada Pardeiro	24 C3
Pousada Porto Imperial	25 C3
Pouso Familiar	26 A3

EATING	(p190)
Beija Flor	27 D2
Brik A Brak	28 C3
Casa do Fogo	29 C3
Hiltinho	30 C3
Miracolo	31 C3
Punto Di Vino	32 C3
Sabor da Terra	33 B3

DRINKING	(p190)
Amada Para Ti	34 C2
Café Paraty	35 C3
Margarida Café	36 C3

ENTERTAINMENT	(p190)
Academia de Cozinha	37 C3
Teatro Espaço	38 C3

| TRANSPORT | (p190) |
| Bus Station | 39 A3 |

OTHER	
Market	40 B3
Paraty Tours	41 B3

To Villagio; BR-101;
Bus Station &
Banco do Brasil ATMs (800m)

Remédios (Praça Monsenhor Hélio Pires) was built in 1787 on the site of two 17th-century churches. Inside, there is art from past and contemporary local artists. According to legend, the construction of the church was financed by pirate treasure found hidden on Praia da Trindade.

FORTE DEFENSOR PERPÉTUO
Built in 1703 to defend the gold being exported out of Minas Gerais from pirate attacks, Forte Defensor Perpétuo was rebuilt in 1822, the year of Brazil's independence, and was named after Emperor Dom Pedro I. It's on the Morro da Vila Velha, the hill just past Praia do Pontal, a 20-minute walk north of town. The fort houses the **Casa de Artista e Centro de Artes e Tradições Populares de Paraty** (admission free; 10am-5pm Tue-Sun) a combination museum and gallery that has a permanent display of fishing implements and baskets, and sells local handicrafts.

ISLANDS & BEACHES
Paraty has some 65 islands and 300 beaches in its vicinity. To visit the less accessible beaches, many tourists take one of the schooners from the docks. There are signs advertised all over town, tickets average about US$12 per person, with lunch served on board for an additional US$8. The boats make three beach stops of about 45 minutes each.

A more independent alternative is to head out to the small stone quay and rent a *lancha* (small boat) by the hour. If you figure on a one-hour boat ride and an hour at the beach, you need a boat for at least three hours – more if you want to really explore or make a day of picnicking and snorkeling. The average price is about US$15 an hour, but the more people you travel with the less you pay. **Daniel Vieira** (☎ 9916 9774), owner of the Brulu, is a great driver – environmentally conscious and very familiar with all the best spots to snorkel, scuba and splash around. His boat can take up to 16 passengers and is equipped with convenient parasols for the fair-skinned and a pillow-covered deck for sun worshipers. There's a freshwater shower to desalinate after a bathe, and he makes *caipirinhas* (the Brazilian national drink: the sugarcane alcohol *cachaça* with crushed lime, sugar and ice) on demand (abstaining himself, as he's an extremely reliable skipper).

The closest fine beaches on the coast – **Vermelha** and **Lulas** (both northeast of Paraty) and **Saco** (to the east) – are about an hour away by boat. Camping is available on the beaches. The best island beaches nearby are probably **Araújo and Sapeca**, but many of the islands have rocky shores and are private. The mainland beaches tend to be better; small and idyllic; most have *barracas* (stalls) serving beer and fish and, at most, a handful of beachgoers.

Praia do Pontal, about 10 minutes away from town by foot, is Paraty's city beach. There are several *barracas* and a lively crowd, but the beach itself is not attractive and the water gets dirty.

On the side of the hill, hidden by the rocks, **Praia do Forte** is the cleanest beach within a quick walk of the city. It is relatively secluded and frequented by a youngish crowd.

Continue on the dirt road north past Praia do Pontal, over the hill, for 2km to **Praia do Jabaquara**, a big, spacious beach with great views in all directions. There is a small restaurant and a camping ground that's better than those in town. The sea is very shallow, so it's possible to wade way out into the bay.

Tours
Paraty Tours (☎ 3371 1327; www.paratytours.com.br; Av Roberto Silveira 11; ☺ 9am-8pm), located just before you reach the colonial part of town, is a good source of information and offers a range of tours: kayaking, biking, horseback riding and diving. Its schooner tours are the big sellers. The five-hour schooner cruises cost US$9 and depart daily at 10am, 11am and noon. Paraty also rents bicycles for US$1.75 an hour or US$7 per day.

Festivals & Events
Paraty is known for colorful and distinctive festivals (see http://paraty.com/acontece/index.htm for more information). The two most important are the **Festa do Divino Espírito Santo**, which begins nine days before Pentecostal Sunday (the seventh Sunday after Easter), and the **Festa de NS dos Remédios**, on September 8. Both festivals are a little more somber in tone than Carnaval, but you'll still get plenty of dancing and late-night partying.

The **Festas Juninas**, during June, are filled with dances, including the *xiba* (a circle clog dance) and the *ciranda* (a xiba with guitar accompaniment). The festivals culminate on June 29 with a maritime procession to Ilha do Araújo. Paraty is a good option for **Carnaval** – young people come in droves to cover themselves in mud and dance through the streets.

The Paraty region produces excellent *cachaça*, and in 1984 the town council in its wisdom inaugurated the annual **Festival da Pinga**. The pinga *(cachaça)* party is held over an August weekend.

Sleeping

From December to February hotels get booked up and room prices double, so reservations are a good idea. The rest of the year, finding accommodations is easy and not expensive, the town is quiet and some of the boutiques and restaurants close for the winter. The prices quoted here are low-season rates. Paraty is a favorite destination for gay and lesbian crowds and all locations should be considered gay-friendly.

BUDGET

Pouso Familiar (☎ 3371 1475; Rua José Vieira Ramos 262; s/d US$8/16) A friendly place run by Joseph and Lúcia, a Belgian/Brazilian couple, Pouso Familiar is close to the bus station, has good clean rooms and clothes-washing facilities. Joseph speaks English, German, French, Spanish and Dutch (of course), and is very helpful.

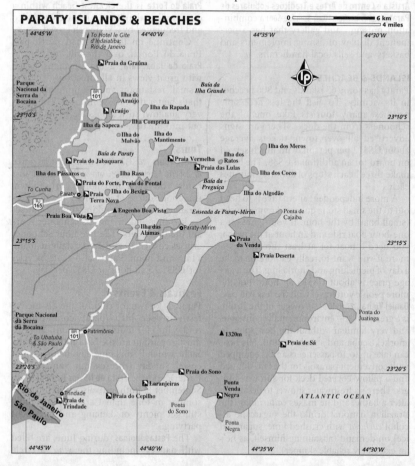

PARATY ISLANDS & BEACHES

0 — 6 km
0 — 4 miles

To Hotel le Gîte d'Indaiatiba; Rio de Janeiro

Praia da Graúna

Parque Nacional da Serra da Bocaina

BR 101

Ilha do Araújo

Araújo

Ilha da Rapada

Baía da Ilha Grande

23°10'S

Ilha da Sapeca   Ilha Comprida

Ilha do Malvão   Ilha do Mantimento

Baía de Paraty   Praia Vermelha   Ilha dos Ratos   Ilha dos Meros

Praia do Jabaquara   Praia das Lulas

Ilha dos Pássaros   Ilha Rasa   Ilha dos Cocos

To Cunha   Praia do Forte, Praia do Pontal   Baía da Preguiça

RJ 165   Paraty   Praia   Ilha do Bexiga   Ilha do Algodão

Terra Nova

Praia Boa Vista   Engenho Boa Vista   Enseada de Paraty-Mirim   Ponta de Cajaiba

Ilha das Alamas   Paraty-Mirim

23°15'S   Praia da Venda

Praia Deserta

Parque Nacional da Serra da Bocaina   Ponta do Juatinga

BR 101   Patrimônio

To Ubatuba & São Paulo   ▲ 1320m   Praia de Sá

23°20'S   Praia do Sono

Rio de Janeiro   Laranjeiras   Ponta Venda

São Paulo   Trindade   Praia do Cepilho   Negra   ATLANTIC OCEAN

Praia de Trindade   Ponta do Sono   Ponta Negra

44°45'W   44°40'W   44°35'W   44°30'W

Pousada da Matriz (☎ 3371 1610; Rua da Matriz; s/d US$10/20) The rooms are small at this old-fashioned pousada, but it is one of the most affordable places in the historic part of town – and it's spotless.

Pousada Marendaz (☎ 3371 1369; pousada-marendaz@uol.com.br; Rua Dr Derly Ellena 9; per person US$13) Run by Rachel and her four sisters, Pousada Marendaz is more of a family home than a hotel and is delightfully welcoming.

Pousada do Careca (☎ 3371 1291; Praça do Chafariz s/n; s/d US$10/17) Right at the edge of the old town, this pousada is a great place to stay. Clean, bright rooms and guests can use the kitchen.

Villaggio (☎ 3371 1870; www.paraty.com.br/villaggio.htm; Rua José Viera Ramos 280; s/d US$10/17; 🏊) About 800m east of town, this newcomer has big airy rooms and a pool around a beautiful garden courtyard.

Pousada Coco Verde (☎ 3371 1039; abiliocarlos@uol.com.br; Rua João Luiz do Rosário 3; s/d US$10/17) Great rooms in a pretty, well built cabin-style pousada that has a very friendly atmosphere.

There are a few camping grounds on the edge of town, just over the bridge.

MID-RANGE

Pousada da Marquesa (☎ 3371 2163; Rua Dona Geralda 69; s/d US$35/50; 🏊) Probably the best deal in town, the Pousada da Marquesa has bedrooms with fabulous views and a lovely inviting pool and garden.

Pousada Art Urquijo (☎ 3371 1362; www.paraty.com.br/urquijo; Rua Dona Geralda 79; s/d US$50/70) This pousada is a true labor of love for owner Luz Urquijo, an artist and local celebrity of sorts. She's put quite a bit of work into each room and used much of her own innovative art to decorate – the results are eye-catching and soul-warming.

Hotel Solar dos Gerânios (☎ 3371 1550; Praça da Matriz; s/d US$25/35) Right on the corner of a plaza that locals call Praça Monsenhor Hélio Pires, this beautiful old hotel has wood and ceramic sculptures, flat brick and stone, rustic heavy furniture and azulejos (Portuguese tiles) in all the rooms. Very beautiful!

Hotel Estalagem (☎ 3371 1626; Rua da Matriz; s/d US$30/36) This is a great location with views, especially if you get an upstairs room.

Pousada Aconchego (☎ 3371 1598; Rua Domingo Gonçalves de Abreu 1; s/d US$33/40; 🏊) This pousada is right on the edge of the old part of

town and has nicely decorated rooms and a cute little garden pool.

Pousada Morro do Forte (☎ 3371 1211; Rua Orlando Carpinelli 21; s/d US40/50; 🏊) For really great vistas of the town and bay, try this pousada, perched on the Morro do Forte. It has comfortable rooms with small balconies opening to gorgeous scenery.

TOP END

There are several splendid colonial pousadas in Paraty.

Pousada Pardieiro (☎ 3371 1370; pp@pousadapardieiro.com.br; Rua do Comércio 74; s/d US$80/100) Owned by a former Brazilian actor, this pousada has a tranquil garden setting, refined service and impeccable décor. One of the best in Brazil!

Pousada do Ouro (☎ 3371 1378; ouro@contracthor.com.br; Rua da Praia 145; s/d US$70/120; 🏊) This is the kind of place where you can imagine bumping into Mick Jagger, Sonia Braga or Tom Cruise, especially when you enter the hotel lobby and see photos of them posing in front of the pousada. The hotel has everything – bar, pool, a good restaurant, and gorgeous garden.

Pousada Porto Imperial (☎ 3371 2323; www.pousadaportoparaty.com.br; Rua Tenente Francisco Antonio s/n; s/d US$60/100) Despite its impressive size, this pousada still manages to feel like a country inn, with simple but attractive rooms (some suites quite elegant) and lovely garden and pool.

Hotel Coxixo (☎ 3371 1460; fax 3371 1568; Rua do Comércio 362; s/d US$50/70) Right in the middle of town on a gorgeous cobblestone street, this hotel has some standard rooms that are a good deal. The décor is cozy and colonial, with lots of medieval-looking stone walls, and rooms are simple, elegant and welcoming.

Hotel le Gite d'Indaiatiba (☎ 3371 1327; fax 3371-2188; bungalow incl breakfast & dinner US$100) Located in the mountains, 16km north of Paraty, this hotel is owned by a Frenchman (if you have any trouble finding the place, ask for 'o hotel do francês'? – everybody knows it). It has small bungalows in a beautiful setting with a great view. You can go horseback riding, trekking or just down to the beach. To get there by bus, take the bus labeled 'Barra Grande via Grauna' and get off at the last stop in Grauna. By car, head toward Rio for 12km, then turn off at the Fazenda Grauna road and follow it for 4km.

Eating

Paraty has many pretty restaurants, but once your feet touch the cobblestones, prices go up.

BUDGET

Sabor da Terra (Av Roberto Silveira 80; meals US$6; 11am-5pm) A great self-serve restaurant just a few feet from the beginning of the historic center, Sabor da Terra has good food at affordable prices.

Miracolo (☎ 3371 1045; Praça da Matriz 80; sandwiches US$5; 11am-midnight) Run by an Italian expat, this small ice cream parlor and snack spot serves creamy gelato in a range of flavors. The outdoor tables in front are a living meeting spot on Friday and Saturday nights.

Beija Flor (☎ 3371 1629; cnr Rua Dr Pereira & Rua Beira Rio; light meals US$5; ☑ 4-11pm Thu-Tue) This pleasant little eatery is in the old part of town and has reasonably priced sandwiches, soups and juices.

MID-RANGE & TOP END

Brik a Brak (☎ 3371 1445; www.paraty.com.br/brikbrak.htm in Portuguese; Rua Dr Samuel Costa 267; US$14; 6pm-midnight) The only thing more inventive than the color scheme at this restaurant is the food – the chefs (all local women) take great pride in creating delicious, out-of-this-world concoctions. A particular winner is the shrimp cooked in passion-fruit sauce with spinach over risotto. Live music complements the food and gorgeous art.

Hiltinho (☎ 3371 1432; Rua Marechal Deodoro da Fonseca 233; plate for 2 US$15; 11am-11pm) This restaurant specializes in seafood dishes, heavy on the prawns (which are divine when stuffed with *farofa* and deep-fried). Dinner is served in an attractive colonial mansion.

Punto di Vino (☎ 3371 1348; Rua Marechal Deodoro da Fonseca 129; meals US$6; 11am-10pm) This quaint little pizzeria sits facing the Praça da Matriz. It also has excellent pasta dishes.

Casa do Fogo (☎ 3371 6359; Rua do Comércio 58; meals US$30; 6pm midnight) The name gives the game away here – everything's on fire! The menu focuses on seafood using the local *cachaça*, and desserts don't escape a fiery death either. You can expect flambéed mango or banana to be ever-present.

Drinking

Café Paraty (☎ 3371 1464; Rua do Comércio 253) This popular hangout attracts a hard-partying crowd with its live music and flashy drinks.

Margarida Café (☎ 3371 2820; Rua Comendador José Luis 11) Located right along the edge of the old town, on the street sometimes known as Rua da Ferraria, this café has live music every night and a cozy, intimate atmosphere.

Amada Para Ti (Rua Tenente Francisco Antonio 14) Young artistic types love this spacious, beautifully decorated bar (that also serves Mexican food). There are all sorts of drinks available, from martinis to *caipiroskas* (a *caipirinha* with vodka instead of rum), and all served with a smile.

Entertainment

Academia de Cozinha (☎ 3371 6468; Rua Dona Geralda 288; all-included dinner US$35) A mix of theater and haute cuisine, the Academia de Cozinha stages cooking shows – in Portuguese and English. Guests learn about regional cuisines, see chef Yara Castro Roberts in action, then enjoy the fruits of her labor. The price includes cocktails, wine, desserts and a wide variety of fare.

Teatro Espaço (☎ 3371 1575; Rua Dona Geralda 327; admission about US$10) This small playhouse has plays, music and dance performances by the resident theater company Contadores de Estórias. Sometimes there are internationally acclaimed puppet shows.

Getting There & Away

The **bus station** (☎ 3371 117; Rua Jango Pádua) is 500m west of the old town. Frequent buses head to Rio de Janeiro (US$13, four hours), Angra dos Reis (US$3, two hours), São Paulo (US$12) and Ubatuba (US$4, one hour).

AROUND PARATY
Praia Barra Grande

About 20km north, on the Rio–Santos highway (BR-101), is Praia Barra Grande, an easy-to-reach alternative to the beaches in Baía de Paraty. To get there take one of the frequent Paraty–Angra buses.

Praia de Paraty-Mirim

For accessibility, cost and beauty, this beach is hard to beat. Paraty-Mirim is a small town 27km east of Paraty. The beach has *barracas* and houses to rent. From Paraty, it's a couple of hours by boat. There's also a municipal bus (US$1) to Paraty-Mirim from the bus station.

Praia do Sono

Beaches don't get much prettier than this. Praia do Sono is about 40km southeast of Paraty, west of Ponta Negra. It's a four- to five-hour boat ride, and the beach can have rough water and is sometimes difficult to land on. It's much cheaper to catch the bus to Laranjeiras beach, and from there get directions for the 1½-hour walk east to Sono. There's food but no formal lodging at the beach. Rough camping is permitted.

Praia da Trindade

About 7.5km west of Sono, this is another beauty. It has lots of simple pousadas so you can stay here for a night or two. The beach is accessible by boat. Alternatively, take the same bus as for Laranjeiras and Praia do Sono and ask the driver to let you off at the entrance to Trindade. From the bus stop, it's 4km downhill.

ITATIAIA REGION

The Itatiaia region is a curious mix of Old World charm and New World jungle. The climate is Alpine temperate and the chalets are Swiss, but the vegetation is tropical and the warm smiles are pure Brazilian. There are neatly tended little farms with horses and goats, and small homes with clipped lawns and flower boxes side by side with large tracts of dense forest untouched by the machete. This is a wonderful place to tramp around green hills, ride ponies up purple mountains, splash in waterfalls and hike trails without straying too far from the comforts of civilization: a sauna, a fireplace, a soft bed, a little wine and a well-grilled trout!

The region lies in the Serra da Mantiqueira's Itatiaia massif, in the northwest corner of Rio de Janeiro, and borders the states of São Paulo and Minas Gerais. This idyllic corner of Rio de Janeiro state was settled by Europeans – and is known as Penedo by Finns, Itatiaia and Visconde de Mauá by Germans and Swiss – but it is now popular among Brazilians of all ethnic groups.

PENEDO

☎ 0xx24 / pop 40,000 / elevation 600m

A little slice of the Old Country has taken root and flourished deep inside the Serra da Mantiqueira's Itatiaia forest, creating an idyllic town on the edge of a national park that's full of Alpine scenery and steaming saunas. In high season this small village is packed full of vacationing Cariocas and Paulistas (from São Paulo), and its great fun!

Information

Petiscos Cyber Bar (Av das Mangueiras 800; per hr US$3) Internet access as well as snacks and drinks.

Tourist office (☎ 3351 1876; Av Casa das Pedras 766; ☻ 1-6pm Mon-Fri, 9am-6pm Sat & Sun) Brochures and information are all in Portuguese.

Sights

Penedo's main attractions are the forest and waterfalls. There are three waterfalls worth visiting: **Três Cachoeiras**, the very pretty **Cachoeira do Roman** which is on private grounds (but accessible to the public), 10 minutes' walk uphill from the Pousada Challenge, and **Cachoeira de Deus** right near the Pousada Challenge.

About one hour of uphill **hiking** from the end of the asphalt takes you into very dense forest, although there are trails inside. Hopefully you will come across the large bands of big monkeys and steer clear of the wildcats.

You can hire horses at **From Penedo** (☎ 3351 1380; Rua Finlândia 150; per person with guide US$20) in Penedo.

Sleeping & Eating

Penedo is expensive, due to the large number of weekend tourists who come up from Rio, but the accommodations are well above average, and you'll find that the food is good. Daily rates usually include breakfast and lunch.

Pousada Challenge (☎ 3351 1389; www.encante-se.com/challenge in Portuguese; Alameda Áustria 43; d US$35; ☻) Tucked into a hilly suburb of Alto do Penedo, this pousada has very clean, prefabricated chalets, with breakfast and use of the pool and sauna.

Pequena Suécia (☎ 2351 1275; www.pequenasuecia .com.br in Portuguese; Rua Toiva Suni; s/d US$20/30) This excellent choice has comfy, clean beds and also houses a delicious Swedish restaurant.

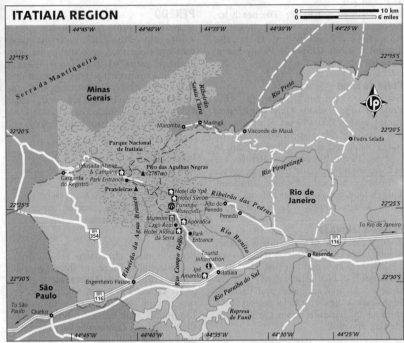

ITATIAIA REGION

Paradiso (☎ 3351 1186; www.paradisohotel.com
.br in Portuguese; Av das Mangueiras 1195; s/d US$30/45)
Individual chalets spread across well-tended
grounds are available for reasonable rates
here, and you have access to a sauna and
other amenities.

Casa do Fritz (Av das Mangueiras 518; lunch US$9;
🕑 noon-midnight Tue-Sun) If you crave some delicious, reasonably priced pasta dishes, this
is the place for you.

Rei das Trutas (Av das Mangueiras 63; dinner US$15;
🕑 11am-11pm) The house speciality at Rei das
Trutas is fresh-grilled river trout, and it's
delectable.

Casa do Chocolate (Av Casa das Pedras 10; sandwiches
US$7) There's more here than just chocolate –
big sandwiches are served, along with 50 different ice-cream flavors if it's hot, and hot
chocolate if it's cold.

Entertainment

Clube Finlandês (Av das Mangueiras 2601; 🕑 9pm-2am
Sat; admission US$4) There is now only a sprink-
ling of Finns among the assortment of Brazilian people, but they all get together for
letkiss and *jenkiss* dances here every Saturday

night. The Finnish dancers put on Old World
togs and do traditional dances.

Shopping

Pequena Finlandia (at Rua das Velas & Av das Mangueiras)
A quaint shopping complex with handicrafts
and a chocolate factory, 'Little Finland' does
its best to convince you that reindeer are
indigenous to Brazil.

Getting There & Away

There are two buses daily from Rio to
Penedo (US$11, 2½ hours) at 1am and
5pm. From Resende, it's much easier to get
one of the frequent buses to Penedo (US$4,
45 minutes) and Itatiaia than to Visconde
de Mauá (in the north of the Itatiaia Region). The bus services the 3km-long main
street and continues to the end of the paved
road.

VISCONDE DE MAUÁ

☎ 0xx24 / elevation 1200m

Mauá is prettier and a little more tranquil
than Penedo, and harder to reach. It's a
lovely place, with streams, tinkling goat

bells, cozy chalets and country lanes graced with wildflowers.

Information

Visconde de Mauá is actually made up of three small villages a few kilometers apart along the Rio Preto. The bus stops first at Mauá, the largest village, and then heads uphill to Maringá, 6km to the west (one side is actually in Minas Gerais). Maromba is farther upstream at the end of the bus route and about 2km west of Maringá. Most travelers stay in Maromba or Maringá.

The **tourist information hut** (8am-noon & 1pm-8pm Tue-Sun) is at the entrance to the village of Mauá.

Sights

The **Santa Clara Cachoeira**, the nicest waterfall in the area, is a 40-minute walk north of Maringá on the Ribeirão Santa Clara. Ask the locals for directions. For a bit of a hike, climb up through the bamboo groves on either side of the falls.

The young and the restless can follow the trail from Maromba to the **Cachoeira Veu de Noiva**, a very beautiful waterfall, in the Parque Nacional de Itatiaia, a full day's hike each way. It's possible to kayak the rapids of the Rio Preto, the cascading river dividing Minas Gerais from Rio state. The river also has small beaches and natural pools.

Sleeping

Most pousadas offer full board with lodging; small signposts at each intersection make them easy to find. If you don't want full board, you can bargain the price down quite a bit.

Barragems Camping (3387 1534; 7km on hwy from Rio; camping per person US$5) Very large sites are available for camping along the river in Maringá. Also available at this complex are big chalet-style apartments, but they'll cost you triple what it does to camp.

Hotel Casa Alpininha (/fax 3387 1390; s/d incl meals US$50) This spartan hotel is in Maringá on the Minas side of the river and makes a great base from which to explore surrounding attractions.

Maromba is less commercial and has a few cheap pousadas next to the bus stop.

Pousada Sonhador (Estrada Mauá-Maromba; s/d incl breakfast US$10/20) This basic hostel-style place is very popular with travelers, despite the

lack of a real address. Just look for it on the right-hand side of the church.

Pousada Casa Bonita (3387 1342; www.pousada casabonita.com.br in Portuguese; d US$50) Right next to a cascading river; 11km along the highway to Rio, this pousada's great for recharging one's batteries and communing with nature in comfort.

Pousada Moriá (3387 1505; www.pousadamoria .com.br in Portuguese; Estrada da Maromba s/n; d US$45) Another beautiful location with gorgeous views, the Pousada Moriá is opposite the Cachoeira do Escorrega in Maromba. It has nice chalets up the hill with views to the valley.

Eating

Restaurante do Moisés in Maromba has good *prato feito* (plate of the day) for US$3. Rua Ponte de Pedestres in Maringá has a couple of good places: Filho da Truta has the ubiquitous per kilo; and Chapeau Noir has home cooking, often accompanied by live music. Restaurante Canto do Rio, next to Bike & Moto in Maringá, has good-value meals in a pleasant location overlooking the river.

Getting There & Around

Visconde de Mauá has no bus station. The two main bus stops are at the shops in Maringá and up at the Praça da Maromba in Maromba.

Three buses from Monday to Saturday and two on Sunday leave Resende for Visconde de Mauá (US$2, 2½ hours) and then continue on to Maringá and Maromba. Two daily buses leave from Maromba, with stops in Maringá and Visconde de Mauá, for Resende (US$2, one hour) at 7:45am and 10am from Monday to Saturday and at 4pm only on Sunday. Buses to Rio (US$13, 4½hrs) leave Maromba, with stops in Maringá and Visconde de Mauá, at 4pm on Sunday and 7:30am on Monday.

PARQUE NACIONAL DE ITATIAIA

0xx24

There are many lovely national parks in Brazil, but perhaps none so ruggedly beautiful as Itatiaia. Its lush, dark foliage contains more than 400 species of native birds, and is also home to monkeys and sloths. It features lakes, rivers, waterfalls, alpine meadows and primary and secondary Atlantic rain forests. Don't let the tropical plants fool you; temperatures drop below freezing in June and, occasionally, the park even has a few snowy days! Bring warm clothes, even in summer.

There is a 24-hour tourist information booth in Itatiaia, 1km north of the Via Dutra, on the road to the park's main entrance. The park entrance is about 5.5km north of that.

Museum

The park headquarters and the museum are 3.7km north of the main park entrance, 10km north of the Via Dutra highway (BR-116). The **Lago Azul** (Blue Lake) is a 400m walk from here. The **museum** (admission free; ☺ 8am-5pm Tue-Sun) is not for the faint of heart; if the smell of formaldehyde doesn't bowl you over, the glass cases of stuffed and mounted animals will.

Activities

Mountain and rock climbing as well as trekking enthusiasts will want to pit themselves against the local peaks, cliffs and trails. Every two weeks a group scales the **Pico das Agulhas Negras**. At 2787m, it's the highest in the area. For more information, contact the **Grupo Excursionista de Agulhas Negras** (☎ 3352 1734).

The best access for walks is from Garganta do Registro on the road from Engenheiro Passos to São Lourenço (near the Minas Gerais and Rio de Janeiro state border). The western park entrance is about 15km from Garganta do Registro along a rough gravel road. From here you can see the dramatic pointy range of the **Agulhas Negras** and from a bit further on, the boulders of the **Prateleiras**. You can hire guides for US$15 a half-day from the Pousada Alsene.

There are simpler hikes on the tamer Itatiaia side of the park, including a 20-minute walk from the main road (6.5km northwest of the main park entrance) to the Poronga waterfalls.

Sleeping

Pousada Alsene (☎ 3363 1773; www.alsene.com.br in Portuguese; per person US$28) Those after an alpine experience will like this remote location. It's up at 2400m, about 12km east of Garganta do Registro near the western entrance to the park. You need to book in advance and,

if you don't have a vehicle, make arrangements to be picked up either from the main road at Garganta do Registro or down at Itatiaia. Camping also available.

Ipê Amarelo (☎ 3352 1232; Rua João Mauricio de Macedo Costa 352; s/d US$13/16) Just north of the Via Dutra in Campo Alegre, a suburb of Itatiaia, you'll find an HI hostel. The hostel has bicycles for rent and will organize day trips to the park (US$20 including meals and transportation). The hostel is a 15-minute walk west of the bus station (US$2.50 by taxi).

Hotel Aldéia da Serra (☎ 3352 1152; d incl breakfast & lunch US$55) Just 1.6km north of the main park entrance is the reasonably priced Aldéia da Serra.

Hotel Simon (☎ 33521122; d US$100) About 7km north of the main park entrance (12km north of Itatiaia) is the very lovely Hotel Simon, which has gorgeous rustic furnishings.

Hotel do Ypê (☎ 3352 1453; fax 3352 1166; d US$110) Also inside the park is the Hotel do Ypê, about 8.5km north of the main entrance, with adorable chalets for rent.

Getting There & Around

Every 20 minutes on weekdays and every 40 minutes on weekends a bus leaves Resende for Itatiaia village. However, there are no regular buses into the park. A taxi ride from Itatiaia town to the places to stay within the main section of the park costs between US$8 and US$13. The park entry fee is another US$2.

NORTH OF RIO DE JANEIRO

PETRÓPOLIS

☎ 0xx24 / pop 270,000 / elevation 809m

A lovely mountain retreat with a decidedly European flavor, Petrópolis is a favorite weekend getaway for Cariocas. Blame it on tradition – this is where the imperial court spent the summer when Rio got too muggy, and it's still the home of the heir to the throne, Dom Pedro II's great-grandson Dom Pedro de Orleans e Bragança. Wander around or ride by horse and carriage through the squares and parks, past bridges, canals and old-fashioned street lamps.

Information

Most of the museums and other attractions are closed on Monday. Useful businesses include the following:

Information booth (Estrada União e Indústria 8764, Itaipava; ☼ 9am-7pm)

Information office (Av Ayrton Senna; ☼ 9am-7pm) At the town entrance.

Petrotur (☎ 0800-241 516; Praça Dom Pedro; ☼ 9am-5pm Tue-Sun) Handy information booth with brochures and maps.

Trekking Petrópolis (☎ 2235 7607; www.rioserra.com.br/trekking) For treks into the nearby Parque Nacional Serra das Órgãos. For details on Trekking Petrópolis and how to book tours, contact Pousada 14 Bis (p196).

Sights

Petrópolis' main attraction is the **Museu Imperial** (☎ 2237 8000; Rua da Imperatriz 220; admission US$3; ☼ noon-5:30pm Tue-Sun), housed in the perfectly preserved and impeccably appointed palace of Dom Pedro II. One interesting exhibit is the 1.7kg imperial crown, with its 639 diamonds and 77 pearls. While you're there, you might want to hire a horse and carriage and go for a ride.

The **Catedral São Pedro de Alcântara** (☎ 2242 4300; Rua Sao Pedro de Alcantara 60; ☼ 8am-noon & 2-4pm Wed-Mon) houses the tombs of Brazil's last emperor, Dom Pedro II, his wife Dona Teresa, and their daughter, Princesa Isabel.

Along Av Koeller are some fine mansions including the **Palácio da Princesa Isabel** (9am-5pm Wed-Mon; admission to the grounds free).

Across Rio Piabanha is the **Casa do Barão de Maua** (☎ 2246 9300; Praca da Confluencia 3; ☼ 9am-6:30pm Mon-Sat, to 7pm Sun). The house of the Baron of Maua features displays devoted to the baron, who was known for playing a crucial role in the construction of Brazil's first railway.

The **Palácio Cristal** (Alfredo Pachá) is an iron and glass structure built in France and imported in 1879 to serve as a hothouse in which to grow orchids.

West of the Praça Rui Barbosa (which has numerous drink stands), the **Casa de Santos Dumont** (admission US$1; ☼ 9am-5pm Tue-Sun) is the summer home of Brazil's diminutive father of aviation and inventor of the wristwatch.

The **Trono de Fátima** is a 3.5m sculpture of NS de Fátima Madonna, imported from

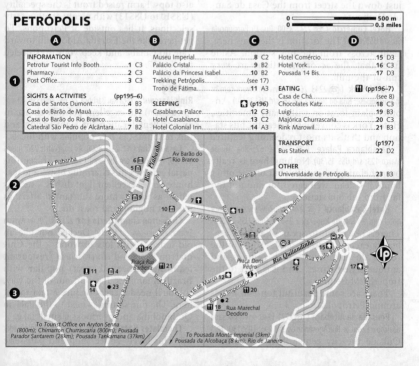

PETRÓPOLIS

0 — 500 m
0 — 0.3 miles

To Tourist Office on Ayrton Senna (800m); Chimarron Churrascaria (800m); Pousada Parador Santarem (28km); Pousada Tankamana (37km)

To Pousada Monte Imperial (3km); Pousada da Alcobaça (8 km; Rio de Janeiro)

Italy. From here you have a great view of the town and surrounding hills. To reach it, turn right as you leave the Casa de Santos Dumont and start walking uphill, then turn right at the first street on your right. There's a sign advertising the Hotel Margaridas. Keep walking uphill, always taking the right fork.

Sleeping

Pousada 14 Bis (☎ 2231 0946; www.pousada14bis.com .br; Rua Santos Dumont 162; s/d from US$15/20) One of the most charming hotels in Petropolis – if not Rio state – the restored colonial Pousada 14 Bis has handsome, well-appointed rooms with lovely wood floors, blue-shuttered windows and comfortable beds. The best rooms have balconies overlooking the peaceful street or garden out back. The French and Brazilian owners have a wealth of information about the city.

Hotel Colonial Inn (☎ 2243 1590; www.colonial inn.com.br in Portuguese; Rua Monsenhor Bacelar 125; d from US$46) Rooms here feature a mix of antique and art-nouveau furnishings, with a friendly, homelike feel to the place. Located just down the street from the Casa de Santos Dumont.

Hotel Comércio (☎ 2242 3500; Rua Dr Porciúncula 56; s/d US$20/30) The location is the draw here, right across from the bus station. Aside from that, the accommodations are very run-of-the-mill.

Hotel York (☎ 2243 2662; www.hotelyork.com.br in Portuguese; Rua do Imperador 78; s/d US$20/30) Another plain location with many amenities, Hotel York is conveniently near the bus station and that's its most redeeming feature.

Casablanca Palace (☎ 2242 0162; Rua 16 de Março 123; s/d US$ 15/30) Nothing here is really overwhelmingly beautiful, but on the other hand, it's clean, well cared-for and not too far from the bus station.

Hotel Casablanca (☎ 2242 6662; www.casablanca hotel.com.br; Rua da Imperatriz 286; d from US$48; 🕿) There's not much to speak of at the Casablanca except its pretty pool – some of the rooms do have lovely, high ceilings and antique-style fixtures. And it is next to the Imperial Museum.

There are some beautiful top-end hotels around Petrópolis.

Pousada da Alcobaça (☎ 2221 1240; www.pousada daalcobaca.com.br; Rua Agostinho Goulão 298; d US$130; 🕿) Outside the city center in the suburb of Corrêas, this beautiful hotel has a pool, a sauna, a tennis court and lovely gardens crossed by a small river. There's also an excellent restaurant in the building.

Pousada Monte Imperial (☎ 2237 1664; Rua José Alencar 27; s/d US$55/75) With the air of a lovely country farm, this pousada is a bit of a walk from the city but well worth the exercise. Rooms are small but very appealing.

Parador Santarém (☎ 2222 9933; www.parador santarem.com.br; Estrada Júlio Cápua, Vale do Cuibá; chalets from US$150; 🕿) A vast amount of greenery – complete with hiking, swimming, fishing opportunities. Palatially decorated rooms (canopy beds being a common feature), live music in the restaurant on Saturday nights, private theater; the list goes on…

Pousada Tankamana (☎ 2222 9181; Estrada Júlio Cápua, Vale do Cuibá; chalets from US$150) Absolutely stunning setting, with 16 chalets surrounded by 900,000 sq meters of forest, mountains and streams. Features include a pool, sauna, outdoor bar, games room (with pool table) and heliport. Guests can make excursions on horseback or go hiking into the mountains. The restaurant here is also tops. Farm raised trout is the speciality (US$10 to US$13) with plenty of other tasty selections. It lies outside of Petrópolis. To get here take the Estrada Aldo Gelli toward Vale do Cuiaba and keep your eyes peeled for Km 37.

Eating

Rink Marowil (Praça Rui Barbosa 27; per kg US$6; 11am-4pm & 6-9pm) An excellent per-kilo choice in an excellent location for sight seeing and this restaurant is very popular with locals.

Casa de Chá (☎ 2237 8000; Av Imperatriz 220; mains US$5-9; 🕑 noon-7pm Tue-Sun) On the Museu Imperial complex this charming bistrô and teahouse serves excellent light dishes – such as pâté – as well as more substantial offerings like filet mignon and roast duck.

Chimarron Churrascaria (☎ 2237 3779; Av Ayrton Senna; all-you-can-eat US$10) Decked out like an old lodge – with lots of wood – the Chimarron is a good *churrascaria* (restaurant featuring barbequed meat) popular with Brazilian families. It's a bit out of the way, so you'll need a car – or hire a taxi to get here. The fine setting is next to the Palácio Quitandinha and overlooks a small lake.

Chocolates Katz (☎ 2245 1818; Rua do Imperador 912) This lovely coffee shop and patisserie makes a fine stop for cappuccinos and chocolate torte.

Luigi (☎ 2246 0279; Praça Rui Barbosa 185; mains US$5-10; ⊙ lunch & dinner Mon-Sat) A charming Italian restaurant set in an old house with tall ceilings and creaky floors. It packs crowds on Friday and Saturday nights, with live music and candlelit ambience.

Majórica Churrascaria (☎ 2242 2498; Rua do Imperador 754; mains US$7-10; ⊙ lunch & dinner Tue-Sun) Within a short distance from the Museu Imperial, Majórica has excellent cuts of meat – served à la carte.

Getting There & Around

There are buses back and forth between Rio and the **Petrópolis bus station** (☎ 2237 6262; Rua Doutor Porciúcula 75) every half-hour, from 5:15am onward. The journey costs US$6 and takes 1½ hours.

VASSOURAS

☎ 0xx24 / pop 20,000 / elevation 434m

Vassouras, a quiet resort 118km north of Rio, was the most important city in the Paraíba valley in the first half of the 19th century. Surrounded by the huge *fazendas* (farms) of the coffee barons of the time, the town still wears the money they poured into it. They actually were barons, for 18 of them were given titles of nobility by the Portuguese crown. With the abolition of slavery in 1888 and the resulting decline in coffee production, the importance of Vassouras diminished, and this preserved the town.

Information

Casa de Cultura (☎ 2471 2765; Praça Barão do Campo Belo) Next to the local cinema.

Tourist office (Rua Barão de Capivari 20; ⊙ 9am-6pm Mon-Fri) Gives out information on which privately owned *fazendas* are open to visitors.

Sights

The beloved grande dame of Vassouras was the aristocratic heiress Eufrásia, who claimed to be devoted to the town despite having palaces in London, Brussels and Paris. **Museu Chácara da Hera** (Rua Dr Fernandes Jr 160; admission free; ⊙ 11am-5pm Wed-Sun) was her former home. Items on display include old furniture, colonial relics, beautiful hardwood floors and handcarved chairs.

There are a few old churches in the town center, as well as old buildings of the schools

of medicine, philosophy and engineering, but the real attractions of Vassouras are the coffee *fazendas*.

Although the *fazendas* are protected by the historical preservation institutes, permission must be obtained from the owners before touring the grounds. For more information, ask at the Casa de Cultura or the tourist office.

Sleeping & Eating

Mara Palace (☎ 2471 1993; Rua Chanceler Dr Raul Fernandes 121; s/d US$48/52) A centrally located hotel with attractive rooms, the Mara is one of the best options in town.

Hotel Parque Santa Amália (☎ 2471 1897; Av Sebastião Manoel Furtado 526; d US$55) A very large, old hotel in the center of town, the Santa Amália also has rates that include lunch and dinner.

Pensão Tia Maria (Rua Domingos de Almeida 134; per person US$10) Just up from the bus station, this very basic hotel is a good deal but doesn't have any double beds. Its **restaurant**, and a few other places nearby, offer reasonably priced *comida caseira* (home-style cooking). But for top restaurants, you're about a hundred years too late.

Getting There & Around

The **bus station** (☎ 2471 1055; Praça Juiz Machado Jr) has frequent buses to Rio (US$6, 2½ hours).

Unfortunately, if you don't have a car, you're in for some long hikes heading out to the *fazendas*.

TERESÓPOLIS

☎ 0xx21 / pop 115,000 / elevation 871m

Do as Empress Maria Tereza used to do and escape from the steamy summer heat of Rio to the cool mountain retreat of Teresópolis, the highest city in the state, nestled in the strange, organ-pipe rock formations of the Serra dos Órgãos. The road from Rio to Teresópolis first passes the sinuous curves of a padded green jungle, then winds and climbs past bald peaks which have poked through the jungle cover to touch the clouds.

The city's principal attraction is the landscape and its natural treasures, which include the amazing Dedo de Deus visible from the main street. Teresópolis is not, however, simply for alpinists: it's a center for sports lovers of all varieties. There are facilities for volleyball, motocross and equestrian activities – many of Brazil's finest thoroughbreds are raised here – not to mention soccer. Teresópolis also bears the distinction of being the training base of Brazil's World Cup squad.

Information

Post office (Av Lúcio Meira)

Telemar (Av Lúcio Meira) The telephone office is a couple of blocks southeast from the post office.

Tourist office (☎ 2742 3352; Praça Olímpica; 🕑 8am-6pm) In the town center.

Sights

The area's main attraction is the Parque Nacional da Serra dos Órgãos. The **Dedo de Deus** (God's Finger) can be seen from the main street, Av Feliciano Sodré, however, the best place for viewing the peak is the suburb of Soberbo.

The **Mulher de Pedra** (Rock Woman) rock formation, 12km from Teresópolis toward Nova Friburgo, really does look like a reclining woman. **Colina dos Mirantes**, south of the center in the suburb of Fazendinha, is

a good place to view the Serra dos Órgãos range and the city. On clear days you can see as far as the Baía de Guanabara. To get there from town, head southeast along Av Feliciano Sodré, turn left at Av Tenente Luiz Meireles and right at Rua Jaguaripe. The Quebra Frascos, the royal family of the Second Empire, had a residence in this neighborhood.

Sleeping

BUDGET & MID-RANGE

Várzea Palace Hotel (☎ 2742 0878; Rua Prefeito Sebastião Teixeira 41/55; s/d US$23/33) This grand old white building with red trim has been a Teresópolis institution since 1916. Classy *quartos* and *apartamentos* are a big hit with the young crowd.

Hotel Comary (☎ 2742 3463; Av Almirante Lúcio Meira 467; s/d US$9/20) Probably the cheapest option in town, the Comary's unattractive exterior is mitigated by the proximity of a *padaria* (bakery) next door, behind the Igreja Matriz.

Center Residence Hotel (☎ 2742 5890; Sebastião Teixeira 245; US$30/40) The Center Residence offers basic rooms, nothing special, but clean and inoffensive.

Hotel Avenida (☎ 2742 2751; Rua Delfim Moreira 439; s/d US$22/35) Although this hotel is in front of the Igreja Matriz, its somewhat outdated, plain *apartamentos* seem a bit overpriced, although it certainly could do in a pinch.

TOP END

The more expensive hotels are out of town.

Hotel Alpina (☎ 2742 5252; d US$85) The Hotel Alpina has spacious *apartamentos* and is across the street from a swanky golf course – nice digs. It's 4km out of town on the road to Petrópolis.

Pousada Vrajabhumi (☎ 2644 6220; d US$90) Run by the Hare Krishnas, this popular pousada can be found along the Teresópolis to Nova Friburgo road, in the middle of a forest reserve. There are chalets and natural swimming pools, and rates include all meals, which are vegetarian.

Hotel Rosa dos Ventos (☎ 2642 8833; d US$150) This is the only Brazilian hotel in the international Relais & Châteaux chain, and it has everything except children, because no one under age 12 is allowed. Big spacious rooms with beautiful decorations abound.

TERESÓPOLIS

0 ——————— 300 m
0 ——————— 0.2 miles

SLEEPING	(pp198–9)
Center Residence Hotel..6	B2
Hotel Avenida............7	B2
Hotel Comary............8	A2
Várzea Palace Hotel 9	B2

EATING	(p199)
Cheiro de Mato..........10	B2
Sand's.................11	A2
Supermarket...........12	B1

TRANSPORT	(p199)
Bus Station.............13	A2
Gas Station............14	B1

INFORMATION		
ATM (24 hours)...........1	B2
Banco do Brasil..........2	B1
Pharmacy (24 hours)...(see 7)	
Post Office..............3	A2
Telephone Office........4	A2
Tourist Office...........5	B1

It's 27km out of town along the road to Nova Friburgo.

Eating

Restaurante Irene (☎ 2742 2901; Rua Tenente Luís Meireles 1800; dinner US$35) In the suburb of Bom Retiro, Irene basks in its reputation for providing the best haute cuisine in Teresópolis. Reservations are required.

Cheiro de Mato (Rua Delfim Moreira 140; lunch US$8) This is a favorite among vegetarians for its innovative cooking and huge buffet of salads.

Sand's (Av Almirante Lúcio Meira; lunch US$5; ☽ lunch) Just a few steps from the bus station, this cheap self-serve lunch spread is popular with travelers.

Pousada Vrajabhumi (☎ 2644 6220; ☽ lunch & dinner) The restaurant at this popular pousada is open to the public for meals.

For self-caterers, there's a supermarket on Av Almirante Lúcio Meira.

Getting There & Around

The **bus station** (Rua Primeiro de Maio) is not too far from Av Tenente Luiz. Buses head to Rio (US$5, 1½ hours) every 30 minutes, from 5am to 10pm, Petrópolis (US$4, one hour, frequent) and Novo Friburgo (US$4, two hours, four daily).

PARQUE NACIONAL DA SERRA DOS ÓRGÃOS

Created in 1939, this national park covers 118 sq km of mountainous terrain between Teresópolis and Petrópolis. A distinctive feature of the park is the strangely shaped peaks of the **Pedra do Sino** (2263m), **Pedra do Açu** (2230m), **Agulha do Diabo** (2020m), **Nariz do Frade** (1919m), **Dedo de Deus** (1651m), **Pedra da Ermitage** (1485m) and **Dedo de Nossa Senhora** (1320m). With so many peaks, it's no wonder that this is the mountain-climbing, rock-climbing and trekking center of Brazil. The region has extensive trails, and it's possible to trek over the forested mountains from Teresópolis to Petrópolis. Unfortunately, most of the trails are unmarked and off the available maps. Hiring a guide, however, is easy and inexpensive. Inquire at the **national park entrance** (☎ 2642 1070; admission US$4; ☽ 8am-5pm Tue-Sun) or go with a group organized by one of the hiking and mountaineering clubs in Rio. The best time for walks is from May to October (the drier months).

The main entrance to the national park is at the southern edge of the township of Teresópolis, off Hwy BR-116 from Rio, about 4km from the center. Walking trails, waterfalls, natural swimming pools and tended lawns and gardens make this a very pretty place for a picnic. A few kilometers up from the main entrance, accommodations can be found at the **Pousada Refúgio do Parque** (☎ 9221 9147; per person US$15). Rates include breakfast, and soup for dinner.

From the main entrance, the road extends into the park as far as Barragem Beija Flor. There are several good walks from near here. The highlight is the **Trilha Pedra do Sino** – a round-trip of about eight hours from the end of the park road. The trail passes Cachoeira Veu da Noiva, the vegetation changes from rain forest to grassland, and the reward is a panoramic view stretching all the way to Rio de Janeiro and the Baía de Guanabara. It costs US$8 to use the trail. For a shorter walk, head up to the **Mirante Alexandre Oliveira** (1100m), from where there is a good view of Teresópolis – it is about a one-hour round-trip from the park road.

There is another, secondary entrance down in the southeast corner of the national park, off the road from Rio. It also has an information center, walking trails and waterfalls.

Tours are also available from Petrópolis (see p195).

Getting There & Around

To get to the park's main entrance from the city center of Teresópolis, take the hourly 'Soberbo' bus (US$0.70). Alternatively, take the more frequent 'Alto' bus and get off at the Praçinha do Alto, from which it's a short walk south to the park's main entrance. A taxi ride from town to the park entrance costs US$10.

NOVA FRIBURGO

☎ 0xx24 / pop 152,000 / elevation 846m

Once upon a time not too long ago (1818, to be exact), about 300 families from the Swiss canton of Friburg decided to emigrate to Brazil to avoid a nasty little dust-up that's now known as the Napoleonic Wars.

The passage to Brazil was horrible and many died, but upon arriving in the New World a handful of surviving Swiss set out to create a perfect little village that reminded them of their home country. Being a resourceful people they had great success, and today visitors to Nova Friburgo still marvel at the town's quaint architecture and apparently perpetually blooming flowers. There are also plenty of resplendent natural attractions: waterfalls, woods, trails, sunny mountain mornings and cool evenings.

Information

Post office Opposite Praça Getúlio Vargas.
Telephone office (Av Alberto Braune)
Tourist office (☎ 2523 8000; Praça Dr Demerval B Moreira; ☒ 8am-8pm) Has maps and a complete list of hotels, including the cheapest, with updated prices.

Sights

Most of the sights are a few kilometers out of town. Survey the surrounding area from **Morro da Cruz** (1800m). The chairlift to Morro da Cruz runs on weekends and holidays from 9am to 6pm. Its station is in the center of town at Praça Teleférico. **Pico da Caledônia** (2310m) offers fantastic views, and launching sites for hang gliders. It's a 6km uphill hike, but the view is worth it.

You can hike to **Pedra do Cão Sentado** and explore the **Furnas do Catete** rock formations. Visit the mountain towns of **Bom Jardim** (23km northeast on Hwy RJ-116) or **Lumiar** (25km east of the turnoff at Mury, which is 9km south of Nova Friburgo). Hippies, cheap pensions, waterfalls, walking trails

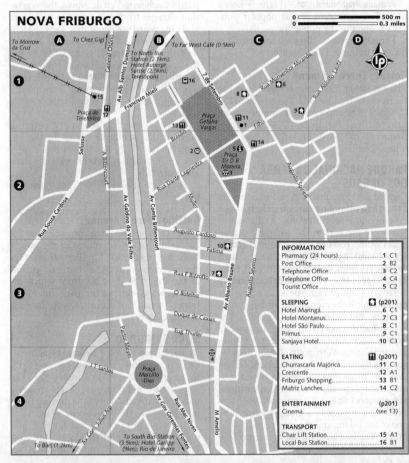

NOVA FRIBURGO

0 _____ 500 m
0 _____ 0.3 miles

INFORMATION	
Pharmacy (24 hours).................................1	C1
Post Office...2	B2
Telephone Office......................................3	C2
Telephone Office......................................4	C4
Tourist Office...5	C2

SLEEPING	🏠 (p201)
Hotel Maringá..6	C1
Hotel Montanus.......................................7	C3
Hotel São Paulo..8	C1
Primus..9	C1
Sanjaya Hotel...10	C3

EATING	🍴 (p201)
Churrascaria Majórica.............................11	C1
Crescente..12	A1
Friburgo Shopping..................................13	B1
Matriz Lanches.......................................14	C2

ENTERTAINMENT	(p201)
Cinema..(see 13)	

TRANSPORT	
Chair Lift Station...................................15	A1
Local Bus Station...................................16	B1

and white-water canoe trips abound in Lumiar. If you have wheels, visit the **Jardim do Nêgo** (admission US$4), 13km from town on Hwy RJ-130, northwest of Nova Friburgo between Campo do Coelho and Conquista. It's a fantastic sculpture garden with huge moss-covered sculptures of human and animal forms.

Sleeping

Primus (☎ 2523 2898; hprimus@hotelprimus.com.br; Rua Adolfo Lautz 128; s/d US$22/35; ☒) This is up on a very steep hill, but the breakfast alone is worth the hike. There's a pool, pet birds, and great views. What's not to like?

Hotel São Paulo (☎ 2522 9135; Rua Monsenhor Miranda 41; s/d US$30/40) Some rooms are in the more modern part of the building but the real winners are in the old section – bargain to get one of those if you can, although you may end up having to pay a few dollars more.

Hotel Maringá (☎ 2522 2309; Rua Monsenhor Miranda 110; s/d apartments US$20/30) There are simple *quartos* and more expensive *apartamentos*, but both choices are clean and nicely decorated.

Hotel Montanus (☎ 2521 1235; Rua Fernando Bizzotto 26; s/d US$23/30) Things are basic and barebones at the Montanus, but prices can be bargained down, especially in low season.

Sanjaya Hotel (☎ 2522 6052; Av Alberto Braune 58; s/d US$45/60) A good, mid-range place in the center of town, the Sanjaya charges reasonable rates for what it offers.

Hotel Garlipp (☎ 2542 1330; d US$125) Full board can be had at this big hotel in Mury, 9km south of town on the road to Niterói.

Hotel Auberge Suisse (☎ 2541 1270; Rua 10 de Outubro, Amparo; cabins from US$40) Serving traditional Swiss cuisine: raclettes, fondues, as well as trout, it's in the Amparo district, north of Nova Friburgo. Take the right branch in the road and look for the sign.

Eating

Crescente (☎ 2523 4616; Rua General Osório 4; meals US$5; 11:30am-11pm Thu-Tue, to 5pm Sun) This is a classy little place serving, among other things, some very tasty trout dishes.

Churrascaría Majórica (☎ 2523 1510; Praça Getúlio Vargas 74; meals US$20) For meat and more meat, this is the place. The restaurant serves a decent filet mignon – it's enough for two.

Matriz Lanches (Rua 7 de Setembro; light meals US$3) A great choice for a quick snack, Matriz has sandwiches, miniquiches and sometimes pizza.

Friburgo Shopping (Praça Getúlio Vargas) Has a few bars and cafés.

Entertainment

There are a few **bars** in Baixo Friburgo, southwest of the center along the front of Friburguense Football Clube Stadium, about 2km along Av Conselheiro Julius Arp from Praça Marcilio Dias. These bars get packed on Friday and Saturday nights. Another recommended bar is the **Far West Café** north of the city in Córrego Dantes. There is a **cinema** (Friburgo Shopping, Praça Getúlio Vargas).

Getting There & Around

Nova Friburgo is a short jaunt from Rio, via Niterói, on bus line 1001. The ride is along a picturesque, winding, misty jungle road.

Novo Friburgo has two long-distance bus stations. The **north bus station** (Rodoviária Norte; ☎ 2522 6095; Praça Feliciano Costa), 2.5km north of the center, has buses to Petrópolis and Teresópolis (US$5, two hours, four daily). The **south bus station** (Rodoviária Sul; ☎ 2522 0400; Ponte da Saudade), 4km south of the center, has frequent buses to Rio (US$7). You'll need to catch a local bus to the central, local bus station just north of Praça Getúlio Vargas. Local buses go to just about all the tourist attractions. Ask for details at the tourist office.

EAST OF RIO DE JANEIRO

SAQUAREMA

☎ 0xx24 / pop 44,000

A laid-back little town with stunning stretches of unmarred beaches, Saquarema is 100km east of Rio de Janeiro. Polluting industries are forbidden in the municipality; the waters are clean and fish and shrimp are abundant. The shoreline attracts surfers, sportfishing enthusiasts and sun worshipers. To the west are Boqueirão, Barra Nova (8km) and Jaconé (15km, reachable by local buses). About 3km east of town is **Praia Itaúna**, probably Saquarema's most beautiful beach and one of the best surf spots in Brazil (US$3 by taxi from center).

A gorgeous **church** (1837) perched on the hill near the entrance to the lagoon is the town's focal point. From this strategic spot you can survey the long, empty beaches and view the mountains beyond the lagoon. Saquarema is a horse-breeding and fruit-growing center; you can visit the orchards and pick fruit, or rent horses or a jeep and take to the hills. Most of the pousadas can arrange these activities.

Saquarema hosts mass at NS de Nazaré on September 7 and 8. It attracts around 150,000 pilgrims, second only to the Nazaré celebrations of Belém.

History

On March 17, 1531, Martim Afonso de Sousa founded a Portuguese settlement here and met with the Tamoio Indian chief Sapuguaçu. Nonplussed by de Sousa's five ships and 400 sailors, Sapuguaçu chose to ally the Tamoios with the French. In 1575 Antônio Salema, then Governor of Rio de Janeiro, decided to break the Tamoio–French alliance and, with an army of over 1000 men, massacred the Indians and their French military advisers.

The next big event in Saquarema's history was the slave revolt of Ipitangas, in which 400 slaves took over the plantation mansion and kicked out their master. For a few days the slaves held the town and fought against cavalry that rode out from Niterói. The town pillory, Bandeque's Post (named after the leader of the slave revolt), was in use as recently as the end of the 19th century. Now it's a small, sleepy village given over to holidaymaking and surfing; in mid-May Praia Itaúna hosts the National Championships.

Information

Banco do Brasil (Av Saquarema 539) It doesn't have currency exchange, but you can get cash advances using a credit card. The nearest place for exchange is in Cabo Frio.

Lakes Shopping This tiny mall, built to look like a log cabin on the road to Praia Itaúna, has an ATM, lots of eateries and Internet access at the computer-repair shop on the first floor.

Post office (Praça Oscar de Macedo Soares) Close to the bus stop.

Secretaria de Turismo (☎ 2651 2178; Prefeitura Bldg; ◷ 9am-8pm) Has friendly staff providing useful information.

Telephone office (Praça Santo Antonio in Bacaxá) About 7km north of Saquarema.

Sleeping

Prices in Saquarema rise by 30% in high season. Prices quoted here are for low season.

BUDGET

Pousada da Titia (☎ 2651 2058; Av Salgado Filho 774; s/d US$9/13) Very popular with both surfers and beachcombers, this pousada has pretty rooms that are reasonably comfortable, considering the simple furnishings and the surroundings.

Costa do Sol (☎ 2651 1233; Av Salgado Filho 5720; s/d US$10/18) Costa do Sol is a tidy little spot not far from the action in town, with comfy beds and clean bathrooms.

Hotel Saquarema (☎ 2651 2275; s/d US$13/20) This hotel is right next to the bus stop on the main praças (town square), but aside from its convenient location it has little of value to offer. Best try your luck elsewhere first.

MID-RANGE & TOP END

Pousada Canto da Vila (☎ 2651 1563; Av Salgado Filho 52; s/d/tr US$30/40/55) A pleasant little place across the road from the beach, spotless *apartamentos* are a bargain, even in high season.

Pousada do Suíço (☎ 2651 2203; Rua das Pitangas 580) Out at Itaúna beach, this cute little pousada is a big favorite with foreigners. The owner speaks German and English. A taxi ride from town should cost about US$3.

Pousada Itaúna Inn (☎ 2651 5147; Av Oceanica 1764; s/d US$20/35) Surfers love this pousada, despite its ugly access at the back, because it has a lovely view to the surf break. The best rooms with sea views are upstairs at the back.

Espuma da Praia (☎ 2651 2118; Av Oceanica; d US$60; ☒) Right next door to the Itaúna Inn is the lovely Espuma da Paraia, which is a converted colonial-style farmhouse with gorgeous and ample frontage facing the beach. It also has a cute swimming pool in the front garden and darling private cabins to rent.

Maasai Hotel Beach & Resort (☎ 2651 1092; www.maasai.com.br; Travessa Itaúna 17; d US$90; ☒) A beautiful full-size resort, the Maasai has a restaurant, swimming pool, and a pretty bar and sitting area facing the beach.

Hotel Fazenda Serra da Castelhana (☎ 2653 3443/2719 5471; Rua Latino Melo; d with meals US$95; ☒) Located about 4km out of town, this romantic getaway throws three square meals a day into its room rate. It has a swimming pool, sauna, games, horseback riding and other organized activities. A day trip including lunch will set you back US$15 per person.

Eating

Crepe e Cia (Av Nazareth 160; light meals US$5; 6-10pm Mon-Fri, to midnight Sat & Sun) The place to come if you crave a delicious crepe.

Pizza na Pedra (Av Nazareth 487; meals US$7) A local favorite for good pizzas and pasta.

Lakes Shopping in the center of town has a few *lanchonetes* and a café.

Garota da Itaúna (Av Oceânica 165; meals US$15; 11am-11pm) Right on the beach, this restaurant is a local favorite for big seafood dishes. It has gorgeous views but hang on to your beers – the wind can be vicious.

Le Bistro (2651 4594; Av São Rafael 1134; meals US$9; 11am-11pm) A very attractive restaurant, Le Bistro has quality comfort food at reasonable prices.

Restaurante Tropical (Av Vila Mar 17; per kg US$5; 11am-4pm & 6-11pm) Everybody's favorite self-serve is just one block inland from the beach. A perfect place to fuel up before returning to the waves.

Getting There & Around

Buses from Rio leave foe Saquarema (US$6, two hours) every hour from 6:30am to 8pm.

To get to Cabo Frio, take a local bus to Bacaxá. From there, buses depart for Cabo Frio every half-hour. The bus stop in Saquarema is on the main praças in the town center.

Walking is the best way to get around Saquarema. There are local buses to Jaconé beach, 15km west of the church.

ARRAIAL DO CABO

0xx24 / pop 24,000

Arraial do Cabo, 45km east of Saquarema, is surrounded by gleaming white sand dunes and offers all the beauty of Búzios with half the fuss. Lately it's become a favorite for fishing enthusiasts, which has somewhat lessened the area's charm (not to mention fish supply), but overall it still maintains a welcoming working-class demeanor. Some of the best beaches – pristine swaths of gorgeous sand and bright-green waters – are within an easy 15-minute stroll, while others are just a short boat ride away.

History

Local history says that before the Portuguese came to town, warring Tamoio and Goitacazes tribes held sway in what's now Cabo Frio. In 1503 a Portuguese fleet under the command of Amerigo Vespucci landed at Praia dos Anjos in Arraial do Cabo, and 24 men were left behind to start a settlement, one of the first in the Americas. Fantastic reports about this community became the model for Thomas More's Utopia.

The economy of the Portuguese settlement was based on coastal brazilwood, which was felled and shipped back to Europe. Portuguese vessels were at the mercy of Dutch and French corsairs until 1615, when the Portuguese defeated these foes. Arraial do Cabo is now mostly dependent on tourism for its livelihood.

Information

There's a **tourist office** (2620 5039; Estrada de Arraial do Cabo) at the town's formal entry portico, known as the Portal, about 3km from the center. There you can get brochures and a map, but the layout is fairly straightforward and the attractions are the beaches. There is also a **post office** (Av Getúlio Vargas) and a **Telemar** telephone office next to the Hotel Praia Grande.

Beaches

Praia dos Anjos has beautiful turquoise water but a little too much boat traffic for comfortable swimming. Favorite beaches within short walking distance of town are: **Prainha** to the north of town; **Praia do Forno** (accessed by a 1km walking trail from Praia dos Anjos) to the northeast; and the vast **Praia Grande** to the west.

Ilha de Cabo Frio is accessed by boat from Praia dos Anjos. **Praia do Farol** on the protected side of the island is a gorgeous beach with fine white sand. From here there is a 2½-hour walk to the lighthouse. The **Gruta Azul** (Blue Cavern), on the southwestern side of the island, is another beautiful spot. Be alert, though: the entrance to the underwater cavern is submerged at high tide. Tour operators who organize dives in these waters abound – the tourist office keeps a complete list.

Sleeping

Expect prices to rise by 30% in high season. Prices quoted here are for the low season.

Hotel Praia Grande (☎ /fax 2622 1369; Rua Dom Pedro 41; s/d US$9/15) A nice budget option right in the center of town, Hotel Praia Grande has clean, spartan rooms available.

IYHF Youth Hostel (☎ /fax2622 4060; Rua Bernardo Lems 145; per person US$8) Located near Praia dos Anjos, this youth hostel is quite a good deal with dorms and private rooms available, and a helpful staff to rent bicycles, canoes and diving equipment.

Porto dos Anjos (☎ /fax2622 1629; Av Luis Correa 8; d US$20) A former house that's been converted into a pousada, Porto dos Angos's rooms have lovely sea views.

Pousada da Prainha (☎ 2622 2512; pousada -da-prainha@alohanet.com.br; Rua D 90; d US$35) Out on Prainha beach, this simple but attractive pousada has nice *apartamentos* designed for couples.

Estalagem dos Corais (☎ 2622 2593; fax 2622 2182; Rua E 101; d US$40) Also on Prainha beach, this pousada is a great deal with a pool, sauna and fresh airy rooms.

Estalagem do Porto (☎ 2622 2892; www.esta lagemdoporto.com.br in Portuguese; Rua Santa Cruz 12; s/d US$25/35) Located on Praia dos Anjos, this place has rooms large enough to hold up to six people. Overall a great place to stay, with comfortable surroundings.

Capitão n'Areia Pousada (☎ 2622 2720; www .capitaopousada.com.br in Portuguese; Rua Santa Cruz 7; s/d US$50/90; ☒) Probably one of the nicest establishments in town, rooms here are elegant and big, just like the pool.

Hotel Pousada Caminho do Sol (☎ 2622 2029; www.caminhodosol.com.br; Rua do Sol 50; d US$50) Right on Praia Grande, this pretty resort hotel with a pool and beautiful views is a big hit with visiting Brazilians looking for a romantic weekend.

Eating

Garrafa de Nansen Restaurante (☎ 2622 1553; Rua Santa Cruz 4; meals US$10; noon-10pm) A classy place for seafood, this local favorite isn't going to break the bank.

Todos as Prazeres (☎ 2622 2365; Rua José Pinto Macedo 5; meals US$10 ☺ 1-8pm) This restaurant, located near the southeastern end of Prainha, is a great place to eat. It serves creative dishes such as fish in orange sauce with coconut *farofa* and apple and gorgonzola soup.

Viagem dos Sabores (☎ 2622 2892; Rua Santa Cruz 12; meals US$12; ☺ 1-9pm) Inside the Pousada Estalagem do Porto, this well-run restaurant serves up delectable dishes with all sorts of eclectic influences. Bahian flavors, Italian and French are prominent.

Getting There & Away

From Rio, there are several buses daily (US$10, three hours).

An alternative is to catch one of the more frequent buses to Cabo Frio, then take the municipal bus from Cabo Frio (US$0.90), which loops around Arraial and returns to Cabo Frio every 20 minutes. Catch it at the Arraial do Cabo **bus station** (☎ 2622 1488; Praça da Bandeira), which is situated in the town center.

CABO FRIO

☎ 0xx24 / pop 102,000

Built up around sand dunes and beaches, with plenty of fresh breezes, Cabo Frio's naturally gorgeous settings have been slightly stunted by the salt and tourism industries that dominate in the area. If you are able to overlook some of the encroaching overdevelopment, Cabo Frio remains a relaxed little beach town, ready to greet newcomers with a smile. Every weekend it attracts scores of visitors and during the holiday months many people come to stay here for weeks at a time – the bars are invariably filled with happy-go-lucky Brazilians whooping it up, and the merrymaking spirit here is clearly Cabo Frio's strongest attraction.

History

Santa Helena de Cabo Frio, as it was originally known, was founded in 1615 after the Portuguese had defeated their European foes in the area. The fort of São Mateus was built to protect the lucrative brazilwood trade. In time, the Franciscans joined the settlement and built the NS dos Anjos convent. They were followed by the Jesuits, who settled at Fazenda Campo Novo. By the 1800s, with the brazilwood stands completely destroyed, the economy was geared toward fishing. More recently, tourism, saltworks and chemical industries have become important.

Ipanema (p123), Rio de Janerio

JOHN MAIER JR

JOHN PENNOCK

Copacabana Beach (p127), Rio de Janerio

Restaurant, Centro (p134), Rio de Janeiro

JOHN PENNOCK

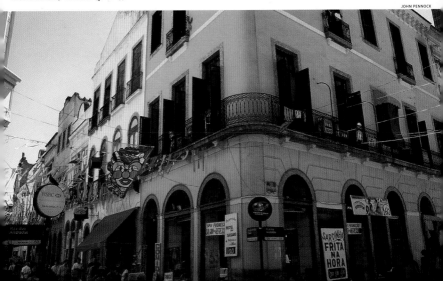

LEE FOSTER

Nightclub performer (p170), Rio de Janeiro

JOHN MA

Carnaval float (p106), Sambódromo, Rio de Janeiro

Samba performers (p55), Copacabana Beach, Rio de Janerio

JOHN MA

Orientation

The town of Cabo Frio is at the end of the long sweeping beach that extends northward from Arraial do Cabo. Cabo Frio lies to the west of the Canal do Itajuru, which links the Lagoa de Araruama to the Atlantic Ocean. Near the bridge is the town's focal point – a hill with a small white chapel. The town center is east of here, and the bus station is to the west (about 2km from the center) near the end of Av Júlia Kubitschek. This road runs almost parallel to the Praia do Forte, named after the fort at its eastern end. There's a small map of Cabo Frio on the wall of the bus station.

Information

Banco do Brasil (Praça Porto Rocha 44)
Bradesco ATM (Av Assunção 904)
Post office (Largo de Santo Antônio 55)
Telemar (Praça Porto Rocha) Telephone office.
Tourist office (☎ 2647 1689; Praça Cristóvão Colombo; 🕑 8am-6pm Mon-Fri, 9am-6pm Sat & Sun) Directly south of the hill, at the end of Av João Pessoa near Praia do Forte. It has hotel information and maps; English, Spanish and French are spoken.

CABO FRIO AREA

Forte São Mateus

This **stone fortress** (admission free; 🕑 10am-4pm Tue-Sun), a stronghold against pirates, was built between 1616 and 1620 to replace the original French-built fort. You will find the fort at the eastern end of Praia do Forte.

Dunes

There are three sand-dune spots in and about Cabo Frio. The dunes of **Praia do Peró**, a super beach for surfing and surf casting, are 6km north in the direction of Búzios, near Ogivas and after Praia Brava and Praia das Conchas. The **Dama Branca** (White Lady) sand dunes are on the road to Arraial do Cabo. The **Pontal** dunes of Praia do Forte town beach stretch from the fort to Miranda hill. Robberies can pose a danger at the dunes, so get advice from the locals before you head out to remote beaches and dunes.

Sleeping

Cabo Frio is a bit built-up, but it's possible to find some good accommodations in the town center.

BUDGET

Porto Fino (☎ /fax 2643 6230; Rua Jorge Lóssio 160; s/d US$20/35) A pretty pousada, Porto Fino is a great option.

Atlantico (☎ /fax 2643 0996; Rua Jose Bonifacio 302; s/d US$20/30) One of the most popular budget hotels in town, Atlantico has large rooms at bargain prices.

Pousada Costa do Sol (☎ 2644 6596; Rua Maria Duarte de Azvedo 85; s/d US$15/28) In the neighborhood known as Jardim Flamboyant, this pousada has simple clean rooms. From the bus station, walk three blocks southwest along Rua Inglaterra and turn right.

Camping Club do Brasil (☎ 2643 3124; Rua dos Passageiros 700; per person US$9) A favorite camping site for youngsters, you get to choose: sling a hammock between scrubby pines or pitch a tent.

MID-RANGE & TOP END

La Plage (☎ 2645 4658; Rua dos Badejos 40; s/d US$60/80) Considered one of Cabo's best hotels, La Plage fills up quickly on the weekends. Book ahead, and try to get a room with a view.

Porto Peró (☎ 2644 5568; www.pousadaportopero .com.br; Av dos Pescadores 2002; s/d US$20/30; 🐾) This pousada is on one of the prettiest stretches of beach around. It has clean, pretty rooms, very light and airy, and a lovely pool area.

Eating

There are some good eateries around Praça Porto Rocha, in the center of town.

Bacalhauzinho (Praça Porto Rocha 27; dinner US$12; 6pm-midnight) An excellent place to try some *bacalhau* (cod), this restaurant has a particularly enjoyable atmosphere.

Confeitaria Branca (Praça Porto Rocha 15; dessert US$1-4) This is where the Brazilians come for their post-*cafezinhos* (coffee) sugar fix every afternoon. The desserts are splendid.

Getting There & Away

The **bus station** (☎ 2643 2291; Av Júlia Kubitschek) is 2km west of the center.

To get to Arraial do Cabo from Cabo Frio, catch a local bus from the bus stop just to the left as you leave the bus station. To get to Búzios, catch a bus from the stop across the road. Local buses cost US$0.90. There are regular, air-conditioned buses from Rio de Janeiro and Niterói along Hwy BR-101 (US$10, three hours, five a day from 7am to 10pm).

BÚZIOS

☎ 0xx24 / pop 8600

Búzios is considered one of the most charming places in Brazil and it is indeed lovely, sitting on a peninsula scalloped by 17 beaches that juts into the Atlantic. A simple fishing village until the early '60s, when it was 'discovered' by Brigitte Bardot and her Brazilian boyfriend, Búzios is now littered with boutiques, fine restaurants, fancy villas, bars and posh pousadas. The Mediterranean touch introduced by the Portuguese has not been lost – in fact the narrow, winding cobblestone streets help make Búzios all the more beautiful – it *is* known as Brazil's St Tropez, after all.

Orientation

Búzios is not a single town but rather three settlements on the peninsula – Ossos, Manguinhos and Armação de Búzios – and one on the mainland called Rasa. Ossos (Bones), at the northern tip of the peninsula, is the oldest and most attractive. It has a pretty harbor and yacht club, a few hotels and bars, and a tourist stand. Manguinhos, on

the isthmus, is the most commercial; it even has a 24-hour medical clinic. Armação, in between, has the best restaurants, along with city necessities such as international phones, a bank, gas station, post office and a pharmacy. Northwest along the coast is Rasa and Ilha Rasa (the island of Rasa), where the political dignitaries and rich of Brazil relax.

Information

From any newsstand, pick up a copy of *Guia Verão Búzios* (US$3). It has information in English as well as Portuguese, including a list of places to stay (but no prices). Other useful places include the following:

Banco do Brasil (Rua Manoel de Carvalho 70) In Armação.

Internet Café (Av José Bento Ribeiro Danta) Next door to the Meu Sonho hotel.

Main tourist office (☎ 0800-249 999; www.buziosturismo.com; 24hr) At the town's main entrance.

Malízia Tour (☎ 2623 1226; Shopping Praia do Canto, loja 16, Rua das Pedras) Will change money; there is an ATM at Praça Santos Dumont.

Secretaria de Turismo (☎ 2623 2099; Praça Santos Dumont; 9am-9pm) Keeps an office in Armação.

Beaches

In general, the southern beaches are trickier to get to, but they're prettier and have better surf. The northern beaches are more sheltered and closer to the towns.

Going counterclockwise from south of Manguinhos, the first beaches are **Geribá** and **Ferradurinha** (Little Horseshoe). These are beautiful beaches with good surf, but the Búzios Beach Club has built condos here. Next on the coast is **Ferradura**, which is large enough for windsurfing, and **Lagoinha**, a rocky beach with rough water. **Praia da Foca** and **Praia do Forno** have colder water than the other beaches. **Praia Olho de Boi** (Bull's Eye) was named after Brazil's first postage stamp. It's a pocket-size beach reached by a little trail from the long, clean beach of **Praia Brava**.

Both **João Fernandinho** and **João Fernandes** are good for snorkeling, as are the topless beaches of **Azedinha** and **Azeda**. **Praia dos Ossos**, **Praia da Armação**, **Praia do Caboclo** and **Praia dos Amores** are pretty to look at, but a bit public and not so nice for lounging around on. **Praia da Tartaruga** is quiet and pretty. **Praia do Gaucho** and **Manguinhos** are town beaches further along.

Tours

The schooner *Queen Lory* makes daily trips (US$20 for 2½ hours) out to Ilha Feia, and to Tartaruga and João Fernandinho beaches. These trips are a good value, especially since *caipirinhas*, soft drinks, fruit salad and snorkeling gear are included in the price. To make a reservation, ask at your pousada or visit **Queen Lory Tours** (☎ 2623 1179; Rua Angela Diniz 35) in Ossos.

Sleeping

Búzios is a romantic place, and solo travelers are unusual, so things can get pricey if you're not traveling in numbers. In general, rooms to rent are cheaper than pousadas. Rates quoted here are for the low season. The high season is December to March and again in July.

BUDGET

Albergue da Juventude Praia dos Amores (☎ 2623 2422; Av Bento Riberio 92; s US$13) Some 20 minutes walking distance from Praia da Tartaruga, this *albergue* (hostel) fronts a busy road and has fairly simple facilities. Nevertheless, it offers OK accommodations in beautiful Búzios and doesn't attempt to price-gouge unaccompanied travelers.

Meu Sonho (☎ 2623 0902; www.meusonho-buzios .8k.com in Portuguese; Av José Bento Ribeiro Dantas 1289; s/d US$20/30) Just a block away from the beach, with an attractive dipping pool, Meu Sonho is clean and affordable.

Seria Dourada (☎ /fax2623 1131; Praia dos Ossos; s/d US$20/35) On the beach but affordable, this cute and quiet pousada is a great deal.

Country Camping Club (☎ /fax 2629 1122; Rua Maria Joaquina 895; per person US$5) Located on Praia Rasa, Country Camping Club has great facilities but is a bit out of the way.

MID-RANGE & TOP END

Pousada Mediterrânea (☎ 2623 2353; Rua João Fernandes 58; s/d US$30/45) A whitewashed little hotel, most rooms have lovely inland views.

Pousadinha em Búzios (☎ /fax 2623 1448; Rua Turíbio de Farias 202; d US$43) A small cutie in the town center, Pousadinha has very attractive rooms in a very scenic section of town.

Pousada do Corsário (☎ 2623 6443; fax 2623 6403; Rua Agripino de Souza 50; d US$60) This pousada is quite pleasant, with beautiful sea views from some of its rooms and really gorgeous grounds leading down to the beach.

Pousada la Chimere (☎ 2623 1460; www.lachimere .com.br; Praça Eugênio Harold 36; s/d US$55/75) What an excellent place for a night of luxury. La Chimere has a lovely courtyard, and large, well-appointed rooms with a view over the square. The surroundings are tranquil and soothing.

There is a couple of top-end places in Alto do Humaitá in Armação with stunning views.

El Cazar (☎ 2623 1620; elcazar@uol.com.br; Rua A No 6; d US$115; ﹩) A stylish place, El Cazar has a rooftop pool, sauna, Jacuzzis, tennis court, gym, and a games room. Very elegant and posh furnishings create a romantic atmosphere.

Eating

For good, cheap food, eat grilled fish right on the beaches. Brava, Ferradura and João Fernandes beaches have little thatched-roof fish and beer restaurants. Most of the better restaurants are in or near Armação.

Bananaland (☎ 2623 2666; Rua Turíbio de Farias 50; meals US$6; ﹩ 11am-midnight) Touted as the largest self-serve around, this place will have something for everyone. The range of choices is simply astounding.

Botequim do Baiano (☎ 9214 0317; Rua Luis Joaquim Pereira 265; meals US$5; ﹩ 11am-11pm) Near Praça Santos Dumont, Botequim has some of the best *prato feitos* in town, which usually includes fish or meat with rice, beans and salad.

Restaurante Boom (☎ 2623 6254; Rua Turíbio de Farias 110; per kg US$10; ﹩ noon-10pm) Another excellent and varied buffet for bargain prices.

For fancier and more expensive fare, go for a stroll on Rua das Pedras.

As Bruxas (☎ 9953 0246; Rua das Pedras 21; US$10; ﹩ 6pm-midnight) A delectable combination of Brazilian and northern Italian dishes is served here.

Shiro uma Shushi (☎ 2623 7445; Rua das Pedras 181; dinner US$12; ﹩ noon-11pm) You've got sushi and sashimi galore at this lovely restaurant.

Chez Michou Crêperie (☎ 2623 2169; Rua das Pedras 90; meals US$6; ﹩ 1pm-late) A popular hangout thanks to the incredible crepes – any kind you want. Of course, the outdoor bar serving delicious *pinha coladas* might also be bringing in the crowds.

Sawasdee (☎ 2623 4644; Orla Bardot 422; mains US$7-10) One of the newest places in Búzios features Thai cuisine that showcases the fresh seafood from the area. The *kaipilychia* (lychee caipirinhas) are quite tasty.

Sorvetes Mil Frutas (☎ 2623 6436; Rua das Pedras 59) A great spot to feast on refreshing ice cream, Mil Frutas offers dozens of flavors.

Entertainment

The center of action in Búzios is the Rua das Pedras in Armação. And it all starts rather late – don't even think of getting here before midnight.

Patio Havana (Rua das Pedras 101) is worth checking out if you're a jazz aficionado, at least for one drink (but the food is great, too). Fabulous musicians from all over Brazil (and the world) regularly pop in here.

Fashion Café (Rua das Pedras s/n) is across the street from Michou's Crêperie. At the hottest spot in town for disco sounds and pop music, a young crowd gathers to dance the night away on weekends.

Takatakata (Rua das Pedras 256) is a lively bar that's a popular place for sampling one of expat owner Kijzer Van Derhoff's fiery concoctions.

Getting There & Around

From Cabo Frio to Búzios (Ossos), take the municipal bus (a 50-minute, 20km trip). The Búzios **bus station** (☎ 2623 2050; Estrada da Usina Velha 444) is easily reachable on foot. Seven buses daily head to Rio (US$10, three hours) from 6:30am to 7:15pm.

Espírito Santo

HIGHLIGHTS

- Climbing **Morro da Penha** (p211) in Vitória for spectacular views

- Dancing to *forró* (popular music of the Northeast) in the village of **Itaúnas** (p216)

- Exploring the **Parque Estadual de Itaúnas** (p215), with its sand dunes, beaches and turtles

- Driving the coastal highway connecting Vitória to the beaches of **Guarapari** (p216), **Anchieta** (p217) and **Piúma** (p219), and stopping to picnic and swim along the way

- Hiking to the Blue Rock at the **Parque Estadual da Pedra Azul** (p220)

Parque Estadual de Itaúnas

Parque Estadual da Pedra Azul

Vitória

Guarapari

Anchieta

Piúma

■ POPULATION: 2.7 MILLION   ■ AREA: 46,184 SQ KM

Espírito Santo

Home to a long, winding coastline dotted with sleepy fishing villages and calm blue waters that sometimes turn violent with bad weather, Espírito Santo is the wallflower of Brazil – often overlooked but not bad upon closer inspection. Some parts of the state are heavily industrialized, but in other locations the beaches are truly divine – the long, sweeping stretches of sand and family-friendly atmosphere are reminiscent of Mediterranean fishing villages. To the north, the sand dunes of the Parque Estadual de Itaúnas are the state's highlight. Espírito Santo has long been a favorite destination for Brazilians and here your fellow beachgoers will likely be from Minas Gerais, southern Bahia or northern Rio state.

Inland, the lush and mountainous coffee- and strawberry-producing regions have interesting towns populated by Italian and German immigrants, along with ecological reserves and the splendid Parque Estadual da Pedra Azul.

History
Colonized in the 16th century, Espírito Santo became an armed region to prevent gold from being smuggled out of Minas Gerais. Coffee plantations, the prime source of income up until the 1960s, have been superseded by mining and shipping. Vitória serves

as headquarters to Garoto, Brazil's famous (and delicious) chocolate, as well as several chemical and agribusiness concerns.

Climate
Not quite as searingly hot as equatorial Bahia or wiltingly humid as São Paulo, Espírito Santo can nonetheless get quite uncomfortable in the summer months. Villages along the rather damp, low-lying seaboard used to be regularly plagued by malaria and it's still a good idea to take basic precautions. Inland, especially in the mountainous Serra da Chibata, temperatures are pleasantly warm year-round. Rains are common, especially in the north, but rarely last long.

Getting There & Around
Vitória is the biggest city in Espírito Santo and as such boasts a domestic and international airport. Air service is offered to all major cities throughout Brazil and the rest of South America. A well-run bus service connects Vitória to Rio, São Paulo, and neighboring cities throughout Minas Gerais, as well as Bahia to the north. Regular buses also run up and down Espírito Santo's coastline.

VITÓRIA
☎ 0xx27 / pop 292,000
Vitória doesn't have much to show of its colonial past and is often dismissed as a being aesthetically unappealing (despite having the same lush backdrop of moun-

ESPÍRITO SANTO

0 ___ 50 km
0 ___ 30 miles

| 42°W | 41°W | 40°W |

18°S

Teófilo Otoni

BR 116

Rio Doce

Governador Valadares

Espírito Santo

Reserva Biológica do Córrego do Veado

Parque Estadual de Itaúnas

BR 101

Itaúnas

Conceição da Barra

São Mateus

Reserva Biológica de Sooretama

19°S

Minas Gerais

Colatina

Linhares

Reserva Biológica Nova Lombardia

Santa Teresa

Fundão

Reserva Biológica de Comboios

Santa Cruz

20°S

Venda Nova do Imigrante

Domingos Martins

VITÓRIA

Vila Velha

BR 262

Parque Nacional do Caparaó

Parque Estadual da Pedra Azul

ES 060

Guarapari

Ubu

Iriri

Anchieta

Cachoeiro de Itapemirim

BR 101

Piúma

Bom Jesus do Itabapoana

Itapemirim

Marataízes

21°S

Itaperuna

BR 356

Rio de Janeiro

ATLANTIC OCEAN

Campos dos Goitacazes

| 42°W | 41°W | 40°W |

Bahia 18°S

19°S

20°S

21°S

tains rushing down to meet sandy beaches that so characterizes Rio). It's true that this capital city is a port town; export coffee and timber pass through here, and the port at nearby Tubarão is the outlet for millions of tons of iron ore. But that doesn't mean Vitória is devoid of all charm. Local residents, known as Capixabas, are warm and friendly and the city has a flourishing economy, which translates into many bars, universities, nightclubs, restaurants and hotels. Plus, the heart of the city is built on an island just off the coast, which gives it an attractive and exotic air.

Orientation

Old Vitória, such as it is, connects to the mainland via a series of bridges. The parts of the city that run along the coast have the best beaches – Canto and Camburí to the north, and Vila Velha to the south has the renowned Praia da Costa. The teeming, modern **bus station** (☎ 3222 3666) is on Ilha do Principe in the center of the old town (don't let the name fool you – it's not a separate island). Trains from Belo Horizonte (see p230) arrive at Estação Ferroviária ria Pedro Nolasco, 1km west of the bus station in the mainland district of Cariacaca.

Information

Traveler's checks are widely accepted and can be cashed at any of the numerous banks around town. There are three telephone posts: two in the center, on Rua do Rosário and at Praça Costa Pereira, and a third at the airport. Other helpful places:

Main post office (Av Jerônimo Monteiros) In the center of town (there's also a branch at the bus station).

Miami souvenir shop (☎ 3222 5973; Av Marechal Mascarenhas; ⊙ 9am-5pm Mon-Fri) The best cash exchange rate.

SETUR (☎ 3325 1899; Shop 4, Rua Celso Calmon 135; ⊙ 8:30am-6:30pm Mon-Fri) The state-run tourism office, located right on Praia do Canto, has great maps and helpful staff.

Tourist booths (⊙ 8am-9pm Mon-Fri, 9am-4pm Sat) Located at the bus station and airport.

Sights

CITY CENTER

The yellow **Anchieta Palace**, on Praça João Climaco, is a 16th-century former Jesuit college and church. It's now the seat of state government, and the only part you can enter is the **tomb of Padre José de Anchieta** (1534-97; admission free), the cofounder of São Paulo and an early missionary who was hailed as the 'Apostle of Brazil.'

Close by is the **Catedral Metropolitana**, with its neo-Gothic exterior and interesting stained-glass windows. **Teatro Carlos Gomes** (Praça Costa Pereira) is a replica of La Scala in Milan. Capixabas like to walk and relax in the **Parque Moscoso**, just west of the city center along Av Cleto Nunes.

VILA VELHA

Across the river and south of Vitória sits Vila Velha, the first place in Espírito Santo to be colonized. Don't miss seeing the **Convento da Penha**, atop the 154m granite Morro da Penha. The panoramic city views are magnificent and the chapel (founded in 1558) isn't too bad either. It's a major pilgrimage destination – around Easter, expect massive crowds all paying homage to NS da Penha, some climbing the hill on their knees.

Beaches

Praia do Camburí, a 5km stretch of beach, is punctuated by kiosks, restaurants, nightspots and mid-range hotels. Don't swim near the bridge – it's polluted here. **Praia da Costa**, the main Vila Velha beach, has fewer hotels and restaurants than Camburí, but you can swim and bodysurf. Keep a close eye on the horizon – huge supertankers often pop up with surprising speed!

Sleeping

BUDGET

Pousada Itatiaia (☎ 3329 6513; Av Antônio Gil Veloso 2728; www.pousadaitatiaia.com.br in Portuguese; s/d US$10/28) Pousada Itatiaia is a simple but pleasant hotel right in the middle of Praia de Itapuã in Vila Velha, exactly the place you want to be.

Principe Hotel (☎ 3322 2799; Av Dario L Souza 120; dm/s/d US$5/7/14) One of many good budget options in the center of town, the Principe Hotel youth hostel is just steps away from the bus station and offers cheerful *quartos* (rooms with shared bathroom) or *apartamentos* (rooms with private bathroom) at good prices.

Hotel Cidade Alta (☎ 3233 3346; Rua Pedro Palácios 213; s/d US$7/15) A decent hotel with clean affordable beds, the Cidade Alta is in the so-called 'historic district.'

MID-RANGE

Ibis Vitória (☎ 3345 8600; www.accorhotels.com.br; Rua João da Cruz 385, Praia do Canto; s/d US$20/30) Usually this hotel caters to business travelers but there's absolutely no reason why the footloose and fancy-free can't enjoy the fully-equipped rooms and great location as well. The Ibis is near Praia do Canto, the beach a short walk away, and there's lots of dining and nightlife right around the corner.

Hotel Praia (☎ 3227 8777; Av Dante Michelini 207; s/d US$34/44) Out at Camburí, this pretty hotel has good rooms in a fun area, not too far from the water.

Comfort Vitória Praia (☎ 3334 9898; Av Dante Michelini 1057; s/d US$30/45) As the name would

suggest, this is a very comfortable place to hang your hat. Although basic, the rooms are welcoming.

Praia da Costa in Vila Velha, although more expensive than other beaches, is the best one near Vitória.

Hostess (☎ 3329 2111; Av Antônio Gil Veloso 412; s/d US$44/53) This three-star hotel has been freshly painted and spruced up, and rooms reflect the new modern approach.

Hotel Costa Mar (☎ 3200 4688; Av Antônio Gil Veloso 1480; s/d US$50/60) This three-star hotel looms up from the pavement just a few short blocks away from Hostess, but the somewhat boring exterior doesn't do the inside justice. Plus, this hotel is well positioned and has rooms with balconies.

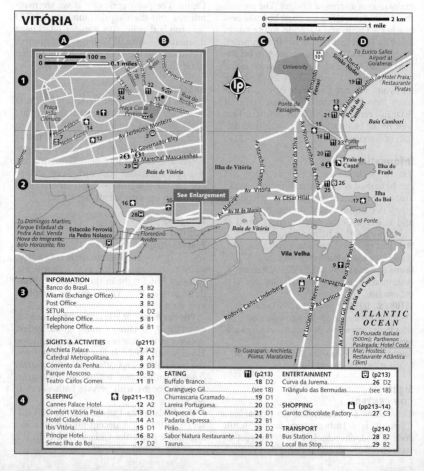

VITÓRIA

0 _____ 2 km
0 _____ 1 mile

Parthenon Pasárgada (☎ 3399 6500; Av Antônio Gil Veloso 1856; s/d US$90/120) Not quite a full splurge but definitely in the high end of the mid-range hotels is the Parthenon in Vila Velha near Praia da Costa. It's got spacious, airy rooms and is supremely comfortable.

TOP END

Senac Ilha do Boi (☎ 3345 0111; Rua Bráulio Macedo 417; www.hotelilhadoboi.com.br; s/d standard US$65/85, luxury US$100/120; P Q ☎) This place will blow your mind. Located on top of a hill with fabulous views of the surrounding bay, the service is impeccable and the amenities delightful, especially the saunas. If you are in need of a real night of luxury, this is a very good choice.

Eating & Drinking

Don't forget to try the regional specialty known as *moqueca capixaba*, a savory mixture of local seafood cooked in a delicious casse-rolelike dish. For drinks, dancing, people-watching and all kinds of fun head to the Triângulo das Bermudas (see right).

BUDGET & MID-RANGE

Buffalo Branco (☎ 3227 2933; Rua Joaquim Lírio 723; meals US$10; ☺ dinner) Along with Caranguejo Gil this is one of the hottest places to eat in town. It serves varied dishes, heavy on meat and seafood, at good prices.

Caranguejo Gil (Rua João da Cruz 80; meals US$10; ☺ dinner) Opposite Buffalo Branco in the very popular Triangulo area, Caranguejo Gil has a similar menu and atmosphere.

Sabor Natura Restaurante (Rua 13 de Maio 90; meals per kg US$4; ☺ 11am-9pm) A veggie-friendly self-serve place that's very popular with students, Sabor always has fresh, delicious food.

Padaria Expressa (Rua Graciano Neves 22; meals per kg US$4; ☺ 11am-7pm) Just off Praça Costa Pereira, this is an excellent place to stock up on bread, cheese and snacks. It also has a good per-kilo buffet lunch.

Restaurante Atlântica (Av Antônio Gil Veloso 80; meals US$8; ☺ lunch Sat & Sun, dinner daily) Head for this place when you're ready for some excellent *moqueca capixaba* for two and local seafood dishes.

Restaurante Piratas (☎ 3235 1622; Av Dante Michelini 747, Praia do Camburí; meals US$10; ☺ 11am-2pm) A decent seafood place, the real attraction at Piratas is the air-conditioning (during summer, at least).

Churrascaria Gramado (☎ 3225 1311; Av Rosendo Serapião Souza Filho 43; meals US$10; ☺ 11am-3pm & 6:30-10:30pm Mon-Sat, 11am-5pm Sun) A haven for meat lovers with big appetites, patrons wad-dle away from their tables and groan their way out the door after a meal here.

Moqueca & Cia (☎ 3227 6899; Av Dante Michelini 727, Praia do Camburí; meals US$12; ☺ 11-1am) Another great place for seafood dishes, the emphasis here is on traditional recipes and dishes.

Taurus (☎ 3225 4888; Rua Madeira de Freitas 174-A, Praia do Canto; meals US$15; ☺ 11:30am-3:30pm & 6:30-11:30pm Mon-Fri, 6:30pm-1am Sat) There are lots of varied dishes, from Italian pastas to American burgers, available at Taurus. A nice change of pace when you've reached your *moqueca* limit.

TOP END

Lareira Portuguesa (☎ 3345 0329; Av Saturnino de Brito 260, Praia do Canto; mains US$9-18; ☺ 11:30am-3pm & 6:30pm-midnight Mon-Sat, 11:30am-4pm Sun) A gorgeous garden and beautiful Portuguese tiles adding splashes of color here and there make this a very sexy and sophisticated location. Delicious fish dishes form the back-bone of the menu, but there are also risottos with a variety of ingredients (broccoli, shrimp, chicken to name a few), some nice grilled, fried or baked shrimp mains, and inventive desserts. A particular standout main is the *bacalhau à Lareira* (cod deep-fried with a crushed-almond coating).

Pirao (☎ 3227 1165; Rua Joaquim Lirio 753, Praia do Canto; meals US$20; ☺ 11am-3pm & 6:30-11pm Tue-Fri, 11am-5pm Sat-Mon) Known for its *moquecas* and *capixabas*, Pirao also does another regional specialty – grouper prepared with banana *à terra*. It's delicious! But only served Friday and Sunday.

Entertainment

Capixabas like the nightlife – check out the **Triângulo das Bermudas**, a stretch of road packed with bars, eateries and nightclubs between Rua Joaquim Lírio and Rua João da Cruz. Hip crowds also gather at Curva da Jurema, populated by shacks that serve snacks and food into the wee hours.

Shopping

Garoto chocolate factory (☎ 3320 1200) Visit the factory store, where the best chocolate in Brazil is really fresh. It's located at Praça

Meyerfreund Glória, off Rodovia Carlos Lindenberg in Vila Velha – you can take bus No 500 from the city center.

Getting There & Away

Buses leave the bus station for Belo Horizonte (US$22, eight hours, nine daily), Ouro Prêto (US$20, eight hours, direct bus at 10:45pm), Porto Seguro (US$25, nine hours, one a day at 9am) and Rio (US$22, nine hours, 11 a day from 6am to 11pm).

There is also a daily train to Belo Horizonte (see p230).

Flights leave regularly for Belém, Belo Horizonte, Brasília, Porto Alegre, Recife, Rio, Salvador and São Paulo.

Getting Around

Eurico Salles airport (☎ 3327 0811) is 10km northeast of the city center, in Goiaberas. Take the local bus marked 'aeroporto/ rodoviária' to and from the center. Taxis cost about US$10.

All local buses (US$0.55) run from the various stops outside the bus station; the

---

THE STEPS OF ANCHIETA

José de Anchieta arrived in Brazil as a Jesuit missionary in 1553. Along with Manoel da Nóbrega he founded the village of Piratininga (today the megacity of São Paulo). On a trip down the São Paulo coast, he was captured by Tamoio Indians. While held hostage he began one of his most famous poems, the 'Poema da Virgem,' by tracing words on the beach sand. In addition to being a priest and poet, he was a teacher, nurse and church-builder, and he was regarded as the 'Indian expert' of his time.

Anchieta walked along the coast of Espírito Santo in his mission to convert all the Indian tribes he met. He ended up at Reritiba, today the town of **Anchieta** (p217), where he chose to spend the last few years of his life. In 1980 he was beatified by the Pope and is now a candidate for sainthood.

A group of devoted followers of Padre Anchieta organizes an annual pilgrimage that retraces his 'steps.' The popular 100km walk along the beach from Vitória to Anchieta takes place in June (exact dates vary each year) and lasts three days. Contact the state tourism office in Vitória for specifics.

---

route is written on the side of each bus. For the center, catch any bus that goes along Av Vitória. When you pass the yellow palace on the left-hand side, get out and you will be at the Anchieta Palace.

For Praia do Camburí, catch any bus that goes along Av Dante Michelini. To Vila Velha and Praia da Costa catch an all-yellow Transcol bus (US$0.80). Look at the place placards on the bus – usually pretty self-explanatory. All those with Praia da Costa on top, for example, are indeed headed to Praia da Costa.

THE COAST

CONCEIÇÃO DA BARRA
☎ 0xx27 / pop 22,000

If you arrive in the off season, Conceição da Barra looks a little run-down – the small town is dominated by a long stretch of beautiful water (not much beach to lie on, though) and without the usual swarm of visitors from Minas Gerais and São Paulo states it can seem a little desolate. Praia da Barra and Guaxindiba are the best beaches and during the Brazilian summer months things are really hopping. At other times though, it's simply a quiet fishing village populated by working-class folk and weekend retirees from Vitória looking to get out of the city.

For a great sight, follow Av Atlântica all the way down to the end, beyond the string of pousadas (guesthouses) until you reach the spot where the River Itaúnas meets the ocean and the waters churn powerfully against the surrounding rocks. Quite a visual feast!

From Conceição da Barra you can go on day trips to the main attraction in the region: the Parque Estadual de Itaúnas, 23km north of Conceição.

Sleeping & Eating

There are several hostels and pousadas lining Av Atlântica, which parallels the beach and has a beautiful esplanade to stroll along.

Praia da Barra (☎ 3762 1100; Av Atlantica 350, Praia de Guaxindiba; s/d US$20/34; P ⊠ ⊠) One of the more attractive options just outside of the city center, Praia da Barra's building isn't all that engaging, but it is right on the beach and offers tons of amenities.

Pousada Varanda da Praia (☎ 3762 1654; Av Atlantica 718; s/d US$15/25) A pousada with very beautiful surroundings and a nice rustic atmosphere, this place serves tea in the garden during the afternoon.

Piramide Hostel (☎ 3762 1983; Rua 26 de Maio 89; s/d per person US$7) Right next to the bus station, the Piramide has basic rooms with bunk beds without fans or breakfast.

Rustico's Hotel (☎ 3762 1193; Rua Muniz Freire 299; s/d US$17/25; ✖) A cut above the rest, Rustico's has rooms around a courtyard and small pool. Prices tend to drop from March through November.

The best places to eat are the kiosks on the beaches, which serve the local speciality *puã de caranguejo*, a tasty crab stew. These shacks also serve coconut milk, fried fish and killer *batidas* (alcoholic fruit shakes). Most regular restaurants close during the slow season, from March through November and December.

Getting There & Away

Buses leave Vitória for Conceição da Barra daily at 6:40am and 11:40am and 4pm. Returning to Vitória, buses (US$12) depart daily from the **bus station** (☎ 3762 1159; Rua 26 de Maio) at 6am, 2pm and 6pm. A local bus heads for Itaúnas five times a day (US$2, 40 minutes).

ITAÚNAS

☎ 0xx27 / pop 2500

Love dancing? Swimming? Fishing? Surfing? Are you like a fly to honey when it comes to being in the great outdoors, consuming potent sugary concoctions and staying up all night with good music? Then you've found your Shangri-La! Itaúnas masquerades as a sleepy fishing village eight months a year, but from early December through early March it's a party-mad town surrounded by a majestic state reserve and ever-encroaching sand dunes.

In fact, those same dunes once engulfed the original village of Itaúnas, which was set about 1km closer to the ocean than it is now – you can even walk on the remains of the top of the old church tower. From atop the dunes you have a great view of the Atlantic Ocean and the neighboring reserve, with its gorgeous mangrove forest.

Until just a few years ago, the rebuilt Itaúnas was simply the gateway to the

fabulous **Parque Estadual de Itaúnas** and only had a couple of places to stay. Now it has about 50 pousadas, and during the Brazilian summer months and holidays is filled with young students who come from all around for the lively *forró* dance parties and nightlife as much as for the beautiful surroundings. In July there's a huge *forró* festival with music and dancing all day and all night. From March to July and August to early December it's very quiet and tranquil – an excellent time to commune with nature at bargain prices.

Things are made somewhat confusing by the lack of street names in Itaúnas, but this is basically a four-road town. Buses stop at the bus depot (a flimsy-looking shack), just a few yards from the village square; around this area are the majority of stores, restaurants and pousadas. In the high season it will be packed; in the low season unbelievably quiet. The main road leading into town loops around the square and back out again. The other roads feed off the main square but don't go far. To get to the beach, ask a local to point you in the right direction and start walking. It's a 1km straight line all the way to the dunes.

Parque Estadual de Itaúnas

This 3674-hectare state reserve extends for 25km along the coast and has impressive 20m- to 30m-high sand dunes. The wilderness here is home to monkeys, sloths and jaguatiricas (wild cats). The park is also a base for the Tamar Project (see p441). From September to March you can view sea turtles hatching. It happens two to three times per week at about 5:30pm.

The Itaúnas **park office** (☎ 3762 1447; peitaunas@ escelsa.com.br) is in the village next to the bridge over the Rio Itaúnas. It has a souvenir shop, as well as informative displays about the local flora, fauna and culture.

Sleeping & Eating

Some addresses in this chapter use the term s/n (*sem número*; without number).

Casa da Praia (☎ 3762 5028; Rua Dercilio Fonseca; www.casadapraiaitaunas.com.br; s/d US$15/30) This is among the loveliest of pousadas that you'll find in this region, although to locate it you'll have to ask for directions once you get down from the bus. There are only a few dirt roads winding around the main square though, so don't worry too much. The beautiful buildings are managed by Lico, an exceptionally friendly Brazilian who takes great pride in keeping the grounds and rooms spotless.

Pousada Albergue Sol das Dunas (☎ 3762 5334; Rua Honório Pinheiro da Silva s/n; dm US$8, d US$16) You'll find clean dorms or private doubles here, with a good breakfast included. It has a nice lounge with a TV and videos, and the friendly owner is fluent in English and German.

Camping da Vila (☎ 3964 2462; Rua Honório Pinheiro da Silva s/n; campsite per person US$3) Right behind the Pousada Albergue Sol das Dunas, this is a pleasant but basic facility.

Pousada Ponta de Areia (☎ 3762 1644; Rua Honório Pinheiro da Silva s/n; d US$30) A supercozy option. The owner, an artist and a great cook, pays attention to the small details.

Pousada das Araras (☎ 3969 0282; Rua Honório Pinheiro da Silva s/n; d US$30) If Ponta de Areia is full, try this place next door. It is similarly priced with *apartamentos* around a courtyard garden. The rooms downstairs also have a nice little garden at the back.

Pousada Arco Íris (☎ 3988 8282; Rua Teófilo Cabral; s/d US$15/25) A friendly atmosphere, this pousada offers simple rooms with balconies.

Pousada A Nave (☎ 3762 1644; Rua Ítalo Vasconcelos; d US$30) Rustic rooms with wooden doors carved by the sculptor/owner (who is a real character) abound here. The round, open-sided thatched bar is a great place for a few late-night drinks. The place overlooks a mangrove forest and sand dunes.

Pousada Gajirú (☎ 3918 5292; Rua Dercílio Ferreora da Fonseca; s/d US$35/45; ✼) If you are suffering from the heat, try this pousada with its air-con rooms and shaded gardens; prices are negotiable for longer stays.

There are plenty of inexpensive options for eating around Itaúnas. Both **Restaurante do Cizinho** (Rua Adolfo Pereira Duarte) just off the plaza, and Pargos, on the plaza, have great per-kilo buffets. The *refeiçaões* (meals) at the simpler restaurants Dona Pedrolina and Dona Teresa, both just a block away from the plaza, are excellent value. Note that opening hours are seasonal and prone to change. In the high season these places are generally open from 11am to 4pm and 6:30pm to 10pm or 11pm. In the low season many open just for dinner or are closed.

Entertainment

During high season the pounding beats of *forró* and *axé* (an Afro-Brazilian pop style, incorporating samba, rock, soul and other influences) spill from every open window and doorway in Itaúnas. You'll have no problem finding a place to cut loose (things don't really start swinging 'til after midnight) but when in doubt head for Casa da Praia (see p215), which opens up its whole veranda for dancing and gives strong encouragement to beginners.

Ask locals to point you toward Baruco do Tatu and Bar Forró (festive little shacks that get packed full of dancers at night during the high season), on the dirt track that heads out to the beaches.

Getting There & Away

From the bus stop in the plaza, there are five buses daily between Conceição da Barra bus station and Itaúnas. Tickets cost US$2.

GUARAPARI

☎ 0xx27

There are some lovely, untrammeled beaches just waiting to be enjoyed about 30 minutes south of Vitória. This stretch of coast is usually passed over by foreigners, but Guarapari is a favored resort destination for Brazilians and as such, retains a relaxed, fun and family-friendly atmosphere. There are 23 beaches in the municipality, each with a lovely mountain backdrop.

The best beach is **Praia do Morro**, north of the city (be aware that its so-called 'healing' black monazitic sand is, in fact, said to be radioactive!), but also consider **Praia dos Namorados** (small but surrounded by rocks that create beautiful pools), **Praia Castanheiras** (more radioactive sand but crystal-clear waters), **Praia do Meio**, aka Siribeira (great rock pools with gorgeous snorkeling), **Praia Enseada Azul** (a long stretch with lots of natural beauty), and **Praia dos Padres** (accessible only by trail from Enseada Azul) with stunning green waters. Right after that comes **Meaípe**, another good place to spend the night. This is a beautiful area to get to know by car (although there are frequent bus connections through the towns) because for most of the trip the highway follows the rough and rugged coastline – what a treat to be able to pull over and take a dip at will!

The only exception is a series of hulking eyesores just above Anchieta; one of the region's largest industrial companies has set up shop there.

Orientation & Information

The center is 500m south of the bus station, across the bridge; the beach is 200m further on. The **tourist office** (☎ 3361 2322; Praça Jerônimo Monteiro) has maps and information in Portuguese. The **telephone post** (Av Des Lourival de Almeida) is on the main drag on the waterfront.

Sleeping

BUDGET

Guaracamping (☎ 3261 0475; Av Antonio Guimarães, QD 40; campsite per person US$6, s/d US$10/20) There are tent sites aplenty on large, walled grounds within walking distance to the beach. Guaracamping also has reasonable *apartamentos* and *quartos* for a bit more money. It's a two-minute walk west of the bus station – cross the main road, take the next left and it's one block down on the right-hand corner. This area is known as Muquiçaba (Mosquito Nest), so bring repellent!

Hotel do Ângelo (☎ 3261 0230; Rua Pedro Caetano 254; s/d US$13/30) Pleasant rooms and a friendly staff are what make this place worth staying in.

Solar da Ruth (☎ 3261 1836; Rua Dr Silva Melo 215; s/d US$10/25) A one-star hotel not too far from the beach, Solar da Ruth has plain rooms but is clean and pleasant.

MID-RANGE & TOP END

Mariner (☎ 3361 1100; Av Beira Mar 1; s/d US$45/60; 🗲) Right by Praia do Morro, the Mariner is a well positioned architectural beauty from the 1970s, atop a big boulder on a point. It has spacious grounds, a swimming pool and nice views throughout. Rooms with sea views are a good deal during low season, but prices double at the peak season (in January and during Carnaval).

Porto do Sol Guarapari (☎ 4336 1100; Av Beira Mar 1; s/d US$50/75) Another beauty on Praia do Morro, the Porto do Sol has a lovely location and large, attractive rooms surrounded by a pretty garden.

Pousada Enseada Verde (☎ 3272 1376; Rua Duarte Mattos 27; s/d US$23/30) A great option further down the coast, Pousada Enseada Verde is closer to Meaípe and has vibrantly colored rooms not far from the beach.

Eating

Delícia Mineira (Rua Joaquim da Silva Lima; meals per kg US$5; ☯ 11:30am-4pm) This is one of the best self-serves in town, heavy on the *comida mineira* (the cuisine of Minas Gerais).

Pizzaria do Ângelo (Rua Pedro Caetano 254; meals from US$9; ☯ lunch & dinner) Located inside the Hotel do Ângelo, this is good and cheap at lunch but more expensive at dinner.

Peixada do Irmão (Rua Jacinto de Almeida 72; meals US$13; ☯ 11:30am-midnight) With such an excellent reputation for seafood dishes, it's no wonder Peixada's gets a little pricey in the high season.

Up and down all the beaches but particularly on Praia do Morro you'll find a slew of *barracas* (stalls) all selling inexpensive, fresh, delicious seafood and regional dishes.

Getting There & Away

Buses run between Vitória and Guarapari's **bus station** (☎ 3261 1308; Rua Araxa 50) very frequently (US$2, 1¼ hours, every hour from 6am to 9pm). Frequent buses make the 28km trip to Anchieta (US$2.50, two hours, every two hours).

ANCHIETA

☎ 0xx27 / pop 15,000

About an hour south of Vitória, Anchieta is one of the oldest settlements in Espírito Santo and, as the name would suggest, contains many relics dedicated to the work of famed 16th-century priest José de Anchieta (see p214). The beaches aren't as attractive as those leading up to Guarapari (20km to the north) or neighboring Iriri and Ubu (to the south and respectively), but this small port town does have its own relaxed appeal – the quiet, rhythmic life of a fishing village is still very much apparent and the atmosphere doesn't feel too far removed from that of a 16th-century Mediterranean colony.

Sights

Tourism is not the major industry in Anchieta so you are pretty much on your own when it comes to finding your way around, but you'll have no problem locating the **Santuário Nacional Padre Anchieta** (☯ 9am-noon Mon-Fri, 2-5pm Sat, 9am-5pm Sun), which dominates the town from its impressive hillside location. The complex includes the **Museu Padre Anchieta** (admission US$0.75), highlighting the evangelical work of the Jesuit priest José de Anchieta among indigenous peoples. The church walls, built by local Indians and Padre Anchieta, are original. The museum contains relics uncovered during restoration. If you'd rather get your history at the seashore, then stroll to the end of Anchieta beach. Just before road goes over a small, white, wooden bridge you'll find a gold-colored statue of José de Anchieta giving blessings to a Goitacá warrior (see p218).

Sleeping & Eating

The prettiest accommodations are to be found either heading into Anchieta from the Guarapari/Meaípe coast or on the way out of town toward Iriri and Piúma.

Hotel Anchieta (☎ 3536 1258; Av Carlos Lindenberg; s/d US$20/30) If you are spending the night in Anchieta, this is your best bet, 100m south of the bus stop. Built in 1911, it is a bit run-down but still retains some charm.

Hotel Porto Velho (☎ 3536 1181; s/d US$30/40; 🖎) Right above the bus stop, the Velho

THE GOITACÁ WARRIORS

Early European explorers reported encounters with the fearsome, long-haired, tall, robust and formidable Goitacá warriors, coastal dwellers of the Rio state–Espírito Santo border region. The tribe had long resisted invasions by rival Tupi nations and, despite the technological advantage of guns, the Europeans found the Goitacá almost impossible to capture. The Goitacá were excellent runners and swimmers, and seemed by all reports to be equally at home on land and in the water. When chased, they were so fast through the waters and jungle that nobody could catch them on foot, on horseback or by boat.

According to legend, a Goitacá could run after a wild deer and capture it with his arms, and could catch a shark using only a piece of wood. (This was accomplished by forcing a stick inside the shark's mouth to stop the jaws from closing, and pulling its guts out by hand until it died.) The Goitacá nation (around 12,000 people), never defeated in battle, was exterminated at the end of the 18th century by an epidemic of small-pox – an epidemic deliberately introduced by the Portuguese for that very purpose.

has rooms with TV and refrigerator. Try to get a room facing the beach and definitely bargain in the low season.

Restaurante Doce Prazer (lunch buffet per kg US$4, dinner US$3; 🕑 lunch & dinner) About 1km north of the bus stop on the main road.

There are a couple of *lanchonetes* (snack bars), with sandwiches and cheap burgers, near the bus stop.

Getting There & Away

To Guarapari, buses (US$1) run every 20 to 30 minutes from 6am to 6:50pm. To Vitória (US$3) they run five times daily. The **bus stop** (☎ 3536 1150; Av Carlos Lindenberg 183), is on the main road through town.

AROUND ANCHIETA
Iriri
☎ 0xx27

This delightful beach town is one of Brazil's best-kept secrets. The small, curved shoreline is capped by an outgrowth of rocks at either side, perfect for exploring and clambering when you're tired of paddling in quiet waters. Iriri's very popular with Mineiros who come in droves during the summer months and turn the tiny little town into an upbeat, family-focused resort area.

SLEEPING & EATING

Hotel Morubixaba (☎ 3534 1180; Rua Joffre Ferrari 100; s/d US$10/20; 🖎) One of the best budget choices around, this hotel is about 100m from the beach with large, spacious rooms cooled by big fans. Air-conditioning is in some of the more modern rooms.

Hotel Pontal das Rochas (☎ 3534 1369; Av Beira Mar s/n; s/d US$40/50) Fabulous accommodations are available at this first-rate hotel on the rocky point overlooking the beach. Expect to pay 40% more during peak season. Among the many amenities is a gorgeous pool built into the rocks overlooking the waters – it's small but very beautiful.

Recanto da Pedra (☎ 3534 1599; Av Beira Mar s/n; s/d US$40/50) Two steps away from Hotel Pontal das Rochas is the adorable Recanto, which offers lovely rooms but also boasts a restaurant of the same name that's built overlooking another outgrowth of rock. It's great fun to lounge on the deck and greet swimmers as they rise up out of the waters for a refreshing libation. And the food is good, too!

Lanchonetes, pizzerias and ice-cream shops abound on the main drag just a few blocks behind the sandy beach.

Ubu
☎ 0xx28

A very small, very undiscovered little town some 9km north of Anchieta, Ubu is characterized by great seafood and strange little mermaid statues that dot the shoreline. The usual Brazilian hospitality is muted somewhat here by the locals' desire to keep their low-key haven from being overrun by developers (something that can happen all too quickly in Brazil), but as long as you don't talk about buying up huge tracts of land and building superhotels, you will eventually be embraced with customary warmth.

There's little nightlife to speak of but that's to be found in some of the larger towns nearby.

SLEEPING & EATING
Hotel Pontal de Ubú (☎ 3536 5065; www.hotelpon taldeubu.com.br; s/d US$30/40) Lift up your eyes as you enter the village and you'll see a huge white edifice perched on a massive cliff at the end of the beach. That's the Pontal, a new luxury hotel that has absurdly low prices in the off season. It's got tons of amenities, including saunas, private beaches and a first-rate restaurant onsite. Expect prices to double in high season. Its entrance is from the Rodovia do Sol highway.

Pousada Aba Ubu (☎ 3536 5067; Rua Manoel Miranda Garcia; s/d US$25/35; 🏊) There are also good accommodations at the Swiss-run Aba Ubu, just uphill from the beach. It has a tennis court and nice rooms around a garden.

Peixada do Garcia (☎ 3536 5050; Av Magno Ribeiro Muqui; meals US$12) There are a few good places on the beach to have seafood, and the place with the best reputation is the 40-year-old Peixada do Garcia. Don't miss it!

PIÚMA
☎ 0xx28 / pop 15,000

The rarest shell in the world, the oliva zelindea, is occasionally found in Piúma, 100km south of Vitória. Nice beaches and some nearby offshore islands make this area worth a look.

The coastline is dominated by the 300m cone-shaped **Monte Aghá**, which is a good place for hang gliding and climbing.

Islands & Beaches
Ilha do Gamba, an ecological reserve, is connected to the mainland by a thin isthmus. At low tide, you can walk from it to **Ilha do Meio**, which is a preserve for wild orchids and native trees. The next island is **Ilha dos Cabritos**. In summer, boats (US$5) run from the first island to the latter two; otherwise, pay a fisherman to take you over.

There are beaches along the main road, within walking distance from the center. Praia Acaiaca to the north has calm water, while Praia Maria Nenen is a little more agitated. Avoid Praia da Boca da Barra – it's polluted.

Sleeping & Eating
Be warned that hotel prices in Piúma double during summer.

Solar de Brasília (☎ 3520 1521; Av Eduardo Rodrigues 15; s/d US$15/25) A nice place with small rooms and a cute little pool, Solar is a favorite with young travelers.

Dom Manuel Pousada e Camping (☎ 3520 1370; Av Eduardo Rodriques 17; campsite per person US$3; s/d US$10/16) This pousada offers attractive rooms for those who like beds and camping for those who prefer to sleep under a blanket of stars.

Coliseu Hotel (☎ 3520 1273; Av Beiramar; s/d US$20/28) A nice mid-range hotel, the Coliseu has rooms with sea views.

Most of Piúma's restaurants are located along the beachfront on Av Beiramar. Try the extremely popular, inexpensive self-serve lunch at **D'Angelus** (🕙 11am-4pm Mon-Sat). Further south along the beach, **Ancoradouro** (🕙 11am-midnight Mon-Fri & 6pm-midnight Sat & Sun, closed Mon & Tue Mar-Dec) has better quality, reasonably priced à la carte meals.

Getting There & Away
Four buses daily connect Piúma to Vitória (US$5), passing through Iriri and Ubu along the way. There are also frequent buses to Anchieta (US$1).

INLAND

DOMINGOS MARTINS
☎ 0xx27 / pop 5800 / elevation 620m

Tucked into the highlands of Serra Capixaba, this pretty little German-style town has bracingly cold nights and gorgeous panoramic views of surrounding forests. Also referred to as Campinho by locals, it makes a good base for exploring the nearby streams and mountains.

Sights

Casa da Cultura (Av Presidente Vargas 520; admission US$2; ⊗ 8am-5pm), opposite the bus stop, has interesting documents, relics and artifacts dating from 1847, when this colony was first developed by Pomeranians.

Further along the same road you'll find the **Recanto dos Colibris**, near the main plaza and Lutheran church, is a pretty gathering spot. Flora lovers should definitely head out to the **Reserva Kautsky** (☎ 3268 1209; ⊗ 10am-noon & 2-5pm), run by dedicated botanist Roberto Kautsky, who has cultivated more than 100 species of orchids at his home at the south end of town (ask anyone) and on his mountainside reserve. He'll drive you, free for the asking, to the reserve in his ancient jeep and talk your ear off in German, 'bad English' or Portuguese – people come from miles around and it's a great experience.

Sleeping & Eating

Hotel e Restaurante Imperador (☎ 3268 1115; Rua Duque de Caxias 275; s/d US$15/30) An oldish hotel with traditional German architecture, the Imperador nonetheless has a quirky charm. It has a pool and sauna and is opposite a cute plaza and the Lutheran church.

Solar da Serra (☎ 3268 1691; Rua Pedro Gerhard 191; s/d US$30/40) Modern and comfortable doubles with views are available at Solar da Serra, which is decidedly more upmarket.

Bigosch (Rua Francisco dos Santos Silva; meals US$6; ⊗ 11am-10pm) Just opposite the Casa da Cultura, Bigosch does good German at cheap prices.

Restaurante dos Imigrantes (meals per kg US$6) For a delicious and inexpensive per-kilo buffet, head to the pedestrian mall in the center.

Adega Alemã Schwambach (☎ 3268 1423; pizzas US$10; ⊗ 11am-6pm) Just inside the city limits, Adega Alemã Schwambach has huge pizzas that come with free samples of local wines. The Jubuticaba wine (per liter US$4) is simultaneously sweet and bitter.

Getting There & Away

Ten buses daily on Monday through Friday and six on Saturday and Sunday make the 41km trip (US$3, one hour) from Vitória bus station to Domingos Martins **bus station** (☎ 3268 1243; Av Presidente Vargas 380). Any bus between Vitória bus station and Belo Horizonte will stop here on request, too.

AROUND DOMINGOS MARTINS
Parque Estadual da Pedra Azul

Vitória–Belo Horizonte buses also stop at the best reason to come inland: the 500m Pedra Azul, 50km west of Domingos Martins down Hwy BR-262. The rock, tinted by a bluish moss, is at the center of **Parque Estadual da Pedra Azul** (☎ 3248 1156). Rangers escort hikers to the rock's nine **natural pools**, a moderately difficult hike from the base trail that takes about 1½ hours. It's free, but you must book a week in advance.

SLEEPING & EATING

Serious climbers are permitted to camp in the park free, but you'll need to prove to the rangers that you know what's what. In winter, it is near freezing during the day and below freezing at night, so pack wisely and bring your supplies, as there are not many stores around catering to hard-core campers. In summer bring a bathing suit, as there are natural pools to swim in. The area is dotted by fancier resort hotels that all have horses for rent.

Aroso Paço Hotel (☎ 3248 1147; off Hwy BR-262 at Km 90; s/d US$75/100) Right near the park headquarters, the spectacular, amenity-packed Aroso has beautifully detailed, immaculate rooms; three meals a day are included in the prices. Ask for a room with a view of the rock.

Pousada Peterle (☎ 3248 1243; s/d US$45/60) Also right at the park entrance, Pousada Peterle has attractive rustic log cabins with fireplaces and balconies.

Italiano (☎ 3268 1420; Rua Duque de Caixas 16; mains US$8; ⊗ 11am-3pm Mon-Thu, to midnight Fri & Sat, to 6pm Sun) Hearty Italian fare, made from old country recipes, goes down easily in this quaint eatery, especially when accompanied by something from the excellent wine list.

Minas Gerais

HIGHLIGHTS

- Walking the **Caminho dos Escravos** (Slave Road; p254), which once linked Diamantina to the coast

- Standing eye-to-eye with renowned artist Aleijadinho's 12 statues, **Os Profetas** (*The Prophets*; p240), in Congonhas

- Taking a picturesque ride on the **Maria-Fumaça** (Smoking Mary; p247) steam engine from São Jão del Rei to Tiradentes

- Touring the **Circuito das Aguas** (Water Circuit; p260) spa towns in the southwest

- Soaking up the baroque architecture while enjoying excellent *comida mineira* (typical cuisine of Minas Gerais) in **Ouro Prêto** (p231)

Diamantina ★

Ouro Prêto ★★
Congonhas ★★
★ Tiradentes
São Jão del Rei ★
Circuito das Aguas ★

■ POPULATION: 17 MILLION   ■ AREA: 588,384 SQ KM

Nowhere else in Brazil do the new and the old blend with such intriguing results. Minas Gerais is a region of tremendous artistic and cultural wealth, despite being cut off from lowland neighbors by a surrounding ring of dramatic and continuous mountains. Thanks to an 18th-century gold rush that brought new settlers in droves, there're plenty of *cidades históricas* (historic colonial towns) far up in the hills that startle visitors with their perfectly preserved baroque grandeur. Modern cities such as Belo Horizonte, fast becoming a regional center of commerce, continue to be trendsetters in the arts, particularly where music, literature, architecture and the avant-garde are concerned.

Minas is as large as France, part of a vast plateau that crosses Brazil's interior. Rising along the state's southern border with Rio and São Paulo is the Serra da Mantiqueira, with some of Brazil's highest peaks. Its rich, red earth still attracts prospectors and multinational mining companies, and produces 95% of Brazil's gemstones.

The most famous of the historical towns, Ouro Prêto, was the stage for the Inconfidência Mineira, an uprising against Portuguese colonization led by local hero Joaquim José da Silva Xavier, more commonly known as Tiradentes (Tooth Puller). Today, like Diamantina and parts of nearby Congonhas, Ouro Prêto has been recognized as a Unesco World Heritage site.

Folklore-inspired tales of magical healing waters have helped create several hydro-mineral spa towns in the mountainous southwest corner, and adventure seekers enjoy the numerous prehistoric caves close to Belo Horizonte.

The roads are mostly good, but travel is usually a sinuous affair. Terrain is largely hilly, with deep valleys and plateaus running off the large mountain ranges.

History

Sometime around 1695, groups of explorers from São Paulo began to make regular excursions into Brazil's untamed interior. These *bandeirantes* (frontiersmen who roamed the interior lands, enslaving indigenous people and taking hold of precious gems and stones as they traveled) are now remembered as heroes, but their original intentions were far from noble – they were essentially searching for indigenous people to enslave. It didn't take long for *bandeirantes* to fix upon the large chunks of *faisqueiras* (sparkles) that lined the beds of rivers flowing down from surrounding mountains. There was gold to be had in them there hills.

Word got out and Brazilians flocked to Minas, while Portuguese flocked to Brazil. These two groups soon fought over land claims in the war known as the Emboabas

War. Slaves were brought from the sugar fields of Bahia and the savannas of Angola, as few Whites did their own mining. Until the last quarter of the 18th century, the slaves of Minas Gerais were digging up half the world's gold. Some of them escaped and created their own *quilombos* (fugitive slave communities) deep in the jungle – until local miners began hiring *bandeirantes* to hunt them down.

Minas set the gold-rush standard – crazy, wild and violent – more than 100 years before the Californian and Australian gold rushes. Disease and famine were rampant. The mine towns were known for their licentiousness, and prostitutes such as the infamous Chica da Silva (see p254) in Diamantina have been immortalized in film.

Minas's gold was siphoned off to Portugal, so the only lasting benefits to come to Brazil were the development of Rio de

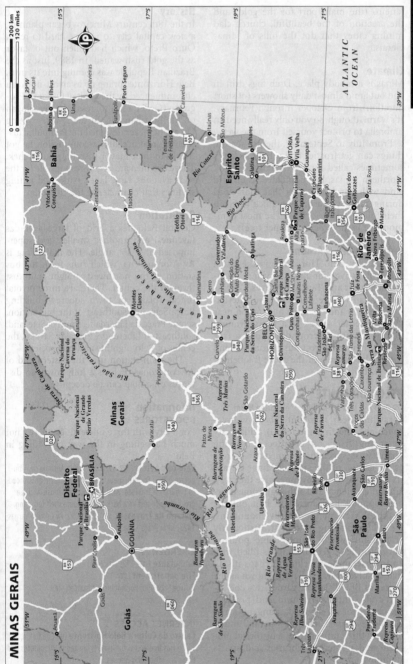

MINAS GERAIS

Janeiro (the main port for the gold) and the creation of the beautiful, church-clad mining cities that dot the hills of Minas Gerais.

Climate

Minas is a moody place. Drab fogs drift in and out amid almost daily showers (of short duration) from October through February. It's warm, though, so you only really need an umbrella to protect yourself from the wet.

From July to September, the dry season, things can get frostier and a light jacket is sometimes called for, particularly at night. Northern Minas, less populated, is an arid land with shrublike trees that look dead during the dry season but quickly regain their foliage when it rains. The most common tree is the *aroeira* (pepper tree).

Getting There & Around

Capital city Belo Horizonte is the usual point of arrival for most travelers. Pampulha airport and Tancredo Neves/Confins airport can handle domestic and international flights and the large bus station near the city center serves as a transportation hub for many surrounding towns (see p229). There are direct buses from Rio and São Paulo to some of the more frequented historic towns.

BELO HORIZONTE

☎ 0xx31 / pop 2.5 million / elevation 858m

Sprawling Belo Horizonte (bell-ow-hree-*zonch*-eh), the first modern Brazilian city to spring from an architect's drawing board, was especially designed for its role as the capital of the state of Minas Gerais. Its wide, landscaped avenues give the city a vibrant efficiency and although some overdevelopment has started to blot out the beautiful view of the nearby mountains, it's still fascinating to look at. Particularly at twilight, when people come pouring out onto the streets, the city is filled with an intense, upbeat feeling. Perhaps it's all that creative energy – Belo is known as the center of Brazil's avant-garde art scene.

It's also the distribution and processing center for all the gold, manganese and gemstones mined in Minas Gerais, and is home to three universities, a historical museum and numerous libraries and sports stadiums.

History

In the 18th century Mineiros began planning a new capital city to replace hard-to-reach Ouro Prêto, which had fallen out of favor as the gold rush waned. In 1889, just as the Brazilian Republic was coming into its own, Belo Horizonte sprang up as an art-nouveau city, influenced by the spirit of Ordem e Progresso (Order and Progress), the new slogan on the Brazilian flag. In the 1940s, a young Oscar Niemeyer designed the Pampulha district to great acclaim, a commission he got thanks to then-mayor Juscelino Kubitschek. These two men are largely responsible for the wide avenues, large lakes, parks and jutting skylines that characterize the city today.

Orientation

Central Belo has a grid of large avenidas (avenues) and another smaller grid superimposed at a 45° angle. The main drag is Av Afonso Pena, which runs from the bus station in the northwest straight southeast through the center. There are three pivotal praças (plazas or town squares): bustling Praça Sete, just southeast of the bus station; serene Praça da Liberdade, south of Sete; and, southeast of Liberdade, Praça da Savassi, the center of Belo nightlife and café society.

The train station is at the eastern end of Av Amazonas. Belo is a hilly town, so distances on a map can be deceptive.

Information

BOOKSTORES

For a city with three universities, there's not much happening in the way of reading in Belo.

Café com Letras (☎ 3225 9973; Rua Antônio de Albuquerque 785) English-speaking, in the same neighborhood as Livraria da Travessa. Also has good live music and is a great place to just kick back and do some shelf browsing.

Livraria da Travessa (☎ 3223 8092; Av Getúlio Vargas 1427) Near Praça Savassi.

EMERGENCY

Ambulance (☎ 192; ☼ 24hr)
Fire department (☎ 193)
Police (☎ 190) For nonurgent matters, call ☎ 3330 5200.

INTERNET ACCESS

Centro de Cultura Belo Horizonte (Rua da Bahia 1149) Has free access but time is limited to 30 minutes and there are often long queues.

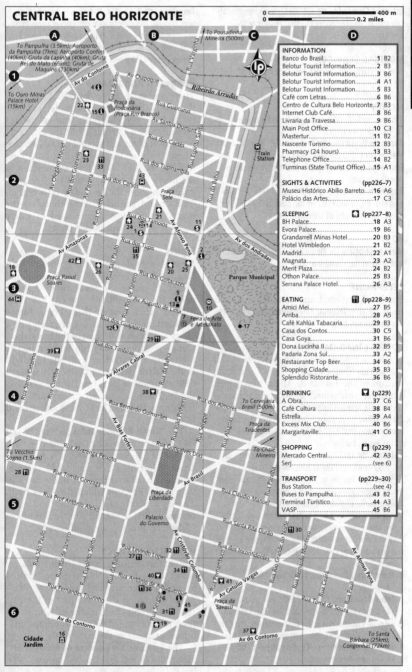

CENTRAL BELO HORIZONTE

0 — 400 m
0 — 0.2 miles

INFORMATION	
Banco do Brasil	1 B2
Belotur Tourist Information	2 B3
Belotur Tourist Information	3 B6
Belotur Tourist Information	4 A1
Belotur Tourist Information	5 B3
Café com Letras	6 B6
Centro de Cultura Belo Horizonte	7 B3
Internet Club Café	8 B6
Livraria da Travessa	9 B6
Main Post Office	10 C3
Mastertur	11 B2
Nascente Turismo	12 B3
Pharmacy (24 hours)	13 B3
Telephone Office	14 B2
Turminas (State Tourist Office)	15 A1

SIGHTS & ACTIVITIES	(pp226–7)
Museu Histórico Abílio Barreto	16 A6
Palácio das Artes	17 C3

SLEEPING	(pp227–8)
BH Palace	18 A3
Evora Palace	19 B6
Grandarrell Minas Hotel	20 B3
Hotel Wimbledon	21 B2
Madrid	22 A1
Magnata	23 A2
Merit Plaza	24 B2
Othon Palace	25 B3
Serrana Palace Hotel	26 A3

EATING	(pp228–9)
Amici Mei	27 B5
Arriba	28 A5
Café Kahlúa Tabacaria	29 B3
Casa dos Contos	30 C5
Casa Goya	31 B6
Dona Lucinha II	32 B5
Padaria Zona Sul	33 A2
Restaurante Top Beer	34 B6
Shopping Cidade	35 B3
Splendido Ristorante	36 B6

DRINKING	(p229)
A Obra	37 C6
Café Cultura	38 B4
Estrella	39 A4
Excess Mix Club	40 B6
Margaritaville	41 C6

SHOPPING	(p229)
Mercado Central	42 A3
Serj	(see 6)

TRANSPORT	(pp229–30)
Bus Station	(see 4)
Buses to Pampulha	43 B2
Terminal Turístico	44 A3
VASP	45 B6

Internet Club Café (☎ 3282-3132; www.Internetclub café.com.br; Rua Fernandes Tourinho 385; per hr US$2; ◯ 9am-8pm Mon-Fri, to 6pm Sat)

MEDICAL SERVICES
For nonurgent health matters call ☎ 3222 3322.

MONEY
There are lots of banks and exchange offices in the city center.
Banco do Brasil (Rua Rio de Janeiro 750) Near Praça Sete.
Mastertur (☎ 3330 3655; Rua da Bahia 2140; ◯ 9am-5pm Mon-Fri) The only American Express (Amex) representative in town.
Nascente Turismo (Rua Rio de Janeiro 1314; ◯ 9am-6pm Mon-Fri, to noon Sat) Try this place to skip long queues and the hefty US$20 commission.

POST
Main post office (Av Afonso Pena 1270) There's another post office at the bus station.

TELEPHONE
For local, national and international calls head to the **Telemar telephone post** (Praça Sete, Rua dos Tamoios 311).

TOURIST INFORMATION
If you can read a little Portuguese, check out the weekly listings in the daily Espetáculo section of the *Estado de Minas* newspaper. Another great source of local information is the Roteiro Cultural supplement of the *Pampulha* paper, published every Saturday.
Alo Turismo (☎ 3277 9777; ◯ 8am-10pm) Belotur's tourist-inquiry hotline.
Belotur (☎ 3277 7666; www.belohorizonte.mg.gov .br; 1055 Av Afonso Pena at Mercado das Flores; ◯ 8am-7pm Tue-Fri, to 3pm Sat & Sun) This municipal tourist organization puts out an excellent monthly guide in Portuguese, English and Spanish. It lists the main tourist attractions and how to get to them using local buses, and includes a city map, flight times, accurate long-distance bus schedules and everything and anything else you wanted to know about Belo Horizonte but didn't know how to ask.
Beltour Pampulha airport (☎ 3277 7400; ◯ 8am-10pm)
Belotur Rodoviaria (☎ 3277 6907; Praça Rio Branco; ◯ 8am-8pm Mon-Fri, to 4pm Sat & Sun) Right in front of the main exit/entrance inside the bus station. There are also Belotur information desks scattered around the city.
Beltour Tancredo Neves/Confins airport (☎ 3689 2557; ◯ 8am-10pm)

Turminas (☎ 3212-2134; 50 Av Bias Fortes; ◯ 9am-6pm Mon-Fri) This state tourism office never knows from one moment to the next if it's going to be shut down, but is currently still dispensing great advice on trips to the interior from an office near Praça da Rodoviária.

Dangers & Annoyances
There are much more dangerous places in the world than Belo Horizonte, but you certainly do need to watch your belongings carefully when moving about the city, particularly at night and around the bus station. There's been an increase in drug trafficking through the area and it's not uncommon to see heavy (and heavily armed) police presence throughout the city and flying overhead. That's mostly muscle-flexing, though – the biggest thing most people need to worry about is getting their pocket picked.

Sights
Most visitors drop in or drop out of Belo Horizonte en route to nearby colonial towns. If you've got some time to spare, definitely stick around – the city has a few hidden gems, one of them being **Parque Municipal**, an enormous sea of green just a 10-minute walk southeast of the bus station along Av Afonso Pena (on Sunday there's a huge food market as well). Its highlight is the **Palácio das Artes** (☎ 3237 7234; www.pala ciodasartes.com.br; Av Afonso Pena 1537; ◯ 10am-10pm Mon-Sat, 2-10pm Sun), an art gallery and performing arts center near the southern end of the park.

The **Museu Histórico Abílio Barreto** (☎ 3277 8861; Av Prudente de Morais 202, Cidade Jardim; ◯ 10am-5pm Tue-Thu & Fri-Sun, to 9pm Wed) is a free museum featuring a renovated old colonial farmhouse, all that remains of the town of Curral del Rey, on which Belo was built. There's a photographic archive and other historical bric-a-brac. It's in the suburb of Cidade Jardim, just south of Savassi.

PAMPULHA DISTRICT
Fans of modernist architect Oscar Niemeyer won't want to miss his creations dotted around a huge artificial lake in the Pampulha district, in the north part of the city. Juscelino Kubitschek, mayor of Belo at the time, commissioned the recent architectural-school graduate in the early 1940s.

The **Igreja de São Francisco de Assis** (☎ 3441 9325; Av Otacílio Negrão de Lima; ◯ 8am-6pm) is an architectural delight and the paintings by Portinari are beautiful. The **Museu de Arte de Belo Horizonte**, with its cute garden designed by landscape architect Roberto Burle Marx, is also worth a look. It was designed as a casino and shows the obvious influence of the modernist work of Le Corbusier.

The **Casa do Baile**, a former dance hall, has finally reopened after extensive renovations and now holds all types of temporary art exhibits. Its lovely on-site café is a great place to take a break.

Sleeping

Accommodations in Belo Horizonte mostly cater to two distinct crowds: students just barely scraping by and well-heeled executives who can afford to splurge. For travelers that means lots of decent low-budget and mid-range options and a few really blowout locations with first-class service. Most places add on a service tax to your room rate – amounts vary depending on the class of hotel. Be sure to get a figure when you check in. Some places will go as high as 20%, although the norm is between 5% and 10%.

Note that in addresses, the abbreviation 's/n' stands for *sem número* (without number).

BUDGET

Madrid (☎ /fax 3201-1088/6330; Rua dos Guaranis 12; s/d US$13/18) Directly across from the bus station, Madrid is surrounded by a lot of noise early in the morning but the bright curtains and decorative touches in rooms make this a practically perfect place to stay.

Albergue de Juventude Chalé Mineiro (☎ /fax 3467-1576; Rua Santa Luzia 288; s/d US$10/13; 🏊) Good dorm rooms available here, with discounts for HI members. It's about 2km east of Parque Municipal. You can get there by bus No 9801 'Saudade/Santa Cruz' from Rua dos Caetés near the bus station, or the metro to Santa Teresa station, from which you cross a pedestrian bridge to Rua Santa Luzia. A well-tended pool adds a nice feeling of luxury to an otherwise no-frills experience.

Magnata (☎ /fax 201 5368; Rua dos Guaranis 124; s/d incl breakfast US$15/24) You'll get a breakfast worthy of a miner in the morning and steaming hot water in each room – something that makes Magnata very handy during the cool season.

Pousadinha Mineira (☎ 3446 2911; pousadin hamineira@terra.com.br; Rua Araxá 514; s US$9) This youth hostel has very bare-bones accommodations with shared bathroom. From the bus station, follow Av Santos Dumont to Rua Rio de Janeiro, then head left to Av do Contorno. Cross it and follow Rua Varginha a few blocks to Rua Araxá.

MID-RANGE

Hotel Wimbledon (☎ 3222 6510; www.wimbledon .com.br; Av Afonso Pena 772; s/d US$56/70; 🍴 🖥️) A great central location with warm, welcoming rooms, hardwood floors, Mineiro art and modern bathrooms (spa baths in the luxury rooms) give Wimbledon a distinct edge over the competition. Drinks are served by the pool at the rooftop bar by a friendly, professional staff. A delightfully comfortable place.

Serrana Palace Hotel (☎ 3271 0200; www.hotel serrana.com.br; Rua Goitacazes 450; s/d US$25/32; 🍴 🖥️) This big high-rise in downtown Belo still manages to exude a lot of charm. There's plenty of bang for your buck with these rooms – although at times the hotel can feel a little overrun with conventioneers.

Evora Palace (☎ 3327 6220; www.orgbristol.com .br; Rua Sergipe 1415; s/d/tr US$30/40/50; 🍴 🖥️ 🏊) In the heart of Savassi, the dining and drinking center of Belo's nightlife, Evora stands out as a great mid-priced choice. Rooms are large and comfortable and the hotel itself is pretty and well-appointed. Discounts are sometimes available on weekends.

BH Palace (☎ 3330 6500; www.hotelbhpalace.com .br; Av Augusto de Lima 1147; s/d US$22/28; 🍴) This place straddles the line between budget and mid-range. Very basic but pretty and clean rooms and all the amenities of a larger hotel at much lower rates, especially if the exchange rate is working in your favor.

TOP END

Ouro Minas Palace Hotel (☎ 3429 4001; www.ourom inas.com.br; Av Cristiano Machado 4001; s/d US$200/250; 🅿️ 🍴 🏊 🖥️ 🏊) Staying at the Minas Palace is a fabulous, wonderful splurge – the beautiful grounds are so well-kept and gorgeous that it's difficult to go inside – even for an indulgent massage. The rooms are very appealing, the pools have waterfalls and even the tennis courts are aesthetically pleasing! It's not centrally located, being in the Ipiranga neighborhood, but the hotel does offer transportation to guests, including to and from airports.

Othon Palace (☎ 3273 3844; www.hoteis-othon .com.br; Av Afonso Pena 1050; s/d/tr US$100/115/ 140; ❖ ❑ ❑) The four-star Othon has a great location in downtown Belo, directly opposite Parque Municipal and ringed by several great shopping locations. The building is a little old but currently undergoing renovations, and the staff is superamenable and attentive. Rooms are a tad bland but the views are spectacular. Don't miss the rooftop pool and bar, one of the best in the city. Prices on the website are often higher than what's offered if you walk in the door or call the hotel directly – don't be afraid to try to bargain a little.

Merit Plaza (☎ 3201 9000; www.meritplaza .com .br; Rua dos Tamoios 341; s/d US$75/90; ❖ ❑ ❑) Particularly popular among business travelers, the Merit is a wonderful find for anyone who likes quick, efficient, quiet service. Granite-covered walls in the atrium and soundproofed guest rooms create a lovely atmosphere of invincibility – no matter what's going on outside on the crowded city streets, the noises won't penetrate beyond the front doors.

Grandarrell Minas Hotel (☎ 3248-1000; www .grandarrell.com.br; Rua Espirito Santo 901; s/d US$80/95; ❖ ❑ ❑) Lots of business travelers stop here because the Grandarrell is considered one of Belo's oldest and most prestigious downtown establishments. Rooms offer gorgeous panoramic views of the surrounding mountains. Similar views can be had from the rooftop bar and pool.

Eating
BUDGET
Comida mineira (the typical cuisine of Minas Gerais) is both filling and delicious, featuring hearty stews, *feijoadas* (bean-and-meat stews) and delicately spiced meat dishes. Lots of *lanchonetes* (snack bars) and fast-food places are clustered around Praça Sete.

Padaria Zona Sul (Av Paraná 163; meals US$5; ❍ 11am-9pm) You'll get super slow-roasted chickens and freshly cooked vegetable dishes at this cheeky little downtown shop.

Dona Lucinha II (☎ 3261 5930; ☎ Rua Sergipe 811; meals US$7; ❍ 11am-11pm) This huge restaurant has about 35 traditional Mineiro dishes available on any given day. The cafeteria-style serving comes in handy if

you're traveling with children, and families appreciate the kiddie discounts.

Arriba (Rua Curitiba 2202; meals US$10; ❍ 5:30pm-2:30am Mon-Sat, 11am-midnight Sun) For great Mexican food with Brazilian flair, check out Arriba. Tacos, burritos and such are given a special flavor from the wood-burning stove in the back.

Shopping Cidade (☎ 3271 3707; Rua Rio de Janeiro 910) Inside an immense food court that goes well beyond the usual fast-food offerings, you'll find many full-service restaurants that have mains as well as buffet-style dishes in a congenial atmosphere.

MID-RANGE
Café Kahlúa Tabacaria (Rua dos Guajajaras 416; coffee with roll or sandwich US$2-5; ❍ 8am-9:30pm, closed Sun) There's a lot more brewing here than java. Locals pop in and out all day, attracted by the delicious sandwiches, the fully enclosed smoking room in the back (cigars and other types of tobacco sold), the bright chatter of the young, artistic clientele and the chance to trade a few quips with the owners. It's particularly popular around 3pm, when it seems almost all of Belo is out looking for a *cafézinho* (small coffee). A wide selection of teas, green and otherwise, is also available.

Casa dos Contos (☎ 3261 5853; Rua Rio Grande do Norte 165; meals US$9; ❍ 11am-midnight) A hangout for journalists, artists and intellectuals, this is a good place to fill up on tasty Mineiro dishes and watch locals break bread.

Restaurante Top Beer (☎ 3221 1116; Rua Tomé de Souza 1121; meals US$10; ❍ 10-1am) The outdoor patio at Top Beer is great for people-watching on a summer night. Inside is an inviting enclave of serenity, with lots of greenery and faux waterfalls scattered about. The pasta and steak dishes are particularly good, but you needn't come just to eat. Plenty of people gather at the bar for a drink with their friends while planning where they're going to party for the rest of the night.

Amici Mei (☎ 3282 4992; Rua Tomé de Souza 1331; meal & drink US$15; ❍ noon-11pm) Hugely popular with young Brazilians looking to get a quick bite on the way home from work, Amici Mei's outside patio gets jam-packed – but more people can always be accommodated if you give the waiters a minute to shuffle things around. There are lots of delicious Italian dishes, replete with garlic, olive oil, prosciutto and other traditional delectables.

Cervejaria Brasil (☎ 3287 3262; Rua dos Aimorés 90; á la carte lunch US$8; ☺ 11:30-2am, closed Mon) This is a hard-core *churrascaria* (restaurant featuring barbecued meat) absolutely overflowing with options for meat lovers.

TOP END

Just about all of Belo Horizonte's standout restaurants are in Savassi.

Splendido Ristorante (☎ 3227 6446; Rua Levindo Lopes 251; dinner & drinks US$25-80; ☺ 3pm-2am) Visiting dignitaries and celebrities always stop by this Savassi eatery when they're in town, and the local beautiful people seem to treat it as their home away from home. Tender veal dishes go well with imported wines from Tuscany and local vegetables are used to surprising effect as fillers for tortellinis and other pasta entrees. The kitchen blends Italian and French cuisines, resulting in innovative and delectable dishes.

Casa Goya (☎ 3281 2162; Rua Fernandes Tourinho 390; dinner & drinks US$30; ☺ noon-midnight Wed-Sat, 12:30-4pm Sun, noon-2:30pm Mon-Tue) For a new spin on traditional Spanish dishes such as paella and *tortilla española*, come to Casa Goya, which uses spices and ingredients not traditionally found on the Iberian Peninsula. The results are surprising but delicious.

Vecchio Sogno (☎ 3292 5251; Rua Martim de Carvalho 75; dinner for 2 US$100; ☺ noon-midnight Mon-Sat, 5pm-midnight Sun) Considered Belo's best Italian restaurant, Vecchio's can set you back a pretty penny. It certainly offers a wide variety of entrees, ranging from lamb and saffron risotto to delicate grilled fish specialities. Reservations are usually required.

Entertainment

Belo is a cosmopolitan town with a vibrant arts scene and plenty of nightlife, most of it in Savassi.

Café Cultura (☎ 3222 1347; Rua da Bahia 1416) This place is pretty packed on weekends, when the bar features live music.

Estrella (☎ 3222-6252; Rua Curitiba 1275) Another great place in town, check out the *forró* (music and dance style of the Northeast) dancing on Saturday night.

Margaritaville (Rua Tomé de Souza 851) In Savassi, this bar is home to a chic, flirty crowd that fills the streets and spills into the many other neighboring bars, all equally as high-volume and fun.

Excess Mix Club (☎ 3225-2353; Rua Antônio de Albuquerque 729; ☺ 8pm-2am or 3am) Also in Savassi, Excess is popular with gay, lesbian and straight revelers for its loyalty to techno and house beats and sometimes the crowd gets so frenetic the club just keeps rockin' into the wee hours.

A Obra (☎ 3215-8077; www.aobra.com.br; Rua Rio Grand do Norte 1168) A great dance bar that's partially located in a basement, this is a fabulous place to hear live music and meet some locals.

Shopping

Feira de Arte e Artesanato (Av Afonso Pena, btwn Rua da Bahia & Rua das Guajarajas; ☺ 6am-noon, but often still going at 3pm) This Sunday fair attracts massive crowds looking over stalls selling all sorts of imported rubbish. In between the junk you can find the odd one with some good local crafts. The food stalls are worthwhile.

Centro de Artesanato Mineiro (☎ 3272 8572; Av Afonso Pena 1537; ☺ 9am-6pm Mon-Fri, to 1pm Sat, 10am-2pm Sun) Inside the Palácio das Artes at the edge of Parque Municipal, this government store has a varied assortment of Mineiro crafts: ceramics, jewelry, tapestries, rugs, quilts and soapstone sculptures. It's probably worth holding off buying, though, if you are heading to the colonial towns.

Serj (Rua Antônio de Albuquerque 749) A great place for quality crafts, Serj can yield the occasional bargain.

Mercado Central (cnr Rua Curitiba & Rua dos Goitacazes) You can buy just about anything at the *mercado* (market), and it's a good place for wandering, sampling the delicious local produce or socializing with locals at one of the bars.

Getting There & Around

AIR

Belo Horizonte has two airports. Most planes use the international **Aeroporto Confins** (CNF; 40km north). The **Aeroporto da Pampulha** (PLU; 7km north) is much more conveniently located.

There are flights from the two airports to just about anywhere in Brazil. Flights to/from Rio, Brasília, Vitória and São Paulo by VASP and Varig are frequent.

City airline offices include:

Varig (☎ 0800-992 004; www.varig.com; Av Getúlio Vargas 840)

VASP (☎ 0800-998 277; www.vasp.com; Av Getúlio Vargas 1492)

Offices at Confins airport include these two:

Varig (☎ 3689 2350)
VASP (☎ 3689 2266)

BUS
There are daily frequent departures for just about every colonial and mineral spa town out of Belo's **bus station** (☎ 3271 3000) at the northern end of the city center on Praça da Rodoviária (also known as Praça Rio Branco), near the end of Av Afonso Pena. The Belotur tourist guide has handy schedules and phone numbers in the back pages.

Destinations include: Brasília (US$30, 12 hours, nine daily, three additional services on Sunday, from 8am to 10:30pm); Caxambú (US$20, five hours, three daily from 7am to 1pm); Diamantina (US$17, six hours, six daily from 5:30am to noon); Mariana (US$6, two hours, 21 daily from 5:30am to noon); Ouro Prêto (US$8, four hours, 11 daily from 6am to 11pm); Rio de Janeiro (US$18, seven hours, 17 daily from 8am to 12:30am); Sabará (US$3, 30 minutes, every 15 minutes from 5am to 11pm); Salvador (US$50, 22hrs, two daily at 6pm and 7pm); São João del Rei (US$7, four hours, 10 daily from 6am to 7pm, to 8pm Friday); São Lourenço (US$20, five hours, two daily, Sunday to Friday, 12:30pm and 11pm); São Paulo (US$25, 10hrs, 22 daily from 8am to midnight); Vitória (US$20, nine hours, seven daily from 8am to 11:45pm).

LOCAL BUSES
Belo Horizonte has a good bus network (newspaper stands sell Peg Bus, which lists all of the timetables, for about US$2,). There's a conventional bus (US$1.50, one hour, every 30 minutes, from 4:45am to 10:45pm) from the bus station to Confins airport. An *executivo* (express) bus (US$5, 30 minutes, every 45 minutes to one hour, from 6am to 10pm) to Confins leaves from the **Terminal Turístico** (☎ 3271 4522; Rua dos Guajajaras), just southwest of Praça Raoul Soares.

Local buses are color-coded, with blue buses going up and down main avenues in the city center. White buses go express and stop only at select points, red buses connect outlying suburbs and *favelas* (slums, shantytowns) to downtown, and yellow buses have circular routes through the city.

Belo Horizonte also has a metro system, which has two lines extending from the main railway station. From Praça da Estação, one extends north to Minas Shopping (via Santa Teresa), and the other to the western suburbs via Estação Lagoinha (near the bus station).

TRAIN
Trains run to Vitória (regular/executivo class US$12/16, 15 hours, two daily, one Sunday) from Belo's main **train station** (☎ 3218 2255) at Praça da Estação just north of Parque Municipal. It is a beautiful trip. This train also stops in Santa Bárbara (US$3, three hours) and Sabará.

AROUND BELO HORIZONTE
Caves
Three fascinating caves are within two hours of downtown Belo and make great day jaunts. The guided trips through some of the larger chambers are quite informative and fun, and the prehistoric petroglyphs are well worth the trip.

GRUTA DE MAQUINÉ
The most famous, and crowded, of the caves is **Gruta de Maquiné** (☎ 3715 1078; adult/child under 5 US$3/free; ☼ 8am-5pm). Maquiné's seven huge chambers are well lit to allow guided tours to pass through. There are cafés at the cave.

Buses (US$6, 2¼ hours, from 8am to 4:20pm) to the caves depart from the bus station in Belo Horizonte three times daily, which gives you ample viewing time.

GRUTA DA LAPINHA
Gruta da Lapinha (☎ 3681 1958; adult/child under 5 US$4/1; ☼ 9am-4:30pm) The highlight here is the Véu da Noiva, a crystal formation in the shape of a bride's veil.

Buses (US$3, every 45 minutes from 6:50am to 5pm) leave Belo's bus station four times daily.

GRUTA REI DO MATO
Gruta Rei do Mato (Cave of the Forest King; ☎ 3773 0888; adult/child US$1/free; ☼ 8am-7pm), near Sete Lagoas north of Belo, has prehistoric paintings and petroglyphs.

Buses from Belo leave frequently (US$3, 1½ hours, every 30 minutes from 6:30am to 11pm).

COLONIAL TOWNS

History comes to life in surprising ways in Minas Gerais, especially among the quaint and archaic colonial towns that sprang up during the gold rush. On quiet days you can almost believe that time stands still on this immense central plateau – church bells peal loudly from atop fragile spires, the aroma of handpicked coffee beans still flavors the air, and everywhere the baroque works of master artist Aleijadinho (see the boxed text below) capture the eye.

The **Estrada Real** (Royal Rd), built hundreds of years ago by slaves, no longer links these towns on Rio coast, but its remnants are still visible amid the low-lying bushes in a few areas. Modern Mineiros, many of whom are descended in some form or another from those slaves, take great pride in displaying the huge cobblestone slabs set deeply into the earth. For more than 150 years their forebears laboriously carted the gold and precious stones of Minas down to European ships waiting near Rio and Paraty.

The region's tremendous legacy of baroque art and architecture is spread out over large distances, but it's quite easy to travel between the colonial towns – there are regular buses between them. It is possible to give Belo Horizonte a miss, and head north from Ouro Prêto through to Diamantina via Mariana and Santa Bárbara, Guanhães and Serro.

OURO PRÊTO

☎ 0xx31 / pop 65,000 / elevation 1179m

Of all the exquisite colonial towns scattered around Minas Gerais, Ouro Prêto might be the jewel in the crown. Built upon the lower slope of a spur of the Serra do Espinhaço range, the city is deeply cut by ravines and divided into a number of irregular hills, upon which narrow, crooked streets are built.

The roads of the upper and lower towns tangle together and in places are too rough and steep for vehicles. That leaves the way clear for visitors to leisurely navigate vertiginous cobblestone streets while taking in the spectacular view of 23 churches spread out across the hilly panorama. Some of Aleijadinho's best works can be found here, as well as many other examples of outstanding Mineiro artwork.

ALEIJADINHO

Antônio Francisco Lisboa (1738–1814), known worldwide today as Aleijadinho (Little Cripple), was the son of a Portuguese architect and a Black slave. His nickname was given to him sometime in the 1770s when the artist began to suffer from a terrible, debilitating disease. It might have been syphilis or possibly leprosy – either way, he lost his fingers, toes and the use of his lower legs.

Undaunted, Aleijadinho strapped hammers and chisels to his arms and continued working, advancing the art in his country from the excesses of the baroque to a finer, more graceful form known as Barroco Mineiro.

Mineiros have reason to be proud of Aleijadinho – he is a figure of international prominence in the history of art. He studied European baroque and rococo traditions through pictures, but went on to develop his own unique style, using only native materials like soapstone and wood. Aleijadinho's angels have his stylistic signature: wavy hair, wide-open eyes and big, round cheeks.

For many years Manuel da Costa Ataíde, from nearby Mariana, successfully collaborated with Aleijadinho on many churches. Aleijadinho would sculpt the exterior and a few interior pieces, and Ataíde would paint the interior panels. With his secretly concocted vegetable dyes, Ataíde fleshed out many of Aleijadinho's creations.

Aleijadinho was buried in the Matriz NS da Conceição, within 50 paces of his birth site. He was named patron of Brazilian arts by federal decree in 1973. *The Prophets* in Congonhas, the Igreja de São Francisco de Assis and the facade of the Igreja de NS do Carmo, both in Ouro Prêto, were all carved by Aleijadinho, as were innumerable relics in Mariana, Sabará, Tiradentes and São João del Rei. The best places to see Aleijadinho's work are Congonhas, Ouro Prêto, Sabará and São João del Rei.

History

Legend has it that a mulatto servant in an early *bandeirante* expedition pocketed a few grains of an odd black metal he found while drinking from a small river near the current site of Ouro Prêto (Portuguese for 'black gold'). It turned out to be gold, but the exact location of the river was forgotten during the long expedition back down to the coast.

In 1698 Antônio Dias de Oliveira rediscovered the area, and was convinced he had found the fabled El Dorado. The mines were the largest deposits of gold in the Western Hemisphere, and the news and gold fever spread fast. Stories abound of men who acquired fabulous wealth from one day to the next, and others who died of hunger with their pockets full of gold.

Portuguese King Dom João V was quick to claim a royal fifth in tax, and a chain of posts was established to ensure that the crown got its cut. In theory, all gold was brought to these *casas de intendéncias* (weighing stations) to be weighed and turned into bars, and the royal fifth was set aside. Tax shirkers were cast into dungeons or exiled to Africa. One common technique used to avoid the tax was to hide gold powder in hollow images of the saints.

Bitter about the tax, the Paulista miners rebelled unsuccessfully against the Portuguese. Two years later, in 1711, Vila Rica de Ouro Prêto, the predecessor of the present town, was founded.

The finest goods from India and England were made available to the simple mining town. The gold bought the services of baroque artisans, who turned the city into an architectural gem. At the height of the gold boom in the mid-18th century, there were 110,000 people (mainly slaves) in Ouro Prêto, as contrasted with 50,000 in New York and about 20,000 in Rio de Janeiro.

The greed of the Portuguese led to sedition by the inhabitants of Vila Rica (1720). As the boom tapered off, the miners found it increasingly difficult to pay ever-larger gold taxes. In 1789 poets Claudio da Costa and Tomás Antônio Gonzaga, Joaquim José da Silva Xavier (nicknamed Tiradentes, meaning Tooth Puller, for his dentistry skills) and others, full of French-Revolutionary philosophies, hatched the Inconfidência Mineira.

The rebellion was crushed in its early stages by agents of the crown. Gonzaga was exiled to Mozambique and Costa did time in prison. Tiradentes, the only man not to deny his role in the conspiracy, was abandoned by his friends, jailed for three years without defense, then drawn and quartered in Rio de Janeiro.

By decree of Emperor Dom Pedro I, Vila Rica, capital of Minas Gerais since 1721, became the Imperial City of Ouro Prêto. In 1897 the state capital was shifted from Ouro Prêto to Belo Horizonte. This was the decisive move that preserved the colonial flavor of Ouro Prêto.

The former capital assumes the symbolic role of state capital once a year, on June 24. The city was declared a Brazilian national monument in 1933, and in 1981 Unesco proclaimed the town of Ouro Prêto a World Heritage site.

Climate

The city is 1km above sea level, and temperatures vary from 2°C to 28°C (36°F to 82°F). Winters are pretty cold. It can be rainy and foggy all year round, but you can definitely expect daily showers in December and January.

Orientation

Praça Tiradentes is the town center. Ouro Prêto is divided into two parishes. If you stand in Praça Tiradentes facing the Museu da Inconfidência, the parish of Pilar is to the right, the parish of Antônio Dias to the left.

All of Ouro Prêto's streets have at least two names: the official one and the one used by the locals because the official one is too much of a mouthful. Rua Conde de Bobadela, the street leading off to the right from Praça Tiradentes as you're facing the Museu da Inconfidência, is commonly known as Rua Direita. Rua Conselheiro Quintiliano is known as Rua das Lajes and Rua Senador Rocha Lagoa as Rua das Flores. To add to the confusion, the names are rarely posted. Lately the town's gotten a bit seedy at night, particularly around the bus station high on one of the main hills. Anyone lodging near there should absolutely not walk around after dark, especially if you've been in the center having a few drinks.

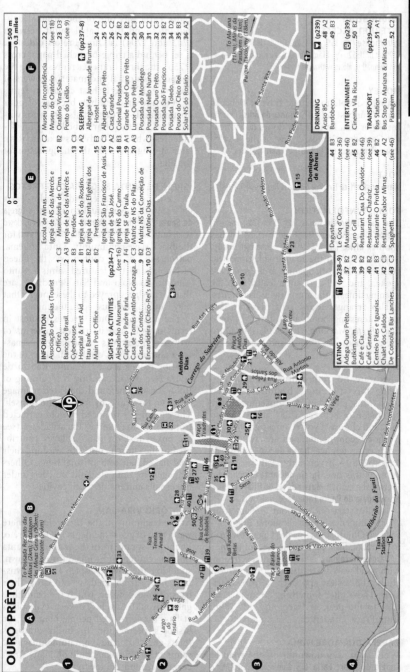

OURO PRÊTO

Information

INTERNET ACCESS

Cyberhouse (☎ 3552 2808; Rua Conde de Bobadela 109; per hr US$2; ☯ 11am-10pm) A great place for tea and sympathy, along with web surfing.

MONEY

It isn't possible to change traveler's checks here. Your best bet is the **Banco do Brasil** (Rua São José 195) or Itaú Bank, a few doors down near the Casa dos Contos. Many of the jewelry stores in town will change cash dollars.

POST

Main post office (cnr Rua Direita & Rua Coronel Alves)

TOURIST INFORMATION

The **Associação de Guias** (☎ 3559 3269; Praça Tiradentes 41; ☯ 8am-6pm Mon-Fri, to 5pm Sat & Sun) has another **office** (☎ 3551 2504; ☯ 8am-6pm Mon-Fri, to 5pm Sat & Sun) on the main road from Belo Horizonte. English, Spanish and French are spoken, and staff give out a leaflet with the opening times of the museums and churches. It also arranges tours, sells maps (US$4) and interesting books including *Visitando Ouro Prêto, Mariana e Congonhas*, by Ouro Prêto Turismo, in English and Portuguese.

Sights

There are no 20th-century buildings to defile this stunningly beautiful colonial town. Most churches and museums charge admission of between US$1 and US$3, so pick and choose if you're on a tight budget. Author recommendations are, roughly in order of preference: **Igreja de São Francisco de Assis** (p236) – if you only visit one, make sure it's this one; **Igreja de Santa Efigênia dos Pretos** (see right); **Matriz de NS do Pilar** (p236); and **Capela do Padre Faria** (see below).

Ideally, start out at about 7:30am from Praça Tiradentes and walk along Rua Conselheiro Quintiliano (Rua das Lajes), the road to Mariana, for a panoramic view of town.

Parque Itacolomy is a pleasant excursion, with good walking trails, waterfalls and orchids (the easiest approach is from Mariana). Those after something strenuous can hike to the peak of Itacolomy; it's 18km from Praça Tiradentes.

CAPELA DO PADRE FARIA

Work your way downhill off the road to **Capela do Padre Faria** (☯ 8am-noon, closed Mon).

Padre Faria was one of the original *bandeirantes*, and the chapel (built between 1701 and 1704) is Ouro Prêto's oldest. It is set behind a triple-branched papal cross (1756), the three branches representing the temporal, spiritual and material powers of the Pope. It's the richest chapel in terms of gold and artwork but, because of poor documentation, the artists are anonymous. In 1750 the church bell rang for Tiradentes (when his body was taken to Rio); later, it rang again for the inauguration of Brasília.

IGREJA DE SANTA EFIGÊNIA DOS PRETOS

Descending the Ladeira do Padre Faria back toward town, you'll come to the **Igreja de Santa Efigênia dos Pretos** (☯ 8am-noon, closed Mon), built between 1742 and 1749 by and for the Black slave community. Santa Efigênia, patron saint of the church, was the queen of Nubia, and the featured saints – Santo Antônio do Nolo and São Benedito – are Black. The slaves prayed to these images that they wouldn't be crushed in the mines.

The church is Ouro Prêto's poorest in terms of gold and its richest in terms of artwork. The altar is by Aleijadinho's master, Francisco Javier do Briton. Many of the interior panels are by Manuel Rabelo de Souza (see if you can find the painting of Robinson Crusoe), and the exterior image of NS do Rosário is by Aleijadinho himself. The church was financed by gold extracted from Chico-Rei's mine, Encardadeira (see the boxed text on p235). Slaves contributed to the church coffers by washing their gold-flaked hair in baptismal fonts. Others managed to smuggle gold powder under fingernails and inside tooth cavities.

ORATÓRIO VIRA-SAIA

At the beginning of the 18th century there was a rash of ghost incidents in Ouro Prêto. Phantoms sprang from the walls near Santa Efigênia church and winged through town, spooking the townspeople. These townsfolk, badly frightened, would drop their bags of gold powder, which the banditlike ghosts would snatch. To keep evil spirits at bay, the terrorized people obtained the bishop's permission to build oratories (glass-encased niches containing images of saints). Oratories were built on many street corners around the town.

Not many of them remain, but there's one on Rua dos Paulistas (also called Bernardo Vasconcelos) and another on Rua Antônio Dias; the most famous one of all is the **Oratório Vira-Saia**. Nowadays, these few remaining oratories are used to scare off evil spirits during Holy Week. The small oratory of Vira-Saia is at the bottom of the Ladeira de Santa Efigênia (also known as Vira-Saia), on the corner with Rua Barão do Ouro Branco. 'Vira-Saia' has a double meaning: it originates from the Portuguese *virar* (turn) and *sair* (depart), and is also the word for 'turncoat' or 'traitor.'

In the latter part of the 18th century, gold caravans destined for the Portuguese crown were robbed on a regular basis, despite measures to conceal shipments by altering dates and routes. It didn't take long to surmise that the rash of robberies was an inside job and that someone working in the Casa de Fundição (gold smelter) was leaking information.

No one suspected that Antônio Francisco Alves – pillar of the community, upstanding citizen, mild-mannered businessman and gentle father – was the brains behind the Vira-Saia bandits who were looting the government's gold caravans. After a caravan's route was planned, Alves would steal out to the oratory and turn the image in the sanctuary of NS das Almas to face the direction of the gold traffic.

A reward was posted for the identity of the criminal. Finally a member of Alves' own band, Luis Gibut, turned him in. Gibut was a French Jesuit who fell in love with a beautiful woman, abandoned the order, became a highway bandit and, eventually, the turncoat's turncoat. This same Luis Gibut was responsible for teaching Aleijadinho

the misspelled Latin phrases that the artist incorporated into many of his works.

Alves, his wife and his daughters were dragged off into the jungle to meet their fate. Sra Duruta, a good neighbor, came to the rescue and saved Alves, but it was too late for his wife and children. Alves was one step ahead of the long arm of the law, but he didn't get off scot-free. Shortly afterward, he was plugged by another unnamed *vira-saia*. The criminal gang continued to do successful robberies without its first chief. Luis Gibut, ex-Jesuit, traitor and poor speller, is probably still doing time in purgatory.

MATRIZ NS DA CONCEIÇÃO DE ANTÔNIO DIAS

The parish church of the Antônio Dias parish, **Matriz NS da Conceição de Antônio Dias** (8:30-11:45am & 1:30-4:45pm Tue-Sat, noon-4:45pm only on Sun; closed Mon) was designed by Aleijadinho's father, Manuel Francisco Lisboa, and built between the years 1727 and 1770. Note the painting of the eagle; its head points downward, symbolizing the domination of the Moors by the Christians. Aleijadinho is buried by the altar of Boa Morte.

The **Museu do Aleijadinho** (Rua do Aleijadinho) is opposite the church and has the same hours.

Nearby is the abandoned mine Encardadeira or **Mina do Chico-Rei** (Rua Dom Silvério 108; admission US$3; 8am-5pm). It's fantastic but dangerous, full of crumbling secret passageways and rumored to be haunted. Ask around for directions on your way; it can be difficult to find.

CASA DE TOMÁS ANTÔNIO GONZAGA

Tomás Antônio Gonzaga's **house** (Rua do Ouvidor 9) is now the seat of the municipal

---

CHICO-REI

Brazil's first abolitionist was Chico-Rei, an African tribal king. In the early 1700s, amid the frenzy of the gold rush, an entire tribe, king and all, was captured in Africa, sent to Brazil and sold to a mine owner in Ouro Prêto.

The king, Chico-Rei, worked as the foreman of the slave miners. Working Sundays and holidays, he finally bought his freedom from the slave master, then freed his son Osmar. Together, father and son liberated the entire tribe.

This collective then bought the fabulously wealthy Encardadeira gold mine, and Chico-Rei assumed his royal functions once again, holding court in Vila Rica and celebrating African holidays in traditional costume. News of this reached the Portuguese king, who immediately prohibited slaves from purchasing their freedom. Chico-Rei is now a folk hero among Brazilian Blacks.

government. This is where Gonzaga, his poet friend Claudio da Costa (author of 'Vila Rica'), Tiradentes and others conspired unsuccessfully to put an end to Portuguese rule in Brazil. The sad little event came to be known as the Inconfidência Mineira.

IGREJA DE SÃO FRANCISCO DE ASSIS
Across the street from Gonzaga's house is the artistry of **Igreja de São Francisco de Assis** (☉ 8:30-11:45am & 1:30-4:45pm Tue-Sun). After *The Prophets* in Congonhas, Aleijadinho's masterpiece, this is the most important piece of Brazilian colonial art. It was lovingly restored in 1992. The entire exterior, a radical departure from military baroque style, was carved by Aleijadinho himself, from the soapstone medallion to the cannon waterspouts and the military two-bar cross. The interior was painted by Aleijadinho's long-term partner, Manuel da Costa Ataíde.

The sacristy is said to be haunted by the spirit of an 18th-century woman. In the dead of night, her head reportedly dissolves into a skull and she screams, 'I'm dying, call Father Carlos'. The annex of the church holds some works from the Museu do Aleijadinho.

PRAÇA TIRADENTES
Praça Tiradentes is the center of town. It's a good place to have lunch, catch your breath by the statue of Tiradentes, or take in some museums before the churches of the Pilar parish open in the afternoon.

The **Museu da Inconfidência** (☉ noon-5:30pm Tue-Sun), formerly the old municipal headquarters and jail, is an attractive building that was built between 1784 and 1854. Used as a prison from 1907 until 1937, the museum contains the tomb of Tiradentes, documents of the Inconfidência Mineira, torture instruments and important works by Ataíde and Aleijadinho.

IGREJA NS DO CARMO
From Praça Tiradentes, head down Rua Brigadeiro Musqueira to the **Igreja NS do Carmo** (☉ 1-4:45pm Tue-Sun). This church, built between 1766 and 1772, was a group effort by the most important artists of the area. The church features a facade by Aleijadinho.

MUSEU DO ORATÓRIO
This new **museum** (www.oratorio.com.br; admission US$1; ☉ 9am-noon & 1-5pm) is in a triple-level colonial house next to the Igreja NS do Carmo. It has a fabulous collection of oratories. The display is well organized and multilingual.

CASA DE TIRADENTES
The home of Joaquim José da Silva Xavier (Tiradentes) was also near the Igreja NS do Carmo. After the failed rebellion against the Portuguese, Tiradentes was executed in Rio and his head was paraded around his hometown. His house was demolished, and its grounds were salted to ensure that nothing would grow there.

ESCOLA DE MINAS
The **Escola de Minas** (☉ noon-5pm Mon-Fri, 9am-1pm Sat & Sun) in the old governor's palace in Praça Tiradentes has a very fine museum of metals and mineralogy.

CASA DOS CONTOS
From Praça Tiradentes head west down Rua Senador Rocha Lagoa to Praça Reynaldo Alves de Brito at the bottom of the hill. Here you'll find the **Casa dos Contos** (☉ 12:30-5:30pm Tue-Sat, 8:30am-1:30pm Sun), now a public library and art gallery. Claudio da Costa was imprisoned here after participating in the Inconfidência Mineira. Next door is the **Ponto do Leilão**, where slaves were taken to be tortured.

MATRIZ DE NS DO PILAR
Head west across the bridge, round along Rua São José and south along Rua Randolfo Bretas to the **Matriz de NS do Pilar** (☉ 9-10:45am & noon-4:45pm Tue-Sun) This is the second-most opulent church in Brazil (after Salvador's São Francisco) in terms of gold. It has 434kg of gold and silver and is one of Brazil's finest showcases of artwork. Note the wild-bird chandelier holders, the laminated beaten gold, the scrolled church doors, 15 panels of Old and New Testament scenes by Pedro Gomes Chaes, and the hair on Jesus (the real stuff, donated by a penitent worshipper).

Legend has it that the Pilar and Antônio Dias parishes vied for the image of NS dos Passos. In order to settle the argument, the image was loaded onto a horse standing in Praça Tiradentes and rockets were fired to scare the horse; the idea was that the image would belong to the parish to which the

Indigenous Brazilians (p48)

JOHN MAIER JR

Afternoon snacking, Rio de Janeiro

JOHN MAIER JR

RICARDO GOMES

Traveling by *bonde* (p138), Santa Teresa, Rio de Janeiro

JOHN MAIER JR

Boy meets girl, Rio de Janeiro

Women in Bahian dress, Salvador (p412), Bahia

Rasta, Salvador, Bahia

The girl from Banda de Ipanema (p107), Rio de Janeiro

Boy, Salvador, Bahia

horse bolted. Since the horse knew only one path, it galloped straight to the Matriz de NS do Pilar.

TEATRO MUNICIPAL

Built in 1769 by João de Souza Lisboa, the **Teatro Municipal** (Rua Brigadeiro Musqueira; concerts US$2-15; 🕑 1-5:30pm) is the oldest theater in Minas Gerais and perhaps in Brazil.

Tours

Official guides (US$30 for four-hour tours, US$40 for four to eight hours for up to 10 people) and interpreters (US$40) can be booked at the tourist office (see p234). Beware of unofficial guides, as there are some nasty characters hanging around.

The tourist office also organizes treks into the surrounding hills and horseback rides to Itacolomy. The cost is around US$60 for the day. Speak to João, Alexandre or Renaldo a day before you go, to give them enough time to get the horses ready. Take care and make sure you have an official guide: there have been problems with robberies on some of the trails of late.

Festivals & Events

Semana Santa (Holy Week) processions in Ouro Prêto, held on the Thursday before Palm Sunday and sporadically until Easter Sunday, are quite a spectacle.

The Congado is to Minas what Candomblé is to Bahia and Macumba is to Rio: the local expression of Afro-Christian syncretism. The major **Congado celebrations** are for NS do Rosário (October 23 to 25, at the Capela do Padre Faria), for the New Year and for May 13 (the anniversary of abolition).

You'd also be wise to reserve a pousada (guesthouse) in late July, when a weeklong annual **winter festival** is held. This involves two universities and the town floods with students participating in 24-hour classes, exhibitions and parties.

Carnaval in Ouro Prêto is also popular. A special feature is the *janela erótica* (erotic window) on Rua Direita, where people dance naked behind a thin curtain.

The **Cavalhada**, held in Amarantina (near Ouro Prêto) during the Festa de São Gonçalo from September 17 to 23, isn't as grand as the one in Pirenópolis, but is impressive nonetheless. The Cavalhada is a reenactment of the battles between Christians and Muslims in Iberia.

Sleeping
BUDGET

Ouro Prêto is a university town, with schools of pharmacy, biochemistry, mineralogy, geology and engineering. Student lodging, known as *repúblicas*, makes up 20% of the housing here. They are not recommended, although they are the cheapest places to stay in town; they're closed from Christmas to Carnaval, they're loud, and they stack as many people as possible into rooms with mattresses on the floor.

Pousada Nello Nuno (☎ 3551 3375; Rua Camilo de Brito 59; s/d US$20/27) In a quiet location just northeast of Praça Tiradentes, this pousada is highly recommended. It has clean and airy *apartamentos* with lots of artwork and a cute courtyard.

Pousada São Francisco (☎ 3551 3456; Rua Padre José Marcos Penna 202; dm/s/d incl breakfast US$10/20/27) Not far from the Igreja de São Francisco de Paula (not São Francisco de Assis), this pousada has good views and a friendly multilingual staff. From the bus station, head toward the church; facing downhill, look for the break in the fence on the left and follow the path down to the pousada. If you pass the church you've missed the turn. If you arrive late at night call from the bus station and someone will pop over to accompany you. Don't try to go it alone – it's close, but impossible to see in the pitch dark.

Albergue de Juventude Brumas Hostel (☎ 3551 2944; Rua Padre José Marcos Penna s/n; s/d US$8/12; 🖳) Just a few meters down the road from Pousada São Francisco, this is another place with clean rooms, great views and a friendly, multilingual staff. Kitchen facilities also available.

Albergue Ouro Prêto (☎ 3551 6705; Rua Costa Sena 30, Largo de Coimbra; dm/s/d US$10/16/23) This wonky-floored hostel faces the lovely Igreja São Francisco de Assis. Discounts apply for HI cardholders.

MID-RANGE

Pouso do Chico Rei (☎ 3551 1274; Rua Brigadeiro Mosqueira 90; s/d US$27/40) This is a charming place with wonderful big beds and great views. Completely furnished in antiques, it's one of the oldest pousadas in the city.

Although bathrooms are in short supply and usually must be shared, it's a delightful experience.

Casa Grande (☎ 3551 4314; Rua Conselheiro Quintiliano 96; s/d US$36/48) Casa Grande has rooms with balconies from which almost the entire town can be seen. Rooms are spacious and well appointed.

Pousada Toledo (☎ 3551 3366; Rua Conselheiro Quintiliano 395; s/d US$33/48). Rooms at this pousada are furnished with antiques and beautiful hand-sewn quilts. Ask for a room in the back to avoid the street noise, which can be intrusive.

Pousada Ouro Prêto (☎ 3551-3081; Largo Musicista José dos Anjos Costa 72; www.pousadaouropreto.com.br; s/d US$20/30) This pousada is at the end of a narrow little street (also called das Mercês), right behind the Igreja de NS das Mercês e Perdões. It's a friendly place, and Gerson, who runs it, speaks English. It has a fantastic view too, and all the comforts that delight the traveler.

Colonial (☎ 3551 3133; www.hotelcolonial.com.br; Travessa Padre Camilo Veloso 26; s/d US$25/35) Situated in an 18th-century building, the Colonial is considered one of the town's most beautiful landmarks. The rooms are somewhat basic but very clean and atmospheric, with big windows that fill the place with natural light. And it's close to the main square.

Pousada Recanto das Minas (☎ 3551 3003; Rua Manganês 287; s/d r US$30/50, s/d apt US$70/100) Perched on a hill just on the edge of town, this pousada has lovely views, but the walk to and fro can get a bit strenuous. Lots of families and large groups favor this pousada because of its simple but cozy chalets scattered around the main building.

Grande Hotel Ouro Prêto (☎ 3551 1488; Rua Senador Rocha Lagoa 164; s/d US$55/66, with views US$66/89) Oscar Niemeyer's Grande Hotel is in a great position, with a pool and bar area overlooking the town. It's an immense hotel (by local standards) and is also the only modernist structure for miles. Most Mineiros, however, consider it an absolute eyesore.

TOP END
Pousada do Mondego (☎ 3551 2040; fax 3551 3094; Largo do Coimbra 38; s/d US$80/110) An intimate, cozy inn close to Igreja São Francisco de Assis, this 18th-century colonial mansion has period furnishings and outstanding service. The hotel can arrange two-hour city tours in a private minivan. This is an excellent top-end choice.

Solar NS do Rosário (☎ 3551 5200; www.hotelsolardorosario.com.br; Rua Getúlio Vargas 270; s/d US$100/120) The five-star Solar feels like a boutique inn. It has a world-class restaurant on site, elegant and comfortable décor and charming guest rooms. Afternoon tea is served in the atrium, cocktails by the pool. The hotel even has its own mine, discovered during renovations a few years ago.

Luxor Ouro Prêto Pousada (☎ 3551 2244; Rua Dr Alfredo Baeta 16; www.luxor.hotels.com; s/d US$140/200) The Luxor has stone walls dating back 200 years, period antique furnishings, hardwood floors, and a small romantic restaurant serving delectable dishes. Guest rooms have gorgeous views, some with original paintings by Chanina, a famous Minas artist.

Estalagem das Minas Gerais (☎ 3551 2122; Rodovia dos Inconfidentes, Km 90; s/d apt US$40/70, chalets US$140) Abutting a nature preserve, this *estalagem* (inn) is perfect for those who like to spend time in the great outdoors. Rooms are modern, with nice views of the surrounding valley, and the chalets are really like small houses, accommodating as many as five people. A restaurant serves plain but fresh regional dishes.

Eating
BUDGET
Most of the restaurants are clustered along two streets: the lively Rua Conde de Bobadela (popularly known as Rua Direita) and Rua São José.

Spaghetti (☎ 3552 5090; Rua Direita 138A; lunch mains US$3-7; ✆ 10-1am) A huge hit with the many students in Ouro Prêto, Spaghetti serves Italian-style pancakes in the morning and pizza all the time, and features live music nightly.

Maximus (☎ 3551 3143; Rua Direita 151; per kg US$6; ✆ 11am-4pm) This is where locals go to serve themselves hearty dishes like *tutu a mineira*, a delicious black-bean *feijoada*.

Ouro Grill (☎ 3551 1188; Rua Senador Rocha Lagoa 61; lunch US$9; ✆ 11am-6pm) Every kind of meat dish you could imagine – grilled, fried, baked and stewed – is served here, each more delectable than the next.

Adega Ouro Prêto (☎ 3551 4171; Rua Teixeira Amaral 24; per kg US$6; ✆ 11:30am-4pm) This vegetarian's delight serves a plethora of fresh dishes daily. It's on the steep street off Rua São José, on the way to Pousada São Francisco.

Butikim.com Arte (Rua Gabriel Santos; lunch US$5; ☎ 11:30am-4pm & 8pm-midnight) Way off the beaten track, Butikim.com Arte is a new 'cultural night bar' that also does lunch. It's run by Pousada São Francisco.

Café e Cia (☎ 3551 4154; Rua São José 187; per kg US$6; ☎ noon-midnight) An old favorite for lunch and dinner, there are lots of good things to eat here, including crepes.

MID-RANGE

Restaurante Chafariz (☎ 3551 2828; Rua São José 167; per kg US$10; ☎ 11am-4.30pm) This restaurant does an incredibly sumptuous all-you-can-eat buffet of *cozinha mineira*, and throws in a free shot of *cachaça* (sugarcane spirit) to aid digestion.

Deguste (☎ 3551 6363; Rua Coronel Alves 15; dinner US$12; ☎ 11am-midnight) Just opposite the theater, Deguste has good food and live music on weekends.

Down on Rua São José there are a few good options:

Restaurante Sabor Minas (Rua São José No 202A; dishes US$6-15; ☎ 11am-midnight) Sabor Minas has phenomenal pizzas and also has various regional dishes that are large enough to share.

De Consola's Bar Lanches (Rua da Conceição 18; lunch with coffee & dessert US$12; ☎ 11am-4pm) On the other side of town, on Praça Antônio Diaz, De Consola's is a cozy informal place with a good wine selection.

Chalet dos Caldos (☎ 3551 3992; Rua Carlos Tomaz 33; mains US$7-12; ☎ 7pm-midnight, closed Mon) For delicious soup and *pratos típicos* (local dishes) large enough to share, head for Chalet dos Caldos. A local speciality is chicken or steak baked with bananas and cheese on top – delicious!

Centeio Pães e Iguarias (Praça Barão do Rio Branco; snacks & coffee US$2-8; ☎ 6am-10pm) If you are after a late-night or early-morning snack, try this bakery at the southeastern end of the center.

TOP END

Le Coq d'Or (☎ 3551 5200; Rua Getúlio Vargas 270; dinner with drinks US$25-60; ☎ noon-3pm & 7-11pm Tue-Fri, noon-midnight Sat & Sun) Probably the finest restaurant in town, if not the region, Le Coq d'Or is extremely elegant, with for-mal place settings, gentle music, attentive waitstaff and an executive chef who trained in Paris. The menu changes seasonally but always includes an innovative selection of fish and meat dishes, complemented with a full wine list.

Restaurant Casa Do Ouvidor (☎ 3551 2141; Rua Direita 42; dinner with drinks US$20; ☎ 11am-3pm & 7-10pm) On top of a jewelry store in the heart of the historical district, Ouvidor has garnered numerous awards for its *comida mineira* entrees. It's very popular, so be pre-pared for a crowded room, and definitely come with an empty stomach – portions are immense.

Restaurante O Profeta (☎ 3551 4556; Rua Conde de Bobadela 65; dinner with drinks US$20; ☎ 11am-11pm Sun-Thu, 11-1am Fri & Sat) If you like live music while you eat, you'll like this very cozy place with a laid-back vibe and great food.

Café Geraes (☎ 3551 1405; Rua Direita 122; dinner with drinks & dessert US$15; ☎ 11am-11pm Sun-Thu & to 1am Fri & Sat) Well-heeled students and art-ists like to congregate here to sip wine and talk shop, or final exams, or whatever is on their minds on any given day. Sandwiches and soups are the main fare, and they are good indeed.

Entertainment

A young crowd hangs out in Praça Tira-dentes at nights and on weekends, but usu-ally after midnight head for some nearby club for a spot of dancing. There's a lot of spontaneous music in the bars and from buskers along Rua Direita.

Bardobeco (Travessa do Arieira 15; ☎ 8-11pm Mon-Fri) This very popular bar has more than 40 brands of *cachaça* – look out! – and is replete with gorgeous furnishings.

Acaso 85 (Largo do Rosário) This club, oppo-site the Hotel Rosário, attracts a late-night crowd. The stone walls and high ceilings impart a medieval feeling to the split-level building.

Getting There & Away

There are frequent buses from Brazil's closest big cities to the **Ouro Prêto bus station** (☎ 3559 3252; Rua Padre Rolim 661), particularly to and from Belo Horizonte. During peak periods, buy your tickets a day in advance – they sell out fast.

Destinations include: Belo Horizonte (US$5, 2¾ hours, eight daily, four Sunday from 7am to 9:30pm); Rio de Janeiro (US$18, seven hours, once daily at 11pm); São Paulo (US$22, 11 hours, twice daily at 6:45am and 5pm, plus a third at 5:25pm Sunday); Santa Bárbara (US$6, three hours, twice daily at 7:30am and 5:45pm); Conselheiro Lafaiete (US$5, five daily Monday to Friday from 5am to 6pm, four daily on Saturday from 9am to 6pm, four daily Sunday from 6am to 6pm).

From Conselheiro Lafaiete you can catch buses to Congonhas.

The bus station is at the northwest end of town. To get to Mariana or Minas de Passagem you can catch a local bus from the bus stop, which is just northeast of Praça Tiradentes.

Getting Around

The town is hilly, but you can go everywhere on foot. A small bus (US$0.30) circulates between the bus station and Capela do Padre Faria on the eastern side of town, making various stops along the way.

AROUND OURO PRÊTO
Minas de Passagem

You will get a kick out of this place, probably the best gold mine to visit in the Ouro Prêto region. There's an immense system of tunnels that goes down very deep and then spreads horizontally. Only a fraction of the mine is open to the public, but for most terrestrials, it's enough.

The descent into the mine is made in a rickety antique cable car (the guide is quick to assure you that the cable itself is new), giving you a firsthand idea of just how dangerous mining can be.

The mine opened in 1719. Until the abolition of slavery it was worked by Black slaves, many of whom died dynamiting into the rock. Even after abolition, the life of the 'free' miner was little improved.

The mandatory guided tour, led by former miners and given in English where possible, is short and quite informative. It covers the history of the mine and details the methods used to extract the gold, quartz and other metals. There's a **shrine** to dead miners at the bottom.

The **mine** (☎ 3557 5000; minadapassagem@bol.com.br; admission US$10; ☉ 9am-5:30pm) has a shallow, sparkling-clear 2km-wide **subterranean lake**, in which you are free to swim. The water's cold, averaging 16°C to 18°C (61°F to 65°F), but blue and pure. It's great fun, so bring a bathing suit.

The mine is between Ouro Prêto and Mariana. Take any local bus that runs between the two (US$0.50 from either town) and ask the driver to let you off at Minas de Passagem.

CONGONHAS

☎ 0xx31 / pop 39,000 / elevation 871m

This small industrial town has been saved from complete obscurity by the beautiful, brooding presence of Aleijadinho's extraordinary *Prophets* at the Basílica do Bom Jesus de Matosinhos. The dramatic statues almost seem to be performing a balletic dance and it's a wondrous experience to be able to walk freely among them. They are Aleijadinho's masterpiece and Brazil's most famed work of art. It's worth taking the trouble to get to Congonhas just to see them.

Congonhas is 72km south of Belo Horizonte, 3km off Hwy BR-040. The city grew up with the search for gold in the nearby Rio Maranhão, and the economy today is dominated by iron mining in the surrounding countryside.

Sights
THE PROPHETS & THE CHAPELS

Already an old man, sick and crippled, Aleijadinho sculpted *The Prophets* between 1800 and 1805. Symmetrically placed in front of the **Basílica do Bom Jesus de Matosinhos**, each of the prophets from the Old Testament was carved out of one or two blocks of soapstone. Each carries a Latin message: some of them are hopeful prophecies, others warn of the end of the world.

Much has been written about these sculptures – their dynamic quality, the sense of movement (much like a Hindu dance or a ballet), how they complement each other and how their arrangement prevents them from being seen in isolation. The poet Carlos Drummond de Andrade wrote that the dramatic faces and gestures are 'magnificent, terrible, grave and tender' and commented on 'the way the statues, of human size, appear to be larger than life as they look down upon the viewer with the sky behind them.'

Before working on *The Prophets*, Aleijadinho carved (or supervised his assistants in carving) the wooden statues that were placed in the six little **chapels**, also designed by Aleijadinho. The chapels and their placement on the sloping site are superb in themselves and just as impressive as the prophets. The way the light falls on the pale sculpted domes against the dark mountain backdrop is truly beautiful. The sets in the chapels represent the Passion of Christ: the Last Supper, Calvary, Imprisonment, Flagellation and Coronation, the Carrying of the Cross and the Crucifixion. Some of the figures, such as the Roman soldiers, are very crude and clearly done by assistants, while others are finely chiseled, with muscles bulging and veins popping.

ROMARIA

From *The Prophets*, wander downhill for about 200m to the **Romaria**, an unusual building where a long loop of rooms surrounds a huge oval courtyard. Originally designed as a pousada for pilgrims, it's now used as a cultural space. Among other things it has museums and a souvenir shop.

Festivals & Events

Held September 7 to 14, the **Jubileu do Senhor Bom Jesus do Matosinhos** is one of the great religious festivals in Minas Gerais. Every year approximately 600,000 pilgrims arrive at the church to make promises, do penance, receive blessings and give and receive alms. The **Holy Week** processions preceding Easter

in Congonhas are also famous, especially the dramatizations on Good Friday.

Sleeping
BUDGET

It's possible to catch an early bus into Congonhas and another one out that same afternoon, and as there's little to see beyond Ajeijadinho's artwork, most people don't spend the night. That's a shame, because to catch the statues in the early-morning light is a joyful experience. That said, there are very few sleeping options available.

Colonial Hotel (☎ 3731 1834; Praça da Basílica 76; s/d US$12/19) Now somewhat faded, remnants of the Colonial's former glory are apparent in the huge hallways and immensely high ceilings. Most of the rooms are spacious and the bathrooms surprisingly modern. Quite a good deal, and it's across the street from Aleijadinho's masterpieces.

Freitas (☎ 3731 1543; Rua Marechal Floriano 69; s/d US$8/12) This hotel has very basic rooms, some without private bathrooms.

MID-RANGE

Dos Profetas (☎ 3731 1352; www.hoteldosprofetas.com .br; Av Júlia Kubitschek 54; s/d US$18/24) A pretty little hotel in the center of town, Dos Profetas is about a 15-minute walk from the actual *Prophets* (and it's mostly uphill). Rooms are clean but sparse, with dark wood furniture and gleaming, modern bathrooms.

THE WAY OF THE CROSS

Aleijadinho and his assistants labored feverishly in Congonhas to complete what has become his masterpiece. One unfortunate soul named Mauricio was actually crushed to death by a large chunk of soapstone, but Aleijadinho continued to work like one possessed, strapped to wooden scaffolding, with hammer and chisel attached to the stumps of his arms. It's possible his fervor was more political than religious. More than once in the chapel figures Christ is depicted with a red mark on his neck, which some local historians believe meant the martyred figure also represented slain independence fighter Tiradente. The theory gains support when one looks at the Roman soldiers Aleijadinho sculpted – they all have two left feet and sport ankle boots, a shoe style then favored by the colonizing Portuguese. Little is known of Aleijadinho's politics, but he lived through the uprising in Ouro Preto and probably knew Tiradentes by sight.

Basílica do Bom Jesus de Matosinhos itself owes its existence to Feliciano Mendes, reportedly a descendant of the Portuguese Royal House of Bragança. Mendes believed that Jesus of Matosinhos had cured him of a serious disease and consequently vowed to commission a church in his honor. After years were spent amassing the necessary funds, work began on the church in 1758, and it was completed by 1761. Ever since, pilgrims (most of them hoping to be cured of a disease) have come from every corner of Brazil on September 14, the anniversary of the miracle cure. Many visitors also come to the church throughout the year to marvel at the last great work of the 'little cripple.'

Max Mazza (☎ 3731 1970; Av Júlia Kubitschek 410; s/d US$16/29) Also about 15 minutes away from the big attraction, Max Mazza is a basic but appealing option.

Eating

There's not too much variety in this town, but some eateries are clustered in the industrial center near Av Júlia Kubitschek.

Cova do Daniel (☎ 3731 1834; Praça da Basílica 76; lunch US$7; ⏰ 11am-3pm) In the basement of the Colonial Hotel, this is an interesting restaurant serving an assortment of Mineiro dishes.

Casa da Ladeira (☎ 3731 2913, 3731 1746; Rua Dr Paulo Mendes 649; dinner US$7; ⏰ 6-10pm) Right across the road from Cova do Daniel, Casa da Ladeira offers much the same type of cuisine as the Cova.

Getting There & Away

Congonhas is a little off the beaten track – it's not too far as the crow flies from neighboring colonial towns, but there's not always a direct bus. The best bet is to return to Belo Horizonte (US$3, 1¾ hours, three daily from 6:15am to 5pm) if you are in a hurry.

To get to Ouro Prêto you must first go to Conselheiro Lafaiete (US$1, 30 minutes, every 45 minutes from 5:30am to 10:30pm) and then from there catch a bus to Ouro Prêto (US$4, 2½ hours, five daily from 7:05am to 6pm, three on Sunday from 6am to 6pm). Try to get to Conselheiro Lafaiete a bit early to make sure you get a bus; if you do miss the last bus, there are a couple of hotels across from the bus station.

There are two buses a day to Rio (US$13, eight hours, 6:45am and 12:30am). To São João del Rei, catch one of the Belo Horizonte to São João del Rei buses that stop off at Congonhas (US$5, two hours, seven daily from 7:30am to 8:20pm).

Getting Around

The bus station is on Av Júlia Kubitschek, across town from the sites of interest. From here the Basílica buses leave every half-hour to 40 minutes and cost US$0.50. It's a 15-minute ride up the hill to the basilica and *The Prophets*. For the best approach and first view of the statues, get off just after the bus passes the church (as it heads downhill). The same bus returns you to the bus station,

or you can have the Colonial Hotel staff call you a taxi (US$5).

SABARÁ

☎ 0xx31 / pop 136,000 / elevation 713m

Sabará is filled with houses, mansions, churches, statues, fountains and sacred art, all dating from the town's glory days in the early 18th century when it was the first major gold-mining center in the state and one of the world's wealthiest towns.

Now Sabará is a poor town dominated by a Belgian metalworks, sitting on the muddy banks of the Rio das Velhas (Old Ladies River), 25km southeast of Belo. In the boom years, when the Rio das Velhas was 15 times wider, slave boats would sail all the way up the Rio São Francisco from Bahia. Sabará produced more gold in one week than the rest of Brazil produced in a year. You can still pan the river bed for gold flakes, but the nuggets are long gone.

Since it's only half an hour by bus from Belo, Sabará makes an easy and interesting day trip. Don't bother visiting here on a Monday – all the sites are closed.

There's an information booth at the entrance to town, but major attractions are easy to find, since there are signposts at Praça Santa Rita telling where everything is.

Sights

Most of the churches, museums and other colonial attractions charge small admission fees (from US$1 to US$3), payable as you come through the door.

A testament to the wealth of bygone days, the elegant opera house of Sabará, **O Teatro Imperial** (Rua Dom Pedro II; ⏰ 8am-noon & 1-6pm Tue-Sun), was built in 1770. It has crystal lamps and three tiers of seats made of carved wood and bamboo.

Housed in an old gold foundry (1730), the **Museu do Ouro** (Rua da Intendência; admission US$1.50; ⏰ noon-5:30pm Tue-Sun) contains art and artifacts of the glory years of Sabará.

MATRIZ DE NS DE CONCEIÇÃO

The Jesuits, cultural ambassadors of the far-flung Portuguese empire, were among the first Westerners to make contact with the Far East. A tangible result is the **Matriz de NS de Conceição** (Praça Getúlio Vargas; ⏰ 9am-noon & 1:30-5pm, closed Mon), finished in 1720 and located at the eastern end of town. It is a fascinating blend of Asian arts and Portuguese baroque – overwhelming with its gold-leaf and red Chinese scrolls.

There are even pagodas on some of the church door panels by the sanctuary, and several other interesting little details in the church. Floorboards cover the graves of the early parishioners; the gold and silver nuggets nailed on these tablets indicate whether the deceased was rich or poor.

On the ceiling of the church is the patron saint of confessors, John Nepomuceno of 14th-century Czechoslovakia, depicted holding his severed tongue. King Wenceslau ordered St Nepomuceno's tongue cut out because the saint refused to reveal whether or not the Moldavian queen was faithful. Nepomuceno died of his terrible wound, but became very popular posthumously in Czechoslovakian cult circles and, inexplicably, in Minas Gerais during the gold era. Look for the little angel at his side who gently shushes churchgoers with a finger to his lips.

IGREJA DE NS DO Ó

After surviving an attack by his own troops in 1720, Captain Lucas Ribeiro de Almeida built a chapel on the east side of town in thanks to the Virgin Mary. He called it the **Igreja de NS do Ó** (Largo NS do Ó; ☿ 9-11:30am & 2-5pm Tue-Sun). Like NS de Conceição, the chapel has Oriental details and an ornate golden interior. It's popular with pregnant women and those who pray for fertility.

IGREJA DE NS DO ROSÁRIO DOS PRETOS

This half-built **church** (Praça Melo Viana; ☿ 8-11am & 1-5pm) was started and financed by slaves but never finished. It now stands as a memorial to the abolition of slavery in 1888.

IGREJA NS DO CARMO

Aleijadinho had a lot to do with the decoration of this **church** (Rua de Carmo; ☿ 9-11:30am, closed Mon). His touch is everywhere, especially in the faces of the statues of São Simão and São João da Cruz.

Getting There & Away

From Belo, buses leave every 15 minutes from the local section behind the bus station. Return buses leave the bus stop on Av Victor Fantini in Sabará; you can also catch one on the road out of town.

MARIANA

☎ 0xx31 / pop 42,000 / elevation 712m

Mariana is a pleasant old mining town with row upon row of fine colonial houses, many of which have now transformed the ground floors into stores and boutiques. It's retained the high-altitude tranquility of many of the mining towns and can really transmit a glimpse of what life was like during the early days of the gold rush. Every July 16, the date of its founding, the town receives the governor of Minas and for 24 hours everyone pretends Mariana is still the state capital.

Information

INTERNET ACCESS

Celeiro das Artes Cybercafé (☎ 3557 1336; Praça Gomes Freire; per hr US$2; ☿ 10am-10pm) This place has relatively fast connections and very beautiful surroundings filled with Mineiro crafts. Consider it an art gallery with computers.

TOURIST INFORMATION

Associação dos Guias (☎ 3557 1158; Rua Antônio Olinto) Next door to the state information office, this place is more useful, and gives away excellent free maps.

State information office (☎ 3557 9044; Rua Antônio Olinto) In the tourist terminal near the river and where the bus from Ouro Prêto stops.

Sights

The 18th-century churches are all worth visiting. The **Catedral Basílica da Sé** (Praça Cláudio Manuel; ☿ 7am-6pm Tue-Sun), with its fantastic German organ dating from 1701, holds **organ concerts** (admission US$7; ☿ 11am Fri, 12:15pm Sun). The **Museu Arquidiocesano de Arte Sacra**

GARIMPEIROS

If you want to try your hand at some old-style prospecting, then head for the *garimpo* (mining camp), just over the last bridge at Carmo Creek, a short walk from town. Look upstream and you'll see people digging and panning. They're *garimpeiros*, gold miners using methods almost unchanged since 1696. The only difference is that pans are now made of metal and not wood. To get a really good look follow Rua Rosario Velho until you reach the stream. The *garimpeiros* enjoy sharing their expertise with novice panners.

(Rua Frei Durão 49; ⏰ 9am-noon & 1-5pm), behind the cathedral, is also worth a look. It has sculptures by Aleijadinho, paintings by Ataíde, and other religious objects.

There are two lovely churches on Praça Minas Gerais. **Igreja NS do Carmo** is slowly being renovated after a fire broke out and caused severe damage some years ago. **Igreja São Francisco de Assis** (⏰ 8:30am-5pm) is the final resting place of the painter Ataíde, Aleijadinho's partner, and 94 other lucky souls.

Further up the hill is the **Basílica de São Pedro dos Clérigos** (Rua Dom Silvério; ⏰ 9am-5pm), which was never completed. There is a great view from the elevated site. The town gallows, long since gone, used to be beside the church. While walking through the old part of town, you'll come across painters and wood sculptors at work in their studios.

Sleeping

There's not much in the way of luxury accommodations, but more than enough comfortable pousadas to go around.

Hotel Providência (☎ 3557 1444; www.hotelprovidencia.com.br; Rua Dom Silveiro 233; s/d/apt US$10/16/20) Originally the living quarters of the nuns who still run a school next door, this hotel has a chapel and an excellent swimming pool, which you are free to use if you don't mind walking through the school to get to it (although strolling there in skimpy swim gear is frowned upon by management). The building is very lovely, with gorgeous colors, and wardrobe restrictions notwithstanding, the nuns maintain a very welcoming vibe.

Pousada do Chafariz (☎ 3557 1492; www.pousadadochafariz.hpg.com.br; Rua Côn Rego 149; s/d/tr US$15/23/35) This pousada has modern rooms with TV and minibar. It's on a tranquil little street very close to the historic center and can be hard to find. Ask around as you go lest you get lost in the winding, narrow staircases. Popular with families.

Pouso da Typographia (☎ 3557 1577; Praça Gomes Freire 220; s/d US$22/30) It's worth staying here just to see the antique printing presses in the foyer. The front rooms overlooking the praça can get noisy on the weekends. Discounts can be had during the week.

Pousada Ladim Gamarano (☎ 3557 1835; Rua Raimundo Gamarano; s/d US$20/28) A beautiful old house adapted to modern tastes and conveniences, the Pousada Ladim is quite a treat. Owner Ladim Gamarano incorp-

ates furniture designed in his atelier into the overall decoration.

Pousada Solar dos Correa (☎ 3557 2080; Rua Josafa Macedo; s/d US$25/35) Pousada Solar has nice airy apartments on top of a colonial restaurant built in 1744.

Eating

If you've had enough Mineiro cooking for the moment, check out the several Italian restaurants that have popped up near the city center. Otherwise, the best dishes are those from the region.

Lua Cheia (Rua Dom Viçoso 23; per kg US$6; ⏰ 11am-4pm) Plentiful good food served by the kilo or all you can eat from the buffet is the norm at this pretty restaurant.

Engenho Novo (Praça da Sé 26; lunch US$8; ⏰ 11am-4pm & 7-11pm) This restaurant serves great regional dishes by day, and doubles as a funky little bar at night. English is spoken by the owners and every effort is made to make visitors feel at home.

Restaurante Tambaú (☎ 3558 2370; Travessa São Francisco 26; lunch buffet US$8; ⏰ 6pm-midnight Mon-Fri, noon-3pm & 6pm-1am Sat, noon-1am Sun) Everybody's favorite place for dinner on weeknights and lunch on Saturday, the Tambaú offers a variety of dishes, some with Bahian influences.

Dom Silvério (☎ 3557 2475; Rua do Seminário 290; pizza with drink US$6; ⏰ 6.30pm-midnight) Delicious and rapid pizzas and snacks.

Portão da Praça (Praça Gomes Freire; sandwiches US$4; ⏰ 11am-6pm) The *beirutes* (pita breads stuffed with meat and salad) here are terrific (almost as good as the ones in São Paulo!).

Getting There & Away

There are regular buses between Ouro Prêto and Mariana (US$0.50, 35 minutes, every 30 minutes, from 6.30am). In Ouro Prêto, the bus stop for Mariana is near the Escola de Minas, just northeast of Praça Tiradentes. In Mariana, the bus stop is next to the tourist information office on Rua Antônio Olinto. Mariana's bus station, Rodovia dos Inconfidêntes, located at Km 72, on the edge of town, services more distant destinations such as Belo Horizonte, Rio de Janeiro and São Paulo.

LAVRAS NOVAS

☎ 0xx31 / pop less than 1000

This is stunningly beautiful mountain country, perfect for a weekend or weekday getaway for nature lovers. The very off-the-beaten-track village of Lavras Novas is 22km south of Ouro Prêto and there are two waterfalls within easy hiking distance.

The town was founded as a *quilombo* (see p31). Today it's a peaceful little place, a favorite hangout for ecotourists and fun-seekers looking to do some climbing, hiking and swimming. The focal point is the **Igreja Cristo Redentor**.

Activities

You can ride or trek to the two closest waterfalls: **Chapada**, 9km west, with natural swimming pools, and **Moinho**, 2km north, which is peaceful and less frequented. Ask at **Taberna Casa Antiga** about hiring horses (US$15 to US$23 a half-day). There are buses to Chapada from Ouro Prêto but none from Lavras Novas.

Sleeping & Eating

Pousadas are generally empty during the week but reservations are a good idea if you'll be here on a weekend or during a holiday.

Pousada Carumbé (☎ 3554 2105; www.carumbe .com.br; Rua Projetada 220; s/d US$12/19; 🏊) This is one of the best options you'll find in this rustic town. Beautiful apartments with relatively modern amenities.

Pousada da Pedra (☎ 9965 1133; Rua da Fonte 102; d incl breakfast & nighttime soup US$40) At the western end of town, Pousada da Pedra is a good option. The three different bohemian-influenced cottages face a majestically serene landscape. As you enter the town, turn right as you pass the cross.

Palavras Novas (☎ 3554 2025; www.palavrasno vas.com.br; Rua NS dos Prazeres 1110; s/d US$10/17; 🏊) This quirky little place is delightful in its idiosyncracies. A few of the rooms are designed like train compartments, with beds to match.

Villa Kokopelli Pousada Restaurante (☎ 9961 1331; Rua Nossa Senhora dos Prazeres 110; s/d US$28) Basic rooms and a restaurant with a good atmosphere; Villa Kokopelli has lots of meat and pasta dishes, and live music on weekends.

Serra do Luar (☎ 9961 2474; Rua Nossa Senhora dos Prazeres 119; s/d US$14/24) These are simple *apartamentos* in rustic cabins, and the on-site restaurant serves hearty *prato feitos* (plates of the day) for under US$7.

Taberna Casa Antiga (Rua Alto do Campo 215; prato feito US$5; 🕙 10am-midnight) At the east end of town, behind the church, you'll find the excellent Taberna Casa Antiga, which features a cozy bar and restaurant with a fireplace, live music and great food.

Getting There & Away

Local bus services are such that you'll have to spend at least a night here – a bus to Lavras Novas (US$2, around 30 minutes) leaves Praça Tiradentes in Ouro Prêto daily at 5:15pm and returns the following day at 6:45am. Hitching is possible, but difficult and not necessarily safe. If driving, from the suburb of Barra (southeast of the center of Ouro Prêto), take the road up along the southern ridge past the university, the town's newer residential suburbs and the aluminum factory. At the intersection with the main road, ignore signs to turn left or right, and go straight across. Of the 17km to Lavras Novas, 9km is unpaved. While the way is sometimes bumpy and precipitous, the trip is scenic.

SÃO JOÃO DEL REI

☎ 0xx32 / pop 74,000 / elevation 910m

São João del Rei affords a unique look at a *cidade historica* that didn't suffer a great decline at the end of the gold boom in the 1800s. São João remains a bustling, flourishing city where the old and the new sit cheek-to-jowl, and not always harmoniously. The historic city center, which is protected by Brazil's Landmarks Commission, features several of the country's finest churches and some gorgeous colonial mansions – one of which belonged to the late and still-popular never-quite-president Tancredo Neves. It also has a good museum and a variety of other sites and activities, and is the gateway for excursions to the stunningly beautiful village of Tiradentes. While Tiradentes is busy on weekends and generally quiet during the week, São João is pretty empty on Sunday.

Floodlights illuminate the churches every night and give them a fantastic appearance. Opening times tend to be unpredictable, but most will at least be open in the late afternoon. Monday is not a good day to visit São João – all the churches are closed; in Tiradentes the attractions are closed on Tuesday.

SÃO JOÃO DEL REI

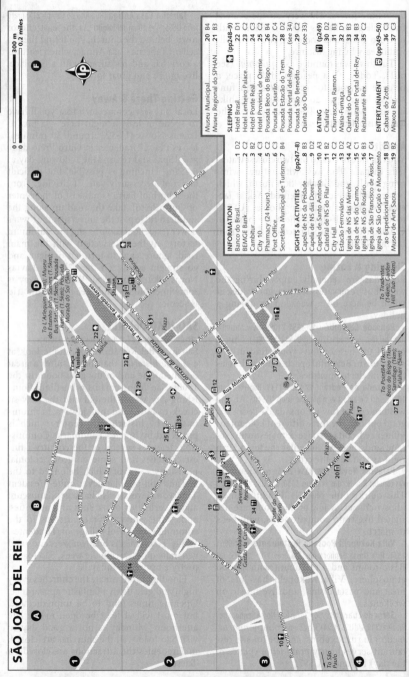

0   300 m
0   0.2 miles

INFORMATION
Banco do Brasil................................	1 D2
BEMGE Bank.....................................	2 C2
Cambitur..	3 B2
City 10..	4 C3
Pharmacy (24 hours).......................	5 C3
Post Office..	6 C3
Secretaria Municipal de Turismo.....	7 B4

SIGHTS & ACTIVITIES   (pp247–8)
Capela de NS da Piedade.................	8 B3
Capela de NS das Dores...................	9 D2
Capela de Santo Antonio................	10 A3
Catedral de NS do Pilar..................	11 B2
City Hall...	12 C2
Estação Ferroviário..........................	13 D2
Igreja de NS das Mercês.................	14 A2
Igreja de NS do Carmo....................	15 C1
Igreja de NS do Rosário...................	16 B3
Igreja de São Francisco de Assis.....	17 C4
Igreja de São Gonçalo e Monumento	
ao Expedicionário........................	18 D3
Museu de Arte Sacra.......................	19 B2

SLEEPING   (pp248–9)
Hotel Brasil.......................................	22 D1
Hotel Lenheiro Palace......................	23 C2
Hotel Ponte Real..............................	24 C3
Hotel Provincia de Orense..............	25 C2
Pousada Beco do Bispo....................	26 B4
Pousada Casarão..............................	27 C4
Pousada Estacão do Trem................	28 D2
Pousada Portal del-Rey....................	(see 34)
Pousada São Benedito......................	29 C2
Quinta do Ouro................................	(see 33)

EATING   (p249)
Chafariz..	30 D2
Churrascaria Ramon.........................	31 B3
Maria-Fumaça...................................	32 D1
Quinta do Ouro................................	33 B3
Restaurante Portal del-Rey..............	34 B3
Restaurante Rex...............................	35 C2

ENTERTAINMENT   (pp249–50)
Cabana do Zotti...............................	36 C3
Mixxou Bar.......................................	37 C3

Museu Municipal............................... | 20 B4 |
Museu Regional do SPHAN............. | 21 B3 |

Orientation

São João sits between the Serra de São José and the Serra do Lenheiro, near the south end of the Serra do Espinhaço. The town is bisected by the Rio Lenheiro, which has several bridges, including two 18th-century stone ones. The bus station is a 15-minute walk northeast of the railway station.

Information

INTERNET ACCESS

City 10 (Av Andrade Reis 120; per hr US$5) A tight squeeze and only has a few computers, but close to the old city center.

MONEY

ATMs can be found at Banco do Brasil, Banespa and HSBC branches on Av Presidente Tancredo Neves.

BEMGE bank (Av Presidente Tancredo Neves 213; ◷ 11am-4pm Mon-Fri) Quick and efficient.

Cambitur (Rua Marechal Deodoro 40; ◷ 8am-5pm Mon-Fri) A convenient and easy place to change cash.

POST

Post office (Av Tiradentes)

TELEPHONE

Telephone posts (Rua Amelia Ribeiro Guedes) There are also telephone posts at the bus station.

TOURIST OFFICES

Main tourist office (☎ 3379 2952; Praça Frei Orlando 90; ◷ 8am-5pm) On the 2nd floor, in a building just opposite the São Francisco church. There is also tourist information at the bus station.

Sights

IGREJA DE SÃO FRANCISCO DE ASSIS

This 1774 baroque **church** (Rua Padre José Maria Xavier; ◷ 9-11am & 2:30-5pm Tue-Sun) is exquisite. This was Aleijadinho's first complete project, but much of his plan was not realized. Still, the exterior, with an **Aleijadinho sculpture** of the Immaculate Virgin and several angels, is one of the finest in Minas.

Records are sketchy; Aleijadinho probably did the main altar, but his work was completely changed. In the second altar to the left, there is an image of São João Evangelista that is the work of Aleijadinho, as is the Santo Antônio. There's particularly fine woodwork in the rear of the church.

Politician Tancredo Neves is buried in the church graveyard. He was the first elected president after the 1960s-to-'80s period of military dictatorship in Brazil, though he died before he could take office.

On Sunday the local Ribeiro Bastos, or Rapadura (women's), orchestra and choir perform sacred baroque music at the 9:15am mass. It is on the south side of the river and faces a lyre-shaped plaza. The best view of the church is from up the hill, behind it.

IGREJA DE NS DO ROSÁRIO

This simple **church** (◷ 8-10am & noon-5pm Tue-Sun) was built in 1719 to honor the patron saint who was protector of the slaves.

MUSEU REGIONAL DO SPHAN

This **museum** (Rua Marechal Deodoro 12; admission US$1; ◷ noon-6pm, closed Mon) is one of the best

---

SMOKING MARY

Sure, there are buses that will get you back and forth between São João del Rei and Tiradentes, but how can they compare to a trip on a 19th-century steam train in pristine condition? Jump aboard as this little engine hisses and belches its way through the winding valley of the Serra de São José, which gradually gets rockier and bleaker as you approach Tiradentes. The trail goes through one of the oldest areas of gold mining in Minas and you'll see the remnants of 18th-century mine workings all around. Keep a sharp eye out for modern *garimpeiros* (see the boxed text on p243) still hoping to strike it rich.

Built in the 1880s as the textile industry began to take hold in São João, the *Maria-Fumaça* (Smoking Mary to locals) was one of the first rail lines in Brazil. More history is available at the **Estacão Ferroviária** (☎ 3371 8485; Av Hermílio Alves; ◷ museum 9-11am-1-5pm Tue-Sun). The trains run out of the same location on Friday, Saturday, Sunday and holidays, leaving São João at 10am and 3pm, returning from Tiradentes at 1pm and 5pm (one-way/round-trip US$5/8). When leaving São João the best views are on the left side, and sit as far back as you can from the actual engine – cinders often come spitting out. If you need more time in Tiradentes than the train schedule allows, you can always bus back (there are eight per day between the two cities).

in Minas Gerais – full of antique furniture and sacred art and housed in a colonial mansion built around 1859.

MUSEU DE ARTE SACRA

This building served as the public jail between 1737 and 1850. The **museum** (Praça Embaixador Gastão da Cunha 8; admission US$1; 9am-5pm Tue-Sun) has a small but impressive collection of art from the city's churches. The drops of blood on the figure of Christ mourned by Mary Magdalene are represented by rubies.

CATEDRAL DE NS DO PILAR

Begun in 1721, this **church** (8-11am & noon-5pm Tue-Sun) has exuberant gold altars and fine Portuguese tiles. On Wednesday the Lira Sanjoanense, or Coalhada (all-White), orchestra and choir accompany the 7pm mass.

IGREJA DE NS DO CARMO

Begun in 1732, this church was also designed by Aleijadinho, who did the frontispiece and the sculpture around the door. In the second sacristy is a famous unfinished sculpture of Christ. **Igreja de NS do Carmo** (Rua Getúlio Vargas; 8-11am & noon-5pm Tue-Sun) is on the northern side of the river and dominates a lovely triangular praça at the end of the road.

Festivals & Events

Someone's always celebrating something in São João. The list of festivals just goes on and on – 15 religious and 10 secular on one calendar – so stop by the tourist office for a schedule of events.

Locals boast, credibly, that their **Carnaval** is the best in Minas Gerais. The **Semana da Inconfidência**, from April 15 to 21, celebrates Brazil's first independence movement and the hometown boys who led it.

Sleeping

BUDGET

There is a good stock of inexpensive hotels in the old section of the city, right where you want to be. Be sure to book ahead in December, when the town is filled with students sitting for exams, and during holidays such as Carnaval and Easter.

Hotel Provincia de Orense (3371 7960; Rua Marechal Deodoro 131; s/d/apt US$15/25/36) Tucked away on a cobblestone street in a great part of town, the Orense's rooms are spacious, modern and welcoming. Breakfast is served in a large room with windows facing the river.

Pousada São Benedito (3371 7381; Rua Marechal Deodoro 254; s US$10) This is really more of a large home than a pousada. Rooms are warm and welcoming, as is the family running the establishment.

Pousada Portal del-Rey (3371 2565; Praça Severiano Resende 134; s/d US$15/24) Many of the city's best sights are in easy walking distance from this pousada. The rooms are basic and a bit plain, but the establishment has the added plus of being built directly over a per-kilo restaurant.

Hotel Brasil (3371 2804; Av Presidente Tancredo Neves 395; s/d US$10/20) The rooms here are large but a bit shabby. However, the Hotel Brasil faces the river (pretty views) and is a convenient walk from the bus station.

Pousada Ramon (3371 5740; Rua Frei Cândido 42; s US$10) Clean and inexpensive dorm rooms are the best Pousada Ramon can offer, as well as being directly in front of the bus station.

MID-RANGE

Pousada Casarão (3371 7447; Rua Ribeiro Bastos 94; s/d US$30/45;) Behind the Igreja de São Francisco, the lovely Pousada Casarão, like many of the elegant mansions-turned-pousadas of Minas, is exquisite.

Pousada Morada do Sol (3371 7686; conecta.mgconecta.com.br/moradadosol; Rua Jovita Giarola, 74, Colônia do Marçal; s/d US$30/70;) While this pousada isn't in the city center, it is well worth the seven-minute taxi drive it takes to get there. Brightly painted in blues and greens, the exterior buildings sit on the edge of a quiet plaza. The rooms are very lovely, with gorgeous bedspreads and beautiful carved headboards. A real treat.

Hotel Lenheiro Palace (3371 8155; Av Presidente Tancredo Neves 257; s/d US$35/56) This multistory hotel faces the river and has basic rooms. Discounts can be had in the low season.

Quinta do Ouro (3371 2565; Av Tancredo Neves at Praça Severiano Resende 4; s/d US$30/45) The Quinta do Ouro has four truly gorgeous rooms, most of which have private salons. Reservations are strongly recommended.

Hotel Ponte Real (3371 7000; Av Eduardo Magalhães 254; s/d US$38/55) The Ponte Real is São João's most modern four-star offering. It has a nice pool and bar area and a very friendly staff.

Pousada Estacão do Trem (☎ 3372 1985; Praça Estacão 45; s/d with breakfast US$40/90) This pousada is just a short walk from the train station, has whimsical rooms – a bit on the small side – and serves breakfast, lunch and nighttime tea onsite.

TOP END

Garden Hill Club (☎ 3371 2551; www.gardenhill .cjb.net; Km 96 on BR-383 in Colônia do Marçal; s/d/tr US$90/115/150; 🕱 🖳 🕱) This full-scale resort is situated between Tiradentes and São João del Rei. Large airy rooms with French doors that open onto balconies make for a blissful stay, and the grounds have swaying hammocks that beckon from under shady trees. A free round of golf or tennis comes with an overnight stay, and afternoon tea is included. Splurge on this if you can!

Pousada Beco do Bispo (☎ 3371 8844; www.beco dobispo.com.br; Beco do Bispo 93; s/d US$40/50; 🕱 🕱) Also outside of the city center but within walking distance for most people, this pousada has warm, cozy rooms gently lit with wall sconces and scented with fresh flowers. Beautiful linens adorn each bed and the ambience is so calming it almost feels like staying in a spa. Deferential service adds the finishing touch.

Eating

BUDGET

Of the town's many self-serve places, a few really stand out.

Chafariz (Rua Quintino Bocáiuva 100; per kg US$5; 🕑 11am-4pm) Chafariz, just behind the train station, is everybody's favorite – it seems half the town is in there for lunch on any given day. Regional dishes, heavy on the *feijoadas*.

Restaurante Portal del-Rey (Praça Severiano Resende 134; per kg US$4; 🕑 11am-4pm), Very good food is available at Portal del-Rey, but get there before mid-afternoon (after a few hours the wood-burning warmer starts to overcook all the food). The desserts are particularly fabulous.

Restaurante Rex (Rua Marechal Deodoro 124; per kg US$5; 🕑 11am-4pm) Rex is an inexpensive and delicious little Italian place in what can be a slightly overpriced part of town.

Maria-Fumaça (Av Presidente Tancredo Neves 437; per kg US$5) Just a block or two east of the bus station, the Maria Fumaca does an excellent per-kilo lunch and also serves dinner, although that can cost a bit more. Frequently features live music at night and is a popular place.

MID-RANGE

Quinta do Ouro (☎ 3371 7577; Av Presidente Tancredo Neves, on Praça Severiano de Resende 4; dinner with drinks US$15; 🕑 11am-3pm & 6-10:30pm) Regional dishes are served with a lot of attention and flair at Quinta. Many say this is the best Mineiro food in town and it's doubtful you'll find any reason to disagree.

Churrascaria Ramon (Praça Severiano Resende; all-you-can-eat deal US$10; 🕑 11am-10pm) Ramon prides itself on its tender, juicy, perfectly cooked meats. It's an all-you-can-eat deal, so make sure you arrive hungry, because you are guaranteed to leave feeling very full.

L'Arlequim (☎ 3371 5246; Americao Brighenti 20, Colonial do Marçal; dinner with drinks US$15; 🕑 7pm-midnight Tue, Thu & Fri, 11am-midnight Sat, to 5pm Sun) Outside the city center, L'Arlequim attracts a loyal following with its mixture of Italian, Brazilian and French dishes.

Entertainment

Most of the city's nightlife is on the south side. Head for the bars crammed together at the end of Av Tiradentes near the Igreja de São Francisco de Assis.

Cabana do Zotti (Av Tiradentes 805; 🕑 9pm-late) Lots of people pack in here every night, as much for the delicious nibbles as the drinks and dancing.

Down Av Tiradente near Rua Ministro Gabriel Passos there is another cluster of activity.

Miaxou Bar (Rua Ministro Gabriel Passos 299; 🕑 5pm-late) Many favor Miaxou, which is popular with all generations. Families welcome, especially on weekends when wild samba dancing is the norm.

Kalahari (Alto da 8 de Dezembro s/n; cover US$2; 🕑 9pm-6am Fri & Sat) A very popular hot spot despite being a bit of a hike up a hill, Kalahari's very big on weekends.

Point84 (Rua Kleber Figueiras 84; 🕑 7pm-5am Thu-Sun) If you are a lover of live music, Point84 is where you want to be.

Sarcofogo (Rua Aureliano Pimentel 49; 🕑 9pm-4am Thu-Sun) This beautifully decorated bar has a slightly 'goth' look and is an entertaining place for a drink, with good music. If the door won't open, ring the bell inside the gate on the right.

Getting There & Away

The **São João bus station** (☎ 3371 5617; Rua Cristóvão Colombo) is about 1.5km northeast of town. Direct buses go to major cities just about every day.

Destinations include: Rio (US$15, 5½ hours, four daily from 8:30am to noon Monday to Saturday, three daily from 4pm to 1:30pm Sunday); Belo Horizonte (US$10, 3½ hours, seven daily from 6am to 6:30pm Monday to Friday).

A few extra buses to Belo Horizonte run on Saturday night, stopping at Congonhas (US$7, two hours).

Ouro Prêto is serviced by the buses going to Mariana from São João (US$14, four hours, twice daily at 5:30pm and 3:30am). To get the 3:30am bus you need to buy tickets the day before.

Getting Around

There are local buses (yellow) between the bus station (US$0.30, 10 minutes) and the center. The local bus stop in the center is in front of the train station.

The local bus stop at the bus station is to your left as you walk out of the station (in front of the butcher), not from the one directly in front of the door.

From the main bus station, you have two taxi options – traditional taxis (US$4) or the cool and totally cheap **motorbike taxi** (☎ 3371 5278; US$1.50). The information booth at the bus station will call one if you ask. Drivers are safe and carry a helmet for the passenger. Use it!

TIRADENTES

☎ 0xx32 / pop 10,000 / elevation 927m

They don't make towns any prettier than Tiradentes, São João del Rei's gold-era rival, 14km down the valley. Quaint colonial houses, fringed by bright-pink wildflowers, stand out against a backdrop of blue Serra de São José mountains. It really is undeniably gorgeous, although some may find the recent influx of antique stores and whimsical boutiques a little too cloying. The town is comprised of a few dozen streets and on weekends gets very lively. Stick to weekdays if you prefer the quiet.

History

Originally called Arrail da Ponta do Morro (Hamlet on a Hilltop), Tiradentes was renamed to honor the martyred hero of the Inconfidência (see p34), who was born at a nearby farm.

The town's colonial buildings run up a hillside, where they culminate in the beautiful **Igreja Matriz de Santo Antônio**.

If you stand between the church's Aleijadinho facade and the famous sundial, there is a colorful view of the terracotta-tiled colonial houses, the green valley, and the towering wall of stone formed by the Serra de São José.

Information

The **Secretária de Turismo** (☎ 3355 1212; Rua Resende Costa 71; ☯ 9am-4pm Mon-Fri) is located on Largo das Forras; it's the only three-story building in sight. Stop by to pick up a map – for a small town, Tiradentes can be very confusing. The staff swore up and down that there is an Internet café somewhere in town, but at the time of writing it had apparently not gotten up and running yet.

For English-language information about excellent hiking and horseback-riding opportunities, try John Parsons, the owner of the **Hotel Solar da Ponte** (☎ 3355 1255; www.solardoponte.com.br), or try **Adriano** (☎ 9966 5864).

Note that all of the churches are closed on Tuesday. The usual hours are 9am to 5pm Wednesday to Monday, with two hours taken for lunch between noon and 2pm.

Sights

IGREJA MATRIZ DE SANTO ANTÔNIO

Named for the town's patron saint, with two bell towers and a frontispiece by Aleijadinho, this **church** is one of Brazil's most beautiful. It is one of the last that Aleijadinho completed. Leandro Gonçalves Chaves made the sundial in front of the church in 1785.

The all-gold interior is rich in Old Testament symbolism. There is a painting by João Batista illustrating the miracle of Santo Antônio making a donkey kneel before the Pope. The polychrome organ was built in Portugal and brought to Tiradentes by donkey in 1798.

IGREJA NS ROSÁRIO DOS PRETOS

A beautiful stone **church** (Praça Padre Lourival on Rua Direita) with paintings on the ceiling and images of Black saints, the existing structure was built in 1708 to replace the original chapel on this site.

MUSEU DO PADRE TOLEDO
This **museum** (Rua Padre Toledo 190; admission US$0.50; 9am-4pm Wed-Mon) is dedicated to another hero of the Inconfidência, Padre Toledo, who lived in this 18-room house where the Inconfidêntes first met. It features regional antiques and documents from the 18th century.

IGREJA DA SANTISSIMA TRINDADE
This simple pilgrimage **church** dates from 1810, when it was built on the site of a small chapel where Tiradentes officials chose the

triangle (representing the holy trinity) as the symbol for the flag of the new nation. Walk along Rua da Santissima Trindade until you see the church.

CHAFARIZ DE SÃO JOSÉ
Constructed in 1749 by the town council, this beautiful **fountain** (Rua do Chafariz, north of Córrego Santo Antônio) has three sections: one for drinking, one for washing clothes and one for watering horses. The water comes from Mãe d'Agua via an old stone pipeline.

SERRA DE SÃO JOSÉ
At the foot of these mountains there is a 1km-wide stretch of protected Atlantic rain forest, and you can hike along several trails.

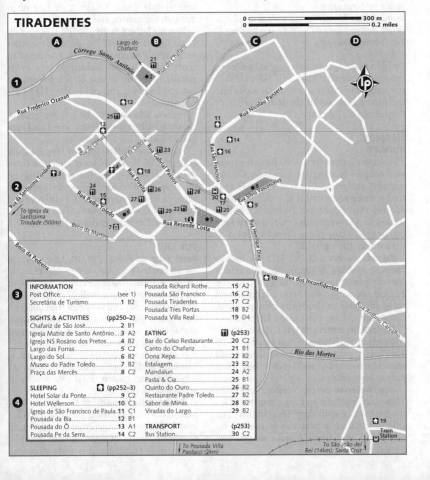

TIRADENTES

0 — 300 m
0 — 0.2 miles

INFORMATION	
Post Office	(see 1)
Secretária de Turismo	1 B2

SIGHTS & ACTIVITIES	(pp250–2)
Chafariz de São José	2 B1
Igreja Matriz de Santo Antônio	3 A2
Igreja NS Rosário dos Pretos	4 B2
Largo das Forras	5 C2
Largo do Sol	6 B2
Museu do Padre Toledo	7 B2
Praça das Mercês	8 C2

SLEEPING	(pp252–3)
Hotel Solar da Ponte	9 C2
Hotel Wellerson	10 C3
Igreja de São Francisco de Paula	11 C1
Pousada da Bia	12 B1
Pousada do Ô	13 A1
Pousada Pe da Serra	14 C2

Pousada Richard Rothe	15 A2
Pousada São Francisco	16 C2
Pousada Tiradentes	17 C2
Pousada Tres Portas	18 B2
Pousada Villa Real	19 D4

EATING	(p253)
Bar do Celso Restaurante	20 C2
Canto do Chafariz	21 B1
Dona Xepa	22 B2
Estalagem	23 B2
Mandalun	24 A2
Pasta & Cia	25 B1
Quinto do Ouro	26 B2
Restaurante Padre Toledo	27 B2
Sabor de Minas	28 B2
Viradas do Largo	29 B2

TRANSPORT	(p253)
Bus Station	30 C2

To Pousada Villa Paolucci (2km)

To São João del Rei (14km); Santa Cruz

Train Station

Rio das Mortes

The most popular and simple is to **Mãe d'Agua**, the source of the spring at Chafariz de São José. From Chafariz, follow the trail north for about 25 minutes into the Bosque da Mãe d'Agua. It is lush with moss and plants and the waters are clear and fresh.

Other walks include the following:

A Calçada This hike covers a stretch of the old road that linked Ouro Prêto with Rio de Janeiro.

Cachoeira do Bom Despacho This is a waterfall on the Tiradentes–Santa Cruz road, which can be reached by car and is therefore far more visited and littered than the other walking destinations.

Caminho do Mangue This walk heads up the *serra* (mountain range) from the west side of town to Aguas Santas, and takes about two hours. There you'll find a mineral-water swimming pool and a very good Portuguese-owned *churrascaria*.

Round Robin A fine six-hour walk would be up to A Calçada, then west across the top of the serra and down from Caminho do Mangue.

Locals advise against carrying valuables or trekking alone. For guides (US$8 to US$15 per walk) and information about walks into the mountains, ask at the tourist office or the Hotel Solar da Ponte.

Sleeping
BUDGET
Tiradentes caters to a well-heeled crowd and couples looking for romance. Consequently, budget and/or solo travelers may find it more economical to commute from São João del Rei or ask around for homes to stay in. On weekends prices quoted here can double. Many places do not accept children under the age of 12.

Pousada da Bia (☎ 3355 1173; Rua Frederico Ozanan 30; s/d US$20) A simple but delightfully friendly place, thanks to the efforts of the English-speaking owner, Pousada da Bia will make your stay in Tiradentes extra pleasant. Guests are welcome to use the kitchen.

Pousada Tiradentes (☎ 3355 1232; www.pousada tiradentes.com; São Francisco de Paula 41; s/d US$14/25) This lovely pousada has good service and attractive rooms but also tends to fill up fast during high season.

Hotel Wellerson (Rua Fogo Simbólico 218; s/d US$25) This place has little to brag about but does the best it can with very basic rooms. The chief attraction is that this is one of the few places that doesn't make singles pay for a double.

MID-RANGE
Pousada do Ô (☎ 3355 1699; Rua do Chafariz 25; s/d US$25/40) On a lovely plaza and boasting a fabulous garden, this pousada has seven rooms, all with private bathrooms. All rooms but one overlook the street – No 7 is set apart from the rest of the house and has a garden view. Book ahead if you want it – it's the most popular one. Children under 12 not accepted here.

Pousada Pe da Serra (☎ 3355 1107; www.pedaserra .com.br; Rua Nicolau Panzera 51; d US$40; ☒ ☒) This family-run, friendly little place is very close to the bus station, behind Igreja Sao Francisco de Paulo. Sitting up on a ridge, the nine small but spotless rooms have panoramic views – the location makes up for the otherwise simple décor. Guests have free reign through the garden and sitting rooms.

Pousada Richard Rothe (☎ 3355 1333; Rua Padre Toledo 124; s/d US$50/80) An excellent option with stylish rooms (although a bit hard to find), this pousada's hidden down a street popularly known as Rua do Sol. Rooms are big and relaxing, and children under 12 are not accepted.

Pousada Villa Real (☎ 3355 1292; Rua Antônio de Carvalho 127; s/d US$30/45) A very warm and nice place right by the train station.

Pousada Tres Portas (☎ 3355 1444; Rua Direita 280A; s/d US$50/95; ☒) Named after the three double doors forming the entrance, some of these rooms have four-poster beds and great views – all have beautiful antiques and hardwood floors. Discounts of up to 30% on weekdays. Children under two stay free.

TOP END
Hotel Solar da Ponte (☎ 3355 1255; www.solar doponte.com.br; Praça das Mercês; s/d US$70/90; ☒ ☒ ☒) This magnificent re-creation of a colonial mansion actually sits on the site of a former one, and is one of the country's best hotels. The rooms have fresh flowers, comfortable chairs, tables and beds, and beautiful antiques scattered about. There's a reading room, complete with fireplace, breakfast and complimentary afternoon tea served in the garden. First-rate food and service across the board.

Pousada Villa Paolucci (☎ 3355 1350; www.villa paolucci.cjb.net; Rua do Chafariz; s/d US$80/120) This mid-18th-century converted house, sitting on the outskirts of town, is also a working *fazenda* (ranch) and is truly stunning.

Rooms are immense, with dark, antique furniture and gleaming mirrors everywhere. Particularly winsome are the lights in a few of the rooms – angels with bulbs on them. Reservations strongly recommended.

Eating

BUDGET

Pasta & Cia (☎ 3355 1478; Rua Frederico Ozanan 327; lunch with coffee & dessert US$8; 11am-10pm Wed-Mon) Good Italian-style cooking and inventive pastas are a nice change from the usual Mineiro dishes.

Restaurante Padre Toledo (☎ 3355 1222; Rua Direita 250; lunch US$10; 11am-10pm) A favorite with locals, Padre Toledo is renowned for its excellent *bife acebolado* (beef with onions).

MID-RANGE

Estalagem do Sabor (☎ 3355 1144; Rua Ministro Gabriel Passos 280; dinner US$12; 11am-4pm & 7-10pm Mon-Sat, 11am-6pm Sun) Estalagem does a mean *feijão com lombo* (beans with pork) – probably the best in town.

Sabor de Minas (☎ 3355 1546; Rua Ministro Gabriel Passos 62; dinner US$12; 11am-4pm & 6-10pm Mon-Sat) On the street popularly known as Rua da Praia, Sabor de Minas does hearty meat and potato dishes.

Bar do Celso Restaurante (☎ 3355 1193; Largo das Forras; lunch US$11; 11am-9pm Thu-Sat, 11:30am-5pm Sun) Near the tourist office in the main square, this is another Mineiro restaurant that has reasonable prices.

Canto do Chafariz (☎ 3355 1377; Largo do Chafariz 37; lunch US$9; 11:30am-10pm, closed Mon) Right near the São José fountain, the Canto do Chafariz does straightforward Mineiro fare that's oh-so-delicious.

Mandalun (☎ 3355 1212; Rua Padre Toledo 172; dinner US$10; 8pm-midnight Tue-Fri, 1-4pm & 8pm-2am Sat & Sun) For a change of pace, try Mandalun, which serves delicious Lebanese *esfihas* (ground beef pastries with veggies).

TOP END

Viradas do Largo (☎ 3355 1111; Rua do Moinho 11; noon-midnight) Pricey but delicious, Viradas is a local favorite, with savory, rich Mineiro dishes of all types.

Quinto do Ouro (☎ 3355 1197; Rua Direita 15; buffet lunch US$12; 12:30-4pm Wed-Mon) This is one of the town's most upmarket self-serve restaurants, with both regional and international dishes.

Dona Xepa (☎ 3355 1767; Rua Ministro Gabriel Passos 26A; dinner US$8; 11am-9pm Thu-Tue) A really fun place to get fabulous and flamboyant food and drink. The *cachaça* menu is twice as long as in most places, and each flavor is more delectable than the last.

Getting There & Away

Tiradentes is 20 minutes by bus from São João del Rei, and buses come and go every 40 minutes. The bus station is just north of the main square, across the stream. The train station is about 700m southeast of the main square.

Buses to Tiradentes (US$2) start at 5:50am on weekdays, at 7am on Saturday, and 8:15am on Sunday.

From Tiradentes, the last bus back to São João del Rei leaves at 6:20pm from Monday to Saturday and at 8:30pm on Sunday.

DIAMANTINA

☎ 0xx38 / pop 40,000 / elevation 1113m

Isolated but fabulous, Diamantina is one of Brazil's prettiest and least-visited colonial towns. Surrounded by desolate mountains (which make for great hiking), Diamantina's fine mansions and winding streets haven't changed much in the last 200 years. Designated a Unesco World Heritage site in 1999, this *cidade histórica* is also the birthplace of Juscelino Kubitschek, former Brazilian president and founder of Brasília.

Getting up here usually involves a winding and lengthy bus ride. Beyond the town of Curvelo (geographical center of Minas), the stark landscape of northern Minas, with its rocky outcrops and barren highlands, poses a sharp contrast to the lush hills in the south. Don't miss the **Caminho dos Escravos**, the old Slave Rd hewed out of the mountains by the sweat, blood and tears of thousands of African slaves and used to ferry Diamantina's vast mineral wealth down to waiting European ships on the Brazilian coast.

Information

As with most Mineiro cities, Diamantina is built on precipitous slopes. The bus station, for example, is high up on a bluff and although it is only a short distance from the town's center (500m), you've got to be in pretty good shape to hump bags back and forth. Taxis (US$2) are an easier option. The central square is Praça Conselheiro Mota,

THE SOUTHEAST

dominated by **Santo Antônio** cathedral – both colloquially known as Sé.

Money can be changed at **Itaú bank** (directly on the Praça Correal Rabelo), but Mauricio, a moneylender who runs Mauricinho, right above the bank on the 2nd floor, generally offers better deals. At the time of writing, a new Internet café was in the works two doors down.

Staff at the **municipal tourist office** (☎ 3531 1857; pmdiamantina@dnet.br; Praça Monsenhor Neves 44) will give you a guide in Portuguese that includes a map. There is a post office opposite the tourist office.

Sights

Expect to pay an entry fee at most **churches** (admission US$0.75; ⊙ 2-5:30pm Tue-Sat, 9am-noon Sun, closed Mon). Hours are generally the same at most attractions.

From Praça Correa Rabelo, head down to Rua do Carmo to see the **Igreja de NS do Carmo**. It's the most opulent church in Diamantina, and is worth a look. Constructed between 1760 and 1765, this church had its tower built at the rear – lest the bells should awaken Chica da Silva. The organ was made in Diamantina and wrought in gold; it is adorned with rich, golden carvings.

The oldest church in town is the **Igreja de NS do Rosário dos Pretos**, which dates from 1731. It's downhill on Largo do Rosário.

The fine colonial mansion known as **Casa da Chica da Silva**, on Praça Lobo de Mesquita, was the home of diamond contractor João

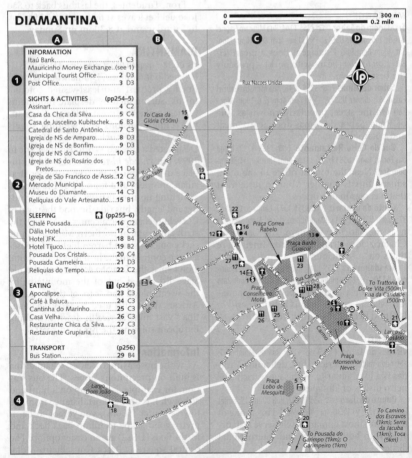

DIAMANTINA

Fernandes de Oliveira and his mistress and former slave, Chica da Silva. Here it is possible to get an idea of the lifestyle of the extravagant mulata. The huge colonial door leads to her private chapel.

Between Praça JK and the cathedral is the house of Padre Rolim, one of the Inconfidêntes. It's now the **Museu do Diamante** (admission US$1; noon-5.30pm Tue-Sat, 9am-noon Sun & holidays), exhibiting furniture, coins, instruments of torture and other relics of the diamond days.

The **Mercado Municipal** (Municipal Market), built by the army in 1835, is in Praça Barão Guaicuí. The building's wooden arches inspired Niemeyer's design for the presidential palace in Brasília. On Saturday it has a food and craft market and live music. People from the Vale de Jequitinhonha still arrive on horseback with their wares. There is a small museum here, the Centro Cultural David Ribeiro, which has some fascinating old photos.

Consisting of two houses on opposite sides of Rua da Glória connected by an enclosed, vivid-blue 2nd-story passageway, **Casa da Glória** was originally the residence of the diamond supervisors and also the official palace of the first bishop of Diamantina. Today, appropriately, the building houses the Institute of Geology.

Casa de Juscelino Kubitschek, a small house at Rua São Francisco 241, reflects the simple upbringing of the former president, whose grandparents were poor Czech immigrants. Kubitschek himself believed that his early life in Diamantina influenced him greatly. There are some good photos of JK along the staircase in the Hotel Tijuco (see p255).

While you are in Diamantina, walk a couple of kilometers down the **Estrada Real** or **Caminho dos Escravos** to the **Serra da Jacuba**. This paved road, built by slaves, linked Diamantina with Paraty on the Rio de Janeiro coast. From Praça JK, head along Rua Macau do Meio and Rua Arraial dos Forros. There are **waterfalls** at Toca, 5km south of town along Hwy BR-259. **Paulo Santos** (3531-2462), a local guide, leads city tours (US$18 per person; 3½ hours) and can organize regional tours.

Sleeping

BUDGET

Pousada Gameleira (3531 1900; Rua do Rosário 209; s/d US$9/15) An inexpensive choice with a quaint atmosphere in the old part of town, some of the pousada's rooms face the Igreja de NS do Rosário.

Chalé Pousada (3531 1246; Rua Macau de Baixo 52; s/d US$10/16) An attractive old house in a great location, this place has friendly staff and simple quartos and apartamentos.

Lost of inexpensive options are available around the bus station in the upper part of town (and you don't have to lug your packs uphill when it's time to leave), with basic rooms going for about US$5 per person.

Hotel JFK (3531 1142; Largo Dom João 135; s/d US$5/9) One of the better places, the Hotel JFK has the added distinction of being directly across from the bus station.

MID-RANGE

Dália Hotel (3531 1477; Praça JK 25; s/d US$20/32) Right next to the Museu do Diamante, the quaintly eclectic Dália has lovely views over the square and a laid-back, welcoming vibe. Probably the best location in town – attractions are just a few steps away in either direction.

Reliquías do Tempo (3351 1627; Rua Macau de Baixo 104; s/d US$35/50) Take a trip back in time at Reliquías do Tempo, a gorgeous historical house with lots of character, great views and local artwork. Tea is served in the late afternoon and the rustic downstairs dining room is a real treat. Ask to look at the chapel in the back. The furnishings are all antiques and the only flaw might be the somewhat stiff and narrow beds.

Pousada Dos Cristais (3531 2897; Rua Jogo do Bola 53; s/d US$25-35) Several recently renovated rooms have verandas and some have a mezzanine at this pousada, and the ambience is very romantic. The kitchen is available for guests and there's a 24-hour bar.

Hotel Tijuco (3581 1022; Rua Macau do Meio 211; s/d US$25/50) The modernist Tijuco is a fine Niemeyer creation with spacious, airy rooms. It charges US$6 more per person for a veranda and great view. Go for it – the upgrade is worth the money!

TOP END

Pousada do Garimpo (3531-2523; Av da Saudade 265; s/d US$60/75;) Just outside the historical center, at the west end of town, this tasteful place has an excellent restaurant, but the rooms, while comfortable, are nothing spectacular.

Eating

BUDGET

Café à Baiuca (Rua Campos Carvalho; ☯ 11am-10pm) Head here for some scrumptious coffee and cakes, fresh from the oven.

Restaurante Grupiaria (☎ 3531 3887; Rua Campos Carvalho 12; per kg US$8; ☯ 11am-11pm Mon-Sat, to 3pm Sun) A popular place, the Grupiaria has the usual assortment of Mineiro food.

Apocalipse (Praça Barão Guaicuí; lunch buffet US$7; ☯ 11am-4pm) Opposite the Mercado Municipal, the Apocalipse has excellent per-kilo meals served in a pleasant room upstairs.

Cantinha do Marinho (Rua Direita 113; lunch dishes US$5; ☯ 11am-4pm & 6-8pm) Stop by for a filling buffet lunch including a drink, and at dinner don't be afraid to try the *lombo com feijão tropeiro* (pork with beans).

MID-RANGE/TOP END

Trattoria La Dolce Vita (☎ 3531 8485; Rua da Caridade 147; dinner US$12; ☯ 6pm-midnight Mon-Fri, noon-midnight Sat, to 11pm Sun) A big hit with visting Brazilians, this trattoria does delicious fresh pastas and meat dishes for very innocuous sums of money! Patrons like to sit in the rustic garden out back. The friendly owner and his Swiss wife love to show off the hand-made noodles drying in the back and are known to treat customers to complimentary shots of *cachaça*.

O Garimpeiro (☎ 3531 1044; Av da Saudade 265; mains US$20; 6-11pm Mon-Fri, noon-midnight Sat & Sun) For a knockout meal, there's no better place than this restaurant in the Pousada do Garimpo. It's out of the way and a bit pricey, but the chef is famous for his regional dishes.

Restaurante Chica da Silva (☎ 3531 3059; Praça JK 27; dinner US$10; ☯ 11am-4pm & noon-10pm Sat & Sun) Right behind the Dália Hotel and more moderately priced, Chica da Silva is also a good choice.

Casa Velha (☎ 3531 3538; Rua Direita 106; pizzas US$3, buffet lunch US$5) Across from Cantinha do Marinho, this place has a terrific per-kilo lunch and very good Mineiro food at dinner.

Getting There & Away

Buses travel back and forth between Belo Horizonte and Diamantina (US$15, six hours, six daily from 5:30am to noon) frequently. The buses take the Hwy BR-040 (the road to Brasília) and then head to Diamantina via Curvelo. The road surface is sealed, but some sections have atrocious potholes.

There are also daily buses to the neighboring historical town of Serro (US$4).

MINERAL SPA TOWNS

Such unexpected surprises lurk in this corner of Brazil! Who knew that tucked away in Minas Gerais sits one of the world's foremost spa locations? For anyone who has overdosed on baroque architecture, or burned themselves to a crisp at the beach, these blissful little towns are the perfect remedy.

History

Springs were first tapped in Caxambu in 1870 and medical practitioners were quick to realize the curative properties of the waters. In 1886 Dr Policarpo Viotti founded the Caxambu Water Company, which was nationalized in 1905.

Long before Perrier hit Manhattan singles bars, Caxambu water was being celebrated on the international water circuit, winning gold medals. It took the gold in the 1903 Victor Emmanuel III Exposition in Rome, and again in the St Louis International Fair of 1904. It was also awarded the Diploma of Honor in the University of Brussels Exposition of 1910.

These water Olympics were discontinued during WWI, and Caxambu's history was uneventful until 1981, when the private firms Supergasbras and Superagua took over the government concession. Caxambu water is now sold throughout Brazil.

CAXAMBU

☎ 0xx35 / pop 22,000 / elevation 895m

Caxambu is a tranquil resort for the middle class and the elderly, who come here to escape the heat of Rio and the madness of Carnaval. Some couples have been coming here every summer for 30 years or more.

Information

Banco do Brasil (Rua Oliveira Mafra) Will do cash advances – try the larger hotels for changing cash dollars. Forget traveler's checks.

Post office (Av Camilo Soares) Next to Hotel Glória.

Tourist office (☎ 3341 9055; axambu@netzoom.psi.br; Praça Cônego José de Castilho Moreira; ☯ 1-6pm Mon-Fri) Obtain maps and other information from this helpful office. It's next to the bus station.

Sights & Activities

The **Parque das Aguas** (admission US$5, separate fees for attractions inside from US$2 to US$6; 8am-6pm) is a rheumatic's Disneyland; people come to take the waters, smell the sulfur, compare liver spots, watch the geyser spout, rest in the shade by the canal and walk in the lovely gardens. There is an outdoor **swimming pool** where you can do laps in the spring water, and the **Balneário Hidroterápico**, a bath house where you can soak in a hot bath, take a shower or relax in a sauna. The ornate building dates from 1912.

It has 12 founts, each housed in its own architectural folly, and each with different properties. Liver problems? Drink from the Dona Leopoldina **magnesium fountain**. Skin disorders? Take the **sulfur baths** of Tereza Cristina. Itchy trigger finger? Hit the **rifle range**. VD? The **Duque de Saxe fountain** helps calm the bacteria that cause syphilis. And there's much more, from kidney-stone cures to stomach-ailment alleviators, and from eyebaths to anemia fixers.

There is an image of Jesus on top of the **Morro Cristo** hill (chairlift ride available for nominal fee), 800m above sea level. The town gained notoriety after Princesa Isabel (daughter of Brazil's last emperor, Dom Pedro II) visited in 1868. After trying various treatments for infertility, she finally managed to conceive after taking the miraculous waters of Caxambu. In thanks she built the **Igreja de Santa Isabel da Hungria** on Rua Princesa Isabela.

Locally produced honey, homemade fruit liqueurs including *jaboticaba* (a local plant) and tangerine, and preserves are sold all over town.

Many of the hotels have spas and offer massages.

It's also possible to rent **horses** in Caxambu (about US$10 per hour; check with the tourist office for a list of horse owners) and ride to some of the surrounding spa towns.

Sleeping

Caxambu is geared to prosperous travelers, but if you're here outside peak holiday times you can get some good deals. Most hotel prices include all meals.

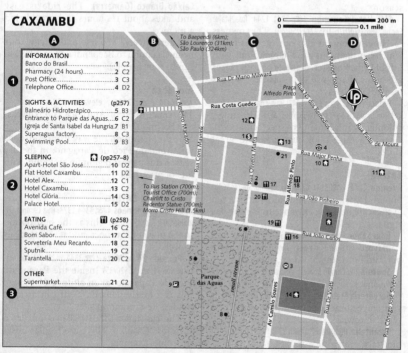

CAXAMBU

0 ———— 200 m
0 ———— 0.1 mile

INFORMATION	
Banco do Brasil	1 C2
Pharmacy (24 hours)	2 C2
Post Office	3 C3
Telephone Office	4 D2

SIGHTS & ACTIVITIES	(p257)
Balneário Hidroterápico	5 B3
Entrance to Parque das Aguas	6 C2
Igreja de Santa Isabel da Hungria	7 B1
Superagua factory	8 C3
Swimming Pool	9 B3

SLEEPING	(pp257–8)
Apart-Hotel São José	10 D2
Flat Hotel Caxambu	11 D2
Hotel Alex	12 C1
Hotel Caxambu	13 C2
Hotel Glória	14 C3
Palace Hotel	15 D2

EATING	(p258)
Avenida Café	16 C2
Bom Sabor	17 C2
Sorveteria Meu Recanto	18 C2
Sputnik	19 C2
Tarantella	20 C2

OTHER	
Supermarket	21 C2

To Baependi (6km);
São Lourenço (31km);
São Paulo (324km)

Rua Dr Mano Milward

Praça Alfredo Pinto

Rua NS dos Remédios

Rua Manoel João

Rua Alonso Pena

Rua Pinto de Moura

Rua Costa Guedes

Rua Américo Macedo

Rua Cons Mayrink

Rua Oliveira Maria

Rua Major Penha

Rua Alfredo Pinto

Rua João Pinheiro

Rua João Carlos

To Bus Station (700m);
Tourist Office (700m);
Chairlift to Cristo
Redentor Statue (700m);
Morro Cristo Hill (1.5km)

Parque das Aguas

small stream

Av Camilo Soares

Rua Dr Viotti

Rua Córrego José Silvério

BUDGET

Apart-Hotel São José (☎ 3341 3133; Rua Major Penha 264; s/d US$14/35) Quite a lot of amenities are offered at this budget location – the sauna room is gorgeous.

Hotel Alex (☎ 3341 1331; Rua Oliveira Mafra 233; s/d US$25/34) Hotel Alex is simple but a good value. Rooms are nice and airy – ask for one with a balcony.

MID-RANGE/TOP END

Hotel Glória (☎ 3341 3000; Av Camilo Soares 590; s/d US$90/130; ✂ ☎) Absolute top of the line is the magnificent Glória, a posh resort complex with a range of activities for the leisure set. Rooms are complete with TV, bathroom, bar, telephone and three meals a day. Facilities include a large gym with indoor basketball court, a physical rehabilitation center and a sauna. Tennis is played on clay courts in the park opposite the hotel.

Hotel Caxambu (☎ 3341 3300; Rua Major Penha 145; s/d US$50/65) This lovely place has a pool, playground and a good restaurant, and is right in the center of town. Luxury rooms in particular are a great deal in the off season.

Flat Hotel Caxambu (☎ 3341 1244; Rua Major Penha 386; s/d/tr/q US$22/29/50/60) The owners of Hotel Caxambu also operate this hotel, which has plain but good, large rooms with lots of beds. Registered guests of both places are allowed the use of a leisure complex located 3km away.

Palace Hotel (☎ 3341-3341; www.palacehotel.com .br; Rua Dr Viotti 567; s/d US$50/65; ☎) This huge, colonial establishment is a spectacular deal. There's a huge pool out back with great slides.

Eating

Avenida Café (☎ 3341 4363; Av Camilo Soares 648) Superb pastries, pies and juices are served at this café near the entrance to Parque das Aguas.

Bom Sabor (Rua João Pinheiro 329) Hidden in a courtyard off the street, Bom Sabor has a per-kilo lunch that is an excellent value.

Sputnik (Av Camilo Soares) A good *lanchonete* for a snack.

Sorveteria Meu Recanto (Av Camilo Soares 756) If you crave some ice cream, this is the best place in town.

Tarantella (Rua João Pinheiro 326) For a taste of old Italy, grab a slice at Tarantella.

Getting There & Away

The **bus station** (☎ 3341-9048) is about 1km south of the center on Praça Cônego José de Castilho Moreira. A horse and buggy from there to your hotel costs US$5.

There are two daily buses (8:25am and 11pm) from Belo Horizonte (see p230). Ten daily buses (US$2) make the 49km trip between Caxambu and São Lourenço on a winding, wooded road. There are six direct buses a day to São Paulo (US$12, 6½ hours), the first at 8am and the last at 11:15pm; two to Rio de Janeiro (US$10, 5½ hours), at 8am and midnight; and, on Sunday, there is one Rio bus only, running at 4pm.

AROUND CAXAMBU
Baependi

☎ 0xx35 / pop 20,000 / elevation 893m

Baependi's treasure is the baroque **Catedral Santa Maria** (1752), but its real attraction is the river and the peaceful waterfall 13km south of town. Rent horses in Caxambu (see p257) and set out. Skip the first, more developed falls in favor of the second, **Caixão Branco (Gamarra)**. The ride is easy and takes about 1½ hours each way. Bring a picnic.

Alternatively, a horse-and-buggy tour from Caxambu to Baependi will cost US$40 (up to four people).

Aiuruoca

☎ 0xx35 / pop 3000 / elevation 979m

The small town of Aiuruoca is 45km east of Caxambu. The main attraction is the Vale do Matutu on the way from Aiuruoca to Parque do Pico do Papagaio; in the dry season it is a great region for trekking, with lots of waterfalls.

SLEEPING & EATING

Pousada Dois Irmãos (☎ 3344 1373; Rua Coronel Os-waldo 204; s/d US$15/30) This is the best option in the town of Aiuruoca, and it serves meals as well.

Pousada Pé da Mata (☎ 3344 1421; Vale do Matutu, Km 14; s/d US$20/35) Inside the Parque do Pico do Papagaio, at an altitude of 1260m, this is a lovely pousada. Staff can arrange guides. Restaurant on site.

The **bus station** (☎ 3341 3839) is on Praça Côn José Castilho. There are regular buses to/from Caxambu.

SÃO LOURENÇO

☎ 0xx35 / pop 40,000 / elevation 874m

São Lourenço, a short distance south of Caxambu, is another city of mineral waters, though a bit more developed, smoggy and traffic-clogged. It makes a good jumping-off place for the surrounding attractions, all much more enjoyable.

Sights

The **Parque das Aguas** (admission US$3; ☺ 8am-5:20pm, mineral-water fountains closed 11:30am-2pm) boasts healing waters, a lake with paddle-boats, and an amphitheater enclosed by giant living bamboo. There are also lots of lovely 1940s pavilions and a gorgeous bathhouse in the middle, known as the Bal-

neário, where baths, saunas and massages (US$3 to US$10) are offered. It has separate facilities for men and women.

Members of the Brazilian Society of Euboise believe that a new civilization will arise in the seven magic cities of the region: São Tomé das Letras, Aiuruoca, Conceição do Rio Verde, Itanhandu, Pouso Alto, Carmo de Minas and Maria da Fe. You can visit the edifice erected by this society, the **Templo da Euboise** (☺ 2-4pm Sat & Sun) which is north of the parque on Rua Rui Barbosa.

Sleeping

Hotel Colombo (☎ 3331 1577; Av Dom Pedro II 611; s/d US$10/18) This hotel has the best budget price in town for its clean, carpeted rooms.

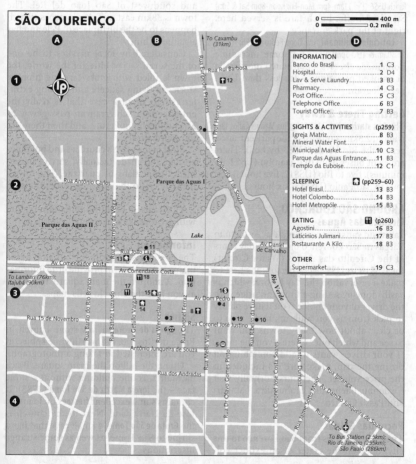

SÃO LOURENÇO

INFORMATION	
Banco do Brasil	1 C3
Hospital	2 D4
Lav & Serve Laundry	3 B3
Pharmacy	4 C3
Post Office	5 C3
Telephone Office	6 B3
Tourist Office	7 B3

SIGHTS & ACTIVITIES	(p259)
Igreja Matriz	8 B3
Mineral Water Font	9 B1
Municipal Market	10 C3
Parque das Aguas Entrance	11 B3
Templo da Euboise	12 C1

SLEEPING	(pp259–60)
Hotel Brasil	13 B3
Hotel Colombo	14 B3
Hotel Metropóle	15 B3

EATING	(p260)
Agostini	16 B3
Laticinios Julimani	17 B3
Restaurante A Kilo	18 B3

OTHER	
Supermarket	19 C3

Hotel Brasil (☎ 3331 1313; Rua João Lage 87; s/d with full board US$74, with breakfast only US$50) The four-star Hotel Brasil faces the park and is the top-of-the-line hotel in São Lourenço. In a gorgeous location, and has delicious food.

Hotel Metropóle (☎ 3332 6000; Rua Wenceslau Brás 70; s/d US$24/40; 🔀 🏊) This place is spotless, with lots of facilities including a sauna.

Eating

Most of the restaurants in town can't compete with the food in the hotels.

Agostini (☎ 3331 1818; Av Comendador Costa; pizzas US$7; 🕙 11am-4pm) Opposite the park, Agostini has great pizza, pasta, trout and wood-fired oven dishes.

Restaurante A Kilo (Av Comendador Costa; buffet lunch US$6; 🕙 11am-4pm Mon-Fri, noon-8pm Sat & Sun) Standard buffet-lunch fare is served here, right at the park entrance.

Laticinios Julimani (Av Dom Pedro II 696; 🕙 9-11:30am & 1:30-5pm) Pick up some incredible homemade cheeses – marinated mozzarella or smoked provolone – for less than US$4 per kilogram.

Getting There & Away

The **bus station** (☎ 3332 5966; Rua Manuel Carlos 130) is about 2.5km southeast of the park entrance, across the Rio Verde (US$3 by taxi). There are eight buses daily to Caxambu (US$2, 45 minutes), five to Rio (US$12, five hours) and four to São Paulo (US$13, six hours).

AROUND SÃO LOURENÇO
Circuito das Aguas

Taxis and vans that congregate at Av Getúlio Vargas in São Lourenço offer half-day tours of the Circuito das Aguas (Water Circuit) for US$16 to US$27 per person; it's best to make a reservation the day before, which is easily done by setting a time and price with the driver of your choice. You'll have plenty to pick from as you walk up; make sure to be clear about how many towns you want to see and which ones interest you the most. If your driver wants to add something on during the trip, make sure it's included in the price you set. The tours normally visit Caxambu, Baependi, Cambuquira, Lambari and Passo Quatro.

Poços das Caldas

There are day trips from São Lorenço to this city, built on the crater of an extinct vol-

cano. A mineral-spring town, it was settled by glassblowers from the island of Murano, near Venice. There are full-day tours to Poços das Caldas from São Lourenço (US$30 per person), which leave from in front of the Parque das Aguas at 7am. Check with the tourist office to see if the day trips are still running.

SÃO TOMÉ DAS LETRAS
☎ 0xx35 / pop 4000 / elevation 1291m

If you're into mysticism or superstition, or just looking for a cheap, fun and idyllic place to rest up for a few days, the quaint village of São Tomé das Letras may be where you need to go. It's a remote place in the hills, north of the mineral spa towns and southwest of São João del Rei. The town is 38km east of Três Corações (which happens to be the birthplace of Pelé and has a statue of him).

Considered by local mystics to be one of the seven sacred cities of the world, the town is filled with grass-carrying hippies, stories of flying saucers and visiting extra-terrestrials or of a cave that is really the entrance to a subterranean passageway to Machu Picchu in Peru... and then there are the weird stories.

Most of the town's churches and buildings are old and made (actually, sort of home-made) from slabs of quartzite. The town's name refers to the puzzling inscriptions on some of the many caverns in the region.

This is also a beautiful mountain region, with great walks and several waterfalls.

Information

The city hall is opposite the bus stop in the main square, but will provide little information. A shop in the main square, to the left as you face the church, sells maps.

Sights

The **Igreja de Pedra**, a raw-stone church in Praça do Rosário, is a worthwhile subject if you are interested in taking a photograph.

Up on the hill on the main square, Praça da Matriz, is one building without a stone face – the **Igreja Matriz de São Tomé** (1785). It contains some excellent **frescoes** by Joaquim José da Natividade. Next to the church is the **Gruta de São Tomé**, a small cave that has a shrine to São Tomé, as well as some strange inscriptions.

The lookout, only 500m from town, provides great views at sunset or sunrise, and it's the place to go for viewing flying saucers.

The caves **Carimbado** (3km away) and **Chico Taquara** (3.5km) both contain additional puzzling inscriptions. The popular waterfalls to walk to are **Euboise** (3km), **Prefeitura** (7km) and **Véu de Noiva** (12km). The army boys have been playing at Pico do Papagaio and have left unexploded mines there, so don't stroll off in that direction!

In August the **Festas de Agosto** attract lots of pilgrims. The **Mystic Festival**, from late December to early January, attracts students and teachers of mysticism – it's a scene. Contact the city hall for more information.

Sleeping & Eating

Gruta do Leão (per person US$5) Camping here allows you to enter a cave that is supposedly stocked with enchanted water.

Pousada Reino dos Magos (☎ 3237 1300; Rua Gabriel Luiz Alvarez 47; s/d US$13/20) The spotless Pousada Reino provides clean, fan-cooled rooms.

Hospedaria dos Sonhos I (☎ 3237 1235; Rua Gabriel Luiz Alvarez 28; per person US$14) The Hospedaria has cute private rooms with breakfast included.

Pousada Arco Iris (☎ 3237 1212; Rua João Batista Neves 19; per person US$20) Popular with travelers, the Pousada Arco Iris is a good value – discounts available during the week.

Pousada e Restaurante Serra Branca (☎ 3237 1200; Rua Capitão João de Deus 7; US$20) This pousada and restaurant is a great deal, offering apartamentos with saunas and pools.

Ximana (☎ 3236 1345; Rua Camilo Rios 12; per kg US$6; ☑ 11am-4pm) Delicous hot foods and salads are the main fare at Ximana.

Getting There & Away

There are three buses (US$3) daily on weekdays and four on weekends to São Tomé das Letras from **Três Corações bus station** (☎ 5232 1311; Praça dos Ferroviários).

From Caxambu, buses leave six times a day from 6:30am to 8:45pm (US$3, 1½ hours).

There are several buses a day from São João del Rei to Três Corações (US$4, 2¼ hours).

Outbound buses depart from Praça Barão de Alfenas in São Tomé das Letras.

PARKS

PARQUE NATURAL DO CARAÇA

☎ 0xx31

The Santa Bárbara region, 105km east of Belo Horizonte, is a gorgeous transition area between Mata Atlântica and some wild mountain vegetation. The 110-sq-km park (admission US$7) includes several mountains – these are **Pico do Sol** (2070m), **Alto do Infficionada** (2068m), **Morro do Piçarrão** (1839m), **Pico da Conceição** (1803m) and **Pico da Trindade** (1908m). The hillsides are lined with easily accessible hiking trails and creeks that form waterfalls and natural swimming pools.

The town of Santa Bárbara itself (population 21,300) has a collection of lovely baroque colonial churches, including the **Igreja Matriz do Santo Antônio** and the **Igreja de Nossa Senhora das Mercês**.

The area's main attraction, 26km southwest of the town and inside the natural park, is a former monastery and boarding school that has been converted to a highly recommended pousada, the **Hospedaria do Colégio Caraça**. It is still owned and run by the Catholic congregation who use the neo-Gothic church for services. The padres offer very friendly advice on hikes and treks into the surrounding countryside. A highlight is when staff feed a couple of relatively tame wolves, which appear most nights for the feeding.

Sleeping & Eating

Hospedaria do Colégio Caraça (☎ 3837 2698; s/d with meals US$23/40) Inside the park, rooms at this place range from bare-boned *quartos* off the courtyard down near the catacombs, to swank private doubles with bathroom. Rates include three meals. The kitchen serves awesome Mineiro cuisine – all ingredients are grown locally. You can fry your own eggs on the wood-fired stove. You need to make reservations if you're going for the weekend, as the place gets packed with escapees from Belo taking in the air. During the week, schoolkids come to visit the museum.

Pousada Pico do Sol (☎ 3832 1836; 14km southwest of Santa Bárbara; s/d US$25/35) Just outside the park gates, this pousada is clean, has a gorgeous pool, and Antonio speaks excellent English. From here you can catch a free ride

12km up to the monastery with the 6am workers bus, and back at about 4:30pm.

Hotel Karaíba (☎ 3832 1501; Praça Pio XII 281; s/d US$12/16) In Santa Bárbara itself, accommodations are available at this hotel. Cheaper rooms have shared bathrooms.

Getting There & Away
The Belo–Vitória train stops in Santa Bárbara (see p230) and there are five to 10 buses a day from Belo Horizonte (US$4, 2½ hours). From Santa Bárbara, a taxi to the Hospedaria do Colégio Caraça will cost US$16 to US$20 plus the US$6 admission fee for the car to the natural park (open 7am to 5pm or to 9pm for guests of the hospedaria).

PARQUE NACIONAL DE CAPARAÓ
☎ 0xx32

This 250-sq-km national park is popular with climbers and hikers from all over Brazil. The panoramic views are superb, taking in the Caparaó Valley that divides Minas Gerais and Espírito Santo. Caparaó contains the highest mountains in southern Brazil, including **Cristal** (2798m) and **Calçado** (2766m), as well as the third-highest peak in the country, **Pico da Bandeira** (2890m). All three can be reached via the park's good network of trails. Climbing gear isn't necessary.

Despite being ravaged by fire in 1988 and by human interference for the last 300 years, the park has a few lush remnants of Mata Atlântica (Atlantic rain forest), mostly in Vale Verde, a small valley split by the Rio Caparaó.

Wildlife in the park is not exactly plentiful, but there are still some opossums, agoutis and spider monkeys to be seen. Bird life includes various eagles, parrots and hummingbirds.

Between November and January there's lots of rain and it's too cloudy for good views. The best time to visit the park is between June and August – although these are the coldest months, the days are clear. Bring warm clothes!

The park is open daily from 7am to 10pm and costs US$4 to enter. The entrance is 4km from Alto Caparaó. Make sure you pick up a map here.

Sleeping
There are two official campsites inside the park: Tronqueira, 8km from the park entrance, and Terreirão, another 4.5km away, halfway to the summit of Pico da Bandeira. It's a good idea to reserve a site about a week before you arrive by calling **IBAMA** (☎ 3747 2555; per camp site US$9).

Caparaó Parque Hotel (☎ 3747 2559; Rua Vale das Hortências; s/d US$60/85) The closest place to the park where you can stay is this hotel, which is a short walk from the entrance. It's pleasant and you'll pay less if it is not peak season.

Pousada do Bezerra (☎ 3747 2628; Av Pico da Bandeira; s/d with full board US$60/84) In Alto Caparaó, the town closest to the park, this pousada has clean basic rooms.

Getting There & Away
Caparaó can be reached via Belo Horizonte (370km), or from Vitória, in Espírito Santo. You'll need to catch a bus to the town of Manhumirim, and then another local bus to Alto Caparaó, an additional 25km away and 4km from the park.

There are only two local buses a day from Manhumirim to Alto Caparaó, at 8am and noon. Unless you want to hitchhike the last leg or pay for a taxi from Manhumirim to Alto Caparaó (US$20 to US$30, depending on the mood of the driver and your bargaining ability), plan on spending the night in Manhumirim.

PARQUE NACIONAL DA SERRA DO CIPÓ
☎ 0xx31

Formed by mountains, rivers, waterfalls and open grasslands, the Parque Nacional da Serra do Cipó, about 100km northeast of Belo Horizonte, is one of the most beautiful parks in Minas. Its highlands, together with an arm of the Serra do Espinhaço, divide the water basins of the São Francisco and Doce rivers.

Most of the park's vegetation is cerrado (savanna) and grassy highlands, but the small river valleys are lush and ferny and contain a number of unique orchids. Fauna here includes the maned wolf, tamarin monkey, banded anteater, tree hedgehog, otter, jaguar and large numbers of bats. Bird life includes woodpeckers, blackbirds and hummingbirds. The highland park is also home to a small, brightly colored frog that secretes deadly toxins from its skin. Brazilians call it *sapo de pijama* (pajama frog).

Other attractions of the park include a 70m waterfall called **Cachoeira da Farofa**, and the **Cânion das Bandeirantes**, named after the early adventurers from São Paulo who used the area as a natural road to the north in their search for riches.

Getting There & Away

From Belo's bus station, take a **Saritur** (☎ 3201 6064) bus for Conceição do Mato Dentro.

For the camping grounds, ask the driver to drop you off at Véu da Noiva. The road to Conceição do Mato Dentro passes through Cardeal Mota, the nearest town to the park entrance, which is 3km north of the bridge over the Rio Cipó.

Various Belo Horizonte trekking companies also take excursions to the park, including **Brasil Aventuras** (☎ 3261 9423) and **Serras de Minas** (☎ 3227 8397).

São Paulo State

HIGHLIGHTS

- Taking in the **Memorial do Imigrante** (p271) in São Paulo
- Hiking the peaceful Brazilian Atlantic Forest in **Iporanga** (p289), a region of international importance for its biodiversity
- Sampling some amazing nightlife in **Vila Olímpia** (p280) in Sampa (an affectionate local nickname for São Paulo)
- Checking out the wild, deserted beaches just north of **Ubatuba** (p283)
- Bundling up for a weekend in the **Serra da Mantiqueira** (p290), known as 'Brazil's Switzerland'

- POPULATION: 38 MILLION
- AREA: 248,800 SQ KM

As the industrial engine that powers the Brazilian economy – or so Paulistas say, at least – not everybody can separate São Paulo state from São Paulo the city. It's understandably difficult, considering it's the largest urban area in all of South America. But lifting your eyes from that teeming megalopolis (just for a moment), it's worth noting that the state's beaches are in surprisingly good shape and make a nice break if you're meandering your way up to Rio. Charming Campos do Jordão – with the country's highest cable car – is a great weekend getaway any time of year. And have you heard of Ilhabela? It's a fabulous island just off the Paulista coastline that attracts scores of visitors every holiday season. Nearby Iporanga, one of the least disturbed areas of Brazilian Atlantic Forest, is a perfect base for exploring the Parque Estadual do Alto do Ribeira, a 360-sq-km national park with 280 cataloged caves that's known as Brazil's Capital das Grutas (Cave Capital). There's ample proof up and down the São Paulo coastline and in the national parks inland that contrary to popular opinion, Paulistas do, in fact, know how to have fun.

History

Looking at the well-developed infrastructure and relatively high quality of life enjoyed by many living in São Paulo state these days, you'd never guess that the region was a mosquito-infested backwater for much of its colonial past. In 1507 São Vicente (now called Santos) was founded on the coast; it was the second Portuguese settlement in Brazil. Until the 17th and 18th centuries the newcomers lived (sometimes peacefully and sometimes not) with the local tribes – the resulting mix spawned a new type of frontiersmen, known as *bandeirantes*. They roamed the interior lands, enslaving indigenous people and taking hold of precious gems and stones as they traveled.

São Paulo state didn't start to become wealthy until the mid-19th century, when cotton producers from North America arrived. Cotton failed as a crop, but intrepid farmers soon discovered the joys of coffee, and that quickly became the state's biggest moneymaker. Brazil had abolished slavery around the time of its independence in 1822 and the flood of Eastern European and Japanese immigrants looking for work gave the São Paulo state a competitive edge. Soon investors from around the world were looking to sink money into development ventures, turning São Paulo city into the vast, sprawling entity that it is today, and São Paulo state into a well-paved, patrolled and developed backdrop for wealthy Paulistanos (inhabitants of the city; inhabitants of São Paulo state are called Paulistas) to enjoy.

Climate

São Paulo's coastline is skirted closely by the Sierra do Mar, below which is a narrow coastal zone broken by lagoons, tidal channels and mountain spurs. In the mountains the state has a mild, temperate climate that can be very bracing – jackets needed in winter. In the coastal zone and São Paulo city the temperatures are moderate in winter and boiling in summer, when the mugginess also gets quite extreme. Heavy rainfall sometimes occurs in December/January and malaria outbreaks do occur in areas with insufficient drainage.

Getting There & Around

São Paulo state has several great highways leading to its coastline and mountain retreats; horrible urban traffic and maniac drivers aside, getting around by car is pretty easy in this region. There are two large airports in São Paulo city – one domestic and the other international – from which it's possible to travel anywhere in the country, on the continent, or in the world. Every major bus carrier comes through the city's bus station and it's possible to catch buses into neighboring Argentina, Paraguay and Uruguay very easily.

SÃO PAULO STATE

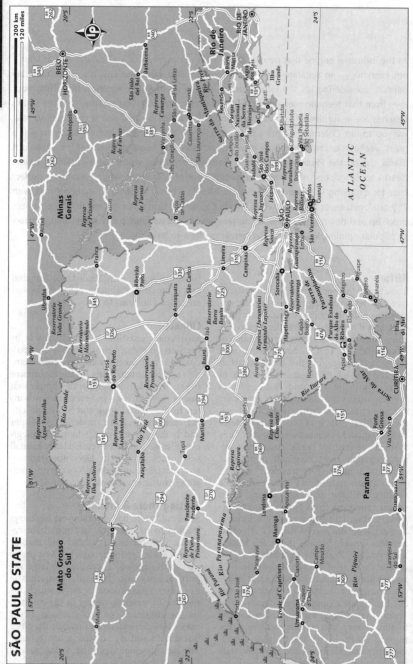

SÃO PAULO CITY

☎ 0xx11 / pop 11 million / elevation 760m

Talk about a city within a city! An estimated 17 million people live in 'Greater São Paulo' (the city proper and its environs), making it the third-largest metropolis on earth. It's home to more ethnic groups than any other part of the country, and contains Brazil's biggest and best-educated middle class. Sampa – as the city is known to locals – is an intoxicating place, with art and entertainment on par with any world capital. Paulistanos believe in working hard and playing harder, and despite constantly complaining about street violence, clogged highways and pollution, most wouldn't dream of living anywhere else.

São Paulo is on a high plateau; it's cold in the Brazilian winter and smoggy-hot in the summer. It can be an intimidating place, but if you know someone who can show you around or if you just like the challenge of navigating urban jungles, then it's worth a visit. At its best it offers the excitement and nightlife that you would expect from one of the world's great cities, and despite moving at a much faster pace than the rest of the country, the usual Brazilian warmth and joie de vivre is still apparent at every turn.

HISTORY

São Paulo was really nothing more than a Jesuit backwater (founded by Manoel da Nóbrega and José de Anchieta in 1554) on the Piratininga plateau called São Paulo for quite a long part of its history.

Things started getting more interesting around the 17th century, when the town became the headquarters for groups of *bandeirantes* – slave-trading pioneers who inadvertently explored and opened up much of Brazil's interior while hunting indigenous people to sell into forced labor.

By the 18th century the *bandeirantes* had turned their attention to mineral exploration and had discovered gold mines in Minas Gerais, Goiás and Mato Grosso. São Paulo was used as a stopover by the increasing number of pioneers, explorers and fortune hunters heading for the interior, as well as by sugar dealers taking their shipments to the port of Santos.

During the early 19th century, two events significantly changed São Paulo. The first was the declaration of Brazilian independence, which led to the city's becoming a provincial capital. The second occurred a few years later with the founding of the Law Faculty, which attracted a new, transient population of students and intellectuals. As a political and intellectual center, São Paulo became a leader both in the campaign to abolish slavery and in the founding of the republic.

The last decades of the 19th century brought dramatic change. The rapid expansion of coffee cultivation in the state, the construction of railroads and the influx of millions of European immigrants caused the city to grow rapidly. São Paulo's industrial base began to form, and the import restrictions caused by WWI meant rapid industrial expansion and population growth, which continued after the war. The city's population reached 580,000 by 1920, 1.2 million by 1940, two million by 1950, 3.1 million by 1960 and 5.2 million by 1970. By 2025 the population of greater São Paulo is expected to top 25 million.

ORIENTATION

The efficient metro (see p282) means that navigating this city is easy. Parks, museums, art galleries, zoos, you name it – are spread throughout the metropolitan area.

As a city of immigrants, São Paulo hosts certain districts that are associated with the nationalities that settled there. **Liberdade**, just south of Praça da Sé, is the Asian area. **Bela Vista**, east of Liberdade (also known as Bixiga) is Italian. **Bom Retiro**, near the Estação da Luz train station (the Luz metro also runs through here), is the old Jewish quarter. The large Arab community is based around Rua 25 de Março, to the north of Praça da Sé. In all these areas you'll find restaurants to match the tastes of their inhabitants.

Avenida Paulista, to the southwest of the center, is an avenue of skyscrapers, and the adjoining district of **Cerqueira César** contains the city's highest concentration of good restaurants, cafés and nightclubs. When people refer to São Paulo as the 'New York of the Tropics,' this is the area they have in mind. Farther west, adjoining Cerqueira César, is the stylish **Jardim Paulista** district,

THE SOUTHEAST

SÃO PAULO

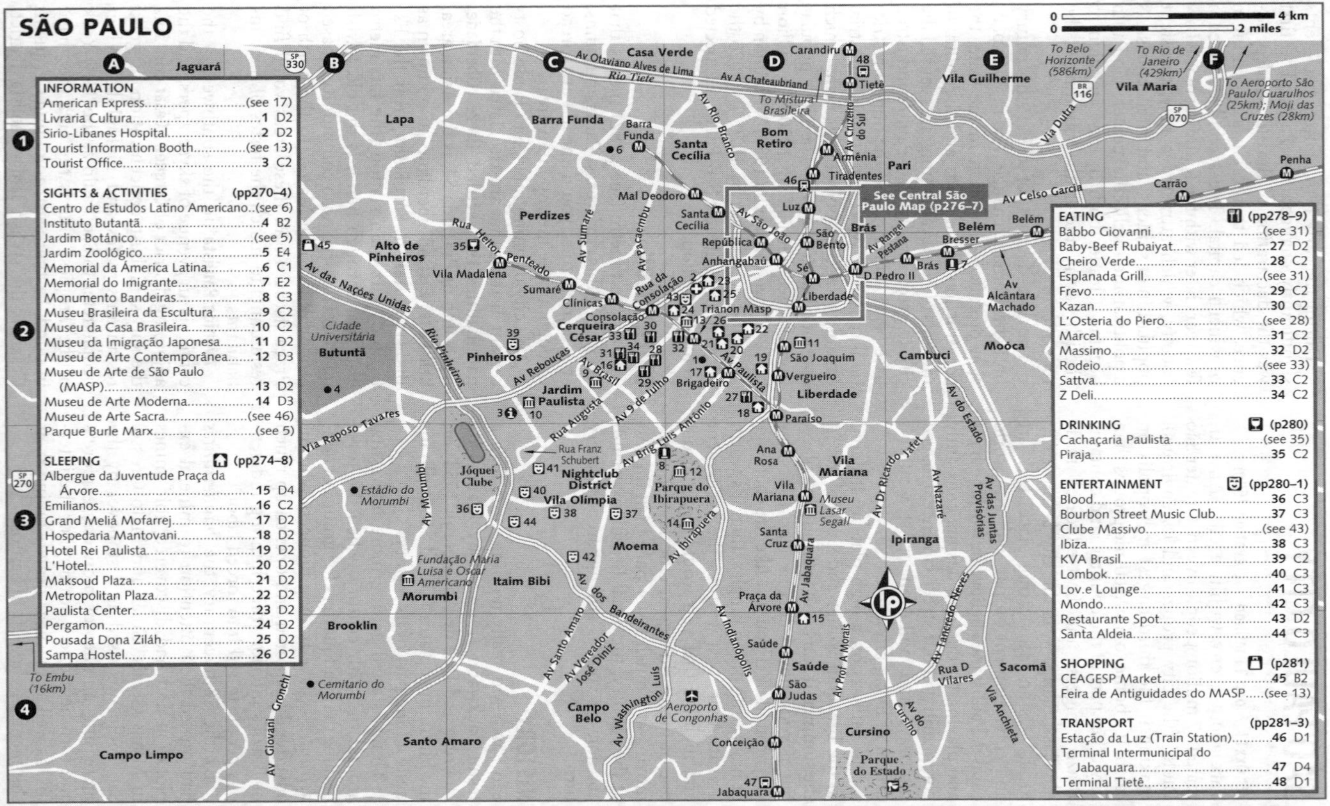

To Belo
Horizonte
(586km)

To Rio de
Janeiro
(429km)

To Aeroporto São
Paulo/Guarulhos
(25km; Moji das
Cruzes (28km)

0   2 miles
0   4 km

home to many of the city's middle- and upper-class residents.

Maps

The *Guia São Paulo* by Quatro Rodas is probably the best all-round guide to the city, with street maps, hotel and restaurant listings and bus lines. *O Guia* has the clearest presentation of any street directory, and it also lists tourist points. Pick them up at any kiosk around town for about US$3.

INFORMATION
Bookstores

Book Centre (Map pp276-7; Av Ibirapuera 1789) Everybody's favorite place for English books – second-hand and brand-new.

Livraria Cultura (Map p268; Av Paulista 2073) Right in the thick of things on Av Paulista, this store is a big favorite with students and artists.

Saraiva Megastore (Map pp276-7; Praça da Sé 423) A wide variety of books and titles available, mostly in Portuguese and Spanish.

Emergency

Deatur (Map pp276-7; ☎ 214 0209; Av São Luís 95; ☼ 9am-5pm Mon-Fri, on call 24hr) is a special police force just for tourists. It has English-speaking officers available 24/7; a **second office** (☎ 3107 5642/8332; Rua São Bento 380) is located on the 5th floor of an office building downtown.

Internet Access

Monkey Lan House (☎ 3253 8627; main office Alameda Santos 1217; per hr US$1.25; ☼ 24hr) The most popular place to surf, Monkey Lan has Internet cafés all over the city.

Medical Services

Einstein Hospital (☎ 3747 1233; Av Albert Einstein 627) Located on a southwestern corner of the city (catch bus No 7241 to Jardim Colombo from Rua Xavier de Toledo), Einstein is one of the best in Latin America.

Sírio-Libânes (Map p268; ☎ 3155 0200; Rua Dona Adma Jafet 91) Another recommended hospital is Libânes in Bela Vista.

Money

Except on weekends, changing money is easy. Many travel agencies and exchange offices around the city offer good rates, but avoid the smaller ones downtown – some are illegal and will rip you off. ATMs are available up and down Av Paulista, which is home to a range of banks from around the world.

Action Cambio (Shopping Light; ☼ 10am-7pm Mon-Fri, to 4pm Sat) Changes money.

American Express (☼ 9:30am-5:30pm Mon-Fri) airport (☎ 6412 3515); central branch (Map p268; ☎ 3251 3383; Gran Meliá Mofarrej, Rua Alameda Santos 1437); Centro Empresarial (☎ 3741 8478; 8th fl, Av Maria Coelho Aguiar 215) The central branch of American Express is located near the Trianon-Masp metro. It changes American Express checks without charging any commission on them and sells US-dollar traveler's checks to American Express cardholders.

Post

Post office (Map pp276-7; Rua Líbero Badaró) This main branch is the safest place to send letters.

Telephone

Cabinas (Map pp276-7; Rua 7 de Abril) Long-distance phone calls can be made from Cabinas, about 200m from Praça da República.

Tourist Information

The **state tourist office** (Map pp276-7; ☎ 3239 5822; Praça Antônio Prado 9; ☼ 9am-6pm Mon-Fri) is in the art-deco Banespa building. It provides information about São Paulo state as well as the city.

Pick up a *Guia da Folha* at any newsstand for reviews of the city's newest restaurants, and *Veja São Paulo* also has great listings.

Tourist information booths (☎ 6224 0400; www.cidadedesaopaulo.com; ☼ 9am-6pm; city tours on Sun US$5) all have excellent city and state maps. They are also good for bus and metro information. English is spoken as are a variety of other languages. Locations include the following:

Av Brigadeiro Faria Lima (Map p268) In front of Shopping Iguatemi.

Av Paulista (Map p268) Near the Museu de Arte de São Paulo (MASP).

Av São Luís (Map p268) On the corner of Praça Dom José Gaspar.

Praça da República (Map pp276-7; ☎ 6224 0620/6224 0621; Av Ipiranga) The best in the city, it has great maps and a friendly, well-informed staff; there's a post office in the building too.

Viaduto do Cha (Map pp276-7) Ground floor of the new Shopping Light in the city center.

Visas

Polícia Federal (Map pp276-7; ☎ 3225 5080; Av Prestes Maia 700; ☼ 8am-4pm) For visa and entry/exit card extensions, head to this office.

DANGERS & ANNOYANCES

Reports of crime in the city have increased, and São Paulo is said to be less safe than Rio. Be especially careful in the center at night, as well as in the cheap-hotel area around Rua Santa Efigênia. Watch out for pickpockets on buses and at Praça da Sé. If you're driving, be aware that carjackings and red-light robberies are common after dark. It's so bad that São Paulo recently changed a traffic law – it's now legal (and recommended) to just slow down at red lights at night. If there's no traffic, continue without stopping. The subway is generally safe, although you want to keep your eyes open; on buses, look out for pickpockets and at night consider taxis over public transportation.

SIGHTS

Museu de Arte de São Paulo

The **São Paulo Museum of Art** (MASP; Map p268; ☎ 251-5644; Av Paulista 1578; metro Trianon-Masp; adult/student US$10/5; ☻ 11am-6pm Tue-Sun) has Latin America's best collection of Western art in, some would say, its ugliest building. Some, though, will find the startlingly simple, confident design by architect Lina Bo Bardi a great example of modern architecture. As well as the work of many French impressionists, there are a few great Brazilian paintings; Cândido Portinari's work alone is worth the trip. There are also temporary exhibits, as well as a pleasant cafeteria on the 1st floor.

Pinacoteca do Estado

The neoclassical building housing the **Pinacoteca do Estado** (☎ 229 9844; Praça da Luz; adult/student US$1.50/0.75; ☻ 10am-6pm) has undergone an interesting renovation and was opened to the public in 1998. It has a good collection of modern art on display, including a few paintings by some of Brazil's big names such as Portinari and Di Cavalcanti.

Parque do Ibirapuera

There's lots to do in this park, and many people doing it on weekends. Take the metro to Santa Cruz and then bus No 775-C 'Jardim Maria Sampião', or bus No 5121 'Santo Amaro' from Praça da República. The large edifice across the street from the park is the São Paulo state legislature. Just outside the park, at the end of Av Brasil, is

Victor Brecheret's huge **Monumento Bandeiras** (Map p268), built in memory of the pioneers of the city.

Inside the park is the **Museu de Arte Moderna** (Map p268; ☎ 5549 9688; admission US$2; ☻ noon-6pm Tue-Sun), the oldest museum of modern art in the country, with a huge collection of works from the 1930s to the '70s.

The **Museu de Arte Contemporânea** (Map p268; ☎ 3091 3039; Rua da Reitoria 160, Cidade Universitária; ☻ 10am-7pm Mon-Fri, to 4pm Sat) is housed in Ibirapuera's Bienal building. This art museum has works by many of the big international names in modern art as well as possessing a good collection of modern Brazilian artists.

The Bienal international art exhibition (see p272) is the largest in Brazil, and if you happen to be in town when it's on, don't miss it. It takes place every even-numbered year.

Museu de Arte Sacra

The best of Brazil's many museums of sacred art is the **Museu de Arte Sacra** (Map p268; ☎ 3326 1373; Av Tiradentes 676, metro Tiradentes; admission US$1.30; ☻ 11am-6pm Tue-Fri, to 6pm Sat, 10am-7pm Sun). Built in 1774 it's a beautiful example of colonial architecture and offers numerous views on how sacred art has evolved over the years.

Museu da Imigração Japonesa

This fascinating **museum** (☎ 3279 5465; Rua São Joaquim 381; admission US$1; ☻ 1:30-5:30pm Tue-Sun), is three blocks east of the São Joaquim metro station. It has exhibitions on the exploits of the Japanese community, from the arrival in Santos of the first 781 settlers aboard the *Kasato-Maru* in 1908 through to today.

Instituto Butantã

The Butantã **snake farm** (Map p268; ☎ 3726 7222; Cidade Universitária; admission US$1.60; ☻ 9am-4:30pm Tue-Sun) is one of the most popular tourist sights in town. It keeps over 1000 serpents, from which it milks venom for the production of antivenin to treat snake and spider bites, as well as for vaccines against a number of diseases, including typhoid fever, typhus and diphtheria.

Memorial da América Latina

Another Niemeyer creation, the Memorial da América Latina is easily identifiable by the 7m-high cement hand slashed with red just outside the front door. Inside is the **Centro de Estudos Latino Americano** (Map p268; ☎ 3823 460; Rua Mario de Andrade 664, metro Barra Funda; ☺ 9am-6pm Tue-Sun), an auditorium that stages free concerts, and various interesting handicraft exhibits from regional Brazil and other Latin American countries. Portinari's painting *Tiradentes* hangs in the Salão de Atos, and huge panels by Carybé and Poty represent the people of South America.

Museu da Casa Brasileira

This former coffee baron's **house** (Map p268; Av Brigadeiro Faria Lima 2705; admission US$2; ☺ 1-6pm Tue-Sun), in Jardim Paulista, has furniture from the 17th to 20th centuries. There is also a good restaurant on-site.

Museu Brasileira da Escultura

As this museum is popularly known, **Mube** (Map p268; ☎ 3081 8611; Rua Alemanha 221; admission US$2; ☺ 10am-7pm Tue-Sun) is in Jardim Europa and is worth a look. The modern building was designed by architect Paulo Mendes da Rocha, the gardens by landscape architect Roberto Burle Marx. Mube features temporary exhibitions by contemporary artists.

Parque do Estado

The Parque do Estado (Map p268) is a vast park south of the center in the suburb of Cursino. It includes three interesting sections: the **Jardim Botânico** (☎ 5073 6300; ☺ 9am-5pm Wed-Sun), a lovely 100-year-old park with a promenade of imperial palms; the **Parque Burle Marx** (☎ 3746 7631; ☺ 6am-7pm); and the

---

THE FUTURE OF THE PAST

Brazil's tremendous ethnic and cultural diversity can be seen at its best in São Paulo – a place that's been dubbed 'the city of the future' by some researchers. Sampa is a living petri dish, they say, with a lot of important genetic splicing and dicing going on, thanks to the various races that have been mixing it up for several generations now. Whether Paulistanos are really preoccupied with creating übergenes or just out doing what comes naturally, the results certainly are mystifying, amazing and breathtaking. Some of the most beautiful people in the world, it seems, can be found strolling the city streets.

But where did all that tremendous diversity come from? For a better understanding of São Paulo's future, one must look towards its past, at the Immigrant Memorial Museum, in the eastern suburb of Moóca. The museum has a permanent collection of period furnishings, some old documents and photographs, and often hosts visiting exhibitions that explore the nature of emigration and national identity.

The biggest attraction, however, is the building itself. Originally built in 1887, it was called the **Hospedaria dos Imigrantes**, and it functioned as a holding place for immigrant labor. The dorm rooms are immense, and one can still see the huge sliding rails that were used to bring in truckloads of people and luggage, fresh from the dock. To the millions of immigrants who came to São Paulo hoping for a better life, it must have seemed more of a prison than hostel. Designed to hold up to 4000 people, records show that as many as 10,000 individuals were housed there at one time. Translators had to be brought in to help recent arrivals understand the work contracts they were signing. There were guards and wardens to make sure people didn't slip away in the middle of the night – not everyone who got off the boat wanted to break their back picking coffee. For many, the dream was to escape and head for the growing metropolis nearby – contracts be damned! Of course, a guarantee of work was the only way out of the Hospedaria, and that, ultimately, was the goal.

You'll be surprised to learn just how many different nationalities have emigrated, seemingly en masse, to Brazil in the past 500 years – not to mention the scores of Africans and Indigenous people who were taken unwillingly from their homes and forced to labor in colonial mines and on colonial plantations.

Don't miss a visit to **Memorial do Imigrante** (Map p268; ☎ 6693-0917; www.memorialdoimigrante .sp.gov.br in Portuguese; Rua Visconde de Paraiba 1316; admission US$1.25; ☺ 10am-5pm Tue-Sun). To get there take the metro to Bresser. It's a five-minute walk away, although on weekends a little tram shuttles visitors back and forth. Be aware that a homeless shelter abuts the museum.

Jardim Zoológico (☎ 5073 0811; admission US$3; ☉ 9am-5pm Tue-Sun). The closest metro station is Jabaquara.

WALKING TOUR

If you really want a feel for the historic parts of São Paulo, follow this meandering three-hour stroll that brings you past all the best-known landmarks and sights of Sampa.

The start is at the **Praça da República (1)**, near the subway stop with the same name. Look for the big yellow edifice known as the **Caetano de Campos building (2)** – it used to be a high school but is now the headquarters for the State Department of Education. On Sunday this plaza is the venue for the Feira da República (see p281), which has a huge variety of crafts, paintings, coins and stones.

Head down Av Ipiranga and then turn onto Av São Luís to get a look at what's still one of the tallest buildings in town – the 41-story **Edifício Itália (3)**. There's a restaurant and piano bar at the top, as well as a viewing terrace. Strictly speaking, you're supposed to be a customer to go there; if you're not, act like one.

Continuing down Av São Luís (there're lots of travel agencies and money exchange bureaus on this street) check out the rather squat, grey building at the end of the small park on the left. It looks like a prison, but it's the **Mario de Andrade Municipal Library (4)**, housing the largest book collection in the city.

Turning left onto Rua Xavier de Toledo, keeping the library on your left, follow the road downhill toward the Anhangabaú subway station a few blocks away. Keep a sharp eye out – it's easy to miss in the hustle and bustle. To the right of the subway station and down a few steps into a park is **Ladeira da Memória** (Memory Hill; **5**), where the Chafariz dos Piques fountain used to supply the city and cattle dealers with water. Now it's the site of the Piramide dos Piques, an obelisk-like structure pointing at the sky.

Continue down Rua Xavier de Toledo until the **Teatro Municipal (6)** appears – this baroque building, with its occasional art-nouveau features, is the pride of the city. Across the street from the Teatro is **Shopping Light (7)**, a modern mall that once belonged to the Light English Company. There's a good food court on the 5th floor. Opposite the Teatro, on the right, is the **Viaduto do Chá (8)**, a metal bridge built in 1892 and named after an old tea plantation that used to be in the area. Pedestrian traffic got too heavy for the old bridge and a new one was inaugurated in 1938.

Crossing the Viaduto, look over the **Parque Anhangabaú (9)** on the left. In the Tupi-Guarani language, Anhangabaú means Demon's Valley, because indigenous peoples believed bad spirits once dwelled there. At the other side of the bridge, enter **Praça do Patriarca (10)** straight ahead. Here you'll find the **Igreja de Santo Antônio (11)**, the central church of the settlement of São Paulo at the start of the 17th century. Some 20 paces beyond that is Rua São Bento, a pedestrian street loaded with shops. Turn right onto Rua São Bento

---

THE SÃO PAULO BIENAL

Every two years the Parque do Ibirapuera (Map p268) is the site of an amazing gathering of modern visual art from all around the world – it's called the **São Paulo Bienal** (☎ 5574-5922; www.1.uol.com.br/bienal; Parque do Ibirapuera, Portal 3, 04090-900, Sao Paulo, SP) and it's considered the most important artistic event in Latin America.

Many of the participants are working artists who have been nominated by their country – some standout artists in the past have hailed from Cuba, Argentina, Russia and Germany. Each year a few select artists are chosen to exhibit by the Bienal's curators.

The event takes place in an Oscar Niemeyer building that, true to form, some people find stunning and others find loathsome. Beleaguered by funding problems and political infighting in the recent past, the Bienal nearly shut down in 1993 – an event that Brazilians would have found horrifying, as they take great pride in that fact that there's been a Bienal every other year since 1951. Thanks to the efforts of many in the art world, Brazil's most prominent artistic event only had to skip a year; the bienal debuted anew in 1994, and now takes place on every even-numbered year. At its best, the Bienal offers the world a chance to view mind-bending new art in innovative surroundings, and shouldn't be missed if you're in town from October through December on an even-numbered year.

and eventually you'll step into the **Largo de São Francisco (12)**, a little plaza triangulated by the **Church of St Francis of Assis (13)**, the **Chapel of the Third Order (14)** and the city's well-respected **College of Law (15)**.

The churches contain a vast number of 18th-century paintings and are well worth a look. In front of the law school is one of Brazil's most controversial works of art – a statue by Swiss artist William Zadig that depicts a Frenchman kissing an indigenous woman. If you can read a little Portuguese, the statue's history is well documented by a plaque on its base.

Just beyond the statue is Rua Senador Feijó, leading to the famous **Praça da Sé (16)**. Soak up the joyous atmosphere in Sé, but watch your pockets. Step inside the **Catedral Metropolitana (17)**, which can hold up to 8000 people (reportedly).

As you exit the cathedral, head down the plaza and continue toward the **Caixa Econômica Federal (18)**, home to the city's coffers and also a great cultural center that features Brazilian artists. Turning right onto Rua Floriano Peixoto, walk to the end (it's a dead-end

street) and feast your eyes upon the **Solar da Marquesa (19)**, a pinkish house that is the city's last remaining residential structure from the 18th century. Follow the street around to the left and **Praça Patío do Colégio (20)**, the actual site where São Paulo was founded in 1554, will appear on your right.

Directly in front of this plaza is Rua Boa Vista. Following it away from the Praça da Sé brings you into the heart of the city's financial district. At the end of Boa Vista, you'll find **Largo de São Bento (21)**, the square that launched thousands of *bandeirante* expeditions. Now it is home to the **Monastery and Basilica of São Bento (22)**, built in an eclectic style and still putting on Gregorian-chant concerts.

Leaving the square, walk up Rua São Bento, a pedestrian street, until reaching Av São João. Turn right and follow the avenue downhill. You are now crossing the Vale do Anhangabaú that you saw earlier from the Viaduto do Chá. Ahead is the **Prédio dos Correios (23)**, the largest post office in the country. It's currently being restored and will soon be a cultural center and postal museum.

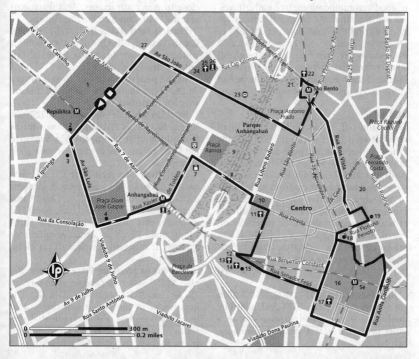

To finish this tour, go up Av São João as far as **Largo de Paiçandú (24)**, where you'll find **NS do Rosário dos Homens Pretos (25)**, a church that was built in 1906 by Black Brazilians on a site where sacred African religious rites were formerly performed. Behind this pretty church, which is painted an unusual yellow/orange tone, is the magnificent **Monumento á Mãe Preta** (Monument to the Black Mother; **26**). This heartwrenching statue depicts an African slave woman suckling a white child, and the poem underneath gives voice to her lament for her own children who must go hungry.

To wrap up a long day, continue forward and you will end up at an intersection point between Av São João and Av Ipiranga, a **corner (27)** that is considered the most famous in all of São Paulo and was immortalized in Caetano Veloso's beautiful ode to the city, 'Sampa.' Turn left and you will be back where it all started, in the Praça da República.

SLEEPING

A city the size of São Paulo has no shortage of good accommodations. Ironically, travelers will find that the biggest discounts are given during the quiet summer months of December, January and February (because Paulistanos are partying at the beaches!) when prices elsewhere in Brazil skyrocket. Weekend discounts of up to 50% can be had at big hotels that cater to business travelers.

Budget

Down-and-out in São Paulo is done in an area between the Estação da Luz and the Praça da República. There are dozens of budget and below-budget hotels on Rua dos Andradas and Rua Santa Efigênia and the streets that intersect them from Av Ipiranga to Av Duque de Caxias. The area is rife with crime and prostitution and is not at all safe at night – women should be especially on guard, or avoid the area completely. If you are going to stay in this area, travel by taxi after dark. There are safer options in better parts of the city, and those we mentioned below.

Hotel Joamar (Map pp276-7; ☎ 3221 3611; Rua Dom Jose de Barros 187; per person US$10) A delightfully quaint place, the Hotel Joamar sits on a quiet pedestrian street and has a friendly, helpful staff.

Galeão Hotel (Map pp276-7; ☎ 3331 8211; Rua dos Gusmões 394; d US$40) Discounts are frequently available at the Galeão, but even paying regular prices you're getting a deal. This is a warm, clean and very welcoming place.

Ikeda Hotel (Map pp276-7; ☎ 3278 3844; Rua dos Estudantes 134; s/d US$14/25) In the quieter, safer and nocturnally more interesting Liberdade area, the Ikeda has great rooms with immense beds.

Hotel Municipal Palace (Map pp276-7; ☎ 3228 7833; Av São João 354; per person US$9) Rooms are basic, but clean and safe, and during downseason you can sometimes bargain for a private bathroom at no extra cost. It's near the square known as Largo do Paissandu.

Hotel Itamarati (Map pp276-7; ☎ 3222 4133; Av Vieira de Carvalho 150; per person US$14) A well-kept but old establishment with helpful staff, the Itamarati makes a stab at supplying amenities by putting TVs and telephones in each room.

Hotel Rei Paulista (Map p268; ☎ 3885 1362; Alameda Lorena 21; per person US$15) This is a slightly more upscale option, but it does sit on Av Paulista, one of the best parts of town and close to many attractions. And the rooms are nice, with comfortable furnishings.

Pauliceía Hotel (Map pp276-7; ☎ 3220 9733; Rua Timbiras 216; s/d US$5/10) One of the best options you can find on Rua Santa Efigênia, this hotel is clean and safe.

In the pedestrian streets close to Praça da República there are a few places that are worth a mention.

Hotel São Sebastião (Map pp276-7; ☎ 3257 4988; Rua 7 de Abril 364; s/d US$13/18) A stone's throw from the tourist booth, the São Sebastião has basic rooms that are in need of a good airing.

Hotel Rivoli (Map pp276-7; ☎ 3231 5633; hotel rivoli@uol.com.br; Rua Dom José de Barros 28; s/d quartos US$10/15, s/d apartamentos US$15/25) Good-value *quartos* (rooms with shared bathroom) and *apartamentos* (rooms with private bathroom) make Rivoli an attractive option for a range of different travelers. It's a clean, friendly place.

Albergue da Juventude Praça da Árvore (Map p268; ☎ 5071 5148; info@spalbergue.com.br; Rua Pageú 266; per person US$12, nonmembers US$16; 🖳) The best hostel in the city is actually located in Chácara Inglesa, a quiet residential area south of the center. It is in a large, modern house that's been converted into a hostel. It has excellent rooms upstairs with bunk beds and balconies. It also offers a well-equipped kitchen and pleasant lounge downstairs, and an area out back for barbecues. To get there take the north–south (Tucuruvi–Jabaquara) metro line and get off at the Praça da Árvore station. Walk north for a block and turn right at Rua Orissanga and left at Rua Caramurú. Continue north until you get to No 260 and turn onto Rua Pageú.

Sampa Hostel (Map p268; ☎ 3288 1592; Rua dos Franceses 100; per person US$10) This hostel, within walking distance of Av Paulista where you can find several good restaurants, cafés and nightclubs, isn't an official HI hostel, and its rooms are pretty basic and in need of renovation. Nevertheless, it offers reasonable lodgings, security and cooking facilities in a very good location. To get there, take the North (Tucuruvi)-South (Jabaquara) metro line to Paraiso station, change lines and get off at the next station of Brigadeiro. Walk northwest along Av Paulista (toward MASP for two blocks) and turn right down Rua Joaquin Eugênio de Lima, until Rua dos Franceses, the third street on your left.

Mid-Range
AROUND PRAÇA DA REPÚBLICA
There are lots of mid-range hotels on the streets around Praça da República. They come in clusters, by price, along certain streets.

Excelsior (Map pp276-7; ☎ 3331 0942; vendas@hotel excelsiorsp.com.br; Av Ipiranga 770; d US$50) One of the city's nicer places, the Escelsior is in a great location, just a few steps from the Praça da República, and the rooms, while not luxurious, are certainly comfortable and pleasant.

São Paulo Othon Classic (Map pp276-7; ☎ 3291-5000; fax 3291 5504; Rua Líbero Badaró 190; d US$55) One of the city's oldies but goodies, the Othon has a great location across from the Teatro Municipal and Viaduto da Chá, and it offers great service and amenities inside its large, rather imposing multistory edifice. During slow times you can often score a nice discount, so don't be afraid to ask for the lowest rate.

AROUND AVENIDA PAULISTA
Pousada Dona Ziláh (Map p268; ☎ 3062 1444; www.zilah.com; Alameda Franca 1621; s/d US$15/30) A rare find in busy Sampa, this lovely pousada (guesthouse) was once a private home and has now been converted into simple but attractive guest rooms for visitors. It's a very friendly and affordable place in an otherwise upmarket (and somewhat soulless) part of town, and the staff love to dole out advice on the city's numerous attractions.

Metropolitan Plaza (Map p268; ☎ 3288 0369; Alameda Campinas 474; s/d US$55/85) A real bargain, the rooms here have individual kitchenettes where you can make simple meals and save a bundle from your food costs. There's a very high standard of care and cleanliness at the Metropolitan and it's a delightful place. For an extra five bucks a night, you can upgrade to a deluxe room that has a separate lounge area and larger bathrooms.

THE AUTHOR'S CHOICE

L'Hotel (Map p268; ☎ 3283 500; www.lhotel.com.br; Alameda Campinas 266; d US$200; P ✖ ✖ 🖥 🖵) If you're going to splurge, then certainly you want to do it at a place that has soundproofed windows, classic and antique furniture, and a 16th-century tapestry on display in the lobby. L'Hotel has all that and more, including lovely restaurants, bars and salons scattered about the complex. And the rooms are divine too.

Pergamon (Map p268; ☎ 3120 2021; www.pergamon.com.br; Rua Frei Caneca 80; d US$125) Such chic, effortless elegance is always a joy to behold and Pergamon is a cut above many of the more well-known and expensive hotels in town. Rooms are relaxing and refreshing, and if you're lucky enough to score a spot on an upper floor you'll have a magnificent view of the city at night.

Eldorado Boulevard (Map pp276-7; ☎ 3214 1863; www.hoteiseldorado.com.br in Portuguese; Av São Luis 234; r US$50) There obviously are prettier, more traditional hotels to be had in Sao Paulo, but Eldorado Boulevard attracts such an interesting crowd. The real draw is probably the on-site, 24-hour coffee shop that's always full of whispering foreign diplomats, rakish actors and stagehands from the nearby theatres, and muckraking journalists. What could be better than getting in some first-rate people-watching without having to stray far from your home away from home?

CENTRAL SÃO PAULO

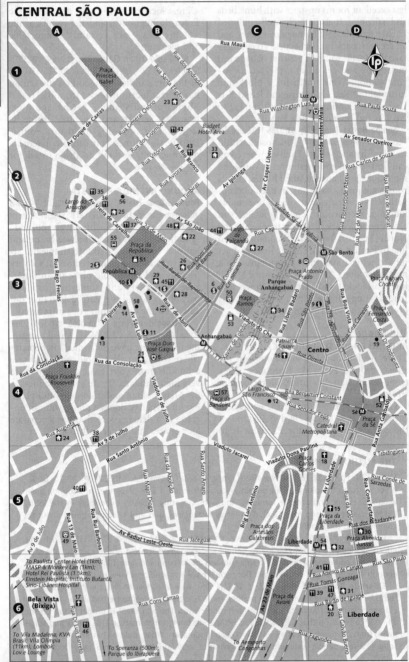

Map markers and labels: 0 – 300 m / 0 – 0.2 miles; To Museu de Arte Sacra (3km); Pinacoteca do Estado; Terminal Tietê Bus Station (5km); Rua da Cantareira; Rio Tamanduateí; Av do Estado; Mercado Municipal; Av Mercurio; Viaduto Diario Popular; Parque Dom Pedro II; Av do Estado; Parque Dom Pedro II; Av Angel Pestana; Rua de Carmo; Rua Helena Zerreno; Av Radial Leste-Oeste; Rua Cincero; Rua Teixeira Leite; Rua Juno Freire

Paulista Center (Map p268; ☎ /fax 3852 0733; Rua Consolação 2567; s/d US$15/35) Right on the edge of the Jardins section of town, Paulista is a good choice if you want to stick on the lower end of the mid-range options. It's got nice rooms and is surrounded by lots of good bars and restaurants.

Hospedaria Mantovani (Map p268; ☎ /fax 3889 8624; Rua Eliseu Guilherme 269; d US$50) Another large house that's been converted into a small hotel, the Hospedaria is clean, well kept, and staffed with amazingly friendly people.

LIBERDADE
This is a really wonderful neighborhood to stay in while in São Paulo – not only is it fascinating and fun, but it's safe.

Barão Lu (Map pp276-7; ☎ 3341 4000; www.hotel baraolu.com.br in Portuguese; Rua Barão de Iguape 80; s/d US$22/35) Decorated with Chinese touches and housing an excellent restaurant serving Shanghai food, Barão Lu does indeed make you feel like 'a very important person,' as its sign in the lobby promises.

Nikkey Palace (Map pp276-7; ☎ 3207 8511; www .nikkeyhotel.com.br; Rua Galvão Bueno 425; s/d US$50/70) Geared toward Japanese business travelers, Nikkey is nonetheless a good option for the leisure crowd. It's unlikely you'll need all the high-tech gadgetry available, but certainly the sauna and health club can be put to good use – and they're free for guests. Rooms are spare, elegant and quite beautiful.

Osaka Plaza (Map pp276-7; ☎ 3270 1311; fax 3270-1788; Praça da Liberdade149; s/d US$25/40) Right across the street from the Liberdade *metrô*, Osaka has modern amenities and spacious rooms. It's a little lacking in originality or charm, but certainly is clean and safe.

Top End
If you've got the bankroll, there are plenty of first-class establishments to enjoy around the city.

Emilianos (Map p268; ☎ 3069 4369; www.emiliano .com.br; Rua Oscar Freire 384; d US$200; P ⊠ ☒ ☐ ☒) With only 57 rooms, this boutique hotel fills up fast with jetsetters from around the world. Gorgeously appointed accommodations await you, with the discreet, attentive service one would expect at these prices. If you're really styling, arrange to be transported to and from Guarulhos

Airport in the hotel's helicopter (there's an extra charge, of course).

Maksoud Plaza (Map p268; ☎ 3145 8000; www .maksoud.com.br; Alameda Campinas 150; s/d US$90/150; P ✕ ✕ ⬛ ✕) Long touted as the city's best hotel, the Maksoud has several good restaurants on site as well as a slew of high-end amenities. Rooms are luxurious, as is the lobby and bar.

Grand Hotel Ca'd'Oro (Map pp276-7; ☎ 3236 4300; www.cadoro.com.br; Rua Augusta 129; s/d US$100/150; P ✕ ✕ ⬛ ✕) Known to give some good discounts, rates at this hotel sometimes can go as low as US$50 per room – an unbelievable steal. The décor is reminiscent of the 1950s, and rooms are quite spacious.

Gran Meliá Mofarrej (Map p268; ☎ 3146 5900; fax 3146 5901; Alameda Santos 1437; s/d US$250/350; P ✕ ✕ ⬛ ✕) This longtime-favorite, luxury hotel is still one of the best places in town to blow some cash. The pool is particularly lovely, surrounded by intense greenery, and it makes you feel like you're swimming in the Amazon. All rooms are large and beautifully decorated.

EATING

Eating is a much-loved activity in Sampa and one of the best reasons to visit this city is to sample the amazing food. Because of the city's ethnic diversity, you can find every kind of cuisine at reasonable prices. There are also a million cheap *lanchonetes* (snack bars), pizzerias and great *churrascarias* (restaurants featuring barbecued meat), and some of the best Italian and Japanese food that you'll find.

Paulistanos love to dine out, and they leave late. Although restaurants open earlier, most don't fill up until 9pm or 10pm on weekdays, and later on weekends, when many stay open until 2am or 3am.

Most of the suggested establishments listed below are easily reached by public transportation. If you have a car, or don't mind grabbing a taxi, you can choose from hundreds of other great eateries. The best listing of good restaurants is in the São Paulo pullout section of the weekly *Veja* magazine.

City Center

Ponto Chic (Map pp276-7; ☎ 3289 1480; Largo Paissandu 27; light meals US$5; ⏰ 11am-midnight) A friendly, informal restaurant only a few blocks from Praça da República, the main reason to stop here is for the famous Brazilian sandwich, the *bauru*, which Ponto Chic invented many moons ago. The *bauru* consists of beef, tomato, pickle and a mix of melted cheeses, served on French bread. Not only is it popular in urban and backland Brazil, it is also served in Paris.

Lanches Aliados (Map pp276-7; Av Rio Branco & Rua Vitória; light meals US$5; ⏰ 11am-4pm Mon-Fri, to 6pm Sat & Sun) A cheap and cheerful spot with excellent food and friendly service, Aliados packs in a whopping lunchtime crowd.

Casa Ricardo (Map pp276-7; Av Vieira de Carvalho 48; light meals US$6; ⏰ 11am-midnight) There are 20 different sandwiches at this reasonably priced establishment, each one with its own distinctive ethnic flavor.

Baby-Beef Rubaiyat (Map p268; ☎ 3141 1188; Alameda Santos 86; meals US$10; ⏰ noon-3:30pm & 7pm-midnight) If it's lean meat you seek, this great eatery in Paraiso offers the best you can get in town; near Brigadeiro metrô.

Carlino (Map pp276-7; Av Vieira de Carvalho 154; meals US$10; ⏰ 6pm-1am) An affordable Italian restaurant that's been around for more than a century, Carlino's is a good deal.

Arroz de Ouro (Map pp276-7; ☎ 3223 0219; Largo do Arouche 88; meals US$8; ⏰ 11am-3pm & 6-10pm) A great macrobiotic restaurant and shop, Arroz has vegetarian and nonvegetarian meals, all delicious.

Rei do Mate (Map pp276-7; Rua São José; sandwich & drink US$5; ⏰ 11am-9pm) Keep your eyes peeled for this chain of small *lanchonetes*, with delicious fruit juices mixed with maté (a kind of Brazilian tea) and good *salgadinhos* (snacks). This one is near Praça da República, opposite the Hotel Rivoli.

Bela Vista

This district, also known as 'Bixiga,' is loaded with Italian restaurants and bars, and has some of the city's best nightspots.

Il Cacciatore (Map pp276-7; ☎ 3120 5119; Rua Santo Antônio 855; meals US$12; ⏰ 6pm-midnight) A hugely popular Italian place, the pastas and pizzas are out of this world! It's possible even the pizza in Italy isn't this good. Open late into the evening, this is a great after-theater hang out.

Famiglia Mancini (Map pp276-7; ☎ 3256 4320; Rua Avanhandava 81; meals US$13; ⏰ 6pm-midnight) Large selection of pasta and wine means this family-run establishment is always hopping.

There are stacks of Italian restaurants on Rua 13 de Maio.

Roperto (Map pp276-7; ☎ 3284 2987; Rua 13 de Maio 634; meals US$9; ☺ 5pm-midnight) Another fabulous Italian place with big hearty pasta dishes.

Speranza (☎ 3288 8502; Rua 13 de Maio 1004; pizzas US$10) It seems this is everybody's favorite pizzeria, and it comes highly recommended by discerning patrons.

Cerqueira César Map p268

There are lots of restaurants and bars in the area bounded by Av Paulista, Rua da Consolação, Rua Estados Unidas and Alameda Ministro Rocha Azevedo. Most are fairly expensive, but there are also quite a few reasonable ones.

Frevo (☎ 3082 3434; Rua Oscar Freire 603; meals US$12; ☺ 11am-10pm) If you want to be really Paulistano, order a *beirute á moda* (a thick, hearty sandwich with different meats) along with a *chope* (draft beer). Servers calling for a *chope* yell for a *rabo de peixe* (fish tail).

Rodeio (☎ 3083 2322; Rua Haddock Lobo 1498; meals US$20; ☺ 11-1am) This is an excellent *churrascaria* and although there are cheaper places for plentiful meat in town, Rodeio is known as the best.

Esplanada Grill (☎ 3081 3199; Rua Haddock Lobo 1682; meals US$20; ☺ 11-1am) Giving the Rodeio a run for its money, the Esplanada does some mean meats as well.

Kazan (☎ 3064 3672; Rua Doutor Melo Alves 343; meals US$17; ☺ noon-1am) A favorite Japanese restaurant for Paulistanos, Kazan has sumptuous and well-presented dishes.

There are a few French restaurants in the area, but nothing cheap.

Marcel (☎ 3064 3089; Rua da Consolação 3555; meals US$25; ☺ 6pm-1am) If bucks aren't a worry, try these famous soufflés – they're very good.

Of course, almost every area has at least a few fine and reasonably priced Italian restaurants.

L'Osteria do Piero (☎ 3085 1082; Alameda Franca 1509; meals US$12; ☺ 11:30am-3pm Wed & Thu, 11:30am-3pm & 7pm-2:30am Fri, 11:30-2:30am Sat, to midnight Sun) Locals come here for the rotating specials, which range from traditional pastas to exotic pizzas and delicately grilled fish entrees.

Babbo Giovanni (☎ 3085 6363; Rua Haddock Lobo 1002; pizza for 2 US$12) Good, inexpensive pizza is the draw at Babbo's.

Massimo (☎ 3284 0311; Alameda Santos 1826; meals US$30; ☺ noon-3pm & 7:30pm-midnight Mon-Fri, noon-4:30pm & 7:30pm-1am Sat; noon-4:30pm & 7:30-11:30pm Sun) Many say this is the city's best Italian restaurant – they may be right, because the food is delicious.

Z Deli (☎ 3088 5644; Alameda Lorena 1689; light meals US$9; ☺ 11am-4pm & 6-11pm) This is a hugely popular Jewish deli that's always jam-packed.

Vegetarians will be happy to know that this neighborhood gives them many choices.

Cheiro Verde (☎ 3289 6853; Rua Peixoto Gomide 1413; light meals US$7; ☺ noon-10pm) There's a healthy fixed menu at this veggie-friendly location.

Sattva (☎ 3083 6237; Rua da Consolação 3140; light meals US$8) Lots of imaginative and plentiful vegetarian dishes are served here, and the owner puts a lot of emphasis on using fresh ingredients.

Liberdade Map pp276-7

Liberdade has lots of inexpensive Asian restaurants and spectacular food at the Sunday street fair, when stalls at the southern side of Praça da Liberdade have *gyoza* (dumplings; US$4), *sukiyaki* (US$6) and much more.

There are several good Japanese restaurants on Rua Tomás Gonzaga.

Gombe (☎ 3209 8499; Rua Tomás Gonzaga 22; meal for 2 US$25; ☺ 11:30am-2pm & 6:30-11:30pm Mon-Thu) This restaurant is always full. It has great sushi and sashimi, and excellent sukiyaki.

Kaburá (☎ 3277 2918; Rua Galvão Bueno 346; meals US$14; ☺ 7pm-2am Mon-Sat) Another local favorite, Kaburá also serves sushi, sashimi and other Japanese dishes.

Sushi-Yassu (☎ 3209 6622; Rua Tomás Gonzaga 98; meals US$18; ☺ 11am-midnight) Probably the most famous – and expensive – restaurant in Liberdade, Sushi-Yassu is a must-visit for anyone who considers themselves a connoisseur of sushi.

Self-Catering

Pão de Açúcar (Map pp276-7; Av Rio Branco) This is a well-stocked supermarket, right in the center of the city, that accepts Visa, MasterCard and American Express credit cards.

The Asian markets you can go to in Liberdade are open Sunday, when most other city supermarkets are closed.

DRINKING

Bar Brahma (Map p268; Av São João 677; ☽ 11am-midnight) Right in the heart of the central hotel district, this is the city's oldest drinking establishment, and the antique surroundings host equally dated live music. The best tables are upstairs. It's friendly and relaxing and a popular after-work hangout for many Paulistano professionals.

Pirajá (Map p268; ☎ 3815 6881; Av Brigadeiro Faria Lima 64; ☽ 5pm-2am Mon-Fri, noon-2am Sat & Sun) Inexpensive and unassuming, this is a great place to have some drinks and relax with a friend.

Cachaçaria Paulista (Map p268; ☎ 3815 4756; Rua Mourato Coelho 593, Vila Madalena; ☽ 6pm-2am Tue-Sun) There's live music every day at this bar, and of course *cachaça* (sugarcane spirit; Brazil's national drink) are the best thing on the menu, although plenty of other libations are available.

ENTERTAINMENT

Break out your dancing shoes – you're going to need them! São Paulo's nightlife rivals the excitement of New York's (and costs almost the same, too). Everyone is out playing until the wee hours, and you can get stuck in traffic snarls at 3am! You'll need money and transport to get the full effect, but luckily Paulistanos have also begun to embrace the joys of the pub crawl – British-style pubs populate the Jardins area and Rua Franz Schubert. For the best list of constantly-changing events, check out www.baladas .com.br and www.obaoba.com.br (both in Portuguese).

Nightclubs

Expect cover charges (ranging from US$7 to US$20 depending on the location) at most nightclubs. Drinks can be expensive – most locals do their imbibing in the street outside, buying from enterprising vendors who have set up makeshift bars (sometimes out of the back of a car) and are selling libations at bargain prices. Tipping bartenders and wait staff is optional at most clubs (meaning it's usually not done). If you choose to sprinkle a few modest tips around, you will certainly be thanked with special service.

Kissing is a common sight at these clubs – young Brazilians sometimes exchange kisses after just a few words. It's viewed as harmless flirtation as long as neither party strenuously objects. Don't be offended if someone you just met moves in for a smooch – just politely pull back and they'll get the message. If someone persists in trying to get some contact, distance yourself as quickly as possible.

The hottest district for clubbing these days is Vila Olímpia, mobbed by the young and beautiful 24/7.

Ibiza (Map p268; ☎ 3045 0388; Rua Casa do Ator 1169; admission US$7; ☽ 10pm-4am Thu-Sat, 7pm-4am Sun) Three huge dance floors, each with its own type of music, translates into a lot of late-night dancing for young Paulistanos. Preferred by those in their late teens and very early 20s.

Mondo (Map p268; ☎ 3045 0303; Av Doutor Cardoso de Melo 1261; admission US$15; ☽ 11:30pm-5am Tue-Sat) One dance floor plus three bars equals some tight and sweaty dancing. Mondo caters to a slightly older crowd – say mid-to-late 20s – and plays a lot of popular tunes.

Blood (Map p268; ☎ 5641 0653; Rua Castro Verde 480, in Morumbi; admission US$13; ☽ 10pm-5am Tue-Sat) Blood was once an old factory and the space has been put to good use. There's a pool table, two dance floors and a big bar. The average age range is 18 to 30.

Santa Aldeia (Map p268; ☎ 3845 9235; Rua Beira Rio 113; admission US$15; ☽ 6pm-3am Tue-Sat, 3pm-3am Sun) Lots of options here – techno, pop, rock, and on Sundays, Brazilian music. Two dance floors, and a crowd that tends to be between 18 and 24 years old.

Café Piu-Piu (☎ 3258 8066; Rua 13 de Maio 134; admission US$7; ☽ 9pm-3am Tue-Thu, 10pm-3am Fri & Sat) One dance floor with a combination of rock songs, Brazilian pop music, and blues from North America. Popular with young twentysomethings.

Lombok (Map p268; Rua Olimpiadas 272; admission US$12; ☽ 9pm-4am Tue-Sun) This place has great electronica beats on three pulsating floors crammed with up to 3500 18-to-25-year-olds per night.

KVA Brasil (Map p268; Rua Cardeal Arco Verde 2978; admission US$10; ☽ 8pm-4am Tue-Sun) Barflies should head to the Vila Madalena district to check out KVA Brasil (one floor plays *forró* and samba, the other techno).

Live Music

Bourbon Street Music Club (Map p268; ☎ 5095 1643; Rua dos Chanés 127; admission US$12; ☽ 9pm-3am Tue-Sun)

A classic spot in the Moema district, Bourbon Street features jazz and Dixieland.

Mistura Brasileira (☎ 3299 8866; Rua Alfreres de Magalhães 103; admission US$5; ☺ 9pm-3am Thu-Sun) For great samba music and dancing, head out to the Santana district and check out Mistura.

Classical Music

There's a steady stream of opera and classical concerts in the Teatro Municipal; check there or at the tourist office to get tickets. Free classical concerts are held every Sunday at 11am in the Parque do Ibirapuera.

Gay & Lesbian Venues

São Paulo has a lively gay scene, and the straight/gay mix in gay places is pretty good. Rua Frei Caneca in Cerqueira César is home to many stores, restaurants and clubs that are frequented by gay, lesbian, bisexual and transgendered people.

Lov.e Lounge (Map p268; ☎ 3044 1613; Rua Pequetita 189; admission US$9; ☺ 11pm-5am Thu-Sun) This place opens its doors to straight and gay alike for nightly raves, with techno music blaring into the wee hours.

Restaurante Spot (Map p268; ☎ 3284 6131; Alameda Maestro Rocha Azevedo 72; admission US$12) This is a popular meeting place near Consolação *metrô*. People come to see and be seen, and sample the delicious salads.

Clube Massivo (Map p268; ☎ 3085 5830; Alameda Itu 1548; admission US$6; ☺ midnight-8am Tue-Sun) A favorite place for gay, lesbian and straights, Clube Massivo is always a big stop on the late-night dance circuit.

SHOPPING

Shopping is almost as important to Paulistanos as eating out. Those who can afford it like to shop in one of the many large malls that dot the city. More interesting are the many markets and fairs that take place around town, especially on weekends.

Feira da República (Map pp276-7; Praça da República; ☺ 8am-2pm Sun) The most popular market, this is a great place for people-watching (and getting pickpocketed). Offerings include Brazilian precious stones, leather gear, wood carvings, handmade lace and paintings. Some of the local painters are excellent.

Street fair (Map pp276-7; ☺ all day Sunday) Liberdade, the Asian district, has a big fair in the area surrounding the Liberdade metro sta-

tion; it's only five minutes from the center by metro.

CEAGESP market (Map p268; Av Doutor Gastão Vidigal) In the district of Jaguaré, this huge market is the center of food distribution for the whole city, and it's quite a sight. The best time to go is Tuesday to Friday 7am to noon, when there's a flower market as well. On other days, it just has lots and lots of fresh produce.

Feira de Antiguidades do MASP (Map p268; ☺ 9am-5pm Sun) This is a popular market full of old odds and ends held below the massive underbelly of the MASP building.

An excellent market takes place every weekend in **Embu**, 28km west of São Paulo, just off Hwy BR-116 toward Curitiba. It's renowned for its rustic furniture, ceramics, paintings and leather items, and you'll find things here from all over Brazil. If you can't make it to the fair on the weekend, it's still worth coming during the week, as most of the artists have permanent shops and there are stacks of handicrafts stores. While there, have a look at the **Igreja Jesuítico NS do Rosário** on Largo dos Jesuítas, in the main square; it contains a small sacred-art museum, as well as the first organ ever made in Brazil.

GETTING THERE & AWAY
Air

From São Paulo's airports there are flights to everywhere in Brazil and to many of the world's major cities. São Paulo is the Brazilian hub for many international airlines and thus the first stop for many travelers. The international airport is **Aeroporto Guarulhos** (☎ 6445 2945; 30km east of the center; airport code GRU). Most domestic flights go from **Aeroporto Congonhas** (Map p268; ☎ 5090 9000; 14km south of the center; airport code CGH).

Most of the major airlines have offices on Av São Luís, near the Praça da República. They include the following:

TAM (Map p268; ☎ 3256 1515; Av São Luís 276)
Varig (Map p268; ☎ 3258-4020; Rua da Consolação 362)
VASP (Map pp276-7; ☎ 3255-3131/ 0800-998277; Av São Luís 123)

Bus

São Paulo has four different bus stations, all accessible by *metrô*. If you need to check which terminal services your destination consult www.socicam.com.br (in Portuguese) or, in São Paulo, call ☎ 3235 0322.

The **Terminal Tietê bus station** (Map p268; ☎ 32 35 0322; Tietê metrô station) is quite easy to reach. The *metrô* is connected to it. It's an enormous building but quite easily navigated. There is an information desk in the middle of the main concourse. Buses leave for destinations throughout Brazil and for international destinations. Bus tickets are sold on the 1st floor, and international ticket booths are at the southern end of the terminal – turn left from the *metrô*. Some of the international destinations served are Asunción in Paraguay (US$50, 20 hours), Buenos Aires in Argentina (US$125, 36 hours), Montevideo in Uruguay (US$100, 30 hours) and Santiago in Chile (US$120, 56 hours).

Domestic buses leave from the Terminal Tietê for Belém (US$114, 46 hours), Belo Horizonte (US$21, eight hours), Brasília (US$37, 14 hours), Cuiabá (US$40, 13 hours), Curitiba (US$15, six hours), Florianópolis (US$30, 12 hours), Foz do Iguaçu (US$40, 15 hours), Porto Velho (US$109, 46 hours), Rio (regular/*leito* (sleeper) US$15/25, six hours), Salvador (US$68, 32 hours) and Ubatuba (US$14, four hours).

Buses to Santos, Guarujá and São Vicente leave every half-hour from a separate bus station – the Terminal Intermunicipal do Jabaquara (Map p268), which is at the end of the southern metrô line (metrô Jabaquara). There is also the Bresser Terminal in the east zone district of Brás, with services to the south of Minas Gerais state and Belo Horizonte, and the Barra Funda Terminal in the west zone, near the Latin America Memorial. All stations have or are close to metrô stops.

GETTING AROUND

Stay away from Kombis, illegal vans that charge through the city streets at amazing speeds – they're illegal, dangerous and frankly, just not worth the hassle.

To/From the Airport

Aeroporto de Congonhas (Map p268; ☎ 5090 9000) is the city's closest airport – 14km south of the city center. Taxis at the front of the terminal charge about US$15 to the center. For buses to the center, walk out of the terminal and then to your right, where you'll see a busy street with a pedestrian overpass. Head to the overpass but don't cross; you should see a crowd of people waiting for the buses

along the street. Alternatively, ask for the bus to Terminal Bandeiras. The trip takes about an hour and the last bus leaves at around 1am.

Aeroporto São Paulo/Guarulhos, São Paulo's international airport, is 30km east of the city. There are 'Airport Service' buses to Praça da República, the Terminal Tietê bus station and Congonhas airport every 30 to 40 minutes. All cost US$10 and leave from the stop just in front of the arrivals terminal. Another bus service from São Paulo's international airport (about US$10), does a circuit of 11 four- and five-star hotels in the center and the Jardim Paulista area. From the international airport to the center, a taxi will cost about US$15.

To get to the Guarulhos airport, you can catch 'Airport Services' buses from Praça da República, the Terminal Tietê bus station and Aeroporto de Congonhas. Alternatively, take the *metrô* to Bresser and grab a shuttle bus (US$0.30, 40 minutes) from the small **bus terminal** (☎ 6692 5191) on Rua do Hipódromo.

Bus

Buses are slow, crowded during rush hours and not too safe. The tourist information booths are excellent sources of information about buses. Bus transfer points are at Praça da República and bustling Terminal Bandeiras, where you can catch buses to far-flung destinations within the city.

Car

There are many car-hire offices in town, but the enormous and continuous traffic is perhaps best avoided. Rely on buses and the metro instead.

Subway

A combination of subway and walking is the easiest way to see the city. São Paulo's efficient **metro** (www.metro.sp.gov.br/ingles/index.asp; one-way US$0.55, round-trip US$0.90, 10-trip pass US$3; ☉ 5am-midnight) is one of the best in the world and its clean, modern stations, often decorated with huge murals by local artists, could be considered attractions in their own right. And it's cheap, too.

Taxi

Usually taxi services are metered, make sure it goes on or you could get a nasty surprise when it's time to pay – a five-minute cab ride is usually around US$3 to US$5. **Radio taxis** (☎ 3146 4000) will pick you up from anywhere in the city. **Associação São Paulo de Taxi** (☎ 5073 2814) and **Use Taxi** (☎ 5583 2000) are two other reliable car services that will make arrangements to chauffeur people around town and to certain nearby attractions in São Paulo state.

PAULISTA COAST

UBATUBA

☎ 0xx12 / pop 65,000

Ubatuba is a stunning length of shoreline on the northern São Paulo coast. The preeminent beach resort for well-to-do Paulistanos, it has elegant beach homes and hotels, especially south of the town of Ubatuba, which is really not a very attractive city. To the north, all the way to Paraty, the beaches are wilder and cleaner – and often deserted.

Orientation & Information

The town is centered on Praça 13 de Maio, which is just a few blocks from the **bus station** (Rua Conceição). Useful businesses include the following:

Banco do Brasil (cnr Rua Dona Maria Alves & Rua Carvalho)

Post office (Rua Dona Maria Alves)

Telephone post (Rua Professor Thomaz Galhardo 81)

Tourist office (☎ 3832-4255; 🕑 8am-6pm) Where Rua Professor Thomaz Galhardo hits the bay; it has useful maps of surrounding beaches.

Beaches

Within the district of Ubatuba, there are some 74 beaches and 15 islands. Praia Vermelha, a couple of kilometers southeast of town, is a fine beach with *barracas* (kiosks) and some surfing.

Regular buses run along the coastal road. Other recommended beaches south of Ubatuba include **Enseada** (8km), **Flamengo** (12km, on the Ponta do Flamengo), and **do Lázaro** (16km) and **Domingos Dias** (18km), both just off the highway. The big, loud party scene is 6km south of Ubatuba at **Praia Grande**.

North of town, the beaches are hidden away down the steep hillside. They're harder to find, but good for boogie boarding and

surfing and well worth the effort. The best are **Vermelha do Norte** (9km); **Itamambuca** (15km), where the river meets the sea, **Promirim** (23km), and **Ubatumirim** (33km).

Port

The port is at Praia de Saco da Ribeira, 12km south of Ubatuba. You can book daily cruises (US$16, four hours) into the Baía da Enseada and out to the Ilha Anchieta. Ilha Anchieta is a lovely island, now protected by the national government, which offers rare glimpses of beautiful fish and birds undisturbed in their natural habitats. You can also see the local Tamar Project, which protects native turtles and their eggs. These mini-cruises offer a great view of Brazil's coastline and beautiful deep-green waters.

Cruise reservations can be made at the tourism office and many hotels and pousadas also offer such services, but most of the time you can mosey down to the docks and talk to the boat owners directly. This is not a state-run deal; like much of the water-based fun on this coastal area, it's pretty informal. The best way, and generally the cheapest, for people to do a cruise is to ask around down at the port – it won't be hard to find people who are willing to set you up for a run around the nearby islands.

Sleeping

If you don't have a car, the center is the most convenient place to stay. From here you can catch local buses to some of the beaches.

BUDGET

Pousada Columbus (☎ 3423 2136; Rua Gurany 536; s/d US$10/18) About 15 minutes by foot or US$4 by taxi from the town center, this pousada is clean and organized, and rooms are a good value.

Hotel Xareu (☎ 3432 1525; Rua Jordão Homem da Costa 413; s/d US$16/27) A slightly pricier option near the bus station, but still a good deal.

Hotel São Nicolau (☎ 3432 3310; Rua Conceição 213; s/d US$16/30) Another clean, safe option near the bus station, this hotel includes breakfast.

Camping Guarani (☎ 3442 0076; on Praia do Lázaro; campsite per person US$7) The facilities for campers are good and secure here, and there are also cabins for five to eight people. Be sure to bring mosquito repellent.

MID-RANGE & TOP END

Ubatuba Palace (☎ 3432 1500; Coronel Domiciano 500; s/d US$60/90) The town's finest hotel, the Ubatuba Palace has lovely rooms at bargain prices, including breakfast and dinner.

Pousada Ana Doce (☎ 3442 0102; Travessa JK 54; s/d US$30/45) A small and very pleasant pousada just a couple of blocks from the beach, the Ana Doce offers spotlessly clean and comfortable rooms; try to get one with a little deck where you can dangle your feet in the pool.

Hotel Solar das Águas Cantantes (☎ 3442 0178; Praia do Lázaro; s/d US$35/48; 🐾) This hotel has stylish rooms, a lovely courtyard garden, a large lounge and games room upstairs, and a good swimming pool. The highlight here is the hotel's restaurant.

Recanto das Toninhas (☎ 3842 1410; Praia das Toninhas; s/d US$100/125; 🐾) This is an immense resort with gorgeous rooms overlooking either the pool or the ocean. Beautiful grounds, great tennis court.

Eating

Buchneiros (Rua Conceição 61; pizzas US$6; ⏲ 11am-4pm & 6-10pm) A quaint pizzeria with a huge wood-burning oven, Buchneiros has all sorts of tasty treats.

Cantina Perequim (Rua Guarani 385; dinner US$8; ⏲ 11am-4pm & 6-9pm Tue-Sat, 11am-3pm Sun) Another Italian restaurant and very popular with locals.

Kilo & Cia (Rua Dona Maria Alves 393; lunch US$5; ⏲ 11am-4pm) One of the best self-serve buffet lunches in the center is done at Kilo & Cia.

Refúgio da Louca (Rua Guarani 737; buffet dinner US$9; ⏲ 6-11pm Tue-Fri, to midnight Sat & Sun) For dinner, the best place to eat is this little self-serve place, about 15 minutes' walk south of the center in the suburb of Itaguá.

Peixe com Banana (☎ 3832 1712; Av Guarani 255; dinner US$14; ⏲ noon-11pm Mon, Tue & Thu-Sun, closed Apr, Jun & Aug) For great seafood head to Peixe com Banana. The signature dish, after which the hotel is named, is fish wrapped in banana leaves and cooked in an earthen oven, then topped with fresh bananas. It's delicious.

Hotel Solar das Águas Cantantes (☎ 3442 0178; Praia do Lázaro; dinner with drinks US$20; ⏲ noon-10:30pm daily, 6-10pm Apr-Jun & Aug-Nov, sometimes closed Tue) An outstanding seafood restaurant, the Solar is known for delicious *moquecas*!

Getting There & Around

There are two bus stations in Ubatuba, less than two blocks apart. The main **bus station** (☎ 3432-6912; Rua Professor Thomaz Galhardo 513) is between Rua Hans Staden and Rua Cunhambebe and has buses to Paraty (US$3, 1½ hours, three a day from 9:40am to 8:40pm), Rio (US$14, five hours, five a day from 6am to 11pm) and São Paulo (US$14, four hours, eight a day from 12:30pm to 6:30pm).

The other bus station, on Rua Conceição between Rua Hans Staden and Rua Ap Santos Velloso, serves local destinations.

For São Sebastião, get a local bus to Caraguátatuba (US$1.20, 40 minutes), then change in front of the main bus station in Caraguátatuba to a São Sebastião bus.

Heading southwest along the coast from Ubatuba, you reach Caraguátatuba (54km), São Sebastião and Ilhabela (75km) and Santos (205km). After Caraguátatuba the road begins to deteriorate and an unending procession of speed bumps rears its ugly head.

SÃO SEBASTIÃO

☎ 0xx12 / pop 58,000

The coastal town of São Sebastião faces the Ilha de São Sebastião (popularly known as 'Ilhabela'), a 15-minute ferry trip away (see p268). Huge oil tankers anchor in the calm channel between the island and mainland, waiting to unload at São Sebastião. Most visitors who stay here do so either because they can't find lodging at Ilhabela or in order to enjoy the channel's excellent windsurfing conditions.

Information

Banco do Brasil (Rua Duque de Caxais 20) It has a Visa Plus ATM.

Tourist office (☎ 3452-1808; Av Doutor Altino Arantes 174; ⏲ 8am-6pm Mon-Fri, 10am-6pm Sat & Sun) On the waterfront.

Sleeping & Eating

Hotel Roma (☎ 3452-1016; Praça Major João Fernandes 174; s/d US$20/33; 🐾) Simple rooms with rickety beds are all you're going to get here, but it's clean.

Pousada da Sesmaria (☎ 3452-2347; Rua São Gonçalo 190; s/d US$40/50) In the center of town, this is more of a mid-range option, with prettier rooms and more amenities.

Pousada da Ana Doce (☎ 3452-1615; Rua Expedicionários Brasileiros 196; s/d US$25/38) Probably one of the best places in town is the lovely and spotless Ana Doce, which has lovely rooms.

Along the waterfront you'll find several good fish restaurants, including **Super Flipper** (mains from US$10) and, next door, **El Greco** (mains from US$10); both have main courses that are usually big enough for two.

Getting There & Away
The **bus station** (Praça da Amizade 10) has regular service to São Paulo (US$14), Rio (US$20), Santos (US$7) and Boiçucanga (US$5).

The Rio–Santos highway is slow going between São Sebastião and Santos as there are a zillion speed bumps along the coastal road. The quickest route to São Paulo (200km) is to head north from Caraguátatuba on Hwy SP-099.

ILHABELA
☎ 0xx12 / pop 28,000 (winter), 120,000 (summer)
This is the biggest island along the Brazilian coast and its volcanic origins are evident from the steeply rising peaks, which are beautifully covered by dense tropical jungle. There are 360 waterfalls, and the flatlands are filled with sugarcane plantations. The island is known for its excellent jungle hiking and its fine *cachaça*. Be aware that in the height of summer the bugs are murder, especially the little bloodsuckers known as *borrachudos*. Use plenty of insect repellent at all times. That's also when the island is packed with vacationing Paulistas – there's lots of nightlife and good times, but if you're looking for solitude come at another time of year.

Information
The **tourist office** (☎ 3896 1091; Rua Bartolomeu de Gusmão 140; ⏰ 9am-6pm Mon-Fri, 10am-4pm Sat, to 2pm Sun) is located on the outskirts of the village. Stop by to pick up its excellent map of the island. For those bringing a car to the island, avoid huge lines at the **ferry** (☎ 0800-55 5510) by booking in advance.

Sights
Vila Ilhabela, on the northwestern part of the island, has quite a few well-preserved colonial buildings, including the slave-built **Igreja NS da Ajuda** (dating from 1532); the **Fazenda Engenho d'Agua** (1582), in Itaquanduba; and **Fazenda Santa Carmen**, at Feiticeira beach.

Beaches
There are more than 50 beaches on the island, but most of them are accessible only by boat or on foot.

Of the sheltered beaches on the north side of the island, **Praia Jabaquara** is recommended; it's accessed by a 5km-long walking trail. On the east side, where the surf is stronger, try **Praia dos Castelhanos** (good camping and surf), **Praia do Gato** and **Praia da Figueira**. From Borrifos you can take a four-hour walk to **Bonete**, a windy surf beach lying on the southern side of the island.

Waterfalls
Two kilometers inland from Perequê beach (near the ferry terminal), **Cachoeira das Tocas** is made up of various small waterfalls with accompanying deep pools and water slides. It costs US$5 to get in; the price includes insect repellent. It's a great place to go if you're sick of the beach. **Cachoeira de Água Branca**, in the middle of the jungle at the southern end of the island, is another waterfall to check out. Access is from Veloso beach.

Sleeping & Eating
Reservations are a good idea, especially on weekends. Many choose to stay in São Sebastião, where hotels are cheaper.

Pousada Caravela (☎ 3472 8295; www.caravela residence.com.br in Portuguese; Rua Carlos Rizzini 70; ste US$40) Near the ferry terminal, this pousada has delightful two-room suites with cooking facilities; it's best to book in advance.

Pousada dos Hibiscos (☎ 3896 1375; www.pousada doshibiscos.com.br; Av Pedro Paula de Morais 714; s/d US$45/70) Out on the beach, this place has lovely rooms just 800m from town, south of the yacht club.

Hotel Costa Azul (☎ 3472 1365; www.hotelcosta azul.com.br in Portuguese; Rua Francisco Gomes da Silva Prado 71; s/d US$50/70) Just north of town is the Costa Azul, with big rooms and attractive surroundings.

There are lots of camping grounds near Barra Velha, where the ferry stops, and just a bit further south, at Praia do Curral.

There is certainly no lack of expensive hotels on the island; the tourist office has a comprehensive list.

Maison Joly (☎ 3896 1201; www.maisonjoly.com.br; Rua Antonio Lisboa Alves 728; d US$200; ✗ 🖭 🖳 🖭) In a sublime location, the Maison Joly offers every amenity imaginable. Children under 12 not accepted; perfect for romantic couples looking for a getaway.

At the traffic circle near the tourist office is a good self-serve ice-cream place. For self-catering, hit the **Ilha da Princesa supermarket** (Av Princesa Isabel 2467) in Barra Velha. In Vila Ilhabela itself there are a few good, cheap *lanchonetes*: two in the pedestrian mall, and a couple on Rua da Padroeira.

Cheiro Verde (Rua da Padroeira 109; meals US$5) The best place in town for a massive *prato feito* (plate of the day).

Convés (Rua da Padroeira 139; sandwich US$6; 11am-10pm) This is a popular and tasty sandwich shop.

Deck (3472 2307; Av Almirante Tamandaré 805; dinner US$12; noon-10pm Tue-Sun) A bit further from Vila Ilhabela is Deck, a popular seafood restaurant that also makes good pizzas. It sometimes closes at 9pm in the low season.

There are lots of great places along the waterfront and near the dock to nurse a *chope* and stare over the ocean.

Getting There & Around

The 15-minute ferry between São Sebastião and Ilhabela runs every half-hour from 5:30am to midnight (often until much later in summer). Cars cost US$4.50, motorcycles US$2.50 and it's free for pedestrians. There are direct buses to São Paulo; the **ticket office** (3472-1869) is on the same street as the tourist office near the old airstrip, Campo de Aviação.

A road runs the length of the western coast. Another unsealed road (22km) crosses the island. To get to the other side of the island requires either a 4WD, **taxi** (3974 1046), a boat trip or a good strong pair of hiking legs.

BOIÇUCANGA & AROUND

 0xx12 / pop 5300

A laid-back surfer town, charming Boiçucanga is well served by simple hotels and decent restaurants. There's good surf at nearby Maresias and Camburi, plus friendly people and some good walks into the Mata Atlântica (Atlantic rain forest).

Information

A good source of information here is José Mauro B Pinto e Silva, who runs a tourist information service called **Amart** (3465 1453; zemauro@boicucanga.com.br; Av Walkir Vergani 319).

An English-speaking budget traveler, José is a friendly guy who can help you out with just about anything, including cheap places to stay, Internet access, surfing and windsurfing information and details on treks into the forest.

Beaches

Some great beaches are strung along this stretch of coastline, all accessible by bus. Both **Maresias** (7km east), and **Camburi** (5km west) are great surf beaches. A creek and a small island divide Camburi – the western end is bigger, rougher and good for surfing, and the eastern end is calmer and good for swimming. **Barra do Sahy** (10km west) also has calmer water.

Islands

There are many nearby offshore islands you can visit (one called Alcatraz). **José Benedito dos Santos** (9715 1879) or **Lili** (9714 3732) can arrange to drop you off in the morning and pick you up at night. You can't camp. Trips average US$20 round-trip per person or US$13 per person for three or more people.

Sleeping

The abbreviation s/n (*sem número*; not numbered) is sometimes used here.

BUDGET

There are camping grounds at all the beaches.

Camping do Vovô Kido (3465 1157; campsite US$2, s/d US$6/10) In Boiçucanga, this place is a popular campsite and also has very simple bed-in-a-box *quartos*. To get here, head to Boiçucanga beach, which is just a few minutes from the bus station. As you approach, you'll see signs for this and other campsites popping up on the road.

Pousada Boiçucanga (3465 1910; Av Walkir Vergani 522, Boiçucanga; s/d US$13/23) One of the simpler hotels in town, just opposite the Casa Pedra restaurant, this pousada is still of very good value.

Dani Hotel (3465 1299; Av Walkir Vergani 455, Boiçucanga; s/d US$24/30) You'll get clean rooms in attractive surroundings at Dani, but not too much more.

MID-RANGE & TOP END

Picturesque Camburi is very popular and fun. There are several places to stay, but off-season weekdays can be very quiet and some places close; call in advance.

Pousada das Praias (☎ 3865 1474; www.pousada daspraias.com.br; Rua Piau 70, Camburi; d US$40) An enjoyable top-end place just off the main road near the eastern end of the beach, this pousada has good rustic-style rooms that go as high as US$100 on weekends.

Maresias tends to be pricier than Boiçucanga, but it may be well worth spending the extra money to have access to the beautiful beach, especially if you intend to surf.

Tubes Maresias (☎ 3465 6107; Rua Silvina Auta Sales 44, Maresias; s/d US$20/30) Spacious chalets with cooking facilities, but a little challenging to get to, Tubes is a great place. Ask to get off the coastal bus at the bridge on the eastern end of the beach. Walk along Rua Nova Iguaçu, just east of the bridge and keep going until you get to Rua Silvina Auta.

There are two hotels, also near the eastern end of the beach, that are worth a look.

Pousada Azul Banana (☎ 34657167; www.pousada daspraias.com.br in Portuguese; Rua da Barra 15, Maresias; d US$53) Spotless doubles that are very affordable during low season are the big attraction at this pousada.

Hotel Villa del Mare (☎ 3465 6744; Rua Nova Iguaçu 349, Maresias; s/d US$50/70; 🏊) Another option is this hotel, which has pleasant *apartamentos*, a pool, spa and sauna; rates are higher at peak times.

Eating
Big Pão (snacks US$1-5; 🕐 until late) In Boiçucanga this bakery, on the bend in the main road opposite the Dani Hotel, has good snacks.

Casa Pedra (☎ 3465 1675; Av Walkir Vergani s/n, Boiçucanga; mains US$9-15; 🕐 11am-4pm & 6-10pm Tue-Sun) Across the street from the bakery, Casa Pedra is a pleasant little restaurant backing on to the beach.

Maresias has lots of restaurants on the beachfront.

Getting There & Around
Buses run along the coast every 30 to 40 minutes from about 6am to about 8pm. There are a few bus stops along the main road, one right in front of the Big Pão bakery.

GUARUJÁ
☎ 0xx13 / pop 285,000
Guarujá, 87km southeast of São Paulo, is the biggest beach resort in the state. The beaches are urban and often get crowded because the town happens to be the closest resort to São Paulo. Plenty of hotels, restaurants and boutiques run along the beachfront. There's surf along **Praia do Tombo**.

Information
The **tourist information office** (☎ 3387 7199; Rua Quintino Bocaiúva 183; 🕐 7am-6pm) is helpful, with maps and accommodation suggestions.

Sleeping & Eating
Pensão Europa (☎ 3386 6879; Rua Rio de Janeiro 193; s/d US$13/25) A great budget option one block from Praia das Pitangueiras, this pension has simple rooms that double in price at peak time.

Hotel Rio (☎ 3386 6081; Rua Rio de Janeiro 131; s/d US$30/50) Down the street is the small and popular Rio, with comfortable rooms.

Pousada MiraMar (☎ 3354 1453; Rua Antônio Marques 328; s/d US$30/40) Inside a lovely little house a couple of blocks from Praia do Tombo; some of the rooms have balconies.

Restaurants and bars line the waterfront area.

Nutris (Av Leomil 538; meals US$5; 🕐 11am-5pm) A good self-serve place with a decent assortment of vegetarian dishes, Nutris also has some meatier stuff.

Restaurante do Joca (Av Miguel Stéfano 3035, Praia da Enseada; dinner for 2 US$15; 🕐 11am-midnight high season, 6-10pm Wed-Sun low season) Great seafood dishes that are large enough for two to share always draw big crowds to Joca.

Getting There & Around
Guarujá is on a large island separated from the mainland by the Canal de Bertioga. The **bus station** (☎ 3386 2325) is on the edge of town on Via Santos Dumont. From there, catch local bus No 1 or 15 (US$2) to the beach. Buses 52 and 25 are good for getting around the town.

Buses leave every half-hour for São Paulo – the US$6 trip takes just over an hour. You'll pass through Cubatão, one of the most polluted places in the world. Depressed? Just think – it used to look even worse than it does now.

IGUAPE & AROUND
☎ 0xx13 / pop 28,000
Founded by the Portuguese in 1538, Iguape is one of the oldest towns in Brazil. It

retains some of its colonial charm, mainly in the form of somewhat dilapidated 19th-century mansions.

Information

Tourist information is available from the **Prefeitura** (Rua 15 de Novembro 272; 8-11am & 1-5 pm).

Sights

The town attractions are the **Museu de Arte Sacra**, in the Igreja do Rosário, and the **Mirante do Morro do Espia**, a lookout with a good view of the port and surrounding area. Iguape's **Museo Histórico e Arqueológico** (Rua das Neves 45) has samples of bones, ceramics and other objects from 5000-year-old civilizations.

Barra do Ribeira, the closest beach that is good for swimming on the mainland, is very popular with surfers. You'll have to grab a boat from Iguape to get there unless you have a car.

Also of interest is **Ilha Comprida**, a small island (86km long but only 3km wide) that faces Iguape. The island is covered with gorgeous forest and an uninterrupted beach stretches the entire Atlantic-facing length of the island. There are always ferries (US$1.25) doing the five-minute crossing to the northern part of the island and, until 7pm, buses take passengers across the island to the beach. It's also now connected to the mainland by a bridge (US$1.25 to cross) and in the summer months it can get really crowded. To go even further off the beaten track, head for the beautiful **Praia da Juréia**, 40km northeast of Iguape.

Iguape also serves as a great base for visiting the **Estacão Ecologica Juréia-Itatins**. For information on organized tours to Juréia contact the **park officer** (3849 1293; Av São Pedro 189, Barra do Ribeira).

Sleeping & Eating

Pousada Solar Colonial (3841 1591; Praça da Basílica 30; s/d US$15/25) A colonial building right on Largo da Basílica (the main church and plaza), this pousada offers good, clean rooms.

Silvi Hotel (3841 1421; Rua Candida Trigo 515; s/d US$10/20) Near the main plaza with clean and spacious accommodations, Silvi is a fair bargain.

Pousada Casa Grande (3841 1920; Rua Maj Rebello 768; s/d US$10/25) A nice, modern building with bright rooms and comfortable surroundings, Casa Grande is popular with couples and tends to book up on weekends.

Eating in Iguape means seafood, seafood and more seafood.

Panela Velha (3841 1869; Rua 15 de Novembro 190; meals US$13; 11am-4pm & 6:30-10:30pm) Touted as the home of the best seafood in town, with immense main courses, Panela Velha is a must-do.

Itacurumins (Rua Porto do Rosário 2; meals US$7; 11am-4pm & 7-11pm Thu-Tue, closed Wed & Mar-Nov) A favorite for delicious seafood, cooked from the local catch of the day. Packing them in during the high season, this place is apt to be closed at other times of the year.

Getting There & Around

Four buses daily (from 6am to 8pm) travel between Iguape and São Paulo (US$15, four hours).

For Cananéia, take a bus to Pariquero and switch there. Regular buses cross the bridge to Ilha Comprida. If you have a 4WD it is possible to drive along the long, flat beach on Ilha Comprida and take the ferry across to Cananéia (US$1.25). There is a daily bus (US$1.50) to Barra do Ribeira leaving at 6:30am.

THE BACHELOR OF CANANÉIA

One of the more notorious characters of Brazil's past was a man who was known only as the 'Bacharel de Cananéia' (Bachelor of Cananéia). As the story goes, he lived among Brazilian Indians like a white king, with six wives, 200 slaves and more than a thousand Indian warriors ready to defend him. All the coastal indigenous tribes, from São Paulo to Santa Catarina, feared and respected him – he was virtually the ruler of Brazil's southern coast.

No one knows for sure, but historians believe the Bacharel arrived as a convict on one of the first exploratory voyages of Amerigo Vespucci, in 1501. He remained in Brazil for at least 30 years, profiting fabulously from the slave trade. The Bacharel de Cananéia is thought to have been the first European resident in South America.

CANANÉIA

☎ 0xx13 / pop 14,000

This quiet but pretty little town was founded in 1531 and is considered one of the oldest settlements in Brazil. It was the first port of call for Martim Afonso de Sousa's fleet of Portuguese colonists and a few attractions remain from that epoch.

Beaches

The beaches of **Ilha Comprida** are only 10 minutes away by boat. To the south are the popular **Prainha** and **Ipanema** beaches, along with a waterfall.

But the highlight of the area is a two-hour boat ride away: **Ilha do Cardoso**, an ecological reserve with some nice deserted beaches and walking tracks. **Lagamar Boat** (☎ 3851 1613; Rua Silvino D'Araujo 16) runs organized boat trips (US$10) to the Ilha do Cardoso beaches.

Sleeping & Eating

Cananéia gets busy and hotels are often booked up during peak holiday season (January and February) and on weekends all summer long.

Costa Azul Club (☎ 3851 8288; www.hotelcosta zul.com.br; Estrada da Ponte, Km 06; s/d US$20/40; ⓟ ⌧ ⌧) This resort hotel is on the highway leading into town. It's got gorgeous grounds with lovely flowers and trees. Some rooms have four beds, so large groups can get a great deal. Tours and boat rides available.

Beira-Mar (☎ 3851 1115; Av Beira-Mar 219; s/d US$8/17) You won't be overwhelmed by the rather plain exterior, but Beira-Mar has some great rooms for good prices.

Hotel Pousada da Néia (☎ 3851 1580; Av Independencia 150; s/d US$20/25) A basic hotel, da Néia has clean, spacious rooms.

Pousada Caropá (☎ 3851 1601; Av Beira-Mar 13; s/d US$30/36) This renovated, historic building is on the plaza and overlooks the ferry crossing to Ilha Comprida. It offers comfortable air-con rooms.

Ilha do Cardoso is a federally protected island with only 400 people living on it. Most of it is national park, with gorgeous natural pools, waterfalls and untouched beaches. Walking is the mode of transport on the island – to get to some of the best natural treasures, be prepared to hoof it great lengths. Some locals rent basic rooms or have set up simple pousadas – the average price is about US$15 a night or slightly less. These are rustic accommodations, as large-scale tourism is prohibited in this area.

Cananéia is renowned for its oysters. The town also has a couple of excellent Japanese restaurants.

Naguissa (☎ 3851 1341; Rua Teotônio Vilela 38; dinner US$15; ☽ 11am-midnight) This restaurant does fish specialities, Japanese-style.

Restaurant Tia Ines (Rua Bandeirantes 48; meals US$8; ☽ 11am-4pm & 6-10pm) For inexpensive self-serve food, this restaurant is your best bet.

Ararapira (☎ 3851 1310; Rua Paulo Almeida 46; meals US$10; ☽ 11am-midnight Dec-Feb) This local favorite has a varied menu.

Getting There & Around

A direct bus leaves Cananéia for São Paulo twice daily (US$17, five hours).

The ferry terminal to Ilha Comprida is down from the main plaza. The ferry is free and leaves every one to 1½ hours (10 minutes). To get to Ilha do Cardoso, time your transfers with the Lagamar boat excursions or hire a *voadeira* (speedboat) for US$50 each way for up to four people.

INLAND

IPORANGA

☎ 0xx15 / pop 2100

This small town is in the Vale do Ribeira in the hills near the São Paulo–Paraná border. Founded in 1576 after gold was discovered in the region, the area has one of the least disturbed areas of Brazilian Atlantic Forest and is of international importance for its biodiversity. Iporanga is a good base for visiting the Parque Estadual do Alto do Ribeira (Petar). This 360-sq-km state park, with its 280 cataloged caves, is known as Brazil's Capital das Grutas (Cave Capital).

Information

Iporanga has no tourist information office. Try Nilton Rosa Pinto at the **Prefeitura** (☎ 3556 1203). For information on the park call **Petar** (☎ 3552-1528), the state park administration in Iporanga.

Caves

The **Núcleos de Visitação** (☎ 3552 1875) are well-set-up visitors centers with information on cave trips, guides (all in Portuguese) and campsites.

There are four Núcleos. Núcleo Santana (17km northwest of town) has good facilities for visitors and campers, four caves and a 3.5km-long trek to a beautiful waterfall; Núcleo Ouro Grosso (16km northwest of town) has basic accommodations for groups and offers cooking facilities, two caves and a walking trail; Núcleo Casa de Pedra (9km by road plus 3km by walking trail) is the base for visiting the cave Casa de Pedra, famous for its 215m-high entrance and pristine Atlantic Forest; and Núcleo Caboclos (centrally located in the park, 86km by road from town) has good camping facilities, basic visitors' lodgings and several caves.

Sleeping & Eating

Pousada Iporanga (☎ 3556 1132; Rua Cel. Déscio 7; s/d US$ 12/25) Pousada Iporanga has good, clean *apartamentos*.

Albergue da Juventude Capitão Caverna (☎ 3556 1125; Rua João Evilásio Nunes 160; US$9-14) In Alto do Coqueiro, a short walk uphill from the center, this *albergue* (hostel) is highly recommended – the view from up here is great. Spotless rooms with bunk beds, including homemade breakfast. It has caving equipment for rental and will help to organize guided cave tours.

Pousada Casa de Pedra (☎ 3556 1157; r per person with private bathroom & breakfast from US$10) Near the river just west of town, this pousada has rustic dormitory accommodations. The restaurant has tasty homemade meals, but you need to place your order for food a day in advance.

Churrascaria do Abel (Rua Barão de Jundiaí 88; meals US$8; ☼ 11am-3pm & 6-10pm) Large, inexpensive meat dishes are what's available here; not so good for vegetarians.

Pousada das Cavernas (☎ 3814-9153; www.pousada dascavernas.com.br in Portuguese; d US$40) This very popular pousada in Bairro da Serra, 13km toward Núcleo Santana, has a few cottages on a hilly site. Each has a couple of rooms with balconies overlooking the river and mountains. It has a great restaurant/lounge area and includes breakfast and dinner.

Getting There & Away

There is one Intersul bus daily at 6:30am from São Paulo's Barra Funda bus station to Eldorado ($US6, five hours). From El-

dorado you can get the bus to Iporanga, departing at 2:30pm.

CAMPOS DO JORDÃO

☎ 0xx12 / pop 44,000 / elevation 1628m
Nestled in the Serra da Mantiqueira, three hours northeast by bus from São Paulo, is Campos do Jordão. It's a highly popular weekend mountain getaway for Paulistas who enjoy the novelty of wearing sweaters and long johns in the winter months. Campos looks very much like a southern German town – hills, wood smoke, *fachwerk* houses and picture-postcard views.

At almost 1700m, Campos is undeniably pretty, and a good place from which to check out some of the last remaining virgin *araucária* (Paraná pine) forests, and to hike to the top of some high peaks with spectacular views of the Paraíba valley and of the coastal mountain range, the Serra do Mar. The railway line that connects Campos with Santo Antônio do Pinhal (US$8 round-trip per person) is the highest in Brazil.

Orientation & Information

Campos is made up of three main districts: Abernéssia (the oldest), Jaguaribe (where the bus station is located) and Capivari, the center. The three districts are connected by a tram that is an attraction in itself.

The **tourist office** (☎ 3262 2799; setur@ig.com .br; ☼ 8am-8pm) is at the gateway to the valley, on the main road into town about 2km before Abernéssia. Pick up a copy of *Nosso Guia-Turístico* – it lists just about everything and has a useful map. The website www.cam posdojordao.com.br (in Portuguese) has a list of places to stay, restaurants and events.

Sights

The **Horto Florestal state park** (admission US$2) is 14km east from Capivari. It contains the largest *araucária* reserve in the state, and there are some fine walks. The **reception desk** (☎ 3263 3762), near the trout farm, can supply you with maps.

Another spot that deserves a visit is the **Pico do Itapeva**, 15km away. From 2030m it's possible to see almost the whole Paraíba valley, including its industrial cities and the Rio Paraíba.

Close to Capivari is a *miniférico* (chairlift; US$3) to the top of the **Morro do Elefante**, which has a good view of the town.

The **Palácio Boa Vista** (☎ 3262 2966; admission US$3; ⊙ 10am-noon & 2-5pm Wed-Sun), 3.5km north of Abernéssia, is the state governor's summer residence; it contains many antiques.

The 19km **electric train ride** (US$10, 2½hr round-trip) from Campos do Jordão to Santo Antônio do Pinhal is one of the country's best. It allows a 20-minute stopover in Santo Antônio – bring your own snack or you will be at the mercy of vendors. The train leaves Campos (from the Capivari terminal at the end of Av Emílio Ribas) Tuesday to Friday at 2 pm and Saturday, Sunday and holidays at 9:30am, 10am, 1:30pm and 2pm. For the best views, sit on the right-hand side when leaving Campos.

Sleeping

July is peak tourist period in Campos, when the town receives up to a million tourists. It is also in July that Campos hosts the **winter music festival**. Prices double or even triple during these periods.

BUDGET

Pousada Brasil (☎ 3262 2341; Rua Pereira Barreto 22; dm US$12, d US$35) In Abernéssia near the tram stop, this pousada offers good hostel-type accommodations. It has clean and secure rooms with bunk beds or double beds.

Pousada Recanto do Sossego (☎ 3262 4224; Rua Professor Raul Pedroza de Moraes 74; s/d US$20/30) Opposite the convent on the street on the left, on the way up the Palácio Boa Vista, this pousada has lovely views and good rooms.

Pousada Alto da Boa Vista (☎ 3262 4900; Rua das Hortencias 605; s/d US$12/25) Up at a beautiful spot and within walking distance of a forest reserve, you'll find Alto da Boa Vista, about 8km north of town (taxi US$6). It has great chalets, a nice outdoor spa, barbecue facilities and bar services. Prices are almost double on weekends during the high season.

Camping Clube do Brasil (☎ 3263 1130; members/nonmembers US$7/14) This camping ground is about 10km east of Capivari on the road to the Horto Florestal.

MID-RANGE & TOP END

Grande Hotel Campos do Jordão (☎ 3260 6000; Av Frei Orestes Girardi; s/d US$100/150; P 🅿 🗖 🎣) About 2km outside of town, this huge megaresort is set in its own private forest. Full board is available for about $20 more a day per person. It makes a gorgeous base

from where to explore surrounding regions. Prices will go up during high season.

Hotel Toriba (☎ 3262 1566; Av Ernesto Diedericksen 2962; s/d US$90/130; P 🅿 🗖) The oldest and most stylish place to stay is the Toriba, in the hills 4km south of Abernéssia. It's a beautiful alpine structure, with afternoon tea available in the garden.

Frontenac (☎ 3269 1000; www.frontenac.com.br; Av Dr Paulo Ribas 295; s/d US$170/300; P 🅿 🗖) A very sophisticated, elegant modern place, Frontenac is a real favorite with visiting Paulistas. There's a home theater in the communal room, but some rooms have DVDs for those who like their solitude. An excellent restaurant and first-class service add to the Frontenac's charm.

Eating & Drinking

Campos has a good number and variety of eateries. The local specialty is *pinhãou* (pine nuts) fried in butter or served with rice, but it is seasonal – available only in July and August.

Esquina do Pastel (Av Macedo Soares 203) For a quick snack try this *lanchonete* located in Capivari.

Sergio's Restaurante (Av Brigadeiro Jordão 688) In Abernéssia, Sergio's has a good-value per-kilo buffet.

Bia Kaffe (Rua Isola Orsi 33) A favorite place in Capivari for quality coffee, cakes and other sweets.

Restaurante Champignon (Rua Gilia 20; meal for 2 US$15; ⊙ 11am-11pm Fri-Sun) Near the Tennis Club in Capivari, this place is a mushroom-lover's dream come true.

Keller Haus (Av Emilio Ribas 478; lunch US$8; ⊙ 11am-10pm Mon-Thu, to 1am Fri-Sun) A fairly good and reasonably priced German place in Capivari, Keller Haus does seasonal dishes from Rhineland.

Baden-Baden (☎ 3263 3659; Rua Djalma Forjaz 93; dinner with drinks US$20; ⊙ 11am-11pm Mon-Thu, to 2am Fri & Sat) A German place that incorporates some Brazilian touches, Baden-Baden is always busy.

Nearby, in the Boulevard Geneve mall, there's a mock English pub, **Royal Flag**, upstairs in the watchtower, with live music or videos in high season at 9:30pm nightly.

Getting There & Away

The **bus station** (☎ 3262-1996; Av Dr Januário Miraglia) is near Supermercado Roma between

Jaguaribe and Capivari. Buses travel to São Paulo (US$8, seven a day) from 6am to 7pm and to Rio de Janeiro (US$12, five hours, two a day).

To get to Ubatuba, take a bus to Taubaté (US$3, every two hours from 6am to 8pm). From Taubaté catch a bus to Ubatuba (US$5).

AROUND CAMPOS DO JORDÃO

The **Gruta dos Crioulos** (Creoles' Cave) was used as a hideout by slaves escaping from the surrounding farms. It's 7km from Jaguaribé on the road to Pedra do Baú, which is a huge, 1950m rectangular granite block. To get to the top you have to walk 2km north and climb 600 steps carved into the rock. It's about 25km from Campos do Jordão.

For a day trip up **Pedra do Baú**, mountainbike tours or guided hikes to waterfalls around Pedra do Baú, check out the ecofriendly **Altus Turismo Ecologico** (☎ 3263 4122; Av Brasil 108). German and English are spoken.

The South

Clean, well-organized cities. Relatively equal distribution of incomes. Towns inhabited almost exclusively by natural blonds. Welcome to the Região Sul (Southern Regions), Brazil's smallest, richest and least distinctly 'Brazilian' region.

The people of southern Brazil are largely descended from Swiss, German, Italian and Eastern European immigrants. Except for the subtropical flora, cities such as Blumenau and Joinville seem to have been plucked straight from the Rhine Valley. In fact, there are still rural areas where German remains the first language. Perhaps the most refreshing quality of southern Brazil is its relatively equitable distribution of incomes. While the economy of the Amazon was built on the backs of slaves, land in the South tended to be divided into small, family-owned farms.

These days, shipping and manufacturing, powered largely by the controversial Itaipu Dam near Iguaçu Falls, have replaced agriculture as the region's economic driver. Change has also come to the pampas (grassy plains) of the far south. Soybean fields stretch to the horizon where gauchos (cowboys) once drove huge cattle.

While not archetypically Brazilian, the South offers plenty of reasons to detain the traveler. The anthropologically minded will have a field day observing the ways the South both integrates and remains distinct from the rest of Brazil, especially in the well-organized bustle of the region's two largest cities, Curitiba and Porto Alegre.

Nature, too, conspires to please. The South's biggest box-office draw must be the justly famous Iguaçu Falls, which are higher than Niagara, wider than Victoria and arguably more beautiful than either. Brazilians themselves count the beaches of Santa Catarina among the country's most beautiful. Breathtaking mountain hikes can be had in all three states, with trails through the canyons of the Serra Gaúcha as the real standouts. And if you travel in winter, you may even see Brazilian snow around Gramado, Canela and São Joaquim, which, at 1355m, is Brazil's highest city.

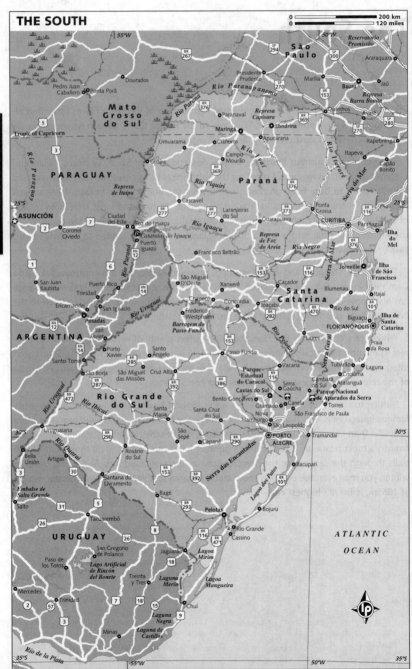

THE SOUTH

Paraná

THE SOUTH

HIGHLIGHTS

- Getting doused during a boat tour of the sublime **Iguaçu Falls** (p310)
- Hiking and surfing on the car-less **Ilha do Mel** (p305), at the mouth of the beautiful Baía de Paranaguá
- Taking the hair-raising **train ride** (p301) from Curitiba to Paranaguá, via the jungle-covered Serra do Mar
- Discovering Curitiba's remarkable **Museu Oscar Niemeyer** (p299), designed by the renowned architect of Brasília
- Dining on *barreado* (the state dish) in the decaying splendor of the colonial port city **Antonina** (p303)

★ Iguaçu Falls

■ POPULATION: 10.2 MILLION   ■ AREA: 10,157,000 SQ KM

Like the other states of the South, Paraná differs markedly from the rest of Brazil. With a population of largely German, Polish and Ukrainian stock, Paraná has a remarkably high percentage of tall, ruddy blonds. The state also boasts a long tradition of savvy public and private investment that makes it, together with neighboring São Paulo, the country's industrial powerhouse. In fact, when pressed, many Paulistas will express envy at the state's more thoughtful approach to economic development.

Both the state capital and largest city, Curitiba combines prosperity, cleanliness and excellent public services, including an innovative public transportation system that is the envy of traffic-clogged cities to the north. Jaime Lerner, who has served as both mayor of Curitiba and governor of Paraná, is largely credited with the enlightened way the city and state have grown and prospered.

Most travelers to Paraná come for one thing: Iguaçu Falls – and for good reason. The falls, which straddle the border with Argentina, are without doubt among the world's most beautiful. At the other end of the state, Ilha do Mel guards the entrance of the beautiful Baía de Paranaguá. The bay, ringed by the peaks of the Serra do Mar, was once an important trading center, evidenced by the decaying splendor of colonial ports such as Antonina and Paranaguá.

Between Curitiba and the Baía de Paranaguá lies a beautiful stretch of the coastal range. You can hike the trails of the Parque Estadual de Marumbi, which afford stunning vistas down to the sea. Or board a train in Curitiba and watch the views unfold in air-conditioned comfort.

History

Like the rest of southern Brazil, Paraná was largely neglected by the Portuguese colonists, and even a brief gold rush in the 17th century died out when bigger finds were discovered in Minas Gerais. When the state seceded from São Paulo in 1853, the economy was based on cattle and *erva maté* tea. To develop the economy, migration from Italy was encouraged. Italians were followed by waves of Germans, Ukrainians and Poles. With immigration and the arrival of the railroad, Curitiba, which had been little more than a stage stop in the cattle trade, grew at a remarkable rate. Today, it is among the country's richest, cleanest and best-organized cities.

Climate

Both the coast and the area around Iguaçu Falls are semitropical regions dominated by the Mata Atlântica (Atlantic rain forest). Summers are very hot and humid, and winters are mild. Curitiba, which lies on an upland plain, is significantly cooler than the coast year-round, though summers are still hot and winters are blustery rather than outright cold.

National Parks

Parque Nacional do Superagüi (p308) is part of a huge, 4700-sq-km reserve of the Mata Atlântica including a few largely uninhabited islands and miles of mangrove swamps.

As well as the famous falls, the 1550-sq-km Parque Nacional do Iguaçu (p310) provides access to the remarkable ecosystem of the Mata Atlântica.

Getting There & Around

Curitiba is the state's transportation hub, with bus and air services to every major city in Brazil. There is also an international airport in Foz do Iguaçu, as well as direct service to São Paulo, Rio de Janeiro and every big city in the South.

As well as the very good bus service that links all major destinations in the state, there are regular flights between Curitiba and Foz do Iguaçu, as well as a passenger train that links Curitiba with the coastal town of Paranaguá.

CURITIBA

☎ 0xx41 / pop 1.67 million

Curitiba possesses neither São Paulo's sophistication nor Rio's sex appeal, yet many a Brazilian dreams of a better life here. With the help of a vibrant local economy, the city has managed to modernize in a relatively sane manner – historic buildings have been preserved, the heart of the city has been closed to cars, and green spaces abound.

In the 1970s and 1980s, long-sighted mayor Jaime Lerner launched a number of progressive incentives, including a drive to get people out of their cars by lowering bus prices and improving service. The strategy worked: today it's easier to get around Curitiba than any other large city in Brazil. Drivers actually stop at red lights, and pedestrians can cross streets without fearing for their lives. The city has also taken innovative approaches to urban ills such as homelessness, pollution and poverty. To help bridge the technological divide, the city even provides free Internet access at more than 20 locations around the city.

At 900m above sea level, Curitiba sits atop the great escarpment along the route from Rio Grande do Sul to São Paulo. It flourished briefly in the 19th century as a pit stop for gauchos (cowboys) and their cattle, but it wasn't until the tremendous growth of the coffee plantations in northern Paraná at the beginning of the 20th century that the modern city of Curitiba began to take shape.

Despite Curitiba's interesting history, it's not a beautiful city, and its appeal to the traveler is limited. However, it's possible to pass a pleasant day walking through the pedestrian streets, noting the way this city differs from others of its size in Brazil. The new Museu Oscar Niemeyer is also a must-see for anyone interested in the country's most-celebrated architect. There's also a large university population, injecting a youthful energy and supporting a good music scene.

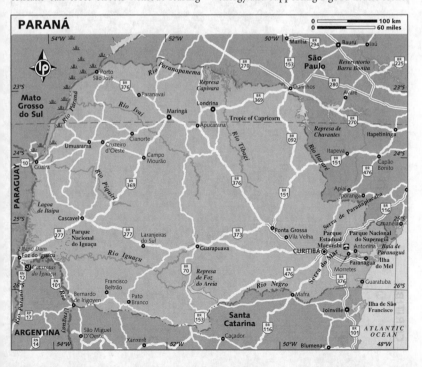

PARANÁ

CURITIBA

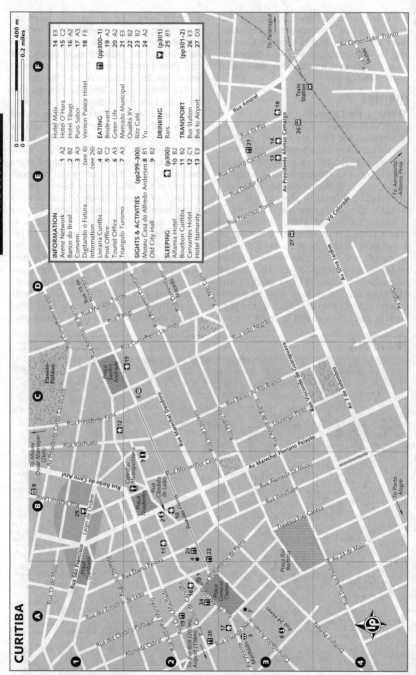

INFORMATION	
Arena Network.................	1 A2
Banco do Brasil................	2 B2
Convem........................	3 A3
Digitando o Futura............	(see 26)
Information....................	(see 6)
Livraria Curitiba...............	4 B2
Post Office....................	5 C2
Tourist Office.................	6 A3
Triangulo Turismo............	7 A3

SIGHTS & ACTIVITIES	(pp299–300)
Museu Casa do Alfredo Andersen.	8 B1
Old City Hall..................	9 B2

SLEEPING	(p300)
Alfamia Hotel.................	10 B2
Bourbon Curitiba..............	11 B2
Cervantes Hotel...............	12 C1
Hotel Itamaraty...............	13 E3

Hotel Maia....................	14 E3
Hotel O'Hara.................	15 C2
Hotel Tibagi..................	16 A2
Puro Sabor...................	17 A3
Vernon Palace Hotel..........	18 F3

EATING	(pp300–1)
Boulevard....................	19 A2
Green Life....................	20 A2
Mercado Municipal............	21 E3
Qualitá XV....................	22 B2
Ritz Café....................	23 B2
Yu..........................	24 A2

DRINKING	(p301)
Bars.........................	25 B1

TRANSPORT	(pp301–2)
Bus Station..................	26 E3
Bus to Airport...............	27 D3

Orientation

The city's downtown and principal area of interest is bounded on one side by Praça Santos Andrade and the nearby Passeio Público, a pleasant city park. At the other end lie Praça General Osório and, a little further, Rua 24 Horas. The two ends are joined by the lively, pedestrian-only Rua das Flores, the city's main *passeio* (promenade). Just to the north of Rua das Flores lies the city's colonial heart along Largo da Ordem, which has become the center of the city's nightlife.

Further afield, the city's long-distance bus station and the adjacent train station are about 2km east of downtown, while the airport lies 18km to the southeast. The largest parks, as well as the Museu Oscar Niemeyer, lie on the city's outskirts.

Information

BOOKSTORES

Livraria Curitiba (☎ 330 5002; Rua das Flores 78) An excellent bookstore with a small selection of foreign-language titles.

EMERGENCY

Federal Police (☎ 362 2313)

INTERNET ACCESS

Arena Network (☎ 233 5181; Rua Cândido Lopes 333; per hr US$3; ☼ 9am-midnight Mon-Sat, 2-9pm Sun) A good option near Praça General Osório.

Digitando o Futuro (☎ 350 6366; shop 16, Rua 24 Horas) Free Internet access provided by the city. Demand can be high, so call ahead to reserve a terminal, especially on evenings and weekends.

INTERNET RESOURCES

Both the state (www.pr.gov.br) and the city (www.viaje.curitiba.pr.gov.br) have websites with extensive information in Portuguese, some of which is also available in Spanish and English.

MEDICAL SERVICES

Medical Emergency (☎ 192)

MONEY

Many travel agencies double as money-exchange houses.

Banco do Brasil (Praça Tiradentes 410) Money exchange and Visa ATMs.

Triangulo Turismo (☎ 233 0311; Praça General Osório 213)

POST

Main post office (Rua XV de Novembro 700) Near Praça Santos Andrade.

TELEPHONE

Convem (☎ 322 8455; Rua Visonde Nácar 1230; ☼ 8am-7pm Mon-Fri, 8am-5pm Sat) For international calls.

TOURIST INFORMATION

Information booth (☎ 352 8000; long-distance bus station)

Paraná Turismo information booth (☎ 324 7036; shop 18, Rua 24 Horas) Handy and very helpful, with maps and glossy brochures. Most staff members speak English.

Sights

In 1972 **Rua das Flores** became Brazil's first pedestrian mall, and it remains the focal point for the city's downtown. Almost 500m in length, it's a great place for walking, shopping and people-watching. At its eastern end sits **Praça Santos Andrade**, a pleasant square dominated by the neoclassical headquarters of the Federal University of Paraná. Two blocks north of the square lies the **Passeio Público** (☼ 6am-8pm Tue-Sun), the park where Curitibanos have relaxed since 1886. Here you'll find shaded walks, a lake and a small zoo.

Just north of Rua das Flores is **Praça Tiradentes**, home of Curitiba's **cathedral**, and **Praça José Borges de Macedo**, home of the former Art Nouveau **city hall**, which at the time of writing was closed for remodeling. Just beyond the cathedral is **Largo da Ordem**, the city's old colonial heart. Its pedestrian-only cobblestone streets are lined with beautifully restored buildings, many of which have been largely converted into trendy art galleries, pubs, restaurants and cafés. **Museu Casa de Alfredo Andersen** (☎ 323 5139; Rua Mateus Leme 336; admission free; ☼ 10am-6pm Mon-Fri, 10am-4pm Sat & Sun) offers a chance to see work by the city's celebrated portraitist, as well as the interior of a typical colonial home.

Praça General Osório, which sits under a majestic canopy of palm trees, guards the western end of Rua das Flores. A bit further west lies **Rua 24 Horas**, which is in fact a block-long, glass-and-steel arcade with gift shops, cafés, bars and Internet kiosks that are open – you guessed it – 24 hours a day. It's another of the city's tireless efforts to keep the urban environment vibrant well after the working stiffs head home for the day.

Unless you're already a fan of architect Oscar Niemeyer, the city's art museum, **Museu Oscar Niemeyer** (☎ 350 4400; Rua Marechal Hermes 999; admission free; ⊙ 10am-8pm Tue-Sun), may at first seem a questionable use of concrete. Try to reserve judgment until you're inside. Every aspect of the museum's design seems to marry beauty with whimsy, the crowning achievement being the playful tower with its eye-shaped main gallery. The museum is a brisk 30-minute walk (about 3km) from the city center, or you can take the Linha Turismo bus (see p302).

Sleeping

Downtown offers a range of hotels in all price ranges. If you arrive late or leave early, there are some very good options right across the street from the train and bus station complex.

BUDGET

Hotel Maia (☎ 264 1684; Av Presidente Afonso Camargo 355; per person with/without private bathroom US$10/7) A no-frills but clean and secure joint just across from the bus station.

Cervantes Hotel (☎ 222 9593; cervanteshotel@ brturbo.com; Rua Alfredo Bufren 66; s/d US$10/17; P) Basic rooms but great value and a central location.

MID-RANGE

Hotel Tibagi (☎ 223 3141; info@hoteltibagi.com.br; Rua Cândido Lopes 318; s/d US$30/40; P ⊠ ⊡) This stylish hotel, one block from Praça General Osório, has smallish but very comfortable rooms, some with great views.

Afamia Hotel (☎ 322 6767; afamiahotel@onda.com .br; Rua Cândido de Leão 15; s/d/tr US$28/34/40) This once-grand hotel on Praça Tiradentes is somewhat shop-worn, but it's still a very good mid-range option with an excellent location. Ask for a room with a view.

Hotel Itamaraty (☎ 362 2022; itamaraty@bbs2 .sul.com.br; Av Presidente Afonso Camargo 279; s/d/tr US$16/23/28, with air-con & cable TV US$19/25/31; P ⊠ ⊡) Just across the street from the train station, what it lacks in charm it makes up in value.

Hotel O'Hara (☎ 232 6044; Rua XV de Novembro 770; s/d/tr US$16/23/28, with air-con US$21/28/34; P ⊠) While the colonial charm does not extend beyond the facade, this offers good value, with an excellent location on Praça Santos Andrade.

TOP END

Vernon Palace Hotel (☎ 362 1222; vernonhotel@ vernonhotel.com.br; Av Presidente Afonso Camargo 455; s/d US$42/53; P ⊠ ⊡) The most luxurious option near the bus station, this marble-heavy hotel attracts a tony business crowd.

Bourbon Curitiba (☎ 221 4600; www.bourbon.com .br; Rua Cândido Lopes 102; s/d US$65/73, ste US$88/98; P ⊠ ⊡ ⊠) This five-star joint is Curitiba's top hotel. The lobby shines with marble and brass, luxurious rooms include a CD player, and the breakfast buffet is a real feast.

Eating

Puro Sabor (☎ 3014 0324; 2nd fl, Av Vicente Machado 18; per kg about US$3; ⊙ 11:30am-2:30pm Mon-Sat) The spotless kitchen of this creative, all-organic per-kilo restaurant is available for all to view behind a glass wall that separates it from the bright dining room. The restaurant began as a joint thesis of two MBA students who were exploring ways for business to support organic farming. Fortunately, the food is as good as their business plan.

Divino Mestre (☎ 3029 1081; Rua Dr Raul Carneiro Filho 25; all-you-can-eat buffet US$14; ⊙ lunch & dinner) The best *churrascaria* (restaurant featuring barbecued meat) in the city, specializing in *filé argentino* (beef tenderloin) and chicken grilled with butter.

Boulevard (☎ 224 8244; Rua Voluntários da Pátria 539; mains US$15-25; ⊙ lunch Mon-Fri, dinner Mon-Sat) The city's top restaurant serves a creative fusion of French, Italian and Brazilian cuisine, with emphasis on the French.

Yu (☎ 232 3500; Praça General Osório 485; per kg about US$5; ⊙ lunch Mon-Sat) This very stylish per-kilo restaurant serves up Asian as well as Brazilian food.

Green Life (☎ 223 8490; Rua Carlos de Carvalho 271; buffet US$3; ⊙ lunch) Most of the ingredients at this all-organic vegetarian restaurant come from the owners' own farm.

Mercado Municipal (cnr Rua General Carneiro & Av Presidente Afonso Camargo; ⊙ 8am-6pm Mon-Sat) Just across from the bus station, the municipal market has some good food stalls on the lower level.

Ritz Café (Rua Ébano Pereira) A Curitiba tradition, this is where the city's movers and shakers get their caffeine fix. Just off Rua das Flores.

Qualitá XV (☎ 224 8730; Rua das Flores 71; per kg about US$3; ⊙ 11am-3pm Mon-Sat) A decent, cheap per-kilo place right on the main drag.

Entertainment

Curitiba has an active live-music and club scene. The streets around Largo da Ordem are packed on warm nights with revelers spilling out of pubs and cafés.

Bin 608 (☎ 225 6541; Rua Carlos de Carvalho 608; cocktails US$1-3; ☼ 10am-midnight) A sophisticated venue for after-work cocktails.

Cats Club (☎ 224 5912; Rua Dr Muricy 949) This place combines a striking pink colonial mansion on the outside with a smoky, underground club on the inside.

Shopping

Feira de Arte e Artesanato (Arts & Crafts Fair; Praça Garibaldi; ☼ 9am-2pm Sun) Offers an excellent variety of arts and crafts.

Getting There & Away

AIR

From Curitiba's **Alfonso Pena Airport** (☎ 381 1515) there are direct flights to São Paulo (45 minutes), Rio de Janeiro (one hour), Foz do Iguaçu (40 minutes), Florianópolis (40 minutes), Porto Alegre (one hour) and Brasília (two hours).

BUS

The long-distance bus station and train station form a single complex called the *rodo-ferroviária* (bus and train station), which is about 2km from downtown.

Within Brazil, destinations include: Paranaguá (US$8, 2½ hours); São Paulo (US$14, 6½ hours); Rio (US$26, 12 hours); Foz do Iguaçu (US$22 to US$42, nine to 10 hours) – several semidirects and *leitos* (overnight sleeper); Joinville (US$6, two hours); and Florianópolis (US$12, four hours).

International destinations by bus include Asunción (US$40, 18 hours), Buenos Aires (US$66, 28 hours) and Santiago (US$120, 52 hours).

TRAIN

The train between Curitiba and Paranaguá via the Serra do Mar (see below) is one of the marvels of travel in Brazil.

Getting Around

TO/FROM THE AIRPORT

Alfonso Pena Airport is 18km from the city (US$15 by taxi). An Aeroporto-Centro bus

---

TRAIN TO PARANAGUÁ

Standing in flat Curitiba, where there is hardly a ripple on the horizon, it's hard to believe that a few dozen kilometers to the west lie sharp, jungle-covered peaks with sweeping views down to the Baía de Paranaguá and the ocean beyond. That's because Curitiba actually sits above the mountains on the so-called Planalto (high plains). As the plains break apart and give way to the sea, they form the stunning Serra do Mar.

Although beautiful to behold, until the 1880s the city's location was a drag on Curitiba's economy, since it took two days to get products from Curitiba to the port of Antonina, only 75km to the east. Finally, in 1885, Brazilian investors turned a common dream into profitable reality, inaugurating a railway that connected Curitiba with the sea. Engineers managed to design and build 67 bridges and viaducts, dig 13 tunnels through granite mountainsides, and lay track along dizzyingly steep heights.

To this day, two daily trains awe tourists as they head down the perilous path from Curitiba to Paranaguá. The view is often sublime and, depending on cloud formations and the quality of the light, surreal, taking in threatening mountain canyons, tropical green lowlands and the vast, blue Atlantic. As you descend the heights, watch as the climate and environment change radically, the weather getting hotter and muggier, the vegetation lusher and greener.

The *litorina* (tourist train) leaves daily from Curitiba at 9am. Features include panoramic windows, air-conditioning, snack and beverage service and a 10-minute stop for the stunning views at Santuário do Cadeado. The ride to Paranaguá takes four hours and costs US$30. The less-luxurious *trem* (regular train) leaves daily at 8am and takes 3½ hours. Two classes are available: *executiva* (US$22) and *turista* (US$13). Prices are high, but you can always return to Curitiba by bus (US$8, two hours).

Reservations are highly recommended during summer, and virtually mandatory on summer weekends and holidays. Prices and times change frequently, so call the **ticket office** (☎ 323 4007; www.serraverdeexpress.com.br) in Curitiba or consult the website

(US$0.70, 35 minutes) leaves every 20 minutes from opposite Hotel Lizon, on the corner of Av Presidente Afonso Camargo near the bus station. From the airport, the bus, which leaves from a nifty tube-shaped station outside the airport, can drop you near the bus station (the fourth stop) or in the center along Rua Conselheiro Laurindo (the fifth stop).

BUS

The Linha Turismo bus is a great way to see the sights that lie outside Curitiba's downtown, including the Museu Oscar Niemeyer. It starts from Praça Tiradentes every half-hour from Tuesday to Sunday – the first bus is at 9am and the last leaves at 5:30pm. You can get off the bus at any of the attractions and hop on the next white Linha Turismo bus that passes. There is a timetable posted at each stop. It costs US$3 for four tickets.

Around Curitiba

PARQUE ESTADUAL MARUMBI

Curitiba may not be visually arresting, but this state park just outside the city sure is. It's very popular with Curitibanos, who get off the train to Paranaguá at the Marumbi station and hike down the old pioneer trails that were the only connections between the coast and the Paranaense highland in the 17th and 18th centuries. The two best walks are the **Graciosa trail**, which passes close to the Estrada da Graciosa, and the **Itupava trail**. Views from both are stunning.

The trails are well signposted from the train station and within the park, so a guide isn't necessary. For more information, contact the **park information center** (☎ 432 2072). You can camp in the park for free, though with the caveat that rains can gather quickly and mosquitoes abound. Plan accordingly.

VILA VELHA

Located in the Campos Gerais region, 93km west of Curitiba, Vila Velha makes an ideal day trip from the city – or a great pit stop if you are driving to Foz do Iguaçu. Known as the 'stone city,' Vila Velha consists of 23 sandstone pillars created by millions of years of erosion. The area also provides great views over the surrounding countryside of the Planalto. Pack your swimsuit: the park has a swimming pool and a 54m-long elevator ride into a crater lake.

You can pick up a map of the trails and sights at the **park center** (☎ 228 1138; 🕑 8am-6pm). There's also a restaurant and kiosks for lunch.

To get there, catch a *semi-direto* (semi-direct) bus to Ponta Grossa from the Curitiba bus station and ask to be let out at the park entrance. There's nowhere to stay in the park, so make sure you get the last bus back, which you can flag down along the road at around 3:45pm.

MORRETES

☎ 0xx41 / pop 7400

Founded in 1721 on the banks of the Rio Nhundiaquara, this tranquil colonial town occupies an emerald-green plain at the foot of the Serra do Mar. *Barreado*, a rib-sticking spiced meat stew that cooks for 24 hours in a sealed clay pot, is the region's culinary gift to the world. Ingredients include beef, salt pork, cumin and onions. It was invented to keep Carnaval-goers nourished over the course of several days of revelry.

Morretes is a relaxing place, especially during the week when Curitibanos are still hard at work. Note that hotels tend to fill quickly on weekends. Diversions include navigating the Nhundiaquara by inner tube and hiking the nearby Parque Estadual Marumbi.

The **Secretaria de Turismo** (☎ 462 1024; Largo Dr Jose Pereira 43) is located in a white colonial-style house on the riverfront.

Activities

RIO NHUNDIAQUARA

Once an important connection between the coast and the highlands, the river is best seen by *boia cross* (inner tube). To rent one (US$2 per day), contact Ibrahim at **Pousada Itupava** (☎ 462 1925; pousada@itupava.com.br), in the village of Porto de Cima, about 5km from Morretes.

Sleeping & Eating

Hotel Nhundiaquara (☎ 462 1228; Rua General Carreiro 13; per person with/without private bathroom US$11/8) A lovely, old-fashioned place right on the river, though with rooms of only moderate comfort. Book well ahead if you plan to arrive on a weekend.

Porto Real Palace (☎ 462 1344; Rua Visconde de Branco 85; d US$23, with air-con US$30; 🅿 🌂) Perhaps as high-end as Morretes manages to get, the rooms are comfortable, if a little threadbare. Watch out for the blindingly bright-red carpet in the halls.

Hotel Bom Jesus (☎ 462 1282; Rua XV de Novembro 281; s/d US$7/9) A bit less expensive, but also far less charming. However, a good budget option when Hotel Nhundiaquara is fully booked.

Most of the restaurants are along Largo Dr Jose Pereira on the riverfront. Here you will find **Restaurante Casarão**, an upmarket place with a balcony on the river. Try the *barreado* (US$6).

Restaurant Nhundiaquara (☎ 462 1228; Rua General Carreiro 13; mains US$5-7; ☽ lunch & dinner) This is the place for *barreado* (US$6). Portions are huge, so plan on spending the rest of the day (and possibly the next) digesting. The dining room is located on a breezy, colonial-style terrace overlooking a lovely bend in the Rio Nhundiaquara.

Getting There & Away
The Morretes train station is on a pretty square right in the center of town. Trains to Curitiba depart daily (see p301).

The bus station is about 1km from the center of town. You can catch the local bus that runs from Antonina (US$1, 30 minutes) to Paranaguá (US$1, one hour) via Morretes every hour. There are also regular nonstop buses to Curitiba (US$4, 1½ hours). At least one bus a day goes to Curitiba via the Graciosa trail, providing views that rival those from the train.

ANTONINA
☎ 0xx41 / pop 16,400

Once an important colonial port, Antonina has, since the 1940s, slipped into charming irrelevance. Fortunately, its economic decline has kept the colonial center intact, and this, together with views of the beautiful Baía de Paranaguá, make it a worthy detour. The pace is languid – except during Carnaval, which is one of the region's best. Be sure to walk along the tree-lined waterfront, then head uphill toward Praça Coronel Macedo, a pretty square lined with homes built with the town's shipping fortunes.

Frequent direct buses link Antonina to Morretes, Paranaguá and Curitiba, but trains no longer stop here.

Sleeping & Eating
Regency Capela Antonina (☎ 432 3267; Praça Coronel Macedo 208; s/d US$27/33; P ☒ ☒) The town's top-end option in a converted, early-19th-century mansion on the main square. There are rooms with breezy balconies and nice bay views.

Hotel Monte Castelo (☎ 432 1163; Praça Coronel Macedo 46; dm US$7, s/d with private bathroom US$10/17) A fine budget option in a modern building on the town's main square.

Restaurante Albatroz (☎ 432 2168; Travessa Marquês do Herval 1000; all-you-can-eat buffet US$4.50; ☽ lunch) Just below the church, this offers a good and very affordable seafood buffet that also includes *barreado*. The upstairs room offers good views of the bay.

Restaurante Caçarola (☎ 432 1286; Praça Romildo Pereira 42; mains for 2 people US$10-12; ☽ 11am-2pm Mon-Wed, Sat & Sun) Considered the best in town, with good *bacalhau* (salt cod) and crab as well as *barreado*.

PARANAGUÁ
☎ 0xx41 / pop 130,600

For most travelers, Paranaguá is merely the last stop on the train from Curitiba, or the place where you catch the boat to Ilha do Mel. However, the colorful old port, which sits serenely on the banks of the Rio Itiberê, has a feeling of tropical decadence that makes it worth a stroll. Commercially important since the late 18th century, the city has a number of well-preserved churches and other public buildings, many of which are being carefully restored. Paranaguá remains an important port, though the primary exports, once gold, *erva maté* (see p347), wood and coffee, are now corn, soy, cotton and vegetable oils.

Information
Banco do Brasil (Largo Conselheiro Alcindino 103) For Visa cash withdrawals, just off Av Gabriel de Lara.
Main tourist office Waterfront (☎ 425 4542; Rua General Carneiro; ☽ 8am-6pm); Train station (☽ noon-4pm)

Sights
MUSEU DE ARQUEOLOGIA E ETNOLOGIA
The **Archeology and Ethnology Museum** (☎ 422 8844; Rua XV de Novembro 567; admission US$1, free Sun; ☽ 9am-noon & 1-6pm Tue-Sat, noon-6pm Sun), housed in a restored Jesuit college that dates to 1736, has indigenous artifacts, primitive and folk art, and some interesting old tools

THE SOUTH

THE SOUTH

and wooden machines. Many Brazilian museums are disappointing; this one isn't.

CHURCHES

The city's churches, built in the Portuguese colonial style, are simple but beautiful. By far the oldest is **Igreja de NS do Rosário** (Rua Marechal Deodoro), parts of which date to 1578. A number of churches were built during the 18th century, including **Igreja São Francisco das Chagas** (Rua XV de Novembro) and **Igreja de São Benedito** (Rua Conselheiro Sinimbu), built specifically for the town's slaves (1784).

Sleeping

Palácio Hotel (☎ 422 5655; fax 423 2518; Rua Correia de Freitas 66; s/d/tr US$13/19/23; [P] [X]) Comfortable rooms at a very good price, a few blocks from the waterfront.

Dantas Executive Hotel (☎ 423 1555; Rua Visconde de Nacar 740; s/d US$28/35; [P] [X]) The city's high-end option has large, comfortable rooms – some of them have views of the port. In the morning, make the most of the generous breakfast buffet.

Hotel Ponderosa (☎ 423 2464; Rua Prescilinio Corrêa 68; d US$12, with view US$15) Occupying a restored colonial building, the interior lacks charm, but the rooms that look out onto the port are a nice option for the price.

Pousada Itiberê (☎ 423 2485; Rua Heitor Ariente 142; r with shared bathroom per person US$5; [P]) A good, secure cheapie right on the waterfront, with very basic but clean single/double *quartos* (rooms with shared bathroom).

Eating

Tres Irmãos (cnr Av Gabriel de Lara & Rua João Eugenio; buffet US$3; ☾ dinner Mon-Sat) The best *churrascaria* near the old port, with all-you-can-eat grilled meats at bargain prices.

Divina Gula (cnr Rua Benjamin Constant & Rua Santa Isabel; ☾ lunch Mon-Fri) A per-kilo joint that's popular with locals.

Mercado Municipal do Café (cnr Rua General Carneiro & Rua 29 de Julho) The lively courtyard of this old public market is a good spot for a cheap coffee, beer, seafood snacks or freshly fried *pastel de carne* (meat-stuffed pastry).

Casa do Barreado (☎ 423 1830; Rua José Antônio da Cruz 9; per kg US$4.50; ☾ noon-3pm Sat & Sun) A short walk from the center, in the Ponta do Cajú neighborhood, this per-kilo restaurant serves excellent local dishes, including – as the name suggests – *barreado*.

Getting There & Away

BOAT

Boats to Ilha do Mel leave in the morning and afternoon, with stops at both Nova Brasília (US$3, one hour) and Praia das Encantadas (US$3, 1½ hours). Exact times vary, so check at the tourist office across from the dock.

There are also daily boats to Guaraqueçaba (US$4.50, three hours), which, along with Ilha do Mel, provides access to Parque Nacional do Superagüi.

BUS

All out-of-town buses leave from the bus station on the waterfront. Destinations include

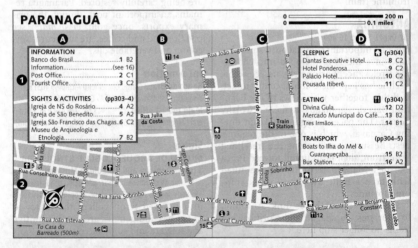

PARANAGUÁ

| 0 | 200 m |
| 0 | 0.1 miles |

INFORMATION
Banco do Brasil..................1 B2
Information.....................(see 16)
Post Office......................2 C1
Tourist Office...................3 C2

SIGHTS & ACTIVITIES (pp303–4)
Igreja de NS do Rosário........4 A2
Igreja de São Benedito.........5 A2
Igreja São Francisco das Chagas..6 C2
Museu de Arqueologia e
   Etnologia....................7 B2

SLEEPING (p304)
Dantas Executive Hotel.........8 C2
Hotel Ponderosa................9 C2
Palácio Hotel.................10 C2
Pousada Itiberê...............11 C2

EATING (p304)
Divina Gula...................12 D2
Mercado Municipal do Café.....13 B2
Tres Irmãos...................14 B1

TRANSPORT (pp304–5)
Boats to Ilha do Mel &
   Guaraqueçaba...............15 B2
Bus Station...................16 A2

Curitiba (US$4, 1½ hours, hourly), Antonina (US$1, 1½ hours, hourly), Morretes (US$1, one hour, hourly), Foz do Iguaçu (US$24, 13 hours, Monday, Wednesday and Friday evening only) and Guaraqueçaba (US$6, 5½ hours, daily).

TRAIN

At the time of writing, the Paranaguá train station was closed. When the station reopens, expect trains to return to Curitiba via Morretes in the late afternoon (see p301).

ILHA DO MEL

☎ 0xx41 / pop 1200

This odd-shaped island at the mouth of the Baía de Paranaguá has one tremendous advantage over every other beach resort in southern Brazil – it lacks even a single car. The result is a sense of calm and isolation that transcends the 40-minute boat ride from the mainland. The fatter, northern half of the island is an ecological preserve, and even a short walk inland from the long, white beaches is forbidden. The hillier southern portion, facing the open ocean, is a surfer's delight. On the other hand, the shallow bay stays warm late into the fall. The towns can grow rowdy during the summer holidays, when a young party crowd descends on the island with surfboards and Rasta gear in tow.

Orientation

Most of the island's hotels are clustered in the town of Nova Brasília, which occupies the isthmus that links its two halves. There is another, smaller settlement known as Encantadas at the southern end of the island, the closest point to the mainland. Both are served by regularly scheduled ferries from Pontal do Sul and Paranguá.

You can get from one town to the other by boat. Or you can take the trail that links them along the island's east coast. On the one-hour hike (about 6km) you will pass a series of completely undeveloped beaches, including Praia de Fora, Praia do Miguel and Praia Grande – the last offering the most challenging surf.

If you find that the towns are too rowdy, head to the pousadas (guesthouses) in the north of the island. Most are found along the long, east-facing beach known as Praia da Fortaleza.

Information

There is no regularly functioning tourist office on the island. However, representatives of the ferry are friendly and can help you find your way to nearby accommodations. There is no place to reliably withdraw money with a foreign bank card. Plan ahead for your cash needs.

For Internet access or international phone calls, head to **Ilha do Mel Online** (☎ 426 8065; per hr US$3.50; ☼ 9am-9pm). It's located in a charming blue house on the path between Nova Brasília and Farol das Conchas. This place is far more than an Internet café or phone kiosk; owner Charles speaks fluent English and is the island's de facto historian and webmaster of its unofficial website (www.ilhadomelonline.com), which has great information in English about food and accommodations, as well as the island's history and ecology. A Carioca by birth, he will make you feel immediately at home. He may even rent you one of the comfortable rooms above the café.

Sights & Activities

BEACHES

The best beaches face the ocean, toward the east. **Praia Grande** is a 20-minute walk (2km) from Nova Brasília and a 40-minute walk (4km) from Encantadas. According to local surfers, it has the best waves in Paraná during winter. **Praia da Fora**, close to Encantadas, also has good waves and a few *barracas* (stalls).

In the north, **Praia da Fortaleza** and **Praia Ponta do Bicho**, which face the shallow bay, have calmer, warmer waters. **Praia das Encantadas**, on the bay side, can get quite dirty; check with locals before swimming.

BOATING

In the harbors of Nova Brasília and Encantadas, you can hire a private boat for excursions to the nearby islands, including **Ilha do Superagüi**, **Ilha das Palmas** and **Ilha das Peças**. Prices are negotiable but not cheap. Expect to pay upward of US$35 for a half-day tour for up to six people. If you have the time, money and interest, you can arrange a multiday expedition to the wilder parts of Superagüi and the inland waterway that connects the bay with São Paulo. For more information contact **Pousada das Meninas** (☎ 426 8023).

THE SOUTH

OTHER ATTRACTIONS

Legend has it that the small caves at the island's southern tip, known as the **Grutas das Encantadas**, are inhabited by beautiful mermaids who enchant all who come near. From the main trail between Encantadas and Nova Brasília, signs clearly mark the way to the caves. The **Farol das Conchas** (Conchas Lighthouse), built in 1872 on orders from Dom Pedro II, stands picturesquely atop a hill at the island's most easterly point. It's well worth a visit, since from here you have panoramic views of the island, the bay, and the mountains of the mainland. The picturesque **Fortaleza de NS dos Prazeres** (Fort of Our Lady of the Pleasures; admission free), which dates to the 1760s, is a 30-minute hike (3km) from Nova Brasília via Praia da Fortaleza.

Sleeping & Eating

Accommodations on the island range from somewhat rustic to extremely rustic. You will need to book ahead for holidays, especially New Year and Carnaval, as well as any summer weekend. However, there are almost always places to pitch a tent or sling a hammock in Nova Brasília. Most camping places have electricity and water and cost US$2 per person.

Restaurants abound in Nova Brasília and along the beach in Encantadas, though quality varies. Many pousadas also double as restaurants.

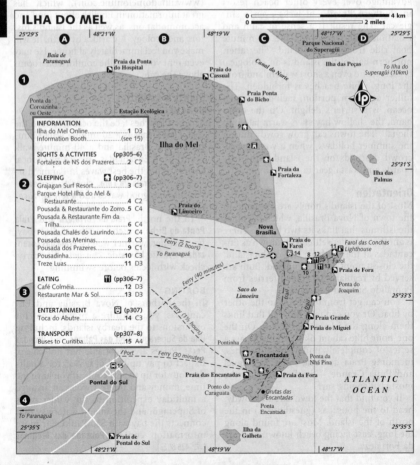

ILHA DO MEL

INFORMATION
Ilha do Mel Online.....................1 D3
Information Booth...................(see 15)

SIGHTS & ACTIVITIES   (pp305–6)
Fortaleza de NS dos Prazeres.......2 C2

SLEEPING   (pp306–7)
Grajagan Surf Resort...................3 C3
Parque Hotel Ilha do Mel &
   Restaurante..........................4 C2
Pousada & Restaurante do Zorro..5 C4
Pousada & Restaurante Fim da
   Trilha.................................6 C4
Pousada Chalés do Laurindo.......7 C4
Pousada das Meninas.................8 C3
Pousada dos Prazeres.................9 C1
Pousadinha.............................10 C3
Treze Luas.............................11 D3

EATING   (pp306–7)
Café Colméia...........................12 D3
Restaurante Mar & Sol.............13 D3

ENTERTAINMENT   (p307)
Toca do Abutre........................14 C3

TRANSPORT   (pp307–8)
Buses to Curitiba.....................15 A4

Prices listed here are for high season. At hotels, expect discounts of 20% to 40% between Easter and early November.

NOVA BRASÍLIA & PRAIA DE FORA

Pousada das Meninas (☎ 426 8023; www.pousada dasmeninas.com.br; r per person US$10, per person with private bathroom US$14, cabins per person US$18) This charming pousada, built largely of driftwood and recycled materials, is set around a small but cozy garden. Suzy – owner, manager and head cook – presides over the place from her inviting kitchen, while her husband organizes boat tours of the surrounding bay. Rooms are simple but tastefully decorated.

Grajagan Surf Resort (☎ 426 8043; www.grajagan .com.br; d US$20, with private bathroom US$35, with ocean view $50; ☒) An accomplished surfer himself, owner Rogério opened this pousada on Praia Grande, the island's best surf beach. The rooms with views of the ocean are arguably the best on the island. Each has a little veranda and hammock facing the sea.

Treze Luas (☎ 426 8067; www.pousadatrezeluas .com; d US$35; ☒) This high-end option has tasteful, well-fitted rooms in a garden setting just steps from the Farol das Conchas lighthouse and Praia de Fora.

Pousadinha (☎ 426 8026; www.pousadinha.com.br; per person US$8, with private bathroom US$14) A simple but decent budget option near the boat landing on the path to Farol das Conchas, with a good restaurant attached.

Restaurante Mar & Sol (☎ 426 8021; mains US$7-10; ☾ lunch & dinner) The best restaurant in Nova Brasília serves simple but very good seafood dishes, including a tasty Bahian crab stew. It's on the path to Farol das Conchas, not far from the lighthouse.

Café Colméia (☎ 426 8029; snacks US$1-3) This stylish little outdoor café serves good coffee, sweets and snacks, to the soothing beat of ambient music.

ENCANTADAS

Pousada & Restaurante Fim da Trilha (☎ 426 9017; www.fimdatrilha.com.br; per person US$8; d with air-con & private bathroom US$33) On the trail to Nova Brasília, this attractive option has both dorms with shared bathrooms and very comfortable rooms with private bathroom and air-conditioning. The restaurant, specializing in paella, is considered the best on the island.

Pousada & Restaurante do Zorro (☎ 426 9052; www.pousadazorro.com.br; HI members/nonmembers US$6/8.50) An HI hostel with clean rooms situated around a pleasant courtyard. It's about 150m from the pier.

Pousada Chalés do Laurindo (☎ 426 9037; www .chalesdolaurindo.com.br; d with breakfast & dinner US$34; ☒ ☒) Small chalets around a courtyard with a small pool, just off the beach 300m from the pier.

AROUND FORTALEZA

Fewer and further between, accommodations around Fortaleza are a good option if you want to escape summer crowds. However, they are a good 40-minute hike (3km) up Praia da Fortaleza from the Nova Brasília pier. Or you can catch a boat across the isthmus for about US$8 for up to four people.

Parque Hotel Ilha do Mel & Restaurant (☎ 426 8075; www.parquehotelilhadomel.com.br; d US$45) Right on the beach a few hundred meters before the fort, this rustic hotel has an outdoor terrace where the general public can enjoy a hearty Brazilian lunch for about US$8. Some of the rooms have balconies with views to the sea. The price includes a huge breakfast and an equally generous dinner buffet.

Pousada dos Prazeres (☎ 243 9649; www.pousada dosprazeres.com.br; s/d US$12/24) A friendly place with basic rooms plus a seafood café on the beach, a few hundred meters past the fort.

Entertainment

The party scene is most active on the path that leads off the Nova Brasília pier. Toca do Abutre, on the beach at the other side of the isthmus, has an outdoor restaurant, a video bar and live music on summer weekends. The beach at Encantadas has a number of outdoor cafés with music, cold *chope* (draft beer) and lively weekend crowds.

Getting There & Away
TO/FROM PARANAGUÁ

See p304 for information on boats to the island.

TO/FROM PONTAL DO SUL

Nonstop buses from Curitiba (US$8, two hours) bypass Paranaguá and head straight to the pier in Pontal do Sul, which is closer to the island and offers more frequent service.

Boats for Encantadas leave at least once an hour between 8am and 6pm, though schedules vary. Some also stop in Nova Brasília. There is an **information booth** (☎ 455 1144) at the port in Pontal do Sul where you can check the latest schedules.

PARQUE NACIONAL DO SUPERAGÜI
☎ 0xx41

Composed of the Superagüi and Peças islands in the Baía de Paranaguá, this national park is renowned for its mangroves and salt marshes, which support an amazing variety of orchids. Jaguars and parrots make the island their home, while dolphins are partial to the waters between Ilha do Superagüi and Ilha do Mel. The national park forms part of the more than 4700 sq km of Atlantic forest reserves in Paraná and São Paulo states that were given Unesco World Heritage listing in 1999.

The village of Barra do Superagüi is inhabited mostly by fishermen, but there are a few pousadas that can serve as a base for exploring the park. Nearby lies Praia Deserta, an 18km-long strip of fine, white sand. You can also hire a boat to explore the north of the island, including a remote village inhabited exclusively by a native tribe.

Sleeping & Eating

All the pousadas in Barra do Superagüi offer very basic accommodations for about US$8 per person. For a little extra, they'll also fix you lunch and/or dinner. At **Pousada Superaguí** (☎ 482 7149, 9978 0821; www.pousada superagui.com.br; s/d US$8/16), friendly owners Dalton and Olga will arrange to pick you up from Ilha do Mel or Paranaguá for an extra cost (see below). Other options for the same price and level of comfort include **Pousada Crepúsculo** (☎ 9959 6709) and **Pousada Centaura** (☎ 9959 8427). **Restaurante Golfinos** (☎ 9959 8852; ⊗ 11am-11pm) is the town's best seafood restaurant.

Getting There & Away

There are no regular boats to Ilha do Superagüi. The closest town is Guaraqueçaba, which is accessible by bus from Curitiba. In Guaraqueçaba, boats anchor in front of the old municipal market, and it's possible to negotiate a ride to the island. Boats from the island have 'S.AGUI' painted on the bow or stern. Note that the road to Guar-

aqueçaba is slow going, taking up to five hours from Curitiba or Paranaguá.

The fastest way to get there is to hire a private boat at the harbor in Paranaguá (US$50 for up to six people, one hour) or in Nova Brasília on Ilha do Mel. Contact **Dalton** (☎ 482 7149, 9978 0821), proprietor of Pousada Superaguí.

FOZ DO IGUAÇU & AROUND
☎ 0xx45 / pop 277,400

Rising in the coastal mountains of Paraná and Santa Catarina, the Rio Iguaçu snakes west for 600km, picking up a few dozen tributaries along the way. It widens majestically and sweeps around a magnificent forest stage before plunging and crashing in the tiered falls known as Iguaçu Falls. A total of 275 individual falls occupy an area more than 3km wide and 80m high, which makes them wider than Victoria, higher than Niagara and more beautiful than either. Neither words nor photographs do them justice – they must be seen and heard.

Thousands of years before they were 'discovered' by Europeans, the falls were a holy burial place for the Tupi-Guarani and Paraguas tribes. Spaniard Don Alvar Nuñes happened upon the falls in 1541 in the course of his journey from Santa Catarina, on the coast, to Asunción. He dubbed the falls the Saltos de Santa María, but this name fell into disuse and the Tupi-Guarani name, Iguaçu (Great Waters), was re-adopted. In 1986 Unesco declared the region a World Heritage site.

The Brazilian city of Foz do Iguaçu (known as 'Foz') went through a period of frenzied growth during the 18 years that Itaipu Dam was under construction, the population increasing from 35,000 in 1973 to 190,000 in 1991. It was an edgy place then, but it's settled down in the years since. That said, you should avoid the riverfront area at night. And don't walk across the bridge to Paraguay at any time. Thieves assume you are returning with duty-free goods, and muggings are regrettably common.

Orientation

Av Brasil is the town's main street. Av Jorge Schimmelpfeng and Av República Argentina form the south and north borders of the center, respectively. The bus station is located 4km to the northeast, while the airport is 18km to the southeast. Just south of town, the junction of the Paraná and Iguaçu rivers forms the tripartite Paraguayan, Brazilian and Argentine border (marked by obelisks). The falls themselves are another 20km to the southeast.

The Ponte Presidente Tancredo Neves, which crosses the Rio Iguaçu about 6km from the center of town, connects Brazil with the Argentine town of Puerto Iguazú. It is smaller and mellower than its Brazilian counterpart. The Rio Paraná, which forms the border with Paraguay, is spanned by the Ponte da Amizade, which is located just north of the center. Across the bridge is the shabby but lively Paraguayan town of Ciudad del Este.

Itaipu Dam – the world's largest hydroelectric project – is located 5km north of Foz do Iguaçu.

Information

EMERGENCY
Bombeiros (☎ 193) Handles fires as well as medical emergencies.
Federal Police (Map below; ☎ 523 1828)

INTERNET ACCESS
NetPub (Map below; ☎ 572 5773; Rua Ruí Barbosa 549; per hr US$2; ☉ 8am-midnight) Internet access and international phone calls.
US Net (Map below; ☎ 523 2289; Av Brasil 549; per hr US$2; ☉ 9am-10pm) Internet access and international phone calls.

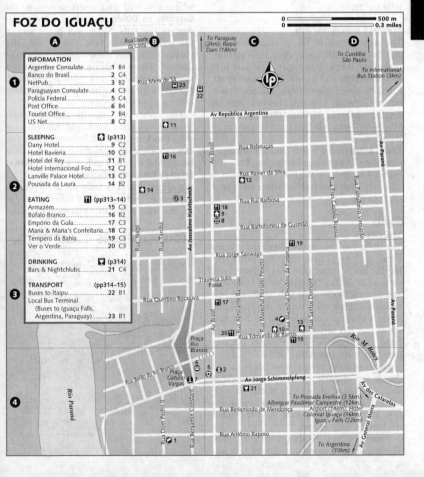

FOZ DO IGUAÇU

INFORMATION	
Argentine Consulate	1 B4
Banco do Brasil	2 C4
NetPub	3 B2
Paraguayan Consulate	4 C3
Policía Federal	5 C4
Post Office	6 B4
Tourist Office	7 B4
US Net	8 C2

SLEEPING ⌂	(p313)
Dany Hotel	9 C2
Hotel Bavieria	10 C3
Hotel del Rey	11 B1
Hotel Internacional Foz	12 C2
Lanville Palace Hotel	13 C3
Pousada da Laura	14 B2

EATING ⌑	(pp313–14)
Armazém	15 C3
Búfalo Branco	16 B2
Empório da Gula	17 C3
Maria & Maria's Confeitaria	18 C3
Tempero da Bahía	19 C3
Ver o Verde	20 C3

DRINKING ⌂	(p314)
Bars & Nightclubs	21 C4

TRANSPORT	(pp314–15)
Buses to Itaipu	22 B1
Local Bus Terminal	
(Buses to Iguaçu Falls, Argentina, Paraguay)	23 B1

MEDICAL SERVICES
Hospital Internacional (Map p311; ☎ 523 1404; Av Brasil 1637) For medical emergencies.

MONEY
There are dozens of money-exchange houses all over town and most give a better rate for cash than the banks.

Banco do Brasil (Map p311; Av Brasil) Visa ATMs and money exchange near Av Jorge Schimmelpfeng.

Caribe Turismo (Map p311; ☎ 529 7173) Located in the airport, this travel agency exchanges Visa and American Express traveler's checks. It's the only place in town open on Sunday.

POST
Post office (Map p311; Praça Getúlio Vargas) Very close to the tourist office.

TOURIST INFORMATION
The region's tourist board maintains various booths with up-to-date information, including maps, bus timetables and lists of restaurants and hotels. Most staff speak English; some also speak Italian, Spanish or German. You can also talk with an English-speaking **representative** (☎ 0800-451 516; ⏱ 7am-11pm) toll-free from anywhere in Brazil.

Tourist board Airport (⏱ noon-7pm, 10pm-midnight); center (Map p311; cnr Av Jorge Schimmelpfeng & Av Juscelino Kubitscheck; ⏱ 7am-11pm); long-distance bus station (⏱ 7:30am-6pm) The office in the center is open 365 days a year.

Sights
THE FALLS
The falls are unequally divided between Brazil and Argentina, with Argentina taking the lion's share. Like fans of New York versus fans of Los Angeles, or of São Paulo and Rio, each side of the falls has its staunch defenders. This much is true: the Brazil side offers a more panoramic view of the totality of the 275 separate falls. On the other hand, the Argentine side provides a closer, more intimate experience of the falls, and a greater variety of perspectives. See both and decide for yourself which you prefer. That said, it's not possible to do justice to both sides of the falls in a single day – plan for two, and more if you want to visit Ciudad del Este or Itaipu Dam.

Remember that it's always wet at the falls. The region gets more than 2m of rain annually, and the falls create a lot of moisture themselves. Pack raingear. Also note that lighting for photography is best in the morning on the Brazilian side and in the late afternoon on the Argentine side.

On both sides of the falls, you will receive detailed maps to help you navigate the parks.

Brazilian Side
If you drive to the falls, you must leave your car at the entrance of the **Parque Nacional do Iguaçu** (Map below; ☎ 521 4400; admission US$4, plus US$2 per vehicle; ⏱ 1-5pm Mon, 8am-5pm Tue-Sun, until 6pm Oct-Mar). Once you've paid your admission, you'll board a free double-decker bus. Take it straight to the last stop, where you will find yourself next to the **Garganta do Diablo**, the most spectacular part of the falls. Signs will point you to the walkways that take you to the falls' very edge. Expect to be dazzled – and also doused. There is also a restaurant at this stop that serves a very good buffet lunch (US$8), with seating on a pleasant outdoor terrace right on the river.

Once you have gotten the visual overview from above (plus a good, cold shower), consider checking out the falls from below. You can catch a boat from the boat ramp 3km back along the road to Foz. Contact **Macuco Safari de Barco** (☎ 574 4244; per person US$30). It's not cheap, but it is truly an unforgettable experience and an entirely different way to see the falls. If you don't have an extra day

IGUAÇU FALLS
0 - 6 km
0 - 4 miles

To Asunción; Ciudad del Este
BR 7
To Itaipu Dam
BR 277
BRAZIL Paraná
To São Paulo; Curitiba
Ponte da Amizade
Foz do Iguaçu
Ponte Presidente Tancredo Neves
Ponto Meira
Albergue Paudimar Campestre
International Airport
PARAGUAY
Puerto Iguazú
Camping Clube do Brasil
Parque Nacional do Iguaçu
Rio Iguaçu
RN 12
Reserva Nacional
Parque das Aves
Hotel Tropical das Cataratas
Hotel Cataratas
Rio Paraná
ARGENTINA
Aeropuerto Internacional de Iguazú
Cataratas do Iguaçu
Parque Nacional Iguazú
RN 12
To Posadas; Buenos Aires
RN 101

to spare for the Argentine side, the boat trip is particularly recommended.

For a real splurge, treat yourself to a helicopter ride over the waterfalls. For US$60, you get 10 minutes in the air. The choppers will take up to three passengers; it's best to sit by the edge of the bubble. **Helisul Taxi Aereo** (☎ 529 7474; www.helisul.com) operates from just outside the park entrance.

Argentine Side

The entrance to the **Parque Nacional Iguazú** (Map opposite; ☎ 0xx54-3757 420 722; www.iguazu argentina.com; admission US$6.50, plus US$4.50 per vehicle; ☼ 8am-7pm, until 6pm Sep-Mar) is 18km from Puerto Iguazú. You must leave your car at the entrance and walk to the various parts of the park. Or you catch a free train (every 30 minutes) that connects the entrance with the Garganta do Diablo walk. There are several restaurants (buffet US$5 to US$10) just inside the entrance of the park, as well as snack bars.

As well as the **Passeio Garganta do Diablo**, there are the **Passeios Inferiores** and the **Passeios Superiores**. Save Garganta until last, both for dramatic effect and because in the morning it tends to be packed with bus tours.

Start with Passeios Superiores. The concrete catwalks behind the waterfalls used to go as far as the Garganta do Diablo, until floods swept them over the edge. It is the least spectacular of the three, but a great way to build suspense.

The Passeios Inferiores is a 1.5km circuit offering a view of the falls from below. From here you can take the free boat (every 15 minutes 9am to 5:30pm) to **Isla San Martín**, which has trails that offer more close-up views of the falls.

The Garganta do Diablo catwalk begins at a quiet point upstream from the falls, passing a number of tranquil islands before reaching its final, stunning destination. At the Garganta, the serene river suddenly turns violent as 13,000 cu meters of water per second plunge 90m in 14 falls around a horseshoe-shaped canyon. It's a hypnotizing, multisensory experience to see the roaring falls, huge rainbow arcs, drenching mist and, in the distance, parrots and hawks cruising over the deep, green forest. Watch for the swifts, which drop like rocks into the misty abyss, catch insects in mid-air,

shoot back up and dart to perch on the cliffs behind the falls.

THE RAIN FOREST

The Brazilian and Argentine parks, occupying 550 sq km and 1550 sq km respectively, encompass much more than the falls themselves. Much of the parkland is inaccessible, but near the falls you can explore the region's remarkable ecosystem. The foliage is lush and lovely: 2000 species of plants growing in four different layers, from forest-floor grasses, ferns and bushes, to low, middle and treetop canopies. Look for the fantastic butterflies (they congregate around pools of urine and on sweaty handrails), parrots, parakeets, woodpeckers, hummingbirds, lizards, 3cm-long ants, beautifully colored spiders and countless varieties of orchids, lianas and vines. There are also four species of toucan in the park. Their long beaks are deceptive; they're actually so light and spongy that the birds are back-heavy and therefore clumsy fliers.

Other creatures in the park include monkeys (there's a large colony of the mono caí variety), deer, sloths, anteaters, raccoons, jaguars, tapirs, caimans and armadillos. Encounters with mammals are less likely, since in rain forests large animals are less abundant and tend to be nocturnal. While daytime encounters with large cats are rare, the park administration provides a leaflet with some safety hints. If you do meet one, you're advised to stay calm, try to appear bigger than you are and do not get close to the cats (especially if they are feeding cubs).

There are a number of simple tips to make your explorations more enjoyable. First, arrive early in the morning, before it gets too hot and when birds and wildlife are easier to spot. Try to gather as much information as possible about the flora and fauna beforehand so you will know what to keep your eyes peeled for. Go in a small group and remain as quiet as possible. Bring binoculars. And finally, carry bug repellent, sunscreen, a hat, water and, depending on how long you will be out, some lunch for the hike.

Argentine Forest

For an excellent introduction to the rain forest, check out the **Sendero Macuco** trail. Ask guides at the **visitors center** (☎ 0xx54-3757 491 469) for a map of the park and to point you to the trail. They may seem more interested in nudging you toward one of the expensive tours (p312), which is one – but not the only – option.

The Sendero Macuco trail begins about 2.5km from the visitors center. About 3km along the trail, there is another short trail to a smaller set of falls at Salto Arrechea. There is a bridge across the falls – don't cross it, as it's in a poor state of repair. Instead, double back and continue on down to the Rio Iguazú Inferior.

Brazilian Forest

On the Brazilian side, the **Trilha Poço Preto** (9km) is another good introduction to the forest. The trailhead is not far from the entrance (ask the driver of the park bus to stop at the trailhead) and goes all the way to **Rio Iguaçu**, several kilometers upriver from the falls. At the river, another short path leads to the **Lagoa do Jacaré**, a popular watering hole for local birds that is particularly lovely in the early morning and late afternoon.

ITAIPU DAM

How did Brazil manage to run up such a huge foreign debt? Part of the answer can be found in mammoth projects such as Itaipu Dam, the world's largest hydroelectric works (see p314).

The dam, which is 19km down the Rio Paraná river from Foz, offers six 1½-hour guided tours a day (8am to 3:30pm Monday to Saturday). From Monday to Friday, the tourist office in Foz can arrange more in-depth, technical tours for small groups. On Friday and Saturday nights at 8pm, there is a **sound-and-light show** (US$2). All tours are free. For information, call the dam's **visitor information service** (☎ 520 6999; www.itaipu.gov.br) or visit the website.

To get to Itaipu Dam, catch a Conjunto C bus from any stop along Av Juscelino Kubitschek in the center of Foz. There's one every 15 to 20 minutes from 6am until midnight (US$0.50, 30 minutes). Head all the way to the last bus stop at the Ecomuseu (worth a look), then walk the final 400m to the Itaipu visitors center.

PARQUE DAS AVES

This five-hectare **bird park** (Map p310; ☎ 529 8282; www.parquedasaves.com.br; admission US$5; ⏰ 8:30am-5:30pm), located 300m from the

entrance to the Brazilian falls, is home to some 800 different species of birds. You can actually enter the 8m-high aviaries that are constructed in the forest itself. There are also exhibits devoted to native snakes and butterflies. It's a good place to identify birds that can be seen in their natural habitat on a forest walk at the falls.

CIUDAD DEL ESTE (PARAGUAY)

Across the Ponte da Amizade, at Ciudad del Este, you can play roulette or baccarat at the Casino de Leste, or purchase duty-free imported goods (no great deals) or some nifty Paraguayan lacework and leather goods.

From the local bus terminal in Foz, buses run to Ciudad del Este (US$1) every 10 minutes (every 30 minutes on Sunday) from 6:15am to 7:30pm.

Tours

To visit the falls efficiently, it's worth hooking up with a guide, especially for the Argentine side. You can save significant time and effort with transportation and border formalities. Generally, costs (about US$10 to US$15 per person plus park fees) end up being lower than renting a car, and relying on public transportation to the Argentine side can be a headache. And if you want to see both sides of the falls in a single day, an organized tour is the only way to make it happen.

You can organize a tour at your hotel's front desk or at any of the myriad travel agencies along Av Brasil, but spend some time shopping around as prices and service vary considerably. **Jaha Iguassu** (Map p309; ☎ 572 4158, 9106 6985; www.jahaiguassu.bio.br; Rua Taborá 1020), run by the friendly and very knowledgeable Luis, is a good option, with a range of options and competitive prices. Guides speak English and Spanish as well as some French and German. Offices are located in the Hotel del Rey.

The parks on both sides of the falls have a number of organized adventure options, including rafting, rappelling, kayaking, biking and guided nature walks. On the Argentine side, **Iguassu Jungle Explorer** (☎ 0xx54-3757 421 600) runs a range of adventure tours. Its main offices are in the Sheraton Hotel inside the park. Inside the Brazilian park, try **Macuco Ecoaventura** (☎ 529 9626) for rafting, rappelling and other organized adventure activities.

Sleeping

There is a wide range of accommodations in Foz, and, because of stiff competition, prices are surprisingly reasonable. You'll get more bang for your buck here than in most other tourist areas in southern Brazil. Prices listed are for high season. You can successfully negotiate discounts at other times.

BUDGET

Pousada da Laura (Map p309; ☎ 574 3628; Rua Naipi 629; per person about US$10) The best budget option in town, this pousada is definitely not lavish but the owner is very friendly. She refuses to provide Internet access on principle – it keeps guests from getting to know one another, she says, which she feels is part of her duty. Communal cooking facilities are available, as is a friendly dog for those homesick for pets.

Hotel del Rey (Map p309; ☎ 523 2027; www.hoteldelreyfoz.com.br; Rua Tarobá 1020; s/d US$12/17; P ⊠ ⊠) The most comfort for your dollar in town. Large, clean rooms with air-con and fridge, plus a pool and a convenient location in the center near the local bus terminal.

Albergue Paudimar Campestre (Map p310; ☎ 572 2430; www.paudimar.com.br; US$7; P ⊑ ⊠) Located 12km from town, on the way to the falls along Av das Cataratas, this is more a mini-resort than a hostel, with a swimming pool, bar and cheap meals.

Camping Clube do Brasil (Map p310; ☎ 523 8599; per person US$5; P ⊠). The closest camping facilities to the Brazilian falls, located just before the entrance to the park, 600m down a dirt road on your left.

MID-RANGE

Hotel Bavieria (Map p309; ☎ 523 5995; www.hotel bavieraiguassu.com.br; Av Jorge Schimmelpfeng 697; s/d/tr US$22/27/34; P ⊠) As the hotel's mock-Germanic facade suggests, this is a very clean and orderly option. It's located within crawling distance of the town's restaurant and nightclub district.

Lanville Palace Hotel (Map p309; ☎ 523 1511; lanville@onda.com.br; Av Jorge Schimmelpfeng 827; s/d US$25/33; P ⊠ ⊑ ⊠) It's no beauty, but this hotel is comfortable and good value, and also close to the town's nightspots. The large pool in back is a welcome relief on hot days.

Dany Hotel (Map p309; ☎ 523 1530; danyhotel@danyhotel.com.br; Av Brasil 509; s/d US$24/48; P ⊠) The rooms are less attractive than the lobby would indicate, but this hotel has decent quarters with fridge, TV and air-con.

TOP END

The falls attract visitors from around the world, including those with cash to burn. There are a number of places that cater to more evolved needs.

Hotel Tropical das Cataratas (Map p310; ☎ 521 7000; www.tropicalhotel.com.br; d US$145-230; P ⊠ ⊑ ⊠) This deluxe, colonial-style hotel is actually inside the park, a few hundred meters from the falls. Service is top-notch. It's the place to stay on someone else's dime. The price is high, but, hey, at least you'll save on park entrance fees and bus fares. Reservations recommended.

Hotel Internacional Foz (Map p309; ☎ 521 4100; www.internacionalfoz.com.br; Rua Almirante Barroso 2006; d US$130; P ⊠ ⊑ ⊠) The fanciest place in the center, this marble-heavy hotel also boasts a gym, a sauna, a chic nightclub, a restaurant-in-the-round with panoramic views, and Internet access in every room.

Eating

Maria & Maria's Confeitaria (Map p309; ☎ 523 5472; Av Brasil 505; mains US$3; ⊗ 8am-10pm) Good bakery with *empadoês* (meat- and cheese-stuffed pastries), sandwiches and pastries, plus a dining room with standard Brazilian lunch fare.

Ver o Verde (Map p309; ☎ 574 5647; Rua Almirante Barroso 1713; fixed-price buffet US$3; ⊗ 11:30am-3pm) The best vegetarian place in town, with simple but tasteful décor and a very good buffet.

Búfalo Branco (Map p309; ☎ 523 9744; Rua Rebouças 530; buffet US$12; ⊗ noon-11:30pm) The best known – and most expensive – *churrascaria* in town, with indisputably good grilled meat and fine service.

Empório da Gula (Map p309; ☎ 574 6191; Av Brasil 1441; buffet US$6; ⊗ lunch Sat & Sun, dinner) A more reasonably priced competitor of Búfalo Branco, also with excellent meat straight from the grill.

Tempero da Bahía (Map p309; ☎ 572 9187; Rua Marechal Deodoro da Fonseca 1228; mains US$8-10; ⊗ 6pm-1am) It's far from Bahia, but the food tastes like the real thing. Live music nightly from 8pm.

Armazém (Map p309; ☎ 572 7422; Rua Edmundo de Barros 446; mains US$10; 🕑 6pm-2am) This cozy restaurant/bar occupies an attractive, colonial-style house on a tree-lined street. Gourmet Brazilian food and a festive atmosphere attract an upscale crowd of both tourists and locals.

NetPub (Map p309; ☎ 572 5773; Rua Ruí Barbosa 549; buffet US$1.50; 🕑 lunch Mon-Fri) If your funds are running low, head to this no-frills but super-cheap all-you-can-eat buffet, which is meant to snag business for the Internet café attached.

Entertainment

The main strip for nightlife is Av Jorge Schimmelpfeng, which is kept safe late into the night by plentiful foot traffic and an adjacent police station. There are lots of open-air beer gardens to start the night off, as well as chill nightclubs that stay open to the wee hours. The names and owners change frequently – peruse the avenue for the crowd that most appeals. The beautiful/rich crowd currently congregates at the nightclub at the **Hotel Internacional Foz** (Map p309; ☎ 521 4100; www.internacionalfoz.com.br; Rua Almirante Barroso 2006).

Getting There & Away

AIR

There are daily direct flights from Foz do Iguaçu to Asunción (one hour), Buenos Aires (two hours), Rio, São Paulo (one hour) and Curitiba (40 minutes).

In Puerto Iguazú, **Aerolineas Argentinas** (☎ 0xx54-3757 420 194; Aguirre 295) offers daily services to Buenos Aires Aeroparque for US$145.

LAND

Border Crossings

Since the events of September 11, border crossings have gotten significantly tighter. You must have a passport and, if required for your country, a visa in order to enter Argentina or Paraguay, even for the day. Argentina is particularly strict. Expect delays at the border.

If you return the same day, you will not receive an entry or exit stamp (unless you ask). Instead, you'll receive a small receipt that you must keep until it is collected on your return in the evening. If you plan to spend more than one day in Argentina or Paraguay, you should advise the immigration officers and ensure that you receive both

A DAM SHAME?

For some, it's a wonder of the modern world. For others, it's a man-made disaster of epic proportions. But there's is no doubt that Itaipu Dam – the world's largest – has permanently changed the face of southern Brazil.

First, the startling statistics. The dam's structures stretch for almost 9km and reach a height of more than 200m. The concrete used in its construction would be sufficient to build a two-lane highway from Moscow to Lisbon, and at the height of construction activity, crews worked at a blinding pace equivalent to building a 20-story office building every 55 minutes. No wonder it cost US$18 billion.

So was it worth it? The answer is not easy. Its generating capacity is 12,600 megawatts – enough to supply both a quarter of Brazil's electricity needs and 90% of Paraguay's. To produce an equivalent amount in oil-burning thermoelectric plants, you'd need 434,000 barrels of oil per day. That's a lot of carbon dioxide emissions.

At the same time, critics of the dam estimate that 700 sq km of forest has been lost or seriously compromised. Several species of plant life have been driven into extinction, including a rare orchid. Many native Guaraní and Tupi settlements were destroyed, as well as important archaeological sites and the impressive Sete Quedas falls. Some speculate that changes in the climate brought about by the huge, new body of water have yet to be determined. For its part, the Itaipu Binacional – a joint Brazilian–Paraguayan agency that administers the dam – has been sensitive to such criticisms. It launched innovative programs to relocate animals displaced by flooding, and has funded extensive reforestation projects on land along the reservoir's banks.

It's tough to come up with a final tally of costs and benefits – especially as you watch the sound-and-light show, dreamed up by the dam's publicity department to illuminate the dam's dramatic, concrete face.

entry and exit stamps from both countries to avoid potential problems. The process should be automatic at the Argentine border, but not necessarily at the Paraguayan border – you may need to be proactive. It generally takes 24 hours to procure either an Argentine or Paraguayan visa.

Argentine consulate (Map p309; ☎ 574 2969; Rua Dom Pedro II 28; ◷ 10am-2:30pm Mon-Fri)

Paraguayan consulate (Map p309; ☎ 523 2898; Rua Marechal Deodoro da Fonseca 901; ◷ 8:30am-4:30pm Mon-Fri)

Bus

All long-distance buses arrive at and depart from the international bus station, 6km from the center of town. For service to Buenos Aires (US$26, 20 hours), head to the station in Puerto Iguazú. For Asunción in Paraguay (US$8, five hours), head to Ciudad del Este. Other destinations include Curitiba (US$20, *leito* US$41, 10 hours), São Paulo (US$28, *leito* US$65, 16 hours) and Rio de Janeiro (US$36, *leito* US$82, 22 hours).

Getting Around
TO/FROM THE AIRPORT

The airport is 16km from the center. To go there, catch a bus marked Aeroporto/P Nacional (US$0.50, 40 minutes) from any stop along Av Juscelino Kubitschek. Buses run every 22 minutes from 5:30am to 7pm

and then every hour until 12:40am. A taxi from the center costs around US$12.

TO/FROM THE BUS STATION

From outside the bus station, catch any Centro bus to town (US$0.50). A taxi costs around US$4.

TO/FROM THE FALLS

For the Brazilian side of the falls, catch the Aeroporto/P Nacional bus (US$0.50, 50 minutes) right to the park entrance. You can catch it in the local bus terminal, or at stops along Av Juscelino Kubitschek and Av Jorge Schimmelpfeng. Transportation within the park is included in the admission fee.

To get to the Argentine side of the falls, catch a Puerto Iguazú bus from the local bus terminal or any stop along Av Juscelino Kubitschek. Buses start running at 6:30am and leave every 20 minutes (every 50 minutes on Sunday) until 7:30pm. The fare is US$1.50.

At the bus station in Puerto Iguazú, transfer to a Cataratas bus to the falls. You can pay in Argentine pesos or Brazilian reais: the bus costs US$2.50 and park entry costs US$10. Buses return to Puerto Iguazú from the visitors center at the falls on the hour. The bus back to Foz leaves Puerto Iguazú approximately every 30 minutes until 7:30pm.

THE SOUTH

Santa Catarina

HIGHLIGHTS

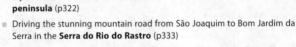

- Seeing mother whales and their calves sport and feed just off the stunning **Praia da Rosa** (p332)

- Following mountain trails to the hidden beaches of southern **Ilha de Santa Catarina** (p331)

- Checking out the colorful marine life in the crystal-clear waters off the **Porto Belo peninsula** (p322)

- Driving the stunning mountain road from São Joaquim to Bom Jardim da Serra in the **Serra do Rio do Rastro** (p333)

- Downing *chopes* (draft beers) at Blumenau's no-holds-barred **Oktoberfest** (p323)

■ POPULATION: 5.8 MILLION   ■ AREA: 95,433 SQ KM

To win the approval of a Rio native, a beach has to be awfully good. Santa Catarina manages to pull it off, attracting hundreds of thousands of Cariocas, as well as Paulistas (residents of Rio and São Paulo state, respectively), Argentineans and Uruguayans, in the summer months of January and February. The mountainous and beautiful Ilha de Santa Catarina is home to an amazing variety of beaches as well as the state's major transport hub and capital city, Florianópolis. South of Florianópolis you can find pumping surf as well as the sophisticated resort town of Praia da Rosa. To the north, the Caribbean-like bays around Porto Belo, with their clear, turquoise waters, are a diver's delight.

Inland from the beaches, Santa Catarina reveals the profound influence of the region's German and Eastern European immigrants. The cities of Blumenau and Joinville combine tidiness and industry with a love of beer, sausage and sauerkraut. A legacy of small, family-owned farms and cooperative social action, as opposed to the plantation culture of northern Brazil, have led to a relatively equitable distribution of incomes. In another un-Brazilian touch, the stunning mountains around São Joaquim, Brazil's highest city, regularly receive snowfall during the winter months of July and August.

As you plan your travel to Santa Catarina, remember that crowds, as well as temperatures and prices, run high all along the coast during January and February. Instead, March and April, or November and December are great times to visit – unless you're specifically looking for the party atmosphere of high summer. Winters are not outright cold, but blustery weather can take the pleasure out of beachgoing. One consolation is that winter is whale-watching season, which is especially good around Praia da Rosa. Beer lovers should consider Blumenau's Oktoberfest, Brazil's biggest street party after Rio's Carnaval.

History
Sitting at the frontier of Spanish and Portuguese Americas, Santa Catarina remained largely undeveloped until the 1820s, when the newly independent Brazil realized the strategic importance of the region. The emperor invited German-speaking immigrants to develop the land and help serve as a buffer against Spanish insurgency. The German immigrants, as well as the Italians who followed them, never adopted the plantation culture of the Northeast. Instead, the economy was based on small, family-owned farms, a legacy that lives on in the region's egalitarian politics and relatively equitable distribution of income (see the boxed text, p321).

Climate
The coastal lowlands of Santa Catarina enjoy a semitropical climate, with hot, humid summers and winters that don't get much colder than chilly – around 15°C (59°F). The central highlands are drier in the summer and colder in the winter, with temperatures sometimes dropping to 5°C (41°F) or even lower. At the higher elevations of the Serra Geral near the border with Rio Grande do Sul, snow is surprisingly common.

Getting There & Around
Florianópolis is the state's transportation hub, with direct bus and air services to every major city in Brazil. The economically important Joinville also has direct air services to São Paulo, with connections to other major cities.

Most destinations of interest to the traveler are within a few hours of Florianópolis by car or bus. Bus service is extensive and quite dependable.

JOINVILLE

☎ 0xx47 / pop 445,900

Imagine a city where natural blonds stroll and cycle through clean, well-lit streets. Where every lawn is well manicured and every park is litter-free. Where drivers – even bus drivers – respect bike lanes and crosswalks. Now here's the hard part: imagine this city in Brazil.

Joinville's citizens, largely of German origins, are proud of their prosperous, ordered home. Though it's Santa Catarina's largest city, it retains a small-town feel with industrial activity tucked neatly away from the center. Interest for the traveler lies mostly in the way it contrasts with the rest of Brazil. At the very least, this clean, safe, pedestrian-friendly city makes a fine stopover.

Information

The city's official website (www.promotur .com.br) is good for general information.

Banco do Brasil (cnr Rua Luiz Neimeyer & Rua do Principe) Money exchange and Visa ATMs.

Information posts (long-distance bus station ☽ 8am-noon & 2-6pm; Shopping Mueller cnr Rua Pedro Lobo & Rua Senador Felipe Schmidt; ☽ 10am-6pm Mon-Fri, 8am-noon & 2-6pm Sat & Sun) Conveniently located in the long-distance bus station and in front of Shopping Mueller.

Main tourist office (☎ 453 2663, Av Beira Rio 315) On the riverfront in the convention center, around 1.5km from the center.

Post office (Rua Princesa Isabel)

Telephone (Shopping Cidade das Flores, cnr Rua Mário Lobo & Rua Princessa Isabel) For international calling there is a shop in the mall.

Museu Nacional da Imigração

This interesting little **National Museum of Immigration** (☎ 433 3736; Rua Rio Branco 229; admission US$1; ☽ 9am-5pm Mon-Fri, 11am-5pm Sat & Sun) documents the history of German immigration to Joinville and the surrounding region. It's housed in a simple but elegant palace, built in 1870 for the sister of Brazil's Emperor Dom Pedro II and her husband – France's Prince of Joinville. The museum grounds also include a well-preserved enxaimal house typical of the region's first immigrants. It's approached by an impressive stand of palms along Alameda das Palmeiras.

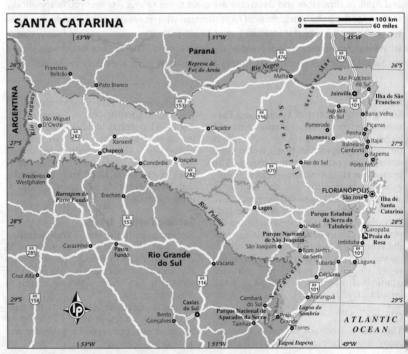

Tours

The popular **Barco Príncipe** (☎ 455 4444) sets out each morning for a daylong tour of the picturesque Baía Babitonga, passing the bay's 14 islands and ending up at the old port city of **São Francisco do Sul**. The boat leaves at 10am from the Espinheiros neighborhood about 10km, or a US$4 taxi ride, from the center. The trip costs US$12 per person including lunch. The boat fills up quickly with tour groups, so book ahead. Pack a swimsuit and your dancing shoes, as the boat has both a swimming pool and a miniature nightclub.

Festivals & Events

During the second half of July, Joinville – the only city in Brazil with an affiliate school of the Bolshoi Ballet – hosts Latin America's largest **dance festival**. Contact the **Instituto Festival de Dança de Joinville** (☎ 423 1010) or check the festival website (www .festivaldedanca.com.br).

The **Festival of Flowers** (☎ 453 2263; promotur@ promotur.com.br) is in mid-November.

Sleeping

Hotel Germânia (☎ 433 9886; www.hotelgermania .com.br; Rua Ministro Calógeras 612; s/d with breakfast & afternoon tea US$32/42; P ⊠ 🖳 🛋) It looks like a chain hotel from the outside, but inside it's anything but. As the name suggests, it is spotlessly clean, but also warm and tastefully appointed. The price includes afternoon tea as well as an excellent breakfast, and it may be the only hotel in Brazil with carpeted rooms that lack even a remote smell of mildew. A friendly staff, English-speaking owner, and a rooftop pool complete the picture.

Hotel Trocadero (☎ 422 1469; Rua Visconde de Taunay 185; s/d US$10/14, with ⊠ US$14/21) Housed in a colonial-style building with comfortable, spick-and-span rooms, this hotel is perennially popular with groups, so try to book ahead if possible.

Anthurium Parque Hotel (☎ 433 6299; www .anthurium.com.br; Rua São José 226; s/d $34/40; P 🖳 🛋) Very elegant for the price, this four-star joint consists of a fine colonial building set around a green courtyard with a pleasant pool. It also has a good, if relatively expensive, dining room.

Tannenhof Othon (☎ 433 8011; www.tannenhof .com.br; Rua Visconde de Taunay 340; s/d/tr with breakfast US$43/43/60; P ⊠ 🖳 🛋). One of the town's

top hotels, the Tannenhof is Germanic in both its architecture and its crisp, if rather formal, service. It offers all the amenities, including a gym and sauna. The breakfast buffet, included in the price of your room, is lavish.

Hotel Atlântica (☎ 3062 6933; Rua 15 de Novembro 811; s/d/tr US$4/8/12, with bathroom US$5.50/11/16; P) Rather rundown and with rooms around a bleak courtyard, but the price is right.

Hotel Mattes (☎ 422 3582; Rua 15 de Novembro 801; s/d US$10/17, with ⊠ US$13/29; P) A good budget option a couple of blocks from the center, with decent rooms around a lacklustre courtyard.

Eating

As in much of Santa Catarina, Italian and German food dominate Joinville's culinary life.

Delicatesse Viktoria (☎ 422 0570; Rua Senador Felipe Schmidt 400; afternoon buffet per person US$4.50; 🕑 9am-8pm Mon-Sat) Come in the morning for coffee and freshly baked sweets, or wait for the afternoon buffet, called *café colonial*, which includes excellent cakes as well as savory items such as soups, quiches and *salgadinhos* (savory snacks). Housed in a former German, colonial-style home, it feels like you've finally returned to the old country to see your beloved German auntie.

Biergarten (☎ 423 3790; Rua Visconde de Taunay 1183; lunch buffet US$6, mains US$7-10; 🕑 lunch & dinner) The main dishes are very good, but the lunch buffet, featuring German as well as Brazilian dishes, is excellent, as is the choice of beers on tap. The bright, cheerful dining room and large terrace are both equally attractive options.

Fatirella (☎ 423 1616; Rua Visconde de Taunay 299; all-you-can-eat pizza US$4; 🕑 lunch daily, dinner Mon-Sat) A lively, relaxed place for a *rodízio* (smorgasbord) of pizza and pasta.

Restaurante Cozinha Natural (☎ 422 7897; Rua Jacob Richlin 12) The town's best all-vegetarian option, with a per-kilo lunch.

Expresso (☎ 433 9451; Av Juscelino Kubitschek 536; mains US$7-10; 🕑 5pm-1am) More bar than restaurant, this pleasant, open-air establishment hosts a prosperous after-work crowd. The food is uninspired, but the beer is good.

Paviloche (☎ 433 9171; Rua 9 de Março nr Rua Eng Niemeyer; 🕑 11am-11pm Mon-Sat, 1-11pm Sun) This

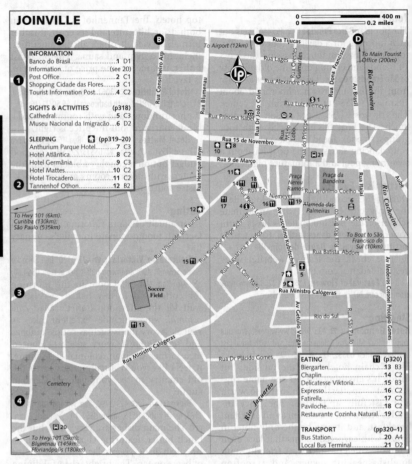

JOINVILLE

INFORMATION	
Banco do Brasil.....................**1** D1
Information.........................(see 20)
Post Office.........................**2** C1
Shopping Cidade das Flores.......**3** C1
Tourist Information Post...........**4** C2

SIGHTS & ACTIVITIES	(p318)
Cathedral...........................**5** C3
Museu Nacional da Imigração...**6** D2

SLEEPING	(pp319–20)
Anthurium Parque Hotel..........**7** C3
Hotel Atlântica.....................**8** C2
Hotel Germânia.....................**9** C3
Hotel Mattes.......................**10** C2
Hotel Trocadero....................**11** C2
Tannenhof Othon...................**12** B2

EATING	(p320)
Biergarten..........................**13** B3
Chaplin.............................**14** C2
Delicatesse Viktoria...............**15** B3
Expresso............................**16** C2
Fatirella............................**17** C2
Paviloche...........................**18** C2
Restaurante Cozinha Natural....**19** C2

TRANSPORT	(pp320–1)
Bus Station.........................**20** A4
Local Bus Terminal................**21** D2

high-tech café serves sandwiches, but its main claim to fame is its do-it-yourself sundaes.

Chaplin (cnr Rua Visconde de Taunay & Rua Pedro Lobo) Catering to this conservative city's small alternative community, this is a good spot for a late-night snack and beer.

Getting There & Around

AIR

The **airport** (☎ 467 1000) is 12km from the city; Aeroporto buses leave from the local bus terminal on Praça da Bandeira. There are regular flights from Joinville to Curitiba (40 minutes), Florianópolis (30 minutes), Brasília (2½ hours), Rio (1½ hours) and São Paulo (one hour).

BUS

The bus station is 2km southwest from the city center. Local buses to the city center leave roughly every 10 to 15 minutes from outside the bus station. There are also regular buses to the beaches of Ilha de São Francisco.

Destinations include: Curitiba (US$4, 2½ hours, hourly); São Paulo (US$18, nine hours, daily); Paranaguá (US$6.50, 3½ hours, twice daily); Florianópolis (US$8, 2½ hours, hourly) – *semi-direito* (semi-direct) buses run along the coast via Itajaí and Balneário Camboriú; Blumenau (US$5, 2½ hours, hourly); Porto Alegre (US$18, nine hours, daily); and Foz do Iguaçu (US$22, 16 hours, daily).

JOINVILLE TO FLORIANÓPOLIS

Varied and beautiful, the beaches along this stretch of coast are both its blessing and its potential downfall. Concrete-bound Balneário Camboriú, known as the Copacabana of the South, is an excellent example of the latter. Other resorts around it are catching up fast, hoping to catch package-travel business from Paraguay, Uruguay and Argentina. The peninsula around Porto Belo, on the other hand, is a relatively undeveloped place with calm bays and crystal-clear waters.

São Francisco do Sul

☎ 0xx47 / pop 31,400

Brazil's third-oldest city after Bahía and São Vicente, São Francisco was 'discovered' by the French explorer Binot Paulmier de Gonneville in 1504. It took another century for the Portuguese to exploit its strategic position at the mouth of Baía Babitonga. Later, it became the port of entry for German immigrants who settled the land around Joinville. The historical center, with its decadent, colonial feel, has been added to the Patrimônio Histórico (National Heritage list).

BEACHES

The beaches on Ilha de São Francisco are good, but their proximity to Joinville (and

even Curitiba) makes them some of the most crowded in the state. On the positive side, they are accessible by local buses, and there are some good point and beach breaks for surfing.

Both **Prainha** and (to the south) **Praia Grande** are ocean beaches exposed to a lot of swell. They are good for surfing, but not safe for swimming. Closer to the city, **Praia da Ubatuba** and **Praia de Enseada** are pretty bays and safe for swimming, but they're developed and get very crowded on weekends. Some of the more secluded beaches are **Praia Itaguaçu** and **Praia do Forte** on the island's northern tip. All the beaches are served by local bus from São Francisco do Sul or Praia de Enseada.

TOURS

In town, boats leave the port for tours of the Baía de São Francisco do Sul at 10:30am, stopping for lunch at the historic town of Vila da Glória on the mainland, returning at 2:30pm. The tour costs US$10, including lunch. Contact **Marakie Tours** (☎ 444 1260) for reservations.

SLEEPING & EATING

In town, try **Kontik** (☎ 444 2232; Rua Camacho 33; s/d US$24/32). Located in the city center, it has

---

THE MICROECONOMIC MIRACLE

When Brazilians speak of the 'Economic Miracle,' they are usually referring to the runaway growth of the late 1960s and early 1970s, when the country's economy grew 10% year after year. The costs of the miracle were high, however: hyperinflation, social dislocation and massive foreign debt.

Since the early 1990s, a smaller but in many ways more impressive microeconomic miracle has been taking place in Santa Catarina. With little fanfare, the state has seen a startling reduction in poverty despite only modest overall economic growth. The statistics speak for themselves. Between 1992 and 2002, the number of people living below the poverty line was slashed by 46%. Results for the very poor are even more astounding: a 64% reduction in the number of people considered 'indigent.'

The state has always enjoyed a much more equitable distribution of wealth than the rest of Brazil. Unlike the plantation culture to the north, Santa Catarina's economy was largely based on small, family-owned farms. Still, the drastic reduction in poverty rates is unprecedented. Brazilian economists have a number of explanations, all of them centering on the recent growth of very small businesses – egg farmers and jelly makers, independent craftspeople producing furniture, fabrics, tiles and glassware, all at competitive prices.

What has fostered the growth of these small *microempresas* (very small businesses)? First, the state has provided active support, helping to provide very small loans and offering training in business skills such as budgeting and accounting. The strong social support that the state offers has, in turn, been an example to small entrepreneurs. They have organized a wide variety of cooperatives, sharing tools and expertise in order to lower costs and boost production. Together, they are able to remain independent – and make a decent living – even amid Brazil's increasingly global markets.

comfortable rooms, some with views over the bay. Praia de Enseada has several hotels, and you can catch a direct bus there from Joinville. **Pousada Estrela do Mar** (☎ 442 3104; Rua Corupá 180; d with bathroom & kitchenette US$14) is a good budget option 100m from the beach. You're on your own for breakfast, but there is a nice bakery just down the street. Also nearby is Pedrinho's, a decent seafood place.

Penha
☎ 0xx47 / pop 16,600
Still a working fishing village, Penha is one of the least developed resorts in the region. However, it does get seriously crowded on weekends in summer, when the main beach-front turns into one big *festa* (party). The ocean, by contrast, is calm along the pretty, tree-lined town beaches: **Praia da Armação** and **Prainha**. The beaches to the south – in particular **Praia Grande** (5km) and **Praia Vermelha** (9km) – are beautiful and much less crowded.

At the nearby **Praia Barra Sul de Piçarras**, you can catch a boat to the nearby islands of **Itacolomi** and **Feia** with Alexandre (☎ 9997 3568), captain of the *Capitão Gato*, among others. The going rate is about US$3 per person for a 90-minute tour.

SLEEPING & EATING
There are camping grounds and some good hotels and seafood restaurants on Praia da Armação.

The friendly **Hotel Itapocoroi** (☎ 345 5015; Rua Maria da Costa 62; d with bathroom US$18) is 50m from the beach. Rooms cost a little more on weekends. Ask if a room with an ocean view is available. **Costamar Praia Hotel** (☎ 345-6861; Av Elizabeth Kondor Reis 556; d with bathroom & ❄ US$20-30) is nearby on the beachfront.

Immigrants from the Portuguese Azores Islands have created a unique regional cuis-ine that blends indigenous and Azorean flavors. The best place to try it (washed down with a dizzying variety of *cachaça*, a white spirit made from sugarcane) is Pirão d'Agua on the beachfront at Av São João. Close by, **Restaurante do Alírio** (Av Elizabeth Kondor Reis 26) has excellent, cheap seafood meals.

GETTING THERE & AWAY
Intercity buses don't stop in Penha. There is a bus terminal at Piçarras (6km north),

where you can take a local Circular or Nava-gantes bus to Penha.

Balneário Camboriú
☎ 0xx47 / pop 83,700
This little Copacabana is complete with its namesake's nightclubs, 'professional companions,' dramatic hills and even an oceanfront boulevard called Av Atlântica. In summertime, the population increases tenfold.

Balneário Camboriú is also Santa Cata-rina's most expensive town. Here you can meet well-heeled Argentines, Paraguayans and Paulistas who spend their summers in beach-hugging high-rise buildings.

Porto Belo
☎ 0xx47 / pop 10,050
The small peninsula that fans out from Porto Belo boasts the last good mainland beaches before Ilha de Santa Catarina and, thanks to clear, emerald-green waters, some of the best diving opportunities in southern Brazil. Many beaches are only accessible by boat or by foot, which keeps them free from the development that is rapidly trans-forming much of the region. Rather than staying in the town of Porto Belo, move on to **Praia Bombinhas** (9km from town) or the adjacent **Praia Bombas** (3km). They are the best beaches that also offer accommoda-tions, though note that rapid development is well underway. Experienced surfers should check out **Praia do Mariscal**, which faces the open sea.

DIVING
Dive operators in Bombinhas offer half-day diving tours (10am-3pm) to the **Reserva Bio-lógica do Avoredo**, a marine park consisting of three islands: Avoredo, Galés and Deserta. The coral reefs surrounding the islands are home to a variety of exotic fish, dolphins, stingrays and turtles. Half-day tours leave from the pier at Praia Bombinhas Thursday through Sunday and cost around US$35 per person, including all equipment. For reservations contact **Submarine** (☎ 369 2223; submarin@melim.com.br) at Rua Manoel Dos Santos in Bombinhas.

SLEEPING & EATING
The peninsula offers plentiful opportunities for camping, of which the best equipped

and easiest to reach is **Camping Bombinhas** (☎ 369 2322), located at the end of Bombinhas beach on Av Manoel José dos Santos.

Pousada do Holandês (☎ 369 1281; Rua Albatrôs 553) in Bombas has double rooms with kitchenettes for US$20. On the other side of the island from the town of Porto Belo, **Pousada Zimbros** (☎ 369 3225; Rua da Praia 527; s/d US$26/38), in the village of the same name, sits on Praia Cantinho. A high-end option in Bombinhas is the lovely **Pousada do Arvoredo** (☎ 369 2355; Rua Tilápia 99; s/d US$90/102), with balconies with ocean or garden views.

In Bombinhas, **Restaurante Comandante Dória** (Rua Tainha 129), in the hotel of the same name, is a reasonably priced seafood restaurant. **Portofino** (Av Manoel José dos Santos 120) has cheap *parrillada* (grilled meat) to cater to homesick Argentine tourists.

GETTING THERE & AWAY
There are 12 buses a day from Balneário Camboriú to Bombinhas (US$3.50, 1½ hours) that stop in Porto Belo and Bombas. During the day there are hourly *semi-direito* buses (US$5, one hour) from Florianópolis and Joinville that stop at Camboriú.

BLUMENAU
☎ 0xx47 / pop 256,100
If you're a fan of either humidity or beer, Blumenau is the place for you. Because of its position in the lowlands of the Vale do Itajaí, Blumenau is among the hottest and wettest places in southern Brazil. It's hard to imagine how German settlers, who arrived in 1850, made it through that first summer. However, they not only persevered but also managed to convince thousands of compatriots to settle the humid valley. Today Blumenau is, like Joinville, a clean, prosperous and serene little city with a population that is, for Brazil, atypically tall and fair.

Blumenau prides itself on its strongly Germanic identity, yet with a distinctly Brazilian flair. The architecture is dominated by Germanic themes, though without a serious attempt at realism. The result has been described more or less aptly as 'Disneyfication.' Still, it's an interesting study in contrasts with the rest of Brazil.

Within Brazil, Blumenau is best known for its no-holds-barred **Oktoberfest**, which has developed into Brazil's largest street party after Rio's Carnaval. For a more profound insight

into the region's Germanic roots, head 30km north to **Pomerode**, where an estimated 80% of the population still speaks German.

Information
Banco do Brasil (Rua 15 de Novembro at Rua Amadeu da Luz) Money exchange and Visa ATMs.

Casa Roweder Cambio e Turismo (Rua Dr Curt Hering 20) Changes cash and traveler's checks at a good rate.

Information booth (☎ 322 6933; cnr Rua 15 de Novembro & Rua Nereu Ramos) In the center. The staff speaks German, and has useful maps and information about other towns in the Itajaí region. It can also help you arrange a stay with a German-speaking family in the region.

Post office (Rua Padre Jacobs) Near Rua 7 de Setembro.

Shopping Neumarket (Rua 7 de Setembro nr Rua Padre Jacobs; per hr US$4.50) For Internet access, head here.

Festivals & Events
Serene, well-behaved Blumenau loses it cool during **Oktoberfest**, which takes place during the middle two weeks of October. The party starts off in traditional fashion, with lederhosen-clad locals singing folk songs and downing sausages and beer. But as the evening wears on, the sounds of samba and *frevo* begin to be heard, and eventually the bump-and-grind of the Northeast takes over until dawn. Check the website (www.oktoberfestblumenau.com.br) for a full program of events, most of which revolve around the consumption of beer.

Sleeping
Be sure to book accommodations well in advance if you plan to be in Blumenau during Oktoberfest.

Hotel Glória (☎ 326 1988; www.hotelgloria.com.br; Rua 7 de Setembro 954; s/d US$20/30; P ⊠ ⌐) With its wood-paneled entrance and a traditional German *kaffeehaus* (coffeehouse) attached, this hotel offers comfortable rooms and a certain old-world flair.

City Hotel (☎ 322 2205; Rua Ângelo Dias 263; s/d US$8/12, with bathroom & ⊠ US$13/19) The rooms are very clean, and considering the price, quite attractive – many have nice hardwood floors. A good value.

Hotel Garden Terrace (☎ 326 3544; Rua Padre Jacobs 45; s/d US$36/48; P ⊠ ⌐) Just across from the city's modern cathedral, this is one of Blumenau's most comfortable hotels. From the higher floors, you'll get some lovely views of Blumenau and the surrounding valley.

THE SOUTH

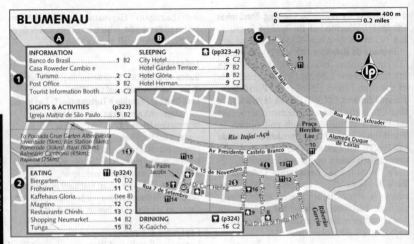

BLUMENAU

0 — 400 m
0 — 0.2 miles

INFORMATION
Banco do Brasil.................................1 B2
Casa Roweder Cambio e
Turismo..2 C2
Post Office.......................................3 B2
Tourist Information Booth.........4 C2

SIGHTS & ACTIVITIES (p323)
Igreja Matriz de São Paulo..........5 B2

EATING (p324)
Biergarten.....................................10 D2
Frohsinn..11 C1
Kaffeehaus Gloria.................(see 8)
Magnino.......................................12 C2
Restaurante Chinês......................13 C2
Shopping Neumarket...................14 B2
Tunga...15 B2

SLEEPING (pp323–4)
City Hotel..6 C2
Hotel Garden Terrace....................7 B2
Hotel Glória....................................8 B2
Hotel Herman.................................9 C2

DRINKING (p324)
X-Gaúcho......................................16 C2

Rua Cedro Alex
Rua Itajaí
Rua Alwin Schrader
Praça Hercílio Luz
Alameda Duque de Caxias
Rio Itajaí-Açú
Av Presidente Castelo Branco
Rua Padre Jacobs
Rua 15 de Novembro
Rua Dr Curt Hering
Rua 7 de Setembro
Rua Floriano Peixoto
Rua Angelo Dias
Rua Nereu Ramos
Rua Rio Branco
Ribeirão Garcia
Rua Dr Luiz de Freitas Melro

To Pousada Grun Garten Albergue da Juventude (5km); Bus Station (6km); Pomerode (30km); Itajaí (60km); Balneário Camboriú (65km); Itapema (75km)

Pousada Grun Garten Albergue da Juventude
(☎ 323 4332; www.grungarten.com.br; Rua São Paulo 2457; s/d US$5/10, with bathroom US$8/16) This clean, attractive HI youth hostel has only one potential drawback – it's 6km from the center, in the suburb of Itoupava Seca. There is a very reasonably priced restaurant attached.

Hotel Hermann (☎ 322 4370; Rua Floriano Peixoto 213; s/d US$7/12, with bathroom & ✗ US$11/18) The lowest-priced hotel in the town center, with a pretty German facade but only the basic comforts inside. No breakfast.

Eating & Drinking

For good German fare, plus lovely views over the town from a nearby hillside, head 2km from the center to **Frohsinn** (Rua Gertrud Sierich; mains US$8-12).

Kaffeehaus Gloria (☎ 326 1988; Rua 7 de Setembro 954) For either a hearty breakfast buffet (US$3) or equally hearty afternoon coffee klatch (coffee break; US$4), head to the old-fashioned dining room of Hotel Gloria. Both meals feature excellent cakes and pastries, savory tortes, German-style sandwich fixings and fresh fruit juices like passion fruit and cashew fruit – neither of which is readily available in the Old Country.

Magnino (25 Rua Nereu Ramos) is the town's best per-kilo restaurant. **Shopping Blumenau** on Rua 7 de Setembro offers plenty of variety in its food hall – pizza, Italian, Chinese and Lebanese. For à la carte Chinese food, head to **Restaurante Chinês** (☎ 322 5753; cnr Rua

15 de Novembro & Av Rio Branco; mains US$8-10; ✾ lunch & dinner). The restaurant also offers delivery service.

At night, the *chopperias* (beer gardens) near the Rua República Argentina bridge, such as **Tunga**, have cheap pizza, *chope* (draft beer) and some live music. **Biergarten**, located on the attractive, tree-lined Praça Hercílio Luz, is another good spot for a beer and snack overlooking the river. **X-Gaúcho** (Rua Floriano Peixoto 55) is a good spot to meet members of Blumenau's young and blond set.

Getting There & Around

There is one bus at least every hour to Florianópolis (US$7, 2½ hours). If you're traveling to the coastal towns north of Florianópolis, catch a *semi-direito* for stops at Itajaí, Balneário Camboriú and Itapema. There are also hourly buses to Joinville (US$5, 2½ hours), and 10 per day to Curitiba (US$9, 4½ hours).

For a local bus into the center of town, head out of the bus station to the far side of Av 2 de Setembro and take the bus marked Fonte (US$0.50) to Rua 7 de Setembro in the center. A taxi costs US$4.

FLORIANÓPOLIS
☎ 0xx48 / pop 358,200
Florianópolis, state capital and gateway to the remarkable Ilha de Santa Catarina, has two distinct sides to its character. The industrial zone occupies the mainland, while the

SPRECHEN SIE PORTUGUES?

Fala Deutsch? It's hard to imagine, but in the 21st century, there are towns in Brazil where German is still the mother tongue.

The first German immigrants began to arrive in the 1820s at the behest of the emperor of a newly independent Brazil. The southern part of Dom Pedro I's empire was still disputed by Argentina and Uruguay, and he wanted to populate the region with a people beholden to his good graces. A second wave of immigrants arrived in the 1850s, mostly in Santa Catarina. They were followed by many more in the 1890s, then again during and after the two world wars. However, contrary to popular imagination, of the Germans who arrived in the 1940s, many more were political and economic refugees than Nazi leaders on the run.

For a century, German was the dominant language in many parts of southern Brazil, though even within their own communities, German speakers, who came from various regions of Germany and spoke a variety of dialects, faced their own kind of linguistic Babel. They often resorted to a kind of Creole, which incorporated Portuguese and even local Indian languages. Italians, facing a similar problem, relied on 'Taliã,' an amalgamation of various dialects, with that of the Veneto region taking dominance.

The 20th century took a mighty toll on the German language in Brazil. The world wars led to the suppression of German in public institutions like schools and government. Industrialization and increasing economic integration brought the region into closer contact with Portuguese speakers. Finally, the arrival of radio and television, dominated by national networks, reinforced the use of Portuguese, especially among the young.

The town of Pomerode remains an exception to the rule. Eighty percent of the population still speaks German fluently. A confluence of forces has ensured the preservation of the language. First, it remained physically isolated from its neighbors for a longer time; only in the last generation have decent roads linked it to Blumenau. In addition, nearly all of its original settlers spoke the same dialect (Pomeranian), so there was no need to resort to Portuguese as a lingua franca. Finally, the settlers were largely Lutheran rather than Catholic, so German remained their language of worship.

These days, there is a growing movement to preserve Brazil's bilingual communities. If you're interested in living with a German-speaking family while in Brazil, contact the Blumenau **tourist office** (☎ 322 6933).

---

quaint colonial center, as well as the chic, modern Beira-Mar Norte district, sit across the bay on the island itself. The bridges that picturesquely join the two halves of the city – the now-closed Ponte Hercílio Luz and the newer Ponte Colombo Machado Salles – are particularly beautiful at night.

For the traveler, Florianópolis – known affectionately as 'Floripa' – serves mostly as a convenient transportation hub, with all of the island's 42 beaches within an hour's drive from the city center. However, the city offers reasons to linger for an afternoon or evening. The colonial, cobblestone streets that fan out from the recently renovated Praça 15 de Novembro are worthy of exploration. And the city increasingly attracts residents of Rio and São Paulo in search of calmer, safer climes; sophisticated hotels, restaurants and nightclubs are popping up to serve an expanding clientele.

Orientation

Just across the bridges from the mainland, you will find the city's major sights, as well as the long-distance and local bus stations and a range of hotels and restaurants, all within a few kilometers of each other. The upscale Beira-Mar Norte neighborhood sits on the bay about 2km north of the center.

Lots of touts wait at the bus station. Remember that they're more likely to send you to a hotel that pays a good commission than one where you would actually like to stay. However, they may have deals on rental cars that are worth considering.

Information
BOOKSTORES

Livraria Catarinense (Rua Felipe Schmidt 60;
🕑 10am-8pm Mon-Sat; Internet access per hr US$2.50)
Internet access as well as a small selection of foreign-language titles.

EMERGENCY
Bombeiros (☎ 193) For fire and medical emergencies.
Federal Police (☎ 281 6500)

INTERNET ACCESS
Moncho (☎ 2106 2775; Rua Tiradentes 181; per hr
US$2.50; ☺ 9am-10pm Mon-Fri, to 8pm Sat)

MONEY
There's an active black market for cash dollars in the pedestrian mall on Rua Felipe
Schmidt – even the tourist office will tacitly
direct you there! Otherwise, change your
cash at one of the money-exchange houses
along the same street.
Banco do Brasil (Praça 15 de Novembro 20) To change
traveler's checks and make Visa withdrawals.

POST & TELEPHONE
Moncho (☎ 2106 2775; Rua Tiradentes 181) Has booths
for international calls as well as Internet access.
Post office (Faces Praça 15 de Novembro)

TOURIST INFORMATION
Information booths (long-distance bus station ☎ 212
3127; ☺ 8am-10pm; customs house ☎ 222 4906; ☺ to

6pm Mon-Fri, to 1pm Sat) In the long-distance bus station
and next to the old customs house. Provides good maps
and information about transport and accommodations.
Staff can make reservations for island lodging and tours.
Spanish is spoken.

Sights
The inviting **Praça 15 de Novembro**, with its
shady walks and 100-year-old fig tree, is
a fine place for a cool drink on a hot day.
To one side of the square sits the **Museu
Histórico de Santa Catarina** (☎ 221 3504; Praça 15
de Novembro 227; admission US$1; ☺ 10am-6pm Tue-
Fri, to 4pm Sat & Sun). Its collection of indigenous and colonial artifacts is perhaps less
interesting than the building itself, which
served as the colonial governor's palace.
The ornate parquetry floors and outrageous 19th-century ceilings are worth the
admission price.

Catedral Metropolitana sits grandly at the
high end of the square. However, major
remodeling in the 1920s means that little
of its colonial aspect remains. **Igreja de NS do
Rosário**, the best-preserved colonial church,
sits at the end of Rua Trajano at the top

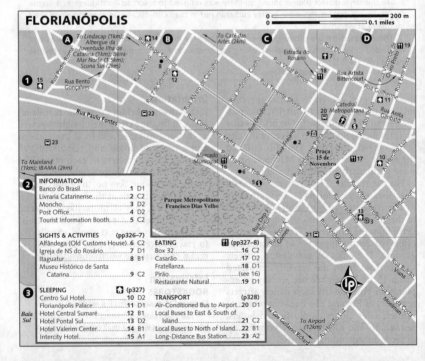

FLORIANÓPOLIS

0 _____ 200 m
0 _____ 0.1 miles

of a flight of stairs vaguely reminiscent of Rome's Spanish Steps.

From the other end of the square, you can head down the busy, pedestrianized **Rua Felipe Schmidt**, a fine place for people-watching and window-shopping. Or continue down toward the waterfront, where another pedestrianized zone links the well-preserved **Alfândega** (customs house) and the **Mercado Municipal** (municipal market), both on Rua Francisco Tolentino. The market's courtyard fills up after work with a lively crowd that comes to snack on seafood, sip *chope* and listen to live music.

Tours

If your time is short, or you'd like to survey the entire island before choosing where to settle, consider a tour with **Itaguatur** (☎ 225 3939; www.itaguatur.com.br; ste 208, Rua Felipe Schmidt 515). A three-hour outing (US$10) includes the city center as well as the beautiful Lagoa da Conceição and nearby beaches. The full-day 'Floripa Total' (US$14) tour takes in the above as well as the beaches at both the north and south ends of the island.

Scuna Sul (☎ 225 1806; www.scunasul.com.br) offers a variety of boat tours of the bay between the island and the mainland, including stops at some pretty 18th-century Portuguese forts, starting at US$10.

Sleeping

Except for by-the-hour places near the waterfront, Floripa has a limited range of budget accommodations, and these fill up quickly during peak times. However, there is a wide choice of good mid-range options.

Hotel Pontal Sul (☎ 224 0810; www.pontalsulhotel .com.br; Rua Tiradentes 167; s/d/tr US$19/25/30; 🍴 🖵) Recently renovated, this hotel has a bright, inviting reception area as well as pleasant rooms, all with cable TV.

Centro Sul Hotel (☎ 222 9110; www.centrosulhotel .com.br; Av Hercílio Luz 652; s/d US$22/29; 🍴) A great value a couple of blocks from Praça 15 de Novembro. Well-appointed rooms, friendly service and large breakfast.

Hotel Central Sumaré (☎ 222 5359; Rua Felipe Schmidt 423; s/d US$9/16, with bathroom US$14/19) Close to the bus station and colonial center, the location is good. The rooms are clean and have attractive hardwood floors. However, the beds are of questionable comfort – test one out before agreeing to the price.

Hotel Valerim Center (☎ 225 1100; www.hotel valerim.com.br; Rua Felipe Schmidt 554; s/d US$19/26; 🅿) A very good value, with few frills but comfortable rooms and a good location between the bus station and the colonial center.

Intercity Hotel (☎ 3027 2200; www.intercityhotel .com.br; Av Paolo Fontes 1210; d US$62; 🅿 🍴 🖵) This shiny new hotel just across from the long-distance bus station affords excellent views of the bay and mainland from the higher floors. Services include a gym and sauna. The hyper-air-conditioned lobby sparkles with white marble.

Florianópolis Palace (☎ 224 9633; floph@iaccess.com .br; Rua Artista Bittencourt 14; s/d US$53/58; 🅿 🍴 🖵) A five-star hotel with the works, including sprawling breakfast buffet, thermal spa and massage, and some rooms with panoramic views of the city.

Albergue da Juventude Ilha de Catarina (☎ 222 3781; Rua Duarte Schutel 227; dm per person US$10) A clean, orderly youth hostel 1km north of the town center. Only a 10-minute walk from the bus station.

Eating

While the more chic establishments are clustered in the Beira-Mar Norte neighborhood, the center of town has a wide range of budget options as well as some classic Floripa watering holes.

Box 32 (☎ 224 5588; Mercado Municipal; mains US$10; 🕑 10am-10pm Mon-Sat, to 5pm Sun) The excellent, if expensive, seafood here attracts the city's movers and shakers during happy hour.

Pirão (☎ 228 7354; Mercado Municipal; mains US$8-14; 🕑 lunch) Upstairs from Box 32, this is another Floripa classic specializing in seafood, with a view onto the busy courtyard of the Mercado Municipal.

Fratellanza (Estrada do Rosário; mains US$10; 🕑 lunch & dinner) Another traditional hangout, with a hearty, Italo-Brazilian menu. Try to get a seat outside on the steps that lead up picturesquely to the Igreja de NS do Rosário.

Restaurante Natural (☎ 223 4507; Rua Visconde de Ouro Preto 298; fixed-price buffet US$2.50; 🕑 11am-3:30 Mon-Fri) This all-vegetarian joint offers a large and appetizing buffet in a handsome, colonial-style home.

Casarão (☎ 222 9092; Praça 15 de Novembro 320; mains US$5-8; 🕑 11am-11pm Mon-Fri, to 3pm Sat) Housed in an old colonial building on the main square, this breezy place offers a good per-kilo lunch buffet. You can also come in the evening for a la carte Brazilian food, seafood snacks and *chope*.

Café das Artes (☎ 322 0690; Rua Esteves Júnior 734; sandwiches US$2-4; ◷ 11:30am-11pm Mon-Sat, 4-11pm Sun) An artsy, upscale café in the Beira-Mar Norte neighborhood, this cozy option offers good coffee and baked goods as well as light fare such as salads and sandwiches.

Lindacap (☎ 222 4002; Rua Felipe Schmidt 1162; mains for 2 US$10-15; ◷ lunch daily, dinner Mon-Sat) One of the city's upmarket addresses in the Beira-Mar Norte neighborhood, this large, comfortable restaurant serves dependable grilled meats as well as seafood dishes.

Getting There & Away

AIR

There are daily direct flights from Florianópolis to São Paulo (one hour), Porto Alegre (one hour), Rio de Janeiro (1½ hours) and Curitiba (40 minutes), with connections to most other cities.

The airport is 12km south of the city (US$12 by taxi). Red local buses marked Correador Sudoeste run to the airport (US$0.50, 45 minutes) every 15 minutes until midnight. They leave from the local bus terminal on Rua Antônio Luz. A special air-conditioned Correador Sudoeste bus to the airport (US$1, 30 minutes) leaves every 20 minutes from the bus stop next to the cathedral on Praça 15 de Novembro.

BUS

Long-distance buses link Florianópolis with every major city in southern Brazil, as well as Uruguay and Argentina. Destinations include: Blumenau (US$10, two hours); Joinville (US$12, three hours); Porto Alegre (US$14, 6½ hours); Curitiba (US$12, 4½ hours); São Paulo (US$28, 12 hours); Rio de Janeiro (US$42, 18 hours); Foz do Iguaçu (US$32, 15 hours); Buenos Aires (US$88, 24 hours); and Montevideo (US$62, 20 hours).

Getting Around

All of Floripa's sights and amenities are a 15-minute hoof from the long-distance bus station. The city is also the transportation hub for the rest of the island, all of which lies within an hour by car or bus.

BUS

The island of Santa Catarina has an extensive and remarkably efficient bus service (US$0.50). Buses for the east and south of the island (including Lagoa and Joaquina) leave from the local bus terminal on Rua Antônio Luz. Buses for the north leave from the local bus terminal across from the long-distance bus station on Rua Francisco Tolentino. Destinations are clearly marked.

Additional yellow microbuses (US$1 to US$2) leave from Praça 15 de Novembro as well as the local terminals. They are generally air-conditioned, make fewer stops, often head straight for the beaches, and accommodate surfboards (which public buses don't).

CAR

If you're going to hire a car anywhere in Brazil, Ilha de Santa Catarina is the place to do it. Roads are well marked, drivers are civilized, and you can explore the island's beaches at will. On the down side, prices are generally high (upwards of US$40 per day). A good alternative is **Latina Rent a Car** (☎ 9101 1570; latinarentacar@ig.com.br). The prices are very reasonable (US$25 per day), and the owners will pick you up and drop you off at the airport, bus station or your hotel – for no extra cost. **Yes Rent a Car** (☎ 236 0229) generally offers the best rates (US$30 a day and up) among the chains, with offices at the airport, in central Floripa and in Canasvieiras. It will deliver a car to any hotel on the island.

ILHA DE SANTA CATARINA
☎ 0xx48

Ilha de Santa Catarina has a gorgeous and remarkably varied coastline, from the calm, well-touristed bays of the north, to the wild, cliff-hugging beaches of the south. But it's the totality of the island's natural beauty, not just its beaches, that make it so enchanting. An extensive forest of protected pines gives much of the east coast an alpine feel, whereas the dunes near Praia da Joaquina, some of them hundreds of feet high, create an almost lunar landscape. A spine of mountains, luxuriant with the flora and fauna of the Mata Atlántica (Atlantic rain forest), runs the length of the island. Near the island's center, the mountains drop precipitously down to the stunning Lagoa da

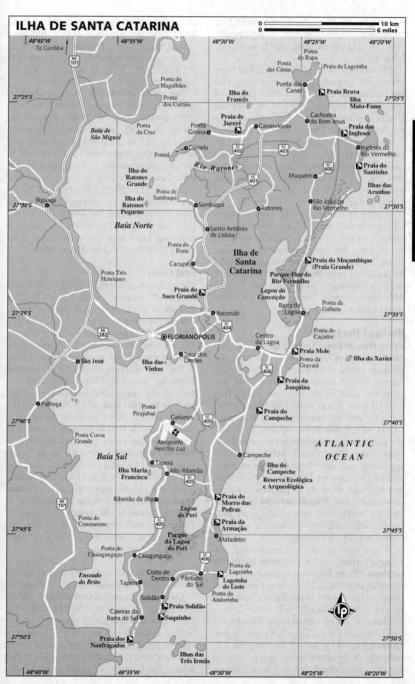

ILHA DE SANTA CATARINA

| 0 | 10 km |
| 0 | 6 miles |

Conceição. It's like a Swiss mountain lake transported to warmer climes. Amazingly, you can take in all these sights in a two-hour drive.

The northern part of the island has been given over to package-tour operators, and the beaches along the west coast can be of questionable hygiene. The best and cleanest beaches lie along the east coast, with several – particularly Praia Mole – offering excellent surfing opportunities. In general, the further south you go, the less developed the island becomes, though the shores of Lagoa da Conceição, in the middle of the island, are crowded with restaurants, hotels and summer homes.

If your travel brings you here between Christmas and early March, plan on big crowds – especially at the northern end of the island – and significantly higher prices. Book in advance where possible. Hotel prices listed here are for high season and holiday weekends. Prices can fall 20% to 40% outside peak times – you probably won't even have to bargain.

North of the Island

From **Praia de Jurerê** to **Praia dos Ingleses**, the northern tip of the island is designed for package tours, with calm, family-friendly waters, lots of anonymous hotels and restaurants, and newly widened roads that provide easy access to and from the international airport. Protected by a hilly peninsula at the northeast tip of the island, the small **Praia da Lagoinha** is ritzier and less densely developed than its neighbors. Moving south and east, **Praia dos Ingleses**, once among the choicest beaches on the island, has suffered from its popularity. Moving down the coast, **Praia do Santinho** is quieter, and the beach itself feels wilder since protected dunes and wetlands form a welcome buffer against civilization.

If you need to stay in Canasvieiras, the most affordable option is **Hotel Residencial Lacabana** (☎ 266 0400; www.lacabana.com.br; Av das Nações 525; d/q US$28/37; ❄), a decent residential hotel on the town's main street a couple of blocks from the beach. All rooms have a kitchenette. An exception to the bland tourist fare in town is the large but pleasant **Restaurante Tropical** (☎ 266 1498; Rua Madre Villac 1129; mains US$7-10; ❄ lunch & dinner), specializing in Bahian and seafood dishes. The restaurant

closes from Easter until November. With lovely views down to Praia da Lagoinha from almost every room, **Pousada da Vigia** (☎ 284 1789; www.pousadadavigia.com.br; Rua Côn Walmor Castro 291; d US$125-200; P ❄ 🖳 🖭) is among the island's poshest, with prices to match.

Pousada do Santinho (☎ 269 2836; www.pousada santinho.hpg.com.br; Rodoviaria Vereador Onildo Lemos 1259; s/d/tr US$27/35/40; P ❄ 🖭) Located on the beach of the same name, this is the place to stay in the north. The owner and her granddaughter make a study of how to best welcome travelers of various cultures, but always extending a warm, Brazilian welcome. The rooms are comfortable, the prices reasonable, the grounds pleasant, the food delicious, and the beach just across the dunes. Depending on the season, your morning juice may come from the pousada's (guesthouse's) small orchard.

East Coast

Facing the open ocean, the east coast boasts the island's cleanest waters, longest beaches and most challenging surf. In the north, **Praia do Moçambique** merges indistinguishably with **Praia Barra da Lagoa** to form a stunning, 14km strand. The beach is hidden from the road by a protected pine forest that thrives in the sandy soil that divides the ocean from Lagoa da Conceição. There is little construction on the beach itself, except around the town of **Barra da Lagoa**, which borders on the shabby but has direct access to the beach.

To the south, **Praia da Joaquina**, whose huge dunes are visible for kilometers, blends into **Praia do Campeche** to a form a single beach that rivals Moçambique in both size and beauty. There are a few hotels and restaurants in Joaquina, and you can rent a **sand board** (per hr US$2) to surf the dunes. There is another cluster of restaurants and hotels in Campeche, with views to Ilha do Campeche, an ecological reserve that sits picturesquely a few kilometers offshore.

Between Barra da Lagoa and Joaquina lies **Praia Mole**, a favorite both of surfers and Florianópolis' gay and lesbian community.

Owner Altamiro of **Chez Altamiro** (☎ 269 7727; Estrada Geral do Rio Vermelho 7742; mains US$10-15; ❄ dinner daily, lunch Sun) is also chef, waiter, maître d' and sommelier. You will see him run outside to pick fresh herbs as he whips up, then serves, classic Cordon Bleu dishes with a combination of Brazilian amiability and French savoir faire. There are just a few tables, so make reservations on summer weekends.

At the northern end of Praia do Moçambique, **Pousada Rio Vermelho** (☎ 296 1337; www.riovermelhopousada.com.br; s/d US$30/40; P ⚇ ⚈), in São João de Rio Vermelho, is a great option. It has large grounds, country-chic chalets, a pool and easy access to the beach.

The town of Barra da Lagoa is packed with pousadas, though they tend to be ratty without being cheap. **Pousada 32** (☎ 232 4232; www.pousada32.com; Rua Angelina Joaquin dos Santos 300; s/d/q with kitchen US$24/34/54; P) is a decent option a block from the beach. Across the main road in the pine forest is **Pousada dos Pinhais** (☎ 232 3662; www.pousadaddospinhais.odi.com.br; Rodoviaria João Gualberto Soares 17370; s/d/tr US$20/40/50; P ⚇ ⚈), offering comfortable and spotless rooms around a tranquil courtyard.

In Joaquina, **Cris Hotel** (☎ 232 5380; www.crishotel.com; s/d US$27/30; P ⚇) could use a facelift inside and out, but wins a mention for its reasonable rates and convenient location right up from the beach and a short walk from the dunes. Down the beach in Campeche, **Pousada Vila Tamarindo** (☎ 237 3464; www.tamarindo.com.br; Av Campeche 1836; d US$28, with air con US$34; P ⚈) is a great option. This friendly, well-run pousada has generous gardens, airy rooms, an excellent breakfast, and views across the dunes to the open ocean.

Lagoa da Conceição

Whether it's to gawk at the views or enjoy water sports in warm, protected waters, **Lagoa da Conceição** is a great alternative to the beaches. The town of **Centro da Lagoa**, which sits largely on a sandbar that divides the two halves of the lagoon, is packed with tourists. However, you can rent a boat (three hours for up to 6 people around US$25) next to the bridge in the middle of town. In the same place, you can catch one of the regularly scheduled water taxis (US$1) used by local residents whose homes are only accessible by boat.

Hotel Cabanas Ilha da Magia (☎ 232 5468; www.pousadailhadamagia.com.br; Av Santiago 23; d US$36, cabins for up to 5 US$80; P) has small, brightly colored cabins across the street from the lagoon. **Chalés do Canto** (☎ 232 0471; www.chalesdocanto.com.br; Rua Silveira 2212; d US$44; P ⚇) is another option, with cabins of varying size, amid a verdant, hillside garden.

While the hotspots vary from season to season, Lagoa has some of the island's best nightclubs.

South of the Island

With white-sand beaches and mountains that drop straight down to the sea, the south is at once the most beautiful and least developed part of the island. The long, curving **Praia da Armação** is a surfer's delight, though currents can be relentless. On the pretty, green jut of land at the southern end of the beach, you can catch a boat to **Ilha do Campeche**, an ecological reserve with a gorgeous beach and opportunities for hiking and snorkeling. Boats head to the island all morning (US$8 round-trip). Just head to the dock and ask when the next group is headed out. Further south, the beach village of **Pântano do Sul**, still largely inhabited by fishermen of Azorean descent, looks out on a protected cove ringed by mountains. A number of small but stunning beaches can be reached only by foot, including **Lagoinha do Leste**, **Saquinho** and, at the very tip of the island, **Naufragados**.

Pousada Sítio dos Tucanos (☎ 237 5084; www.pousadasitiodostucanos.com; s/d US$28/40; P ▢) This splendidly situated pousada offers sweeping views down to the ocean from its secluded hillside gardens. Rooms are rustic but elegant, most with balconies that open onto a gurgling mountain stream. The gracious owner, who speaks English, French and German, organizes hiking expeditions, and will serve dinner as well as breakfast if you let her know in advance. If you are coming by bus, call ahead and arrange to be picked up at the nearest bus stop.

Across the highway from Armação, **Pousada Alemdomar** (☎ 237 5600; www.alemdomar.com.br; Rua Lagoa do Peri 403; s/d US$40/55) is a classy place with a hint of the new age. Attributes include pretty gardens, tastefully decorated rooms and a candlelit sauna and spa. In the village of Pântano do Sul, **Pousada do Pescador** (☎ 237 7122; www.pousadadopescador.com.br; Rua Manoel Vidal 257; s/d/tr US$30/37/44; P) offers decent chalets in a garden setting 100m from the water. Continuing on the main road past the village and an exclusive housing development, you will arrive at the unpaved Rua Rosália P Ferreira. About a kilometer down the road is **Albergue do Pirata** (☎ 389 2727; www.megasites.com.br/pirata; dm per person US$5), an HI youth hostel. Rooms are spartan but the Argentine owners are friendly, and it's the cheapest place on the island.

Right on the beach along the town's main street, **Arante** (☎ 237 7022; mains for 2 US$10-14; ☾ lunch & dinner) is an island institution. The seafood couldn't be better or fresher, and the atmosphere is bohemian, with walls covered with handwritten messages, poetry and art contributed by its patrons. The grilled *tainha* (meaty but tender local fish), fresh from the sea in fall and early winter, is exquisite, and the tradition is to wash it down with locally made *cachaça*.

SOUTH OF FLORIANÓPOLIS
Garopaba
☎ 0xx48 / pop 11,900
Once a quiet Azorean fishing village, Garopaba has turned into Brazil's unofficial surfing capital. In summer, it's packed with feisty, well-heeled *surfistas* (surfers) who come to test their mettle at nearby Praia do Silveira. The town itself is not beautiful, but its beach is quaint.

Located 95km from of Florianópolis, including a 15km drive from Hwy BR-101, it's the first resort town south of the state capital. Regular buses connect the town of Garopaba with Florianópolis (US$4, two hours). For other destinations, head first to the nearby town of Imbituba.

SLEEPING & EATING
For a cheap sleep, there are a number of campgrounds along the town beach. **Lobo Hotel** (☎ 254 3745; www.gtn.com.br/lobohotel; Rua Marques Guimarães 81; s/d US$14/20) is an excellent value, with basic but clean, airy rooms one block back from the beach. **Pousada da Praia** (☎ 254 3334; pousadadapraia@terra.com.br; Av dos Pescadores 121; d US$35, with ocean view US$55; P X) is pretty bland, but it's family-run and sits right on the beach.

One of the region's finer dining options is **Bistro do Cais** (☎ 254 3325; Praça 21 de Abril 2; mains US$8-14; ☾ dinner). It's located in an old Azorean-style house on the town's old main square at the end of the town beach, and serves very good Mediterranean-style seafood. For a good, all-you-can-eat buffet near the beach, try **Recanto Tio Tia** (☎ 354 1354; Rua Marques Guimarães 157; fixed-price buffet around US$3; ☾ 11:30am-3pm). For snacks, coffee or Internet access, check out the café at **Mormaii**

Surf Shop and Café (☎ 254 3733; ☾ 10am-10pm), which doubles as the flagship store for Brazil's most chic surf gear. It's located on the main highway just as you enter town.

Praia da Rosa
☎ 0xx48 / pop 900
Santa Catarina's plushest seaside town, Praia da Rosa has two things going for it: a stunning set of beaches and genuinely sophisticated hoteliers. The pousadas, some of them quite beautiful in themselves, are set well back from the beach. Opportunities for surfing abound, though swimmers need to take care of potentially dangerous currents.

From June to October, the bay turns into a breeding ground for southern right whales, when mothers and calves can be seen from the beach. Projeto Baleia Franca, a conservation group created to protect and study these unique mammals, is based here.

SLEEPING & EATING
Most of the accommodations are on cliffs overlooking the bay. There are no street signs, but placards will direct you to all the pousadas. For longer stays, look around for houses to rent (with 'Aluga-se' signs). Prices are for summer; expect discounts of 20% to 50% at other times. Reservations are recommended in summer, and are a must for summer weekends and holidays.

On Caminho do Rei, the highest road in town, there is a number of higher-end options with sweeping views.

Pousada Caminho do Rei (☎ 355 6062; www.caminhodorei.com.br; d US$63-85; P X) Rustically elegant and offers the best views in town from its hillside pool.

Rosebud (☎ 355 6101; www.therosebud.com.br; s/d US$40/60; P X) With similar views to those from nearby Pousada Caminho do Rei, this place has an orchid garden tended by the English-speaking owner.

Albergue Dinda Rosa (☎ 355 7139; www.gsurf.com.br/dindarosa; dm per person US$5) Head here for cheap digs in the middle of town. This is part of a complex that also includes an **Internet café** (per hr US$3) and a 24-hour convenience store and snack bar

Fazenda Verde do Rosa (☎ 355 6006; www.fazendaverdedorosa.com.br; chalets for 4 US$155, chalets for 6 with ocean views US$220; P X) At the high end, this place is spread across a stunning bluff just above the beach. Its horseback-riding facilities, run by the friendly and knowledgeable Luciane, are open to the public (three-hour ride US$15). It's an excellent way to get to know the area. The hotel's restaurant, **O Pirata** (mains US$10-12; dinner), serves very good French-inspired gourmet food.

Alma Zen (mains US$8-10; dinner) Another casual-chic dining option, which serves good tapas in a stylish garden setting.

Aquarius (355 7009; buffet US$3.50; 11am-10pm) Head here for a tasty feed, with fresh salads and grilled chicken and fish.

GETTING THERE & AWAY

There are two buses a day from Florianópolis to Praia da Rosa (US$4, two hours). The bus drops you off on Hwy BR-101 at the turnoff to Praia da Rosa, around 7km from the beach. Local buses run from here into Praia da Rosa about every hour. A taxi costs about US$7.

Laguna

 0xx48 / pop 37,200

Located at the boundary that, according to the 1494 Treaty of Tordesillas, divided Spanish from Portuguese America, Laguna was not actually settled until the 1670s. Today, it's southern Santa Catarina's principal seaside resort, with a small but well-preserved colonial town and, across a steep hill, a fine, if overly developed, beach known as Mar Grosso. For more elbow room, head to the terrific beaches around Farol de Santa Marta, 18km south of town on a dirt road followed by a 10-minute ferry ride.

While wandering the quaint streets and cobblestone squares of the old town, you can take a brief gander at **Museu Anita Garibaldi** (admission $1; 8am-6pm), which honors the Brazilian wife of the Italian leader and the town's favorite daughter. Nearby, the **Casa de Anita Garibaldi** (Praça Vidal Ramos; admission US$1; 8am-6pm) offers the chance to see inside a colonial home.

For your cash needs, **Banco do Brasil**, across from the old cathedral on Rua Cons Jerônimo Coelho, has Visa ATMs.

SLEEPING & EATING

Many hotels in Laguna are only open on weekends from March to November.

In the old town, **Hotel Recanto** (644 0902; Rua Engenho Colombo Salles 108; s/d US$15/30) offers no-frills rooms. In Mar Grosso, there's a de-

cent **youth hostel** (647-0675; Rua Aurélio Rótolo; dm per person US$6) that is open only in summer. A block back from the ocean, the family-owned **Laguna Palace Hotel** (647 0548; Av Senador Galotti 635; s/d US$25/33) is a good mid-range option. Some rooms have ocean views. The town's top hotel is the **Laguna Tourist Hotel** (647 0022; www.lagunatourist.com.br; s/d US$74/79;). It's located on the coastal road about 1km north of Mar Grosso.

Gastronomically, seafood is the order of the day. In Mar Grosso, there are several old-fashioned but very good seafood restaurants, including **Arrastão** (Av Senador Galotti 629; mains US$8-12). In the old town, the per-kilo **Restaurante Praç de Anita** (Praça República Juliana; per kg about US$3; lunch Mon-Sat) is a great option, with excellent, Azorean-influenced food served in an airy colonial house. The **Esmeralda Café** (646 0875; Rua Conselheiro Jerônimo Coelho 90; sandwiches US$2) serves sandwiches and espresso on the site of an old-fashioned pharmacy.

GETTING THERE & AROUND

The long-distance bus station is located a few blocks from the old town, with direct routes to destinations up and down the coast, including Porto Alegre (US$12, six hours) and Torres (US$9, four hours) to Florianópolis (US$6, two hours).

São Joaquim

 0xx49 / pop 16,800

Came to Brazil to see snow? At 1355m above sea level, São Joaquim is your best bet. Brazil's highest city is tucked in the mountains of the Serra do Rio Rastro. The region is also known for its apple orchards, many of which were founded in by Brazilians of Japanese descent. **Nevada Hotel** (233 0259; Rua Manoel Joaquim Pinto 190; s/d US$9/18;) is the city's best budget option. There are daily buses to and from Florianópolis (US$13, 5½ hours).

Bom Jardim da Serra

In the middle of the Serra do Rio do Rastro, Bom Jardim da Serra is a hair-raising but spectacular 45km drive from São Joaquim. Parque Nacional de São Joaquim, known for its araucaria forests, is a few kilometers north of the town. The park is undeveloped, but if you want to explore it, contact **IBAMA** (0xx48-212 3303; Av Maro Ramos 1113) in Florianópolis.

Rio Grande do Sul

THE SOUTH

HIGHLIGHTS

- Listening in on the vibrant artistic and political discussion at Porto Alegre's beaux-arts **Casa da Cultura Maria Quintana** (p339)

- Peering over the edge of the 700m-deep **Cânion do Itaimbezinho** (p344) in Parque Nacional de Aparados da Serra

- Tapping into history at the sound-and-light show at the stunning 18th-century ruins of the Jesuit mission at **São Miguel das Missões** (p350)

- Sipping *erva maté* (tea-like beverage made from the leaves of the maté tree) in the old colonial port town of **Rio Grande** (p347)

- Exploring the beautiful state parks around the quaint mountain resorts of **Canela** (p342) and **Gramado** (p341)

★ São Miguel das Missões
★ Parque Nacional de Aparados da Serra
★ Gramado ★ Canela
★ Porto Alegre
★ Rio Grande

| ■ POPULATION: 10.8 MILLION | ■ AREA: 282,062 SQ KM |

If the South ever decides to secede from the rest of Brazil, Rio Grande do Sul will no doubt lead the charge. Residents proudly call themselves *gaúchos* after the independent-minded cowboys who once drove great herds of cattle across the pampas – grassy plains that dominate much of the state's geography.

These days, cowboy culture is mostly a matter of nostalgia, with great stretches of the pampas now yielding bumper soybean crops. However, grilled meats still dominate *gaúcho* menus, and even urban dwellers prize the distinctive *gaúcho* tea made from the maté plant. Happily for the traveler, *gaúchos* preserve another fine cowboy tradition; in a country remarkable for its hospitality, they stand out for their warm welcome.

Except around Torres, Rio Grande do Sul's coast lacks inviting beaches, but nature has provided the Serra Gaúcha by way of recompense. Rising in the northeastern part of the state, the mountains are home to pleasant mountain resorts and extraordinary hiking, especially around the canyons of Parque Nacional de Aparados da Serra. The sleepy coastal towns of Pelotas and Rio Grande, once vital to the beef trade, retain vestiges of their former prosperity. And in the northwest, near the Argentine border, you can visit the ruins of 18th-century Jesuit missions that once formed an impressive 'nation within a nation'.

History

Living on land long disputed by the Spanish and Portuguese crowns, the people of Rio Grande do Sul used the conflict, together with their distance from central authorities, to carve out an identity distinct from the rest of Brazil. The region even declared its independence during the ill-fated Guerra dos Farrapos, a decade-long civil war ending in 1845. A wave of immigrants, mostly German, Italian and Swiss, began arriving in the latter half of the 19th century, reinforcing the region's cultural differences from the rest of the country. Today, the state is among the most prosperous in the nation. Porto Alegre is a key port for trade with Argentina and Uruguay, Brazil's partners in the free trade zone known as Mercosul. The state is also the country's most politically progressive (see the boxed text, p340).

Climate

Sitting furthest from the equator, Rio Grande do Sul has the most temperate climate in Brazil, with hot summers and relatively cool winters – the mountains of the Serra Gaúcha north of Porto Alegre even see occasional snow. That said, summers can be uncomfortably hot and humid, especially along the coastal lowlands.

National Parks

Parque Nacional Aparados da Serra (p344) preserves one of the country's last araucaria forests, as well as the famous Cânion do Itaimbezinho, a narrow, 5800m-long canyon with sheer 600m to 720m parallel escarpments.

Getting There & Around

Porto Alegre is the state's transportation hub, with air and bus services to every major city in Brazil. Most flights have connections via São Paulo. Within the state, excellent roads make driving easy, and there are also very good regional bus lines, with most longer-distance routes beginning or ending in Porto Alegre.

PORTO ALEGRE

☎ 0xx51 / pop 1.35 million

Built on the banks of the huge, freshwater Lagoa dos Patos, Porto Alegre remained a colonial backwater until the late 19th century, when the arrival of Italian and German immigrants transformed the city. Today it's southern Brazil's most important port city. No surprise, then, that its residents are aggressive supporters of Mercosul, the South American free trade zone.

Though not beautiful at first glance, Porto Alegre is one of Brazil's most sophisticated cities. Alegrenses, as residents are known, have made a concerted – and very successful – effort to preserve the downtown area, from the creation of transportation hubs to the preservation of its grand, neoclassical buildings. As well as creative social policies, a long tradition of progressive politics in the city has helped nurture vibrant arts and alternative music scenes. Likewise, the well-organized gay and lesbian community recently won the right to register domestic

partnerships. Unfortunately, it should be noted that crime levels in the city have risen in recent years. Exercise caution downtown after dark.

Orientation

All of Porto Alegre's sights and amenities are in the downtown area and lie within a 15-minute walk from the Mercado Público (public market). The market is also the city's transportation hub, with both a metro station and a local bus terminal just outside its doors. The cathedral sits at the top of the hill that divides downtown from a series of prosperous residential neighborhoods that are clustered around Parque Farroupilha, the city's largest green space.

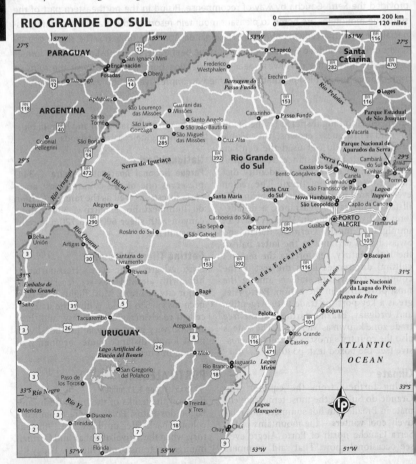

Information

BOOKSTORES
SBS (Rua Caldas Júnior at Av Mauá) Small selection of English-language classics.

EMERGENCY
Bombeiros (☎ 193) Handles both fire and medical emergencies.
Polícia Municipal (☎ 190)

INTERNET ACCESS
.com Cyber Café (☎ 3286 4244; Rua dos Andradas 1001; per hr US$1.50; ☺ 9am-10pm Mon-Sat, 1-10pm Sun)

INTERNET RESOURCES
The state tourist board has a reasonable Portuguese-only site at www.turismogaucho.rs.gov.br. The city tourist board also has an extensive, Portuguese-only site at www.portoalegre.rs.gov.br/turismo/cidade.htm.

MEDICAL SERVICES
Medical emergencies (☎ 192)

MONEY
Aerotur (☎ 3228 8144; Rua dos Andradas 1137) Exchanges traveler's checks and cash.
Banco do Brasil (Av Uruguai 185) Exchanges cash and has Visa ATMs.
Citibank (Rua 7 de Setembro 722) Visa ATMs.
Prontur (☎ 3221 6566; Av Borges de Medeiros 445) Exchanges traveler's checks and cash.

POST
Main post office (Rua Siqueira Campos 1100)

TELEPHONE
Integração (☎ 3212 6444; Av Borges de Medeiros 332) Good prices for international phone calls.
Phone Express (Rua Uruguai 279; ☺ 8:30am-7pm Mon-Fri) International phone calls.

TOURIST INFORMATION
Aeroporto Internacional Salgado Filho Tourist Office (☎ 3358 2000; ☺ 7:30am-midnight) In the luggage-claim area.
Mercado Público Tourist Office (☺ 9am-8pm Mon-Sat) Located just inside the main entrance of the Mercado Público.

Sights
The **Mercado Público**, constructed in 1869, together with the adjacent **Praça 15 de Novembro**, make up the heart of Porto Alegre's city center. The market houses a number of cafés and restaurants as well as stalls that sell everything from meat and produce to *erva maté*, the bitter tea close to the *gaúcho* heart. Nearby lies **Rua dos Andradas**. Closed to cars, it is the city's main *passeio* (promenade) and bears a constant flow of foot traffic, especially from about 4pm to 8pm.

Rua dos Andradas runs into **Praça Alfândega**, a leafy square that is home to the **Museu de Arte do Rio Grande do Sul** (☎ 3227 2311; Praça Alfândega; admission free; ☺ 10am-7pm Tue-Sun), which has a small but interesting collection of regional artists in an impressive neoclassical building. The rooftop café offers an interesting view of downtown.

Continuing down Rua dos Andradas, you will pass the pink **Casa da Cultura Maria Quintana** (see Entertainment, p339), then the colonial church of **NS das Dores**, which sits atop an impressive flight of steps. On the banks of the Lagoa dos Patos, the **Centro Cultural do Usino Gasômetro** (☎ 3212 5979; Av Presidente João Goulart 551; admission free) once served as the city's main power source but now houses art cinemas, temporary art exhibitions and a pleasant café.

Uphill from downtown lies the picturesque **Praça da Matriz**. The square is home to both the early-20th-century, neoclassical **Catedral Metropolitana**, along with the elegant, mid-19th-century **Teatro São Paolo**. Nearby is the **Museu Júlio de Castilhos** (☎ 3221 3959; Rua Duque de Caxias 1231; admission free; ☺ 10am-7pm Tue-Fri, 1:30-5pm Sat & Sun), with an interesting collection of gaúcho artifacts housed in a typical, 19th-century bourgeois home. About 2km past the cathedral lies **Parque Farroupilha**, the city's largest park and home to a sprawling flea market on Sunday morning, from 9am.

River Cruises
Cisne Branco (☎ 3224 5222; Av Presidente João Goulart 551) runs tourist cruises that leave from Centro Cultural do Usino Gasômetro and head up the Rio Guaíba delta, passing many of the uninhabited islands along the way. Trips range from 'happy hour' cruises (US$5) to three-hour dinner cruises (US$14). Timetables change frequently, so check with the tourist office.

Sleeping
BUDGET
Hotel Palácio (☎ 3225 3467; Rua Vigário José Inácio 644; s/d US$8/13, with bathroom s/d/tr US$12/17/22)

Clean and friendly with large, well-kept rooms, the Palácio is the best of the city's budget hotels.

Marechal Hotel (☎ 3228 3076; Rua General Andrade Neves 123; s/d/tr US$5/9/12, with private bathroom US$10/14/18) The hotel could use a major facelift, but price and hospitable owners make the Marechal a reasonably good choice if the Palácio is full. It is also in a great location

Hotel Praça da Matriz (☎ 3225 5772; Largo João Amorim de Albuquerque 72; s/d/tr US$5/10/15, with bathroom US$12/16/20) Housed in a neoclassical mansion, this hotel has definitely seen better days, but there are a few rooms with French doors that open picturesquely onto Praça da Matriz.

MID-RANGE

Lido Hotel (☎ 3228 9111; www.lidohotel.com.br; Rua General Andrade Neves 150; s/d/tr US$29/35/45; P 🅿 🖭) A business traveler's favorite, the Lido combines the three biggies: value, comfort and location. Rooms are cheerful, and the hotel is just a block from both Rua dos Andradas and Av Borges de Medeiros.

Hotel Lancaster (☎ 3224 4737; www.hotel-lancaster-poa.com.br; Travessa Eng Acelino de Carvalho 67; s/d/tr US$20/28/35; 🅿) Set on a quaint, pedestrian passage a half-block above busy Rua dos Andradas, the Lancaster is a decent, two-star joint in a remodeled art-deco apartment building.

Conceição Center Hotel (☎ 3227 6088; www.hotel sconceicao.com.br; Av Senador Salgado Filho 201; s/d/tr

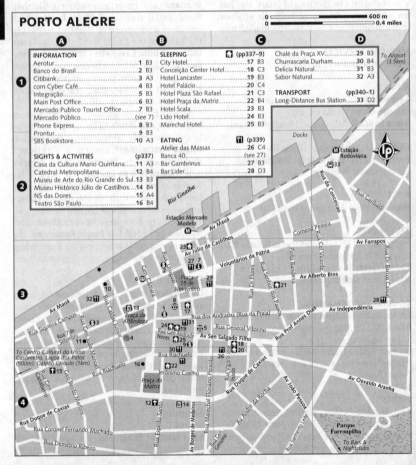

PORTO ALEGRE

0   600 m
0   0.4 miles

INFORMATION
Aerotur...1 B3
Banco do Brasil................................2 B3
Citibank...3 A3
com Cyber Café...............................4 B3
Integração..5 B3
Main Post Office.............................6 B3
Mercado Publico Tourist Office.......7 B3
Mercado Público.........................(see 7)
Phone Express.................................8 B3
Prontur..9 B3
SBS Bookstore...............................10 A3

SIGHTS & ACTIVITIES (p337)
Casa da Cultura Mario Quintana....11 A3
Catedral Metropolitana..................12 B4
Museu de Arte do Rio Grande do Sul.13 B3
Museu Histórico Júlio de Castilhos...14 A4
NS das Dores..................................15 A4
Teatro São Paulo...........................16 B4

SLEEPING 🛏 (pp337–9)
City Hotel......................................17 B3
Conceição Center Hotel................18 C3
Hotel Lancaster.............................19 B3
Hotel Palácio.................................20 C4
Hotel Plaza São Rafael..................21 C3
Hotel Praça da Matriz....................22 B4
Hotel Scala....................................23 B3
Lido Hotel.....................................24 B3
Marechal Hotel..............................25 B3

EATING 🍴 (p339)
Atelier das Massas 26 C4
Banca 40...................................(see 27)
Bar Gambrinus...............................27 B3
Bar Lider..28 D3

Chalé da Praça XV.........................29 B3
Churrascaria Durham.....................30 B4
Delicia Natural...............................31 B3
Sabor Natural................................32 A3

TRANSPORT (pp340–1)
Long-Distance Bus Station............33 D2

To Airport (3.5km)

Estação Rodoviária
🚇 33

Rio Guaíba

Docks

Av Farrapos
Av Alberto Bins
Av Independência
Av Osvaldo Aranha

Estação Mercado Modelo
Av Mauá
Av Júlio de Castilhos
Voluntários da Pátria
Praça 15 de Novembro
Rua dos Andradas (Rua da Praia)
Rua Gen Andrade Neves
Av Sen Salgado Filho
Rua Riachuelo
Jerônimo Coelho
Praça da Matriz

To Centro Cultural do Usina Gasômetro, Lagoa dos Patos (500m); Galpão Crioulo (1km)

Rua 7 de Setembro
Av Mauá
Praça da Alfândega
Rua Siqueira Campos
Rua Gen Câmara
Rua Cel Bento Martins

Rua Duque de Caxias
Rua Coronel Fernando Machado
Rua Demétrio Ribeiro
Rua Espírito Santo
Av Borges de Medeiros
Rua Marechal Floriano Peixoto
Av André da Rocha
Av João Pessoa
Rua Sarmento Leite

Parque Farroupilha

To Bars & Nightclubs

US$26/34/40; (P) (□)) Impersonal but comfortable.

Hotel Scala (☎ 3227 5522; www.hotelscala.com.br; Av Júlio de Castilhos 34; s/d/tr $23/34/45; (P) (X) (□)) Clean, bright rooms, with all the basic comforts. Avoid rooms facing the busy street.

TOP END

City Hotel (☎ 3212 5488; www.cityhotel.com.br; Rua Dr José Montaury 20; s/d/tr US$40/42/50; (P) (X) (□)) A grand, old hotel but with completely modernized rooms, this beaux-arts classic is located in the heart of downtown. Considering all these benefits, the prices are remarkably reasonable.

Hotel Plaza São Rafael (☎ 3220 8000; www.plaza hoteis.com.br; Av Alberto Bins 514; s/d $62/69; (P) (X) (□)) This modern hotel is impersonal, but it's the most luxurious option in the city center, with all the amenities.

Eating

The city is filled with *churrascarias* (restaurants featuring barbecued meat) serving up tender, gaúcho beef, making it a great place to boost your iron levels. On the other hand, a large alternative community supports some good vegetarian options.

Galpão Crioulo (☎ 3226 8194; Parque Maurício Sirotsky Sobrinho; all-you-can-eat buffet US$12.50; ☺ lunch & dinner) Billing itself as the meeting place of the Mercosul, this high-end *churrascaria* is considered the city's best. As well as some 20 different cuts of grilled meats, there is a buffet with dozens of hot and cold dishes.

Churrascaria Durham (Rua Riachuelo 1300; fixed-price buffet US$4.50; ☺ lunch & dinner) A standard *churrascaria* with all-you-can-eat beef, chicken and pork straight off the grill. Close to downtown.

Atelier das Massas (☎ 3225 1125; Rua Riachuelo 1482; dishes for 2 US$10-12; ☺ lunch & dinner Mon-Sat) Modern, downtown joint with good pasta and original paintings on the walls.

Sabor Natural (☎ 3286 4544; Rua Siqueira Campos 890; all-you-can-eat buffet US$3; ☺ lunch Mon-Fri) This lunch-only restaurant delivers good, dependable vegetarian fare.

Banca 40 (Mercado Público; ☺ 9am-7pm) This family-owned bakery and creamery serves up distinctive ice cream made using 50-year-old recipes. Try a scoop (US$0.50) of the surprisingly delicious *milho* (corn) ice cream.

Bar Gambrinus (☎ 3226 6914; Mercado Público; mains US$10-15; ☺ lunch daily, dinner Mon-Fri) For lunch, this Portuguese restaurant in the Mercado Público attracts the city's movers and shakers with its old-world aura and extremely fresh seafood. The signature dish is *tainha* (meaty but tender local fish) stuffed with shrimp.

Chale da Praça XV (☎ 3225 2667; Praça 15 de Novembro; mains US$8-15; ☺ noon-midnight) Housed in a pleasant, Victorian-style garden house and surrounded by a sprawling terrace, this Porto Alegre institution buzzes with activity starting around happy hour. The food is only decent, and the prices are higher than average, but the atmosphere is worth the slight premium. There's also a small cybercafé inside the main building.

Delicia Natural (☎ 3225 4970; Rua dos Andradas 1325; all-you-can-eat buffet US$2.75; ☺ lunch Mon-Fri) A favorite lunchtime stop among the downtown lunch crowd, this place is easy to miss. Upstairs from the discreet entrance is a large, cheerful, if simple, dining room with an extremely fresh, vegetarian-friendly buffet. The low price includes dessert, fresh juices, coffee and freshly grilled chicken and fish.

Entertainment

For insight into cultural happenings in the city, head to the information desk in the **Casa da Cultura Mario Quintana** (☎ 3221 7147; Rua dos Andradas 736). You'll find comprehensive information about theater, music, cinema and art exhibitions. The cultural center also has a cinema and two busy cafés – one at street level and one on the 7th floor called Café Concerto Majestic. This café is a great place from which to watch the sunset over Lagoa dos Patos. Most nights, there's live music starting at 7pm.

Bars and clubs are concentrated around two streets: Av Goethe and Rua Fernando Gomes (known as 'The Walk of Fame'). **Dado Pub** (☎ 3395-1468; Rua Fernando Gomes 80) is a perennial favorite of the 20-something crowd. On Tuesday, **Bar do Goethe** (☎ 3222 2043; Rua 24 de Outobro 112) hosts an international student cultural exchange. With 40 different kinds of wine, and original art on the walls, **Ossip** (☎ 3224 2422; Rua da República 677) is a good option.

Liquid (☎ 3312 4432; Rua João Telles 54) is a big dance club with juggling bartenders and pumping techno and electronica. **Dr Jekyll** (☎ 3226 9404; Travessa do Carmo 76) hosts mostly alternative rock bands.

Porto Alegre has an active gay and lesbian social scene. Pick up a copy of *Jornal do Nuances*, available at Casa da Cultura Mario Quintana, for community news as well as listings for nightlife and special events.

Getting There & Away

AIR

Porto Alegre's attractive, modern **Aeroporto Internacional Salgado Filho** (☎ 3358 2000) is located 6km from downtown. A taxi to the center of the city costs about US$8. The airport is also connected to downtown by the city's efficient metro (US$0.25, 30 minutes).

There are direct domestic flights via Tam and Varig to São Paulo (one hour), Rio de Janeiro (1½ hours), Florianópolis (40 minutes), Curitiba (one hour) and Brasília (2½ hours). There are also direct flights via both Varig and Aerolineas Argentinas to Montevideo and Buenos Aires.

BUS

The busy long-distance bus station, on Largo Vespiano Júlio Veppo, is connected by a short pedestrian bridge to the city's efficient aboveground metro. For all downtown destinations, head to the Mercado Púb-

lico stop, about a 10-minute ride. A taxi to downtown costs US$3 to US$4.

International destinations include: Montevideo (US$45, 12 hours); Buenos Aires (US$51, 18 hours); and Santiago (US$105, 36 hours). Buses travel interstate to: Foz do Iguaçu (US$28, 14 hours); Florianópolis (US$14, seven hours); Curitiba (US$21, 11 hours); and Rio de Janeiro (US$57, 26 hours).

For detailed information about prices and times for buses within Rio Grande do Sul, consult www.rodoviaria-poa.com.br. Destinations include: Torres (US$7, three hours); Gramado (US$5, two hours); Canela (US$6, 2½ hours); Pelotas (US$5, two hours); Rio Grande (US$6, three hours); Cambará do Sul ($7, six hours), for access to Parque Nacional de Aparados da Serra; and Santo Ángelo (US$21, six hours), for access to São Miguel das Missões and other nearby missions.

Getting Around

Porto Alegre has a very clean and efficient one-line metro that conveniently connects downtown with both the long-distance bus station and the airport. A ride costs about

---

PROGRESSIVE POLITICS IN RIO GRANDE DO SUL

Rio Grande do Sul has a long history of contrariness. The state's *farroupilhas* – a term roughly equivalent to France's sansculottes (ie shabbily dressed) – revolted against the Brazilian emperor in the 1830s and '40s, declaring a short-lived republic. In the late 1970s, strikes by *gaúcho* trade unions helped weaken the military junta ruling the country. And in March 2004, in a country that is overwhelmingly Catholic (with a strong evangelical Christian minority), the state's high court declared same-sex unions a civil right.

In the rest of the world, the future of democracy seems in question as media behemoths and corporation-funded campaigns produce increasingly feckless electorates. But not so in the capital of Rio Grande do Sul – and the unofficial world headquarters of progressive politics. In 2001, the city hosted the first World Social Forum, the left's answer to the World Economic Forum. Activists from around the world gathered on the banks of Lagoa dos Patos to advance alternatives to unbridled global capitalism. To their surprise, many of the activists discovered that the city of Porto Alegre was itself a model in democratic political organization.

When the Labor Party came to power in the city upon the restoration of full democracy in the late 1980s, its leaders faced a serious problem. They had made myriad promises in the campaign, but found the city had been bankrupted by the previous administration. In a bid to extend democratic institutions as well as create buy-in from a restive population, they set up the Orcamento Participativo, a complex system by which citizen committees are given a direct hand in creating the municipal budget. They set priorities that the city council is then unofficially bound to respect.

Activists at the World Social Forum were impressed by the way the system advanced the needs of working-class and poor communities, and also encouraged their vigorous political participation. Now the system is being replicated in at least 10 other cities throughout Latin America.

US$0.25. Purchase tickets at the booths within the station. Once you are downtown, virtually all the city's main attractions are within a 15-minute walk of the metro's final stop, just behind the Mercado Público.

SERRA GAÚCHA

As you head north from Porto Alegre, you quickly begin to climb into the Serra Gaúcha. The ride is beautiful, particularly the stretch between Nova Petrópolis and Gramado. First settled by Germans (beginning in 1824) and later by Italians (starting in the 1870s), the region is as close as Brazil comes to the Alps.

The mountains don't reach much more than 1000m, but with typical Brazilian exuberance, Gramado and – to a lesser extent – neighboring Canela are built to resemble Swiss villages. The area can become crowded with Porto Alegrenses and Paulistas, particularly during summer weekends when temperatures swelter in the flatlands.

In spring the hills are blanketed with wildflowers, while tens of thousands of hydrangeas keep blooming well into summer. If you come in winter, you may see actual Brazilian snow. Higher altitudes get a couple of inches a year. Hiking is excellent year-round, particularly in the Parque Estadual do Caracol.

Gramado

☎ 0xx54 / pop 25,000

This tony mountain resort, which bills itself as 'naturally European,' is a favorite with well-to-do *gaúchos* as well as Argentines, Uruguayans and Paulistas. The town consists of upmarket shops, cozy restaurants, manicured gardens and expensive Swiss-style chalets/hotels. At times the insistence on Alpine themes crosses over into kitsch, but the overall affect is pleasant.

During the first two weeks in August, Gramado hosts the Festival de Gramado Cinema Brasileiro e Latino. It's among the most prestigious film festivals in Brazil and attracts the international jet set. At Christmas, the town is decked out in full Christmas regalia. At this time, the kitsch factor increases manyfold.

ORIENTATION & INFORMATION

Gramado's bus station is located about 400m from the intersection of the town's two main streets, Av Borges de Medeiros and Av das Hortênsias. All sights and amenities are within 2km of this unofficial center.

Banco do Brasil (cnr Rua Garibaldi & Rua Augusto Zatti) ATM and money exchange.

Centro de Informações (☎ 286 1475; Praça Major Nicoletti; ☼ 9am-7pm) The friendly, helpful tourist office is located 100m from the intersection of Av Borges de Medeiros and Av das Hortênsias.

Posto Telefônico (☎ 286 4727; Av Borges de Medeiros 2889; Internet access per hr US$3; ☼ 9am-9pm Mon-Sat, noon-6pm Sun) Internet access as well as booths for international phone calls.

PARKS

Lago Negro, situated about 1.5km southeast of the town center, is an attractive, man-made lake surrounded by hydrangeas. On sunny days it's crowded with cute swan-shaped boats. Closer to the center, **Parque Knorr**, located at the end of Rua Bela Vista, offers inspiring views of the canyon-like Vale do Quilombo, a beautiful valley that stretches along the road between Gramado and Canela.

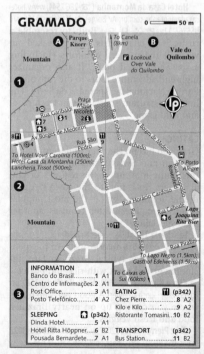

GRAMADO

INFORMATION	
Banco do Brasil..............1	A1
Centro de Informações..2	A1
Post Office.................3	A1
Posto Telefônico.........4	A2

SLEEPING	(p342)
Dinda Hotel..............5	A1
Hotel Ritta Höppner....6	A2
Pousada Bernardete....7	A1

EATING	(p342)
Chez Pierre..............8	A2
Kilo e Kilo..............9	A2
Ristorante Tomasini...10	B2

TRANSPORT	(p342)
Bus Station..............11	B2

THE SOUTH

SLEEPING

Gramado has a surfeit of high-end accommodations, while budget options are few and far between. Prices here are for weekends outside high season. Rates can rise 20% to 30% from around mid-December until early March.

Dinda Hotel (☎ 286 2810; Rua Augusto Zatti 160; s/d US$10/20) This family-owned place lacks charm but is the cheapest place in town.

Hotel Vovó Carolina (☎ 286 2433; www.vovocarolina.com.br; Av Borges de Medeiros 3129; s/d/tr US$24/34/42; P) Clean, bright, and with all the basic comforts.

Pousada Bernardete (☎ 286 1569; www.gramado.com.br/bernardete.htm; Rua Augusto Zatti 200; s/d US$24/45; P) A bright, pleasant bed-and-brekky.

Hotel Ritta Höppner (☎ 286 1334; www.rittahoppner.com.br; Rua Pedro Candiago 305; s/d US$65/74; P ⬛) Situated in a lovely residential district, this plush inn takes kitsch seriously. The breakfast room is a lace-filled affair, and the garden is replete with gnomes and elves. In a surprising touch, every room has a spa bath built for two.

Hotel Casa da Montanha (☎ 286 2544; www.hotelcasadamontanha.com.br; Av Borges de Medeiros 3166; s/d US$76/112; P ⬛ ⬛ ⬛) Built to resemble a rustic Swiss chalet, this hotel is decked out with all the modern comforts (including a spa and heated pool). It also organizes high-end adventure tours to the canyons of Parque Nacional de Aparados da Serra. The hotel's restaurant specializes in fresh trout and wild game.

EATING

Gramado has no shortage of decent Italian, German and Swiss restaurants, reflecting the ethnic makeup of the region's original settlers. In a nod to the town's Alpine theme, fondue is by far the most popular menu item. Freshwater trout is another local speciality.

Lancheria Tissot (Av Borges de Medeiros 3283; mains US$1.50-3; ⊗ lunch & dinner Mon-Sat) An inexpensive option for typical Brazilian fare, including grilled meat with rice and beans.

Kilo e Kilo (☎ 286 1182; Av das Hortênsias 1720; per kg US$4; ⊗ lunch & dinner) A good per-kilo buffet where you can fill up on hearty Brazilian food and fresh veggies.

Chez Pierre (☎ 286 2057; Av Borges de Medeiros 3022; mains US$10-12; ⊗ dinner only Mon-Sat) This cozy Swiss restaurant is the best place in town for fondue, raclettes and local trout.

Gasthof Edelweiss (☎ 286 1861; Rua da Carriérie 1119; mains US$10-15) Situated picturesquely just across from Lago Negro, this homey restaurant is relatively pricey but serves up the town's best German cuisine.

Ristorante Tomasini (☎ 286 4311; Av das Hortênsias 1189; mains US$10-12; ⊗ lunch & dinner) Tasty pasta dishes as well as grilled meats.

GETTING THERE & AROUND

The town is small enough to get everywhere by foot. There are frequent buses to Porto Alegre (US$5.50, two hours). Buses for Canela leave the main bus station every 10 to 20 minutes (US$1.50, 20 minutes).

Canela

☎ 0xx54 / pop 33,200

While lacking Gramado's manicured glamour, Canela is the obvious choice for budget travelers, with cheaper hotels and more convenient access to a series of stunning state parks.

ORIENTATION & INFORMATION

Except for a few pousadas (guesthouses) tucked away in the adjacent forests, all the town's amenities are within a block or two of the main drag, Av Osvaldo Aranha.

Banco do Brasil (Praça João Corrêa) Money exchange and Visa ATMs.

Central de Informações (☎ 282 2200; Lago da Fama 227) The main tourist office provides maps and a list of recommended agencies for half-day tours of the nearby state parks (about US$24 per person), and for rafting trips and mountain-bike adventures. For more information, see the town's comprehensive website (www.canela.com.br).

Post office (Rua Dona Carlinda) Near Rua Batista Luzardo.

Posto Telefônico (☎ 3031 107; Av Julio de Castilhos 319) Provides both Internet access and international phone calls.

PARKS

The major attraction of **Parque Estadual do Caracol** (☎ 278 035; admission US$2; ⊗ 8:30am-5:30pm), 9km from Canela, is the spectacular Cascata do Caracol, a 130m free-falling waterfall. It's particularly stunning in the morning sun – the water sparkles as it cascades over the granite lip. If you're feeling fit, you can walk to the base of the waterfall down (and back up) the 927 stairs.

Parque Floresta Encantada de Canela, a brief 3km drive or a 45-minute hike from Parque do Caracol, has a gorgeous chairlift ride along a canyon that provides a front view of the Cascata do Caracol. Entry to the park (including the chairlift ride) is US$3.

A 6km hike along Estrada Ferradura from the Parque do Caracol entrance brings you to **Parque da Ferradura** (☎ 9969 6785; admission US$2.50; 🕙 9am-5:30pm), which features a stunning 420m horseshoe-shaped canyon formed by the Rio Santa Cruz. There are three lookouts that you can hike to along well-marked trails – the longest takes around two hours. About 3km from town on the road to the park is **Castelinho**. The oldest house in the area, it was built by German pioneers without the luxury of metal nails.

Heading out of town on Rua Felisberto Soares past the cathedral, you will reach **Morros Pelado, Queimado** and **Dedão**. These hills provide stunning views of the Vale do Quilombo, and on clear days you can see the coast. They're 5km, 5.5km and 6.5km from Canela respectively.

ACTIVITIES

Adventure tourism has arrived in Canela, but it's a fairly gentle brand of adventure on the whole. There are opportunities for rock climbing, rappelling, rafting, mountain biking and bungee jumping in the various local parks. A 2½-hour rafting trip along the Rio Paranhana costs around US$25 and rappelling and rock climbing at Ferradura costs around US$15, including transport and equipment.

At!tude Ecologia & Tourismo (☎ 282 6305; atitude@serragaucha.com.br; Av Osvaldo Aranha 391, Shop 16) Adventure tours of nearby parks.

Vida Livre (☎ 282 1518, 9956 9584; www.vidalivretur ismo.com.br; Av Osvaldo Aranha 450) Half-day tours of the local parks (US$24 per person) or full-day expeditions to the spectacular canyons of Parque Nacional de Aparados da Serra (US$45 per person). English spoken.

SLEEPING

Alpes Verdes Parque Hotel (☎ 282 1162; www.alpes verdes.com; Rua Gilda T Bolognese 1001; s/d US$34/52; P 🖳 🐕) In a lovely parklike setting 2km from town, this hotel features private chalets, including two duplex rooms with excellent views of the Vale do Quilombo. It's removed from the center, but the learned and extremely hospitable hosts are happy to ferry you back and forth. They are perfect exemplars of the hospitality for which *gaúchos* are so well known.

Vila Vecchia (☎ 282 1051; Rua Melvin Jones 137; s/d US$18/32) Steps from the bus station, this Swiss-style chalet has decent rooms with television and fridge at very reasonable prices.

Pousada do Viajante (☎ 282 2017; Rua Ernesto Urban 1; s/d/tr US$11/22/33) This clean, pleasant HI youth hostel is right next to the bus station. It has both dorm-style and private rooms.

Hotel Bela Vista (☎ 282 1327; www.canela.tur.br /hotelbelavista.htm; Av Osvaldo Aranha 160; quarto per person US$9, s/d with bathroom US$26/29) Located right in the center of town, the clean but very basic *quartos* are a great deal.

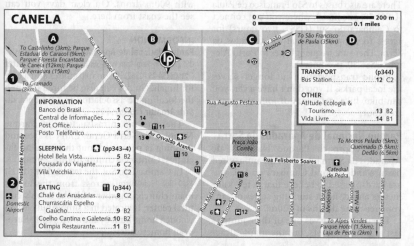

Laje de Pedra (☎ 282 4300; www.lajedepedra.com
.br; Rua dos Flores 222; s/d US$75/90; P ❘❙❘ ⬚ ⬚)
The most luxurious in the region, this hotel
sits at the edge of Vale do Quilombo and
offers spectacular views as well as five-star
comforts and service.

EATING

Olimpia Restaurante (☎ 282 3888; Av Osvaldo Aranha
456; all-you-can-eat buffet US$4; ☷ 11:30am-3am) This
per-kilo restaurant is packed by noon, and
for good reason. The buffet includes grilled
meats as well as fresh vegetables and salads.

Churrascaria Espelho Gaúcho (☎ 282 4348; just
off Av Osvaldo Aranha; mains $US5-7; ☷ lunch & dinner)
A decent *churrascaria* with an all-the-meat-
you-can-eat option.

Coelho Cantina e Galeteria (☎ 282 4224; Av Osvaldo Aranha 287; all-you-can-eat buffet US$6.50; ☷ lunch
& dinner) Though touristy, this is a good place
to fill up on local-style Italian food, including pastas, roast chicken, and pork with
polenta. At dinner, add the fondue buffet
for an extra US$3.50.

Chalé das Aruacárias (☎ 282 8252; across
from Praça João Corrêa; all-you-can-eat buffet US$2.50;
☷ 11am-3pm & 7-10pm) Straightforward Brazilian food in a pleasant garden setting right
next to the tourist office.

GETTING THERE & AROUND

There are frequent buses from Canela to Porto
Alegre via Gramado (US$6.50, 2½ hours).
Buses for Canela leave the main bus station
every 10 to 20 minutes ($1.50, 20 minutes).
There are also buses to São Francisco de Paula
(US$1.50, one hour), where you can connect
to Cambará do Sul (US$7, two hours) for
access to Parque Nacional de Aparados da
Serra. There are frequent buses to Porto Ale-
gre (US$5.50, two hours).

Public transportation no longer serves
the local parks. If you don't have a car, you
can bike, hike, get a taxi or join an organized tour.

Parque Nacional de Aparados da Serra

As you approach Parque Nacional de
Aparados da Serra by way of the uninspired
pasturelands around Cambará do Sul, you
are hard-pressed to believe that, a few kilometers ahead, lies a stunning series of canyons reaching depths of 720m.

The park preserves one of the country's
last araucaria forests, but the main attrac-

tion is the **Cânion do Itaimbezinho**, a narrow,
5800m-long canyon with sheer 600m to
720m parallel escarpments. Two waterfalls
drop into this incision in the earth, which
was formed by the Rio Perdiz's rush to
the sea.

This magnificent national park stretches
across two states: the majority is in Rio
Grande do Sul, while a small part lies in
Santa Catarina. The park is 70km north of
São Francisco de Paula and 18km from the
town of Cambará do Sul, which serves as
the base for visitors.

There are three hiking trails through the
park. **Trilha do Vértice** runs for 2km to an
observation point for the canyon and the
Cascata do Andorinhas. **Trilha Cotovelo** is a 3km
trail (2½ hours round-trip) passing by the
Véu de Noiva waterfall, with wonderful vistas
of the canyon. **Trilha do Rio do Boi** is best approached from the town of Praia Grande
in Santa Catarina. From the Posto Rio do
Boi entrance to the park, the trail follows
the base of the canyon for 7km, much of it
over loose rocks. It's for experienced hikers
and a guide is highly recommended. During rainy season the trail is closed because
of the danger of flooding.

Parque Nacional da Serra Geral was created
in 1992 as an extension of the northern and
southern borders of the Parque Nacional de
Aparados da Serra. The larger northern section contains two more canyons that rival
Itaimbezinho: **Cânion Malacara** and **Cânion
da Fortaleza**, an 8km stretch of escarpment
with 900m drops. On clear days you can
see the coast from here.

INFORMATION

Parque Nacional de Aparados da Serra (admission
US$2.50; ☷ 9am-4pm Wed-Sun). The **visitor's center**
(☎ 0xx54-251 1262) has maps, guides and a café
for lunch. Guides can also be hired through
the local guide association in Cambará do
Sul, **Acontur** (☎ 0xx54-251 1265).

There is no infrastructure in Parque
Nacional da Serra Geral. Entry is free and
camping is permitted, but there are no facilities. Contact Acontur to hire a guide.

In Cambará do Sul, the **tourist office** (☎ 251
1320; Rua 15 de Março), across from the town's
main church, together with the town's cultural center, is located in a simple but elegant
wooden home built by the town's early European homesteaders.

SLEEPING & EATING

Cambará do Sul is the town closest to both Parque Nacional de Aparados da Serra (18km) and Parque Nacional da Serra Geral (23km). It lacks charm but has many economical, family-run pousadas. Outside of town, a number of higher-end options has opened as Brazil's upper class discovers adventure travel. Within Parque Nacional da Serra Geral, there are good spots to camp (without facilities) near the old Paradouro Hotel and near the Cânion da Fortaleza.

Pousada Itaimbeleza (☎ 0xx54-251 1367; Rua Dona Úrsula 648; s/d US$10/20) A block from the train station, this busy pousada has an atmosphere of backpacking bonhomie. Rooms are pretty basic, and you may need to share if business is brisk.

Pousada Alvarado (☎ 0xx54-251 1284; Av Getúlio Vargas 630; s/d US$7/14, with private bathroom US$9/18; **P**) Basic singles and doubles just off the town's main street.

Pousada Corucacas (☎ 0xx54-251 1123, 9956 7042; per person incl breakfast & dinner US$20) Two kilometers from town on the road to Ouro Verde, this pousada is also a working farm, with horseback riding and fishing. Price includes both breakfast and dinner. Reservations are necessary.

Refúgio Ecológico Pedra Afiada (☎ 0xx48-532 1059; www.pedraafiada.com.br; s/d/tr US$60/66/95) Splendidly located within the Canión Malacara, this isolated inn boasts a working fireplace for chilly nights and a rooftop deck with spectacular views.

Parador Casa da Montanha (☎ 0xx54-286 2544; www.paradorcasadamontanha.com.br; d US$110; **P**) Experience rustic chic in the region's most upscale hostelry. Price includes well-appointed cabin-tents, three meals a day, tours of the nearby canyons and adventure activities such as rafting and horseback riding.

Unless your hotel offers board, dining options are mostly limited to pizza, burgers, and meat- and cheese-stuffed pastries. **Galpão Crioulo** (☎ 0xx54-251 1341; Rua Padre João Francisco Ritter 650) is undoubtedly the town's best *churrascaria*.

Getting There & Around

There's one daily bus to and from Porto Alegre to Cambará do Sul (US$6.50, five hours) via São Francisco de Paula. If you're coming from the north, there's a daily bus to and from Torres to Cambará do Sul that comes by a spectacular road from the coast (US$7, three hours). There are also buses from Torres to Praia Grande (in Santa Catarina state) for access to the park's Trilha do Rio do Boi.

No public buses go to the parks. Even if you have a car, the dirt roads are rough and driving is very slow. For a fixed fare, any taxi (about US$20, up to four people) or minivan in town (about US$25, up to six people) will drop you off at the park in the morning and pick you up again at the end of the day.

LITORAL GAÚCHO

On paper, it sounds amazing: a 500km strip of the Brazilian coastline that forms what is essentially one long beach – stretching from Torres, on the border with Santa Catarina, all the way to Chuí at the Uruguayan border. Unfortunately, the reality is less enticing. The water tends to be murky and the beaches are undistinguished, with little geographical variation – wide open, with bushy vegetation and occasional dunes.

There are some decent beaches in and around the resort town of Torres, which fills up in summer with Porto Alegrenses, Uruguayans and Argentines. In winter, currents from the Antarctic bring cold, hard winds to the coast. Bathing suits disappear, as do the crowds, and most hotels shut down from March to November.

Once vital to southern Brazil's cattle industry, the towns of Pelotas and Rio Grande still retain the vestiges of their former 19th-century glory, making them worth a look.

Torres

☎ 0xx51 / pop 29,100
Torres, which lies at the border with Santa Catarina about 205km from Porto Alegre, is the exception to the state's uninviting coastline. The town has fine beaches punctuated in places by beautiful basalt-rock formations. The town is crowded throughout the summer, especially on weekends when Porto Alegrenses descend en masse.

Praia Grande, the town's main beach, is relatively calm, but surfers only need to head about 2km south to **Praia da Cal** for decent waves. A little farther south lie the dunes of **Parque e Praia da Guarita**, which make for fun trekking.

INFORMATION

There's a good **tourist office** (☎ 626 1937; cnr Av Barão do Rio Branco & Rua General Osório). It publishes a list of hotels, including the cheapest ones, and a good city map.

The **Banco do Brasil** (Av Barão do Rio Branco 236) has both a money exchange and Visa ATMs. Nearby are a number of money-exchange offices.

For Internet access, a number of places along Av José Bonifácio between the bus station and Av Barão do Rio Branco includes **Mr Cópias** (☎ 664 2266; Rua José Luiz de Freitas 163; per hr US$3; ⏱ 8:30am-7pm Mon-Sat).

BOAT TRIPS

Barcos Marina and **Flamingo** (☎ 626 2933 for both) offer trips to the ecological reserve on Ilha dos Lobos. Boats leave from Ponte Pênsil on the Rio Mampituba. To get to the jetty, walk to the end of Av Silva Jardim and turn left when you reach the river. The trip lasts about 45 minutes and costs US$3.50 per person.

SLEEPING

For a resort town, Torres has a large selection of reasonably priced accommodations. The prices listed below are for summer season – expect discounts of 20% to 40% between March and November.

Pousada da Prainha (☎ 626 2454; www.pousada daprainha.com.br; Rua Alferes Feirreira Porto 138; s/d US$23/32; ⓟ ☒) An attractive, colonial-style hotel one block from the beach. Reservations recommended for rooms with an ocean view.

Pousada Brisa do Mar (☎ 664 2019; Rua Borges de Medeiros 51; s/d US$20/36; ⓟ ☒) Built around an enclosed courtyard, this is a fine mid-range option close to the beach.

Hotel Costa Azul (☎ 664 3291; Av José Bonifácio 382; s/d US$24/34; ☒) Just a block from the bus station, this is a clean, well-appointed place and a good value.

Dunas Praias Hotel (☎ 664 1011; www.dunas hoteis.com.br; Rua Mal Deodoro 48; s/d US$52/85, with views s/d $80/150; ⓟ ☒ ▢ ☒) An upmarket hotel well located at the point where Praia Grande and Prainha meet, with the best ocean views in town.

Hotel Medusa (☎ 664 2378; Rua Benjamin Constant 828; s/d US$7/12, with bathroom US$8.50/17) It may be set on a grim courtyard, but this family-owned place is clean, friendly and one of the cheapest places in town.

EATING

Doce Art (☎ 664 5591; Av Silva Jardim 295) A pleasant café on Praça 15 serving good espresso and both sweet and savory baked goods.

Bom Gosto (Av Barão do Rio Branco 242) A good *churrascaria* popular with homesick Uruguayans and Argentines.

GETTING THERE & AWAY

The town is small and all conveniences are easily accessible by foot, including the long-distance bus station. Destinations include: Porto Alegre (US$8, three hours, hourly); Cambará do Sul (US$7, three hours, daily); Florianópolis (US$12, five hours, five daily).

Pelotas

☎ 0xx53 / pop 308,700

Once a vital port in Brazil's profitable trade in *charque* (dried beef), Pelotas remains an important industrial center and Rio Grande's second-largest city. However, these days its major exports – sweets and preserved fruits – are sweet rather than savory. The city had its heyday in the late 19th century, and the wealth generated in those years is still reflected in some grand neoclassical mansions around the main square, Praça General Osório. Other than a short walk around the center, there is really no reason to linger.

ORIENTATION & INFORMATION

The intercity bus station sits well outside the city center, with local buses to the city center leaving every 15 minutes. A taxi to the center costs about US$4. A **Banco do Brasil** (cnr Rua General Osório & Rua Lobo da Costa) exchanges money but does not have Visa ATMs. Two blocks from Praça General Osório, there is a small but friendly **tourist office** (☎ 225 7755; 2nd fl, Rua Lobo da Costa 1274; ⏱ 9am-6pm Mon-Fri).

SLEEPING & EATING

Hotel Aleppo (☎ 225 3950, Rua General Osório 708A; s/d/tr US$11/16/21; ⓟ) Centrally located and an excellent value, with cable TV and large rooms with the basic comforts.

Hotel Manta (☎ 225 2411; www.hoteismanta.com .br; Rua General Neto 1131; s/d US$40/49; ⓟ ☒ ▢) A very comfortable business hotel near the center. Considered the best in town.

Lobão Churrascaria (☎ 227 9596; Av Bento Gonçalves 3460) Good *churrascaria* next to the town's largest park.

GETTING THERE & AWAY
Pelotas is a transportation hub for the area, with service to Porto Alegre (US$8, three hours) and Rio Grande (US$4, one hour). There are regular buses to Uruguay and buses to both Porto Alegre and Rio Grande every half-hour.

Rio Grande
☎ 0xx53 / pop 183,400
Strategically located at the mouth of Lagoa dos Patos, Rio Grande was founded by Portuguese colonists in 1737 to guard the disputed southern border of their empire. The region's oldest city, Rio Grande had its flowering at the second half of the 19th century, when its port became a vital link in the highly profitable beef trade. Though smaller than neighboring Pelotas, Rio Grande has an historic center that is both better preserved and more charming, with some interesting Portuguese colonial and neoclassical building. The very well-preserved, colonial Portuguese-style **Catedral de São Paolo** (Praça Dr Pio) dates to the 18th century.

ORIENTATION & INFORMATION
The historic center is a short walk from the bus station and can be seen in its entirety within a few hours. There aren't enough visitors to support a regularly working tourist office. Ask in any of the hotels listed below for a map of the city.

Banco do Brasil (cnr Rua Marechal Floriano Peixoto & Rua Benjamin Constant) has both a Visa ATM and a money exchange. **Netmix Internet Café** (☎ 232 6890; Rua Conde de Porto Alegre 371; per hr US$2; ☑ 10am-noon & 1:30-7pm Mon-Fri, 10am-noon & 1:30-5pm Sat) provides high-speed Internet access.

MUSEU OCEANOGRÁFICO
This **museum** (☎ 232 9107; Rua Capitão Heitor Perdigão 10; admission free; ☑ 9-11:30am & 2 5:30pm Tue-Sun), located on the water 2km north from the center, is small but elegant and one of the most complete of its type in Latin America. On weekends you can cross the bay to a restored colonial **farm** (admission US$0.75; ☑ 2-5:30pm Fri-Sun) that serves as a miniature wetlands reserve.

SLEEPING
Atlântico Rio Grande (☎ 231 3833; Rua Duque de Caixas 53; s/d US$30/45; P ⛽ 🖳) It may not be beautiful to look at, but this is the top hotel in town and very comfortable once you get inside. Ask for a room facing the waterfront and adjacent park – the views are lovely.

Paris Hotel (☎ 231 3866; Rua Marechal Floriano 112; s/d US$8/11, with bathroom US$11/15). What this hotel lacks in the latest comforts, it makes up for in charm. Housed in an elegant, 19th-century building, it has a leafy courtyard

---

ERVA MATÉ

Rio Grande do Sul has modernized at a startling pace. It's among the wealthiest states, per capita, in Brazil – and the most sophisticated. Yet when even the most *moderno gaúcho* needs a lift, he reaches for a gourd rather than an espresso cup.

It was the Guaraní Indians who taught Spanish settlers to the region the pleasures of *erva maté*, and how to sip it not from a cup but through a *bomba* (straw) stuck into a hollowed-out *cuia* (gourd). Also known as *chimarrão* or simply *maté*, this tea-like beverage is made from the leaves of the maté tree, which is native to the pampas (grassy plains) that extend from Argentina and Uruguay through southern Brazil.

The original *gaúchos*, the men who tended the region's vast cattle herds, quickly became addicted to maté's pleasurable effects, which are at once energizing and calming. They even grew to love its bittersweet taste, perhaps because it reflected the lives they led on the empty plains. Indeed, there is something intrinsically nostalgic about maté, both in its taste and its physical effect. Even the act of sucking at the straw seems both to instill and to satisfy an ancient yearning. It's an acquired taste that, once acquired, is very hard to kick.

This ancient tradition is getting a contemporary boost from scientists and pseudo-scientists alike, who make extravagant claims about maté's health benefits, from lower blood pressure and improved digestion to increased intelligence. Hard results are yet to come. In the meantime, you can make a study of the pleasurable, abstracted, almost timeless look in the eye of the *gaúcho* as he is intimately engaged with his *bomba*, *cuia* and *erva maté*.

that makes an excellent place in which contemplate to the glory days of the city.

EATING

Restaurante Marcos (☎ 232 4447; Av Silva Paes 400; mains US$10; ☽ lunch & dinner Mon-Sat) This small, elegant restaurant serves remarkably good seafood. Among the house specialities is the local *congro*, a tender but meaty whitefish.

Pimenta Americana (Rua General Câmara 443; per kg US$4; ☽ lunch Mon-Sat) An excellent per-kilo lunch place with a variety of Brazilian dishes.

Plaza Grill (☎ 232 1190; Rua General Bacelar 457; all-you-can-eat churrascaria US$5; ☽ lunch & dinner) A combination café and *churrascaria* across from the cathedral.

GETTING THERE & AWAY

Buses connect Rio Grande with all major cities in southern Brazil. However, Pelotas (US$4, one hour) is the major transportation hub. Buses leave for Pelotas every half-hour, so you may be better off making a connection there. There are two buses a day to Chuí (US$8, 3½ hours) on the Uruguayan border.

Chuí

☎ 0xx53 / pop 5700

Except maybe for smugglers of contraband perfumes and liquor, the small, dusty border town of Chuí offers few reasons to linger. Located 245km south of Rio Grande on a good sealed road, its major attractions are cheap whiskey and remaindered designer clothing. Av Brasil divides the town into its Uruguayan and Brazilian halves. Portuguese and Spanish are spoken interchangeably.

INFORMATION

Most establishments happily accept Brazilian and Uruguayan currency as well as US dollars. There is a **Banco do Brasil** (cnr Rua Venezuela & Rua Chile) with Visa ATMs and a money exchange, two blocks from the Brazilian bus station. There are also a number of money-exchange offices near the corner of Av General Artigas and Av Brasil.

Nemar Informatica, on the Uruguayan side of Calle Numancia a half-block from Av Brasil, offers Internet access for US$3 per hour.

The **Brazilian consulate** (☎ 265 1011) is located at Calle Tito Fernandez 147. The Uru-

guayan consulate (☎ 265 1151; Rua Venezuala 311) is located a block from the Brazilian bus station. It can take up to 24 hours to get a visa for either country, so plan accordingly.

SLEEPING & EATING

If you're stuck in Chuí, the best cheapie is **Rivero Hotel** (☎ 265 1271; Calle Colombia 163; s/d US$4/8; **P**) on the Brazilian side. If you require air-conditioning, head to **Nuevo Hotel Plaza** (Plaça de Chuy; s/d US$19/30) in Uruguay.

There are some good *churrascarias* on the Uruguayan side of Av Brasil. Try **Jesus** (Av Brasil 603) or **Los Leños** (Av General Artigas nr Av Brasil) for excellent Uruguayan *parrillada* (grilled meats).

GETTING THERE & AWAY
Border Crossings

You do not need a visa or entry or exit stamp if you plan to visit only the town of Chuí. However, if you are continuing on into Uruguay, you will need to tell the driver that you need an exit stamp at the Brazilian Polícia Federal post on Av Argentina, a couple of kilometers north of town. In Uruguay, the bus will stop again for the Uruguayan officials to check your Brazilian exit stamp and Uruguayan visa (if you need one). If you plan to re-enter Brazil, you'll need both an entry and exit stamp for Uruguay. At the time of writing there are plans to construct a single border crossing, which should simplify the process.

Bus

The Brazilian bus station is located on Rua Venezuela about three blocks from Av Brasil. There are regular buses to Pelotas (US$9, four hours) for connections to Porto Alegre, and two daily buses to Rio Grande (US$11, 3½ hours). You can buy tickets to Montevideo (about US$10, five hours) and other Uruguayan destinations from the bus agencies along Calle Leonardo Oliveira just across the Uruguayan side of Av Brasil.

JESUIT MISSIONS

Soon after the discovery of the New World, the Portuguese and Spanish kings authorized Catholic orders to create missions to convert the natives into Catholic subjects. The most successful of these orders were the Jesuits, who established a series of missions in a region that spanned parts of Paraguay, Brazil and Argentina. In effect, it was a nation within a nation that, at its height in the 1720s, claimed 30 mission villages inhabited by more than 150,000 Guarani Indians.

Today, all 30 missions are in ruins. Seven lie in Brazil (in the northwestern part of Rio Grande do Sul), eight are in the Itapuá region of southern Paraguay, and the remaining 15 are in northeastern Argentina.

Santo Ângelo

☎ 0xx55 / pop 66,100

Largely populated by descendants of German and Eastern European immigrants, the small but pleasant city of Santo Ângelo is the regional transportation hub and a good jumping-off point for exploring the Brazilian missions. The town's cathedral, which is a replica of the church at São Miguel, is worth a look. It's situated on the pleasant Praça Pinheiro Machado, where the locals gather in the shade to chat and sip the ever-present *erva maté* tea.

ORIENTATION & INFORMATION

The bus station is about one kilometer from the center. The town lacks a regularly functioning tourist office, but you can ask for a map in one of the hotels listed here. The **Banco do Brasil** (cnr Av Brasil & Rua dos Andradas) has a money exchange and Visa ATMs.

TOURS

Because of difficult bus connections and a ban on driving rental cars across international borders, the most efficient way to visit all the missions is by organized tour. From offices in Santo Ângelo's Turis Hotel, **Missiotur** (☎ 3312 5265; missiotur@terra.com.br; Rua Antônio Manoel 726) organizes two-day tours of the Brazilian missions, as well three-, four- and five-day tours that include the Paraguayan and Argentine missions. The packages include accommodations, transport and entry fees, and cost around US$50 per person per day.

SLEEPING & EATING

Turis Hotel Santo Ângelo (☎ 3313 5255; Rua Antônio Manoel 726; s/d incl breakfast US$11/15, with bathrooms

THE SOUTH

A NATION WITHIN A NATION

In 1608, the governor of the Spanish province of Paraguay ordered the local Jesuit leader, Fray Diego de Torres, to send missionaries to convert the local Tupi-Guarani people. Unlike their brethren elsewhere in the New World, the Jesuits made a concerted effort to convert the Tupi-Guarani people without destroying their culture or language. The missions they established covered a vast region that encompassed much of the present-day Brazilian states of Paraná, Santa Catarina and Rio Grande do Sul, as well as portions of Paraguay and northern Argentina.

The Jesuit missions quickly became centers of culture and intellect as well as of religion. A fascinating hybrid of European baroque and indigenous Guarani arts, music and painting flourished. Indigenous scholars created a written form of Tupi-Guarani and, beginning in 1704, published several works in Tupi-Guarani, using one of the earliest printing presses in South America. The missions also produced remarkably sophisticated sculpture, metallurgy and ceramics. In an age of monarchies and institutionalized slavery, the missions formed a utopian island of progress, where wealth was equally divided and religion, intellect and the arts were honored equally.

Almost from the beginning, the missions faced threats from the outside world. In the 1620s, Portuguese *bandeirantes* (bands of Paulistas who raided the interior of Brazil in search of gold and slaves) found the missionary settlements easy pickings. Thousands of Indians were captured, and the 13 missions of Guayra (a province roughly encompassing the present-day state of Paraná) were eventually abandoned. Beginning in the 1630s, the Jesuits consolidated their position in 30 sites across the northwest corner of present-day Rio Grande do Sul, as well as across the border into Argentina and Paraguay.

It was in large part the success of the missions that brought about their downfall. The independent-minded Jesuits became an embarrassment to Rome, and in turn to the Spanish and Portuguese kings. Secular authorities began to seize control of the missions in the 1750s, destroying the social system that had made them so successful. The wars of independence of the early 19th century spelled a definitive end to what many historians consider a grand and successful experiment in socialism.

US$25/33) is a fine choice for budget travelers, a block from the town's main square. **Hotel Maerkli** (☎ 3313 2127; Av Brasil 1000; s/d US$35/45; **P** 🔀) is the high-end option in Santo Ângelo, with well-appointed rooms and an excellent breakfast.

There are no culinary standouts in Santo Ângelo, but there are some decent places to eat along Rua Marques do Herval between Av Brasil and the main square.

GETTING THERE & AROUND

There are six buses a day from Porto Alegre to Santo Ângelo (US$18, 6½ hours).

From Santo Ângelo, local buses run four times a day to São João Batista and São Miguel das Missões (US$4, one hour). It's possible to rent a car in Santo Ângelo (as well as from Encarnación or Posadas), but driving a rental car over borders is difficult. In Santo Ângelo, call **Sulmive** (☎ 3312 1000).

The most direct route from Santo Ângelo to the Argentine and Paraguayan missions is by car or bus via the border town of Porto Xavier, 145km to the northwest. From here it's possible to cross the Rio Uruguai by barge to the Argentine town of São Tomé, where there are buses to Posadas.

São Miguel das Missões

The most interesting and well-preserved of the Brazilian missions, São Miguel das Missões is 53km from Santo Ângelo. The elegant church, designed by an Italian architect who was also a Jesuit friar, earned Unesco World Heritage listing in 1984. It reveals the remarkable level of sophistication that the missions achieved despite limited means and extreme isolation. Every evening there's a spectacular and informative, if campy, sound-and-light show that illustrates the history of the missions.

Nearby are the missions of **São João Batista** (on the road between Santo Ângelo and São Miguel) and **São Lourenço das Missões** (18km past the turnoff to São Miguel). For information on visiting all the missions (in Portuguese), check out www.rotamissoes .com.br.

INFORMATION

The mission is about 500m down the street from the town's long-distance bus station, and the town's **tourist office** (☎ 3381 1294) is

across from the entrance of the mission on Rua São Luis. Entry to the mission is US$1.50; the sound-and-light show also costs US$1.50.

SLEEPING & EATING

The last bus back to Santo Ângelo leaves before the sound-and-light show, so it's worth sticking around for the night.

Pousada das Missões (☎ 0xx55-3381 1202; www .albergues.com.br; Rua São Nicalau 601; dm per person US$10, s/d/tr with private bathroom & 🔀 US$15/22/27; **P**) This very pleasant HI youth hostel is located just behind the São Miguel mission. Follow signs from the mission entrance. It fills up with school groups, so it's best to book ahead.

Hotel Barichello (☎ 0xx55-3381 1272; Av Borges do Canto 1567; s/d US$15/23; **P** 🔀) Another good budget option, with very small but comfortable rooms. It also has a *churrascaria*-style restaurant that is open to the public.

Wilson Park Hotel (☎ 3381 2000; www.wilson parkhotel.com.br; Rua São Miguel 664; s/d US$28/35; **P** 🔀 🖥 📶) This is the town's new, high-end option, with a vast, mission-style lobby, a fancy pool, rooms with all the comforts, and a decent restaurant.

GETTING THERE & AROUND

From São Miguel das Missões, local buses run four times a day to Santo Ângelo (US$4, one hour) via São João Batista.

Paraguayan Missions

The most important mission to see in Paraguay is Trinidad, 25km northeast of Encarnación. The red-stone ruins are fascinating. Use Encarnación as a base for visiting the missions of Paraguay – it has some cheap, modest hotels and restaurants. If you're looking for something a bit more upscale, you can stay in Posadas, just across the border from Encarnación.

Argentine Missions

In Argentina, Posadas is the best bet as a base for exploring the Argentine missions. It's just across the Rio Paraná from the Paraguayan town of Encarnación, and generally a more pleasant place to stay. Don't miss San Ignacio 60km northeast of Posadas on Hwy RN-12, where there's a sound-and-light show every night.

The Central West

The Central West is Brazil's wild west. Stretching from the southern Amazon to the Paraná River almost 2000km away, it is a sparsely populated region with an abundance of natural wonders – dramatic tablelands rising into Brazil's high plains, deep canyons with high waterfalls, and crystal-clear rivers teeming with fish.

For the traveler, the Central West offers the opportunity to travel in time. Visit the future (or a '60s version of it at least) in the nation's capital Brasília. Enjoy the present in lively, modern cities such as Campo Grande and Cuiabá. Cruise back to 18th-century colonial Brazil

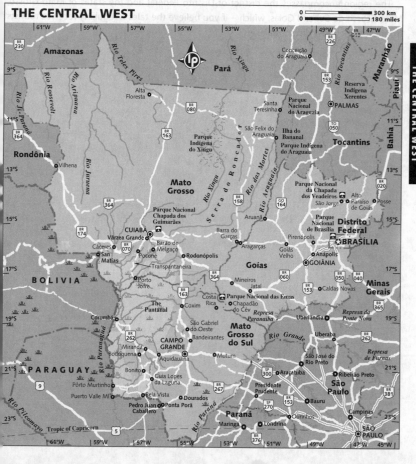

THE CENTRAL WEST

in picturesque cobblestoned towns such as Goiás Velho and Pirenópolis. Or trip back even further to the hot, sticky and dramatic Pantanal, one of the world's greatest natural areas.

An area more than half the size of France that reaches into Paraguay and Bolivia, the Pantanal fills with water for six months every year. It's a wildlife paradise – home to an abundance of birds, fish, alligators and about a million other creatures.

Don't be put off by the long distances between attractions. All major cities are serviced by regular flights and the major road routes are well serviced by good-quality buses. Renting a car is a viable and enjoyable option, as the traffic – apart from the steady stream of trucks – is fairly light compared to the coastal areas of Brazil.

The region encompasses the district of Distrito Federal and the states of Mato Grosso, Mato Grosso do Sul and Goiás, which – if you believe the tales – regularly receives tourists from even the most distant galaxies

Distrito Federal

THE CENTRAL WEST

HIGHLIGHTS

- Visiting the magnificent **cathedral** (p356) with its spectacular stained-glass windows and floating angels
- Walking around on top of Brazil's national congress building, **Palácio do Congresso** (p357)
- Watching the sun set over the monuments from the **TV tower** (p356)
- Experiencing the varied **religious sects** (p357) and rituals around Brasília
- Cruising **Brasília** (p360) and looking at its futuristic architecture and town plan

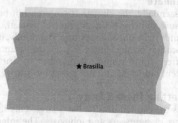

★ Brasília

■ POPULATION: 2.3 MILLION   ■ AREA: 5,814 SQ KM

The Distrito Federal (DF) occupies part of the Brazilian central plateau – the *planalto* – totaling 5814 sq km, with rolling hills and a large artificial lake, Paranoá. Within this smallish (by Brazilian standards) territory is the spread-out environs of the national capital, Brasília, the '60s vision of a third-millennium city. Surrounding Brasília are several satellite cities – Brasilândia, Ceilândia and Taguatinga – their chaotic development a world away from the clean lines of the capital.

Although most travelers will find themselves outside the Distrito Federal quite quickly after leaving the city, those who stay longer can explore some splendid natural areas with waterfalls and forests close to the city, including the Parque Nacional de Brasília.

History

The Distrito Federal resulted from a long-held Brazilian dream to harness the vast resources of its inland territories. Central to this dream, first mooted in 1823 by Brazilian statesman José Bonifácio, was establishing an inland capital to catalyze the economic development of the interior.

Brasília's location was also influenced by Dom Bosco (don't miss his shrine in Brasília), a Salesian priest living in Turin, Italy. In 1883 he dreamed that a new civilization would emerge in the center of Brazil, somewhere between the 15th and 20th parallels. Bosco's dream became well known to Brazilians, and in the 1891 Constitution, land in the region was set aside for the construction of the new capital.

Finally, in 1955, after almost 150 years of debate, President Juscelino Kubitschek proposed that the Distrito Federal be carved out of the state of Goiás to house the new capital, Brasília. You can judge for yourself if the dream has become a reality.

Climate

Essentially, the climate is tropical, but because the city is on the central plateau, it tends to be hot and very dry. Thankfully, its location on the shores of Lago do Paranoá offers some respite. Remember to drink plenty of water and use a skin moisturizer.

Getting There & Away

As the capital, Brasília has a large daily influx of sightseers and lobbyists. The international airport connects with all major Brazilian cities. Most visitors fly in, but those who choose to go overland will cover some long distances if they travel here from Rio, Belem, Belo Horizonte, São Paulo or the Northeastern capitals.

Getting Around

Although the Distrito Federal offers few attractions apart from the capital itself, it is a major transit point for going north into the mountains or west toward Mato Grosso. Regular bus services connect the city with Cuiabá and major eastern and southern cities.

BRASÍLIA

☎ 0xx61 / pop 2.2 million

> I sought the curved and sensual line. The curve that I see in the Brazilian hills, in the body of a loved one, in the clouds in the sky and in the ocean waves.
> *Oscar Niemeyer, Brasília architect*

Brazil's capital is unique. It's one of the 20th century's architectural marvels. In 1987 it was added to the Unesco list of World Heritage sites as a major example of the 20th century's modern movement in architecture and urban planning. Look at Niemeyer's monuments as part of a bigger picture that includes the deep blue sky, the overall city layout and the time of day.

President Kubischek once promised 'fifty years' progress in five.' As its 50th anniversary approaches, Brasília is an affluent city and its residents are well educated and helpful. If you're interested in modern architecture, you'll easily spend a few days visiting the city's impressive buildings and monuments. Otherwise, come here if you must see the capital or as a stopover en route to the Pantanal, Parque Nacional da Chapada dos Veadeiros (Goiás) or Ilha do Bananal (Tocantins).

History

All this is the doing of three famous Brazilians: an urban planner (Lúcio Costa), an architect (Oscar Niemeyer) and a landscape architect (Burle Marx), who were commissioned by President Juscelino Kubitschek to build a new inland capital. With millions of poor peasants from the Northeast working around the clock, Brasília was built, incredibly, in just three years – it wasn't exactly finished but it was ready to be the capital (Niemeyer later admitted that it was all done too quickly). The capital was officially moved from Rio to Brasília on April 21, 1960.

The old Brazilian dream of an inland capital had always been dismissed as expensive folly. What possessed Kubitschek to actually do it? Politics. He made the building of Brasília a symbol of the country's determination and ability to become a great economic power. Kubitschek successfully appealed to all Brazilians to put aside their differences and rally to the cause. In doing so, he distracted attention from the country's social and economic problems, gained enormous personal popularity and borrowed heavily from the international banks.

Orientation

Seen from above, Brasília looks like an airplane, or a bow and arrow. The *plano piloto* (pilot plan) specified that the city would face the giant artificial Lago do Paranoá. In the fuselage (or the arrow) are all the government buildings and monuments. The plaza of three powers – with the Palácio do Planalto, the Palácio do Congresso and the Palácio da Justiça – is in the cockpit. Out on the *asas* (wings) are

THE CENTRAL WEST

ADDRESSES FOR THE LOGICAL MIND

Brasília's addresses are as futuristic as its architecture – a series of numbers and letters that look baffling at first, but are easy to decipher once you know what all the acronyms mean.

For example, the address to Pensão da Zenilda is SQS 704, Bloco Q, Casa 29. That means it's in Super Quadra South 704, building *(bloco)* Q, house *(casa)* 29. The first digit in the address (7) shows the position east or west of the Eixo Rodoviário (the main north–south arterial road) – odd numbers to the west and even to the east, increasing as they move away from the center. The last two digits (04) show the distance north or south of the Eixo Monumental. So Pensão da Zenilda is four blocks to the south of the Eixo Monumental and four blocks east of the Eixo Rodoviário (1, 3, 5, 7). The higher the number of the Super Quadra, the further it is from the center.

Get to know these acronyms:

Asa Norte/Asa Sul The two 'wings' of the city, connected by main roads, *eixo rodoviários*. The N (Norte) or S (Sul) after an acronym indicates which side of the Eixo Monumental it's located.

SBN/SBS (Setor Bancário Norte/Sul) The banking areas either side of the Eixo Monumental.

SCLN/SCLS (Setor Comércio Local Norte/Sul) The main shopping blocks between the *superquadras*.

SCN/SCS (Setor Comercial Norte/Sul) The commercial office block areas next to the main shopping centers.

SDN/SDS (Setor de Diversões Norte/Sul) The main shopping centers *(conjuntos)* either side of the Eixo Monumental.

SEN/SES (Setor de Embaixadas Norte/Sul) The embassy sectors.

SHIN/SHIS (Setor de Habitações Individuais Norte/Sul) The residential areas around the lake. SHIN is reached on the Eixo Norte. SHIS is accessed via the bridges off Av das Nações.

SHN/SHS (Setor Hoteleiro Norte/Sul) The hotel sectors each side of the Eixo Monumental.

SMHN/SMHS (Setor Médico Hospitalar Norte/Sul) The hospital sectors each side of the Eixo Monumental, next to the SCN and SCS respectively.

SQN/SQS (Super Quadras Norte/Sul) The individual *superquadras* in the main residential wings of the *plano piloto*.

If all of this seems too logical, make sure you write down the address, as all these *superquadras* start to look the same after a very short while.

block after numbered block of apartment buildings (known as *superquadras* or *quadras*) but little else.

To get the full effect, you must take a tour of the city by air, bus or foot. See p360 for details.

Information

BOOKSTORES

Livro Siciliano has branches on the 2nd floor in the Conjunto Nacional and Pátio Brasil shopping malls. Both have a good selection of English books and magazines.

EMBASSIES & CONSULATES

This being the national capital you would expect them all to be here. Most are located along Av das Nações between Quadras 801 and 809 in the Setor de Embaixadas Sul (or Embassy Sector South). See p684 for details.

EMERGENCY

Ambulance (☎ 192)
Fire department (☎ 193)
Police (☎ 190)

INTERNET ACCESS

Internet cafés are clustered around 505 Sul and 303 Norte, and at the airport, which has a VIP center with Internet connections all conveniently lined up next to each other – something you won't find again until you leave the city.

CLA (☎ 322 8060; Pátio Brasil Shopping Mall; per hr US$2; ☉ 10am-10pm Mon-Sat, noon-10pm Sun)

MEDICAL SERVICES

Da Base do Distrito Federal (☎ 325 5050; SMHS 101)
Santa Lúcia (☎ 245 3344; SHLS 716, Bloco C)

MONEY

There are banks with money-changing facilities in the Setor Bancário Sul (SBS; Banking Sector South) and Setor Bancário Norte (SBN; Banking Sector North). Both sectors are close to the city bus station. The airport also has a variety of ATMs, most with Cirrus/MasterCard/Visa networking. Travel agencies will change cash dollars and often give better rates.

Banco do Brasil (SCS Quadra 5, Bloco B, loja 158; ☉ 11am-4pm Mon-Fri) Has a Visa ATM, and its handy branch at the airport changes money, has a Visa ATM and is open on Saturday.

POST

Main post office (SHS Quadra 2, Bloco B; ☉ 9am-5pm Mon-Fri) Has *posta restante* (poste restante) and fax facilities.

TOURIST INFORMATION

If all you need is a map or a list of attractions, simply pick up a brochure from the front desk of any large hotel or travel agency. There are information booths at the TV tower, Praça dos Três Poderes and an office at Memorial JK.

Tourist office (☎ 364 9135; airport; ☉ 7am-11pm) This is the best place for information. Staff speak English and can make bookings and organize discounts at city hotels.

TRAVEL AGENCIES

CTR Turismo (☎ 323 1713; Hotel Nacional, SHS Quadra 1; ☉ 8am-6:30pm Mon-Fri, 9am-1pm Sat) Useful for booking flights, renting cars and organizing in and around the city.

Sights

MEMORIAL JK

Along with the tomb of JK (President Juscelino Kubitschek) on Praça do Cruzeiro, the **memorial** (☎ 225 9451; admission US$1; ☉ 9am-5:45pm Tue-Sat) features photographs and documents about the construction of the city.

MEMORIAL DOS POVOS INDIGENAS

This interesting **museum** (☎ 223 3760; admission free; ☉ 9am-6pm Tue-Fri, 11am-5pm Sat & Sun) showcases an excellent collection of indigenous art. There are also some lovely crafts for sale.

TV TOWER

The 75m-high **observation deck** (☎ 325 5735; Eixo Monumental; admission free; ☉ 10am-6pm Tue-Sun) of the TV tower is the best place to get a bird's-eye view of the city (apart from a helicopter ride). There's a handicrafts fair at the base of the tower on weekends and holidays.

CATEDRAL METROPOLITANA

With its 16 curved columns and its stained-glass interior, the **cathedral** (☎ 224 4073; ☉ 8am-7:30pm) is heavenly viewing. At the entrance are the haunting **Four Disciples** statues carved by Ceschiatti, who also made the aluminum angels hanging inside.

PRAÇA DOS TRÉS PODERES

Down by the tip of the arrow you'll find the most interesting buildings surrounding the Praça dos Trés Poderes. It's a synthesis of the ideas of architects Niemeyer and Costa, combining various monuments, museums and federal buildings. The space includes striking sculptures by Bruno Giorgi *Os Candangos*, Alfredo Ceschiatti *A Justiça* and Niemeyer *O Pombal*.

Palácio do Itamaraty (Palace of Arches; admission free; ☽ 3-5pm Mon-Fri, 10am-2pm Sat & Sun) is home to the Foreign Ministry and one of the most impressive buildings – a series of arches surrounded by a reflecting pool and landscaped by Burle Marx. Its rooms are tastefully decorated with antiques and art objects. There's no entry unless your arms and legs are covered – you won't match the décor.

Outside the **Palácio da Justiça** (Supreme Court bldg; admission free; ☽ 10am-noon & 3-5pm Mon-Fri) water cascades between its arches; inside is a lovely internal garden.

Featuring the photogenic 'dishes' and twin towers, the congress building, **Palácio do Congresso** (Parliament; admission free; ☽ 9am-6:30pm Mon-Fri, 10am-3pm Sat & Sun), is beautiful at sunset. And how many places do you visit where you can walk around on top of the seat of government?

The president's office, the **Palácio do Planalto** (☽ 9am-1pm Sun), is another Niemeyer design that's worth seeing, both inside and out. From the curved lines of the exterior to the lustrous columns and sweeping curved ramp inside, it's one of the best examples of architectural Modernism in the world. Unfortunately, it is only open to the public on Sunday, but you can watch the ceremonial changing of the guard outside the gates, usually at 8:30am and 5:30pm every day.

SANTUÁRIO DOM BOSCO

As impressive as the cathedral, the **Santuário Dom Bosco** (Dom Bosco's Shrine; ☎ 223 6542; Via W3 Sul; admission free; ☽ 7am-7pm) is made of concrete

---

BRASÍLIA – CAPITAL OF THE THIRD MILLENNIUM

In 1883 an Italian priest, John Bosco, prophesied that a new civilization would arise between parallels 15 and 20, and that its capital would be built between parallels 15 and 16, on the edge of an artificial lake. Many consider Brasília to be that city, and a number of cults have sprung up in the area. If you tire of Brasília's architectural monuments, a visit to one of the cults may be part of your destiny.

About 45km east of Brasília, near the satellite city of Planaltina, you'll find the **Vale do Amanhecer** (Valley of the Dawn; ☎ 596 1258; ☽ 10pm-midnight), founded in 1959 by a clairvoyant, Tia Neiva. The valley is actually a small town where you can see (or take part in) Egyptian, Greek, Aztec, Indian, Gypsy, Inca, Trojan and Afro-Brazilian rituals. The mediums in the town believe that a new civilization will come during the third millennium. The town's main temple was inspired by spiritual advice received by Tia Neiva. In the center is an enormous Star of David, which forms a lake, pierced by an arrow. Get there by bus No 617 from the center of Brasília.

About 100km west of Brasília, near the town of Santo Antônio do Descoberto (Goiás), is the **Cidade Eclética** (Eclectic City; ☎ 626 1391; ☽ 8-10pm Wed-Fri, 3-6pm Sun). Founded in 1956 by Yokanam, an ex-airline pilot, the group's aim is to unify all religions on the planet through fraternity and equality. You're welcome to attend its ceremonies, but there are strict dress regulations. If you're not dressed suitably, you'll be given a special tunic to wear.

In Brasília itself, the **Granja do Ipê** (Ipê Estate; ☎ 380 1825) at the city's southern exit is the site of the City of Peace and Holistic University. This institution aims to form a new generation with a mentality suited to the needs of the third millennium. There's a lot to be said for peace, love and understanding.

The **Templo da Boa Vontade** (Temple of Goodwill; ☎ 245 1070; No 75/76, 915 Sul; ☽ 24hr) was created by the Legion of Goodwill in 1989 as a symbol of universal solidarity. It incorporates seven pyramids, joined to form a cone that is topped with the biggest raw crystal you will ever see. Inside there's a meditative space. Get there on bus No 105 or 107 from the city bus station.

Some people also believe that in certain regions around Brasília extraterrestrial contacts are more likely – at Km 69 on Hwy BR-351, for instance, or on the plateau in the smaller city of Brasilândia. Believe it, or not!

THE CENTRAL WEST

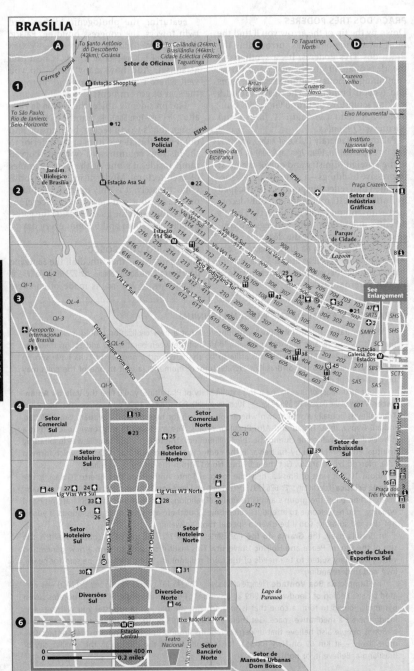

BRASÍLIA

To Santo Antônio do Descoberto (42km); Goiânia
To Ceilândia (26km); Brasilândia (46km); Cidade Eclética (48km); Taguatinga
To Taguatinga North

Córrego Guará
Setor de Oficinas

Estação Shopping
Áreas Octogonais
Cruzeiro Novo
Cruzeiro Velho

To São Paulo; Rio de Janeiro; Belo Horizonte

ESPM
Eixo Monumental

Jardim Biológico de Brasília

Setor Policial Sul

Cemitério da Esperança

Instituto Nacional de Meteorologia

Estação Asa Sul

EPIN
Praça Cruzeiro

Setor de Indústrias Gráficas

Estação 114 Sul

Via W5 Sul
Via W4 Sul
Via W3 Sul
Via W1 Sul

Parque de Cidade

Lagoon

Via L4 Sul
Eixo Rodoviário Sul
Via L1 Sul
Via L2 Sul

Estação Galeria dos Estados

See Enlargement

QI-2
QI-1

Aeroporto Internacional de Brasília

Estrada Parque Dom Bosco

QI-4
QI-3
QI-5
QI-6
QI-8

SRTS SHS
SMHS SHS
SCS
SBS
SAS SAS
SCTS
601
602

Setor Comercial Sul
Setor Comercial Norte

Setor Hoteleiro Sul
Setor Hoteleiro Norte

QL-10

Setor de Embaixadas Sul

Lig Vias W3 Sul
Lig Vias W3 Norte

Av das Nações

Via S-1 Oeste
Via N-1 Oeste
Eixo Monumental

Setor Hoteleiro Sul
Setor Hoteleiro Norte

QI-12

Praça dos Três Poderes

Esplanada dos Ministérios

Diversões Sul
Diversões Norte

Setoe de Clubes Esportivos Sul

Lago do Paranoá

Eixo Rodoviária Norte
Estação Central
Teatro Nacional
Setor Bancário Norte

Setor de Mansões Urbanas Dom Bosco

0   400 m
0   0.2 miles

THE CENTRAL WEST

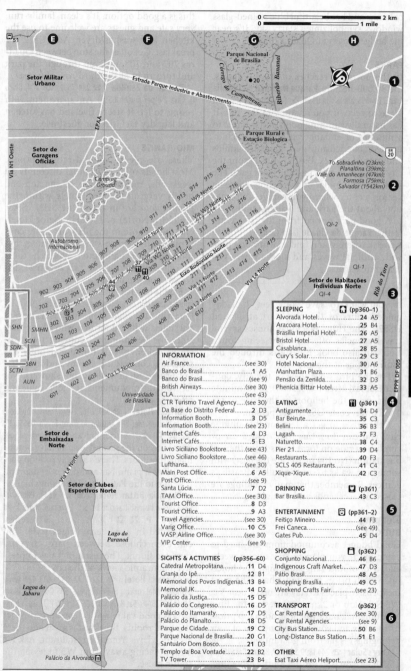

0 — 2 km
0 — 1 mile

Parque Nacional
de Brasília
● 20

Setor Militar
Urbano

Estrada Parque Industria e Abastecimento

Córrego do Campamento

Ribeirão Bananal

Rib do Torto

❶

Parque Rural e
Estação Biológica

Setor de
Garagens
Oficiais

BR
20

To Sobradinho (23km);
Planaltina (39km);
Vale do Amanhecer (47km);
Formosa (75km);
Salvador (1542km)

Camping
Ground

QI-2

❷

Via N1 Oeste

EPAA

Via W5 Norte
Via W4 Norte
Via W3 Norte
Via W2 Norte
Via W1 Norte

911 912 913 914 915 916
910 909 908 907 710 711 712 713 715-716
906 905 807 708 709 610 611 612 515-516
903 904 705 706 707 508 509 510 415-416
902 703 704 505 506 507 308 309 310 313 314 315 316
702 502 503 504 305 306 307 208 209 210 213 214 215 216
502 501 304 305 106 107 108 109 110 113 114 115 116

Eixo Rodoviário Norte

Via L4 Norte
Via L3 Norte
Via L2 Norte
Via L1 Norte

170 171 172 173 213 214 215 216
270 271 272 273 413 412
408 409 410 411 611
208 209 210

QI-1

Setor de Habitações
Individuas Norte

QI-4

❸

Autobromo
Internacional

37

44

40

5

SHN
SMHN
SCN
SDN
SBN
SCTN

102 103 104 105 106
202 203 204 405 406
302 303 304 305
402 403 404

601 602 603

AUN

Via L3 Norte

Universidade
de Brasília

Setor de
Embaixadas
Norte

Via L4 Norte

Setor de Clubes
Esportivos Norte

Lago do
Paranoá

Lagoa do
Jaburu

Palácio da Alvorada 🏛

THE CENTRAL WEST

EPPR DF 005

INFORMATION
Air France.............................(see 30)
Banco do Brasil.........................1 A5
Banco do Brasil.......................(see 9)
British Airways.......................(see 30)
CLA.......................................(see 43)
CTR Turismo Travel Agency.....(see 30)
Da Base do Distrito Federal........2 D3
Information Booth......................3 D5
Information Booth...................(see 23)
Internet Cafés...........................4 D3
Internet Cafés...........................5 E3
Livro Siciliano Bookstore........(see 43)
Livro Siciliano Bookstore........(see 46)
Lufthansa..............................(see 30)
Main Post Office........................6 A5
Post Office.............................(see 9)
Santa Lúcia.............................7 D2
TAM Office............................(see 30)
Tourist Office............................8 D3
Tourist Office............................9 A3
Travel Agencies.....................(see 30)
Varig Office.............................10 C5
VASP Airline Office.................(see 30)
VIP Center............................(see 9)

SIGHTS & ACTIVITIES (pp356–60)
Catedral Metropolitana............11 D4
Granja do Ipê..........................12 B1
Memorial dos Povos Indígenas..13 B4
Memorial JK............................14 D2
Palácio da Justiça.....................15 D5
Palácio do Congresso...............16 D5
Palácio do Itamaraty................17 D5
Palácio do Planalto...................18 D5
Parque de Cidade.....................19 C2
Parque Nacional de Brasília.......20 G1
Santuário Dom Bosco...............21 D3
Templo da Boa Vontade............22 B2
TV Tower................................23 B4

SLEEPING 🛏 (pp360–1)
Alvorada Hotel.......................24 A5
Aracoara Hotel.......................25 B4
Brasília Imperial Hotel.............26 A5
Bristol Hotel...........................27 A5
Casablanca............................28 B5
Cury's Solar...........................29 C3
Hotel Nacional.......................30 A6
Manhattan Plaza....................31 B6
Pensão da Zenilda...................32 D3
Phenicia Bittar Hotel...............33 A5

EATING 🍴 (p361)
Antigamente..........................34 D4
Bar Beirute............................35 C3
Belini....................................36 B3
Lagash..................................37 F3
Naturetto...............................38 C4
Pier 21..................................39 D4
Restaurants............................40 F3
SCLS 405 Restaurants..............41 C4
Xique-Xique...........................42 C3

DRINKING 🍷 (p361)
Bar Brasília............................43 C3

ENTERTAINMENT 🎭 (pp361–2)
Feitiço Mineiro........................44 F3
Frei Caneca..........................(see 49)
Gates Pub.............................45 D4

SHOPPING 🛍 (p362)
Conjunto Nacional..................46 B6
Indigenous Craft Market..........47 D3
Pátio Brasil............................48 A5
Shopping Brasília....................49 C5
Weekend Crafts Fair..............(see 23)

TRANSPORT (p362)
Car Rental Agencies...............(see 30)
Car Rental Agencies.................(see 9)
City Bus Station......................50 B6
Long-Distance Bus Station........51 E1

OTHER
Esat Taxi Aéreo Heliport.........(see 23)

columns and has beautiful blue stained-glass windows symbolizing a starry sky. It's near the budget hotels at Quadra 702.

PARKS

In the northern reaches of the city limits, the 30,000-hectare **Parque Nacional de Brasília** (☎ 233 4055; admission US$1; ☉ 8am-4pm) is a good place to relax if you're stuck in the city. It has natural swimming pools and is home to a number of endangered animals, including deer, banded anteaters, giant armadillos and maned wolves. Bus No 128.1 from the city bus station goes past the front gate. The park is very popular on weekends. There's a visitors center where you can get information about the park and walking trails.

A good park not far from the city center is the **Parque da Cidade** (admission free; ☉ 5am-midnight), where you'll find a swimming pool with artificial waves and kiosks where you can grab a snack.

Tours

If you want to save your feet, half-day guided tours of the city start at around US$20. The Hotel Nacional houses several travel agencies offering sightseeing tours. You can also book bus tours through the tourist office at the airport.

For the bird's-eye view of the city, contact **Esat Taxi Aéreo** (☎ 323 8777). A 10-minute flight, from the heliport at the base of the TV Tower, costs US$36 per person.

Otherwise, to get a feel for this unique city, you can do a bus tour, rent a car or combine a ride on local buses from the city bus station (No 104 or 108 are the best) with some long walks to see the bulk of Brasília's edifices. Remember that many buildings are closed on weekends and at night.

Sleeping

BUDGET

Good budget accommodations are hard to come by. If you plan to stay over a weekend, a lot of mid-range and high-end hotels often slash prices by almost half. The most inexpensive places to stay are on or near Via W3 Sul, 1km or 2km southwest of the Eixo Monumental, but hygiene is not a top priority in many and your safety (and that of your belongings) is far from guaranteed.

Cury's Solar (☎ 244 1899; SQS 707, Bloco I, Casa 15; s/d US$9/16) If you don't mind a little crowding,

this is a good option. It's clean, family-run, very safe and guests are welcome to use the kitchen and washer/dryer. Add US$2 for breakfast. Get off at the stop between Quadras 707 and 708, walk up through the park and turn right at the third row of houses.

Pensão da Zenilda (☎ 224 7532; SQS 704, Bloco Q, Casa 29; per person US$9) An apartment with rooms to let. It sleeps five and has kitchen and laundry facilities for guest use.

MID-RANGE

There are plenty of mid-range options. Most hotels offer substantial discounts on weekends, making some of the top-end hotels very affordable. Hotels within the *plano piloto* are in either the SHN (Setor Hoteleiro Norte) or the SHS (Setor Hoteleiro Sul). Those in the SHN are more conveniently located to shopping centers, but those in the SHS are better value. The tourist office at the airport can organize discounts at these hotels.

Brasília Imperial Hotel (☎ 321 8747; www.brasilia imperialhotel.com.br, in Portuguese; SHS Quadra 3, Blocos E & H; s/d/tr US$30/34/42; ⚡) One of Brasília's original hotels with a doorman who's been here since the beginning. Occupying two two-story buildings, this functional hotel has spacious, comfortable rooms and a central hot-water system for long, hot showers. Not far from the monuments, it's good value and offers discounts.

Bristol Hotel (☎ 321 6162; www.bristolhotel.com .br, in Portuguese; SHS Quadra 4, Bloco F; s/d US$30/35; ⚡ ⚡ ⚡ ⚡) A friendly and relaxed place, the rooms on the second level all have beautiful marble floors. There's a lovely rooftop pool as well as a piano bar and decent restaurant. It's close to the Pátio Brasil shopping mall.

Phenicia Bittar Hotel (☎ 321 4342, 0800-707 5858; www.hoteisbittar.com.br; SHS Quadra 5, Bloco J; s/d US$36/43; ⚡ ⚡ ⚡) This hotel is recently renovated in a modern, bright style. You can even choose between parquetry and carpeted floors. The restaurant has impressive panoramic views of the city.

Alvorada Hotel (☎ 322 1122, 0800-613 424; www .alvoradahotel.com.br, in Portuguese; SHS Quadra 4, Bloco A; s/d US$35/46, Sat & Sun US$26/34; ⚡) The Alvorada is good value, with clean and compact standard rooms. Breakfast is great and there are fine views from the restaurant. Ask for a room facing away from W3 to lessen the traffic noise.

Aracoara Hotel (☎ 328 9222, toll-free 0800-614 881; www.aracoara.com.br; SHN Quadra 5, Bloco C; s/d US$47/59; P ⌧ ☐) This hotel is spacious and comfortable, with funky 1970s décor. Staff are helpful and the cozy bar is a good spot for an early evening cocktail. The only drawback is that this place is a long walk to anywhere of interest.

Casablanca (☎ 328 8586; SHN Quadra 3, Bloco A; s/d/tr US$32/40/48; P ⌧) A friendly hotel not far from the TV tower. All rooms have a double and single bed. The restaurant is pleasant and offers a good variety of local dishes.

TOP END

Hotel Nacional (☎ 321 7575, 0800-616 611; www.hotel nacional.com.br; SHS Quadra 1, Bloco A; s/d/tr US$80/86/96, Sat & Sun US$36/43/53; P ⌧ ⌧ ☐ ⌧) A Brasília institution that has long been a favorite of ex-dictators and soap stars. James Bond would feel at home here. Classic 1960s décor, luxurious spa and sauna and fine restaurants make this a recommended option. Money changers, airline offices, travel agents and car-rental agencies are right outside the front door.

Manhattan Plaza (☎ 319 3543, 0800-614 002; www .manhattan.com.br; SHN Quadra 2, Bloco A; s/d US$60/80, Sat & Sun US$40/60; P ⌧ ☐ ⌧) The Manhattan is luxurious and it's close to the city's main attractions. *Luxo* suites cost a little more but have great views of the monuments from their balconies.

Eating & Drinking

Shopping-mall culture has taken hold in Brasília and while it might not be the travelers' cup of tea, there are two important things to be said for it – air-conditioning and concentration.

With buildings so spread out and few street stalls, finding somewhere to eat and drink out of the heat during the day can require endurance. Not surprisingly, the locals flock to three centrally located oases – Shopping Brasília, Pátio Brasil and Conjunto Nacional – to chow down. All have small cafés and food courts with enough variety to cater to most tastes.

Pier 21 is a new restaurant and shopping development near Setor de Embaixadas Sul. It's in a pleasant location overlooking the Lago do Paranoá – it's a pity the parking lot took precedence over the food hall for prime waterfront position. You'll find seafood, pizza, Chinese and other fast-food outlets along with barn-sized pub/restaurants with a distinctly country 'n' western flavor.

A good selection of restaurants is clustered in SCLS 405. Here you'll find Italian, French, Spanish, Portuguese, Tex-Mex, Korean, Japanese, Chinese, Thai and vegetarian eateries. It's packed on weekends.

There are also many excellent restaurants and bars scattered around the city. In the following addresses, SCL means Setor Comércio Local, which is the space provided in the *quadras* for shops, restaurants etc. The letter N or S immediately after SCL means Norte (North) or Sul (South), and is followed by the *quadra* number, the block number and the *loja* (shop) number.

Antigamente (☎ 323 3245; SCLS Quadra 403, Bloco A, Lojas 12/16; dishes US$5-15; noon-4pm Mon-Thu, noon-6pm Fri-Sun) It has an outstanding Sunday buffet serving regional dishes.

Lagash (☎ 273 0098; SCLN Quadra 308/309, Bloco B, Loja 11; dishes US$5-25; noon-4pm & 7pm-midnight Mon-Sat, noon-6pm Sun; ⌧) Serves the best Middle Eastern food in town. Locals love the lamb dishes.

Belini (☎ 345 0777; SCLS Quadra 113, Bloco D, Loja 35; dishes for 2 US$5-20, sandwiches US$3-5; noon-3pm & 7pm-midnight Tue-Sat, noon-4pm Sun, 7pm-midnight Mon; ⌧) Top spot for both casual outdoor and formal indoor eating. There's also a deli and cooking school.

Naturetto (☎ 242 3532; SCLS Quadra 405, Bloco A, Loja 22; dishes US$2-5; 11:30am-10pm Mon-Fri, 11:30am-3:30pm Sat & Sun) Good-quality vegetarian fare and great soups.

Xique-Xique (☎ 244 5797; SCLS Quadra 107, Bloco E, Loja 2; dishes for 2 US$8-15; 8am-midnight) This place has very good *nordestino* (Northeastern) cuisine.

Bar Beirute (☎ 244 1717; SCLS Quadra 109, Bloco A, Lojas 2/4; dishes for 2 US$10-15; 11-2am) An institution in Brasília. It has some Middle Eastern–themed dishes, and you can sit at outdoor tables under trees. It's a lively bar later in the evening.

Bar Brasília (☎ 443 4323; SCLS Quadra 506, Bloco A, Loja 14; 5pm-2am) Another classic bar, this is a popular watering hole for politicians and eggheads; it has tasty home-brewed beers.

Entertainment

If you're after live music, check the listings in the 'Caderno C' section of the daily *Correio Braziliense* newspaper.

Frei Caneca (☎ 244 6711; Shopping Brasília, SCN; cover US$5) With live music nightly, Frei Caneca is popular with 30- to 40-somethings.

Gate's Pub (☎ 225 4576; SCLS Quadra 403, Bloco B, Loja 34; cover US$7; ☒ 9pm-3am Tue-Sun) Gate's claims to be the longest-established bar in the city. Most nights there's live music with a rock, reggae and funk flavor, followed by dance music until closing.

Feitiço Mineiro (☎ 272 3032; SCLN Quadra 306, Bloco B, Loja 45; cover US$4) This is a restaurant that becomes a live-music venue after 7:30pm; it showcases local talent.

Shopping

The weekend crafts fair at the base of the TV tower is a good place to pick up leather goods, ceramics and art objects. You'll also find a small indigenous craft market outside the FUNAI headquarters.

You should be able to satisfy your other shopping needs in one of Brasília's shopping malls:

Conjunto Nacional (Asa Norte SCN) Brasília's first mall, right across from the bus station. Contains a post office, pharmacies, restaurants and a supermarket.

Pátio Brasil (Asa Sul W3 SCS) More modern than the Conjunto Nacional, with a better restaurant selection.

Pier 21 (Setor de Clubes Esportivos Sul) Brasília's newest mall. Has the largest concentration of restaurants, bars and nightclubs of all the malls. Very popular with the young and well-off. See also p361.

Shopping Brasília (Asa Norte SCN Quadra 5) All amenities, including cinemas and restaurants.

Getting There & Away
AIR

With so many domestic flights making stopovers in Brasília, it's easy to catch a plane to almost anywhere in Brazil. Flying time to Rio is 1½ hours; to São Paulo, it's one hour 20 minutes.

The easiest way to book a flight is through the travel agencies in the Hotel Nacional complex. Major domestic airlines with offices in Brasília include:

TAM (☎ 365 1560)
Varig (☎ 365 1550)
VASP (☎ 321 3636)

International airlines with offices at the Hotel Nacional complex include:
Air France (☎ 223 4152)
British Airways (☎ 226 4164)
Lufthansa (☎ 223 8202)

BUS

From the ginormous **train and long-distance bus station** (rodoferroviária; ☎ 363 2281), due west of the city center, there are buses to places you've never heard of, but no trains. Bus destinations include Goiânia (US$6, three hours), Rio (US$48, 17 hours), São Paulo (US$34, 14 hours) and Salvador (US$44, 21 hours). There are also buses to Cuiabá (US$27, 18 hours) and Porto Velho (US$72, 42 hours). Buses run north along Hwy BR-153 to Belém (US$77, 34 hours, two daily), but the road around the Tocantins border can be impassable during rainy season.

Buses go to Pirenópolis (US$5, three hours, seven daily) and Alto Paraíso (US$7, four hours, two daily) for access to the Parque Nacional da Chapada dos Veadeiros.

Getting Around

The **international airport** (☎ 365 1941) is 12km south of the center. To get to the airport from the city, take a No 102 bus (US$1, 40 minutes) or a No 30 minibus (US$1, 25 minutes) from the city bus station. A taxi to the airport from the center costs US$12.

To get from the city bus station to the long-distance bus and train station, take local bus No 131.

There are car-rental agencies at Brasília's airport and the Hotel Nacional.

The long-awaited Metro DF, which first began construction in 1992, came into operation in late 2001. The metro (one-way ticket US$0.35, 6am to 8pm Monday to Friday) runs from the city bus station under the southern 'wing' of the city to the outer suburbs of Taguatinga and Samambaia. It has little usefulness for travelers.

AROUND BRASÍLIA
Salto de Itiquira

Itiquira is a Tupi-Guarani Indian word meaning 'water that falls.' From the viewpoint at this 170m-high free-fall **waterfall** (☎ 225 6601; ☒ 8am-4pm), you can see the valley of the Paranãs to the south. There's forest, several crystal-clear streams with natural pools for a swim and the requisite restaurants and bars.

Itiquira is 110km northeast of Brasília; you need a car to get there or you can take a bus from the long-distance bus station to the city of Formosa and try your luck organizing a lift from there. If you're driving, leave Brasília on Hwys BR-020 and BR-30, which take you through the satellite cities of Sobradinho and Planaltina to Formosa. The falls are 35km from Formosa at the end of the dirt road.

Cachoeira Saia Velha

This is a pleasant swimming hangout not too far from the city. Take Hwy BR-040 in the direction of Belo Horizonte for about 20km. When you reach the **Monumento do Candango** – a wacky statue created by a Frenchman to honor the people who built Brasília – there's a sign to the waterfall. The road is to the left of the monument. There are also several natural swimming pools, plus restaurants and camping areas but no hotel.

Goiás

CONTENTS

THE CENTRAL WEST

HIGHLIGHTS

- Strolling through the historic colonial towns of **Goiás Velho** (p368) and **Pirenópolis** (p370)

- Soaking in the therapeutic hot springs at **Caldas Novas** (p373)

- Trekking through the unique high-cerrado flora in **Parque Nacional da Chapada dos Veadeiros** (p374)

- Rock-hopping through the **Vale da Lua** (p375), near Chapada dos Veadeiros

- Spotting emas (the biggest birds in Brazil) and anteaters in **Parque Nacional das Emas** (p376)

- POPULATION: 5 MILLION
- AREA: 355,386 SQ KM

Spectacular sunsets in a huge sky, lush, rolling hills and long distances greet the traveler to Goiás. While not usually on the agenda, this sparsely populated state has much to offer. Avoid the large cities such as Goiânia and Anápolis and spend most time exploring the natural beauty of the state. Tourism infrastructure has improved in recent years, and national parks such as Chapada dos Veadeiros and Emas are more accessible than before.

In recent years, Goiás has become the center of a campaign aimed at protecting the cerrado, the savanna-like landscape that sprawls across Brazil's central high plains. Unfortunately, much of it is being ploughed under at a rapid rate to make way for immense soy plantations. Agriculture is big business, and Goiás now boasts more millionaires per capita than any other state.

While Brasília still attracts visitors to its monuments, Goiás is an increasingly popular destination for Brazilians and foreigners. Major attractions include the picturesque colonial villages of Goiás Velho and Pirenópolis, the natural hot springs at Caldas Novas and the rivers, waterfalls and forest trails of the Parque Nacional da Chapada dos Veadeiros. It's also a gateway to the river beaches of the mighty Rio Araguaia, which forms the border with Mato Grosso state, and to the Ilha do Bananal in Tocantins state, the world's largest river island.

You could easily spend a couple of weeks in Goiás. It's not as hectic as Rio or the Northeast, the people and towns are more prosperous and the regional food is excellent.

History

On the heels of the gold discoveries in Minas Gerais, *bandeirantes* (groups of roaming adventurers who explored the interior) pushed further inland in search of more precious metals and, as always, Indian slaves. In 1682, a *bandeira* headed by the old Paulista Bartolomeu Bueno da Silva visited the region. The Goyaz Indians gave him the nickname *anhanguera* (old devil) when, after burning some *cachaça* (sugarcane rum) – which the Indians believed to be water – on a plate, he threatened to set fire to all the rivers if they didn't show him where their gold mines were. Three years later, having been given up for dead, the old devil returned to São Paulo with a few survivors, and with gold and Indian slaves from Goiás.

In 1722, da Silva's son, who had been on the first trip, organized another *bandeira*. The gold rush was on. It followed a pattern similar to that in Minas Gerais: first came the Paulistas, then the Portuguese Emboabas (immigrants who had arrived for the earlier gold rush in Minas Gerais) and soon the Black slaves. With everything imported from so far away, prices in Goiás were high. Many suffered and died, particularly the slaves. The gold rush ended quickly.

Climate

Most of Goiás lies within the Brazilian highlands, which has a tropical climate. Between October and March it's hot and humid. From April to September it's hot and dusty. That said, don't be surprised if you get bogged down during the dry season or eat dust in the wet season. The temperature averages 20°C (68°F) year-round. In the south the state occupies the major part of the central plateau, at an altitude of between 250m to 300m above sea level, so temperatures tend to be cooler, especially in the more mountainous areas.

National Parks

In the mountainous area north of Brasília, the impressive Parque Nacional da Chapada dos Veadeiros (p374) is a 65,000-hectare national park filled with waterfalls and canyons. Scenery is spectacular and wildlife viewing is excellent.

The 131,868-hectare Parque Nacional das Emas (p376) sits on a high plateau surrounded by farmland. Its lack of dense foliage makes it easier to spot a wide variety of plant and animal life, including the wonderful emas – Brazil's biggest birds.

Getting There & Away

The gateway to Goiás is Brasília, with daily flights to all major Brazilian cities. It's also possible to travel overland via some long bus rides. The majority of travelers coming from the coast first pass through Minas Gerais, or come north from São Paulo. Minas is the more scenic and interesting route.

Getting Around

Goiás offers many attractions and is a popular stopover for travelers wanting to break their journey between the coast and the Pantanal. Regular bus services connect all the major towns and cities. Road conditions are generally good (with notable exceptions such as some stretches of the Brasília–Belem highway) and if you don't mind mixing it with the trucks, renting a car is a viable option.

UNIQUE CERRADO

A mosaic of grassland, palm stands (known as *veredas*) and dry gallery forests, the cerrado is the country's second-largest eco-region after Amazonia. It is only now being recognized for its incredible diversity of flora. Of the 10,000 species of plants found in the cerrado, 44% are found nowhere else in the world. It's also home to some of Brazil's most rare and endangered species, including the maned wolf, giant otter, giant armadillo, tapir, pampas deer and giant anteater.

Since the 1970s, vast tracts of native cerrado vegetation have been converted to soybean, rice, corn, wheat and cattle production. The rate of habitat loss is greater than in any of Brazil's other ecoregions, including Amazonia, and this shows no sign of abating.

GOIÂNIA

☎ 0xx62 / pop 1.2 million

The capital of Goiás, Goiânia is the state's other planned city, predating Brasília by almost 30 years. Planned by urbanist Armando de Godói and founded in 1933, it's a pleasant combination of parks, leafy avenues and modern and not-so-modern high-rise buildings laid out around circular streets.

Information

If you're traveling on to the national parks or colonial towns, it is wise to get money in Goiânia.

Banco do Brasil (Av Goiás 980; ☺ 10am-4pm Mon-Fri) The main branch; changes money for its usual hefty commissions.

Bradesco ATM (bus station)

Inamps Hospital (☎ 223 5601; Av Anhanguera 4379)

Information desk (☎ 217 1100; level 2, Centro de Convenções, cnr Rua 30 & Rua 4; ☺ 9am-9pm) It's not always open; there's more likely to be someone attending when a convention is happening.

Online Goiânia (shopping mall, cnr Rua 3 & Rua 21; per hr US$2; ☺ 9am-7pm Mon-Fri, 9am-3pm Sat) Internet access.

Post office (Praça Cívica 11) Right in the center of town; there's also a handy branch at the bus station.

Turisplan Turismo (☎ 224 1941; Rua 8, No 388) A central travel agency selling airline and bus tickets; can be helpful with information.

Sights & Activities

There's not much for the visitor in Goiânia. Our advice is to get out to one of the national parks or nearby colonial towns as quickly as you can. An excursion within 200km of Goiânia includes the Caldas Novas hot springs (p373).

If you have some time to kill, try the **Bosque do Buritis**, a lush central park with fountains and lakes overflowing with birdlife. The **Museu de Arte de Goiânia** (admission free; ☺ 9am-9pm Tue-Sun) is in the northern part of the park and worth a quick look.

The **Parque Zoológico** (Av Anhanguera; admission US$1; ☺ 8am-5pm Tue-Sun), approximately 1km west of the center, contains over 1000 animals from 193 species.

The weekend markets – **Feira da Lua** (Praça Tamandaré) a few blocks west of the Centro Cívico on Saturday afternoon and **Feira do Sol** (Praça do Sol) on Sunday afternoon – are definitely worth a look.

Sleeping

Ask for discounts at all city hotels on weekends. The mid-range and top-end hotels in particular drop as much as 50% off their prices on weekends. Some addresses include 's/n' *(sem número)*, which means 'without number.'

Goiânia Palace (☎ 224 4874; Av Anhanguera 5195; s/d/tr quartos US$6/9/13, apartamentos US$12/15/20; ✷) Inside its pink Deco facade is a friendly, modern hotel, slowly being renovated by its French owner. The French travel posters in the foyer are a nice touch. English is also spoken and the location is central.

Lord Hotel (☎ 3091 2969; Av Anhanguera 4999; s/d/tr apartamentos US$12/18/24) Cheap and comfortable. Rooms at the front with balconies are

light and airy, but the downside is noise from the street.

Principe Hotel (☎ 224 0962; Av Anhanguera 2936; s/d quartos US$9/14, apartamentos US$14/22; ✷) This place has a homier feel than many of the city hotels. Breakfast costs extra.

Hotel Araguaia (☎ 212 9800; www.araguaiahotel .com.br, in Portuguese; Av Araguaia 664; s/d US$15/22; P ✷ ☐) A spotlessly clean and friendly option with a huge breakfast spread.

Vila Rica Palace (☎ 223 2733; Av Anhanguera 5308; s/d US$25/30; P ✷ ☐) Funky, spacious and comfortable, with substantial discounts for longer stays.

Hotel Serras de Goyaz (☎ 224 2310; www.hotel serrasdegoyaz.com.br, in Portuguese; Av Paranaíba 5106; s/d US$28/40; P ✷) Close to the convention

GOIÂNIA

INFORMATION		SIGHTS & ACTIVITIES	(p366)	Lord Hotel	12 C2
Banco do Brasil	1 C1	Museu de Arte de Goiânia	7 A3	Principe Hotel	13 C2
Bradesco	2 B2			Vila Rica Palace	14 B2
Centro de Convenções (Convention		SLEEPING	(pp367–8)		
Center)	3 A2	Goiânia Palace	8 B2	EATING	(p368)
Online Goiânia	4 C2	Hotel Araguaia	9 C2	Argu's Executivo Restaurant	15 B2
Post Office	5 B3	Hotel Karajás	10 B2	Chão Nativo	(see 3)
Turisplan Turismo	6 B2	Hotel Serras de Goyaz	11 B1	Panela de Ferro	16 B2
				DRINKING	(p368)
				Cervejária Brasil	17 D2

center, it features exposed brick walls and offers large, tastefully decorated apartments with good city views.

Hotel Karajás (☎ 224 9666; www.hotelkarajas .com.br, in Portuguese; Rua 3, No 860; s/d US$30/40; P 🍴 🚭 🖳) Karajás offers excellent suites that are bright, spacious and worth the extra expense. It's in a good, central location.

Eating & Drinking

Since they are surrounded by cattle, locals eat plenty of meat. They also like to munch on *pamonha*, a very tasty green-corn snack sold at stands around town.

If you want to taste some typical Goiânian dishes, the best places to head are **Chão Nativo** (☎ 217 2111; Av Paranaíba; buffet US$6; ⏰ 11:30am-3:30pm) in the Centro de Convenções, or **Panela de Ferro** (☎ 225 1514; Rua 8, No 197; dishes US$3-8; ⏰ 11:30am-3:30pm). One favorite dish is the *empadão de Goiás*, a tasty meat, vegetable, olive and egg pie.

Praça Tamandaré, a short ride on the Eixo T-7 or Vila União bus or a long walk from the center, is a good bet at night. It's the pizza capital of Goiânia; just wander around and see what takes your fancy.

Argu's Executivo Restaurant (☎ 224 8429; Rua 4, No 811; meals per kg US$5; ⏰ 11:30am-3pm Mon-Fri & noon-3:30pm Sat & Sun) The best per-kilogram lunch in the center. Get in early when the food is freshest and the crowd is thinnest.

Cervejária Brasil (cnr Rua 4 & Rua Araguaia; ⏰ noon-midnight) Although the center is almost deserted at night, this is one of the livelier spots for a drink and snack.

Modiglianni (☎ 215 4155; Rua 7 No 754; ⏰ 6pm-midnight) This is a popular outdoor place that gets busy late.

Getting There & Around

Aeroporto Santo Genoveva (☎ 265 1500) is 6km northeast of the city center (US$6 by taxi). You can fly to Rio (US$185), São Paulo (US$160) and other major Brazilian cities.

From the huge bus station/shopping mall, hourly buses leave for Brasília (US$6,

three hours, hourly), Cuiabá (US$23, 14 hours, daily), Caldas Novas (US$8, three hours, 10 daily), Pirenópolis (US$7, two hours, two daily) and Goiás Velho (US$7, three hours, hourly). Two of the buses to Goiás Velho continue on to Aruanã (US$12, six hours), for access to the Rio Araguaia.

You can walk from the bus station into town – it takes 15 minutes to get to the corner of Av Anhanguera and Av Goiás, but you might melt along the way. From outside the bus station, take a Rodoviária-Centro bus to town, or grab a taxi (US$4).

GOIÁS VELHO

☎ 0xx62 / pop 27,000

Travel back to the late 18th century in the cobblestone, lamp-lit streets of Goiás Velho. The former state capital once known as Vila Boa is a colonial gem. Straddling the Rio Vermelho and surrounded by the rugged Serra Dourada, the town was awarded Unesco World Heritage status in 2002. Its gorgeous baroque churches shine and the town's population swells during Semana Santa (Holy Week).

After disastrous floods in 2001, Goiás Velho was restored, basic sanitation was upgraded and the power lines were placed underground.

Information

There's no tourist office or money exchange here.

Bradesco (Praça do Coreto; ⏰ 10am-3pm Mon-Fri) Visa withdrawals.

Empadaria do Carmo (Rua Dom Candido 33; per hr US$2; ⏰ 8am-5pm Mon-Fri, 11am-11pm Sat) Internet access, plus tasty snacks and juices.

Metainformatica (Rua Dr Americano do Brasil 10; per hr US$2; ⏰ 8am-5pm Mon-Fri) Internet access.

Sights & Activities

Strolling through town, you quickly notice the magnificent 18th-century colonial architecture. The streets are very narrow, with low houses, and there are seven churches. The most impressive is the oldest, the **Igreja da Paula** (Praça Zaqueu Alves de Castro), built in 1761.

The **Museu das Bandeiras** (Praça Brasil Caiado; admission US$0.50; ⏰ 8am-5pm Tue-Sat & 8am-noon Sun) is in the old town council building (1766) and is filled with a variety of interesting antiques from around the world. The

---

STATE CAPITAL OR NOT?

Every July 25, the anniversary of the town's foundation in 1727, the state governor goes to Goiás Velho and the town becomes the state capital for three days.

building itself is pretty amazing, and the **Chafariz de Cauda fountain** (1778) close by is beautiful. Other interesting museums are the **Museu de Arte Sacra** (admission US$1; ☺ 8am-5pm Tue-Fri, 9am-5pm Sat, 9am-4pm Sun) in the old **Igreja da Boa Morte** (Praça Castelo Branco) with a good selection of 19th-century works by renowned Goiânian sculptor Viega Vale, and the **Palácio Conde dos Arcos** (admission US$0.50; ☺ 8am-7pm Tue-Sat & 8am-noon Sun), the restored colonial governor's residence. **Ateliê de Goi-andeira do Courto** (☎ 371 1303; Rua Joaquim Bonifácio 19; ☺ 9am-noon & 1-5pm Tue-Sun) is well worth a visit. This amazing elderly artist paints using the immense variety of colored sands from the Serra Dourada. She maintains an exposition in her studio and is a delightful character. Best to call in advance to arrange a tour.

Festivals & Events

The big occasion in Goiás Velho is **Semana Santa**, which takes place the week before Easter. The week's highlight is the Wednes-day-night procession reenacting the arrest of Christ. The street lights are turned off and thousands of people march through the streets carrying torches, led by 40 pointy-hooded figures – the *farricocos* – whose dress harks back to the days of the Inquisition.

The other big event on the calendar is the **Festival International de Cinema Ambiental** (International Environmental Film Festi-val), which takes place over five days in

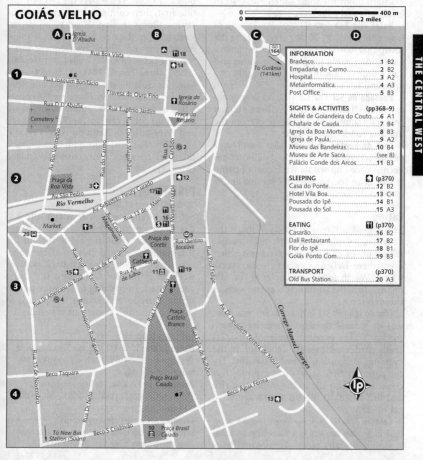

GOIÁS VELHO

0 _____ 400 m
0 _____ 0.2 miles

INFORMATION

Bradesco	1 B2
Empadaria do Carmo	2 B2
Hospital	3 A2
Metainformática	4 A3
Post Office	5 B3

SIGHTS & ACTIVITIES (pp368–9)

Ateliê de Goiandeira do Couto	6 A1
Chafariz de Cauda	7 B4
Igreja da Boa Morte	8 B3
Igreja de Paula	9 A2
Museu das Bandeiras	10 B4
Museu de Arte Sacra	(see 8)
Palácio Conde dos Arcos	11 B3

SLEEPING (p370)

Casa do Ponte	12 B2
Hotel Vila Boa	13 C4
Pousada do Ipê	14 B1
Pousada do Sol	15 A3

EATING (p370)

Casarão	16 B2
Dalí Restaurant	17 B2
Flor do Ipê	18 B1
Goiás Ponto Com	19 B3

TRANSPORT (p370)

Old Bus Station	20 A3

THE CENTRAL WEST

early June. The festival includes film and video screenings, workshops, live shows, lectures and exhibitions – all environmentally themed.

Sleeping

Goiás is a popular getaway from Goiânia, so it's a good idea to book ahead if you're arriving on a weekend. The town is packed during Semana Santa and for the International Environmental Film Festival.

Pousada do Ipê (☎ 371 2065; Rua do Forum 22; s/d apartamentos US$15/25; ⚫) The most pleasant place to stay, with rooms set around a shady courtyard. Newer apartments face a lovely garden with swimming pool and bar /restaurant. They're a little more pricey but worth it. Enjoy the sugar-laden breakfast of local jams and jellies.

Hotel Vila Boa (☎ 371 1000; Morro Chapéu do Padre; s/d US$30/45; P ⚫ ⚫) Overlooking the town, this '60s-style hotel offers expansive views, interesting local art expositions and a welcome swimming pool. We highly recommend it.

Pousada do Sol (☎ 371 1717; Rua Dr Americano do Brasil 17; s/d US$9/12; P) A well-maintained colonial building with nice views from the upstairs rooms. Good value.

Casa do Ponte (☎ 371 4467; Rua Moretti Foggia s/n; s/d US$15/20; ⚫) This '50s-style hotel has been spruced up with a fresh coat of paint. It has clean rooms, friendly service and is close to the center of town.

Eating

The *empadão* reigns in Goiás Velho – the tasty savory pie filled with meat, vegetables, olives and egg is served just about everywhere. Delicious sweets are also everywhere. Watch for them displayed for sale on private house windowsills as you wander through town.

Flor do Ipê (☎ 371 1691; Rua da Boa Vista; dishes US$4-10; ⚙ noon-2:30pm & 7pm-midnight Tue-Sat, noon-3pm Sun) Serves excellent regional food. Its shady garden settings are delightful. In the evenings, one dish will feed two easily. Try the *peixe na telha, com arroz e pirão* (fish cooked on a clay tile in the oven, with rice and fish sauce). It fills up on weekends, so get in early.

Casarão (☎ 371 2874; Rua Moretti Foggia 8; dishes US$2-5; ⚙ 10am-8pm Mon-Fri & 10am-10pm Sat & Sun) A simple upstairs place overlooking Praça do Coreto. It serves great *empadões*. This plaza is also the place to go for music, drinks and snacks at night.

Dalí Restaurant (☎ 372 1640; Rua 13 de Maio 26; dishes US$2-10; ⚙ 11am-11pm Tue-Sun) An intimate place with friendly service and a huge menu, including some of the tasty sweets and cakes the town is famous for.

Goiás Ponto Com (☎ 371 1691; Praça do Coreto 19; dishes US$5-20; ⚙ noon-3pm & 8pm-midnight Thu-Sat, noon-3pm Sun, Tue & Wed) Offers the town's most stylish dining experience, with modern art in a colonial setting. For lunch, there are daily 'executive specials' and in the evenings it's candlelight and a la carte.

Getting There & Away

Buses to Goiás Velho pass the old bus station first, then continue on to the new bus station. Buses leaving Goiás Velho depart straight from the new bus station, without passing the old. There are frequent buses running between Goiás Velho and Goiânia (US$7, three hours, 144km). Direct buses leave for Goiânia at 6am, 8:10am and 4pm and are much quicker. There are two buses a day to Aruanã (US$7, three hours, 11am and 5pm) for access to the Rio Araguaia, and three buses to Barra do Garças (US$9, six hours, 8:40am, 9am and 1pm), where there are frequent connections to Cuiabá (Mato Grosso).

PIRENÓPOLIS

☎ 0xx62 / pop 21,000

Set on striking red earth astride the Rio das Almas, picturesque Pirenópolis is another historic colonial gold town. On the Patrimonio Nacional (National Heritage) register since 1989, it's a laid-back, popular weekend retreat for Goiânians. It's also a good base for exploring the unique terrain of the cerrado and taking the plunge at some of the area's numerous waterfalls.

Information

Banco do Brasil (☎ 331 1182; Rua Sizenando Jayme; ⚙ 11am-4pm Mon-Fri) Visa cash withdrawals; on the main commercial strip.

Bradesco (☎ 331 1044; Rua Sizenando Jayme; ⚙ 11am-4pm Mon-Fri) Visa cash withdrawals; on the main commercial strip.

Ceramica Art (Ponte da Pedra; per hr US$1; ⚙ 9am-6pm) Internet access; next to the small bridge, with a terminal among the artworks. It also rents bikes for US$8 a day.

Delegacía de Polícia (☎ 331 1105; Praça Bernando Sayão)

Hospital Nossa Senhora do Rosário (☎ 331 1897; Av Neco Mendonça) Opposite the bus station.

Tourist office (☎ 331 2729; Rua do Bonfim; ☼ 8am-5pm) Friendly and useful for organizing transportation and accredited guides for local sights. Guides generally charge around US$15 a day, excluding transportation. A two-hour city tour costs US$10.

Sights & Activities
CHURCHES

The town's oldest church, Igreja NS do Rosário Matriz (1732), was tragically gutted by fire in 2001 and is slowly undergoing careful restoration. The **Igreja NS do Bonfim** (1750), with its beautiful altars, con-

tains an image of the Senhor de Bonfim brought here from Portugal in 1755. The **Igreja NS do Carmo** (1750) was built by the Portuguese and today houses the **Museu de Arte Sacra** (admission US$0.50; ☼ 9am-6pm Mon-Sat), which contains a variety of sacred images, some brought from Portugal by the early settlers.

SANTUÁRIO DE VIDA SILVESTRE – FAZENDA VAGAFOGO

Six kilometers northwest of town, the **Vagafogo Farm Wildlife Sanctuary** (☎ 9969 3090; admission US$3; ☼ 8am-5pm Tue-Sun) is a top spot. The nature reserve of cerrado and gallery forests on the margins of the Rio Vagafogo is home to brown capuchin and black

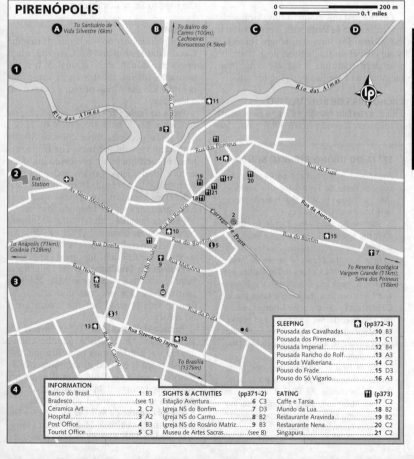

PIRENÓPOLIS

0 ——— 200 m
0 ——— 0.1 miles

To Santuário de Vida Silvestre (6km)
To Bairro do Carmo (100m); Cachoeiras Bonsucesso (4.5km)
Rio das Almas
Rua do Carmo
Rua dos Pireneus
Rua do Fuzil
Bus Station
Av Neco Mendonça
Rua da Aurora
Corrego da Prata
Rua do Rosário
Rua do Bonfim
To Anápolis (71km); Goiânia (128km)
Rua Direita
Rua Nova
Rua do Rosário
Rua Matutina
Rua da Prata
Rua Sizenando Jayme
Rua do Campo
To Brasília (137km)
To Reserva Ecológica Vargem Grande (11km); Serra dos Pireneus (18km)

THE CENTRAL WEST

INFORMATION
Banco do Brasil..................................1 B3
Bradesco.......................................(see 1)
Ceramica Art....................................2 C2
Hospital...3 A2
Post Office.......................................4 B3
Tourist Office...................................5 C3

SIGHTS & ACTIVITIES (pp371–2)
Estação Aventura...............................6 C3
Igreja NS do Bonfim............................7 D3
Igreja NS do Carmo............................8 B2
Igreja NS do Rosário Matriz..................9 B3
Museu de Artes Sacras.....................(see 8)

SLEEPING (pp372–3)
Pousada das Cavalhadas.....................10 B3
Pousada dos Pireneus........................11 C1
Pousada Imperial...............................12 B4
Pousada Rancho do Rolf.....................13 A3
Pousada Walkeriana...........................14 C2
Pouso do Frade.................................15 D3
Pouso do Só Vigario..........................16 A3

EATING (p373)
Caffe e Tarsia....................................17 C2
Mundo da Lua....................................18 B2
Restaurante Aravinda.........................19 B2
Restaurante Nena..............................20 C2
Singapura...21 C2

howler monkeys, armadillos, pampas deer, agouti and many bird species.

There's a café for lunch at the visitors' center, as well as some hammocks for kicking back after your walk. Try some of the colorful homemade preservatives.

To get there from town, head north along Rua do Carmo; you can walk if you're feeling fit, grab a cab or hop on a mototaxi.

PARQUE ESTADUAL DA SERRA DOS PIRINEUS

This park contains three peaks – Pai (Father), the tallest at 1385m, Filho (Son) and Espírito Santo (Holy Spirit). It's 18km northeast of town and there are waterfalls and interesting rock formations to see along the way, some dating back to Gondwanaland.

On the first full moon in July, locals celebrate the **Festa do Morro** with a procession to the Morro dos Pireneus, where there is a small chapel on the highest peak (Pai). It's a modern tradition, more New Age than religious, and serious partying prevails.

CACHOEIRAS DE BONSUCESSO

These **waterfalls** (admission US$3), 4.5km north of town, are a good place to cool off in clear

---

FESTA DO DIVINO ESPÍRITO SANTO

Pirenópolis is famous for performing the story of Festa do Divino Espírito Santo, a tradition begun in 1819 that is more popularly known as Cavalhadas.

Starting 50 days after Easter, for three days the town looks like a scene from the Middle Ages as it celebrates Charlemagne's victory over the Moors. A series of medieval tournaments, dances and festivities, including a mock battle between the Moors and Christians in distant Iberia takes place. Combatants ride decorated horses, wearing bright costumes and bull-head masks. The Moors are defeated on the battlefield and convert to Christianity, proving that heresy doesn't pay in the end.

The festival is a happy one, and more folkloric than religious. The town's population swells during the festival. If you're in the neighborhood, make a point of seeing this stunning and curious spectacle, one of the most fascinating in Brazil.

---

pools. There are six small waterfalls along a 1.5km trail. Be prepared to jump off some cliffs, and take your snorkel.

You can buy food and drinks at the **visitors' center** (☎ 321 1217; ☻ 7am-5pm), where you also pay admission for the waterfalls. To get there, walk north along Rua do Carmo and follow the signs or take a cab or mototaxi from town.

RESERVA ECOLÓGICA VARGEM GRANDE

This 3.6-sq-km **park** (☎ 331 1171; admission US$3; ☻ 8.30am-5pm) on private land contains two impressive waterfalls – **Caldeirão do Inferno** and **Caldeirão do Lázaro**. There are small river beaches and natural pools for swimming in.

The reserve is 11km northeast of town on the road to Serra dos Pireneus.

Sleeping

Pirenópolis is busy on weekends, during the Cavalhadas festival and for Carnaval, when prices can double these quoted. When the pousadas fill up, most visitors camp out near the Rio das Almas or rent a room from a local.

Pouso do Frade (☎ 331 1046; www.pousadaspiren opolis.com.br; Rua do Bonfim 37; s/d US$30/45; ☢ ☛) This place occupies three colonial houses with centuries-old gardens. The characteristics of each house are preserved but open onto a lovely, large garden and pool area surrounded by a veranda from which you eat a delicious breakfast. An upstairs apartment has a great view of the Igreja da Matriz.

Pousada Imperial (☎ 331 11382; Av Sizenando Jayme 21; s/d apartamentos US$14/28; ☢ ☛) An extremely friendly, comfortable place. The room on the top floor has great views.

Pousada das Cavalhadas (☎ 331 1261; Praça da Matriz 1; s/d apartamentos per person US$10; ☢) This pousada is in a good, central location. The lounge area is good but the rooms are a bit musty.

Pousada Walkeriana (☎ 331 1260; Rua do Rosário 37; s/d US$40/45; ☢ ☛ ☛) A popular choice among weekend visitors from Brasília, this stylish place is housed in an immaculately restored century-old building. Rooms are tastefully decorated in colonial style and there's a spacious garden with a pool.

Pousada Rancho do Rolf (☎ 331 1162; Rua Benjamin Constant 17; s & d US$50; ☢ ☛) Set in a large, lush garden with a lovely shaded pool area, this place has a pseudo-colonial feel to it, thanks to the old gold-mining implements and wagon wheels hanging on the walls. The clean, spacious rooms are food value and there's even a mini-chapel.

Pouso do Só Vigario (☎ 331 1206; www.pousada spirenopolis.com.br; Rua Nova 25; s/d US$25/40; 🗷 🖭) Another pousada set in a converted colonial house. A very tasteful renovation, incorporating colonial stylings, mixes well with the colorful modern artwork on the walls. It also has a pleasant pool area.

Pousada dos Pireneus (☎ 331 1345; www.pousa dadospireneus.com.br, in Portuguese; Rua do Carmo 80; s/d US$50/65; 🅿 🗷 🖳 🖭) Cross the bridge and follow the signs – this place is the most upmarket in town and popular with politicians seeking privacy. Rooms are large and well appointed. There are lots of recreational activities, including donkey rides for the kids! The sprawling gardens contain a small water park. Tariffs include dinner.

Eating

Most restaurants close on Monday – some only open on weekends. Rua do Rosário, aka. Rua do Lazer, is the main restaurant /café strip.

Restaurante Aravinda (Rua do Rosário 25; dishes US$2-8; 🕑 lunch & dinner Thu-Sun) Has an extensive menu with some vegetarian dishes.

Mundo da Lua (Rua do Rosário 20; dishes for 2 US$10; 🕑 6pm-midnight Tue-Sun) A busy place in a busy street, specializing in fast grills served quickly.

Caffe e Tarsia (☎ 331 1274; Rua do Rosário 34; dishes US$10) A more upmarket Italian restaurant with live music on weekends.

Singapura (☎ 331 3779; Rua do Rosário 22; dishes US$10-20; 🕑 7pm-midnight Thu-Sun) The best place in town for Asian food.

Restaurante Nena (☎ 331 1470; Rua da Aurora 4; 🕑 noon-3pm Tue-Sun) Great spot for some regional cooking. Good selection of salads.

Getting There & Away

There are buses to Brasília (US$5, three hours, 165km, seven daily), and one to Goiânia (US$6, two hours, 128km, 6am) There are more frequent local buses to Anápolis, where you can catch a connection to Goiânia.

Getting around town is easily done on foot or by mototaxi.

CALDAS NOVAS

☎ 0xx62 / pop 50,000

Suffering from high blood pressure after your visit to Brasília? Poor digestion after your visit to a truck-stop café in Minas? Exhausted after your extended Carnaval in Salvador? If your answer is yes to any or all of these questions, then Caldas Novas, with more than 30 curative hot springs, may be just the place for you. Now an upmarket, high-rise resort, the town's population swells to around 200,000 during holidays.

Information

Banco do Brasil (Rua Capitan João Crisostomo 325) Has a 24-hour Visa ATM but there are no exchange facilities in town.

City On Line (Rua Antônio Godoy 421; per hr US$1; 🕑 8am-9pm Mon-Fri, 8am-3pm Sat) Internet access.

Hospital Aparecida (☎ 453 1290; Rua Eça de Queiroz 13) Has medical facilities, but you should be feeling good after a soak in the springs.

Police station (☎ 453 1190; cnr Alameda do Contono & Rua Crisostómo)

Post office (Rua Crisostómo 361)

Tourist information booth (☎ 453 1868; Praça Mestre Orlando; 🕑 8am-6pm Mon-Fri, 8am-noon Sat) In the center of town; provides plenty of water-park brochures. Staff are helpful and some speak English.

Sleeping & Eating

During holidays and long weekends the town is packed, so reservations are advisable. Prices quoted here are for low season.

Camping Lagoa Quente (☎ 453 1250; per person US$8; 🅿 🖭) Has two thermal swimming pools. It's in a beautiful spot 6km from the city, on the road to Pires do Rio.

Hotel Roma (☎ 453 1335; www.hotelroma .br; Praça Mestre Orlando 368; s & d US$40; 🅿 🗷 🖭) Prepare to get wrinkly – it has six thermal pools, hydromassage and a whirlpool. It also has live music and a view of the town square in the evenings. Rates include breakfast and lunch.

Hotel Aguas Claras Thermas (☎ 453 1738; Rua São Cristovão 1; s/d US$20/25; 🅿 🗷 🖭) This hotel has two thermal pools and a sauna; it's a good mid-range option.

SESC Caldas Novas (☎ 453 1500; www.sescgo.com .br, in Portuguese; Rua do Balneário 600; per person US$15-30; 🅿 🗷 🖭) Large recreation area includes eight thermal pools. Recreation facilities are open to the public (US$5).

Thermas di Roma (☎ 453 1718; www.diroma.com .br; Rua São Cristovão 1110; s & d US$65; P ✖ ❑ ♻) A few kilometers out of town on the road to Mineiros, this huge luxury resort complex boasts great views. Hot-spring action here includes nine thermal pools. It's great for kids. In January and July there's a three-day minimum stay. Rates include breakfast.

Paneteria Famigli Amoroso (cnr Rua do Turismo & Rua da Madalena; pizzas US$5; ✆ 6pm-midnight) This small bakery makes excellent pizzas in a wood-fired oven. Try the *mussarela*, *catupiry* and *peru* combination.

Girrassol (Rua do Turismo 240; dishes US$1-8; ✆ 11:30am-3pm & 6:30-10pm Tue-Sun) Has a varied lunch buffet and serves tasty soups in the evenings.

Chão das Goianas (☎ 453 6715; Av Orcalino Santos 7140; meals per kg US$3; ✆ 11am-midnight) This place has an enormous buffet selection – start hungry.

Getting There & Away

The bus station is at the end of Rua Antônio Coelho de Godoy. Regular buses run to Brasília (US$9, six hours, 393km, two daily) and Goiânia (US$6, three hours, 187km, 10 daily), as well as to Rio de Janeiro and São Paulo.

PARQUE NACIONAL DA CHAPADA DOS VEADEIROS

☎ 0xx61

This spectacular national park in the highest area of the Central West showcases the unique landscape and flora of high-altitude cerrado.

With high waterfalls, natural swimming pools and oasis-like stands of wine palms, the park is a popular destination for ecotourists. In fact, the whole area is beautiful, with its big skies, exotic flora and dramatic hills rising up like waves breaking across the plains.

The sublime landscape, much of it based on quartz crystal, has also attracted New Agers who have established alternative communities and a burgeoning 'esoturismo' industry in the area.

The town of **Alto Paraíso de Goiás** (commonly known as Alto Paraíso), 38km from the park, is the center of these communities, but most travelers will use the former crystal-mining hamlet of **São Jorge** (2km from the national park entrance) as a base. You'll need two or

three days to see the main attractions within the park, but it's easy to spend longer soaking up the atmosphere of the area.

Mammals in the area include maned wolves, banded anteaters, giant armadillos, deer, capybaras and tapirs. Birds include rheas, toucans, macaws, hawks and vultures. The best time to visit the park is between April and October, before the rivers flood during the rainy season and access becomes very slippery.

Information

There's an excellent **tourist office** (☎ 446 1159; Av Ari Valadão; ✆ 8am-5pm Tue-Fri, 8am-8pm Sat & 8am-2pm Sun) in Alto Paraíso. It's 200m from the bus station, on the town's main street. It can arrange experienced guides and transportation to the surrounding attractions, not all of which are inside the park.

Sights & Activities

All visitors to the **park** (☎ 459 3388; admission US$1; ✆ 8am-5pm Tue-Sun) must be accompanied by an accredited guide. Guides can be organized at the park entrance, through the local guide association, **ACVCV** (☎ 446 1690), or at most hotels in São Jorge. Guides usually cost US$10 a day, US$30 with car.

The guides run separate six-hour tours to each of the park's three main attractions – the *canions* (canyons), *cachoeiras* (waterfalls) and *cariocas* (rocks). The tours cost US$15 for up to 10 people.

The **canions tour** weaves along the Rio Preto, which runs through the middle of the park. The river has cut two large canyons (imaginatively named Canion I and Canion II) through rock with sheer 20m-high walls on either side. There are natural platforms for diving into the cold water.

The **cachoeiras tour** takes in Salto do Rio Preto I and II, two beautiful waterfalls (80m and 120m respectively) that cascade to the ground just 30m apart. The falls are set in a picturesque valley at the end of a trail that weaves through classic cerrado landscape of meadows and gallery forests.

The **cariocas tour** runs through a river valley with interesting rock formations. There's also a small white-sand river beach for cooling off, and cascading waters for a natural spa massage.

There are several sights adjacent to the road between Alto Paraíso and São Jorge

Because they are inside the park, you're obliged to hire a guide to access them, but there are no regular tours. **Morro da Baleia** (Whale's Hill), with its humpback rising from the plain, is ideal for hiking and there's a spot for a swim on the first plateau. There's a 2.5km hiking trail to the top – it takes about two hours each way.

The imposing **Morro do Buracão**, made up of craggy outcrops of quartz rock, lies close to the road but is difficult to access.

VALE DA LUA

A unique sight in the Chapada dos Veadeiros area is the **Vale da Lua** (Valley of the Moon; admission US$2). Over millions of years, the rushing waters of the Rio São Miguel have sculpted rock formations and craters with a striking resemblance to a lunar landscape. Shades of silver, gray and white reflect from rocks and the chilly emerald waters add to the otherworldly atmosphere.

Vale da Lua is outside the national park, so you don't need a guide, but the area is subject to flash flooding during the rainy season, so check with locals before you head off. It's around 5km from São Jorge on a well-marked walking trail that follows the Rio São Miguel. Take sunscreen and water with you. Pay the admission fee at the gate at the entrance to the property.

AEROPORTO DE UFO

The best offbeat attraction is the **Aeroporto de UFO** (☎ 446 1681), 4km north of Alto Paraíso. Local myth has it that a wealthy believer built the runway to receive UFOs. It's a popular spot for mystic rituals, meditations and concerts – especially during a full moon.

Tours

Trans Chapada Tourismo (☎ 446 1345; Rua dos Cristais 7; ⏰ 8am-7pm Mon-Fri) is directly opposite the bus station in Alto Paraíso. It organizes transportation and guides for a variety of tours and activities, including trekking, mountain biking and canyoning. It also rents cars for US$35 per day.

Travessia Ecoturismo (☎ 446 1595; www.travessia tur.br, in Portuguese; Av Ary Filho 979; ⏰ 8am-7pm Mon-Fri, 10am-2pm Sat & Sun) offers some more adventurous jeep tours, and canyoning and rappeling trips.

Alpatur (☎ 446 1820; www.altoparaiso.com; Rua das Nascentes 129; ⏰ 8am-7pm Mon-Fri & 10am-2pm Sat &

Sun) offers therapy tours as well as adventure activities.

Sleeping & Eating

Alto Paraíso has a wide range of accommodations, including upmarket options, but most travelers stay in the village of São Jorge because it is prettier, closer to the park and has more of a village atmosphere. Prices quoted below are for weekdays; they rise by up to 30% on weekends.

There are three good pousadas close together two blocks from São Jorge's main street.

Pousada Trilha Violeta (☎ 9985 6544; s/d US$10/20) A friendly place with gorgeous apartments facing onto a lovely garden. All rooms have a small veranda with hammock and the upstairs ones are reached via an ornate spiral staircase. Breakfast is included, and the managers can organize guides and transport.

Pousada Aguas de Marco (☎ 347 2082; s/d US$15/30; 🛁) A rustic, ambient little place with a Japanese bath and a cozy sauna.

Pousada Casa das Flores (☎ 234 7493; s/d US$45/58; 🛏 🛁) It's a charming, mini–New Age resort with a pool and small chalet-style apartments. Lighting is all from candles or gas lamps, making it ideal for romance, plus it has a sophisticated restaurant.

Cristal da Terra (☎ 455 1052; s/d US$30/40; P 🛏 🛁) Enter the comfort zone; this place has lovely chalets around a lush pool area.

Villa São Jorge (pizzas US$7) A laid-back outdoor restaurant and bar with a great atmosphere. The pizzas made from natural ingredients are wood-fired.

Restaurante da Nenzinha (buffet US$4) Owner Dona Nenzinha offers a hearty, home-cooked buffet of regional food.

Two great bars in town are the traditional Bar do Pelé and the cool Casa da Jia café/bar near the Trilha Violeta, an ideal place to relax after a day on the trails.

Getting There & Away

From Goiânia, there's a daily bus to Alto Paraíso (US$18, six hours, 420km, 8:30am). There are three buses a day from Brasília to Alto Paraíso (US$9, 3½ hours, 220km, 10am, 3pm, 10:30pm). From Palmas (in Tocantins), Expresso União runs via Natividade (US$16, seven hours, daily 9:30pm).

There is one daily bus from Alto Paraíso to São Jorge (US$2, one hour, 4pm) for access to the park. The bus returns from São Jorge to Alto Paraíso daily at 9am. An alternative is to get a ride on the school bus. It leaves São Jorge on weekdays at 6am and returns from Alto Paraíso to São Jorge at noon. From Alto Paraíso, the best place to catch it is at the São Jorge turnoff. Yes – it takes paying passengers.

PARQUE NACIONAL DAS EMAS

Parque Nacional das Emas is a relatively small (1300-sq-km) park in the remote southwest corner of Goiás, where it meets the states of Mato Grosso and Mato Grosso do Sul.

Situated on a high plateau surrounded by farmland, this park is considered the best-preserved cerrado in the country. There's not much foliage to obstruct the sighting of wildlife, including tapirs, anteaters, deer, capybaras, foxes, peccaries, armadillos, blue and yellow macaws and the emas (South American rheas) that give the park its name. The flightless ema is Brazil's biggest bird, growing to a height of 1.4m and weighing around 30kg. The park is also the exclusive sanctuary of the jacamari (a species of wolf) and other endangered wolves.

An interesting spectacle is the 2m-high termite mounds that 'glow' in the dark (most often at the start of the rainy season in October) – the result of bioluminescence (say it fast after three *caipirinhas*) produced by the termite larvae.

The park is a long way from any major city – 480km from Goiânia and 375km from Campo Grande, the capital of Mato Grosso do Sul. There are two entry points: Portão Jacuba (85km from Mineiros) and Portão Guarda da Bandeira (25km from Chapadão do Céu).

The area gets seriously hot and there are few trees for shade within the park. It's recommended that you visit in the early morning or late afternoon – take sunscreen, a hat, water and food as there is no infrastructure within the park.

The park lies along the Brazilian great divide, between the Amazon and Paraná river basins, at the headwaters of the Araguaia, Formoso and Taquari Rivers. Despite all the surrounding rivers, during dry season (July to October) the area is dry enough for fires to ignite spontaneously. Be careful with sparks!

Information & Tours

No public transportation goes to the park, so your options for getting there are to hire a car, either in Brasília or Campo Grande, or to go on a guided tour. You aren't obliged to enter the park with a guide, but guides aren't expensive and they can organize transport.

In Goiânia, you can contact **IBAMA** (☎ 0xx62-224 2441) and the **Fundação Emas** (☎ 0xx62-661 4407) for information about the park and guides. In Mineiros the **guides association** (☎ 0xx62-661 1547; Praça Marcelino Roque) is your point of call for IBAMA-accredited guides. The **tourist office** (☎ 0xx62-634 1228; Praça do Sol) in Chapadão do Céu can do the same.

In Chapadão do Céu, recommended guides include **'Seu' Rubens and Elaine Peixoto** (☎ 0xx62-634 1309). There are two accredited guides at Fazenda Santa Amelia (see below) – Nadir (who is the owner) and **João Pereira** (☎ 0xx62-634 1215). Rates start at around US$15 per day for groups of up to six, not including transport, which costs an extra US$20 a day for groups up to four.

Sleeping

In Mineiros, the cheap and basic places to stay are **Boi na Brasa** (☎ 0xx62-661 1532; Rua 11, No 11; s/d US$8/15) and **Hotel Pinheiros** (☎ 0xx62-661 1942; Rua 8, No 90; s/d US$5/11).

Pilões Palace (☎ 0xx62-661 1547; Praça Jose Alves de Assis; s/d US$20/30; **P ⊠**) The best hotel if you want to stay in Mineiros. It's far from flashy, but has a decent bar and restaurant.

Fazenda Santa Amelia (☎ 0xx62-634 1380; www .brazilnature.com/emas/santaameliaacomodacao.html, in Portuguese; s/d quartos US$15/30, s/d chalet apartamentos US$20/35; **P ⊠ ⊠**) A more interesting place to stay for organizing park visits, this working cattle ranch on Hwy G0-302 12km from Chapadão do Céu has clean and basic rooms and great home cooking over a wood-fired stove. Rates include all meals.

Getting There & Away

Access to the park is tough: there are no paved roads or regular bus routes. Buses go daily from Goiânia to Mineiros (US$13, seven hours, 425km) and Chapadão do Céu (US$15, eight hours, 490km).

RIO ARAGUAIA

For information on places along this large river, which forms a long stretch of the Goiás–Mato Grosso state border, see p615.

Mato Grosso & Mato Grosso do Sul

THE CENTRAL WEST

HIGHLIGHTS

- Spotting wildlife and fishing for piranha in the **Pantanal** (p388)

- Enjoying the breathtaking vistas of **Parque Nacional da Chapada dos Guimarães** (p384)

- Experiencing safaris in **Alta Floresta** (p386) in the southern Amazon rain forest

- Swimming with exotic fish in **Bonito's** (p402) crystal-clear rivers

- Exploring lively frontier towns such as **Poconé** (p387) and **Corumbá** (p399)

★ Alta Floresta

Parque Nacional da Chapada dos Guimarães ★

★ Poconé

Corumbá ★   ★ Pantanal

★ Bonito

- POPULATION: 3.7 MILLION
- AREA: 1,231,549 SQ KM

In the past, Mato Grosso was the destination of choice for explorers, Indian hunters, gold seekers and naturalists. Formed into the separate states of Mato Grosso and Mato Grosso do Sul in the late 1970s, the region today is a prime destination for ecotourists and anglers. This chapter contains a separate section on the Pantanal, the vast wetlands that extend across parts of both states.

The star attraction of the region, the Pantanal is a wildlife paradise that spreads its watery tentacles across both states and into Bolivia and Paraguay, in an area more than half the size of France. It's one of the most important ecosystems on the planet, full of alligators, anacondas, jaguars and an immense variety of birds such as the macaw and jabiru stork. You can tackle it by boat, car, horseback or on foot – whichever way you choose, you're guaranteed a large dose of natural beauty. Ecotourists flock to the Pantanal through the gateway towns of Cuiabá, Corumbá and Campo Grande.

Anglers from all over the world stream into the Pantanal because it's one of the best freshwater fishing areas in the world, renowned for the quantity and diversity of its fish. Cáceres in the northern Pantanal hosts the International Fishing Festival in the last week of September. It's considered by Guinness World Records to be the largest freshwater contest in the world, with more than 2000 participants.

Another lovely area is the Serra do Bodoquena surrounding Bonito in the southeast of Mato Grosso do Sul. The high waterfalls, deep canyons, caves and crystal-clear rivers, where you can float downstream with the fish, are all popular with travelers.

History

According to the Treaty of Tordesillas, the state of Mato Grosso belonged to Spain. For years its exploration was limited to occasional expeditions by adventurers and Jesuit missionaries.

With the discovery of gold in the early 18th century, the region was invaded by thousands of fortune hunters. To reach Cuiabá, they had to cross the lands of several groups of Indians, many of whom were formidable warriors. They included the Caiapó (who even attacked the settlement at Goiás), the Bororo of the Pantanal, the Parecis (who were enslaved to mine gold), the Paiaguá (who defeated several large Portuguese flotillas and caused periodic panic in Cuiabá) and the Guaicuru (skilled riders and warriors who gained many years of experience fighting the Europeans).

As the gold cycle declined, Mato Grosso again became just another isolated province, with its inhabitants eking out a living from subsistence farming and fishing. In the 19th century, the only way to get from Mato Grosso to Rio de Janeiro was by ship via the Rio Paraguay, a journey of several weeks.

This isolation from the capital fuelled several separatist movements, but with the coming of the republic in 1889, the arrival of the telegraph in the early 20th century and the opening of a few rough roads, Mato Grosso slowly emerged from its slumber.

The government policy of developing the interior in the 1940s and '50s and the construction of Brasília in 1960 brought huge waves of migrants from both the Northeast and the south of the country. Today, using modern agricultural methods, the area is fast developing into Brazil's breadbasket, cultivating soy, corn, rice and cotton in vast plantations. Huge cattle ranches also abound.

Mato Grosso is still home to a large population of indigenous Brazilians. Several tribes remain in northern Mato Grosso, living as they have for centuries. The Erikbatsa, noted for their fine featherwork, live near Fontanilles and Juima; the Nhambikuraa are near Padroal; and the Cayabi live near Juara. The only tribe left in the Pantanal still subsisting by hunting and fishing is the Bororo. There are also the Cinta Larga Indians of Parque Indígena Aripuanã and the tribes under the care of FUNAI in the Parque Indígena do Xingu, which was set up in the 1950s as a safe haven for several groups of Indians.

Climate

Given its geographic diversity, the climate varies considerably throughout Mato Grosso. In the north, Cuiabá remains hot and humid year-round, with marked rainfall from October through to March. Just 1½ hours north, in the higher Chapada dos Guimarães, you can expect much cooler temperatures year-round. In Mato Grosso do Sul, cold fronts coming up from the south during winter can cause dramatic temperature drops. In the Pantanal, expect the most rainfall from October to March. The climate here is generally hot and humid, but it can get cold at night during winter as cold fronts push up from the south.

National Parks

Deep in the Pantanal is the isolated Parque Nacional do Pantanal, a 135,000-hectare national park encompassing the confluence of the mighty Paraguay and Cuiabá Rivers. It's usually only visited by researchers, as access is by boat only. Most foreign travelers experience the Pantanal outside the park.

The 33,000-hectare Parque Nacional Chapada dos Guimarães (p384) is located in the tablelands that mark the western edge of the Brazilian central plateau. It has several excellent walks to waterfalls and caves, or you can hire guides to lead you on overnight excursions. The park is only 1½ hours from Cuiabá.

Getting There & Away

The gateway cities to Mato Grosso are Cuiabá and Campo Grande, with daily flights to Rio, São Paulo and Brasília. The majority of travelers coming from Bolivia take the scenic (though white-knuckled) train journey from Santa Cruz to Quijarro and cross into the Brazilian town of Corumbá, which is connected by road to all points east. Mato Grosso also borders Paraguay in the south. There are regular bus services to the Paraguayan border from Campo Grande.

Getting Around

Although distances are great, Mato Grosso has a well-developed road network and regular bus services connect its towns and cities. Most travelers visiting the Pantanal will travel on either the Estrada Parque in Mato Grosso do Sul or the Transpantaneira in Mato Grosso. Both are dirt roads and conditions can be precarious. See p395 for details.

MATO GROSSO

Mato Grosso means *bundu*, savanna, bush, outback; an undeveloped thick scrub. Part of the highland plain that runs through Brazil's interior, Mato Grosso is a dusty land of rolling hills and some of the best fishing rivers in the world, such as the Araguaia.

To begin to appreciate the Mato Grosso's inaccessibility and vastness, read Peter Fleming's classic *Brazilian Adventure*, which also happens to be one of the funniest travel books ever written. Fleming tells the story of his quest to find the famous British explorer Colonel Fawcett, who disappeared in Mato Grosso in 1925 while searching for the hidden city of gold.

CUIABÁ

☎ 0xx65 / pop 481,000

Cuiabá is a frontier boom town. During the 1970s and '80s, the population grew at 14% annually (a national record) as vast tracts of land were opened up for agriculture. The population explosion has tailed off in recent years, but Cuiabá is still one of Brazil's fastest-growing cities. It has been named the *boca de sertão* (mouth of the backlands).

Cuiabá is a lively place and a good starting point for excursions to the Pantanal and Chapada dos Guimarães. It also has some interesting historic and cultural attractions.

History

In 1719 a Paulista, Pascoal Moreira Cabral, was hunting Indians along the Rio Cuiabá when he found gold. A gold rush followed, but many of those seeking gold never reached the new settlement at Cuiabá. Traveling more than 3000km from São Paulo by river took five months; along the way, gold seekers found little food, many mosquitoes, dangerous rapids, lengthy portages, disease and incredible heat.

With the end of the gold boom and the decay of the mines, Cuiabá would have disappeared, except that the soil along the Rio Cuiabá allowed subsistence agriculture, while the river itself provided fish.

By 1835 the town was the capital of Mato Grosso but, apart from a brief resurgence as a staging point for the war against Paraguay in the 1860s, it remained a backwater. Today, thanks mostly to the construction of Brasília and the consequent land development, Cuiabá has finally been propelled into the modern world.

Orientation

The city is actually two sister cities separated by the Rio Cuiabá: Old Cuiabá and Várzea Grande (where the airport is located, by the Rio Cuiabá). The center of the city is approximately 2.5km north of the river. The bus station is 3km north of the center.

Information

EMERGENCY
Ambulance (☎ 192)
Fire department (☎ 193)
Police (☎ 190)

INTERNET ACCESS
Point One (Map p382; ☎ 623 5120; Av Mato Grosso 96A; per hr US$1; ☺ 8:30am-midnight Mon-Sat, 1pm-1am Sun) You'll love the air-con.

MEDICAL SERVICES
Hospital Geral (☎ 616 7000; Rua 13 de Junho 2101)

MONEY
There are ATMs at the airport for Visa cash withdrawals. In town, you're better off changing at one of the currency exchanges than paying the Banco do Brasil's hefty commissions.
Banco do Brasil (Map p382; Rua Getúlio Vargas 915; ☺ 11am-4pm) Has Visa and MasterCard ATMs.
Bradesco (Rua Barão de Melgaço 3475; ☺ 11am-4pm Mon-Fri) Has a Visa ATM.
Mato Câmbio (Map p382; Rua Comandante Costa 465; ☺ 8am-6pm Mon-Fri, 8am-noon Sat)
Ourominas (Map p382; Rua Cándidi Mariano 401; ☺ 8am-5pm Mon-Fri, 8am-noon Sat)

POST
Post office (Map p382; Praça da República 101; ☺ 9am-5pm Mon-Fri, 9am-noon Sat)

TOURIST INFORMATION
The tourist office in the Praça da República is now closed. Your best sources of information are the travel agencies.

TRAVEL AGENCIES
Anaconda (☎ 624 4142; www.anacondapantanal.com .br; Av Isaac Povoas 606; ☺ 9am-6pm Mon-Fri, 9am-noon Sat) Organizes city tours as well as tours to the Pantanal, Chapada dos Guimarães and the Amazon.

CUIABÁ

0 ___ 8 km
0 ___ 4 miles

To Chapada dos Guimarães

MT 010
MT 251

Bus Station

Av do Líbano
Av Hist Rubens de Mendonça
Av Getúlio Vargas
Av João G Monteiro
Av Sen Metello
Av Miguel Sutil

See Central Cuiabá Map (p382)

Rio Coxipó
Contorno Rodoviária
Av Fernando Cda Costa

Várzea Grande

To Poconé
Av Ulisses Pompeu de Campos

Marechal Rondon Airport

MT 163
MT 364
MT 040

To Brasília; Campo Grande

Est do Capão Grande
Av Archia Santana
Rio Cuiabá

SIGHTS & ACTIVITIES	(p381)
Aquário Municipal	(see 3)
Mercado de Peixes	1 A2
Museu do Índio	2 B2
Museu do Rio Cuiabá	3 A2

| SLEEPING | (pp381–3) |
| Skala Palace Hotel | 4 A1 |

| EATING | (p383) |
| O Regionalíssimo | 5 A2 |

| ENTERTAINMENT | (pp383–4) |
| Haus Bier | 6 A2 |

| SHOPPING | (p384) |
| Casa de Artesão | (see 5) |

Confiança (☎ 314 2700; Av São Sebastião 2852; ☼ 9am-5pm Mon-Sat) Good for airline and bus tickets. Also books Pantanal lodges.

Sights

PALÁCIO DA INSTRUÇÃO
An interesting colonial mansion on the Praça da República houses three **museums** (Map p382; ☎ 321 3391; admission US$0.50; ☼ 8am-noon & 2-5pm Mon-Fri): history, natural history and anthropology. The history museum has some fascinating old photos of the 1860s war between Brazil and Paraguay; the natural history museum has lots of rocks and stuffed animals; but the anthropology section is the best, with lots of colorful Indian headdresses, clubs and arrows.

MUSEU DO ÍNDIO
The **Indian museum** (Map p380; ☎ 615 8489; Av Fernando Correia da Costa; admission US$1; ☼ 7:30-11:30am & 1:30-5:30pm Tue-Fri, 7:30-11:30am Sat) has exhibits of the Xavante, Bororo and Karajá tribes and is well worth a visit. It is in the grounds of the university, which also has a small **zoo**, where you can check out the Pantanal creatures, including some you may not see easily in the wild, such as otters. To get there, catch a No 406 Jd Universitário bus, on Av Tenente Coronel Duarte.

AQUÁRIO MUNICIPAL
The **old fish market** (Map p380; ☎ 623 1440; Av Beira Rio s/n; ☼ 9am-6pm Tue-Sun) along the riverfront has been restored and now houses an aquarium, museum and art gallery. The **aquarium** (admission US$0.50) houses around 45 species of the region's fish, including pintado, piranha and curimatá. It's about 2.5km from the center.

MERCADO DE PEIXES
Close to the aquarium, the **fish market** (Map p380) by the bridge is worth a visit, at least before the heat of the day. It's interesting not so much as a place to shop but as a venue to look at the people and their products.

SANTO ANTÔNIO DE LEVERGER
Cuiabános go to enjoy the river beaches from June to October at **Santo Antônio de Leverger**, also the site of Mato Grosso's best Carnaval. It's on the Rio Cuiabá, 28km south of Cuiabá in the direction of Barão de Melgaço. To get there, take a 'Santo Antônio' bus from Av Isaac Póvoas in the center.

Tours
For details about excursions from Cuiabá into the Pantanal, see p391.

Anaconda (☎ 624 4142; www.anacondapantanal.com.br; Av Isaac Povoas 606; ☼ 9am-6pm Mon-Fri, 9am-noon Sat) is a travel agency that offers a wide variety of tours apart from its Pantanal ones, including one that takes in three different ecosystems – the Pantanal, *cerrado* (savanna) and the Amazon. If you don't have time to visit Bonito in the south or don't like crowds, an excellent alternative is to spend a couple of days at the Recanto Ecológico Lagoa Azul. You can snorkel with the fishes in the crystal waters of the Rio Salobra and visit a blue lake that's as spectacular as the one near Bonito.

Festivals
The **Festa de São Benedito** takes place during the first week of July at the Igreja NS do Rosário and the Capela de São Benedito. The holiday has a more Umbanda than Catholic flavor; it's celebrated with traditional foods such as *bolos de queijo* (cheese balls) and *bolos de arroz* (rice balls), and colorful regional dances.

Sleeping
Some addresses include 's/n' *(sem número)*, which means 'without number.'

Pousada Ecoverde (Map p382; ☎ 624 1386; www.ecoverdetours.com; Rua Pedro Celestino 391; s/d/tr US$7/10/14) Run by local guide Joel Souza and his family, this is a rustic but comfortable old house. It's a small oasis in the middle of the city, with a shady courtyard and garden, a library and laundry facilities. It's centrally located, two blocks north of Praça Alencastro in the old part of town.

Amazon Plaza Hotel (Map p382; ☎ 2121 2000; www.amazonph.com.br; Av Getúlio Vargas 600; s/d US$35/42; P ✗ ☐ ☎) Recently refurbished and in an excellent location. Highly recommended.

Mato Grosso Palace (Map p382; ☎ 614 7000; www.hotelmatogrosso.com.br; Rua Joaquim Murtinho 170; s/d US$45/60; P ✗ ✗ ☐) Recently renovated, this is the best hotel in the center of Cuiabá. It has everything but a pool.

CENTRAL CUIABÁ

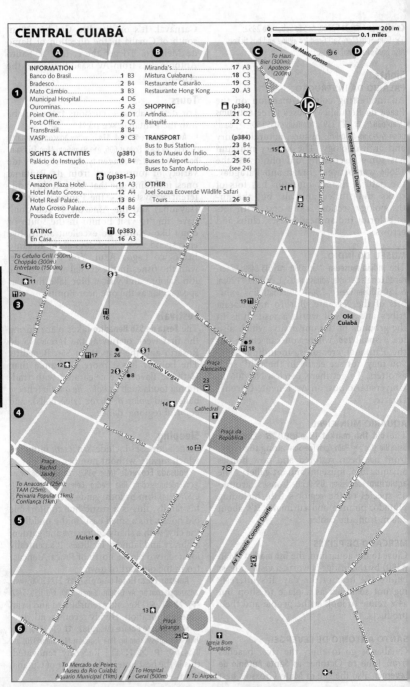

0 ──────── 200 m
0 ──────── 0.1 miles

A **B** **C** **D**

INFORMATION
Banco do Brasil.............................1 B3
Bradesco.......................................2 B4
Mato Câmbio.................................3 B3
Municipal Hospital........................4 D6
Ouriminas......................................5 A3
Point One......................................6 D1
Post Office.....................................7 C5
TransBrasil.....................................8 B4
VASP..9 C3

SIGHTS & ACTIVITIES   (p381)
Palácio do Instrução......................10 B4

SLEEPING   (pp381–3)
Amazon Plaza Hotel.......................11 A3
Hotel Mato Grosso.........................12 A4
Hotel Real Palace...........................13 B6
Mato Grosso Palace.......................14 B4
Pousada Ecoverde.........................15 C2

EATING   (p383)
En Casa..16 A3

Miranda's.......................................17 A3
Mistura Cuiabana............................18 C3
Restaurante Casarão......................19 C3
Restaurante Hong Kong.................20 A3

SHOPPING   (p384)
Artíndia...21 C2
Baiquité...22 C2

TRANSPORT   (p384)
Bus to Bus Station..........................23 B4
Bus to Museu do Índio...................24 C5
Buses to Airport.............................25 B6
Buses to Santo Antonio...........(see 24)

OTHER
Joel Souza Ecoverde Wildlife Safari
   Tours...26 B3

To Haus
Bier (300m);
Apoteose
(200m)

Av Mato Grosso

Rua Pedro Celestino

Rua Tenente Coronel Duarte

Rua Bandeirantes

Rua Erik Ricardo Franco

Rua Voluntários da Pátria

Old
Cuiabá

To Getúlio Grill (500m);
Choppão (300m);
Entretanto (1500m)

Rua Barão de Melgaço

Rua Campo Grande

Rua Cândido Mariano

Rua Pedro Celestino

Rua Batista das Neves

Rua Comandante Costa

Av Getúlio Vargas

Praça
Alencastro

Rua Erik Ricardo Franco

Rua Galdino Pimentel

Cathedral

Travessia João Diaz

Praça
Rachid
Jaudy

To Anaconda (25m);
TAM (25m);
Peixaria Popular (1km);
Confiança (1km)

Rua Antônio Maria

Praça da
República

Rua Manoel Coimbra

Market

Avenida Isaac Póvoas

Rua 13 de Junho

Av Tenente Coronel Duarte

Rua Domingos Ferreira

Rua Manoel Garcia Velho

Rua Joaquim Murtinho

Praça
Ipiranga

Igreja Bom
Despácho

Rua Francisco de Siqueira

Travessia Tereira Mendes

To Mercado de Peixes;
Museu do Rio Cuiabá;
Aquario Municipal (1km)

To Hospital
Geral (500m)

To Airport

Hotel Mato Grosso (Map p382; ☎ 614 7000; Rua Comandante Costa 2522; s/d US$15/20; 🔌 🍴 🐾) A good choice and a favorite with travelers, this place has small but clean *apartamentos* (rooms with private bathroom).

Skala Palace Hotel (Map p380; ☎ 621 3067; Av Jules Rimet 26; s/d US$12/15; 🐾) It's directly opposite the bus station and a good option if you're just overnighting or arrive late on the bus. The comfortable *apartamentos* are good value. It's worth asking about discounts.

Hotel Real Palace (Map p382; ☎ 321 5375; Praça Ipiranga 102; s/d US$15/20) Has enormous *apartamentos* and a good breakfast.

Eating & Drinking

The center is almost deserted at night, but there are good restaurants nearby on Av Getúlio Vargas.

Mistura Cuiabana (☎ 624 1127; cnr Rua Padre Celestino & Rua Candido Mariano; meals per kg US$2; 🕐 11am-2pm Mon-Fri) A good cheap lunch spot right in the center.

Peixaria Popular (☎ 322 5471; Av São Sebastião 2324; dishes US$5-15; 🕐 11am-midnight Mon-Sat) An award-winning restaurant specializing in fish. The US$10 lunch special for two is five courses!

O Regionalissimo (Map p380; ☎ 623 6881; Rua 13 de Junho 27; meals per kg US$4; 🕐 11:15am-2pm Tue-Sun) Serves excellent regional food per kilogram – lots of fish and the sweetest of sweets. Next to the Casa do Artesão.

Restaurante Hong Kong (Map p382; ☎ 622 0535; Av Getúlio Vargas 647; dishes US$4-8; 🕐 11am-3pm & 6-11pm Tue-Sun) Offers a tasty all-you-can-eat Chinese buffet for US$4 per person.

Getúlio Grill (☎ 624 9992; Av Getúlio Vargas 1147; dishes US$10-25; 🕐 11:30am-2:30pm & 5:30pm-1am Tue-Fri, 11:30am-1am Sat & Sun) An upmarket bar/restaurant popular with young Cuiabános. There's a sushi bar, too, if you're craving raw fish.

Choppão (☎ 623 9101; Praça 8 de Abril s/n) A classic Cuiabá eatery. Obscenely large meals of meat or fish with salad cost US$11 for two people, and you can drink the coldest *chope* (draft beer) in town in specially iced tankards.

Entertainment

There are two main nightlife clusters in town, along Av Getúlio Vargas and around Av Mato Grosso.

Apoteose (☎ 623 5159; Av Mato Grosso 442; cover charge US$3; 🕐 11:30pm-5am Thu-Sat) A popular dance club for teens and 20-somethings.

Deck Avenida (☎ 623 7776; Av Rúbens de Mendonça 635; 🕐 6pm-late Mon-Fri, noon-late Sat & Sun) Lively place. Good for a meal as well.

Haus Bier (Map p380; ☎ 621 5296; Av Mato Grosso 1000; 🕐 4-11:30pm) This place is good for a beer and has live music. Avoid the mint-flavored *chope*.

Entretanto (☎ 623 3786; Rua Marechal Floriano 401; cover charge US$1; 🕐 7pm-1am Wed-Sun) Trendy

---

PANTANAL CUISINE

Pantaneiros – the local Pantanal folk – make good use of regional ingredients in preparing their delicacies. You'll find lots of restaurants offering regional specialties on your travels in the area – stop in and try some.

In the northern Pantanal, the cuisine is decidedly fishy. Pacu, dourado and pintado are the most consumed fish, and they come *frito* (fried), *grelhado* (grilled), *assado* (baked) or *defumado* (smoked). Both dourado and pacu have lots of small bones, but they separate easily when baked slowly. Pacu is often baked and served with an *escabeche* sauce consisting of onions, tomatoes and peppers. Another favorite fish is pintado, excellent when spiced with rough salt and pepper and grilled. One specialty is *peixe á urucum*, where the chosen fish is served topped with spices, condensed milk, coconut milk and melted mozzarella. Piranha soup is another exotic favorite, considered an aphrodisiac by the Pantaneiros.

In the southern Pantanal, the dishes are more strongly influenced by the cattle and grains produced in the area. A specialty here is *arroz de carreteiro* – rice with sun-dried beef served with fried manioc and banana. Another typical dish is *galinha caipira* – chicken served with white rice and pequi, a small yellow fruit of the *cerrado*. Don't bite into the pequi – its seed contains lots of spines!

Pantanal desserts are sweet and tasty. Some popular ones are *furrundu* – a mixture of papaya and sugarcane – and ice cream made from bocaiúva, another local fruit.

THE CENTRAL WEST

bar filled with Cuiaba's young, restless and wealthy. On Wednesday night, ladies get in free.

Shopping

Artíndia (Map p382; ☎ 623 1675; Rua Pedro Celestino 301; ⏰ 8-11am & 1:30-5pm Mon-Fri) Good range of Indian baskets, bows and arrows, and jewelry.

Casa do Artesão (Map p380; ☎ 316 3151; cnr Rua 13 de Junho & Rua Senador Mello; ⏰ 8am-6pm Mon-Fri, 9am-4pm Sat & Sun) Local handicrafts, including ceramics, woodcarvings, straw baskets, paintings and woven hammocks.

Baiquité Artesanato (Map p382; ☎ 624 9480; Rua Pedro Celestino 300; ⏰ 8am-6pm Mon-Fri, 8am-3pm Sat) Large variety of local handicrafts at reasonable prices.

Getting There & Away

There are flights between Cuiabá and many airports in Brazil (with the notable omission of Corumbá in Mato Grosso do Sul) by **TAM** (☎ 682 3650), **Varig** (☎ 682 1140), **Gol** (☎ 682 1666), **VASP** (☎ 682 3737), and **Trip** (☎ 682 2555) for flights to Alta Floresta.

Frequent buses make the trip to Poconé (US$5, 2½ hours, six daily); the first leaves at 6am. To Barão de Melgaço (US$7, 4½ hours, two daily), buses leave at 7:30am and 3pm. For Chapada dos Guimarães (US$9, two hours, 12 daily), there are buses every hour from 7am, but take an early bus if you're doing a day trip.

Buses go to Cáceres (US$9, 3½ hours, six daily), with connections to Santa Cruz in Bolivia. Porto Velho is a long (US$22, 24 hours, two daily) ride. There are buses daily to Goiânia (US$27, 13 hours, four daily) and Brasília (US$33, 16 hours, four daily) – most of them stop in Barra do Garças (US$18, seven hours), where you have access to the Rio Araguaia. Most of the buses to Campo Grande (US$24, 10 hours, eight daily) stop at Coxim (US$14, seven hours). To Alta Floresta (US$35, 13 hours, four daily), the first bus leaves at 8am.

Getting Around

Marechal Rondon airport (☎ 614 2500) is in Varzea Grande, 7km from Cuiabá. To catch the local bus to town, turn left as you leave the airport and walk to the Las Velas Hotel. Opposite the hotel entrance, catch a Jardim Marajoara, 24 de Dezembro or Pireneus bus. A taxi costs US$8.

Cuiabá's **bus station** (☎ 621 3629) is 3km north of the center on the highway toward Chapada dos Guimarães. From inside the bus station, you can get a Centro bus to Praça Alencastro. More frequent buses marked 'Centro' leave from outside the bus station and can drop you along Av Isaac Póvoas. A ticket taxi from inside the bus station costs US$4 – or if you're traveling light, grab a mototaxi outside for around US$2.

All the car-rental places have branches in the center and in or near the airport. There are often promotional rates, so shop around. **Unidas** (☎ 682 4052) and **Localiza** (☎ 624 7979) are a couple of reliable companies. The best car for the Pantanal is the Volkswagen Gol. On average, a rental car with unlimited kilometers will cost around US$30 a day.

CHAPADA DOS GUIMARÃES

☎ 0xx65 / pop 15,700

After the Pantanal, the Parque Nacional da Chapada dos Guimarães is Mato Grosso's leading attraction. The park is located on a rocky plateau 64km northeast of Cuiabá and 800m higher, offering a cool change from the state capital. The region is reminiscent of the American Southwest and surprisingly different from the typical Mato Grosso terrain. The town of the same name is a convenient base for exploring the park and surrounding areas.

The area surrounding the park has numerous attractions. About 41km northeast of Chapada town is the 1100m-long **Aroe Jari** cavern and, in another cave close by, the **Lagoa Azul** (Blue Lake). On the way from Cuiabá to Chapada town, you pass **Rio dos Peixes**, **Rio Mutaca** and **Rio Claro**, which are popular weekend bathing spots for Cuiabános. The sheer 80m drop called **Portão do Inferno** (Hell's Gate) is also unforgettable. Take a waterfall shower at **Salgadeira**, on the road to Cuiabá, and peek into the chapel of **NS de Santãna**, a strange mixture of Portuguese and French baroque.

Parque Nacional da Chapada dos Guimarães

The two exceptional sights inside the park are the 60m **Véu de Noiva** (Bridal Veil) falls and the Cidade de Pedra (Stone City). There is a **visitors' center** (☎ 301 1133; admission US$1; ⏰ 8am-5pm Tue-Sun) at the park entrance.

The major attraction is the impressive **Véu de Noiva**, an 86m free-falling waterfall. It is around 15km west of the town of Chapada dos Guimarães. You can get off the bus from Cuiabá and walk from the road, spend a couple of hours there, then flag down the next bus coming through to the town of Chapada dos Guimarães. Start walking downhill over the bluff, slightly to your right. A small trail leads to a magical **lookout**, perched on top of rocks with the canyon below. This is Chapada's most dazzling place.

The **Cidade de Pedra** has wonderful vistas and rock formations reminiscent of stone temples. It's 20km north of Chapada town along the road to Água Fria. The turnoff to Água Fria is 6km west of Chapada town on Hwy MT-251.

Mirante

The Mirante (Lookout) is the unofficial geographic center of South America. It's outside the national park, 8km from the town of Chapada dos Guimarães. Take the last road in Chapada on your right and go 8km; you'll see a dirt road. The rim of the canyon is a couple of hundred meters away. The view is stupendous; off to your right you can see the Cuiabá skyline. There is no public transportation to Mirante.

Tours

If you don't have a car, your best bet is to take an excursion with **Eco Turismo Cultural** (☎ 301 1393; www.chapadadosguimaraes.com.br, in Portuguese; Praça Dom Wunibaldo 57, Chapada dos Guimarães; ☉ 8am-noon & 1-5pm Mon-Sat, 8-11:30am Sun). It runs four excursions: to the national

park (which contains the most spectacular waterfalls); to the Lagoa Azul and Aroe Jari cavern; to the Cidade de Pedra; and to Água Fria, a diamond-mining town 40km from Chapada. All tours cost US$100 for up to five people (US$20 per person), except Aroe Jari cavern, which is US$115 (US$23 per person) for up to five people. Prices don't include lunch or park entrance fees.

If you're driving, drop by the **Secretária de Turismo** (☎ 301 2045; Rua Penn Gomes s/n; ☉ 8am-6pm Mon-Fri, 8:30-11:30am & 2-5pm Sat & Sun). A useful map is available – you'll need it!

Sleeping & Eating

There is camping with good facilities at Salgadeira, just before the climb into the Chapada park. Chapada town has plenty of accommodations.

Pousada Bom Jardim (☎ 301 1244; Praça Dom Wunibaldo 641; s/d US$12/22; **P**) This is the best cheapie in town. It's right on the main square, with friendly service and a decent breakfast. It's a favorite with backpackers.

Turismo Hotel (☎ 301 1176; www.chapadadosguimaraes.com.br/hotelturismo, in Portuguese; Rua Fernando Correo Costa 1065; s/d US$10/20; **P** **X** **R**) A spotless place run by a German family. The traditional *café colonial* breakfast spread is excellent.

Solar do Inglês (☎ 301 1389; www.chapadadosguimaraes.com.br/solardoingles, in Portuguese; Rua Cipriano Curvo 142; s/d US$43/55; **P** **X** **R**) A charming place with an English flavor. Décor includes English carpets and displays of fine china. It even serves afternoon tea (included in the price). This hotel doesn't accept anyone under 14 years old.

THE HARPY EAGLE'S FIGHT FOR SURVIVAL

The harpy eagle is the world's largest eagle and the most powerful predatory bird in South America. It's threatened by deforestation, destruction of nesting sites and poaching, and since 1992 just nine nests have been confirmed in Guyana, 10 in Venezuela, eight in Panama – and one in Brazil, in northern Mato Grosso. Harpy eagles are about 85cm long and have a wingspan of almost 2m. Females are one-third larger than males and weigh from 7kg to 9kg. The female's powerful talons are up to 12cm long – as long as the claws of a grizzly bear – all the better to hunt their prey, which includes sloths, monkeys, deer and reptiles. Harpy eagles mate for life and build large nests very high (40m and above) in the forest canopy. Females lay one or two eggs in a clutch, but only one survives. Both parents care for the young. Sure, they're hunters, but they love their kids!

If you're serious about your birds, you'll want to see the harpy eagle nest, which is close to **Pousada Currupira das Araras** (☎ 0xx65-321 1066), near the town of Barra do Bugres in the Serra das Araras, 169km northwest of Cuiabá.

Pousada Penhasco (☎ 301 1555; www.penhasco .com.br; Av Penhasco; s/d US$60/65; P ✻ ⌧) This resort hotel, 2.5km from town, has great views and all the amenities, including a swimming pool with waterfall and video karaoke.

Cheiro Verde (☎ 301 3078; Rua Cipriano Curvo 729; meals per kg US$3; ☺ 10:30am-4pm) A decent perkilo joint with a good variety of salads. It's run by a nutritionist.

Samambaia (☎ 301 1843; Rua Dr Penn Gomes 532; dishes US$2-10; ☺ 11am-8pm Mon-Sat & 8am-5pm Sun) A good place for some regional home cooking. Most dishes will do for two easily.

Restaurante Morro dos Ventos (☎ 301 1030; dishes US$5-15; ☺ 8am-6pm) Worth a splurge. It's 4km east of town along Hwy MT-251 in the direction of Campo Verde. It has spectacular views across the Morro dos Ventos, as well as excellent regional cuisine.

Getting There & Away

Buses leave Cuiabá's bus station for Chapada town (US$9, two hours) hourly from 7am to 7pm. In the other direction, the first bus leaves Chapada town at 6am and the last at 6pm.

ALTA FLORESTA

☎ 0xx65 / pop 47,000

Alta Floresta, 873km north of Cuiabá, is situated in the extreme north of Mato Grosso, at the edge of the pristine southern Amazon rain forest. The area is considered one of the best in the Brazilian Amazon for spotting rare birds and mammals, including the endangered white-nosed bearded saki monkey, brown titi monkey, tapir, giant river otter, three-toed sloth and five species of macaws.

Alta Floresta is the end of the road: beyond it to the north is the vast expanse of the jungle. The town itself has no attractions and has grown rapidly as an agricultural and logging center since its foundation in the early 1970s.

Sleeping & Eating

Many visitors to the area are naturalists on expensive package tours to isolated jungle lodges, but independent travelers will find a few good accommodations in town.

Lisboa Palace (☎ 521 2876; www.hotellisboa.com .br; Av Jaime Verríssimo de Campos 251, Setor C; s/d US$18/25; P ✻) This is a clean, modern hotel; its VIP suite (US$40) has a spa bath.

Floresta Amazônica (☎ 512 7100; www.crista linolodge.com.br/fah/english/apresentacao.htm; Av Perimetral Oeste 2001; s/d US$23/26; P ✻ ⌧ ☺) This place has a gorgeous garden and lovely apartments with balconies. Highly recommended. It's affiliated with the Cristalino Jungle Lodge.

Cristalino Jungle Lodge (☎ 521 1349; www.crista linolodge.com.br; s/d quartos US$40/80, s/d apartamentos US$53/90) On the banks of the Rio Cristalino (38km north of Alta Floresta) in a region rich in Amazon flora and fauna, the lodge offers a 50m-high observation tower and a number of small, well-maintained birdwatching trails. The lodge also employs bilingual guides for boat and hiking expeditions. Rates include all meals.

Papagaio Grill (☎ 521 1651; Av Ariosto da Riva 2905; dishes for 2 US$10; ☺ 11am-2pm & 5pm-midnight) On the main street, this restaurant is popular with locals and one of the better dining options in town. It has a varied menu, including tasty set lunches, delicious fish dishes and a choice of high-calorie cakes and pastries.

Getting There & Away

From Cuiabá, there are frequent buses to Alta Floresta (US$30, 13 hours, eight daily). **Trip** (☎ 0xx65-682 2555) flies from Cuiabá to Alta Floresta (US$130) Monday to Friday at 11:50am.

CÁCERES

☎ 0xx65 / pop 66,000

Languishing on the banks of the Rio Paraguay, Cáceres is a sleepy little town that's a favorite destination for anglers. It's an access point for a few Pantanal lodges and for Bolivia, but mostly it's a fishing town, especially during September, when it attracts 100,000 visitors for the world's biggest fishing competition.

Information

If you're traveling on to Corixio and the Bolivian border, get a Brazilian exit stamp from the **Federal Police** (☎ 223 1110; Av Getúlio Vargas; ☺ 7am-8pm), 4km from town, next to the *prefeitura* (city hall). If you need a yellow fever vaccination (you'll need one to get into Bolivia – also it would be a shame to get yellow fever, wouldn't it?), they are free at the **small clinic** (☺ 7:30am-8pm) next to the bus station.

Banco do Brasil (Rua José Dulce 234; 🕑 9am-3pm Mon-Fri) For currency and traveler's checks.

Bradesco (Rua José Dulce 183) Has Visa ATM.

Ontop Cybercafe (Praça Barão do Rio Branco 27; per hr US$1; 🕑 noon-11pm) Right in the main square, for Internet access.

Post office (Av 7 de Setembro; 🕑 9am-5pm Mon-Fri, 9am-noon Sat)

Sematur (☎ 223 5918; Rua Riachuelo 1; 🕑 7am-6pm Mon-Fri) For help hiring boats and arranging accommodations in the Pantanal, this local tourist office is a good place to start.

Sleeping & Eating

Capri Hotel (☎ 223 1771; Rua Getúlio Vargas 99; s/d US$5/10; 🕮) Basic and clean. Spacious rooms. It's the best place near the bus station.

Rio Hotel (☎ 223 3084; Praça Major João Carlos; s/d with private bathroom US$12/20; 🕮) A good choice closer to the river and the center. Also has cheaper *quartos* (rooms without private bathroom).

Turbo (☎ 223 1984; Av São Luís 1399; s/d US$15/23; 🅿 🕮 🍸) It's 4km from the center at the turn-off from the BR-70 and a great option if you have transport. You'll be loving that pool.

Ipanema (☎ 223 1177; Rua General Osório 540; s/d US$23/38; 🅿 🕮 🍸) Closer to the center with all the amenities needed to keep cool in the tropics. Highly recommended.

All the action happens around the riverfront and nearby Praça Barão do Rio Branco, where there are many restaurants and bars.

Restaurante Kaskata Flutuante (☎ 223 2916; Rua Coronel José Dulce; dishes per person around US$10; 🕑 11am-midnight) The best floating restaurant in town, with an extensive menu of regional fish dishes.

Corimba (☎ 223 3002; Rua 6 de Outubro 27; pizzas US$4; 🕑 10:30am-midnight) An upmarket pizzeria and *chopperia* (beer hall) with tables set up outside overlooking the river.

Restaurant Hispano (☎ 223 1486; Praça Barão do Rio Branco 64; meals per kg US$4; 🕑 7am-3:30pm Mon-Sat) In the center, it's a decent per-kilo restaurant with river views.

Getting There & Away

The bus station is 10 blocks north of the riverfront. Frequent buses make the journey between Cuiabá and Cáceres (US$8, 3½ hours, six daily). There are also bus services to Porto Velho. For information on buses to Bolivia, see p701.

In the past, a steady stream of travelers arrived in Cáceres to take cement barges along the Rio Paraguay to Corumbá. These days, you'll need a lot of luck and plenty of time to hang around: there are no regular itineraries and passenger travel on cargo boats is officially not allowed. Your best bet is to ask around the port; if you do find someone willing to take you downstream to Corumbá, the trip takes three to six days.

POCONÉ

☎ 0xx65 / pop 22,000

The main entry point to the Pantanal for travelers heading south from Cuiabá, Poconé marks the beginning of the Transpantaneira 'highway.' Poconé still has a frontier feel, and stories of finding nuggets after heavy rains and hunting jaguar abound. The locals, many of whom are descended from the original tribe in the area, the Beripoconeses, have a strong sense of tradition.

In May, Poconé celebrates the week-long **Semana do Fazendeiro e do Cavalo Pantaneiro** with a cattle fair and rodeos.

ALLIGATOR'S BACK ON THE MENU

Long a staple of Indians and river folk, *jacaré* (alligator) is back on the menu for the rest of us. Its chicken-like texture and lack of strong flavor means it readily absorbs spices and can be used in many dishes. It's on the menu at many regional restaurants in the Pantanal and Bonito.

Farmed legally since 2000, *jacaré* are proving to be a lucrative business. There are now 50 *jacaré* farms around Cáceres in Mato Grosso and they have big plans to increase production, claiming it is more lucrative than cattle farming. At present there are approximately 45,000 *jacaré* in captivity. Farms 'process' 100 animals daily, exporting 2000 skins and 3000kg of meat each month to domestic and international markets such as the USA and Europe.

At the last fishing festival in Cáceres they were promoting such gastronomic delights as *jacaré* with banana and *jacaré* pâté. While others were also promoting soy products such as soybread and soy pâté, locals preferred the *jacaré* meat.

Orientation

When you arrive at the bus station, you are 2km from the start of the dirt road that becomes the Transpantaneira; the center of town is about halfway. To get there, grab a cab or mototaxi. If you feel like walking, turn left as you leave the bus station, walk two blocks down Av Anibol de Toledo to Rua Antônio João, then turn right. Walk up seven blocks – you'll be in the large town square (more like a rectangle). The Hotel Skala is 100m to your right. On your left, behind the church, is the road that leads to the beginning of the Transpantaneira. There are a few pousadas (guesthouses) here.

Information

Banco do Brasil (Rua Campos Sales 449) Has a Visa ATM.
BiLink Informatica (Rua Cel Salvador Marques 316; per hr US$2; ⊗ 8am-9pm Mon-Fri, 8am-4pm Sat) Internet access.
Hospital (☎ 345 1963; Rua Dom Aquino s/n)
Police (☎ 345 1456) Situated at the beginning of the Transpantaneira.
Post office (Rua Cel Salvador Marques 335)

Tours

Local boat captain **Gonçalo de Arruda** (☎ 345 1460; Rua 13 de Junho 50) offers boat trips from Poconé along the Rio Cuiabá as far as Porto Cercado. The *Laura Vicuña* sleeps around 20 people and trips cost US$30 per day per person (not including food and drinks). Drop a line over the side and you might end up with a big pintado (catfish) on your plate.

The boat is smallish and caters mostly to fishing tours. Take plenty of insect repellent, a mosquito net and water.

Sleeping & Eating

The best places to stay, especially if you're trying to organize a lift down the Transpantaneira, are a couple of kilometers out of town near the beginning of the road.

Hotel Skala (☎ 345 1407; Praça Bem Rondon 64; s/d US$10/14; ❄) In the middle of town, this is a reasonably comfortable option, with cool, dark rooms and a decent restaurant specializing in fish dishes.

Pousada Pantaneira (☎ 345 1630; per person US$8) The first place you'll pass heading out of town, Pantaneira is pretty basic, but the hotel restaurant serves a good *rodízio* (smorgasbord) for US$5.

Hotel Santa Cruz (☎ 345 1439; s/d US$14/25) This is just up the road, on the same side as Pousada Pantaneira. It is an attractively rustic place.

Petiscaria Shanandoah (☎ 345 2634; Praça Matriz) A popular pizza and burger joint with a dance floor upstairs where the town's young and restless dance the lambada Poconé-style – slower but still sexy.

Getting There & Away

There are buses from Cuiabá to Poconé (US$4, 2½ hours, six daily) from 6am to 7pm, and six in the opposite direction from 6am to 7:30pm. Get a window seat if you want to appreciate the vegetation typical of the Pantanal's outskirts: *pequís* (a five- to 15m-tall plant with a thick, twisted trunk, the fruit of which is used in lots of local dishes); *piúvas* (one of the Pantanal's commonest trees, covered in pink flowers between July and September); *babaçus* (palm trees covered in spines, the fruit, wood and fiber of which are highly valued by locals); *ipês* (another common tree of the Pantanal that's covered in yellow flowers between August and September); and *buritis* (a variety of palm that's frequently used as an ornamental tree in Brazil's parks).

THE PANTANAL

The Amazon may attract more fame and glory, but the Pantanal is a better place to see wildlife. In the Amazon, the animals hide in the dense foliage, but in the open spaces of the Pantanal, wildlife is visible to the most casual observer. If you like to see animals in their natural environment, the Pantanal – with the greatest concentration of fauna in the New World – should not be missed.

A vast wetlands in the center of South America, the Pantanal is more than half the size of France – some 230,000 sq km. Something less than 100,000 sq km of this is in Bolivia and Paraguay; the rest is in Brazil, split between the states of Mato Grosso and Mato Grosso do Sul.

The Pantanal has few people and no towns. Distances are so great and ground transport so poor that people get around in small airplanes and motorboats; 4WD travel is restricted by the seasons. The only

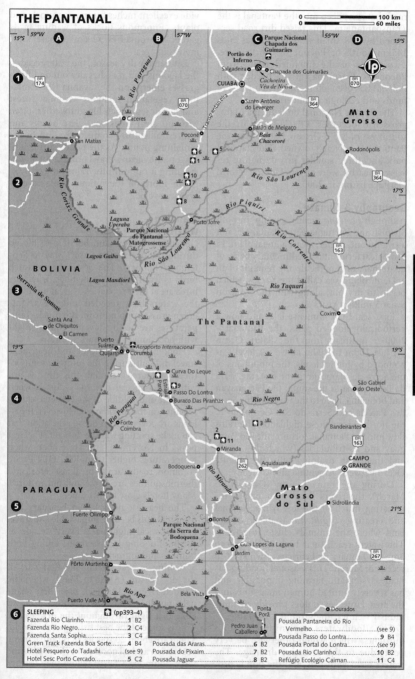

THE PANTANAL

| 0 | 100 km |
| 0 | 60 miles |

SLEEPING (pp393–4)

Fazenda Rio Clarinho	1 B2
Fazenda Rio Negro	2 C4
Fazenda Santa Sophia	3 C4
Green Track Fazenda Boa Sorte	4 B4
Hotel Pesqueiro do Tadashi	(see 9)
Hotel Sesc Porto Cercado	5 C2
Pousada das Araras	6 B2
Pousada do Pixaim	7 B2
Pousada Jaguar	8 B2
Pousada Pantaneira do Rio Vermelho	(see 9)
Pousada Passo do Lontra	9 B4
Pousada Portal do Lontra	(see 9)
Pousada Rio Clarinho	10 B2
Refúgio Ecológio Caiman	11 C4

road that runs deep into the Pantanal is the Transpantaneira. This raised dirt road sectioned by 118 small wooden bridges ends 145km south of Poconé, at Porto Jofre. Two-thirds of the intended route from Poconé to Corumbá (at the border with Bolivia) has been left incomplete for lack of funds and ecological concerns.

The Parque Nacional do Pantanal Matogrossense occupies 1350 sq km in the southwest of Mato Grosso, but most of the Pantanal is privately owned. The national park and three smaller private nature reserves nearby were given Unesco World Heritage listing in 2000.

Geography & Climate

Although *pantano* means 'swamp' in both Spanish and Portuguese, the Pantanal is not a swamp but, rather, a vast alluvial plain. In geological terms, it is a sedimentary basin of quaternary origin, the drying remains of an ancient inland sea called the Xaraés, which began to dry out, along with the Amazon Sea, 65 million years ago.

First sea, then immense lake and now a periodically flooded plain, the Pantanal – 2000km upstream from the Atlantic Ocean yet just 100m to 200m above sea level – is bounded by higher lands: the mountains of the Serra de Maracaju to the east, the Serra da Bodoquena to the south, the Paraguayan and Bolivian Chaco to the west and the Serra dos Parecis and Serra do São Geronimo to the north. From these highlands, the rains flow into the Pantanal, forming the Rio Paraguay and its tributaries (which flow south and then east, draining into the Atlantic Ocean between Argentina and Uruguay).

During the rainy season (October to March), the rivers flood their banks, inundating much of the low-lying Pantanal and creating *cordilheiras* (patches of dry land where the animals cluster together). The waters reach their high mark – up to 3m – in January or February, then start to recede in March. This seasonal flooding has made systematic farming impossible and has severely limited human incursions into the area. However, it does provide an enormously rich feeding ground for wildlife.

The floodwaters replenish the soil's nutrients, which would otherwise be very poor, due to the excessive drainage. The waters teem with fish, and the ponds provide excellent niches for many animals and plants. Enormous flocks of wading birds gather in rookeries several square kilometers in area.

Later in the dry season, the water recedes, the lagoons and marshes dry out and fresh grasses emerge on the savanna (the Pantanal's vegetation includes savanna, forest and meadows, which blend together, often with no clear divisions). The hawks and *jacarés* (alligators) compete for fish in the remaining ponds. As the ponds shrink and dry up, the *jacarés* crawl around for water, sweating it out until the rains return.

For more on the unique Pantanal ecosystem, see p62.

Planning
WHEN TO GO

Go whenever you can, but if possible go during the dry season (April/May to September/October). The best time to watch birds is from July to September, when the birds are at their rookeries in great numbers, the waters have receded and the bright-green grasses pop up from the muck. Temperatures are hot by day and cool by night with occasional short bursts of rain.

Flooding, incessant rains and heat make travel difficult during the rainy season (October to March), though this time is not without its special rewards – this is when the cattle and wildlife of the Pantanal clump together on the *cordilheiras*. However, the islands are covered with dense vegetation that can make spotting wildlife difficult. The heat peaks in November and December, when temperatures higher than 40°C (104°F) are common, roads turn to breakfast cereal, and the mosquitoes are fierce and out in force. Many hotels close at this time.

The heaviest rains fall in February and March. Roads become impassable and travel is a logistical nightmare. Every decade or so, the flooding is disastrous, killing both humans and animals.

Fishing is best during the first part of the dry season (April to May), when the flooded rivers settle back into their channels, but locals have been known to lasso 80kg fish right throughout the dry season. This is some of the best fishing in the world. There are about 20 species of piranha, many vegetarian and all good eating, as well as the tasty dourado, a feisty fellow that reaches upwards of 9kg. Other excellent catches include pacu, suribim, bagre, giripoca, piraputanga, piapara, cachara, pirancajuva and pintado, to name but a few.

Although hunting is not allowed, fishing – with the required permits – is encouraged between February and October. It is, however, prohibited during the *piracema* (breeding season) from November to the end of January. The Banco do Brasil branches in Cuiabá, Campo Grande and Coxim issue permits (US$7) valid for three months for fishing in the Pantanal. National fishing permits valid for one year are also available from **IBAMA offices** (Cuiabá ☎ 0xx65-644 1200, Campo Grande ☎ 0xx67-382 2966, Corumbá ☎ 0xx67-231 6096, Coxim ☎ 0xx67-291 2310).

WHAT TO BRING

You can't buy much in the Pantanal, so come prepared. The dry season is also the cooler season. Bring attire suitable for hot days, coolish nights, rain and mosquitoes. You'll need sunscreen, sunglasses, a hat, lightweight clothes, sneakers or boots, light rain gear and something warmer for the evening. Mosquito relief means long pants and long-sleeved shirts, vitamin B-12 and insect repellent.

Binoculars are your best friend in the Pantanal. Bring an alarm clock (to get up before sunrise), an audio recorder (for recording the wonderful bird calls) and a strong flashlight (to go searching for owls and anacondas after dark). Don't forget plenty of film, a camera and, if you're serious about photography, a tripod and a long lens (300mm is about right for wildlife).

HEALTH

According to local authorities, malaria has been eradicated from the Pantanal. There's probably still a very low risk of contracting malaria, so consult with a travel health expert for the latest information before you leave home. For more on malaria and other traveler's health concerns, see p708, or check out Lonely Planet's *Healthy Travel – Central & South America* by Isabelle Young.

There are medical services available in Cuiabá, Corumbá and Campo Grande.

Tours

There are three main approach routes to the Pantanal: via Cuiabá in Mato Grosso and via Corumbá or Campo Grande in Mato Grosso do Sul. You can arrange guided tours (or head off on your own) from any of these three towns.

Bringing tourists into the Pantanal is now a big business, and whether you arrive in Cuiabá, Corumbá, or Campo Grande you can expect to be approached by a guide fairly rapidly – at peak times you might even be stampeded. Some of these individuals are simply opportunists looking to make a buck out of Brazil's ecotourism, but there are still a few old-timers out there who work to protect the environment while sharing its tremendous diversity with visitors.

A good guide can enhance your Pantanal experience by spotting and identifying animal and bird species, explaining the diverse ecology and taking care of any hassles you may encounter along the way. Plus, if you're hoping to catch a glimpse of rarer animals such as anteaters, anacondas, otters, iguanas and jaguars, a guide is indispensable. A guide who is familiar with the area will also know the location of nests of rare birds.

It can be hard to tell the good from the bad, but here are some suggestions to ensure you have a safe and enjoyable trip:

- Resist making a snap decision, especially if you've just climbed off an overnight bus.
- Go to the local tourism office. Most can't give independent advice because they're government funded, but they do keep complaints books that you're free to peruse. There's a lot to be gleaned from other travelers' experiences.
- Remember that the owner or salesperson is not always your guide, and it's the guide you're going to be with in the wilderness for three to five days. Ask to meet your guide if possible.
- Try to get things in writing and don't hand over your cash to any go-betweens.
- Compare your options. Most operators work out of the local bus station or airport, so it's easy to shop around.

Of course there's no obligation to go with a tour operator. You can drive or hitchhike across the Transpantaneira road that starts in the northwest (Mato Grosso), or the Estrada Parque that loops around the south (Mato Grosso do Sul). You'll still see plenty of wildlife – many species of birds, jacarés, capybaras and the occasional deer – close to the road.

If time is a problem and money isn't, or if you'd just like a quality guide, contact **Focus Tours** (www.focustours.com) in the USA. Focus Tours specializes in nature tours and is active in trying to preserve the Pantanal. It can also offer advice if you're interested in volunteering to teach English to potential guides and help build rain-forest towers (minimum two-week commitment is required).

CUIABÁ

From Cuiabá, the capital of Mato Grosso, small tour operators arrange safaris into the Pantanal that include transportation, accommodations on farms, and guides.

Fortunately, while there is healthy competition between tour operators in Cuiabá, it's not as intense as in Mato Grosso do Sul. Tours from Cuiabá are generally well-organized trips.

Joel Souza Ecoverde Wildlife Safari Tours (Map p382; ☎ 0xx65-624 1386; www.ecoverdesafaritours.com; US$50 a day) offers bird-watching and nature tours, including accommodations on farms, meals, hikes and boat rides. You can also contact him at Pousada Ecoverde (p381). He speaks English, German and Spanish, and the tours are excellent.

Munir Nasr's Natureco (☎ 0xx65-321 1001; www.natureco.com.br; Rua Benedito Leite 570) is another highly recommended guide who organizes tours into the Pantanal.

Anaconda (☎ 0xx65-624 4142; www.anacondapantanal.com.br, in Portuguese; Av Isaac Póvoes 606) provides more upmarket Pantanal programs. It's highly organized and recommended.

CAMPO GRANDE

Many budget travelers choose to go on cheap three- to four-day tours into the southern Pantanal from Corumbá or Campo Grande. Most trips are better organized than in the past, but they are still rough-and-ready affairs. Accommodations are at basic lodges or bush camps in netted communal huts with hammocks or in tents. Food is generally OK, though you should take some extra snack food and water. You'll see lots of birds, capybaras and jacarés, but larger mammals are harder to spot.

All the budget tour operators operating in Mato Grosso do Sul offer similar packages at camps along Estrada Parque, a 117km stretch of dirt road through the region known as Nhecolândia. Estrada Parque runs off the main Campo Grande–Corumbá road (Hwy BR-262) at Buraco da Piranha, 72km from Corumbá and 324km from Campo Grande. The first stretch of Estrada Parque penetrates 47km into the Pantanal, before it doglegs back toward Corumbá. At Porto da Manga, a barge ferries vehicles over the Rio Paraguay before Estrada Parque rejoins Hwy BR-262 at Lampião Aceso, about 12km from Corumbá.

Estrada Parque is much closer to Corumbá than to Campo Grande. And even though Corumbá is a more pleasant place to hang out than Campo Grande, unless you're traveling to or from Bolivia, there's no real need to travel all the way to Corumbá to join a tour. Campo Grande is a travel hub and more convenient for onward travel to other parts of Brazil.

Pantanal Discovery (☎ 0xx67-383 9791; www.gilspantanaldiscovery.com.br) is based on the ground floor of the Campo Grande bus station. Packages start at US$125 for three days and two nights; extra days are US$30 per day, and you can negotiate discounts for longer stays. The price includes bus fare to the pickup point (Buraco da Piranha) at the entrance to Estrada Parque, meals and accommodations at the rustic Portal do Lontra lodge.

Ecological Expeditions (☎ 0xx67-782 3504; ecoexpeditionsbr@hotmail.com; Rua Joaquim Nabuco 185) is a well-organized operation with an office just opposite the bus station. In a short time it has established a good reputation, and now attracts the majority of backpackers. Free nights in the hotel help sweeten the deal. Tour prices are the same as for Pantanal Discovery. It also has an office in Corumbá.

CORUMBÁ

In Corumbá, the number of tour companies has declined due to competition from the Campo Grande operators. A couple of companies operate budget tours to camps in Nhecolândia around Estrada Parque.

Green Track (☎ 0xx67-231 2258; http://mitglied.lycos.de/greentrack/; Rua Antonio João 216) runs out of the pousada of the same name. Operated by Murilo, head of the guides association and one of the most experienced guides around, it specializes in hiking and offers a range of itineraries from two-night/three-day tours to five-day hiking tours based out of Fazenda Boa Sorte, a working Pantanal farm on the Estrada Parque. Costs are US$30 per day.

Ecological Expeditions (☎ 0xx67-232 4775; www .pantanaltrekking.com; Rua Antonio Maria Coelho 78) is a branch of the large Campo Grande tour operator.

Sleeping

Pantanal accommodations are divided into three types: pousadas include all meals and range from simple to top-end; fazendas are ranch-style hotels that usually have horses and often boats for rent; and pesqueiros cater for anglers and usually have boats and fishing gear for rent. Typical rental costs would be US$30 to US$40 a day for boats and US$10 for a couple of hours on horseback.

If you have doubts about roughing it on the budget tours, it is probably better for you to spend a bit more money for basic comforts – a bed, running water and some hope of avoiding a million mosquito bites, for example.

Rates will usually include transportation by 4WD, boat or plane from Corumbá or Cuiabá, good food and modest lodging. Reservations are often handled by a travel agent, but in many cases you can make reservations directly via email.

Reservations are needed for all accommodations in July, when lots of Brazilians vacation here.

MATO GROSSO

Accommodations along the Transpantaneira are plentiful.

Pousada das Araras (☎ 0xx65-682 2800; www.araras lodge.com.br; Transpantaneira Km 32; s/d/tr US$45/65/90; 🕸 🐾) Rents boats and horses. It also prepares macrobiotic food if you wish. There are treetop towers for bird-watching and a very informative wildlife and bird list is available. The lodge also organizes package tours to other natural areas in Mato Grosso. For more information and reservations, check out the website.

Pousada Rio Clarinho (☎ 0xx65-9977 8966; Transpantaneira Km 42; per person with full board US$30) A charmingly rustic fazenda offering boat and horse rides. The food is authentic Pantanal; check out the old-time kitchen and the wood-fired stove. Cheerful and friendly.

Pousada do Pixaim (☎ 0xx65-345 2091, 0xx65-9973 1801 for reservations; Transpantaneira Km 65; s/d US$30/60; 🕸) A rustic place, this is a classic wooden Pantanal building on stilts next to the Pixaim River. It has air-conditioning, tasty meals (included in the accommodations price) and the last gas pump until you return to Poconé – so fill up.

Pousada Jaguar (☎ 0xx65-345 1545; Transpantaneira Km 105; s/d US$40/45) Situated on the Jaguar Ecological Reserve, where jaguar sightings are frequent, the owners are active in trying to preserve the Pantanal. They have a program where with just US$15 they are able to pay Pantaneiros to put an acre of land into permanent protection as a private reserve. So far they have had over 3500 acres preserved. To show their support for conserving the region, for each room filled each night the Pousada Jaguar will preserve one acre.

Porto Jofre is where the Transpantaneira meets its end, at the Rio Cuiabá. It's a one-hotel town – in fact, it's not even a town, just a few buildings strung out along the river and a small port.

Hotel Porto Jofre Pantanal (☎ 0xx65-623 0236; www.portojofre.com.br, in Portuguese; s/d US$60/110; 🕸 Mar-Oct; 🕸 🐾) It's the only hotel at the end of the road. You can also camp on the grounds for US$5 per person and buy meals at the hotel restaurant (US$5 to US$10). The hotel has boats for hire.

Hotel Sesc Porto Cercado (☎ 0xx65-688 2001; www.sescpantanal.com.br; s/d with full board US$70/110; 🕸 🐾) In a beautiful setting along the Rio Cuiabá, 42km from Poconé. The hotel is within the 90,000-hectare Reserva Particular Patrimônio Natural (RPPN) do Sesc, which is an ecological station dedicated to preserving the natural flora and fauna of the area. It's comfortable and a great spot for walks and horseback rides.

MATO GROSSO DO SUL

Southern gateways to the Pantanal are the cities of Corumbá, Campo Grande, Aquidauana and Miranda. Most travelers head to Campo Grande or Corumbá, while Aquidauana and Miranda are popular with Brazilian anglers.

DRIVING IN THE PANTANAL

Only two roads penetrate deep into the Pantanal, the Transpantaneira and the Estrada Parque.

Estrada Parque

Also known as the Rodóvia do Integração – Road of Integration – the Estrada Parque was first opened by Marechal Candido Rondon toward the end of the 19th century as he extended the telegraph line to the western reaches of the country. Until the middle of the 1980s it was the only road to Corumbá. It consists of 117km of dirt road in variable conditions, passing over 87 small, poorly maintained wooden bridges. Along the way you'll come into direct contact with the flora and fauna of the Pantanal, such as *jacarés*, capybaras, jabiru storks, macaws and white egrets surrounding the bridges and other watery areas.

Along the road are various fishing hotels and pousadas of varying quality. The best time to hit the road is between May and October, when it rains less. The best vehicle is a 4WD but you can make it in a rental car if conditions allow. Make sure to get an update from someone who's not a professional guide – guides will always say it's *muito ruím* (really bad). The road is full of holes, sand banks and corrugations. Take plenty of repellent and refreshments. The only stores are at Curva do Leque and Passo do Lontra. The latter also has a gas station.

Access from the east is via the BR-262. Turn off at the Buraco das Piranhas toward Passo do Lontra. From Corumbá, access is via Porto da Manga. The ferry across the Rio Paraguay at Porto da Manga operates daily from 6am to 6pm.

From the airport in Campo Grande, **Unidas** (☎ 0xx67-368 6120), **Localiza** (☎ 0800-992 000) and **Interlocadora** (☎ 0xx65-363 4005) rent cars from around US$30 per day.

Transpantaneira

In 1973 the government decided to push a road through the Pantanal from Cuiabá to Corumbá. After they had arrived at Porto Cercado, 145km from Poconé, they then made the wise choice of stopping and questioning the wisdom of putting a road through an area that was under water for six months a year. The result, or remnant, is the Transpantaneira, a raised dirt road pushing deep into the Pantanal. Wildlife is plentiful along the roadside and you'll typically see *jacaré*, capivara and lots of birds. Once you get off the Transpantaneira onto some of the farms, the wildlife becomes even more varied. There are several places to stay along the Transpantaneira, all offering horseback riding, walking and boating expeditions (p393).

If you are driving from Cuiabá, head out early. Leave at 4am to reach the Transpantaneira by sunrise, when the animals come to life. The Transpantaneira officially starts 17km south of Poconé. There's a sign and a guard station, where you pay a small entrance fee. Don't forget to fill up your fuel tank in Poconé and at the Pousada do Pixaim. They are the only gas stations en route.

Stopping to see wildlife and slowing down for 118 little wooden bridges and meter-wide potholes, it's possible to pass the whole day driving the Transpantaneira. Weekdays are better for driving, as there's less traffic kicking up dust.

In Cuiabá, there are car-rental agencies just outside the airport grounds, and they're often cheaper than the agencies inside the airport. No matter what anyone tells you, you don't need a 4WD vehicle to drive the Transpantaneira. The best car is a VW Gol or a Fiat Uno.

Around Aquidauana are a number of excellent but expensive hotel-*fazendas*.

Fazenda Santa Sophia (☎ 0xx67-686 2025; www .fazendasantasophia.com.br; s/d US$80/100) Situated 120km from Aquidauana on one of the oldest cattle ranches in the area, it specializes in horseback tours. The accommodations in the farmhouse are very comfortable and the food

is excellent. The maximum number of guests is eight, so you won't feel crowded. Access by road is only possible from June to October. The rest of the time you'll need to fly in.

Fazenda Rio Negro (☎ 0xx67-326 0002; www .fazendarionegro.com.br; s/d US$120/150; 🖳) On the banks of the Rio Negro, 40 minutes by plane from Aquidauana (one hour from Campo

Grande), Fazenda Rio Negro is rustic and beautiful. It offers horseback rides, boat rides and walks. Highly recommended.

Refúgio Ecológico Caiman (☎ 0xx11-3079 6622; www.caiman.com.br; d incl meals & tours US$200, 3-day minimum stay) The most luxurious place in the southern Pantanal. Harrison Ford visited a few years ago and loved it. It's a working ranch 36km north of Miranda. Caiman was a pioneering ecotourism destination in the southern Pantanal and is the base for Project Blue Macaw, which focuses on the preservation of this magnificent, endangered bird. There are five lodges in different areas of the 530-sq-km *fazenda*. Caiman offers a wide variety of hiking, horseback and boat tours. All tours are led by multilingual guides who live on the *fazenda*.

To get to Estrada Parque you can take the Campo Grande–Corumbá bus and arrange for your lodge to pick you up (for a small fee) by the Posto Florestal guard station at the Buraco das Piranhas intersection.

At Passo do Lontra, 7km from the Buraco das Piranhas, you cross the Miranda river. There are lots of decent accommodations here.

Pousada Portal do Lontra (☎ 0xx67-231 6136; per person incl meals US$15) Another classic Pantanal wood-on-stilt structure, with lots of wildlife around. It's well worn but highly recommended. Activities cost extra.

Hotel Pesqueiro do Tadashi (☎ 0xx67-231 9400; per person incl meals US$30) Friendly, clean and very comfortable *pesqueiro* on the riverbank close to the bridge. Excellent food with a Japanese touch; boat and rod rental is US$40 per day. Highly recommended and good value.

Pousada Pantaneira do Rio Vermelho (☎ 9987 4373, 0xx67-321 4737; per person incl meals & activities US$50; ❷) On the bank of the Vermelho (Red) River, this comfortable pousada offers horseback rides, boat trips and some fine walking trails. Best accessed by boat from Cabana do Lontra or you can arrange to be picked up at Buraco das Piranhas for US$50.

Pousada Passo do Lontra (☎ 0xx67-231 6569; www.passodolontra.com.br; campsites per person US$4, d quartos/apartamentos US$20/30, chalets US$70; ❷) A comfortable place that offers horseback rides and walking, but the main focus is the river safaris. Food is excellent, but note that meals and activities are not included.

Green Track Fazenda Boa Sorte (☎ 9611 3862, 0xx67-231 2258; dm US$10) A popular option with budget travelers, this rustic *fazenda* offers horseback rides, fishing and walking tours. You can even help around the farm if you want. The accommodations are huts with mosquito netting. The *fazenda* is 36km from the Buraco das Piranhas turnoff.

Getting There & Away

From Cuiabá, the capital of Mato Grosso, there are three gateways to the Pantanal – Cáceres, Barão de Melgaço and Poconé.

Campo Grande, the capital of Mato Grosso do Sul, is a transportation hub, while Corumbá is best accessed by bus from Campo Grande. The route to Corumbá from Campo Grande runs via Aquidauana and Miranda. For transportation details, see the relevant city and town sections.

There are direct flights to Cuiabá and Campo Grande from Brasília and connecting flights from Rio and São Paulo. TAM is the only major Brazilian airline connecting other capitals, including Campo Grande and São Paulo to Corumbá.

Getting Around

Since the lodges are the only places to sleep, drink and eat, and public transportation is very limited, independent travel is difficult here. Driving is not easy. Only a few roads reach into the periphery of the Pantanal; they are frequently closed by rains, and reconstructed yearly. Only the Transpantaneira in Mato Grosso and Estrada Parque in Mato Grosso do Sul go deep into the region. See the boxed text opposite.

Hitching, though never entirely safe, may be the cheapest way to go, but it doesn't allow you to stop whenever you want along the road to observe wildlife. There's quite a bit of traffic going up and down the Transpantaneira, during the dry season at least, and if you make your way to one of the pousadas, you can then do walks or rent a horse or boat. The best time to hitch is on the weekend, when locals drive down the Transpantaneira for a day's fishing.

MATO GROSSO DO SUL

Mato Grosso do Sul was created in 1979 when the military government decided it would be the best way to administer and develop such a large region (cynics claimed it was to provide more high-paying bureaucratic jobs for cronies). But even before the split, the area had a different economic and social make-up from the northern Mato Grosso.

In the late 19th century, many migrants from the south and southeast of Brazil arrived in the area, so the south has a greater number of smaller farms and a much more intensive agriculture when compared to the large farms and ranches in the north. All this is thanks to the rich, red earth, known as *terra rocha*.

The wealth created by the *terra rocha* has helped develop the state's modern agriculture sector. The main crop is soy, but there's also lots of corn, rice and cotton production. Mato Grosso do Sul also contains two-thirds of the Pantanal and the Serra da Bocaina, two wonderful natural areas that are popular with both Brazilian and foreign travelers.

CAMPO GRANDE
☎ 0xx67 / pop 663,000

The capital of Mato Grosso do Sul, Campo Grande is developing as a major gateway to the Pantanal and with good reason: it's a transportation hub and has an excellent tourist office that tries hard to give independent advice. There's not much to see in the city itself, but it's a lively place with a young population.

It is known as the Cidade Morena because of its red earth. Manganese, rice, soy and cattle are the traditional sources of its wealth, while education (there are four universities in the city), commerce and tourism are growing industries. Campo Grande lies 716km south of Cuiabá and 403km southeast of Corumbá.

History
Founded around 1875 as the village of Santo Antônio de Campo Grande, Campo Grande's growth spurt really began when the railway came through in 1914. By decree of military president Ernesto Giesel, the city became the capital of Mato Grosso do Sul in 1977 when the new state splintered off from Mato Grosso.

Orientation
The downtown area of Campo Grande is compact and easy to get around on foot. Av Afonso Pena, the main boulevard, runs

east-west. Going west, it becomes Av Duque de Caxias and then Highway BR-262 before passing the airport (7km) and heading on to Corumbá. To the east, it runs past the Eldorado shopping complex and the Parque das Nações Indígenas. The center of the city is a grid, with the main commercial area concentrated around Afonso Pena and cross-streets Av Calógeras and Rua 14 de Julho.

Information

EMERGENCY
Ambulance (☎ 192)
Fire department (☎ 193)
Police (☎ 190)

INTERNET ACCESS
Café Iris (☎ 384 6002; Av Afonso Pena 1975; per hr US$1; ☻ 8am-11pm Mon-Sat) A newsstand, bar, acoustic venue and Internet café rolled into one small, friendly space.

MEDICAL SERVICES
Clínica Campo Grande (☎ 327 9000; Rua Candido Mariano Rondon 1703)
Santa Casa (☎ 321 5151; Rua Edward Santos Pereira 88)

MONEY
Banco 24 hr Has an ATM beside the bus station that accepts Amex/Cirrus/MasterCard/Maestro cards.
Banco do Brasil (Av Afonso Pena 2202; ☻ 11am-4pm Mon-Fri) Has its usual hefty commissions.
Bradesco (Rua Barão do Rio Branco 1582) Has a visa ATM with 24 hour access.

POST
Post office (cnr Rua Dom Aquino & Av Calógeras; ☻ 8:30am-5pm Mon-Fri, 8-11:30am Sat) There's also a branch opposite the bus station that stays open until 6pm weekdays.

TOURIST INFORMATION
Tourist office (☎ 724 5830; Av Noroeste 5140; ☻ 8am-7pm Tue-Sat, 9am-noon Sun) The best tourist office in the region, on the corner of Av Afonso Pena. Friendly staff (most are tourism students), an excellent city map and an extensive database with information about hotels and attractions throughout the state.

Sights
The **Museu Dom Bosco** (Rua Barão do Rio Branco 1843; admission US$1; ☻ 8-11am & 1-5pm) is the only museum in town that's worth a look. It has an excellent collection of over 10,000 insects,

including 7000 butterflies. There are lots of stuffed animals and interesting exhibits about the Bororo, Moro, Karajá and Xavante Indians. Reasonably priced handicrafts are also available.

Tours

If you don't want to rough it on a camping tour of the Pantanal, travel agencies in Campo Grande sell packages at farm hotels, but you'll probably get a better deal by booking direct.

N & T Japan Tour (☎ 784 2820; www.japantour.com.br, in Portuguese; rm 20, Av Afonso Pena 2081; ⏲ 9am-6pm Mon-Fri, 9am-2pm Sat)

Palm Tour (☎ 324 6012; Rua Joaquim Nabuco 169-b; ⏲ 6am-8pm Mon-Fri)

Sleeping

Most budget accommodations are clustered around the bus station. Some of the dives have pulled their act together recently, but the area is still a bit seedy at night.

Pousada Dom Aquino (☎ 382 9373; pousada@domaquino.com.br; Rua Dom Aquino 1806; s/d apartamentos US$15/20; 🖳) Tastefully decorated with artworks depicting Pantanal settings, this relaxed pousada is an oasis in the city, with a lovely garden and friendly staff. Book ahead, because it's often full, especially on weekends.

Hotel Iguaçu (☎ 384 4621; www.hoteliguacu.com.br; Rua Dom Aquino 761; s/d quartos US$10/15, s/d apartamentos US$15/20; 🖳 🖳) It's popular with students and travelers. Opposite the bus station, it's clean, friendly and comfortable, with small balconies on the front rooms and an Internet terminal in the lobby.

Nosso Novo Hotel (☎ 321 0505; Rua Joaquim Nabuco 185; dm US$6, s/d US$8/10; 🖳) This hotel is affiliated with YHI and Ecological Expeditions. Staff have lots of information on the Pantanal and Bonito, and you get a free night if you sign up for a tour.

Hotel Colonial (☎ 382 6061; Rua Allan Kardec 211; s/d apartamentos US$15/21; 🖳) Small, spotless rooms. The big advantage of staying here is that you get to use the pool and eat breakfast at the more upmarket Hotel Internacional next door (they have the same owner).

CAMPO GRANDE

0 — 1 km
0 — 0.5 miles

INFORMATION	
Banco 24 hr ATM	1 A3
Banco do Brasil	2 C3
Bradesco	3 B3
Café Íris	4 B3
Post Office	5 B3
Santa Casa	6 C1
Tourist Office	7 B3

SIGHTS & ACTIVITIES	(pp396-7)
Museu Dom Bosco	8 D3

SLEEPING	(pp397-8)
Hotel Colonial	9 A3
Hotel Iguaçu	10 A2
Hotel Internacional	11 A3

Jandaia Hotel	12 C3
Nosso Novo Hotel	13 A3
Palace Hotel	14 B2
Pousada Dom Aquino	15 C3

EATING	🍴 (p398)
Morado de Bais Restauranre e Chopuria	16 A3
Sabor en Quilo	17 C3
Viva a Vida	18 B3

ENTERTAINMENT	🎭 (p398)
Acustic Bar	19 D2

SHOPPING	🛍 (pp398-9)
Centro de Artesão	20 B3

Feíra Indígena	21 B3

TRANSPORT	(p399)
Bus Station	22 A3
VARIG	23 C3

OTHER	
Ecological Expeditions	24 A3
N & T Japan Tour	25 B3
Palm Tour	26 A3
Pantanal Discovery	(see 22)

Hotel Internacional (☎ 324 6061; www.hotelinter metro.com.br, in Portuguese; Rua Allan Kardec 223; s/d apartamentos US$25/40; 🅿 🆒 🄿 🖥) The plush-est hotel close to the bus station. Great breakfast spread.

Palace Hotel (☎ 384 4741; Rua Dom Aquino 1501; s/d apartamentos US$15/19) Not exactly a palace, but it's a comfortable, centrally located place that's popular with sales representatives.

Jandaía Hotel (☎ 321 7000; www.jandaia.com.br; Rua Barão do Rio Branco 1271; s/d US$55/74; 🄿 ✕ 🆒 🖥 🄰) The most luxurious in town. In the heart of the city, it has two good restaurants and lots of amenities.

A couple of kilometers west on Av Afonso Pena are two excellent mid-range options:

Hotel Vale Verde (☎ 321 3355; www.hotelvale verde.com.br, in Portuguese; Av Afonso Pena 106; s/d apartamentos US$33/45; 🄿 🆒 🄰 🆒) This hotel has clean, spacious apartments and a lovely garden.

Indaia Park Hotel (☎ 312 9400; www.indaia-hotel .com.br, in Portuguese; Av Afonso Pena 354; s/d apartmentos US$30/38; 🄿 🆒 🖥 🄰) Kitsch decorations but welcoming box-spring mattresses and goose-feather pillows.

Eating & Drinking

Viva a Vida (☎ 384 6524; 1st fl, Rua Dom Aquino 1354; ☾ lunch Mon-Fri) A good natural-food place that's popular with locals.

Fogo Caipira (☎ 324 1641; Rua José Antônio 145; dishes US$5-10; ☾ 5-11pm Mon-Thu, 11am-midnight Fri & Sat, 11am-4pm Sun) Huge servings of top-quality regional food. Try the *galinhada* (chicken stew) or *pacu recheado* (a tasty fish stuffed with manioc and spices). Tasty regional desserts are complementary.

Sabor en Quilo (☎ 325 5102; Rua Dom Aquino 1786; meals per kg US$5; ☾ 11am-2:30pm Mon-Fri, 11am-3pm Sat & Sun) Classy self-serve, including sushi, pasta and curries.

If you feel like a stroll before dinner, there are a couple of upmarket restaurants in the suburb of Jardim dos Estados, 2km east of the city center along Av Afonso Pena.

Casa Colonial (☎ 383 3207; Av Afonso Pena 3997; dishes US$5-10; ☾ 6:30-11pm Mon, 11am-2pm & 6:30-11:30pm Tue-Sat, 11am-4pm Sun) A stylish place with a good *rodízio* for US$7 per person or à la carte regional and Italian food. It has a breezy courtyard out the back.

Barroarte (☎ 324 1355; Av Afonso Pena 4329; ☾ 9am-10pm) A gallery and bar with live music at night and small meals.

Morado de Bais Restaurante e Choperia (☎ 383 1227; Av Afonso Pena s/n; ☾ 11am-2:30pm & 7pm-mid-night) Next to the tourist office, this has a good selection of regional dishes and live music nightly.

Entertainment

From Friday to Sunday night, Campo Grande's nightlife is jumping.

Acustic Bar (☎ 385 5500; Rua 13 de Junho 945; cover US$4; ☾ 11pm-late Fri & Sat) Has live music nightly but on Friday and Saturday it's a happening place to check live bands.

Stones (☎ 326 4957; Av Ceará 2114; ☾ 10am-10pm Tue-Thu, 6pm-midnight Fri-Sun) Classic jazz, blues and rock.

For happy hour try the **Tamba Bar** (Rua 15 de Novembro 2283; ☾ 10am-10pm Tue-Thu, 10am-midnight Fri-Sun) or **Café Mostarda** (☎ 382 8468; Av Afonso Pena 3952; dishes US$5-10; ☾ 10am-midnight), which is seriously trendy and always filled with smart young locals.

Shopping

Centro de Artesão (☎ 383 2633; Av Calógeras 2050; ☾ 8am-6pm Mon-Fri, 9am-3pm Sat & Sun) Sells color-ful Indian ceramics, wooden crafts, sacred art, carpets and locally brewed liquor.

Barroarte (☎ 324 1355; Av Afonso Pena 4329; ☾ 9am-6pm Mon-Fri) About 2km east of the center, Barroarte has beautiful clay pieces.

Feira Indigena (Praça Oshiro Takemori; ☾ 6:30am-8pm) The Terena Indians sell their native products here. The proceeds help maintain

---

RETURN OF THE DEATH TRAIN

Good news for train buffs is the announce-ment that the rail service between Campo Grande and Corumbá is going to be reacti-vated. This means it will again be possible to go most of the way between Campo Grande and Santa Cruz, Bolivia, on the so-called 'Trem del Morte' (Death Train). It's is one of the world's great train rides, and passes through the southern Pantanal be-tween Miranda and Corumbá.

To restore the trains and stations will cost about US$4.5 million, and to repair the tracks will cost US$26 million. The proposed plan includes tourist cars, as well as normal passenger cars. All they're waiting for is the money to come from the federal and state governments and private sources.

their economic and cultural independence, so don't bargain too hard.

Getting There & Around

AIR

Daily connections link Campo Grande to São Paulo (US$120), Cuiabá (US$35), Corumbá (US$77), Rio (US$187), Brasília (US$192) and Porto Velho (US$296). For additional information call **TAM** (☎ 384 0100), **Varig** (☎ 325 1112) or **VASP** (☎ 363 2389).

There are several air-taxi companies at the airport for trips into remote areas of the Pantanal. Try **Táxi Aéreo Pantanal** (☎ 363 3859).

Aeroporto Internacional de Campo Grande (☎ 368 6000) is 7km from town; to get there, take the Indubrasil bus from the bus station. To get a bus to the center from the airport, walk out of the airport to the bus stop on the main road. A taxi costs US$9.

BUS

The bus station is huge, with lots of bars, barbers and travel agencies. There are frequent buses to Corumbá (US$24, six hours, seven daily); four are direct. Non-direct buses to Corumbá stop in Miranda and Aquidauana, and can drop you at the intersection with Estrada Parque.

Regular buses make the trip to Cuiabá (US$21, 10 hours, 10 daily) and there are buses to Bonito (US$12, five hours, three daily at 6am, 11am and 3pm). The route to Bonito via Sidrolândia and Jardim is paved all the way. There are frequent buses to Ponta Porã (US$13, seven hours, 11 daily) on the Paraguayan frontier. There are also buses to São Paulo (US$45, 14 hours, 10 daily) and Foz do Iguaçu (US$22, 16 hours, one daily at 7:30pm).

CORUMBÁ

☎ 0xx67 / pop 88,000

This port city close to the Bolivian border is a southern gateway to the Pantanal. The city sits atop a steep hill overlooking the Rio Paraguay; on the far side of the river, the huge expanse of the Pantanal stretches to the horizon.

Corumbá is 403km northwest of Campo Grande by road. It's location near the Paraguayan and Bolivian borders (Puerto Suárez, Bolivia, is 19km away), and has a reputation for poaching and drug smuggling, but travelers are generally left alone.

CORUMBÁ

INFORMATION	
Banco do Brasil	1 A2
Bolivian Consulate	2 B3
Bradesco	3 A1
Hospital Caridade	4 A3
HSBC Bank	5 A1
Mutum Turismo	6 A1
Pantur Travel Agency	7 A3
Policia Federal	8 B2
Post Office	9 B1
Sematur Tourist Office	10 A1
Telephone Office	11 A2
Terra Net	12 B3

SIGHTS & ACTIVITIES	(pp400–1)
Art Izu	13 B2
Casa de Artesão	14 B2
Museu do Pantanal	(see 8)

SLEEPING	(p401)
Hotel Laura Vicuña	15 B2
Hotel Nelly	16 A1
Internacional Palace	17 A2
Nacional	18 A3
Pousada Green Track	19 B2
Santa Monica Palace	20 B2

EATING	(p401)
Churrascaria e Restaurante Rodeio	21 B2
Laço do Ouro	22 A2
Peixaria do Lulu	23 B2
Vivabella	24 A1

DRINKING	(p401)
Baís do Chopp	25 A1

TRANSPORT	(pp401–2)
Bus to Bolivian border	26 A2
Local Bus Terminal	27 B2
Local Bus Terminal	28 B2

OTHER	
Ecological Expeditions	29 B1
Green Track (tours to the Pantanal)	(see 19)

THE CENTRAL WEST

History

Corumbá, also known as Cidade Branca (White City), was founded in 1776 by Captain Luis de Albuquerque. By 1840 it was the biggest river port in the world, boasting a dozen foreign consulates. Ships would enter the Rio de la Plata in the South Atlantic, sail up the Rio Paraná to its confluence with the Rio Paraguay, then continue up to Corumbá. The impressive buildings along the waterfront reflect the wealth that passed through the town in the 19th century. With the coming of the railway, Corumbá lost its importance as a port and went into decline.

Orientation

The city is divided into the upper and lower. The upper city contains most of the commerce. The lower city takes in the port. The streets are laid out in a grid pattern and are easy to navigate.

Information

EMERGENCY

Federal Police (☎ 231 5848; Praça da República 51; ⊙ 7:30am-5:30pm Mon-Fri) There's also an office at the bus station.

IMMIGRATION

At present all Brazilian border formalities (including entry and exit stamps) must be completed at the **Federal Police office** (☎ 231 1224; ⊙ 8-11am & 2-5:30pm) at the long-distance bus station. Bolivian entry/exit formalities can all be completed at the border post. If you're just crossing over to Bolivia for a few hours to buy train tickets, you don't need to get a Brazilian exit stamp.

Moneychangers at the border accept cash only and will change both reais and dollars.

You won't be allowed to enter Bolivia without a current yellow-fever vaccination certificate, so organize one well in advance.

INTERNET ACCESS

Terra Net (☎ 231 1221; Rua América 677; per hr US$1.50; ⊙ 8-11:30am & 1:30-6pm Mon-Fri, 8am-noon Sat)

MEDICAL SERVICES

Hospital Candade (☎ 231 2993; Rua 15 de Novembro 854)

MONEY

Most shopkeepers on Rua 13 de Junho change Brazilian, Bolivian and US money.

Banco do Brasil (Rua 13 de Junho 914; ⊙ 10am-3pm Mon-Fri) Usual high commissions for cash and traveler's checks.

Bradesco (Rua Delamare 1067; ⊙ 10am-3pm Mon-Fri) Has Visa ATMs.

HSBC (Rua Delamare 1067; ⊙ 10am-3pm Mon-Fri) 24-hour Cirrus and MasterCard ATMs.

POST

Post office (Rua Delamare 708; ⊙ 8:30am-5pm Mon-Fri, 8-11:30am Sat)

TOURIST INFORMATION

Sematur tourist office (☎ 231 7336; Rua Manoel Cavassa 275; ⊙ 1:30-6pm Mon, 8:30-11:30am & 1:30-6pm Tue-Fri) On the right as you begin the descent to the port. It's not well marked and the building looks derelict from the street. Staff can provide a list of Pantanal guides and tour companies, hotels and boat trips.

TRAVEL AGENCIES

Pantanal tours and boat and fishing tours of the Corumbá environs are available from all travel agencies. Recommended agencies include **Mutum Turismo** (☎ 231 1818; mutum@pantanalnet.com.br; Rua Frei Mariano 17; ⊙ 7:30am-6pm Mon-Fri, 7:30am-noon Sat) and **Pantur** (☎ 231 2000; Rua Frei Mariano 1013; ⊙ 8am-6pm Mon-Fri, 8am-noon Sat, 9am-noon Sun).

Sights & Activities

Corumbá's star attraction is the Pantanal; you can get a preview of it from the highest point in the area, **Morro Urucum** (1100m), 20km south of Corumbá. Otherwise, you may enjoy a boat trip on the Rio Paraguay. Between three and nine hours long, these cruises usually take in the **Base Fluvial de Ladário**, Brazil's first river arsenal dating from 1872, and **Porto Qijarro** on the Bolivian border. They also stop for a while to allow you to throw in a line. These tours can be booked through any travel agent and usually cost between US$10 and US$20.

Around town, a pleasant spot to visit is the **Casa de Artesão** (Rua Dom Aquino 405; ⊙ 8-11:30am & 2-5:30pm Mon-Fri, 7:30-11:30pm Sat), which has an excellent selection of indigenous and local art and artifacts. Each cell is a small gallery for an individual artist and, despite its bleak past, the old prison is a peaceful haven in the town. **Art Izu** (Rua Cuiabá 558; ⊙ 8-11am & 1:30-5pm Mon-Fri) is home to one of Corumbá's premier artists. You can't miss it – the giant bird sculptures and bronze

statue of Jesus out the front are amazing.
Museu do Pantanal (☎ 231 5757; Praça da República; 🕒 8am-noon & 2-5:30pm Mon-Fri) contains a reasonably interesting collection of stuffed local wildlife and Indian artifacts. It also displays modern local art.

Forte de Junqueira (☎ 231 5828; Rua Cáceres 425; 🕒 8am-5pm) is the only intact fort left near the city. A hexagonal fort with 50cm-thick walls, the real attraction is the excellent view of the Rio Paraguay and the Pantanal in the distance. To get there, go east along Rua Dom Aquino and turn left at the athletic ground. Once you hit the waterfront, continue east for another 10 minutes.

Sleeping

There are some cheap hotels close to the long-distance bus station that are OK if you're just spending a night in Corumbá before heading out. Otherwise, there are better places closer to the waterfront and the restaurants and bars in the center of town.

Pousada Green Track (☎ 231 2258; Rua Antônio João 216; dm US$5; 🖳) Set up in a large old house, it's a friendly place that's popular with backpackers. There's a laundry and you can swim at a nearby club's pool.

Hotel Nelly (☎ 231 6001; Rua Delamere 902; s/d quartos US$3/5, with air-con US$6/9; 🗙) Offers the best value of a cluster of cheapies on Rua Delamare between Rua Frei Mariano and Rua Antônio Maria Coelho.

Nacional (☎ 231 6868; www.hnacional.com.br, in Portuguese; Rua América 936; s/d US$30/40, ste US$45; 🅿 🗙 🖳 🏊) This is the plushest hotel in town. It has a lovely pool area and restaurant, and is very good value.

Hotel Laura Vicuña (☎ 231 5874; Rua Cuiabá 775; s/d quartos US$10/15, apartamentos US$12/18; 🅿 🗙) A clean, comfortable hotel in a quiet spot close to the center.

Santa Monica Palace (☎ 231 3001; Rua Antônio Maria Coelho 345; s/d US$20/28; 🅿 🗙 🖳 🏊) A favorite with group tours, this is a good-value, modern hotel in the center of town.

Internacional Palace (☎ 231 6343; Rua Dom Aquino Correia 1457; s/d US$20/30; 🅿 🗙 🏊) Another comfortable mid-range hotel a bit further from the center.

Eating & Drinking

Churrascaria e Restaurante Rodeio (☎ 231 6477; Rua 13 de Junho 760; meals per kg US$5; 🕒 11am-3:30pm

& 7pm-midnight Mon-Sat, 11am-4pm Sun; 🗙) It has 43 different salad dishes (go on, count 'em) to choose from and plenty of tasty meat as well.

Peixaria do Lulu (☎ 232 2142; Rua Dom Aquino 700; dishes for 2 US$5-10; 🕒 10am-3pm & 6pm-midnight Mon-Sat, 11am-4pm Sun) The best fish restaurant in town. Don't let the humble appearance fool you – it serves superb regional fish dishes such as *pacu frito com pirão e arroz* (fried pacu with tapioca pudding and rice). It's a friendly, family-run place – they're big Vasco fans.

Vivabella (☎ 232 9464; Rua Arthur Mangabeira 1; dishes US$5-10; 🕒 noon-2pm) This small bar/restaurant has the best views over the Pantanal (and good Italian food). The pizza, pasta and salad dishes are enough for two. If you are *sozinho* (alone) ask for half a portion.

Laço do Ouro (☎ 231 7371; Rua Frei Mariano 556; self-serve lunch US$5; 🕒 10:30-1am) For an early lunch (before 1pm) try the self-serve here. At night, the restaurant becomes a bar, with live music from Thursday to Saturday.

Baís do Chopp (☎ 231 1079; Rua Manoel Cavassa 275; dishes US$5-15; 🕒 5:30-10pm Tue & Wed, 5:30pm-1am Thu-Sat) A very stylish bar with a chic restaurant, it has live music on weekends.

Getting There & Away

Corumbá is a transit point for travel to/from Bolivia and Paraguay.

AIR

Corumbá **airport** (☎ 231 3322) is 3km east of the town center. **TAM** (☎ 231 7099), **Pantanal Linhas Aéreas** (☎ 231 1818) and **VASP** (☎ 231 4441) all fly regularly to Campo Grande (US$77). Flights are also available to Rio (US$180), Brasília (US$180) and other major cities.

BOAT

Passenger boat services between Corumbá and Asunción (Paraguay) have been discontinued. Boat transportation through the Pantanal is infrequent – inquire at the port.

BUS

From the **long-distance bus station** (☎ 231 2033; Rua Porto Carrero), buses run to Campo Grande (US$16, six hours, 11 daily) from 8:30am to 11:30pm; and to Bonito (US$22, eight hours) at 1:30pm Monday to Saturday.

THE CENTRAL WEST

TO/FROM BOLIVIA

If you're heading from the city to the border, catch the Fronteira bus on Praça Independência on Rua Dom Aquino (US$0.50, every 30 minutes). If you're in a hurry, grab a mototaxi for US$2. Taxis want US$5.

The Bolivian border town of Quijarro is not much more than a muddy little collection of shacks around the train station. Taxis operate between the border and Quijarro station (trains travel to Santa Cruz in Bolivia from this station), a distance of about 4km – the going rate is around US$2.50.

Getting Around

The cost of a taxi from Corumbá's long-distance bus station to the center is US$4.

From the bus stop outside the long-distance bus station, the Cristo Redentur bus (US$0.50) runs to the **local bus terminal** (Rua 13 de Junho). Going to the long-distance bus station, you can take a mototaxi (US$1) from the local bus station on Rua Antônio Maria Coelho if you're light on luggage.

From the local bus terminal, the Aeroporto bus runs (spookily) to the airport. Taxis usually cost US$5 for the 3km trip to town – make sure the taxi has a meter or establish a price before you get in, as some drivers like to play gringo rip-off.

COXIM

☎ 0xx67 / pop 31,000

Coxim is a small town about halfway between Cuiabá and Campo Grande, on the eastern border of the Pantanal. The town's main draw is the Piracema, when fish migrate up the Taquari and Coxim Rivers, leaping through rapids to spawn. The Piracema takes place from November to January; fishing is not allowed during this period, but if you're traveling through it's worth stopping off to have a look.

The fishing – for pacu, pintado, curimbatá, dourado and jaú – is best from August to October. Coxim is also an entry point to the Pantanal, but it has limited infrastructure for wildlife-spotting tours, with most operators catering exclusively to fishing tours.

Information

If you get the urge to wet a line, a fishing permit is required – you can pick one up at **IBAMA** (☎ 291 2310; Rua Floriano Peixoto 304) or

at the **Banco do Brasil** (Rua Antônio de Alberqueque 248). A permit valid for three months costs US$9. In the center, **Peixe Viva** (☎ 291 1798; Rua Getúlio Vargas 350; ⏲ 6am-7pm Mon-Fri) is the place to rent boats, fishing rods and buy bait.
Bradesco (Rua Flint Muller 85; ⏲ 10am-3pm Mon-Fri) Visa ATM.
Comtur (☎ 291 2669; ⏲ 7am-6pm) Next to the river in the Anexo Taquari; can arrange guides to the local waterfalls as well as fishing trips and farm stays.
Hospital (☎ 291 1398; Av Virginia Ferreira 2415)
Post office (Rua Antônio João 111; ⏲ 8:30am-5pm Mon-Fri, 8-11:30am Sat)

Sleeping & Eating

There are a number of cheap hotels in town.

Hotel Neves (☎ 291 1273; Av Gaspar Ries Coelho 1931; s/d apartamentos with fan US$5/8, with air-con US$7/12; 🌊) If you arrive late at night, this is next to the bus station. It's also clean and friendly and the best budget option in town. The town is 3km away, on the banks of the river.

Coxim Hotel (☎ 291 1480; s/d US$13/23; P 🌊 🏊) About 4km from town on the road to Campo Grande, the Coxim Hotel is well set up for fishing tours.

Santa Ana (☎ 291 1602; Rua Miranda Reis 931; s/d US$15/28; P 🌊 🏊) A comfortable hotel with a river frontage close to town.

Ki-xodó (☎ 291 3556; Av Virginia Ferreira 1523; dishes US$3-6; ⏲ 11am-2pm & 6:30-11pm Mon-Fri, 11am-2:30pm Sat & Sun) Situated next to the river, this restaurant's home cooking is fresh and tasty. It's nothing sophisticated, but the portions are huge. Obviously, fish is the best option.

Getting There & Around

There are plenty of buses from both Cuiabá (US$12, seven hours, five daily) and Campo Grande (US$9, four hours, six daily) to Coxim. To get to the bus station, you can walk or catch a mototaxi (US$2).

All the hotels along the river have small outboard boats for hire; daily rates start at about US$50.

BONITO

☎ 0xx67 / pop 18,000

Bonito is an ecotourism boom town. This small town in the southwestern corner of Mato Grosso do Sul has no attractions itself, but the natural resources of the area are spectacular. There are caves with lakes and amazing stalactite formations, beautiful waterfalls and incredibly clear rivers surrounded by lush forest where it's possible for divers to swim eyeball to eyeball with hundreds of fish. Since Bonito was put on the ecotourism map in the early 1990s, the number of visitors has risen dramatically every year. Despite its popularity, it's still a great place to kick back outside peak holiday periods (December to February and July).

Orientation & Information

Bonito's main street is Rua Coronel Pilad Rebua.

EMERGENCY

Police station (☎ 661 2132; Rua Nova Mato Grosso)

INTERNET ACCESS

Central de Aventuras (☎ 255 2026; Rua Coronel Pilad Rebua 1861; per hr US$2; ☷ 8am-midnight)

MEDICAL SERVICES

Hospital (☎ 255 3448; Rua Pedro Apóstolo 201)

MONEY

Banco do Brasil (Rua Luiz da Costa Leite 2279) Just off the main plaza.
Bradesco (Rua Coronel Pilad Rebua 1942) Visa ATMs.

POST

Post office (Rua Coronel Pilad Rebua 1759)

TOURIST INFORMATION

Setur (☎ 255 1850; Rua Coronel Pilad Rebua 1780; ☷ 8am-5pm Mon-Fri)

TRAVEL AGENCIES

Muito Bonito Tourismo (☎ 255 1645; www.muito bonito.com.br, in Portuguese; Rua Coronel Pilad Rebua 1448; ☷ 7am-9pm Mon-Fri) Travel agency located in the pousada of the same name. Multilingual and very helpful. Go here first.
Tamanduá Viagems & Turismo (☎ 255 5000; www .tamandua.com.br, in Portuguese; Rua Coronel Pilad Rebua 1890; ☷ 7am-9pm Mon-Fri)
Ygarapé Tour (☎ 255 1733; www.ygarape.com.br, in Portuguese; Rua Coronel Pilad Rebua 1956; ☷ 7am-10pm Mon-Fri) Well-established and reputable.

Sights

The only sight in Bonito that doesn't need a guide is the **Balneário Municipal** (☎ 255 1850; admission US$4; ☷ 7am-6pm), a natural swimming pool with clear water and lots of fish on the Rio Formoso, 7km southeast of town. You can spend the whole day there and have lunch at the kiosk. A shuttle bus (US$0.50) runs there on weekends, but during the week you're on your own. To experience anything else of the pristine nature on Bonito's doorstep, you need to join a tour.

Tours

The local government has strict regulations in place for visiting the area's natural attractions, partly because many are on private land and partly to minimize the impact on some pristine areas. Most attractions have a daily limit on the number of visitors they will accept, and visitors at all sites must be accompanied by a guide.

Only guides from local travel agencies are authorized, so you're obliged to book tours

THE CENTRAL WEST

IT'S CLEAR TO SEE: BONITO IS BEAUTIFUL

Bonito's incredibly clear rivers were produced by a happy accident of nature. The river waters spring from subterranean sources in a limestone base, which releases calcium carbonate into the water. The calcium carbonate calcifies all impurities in the water, which then sink to the riverbed (this is the reason you're asked to stay afloat and not touch the bottom during river tours). The result is an area filled with natural aquariums surrounded by lush forest; a beautiful environment in which to study the abundant numbers of fascinating fish in the rivers. The robust *dourado* (gold) fish is known as the 'shark of the river' – a sinister-looking creature, it cruises the river eating its fellow fish. Meter-long catfish lurk in grottoes, while the huge, black *pacu* move with surprising quickness along the river in large schools.

The river tours are a unique experience and not to be missed – the only drawback is that the area's popularity brings its own challenges. While there are limits on the number of daily visitors to most of the area's natural attractions, those limits are being reached most days. At some attractions, 'rest periods' of two to three months each year are being introduced to allow the fragile vegetation to regenerate.

through them. There are about 25 travel agencies in Bonito offering about 30 different tours. Unfortunately, few tours are cheap and they don't include transport, which you have to arrange yourself. See opposite for more information. For this reason, you might find it easier to tack onto a group that has already organized transportation through the more popular agencies. Don't bother shopping around – all prices are fixed.

There are over 30 attractions in the area now, but few are exceptional. There have been exciting developments in adventure tours (including rappelling down to and diving in underground lakes), but these are also the most expensive. Prices quoted here are for low season – they rise by around 25% in high season. In the high season, many of these tours are booked up months ahead. If you're traveling during these times, it's a good idea to book well in advance.

Seven kilometers southeast of Bonito, **Aquário Natural Baía Bonita** (3hr tour US$25; ⏰ 7:30am-3:30pm) is a beautiful natural spring where you can swim among 30 different varieties of fish and then float gently downstream to small waterfalls. The price includes wetsuits and snorkels. A wetsuit will take the edge off the cold water and also protect you from the sun – you aren't allowed to wear sunscreen in any of the river tours because it taints the water.

Rio Sucuri (3hr tour US$23; ⏰ 8:30am-3pm), 20km southwest of Bonito, is similar to Aquário Natural – with springs and a crystal-clear

river full of fish and subaquatic gardens, surrounded by lush forest – but it's further out in the wild.

Within a *fazenda*, 50km south of Bonito, the marvelous **Rio da Prata** (5hr tour US$28; ⏰ 8am-3pm) program includes a short trek through rain forest and a 3km swim downstream along the river. This place should be on top of your list. The tour includes a buffet lunch.

A bargain attraction is the **Gruta do Lago Azul** (admission US$8; ⏰ 7am-1pm), a large cave with a luminous underground lake and stalactite formations 20km west of Bonito.

Abismo de Anhumas (rappelling US$105, scuba diving US$50; ⏰ 7am-5pm), 22km west of Bonito, is a 72m abyss that descends to a lake underground. It has incredible stalactite formations, including Os Dedos (The Fingers), O Vigilante (The Vigilant) and Cascatas (Cascades). The tour involves rappeling (abseiling) down to the bottom and snorkeling in the lake (or you can opt for scuba diving if you have a basic certificate).

Lagoa Misteriosa (snorkeling US$14, scuba diving US$50; ⏰ 7am-5pm), 42km south of Bonito, is a small 'bottomless' lake (its depth is estimated at 180m to 200m) with submerged rock and stalactite formations. Snorkeling or diving to a depth of 25m to 30m is allowed on tours.

Sleeping

Accommodations in Bonito are tight and more expensive during the high season and on weekends throughout the year.

MOONIES IN THE PANTANAL

One of the biggest landowners in the southern Pantanal is the Unification Church, whose members are known as Moonies and follow the teaching of Sun Myung Moon, self-styled leader of the sect and huge fishing fan. On a fishing trip to the area in the mid '90s, Moon fell in love with the Pantanal because of its resemblance to his vision of the Garden of Eden, and started buying up land in the area. So far the church owns 40,000 hectares. Its farm near Jardim is called New Hope, and includes the fork of the Miranda and Silver (Prata) Rivers. Those who take the fantastic Rio da Prata river swim will know how crystal those waters are. Unfortunately, it was discovered in 1998 that the New Hope Farm was pumping raw sewage into the river.

The Moonies presence in the area has met with some suspicion from local townspeople, government and church groups, mainly because of past bad publicity (Moon served a year in jail in the USA for tax evasion) and the lack of information about what is actually going on there. Comparisons have been made with that other famous religious settlement in South America – Jonestown, where sect leader Jim Jones and 912 followers committed ritual suicide in 1978. But since suicide is against Moonie teachings, it seems unlikely the 80-something Moon is about to order his followers to drink some poison Kool-Aid, especially since the Moonie-sponsored Jardim football team has started winning state championships!

Pousada Muito Bonito (☎ 255 1645; www.muito bonito.com.br, in Portuguese; Rua Coronel Pilad Rebua 1448; per person US$10; **P** **✗**) Located close to the center, this is an excellent option. Comfortable *apartamentos* with a good breakfast included. The owner, Mario Doblack, speaks English, French, Spanish and Italian and is very helpful with information.

Albergue da Juventude do Ecoturismo (☎ 255 1462; www.ajbonito.com.br; Rua Lúcio Borralho 716; dm US$7) The town's youth hostel is approximately 1.5km from the center, but staff meet buses, and bikes are available for trips to town. You can buy meals there for around US$4 or cook in the kitchen. The hostel can also book tours and arrange transport.

Hotel e Pousada Águas de Bonito (☎ 255 2330; www.aguasdebonito.com.br; Rua 29 de Maio 1679; d US$40; **✗**) Modern, spacious rooms.

Marruá Hotel (☎ 255 1040; www.marruahotel .com.br, in Portuguese; Rua João Sorta 1173; s/d US$35/50; **P** **✗** **🖵** **🛈**) A comfortable hotel with all the extras, including 24-hour room service.

Hotel Pirá Miuna (☎ 255 1058; www.piramiunahotel .com.br; Rua Luís Costa Leite 1792; s/d US$35/45; **P** **✗** **🖵** **🛈**) Lovely newer hotel; good value.

Wetega Hotel (☎ 255 1699; www.wetegahotel.com .br; Rua Coronel Pilad Rebua 679; s/d US$75/90; **P** **🖵** **🛈**) Interesting structure with wooden pillars. Rooms overlook a courtyard.

Eating & Drinking

Restaurante da Vovó (☎ 255 2723; Rua Felinto Muller 570; meals per kg US$5; ☽ 11am-2:30pm) An excellent per-kilogram joint serving regional food. Leave some room for the *mousse maracujá* (US$0.70) for dessert – it's special.

O Casarão (☎ 255 1970; Rua Coronel Pilad Rebua 1843; meals per kg US$4; ☽ 10:30am-3pm & 6:30-11pm) A good place to try some of the local fish you swam with during the day!

Cantinho do Peixe (☎ 255 3381; Rua 31 de Março 1918; dishes US$8-15; ☽ 11am-2pm & 6-11pm Mon-Sat) This simple, friendly place is one of the cheapest and best places in town to eat pintado fresh from the Miranda River. It offers 24 different recipes for pintado. Try the *pintado á urucum*, in which the fish is covered in melted mozzarella and condensed milk.

Tapera (☎ 255 1757; Rua Coronel Pilad Rebua 480; dishes US$4-10; ☽ 11am-3pm & 6-11pm) Serves decent meat, chicken and fish dishes for two.

Sale & Pepe (☎ 255 1822; Rua 29 de Maio 971; dishes US$5-10; ☽ 6:30-11pm Tue-Sat) Try this, the best place for Asian dishes.

Castellababe (☎ 255 1713; Rua Coronel Pilad Rebua 2168; pizzas US$5; ☽ 11am-2:30pm & 6-11pm) Inside this fake castle, you'll find really good pizza. It also has cheap *jacaré* (US$12 for two).

Taboa Bar (☎ 255 1862; Rua Coronel Pilad Rebua 1841) Located in the heart of the main street, this Bonito institution is the place where locals and travelers converge for drinks and live music on weekends. Try the house special, *pinga* (sugarcane spirit).

Getting There & Away

There are buses to Bonito from Campo Grande (US$11, five hours, three daily at 6am, 11am and 3pm) via Nioaque and Guia Lopes da Laguna. Buses return to Campo Grande from Bonito at 6am, noon and 4pm. There are buses to Ponta Porã (US$10, six hours, noon) from Monday to Friday and to Corumbá (US$14, seven hours, 6am). If you're in a hurry or can't hack overcrowded buses, private Kombi vans based in town do runs to Campo Grande, Corumbá, Foz do Iguaçu and Anastácio. They cost just a bit more than traveling by bus.

Getting Around

Unfortunately, many of Bonito's attractions are a fair hike from town, and there's no public transportation apart from a shuttle bus that runs on weekends to the Balneário Municipal (US$0.50). Tours booked with travel agencies in Bonito don't include transport. If you book a tour with a busy travel agency, you might be able to scrounge a ride with Brazilian tourists, most of whom are traveling by car or minibus.

Otherwise, your options are to rent a car (around US$25 per day with unlimited kms) from **Yes Rent-a-Car** (☎ 255 1702; www.yes-rentacar .com.br, in Portuguese; Rua Felinto Muller 656) or grab a mototaxi. Mototaxi prices are negotiable: to the Rio Sucuri (40km round-trip) and Gruta do Lago Azul (40km round-trip) and back to town costs US$5 to US$10 per person; to the Aquário Natural (14km round-trip) costs US$3. The drivers wait around for the duration of the tour. To Balneário Municipal (7km) is US$1.50 (one-way).

PONTA PORÃ

☎ 0xx67 / pop 61,000

Ponta Porã is a dusty border town divided from the Paraguayan town of Pedro Juan Caballero by Av Internacional. It was a center

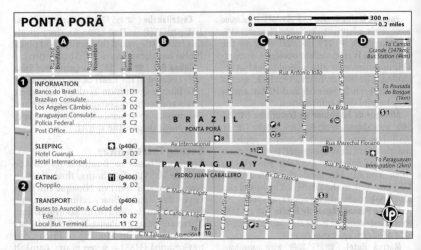

PONTA PORÃ

0 — 300 m
0 — 0.2 miles

INFORMATION
Banco do Brasil.....................1 D1
Brazilian Consulate...............2 C2
Los Angeles Câmbio..............3 D2
Paraguayan Consulate...........4 C1
Policia Federal.....................5 D2
Post Office..........................6 D1

SLEEPING 🏠 (p406)
Hotel Guarujá......................7 D2
Hotel Internacional...............8 C2

EATING 🍴 (p406)
Choppão..............................9 D2

TRANSPORT (p406)
Buses to Asunción & Cuidad del
Este.................................10 B2
Local Bus Terminal..............11 C2

for the *yerba maté* trade in the late 19th century, long before it started attracting Brazilians who like to play in the Paraguayan casinos and shop for perfumes, electronics and musical condoms.

Information

Getting exit/entry stamps involves a bit of legwork, so if you're in a hurry, grab a cab. For Brazilian entry/exit stamps, go to the **Federal Police** (☎ 431 1428; Av Presidente Vargas, Ponta Porã; ⊗ 8am-5pm), near the Paraguayan consulate. For Paraguayan entry/exit stamps, the **Paraguayan immigration office** (☎ 431 6312; Av Dr Francis; ⊗ 7am-noon & 2-5pm Mon-Fri, 7am-noon Sat) is about 2km east of the local bus terminal. It's a large, brown building.
Banco do Brasil (Av Brasil 2623) On the corner of Rua Guia Lopes, with a Visa ATM.
Los Angeles Câmbio (cnr Calle Mariscal López & Calle Curupayty, Pedro Juan Caballero) Changes cash at a reasonable rate.

Sleeping & Eating

This area is now heavily patrolled by Brazilian and Paraguayan authorities. Drug trafficking is on the rise and it's a good idea to limit your nighttime activities.
Hotel Internacional (☎ 431 1243; Av Internacional 2604; s/d quartos US$6/12, apartamentos US$14/24; ⊠) A safe, inexpensive option.
Hotel Guarujá (☎ 431 9515; Rua Guia Lopes 63; s/d apartamentos US$8/12; P ⊠) Large *apartamentos*. Friendly service.

Pousada do Bosque (☎ 431 1181; www.hotelpousada dobosque.com.br, in Portuguese; Av Presidente Vargas 1151; s/d apartamentos US$12/19; P ⊠ ⊠) Extremely good value for a hotel with such extensive facilities. Just outside town.
Choppão (☎ 431 2275; Rua Marechal Floriano 1877; dishes US$5) A popular spot with an extensive menu of meat, fish and pasta.

Getting There & Around

From the **bus station** (☎ 431 4145), about 4km from the center of Ponta Porã, frequent buses go to Campo Grande (US$10, 5½ hours, nine daily). There's one bus to Corumbá via Bonito; it's usually at 6am but it changes frequently.

For Foz do Iguaçu, take a bus from the bus station on Calle Alberdi in Pedro Juan Caballero (on the Paraguayan side) to Ciudad del Este (Paraguay) is just across the border from the Brazilian town of Foz do Iguaçu. There are daily buses to Ciudad del Este (US$8, eight hours, twice daily). You don't need a Paraguayan visa to transit through Paraguay on your way to Foz do Iguaçu. From the same bus station in Pedro Juan Caballero, there are also frequent buses to Asunción, the capital of Paraguay (US$7 to US$9, seven hours).

If you're coming into town from the Brazilian side, the bus can drop you at the local bus terminal on Av Internacional, near the hotels.

The Northeast

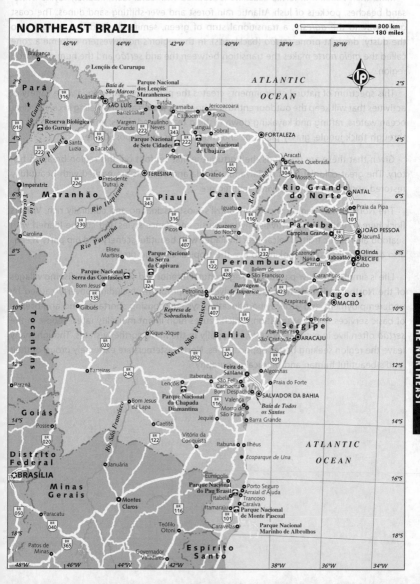

NORTHEAST BRAZIL

Brazil's Northeast is a true tropical paradise of year-round warmth, physical beauty and sensual culture rich in folkloric traditions.

More than 2000km of fertile coastline is studded with coral reefs, insanely idyllic white-sand beaches, pockets of lush Atlantic rain forest and ever-shifting sand dunes. The coast gives way to the *agreste*, a transitional strip of green, semifertile land that merges into the dusty, drought-prone *sertão* (backlands). In the region's northwestern extreme a zone called the *meio norte* makes the transition between the arid *sertão* and the humid Amazon region.

This spectrum of natural environments creates the perfect backdrop for a wide variety of activities that will keep the outdoor enthusiast hopping. Diving and snorkeling in crystal-clear ocean waters, rafting and kayaking down rushing tea-colored rivers, and hiking and biking through thick jungle, grassy plains or arid moonscapes are all possibilities.

Given that these are the lands the Portuguese first set foot on, this region breathes history. The great colonial cities of Salvador, Olinda and São Luís are packed with beautifully restored and satisfyingly decaying architecture.

The Northeastern region is possibly Brazil's most fascinating and culturally rich. Visitors flock here to enjoy lively festivals, myriad music and dance styles and cuisine loaded with seafood and exotic fruit. Magical beach villages with beautiful scenery and hip party scenes also draw yearly crowds looking to live the tropical-vacation dream.

Life is simple and slow-paced in the agricultural interior and simple coastal fishing villages of the Northeast. People here face massive social problems, including poverty caused by underemployment and a decaying education system, housing shortages and an absence of basic services such as sanitation, which causes high infant mortality rates. People in the *sertão* often live in extreme poverty, especially in the more northerly states. Though many leave the region seeking better opportunities, Northeasterners are extremely proud of their land's beautiful human and physical geography.

Bahia

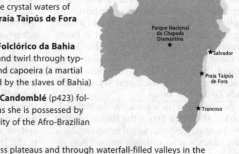

HIGHLIGHTS

- Gazing at the twinkling nighttime lights around Trancoso's magical **Quadrado** (p461)
- Floating in the crystal waters of white-sand **Praia Taipús de Fora** (p448)
- Seeing **Balé Folclórico da Bahia** (p431) whip and twirl through typical dances and capoeira (a martial art developed by the slaves of Bahia)
- Witnessing a **Candomblé** (p423) follower shiver as she is possessed by an *orixá* (a deity of the Afro-Brazilian religions)
- Trekking across plateaus and through waterfall-filled valleys in the **Parque Nacional da Chapada Diamantina** (p471)

Parque Nacional da Chapada Diamantina ★
★ Salvador
★ Praia Taipús de Fora
★ Trancoso

- POPULATION: 13.1 MILLION
- AREA: 567,295 SQ KM

THE NORTHEAST

When you imagine Brazil, if you think of idyllic white-sand beaches, indigenous villages concealed from the outside world by rain forest, drums pounding out rhythms you couldn't name and sweaty bodies moving through forbidden dances, then you are imagining Bahia. If you picture yourself running around day and night in very little clothing, sipping a fruit cocktail on a lounge chair and being taught dance steps by an enthusiastic new friend, you are picturing yourself in Bahia.

Endless stretches of gorgeous beaches line Bahia's dreamy coast. The southern coast is the most sought after, its warm waters ranging from calm (by reefs) to cut (by surfboards). In a few hip villages, beach culture mingles with chic nouveau-hippy, rustic reggae and progressive rave scenes, creating a unique magic that entrances visitors.

Bahia's interior, the dusty *sertão* (backlands), is pure *forró*-dancing cowboys, save for Parque Nacional da Chapada Diamantina, a forested mountain oasis that will keep you trading between your hiking boots and your bathing suit with its alluring treks and waterfalls.

Salvador, Bahia's capital, and the *recôncavo*, a fertile zone nearby, have charming cobblestone streets, colorful colonial facades and endless churches that recall the state's historical importance.

As can be seen in the faces of its people, Bahia received the majority of the African slaves brought to Brazil. The result is a culture rich in hypnotic drum beats, graceful movement, fragrant spices, inherent sensuality and *axé*: divine energy that brings good luck and positive results.

History

Brazil's history since Europeans entered the scene began in Bahia. After sighting Monte Pascoal (in southern Bahia) in April 1500, early explorer Pedro Cabral sailed north for three days in search of a safe port. The landing, officially considered the first Portuguese landfall in Brazil, was not at Porto Seguro as is commonly thought, but 16km north at Coroa Vermelha. The sailors celebrated their first Mass in the New Land, stocked up on supplies, and set sail after only 10 days on shore.

According to the legend, on November 1, 1501 – All Saints' Day – the Italian navigator Amerigo Vespucci sailed into Salvador's bay, which was accordingly named Baía de Todos os Santos. Forty eight years later, Tomé de Souza returned under orders by the Portuguese crown to found Brazil's first capital, Salvador da Bahia.

To fuel this new country, cultivation of sugarcane and tobacco was established in the fertile *recôncavo* region that surrounds the Baía de Todos os Santos. Some of the earliest encounters between Portuguese, African and indigenous peoples, and therefore the establishment of the Brazilian people, occurred in the *recôncavo*.

Sugar cultivation was successful in the *recôncavo*, not only because of the excellent growing conditions but also from its relative proximity to Portuguese sugar markets, favorable winds for sailing to Europe and the excellent harbors afforded by the Baía de Todos os Santos. The sugar-plantation system was firmly entrenched by the end of the 16th century and continued to grow from the sweat of African slaves for another 250 years.

Tobacco came a bit later to the *recôncavo*. Traded to African slave hunters and kings, it was the key commodity in the slave-trade triangle. The big fortunes were made growing sugar, not tobacco, as sugar was a hardier crop and the estates were much larger. On the other hand, tobacco required fewer slaves, making it more attractive to poorer Portuguese settlers. A less-rigid social hierarchy developed on tobacco plantations. Settlers actually worked occasionally!

A second, subsidiary industry in the area was cattle ranching, which provided food for the plantation hands and a means to transport fuel wood to the sugar mills and processed cane to market. Cattle breeding started in the *recôncavo* and spread inland, radiating west into the *sertão* and Minas Gerais, then northwest into Piauí.

Primary products were shipped out, while slaves and European luxury goods were shipped in. Bahia was colonial Brazil's economic heartland.

The first African slaves were brought from Guinea in 1538, and in the end, the largest percentage of the African slaves brought to the New World were brought to Brazil's Northeast. With their numbers, they managed to maintain much of their African culture. Upon finding their own religious practices prohibited, slaves kept their Candomblé *terreiros* (venues) hidden or far from town and syncretized their gods with Catholic saints. African food and music enriched the homes of both Blacks and Whites, and the African culture deeply

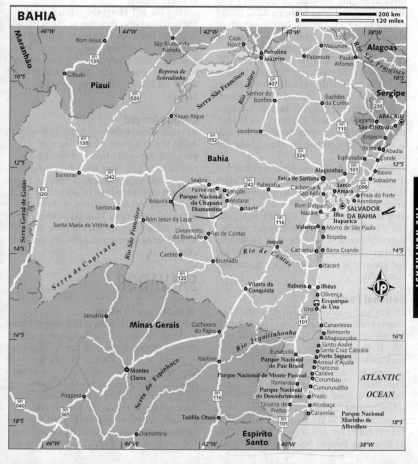

influenced the newly developing Brazilian culture. Actually, the almost equal ratio of Blacks to Whites in colonial Bahia threatened the social hierarchy enforced by the White community, and Quilombos (communities of runaway slaves) terrified the landed aristocracy.

Bahia's capital city, Salvador da Bahia, served as the capital of colonial Brazil from 1549 to 1763, and was the center of the sugar industry, which sustained the prosperity of the country until the decline in international sugar prices in the 1820s.

Climate

Bahia's tropical Atlantic coast remains hot and humid all year long, with high temperatures averaging between 26°C (79°F) and 30°C (86°F) and lows between 22°C (72°F) and 24°C (75°F). The southern coast (from about Porto Seguro south) is cooler during winter months, with low temperatures dropping as low as 17°C (63°F). Monthly rainfall averages on the coast run between 100mm and 350mm, with the period between March and June being the wettest. The southern coast has smaller monthly rainfall averages, between 100mm and 170mm, and though there is more rain from April to July, rain is seen pretty consistently throughout the year.

The Chapada Diamantina remains hot during the day and pleasantly cool at night throughout the year. High temperatures average between 27°C (81°F) and 32°C (90°F), and lows between 16°C (61°F) and 20°C (68°F). Monthly rainfall averages range between 50mm and 170mm, with November to March being the wettest months, making for greener scenery and fuller rivers and waterfalls.

National Parks

Divers and snorkelers will love the clear waters and colorful variety of coral and marine life in the Parque Nacional Marinho de Abrolhos (p465). The 913-sq-km marine park includes an archipelago and expanses of coral reef off the very south of the Bahian coast. Also in southern Bahia, coastal Parque Nacional de Monte Pascoal (p464) offers limited hiking, excellent views from its peak and is overseen by an indigenous Pataxó tribe. Set well west of Salvador, the 1520-sq-km Parque Nacional da Chapada

Diamantina (p471) is by far Bahia's most spectacular national park. A well-developed network of tour providers and guides offer treks and a range of adventure sports in and around the park, which abounds with waterfalls, green valleys, towering peaks and wildlife.

Getting There & Away

Bahia's primary airport is located in its capital, Salvador. If coming from the south, and looking to skip over Espírito Santo, an excellent option is to fly into Porto Seguro, which has regular daily flights and is served by a number of carriers. Ilhéus' airport is Bahia's third most trafficked, but you will probably find fares to be higher than those to Porto Seguro.

Hwy BR-101 skirts the Bahian coastline but remains between 50km to 75km inland. It is the main thoroughfare through the state and the chosen route of most long-distance buses. There are good coastal highways only between Canavieiras and Itacaré and from Salvador north to the border with Sergipe.

Getting Around

As is the norm in the Northeast, throughout Bahia there is always some form of transportation between where you are and where you need to go. Aside from buses, Kombis and *bestas* (vans that run a specific route and will stop anywhere to drop off or pick up passengers) are common in rural areas, as are collective taxis. Mototaxis (motorcycle taxis) are almost always available in small to mid-sized towns and taxis are available everywhere.

SALVADOR

☎ 0xx71 / pop 2.4 million

Salvador da Bahia, often called simply Bahia by locals, is one of the brightest gems in Brazil's crown. Known as the African soul of Brazil, it is the darkest city in terms of skin color and the hottest in terms of culture. Here the descendants of African slaves have preserved their cultural roots more than anywhere else in the New World, successfully transforming them into thriving culinary, religious, musical, dance and martial art traditions. Salvador is famous for combining all of these sacred and secular elements in its wild popular festivals, but even on ordinary days you can still round a corner and bump into a capoeira (a martial art developed by the slaves of Bahia) circle or a drum corps pounding out samba reggae, munch *acarajé* (bean dumplings fried in *dendê* oil filled with dried shrimp, spiced manioc paste and sauces, which is still sold on the streets of Nigeria) and witness a Candomblé follower be possessed by an African deity.

Salvador has a vibrant historic center, which is packed with colonial architecture, much of it renovated and painted in bright pastels. For good reason, its cobblestone streets have become something of a tourist mecca and are rarely empty due to the area's happening nightlife. You may want to dedicate the better part of a week to checking out the churches (one for every day of the year, according to popular belief) and other sights, catching some rays on the beaches and dancing into the night in this incredibly musical city.

HISTORY

In 1549, Tomé de Souza landed on Praia Porto da Barra under Portuguese royal orders to found Brazil's first capital, bringing city plans, a statue, 400 soldiers and 400 settlers, including priests and prostitutes. He founded the city in a defensive location: on a cliff top facing the sea. After the first year, a city of mud and straw had been erected, and by 1550 the surrounding walls were in place to protect against attacks from hostile Indians. Salvador da Bahia remained Brazil's most important city for the next three centuries.

During its first century of existence, the city depended upon the export of sugarcane from the fertile *recôncavo* region at the northern end of Baía de Todos os Santos. Later, dependence shifted as tobacco cultivation and cattle ranching were introduced to the *recôncavo* and *sertão*. These exports, topped off by gold and diamonds mined in the Bahian interior, provided Salvador with immense wealth, as is visible in the city's opulent baroque architecture.

African slaves were first brought to Salvador in 1538, and in 1587 historian Gabriel Soares tallied an estimated 12,000 Whites, 8000 converted Indians and 4000 Black slaves. The number of Blacks eventually increased to constitute half of the city's population, and uprisings of Blacks threatened Salvador's stability several times.

After Lisbon, Salvador was the second most important city in the Portuguese empire and the glory of colonial Brazil, famed for its many gold-filled churches, beautiful mansions and numerous festivals. It was also renowned as early as the 17th century for its bawdy public life, sensuality and decadence – so much so that its bay won the nickname Baia de Todos os Santos e de Quase Todos os Pecados (Bay of All Saints and of Nearly All Sins)!

Salvador remained Brazil's seat of colonial government until 1763 when, with the decline of the sugarcane industry, the capital was moved to Rio.

In 1798, the city was the stage for the Conjuração dos Alfaiates (Conspiracy of the Tailors), which intended to proclaim a Bahian republic. Although this uprising was quickly quelled, battles between those longing for independence and those loyal to Portugal continued in the streets of Salvador for many years. It was only on July 2, 1823, with the defeat in Cabrito and Pirajá of the Portuguese troops commanded by Madeira de Melo, that the city found peace. At that time, Salvador numbered 45,000 inhabitants and was the commercial center of a vast territory.

For most of the 19th and 20th centuries the city stagnated as the agricultural economy, based on archaic arrangements for land distribution, organization of labor and production, went into uninterrupted decline. Today, Salvador is Brazil's third-largest city, the largest in the Northeast. Only recently has it begun to move forward economically. New industries such as petroleum, chemicals and tourism are producing changes in the urban landscape, but the rapidly increasing population is still faced with major economic and social problems.

ORIENTATION

Salvador sits at the southern tip of a V-shaped peninsula at the mouth of the Baía de Todos os Santos. The city can be difficult to navigate as there are many one-way, no-left-turn streets that wind through Salvador's hills and valleys. The center of the city is on the bay

THE NORTHEAST

SALVADOR

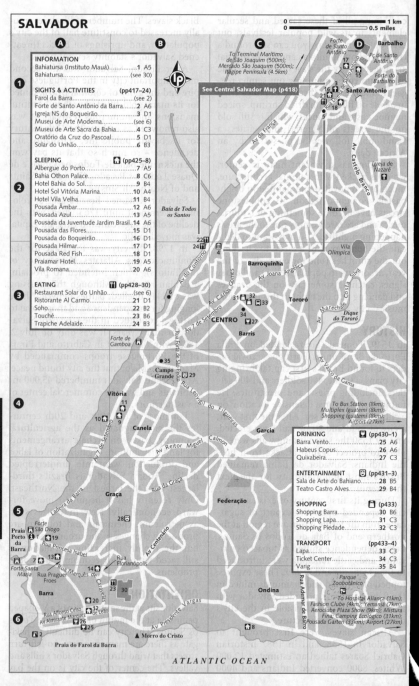

0 ——————— 1 km
0 ——————— 0.5 miles

INFORMATION
Bahiatursa (Instituto Mauá)..............1 A5
Bahiatursa...................................(see 30)

SIGHTS & ACTIVITIES (pp417–24)
Farol da Barra................................(see 2)
Forte de Santo Antônio da Barra........2 A6
Igreja NS do Boqueirão....................3 D1
Museu de Arte Moderna.................(see 6)
Museu de Arte Sacra da Bahia..........4 C3
Oratório da Cruz do Pascoal............5 D1
Solar do Unhão...............................6 B3

SLEEPING (pp425–8)
Albergue do Porto...........................7 A5
Bahia Othon Palace.........................8 C6
Hotel Bahia do Sol..........................9 B4
Hotel Sol Vitória Marina.................10 A4
Hotel Vila Velha............................11 B4
Pousada Âmbar.............................12 A6
Pousada Azul................................13 A5
Pousada da Juventude Jardim Brasil.14 A6
Pousada das Flores........................15 D1
Pousada do Boqueirão....................16 D1
Pousada Hilmar.............................17 D1
Pousada Red Fish..........................18 D1
Praiamar Hotel..............................19 A5
Vila Romana.................................20 A6

EATING (pp428–30)
Restaurant Solar do Unhão.............(see 6)
Ristorante Al Carmo.......................21 D1
Soho..22 B2
Touché...23 B6
Trapiche Adelaide..........................24 B3

To Terminal Marítimo
de São Joaquim (500m);
Mercado São Joaquim (500m);
Itagipe Peninsula (4.5km);

See Central Salvador Map (p418)

Forte
de Santo
Antônio

Barbalho
Pç de Santo
Antônio
Forte do
Barbalho
Santo Antonio

Igreja de
Nazaré

Nazaré

Baía de Todos
os Santos

Vila
Olímpica

Barroquinha

Tororó

Dique
do Tororó

CENTRO

Barris

Forte de
Gamboa

Campo
Grande

Vitória

Canela

Garcia

DRINKING (pp430–1)
Barra Vento..................................25 A6
Habeus Copus...............................26 A6
Quixabeira....................................27 C3

ENTERTAINMENT (pp431–3)
Sala de Arte do Bahiano.................28 B5
Teatro Castro Alves.......................29 B4

SHOPPING (p433)
Shopping Barra.............................30 B6
Shopping Lapa..............................31 C3
Shopping Piedade.........................32 C3

TRANSPORT (pp433–4)
Lapa..33 C3
Ticket Center................................34 C3
Varig..35 B4

Graça

Federação

To Bus Station (8km);
Multiplex Iguatemi (8km);
Shopping Iguatemi (8km);
Airport (27km)

Forte
São Diogo
Praia
Porto
da
Barra

Forte Santa
Maria

Barra

Ondina

Parque
Zoobotânico

To Hospital Aliança (1km);
Fashion Clube (4km); Yemanjá (7km);
Aeroclube Plaza Show (9km); Mistura
Fina; Camping Ecologico (31km);
Pousada Garten (33km); Airport (27km)

Praia do Farol da Barra

Morro do Cristo

ATLANTIC OCEAN

THE NORTHEAST

FOLK ART

Bahia has some of Brazil's best artisans, who usually have small shops or sell in the local market. You can buy their folk art in Salvador, but the best place to see or purchase the real stuff is in the town of origin, as so much of the production is regional and specialized.

The main materials used in Bahian folk art are leather, wood, earth, metal and fiber. The city of Feira de Santana is known for its leatherwork. Maragojipinho, Rio Real and Cachoeira produce earthenware. Caldas do Jorro, Caldas de Cipo and Itaparica specialize in straw crafts. Rio de Contas and Muritiba do metalwork. Ilha de Maré is famous for lacework. Jequié, Valença and Feira de Santana are woodworking centers. Santo Antônio de Jesus, Rio de Contas and Monte Santo manufacture goods made of leather and silver.

---

mostly male crowd, this club heats up with thumping electronica.

Cinemas

The **Cinema XIV** (Map pp418-9; ☎ 331 1279; Rua Frei Vicente 12-14, Pelourinho) and **Sala de Arte do Bahiano** (Map p414; ☎ 331 1279; Clube Bahiano de Tênis, Av Princesa Leopoldina 398, Graça) show international art-house films. In the malls are **Lapa I e II** (Map p414; ☎ 328 1121; Shopping Lapa, Rua Portão da Piedade, Piedade), **Barra I e II** (Map p414; ☎ 264 5795; Shopping Barra, Av Centenário 2992, Chame-Chame), **Multiplex Iguatemi** (☎ 450 6636; Shopping Iguatemi, Av Tancredo Neves, Pituba) and **Multiplex Aeroclube** (☎ 461 0604; Aeroclube Plaza Show, Av Otávio Mangabeira, Boca do Rio).

SHOPPING

Mercado Modelo (Map pp418-9; ☎ 241 2893; Praça Cayru; ☼ 9am-7pm Mon-Sat, 9am-2pm Sun) This two-story, enclosed tourist market has dozens of stalls selling local handicrafts ranging from embroidery to musical instruments. More of the same can be purchased in shops throughout the Pelourinho.

Shopping Iguatemi (☎ 350 5050; Av Tancredo Neves, Pituba; ☼ 9am-10pm Mon-Sat, 2-8pm Sun) Salvador's largest and chicest mall is a convenient place to see a movie while you wait for your bus, since the bus station is right across the road.

The twin malls of **Shopping Lapa** (Map p414; ☎ 328 8200; Rua Portão da Piedade, Piedade; ☼ 9am-9pm Mon-Fri, 9am-8pm Sat) and **Shopping Piedade** (Map p414; ☎ 328 1555; Rua Portão da Piedade, Piedade; ☼ 9am-9pm Mon-Fri, 9am-8pm Sat) are much smaller and less upscale than **Shopping Barra** (Map p414; ☎ 339 8222; Av Centenário 2992, Chame-Chame; ☼ 10am-10pm Mon-Fri, 10am-9pm Sat, 3-9pm Sun) but walking distance from the Pelourinho.

GETTING THERE & AWAY
Air

Aeroporto Deputado Luis Eduardo do Magalhães (code SSA; ☎ 204 1010; São Cristovão) is serviced by **Gol** (☎ 204 1603; airport), **TAM** (☎ 342 0123; airport), **Varig** (Map p414; ☎ 204 1050, 343 3100; Tropical Hotel da Bahia, Av 7 de Setembro 1537) and **VASP** (Map pp418-9; ☎ 204 1304; Rua Miguel Calmon 27, Comércio). There are daily flights to any Brazilian destination – be sure to ask how many stops will be made. It's worth checking up on airline specials as flying can sometimes be nominally more expensive than the bus. One-way fares from Salvador to São Paulo run around US$160, to Rio US$165, to Recife US$75 and to Fortaleza US$115, though there are constant promotional sales and seasonal variations.

Air Europa (☎ 204 1625; airport) and **TAP** (Air Portugal; ☎ 243 6122; Av Estados Unidos 137, sala 401, Comércio) connect Salvador with Europe. Flights to and from other international destinations go via São Paulo or Rio.

Boat

Boats to points on Baía de Todos os Santos leave from the **Terminal Marítimo Turístico** (Map pp418-9; ☎ 326 6603; Av da França), behind the Mercado Modelo, and the **Terminal Marítimo de São Joaquim** (☎ 633 1248; Av Oscar Pontes, Água de Menino). See p435 and p436 for more information.

Boats heading for Morro de São Paulo also leave from the Terminal Marítimo Turístico. Four companies have *lanchas rapidas* (speed boats; US$16.50, two hours) and two run catamarans (US$15, two hours). The number of daily departures varies according to demand.

Bus

Most Salvador buses coming from the south go around the Baía de Todos os Santos, but alternately you can disembark at Bom Despacho on the Ilha de Itaparica,

Destination	Duration (Hours)	Cost	Frequency	Company
Aracaju	4½	US$10-15	10 daily	Bonfim (☎ 460 0000)
Belo Horizonte	24	US$51	daily	São Geraldo (☎ 450 4488)
Fortaleza	22	US$56	daily	Itapamirim (☎ 450 5644)
Ilhéus	8	US$19	3 daily	Águia Branca (☎ 450 5539)
João Pessoa	14	US$24	daily	Bonfim (☎ 460 0000)
Lençóis	6	US$11	2 daily	Real Express (☎ 450 9310)
Maceió	9	US$15-21	4 daily	Bonfim (☎ 460 0000)
Natal	21	US$40-43	2 daily	São Geraldo (☎ 450 4488)
Porto Seguro	11	US$29	daily	Águia Branca (☎ 450 5539)
Recife	11	US$26-31	2 daily	Itapamirim (☎ 450 5644)
Rio	24-28	US$48-59	4 daily	Águia Branca (☎ 450 5539) & Itapamirim (☎ 450 5644)
São Paulo	33	US$59-71	3 daily	São Geraldo (☎ 450 4488)
Vitória	19	US$47	daily	Águia Branca (☎ 450 5539)

and catch a boat (p435) across the bay. Some bus companies sell their tickets at convenient locations throughout the city, usually at malls. Ask Emtursa or Bahiatursa for more information. **Ticket Center** (Map p414; ☎ 329 5433; Rua Portão da Piedade, Piedade), located facing Shopping Piedade, sells tickets for a variety of bus companies. More buses are added during high travel times. (See table above).

GETTING AROUND
To/From the Airport
The airport is located about 30km east of the center. A taxi to the center will cost you around US$11.50. There are also air-conditioned minibuses (US$1.50) to the center marked 'Praça da Sé/Aeroporto.' City buses leave from a depot behind the parking garage.

Buses to the airport depart regularly from the so-called Praça da Sé bus stop (Map pp418-9), actually a block southeast of Praça Municipal. Supposedly they leave every 30 minutes, but the schedule is rather flexible, so leave plenty of time. The bus goes down Av 7 de Setembro to Barra, and continues along the coast before heading inland to the airport. In light traffic, the ride takes about an hour; with traffic allow 1¾ hours.

A municipal Aeroporto bus follows the same route to the airport, but gets very crowded and isn't recommended if you're carrying a bag.

To/From the Bus Station
Salvador's **bus station** (☎ 460 8300) is 8km east of the city center. A taxi to Cidade Alta or Barra runs US$4.50. Air-con minibuses (US$1.50) marked 'Praça da Sé' go to the center from in front of Shopping Iguatemi, just across the footbridge out front. For Barra, catch the Barra 1 bus in front of the bus station. Any bus that goes to Shopping Iguatemi will get you to the bus station.

Public Transportation
Linking Cidade Alta and Cidade Baixa are the **Elevador Lacerda** (Map pp418-9; ☎ 322 7049; US$0.05; ☼ 24hr) and the **Plano Inclinado Gonçalves** (funicular railway; Map pp418-9; US$0.05; ☼ 7am-7pm Mon-Fri, 7am-1pm Sat).

There are two main city bus terminals in the center that can serve as destinations or transfer points: Terminal da França (Map pp418-9) in the Comércio and Lapa (Map p414), behind Shoppings Lapa and Piedade. The air-con minibuses are sometimes four times the cost of a regular fare. Taxis can be taken at meter price (legal) or negotiated.

BAÍA DE TODOS OS SANTOS

The Baía de Todos os Santos is Brazil's largest bay, and was at one time among the hemisphere's most important. The 56 islands contained in the 1000-sq-km bay have lush vegetation and architectural remnants of its historic past.

ILHA DE ITAPARICA
☎ 0xx71 / pop 48,660

Itaparica has long been an escape for the residents of Salvador, whether for the day or the weekend (its shores are lined with vacation homes). It's a place to swim in the calm waters of the bay and hold the city at arm's length. Though the beaches can't compare with those on Salvador's northern coast, and Club Med has privatized the best one, they are still a fine place to get some sun, salt and relative peace. Mar Grande (9km south of Bom Despacho) is perhaps the most likeable town on the island, with lots of bars and restaurants and a relaxed atmosphere.

Sights & Activities

Guarding the northern tip of the island, the **Forte de São Lourenço** (1711) was built by Dutch invaders and figured prominently in Bahia's battle for independence in 1823. Nearby, the city of Itaparica has a few historic constructions, including the **Solar Tenente Botas** (Lieutenant Botas Manor; Praça Tenente Brotas), the **Igreja Matriz do Santíssimo Sacramento** (Rua Luís Gama), built in 1715, and the **Fonte da Bica** (mineral-water fountain), from 1842. In the center of the island, a huge tree wraps its roots around the ruins of the **Igreja Baiacu** and grows right out of them.

BEACHES

Praia Ponta de Areia (2km north of Bom Despacho) is a thin strip of sand with clear, shallow water and *barracas* serving good seafood. **Praia da Penha** (10km south of Bom Despacho) is a nice beach with excellent views of Salvador. **Praia Barra Grande** (7km further south) is Itaparica's finest public beach. It has clear water and weekend homes, and lies in front of its namesake village. Bahians, who love a beach with lots of people on it, consider **Cacha Pregos** (20km further south) the island's best.

Sleeping & Eating

The following are high-season prices.

Zimbo Tropical (☎ 638 1148; zimbo_tropical@zipmail.com.br; Aratuba; s/d with fan US$13.50/23.50) Sweet bungalows are spread through a gorgeously lush garden just 200m from the beach. The laid-back owners offer group meals and excursions to local sights, speak French and English and can make tiny monkeys magically emerge from the trees. If this sounds like the tropical pousada you imagined you'd find in Brazil, a trip to Itaparica just to stay here is highly recommended. Ask the Kombi driver to let you off at the Brazil Gás store at the northern entrance to Aratuba (28km south of Bom Despacho), and walk 200m down Rua Iemenjá toward the beach. A taxi from Bom Despacho or Mar Grande runs US$8.50.

Pousada e Restaurante Koisa Nossa (☎ 633 1028; Av Juvenal João Vinagre 173; s/d with fan & TV US$6.50/10; 🍴) In Mar Grande, 200m straight up from the dock, this pousada has two floors of simple, slightly run-down rooms surrounding a grassy yard. You'll find it to be a friendly, relaxed place and it serves up fresh, tasty seafood.

Pousada Arco-Íris (☎ /fax 633 1130; www.parcoiris.na-web.net, in Portuguese; Estrada da Gamboa 102; d without bathroom with fan US$25.50, d with fan US$29.50, d cabin with fan US$36.50; 🍴) Around the corner from Koisa Nossa, Arco-Íris is set on the unmanicured grounds of an old mango ranch. A variety of rooms are available in the antique-laden main house, which dates back to 1890, and cabins are spread throughout the yard. The whole place has an air of neglect with a few pretty touches. **Manga Rosa** (🕐 lunch & dinner), the attached restaurant, serves large portions of acclaimed Bahian and international cuisine. The bar and dance floor allegedly get going on weekends.

Restaurante Philippe (☎ 633 1060; 🕐 lunch & dinner) Back near the dock, this is as well regarded as Manga Rosa and has a similar spectrum of flavors.

Camping Praia de Berlinque (☎ 638 3746; per person US$2) A camping ground on the beach 30km south of Bom Despacho.

Getting There & Away
BOAT

Schedules change with the seasons, so times below should be verified.

Passenger ferries (US$1, 50 minutes, every 30 minutes from 7am to 6:50pm) leave from Salvador's Terminal Marítimo Turístico for Mar Grande's **terminal** (☎ 633 1248), and return from 6:30am to 7:30pm. Buy your return ticket ahead of time on summer days.

A car ferry (US$1.50, car US$11, one hour, hourly from 5am to 11:30pm) and a catamaran (US$1.50, 30 minutes, seven daily) run between Salvador's Terminal Marítimo de São Joaquim and Bom Despacho. Expect a long wait to get on the ferry on weekends, especially in summer.

BUS
Frequent buses leave from Bom Despacho's **bus/ferry terminal** (☎ 319 2890) for Valença (US$3, two hours, five daily).

Getting Around
Kombis leave from the boat terminals in both Bom Despacho and Mar Grande and run a circuit around the island until about 8pm. Some unscrupulous drivers overcharge tourists, so remember that no fare should be over US$2. Bicycles are widely available to rent (US$6.50 per day).

OTHER ISLANDS
The lesser Baía de Todos os Santos islands include **Ilha Bom Jesus dos Passos**, which has traditional fishing boats and artisans; **Ilha**
dos Frades (named after two monks who were killed and cannibalized there by local Indians), which has attractive waterfalls and palm trees; and **Ilha da Maré** with the quiet beaches of **Itamoabo** and **Bacia das Neves** and the 17th-century **Igreja de NS das Neves**.

Tour companies in Salvador offer boat tours of the bay (US$11.50) to either Ilha da Maré, or Ilha dos Frades and Ilha de Itaparica, from Salvador's Terminal Marítimo Turístico. Alternatively, boats to Ilha da Maré (US$1, 20 minutes, every 40 minutes from 8am to 5:30pm) leave from São Tomé de Paripe's **terminal** (☎ 307 1447), 25km north of the city. To get there, take the Base Naval/São Tomé bus to the end of the line (ask at tourist information about the most convenient place to catch the bus). For Ilha dos Frades, take an Oxalá bus from Salvador's main bus station to Madre de Deus (70km northwest of the city) and catch a boat for Paramana (US$0.50). You could also try your luck at hiring a boat from the small port next to the Mercado Modelo.

RECÔNCAVO

The *recôncavo* is a region of green, fertile lands surrounding the Baía de Todos os Santos, which historically proved to be among Brazil's best for growing sugar and tobacco. The profits reaped off these lands fueled colonial Salvador and built an impressive amount of colonial architecture, which can be seen today in a few pretty, quiet towns through the region. Most travelers pay Cachoeira (west of the bay) a visit to soak in the unique history of this area, but for more of an adventure, hire a boat across Baía de Todos os Santos to Maragojipe, a sweet colonial village, and then catch a bus on to Cachoeira and São Félix.

CACHOEIRA & SÃO FÉLIX

☎ 0xx75 / pop 30,325

Cachoeira, affectionately known as the jewel of the *recôncavo*, is a sleepy place, full of colorful, mostly preserved colonial architecture uncompromised by the presence of modern buildings. The town sits below a series of hills, strung along the banks of the Rio Paraguaçu in a face-off with its twin, São Félix. A steady trickle of tourism flows through the area, attracted by Brazil's best tobacco, a renowned center of Candomblé and a strong wood-sculpting tradition. If you get an early start, Cachoeira and São Félix make a great day trip from Salvador, or stay the night and explore at a more relaxed pace.

History

Diego Álvares, the father of Cachoeira's founders, was the sole survivor of a ship bound for the West Indies that was wrecked in 1510 on a reef near Salvador. This Portuguese Robinson Crusoe was saved by the Tupinambá Indians of Rio Vermelho, who dubbed the strange white sea creature Caramuru, or 'Fish-Man.' Álvares lived 20 years with the Indians and married Catarina do Paraguaçu, the daughter of the most powerful Tupinambá chief. Their sons João Gaspar Aderno Álvares and Rodrigues Martins Álvares killed off the local indigenous people, set up the first sugarcane *fazendas* (ranches) and founded Cachoeira.

By the 18th century, tobacco from Cachoeira was considered the world's finest,

sought by rulers in China and Africa. The 'holy herb' also became popular in Brazil, taken as snuff, smoked in a pipe or chewed.

Early in the 19th century, Cachoeira achieved fame as a center for military operations in Bahia to oust the Portuguese rulers, and was the first to recognize Dom Pedro I as the independent ruler of Brazil.

Information

There is a helpful **tourist office** (☎ 425 1123; Praça da Aclamação; ☉ 8am-noon & 1-5pm Mon-Fri, 1-4pm Sat & Sun) in Cachoeira and banks in both towns.

Sights & Activities

At some sights here, especially at churches, theft has been a problem, so you may have to pre-arrange a visit through the tourist office.

CACHOEIRA

At the **Casa da Câmara e Cadeia** (Prefecture & Jail; Praça da Aclamação) organized criminals ran the show upstairs and disorganized criminals were kept behind bars downstairs. The building dates to 1698 and served as the seat of the Bahian government in 1822. The old marble pillory was removed from out front after abolition.

The municipality's oldest hospital, the **Santa Casa de Misericórdia** (Praça Dr Milton; ☉ 2-5pm Mon-Fri) has a pretty chapel (1734) with a painted ceiling, gardens and an ossuary.

Churches

The **Igreja da Ordem Terceira do Carmo** (Praça da Aclamação; admission US$0.75; ☉ 2-5pm Tue-Sat, 9am-noon Sun) has a gilded baroque altar, paneled ceilings, *azulejos* and dates from 1702. In a side gallery are suffering polychrome Christs, imported from the Portuguese colony in Macao, dripping with bovine blood mixed with Chinese herbs and sparkling rubies.

The **Igreja Matriz NS do Rosário** (Rua Ana Nery) dates between 1693 and 1754. It has beautiful *azulejos* and a ceiling painted by Teófilo de Jesus. On the 2nd floor, the Museu das Alfaias contains remnants from the abandoned 17th-century Convento de São Francisco do Paraguaçu. The church is usually open mornings, but try knocking if you find it closed.

Cachoeira's oldest church is the tiny **Igreja de NS da Ajuda** (Largo da Ajuda), built in 1595 when the town was known as Arraial d'Ajuda.

The climb to the 18th-century Igreja de NS do Conceição do Monte is rewarded only by views as it is closed to visitors.

Museums

The **Museu Hansen Bahia** (Rua 13 de Maio; admission free; ☻ 9am-5pm Tue-Fri, 9am-2pm Sat & Sun) occupies the birthplace and former home of Brazilian heroine Ana Nery, who organized the nursing corps during the Paraguay War. Both Dom Pedro II and Princess Isabel once slept here as well. Today, it houses the work of German-Brazilian artist Hansen Bahia.

Among his powerful block prints and paintings on the theme of human suffering, depicting primarily prostitutes and Christ, is a series of illustrations of Castro Alves' poem *Návio Negreiro* (Slave Ship).

For a small donation, members of the exclusively female Boa Morte (Good Death) religious society will lead you around their barren one-room **Museu da Boa Morte** (Rua 13 de Maio; ☻ 10am-6pm). There are some good photos and usually members sit around in their whites, smoking pipes and gossiping. The society began as a sisterhood of slaves that assured dead slaves a proper burial and bought old slaves freedom, while on the side they passed information regarding slave uprisings and camouflaged events.

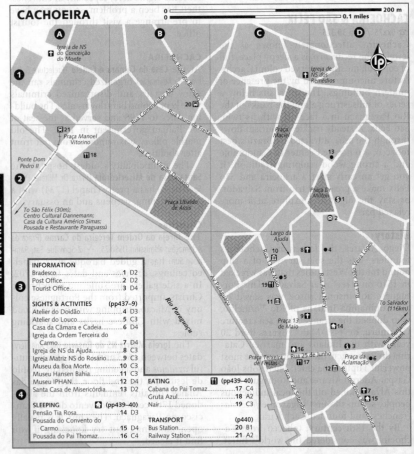

CACHOEIRA

INFORMATION	
Bradesco	1 D2
Post Office	2 D2
Tourist Office	3 D4

SIGHTS & ACTIVITIES	(pp437–9)
Atelier do Doidão	4 D3
Atelier do Louco	5 C3
Casa da Câmara e Cadeia	6 D4
Igreja da Ordem Terceira do Carmo	7 D4
Igreja de NS da Ajuda	8 C3
Igreja Matriz NS do Rosário	9 C3
Museu da Boa Morte	10 C3
Museu Hansen Bahia	11 C3
Museu IPHAN	12 D4
Santa Casa de Misericórdia	13 D2

SLEEPING	(pp439–40)
Pensão Tia Rosa	14 D3
Pousada do Convento do Carmo	15 D4
Pousada do Pai Thomaz	16 C4

EATING	(pp439–40)
Cabana do Pai Tomaz	17 C4
Gruta Azul	18 A2
Nair	19 C3

TRANSPORT	(p440)
Bus Station	20 B1
Railway Station	21 A2

THE NORTHEAST

Housed in an 18th-century colonial mansion, the humble **Museu IPHAN** (☎ 425 1123; Praça da Aclamação; admission US$0.50; ☺ 8am-noon & 2-5pm Mon-Fri, 8am-noon Sat), displays colonial furnishings and priestly vestments.

Woodcarving
Cachoeira has maintained a tradition of woodcarving with a heavy African flavor. Stop in on the *ateliers* (studios) of two of the best sculptors in town, **Doidão** and **Louco**, to get a sense of the local style.

Candomblé
Cachoeira is one of Candomblé's strongest and perhaps purest spiritual and religious centers. The *terreiros* are in small homes and shacks in the hills, where long ceremonies are usually held on Friday and Saturday nights. The tourist office is sometimes reluctant to give out information about Candomblé, but if you show respect for its traditions you may inspire confidence.

SÃO FÉLIX
Watch your footing while crossing the narrow and dilapidated bridge to São Félix, built by the British in 1885. Loose planks have claimed at least one life in recent years. When vehicles pass over the bridge it emits a wild cacophony of sounds not unlike one of those urban/industrial percussion acts.

The riverfront **Centro Cultural Dannemann** (☎ 425 2208; Av Salvador Pinto 29; admission free; ☺ 8am-noon & 1-4:30pm Tue-Sat, gallery only 1-4pm Sun) has modern art – surprisingly provocative for this backwater town – displayed throughout a converted warehouse. In a large room in the rear of the building, heavy with the rich smell of tobacco, women dressed in white with flowered head wraps sit at antique wooden tables rolling *charutos* (cigars), as has been done here since 1873. You are welcome to watch them at work and check out the displays of old machinery. Dannemann cigars are considered Brazil's finest.

Housed in another of Dannemann's old buildings, the **Casa da Cultura Américo Simas** (Rua Celestino João Severino Luz Neto 6; ☺ closed Mon) has rotating art and culture exhibits.

Festivals & Events
Festa de São João (June 22 to 24) The largest popular festival of Bahia's interior, celebrated with folklore, music, dancing and a generous amount of food and drink.

Festa da NS da Boa Morte (the Friday, Saturday and Sunday closest to August 15) Organized by the Boa Morte sisterhood: slave descendants pay tribute to their liberation with dance and prayer in a mix of Candomblé and Catholicism.

NS do Rosário (second half of October) Includes games, music and food.

NS da Ajuda (first half of November) Features a ritual *lavagem* (washing) of the church and a street festival.

Santa Bárbara or **Iansã** (December 4) Candomblé ceremony held in São Félix.

Sleeping & Eating
Expect prices quoted here to almost double during festivals.

Pousada do Convento do Carmo (☎ /fax 425 1716; Praça da Aclamação, Cachoeira; s/d with fan, TV & minibar US$13.50/15; ☒ ☒) The 18th-century convent attached to the Igreja da Ordem Terceira do Carmo has been converted into a lovely pousada with all the attributes and comforts of a modern hotel. The restaurant puts out a major breakfast spread and also serves lunch and dinner. The hotel pitches the adjoining church as its 'meeting room,' which is pure comedy.

Pousada e Restaurante Paraguassú (☎ 438 3386; p-paraguassu@uol.com.br; Av Salvador Pinto 1, São Félix; s/d with fan US$10/15; ☒) Located on the riverfront in São Félix, this modern pousada has fine rooms surrounding a flowery central courtyard. The restaurant is open for lunch and dinner and serves good typical food and pizza overlooking the river.

Pousada do Pai Thomaz (☎ 425 1288; Rua 25 de Junho 12, Cachoeira; s/d with fan US$5/10) Though the rooms are considerably more simple than the downstairs restaurant laden with local wood carvings, they are comfortable and bright.

Cabana do Pai Thomaz (☺ lunch & dinner) Across the street and linked to Pousada do Pai Thomaz, this restaurant serves good Bahian food and is filled with carved wooden panels and furniture, including scraps hanging from the ceiling.

Pensão Tia Rosa (☎ 425 1792; Rua Ana Nery 12, Cachoeira; s/d without bath US$4/8.50) Simple, windowless rooms are available in this family home.

Gruta Azul (☎ 425 1295; Praça Manoel Vitorino 2, Cachoeira; ☺ Sat & Sun) Sit out at a table on the plaza here and enjoy a Boa Morte cocktail and a snack or a bowl of soup at this local bar. Attached is one of the best restaurants

THE NORTHEAST

in Cachoeira, which has been under reforms and a pending ownership change for the past few years.

Nair (Rua 13 de Maio, Cachoeira; ⏾ lunch & dinner) This simple restaurant serves Bahian food and a decent *prato feito* (plate of the day, US$1). Locals delight in turning things around, often calling it Rian.

Getting There & Away

Daily buses depart Salvador for Cachoeira/São Félix (US$3, two hours, hourly from 5:30am to 9:30pm). Hourly return buses can be caught in either town from 4:20am to 6:30pm. You can also continue on to Feira de Santana (US$1, 1½ hours, 12 daily) to make further connections. For Valença, take either the 7:40am or 12:20pm bus from São Félix to Santo Antônio and connect from there.

SANTO AMARO

☎ 0xx75 / pop 58,395

Santo Amaro is a friendly colonial sugar town that sees very few tourists and has an unpretentious charm. It is most well known for being the hometown of the brother-sister pair Caetano Veloso and Maria Betânia, two of Brazil's most popular singers (who often put in an appearance during Carnaval). The center bustles with people, especially around the small outdoor market. Paper production has replaced sugar as the major industry, visible in the invasion of bamboo on the hillsides where sugarcane once flourished, and a large paper mill outside of town.

The decrepit sugar-baron mansions along the old commercial street, Rua General Câmara, and the numerous churches are reminders of Santo Amaro's prosperous days. The ornate **Matriz de NS da Purificação** (1668) is the largest church, with *azulejos* and a painted ceiling. Unfortunately, a gang of thieves stole most of the church's holy images and exported them to France.

The **Lavagem da Purificação** (January 23 to February 2) is celebrated by a procession and ritual washing of the church steps by *baianas* in traditional dress, before bands and *trios elétricos* take over the streets.

Some of the good nighttime local music is played at the sterile **Hotel Lôbo** (☎ 241 1721; Rua Conselheiro Paranhos 52; s/d with fan US$6.50/10; ⯌), with its modern, tiled rooms.

Buses leave Salvador for Santo Amaro (US$2.50, one hour 10 minutes, almost every 30 minutes from 5:30am to 9:30pm). Most continue on to Cachoeira/São Félix (US$1, 50 minutes).

NORTH OF SALVADOR

When Salvadorenos want a day at the beach or a quick getaway, they naturally head for Bahia's northern coast. As a result, proximity to the city dictates how full beaches are on Sundays and the number of weekend homes that crowd the shore. There are a few popular beach towns and a huge resort complex, but if tranquility is what you seek, don't despair: there are kilometers of deserted, pristine beaches. Bahia's northern coast is not as startling as its southern, but tall bluffs with rustling palms, white sands that grow progressively finer as you head north and a range of calm inlets to surfable waves are a recipe for enjoyment.

The Estrada do Coco (Coconut Hwy) runs as far north as Praia do Forte, where the Linha Verde (Green Line, an 'ecologically planned' highway) picks up, continuing all the way to the Sergipe border. You may feel that you are going against the grain if you are trying to access this coast heading north to south. Grassy medians in the highways require buses to pass town entrances and then double back, so few do. Instead, they drop passengers on the highway, leav-

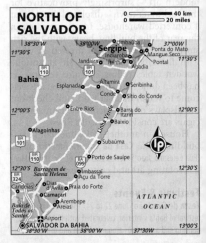

NORTH OF SALVADOR

0 — 40 km
0 — 20 miles

ing you to walk or pick up other transportation into the small towns and fishing communities along this stretch of coast. Traveling from south to north is a much smoother process.

AREMBEPE
☎ 0xx71

Arembepe's proximity to Salvador and its past fame keep visitors packing the beaches on weekends or swinging through to check out the *aldea hippy*, a hippy village that Mick Jagger and Janis Joplin got rolling in the 1960s. Unfortunately, pollution from the giant chemical plant to the south and an abundance of weekend homes detract from the beauty of the rocky coast. If you're looking for a quick escape from Salvador, there are prettier beaches than Arembepe, and more charming coastal villages.

The **Praia de Arembepe Hotel** (☎ 624 1415; Largo de São Francisco; d with fan & TV US$11.50) has simple, good-value rooms without breakfast. Rooms 101 and 201 have sea views. The **Pousada da Fazenda** (☎ 624 1030; Rua Piruí; d with fan & minibar US$13.50) has super-basic beachfront chalets, some with two stories

and veranda, and a bit of that hippy vibe. There is also a camping ground near the *aldea hippy*, which is a few kilometers outside of town.

From Salvador, catch an Arembepe bus from Terminal da França, or a Monte Gordo bus from Lapa (both US$1.50, 1¼ hours). Arembepe is 2km off the highway. Frequent buses continue on to Praia do Forte.

PRAIA DO FORTE
☎ 0xx71

Praia do Forte has been intentionally developed into an upmarket, ecological beach resort. The result is a pleasant and attractive tourist village that has retained something relating to its original size and charm. The main drag (Alameda do Sol) is a pedestrian walkway lined with nice restaurants and boutiques and dotted with trees. It leads to an adorably tiny church, a sea turtle reserve and fantastic, palm-lined beaches with fluffy white sands that fill up on weekends. Surrounding the village are a castle ruins, a lagoon for canoeing, and the Sapiranga forest reserve, which has hiking and biking trails and a zip line. If you can, time your visit

---

THE TAMAR PROJECT TO SAVE SEA TURTLES

Tamar is an abbreviation of the Portuguese name for sea turtles, TArtaruga MARinha. The highly successful Tamar project was created in 1980 by IBAMA (the Brazilian Environment Agency) and as it quickly expanded, a nonprofit foundation (Fundação Pró Tamar) was created to support, raise money and co-administer Tamar with the government. Its goal is to reverse the process of extinction of the five species of sea turtles in Brazil: loggerhead, hawksbill, olive ridley, green and leatherback.

At the Praia do Forte station you can see several small exhibiting pools with marine turtles of various sizes and species, as well as urchins, eels and other sea life. If you visit during the turtles' nesting season (September to March) you will see the hatcheries functioning. A museum featuring videos and multimedia programs shows the life of marine turtles, and a gift shop sells T-shirts and other souvenirs.

Tamar researchers protect around 550 nests a year along 50km of coast close to Praia do Forte. The eggs – moist, leathery, ping-pong-size balls – are buried in the sand when laid and either left on the beach or brought to the hatcheries for incubation. When they hatch, the baby turtles are immediately released into the sea.

Tamar has another 18 stations along the coast and two stations on oceanic islands. The Comboios station (Espírito Santo state, north of Vitória and near Linhares) protects the loggerhead and leatherback turtles. The Fernando de Noronha station protects green and hawksbill turtles. Praia do Forte station protects loggerhead, hawksbill, olive ridley and green turtles. Of the 60km of beach under the jurisdiction of the Tamar Project in Bahia, 13km are patrolled by the scientists alone; the remainder is protected by a cooperative effort in which fishermen – the very ones who used to collect the eggs for food – are contracted to collect eggs for the scientists.

Nowadays, commerce in endangered turtle species is illegal, but unfortunately shells are still sold and turtle eggs are still popular hors d'oeuvres in some areas.

for the full moon and walk along the beach past the resort at sunset, when the sun turns the waters of the Rio Timeantube red as the moon rises over the sea. It's an unforgettable sight.

Sights

The extremely worthwhile **Tamar Project station** (adult US$2, child & student US$1; ☺ 9am-6:30pm) is located on the beach next to the church and lighthouse. See below for a description of the station and details on this national project designed to protect endangered sea turtles.

The **Castelo do Garcia d'Ávila** (☺ 676 1073; admission US$1; ☺ 8:30am-6pm), dating from 1552, was the first great Portuguese edifice in Brazil. Today, it's an impressive ruin that's slowly being restored. Desperate to colonize as a way to control his new territory, the king of Portugal set about granting lands to merchants, soldiers and aristocrats. For no apparent reason, a poor, 12-cow farmer called Garcia d'Ávila was endowed with a tract of land that extended inland all the way to the state of Maranhão, with Praia do Forte as its seat. He became overnight the largest landholder in the Northeast. For the site of his home, Garcia chose an aquamarine ocean-view plot studded with palm trees. It's a 3km walk down the only road out of town and there is a sign indicating where to turn, or you can take a taxi or mototaxi.

Sleeping & Eating

Praia do Forte's accommodations average in the mid-range price level. Budget travelers will find it most accessible mid-week and in the low season when there are substantial discounts. There is a camping ground behind town that has shady, sandy sites.

Pousada Ogum Marinho (☎ /fax 676 1165; www .ogummarinho.com.br; Alameda do Sol; d with fan, TV & minibar US$40; ☒) Quality rooms right in the heart of the action and a few steps from the beach.

Pousada dos Artistas (☎ 676 1147; www.pousada dosartistas.tur.br; Praça dos Artistas; s/d with TV & minibar US$30/36.50; ☒) This is a friendly pousada with lovely rooms with internal hammocks that look out on a lush, tropical garden.

Pousada Balanço do Mar (☎ 676 1059; www .pousadabalancodomar.com.br, in Portuguese; Rua da Aurora; s/d with fan, TV & minibar US$20/26.50) Lots of

greenery, songbirds and a few hammocks make up for the small rooms at this sweet pousada.

Albergue Praia do Forte (☎ /fax 676 1094; www .albergue.com.br; Rua da Aurora 3; 6-bed dm US$9, d US$20; ☐) Fine rooms surround a grassy central courtyard. Guests have use of the kitchen, and bikes and surfboards are available for rent.

Praia do Forte Eco-Resort (☎ 676 4000; www .ecoresort.com.br; Av do Farol; d with TV, minibar & dinner US$66.50; ☒) It's all luxury at this excellent resort, where walkways wind through groomed gardens to the beach out front and the food is fabulous.

For great Bahian home cooking, try **Sabor da Vila** (☎ 676 1156; Alameda do Sol; ☺ lunch & dinner) or **Forte Dream** (☎ 676 1265; Alameda da Felicidade; ☺ lunch & dinner Tue-Sun).

Getting There & Away

Catuense (☎ 450 4004) has buses to Praia do Forte (US$2.50, 1½ hours) from Salvador's bus station at 9:45am daily, and 4:40pm and 6:30pm Monday through Saturday. Return buses depart every 40 minutes from 7am to 6:40pm, or catch a Kombi (US$1.50). **Cacique** (☎ 392 5381) has buses (US$1.25, two hours) to Praia do Forte, departing from the Terminal da Calçada in Salvador's Cidade Baixa every 30 minutes from 5am to 6pm.

Praia do Forte is 3km off the highway.

PRAIA DO FORTE TO SÍTIO DO CONDE

Imbassaí is a rustic beach town 16km north of Praia do Forte with mid-range to top-end accommodation. A tall dune and the Rio Barroso, which runs parallel to the beach, separate the village from a fine beach with choppy, rough surf. North of town are some nice beaches with calm water for swimming. A further 9km north, in Porto de Sauípe, is the immense **Costa do Sauípe** tourist resort complex, consisting of luxury hotels, high-quality pousadas, an 18-hole golf course, an equestrian center and a windsurfing lake, but no good natural beach. **Subaúma** (21km further north) is a developed beach town with a few hotels and lots of weekend beach homes. The beach is decent with strong surf, natural reef pools and moored fishing boats. Continuing 20km north, **Baixio** is a pretty, clean town, but the beach is rocky and not great for swimming. The latter two are 8km off the Linha Verde.

SÍTIO DO CONDE

☎ 0xx75

Wet lowlands full of cattle surround this quiet, working-class beach retreat. A beach break on Sítio's main beach attracts surfers. North or south along the coast are deserted, pristine beaches with churning seas and flat sands backed by bluffs topped with coconut palms. Buses go through a picturesque coconut-palm forest to **Seribinha** (16km north), a small, fishing community with a pretty riverside setting and good beach. From here, boats cross the Rio Itapicuru, from which it is a 30-minute walk to **Cavalo Russo**, a tea-colored lake with a sand dune sliding into it.

Perched overlooking the beach, **Pousada Praiamar** (☎ 449 1150; www.rrtv.com.br/praiamarpousada, in Portuguese; s/d with fan, TV & minibar US$16/25) has comfortable rooms surrounding a sandy, palm-studded yard, a sea-facing breakfast porch with hammocks, and a constant breeze. Between the main plaza and the ocean, the flowery **Pousada Laia** (☎ 449 1254; s/d with fan & TV US$6/10) has well-kept, good-value rooms and great home cooking. **Zecas & Zecas** (☎ 449 1298; Praça Arsênio Mendes; ☼ lunch & dinner), on the main square, is a seafood restaurant with a great *moquecas*.

Direct transportation to Sítio do Conde is infrequent. You will most likely route through Conde on the Linha Verde. From Salvador, São Luís has buses to Conde (US$5, 3½ hours, nine daily) from 6am to 5pm. Buses and more-frequent *topiques* (vans) make the 8km trip on to Sítio until about 5:30pm, or you can get a taxi (US$3).

BARRA DO ITARIRÍ

☎ 0xx75

Prettier than Sítio do Conde, Barra do Itariri (Barra) is a tiny community of weekend homes and beachfront restaurants. The main beach is a wide, white sand bar that curves into the bank of the small Rio Itariri. A tall sand bluff on the facing side and palm trees all around create a picturesque setting. To the north and south are the same style of pristine, attractive beaches that surround Sítio. Outside of Sundays and January through Carnaval, Barra is pretty much deserted.

The German-owned **Hotel das Bougan-villes** (☎ 449 4100; www.itariri.com, in Portuguese; d with TV & minibar US$33; ☒) is a green, flowery place with hammocks on your porch and the beach out front. It has a restaurant and horses available for hire.

Catuense buses from Conde pass through Sítio do Conde at 9am, 11am and 2:30pm on their way to Barra (US$0.50, 20 minutes). The last bus back leaves at 2pm.

MANGUE SECO

☎ 0xx79 / pop 815

Mangue Seco is a tiny, beautifully rustic, riverfront village backed by an endless expanse of tall white sand dunes. It sits at the tip of a peninsula formed by the Rio Real, which delineates the Bahia/Sergipe border. The remote location causes most visitors to come on guided day tours, preventing rapid growth and leaving nights decidedly quiet. Jorge Amado's novel *Tieta do Agreste* and the TV series based on it were set here. Dune buggy trips through the sand dunes are offered (US$11.50 for up to four people), indicating places where filming was done. It's about a 1km walk to the ocean, where simple *barracas* hung with hammocks cluster together. The rest of the beach's flat, wet and fine, dry sands stretch deserted to the south.

Sleeping & Eating

The following pousadas are riverfront.

Pousada O Forte (☎ 9985 1217; www.infonet.com.br/pousadaoforte, in Portuguese; s/d with fan US$13.50/16.50; ☒) Located 300m from the village center on the way to the beach, this pousada is in a prime, isolated spot overlooking the river and mangroves. From your well-kept room on the hillside you'll hear nothing but rustling palms, frogs and a distant ocean rumble.

Village Mangue Seco (☎ 445 9047; s/d with minibar US$23.50/26.50; ☒ ☒) Equally isolated and quiet, and the most upmarket place around. High tides swallow the river-bank 'road' to the village center, further isolating these last two pousadas and leaving you to either wait, wade or go through the sand dunes.

Pousada Suruby (☎ 9121 0803; www.guiaturbahia.com.br; s/d with fan US$8.50/11.50) The last building in town as you head toward the beach, this pousada has small, simple, fairly new rooms that open onto a pleasant front yard.

To try *aratu*, a local shellfish, head for dinner at the seafood restaurants **Asa Branca**

(☎ 445 9054), **Restaurant Frutas do Mar** (☎ 445 9049) or **Suruby** (☎ 445 9061). For dessert, Dona Sula sells sweets, ice creams and liqueurs made from local fruits in her café next to the church.

Getting There & Away

The easiest access to Mangue Seco is through Pontal, though boats also leave from Ponto do Mato, both in Sergipe. Rota Sul has one daily bus to Pontal which leaves Aracaju at 1:30pm, passing through Estância (US$1, 2½ hours) at 3pm, and Indiaroba (US$0.75, 1½ hours) at 4pm. Upon arriving in Indiaroba, you will practically be pulled off the bus by eager taxi drivers, who (should) charge US$5 to Pontal.

Alternately, frequent *topiques* for Pontal leave from in front of Estância's hospital. If coming from the north, ask to be let off at the *posto de gasolina* (gas station) before Estância's bus station and walk one block up into town to the hospital. A taxi from Estância to Pontal costs US$8.50.

From Pontal, speed boats charge US$8.50 for up to six people. Slow boats (US$0.50) leave when they have 15 people together, which could take an entire day outside of the highest seasons.

A scheduled canoe departs Mangue Seco for Pontal at 5am on Monday (US$0.50), or you should arrange a speed boat. *Topiques* depart Pontal (US$1, 40 minutes, hourly from 5:30am to 8:30am Monday to Saturday) and Ponto do Mato (US$1, one hour, every 30 minutes until 6pm) for Estância.

SOUTH OF SALVADOR

VALENÇA

☎ 0xx75 / pop 77,450

Valença is a colonial fishing town on the banks of the Rio Una, historically the site of Portuguese struggles with both indigenous tribes and the Dutch. For most it is simply the gateway to Morro de São Paulo, but it has its own little-known secrets. Local shipbuilders maintain 15th-century techniques to such a degree that the town was chosen to produce a replica of the Spanish galleon *La Niña* for the American epic film *1492* (1992) about Christopher Columbus' journey.

To see the building of *saveiro* fishing boats in action, wander to the far end of the port where the smell of sap and sawdust, old fish and sea salt mingles with the wonderful odor of nutmeg drying in the sun. For a good walk and a beautiful view, follow the river's left bank upstream toward the **Igreja NS de Amparo** (1757) on the hill.

Information

All of the following are within a short walk of the port.

Banco do Brasil (Rua Governador Gonçalves)
Bradesco (Rua Governador Gonçalves 178)
Internauta (☎ 641 7017; Praça da República 34; per hr US$1) Internet access.
Tourist office (☎ 641 0518; Rua Comandante Madureira; ⏰ 8am-noon & 2-5pm Mon-Fri)

Festivals & Events

During Carnaval and at Christmas, people dressed as cowhands accompany Catarina the *baiana* throughout the city while chanting and playing tambourines in the celebration of **Boi Estrela**. **Carnaval** and **Micareta** (held 15 days after the end of Lent) are lively, with *trios elétricos* blasting *axé* music. A weeklong festival in honor of **NS do Amparo**, the patron saint of workers, climaxes on November 8. On New Year's Eve, **Zambiapumba** is celebrated by musical groups running through the streets playing improvised instruments.

Sleeping & Eating

Hotel Valença (☎ 641 3807; Rua Dr Heitor Guedes De Melo 15; s without bathroom with fan US$3, s/d with fan & TV US$5/10; 🅿) A few blocks off Praça da República, this hotel has clean, basic rooms.

Hotel Guaibim (☎ 641 0018; Praça da Independência 74; s/d with fan & TV US$9.50/16; 🅿) Up from the port. This nice, simple hotel may aspire to be more, but the mismatching tiles in the bathrooms blows its cover.

Hotel Portal Rio Una (☎ /fax 641 5050; www.portal hoteis.tur.br/una.html; Rua Maestro Barrinha; s/d with TV & minibar US$51/56.50; 🅿 🖳) A large, proper hotel with top-end rooms with verandas overlooking the river. It offers 30% low-season discounts.

Hotel Rio Mar (☎ 741 3408; fax 741 2714; Av Dendezeiros; s/d with TV & minibar US$16.50/26.50; 🅿 🅿 🖳) A little over 1km from the bridge, with comfortable rooms and slashed low-season prices.

Restaurant Capixaba (Rua Comandante Madureira 88) On the riverfront where the nighttime action concentrates, it serves a wide range of seafood.

Restaurante Ponto Chic (☎ 741 4704; Av Maçonica 11; per kg US$4) Across the bridge from the town center, with a decent self-service buffet.

Getting There & Away

Valença's tiny airport is served only by small air-taxi companies and is 15km from the center.

There is daily boat service to Boipeba, Gamboa and Morro de São Paulo from the port in the center.

The **bus station** (☎ 641 4805) is about 2km from the port; you'll probably want to take a taxi there (US$2). Frequent buses go to Porto Seguro (US$12.50, nine hours, two daily), Ilhéus via Itabuna (US$6, five hours, four daily) and Camamu (US$2, 1½ hours, hourly from 5am to 8pm). For Salvador, take a bus to Bom Despacho (US$3, two hours, hourly from 5am to 11:45pm) on the Ilha de Itaparica and then a ferry (p435) across the bay.

AROUND VALENÇA

The best mainland beach in the vicinity is **Guaibim** (16km north), which is a popular local resort. There are frequent buses there, and the beach packs on weekends. The owner of the beach *barraca* Cabana Nativa, Horácio, speaks English and happily dispenses information on local attractions and activities.

VALENÇA TO ILHÉUS
Morro de São Paulo
☎ 0xx75

For some, the picturesque holiday village of Morro de São Paulo has exceeded acceptable limits of touristiness. For others, it is Bahia's best beach town. All agree it is charming. Remotely perched at the northern tip of the Ilha de Tinharé, Morro's charm stems from its unique geography: three jungle-topped hills on a point at the meeting of the mangrove-lined Canal de Taperoá and a clear, shallow Atlantic. A colonial history and the steep hills have led to wheelbarrows being the primary mode of transportation on a few sand 'roads' lined with pousadas, restaurants and boutiques. During the high season the village booms, and there are parties on the beaches every night. Throughout the year, everyone gathers at night around the main drag and the plaza to visit, sing and see who walks by.

INFORMATION
There are no banks but many establishments accept major credit cards.

Centro de Informações ao Turista (☎ 483 1083; www.morrosp.com.br, in Portuguese) At the top of the hill up from the dock, it sells boat and domestic airline tickets, organizes excursions and is cheerfully helpful.

Internet café (Rua Fonte Grande; per hr US$2) The cheapest Internet access.

SIGHTS & ACTIVITIES
The town's icon is a 17th-century carved-stone **fortress gate**, which welcomes each arrival from its position above the dock. Around the corner at the point are the **fort ruins** (1630). Catching the rare sight of the sun setting over the river and mangroves from the fort is a visitor ritual. The **lighthouse** (1835) above the fort affords a fantastic view over Morro's beaches and has a **zip line** descending to Primeira Praia.

The waters of Morro's four conveniently named main beaches are mostly calm, shallow and warm, and their sands are narrow and swallowed by the high tides. Tiny **Primeira Praia** is lined with pousadas and has a decent surf break. Deep **Segunda Praia** (500m) is the 'action' beach with pousadas, restaurants, nightclubs and a sea of tables and chairs. Pousadas and anchored boats dominate one end of **Terceira Praia** (1km). Once you pass a pair of restaurants, **Quarta Praia** (2km) is a long, lovely stretch of sand graced by tall, swaying palms. For even more isolated peace, continue on at low tide to **Praia do Encanto** (5km) or further down the island to **Garapuá**, which has one pousada.

At low tide, take a walk to **Gamboa**, the next village on the river side of the island. The coast between the villages is filled with nooks to hide in and rocks to climb on. To start, head down Rua Fonte Grande and head right at the crossroads. You can catch the ferry back.

TOURS
A boat trip around the island, with stops at the Garapuá and Moreré offshore reefs and the villages of Boipeba and historical Cairu, is obligatory (US$16.50). You'll fly over waves in a 10-person speedboat (the adrenaline-inducing choice) past gorgeous

THE NORTHEAST

beach and mangrove scenery, swim, snorkel and sample local shell fish. Jeep trips to Boipeba are also possible (US$10). Also worthwhile is a hike to the small Fonte do Ceu waterfall, passing through the neighboring village of Gamboa, with an opportunity to paint yourself from a cliff of colored clays (US$6.50). Horseback rides can also be arranged (US$6.50 per hour). All these tours can be booked through the many local agencies.

SLEEPING

Renting a house can be a great deal for longer stays – just ask around. Reservations for Morro's 100 or so pousadas are required for all major holidays, especially Carnaval and *resaca* (five days of post-Carnaval hangover). Be forewarned that staying on Segunda Praia means sleeping to the nightclubs' pounding beats. Prices below are for the mid- to low-season.

After struggling up the hill from the dock, **Pousada Natureza** (☎ /fax 483 1044; www.hotelnatureza.com; Praça da Amendoeira 46; d with TV & minibar US$40, d bungalow with fan, TV & minibar US$60; 🛇 🔊) is just beyond the huge *amendoeira* tree on your left. Natureza has breezy rooms with verandas overlooking luxury bungalows spread throughout a hillside garden or the sea. On the hill above Natureza, **Pousada Ninho da Águia** (☎ 483 1537; mlso@zipmail.com.br; s/d with minibar US$10/15; 🛇) is a bit of a climb, but modern, well-finished rooms and a view over the beaches await.

Reining over the wide main plaza, the classy **O Casarão** (☎ 483 1049; www.ocasarao.net; Praça Aureliano Lima 190; d with TV & minibar US$50, d chalet with TV & minibar US$60; 🛇 🔊) has large rooms in a renovated colonial house and garden chalets decorated in the theme of foreign countries. Heading through the archway and down Rua Fonte Grande, you'll come to a cemented spring that used to serve as a freshwater source for the village. Just past it on the left, **Pousada Cairu** (☎ 483 1074; pousadacairu@hotmail.com; s/d with fan, TV & minibar US$6.50/10; 🛇) has basic rooms, the best of which have windows and open to the upstairs balcony. Heading right from the spring, up a quiet, forested path, **Pousada Aquarela** (☎ 483 1509; pousadaaquarela@hotmail.com; Rua Porto de Cima; s/d with TV & minibar US$13.50/20; 🛇) has four-room blocks perched on a steep hillside. The gorgeous rooms have

stone floors and a hammock hanging on a breezy porch. Continuing on, the German-run **Pousada Colibri** (☎ /fax 483 1056; www.pousada-colibri.com; d with TV & minibar US$41.50, d chalet with TV & minibar US$28; 🛇) sits in a privileged position atop the facing hill, overlooking the ocean and the Morro do Farol. Its round chalets and well-finished two-room suites have verandas with hammocks to catch the welcome breeze. The surrounding two hectares of jungle assure beauty and quiet.

Heading off the main plaza, the Camino das Praias leads down to the beaches and is Morro's main drag. On it, **Pousada Gaucho** (☎ 483 1305; www.pousadagaucho.com.br, in Portuguese; Caminho da Praia; s/d with fan US$10/16.50; 🛇) has fine cheap rooms that can be a little noisy. Pricier, better rooms on upper floors are considered by the family to be a separate pousada by the same name. At the base of the Camino's steep drop down to the ocean, the well-established **Pousada Ilha do Sol** (☎ 483 1576; d with fan, TV & minibar US$20; 🛇) has open two-room suites catching the ocean breeze, and porches for watching the people streaming by.

The attractive **Morro Praia Hotel** (☎ 483 1244; www.morropraiahotel.com; Terceira Praia; s/d with minibar US$20/26.50; 🛇) has comfortable rooms looking out onto its front yard and to the sea beyond, making it a great beachfront option. Further down, the **Pousada Aradhia** (☎ 483 1099; www.pousadaaaradhia.hpg.com.br, in Portuguese; Terceira Praia; s/d with fan, TV & minibar US$16.50/23.50; 🛇 🔊) is one of the best economical options on this beach. An ocean view is not part of the package since rooms are located behind another building, but a few plants make up for it.

EATING

There is a lot of flash among restaurants on Camino das Praias, but for quality and value, stick to the time-tested favorites. At the top of the road, **Espaguetaria Strega** (☎ 483 1033) has well-priced fresh pastas and over 40 different *cachaça* infusions. Further down, **Sabor da Terra** (☎ 483 1156; 🕑 lunch & dinner) serves seafood prepared simply or with Bahian spice, fish *moqueca* (US$3) being its specialty. For gourmet flavors, continue on to chic **Ponto de Encontro** (☎ 483 1165; 🕑 late lunch & dinner). Though its menu is mostly vegetarian, it throws some white meat into the mix, such as in the chicken salad with grilled fruit and passion fruit dressing (US$5). Right next door, **Oh La La! Crepes** (Camino das Praias) is a hip bar serving genuine French-made sweet and savory crepes. Down the stairs immediately on the right, **Restaurante Tinharé** (Camino das Praias) has portions of fantastically authentic Bahian cuisine that could feed a small country – don't order extra for your third person.

GETTING THERE & AWAY

Both catamarans (US$15, two hours, three daily) and *lanchas rapidas* (speed boats, US$16.50, two hours, daily) sail between Morro and the Terminal Marítimo Turístico in Salvador. The ride is often rough – to avoid feeling queasy embark with a medium-empty stomach and focus on a fixed point on land. Extra departures are added when there's sufficient demand.

If coming from the south, passenger ferries travel upriver to Morro from Valença (US$1, 1½ hours, hourly from 7:30am to 5:30pm), stopping first in Gamboa. At low tide, passengers are bused to Atracadoro, then transferred to a waiting ferry. *Lanchas rapidas* (US$3, 40 minutes) leave whenever they have a full load.

Three daily flights go between Salvador and Morro (US$49, 20 minutes). Contact **Aerostar** (☎ 483 1112, Salvador ☎ 0xx71-377 4406), **Adey Taxi** (☎ 483 1090, Salvador ☎ 0xx71-377 1993) or a travel agent.

Boipeba

☎ 0xx75 / pop 4900

South of the Ilha da Tinharé, across the narrow Rio do Inferno, sits the Ilha de Boipeba. The village of Boipeba, on the northeastern tip of the island, is quiet, rustic and said to be what Morro de São Paulo was 20 years ago. The island's coastline is pristine, with more than 20km of beautiful, deserted beaches, including **Ponta de Castelhanos**, known for its diving.

SLEEPING & EATING

Reservations are recommended in the high season. The prices quoted here are for low season.

Restaurants serving great seafood line the beach where the river meets the sea. Rounding the point, a string of top end pousadas face Praia Boca da Barra.

Small Vila de Moreré, 40 minutes south by boat, has rustic accommodation.

Pousada 7 (☎ 653 6086; www.amabo.org.br/amabo 2003/mfpousada_sete.html, in Portuguese; Praça Santo Antônio; s/d with fan US$8.50/13.50; 🏊) In the village center, this pretty pousada has rooms in good shape.

Pousada Vila Sereia (☎ 653 6054; www.ilhaboipeba .org.br, in Portuguese; d with fan & minibar US$47) Brightly painted, thatched-roof cabins sit raised on stilts throughout a beachfront garden at this extremely special pousada. Breakfast is served right on your porch.

Pousada Pouso da Maré (☎ 9147 1712; www .ilhaboipeba.org.br, in Portuguese; s/d with fan & minibar US$21/30) Large, comfortable rooms facing the beautiful gardens or the ocean.

Raizes Nativas, in the village center, serves tasty Bahian food.

GETTING THERE & AWAY

From Valença, passenger ferries for Boipeba (US$2.50, four hours) leave at noon, 1pm and 2pm. At 11:30am and 2pm, buses leave Valença for Torrinhas, where passengers are transferred to a ferry for Boipeba (US$2.50, bus and ferry 1½ hours). Ferries stop first at the historic town of Cairu, a recommended stopover if you can catch a later boat on to Boipeba.

From Morro de São Paulo, options are to negotiate a boat ride with tour providers, or take a jeep (US$8.50) and then the ferry across the river.

Camamu

☎ 0xx73 / pop 33,620

On the mainland, shielded from the open ocean by the Peninsula de Maraú, Camamu is primarily the jumping-off point for Barra Grande. This picturesque town is the port of call for the many tiny fishing villages in the region and overlooks a maze of mangrove-filled islets and narrow channels. *Saveiro* fishing boats are built and repaired right outside the port. The beautiful **Açaraí Waterfalls** are 5km away by local bus or taxi (US$10 round-trip).

The **Pousada Green House** (☎ 255 2178; Rua Djalma Dutra 61; s/d with fan & TV US$5/10), where the buses stop, is friendly, family-run, and great value. Up a steep road from the port, the **Hotel Rio Açaraí** (☎ 255 2315; www.hotelrioacarai .com.br; Praça Dr Francisco Xavier; s/d with TV & minibar US$17/21; 🏊 🖥) is a garish modern hotel.

THE NORTHEAST

There is no real bus station here; buses stop near the port. **Águia Branca** (☎ 255 2222) goes to Ilhéus (US$4, three hours, four daily) and Bom Despacho (US$4.50, 3½ hours, five daily) via Valença. Three other bus companies also go to Valença (US$2, 1½ hours) from 5am to 6pm, so it's good to ask around before buying a ticket. Cidade do Sol and Águia Branca go to Ubaitaba (US$2, 1¼ hours, four daily) for further connections south.

Barra Grande
☎ 0xx73

Deliciously off the beaten path, Barra Grande is a remote, tranquil fishing village at the northern tip of the Peninsula de Maraú. It has the same charm and tree-shaded magic that originally attracted bohemian types to similar sand-street villages further south, but hasn't yet experienced a tourism boom. With a fair number of pousadas and restaurants, Barra Grande makes a great base for checking out the rest of the peninsula. Much of the village closes in winter.

Separating the peninsula from the mainland is the island-riddled Baía de Camamu, Brazil's third-largest bay. One long, dirt road (often impassable after rain) heads down the peninsula, providing access to stunning beaches with crystal-clear water, such as **Praia Taipús de Fora** (7km, rated among Brazil's top beaches), and a handful of very small fishing villages. Pricey excursions to **Lagoa Azul**, view points, bay islands and down the Rio Maraú are offered by local providers.

SLEEPING & EATING
The first pousada as you leave the pier, **Maria de Firmino** (☎ 255 1628; s/d with fan US$10/13.50) has spacious rooms that are a little rough around the edges. On the following corner, the attractive **Pousada da Barra** (☎ 258 6009; s/d with TV & minibar US$13.50/20; ✱) has comfortable, great-value rooms, including a few cheaper ones with fans. Half a block down, brand-new rooms at the **Pousada Tubarão** (☎ 258 6006; www.barragrandeturismo.com.br; s/d with fan & minibar US$13.50/23.50; ✱) are classy, despite the satin sheets. Its restaurant serves excellent fresh seafood. Nearby, Cafe Latino has excellent pastas, coffee and desserts, as well as a gallery of Juan Pablo's travel pho-

tography. Just off the plaza, **A Tapera** (☎ 258 6119; ✷ lunch & dinner) makes an amazing squid *moqueca* (US$13.50 for two).

By heading left and up the beach as you leave the pier, you pass Dejanira's very basic **Pousada Entrada do Sol** (☎ 258 6056; s/d with fan US$5/10) before hitting the point and the **Pousada Camping Lagosta Azul** (☎ 258 6144; Ponta do Mutá; camping per person US$1.50, s/d with fan US$10/16.50). The latter has fine rooms and a shaded camping area in a gorgeous, quiet, forested setting, just a short walk from the center. At the entrance to town, a 10-minute walk from the center, the **Albergue Barra Grande** (☎ 258 6117; hostelbarragrande@uol .com.br; dm/d US$4/13.50) is modern and well finished. High-end accommodation, such as **Pousada Maraú** (☎ 258 2113; www.pousadamarau .com.br, in Portuguese; Praia de Saquaíra; d US$30), is available at the southern beaches.

GETTING THERE & AROUND
Passenger ferries (US$1, 1¼ hours, hourly from 6am to 9pm) and speed boats (US$5, 25 minutes) depart for Barra Grande from Camamu. Heading to or from Itacaré, you will need to negotiate a ride with a tour provider, or you might consider walking the 50km along stretches of coconut-palm-lined beaches.

Four-wheel-drive *jardineiras* (US$1) park across from Pousada da Barra, leaving for the beaches as soon as they have a full load.

Itacaré
☎ 0xx73 / pop 18,100

At its heart, Itacaré is a quiet, colonial fishing town at the mouth of the Rio de Contas, long sought out by hippies and surfers mesmerized by wide stretches of virgin Atlantic rain forest, postcard-perfect beaches and reliable surf breaks. In recent years, the paving of the road into town and the subsequent tourism boom has made ecotourism the new focus, but the mellow, youthful vibe prevails. Deviating from the Bahian norm, Carnaval here is all about reggae.

There are major bank ATMs, and Internet runs around US$2 per hour.

ACTIVITIES
The coast south of Itacaré is characterized by rough surf (better for surfing than swimming) and cove beaches separated by

rain-forested hills. Some beaches, such as idyllic **Prainha** (reachable by trail from Praia do Ribeira), are private and charge entrance fees. **Praia da Concha** is an ordinary city beach. **Resende**, **Tiririca** and **Ribeira** beaches lie within 1.5km south of town and are frequented by surfers. Highly recommended are the paradisiacal **Engenhoca**, **Havaizinho** and **Itacarezinho** beaches, 12km south of town.

Multiple travel agencies and seemingly every hotel offer canoe trips upriver, rafting, mountain biking, rappelling and excursions on foot or horseback to local sights. The principal excursion is up the Peninsula de Maraú, with stops at **Lagoa Azul** and **Praia Taipús de Fora** (US$21.50). A word of advice: maximize your comfort by assuring that the vehicle's seats face forward. Surfboard rental and surf lessons are easily arranged.

For a do-it-yourself excursion and a swim, catch a bus leaving town and hop off at the **Cachoeira Tijuipe** (admission US$1.50), a wide waterfall of tea-colored water on private, forested land.

SLEEPING

There is plenty of accommodation, from camping grounds to resorts. Everything is a short walk from the action. Reservations are recommended for major holidays.

Sage Point (☎ /fax 251 2030; www.pousadasage point.com.br; d with fan & minibar US$43-132) Perched on a hill overlooking Praia Tiririca are beautiful wooden chalets run by Ana, a friendly Cuban-American. Her breakfast is huge and healthy.

Aldeia do Mar (☎ 251 2230; www.aldeiadomar.tur .br, in Portuguese; Praia da Concha; d with TV & minibar US$62; 🏖) Luxury rooms are spread over a hillside closing Praia da Concha, each with a porch overlooking the manicured green grounds. Low-season discounts offered.

Pousada da Paz (☎ 251 2027; Av Castro Alves 319; s/d with TV & minibar US$16.50/23.50; 🏖) On the bay, just past the gas station, this brand new pousada has very comfortable rooms with porches and hammocks. The breakfast area lies below a tree house–like building and looks out onto vegetation.

Pousada Cores do Mar (☎ 251 3418; Condomínio Conchas do Mar; s/d with fan US$8.50/11.50) A row of comfortable rooms with hammocks strung up in front of them faces a side garden in this simple pousada. Located in a quiet neighborhood of fancy hotels.

Hawaii Aqui (☎ 231 3050; www.hawaiiaqui.com, in Portuguese; Rua Caminho das Praias 169, Pituba; dm/ s/d with fan US$6/8.50/11.50) Fairly new collective and private rooms line an open-air corridor behind this pousada's Internet café, right in the thick of things. It also has a back garden that you can pitch a tent in.

Other recommendations:

Pousada Papa Terra (☎ /fax 251 2137; www.papa terra.com.br, in Portuguese; Condomínio Conchas do Mar; s/d with TV & minibar US$25/33; 🏖 🏖)

Pousada Estrela (☎ 251 2006; www.itacare.com.br; Rua Pedro Longo 50; s/d with fan, TV & minibar US$10/16.50; 🏖)

Pousada do Costinha (☎ 251 2005; pousadacostinha@uol.com.br; Rua Pitubá 170, Pituba; s/d with fan, TV & minibar US$11.50/15; 🏖)

EATING

Itacaré's restaurants concentrate along one road that changes names as it runs from the main plaza out to the beaches. Just off the plaza, **Berimbau Restaurante** (Rua Lodônia Almeida) specializes in *bobó de camarão* (shrimp in spiced manioc cream, US$10 for two). Half a block down, **Boca do Forno** (☎ 251 2174; Rua Lodônia Almeida 134; US$6-11; 🕑 dinner) serves pizzas everyone raves about in a beautiful floral outdoor setting. Further down, **Almazen** (Rua Pedro Longo 69; 🕑 breakfast, lunch & dinner) serves healthy sandwiches on homemade bread, its own yogurt and granola, salads and a delicious vegetarian *prato feito* (US$3). Continuing along, **O Restaurante** (☎ 251 2012; Rua Pedro Longo 150; 🕑 lunch & dinner) serves seafood dishes such as grilled fish and eggplant in cream sauce (US$11 for two) and a creative *prato feito*. Further on and across the road, Mistura Fina has a tasty fish *moqueca* (US$9.50 for two). At the very end of the road, an Italian makes wonderful homemade pastas at Giardino Italiano.

GETTING THERE & AWAY

Itacaré's **bus station** (☎ 251 2200) is just out of the center, but a bit of a hike from many of the pousadas. To get to Itacaré, you will most likely need to connect through Itabuna or Ilhéus. **Rota** (☎ Itabuna 0xx73-613 3462, Ilhéus ☎ 0xx73-634 3161) has hourly buses to Itacaré from Itabuna (US$3, 2½ hours, from 6am to 7:50pm) and Ilhéus (US$2, 1½ hours, from 6:40am to 11:40pm).

A ferry carries cars and passengers across the river to the Peninsula de Maraú (US$3).

THE NORTHEAST

ILHÉUS

☎ 0xx73 / pop 221,880

Bright, turn-of-the-century architecture and oddly angled streets lend a vibrant and rather playful air to Ilhéus.

The town's fame comes from its history as a prosperous cocoa port, as well as being the hometown of Jorge Amado (Brazil's best-known novelist). He used it as the setting of one of his greatest novels *Gabriela, Cravo e Canela* ('Gabriela, Clove and Cinnamon'). When you combine all this with Ilhéus' attractive city geography, its affable people and the nearby Atlantic rain-forest reserves you can argue it's worth a quick stopover.

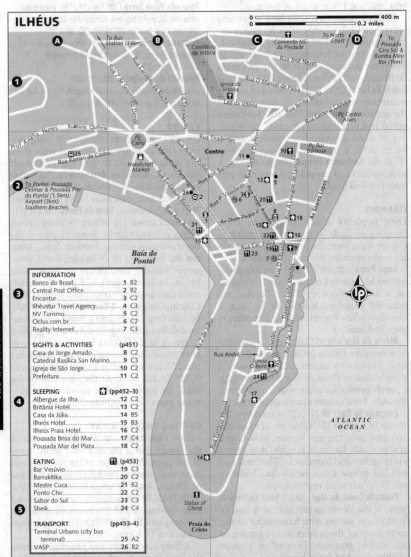

ILHÉUS

INFORMATION
Banco do Brasil	1 B2
Central Post Office	2 B2
Encantur	3 C2
Ilhéustur Travel Agency	4 C3
NV Turismo	5 C2
Oclus.com.br	6 C2
Reality Internet	7 C3

SIGHTS & ACTIVITIES (p451)
Casa de Jorge Amado	8 C2
Catedral Basílica San Marino	9 C3
Igreja de São Jorge	10 C2
Prefeitura	11 C2

SLEEPING (pp452–3)
Albergue da Ilha	12 C2
Britânia Hotel	13 C2
Casa da Júlia	14 B5
Ilhéos Hotel	15 B3
Ilhéos Praia Hotel	16 C2
Pousada Brisa do Mar	17 C4
Pousada Mar del Plata	18 C2

EATING (p453)
Bar Vesúvio	19 C3
Barrakítika	20 C2
Mestre Cuca	21 B2
Ponto Chic	22 C2
Sabor do Sul	23 C3
Sheik	24 C4

TRANSPORT (pp453–4)
Terminal Urbano (city bus terminal)	25 A2
VASP	26 B2

History

Ilhéus was a sleepy place until cacao was introduced into the region from Belém in 1881. Simultaneously, Brazil's behind-the-times sugar estates were reeling from a drop in world sugar prices and the slave system was finally coming to an end. With the sugar plantations in the doldrums, impoverished agricultural workers and freed or escaped slaves flocked from all over the Northeast to the hills surrounding Ilhéus to participate in the new boom: cacao, known as the *ouro branco* (white gold) of Brazil.

Sudden, lawless and violent, the scramble to plant cacao displayed all the characteristics of a gold rush. When the dust settled, the land and power belonged to a few ruthless *coroneis* (so-called 'colonels') and their hired guns. The landless were left to work, and usually live, on the *fazendas*, where they were subjected to a harsh and paternalistic labor system. This history is graphically told by Amado, who grew up on a cacao plantation, in his book *Terras do Sem Fim* (published in English as *The Violent Land*).

In the early 1990s, the *vassoura de bruxa* (witch's broom) disease left cacao trees shriveled and unable to bear fruit, hurting the area's economy dramatically. Though the disease persists to this day, you can still see cacao *fazendas* and rural workers like those Amado described throughout the lush, tropical hills.

Orientation

The city center is located on a beach-lined point that reaches into the mouth of the Rio Cachoeira, and is sandwiched between two hills. On the southern side of the s-curving river mouth is the modern neighborhood of Pontal. The recommended *Mapa Turistico Ilhéus: De Ponta a Ponto* (US$1.50) is available at Ilhéustur or newsstands.

Information

There are ATMs next to the cathedral.
Banco do Brasil (Rua Marquês de Paranagua 112, Centro)
Central post office (Rua Marquês de Paranagua 200, Centro)
Encantur (☎ 234 3907; Rua Jorge Amado 102, Centro; ◷ 9am-4:30pm Mon-Fri, 9am-noon Sat) Changes cash and traveler's checks. Also books bus and airline tickets and local tours.

Ilhéustur (☎ 634 3510; Praça Dom Eduardo, Centro; ◷ 9am-9pm) Tourist office.
NV Turismo (☎ 634 4101; Rua General Câmara 27, Centro) Offers local tours.
Oclus.com.br (Rua Rodolfo Vieira 27, Centro; per hr US$1.50) Internet access; also in the airport.
Reality Internet (Rua Dom Eduardo, Centro; per hr US$1) The cheapest and speediest Internet access.

Sights & Activities

The best thing to do in Ilhéus is just wander. The center is lively, with several old, gargoyled buildings such as the **Prefeitura**. The view over the city and the sunset are fantastic from the **Cemitério da Vitória** hill.

The **Casa de Jorge Amado** (Rua Jorge Amado 21; admission US$0.25; ◷ 9am-noon & 2-6pm Mon-Fri, 11am-5pm Sat & Sun), where the great writer lived with his parents while working on his first novel, has been restored and turned into a Casa de Cultura, complete with an interesting display about the man himself. Not many writers can boast this sort of recognition while still alive, but Amado became a national treasure well before his death in 2001. For more on his work, see the boxed text on p452.

CHURCHES

The **Catedral Basílica San Marino** (Praça Dom Eduardo) is the city's icon and a unique, eclectic mix of architectural styles. The **Igreja de São Jorge** (Praça Rui Barbosa; ◷ Tue-Sun) is the city's oldest church, dating from 1534, and houses a small sacred-art museum.

BEACHES

City beaches such as Praia da Avenida are dirty. Your best bet is to head south, but even then you'll find that area's beaches are best for a *futbol* game (broad and flat), and it takes kilometers for the water to lose the muddy color of the river outflow. **Praia dos Milionários** (7km) has some *barracas* and is popular with locals, as is the prettier **Praia Cururupe** (12km), where a small river curves into the sea.

Tours

Trips to a tree sloth recuperation center, a chocolate factory and Primavera Fazenda, where you'll be taken through the process of cacao production, can all be arranged through local travel agencies. Tours are also given of Lagoa Encantada, a state-protected area of Atlantic rain forest with waterfalls and wildlife, and Rio do Engenho, an estate with Bahia's first sugarcane mill, and the Capela de Santana (1537), Brazil's third-oldest church. For information on the Ecoparque de Una tour, see the boxed text opposite.

Festivals & Events

As any knowledgeable Amado fan would guess, Ilhéus has highly spirited festivals. The best are the **Gincana da Pesca** in early January, **Festa de São Sebastião** (much samba and capoeira) from January 11 to 20, **Festa de São Jorge** (featuring Candomblé) on April 23 and **Festa das Águas** (Candomblé) in December. **Carnaval** has a full complement of *trios elétricos*.

Sleeping

Almost all of Ilhéus' best hotels are located south of the city along the road to Olivença, making them convenient only for those traveling by car. Those accommodations in the center are generally a bit run down, while that in Pontal is more modern.

BUDGET

Pousada Brisa do Mar (☎ 231 2644; Av 2 de Julho 136; s/d with fan, TV & minibar US$8.50/13.50; ✷) A huge step up from the rest, this modern pousada really does have a sea breeze and a privileged view over the river mouth. The walk to the center at night, though short, is dark and desolate.

Albergue da Ilha (☎ 231 8938; Rua General Câmara 31, Centro; 7-bed dm US$5.25, d US$20) This friendly and secure hostel has a mixed-gender dorm room and one pricey double room. Guests have access to the kitchen and a roof patio with fantastic views. English is spoken.

Pousada Mar del Plata (☎ 634 7692; Rua AL de Lemos 3, Centro; s/d without bathroom with fan US$9/13, s/d with fan US$13/19) The old building lends this clean pousada a little charm, but it isn't the best-kept. Rooms can be noisy due to the hardwood floors and high vents to the hallway.

Other recommendation:

Pousada Delmar (☎ 632 8435; Rua Castro Alves 322, Pontal; s/d with fan, TV & minibar US$8.50/11.50; ✷)

MID-RANGE

Ilhéos Hotel (☎ 634 4242; Rua Eustáquio Bastos 144, Centro; s/d with TV & minibar US$18.50/20; ✷) This multistoried 1930s hotel has a fading grandeur and a vintage elevator that was hand-cranked until electrified in 1950. The rooms are fairly comfortable and have views over the bay. Rooms with an internal window are cheaper, and 25% low-season discounts are given.

Britânia Hotel (☎ 634 1722; www.britaniahotel.cjb .net; Rua Jorge Amado 16, Centro; s/d without bathroom with fan US$6.50/10, s/d with TV & minibar US$16.50/26.50; ✷) A large, older hotel with mismatching

---

BAHIA'S FAVORITE SON

Nobody is more responsible for bringing Bahian culture to the rest of the world than Jorge Amado. Brazil's most famous romanticist author, Amado's tales have been translated into 49 languages and read the world over.

Born in 1912, Jorge spent his youth in Ilhéus, the scene of many of his later novels. After secondary studies in Salvador, Amado studied law in Rio, but instead of going into practice he decided to become a writer. He surprised critics and the public by publishing his first novel, *O País do Carnaval*, when he was only 19 years old.

An avowed communist, Amado participated in the rebel literary movement of the time, launching two romances set in the cacao zone around Ilhéus: *Cacau* and *Suor*. The first novel was banned by the fascist-leaning Vargas government, an act that only served to increase his popularity. Sent to prison several times for his beliefs, Amado was elected a federal deputy for the Brazilian communist party (PCB) in 1945, but he lost his seat after a disagreement with the party several years later. He left Brazil and lived for more than five years in Europe and Asia, finally breaking ties with the communist party after the crimes of Stalin were revealed to the world.

With *Gabriela, Cravo e Canela* (Gabriela, Clove and Cinnamon), published in 1958, he entered a new writing phase, marked by a picturesque style that intimately described the colorful escapades of his Bahian heroes and heroines.

Amado died of heart failure in Salvador in August 2001, just short of his 89th birthday.

sheets and funky décor. The *apartamentos* are bright and well-kept. The *quartos* are windowless and have vents to the noisy hallway.

Other recommendations:

Pousada Gira Sol (☎ 634 3400; www.pousadagirasol .com.br; Praça Florêncio Gomes 460, Cidade Nova; s/d with TV & minibar US$15/20; P 🗙)

Pousada Pier do Pontal (☎ /fax 623 4000; www .pierdopontal.com.br; Av Lomanto Jr 1650, Pontal; s/d with TV & minibar US$26.50/33; P 🗙 🖭)

TOP END

Casa da Júlia (☎ 8803 2377; juliaher_99@yahoo; Rua Epitácio Pessoã 333, Alto de São Sebastião; d US$33) Júlia's beautiful house, high above the statue of Christ, has a panoramic view to the south of the city. She rents just one double room, and as you will be staying in her home, she'll want to get a sense of you first.

Ilhéus Praia Hotel (☎ 634 2533; www.ilheuspraia .com.br; Praça Dom Eduardo, Centro; s/d with TV & minibar US$38/43; 🗙 🖭) A standard, high-rise hotel with ocean views in the heart of the center. It has half-price ground-floor rooms and a 30% low-season discount.

Eating

Being a rather humble city, fine restaurants are few in Ilhéus.

Sheik (☎ 634 1799; Rua NS de Lurdes; 🕒 dinner Mon-Sat) One of the few nice restaurants near the center and has great views over the city. It rounds out its menu of typical dishes with Arab and Japanese food, and the bar fills up late in the evening.

Bar Vesúvio (☎ 634 2164; Praça Dom Eduardo, Centro; 🕒 lunch & dinner) Attracts both Amado fans and those simply looking to enjoy a beer and some Arabic food at the outdoor tables facing the cathedral. Across the road, Ponto Chic has ice-cream flavors of more local fruits than you knew existed.

Barrakítika (☎ 231 8300; Praça Antônio Muniz 39; 🕒 lunch & dinner) Another outdoor hangout serving pizza, pastas and meat dishes, including cheap *pratos executivos* (US$2.50). It has live music on weekend evenings.

Bumba Meu Boi (☎ 231 3725; Av Soares Lopes 1546, Cidade Nova; 🕒 lunch & dinner) Northeast of the center, past the convention center, Bumba Meu Boi is the spot for Brazilian *churrasco* (barbeque).

The center is loaded with cheap *lanchonetes*, but for a quality self-service lunch,

head for **Mestre Cuca** (☎ 634 1092; Rua Eustáquio Bastos 126) or **Sabor do Sul** (☎ 231 3031; Rua Coronel Paiva 93). If you can stand the blasting music, there are several reasonably priced seafood stands behind the cathedral with tables right on the sand.

In Pontal, major traffic turns south off the road along the bay, creating a quiet area near the end of the point with great views back to the center. Here there is a pair of frequented restaurants and Larika (munchies), a stand serving fantastic sandwiches and fresh fruit juices.

Getting There & Away

AIR

TAM (☎ 234 5259; airport), **Varig** (☎ 231 3614; airport) and **VASP** (☎ 231 3412; Rua Marques de Paranagua) can fly or connect you to anywhere in Brazil from Ilhéus' **Aeroporto Jorge Amado** (code IOS; ☎ 231 7629).

BUS

The **long-distance bus station** (☎ 634 4121) is 15km from the center. Frequent buses go to Valença (US$6, five hours, four daily), Porto Seguro (US$8, six hours, four daily), Vitória (US$19 to US$28, 13 hours, two daily) and Rio (US$35 to US$44, 22 hours, two to three daily).

ECOPARQUE DE UNA

The **Ecoparque de Una** (☎ 633 1121; admission US$15; 🕒 Tue-Sun) is a lush Atlantic rainforest reserve 63km south of Ilhéus. Here, guides lead visitors on a 2km trail, including four suspended tree-canopy walkways. The tour lasts two hours and ends with a cool pond dip.

Taking refuge in the park are rare species such as the golden-headed lion tamarin (*Leontopithecus chrysomelas*). These unusual monkeys have the look and proud gaze of miniature lions: a blazing yellow, orange and brown striped coat, a golden mane and a long, scruffy tail. If you're lucky you'll also see *tatus* (armadillos), *pacas* (agoutis), capybaras and *veados* (deer), all native to the area.

Visits can be arranged through a travel agency or you can make a direct appointment. If you go on your own, the bus to Canavieiras drops you at the park gate, where a park jeep picks you up.

Buses to Salvador (US$11 to US$29, seven hours, five daily) make a long sweep around the Baía de Todos os Santos, recommended if you are stopping in the *recôncavo* on the way. Otherwise, catch a bus to Bom Despacho on the Ilha de Itaparica, and then a ferry into Salvador. For ferry information, see p435.

More frequent connections can be made in Itabuna, 30km inland. Local buses to Itabuna leave from the local bus terminal in the center and from outside the long-distance bus station (US$0.50, 40 minutes) every 15 minutes.

Getting Around

The *terminal urbano* (city bus terminal) is on the edge of the center in a super-sinister area of abandoned-looking warehouses – not where you want to be at night or with your bags.

TO/FROM THE AIRPORT

The airport is in Pontal, 3.5km from the center. Taxis cost US$2.50.

TO/FROM THE BUS STATION

From the center, Teotónio Vilela, Circular and Santo Brinto buses pass the bus station. Taxis cost US$4.50.

AROUND ILHÉUS
Olivença
☎ 0xx73

Olivença is a charming little beach town 16km south of Ilhéus. Sights include a spa with baths believed to have healing powers and a nearby indigenous village. The town shore is grassy and composed of beautiful cove beaches with rock formations and flat sand, churning waves and a restaurant or two. South of Olivença are deserted beaches and calmer water.

There are great waves just north of town at **Batuba** and **Backdoor**, Brazil's third-best surf break. Marcio of **Pokoloco Surf Shop** (☎ 269 1493) rents long and short boards (per day US$6.50), gives surf lessons (for six hours private US$33) and speaks fluent English, Spanish and Italian.

The artsy **Albergue da Juventude Fazenda Tororomba** (☎ 269 1139; www.fazendatororomba .br; Rua Eduardo Magalhães; 4- or 10-bed dm US$7, s/d with fan & minibar US$8.50/15, d chalet with kitchen US$16.50; 🏊) is spread over a large grassy property

with large trees and a pond. A house with a living room and full kitchen has several collective rooms with lofts. The *apartamentos* are comfortable and have hand-painted designs on the walls. Some of the rustic chalets have outdoor jet bathtubs. **Camping Estância das Fontes** (☎ 269 1480; per person US$2), 15km south of Ilhéus, is close to the beach and has hot showers.

City buses leave every 30 minutes from Ilhéus' bus station (passing the city bus terminal) for Olivença (30 minutes) from 6am to 11pm. The bus travels close to the beaches, so you can hop off when you see one you like.

PORTO SEGURO
☎ 0xx73 / pop 95,660

For decades Porto Seguro (Porto) has epitomized the Bahian tourism attraction of gorgeous beaches with hot music and party scenes day and night. Package tours (bringing southern Brazilians seeking fun in the sun) have lessened in recent years, and Arraial d'Ajuda now lures most foreign tourists across the river, leaving a well-developed tourism infrastructure with – mercifully – no building over two stories. Porto is famous for being the officially recognized first Portuguese landfall in Brazil, as well as the birthplace of lambada, a dance whose sensuality really did lead it to be forbidden at one time. Today, Porto is a great place for anyone wanting to party Brazilian-style and catch some exceptionally skilled dancers and Capoeiristas.

History

Pedro Cabral's landing 16km north of Porto Seguro (Safe Port) at Coroa Vermelha is officially considered the first Portuguese landfall in Brazil. The sailors didn't stay long, just long enough to stock up on supplies. Three years later the Gonçalvo Coelho expedition arrived and planted a marker in what is now Porto Seguro's Cidade Histórica (Historic City). Jesuits on the same expedition built a church, now in ruins, in Outeiro da Glória. In 1526, a naval outpost, convent and chapel (Igreja NS da Misericórdia) were built in the present-day Cidade Histórica.

The Tupininquin, not the Pataxó, were the indigenous tribe around the site of Porto Seguro when the Portuguese landed.

They were rapidly conquered and enslaved by the colonists, but the Aimoré, Pataxó, Cataxó and other inland tribes resisted Portuguese colonization and constantly threatened Porto Seguro. Military outposts were built along the coast in Belmonte, Vila Viçosa, Prado and Alcobaça to defend the Portuguese from European attacks by sea and Indian attacks by land.

The Indians still managed to take Porto Seguro on twice and, according to colonial documents, reduced Porto Seguro to rubble in 1612 (thus undermining the city's claims to have 16th-century buildings).

Information

Adeltour (☎ 288 1888; www.adeltour.com.br, in Portuguese; Shopping Avenida, Av 22 de Abril 100; ☯ 9am-7:30pm Mon-Fri, 9am-3pm Sat) For national and international air travel.Changes cash and traveler's checks. Also in the airport.

Banco do Brasil (☎ 288 2311; Av 22 de Abril; ☯ 10am-3pm Mon-Fri)

Bradesco ATMs (Praça do Relógio & Av dos Navegantes)

Branch post office (☎ 288 5645; Shopping Oceania, Av Getúlio Vargas; ☯ 9am-5pm Mon-Fri)

Brazil Travel (☎ 288 1824; www.braziltravel.tur.br; Av 22 de Abril 200; ☯ 8am-10pm Mon-Fri, 8am-10pm Sun Dec-Feb) Offers local tours. Staff speak English, Dutch, German and Spanish.

Central post office (☎ 288 3117; Rua Itagibá; ☯ 9am-5pm Mon-Fri, 9am-noon Sat)

Clínica NS d'Ajuda (☎ 288 1307; Av dos Navegantes 640) Medical service.

Internet Point (☎ 268 4191; Av dos Navegantes; per hr US$2; ☯ 9am-11pm Mon-Sat, 4:30-10:30pm Sun) Internet access and telephone; it also changes US dollars and euros.

Dangers & Annoyances

It's best to take a taxi or the bus on Av Beira Mar at night as there have been frequent muggings.

Sights & Activities

BEACHES

North of town is one long bay dotted with *barracas* and clubs with invisible divisions creating **Praia Curuípe** (3km), **Praia Itacimirim** (4km), **Praia Mundaí** (6km) and **Praia Taperapuã** (7km). The sands are white and fluffy, backed by green vegetation and lapped by a tranquil sea. **Tôa Tôa** (Praia Mundaí), **Axé Moi** (Praia Mundaí) and **Barramares** (Praia Taperapuã) are

the biggest beach clubs and all have MCs and dancers leading crowds through popular dances. The best advice is to get off the bus at Tôa Tôa and walk north until you find your spot.

CIDADE HISTÓRICA

Motivation is required to climb the stairs to the Cidade Histórica. Rewards include a sweeping view, colorful old buildings, and free and humorous capoeira demonstrations given under the round roof behind the churches (hourly in high season). Gonçalvo Coelho's **marker stone** now sits encased in glass and within a fenced-off area. Other reminders of the past are the **Igreja NS da Misericórdia** (1526) and its **Museu de Arte Sacra**, the **Igreja NS da Pena** (1772), the **Igreja NS do Rosário dos Jesuitas** and the **old fort**.

Warning: the area is beautifully illuminated at night, and definitely worth a look, but the steps from the traffic circle are not safe after dark. Take a bus or taxi.

RESERVA INDÍGENA DE JAQUEIRA

At the **Reserva Indígena de Jaqueira** (☯ 8am-4:30pm Mon-Sat), Pataxós dressed in traditional native gear present dances, pray to their gods and demonstrate how to shoot their bow and arrows. Visitors are also taken along trails through their 8 sq km of Atlantic rain forest and shown medicinal and edible plants used by the tribe. The reserve is 10km north of Porto Seguro, and 2km off the road. To get there, take the Campinho-Barramares or Santa Cruz de Cabrália city buses, a taxi (US$10) or an agency tour (US$21.50).

Courses

The friendly **Capoeira Sul da Bahia** (Rua Benedito Claudio 98; per class US$3; ☯ 6:30-8pm Mon-Fri) welcomes visitors to watch or take a class at its academy.

Tours

Local agencies offer schooner and car trips to Trancoso (US$31.50), Caraíva (US$50) and the Parque Nacional Monte Pascoal (US$16.50). Trips are also offered to Recife de Fora (US$5) and Coroa Alta (US$16.50) offshore reefs, but take note that visitors are encouraged to walk over the reefs in order to enter internal pools. Remember that stepping on coral effectively kills it.

THE NORTHEAST

PORTO SEGURO

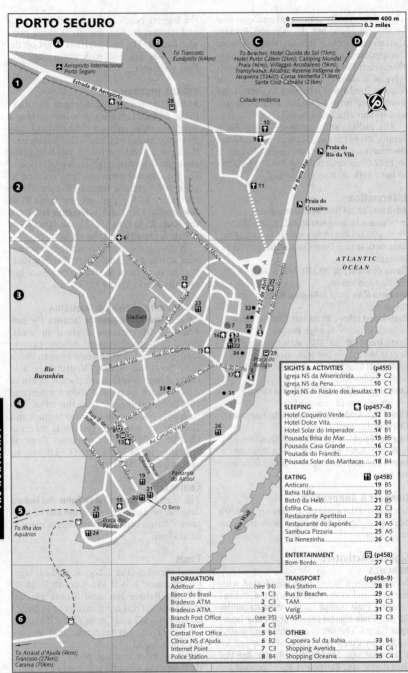

0 — 400 m
0 — 0.2 miles

To Trancoso;
Eunápolis (64km)

To Beaches; Hotel Quinta do Sol (1km);
Hotel Porto Cálem (2km); Camping Mundaí
Praia (4km); Villaggio Arcobaleno (5km);
Transylvania; Alcatraz; Reserva Indígena de
Jaqueira (12km); Coroa Vermelha (13km);
Santa Cruz Cabrália (23km)

Aeroporto Internacional
Porto Seguro

Estrada do Aeroporto

Cidade Histórica

Praia do
Rio da Vila

Praia do
Cruzeiro

Av Beira Mar

Rua Cova da Moça

ATLANTIC
OCEAN

Av dos Navegantes

Rua +5 de Novembro

Av 22 de Abril

Av do Descobrimento

Stadium

Rua Cova da Moça

Rua da Faca

Praça do
Relógio

Rua do Cajueiro

Rua do Golfo

Rio
Buranhém

Rua da Vala

Rua Benecito Cláudio

Rua Pero Vaz de Caminha

Rua 2 de
Julho

Rua Oscar
Oliveira

Av Getúlio Vargas

Rua P. Cabral

Rua São Pedro

Pascarela
do Álcool

Praça dos
Pataxós

O Beco

To Ilha dos
Aquários

Sea Wall

Ferry

To Arraial d'Ajuda (4km);
Trancoso (27km);
Caraíva (70km)

SIGHTS & ACTIVITIES	(p455)
Igreja NS da Misericórdia	9 C2
Igreja NS da Pena	10 C1
Igreja NS do Rosário dos Jesuitas	11 C2

SLEEPING	(pp457–8)
Hotel Coqueiro Verde	12 B3
Hotel Dolce Vita	13 B4
Hotel Solar do Imperador	14 B1
Pousada Brisa do Mar	15 B5
Pousada Casa Grande	16 C3
Pousada do Francês	17 C4
Pousada Solar das Maritacas	18 B4

EATING	(p458)
Anticaro	19 B5
Bahia Itália	20 B5
Bistrô da Helô	21 B5
Esfiha Cia	22 C3
Restaurante Apetitoso	23 B3
Restaurante do Japonês	24 A5
Sambuca Pizzaria	25 A5
Tia Nenezinha	26 C4

ENTERTAINMENT	(p458)
Bom Bordo	27 C3

TRANSPORT	(pp458–9)
Bus Station	28 B1
Bus to Beaches	29 C4
TAM	30 C3
Varig	31 C3
VASP	32 C3

INFORMATION	
Adeltour	(see 34)
Banco do Brasil	1 C3
Bradesco ATM	2 C3
Bradesco ATM	3 C4
Branch Post Office	(see 35)
Brazil Travel	4 C3
Central Post Office	5 B4
Clínica NS d'Ajuda	6 B2
Internet Point	7 C3
Police Station	8 B4

OTHER	
Capoeira Sul da Bahia	33 B4
Shopping Avenida	34 C4
Shopping Oceania	35 C4

THE NORTHEAST

Festivals & Events

Porto Seguro's **Carnaval** is Bahia's most famous after Salvador's. It is pretty small and safe, consisting of a few *trios elétricos* cruising the main drag blasting *axé* music, and lasts until the Saturday after Ash Wednesday, an additional four days. Well-known groups play here after finishing up in Salvador.

On April 19 to 22 the discovery of Brazil is commemorated with an outdoor mass and Indian celebrations on Av do Descobrimento. This seems a rather baffling celebration since the Indians lived here before the 'discoverers' and fared poorly after their arrival. The **Festa de São Benedito** is celebrated in the Cidade Histórica on December 25 to 27. Children blacken their faces and perform African dances, such as *congo da alma*, *ole* or *lalá*, to the percussion of drums, *cuica* and *xeque-xeque*.

Sleeping

Porto Seguro overflows with hotels from its boom days, both in the center and up the northern coastal road. Locals claim the city matches Salvador in sheer numbers. Given this, low-cost, high-quality rooms are easy to find, but reservations should still be made for major holidays. Prices quoted here are for the low season.

BUDGET

Pousada Casa Grande (☎ 288 1259; Av dos Navegantes 151; s/d with fan & minibar US$6.50/13.50) Nicely painted rooms in good shape and hammocks surround a tree-shaded courtyard in an extremely central location. Since the pousada is buried inside a block of shops, almost no one knows it exists! Second-floor rooms recommended.

Pousada do Francês (☎ 288 2469; Av 22 de Abril 180; s/d with TV & minibar US$8.50/13.50; ⚡) Another super-central hidden oasis, with fine, smallish rooms with aging extras and verandas looking onto a side garden.

Hotel Dolce Vita (☎ 288 1058; Rua Itagiba 67; s/d with TV & minibar US$8.50/16.50; ⚡ ⚡) Also a great deal, Dolce Vita has comfortable rooms surrounding a pool area.

Other recommendations:

Pousada Brisas do Mar (☎ 288 2943; Praça Dr Manoel Ribeiro Coelho 188; www.pousadabrisasdomar.hpgvip.com .br, in Portuguese; s/d with fan US$6.50/13.50)

Camping Mundaí Praia (☎ 679 2287; per person US$4; ⚡) Opposite the beach, 4km north of town.

MID-RANGE

Hotel Coqueiro Verde (☎ 288 2621; www.coqueiro verde.com.br, in Portuguese; Rua Oscar da Rosa Teixeira 1; s/d with TV & minibar US$18.50/25.50; ⚡ ⚡) Set off a main road, Coqueiro Verde has two stories of very comfortable rooms with verandas and hammocks looking onto a wide central grassy area and waving palms. The lawn and small play area make it a great place for kids.

Pousada Solar das Maritacas (☎ 288 2082; www .portonet.com.br/maritacas, in Portuguese; Rua dos Periquitos; s/d with TV & minibar US$11.50/16.50; ⚡ ⚡) Maritacas has tall windows that look out on lush landscaping dripping with flowering vines, and lots of varnished dark wood. Rooms are quiet, comfortable and well-maintained. Centrally located.

Hotel Porto Cálem (☎ 268 8400; www.portocalem .com.br, in Portuguese; s/d with TV & minibar US$21.50/23.50; ⚡ ⚡) Located 2km north of town, Cálem has spacious rooms looking across the road to the ocean or over the large pool area. It also has a sauna, games room and that universal modern-hotel feel.

Hotel Quinta do Sol (☎ 268 8500; s & d with TV & minibar US$25.50; ⚡ ⚡) The hotel is creatively designed to fit up against the coastal bluff, but in the pool area and tiny bathrooms it's apparent that architects were on a tight space budget. The rooms are well finished with tile floors, porches with hammocks and wood and stone accents. It's 1km north of town.

TOP END

Hotel Solar do Imperador (☎ 288 1581, 0800 738 686; www.solardoimperador.com.br, in Portuguese; Estrada do Aeroporto 317; s/d with TV, minibar and dinner US$25/29; ⚡ ⚡) From the vines hanging down into the entry courtyard to the sunny pool area with a privileged view out over Porto, crossing the gate of this hotel really does feel like entering an emperor's manor. The hotel is more exotic than the rooms, which have tiny verandas and the classic colonial combination of dark wood floors and white walls. Daily complimentary transportation to town.

Villaggio Arcobaleno (☎ 679 2000, 0800-284 5222; www.hotelarcobaleno.com.br, in Portuguese; s & d with TV & minibar US$62.50/62.50; ⚡ ⚡) Each block of rooms surrounding the wide pool area is painted a different color of the rainbow. The management has ascribed New Agey symbolism to each color, surprising for this conventional hotel 5km north of town. The hotel has spas, saunas, a gym, tennis courts and a beach *barraca* across the road.

Eating

Though Porto is not known for its restaurants, it can't be said that it lacks selection. Most restaurants are clustered around the Passarela do Álcool, where there are also street-food options.

Bistrô da Helô (☎ 288 3940; O Beco; ☽ dinner Tue-Sun) This cute little bistro is the most gourmet in town. Try the balsamic glazed shellfish with basil risotto (US$11.50 for two).

Tia Nenezinha (☎ 288 1846; Passarela do Álcool; ☽ lunch & dinner) The best Bahian food in town is served here.

Restaurante do Japonês (☎ 288 2592; Praça dos Pataxós; ☽ lunch & dinner) The Japonês serves good sushi and great noodle and meat dishes, and is always busy.

Bahia Itália (☎ 288 1820; O Beco; ☽ dinner) Bypass the flashy chain Italian places on the Passarela and come here to fulfill your pasta craving.

Sambuca Pizzaria (☎ 288 2366; Praça dos Pataxós; ☽ dinner) Though the semi-seedy surroundings may give you doubts, Sambuca really does have the best pizza around.

Anticaro (☎ 288 2683; Passarela do Álcool; ☽ lunch & dinner) Some typical Brazilian dishes are served with a little flare here at this friendly restaurant.

Restaurante Apetitoso (☎ 288 1537; Av dos Navegantes 404; per kg US$4.50; ☽ lunch & dinner) This self-service restaurant has a good selection and is always packed.

Esfíha & Cia (☎ 288 5917; Rua Cidade de Fafe; ☽ 9:30am-10pm Mon-Sat) These meat or veggie *esfíhas* (fluffy breads topped or filled) make excellent snacks.

Entertainment

Evening action concentrates on the Passarela do Álcool (Alcohol Walkway), where craft stalls and street performers set up nightly. One section is dominated by fresh-fruit cocktail stands making the infamous *capeta* (*guaraná*, cocoa powder, cinnamon, sweetened condensed milk and vodka), just the thing to get you to finally attempt to samba. There is always live music in front of one restaurant or another and, on weekends, capoeira circles.

Young hipsters selling club and party tickets around the Passarela will let you know what's going on that night. The major beach clubs all put on weekly night time *luaus* (parties), **Barramares**' (☎ 679 2980; Praia de Taperapuã) being the most stunning. Ilha dos Aquários is traditionally a good party, probably because of the novelty of the aquariums and its river-island setting. Up the coast, Transylvania and Alcatraz are clubs in the theme of their namesakes. Each of these venues has separate areas for *axé*, *forró*, samba or MPB and electronic music. Some *luaus* also have lambada and capoeira demonstrations. If the party is up the coast, there are usually round-trip courtesy buses leaving from the *trevo do Cabral* (traffic circle at the entrance of town). For further information about these *luaus* and clubs, call **Porto Night** (☎ 268 2828).

In town, **Bom Bordo** (☎ 288 4113; Av 22 de Abril 151) can be fun when it fills up with people swinging to *axé* and *forró*.

Getting There & Away

AIR

BRA (☎ 288 8917; airport), **Gol** (☎ 268 4460; airport), **TAM** (☎ 288 3399; Shopping Caravelas Boulevard, Av dos Navegantes), **Varig** (☎ 288 3327; shop 45, Av dos Navegantes 69) and **VASP** (☎ 288 1205/1847; sala 102, Av 22 de Abril 1077) can fly or connect you anywhere in Brazil from Porto Seguro's **airport** (code BPS; ☎ 288 1880), about 2km northeast of town. There are no buses to the airport. Taxis run US$5.

BUS

The turnoff for Porto Seguro from Hwy BR-101 is at Eunápolis. The **bus station** (☎ 288 1914) is 1.5km outside the town on the road to Eunápolis. Additional buses are usually added in the high season.

São Geraldo (☎ 288 1198) goes to São Paulo (US$46 to US$59.50, 26 hours, two daily), Rio (US$47, 19 hours, one daily) and Belo Horizonte (US$29 to US$39, 18 hours, three daily), and its tickets can be purchased through travel agents in the center. **Águia Branca** (☎ 288 1039) goes to Vitória (US$17 to US$25, 10 hours, three daily), Valença (US$13.50, nine hours, two daily), Bom Despacho (US$16.50, 12 hours, two daily) and Salvador (US$29.50, 11 hours, one daily). **Rota Sul** (☎ 288 3065) goes to Ilhéus (US$8, six hours, four daily) and shares the Itabuna

(US$6.50, five hours, eight daily) route with Águia Branca. **Brasileiro** (☎ 288 3065) goes to Itamaraju (US$4, three hours, six daily) for access to Corumbau, and Teixeira de Freitas (US$6, five hours, six daily) for access to Caravelas.

For more frequent connections, three companies run buses to Eunápolis (US$2, one hour, every 30 minutes from 5:30am to 10pm).

Getting Around

From Porto Seguro, take the Riacho Doce, Alto do Mundaí, Campinho-Barramares or Cabralia buses to the beach. On the return trip, hop off at the traffic circle if your bus is heading up to the bus station. Taxis and mototaxis are widely available throughout the city.

NORTH OF PORTO SEGURO

The beaches maintain the same look from Porto Seguro north: long, gently curving bays of fluffy sands and gentle seas backed by flowering vines. A good paved road runs along the coast, so it is consequently much more developed than the southern coast.

Coroa Vermelha, a village 13km north of Porto Seguro, has a beach lined with *barracas* and reefs, and several pousadas. A walkway bordered by Pataxó craft stands selling bow and arrow packs and smooth wooden bowls leads to a monument to the discovery of Brazil. Just off the walkway is the **Museu do Índio** (admission US$0.25; 🕙 8:30am-5pm), displaying color photos and traditional objects.

Much more attractive, but still not worth staying overnight in, is **Santa Cruz Cabrália**, 23km north of Porto Seguro. Climb up the bluff to visit the **Igreja NS da Imaculada Conceição**, a small church built by Jesuits in 1630, and for a rewarding view over terracotta roofs, colorful lobster boats and the Rio João de Tiba. Departing with the morning low tide (usually around 9am to 10am), schooners cruise upriver and then out to **Coroa Alta coral platform** (US$4). Santa Cruz Cabrália buses (US$2, 40 minutes, hourly from 6:20am to 7pm) leave from Porto Seguro's bus station and pass through the center.

To continue north, a ferry (pedestrian/car US$0.20/2, every 30 minutes from 6am to 8pm, hourly from 8pm to midnight, every two hours from midnight to 8am) crosses the river. It's 2.5km further along to **Santo André**, a tiny fishing village with a lovely, tree-shaded magic similar to Arraial d'Ajuda's. There are four pousadas ranging from super simple to a deluxe luxury resort, and a pair of bohemian restaurants and bars. **Victor Hugo** (☎ 671 4064; www.portonet.com.br/victorhugo, in Portuguese; s/d with fan & minibar US$21.50/26.50; 🏊) has elegantly simple chalets with décor from the owner's travels, a beachfront garden area and a gay-pride flag in the lobby. Surfers will be interested to know that **Mogiquiçaba** (22km north) has waves.

SOUTH OF PORTO SEGURO

South of Porto Seguro is a series of touristy villages, each with their own unique magic and attractive charms. The comforts of civilization decrease with each kilometer traveled south. The coast from Arraial d'Ajuda to Trancoso is a long stretch of pristine, dreamlike beaches backed by colored cliffs. From Trancoso to south of Corumbau, the beaches remain just as tropically dreamy, and the cliffs begin to flatten out.

Arraial d'Ajuda

☎ 0xx73 / pop 13,000

Arraial d'Ajuda is a beautiful tourist village with an intangible twinkling magic. Stone roads wind beneath large, shady trees atop a bluff overlooking the dreamlike beaches. A traditional plaza is surrounded by squat buildings painted bright colors. In the past, Arraial was the playground of the wealthy and connected, a legacy leaving it with a trickle of upmarket tourism that keeps its slicker pousadas and boutiques afloat. The new wave of international backpackers and nouveau hippies mesh a little better with the relaxed vibe and rustic setting. Contrasting with neighboring Porto Seguro, Arraial has a reputation for attracting a wilder crowd looking to slough off excess brain cells.

INFORMATION

A few places on Broadway (spelled Bróduei by locals) and the Praça São Brás exchange US dollars and euros and offer Internet access for around US$2 per hour. The Banco do Brasil ATM in the bakery at the top of Broadway has a fickle international connection.

THE NORTHEAST

ACTIVITIES

Billed as the largest water park in Latin America, **Paradise Water Park** (☎ 575 1500; Praia d'Ajuda; adult/child US$12.50/6.50; ☽ changes seasonally) has long, twisting water slides, a wave pool and a slow 'river' you can float down on rafts. It brings famous bands from Salvador for summer concerts.

Praia Mucugê is Arraial's main tourist beach and is crowded with *barracas* and blasted by music. As you continue south, **Praia do Parracho** is also built up, but with beach clubs and a few condominium complexes. Both of these beaches are sheltered by offshore reefs. Around the point, beautiful **Praia Pitinga** has red striped sandstone cliffs, pretty, calm waters and a few *barracas*. South of Pitinga, **Praia da Lagoa Azul** and **Praia Taípe** are backed by tall cliffs, pristine and have stronger waves.

COURSES

Newcomers are warmly received and taken seriously at **Capoeira Sul da Bahia** (☎ 575 2981; Rua da Capoeira; per class US$3), which also offers lambada, samba and Afro-Brazilian dance classes. Take a stroll by and at least watch an **advanced class** (☽ 8-9:30pm Mon-Thu & Sat) from the window with all the neighbors.

TOURS

Arco-Iris Turismo (☎ 575 1672; cnr Broadway & Estrada de Mucugê) organizes schooner and van trips to Caraíva, Praias Espelho and Curuípe (both south of Trancoso), Trancoso and the offshore reefs Recife de Fora and Coroa Alta. It also occasionally runs three-day catamaran trips to the Parque Nacional Marinho de Abrolhos.

SLEEPING

The road from the ferry dock to the center is lined with places to stay (some of them quite chic) but you'll find the center to be much more convenient. Prices drop 50% in the low season. Reservations are a must for major holidays.

Vila do Beco (☎ 575 1230; fax 575 1270; Beco do Jegue 173; s/d with fan & minibar US$23/30; ☒ ☒) The location and position couldn't be more privileged: on a side street off Estrada do Mucugê – so right in the heart of things – but set on a tranquil property on the edge of the bluff. White buildings are spread through 1200 sq meters of lush green grounds loaded with fruit trees of every imaginable type. The rooms and two-floor suites are tastefully simple, without a TV in sight. The ocean view from the beautiful pool area is amazing and birds are the only noise you hear.

Saudosa Maloca (☎ 575 1266; www.saudosa maloca.tur.br; Alameda das Eugênias 31; s/d with TV & minibar US$23.50/46; ☒ ☒) Modern, comfortable rooms have balconies with hammocks overlooking a lush pool area. The hotel is large and attractive and located a few blocks from the main drag.

Le Grand Bleu (☎ 575 1272; Beco do Jegue 160; s/d with TV & minibar US$15/20; ☒ ☒) Tucked down a side street off Estrada do Mucugê, this pretty pousada with a green garden has well-kept, unique rooms, some of them two-story suites.

Estalagem Manga Rosa (☎ 575 1252/1423; Rua Jatobá 172; s/d with minibar US$20/26.50; ☒) Tall trees tower over an enclosed courtyard surrounded by a jungly border. Each comfortable room has a hammock and porch. Run by a sweet family.

Pousada Alto Mar (☎ 575 1935; Rua Bela Vista 114; s/d with fan US$3/6.50) Turn down the road on the right side of the church to find this quiet cheapie with clean, basic *apartamentos*. No breakfast.

EATING

There are excellent restaurants in Arraial, serving every type of food imaginable.

Ciboulette & Ciboleto (☎ 575 2050; Estrada do Mucugê; ☽ dinner) Incredible gourmet creations by Belgian chef Pierre are served in an equally pleasing environment beneath a towering tree. Choose from his salmon, filet mignon or crab dishes off the menu or design your own sauce for his fresh pastas. His crème brûlée is divine (US$2).

Rosa dos Ventos (☎ 575 1271; Alameda dos Flamboyants 24; ☽ dinner Thu-Tue) While you may not know what to make of the combination of Austrian and Bahian cuisine, the result is hailed as one of Arraial's best restaurants. Try the fish with shrimp and pineapple wrapped in banana leaves (US$20 for two).

Boi nos Aires (☎ 575 2554; Estrada do Mucugê; ☽ dinner) Red meat lovers go crazy for this place, which serves fine Argentine beef. Sit inside under space-age lamps or outside and watch everyone pass by; either way the tunes are always cool.

Mão na Massa (☎ 575 1257; Rua Bela Vista 125; ☷ dinner) Wonderful salads, fish and fresh pasta dishes are only made better by the sweeping view at this charming restaurant at the edge of the bluff. Behind the church.

Beco dos Cores (Estrada do Mucugê; ☷ Mon-Sat) This beautiful galleria has great sushi, crepes, pizza and fancier food with Asian flavors served in magical ambience.

A Portinha (☎ 575 1289; Rua do Campo; per kg US$6; ☷ lunch & dinner) This is possibly the best self-service restaurant in Bahia. Mashed pumpkin, veggie quiches and meats of all kinds are kept hot over a wood fire.

Paulo Pescador (☎ 575 1242; Praça São Braz 116; dishes US$3; ☷ lunch & dinner Tue-Sun) The choosing couldn't be made easier at this incredibly friendly *prato feito* restaurant: the menu has large photos of each option, and there is only one price. In addition to simply prepared fish and chicken, it also serves stroganoffs and Bahian food. Great quality.

Mary's Salgados (☎ 575 1739; Estrada do Mucugê 157; ☷ 3-10pm) Mary's piping-hot snacks are great after the beach. Her *coxinhas* (fried dumplings) filled with chicken and creamy *catupiry* cheese have a local following.

Soveteria Sumatra (☎ 575 1951; Estrada do Mucugê 118; ☷ noon-11pm) Delicious, creamy ice cream made right here in Arraial. Antonio's creative flavors such as orange and carrot, or guava and cream are great, but his coffee with chocolate chips is famous.

ENTERTAINMENT

Arraial has great nightlife throughout the summer, when beach clubs put on dance parties, and a few nights of the week through the low seasons.

Girasol (☎ 575 1717; Estrada do Mucugê; ☷ 5pm-last client) Here, dancers surround the pool tables on crowded nights, and pillowed window seats offer a comfortable vantage point. The tables out front are great for a drink and the hip place to begin the night.

Beco dos Cores (Estrada do Mucugê; ☷ Mon-Sat) This shop and restaurant galleria has a few bars with magical atmosphere and always attracts a crowd with live music from Thursday through Saturday.

The enclosed **Doc** (Shopping d'Ajuda, Estrada do Mucugê; cover US$6.50) and smaller but more open **Limelight** (☎ 575 2171; Estrada Trancoso; cover US$5) provide more typical dance-club environments with pounding techno.

Sweaty nights spent dancing rootsy lambada and *forró* are an Arraial staple. **Jatobar** (Rua Jatobá) is candle-lit and magical when it's open – ask around for the current hot spot for lambada and *forró*.

GETTING THERE & AROUND

Two ferries travel between Porto Seguro and Arraial d'Ajuda (US$0.60, five minutes). The passenger ferry runs every 30 minutes from 7:30am to 10pm. The car ferry runs every 30 minutes from 7am to midnight, and hourly from midnight to 7am. From the dock, jump on a bus or Kombi van to Arraial. It's also possible to walk the lovely 4km along the beach, but be cautious about carrying valuables or walking alone during hours when the beaches are deserted. Tourist muggings have occurred.

Bicycles and motorcycles are available for hire in the village.

Trancoso
☎ 0xx73

Very hip with the international hippy crowd, Trancoso is a tiny rustic village atop a grassy bluff overlooking fantastic beaches. The town is characterized by its wide, grassy and, most importantly, car-less Quadrado. This central square is crowned by a small church and lined with colorful buildings, nestled under large trees, which house expensive boutiques and casual bars and restaurants. The sight of it lit at night is unforgettable. Rave culture thrives in 'Transe-coso,' famous for its full-moon beach parties. The village fills nicely in summer, but in the low season you'll find it in hibernation.

There are no banks. A couple of places offer Internet access for around US$3 per hour.

SLEEPING

During holidays or for long stays, renting a house is easy to do as locals are quick to abandon their homes in favor of additional income. Young touts acting as go-betweens congregate near the bus stop during holidays. Reservations are a must during January and major holidays. There are a couple of good camping grounds on or just off the Quadrado. Prices quoted here are for low season.

Pousada Puerto Bananas (☎ /fax 668 1017; Quadrado; d with fan & minibar US$29.50; ☷) Lovely rooms with smooth cement floors stained dark blue, bright bathrooms with a window in the shower, and beds sheathed in mosquito netting are spread through a towering green jungle of a garden. The whole scene is honeymoon perfection.

Pousada Mundo Verde (☎ 668 1279; www.porto net.com.br/mundoverde; s/d US$26.50/30; ✂ 🖳) Set on a quiet bluff overlooking the Rio Trancoso and the ocean, blocks of comfortable, spacious rooms sit in a natural garden. A short walk from the Quadrado.

Pousada Jequitibá (☎ 668 1028; www.trancoso bahia.com.br/jequitiba; s/d with fan US$11.50/16.50; ✂) Large rooms with hammocks hung along a common walkway look out onto a pretty side-garden strip. Located on the plaza to the right of the Quadrado.

Pousada Quarto Crescente (☎ /fax 668 1014; www .quartocrescente.net; s/d with fan & minibar US$11.50/16.50; ✂ 🖳) Lovely gardens surround comfortable rooms and a well-stocked library, all with a bohemian edge. On the road into town next to the school, a short walk from the Quadrado.

Other recommendations:

Albergue Café Esmeralda (☎ 668 1527; Quadrado; s/d without bathroom US$8.50/10, s/d US$10/13.50)

Pousada Brilho do Sol (☎ 668 2333; s/d with fan US$10/13.50) A block down from the bus stop.

EATING

Trancoso's restaurants offer a wide variety of flavors and addictively charming ambience. On the road leading to the Quadrado, **Maritaca** (☎ 668 1258; ❨ dinner daily Jul & Dec-Feb, Thu-Tue Mar-Jun & Aug-Nov) serves fantastic gourmet pizzas with service so attentive it verges on comic. Next door, a local character makes the best sweet and savory crepes in the area. Down a little further, the vegetarian restaurant Legume serves two yummy set plates daily.

Moving to the Quadrado, both **Silvana & Cia** (☎ 668 1049; ❨ lunch & dinner) and **Cacau** (☎ 668 1266; ❨ dinner Tue-Sun) are known for their typical Bahian/Brazilian food. **Cantinho Doce** (Quadrado) also serves gigantic portions of typical food, but successfully adds a few creative flavor twists. For possibly the best per-kilo food in Brazil, including mashed pumpkin, quiches and fresh gnocchi, head for **A Portinha** (☎ 668 1054; ❨ lunch & dinner).

On the beach, Barraca do Jonas is known for fresh, tasty seafood.

ENTERTAINMENT

The two main night spots are on the road leading to the Quadrado. Loucos has hiphop, reggae, *axé* and lambada nights, but its Friday-night *forró* is renowned with locals throughout the region. It also has a great sandwich grill. Pára-Raio is an ambient restaurant with outdoor tables under massive trees and an enclosed dance space.

There is always live music somewhere on the Quadrado, but if Elba Ramalho – a local resident and one of Brazil's most wellknown singers – is giving a show, don't miss it. Beach *barracas* such as Pé na Praia (the hippest of them all) sometimes have nighttime parties with pumping trance music and psychedelic décor. Periodically, three-day raves are organized at secluded locations along the beach, complete with bars and sophisticated sound and lighting systems.

GETTING THERE & AWAY

It is possible to walk the entirely beautiful 13km along the beach from Arraial d'Ajuda. If that doesn't appeal, hourly buses depart from Arraial d'Ajuda (catch them on the plaza or at the ferry dock) from 7:20am to 8:30pm (US$2.50, one hour) and return hourly from 6:15am to 10pm. Three buses a day travel between Trancoso and Porto Seguro (US$2.50, two hours). For further connections north or south, head for Eunápolis (US$2.50, 2½ hours, six daily) on Hwy BR-101. Schedules change with the seasons.

TRANCOSO TO CARAÍVA

Rated among Brazil's top-10 beaches, **Praia do Espelho** is 27km south of Trancoso and 14km north of Caraíva. Protective offshore reefs create calm, warm, transparent waters, while reefs closer to shore create natural pools at low tide. The shore is thick with coconut palms. White and orange cliffs divide Espelho from **Praia do Curuípe**, its neighboring beach, which has a collection of top-end pousadas.

Caraíva

☎ 0xx73 / pop 6440

Without electricity, cars, banks or even decent phone lines, the village of Caraíva is remote and beautiful, a combination that has attracted hippies and others looking for a quiet pace of life. The village is strung along the eastern bank of the mangrove-lined Rio Caraíva and a long deserted beach dashed by churning surf. Noisy generators light up the dozen-or-so shops and restaurants lining the sand streets, and most importantly keep the *forró* hopping on Friday night. In the low season, the town all but shuts down.

Boat trips upriver, south to Parque Nacional de Monte Pascoal or Corumbau, and north to Praia do Espelho and Praia do Curuípe are easily organized. Horseback riding along the beach to **Barra Velha**, the Pataxó Indian village, is also an option if walking the 6km isn't appealing. When going to the village, bring lots of water and small bills. On April 19 the village celebrates the **Festa do Indio** with traditional games and dancing.

SLEEPING & EATING

Prices below are for the low season. Due to the lack of electricity, a mosquito net is essential and breakfast is commonly not offered by budget pousadas.

Pousada da Lagoa (☎ /fax 9985 6862; www.caraiva .com.br; d US$30) Surrounding a small pond are brightly painted, nicely decorated cottages with hammocks slung on their porches. There isn't any electricity, except in the bar/restaurant, which is the hip nighttime hangout.

Pousada da Terra (☎ 9985 4417; pousadaterra@ hotmail.com; s/d US$15/22) The absence of electricity in Terra's sweet little bungalows means cold showers and no fan, but mosquito nets and the attractive pousada's charms make the sacrifice easy. An elevated communal space with hammocks and pillows catches the breeze and a café area is lit by generator at night.

Pousada Casinhas da Bahia (☎ 9985 6826; www .caraiva.com.br/casinhas, in Portuguese; d with fan US$20) Tucked around behind the *forró* club, and sharing the same owner, are a grouping of quality rooms in a pretty garden setting. If the music doesn't bother you, the generator noise might, the benefit being 24-hour electricity.

Brilho do Mar (☎ 668 5053; s/d with fan US$8.50/ 16.50) Nice, comfortable rooms and a restaurant serving great Bahian food. It has 24-hour electricity.

Cantinho da Duca (☎ 288 2329; s/d US$5/10) Duca's place is a few wooden hippy shacks on the beachfront, a yard with plants and sculptures, and an area where she paints. She serves a fantastic daily vegetarian *prato feito* from noon to about 8pm and rents a few simple rooms.

Casa da Praia (☎ 575 2747; www.pousadapraia caraiva.com.br, in Portuguese; s/d without bathroom with fan US$6.50/13.50) Small, modern rooms with nothing more than a bed and a mosquito net do the trick for the budget traveler. No breakfast.

GETTING THERE & AWAY

Buses travel twice daily at early morning and early afternoon along a reasonable dirt road (keep an eye out for grazing buffalo) between Trancoso and Caraíva (US$2.50, two hours). The bus stops on the far side of the river in Caraíva, where small dugout canoes ferry passengers across to the village.

As there is no road south along the coast from Caraíva, transportation is by beach buggy or foot along the beach, or via boat. It's a beautiful walk 40km south along the beach to the small town of Cumuruxatiba, passing through the Parque Nacional de Monte Pascoal and Corumbau. Ask around for details.

If heading for other destinations north or south, catch the daily bus to Eunapolis via Itabela, both on Hwy BR-101.

Corumbau

☎ 0xx73

Corumbau sits at the mouth of a river on a sand spit reaching into the ocean. It is barely the semblance of a hamlet, just a charming collection of buildings without electricity. The spit creates calm, blue waters for a long white-sand beach dotted with a few simple restaurants.

The very comfortable, German-run **Jocotoka Eco Resort** (☎ 288 2291; www.jocotoka.com.br; low season s/d with fan & minibar US$32/53; 🅿 🅡) is a collection of round, thatched-roof bungalows 100m from the ocean. Included in the room price is a gourmet buffet dinner served in the stylish dining room. The resort offers activities such as snorkeling, river trips by canoe, kayak or boat, trekking in the national park, a visit to the nearby Pataxó village and whale watching (August to October). There are also a couple of simple pousadas in the village, if you're looking for something less pricey.

A bus leaves Itamaraju on Hwy BR-101 for Corumbau (US$3, three hours) daily at 2:30pm. Otherwise, access is via beach buggy (US$6.50) or boat (US$5, 40 minutes) or a hike along the beach from Caraíva, 12km north.

PARQUE NACIONAL DE MONTE PASCOAL

On April 22, 1500, the Portuguese, sailing under the command of Pedro Álvares Cabral, sighted the broad, 536m-high hump of Monte Pascoal (Mt Easter), their first glimpse of the New World. The sailors called the land Terra da Vera Cruz (Land of the True Cross).

The 225-sq-km national park contains a variety of ecosystems: Atlantic rain forest, secondary forests, swamplands and shallows, mangroves, beaches and reefs. The variety of the landscape is matched by the diversity in flora and fauna: several monkey species, including the endangered spider monkey, two types of sloth, anteaters, rare porcupines, capybara, deer, jaguars and numerous species of bird all inhabit the park.

The northeastern corner of the park, below Caraíva, is home to a small number of Pataxó Indians, who took over control of the park in 2000. They allow visitors access to two trails while accompanied by a guide (settle fees before setting out), one of which climbs the mountain. The **visitors' center** (☎ 294 1110) is 14km from the western (Hwy BR-101) end of the park. The coastal side is accessible by boat or on foot from Caraíva to the north and Corumbau to the south.

There are no direct buses to the park. A taxi from the closest town, Itamaraju, runs about US$10.

CARAVELAS

☎ 0xx73 / pop 20,100

Caravelas is a calm fishing town on the banks of the mangrove-lined Rio Caravelas. Though it has a friendly, down-home Carnaval and a pleasant enough atmosphere, the primary reason it attracts visitors is its status as the gateway to the Parque Nacional Marinho de Abrolhos and other offshore reefs.

Information

Abrolhos Embarcações (☎ 297 1172; Av das Palmeiras 2) Travel agency.

Abrolhos Turismo (☎ 297 1149; Praça Dr Imbassahi) Travel agency; also acts as a kind of unofficial tourist office. Some English spoken.

Banco do Brasil (Praça Dr Imbassahi) ATMs with Visa connections.

Impacto (Rua 7 de Setembro 234) Internet access.

Sights & Activities

To get a feel for the town's thriving fishing industry, check out the **Cooperativa Mista dos Pescadores** (Rua da Cooperativa), opposite the hospital, or wander along the riverfront where the fishers hang out after coming in with the day's catch. The **Instituto Baleia Jubarte** (Humpback Whale Institute; Rua 7 de Setembro 214; ⏱ Mon-Fri) shows videos and offers information about its projects and Abrolhos at its visitors' center.

When the locals go to the beach, most head north for **Praia Grauçá** (10km) or the more isolated **Praia Iemanjá** (20km). Both have calm water colored brown with river silt. Reachable by boat are **Praia Pontal do Sul** (across Rio Caravelas) and the island beach **Coroa da Barra** (30 minutes offshore).

Tours

Travel agencies offer snorkeling day trips (US$41.50) to nearby reefs and islands such as Parcel das Paredes, Sebastião Gomes and Coroa Vermelha. Since most tourists head for Abrolhos, these trips rarely meet the minimum number of people required for departure. River trips up the Rio Caravelas or down the Rio Caribê to the next beach town to the south, Nova Viçosa, are also possible.

Sleeping

Reservations are recommended during Carnaval, when the city fills up with Brazilian tourists.

Pousada Canto do Atobá (☎ 297 1009; www .geocities.com/pousadacantodoatoba, in Portuguese; Av Adalício Nogueira; s/d with fan & TV US$10/20; ⚒ ⚑) A few friendly dogs and cats wander through the garden of this pretty pousada just outside the entrance of town. A back door opening onto a veranda hung with a hammock makes the well-kept rooms airy and bright.

Pousada & Spa da Ilha (☎ 297 2218; www.hotel mais.com.br/c/carav.htm, in Portuguese; s/d US$16.50/30) Across the river, on Ilha da Caçumba, this bohemian pousada has two sweet and simple rooms with furniture built by the owners themselves and solar power. The Uruguayan owner has an in-depth knowledge of the local culture and environment, gives excellent shiatsu massages and natural treatments, cooks creative vegetarian meals and speaks French and English. One daily return boat trip to town is included in the room price; otherwise the cost is US$5. To get there, contact the pousada. Lots of mosquitoes.

Hotel Marina Porto Abrolhos (☎ 674 1082; www .marinaportoabrolhos.com.br; Rua da Baleia 333, Praia Grauça; s/d with TV & minibar US$27/30; ✕ ⚑) The fanciest hotel in town is located 7km from Caravelas, and has round, thatched-roof, beachfront chalets surrounding a gigantic pool.

Pousada dos Navegantes (☎ 297 1799; www.ab rolhos.com.br/caravelas/navegantes; Rua das Palmeiras 45; s/d with fan, TV & minibar US$11.50/23.50; ✕ ⚑) This place is right at the entrance of town.

Pousada Caravalense (☎ /fax 297 1182; Praça Teófilo Otoni; s/d with fan US$6.50/11.50; ✕ ⚑) Located across from the bus station.

Eating

The restaurants at Praia Grauçá have great seafood.

Encontro dos Amigos (☎ 297 1600; Rua das Palmeiras 370; ☽ lunch & dinner) The place in town for seafood.

Carenagem (☎ 297 1280; Rua das Palmeiras; ☽ lunch & dinner) This corner meeting spot has an extensive menu of meat dishes, some fancier than you'd expect from this little town, such as chicken cordon bleu (US$6 for two).

Getting There & Around
AIR

Caravelas' tiny **airport** (☎ 297 1183) is 14km from town, and is served only by Pantanal Linhas Aéreas.

BUS

Access to the town of Caravelas is via Teixeira de Freitas, 74km east. The **bus station** (☎ 297 1151) is in the center of town. Expresso Brasileiro goes to Teixeira de Freitas via Alcobaça (US$2.50, two hours, five daily).

Local buses do a round trip between Caravelas and the neighboring village of Barra (providing access to Praia Grauçá),

leaving every 30 minutes from 6:30am until 10:30pm.

PARQUE NACIONAL MARINHO DE ABROLHOS

It is thought that the name of Brazil's first marine park comes from a sailor's warning: when approaching land, open your eyes *(abre os olhos)*. Abrolhos covers an area of 913 sq km, including reefs noted for the variety of colors and a five-island archipelago that Charles Darwin, aboard the HMS *Beagle*, visited in 1832. These days the primary residents of the archipelago are migrating birds and humpback whales (June to October), which come here to rest and give birth. Only the Ilha de Santa Bárbara has a handful of buildings, including a lighthouse built in 1861. The preservation of the islands is important to IBAMA, so visitor land access is limited to daytime hours on only the Ilha da Siriba. But you didn't come to a marine park for land; you came to snorkel and dive in crystal-clear waters, the visibility of which can reach 20m in the dry season (May to September).

Getting There & Around

Abrolhos is located 80km offshore from Caravelas, the primary gateway, where travel agencies (p464) offer one- to three-day trips to the park. Day trips run US$60 per person, including park fees and lunch. Abrolhos Turismo runs a two-day schooner trip, with an overnight stay on board, starting at US$110 per person including park fees, all meals, soft drinks and water. Snorkel kit rental is US$3 per day. Trips require around a 10-person minimum to go out, but by working together, tour operators usually manage to get trips out even in the low season.

From Arraial d'Ajuda, **Arco Iris Turismo** (☎ 0xx73-575 2736) occasionally organizes three-day catamaran trips that cruise south along the Bahian coast, then on to Abrolhos.

WEST OF SALVADOR

Bahia's interior is primarily made up of the bizarre moonscapes of the *sertão*, a vast and parched land on which a suffering people eke out a meager existence raising cattle and tilling the earth. When the periodic tremendous droughts sweep the land, thousands of Sertanejos (inhabitants of the *sertão*) pile their belongings on their backs and head out in search of jobs. But with the first hint of rain they return to renew their strong bond with this land. Contrasting completely with its dry surroundings, the Parque Nacional da Chapada Diamantina area is lush and green and promises fantastic hiking.

FEIRA DE SANTANA

☎ 0xx75 / pop 480,700

Feira de Santana is the main city of Bahia's interior, and a great cattle center. There's not much to do or see here except the **Feira do Couro**, the big Monday cattle market, which is great fun, with lots of leather bargains, and the **Mercado de Arte Popular** (🕙 Mon-Sat), which has folk art for sale.

Festivals & Events

Feira invented the now widespread concept of **Micareta**, an out-of-season Carnaval. In 1937 a flood caused the city's Carnaval to be celebrated late, a tradition the citizens decided to adopt and rename. In April or early May around 150,000 spectators fill the city to see Salvador's best *trios elétricos* parade for four days along with local samba schools and folklore groups. For those who missed out on Carnaval in Salvador, this could be the next best thing.

Sleeping & Eating

There are several cheap hotels near the bus station, such as the **Hotel Samburá** (☎ 623 8511; Praça Dr Jackson do Amauri 132; s/d with fan, TV & minibar US$8.50/11.50; 🍴).

Feira Palace (☎ 602 9300; www.feirapalacehotel.com.br; Av Maria Quitéria 1572; s/d with TV & minibar US$56.50/60.50; 🅿 🍴 🛋) Feira's nicest hotel often has promotions reducing room prices by up to 60%.

O Picuí (☎ 221 1018; Av Maria Quitéria 2463; 🕙 lunch & dinner) Good regional food.

Getting There & Away

At the crossroads of three major highways, Feira is a major transportation hub. The **bus station** (☎ 623 3667) features an eye-catching mural painted by Lénio Braga in 1967. Frequent buses go to Salvador (US$2, two hours). Buses for Lençóis originating in Salvador pass through Feira de Santana.

LENÇÓIS

☎ 0xx75 / pop 8900

Lençóis is the prettiest of the old diamond-mining towns in the Chapada Diamantina, a mountainous wooded oasis in the dusty *sertão*. While the town itself is a draw – charming cobbled streets, brightly painted 19th-century buildings, nestled between lush green hills – it is the surrounding area bursting with caves, waterfalls and plateaus promising panoramic views that is the real attraction. Most visitors to the area use Lençóis as a base from which to embark on treks within the surrounding Parque Nacional da Chapada Diamantina (p471) and sights outside the park. Lençóis is also noted for Jarê, the regional variation of Candomblé. If you want to see a flip side to surf-and-sand Brazil, or have time for only one excursion into the Northeastern interior, this is it.

History

The history of Lençóis epitomizes the story of the diamond boom and subsequent bust. After earlier expeditions by *bandeirantes* (bands of Paulistas who explored the Brazilian interior while searching for gold and Indians to enslave) proved fruitless, the first diamonds were found in Chapada Velha in 1822. After large strikes in the Rio Mucujê in 1844, a motley collection of prospectors, roughnecks and adventurers arrived from all over Brazil to seek their fortunes.

Miners began searching for diamonds in alluvial deposits. They settled in makeshift tents, which, from the hills above, looked like bed sheets drying in the wind – hence the town's name: Lençóis (sheets). The tents of these diamond prospectors grew into villages: Vila Velha de Palmeiras, Andaraí, Piatã, Igatu and Lençóis. Exaggerated stories of endless riches in the Diamantina mines precipitated mass migrations, but the area proved rich in clouded industrial stones, not display-quality gems.

At the height of the diamond boom, the French – who purchased diamonds and used them to drill the Panama Canal (1881–89), St Gothard Tunnel and London Underground – built a vice-consulate in Lençóis. French fashions and *bons mots* made their way into town, but with the depletion of diamonds, the fall-off in French demand (and subsequently the fall in diamond prices on the international market), the abolition of slavery and the newly discovered South African mines, the boom went bust at the beginning of the 20th century.

But despite these developments, mining held on. Powerful and destructive water pumps were introduced in the 1980s, which increased production until they were finally banned in 1995. The few remaining miners have returned to traditional methods to extract diamonds from the riverbeds. With the establishment of the national park in 1985, the town's economy turned instead to tourism.

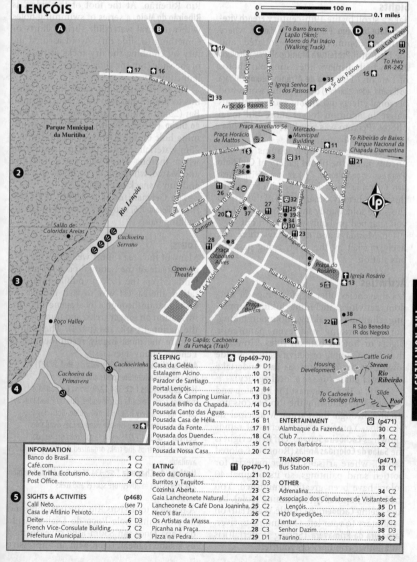

LENÇÓIS

THE NORTHEAST

INFORMATION	
Banco do Brasil	1 C2
Café.com	2 C2
Pede Trilha Ecoturismo	3 C2
Post Office	4 C2

SIGHTS & ACTIVITIES	(p468)
Calil Neto	(see 7)
Casa de Afrânio Peixoto	5 D3
Deiter	6 D3
French Vice-Consulate Building	7 C2
Prefeitura Municipal	8 C3

SLEEPING	(pp469–70)
Casa da Geléia	9 D1
Estalagem Alcino	10 D1
Parador de Santiago	11 D2
Portal Lençóis	12 B4
Pousada & Camping Lumiar	13 D3
Pousada Brilho da Chapada	14 D4
Pousada Canto das Águas	15 D1
Pousada Casa de Hélia	16 B1
Pousada da Fonte	17 B1
Pousada dos Duendes	18 C4
Pousada Lavramor	19 C1
Pousada Nossa Casa	20 C2

EATING	(pp470–1)
Beco da Coruja	21 D2
Burritos y Taquitos	22 D3
Cozinha Aberta	23 C2
Gaia Lancheonete Natural	24 C2
Lancheonete & Café Dona Joaninha	25 C2
Neco's Bar	26 C2
Os Artistas da Massa	27 C2
Picanha na Praça	28 C3
Pizza na Pedra	29 D1

ENTERTAINMENT	(p471)
Alambaque da Fazenda	30 C2
Club 7	31 C2
Doces Barbáros	32 C2

TRANSPORT	(p471)
Bus Station	33 C1

OTHER	
Adrenalina	34 C2
Associação dos Condutores de Visitantes de Lençóis	35 D1
H2O Expedições	36 C2
Lentur	37 C2
Senhor Dazim	38 D3
Taurino	39 C2

Information

Banco do Brasil (Praça Horácio de Mattos) Has ATMs with international connections.

Café.com (☎ 9114 7099; Praça Horácio de Mattos 20; per hr US$2.50) Internet access.

Pede Trilha Ecoturismo (☎ 334 1124; pedetrilha@terra.com.br; Praça Horácio de Mattos) For airline tickets.

Sights

Take a stroll by the 19th-century **French vice-consulate building** (Praça Horácio de Mattos), where diamond commerce was negotiated, and the beautiful **Prefeitura Municipal** (Praça Otaviano Alves), which displays interesting old photos of Lençóis. The **Casa de Afrânio Peixoto** (Praça do Rosário; admission free) displays the works and personal effects of Lençóis' most illustrious native in addition to yet more old town photos. Peixoto was a writer, doctor, politician and academic.

If travel-agency photo albums left you unconvinced, the photo gallery of **Calil Neto** (Praça Horácio de Mattos 82; ◷ 8am-1pm & 6-11pm Wed-Mon, 6-11pm Tue) will leave no doubts about this area's beauty. Small prints of the artist's shots are sold; handy since those cave shots you snapped probably won't turn out.

On Mondays and on Fridays there is a lively market by the river, along past the bus station.

Activities

Local agencies offer a wide range of outdoor activities, including hiking, rappelling, climbing, kayaking, mountain biking, horseback riding and even panoramic flights or hot air balloon rides. However, there are a couple of activities just outside town that the adventurous can undertake without a guide (or see a local agency).

One is a 3km walk past the bus stop and out of town, following the Rio Lençóis upstream through the Parque Municipal da Muritiba. You first pass a series of rapids known as **Cachoeira Serrano**. Off to the right is the **Salão de Coloridas Areias** (Room of Colored Sands), where artisans gather material for bottled sand paintings, so its original 40 colors have been greatly diminished. You then pass **Poço Halley** (Swimming Hole), before seeing **Cachoeirinha** (Little Waterfall) on a tributary to your left. Continuing upriver, **Cachoeira da Primavera** (Spring Waterfall) is on another tributary on your left.

Another relaxing 4km hike is to follow Rua São Benedito (known as Rua dos Negros) out of town, ignoring the left turn 100m after Pousada Lumiar. Continue until the road ends at an upmarket housing development. Continue a short distance, then take a left fork onto a trail that descends and crosses a stream. Keep following the track until you reach a ridge overlooking Rio Ribeirão. At the foot of the ridge, is **Ribeirão do Meio**, a series of swimming holes with a natural waterslide (bring shorts or something to slide on). Avoid assured injury by climbing the dry rocks at the side of the slide (not the slide's wet ones) before launching off.

For more swimming, catch the morning bus to Seabra and hop off at Mucugêzinho Bar (25km). About 2km downstream is **Poço do Diabo** (Devil's Well), a beautiful swimming hole on the Rio Mucugêzinho with a 25m waterfall. About 200m upstream from where the bus drops you, you'll find Rita and Marco, who have set up house in a cave and run a snack bar outside.

The German masseur **Deiter** (☎ 334 1200; Praça do Rosário 156) is highly recommended for walking pains.

Tours

Many of the area's most well-known sights are outside of the national park on private land. Given the lack of public transportation, the easiest way to visit them is by taking a tour through a local agency. For information on longer treks, and tours within the national park, see (p474). The following are the most highly recommended of Lençóis' many agencies:

Andrenalina (☎ 334 1689; Rua das Pedras 121) Specializes in adventure sports and treks.

H₂O Expedições (☎ 334 1229; www.pousadados duendes.com; Pousada dos Duendes, Rua do Pires) Run by Olivia Taylor, a very helpful British guide. Both day trips and treks offered. English-speaking guides available.

Lentur (☎ 334 1271; www.lentur.com.br; Rua da Baderna) Day trips and treks organized. Multilingual guides available.

Nativos da Chapada (☎ 334 1689; Rua Miguel Calmon 29) Specializes in adventure sports and treks.

A popular tour visits Rio Mucugêzinho and its swimming hole Poço do Diabo, Gruta da Lapa Doce (an 850m-long cave, formed by a subterranean river, with an impressive assortment of stalagmites and stalactites), Gruta da Pratinha (a cave and river with clear, light blue waters), Gruta Azul (Blue Cave) and Morro do Pai Inácio (an 1120m peak affording an awesome view over a plateau-filled valley). Though it may sound like a long day in the car, this worthwhile tour includes a lot of walking and swimming and is one you won't forget (US$13.50 plus US$2 admission fees).

Tours to Poço Encantado (the Lençóis poster child: a cave filled with stunningly beautiful blue water) and Poço Azul (another rainwater-filled cave you can swim in) are also offered (US$16.50 plus US$2 admission fees). The caves are guaranteed to stun you with their beauty.

If two wheels is more your speed, contact **Rony** (☎ 334 1700; Rua do Lagedo 68) for mountain bike tours of the area. He speaks English and French. **Senhor Dazim** (Rua São Benedito 27) and **Taurino** (☎ 334 1403; Rua das Pedras 109) both organize horseback tours to various rivers, waterfalls and Morro do Pai Inácio.

Festivals & Events

The **Festa de Senhor dos Passos** begins on January 24 and culminates on February 2 with the Noite dos Garimpeiros (Prospectors' Night). **Lamentação das Almas** is a mystical festival held during Lent. Celebrated from June 23 to 25, the **Festa de São João** is a huge street party with traditional dancing and bonfires outside every house. The **Semana de Afrânio Peixoto** is held from December 11 to 18 and coincides with the municipality's emancipation from slavery.

Sleeping

There is an abundance of very basic, dorm-style accommodations in the dark, old houses in the center, and generally few mid-range options. Reservations are required for all major holidays and suggested for the high seasons (December to February and June and July). For longer stays, ask around about renting a house. Lençóis' pousadas are famous for their fantastic breakfast spreads.

BUDGET

Pousada Casa de Hélia (☎ 334 1143; www.casadehelia.com.br; Rua da Muritiba; 4- or 5-bed dm US$6.50, d US$16.50) This backpacker favorite has beautifully done rooms with floors and, in some

places, walls lined with stone slabs, and furniture fashioned out of twisted branches. The pousada is interspersed between rock walkways bordered by flowering plants, all on the side of a hill affording views over the green river valley below. Some English spoken.

Pousada dos Duendes (☎ 334 1229; www.pousadadosduendes.com.br; Rua do Pires; dm US$5, s/d without bathroom US$6.50/13.50, s/d US$8.50/15) Nicely finished with a very relaxed, social atmosphere, this pretty pousada is perched above town in a quiet neighborhood. It puts on open group dinners with vegetarian options (vegan meals on request), just let them know you're coming. Some *apartamentos* have verandas, and camping is possible. The British owner and guide, Olivia Taylor, has an agency located in the pousada, and is a great source of information about the area. She speaks Spanish and some French. Books are traded.

Pousada da Fonte (☎ 334 1953; www.pousadadafonte.com.br, in Portuguese; Rua da Muritiba; dm/s/d with fan US$6.50/10/16.50) With stone walls, outdoor hammocks and an open breakfast porch surrounded by lush forest, this quaint five-room pousada has the feel of a weekend mountain home. In a quiet green area.

Pousada Lavramor (☎ 334 1280; lavramor@hotmail.com; Praça João Colosso; s/d without bathroom US$5/10, s/d US$8.50/16.50) On the hill across the river from the center of town, Lavramor offers bright, modern rooms with a breeze and a fantastic view.

Pousada Brilho da Chapada (☎ 334 1343; brilhodachapada@bol.com.br; Rua São Benedito 27; s/d with fan & TV or minibar US$6.50/13.50) Granite bathroom counters add class to simple, bright rooms in this modern pousada. Request a 2nd-floor room with an external window.

Pousada Nossa Casa (☎ 334 1258; www.uol.com.br/mochilabrasil/nossacasa.html, in Portuguese; Av 7 de Setembro 62; s/d with fan US$10/13.50) Newly reformed 2nd-floor rooms right in the heart of things make this friendly pousada an excellent option.

Pousada & Camping Lumiar (☎ 334 1241; lumiar@sendnet.com.br; Praça do Rosário; camping per person US$2.50, s/d without bathroom with fan US$11.50/23.50, s/d with fan $13.50/26.50) Lumiar converted his grandparents' colonial family home into a stately pousada and installed an excellent French restaurant (which he chefs) in the beautifully groomed gardens out back.

THE NORTHEAST

Camping in the shady garden is the real draw, as the rooms with their open ceiling vents offer little privacy. Campers have use of the kitchen.

MID-RANGE

Parador de Santiago (☎ 334 1083; www.paradorde santiago.com, in Portuguese; Rua Cel José Florêncio; s/d with fan US$16.50/26.50) In a privileged position beside the river, this beautifully decorated pousada has just four sweet rooms. Though only two have river views, the sound of the water cascading down the rocks fills every room. Even if you don't stay here, you might want to check out its fine restaurant.

Estalagem Alcino (☎ /fax 334 1171; Rua Tomba Surrão 139; s/d without bathroom US$20/26.50, s/d $26.50/ 33) Local artist Alcino offers rooms in his tastefully decorated house. By following only old photos, he built in the likeness of one that once stood in its place. His artwork from his ceramic workshop out back is visible throughout the comfortable rooms and common areas. Alcino speaks a little English and French.

Casa da Geléia (☎ /fax 334 1151; www.casadageleia .com.br; Rua Gal Viveiros 178; s/d US$16.50/26.50) A row of large rooms looks out onto a grassy yard, and has decent views of the surrounding countryside. Host Zé Carlos, a lawyer in town, speaks English and is also a keen birder. Lia's Casa da Geléia (House of Jams) is open to the public and stocks an unbelievable range of homemade jams, chutneys, canned veggies, liqueurs and dried fruits and vegetables. It often appears closed; just ring the bell.

TOP END

Pousada Canto das Águas (☎ /fax 334 1154; www .lencois.com.br, in Portuguese; Av Senhor dos Passos; s/d with TV & minibar US$43/48; ❄ ❄) The location is amazing: at the river's edge, perched level with the water sliding down the gently sloping, burnt-orange rock face. To top it off, the hotel is attractively designed and classily charming, the rooms comfortable to luxurious. The sound of the river can grow to such heights that the staff have trouble hearing the phone in the open-air lobby. At night, huge toads hang around the front entrance, scaring away evil-doers and the skittish. Low-season discounts of 25% are offered.

Portal Lençóis (☎ /fax 334 1233; www.portalhoteis .tur.br; Rua Chacára Grota; s/d with TV & minibar US$81/90;

❄ ❄) This very high-class, luxury hotel has a heated pool with a sunken bar. Panoramic views over Lençóis and the river valley are available poolside or from your veranda. Don't worry about the steep climb from the center, free scheduled shuttles are provided.

Eating

If you delight in a good meal, you may never want to leave Lençóis. Vegetarians will love the many little cafés, most of which can pack lunches for hikes if you pre-arrange it.

Cozinha Aberta (☎ 334 1066; Rua da Baderna 111; ❄ lunch & dinner) The atmosphere is comfortable and cozy in this sweet little bistro, which is just a few tables in the front rooms of an old house. The owner brings the flavors of her travels to Lençóis, with remarkable accuracy and beautiful presentation. A dish of steaming pad Thai or Indian beef-and-vegetable curry over rice, accompanied by a glass of Italian red wine, might satiate your craving for something outside the Brazilian spectrum. Follow your dinner with a brownie and cardamom ice cream and you'll be back the next day. The place tends to fill up, so get there early to stake out a table.

Os Artistas da Massa (☎ 334 1886; Rua da Baderna 49; ❄ lunch & dinner) Fantastically fresh pastas and other Italian dishes are served to the jazz and pop tunes you pick off the menu at this gourmet restaurant.

Picanha na Praça (☎ 334 1080; Praça Otaviano Alves 62; ❄ lunch & dinner Tue-Sun) Choice cuts of beef, chicken and fish are brought to your table sizzling on their own grill at this well-frequented institution. The half-portions, with their heaping side dishes, feed two.

Neco's Bar (☎ 334 1179; Praça Clarim Pacheco; meals US$3; ❄ dinner) Neco's is renowned for having the best regional food in town. Orders must be placed the day before.

Burritos y Taquitos (☎ 334 1105; Rua São Benedito 58; ❄ lunch & dinner Tue-Sun) Ever thought you'd be crunching a Mexican beef taco or sampling sweet, hot tamarind in the Bahian mountains? Make reservations (required for groups over five) for this hot spot or you won't!

Pizza na Pedra (☎ 334 1475; Av Senhor dos Passos; ❄ dinner) Stone slab tables and tree-trunk stools create a rustic atmosphere at this pizzeria tucked away on the road leaving town. The pizzas are agreed to be the best in town, and its serves calzones and pastas as well.

Beco da Coruja (☎ 334 1652; Rua do Rosário 172; ❤ lunch & dinner) This vegetarian restaurant serves salads, soups, *yaki-soba* and pizzas (among other things) to just a few tables in the front room of a small house.

Gaia Lancheonete Natural (Praça Horácio de Mattos 114; ❤ breakfast, lunch & dinner) You pick four items off the menu and they slide them between two thick slices of homemade whole-wheat bread to create healthy, tasty sandwiches (US$2). It also has soups, fruit and granola or egg breakfasts.

Lancheonete & Café Dona Joaninha (Rua das Pedras; ❤ breakfast, lunch & dinner) If breakfast is not included in your accommodations, let Dona Joaninha do you right with her excellent spread (US$2).

Entertainment

Get your predinner or predancing buzz going with an infused *cachaça* (US$0.25) at **Alambaque da Fazenda** (Rua das Pedras 125). On weekends, the dance floor heats up (literally) at **Club 7** (Rua das Pedras). Locals fondly refer to it as Inferninho (Little Hell). You can also get your groove on at **Doces Bárbaros** (☎ 334 1678; Rua das Pedras 85), where there is often a live band on Saturday night. It serves a mean crepe.

Getting There & Away

AIR

The **airport** (code LEC; ☎ 625 8100) is 25km east of Lençóis; a taxi there runs US$6.50. On Saturday, **Varig** (☎ 625 8815) has a flight to Salvador (US$110) and **Pantanal** (☎ 334 1183) flies to São Paulo (US$273).

BUS

If coming from the south, the journey, though indirect, will be a lot quicker if you route through Salvador.

Real Express (☎ 334 1112) buses for Salvador leave at 1:15pm and 11:30pm daily, and at 7:30am on Monday, Wednesday and Friday. All buses to Salvador stop in Feira de Santana (US$7, 4½ hours), where connections can be made to just about anywhere, but are not always well timed. If you arrive by night bus, you will be greeted by tour-company and pousada reps. Tour-company reps are happy to drop you off at the pou-

sada of your choice so they know where to find you later to deliver their pitch. Most pousadas allow you to stay the rest of the night, only charging for breakfast.

CAR

Lençóis is 13km off Hwy BR-242, the main Salvador–Brasília route. There's a gas station 22km east of Lençóis on Hwy BR-242, in Tanquinho. The nearest station to the west is around 30km away. It's not a good idea to rely on the improvised fuel station in Lençóis, which may or may not be open, have fuel or want to sell it.

PARQUE NACIONAL DA CHAPADA DIAMANTINA

☎ 0xx75

Within this national park's 1520 sq km, waterfalls cascade over the Sincora Range's mountains and plateaus, dropping into rivers and streams that wind their way through grassy valleys and clean swimming holes. An endless network of trails is dotted with cactus and strawflowers in some places, and the philodendrons, velosiaceas, orchids and other bromeliads that have escaped poaching in others. Several species of monkey swing through trees where *araras* (macaws) perch. *Veados* (deer) pick their way past gaping caves, while *mocós* (native rodents) and *cutia* (agouti) scurry underfoot. Even an *onça pintada* (jaguar) or two sharpens its claws on a towering tree, but you're much more likely to cross paths with a cute *quati* (small, furry carnivore with a brown-and-yellow-ringed tail).

The region's unique natural beauty and the tranquility of its small, colonial towns have attracted a steady trickle of Brazilian and foreign travelers for several decades; some have never left. These introduced residents, moved by the degradation of the environment and depletion of the wild-animal population, spearheaded an active ecological movement, in direct opposition to the extractive mentality of diamond miners and many locals. After six years of bureaucratic battles, biologist Roy Funch helped convince the government to create the Parque Nacional da Chapada Diamantina in 1985.

The park has little, if any, infrastructure for visitors. Bus service is infrequent and scarce, particularly to the remote parts of

THE NORTHEAST

the park. However, camping or sleeping in the park's small caves is free and can be done without a permit. You'll want gear such as backpacks, sleeping bags or tents, which can easily be rented in town, and reasonably warm clothes.

Geology

According to geologists, the diamonds in Chapada Diamantina were formed millions of years ago near present-day Namibia (Bahia was contiguous with Africa before the continental drift). The diamonds were mixed with pebbles, swept into the depths of the sea that covered what is now inland Brazil, and imprisoned when the seabed turned to stone. Ultimately this layer of conglomerate stone was elevated, and the forces of erosion released the trapped diamonds, which then came to rest in the riverbeds.

Day Hikes & Trips

The most popular day trip into the park is to the top of Brazil's tallest waterfall, **Cachoeira da Fumaça** (Smoke Waterfall), so named because before it has plummeted the entire 420m, the water evaporates into mist. This 6km hike requires a guide, so contact an agency in Lençóis. Alternately, you can originate from the closest village, **Capão** (80km west of Lençóis by road), which has a number of pousadas and a few travel agencies. The nearby mystical Vale do Capão, or **Caeté-Açu**, has attracted an international community of folks interested in an alternative, back-to-the-land lifestyle.

Up the road and outside of the park, **Palmeiras** (54km west of Lençóis by car) is a drowsy little town with a scenic riverside position. The streets are lined with colorful houses and a couple of cheap pousadas.

Hikers may want to take the trail along Barro Branco between Lençóis and **Morro do Pai Inácio**, an 1120m peak affording an awesome view over a plateau-filled valley. Allow four or five hours one way for the hike.

Just southwest of Lençóis, upstream from Ribeirão do Meio (p468), is the lovely **Cachoeira do Sossêgo** waterfall, with a deep pool at its base and rock ledges for diving. The 7km hike involves a great deal of stone-hopping along the riverbed and should not be attempted without a guide, or when rain or high water has made the lichen-covered rocks slippery.

Gruta do Lapão is probably the largest sandstone cave in South America and is just a 5km hike north of Lençóis. A guide is required as access is tricky.

'Chapada's Pantanal', or **Marimbus**, is a marshy microregion 94km south of Lençóis where you can canoe or kayak while fishing for *tucunaré* (peacock bass) and keeping on the lookout for capybaras and *jacarés* (caimans). **H₂O Expedições** (☎ 334 1229; www.pousadadosduendes.com; Pousada dos Duendes, Rua do Pires, Lençóis) is currently the only agency with kayaks running this tour (US$20).

Treks

Navigating the correct routes for these treks can be very difficult, so using a guide is strongly recommended. Treks organized with a guide can last anywhere from two to eight days, and can be custom fitted to the group. They usually involve a combination of camping and staying in local homes and pousadas.

THE BASE OF FUMAÇA

This extremely beautiful yet tiring 36km trek traverses the park from Lençóis to Capão in three days. Detours to other waterfalls are taken along the way, in addition to reaching the base of **Cachoeira da Fumaça**. An extra day can be added walking back to Lençóis or you can continue with the Grand Circuit. Be forewarned that the area around Fumaça's base gets extremely crowded in the highest seasons, so you may find yourself sharing your sleeping cave with unexpected companions. Agencies charge about US$23.50 per day, including meals.

VALE DO PATÍ

Much easier than the Fumaça trek, this highly recommended hike starts and ends in Vale do Capão, and can last from four to six days depending on detours. You are more likely to have the trails to yourself here, and the views over the plains and Chapada's table mountains are spectacular. Stopping in at a local home for a meal or a night is a wonderful possibility. For those who don't want to carry anything, pack mules can be used.

THE GRAND CIRCUIT

The grand circuit of the park covers about 100km, best done in a counterclockwise

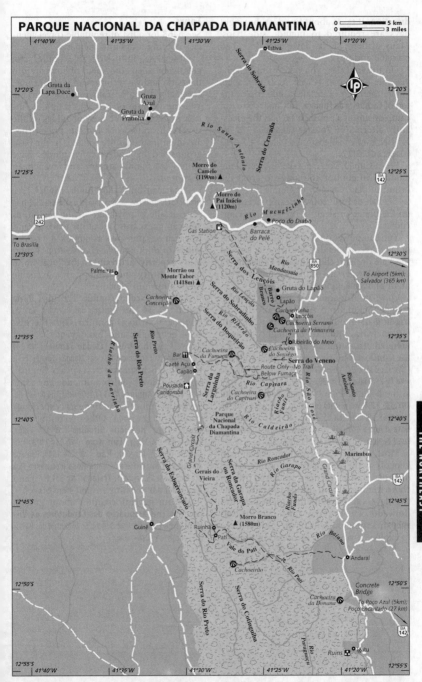

PARQUE NACIONAL DA CHAPADA DIAMANTINA

direction. It takes about five days, but eight days are required to include side trips. Many of these sights have been described on p468 and p472.

On the first day, you hike from Lençóis via Vale do Capão (Caeté Açu) to Capão. While there, you can take a side trip to the top of **Cachoeira da Fumaça**. In Capão, you can camp or stay at a pousada such as the pleasantly alternative **Pousada Candombá** (☎ /fax 344 1102; www.infochapada.com, in Portuguese; Rua das Mangas; s/d US$10/20).

From Capão, you can take one very long day or two comfortable ones to cross the beautiful plains region of Gerais do Vieira to the **Vale do Patí**. You can camp overnight on the plains or sleep in the Toca do Gaucho cave.

You can power on in one day to Andaraí, or take a recommended day to putter around the Vale do Patí, checking out **Cachoeirão** (a delightful waterfall) or the tiny ghost settlement of **Ruinha**, before heading out.

Once in Andaraí, side trips to **Poço Encantado** (56km from Andaraí) and the intriguing diamond-era stone ruins in **Igatu** (12km from Andaraí) are highly recommended. In Andaraí, either camp or try the comfortable, riverside **Pousada Ecológica** (☎ /fax 335 2176; pousada.ecologica@terra.com.br; s/d with TV & minibar US$20/30; ◧ ◪). In Igatu, stay at the beautifully set **Pousada Pedras do Igatu** (☎ 335 2281; www.igatu.com.br, in Portuguese; Rua São Sebastião; s/d with fan US$21/31; ◪) or **Estalagem Gota d'Agua** (☎ 335 2036; www.gotadaguahotel.com; Rua 2 de Julio; s/d with fan US$11.50/23.50).

Most choose to drive from Andaraí to Lençóis as the walk is on an uninteresting dirt road passing scenery destroyed by machine mining. If you decide to walk, allow two days, camping the first night near Rio Roncador. The next day you'll pass the **Marimbus** microregion, which you could arrange to explore if you set it up ahead of time.

Tours

See p468 for a list of reputable travel agencies offering tours into the park.

Otherwise, knowledgeable guides can greatly enhance enjoyment of any trip into the park, and we recommend you take one, especially as park trails are not marked. Whether you do or not, you should definitely not go alone. Be wary of guides off the street who offer rock-bottom prices; they are often insufficiently trained. In the past, groups led by undertrained guides have gotten lost, gone hungry and even been abandoned!

American-born **Roy Funch** (☎ 334 1305; Fundação Chapada Diamantina, Rua Pé de Ladeira 212) has very detailed knowledge of the region, as you can guess from all of his work in, and research on, this area. His book *A Visitor's Guide to the Chapada Diamantina Mountains* expertly demystifies the local flora, fauna, history and geology. It's available around town in Lençóis.

Another excellent guide is British **Olivia Taylor** (☎ 334 1229; Pousada dos Duendes, Rua do Pires, Lençóis), who is familiar with the history, geography and biology of the area, as well as the trails. **Claude Samuel** (☎ 344 1102; Pousada Candombá, Rua das Mangas, Capão) is a native French speaker and speaks English. His treks have been recommended by readers. **Virgínia Aguiar** (☎ 334 1503; Rua Alto da Estrela, Lençóis) has more than 10 years' experience guiding in the area. Other recommended guides are **Henrique Gironha** (☎ 334 1326), **João** (☎ 334 1221), **Luiz Krug** (☎ 334 1102; Pousada de Lençóis, Lençóis), **Rao** (☎ 334 1544; Pousada dos Duendes, Rua do Pires, Lençóis), **Rosa** (Pousalegre, Rua Urbano Duarte 95, Lençóis), **Trajano** (☎ 334 1143) and Zoi (just ask for him around Lençóis).

For further information about guides, contact the **Associação dos Condutores de Visitantes de Lençóis** (☎ 334 1425; Av Senhor dos Passos 61, Lençóis; ◷ 8am-noon).

Sergipe & Alagoas

THE NORTHEAST

HIGHLIGHTS

- Setting out on the **Rio São Francisco** (p491) from colonial Penedo
- Sipping a coconut on tropically idyllic **Praia do Gunga** (p489)
- A sweaty night of *forró* dancing in **Maceió** (p487)
- Lounging at a posh pousada on the remote **Alagoas north coast** (p492)
- Dodging an eel in the **Galés marine reserve** (p494)

Galés Marine Reserve ★
★ Alagoas North Coast
★ Maceió
★ Praia do Gunga
★ Penedo

| ■ POPULATION: 4.6 MILLION | ■ AREA: 49,983 SQ KM |

If Brazil were a person, it would experience major changes in personality, from extroverted Bahia, which catches everyone's eye, to quiet Sergipe, which goes almost completely unnoticed. With their shallow, muddy waters, the beaches in Sergipe, Brazil's smallest state, are not the Northeast's most beautiful, but Sergipe's attractions are interesting on a subtle level, and completely without hype. There is a small amount of colonial architecture, but as it is not polished to its highest shine, bats are more common visitors than tourists.

The largest river in northeastern Brazil, the Rio São Francisco, defines the Sergipe/Alagoas border and was historically an important avenue for moving goods throughout the area. This legacy has left a few charming colonial towns with a unique river culture.

Word hasn't gotten out about Alagoas and its capital Maceió, so a common reaction among visitors is one of pleasant surprise. The state is famous for its deep emerald- and jade-colored ocean waters and picture-perfect tropical beaches. Tiny, one-church fishing villages spaced out along the coast between endless rows of coconut palms, and inland stretches of sugarcane fields, indicate the basis of the local economy and make for gorgeous scenery. Given that there is little tourism infrastructure outside of a few hot spots, Alagoas is a grass-roots, do-it-yourself destination ideal for the independent traveler.

History
During the invasion by the Dutch in 1630, many slaves took advantage of the confusion and escaped to the mountains behind the coasts of northern Alagoas and southern Pernambuco. Where the Alagoan towns of Atalaia, Capela, Viçosa, União dos Palmares and Porto Calvo stand today, virgin forests with fruit and wildlife once provided for colonies of runaway slaves. Palmares, the mightiest republic of escaped slaves, led by the former African king Zumbi, covered present-day Alagoas and Pernambuco.

Climate
The tropical Atlantic coast of Sergipe and Alagoas remains hot and humid throughout the year. High temperatures range from 30°C (86°F) to 36°C (97°F) and low temperatures run between 20°C (68°F) and 25°C (77°F). Monthly rainfall averages run from 60mm in dry months (August to March) to 325mm in the rainy months (April to July). The interior of Sergipe has a semiarid climate and therefore sees less rainfall.

Getting There & Away
Hwy BR-101 skirts the coastline of both Sergipe and Alagoas between 25km and 50km inland. It is the main thoroughfare through the region and the chosen route of most long-distance buses. The main airports in the region are in the capital cities, Aracaju and Maceió.

Getting Around
As is the norm in the Northeast, there is always some form of transportation between where you are and where you need to go. As well as buses, Kombi vans and *bestas* (vans that run a specific route and will stop anywhere to drop off or pick up passengers) are common in rural areas, as are *taxis coletivos* (collective taxis). *Mototaxis* (motorcycle taxis) are almost always available in small to mid-sized towns.

SERGIPE

ARACAJU
☎ 0xx79 / pop 460,900
Aracaju has a friendly, relaxed environment and if you're coming from the south, it's the first city with a real Northeastern feel about it. Pedestrian malls slow the center to walking pace, and many impressive buildings surrounding the leafy main square have

been restored. Though not a major tourist draw, Aracaju is a pleasant enough place to take care of business before continuing on to your next destination.

History
The seat of state government was moved from São Cristóvão to Aracaju in 1855, in part because of its good deep harbor – badly needed to handle large ships transporting sugar to Europe – and because residents of the old capital were on the verge of armed revolt. Within a year an epidemic broke out and decimated Aracaju's population, which the residents of São Cristóvão naturally saw as an omen that the new capital had a doomed future.

Orientation
Aracaju's Centro sits on the Rio Sergipe, guarded from the ocean by a sandy barrier island, the Ilha de Santa Luzia. To the south, past the river mouth, are the city beach neighborhoods of Coroa do Meio, Jardim Atlantico (Praia dos Artistas) and Atalaia, collectively referred to as the *orla*

(waterfront). Most of the action and nightlife concentrates in these suburban neighborhoods, where only the main avenues are paved.

Information

EMERGENCY
Police (☎ 190)

INTERNET ACCESS
Centernet (☎ 213 7039; Rua João Pessoa 64, Centro; per hr US$1; ☒ 8am-7pm Mon-Fri, 9am-3pm Sat)
Timer Web Café (Praça Olimpio Campos, Centro; per hr US$1; ☒ 9am-10pm Mon-Sat, 2-10pm Sun) Even cheaper on weekends.

MEDICAL SERVICES
Hospital Governador João Alves Filho (☎ 216 2600; Av Tancredo Neves, América)

MONEY
Banco do Brasil (Rua Geru 341, Centro)
Bradesco (cnr Rua Geru & Praça Fausto Cardoso, Centro)

POST
Central post office (Rua Laranjeiras 229, Centro)

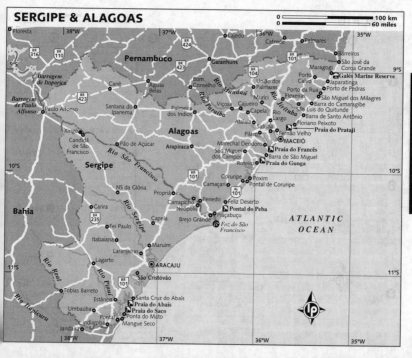

SERGIPE & ALAGOAS

TELEPHONE

Centernet (☎ 213 7039; Rua João Pessoa 64, Centro; ☒ 8am-7pm Mon-Fri, 9am-3pm Sat)

TOURIST INFORMATION

Emsetur (www.emsetur.gov.br); Centro (☎ 3179 1947; Rua Propriá, Centro; ☒ 8:30am-7pm); Rodoviária Nova (☒ 8am-10pm Mon-Fri, 9am-9pm Sat & Sun) The main office of the state tourism authority is in the Centro do Turismo, which includes a few craft shops, and backs the Rua 24 Horas shopping arcade. It has free maps of Aracaju and São Cristóvão.

TRAVEL AGENCIES

Sergitur (☎ 9969 6574; Rua João Pessoa 71/75, Centro) Offers day tours. Enter from Rua Laranjeiras.

Sights & Activities

Tamar Project's small, interesting **Oceanário** (aquarium; ☎ 243 3214; Av Santos Dumont, Atalaia; adult US$2, senior & student US$1, child free; ☒ 2-8pm Tue-Fri, 9am-9pm Sat & Sun) has tanks with sea turtles, rays and eels as well as examples of specific local freshwater environments and their species.

For a more concentrated look at this conservation and education project, go and visit its **biological reserve** (☎ 276 1202; Pirambú; admission free; ☒ 8am-5pm), where you can see tanks of sea turtles and have a talk with the biologists. To get there, catch a ferry to Barra dos Coqueiros (see p480), and then a *topique* (van) to Pirambú (US$1, 30 minutes). If you ask, the driver will take you all the way.

Fruit is peddled, watches are fixed and rabbits find new homes (or pots) at the **Mercado Municipal** (Rua José do Prado Franco, Centro; ☒ 6am-6pm Mon-Sat, 6am-noon Sun), a two-story enclosed market.

BEACHES

With rustling palms and a relative lack of buildings, **Praia Atalaia Nova**, on the Ilha de Santa Luzia, is preferred over the city beaches of **Praia dos Artistas** (7km), **Praia Atalaia** (9km) and **Praia Aruana** (11km) to the south. These beaches are heavily developed but are popular with locals; they are also good sources of inexpensive seafood. Further south, **Praia do Refúgio** (18km) is the prettiest and most secluded nearby beach.

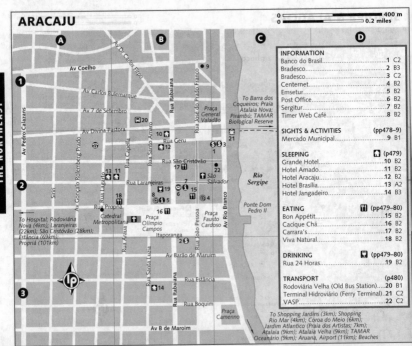

ARACAJU

0 — 400 m
0 — 0.2 miles

INFORMATION	
Banco do Brasil	**1** C2
Bradesco	**2** B3
Bradesco	**3** B2
Centernet	**4** C2
Emsetur	**5** B2
Post Office	**6** B2
Sergitur	**7** B2
Timer Web Café	**8** B2

SIGHTS & ACTIVITIES	(pp478-9)
Mercado Municipal	**9** B1

SLEEPING	(p479)
Grande Hotel	**10** B2
Hotel Amado	**11** B2
Hotel Aracaju	**12** B2
Hotel Brasília	**13** A2
Hotel Jangadeiro	**14** B3

EATING	(pp479-80)
Bon Appétit	**15** B2
Cacique Chã	**16** B2
Carrara's	**17** B2
Viva Natural	**18** B2

DRINKING	(pp479-80)
Rua 24 Horas	**19** B2

TRANSPORT	(p480)
Rodoviária Velha (Old Bus Station)	**20** B1
Terminal Hidroviário (Ferry Terminal)	**21** C2
VASP	**22** C2

Tours

Local travel agencies offer a variety of day tours, including catamaran trips on the Rio São Francisco to the green waters of the canyon of **Xingó** (US$20), or to the **Foz de São Francisco** (US$20), where the river meets the sea. A tour is also a pretty good way to check out difficult-to-reach **Mangue Seco** (US$15, p443) on the border with Bahia.

Festivals & Events

On January 1 a huge fleet of fishing boats sail along the Rio Sergipe following the image of their patron saint to celebrate **Bom Jesus dos Navegantes**. The largest festival of all is the **Festa de São João**, which runs for the entire month of June and includes live *forró* (music and dance style of the Northeast; see p516) bands and *quadrilha* (type of square dancing) presentations. The **Festa de Iemanjá** is celebrated on December 8, when followers perform ceremonies and make offerings to the sea goddess.

Sleeping

The majority of Aracaju's hotels are on the waterfront at Praia dos Artistas and Atalaia. For a short stay, you'll find those in the center more convenient and generally less expensive.

BUDGET

Hotel Amado (☎ /fax 211 9937; www.infonet.com.br /hotelamado; Rua Laranjeiras 532, Centro; s/d with fan & TV US$8.50/13.50; ☒) Potted plants line the porch of this old house adapted and expanded into a hotel, making it almost pretty. Safe and family-run.

Grande Hotel (☎ /fax 211 1383; grandehotel@infonet .com.br; Rua Itabaiana 371, Centro; s/d with TV & minibar US$8.50/16.50; ☒ ☒) The rooms in this large hotel, which knew grander days, are a good size and have stained wood floors.

Hotel Aracaju (☎ 214 2898; Rua Geru 205, Centro; s with shared bathroom US$7, s/d with private bathroom US$12/18) A rock-bottom choice, favored by local clientele as a short-time joint. No breakfast to be had here.

MID-RANGE

Tropical Praia Hotel (☎ 255 2799; www.tropicalpraia hotel.com.br; Rua Renato Fonseca Oliveira 55, Praia dos Artistas; s/d with TV & minibar US$23.50/30; ☒ ☒ ☒) Rooms are spacious and comfortable, and

the hotel is modern and oceanfront. Low-season prices drop by almost 50%.

Pousada do Farol (☎ 255 1513; www.pousadado farol.com.br; Rua Delmiro Gouveia 663, Coroa do Meio; s/d with TV & minibar US$13.50/20; ☒ ☒ ☒) The overall feeling is a little sterile, but the granite fixtures in the bathroom remind you that this place is great value.

Hotel Jangadeiro (☎ /fax 211 1350; www.janga deirose.com.br; Rua Santa Luzia 269, Centro; s/d with TV & minibar US$20/23; ☒ ☒) Grey walls and tiles and narrow windows lend no luxury to this plain hotel, but you'll be comfortable and treated well.

Hotel Brasília (☎ 214 2964; Rua Laranjeiras 580, Centro; s/d with TV US$12/18.50; ☒ ☒) A modern, no-frills but presentable option with a 10% discount for cash payment.

TOP END

Del Mar Hotel (☎ 255 9100, 0800-560 056; www.del marhotel.com.br; Av Santos Dumont 1500, Praia dos Artistas; s/d US$62.50/71; ☒ ☒ ☒ ☒) Rooms have all the comforts you'd expect from an ocean-front, four-star hotel. Out back there's a nice green area with a boat-shaped pool.

Eating & Drinking

Bars and restaurants stretch out along the waterfront in Atalaia, making it a good spot to wander at night, when the center is pretty dead.

O Miguel (☎ 243 1444; Av Antônio Alves 340, Atalaia Velha; ☽ lunch daily, dinner Tue-Sun) The place in town for Northeastern food, specializing in *carne do sol* (a tasty, salted meat, grilled and served with beans, rice and vegetables).

Boigordo (☎ 243 1101; Rua do Boigordo 74, Aruana; ☽ lunch & dinner Wed-Sun) In addition to the regional favorites, the seafood here is quite good. Popular with locals.

Viva Natural (☎ 224 4515; Rua Propriá 10, Centro; per kg US$3; ☽ lunch, closed Sun) A well-stocked health-food store offering a self-service veggie lunch.

Cacique Chá (☎ 214 6854; Praça Olímpio Campos, Centro; ☽ lunch & dinner, closed Sun) The leafy plaza setting of this restaurant makes it a great place to relax with a drink and enjoy live music on Friday and Saturday. It offers a self-service buffet during the day and small bites at night, including tasty soups (US$0.75).

Rua 24 Horas (Rua Laranjeiras, Centro) Tucked in a courtyard between a shopping arcade and the Centro do Turismo are a few bars and cafés offering drinks and snacks, as well as a stage that heats up on weekends.

For self-service, try **Bon Appétit** (☎ 221 1113; Rua João Pessoa 71175, Centro; per kg US$4; ☼ lunch, closed Sun) or **Carrara's** (☎ 224 6866; Rua São Cristóvão 165, Centro; per kg US$4; ☼ lunch, closed Sun).

Entertainment
DANCING
Cariri (☎ 9972 2604; Av Santos Dumont, Atalaia; ☼ 10pm-last client) *Forró* rules the house here, in the traditional style of *pé de serra* (foot of the hills).

Rock (☎ 243 3655; Av Santos Dumont, Atalaia; ☼ 9pm-last client Wed-Sat) This bar and nightclub changes its style nightly from electronic music to live rock to *musica romantica*.

CINEMAS
Both **Cinemark** (☎ 217 5838; Shopping Jardins, Av Tancredo Neves; ☼ 10am-10pm Mon-Sat, noon-10pm Sun) and **Movicom** (☎ 213 8505; Shopping Rio Mar, Av Santos Dumont; ☼ 10am-10pm Mon-Sat, 10am-10pm Sun) run about 10 movies daily.

Getting There & Away
AIR
BRA (☎ 212 8590; airport), **TAM** (☎ 214 5492; airport), **Varig** (☎ 211 1889; Rua Itabaiana 390, Centro) and **VASP** (☎ 214 5801; Rua São Cristóvão, Centro) can fly or connect you to anywhere in Brazil from Aracaju's **airport** (code AJU; ☎ 243 7607)

BUS
Most long-distance buses leave from the **Rodoviária Nova** (New Bus Station; ☎ 259 2848), 4km east of the center.

Bonfim (☎ 259 2788) runs three daily buses to Salvador (US$10 to US$15) along the costal Linha Verde highway (4½ hours), and two along Hwy BR-101 via Entre Rios (six hours). Bonfim buses also go to Maceió (US$7.50 to US$9, 4½ hours, four daily) and Penedo (US$4.50, four hours, one daily). Both **Progresso** (☎ 259 3020) and **Real Alagoas** (☎ 259 2832) go to Recife (US$16, nine hours, four daily). For further access to Penedo, catch a **Santa Maria** (☎ 259 3000) bus to Neópolis (US$2.50, two hours, five to seven daily) and then a ferry from there (see p492).

Coopertalse (☎ 259 3028) and Santa Maria depart for Propriá (US$2.50, two hours,

hourly 6am to 5:40pm) from the **Rodoviária Velha** (Old Bus Station; ☎ 214 2578; Centro).

Getting Around
TO/FROM THE AIRPORT
Aracaju's airport is 11km south of the center. A taxi to the airport from the center will cost about US$5. From the Rodoviária Velha, take the Aeroporto city bus.

TO/FROM THE BUS STATION
City buses depart from a large shelter with a series of triangular roofs beside the Rodoviária Nova. For the center, catch any bus going to the Rodoviária Velha, such as Centro or Terminal Rodoviário/Desembarcador. The Circular Cidade 1 bus goes south to the beach neighborhoods. A taxi to the center costs about US$3.

BOAT
Ferries leave every 15 minutes for Barra dos Coqueiros (US$0.25) and hourly on the hour for Praia Atalaia Nova (US$0.50) – both on Ilha de Santa Luzia – 24 hours a day from the Terminal Hidroviário (Ferry Terminal). Departures are less frequent after midnight. Buses travel between Barra dos Coqueiros and Praia Atalaia Nova.

BUS
The Rodoviária Velha is the terminal for local runs and nearby towns.

Aracaju has a few bus transfer points spread around the city which you pay to enter, effectively paying your bus fare upfront. The money collectors are great sources of bus information.

LARANJEIRAS
☎ 0xx79 / pop 23,400
Nestled between three grassy, church-topped hills, Laranjeiras is the colonial gem of Sergipe. This may not be saying much, but it is still a pretty little town of cobblestone roads lined with colorful colonial facades and terracotta roofs, unblemished by modern development. The town's churches are simple, while the museums are surprisingly good for a town of its size. The surrounding countryside is filled with crumbling ruins of old sugar mills and estates. Laranjeiras can be a pretty quick day trip from Aracaju, or a full day if you want to really explore the surrounding area.

History

First settled in 1605, Laranjeiras became the commercial center for its surrounding rich sugar and cotton region during the 18th and 19th centuries. At one point there were more than 60 sugar mills in and around Laranjeiras sending sugar down the Rio Cotinguiba to Aracaju for export to Europe.

Information

There is usually someone lingering inside the Trapiche building who can answer questions about local sights. Free guides paid by the city, or private guides charging around US$4, can be picked up around the bus station and Trapiche.

Sights

Facing the bus station, the **Trapiche** is an imposing, 19th-century structure that historically held cargo waiting to be shipped down river.

A few kilometers from town is a partly restored sugar mill, known simply as **Engenho** (mill), in a lovely setting. It is privately owned and not generally open to the public, but it may be possible to arrange a visit through a guide.

CHURCHES

At the top of Alto do Bonfim (Bonfim Heights), is the restored 19th-century **Igreja NS do Bonfim** and a fine view. If it is closed, someone around back can likely let you in.

Out at the Engenho Boa Sorte, 4km upriver from town, is the baroque **Igreja de Comandaroba**, constructed by Jesuits in 1734. Only a few guides have keys to it, and unfortunately the church is not well maintained, despite past restoration efforts. A 1km tunnel leads from the church to the **Gruta da Pedra Furada** (a large cave built by the Jesuits to escape their persecutors and used for Mass in the early days).

MUSEUMS

The **Museu de Arte Sacra** (Museum of Sacred Art; admission US$0.75; 10am-5pm Tue-Fri, 1-5pm Sat & Sun) is located in a beautifully restored colonial house next door to the Igreja da Matriz on the main plaza. The house, built in 1897, still has its original wood floors and walls bordered with hand-painted flowers. The museum's collection has been gathered from churches in the area and includes

17th- and 18th-century silver pieces, as well as restored wooden saint statues. The statue of NS das Dores had her quartz-crystal tears stolen when the Igreja NS do Bonfim caught fire. The museum often appears closed when not – just rap on the front door.

Laranjeiras is considered to be the stronghold of Afro-Brazilian culture in Sergipe. At the **Museu Afro-Brasileiro** (Rua José do Prado Franco; admission US$0.75; 10am-5pm Tue-Fri, 1-5pm Sat & Sun), a knowledgeable docent will explain displays on sugar production, slave torture methods, Afro-Brazilian religions and Laranjeiras' cultural traditions.

Festivals & Events

During the second week of January, Laranjeiras hosts the **Encontro Cultural**, a folklore festival full of traditional music and dance.

Sleeping & Eating

Pousada Vale dos Outeiros (281 2434; Rua João Prado Franco 124; s/d with fan US$5/11.50;) The choice is easy since it is the only pousada (guesthouse) in town. The rooms are simple but those in the back have good views of the surrounding hills.

Nice's Restaurant (281 2883; Praça da Matriz) A good place to grab lunch in between your adventures.

Getting There & Away

Both Coopertalse and São Pedro buses make the 21km trip between Laranjeiras and Aracaju's Rodoviária Velha (US$0.50, 35 minutes, hourly from 6am to 10:30pm). There are also unofficial collective taxis running the same route at the same price. If you're coming from the north on Hwy BR-101, get off at the turnoff for Laranjeiras and catch a ride or walk the 4km into town.

If you're continuing on to São Cristóvão, catch Aracaju-bound transportation and ask to be let off at the *trevo* (roundabout, but in this case a highway-side bus stop outside Aracaju) and catch a São Cristóvão bus from there.

SÃO CRISTÓVÃO

0xx79 / pop 64,520

Atop a steep hill with expansive views over rivers winding through lushness, the historic part of São Cristóvão is a sleepy concentration of white 17th- and 18th-century colonial buildings along narrow stone roads and a few wide plazas. Founded in 1590, São Cristóvão is reputedly Brazil's fourth-oldest town and was the capital of Sergipe until 1855. Your sweet tooth will be tempted by local bakers, who are renowned for their homemade confectionery and cakes. Even the Benedictine nuns at the Convento do Carmo join in with their *bricelete*, a yummy lemon-flavored wafer cookie. There are no pousadas in São Cristóvão, but it's an easy and worthwhile day trip from Aracaju.

São Cristóvão does not lack for churches. Of particular distinction are **Igreja de Senhor dos Passos** (1739), with its ceiling painted by José Teófilo de Jesus, and **Igreja e Convento de São Francisco** (1906), with its excellent **Museu de Arte Sacra** (admission US$0.50; 1-6pm Tue-Sun). The **Antiga Assembléia Legislativa** and **Antigo Palácio do Governo** are reminders of the previous political power held here.

During one weekend in the second half of October, the town comes alive for the **Festival de Arte de São Cristóvão**, a festival of fine and popular arts, filled with music and dance.

Frequent buses make the 25km trip between São Cristóvão and Aracaju's Rodoviária Velha (US$0.50, 45 minutes). The town is 8km off Hwy BR-101.

ESTÂNCIA
☎ 0xx79 / pop 58,830

Estância has a certain amount of character, a few historic buildings in the center, and can offer all basic services. However, there's little reason to stop here unless you want to avoid spending the night in Aracaju or are heading to the nearby beaches at Mangue Seco (p443). Estância's **Festas de São João** draw big crowds throughout the entire month of June.

The lobby at the **Hotel Turismo Estanciano** (☎ /fax 522 1404; Praça Barão do Rio Branco 176; s/d with fan & TV US$8.50/11.50;) opens onto the pretty main plaza, and is dotted with potted plants and colored tiles. Rooms are bright, airy and comfortable, some with ceilings so high the walls don't actually reach them! Get a room away from the restaurant.

Estância is a bit off Hwy BR-101, but most long-distance buses still stop at its **bus station** (☎ 522 1466). Bonfim runs buses to Salvador along the coastal Linha Verde highway (US$9.50 to US$15, 3½ hours, 11 daily) or on Hwy BR-101 via Entre Rios (US$8 to US$13.50, 4½ hours, three daily). Take the Linha Verde route for access to Bahia's

northern beaches, but know that although you will be dropped on the highway – where you will have to catch additional transportation into town – you will be charged the full fare to Salvador. For Aracaju (US$1, one hour, 5:30am to 6pm), Rota Sul buses leave frequently from the bus station, and yet more buses and collective taxis leave from the Mini-Rodoviária (Mini-Bus Station).

PROPRIÁ
☎ 0xx79 / pop 27,290

On the banks of the mighty Rio São Francisco, Propriá has the same combination of colonial charm and river culture found in Penedo (p490) and Neópolis further downstream, though perhaps to a lesser degree. To be honest, only those interested in hustling for some river travel should go out of their way to visit. Thursday and Friday are the town's market days, when goods are traded from communities along the river.

River Trips

In recent years there has been a steady decline in long-distance boat travel along the Rio São Francisco. The only known regular boat departure from Propriá leaves at 5am on Wednesday and Saturday and travels downriver to Penedo (US$1, three hours). A word of advice for the tender and claustrophobic – the wooden seats quickly get pretty hard, and the boat is too small to get up and wander around. There is also occasionally a catamaran making Sunday river cruises if there is sufficient interest.

The other option is to try your luck at bargaining your way onto a boat leaving town, which range from powerful motorboats to beautiful sailing boats with long, curved masts and striking yellow or red sails.

Festivals & Events

The colorful and highly recommended **Festa de Bom Jesus dos Navegantes**, held on the last Sunday in January, involves a maritime procession and *reisado*, a dramatic dance that celebrates Epiphany.

Sleeping & Eating

Hotel Imperial (☎ 322 1294; Rua Gouveia Lima 66 s/d with fan US$5/8.50;) The atmosphere throughout the hotel is simple and pleasant with beautiful old floor tiles and high ceilings. Faces the main church.

VELHO CHICO: THE RIVER OF NATIONAL UNITY

For the Brazilian, particularly the Nordestino, it's impossible to speak about the Rio São Francisco without a swelling of pride and emotion. There is no river like the São Francisco, which is the third most important river in Brazil, after the Amazon and the Paraguay. Those who live along its banks speak of it as a friend – hence the affectionate nickname *Velho Chico* or *Chicão* (Chico is a nickname for Francisco).

The geographical situation of the São Francisco gave it a prominence in the colonial history of Brazil that surpassed the Amazon. With its headwaters in the Serra da Canastra, 1500m high in Minas Gerais, the Rio São Francisco flows north across the greater part of the Northeast *sertão* (backlands), and completes its 3160km journey at the Atlantic Ocean after slicing through the states of Minas Gerais and Bahia, and delineating the Bahia/Pernambuco and Sergipe/Alagoas state borders.

For three centuries the São Francisco, also referred to as the 'river of national unity,' represented the only connection between the small towns at the extremes of the *sertão* and the coast. 'Discovered' in the 17th century, the river was the best of the few routes available to penetrate the semiarid Northeastern interior. Thus, the frontier grew along the margins of the river. The economy of these settlements was based on cattle, which provided desperately needed food for the gold miners in Minas Gerais in the 18th century and later fed workers in the cacao plantations throughout southern Bahia.

Although the inhabitants of the region were often separated by enormous distances, cattle ranching proved a common bond and produced a culture that can be seen today in the region's folklore, music and art.

The history of this area is legendary in Brazil: the tough *vaqueiros* (cowboys of the Northeast) who drove the cattle; the commerce in salt (to fatten the cows); the cultivation of rice; the rise in banditry; the battles between the big landowners; and the religious fanaticism of Canudos.

The slow waters of the São Francisco have been so vital to Brazil because, in a region with devastating periodic droughts, the river provides one of the only guaranteed sources of water. Today the river valley is irrigated to produce a huge amount of produce for local consumption and export.

Locals realize the importance of the São Francisco and thus, over the centuries, they have created hundreds of stories, fairy tales and myths about the river. One example is the *bicho da água* (water beast). This creature, part animal and part human, walks on the bottom of the river and snores. The crews on the riverboats placate the *bicho da água* with handfuls of tobacco thrown into the water.

The river's width varies from two hand-spans at its source in the Serra da Canastra, an empty, uninhabitable region where little grows, to 40km at Bahia's Lagoa do Sobradinho, the biggest artificial lake in the world. Nordestinos believe that São Francisco is a gift from God to the people of the *sertão* to recompense all their suffering in the drought-plagued land.

Hotel Velho Chico (☎ 322 1734; velhochico@infonet .com.br; s/d with TV & minibar US$21/23.50; P ☒ ☒) The rooms aren't fancy but are comfortable and have a river view. The hotel has a restaurant and sits at the base of the bridge over the river, just off the highway.

O Veleiro (Av Nelson Melo) Head here for a pleasant meal with a view of the river.

Getting There & Away

Buses stop at a café/ticket agency on the riverfront. Coopertalse and Santa Maria buses make the 81km trip to Aracaju hourly from 6am to 6pm (US$2.50, 1½ hours). A *topique* leaves from the bus stop for Penedo

(US$1.50, two hours, 7:20am and 4:20pm Monday to Saturday). A student bus leaves around 5pm or 6pm for Penedo, or you can catch Santa Maria's 12:30pm bus to Neópolis (US$1) and take a ferry from there.

ALAGOAS

MACEIÓ

☎ 0xx82 / pop 796,840

Maceió is a navigable modern city blessed with both a happening nightlife and a winning restaurant selection, but what really gives it an edge are its great beaches. On the city's beachfronts, vividly green water laps on sands that are lined with palms and brightly painted *jangadas* (traditional sailboats). Here the local people weave on their evening walks in between thatched-roof restaurants and palm-shaded *futebol* (soccer) pitches...try out your skills. Quieter and even more beautiful beaches are located only a short bus ride away. Maceió's sights are relatively few, leaving you plenty of time to enjoy a great meal, catch some warm rays and soak in the relaxed atmosphere.

Orientation

Maceió sits on a jagged peninsula between the Lagoa Mundaú and the ocean. The peninsula features two main points: one is the site of the city's port and the other divides Praia de Pajuçara and Praia dos Sete Coqueiros from the more northern Praia de Ponta Verde and Praia de Jatiúca. The Centro is located near the oceanfront, 2km from Pajuçara and 4km from Ponta Verde. Local phone books will provide you with fantastically detailed maps of the city.

Information

EMERGENCY

Police (☎ 190)
Pronto Socorro (First Aid; ☎ 221 5939)

INTERNET ACCESS

Internet Cybercafé (☎ 327 5305; Av Dr Antônio Gouveia 1113, Pajuçara; per hr US$1.50; ⏰ 8am-10pm Mon-Sat) In the Ana Maria building's shopping arcade.
Monkey (☎ 357 8041; Ponta Verde Center, Av Engenheiro Mário de Gusmão 513, Ponta Verde; per hr US$1; ⏰ 9am-midnight Mon-Thu, 9-3am Fri & Sat, noon-3am Sun) An Internet game place with speedy connections.

MEDICAL SERVICES

Unimed (☎ 215 2000; Av Dom Antônio Brandão, Farol)

MONEY

Major bank ATMs can also be found at the 24-hour Bon Preço grocery store in Pajuçara and at Shopping Iguatemi.
Aeroturismo Centro (☎ 218 2030; Rua Barão do Penedo 61, Centro; ⏰ 9am-noon & 2-6pm Mon-Fri); Mangabeiras (☎ 357 1184; Shopping Iguatemi, Mangabeiras; ⏰ 10am-9:30pm Mon-Sat, 3-9:30pm Sun) Both branches change traveler's checks with no fee.

MACEIÓ

INFORMATION	
Aeroturismo...................................1	A2
Alseturs.......................................2	F2
Banco do Brasil.............................3	B2
Bon Preço....................................4	F2
Bradesco ATM..............................5	H2
Internet Cybercafé.........................6	F2
Monkey.......................................7	G1
Post Office...................................8	B2

To Farol (1km);
Bus Station (3km);
Airport (18km)

Rua Melo Morais
Rua Ladislau Neto
Old Cine Ideal
Av Moreira Lima
Rua do Livramento
Praça do Pirolito
Av Santos Pacheco
Rua Pedro Monteiro
Rua Rosa de Fonseca
Rua Zacarias
Av Duque de Caxias
Centro
Av C da Fonseca
Av Saldanha da Gama
Cathedral
Pc dos Palmares
Train Station
Praça Sinibu
Av Aristeu de Andrade
Rua Barão de Atalaia
Rua Ferroviário
Av Buarue de Macêdo RFFSA
Rua Silvério Jorge
Av da Paz
Canal
Av Comendador Leão
Av Prof Santos Ferraz
Av Maceió
Jaraguá
Rua Santa Albuquerque
Rua Barão de Jaraguá
Rua Ind Cícero de Toledo

To Pontal da Barra (8km);
Lagoa Mundaú (9km);
Massagueira (10km);
Praia do Francês (19km);
Marechal Deodoro (27km);
Barra de São Miguel (34km);
Pontal de Coruipe (95km)

Praia da Avenida

ATLANTIC OCEAN

Porto de Jaraguá

Banco do Brasil (Rua João Pessoa, Centro)
Bradesco ATM (Av Senador Robert Kennedy, Ponta Verde)

POST
Central post office (Rua João Pessoa, Centro)

TOURIST INFORMATION
Alseturs (☎ 315 1503; www.visitealagoas.com.br; Av Dr Antônio Gouveia 1143, Pajuçara; ☼ 8am-6pm Mon-Fri) State tourism authority.

Sights & Activities
The **Museu Théo Brandão** (☎ 221 2651; Av da Paz 1490, Centro; admission by donation; ☼ 9am-noon & 2-5pm Tue-Fri, 3-6pm Sat & Sun) is housed in a beautifully renovated colonial building on the seafront. It has excellent exhibits on the state's history and popular culture, including older, high-quality samples of local crafts. The most impressive are festival headpieces modeled after churches, which are loaded with mirrors, beads and multi-colored ribbons and weigh up to 35kg.

The **Museu do Instituto Histórico e Geográfico de Alagoas** (☎ 223 7797; Rua do Sol, Centro; admission US$0.50; ☼ 8-11:30am Mon-Fri) displays artifacts

of local indigenous peoples – such as head-dresses, arrows and canoe oars – as well as a hodgepodge of historic items. It's worthwhile if you are not bothered by dusty displays and poor lighting.

BEACHES
Protected by an offshore coral reef, Maceió's ocean waters are calm and a deep emerald color. The most popular and beautiful of the city beaches are **Praia de Ponta Verde** (5km from the city center) and **Jatiúca** (6km). Be forewarned that Praia do Sobral and Praia da Avenida, close to the center, are polluted. **Praia de Pajuçara** and **Praia dos Sete Coqueiros** sometimes suffer from pollution as well.

The nicest beaches north of the city are thought to be **Garça Torta** (14km) and **Pratagi** (17km), but **Jacarecica** (9km), **Guaxuma** (12km) and **Riacho Doce** (16km) are also tropical paradises. The Riacho Doce bus runs up the coast to these northern beaches.

Tours
From Praia de Pajuçara, *jangadas* sail out 2km at low tide to natural pools formed by

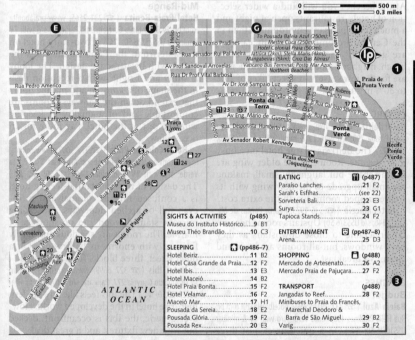

THE NORTHEAST

the reef (US$4). Tickets are sold at a little kiosk next to the tourist information office. On a busy day, the pools fill up with people (clouding the water for those interested in snorkeling) and waiters run around serving drinks from floating bars.

From the nearby village of Pontal da Barra (see Shopping p488), schooners leave at around 9am and 1pm on the Nove Ilhas (Nine Islands) tour (US$5). The trip lasts four hours and, in addition to cruising the Lagoa Mundaú, stops at the outlet of the lake into the ocean. Departures are from Pontal da Barra's lakefront restaurants, such as **O Peixarão** (☎ 325 7011), **Restaurante Maré** (☎ 371 1057) or **Alípio** (☎ 351 9151). A five-person minimum is required, so calling ahead might be a good idea.

Festivals & Events

Maceió Fest, a Salvador-style, out-of-season Carnaval in the third week of November, is the city's largest festival. As for Carnaval, the city empties and locals head for the beaches, especially Barra de São Miguel (p489).

Sleeping

At the beaches you will find a wider selection of hotels, restaurants open at night and a much more pleasant environment than in the Centro. Accommodations in Pajuçara are generally cheaper than in the other beach neighborhoods. Prices quoted here are for the low season – expect hikes of 20% to 30% in summer.

CENTRO

Hotel Beiriz (☎ 221 1080; www.hotelbeiriz.com.br; Rua João Pessoa 290; s/d with TV & minibar US$11.50/13.50; ✺ ⬚) The Beiriz is a large hotel on a busy main avenue. Rooms in the older wing are in fine shape but laughably small, making the small upgrade to the new wing with its well-equipped rooms worth the extra cost.

Hotel Maceió (☎ 336 1975; Rua Dr Pontas de Miranda 146; s/d US$3/6.50) Upstairs rooms here are far preferable to those downstairs as they have windows, but all rooms are basic and clean. No breakfast.

BEACHES
Budget

Baleia Azul (☎ 231 3914; www.hotelbaleiaazul.com.br; Rua Hélio Pradines 450, Ponta Verde; s/d with TV & minibar US$10/16.50; ✺) On a quiet street, just three blocks from the beach, Baleia Azul has huge, comfortable rooms and a hammock hanging on the porch. This pousada is actually an annex of the original by the same name, two blocks away. Though the fixtures in the annex are older, the large rooms and more laid-back environment make it the first choice.

Algamar Hostel (☎ 231 2246; a.j.algamar@ofm .com.br; Rua Pref Abdon Arroxelas 327, Ponta Verde; dm/ d with fan US$7.50/12; ✺) Algamar is not only modern with kitchen, laundry, TV room and an ample front porch for guest use, but it is located on a quiet street just two blocks from the beach. The dorm rooms are separate sex and sleep six. Discount for stays over three days and for HI members.

Other recommendations:

Hotel Velamar (☎ 327 5488; atendimento@hotel velamar.com.br; Av Dr Antônio Gouveia 1359, Pajuçara; s/d with TV & minibar US$8.50/13.50; ✺)

Pousada Glória (☎ 231 3261; Rua Jangadeiros Alagoanos 1119, Pajuçara; s/d with fan & TV US$8.50/8.50; ✺) Surrounded by other cheap pousadas.

Pousada Rex (☎ 231 4239; Rua Dr Antônio Pedro de Mendonça 311, Pajuçara; s/d with fan & TV US$6.50/11.50; ✺)

Mid-Range

Hotel Praia Bonita (☎ 231 2565; www.praiabonita .com.br; Av Dr Antônio Gouveia 943, Pajuçara; s/d with TV & minibar US$23/26.50; ✺) A two-story hotel on the waterfront, the Praia Bonita lures the visitor with its attractive design. The lobby is shiny and bright, with a reception desk in the shape of a *jangada* and marble floors that extend down the hallways. Rooms are comfortable and of a quality in keeping with the rest of the hotel. Pay more for an ocean view.

Hotel Colonial Praia (☎ 377 5007; www.colonial maceio.com.br; Rua Prefeito Abdon Arroxelas 375, Ponta Verde; s/d with TV & minibar US$15/23.50; ✺ ⬚) The design of this substantial-feeling hotel is a confused mix of colonial and medieval, full of arched doorways, misleading mirrors, stained wood and no shortage of marble. The rooms are spacious and nicely finished with enormous bathrooms. On a quiet street, three blocks from the beach.

Hotel Ibis (☎ 327 6699; www.accorhotels.com.br; Av Dr Antônio Gouveia 277, Pajuçara; s/d with TV & minibar US$22/25.50; ✺) The Ibis feels like any modern high-rise hotel in the developed world. However generic, the Ibis is oceanfront, decked out with new fixtures, and a great deal.

Pousada Cavalo Marinho (☎ 355 1247; www.br
.geocities.com/pousadacavalomarinho.com; Rua da Praia
55, Riacho Doce; s/d with fan, TV & minibar US$10/12)
Located 17km northeast of the city in the
fishing village of Riacho Doce, the Cavalo
Marinho is Swiss-owned quality: white walls
and terracotta tile floors, hangout areas, the
ocean lapping at its feet. There are canoes,
bicycles and body boards available for guest
use. Just follow the signs.

Other recommendations:

Hotel Casa Grande da Praia (☎ 231 3332; www.hotel
casagrandedapraia.com.br; Rua Jangadeiros Alagoanos 1528,
Pajuçara; s/d with TV & minibar US$13.50/16.50; ❄)
Pousada da Sereia (☎ 231 0231; www.pousada
dasereia.com.br; Rua Araújo Bivar 57, Pajuçara; s/d with TV
& minibar US$13.50/16.50; ❄ ❅)

Top End
Jatiúca Resort (☎ 327 5959; www.hoteljatiuca.com.br;
Lagoa da Anta 220, Jatiúca; d with TV & minibar US$177;
❄ ❅) Set in a privileged position at the
northern end of the city, bordering both a
lagoon and the ocean, the Jatiúca has expansive grounds with sports facilities and
a tropical-lagoon-like pool. Rooms have
tasteful décor, partial ocean/lagoon views
from the porch, and all the luxury one
would expect. Prices double in high season.

Maceió Mar (☎ 217 8000; www.maceiomar.com.br;
Av Álvaro Otacílio 2991, Ponta Verde; s/d with TV & minibar US$40/43; ❄ ❅ ❅) Rooms in this water-
front, high-rise hotel have marble bathroom
counters and sea views.

Eating
Maceió offers an impressive variety of flavors. The beachfronts of Pajuçara, Ponta
Verde and Jatiúca are packed with stands
and restaurants.

Local seafood specialties worth trying
are *sururu* (small mussels) and *maçunim*
(shellfish) cooked in coconut sauce, served
as main courses or in a *caldo* (soup). Other
seafood treats include *peixe agulha* (needle-
fish) and *siri na casca com coral* (crab in
its shell with roe). Stands clustered on the
Pajuçara and Ponta Verde beachfronts make
the northeastern specialty *beiju de tapioca* by
heating manioc flour until it solidifies, folding it like a taco, then filling it with savory or
sweet fillings. The most traditional is *queijo
coalho* (curd cheese) and coconut (US$1).

Simple restaurants serve up massive portions of extremely tasty and cheap seafood

in Massagueira (10km south), on the southern shore of Lagoa Mundaú. All are good,
but Bar do Pato has gained a following.

Wanchaco (☎ 327 8701; Rua São Francisco de Assis
93, Jatiúca; ☽ lunch Tue-Fri & Sun, dinner Tue-Sat; ❄)
Renowned as one of the finest restaurants
in the city, pricey Wanchaco is also one of
the few Peruvian restaurants in Brazil.

Bar das Ostras (☎ 355 8102; Rua Paulina Mendonça
153, Jatiúca; ☽ lunch & dinner; ❄) A traditional
oyster bar where you can snack or dine on
all types of seafood, raw and cooked.

New Hakata (☎ 325 6160; Rua Eng Paulo B Noque-
ira 95, Jatiúca; buffet $10; ☽ lunch & dinner; ❄) This
Japanese restaurant has an all-you-can-eat
buffet on Tuesday night.

Sarah's Esfihas (☎ 327 8877; Rua Dr Lessa de
Azevedo 59, Pajuçara; ☽ lunch & dinner) Great for
a light snack, Sarah's is a popular Middle
Eastern food stand making *esfihas* (fluffy
breads topped or filled) to order. The *quatro qeijos* (four cheese; US$0.75) is divine.

Divina Gula (☎ 235 1016; Rua Eng Paulo B Nogueira 85,
Jatiúca; ☽ lunch & dinner, closed Mon) Locals will tell
you that 'everything is good' at this Maceió
institution. The house specializes in dishes
typical of Minas Gerais as well as the Northeast, so the flavors are varied and the variety
is wide. Try the *carne do sol* with plantains,
corn, zucchini and *inhame* (a starchy root)
pure (US$5) or grilled beef with broccoli
(US$4). Since it is also a popular spot for
a drink with friends, the outdoor tables in
front of the restaurant are never empty.
The bar boasts 50 different kinds of *cachaça*
(white spirit made from sugarcane).

Other recommendations:

Mestre Cuca (☎ 327 1970; Av Deputado José Lages
593, Ponta Verde; per kg $4.50; ☽ lunch & dinner)
Self-service.
Paraíso Lanches (☎ 231 8446; Av Dr Antônio Gouveia
877, Pajuçara; ☽ lunch & dinner) Innovative sandwiches
and juices.
Sorveteria Bali (☎ 231 8833; Av Dr Antônio Gouveia,
Pajuçara) City's best ice cream – try the *petit gateau*
(US$2).
Surya (☎ 3034 0175; Rua Durval Guimarães 266, Ponta
Verde; ☽ lunch, closed Sun) Vegetarian.

Entertainment
DANCING
Maceió's nightlife mostly concentrates along
Rua Sá e Albuquerque in Jaraguá, a semire-
stored area with lots of trendy bars, nightclubs and a few restaurants.

THE NORTHEAST

Arena (☎ 221 4133; Rua Sá e Albuquerque 168, Jaraguá; ☼ 11pm-last client Thu-Sun) Electronic music dominates the dancefloor at this huge-capacity dance club.

Mai Kai (☎ 325 7565; Rua Alfredo G de Mendonça, Stella Maris; cover US$2.50; ☼ 9pm-last client Thu-Sun) The space is split into bar tables on one side and a stage with a live band playing pop, rock or *axé* (Bahian pop music*)* on the other. The crowd can be very young, especially on *axé* nights.

Lampião (☎ 325 4376; Av Álvaro Otacílio, Jatiúca; cover US$2; ☼ 9pm-last client, closed Mon) Beachfront and always attracts a crowd (including a lot of tourists) for *forró* with a sea breeze.

Virgulino (☎ 221 2423; Rua Sá e Albuquerque 674, Jatiúca; ☼ 7pm-4am Wed-Sat) More of a *forró* spot for locals, and goes all out with décor, costuming, bar food and *cachaça* in the Northeastern style.

CINEMAS

Cine Iguatemi (☎ 357 1193; Shopping Iguatemi, Av Comendador Gustavo Paiva, Mangabeiras; ☼ 1:30-9:30pm), **Cine Farol** (☎ 338 1014; Shopping Farol, Av Fernandes Lima, Farol; ☼ 1:30-8:30pm) and **Cine Art Cidade** (☎ 336 5200; Shopping Cidade, Av Fernandes Lima, Farol; ☼ 2:30-9pm) tend to screen the same few films, but the latter also throws in an arthouse or foreign film.

Shopping

The Mercado Praia de Pajuçara is an enclosed craft market on Pajuçara's waterfront selling lacework, hammocks, baskets and ceramics. However, you'll get a better deal at the **Mercado do Artesanato** (Centro; ☼ 8am-6pm Mon-Sat, 8am-noon Sun). To get there, catch a bus that stops in front of the *antigo* (old) Cine Ideal.

If you are interested in doing some shopping for Alagoas' characteristic *filé* crochet work, head for Pontal da Barra (8km south), a fishing/crafts village beside the Lagoa Mundaú. Women weave outside the shops that line the streets, and prices are generally the lowest around. To get there, catch any bus heading south with Barra in its name.

Getting There & Away

AIR

BRA (☎ 322 1433; airport), **Gol** (☎ 214 4078; airport), **TAM** (☎ 214 4111-6; airport), **Varig** (☎ 214 4100-6;

Av Dr Antônio Gouveia, Pajuçara) and **VASP** (☎ 322 1414/1099/1818; airport) can fly you or connect you to anywhere in Brazil from **Aeroporto Zumbi dos Palmares** (code MCZ; ☎ 214 4000).

BUS

The **bus station** (☎ 221 4615) is 4km north of the city center.

Bonfim (☎ 335 4629, 336 1112) buses go to Salvador on Hwy BR-101 via Entre Rios (US$15, 10½ hours, daily) or along the coastal Linha Verde highway (US$21, nine hours, three daily). There is a direct Linha Verde bus (US$13, eight hours) on Sunday at 8:30am. Bonfim also has a daily *comercial* (US$7.50, six hours) and *executivo* (US$9, 4½ hours) bus to Aracaju.

São Geraldo (☎ 223 4560) goes to João Pessoa (US$12, six hours, Tuesday, Thursday and Sunday), Recife (US$8.50 to US$11.50, four to 5½ hours, 13 daily) and Natal (US$24, nine hours, daily).

For Penedo, **Real** (☎ 356 1324) has normal (Hwy BR-101 via São Miguel; US$5, four hours, two daily), *expresso litoral* (coastal express; US$5, 2½ hours, two daily) and *pinga litoral* (coastal drip; US$5, four hours, two daily) buses. The last two provide access to Barra de São Miguel and Pontal do Coruripe. For more on the *pinga* see p492.

Transportation for the northern coast (except Maragogi) can be caught at the bus station or at the *posto* (gas station) Mar Azul at the northern edge of town, two blocks from the Cruz das Almas/Vaticano city bus terminal.

Getting Around

TO/FROM THE AIRPORT

Maceió's airport is 20km north of the center. To get there, book a shuttle through a travel agent (US$5) or catch a taxi (US$10). The Rio Largo company's buses to the airport run every 50 minutes to every hour and 40 minutes.

TO/FROM THE BUS STATION

To reach the center, take the Ouro Prêto bus; for the beaches, catch the Circular 1. A taxi to the center costs US$2, and around US$4 to the beaches.

SOUTH OF MACEIÓ

This stretch of coast is characterized by small, quaint coastal villages – some with amazing beaches – surrounded by wide stretches of coconut plantations. The tourism hot spots on Alagoas' south coast are Praia do Francês and Barra de São Miguel, though entire neighborhoods of summer homes for Maceió's wealthy pop up in other areas as well.

Praia do Francês
☎ 0xx82

Given its proximity to Maceió (22km), Praia do Francês functions much like a remote city beach: cars and buses roll in on weekend days and completely clear out by 5pm. Everyone concentrates on one end of Francês' fine, white sands where just-offshore reefs create calm green waters and a string of restaurants provide beer and fried shrimp. Arching to the south is an empty stretch of palm-lined beach boasting the best surf in Alagoas. A grouping of weekend homes, pousadas and a few restaurants, Francês lacks the infrastructure of a real town (or even a pharmacy).

SLEEPING & EATING
Prices below are for the low season.

Pousada Miroku (☎ 260 1187; www.pousadamiroku.com.br; Rua Cavalo Marinho 16; s/d with TV & minibar US$8.50/13.50; ✂ 🅡) A few blocks from the beach, Miroku is a modern hotel offering porches with hammocks and a breakfast area looking out onto a small garden.

Pousada Graciosa (☎ 260 1197; www.sempregraciosa.com.br; Rua Cavalo Marinho 21; s/d with TV & minibar US$13.50/16.50; ✂) Just as its name implies, Graciosa (charming) is perfect for those seeking something pretty and quiet; rooms have porches facing an internal lush patio. It's a little dark due to the use of brick inside and out.

Pousada Tortuga (☎ 260 1567; Av dos Arrecifes; s/d with fan US$5/10) Tortuga is the best-value cheapie, with its sealed and colored cement floors. Right on the beach.

Restaurant Chez Patrick (☎ 260 1377; Rua Marisia 15; ✞ lunch Tue-Sun, dinner Tue-Sat) A charming little bistro with a genuine French chef!

GETTING THERE & AWAY
From Maceió, take either a city bus (hourly) or a minibus (US$0.50, 35 minutes, every 15 minutes from 5am to 10:30pm) from the stop outside the train station. From Francês, any minibus destined for Maceió

after 7pm, or coming from Barra de São Miguel, goes to Maceió's bus station after passing through the center.

Marechal Deodoro
☎ 0xx82 / pop 35,820

Small and quiet, Marechal Deodoro is a historic town with some pretty architecture on the banks of the Lagoa Manguaba. It served as capital of Alagoas between 1823 and 1839, and makes an easy day trip from Maceió. The Saturday market, held until noon along the waterfront, is a lively, colorful event.

Bar do Bahia on the river lets you choose your lunch straight from the water.

SIGHTS
Marechal Deodoro has several churches, the most interesting being the **Igreja de NS da Conceição** (✞ 8am-1pm Mon-Sat) and the 17th-century **Igreja e Convento São Francisco** (✞ 8am-1pm Mon-Sat), which houses the **Museu de Arte Sacra** (Sacred Art Museum; ✞ 8am-1pm Mon-Sat).

History buffs will enjoy the **old governor's palace** and the **Museu Deodoro** (✞ 8am-6pm), the house where Brazil's first president was born. The exhibits give a deodorized view of Manuel Deodoro da Fonseca, emphasizing his role as a military hero and president, but omitting to mention that he achieved this position with a military putsch in 1889 and later proved to be a poor politician. The shop next door sells the lace and homemade sweets for which the town is renowned.

GETTING THERE & AWAY
Buses and minibuses for Marechal Deodoro (US$0.50, 50 minutes) via Praia do Francês depart frequently from the bus stop outside the train station in Maceió. Buses, Kombi vans and collective taxis leave from Marechal's plaza for Praia do Francês (US$0.50, 15 minutes) and back to Maceió.

Barra de São Miguel
☎ 0xx82 / pop 6290

Barra de São Miguel is best known as the gateway to **Praia do Gunga**, an incredibly idyllic, white-sand beach that curves to a point at the meeting of the Rio São Miguel and a green sea. The center of this small village sits on the riverbank, facing Praia do Gunga. The river mouth and local beaches are protected by a huge offshore reef, leaving the waters calm for bathing or kayaking.

A daytime destination throughout the year, Barra only explodes with people during the high season and during Carnaval when *trios electricos* (electrically amplified bands playing atop trucks) take over the scene.

Boats for Praia do Gunga (US$6.50) leave in the morning from the town's port, as well as from Praia de Barra de São Miguel.

SLEEPING

Most hotels are located 3km from the center at Praias Niquin and Barra de São Miguel, where there is unfortunately little else.

Pousada Sete Mares (☎ 272 1054; fax 272 1989; Av Leonita Cavalcante, Niquin; s/d with TV & minibar US$16.50 /23.50; ✖ ☒) Spacious (though dark) rooms surround a palm-shaded pool area and have decorative touches such as hand-painted sheets.

Pousada Aconchego (☎ 272 2090; Rua João Florêncio 97, Centro; s/d with TV & minibar US$10/16.50; ✖) is Modern and well-finished.

Hotel Portal Duleste (☎ 272 1089; Rua Projetada MB D2, Niquin; s/d with TV & minibar US$10/20; P ✖ ☒) Drabber but still modern and well-finished.

EATING

The town's two restaurants are in the center and open on weekends only outside of the high season (December to February), but there are plenty of *lanchonetes* (snack bars). Restaurants at Praia do Gunga are infamously overpriced.

La Tablita (☎ 272 1944; Rua Salvador Aprato 30; ⏲ lunch & dinner) Serves Spanish food adapted to local ingredients.

GETTING THERE & AWAY

Buses leave hourly for the 35km trip to Barra de São Miguel from near Maceió's railway station.

From here, buses to Maceió (US$1, one hour) via Praia do Francês (US$0.75, 20 minutes) leave hourly until 7pm. Collective taxis run the same route for the same price, leaving from behind the church in the center. Both buses and taxis pass through Praias Niquin and Barra de São Miguel.

Pontal de Coruripe

☎ 0xx82

Pontal de Coruripe is a relatively untouristy village surrounded by coconut plantations, located on a point of land reaching into the ocean. The point has a lighthouse at its tip and creates a calm cove for fishing boats. Around the point are low rocks that provide great tide pooling at low tide and pools for lounging in at medium and high tides. There is a long, deserted beach with beautiful green water. Women sit in front of their homes gossiping and weaving palm baskets, placemats and handbags.

SLEEPING & EATING

Pousada da Ada (☎ 273 7209; www.geocities.com /adapousada; s/d with fan US$10/15; ✖ ☐) Travelers breathe a sigh of relief upon entering this pousada, with its shelves of books (some for trade), lush, unmanicured garden, pets loafing about and the generally bohemian atmosphere. Ada speaks Italian, French, German and English and offers Portuguese lessons in her garden. Her rooms are tastefully simple and bright, and her breakfast and vegetarian meals are unforgettable.

Of the restaurants clustered at the lighthouse, Peixada da Madalena cooks up the meanest seafood.

GETTING THERE & AWAY

The *pinga litoral* bus heading for Maceió (US$2, two hours) passes through Pontal de Coruripe around 8:30am and 4pm, and around 3:30pm heading for Penedo (US$2, 2½ hours). There are more transportation options out of Coruripe (9km), or you can get a ride up to the highway (1km) and catch a passing *besta*.

PENEDO

☎ 0xx82 / pop 56,750

Penedo, known as the capital of the lower São Francisco, is the colonial masterpiece of the state and is almost unaltered by tourism. Attractions include the city's many baroque churches and colonial buildings and the opportunity to travel the sometimes-jade-colored waters of the Rio São Francisco. Penedo's downtown bustles with a daily market, Saturday being the biggest day, when people from surrounding villages pour in to do their shopping. The market is filled with ceramics, baskets and reed shrimp traps.

History

Penedo was founded sometime between 1535 and 1560 by Duarte Coelho Pereira, who descended the Rio São Francisco in pursuit of Caete Indians responsible for killing a bishop. Penedo is claimed to be the river's first colonial settlement. It was also the scene of a fierce 17th-century battle between the Dutch and Portuguese for control of the Northeast.

Information

You'll find banks with ATMs located on the riverfront.

Tourist office (☎ 551 2727; Praça Barão de Penedo; ⏰ 7:30am-3:30pm) Located in the Casa da Aposentadoria, staff hand out great maps and gives guided walking tours (for a fee and in Portuguese) of the city. Catch the view from the second floor while you are in the office.

Sights & Activities

Penedo has a rich collection of 17th- and 18th-century colonial buildings, including many churches.

CHURCHES

The **Convento de São Francisco e Igreja NS dos Anjos** (Praça Rui Barbosa; ⏰ 8-11am & 2-5pm Tue-Fri, 8-11am Sat & Sun) was under construction for nearly 100 years before its completion in 1759, and is considered the finest church in the state. Even Dom Pedro II (Brazil's second and last emperor) paid a visit. Note especially the gold rococo altar and the saint on the left by Aleijadinho.

The **Igreja de NS da Corrente** (Praça 12 de Abril; ⏰ 8am-6pm Tue-Sun) was completed in 1764. It has some fine Portuguese *azulejos* (tiles) and a rococo main altar.

The **Igreja NS do Rosário dos Pretos** (Catedral do Penedo; Praça Marechal Deodoro; ⏰ 8am-6pm) was built by slaves. The **Igreja de São Gonçalo Garcia** (Av Floriano Peixoto; ⏰ 8am-6pm Tue-Sun) was built at the end of the 18th century and has a small museum with some of the city's finest sacred-art pieces. The small **oratório** (Praça Barão de Penedo) is where the condemned spent their last night praying before being hanged.

MUSEUMS

Occupying the top floor of the house Dom Pedro II once slept in, the **Museu do Paço Imperial** (Praça 12 de Abril 9; admission free; ⏰ 11am-5pm, closed Mon) displays dishes, furniture and religious art from the imperial period (17th and 18th centuries), and is surprisingly well done. The **Casa do Penedo** (Rua João Pessoa 156; admission free; ⏰ 8am-6pm, closed Mon) is a small

museum of relics and photographs from Penedo's rich history.

RIVER TRIPS

Regular ferries depart from the center for **Neópolis**, a colonial town on a hill with some interesting buildings and good crafts for sale, and **Carrapicho** (officially Santana de São Francisco; US$0.50, every 30 minutes), a small town noted for its ceramics.

An organized tour takes visitors to the **Foz do São Francisco** (US$5), where the river meets the sea at a beach with dunes and natural pools. The most frequent departures for this trip leave 28km downriver from Piaçabuçu.

Festivals & Events

The **Festa do Senhor Bom Jesus dos Navegantes** is held over four days from the second Sunday of January, and features an elaborate procession of boats and an exciting sailboat race.

Sleeping

Pousada Colonial (☎ 551 2355; Praça 12 de Abril 21; s/d with fan US$11.50/20; ❄) The spacious rooms in this beautifully converted colonial home on the waterfront have stained wood floors and antique furniture – get one with a view of the river. The overall feeling is clean and simple.

Hotel São Francisco (☎ 551 2273; hotelsaofrancisco@bol.com.br; Av Floriano Peixoto; s/d with TV US$22/29; ❄) The rooms in this 1960s-style hotel have varnished wood floors, trim and furniture and bathrooms full of tiny blue tiles. The place is quiet (could they ever hope to fill so many rooms?), has great hot showers and usually offers a 20% discount for cash payment. The frontal view is worth the upgrade.

Hotel Turista (☎ 551 2237; Rua Siqueira Campos 143; s/d with fan US$5/8.50) Traffic noise fills this simple hotel, and the state of the walls suggests a city-wide paint shortage, but it's the most comfortable budget option.

Eating

Forte da Rocheira (☎ 551 3273; Rua da Rocheira 2; ⏰ lunch & dinner) When the Dutch sweated over building their fort's stone side wall, they would have never dreamed a restaurant would someday hang off it. Don't expect the food to be as awesome as the location or the view and you'll be alright.

THE NORTHEAST

O Laçador (☎ 551 2956; Rodovia Engenheiro Joaquim Gonçalves 17, Cohab; ⏲ lunch & dinner; ⊠) One of the most well-established restaurants in town, O Laçador offers barbecued meats, pastas, pizza and sandwiches.

Esquina Imperial (☎ 551 5858; Av Floriano Peixoto 61; per kg US$4; ⏲ lunch & dinner) This restaurant, commonly known by the owner's name (Menendez), has a simple self-service lunch, and soups and sandwiches at night.

Getting There & Away

The **bus station** (☎ 551 2602) is on a riverfront traffic island. For Maceió, take the normal (Hwy BR-101 via São Miguel dos Campos; US$4, four hours, two daily), the *expresso litoral* (US$4, 2½ hours, two daily) or the *pinga litoral* (US$4, four hours, two daily) bus. The last two provide access to Pontal do Coruripe, Barra de São Miguel and Praia do Francês. For more on the *pinga* see below.

There is one daily bus to Salvador (US$13, nine hours) via Propriá (US$1.50, 1½ hours) and Aracaju (US$3.50, three hours). It could be more convenient to take a ferry to Neópolis (US$0.50, 15 minutes, every 30 minutes from 5:30am to 10pm), where there are more frequent buses.

Topiques also go to Aracaju, Propriá and most frequently to Piaçabuçu (US$0.50,

40 minutes, every 20 minutes from 6am to 6pm). Ask the *topique* drivers hanging out on the riverfront for departure times.

If you're traveling by car, a car ferry runs between Penedo and Passagem (US$2.50, 10 minutes, hourly from 5:30am to 10pm), a short drive from Neópolis.

NORTH OF MACEIÓ

The coast up to Barra de Santo Antônio has fluffy sands, green waters and no shortage of coconut palms. From that point to Maragogi, the ocean takes on a calm, shallow and warm aspect due to the many reefs close to shore. Low tides can allow you to walk 1km out to sea. The stretch from Barra do Camaragibe to Porto de Pedras is a sweet little pocket off the highway and a great place to treat yourself. Strung along one road are tiny villages with barely the basics to support tourism, save for a few luxury pousadas. Maragogi is the seat of tourism in the area.

Barra de Santo Antônio

☎ 0xx82 / pop 11,270

Barra de Santo Antônio is a mellow fishing village built along the mouth of the Rio Jirituba. Across the river, on the narrow Ilha da Croa, is a small settlement known as 'Barra

---

DRIPPING ALONG THE COAST

When traveling from Penedo to Maceió, throw in the extra two hours and opt for the *pinga litoral* (coastal drip) bus. If constant stops and deviations off the main road don't drive you crazy, you'll love the idyllic tropical scenery and glimpses into simple, local life. Adorably tiny churches, children waving as you pass and beautifully rustic fishing huts may make you wish you had your camera handy.

From Penedo, the bus travels along the river toward the coast, passing the thatched huts of the fishermen who live in Piaçabuçu, then swings in from the river and north to Pontal do Peba, where it does a U-turn on the beach. From there it passes through Feliz Deserto, which has lots of cowboys and coconuts, one pousada and plenty of seafood.

The bus turns off Hwy AL-101 a bit further north at Miaí de Cima, where there are no pousadas, but many locals on the beach on weekends. The next time the bus turns off the main road is into Barreiras, also with good beaches but no pousadas. It then comes to pretty Coruripe before continuing to Pontal de Coruripe.

Next stop is Lagoa do Pau, with shrimp cultivation, weekend homes and a couple of pousadas. Then it's on to Poxim, past sugarcane fields and coconut palms. Approaching Maceió, the bus stops at the turnoffs for Barra de São Miguel and Praia do Francês. Passing the huge estuaries of the Mundaú and Manguaba lagoons, it's not long before the bus reaches the capital.

If you plan to stay at Pajuçara or beaches further north, get off the bus after it turns off the coast road into the center of Maceió. This will save you a long ride up to the bus station. As city buses travel through Pajuçara, they don't follow the beach, but run along the first road parallel. Hotels on the beachfront are good points of reference for asking directions.

II' and a collection of weekend houses. The main attraction of the area is the deserted **Praia de Carro Quebrado**, an exotic white-sand beach backed by thick palms. It is a 7km walk or beach buggy ride (US$6.50 per car) from Barra II.

Praia Tabuba is a pretty, tranquil bay with a few bars and a couple of pousadas, 4km south of Barra de Santo Antônio. There are reef tidal pools off the beach – ask at the bars about a ride there by *jangada*.

SLEEPING & EATING
Pousada Arco-Íris (☎ 291 1250; www.tabuba.tk; Rua 10, Praia Tabuba; s/d with fan, TV & minibar US$16.50/20; ❸) Arco-Íris is an attractive, high-quality pousada surrounded by greenery, 30m from the beach. The comfortable rooms are tastefully decorated and open onto a leafy back veranda equipped with hammock. Windsurf rigs, kayaks and bicycles are available for rent and the pousada offers *jangada* trips. Heinz, the friendly Swiss owner, speaks German, English, French and Spanish. Just follow the signs.

Chalés Costa Dourada (☎ 3279327; luizmendonca@ nornet.com.br; s/d with TV & fan US$10/16) Barra II has three pousadas, and the Costa Dourada's two-bedroom brick chalets are surprisingly the most economical. Though they feel a little like government housing, each one has a full kitchen and a hammock hung on the porch. No breakfast.

Peixada da Rita (☎ 291 1544; ⏲ lunch & dinner) Just up from the bus station, Rita serves sensational seafood riverside.

GETTING THERE & AROUND
You can catch minibuses to Barra de Santo Antônio (US$1, one hour, every 30 minutes from 5am to 6:30pm) at Maceió's bus station or *posto* Mar Azul at the northern edge of town. Collective taxis also leave from the Mar Azul, but charge extra to enter the town.

For Maceió, catch one of the frequent buses leaving Barra de Santo Antônio's bus station. To head north, walk or catch a ride to the main highway, where you can flag down a bus, *besta* or collective taxi.

Canoes cross the river from behind the bus station (US$0.25), while the car ferry (US$2 per car) leaves from beside the Banco do Brasil, up the road from the bus station.

Barra do Camaragibe
☎ 0xx82
This idyllic fishing village is strung along the road, on the edge of a small, shallow, reef-laden bay. *Jangadas* make trips south to **Praia do Morro**, a deserted beach with cliffs and clear waters. **Pousada & Restaurante Barra Mar** (☎ 258 5141; s/d with TV & minibar US$8.50/13.50; ❸) has spacious rooms in good shape. The seafood at the town's two restaurant/pousadas is great, but not super-cheap. It's 7km to São Miguel dos Milagres. See p494 for transportation information.

São Miguel dos Milagres
☎ 0xx82 / pop 5850
São Miguel dos Milagres has soft beaches with warm, shallow seas protected by offshore reefs. **Restaurante do Gordo** (☎ 295 1181; s/d with fan US$5/10), on the main road, rents out some super basic rooms tucked behind its kitchen. It's a five-minute walk through coconut palm plantations to the beach and 4km to Porto da Rua. See p494 for transportation information.

Porto da Rua
☎ 0xx82
Much like its neighbors, Porto da Rua is a small and sweet village of colorful houses spread along the road. A stretch of coconut plantation about 2km deep separates the center from the beach, where there are a few bars. The area's accommodations options (including some distinctive spots) concentrate in and around Porto da Rua, but you'll find them spread out and set up for those traveling by car. The nicer pousadas have no problem picking up guests from as far away as Maceió; just call them. See p494 for transportation information.

SLEEPING
Pousada do Toque (☎ 295 1127; www.pousadadotoque .com.br; s/d with TV, DVD & minibar US$40/56.50; ❸ ❹) In the settlement of Toque, a few kilometers south of Porto da Rua, is this exotic pousada. Oceanfronted, surrounded by palms, it offers luxury in thatched-roof bungalows in a lush, tropical garden. Included in the room cost are two meals of your choice.

Pousada do Caju (☎ 295 1103; jeromebresil@hotmail .com; s/d with TV, DVD & minibar US$28/33; ❸) Right 'next door', this estate house with tall doors and a wraparound porch, newly converted

THE NORTHEAST

into a pousada. Caju has successfully achieved the cool, urban-antique look in its comfortable rooms and has gorgeous gardens. The owners speak French and a little English.

Pousada das Acácias (☎ 295 1142; s/d with TV & minibar US$20/20; ❄) On the main road in Porto da Rua, with modern, white rooms that are a little overpriced but in a central location.

Pousada Um Milhão de Estrelas (☎ 298 6223; www.pousadaummilhaodeestrelas.com.br; Praia de Tatuamunha; s/d with TV, DVD & minibar US$47/66.50; ❄ ⬛) A few kilometers north of Porto da Rua, at the entrance of the settlement of Lages, this pousada sits 1800m off the main road, secluded in a sea of palms. Bright-salmon cottages are spread through the grounds, each with its own wooden deck and some with Jacuzzi tubs. Interior décor is creative and chicly simple. Included in the room cost are two meals of your choice.

Porto de Pedras
☎ 0xx82 / pop 10,220
Porto de Pedras is a sweet little fishing town and, as it is the most established on this stretch of road, it boasts a few shops, bars and restaurants. It is located where the Rio Manguaba meets the sea and is watched over by a hilltop lighthouse offering great views.

Pousada Quinta do Coqueirais (☎ 298 1375; Rua Seu Avelinho Cunha 39; s/d with shared bathroom, fan & minibar US$6.50/10) is an older home converted into a pleasant pousada. Its rooms have stained, sealed cement floors, mosquito nets and charming décor.

The Atlantica bus to Porto de Pedras (US$3, 3½ hours, five daily) runs via Barra do Camaragibe, São Miguel dos Milagres and Porto da Rua from the bus station in Maceió. This bus, as well as minibuses, *bestas* and collective taxis traveling the same route, can be caught at the *posto* Mar Azul at the northern edge of Maceió. Due to the wide variety of transportation options, travel between these little towns is extremely easy up until about 7pm.

A pedestrian ferry (US$0.50, 5am to 7pm) and a car ferry (car/pedestrian US$2/free,

7am to midnight) provide access to Japaratinga. Once across the river, you'll need to catch a collective taxi (US$1) the rest of the 9km into Japaratinga.

Japaratinga
☎ 0xx82 / pop 6870
Japaratinga's shallow waters are protected by coral reefs and the beaches are backed by coconut trees and fishing huts. Under the moonlight, you can walk a couple of kilometers into the sea. The town is small, but more touristy than the beach towns to its south, and has a bustle to it. Accommodations on the whole are overpriced, but **Pousada dos Mares** (☎ 297 1398; pousadadosmares@bol .com.br; s/d with fan US$8.50/11.50; ❄) is a cute place with simple, economical rooms. Kombi vans regularly make the 10km trip north to Maragogi (US$0.50).

Maragogi
☎ 0xx82 / pop 21,825
Maragogi is a small town with a waterfront strip along a white-sand beach and amazingly turquoise sea. It is probably the most visited beach in the state, due to its major draw: the sandbars and reefs that make up the **Galés marine reserve**, 6km offshore. Trips to Galés marine reserve (US$5) are easily organized through the beachfront restaurants. It is a very touristy affair, with touts trying to sell you everything from fish food (unnecessary) to underwater photos, but if you grab a mask and snorkel and swim away from the crowd, the reefs are rich with sea life. Maragogi has a Banco do Brasil.

Maragogi's tourism is mostly day-use but, despite this, it has quite a few pousadas and Pernambucano weekend homes. On the waterfront, **Pousada Solar da Praia** (☎ 296 2025; www .solardapraia.com.br; s/d with TV & minibar US$11.50/16.50; ❄) feels new and is excellent value.

Atlantica has buses to Maragogi (US$4, 4½ hours, two daily) from Maceió's bus station. From Recife, Real Alagoas has three daily buses (US$4, two hours). From Maragogi there are five daily buses to Maceió and three to Recife.

Pernambuco

CONTENTS

THE NORTHEAST

HIGHLIGHTS

- Dancing down the street in **Olinda** (p507) and **Recife** (p501) during frenetic Carnaval

- Soaking up the sun at the excellent beaches around **Porto de Galinhas** (p509)

- Wandering around the bizarre sculpture garden at **Oficina Cerâmica Francisco Brennand** (p510) in Recife

- Visiting the fascinating market and artist workshops at **Caruaru** (p516) and **Alto de Moura** (p517)

- Diving in the crystalline waters of the **Fernando de Noronha Marine Park** (p513)

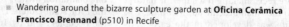

Olinda ★
Recife ★
Caruaru ★
Alto de Moura ★
Porto de Galinhas ★

- POPULATION: 8.2 MILLION
- AREA: 98,938 SQ KM

One of Brazil's major tourist destinations, Pernambuco is at once exciting and relaxed, urban and rural, developed and pristine. You can easily have an entire Brazilian trip in this small state, which extends like a finger from the populated coastline back into the sparse, arid interior.

Most visitors arrive in the large industrial center of Recife, which has some decent beaches and nightlife but is only the tip of what the state has to offer. Just to the north of Recife lies the famous, yet somehow still quaint, colonial town of Olinda, with more nightlife plus a good dose of art, music and historic charm. To the south are the beautiful beaches around Porto de Galinhas, which are good for simply relaxing or for surfing some of the Northeast's better waves. Inland is the bustling provincial market town of Caruaru and the artisan center of Alto de Moura, while a one-hour flight offshore is what locals refer to as 'Brazilian Hawaii,' the exquisite islands and national marine park of Fernando de Noronha. Here you can hike along the tropical coast, snorkel in crystal-clear tide pools, swim with giant sea turtles or visit what are perhaps the best beaches in South America.

Pernambucanos have a rich cultural tradition, from the lively street Carnaval in Olinda to art and handicrafts that are for sale in Caruaru. They have spawned a number of types of music, including *frevó* and the über-popular *forró*. After Bahia, this is one of the most important centers for the Brazilian martial art/dance capoeira. To top it off, the legendary Passion of the Christ play in Nova Jerusalém draws crowds of 80,000 during Semana Santa as locals and TV stars act out the last days of Jesus.

Beyond tourism, sugarcane still dominates the economy and sprawling Recife is a magnet for the poor and destitute from the unforgiving interior.

History

The history of Pernambuco revolves around its cultural and industrial epicenters: Recife and Olinda. When sugarcane was introduced to Brazil, coastal Pernambuco quickly became one of the most important production areas in the country. Much wealth was accumulated and plantation owners built their homes on the hills that were to become the city of Olinda. Recife came along later; it had several rivers and offshore reefs, making it a superior natural port to the small beachhead in Olinda.

Recife was developed in the early 17th century to ship out Olinda's sugar and bring in African slaves to process more sugar. Within a few decades it began to outgrow its wealthier counterpart. By the mid-17th century, Recife and Olinda together were the most prosperous cities in Brazil, with the possible exception of Salvador da Bahia.

The indigenous population had been subdued after brutal warfare, and the colonial aristocracy in Olinda was raking in profits from the many sugar *engenhos* (mills). Of course, all of the hard labor continued to be performed by African slaves.

In 1629, after a previous failed attempt in Salvador, the Dutch invaded Pernambuco and Recife was abandoned. The Dutch took the city and by 1640 they controlled a great chunk of the Northeast. The Catholic plantation owners refused allegiance to the Protestant Dutch. They rebelled against the occupiers and by 1654 the Dutch had retreated.

Recife continued then to prosper, and eventually it eclipsed Olinda as an industrial power. However, the majority of the political strength remained in the hands of the wealthy Olinda aristocrats. In 1710 fighting began between the *filhos da terra* ('children of the land', the sugar planters of Olinda) and the *mascates* (the Portuguese merchants of Recife, who were more recent immigrants). The Guerra dos Mascates (War of the Mascates) was a bloody regional feud between different sections of the ruling class. In the end, with their superior economic resources and the help of the Portuguese Crown, the *mascates* of Recife gained considerable political clout at the expense of Olinda, which then began its long, slow decline (only to be rescued in recent years by the increase in international tourism).

More dependent on sugar than Rio or São Paulo, Recife was surpassed by the southern metropolises as the sugar economy floundered throughout the 19th century. Pernambuco was relegated to being more of a backwater Northeastern state than part of the southern industrial power. Tourism has become a new commodity for the state and Recife is now the port of entry for many Brazilian tourists and charter flights carrying European travelers.

Climate

Pernambuco is hot and dry, and has a light rainy season from December through to March. Temperatures along the coast rarely dip below the high 20°s Celsius (low 80°s Fahrenheit) and the interior is a lot hotter. Anytime of the year is a good time to visit, but the temperatures are a bit more moderate and the foliage greener during the rainy season.

National Parks

Approximately 70% of the 21-island Fernando de Noronha archipelago (p511), 525km from Recife, is part of a national marine park, which features crystalline waters and abundant marine life from iridescent fish to giant sea turtles. The park is tightly controlled by IBAMA and the government of Pernambuco.

Getting There & Away

Recife's airport receives regular flights from all over Brazil and many large Latin American cities, and charter flights from a few European and North American cities.

Recife has a major bus station and has direct connections to all major cities in the country.

Getting Around

Bus transport in and around Pernambuco is straightforward and easy. Expect buses to be more frequent and faster in the coastal areas than in the more provincial interior. To get to to Fernando de Noronha, you must fly.

THE COAST

RECIFE

☎ 0xx81 / pop 2.9 million

Recife ('heh-*see*-fee'), the capital of Pernambuco, is a major port and urban hub, full of glassy high-rises and sprawling suburbs. The city center has a number of rivers and bridges and the beaches are kept calm by offshore *recifes* (reefs).

Amid its rapid development, Recife retains a rich traditional side, with some of Brazil's best folk art, including painting and sculpture, dance, music and festivals. Little of this is packaged for the tourist, so it takes time to discover the cultural side of the city. However, unless you want to be on the beach in Boa Viagem, it is suggested that you stay in Olinda and visit Recife during the day, or venture in during the evening for the animated nightlife in Recife Antigo.

Orientation

Recife is large, modern and more difficult to negotiate than most cities in the Northeast. The city center is a confusing mixture of high-rise offices, colonial churches and popular markets. During the day, traffic and tourists get lost in the maze of winding one-way streets.

The heart of Recife ranges along the riverfront in the Boa Vista area, across the Rio Capibaribe to the Santo Antônio district and then across to Ilha do Recife, which is home to the Recife Antigo neighborhood. All are connected by bridges. Boa Viagem is a wealthier beachside zone, 6km south of the center. Many of Recife's visitors opt to stay in Boa Viagem.

MAPS

Tourist offices have good maps, including *Recife & Olinda Tourism Map – Rota do Sol*, which includes a map of the beaches around Recife.

THE NORTHEAST

Information

BOOKSTORES

There are several bookstalls along Rua do Infante Dom Henrique. The airport bookstore (2nd floor) is your best bet for foreign-language books.

Livraria Brandão (Rua da Matriz 22; 🕙 9am-6pm Mon-Sat) For used books in French and English, this is a good option.

Sodiler (Shopping Recife, Rua Padre Carapuceiro 777, Boa Viagem; 🕙 9am-10pm Mon-Sat) This chain store has international books.

EMBASSIES & CONSULATES

France (☎ 3465 3290; 6th fl, Av Conselheiro Aguiar 2333, Boa Viagem)

UK (☎ 3465 0230; 3rd fl, Av Conselheiro Aguiar 2941, Boa Viagem)

USA (☎ 3424 1840; Rua Gonçalves Maia 163, Boa Vista)

EMERGENCY

Police (☎ 190)

Tourist Police (☎ 3326 9603; 3rd fl; Guararapes Airport) Travelers must deal with the tourist police for most issues.

INTERNET ACCESS

Instituto Porto Digital (Av Barbosa Lima 149, Recife Antigo; per hr US$2; 🕙 11am-10pm Mon-Fri) Offers one-hour free Internet access from 4pm to 6pm.

Internet Point (2nd fl, Shopping Recife, Rua Padre Carapuceiro 777, Boa Viagem; per hr US$2.50; 🕙 9am-midnight)

Net.Station (Empresarial Giriquiti 140, Boa Vista; per hr US$2; 🕙 9am-10pm Mon-Fri, 9am-2pm Sat) Next to Shopping Boa Vista.

Pl@ylink (☎ 3463 8932; shop 4, Av Conselheiro Aguiar 2966, Boa Viagem; per hr US$2; 🕙 9am-11pm Mon-Thu, 24hr Fri-Sun) Full of loud, sometimes raucous video-game players, but the machines, rates and connections are the best in the area.

INTERNET RESOURCES

General Pernambuco site (www.pe360graus.com.br) Portuguese site with all sorts of regional news and other information.

Nightlife listings (www.guiametropole.com.br/show.php)

Official site (www.recife.pe.gov.br)

LAUNDRY

Most hotels here will arrange affordable laundry services for guests. If you are in the

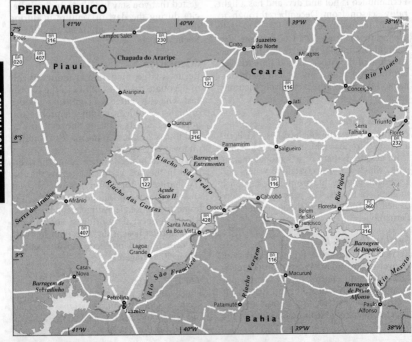

city center, go to **Laundromat** (Rua Gervásio Pires 143, Boa Vista; ☺ 7am-8pm Mon-Fri, 10am-4pm Sat).

MEDICAL SERVICES
Albert Sabin (☎ 3421 5411) Private hospital.
Real Português (☎ 3416 1122) Private hospital.

MONEY
Banco do Brasil Boa Viagem (Av Conselheiro Aguiar 3600); Santo Antônio (Av Dantas Barreto 541). Also at the airport.
Bradesco (cnr Av Conselheiro Aguiar & Félix de Brito, Boa Viagem) Also many ATMs in the center of the city.
Norte Câmbio Turismo Av Boa Viagem (Shop B, Av Boa Viagem 500); Boa Viagem (Shopping Recife, Rua Padre Carapuceiro 777, Boa Viagem) ; Piedade (Shopping Guararapes, Piedade) Changes cash and traveler's checks.

POST
Main post office (Av Guararapes 250, Santo Antônio) The *posta restante* (poste restante) counter is in the basement. There are also post offices at the airport and the bus station.

TELEPHONE
Telemar Boa Vista (Rua do Hospício 148); Terminal Integrado de Passageiros (TIP; combined metro terminal and bus station) Telephone stations with international service; also has a branch at the airport.

TOURIST INFORMATION
Disque Turismo (☎ 3425 8409) is the tourist hotline. *Informativo Pro Lazer* is a bimonthly mini-guide to Recife. *Jornal do Commércio*, a local newspaper, has cultural listings (museums, art galleries, movies) in its daily Caderno C section. All are in Portuguese.
Empetur headquarters (☎ 3427 8183; Centro de Convenções); airport (☎ 3462 4960; ☺ 24hr); Boa Viagem (☎ 3463 3621; Praça de Boa Viagem; ☺ 8am-8pm); Recife Antigo (☎ 3224 2361; Rua Bom Jesus 197; ☺ 9am-9pm); TIP (☎ 3452 2824; Av Central; ☺ 7am-7pm) The headquarters is inconveniently located between the city center and Olinda, but the other information booths are more accessible. The airport booth has English-speaking attendants, sells maps and can book hotels.

TRAVEL AGENCIES
Andratur (☎ 3465 8588; andratur@hotmail.com; shop 5, Av Conselheiro Aguiar 3150, Boa Viagem) This professional agency provides national and international tickets at discounted prices. It also sells package trips and flights to Fernando de Noronha.

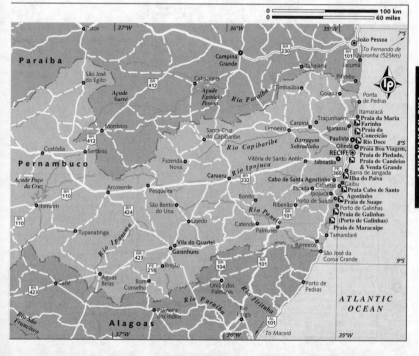

Brasitur (☎ 3465 0426; www.brasitur.com.br; shop 6, Av Conselheiro Aguiar 3150, Boa Viagem) Next door to Andratur, this agency offers competitive prices.

Dangers & Annoyances
Surfing is prohibited in Boa Viagem due to the occasional shark attack. Swimmers are advised to stay inside the reef at Boa Viagem. Recife has a reputation in the Northeast as a bit of a violent town, although it is considerably less violent than major towns in the south.

Much like other popular urban beach destinations, Boa Viagem has an active prostitution scene that caters to tourists and businessmen.

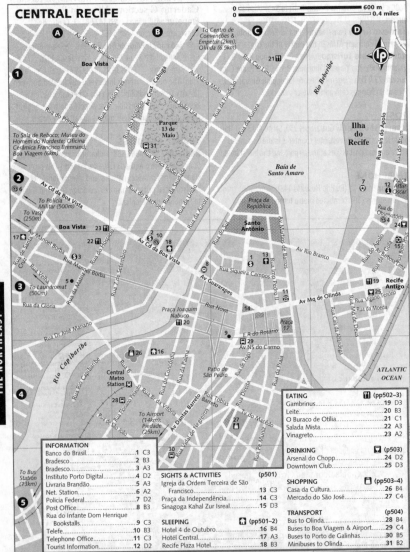

CENTRAL RECIFE

0   600 m
0   0.4 miles

INFORMATION	
Banco do Brasil	1 C3
Bradesco	2 B3
Bradesco	3 A3
Instituto Porto Digital	4 D2
Livraria Brandão	5 A3
Net. Station	6 A2
Policia Federal	7 D2
Post Office	8 B3
Rua do Infante Dom Henrique Bookstalls	9 C3
Telefe	10 B3
Telephone Office	11 C3
Tourist Information	12 D2

SIGHTS & ACTIVITIES	(p501)
Igreja da Ordem Terceira de São Francisco	13 C3
Praça da Independência	14 C3
Sinagoga Kahal Zur Isreal	15 D3

SLEEPING	(pp501–2)
Hotel 4 de Outubro	16 B4
Hotel Central	17 A3
Recife Plaza Hotel	18 B3

EATING	(pp502–3)
Gambrinus	19 D3
Leite	20 B3
O Buraco de Otília	21 C1
Salada Mista	22 A3
Vinagreto	23 A3

DRINKING	(p503)
Arsenal do Chopp	24 D2
Downtown Club	25 D3

SHOPPING	(pp503–4)
Casa da Cultura	26 B4
Mercado do São José	27 C4

TRANSPORT	(p504)
Bus to Olinda	28 B4
Buses to Boa Viagem & Airport	29 C4
Buses to Porto de Galinhas	30 B5
Minibuses to Olinda	31 B2

THE NORTHEAST

Sights

OFICINA CERÂMICA FRANCISCO BRENNAND

A surreal sculpture garden of bizarre sexualized earthworms, frogs and turtles covers the landscape at the unique **Oficina Cerâmica Francisco Brennand** (Várzea; admission US$1; ☺ 8am-5pm Mon-Thu, 8am-4pm Fri). The artist revitalized his family's abandoned roof- and floor-tile factory to create his own line of decorative ceramic tiles. The rest of the huge space is dedicated to a seemingly exhaustive exhibition of his peculiar sculptures, including gardens with Moorish arches and rows of contorted busts. A trip out to this forested suburb is a regional highlight, so set aside an afternoon. To get there, arrange for a round-trip taxi (fix a price of approximately US$10 from Recife, including waiting time) or take the UR7-Várzea bus from the main post office downtown on Av Guararapes to the end of the line (35 minutes). From there, catch a taxi (US$2) as the several-kilometer walk is complicated and not necessarily safe. The scenic, yet overrated, Instituto Ricardo Brennand, the artist's father's museum, is 10 minutes away by taxi. It contains a massive collection of European art, swords and knives in a castle-like building on well-maintained grounds.

MUSEU DO HOMEM DO NORDESTE

The **Museu do Homem do Nordeste** (Av 17 de Agosto 2187, Casa Forte; admission US$2; ☺ 11am-5pm Tue-Fri, 1-5pm Sat & Sun) has anthropological exhibits on Northeastern life ranging from slave chains to Carnaval costumes, with good photos throughout. The museum is extensive and well-done. To get there, catch the Dois Irmãos bus from the main post office on Av Guararapes downtown.

IGREJA DA ORDEM TERCEIRA DE SÃO FRANCISCO

The most important building to visit in the city center is the **Igreja da Ordem Terceira de São Francisco** (Rua Imperador Pedro II; ☺ 8-11am & 2-5pm Mon-Fri, 8-11:30am Sat), a church dating from 1697 with a **Capela Dourada** (Golden Chapel) that is one of the finest examples of Brazilian baroque.

SINAGOGA KAHAL ZUR ISREAL

The first synagogue in the Americas, **Sinagoga Kahal Zur Isreal** (Rua Bom Jesus 197, Recife Antigo; ☺ 9am-5pm Tue-Fri, 3-7pm Sat & Sun) still has a bit of the original structure and interesting murals that depict the role of Jews in the development of the city.

PARQUE 13 DE MAIO

A great place to hang out, especially on a Sunday, is the **Parque 13 de Maio**. There is a lot of action in the park, including capoeira, heated domino games and even more heated political debates.

BEACHES

The only beach worth visiting in Recife is at **Boa Viagem**, but still very few people actually enter the water. It is packed on weekends and is a good place to watch or play beach sports, but you'll find cleaner water 14km to 18km further south at **Praia Enseada dos Corais**, **Praia Gaibu** and **Praia Calhetas**.

Festivals & Events

The Recife **Carnaval** is one of Brazil's most colorful and folkloric festivals, and is arguably the best in the country. The few months leading up to Carnaval, which are filled with parties and public rehearsals, are almost as fun as the actual event. Carnaval groups and spectators deck themselves out in elaborate costumes, such as *maracatu* (warrior with a huge headpiece and a flower in his mouth), *caboclo* (indigenous/African mix), colonial-era royalty, harlequin, bull and *frevo* (crop tops with ruffled sleeves for both genders, and a tiny umbrella), and shimmy for days to frenetic *frevo* music. Recife's action concentrates downtown along Av Guararapes. Galo da Madrugada, Recife's largest *bloco* (themed singing/dancing group), has been known to bring 20,000 people in costume onto the beach at Boa Viagem to dance.

Carnaval in Olinda is so close that you could participate in both on the same day, and there is a lot of crossover in their events.

In the last week in October Recife also hosts an out-of-season Carnaval called **Recifolia**. More than two million people crowd the streets during this Salvador-style Carnaval, dancing to Bahian bands for seven days straight.

Sleeping

Many travelers prefer to stay in neighboring Olinda and visit Recife during the day (if at all). If you want the beach, head to Boa Viagem, where there are accommodations ranging from hostels to five-star hotels. Aside from business travel, the only real reason to stay in the city center is proximity to nightlife in Recife Antigo.

Most Recife accommodations have a 10% surcharge on rooms, which may or may not be discussed beforehand and is not included in the prices below.

CITY CENTER
Budget
There are a few cheap places in central Recife, but you should only consider them if you're on the tightest budget.

Hotél Central (☎ 3423 6411; info@hotelcentral.com .br; Av Manoel Borba 209; s/d US$8/11, s/d with private bathroom US$11/13) Bright rooms with high ceilings and a location on a tree-shaded street make this semi-shabby 1930s hotel the best budget option in the center.

Mid-Range
Hotel 4 de Outubro (☎ /fax 3224 4900; 4deoutubro@uol .com.br; Rua Floriano Peixoto 141; s/d US$28/32; ☒) A wise city-center choice, this modern, functional hotel is in a nice location near the metro station.

Recife Plaza Hotel (☎ /fax 3231 1200; atendimento@ recifeplazahotel.com.br; Rua da Aurora 225; s/d US$27/33; ☒ ☒) The relatively charming Recife Plaza overlooks the Rio Capibaribe in the center of town. With standard amenities and a restaurant, it is a good escape from the urban bustle.

BOA VIAGEM
Budget
Albergue Maracatus do Recife (☎ 3326 1221; albergue maracatus@yahoo.com; Rua Maria Carolina 185; dm/d US$7/13; ☒) This is a well-located, simple place, frequently full of other travelers. Dorm rooms have only four beds and there is a discount for HI members.

Albergue Boa Viagem (☎ 3326 9572; alberguebo a viagem@ieg.com.br; Rua Aviador Severiano Lins 455; dm/s/d US$7/12/13; ☒) A newer hostel with dorms, small rooms for couples and ample common areas. It continues to evolve into an ever-larger backpacker retreat.

Mid-Range
Navegantes Praia Hotel (☎ /fax 326 9609; Rua dos Navegantes 1997; s/d US$17/22; ☒ ☒) Although

it is on an unattractive street, Navegantes is the best value that you will get within a block of the beach, with tidy rooms and a quality breakfast. It does not request the 10% room surcharge.

Hotel Aconchego (☎ 3464 2989; www.hotel aconchego.com.br; Félix de Brito 382, Boa Viagem; s/d US$26/35; ☒ ☒) A few blocks further back from the beach and a bit more expensive than the Navegantes Praia Hotel, Aconchego has immaculate rooms, substantial common areas, an affordable 24-hour restaurant and good service. It is popular with Brazilian tourists.

Hotel Jangadeiro (☎ 3086 5050; www.jangadeiro hotel.com.br; Av Boa Viagem 3114; d US$35-64; ☒ ☒) One of the few mid-range places on the beachfront, the high-rise Jangadeiro isn't exactly luxurious with its low ceilings and overuse of bathroom tiling, but the more expensive rooms have nice views. It is at one of the best parts of the beach.

Top End
Recife Palace (☎ 3465 2500; recifepalace@lucsimhoteis .com.br; Av Boa Viagem 4070; d US$125-150; ℗ ☒ ☒ ☐ ☒) This is a well-known and well-appointed five-star, beachfront spot.

Mar Hotel Recife (☎ 3302 4444; www.marhotel .com.br; Rua Sousa Leão 451, Boa Viagem; d US$133-200; ℗ ☒ ☒ ☐ ☒) Also near the beach, this top-notch place is your best option close to the airport.

Eating
The *barracas* (kiosks) along Boa Viagem have a variety of *salgados* (snacks), *sucos* (fruit juices) and *açaí* (berry-like fruit, prepared as a cold drink or as a sherbet-like frozen liquid, mixed with *guarana* and topped with granola and honey) to keep you going along a long day on the beach.

After a trip to Europe, the mayor of Recife decided that the restaurants and nightclubs of the city were too scattered and tried to create two major leisure areas. One is in Recife Antigo and is called Polo Bom Jesus; the other is at the northern end of Boa Viagem and is known as Polo Pina. Outside of Polo Pina, the restaurants in Boa Viagem are rather scattered.

CITY CENTER
The city center is loaded with self-serve places (most charging around US$4 per kilo-

gram) – try **Vinagreto** (Rua do Hospício 203) or the nearby **Salada Mista** (Rua do Hospício 50).

Gambrinus (☎ 3224 0466; Av Marquês de Olinda 263, Recife Antigo; mains US$4-10; ☯ 6pm-late) In the generally upscale Recife Antigo, Gambrinus offers quality local and regional dishes. It is a good place to go before a night on the town and gets lively enough that you may end up just hanging out at the restaurant.

Leite (☎ 3224 7977; Praça Joaquim Nabuco 147; lunch US$10-15; ☯ 11:30am-4pm Sun-Fri) One of the oldest restaurants in the country, this famous traditional lunch place was opened in 1882. It is a bit expensive, but worth stopping in for a glass of wine, if nothing else.

O Buraco de Otília (☎ 3231 1528; Rua da Aurora 1232; lunch US$6; ☯ 11am-3pm Sun-Fri) For a lunch of great regional cuisine, try the *pouco de tudo* (a little of everything) special. Come prepared with a large appetite.

BOA VIAGEM

Ilha da Kosta (☎ 3466 2122; Rua Bernardino Pessoa 50; mains US$7-12) This attractive and popular, if overly commercial, restaurant, has a good variety from seafood to pizza to steaks. Try the *camarão ao molho de coco* (shrimp in coconut sauce) for US$8.

Ilha Sushi (Rua Maria Carolina 80) The operators of Ilha da Kosta also own this good sushi restaurant nearby.

Nau dos Navegantes (☎ 3465 3869; Rua dos Navegantes 1706; mains US$7-14; ☯ noon-3pm & 6pm-midnight) Good-value Portuguese food in a comfortable restaurant close to the beach.

Sabor de Beijo (☎ 3325 2141; Av Conselheiro Aguiar 2994; per kg US$5; ☯ 10am-11pm) The best self-service place in the area, it's clean, popular with locals and has a good variety of desserts.

Entertainment

People from Recife – Recifenses – are proud of their nightlife and the variety of music that can be found in their city. The main areas to go out are Polo Bom Jesus in Recife Antigo and Polo Pina in Boa Viagem; Polo Bom Jesus is the more interesting area. Every night of the week there is something going on in Bom Jesus. Up-to-date music and nightlife listings can be found online at www.guiametropole.com.br/show.php.

Another favorite part of town is the Patio de São Pedro in the city center, with a night of Afro-Brazilian rhythms such as *afoxé* (traditional Afro-Brazilian rhythm) and *maracatu*, called Terça Negra (Black Tuesday).

POLO BOM JESUS
With more than a dozen small, artsy bars and lots of outdoor tables concentrated along Rua Bom Jesus, Recife Antigo comes alive at night. Head to the neighborhood after 10pm and follow the crowds.

Arsenal do Chopp (☎ 3224 6259; Praça Arsenal da Marinha 59; ☯ 5pm-late) This consistently popular bar and restaurant is always a good place to start or end an evening and enjoy the house beer.

Downtown Club (Rua Vigário Tenório 105; admission US$5; ☯ 10pm-late Thu-Sun) Popular with locals, Downtown is a sure bet to hear good music, meet some Recifenses and not return home until after sunrise.

BOA VIAGEM
Beyond the busy prostitution scene, Boa Viagem is surprisingly quiet at night. Polo Pina, at the north end of the neighborhood, has some action, but pales by comparison to Polo Bom Jesus.

Biruta Bar (☎ 3326 5151; Rua Bem-Te-Vi; ☯ 5pm-late Mon-Thu, noon-late Fri-Sun) This fun bar is a local favorite, with strong drinks, a variety of music and a fun crowd. It's one of the more lively spots in Polo Pina.

Theatro (Av Boa Viagem 760) This place plays everything from *pagode* (popular samba music) to electronica.

Sala de Reboco (Rua Gregorio 264, Cordeiro) Some of the best *forró* (popular music of the Northeast) in the city can be found here.

Shopping

Pernambuco's traditional handicrafts of clay figurines, wood sculptures and leather goods can be picked up at the **Mercado do São José** (Rua da Praia; ☯ 6am-5:30pm Mon-Sat, 6am-11:30pm Sun), before Rua da Santa Rita, or the **Casa da Cultura** (Rua Floriano Peixoto s/n; ☯ 9am-7pm Mon-Sat, 9am-2pm Sun). The latter is a creepy colonial-era prison with market stalls in cells where prisoners languished until 1979. It often has music and dance performances at its entrance at around 3pm on Friday. On Sunday there's an interesting **food and handicraft market** (Rua Bom Jesus) in Recife Antigo.

Recife is full of shopping malls. **Shopping Recife** (Rua Padre Carapuceiro 777, Boa Viagem) bills itself as the largest mall in the country. It's a maze of stores, movie theaters, recreation and event complexes and is a good place to restock on any international goods that you may need to pick up for your trip.

Getting There & Away

AIR

From Recife's **Guararapes Airport** (☎ 3464 4188), there are flights to most major Brazilian cities, New York, Miami and a number of European capitals. The airport code is REC.

The following airlines all have offices in Recife:

Gol (☎ 3464 4793; Guararapes Airport)

TAM (☎ 3464 4257; Guararapes Airport)

Trip (☎ 3464 4610; Guararapes Airport)

Varig/Nordeste (☎ 3464 4809; Av Conselheiro Aguiar 456, Boa Viagem)

VASP (☎ 3462 4931; Av Manoel Borba 488, Boa Vista)

BUS

The **Terminal Integrado de Passageiros** (TIP; ☎ 3452 2824) is a combined metro terminal and bus station, 14km southwest of the center. The TIP handles all interstate buses as well as many connections for local destinations. You can purchase any bus tickets at outlets in town, or by calling **Disk Rodoviária** (☎ 3452 3990) – a bus-ticket delivery service.

Destinations include Caruaru (US$5, two hours, 138km, 14 daily), Fortaleza (US$23 to US$33, 12 hours, 799km, four daily), João Pessoa (US$4, two hours, 125km, hourly 5am to 7:30pm), Maceió (US$6 to US$9, four hours, 253km, eight daily), Natal (US$10, 4½ hours, 288km, nine daily), Rio (US$58 to US$70, 42 hours, 2392km, five daily) and Salvador (US$26 to US$30, 11 to 12 hours, 842km, two daily).

Getting Around

Recife is spread out and hard to navigate. If you can afford taxis, they will save you a fair amount of time and stress.

TO/FROM THE AIRPORT

Taxis cost approximately US$7 from the city center to the airport, 10km south of the center. The trip from the airport will cost US$3 to Boa Viagem, US$8 to the bus station and US$10 to Olinda – catch a regular taxi, not a special airport taxi, which is almost twice as expensive.

From the airport, there are also regular buses and microbuses (minibuses). The Aeroporto bus runs to Av Dantas Barreto in the center of Recife, stopping in Boa Viagem on the way. To Olinda, take the Aeroporto bus to Av NS do Carmo in Recife and pick up a Casa Caiada bus from there. Another option is to get off in Boa Viagem and take a Piedade/Rio Doce bus from there to Olinda.

TO/FROM THE METRO/BUS STATION

From the TIP to all Recife and Olinda destinations, catch a metro train to the Estacão Recife stop (US$0.30, 25 minutes) and take a bus or Kombi van from there.

TO/FROM OLINDA

From the city center to Olinda, catch any bus marked 'Rio Doce.' From outside the central metro station, known as Estacão Recife, catch a Rio Doce/Princesa Isabel bus. The main bus stop in Olinda is Praça do Carmo. Ask the conductor to let you know when you get there, as it's easy to miss. The Rio Doce/Piedade and Barra de Jangada/Casa Caiada buses run between Olinda and Boa Viagem. Taxis from the center of Recife to Olinda cost US$6 and take 20 minutes. A taxi from the airport to Olinda will cost US$10.

TO/FROM BOA VIAGEM

From the center to Boa Viagem, take any bus marked 'Aeroporto,' 'Shopping Center,' 'Candeias' or 'Piedade' from Av NS do Carmo. To return to the center, take any bus marked 'Dantas Barreto.' Buses run along Av Engenheiro Domingos Ferreira in Boa Viagem, three blocks from the beach. A taxi from the center to Boa Viagem costs around US$4; Kombi vans cost the same as buses (US$0.60).

OLINDA

☎ 0xx81 / pop 360,000

While Recife plays the role of an industrial center, Olinda is recognized as its cultural counterpart: a living city with bohemian quarters, art galleries, museums, music in the streets and always some kind of celebration in the works. The beautiful historic center of Olinda sits on a hill overlooking Recife and the Atlantic Ocean. It is one of the largest and best-preserved colonial cities in Brazil, with twisting streets of colorful old houses and a plethora of scenic churches in various states of decay and repair. It is a touristy destination, but Olinda does not disappoint, as it remains charming, fun and friendly.

Although many buildings were originally constructed in the 16th century, the Dutch burnt almost everything in 1631. Consequently, the majority of what you now see was actually reconstructed at a later date.

Orientation

Olinda is about 6km north of Recife. The historic district, which constitutes about 10% of the city, is concentrated around the upper streets of the hill and is easily visited on foot. The beaches that are immediately adjacent to the city – Milagres, for example – suffer from pollution and swimming is not recommended.

Information

Whatever services you don't find in Olinda you can secure during a short day trip to central Recife.

INTERNET ACCESS

Olinda Net Café (Praça do Carmo 5-B; per hr US$2)
Olind@.com (Praça João Pessoa 15; per hr US$2)

INTERNET RESOURCES

Official site (www.olinda.pe.gov.br)
Olinda information (www.olinda.com.br) Detailed Carnaval info.

MEDICAL SERVICES

Prontolinda (☎ 3432 8000) Local private medical service.

MONEY

There are no ATMs in the old town, but there is a **Banco do Brasil** (Av Getúlio Vargas) just northeast of Olinda. Catch any Kombi van heading up the road from Praça do Carmo and it'll drop you at the door, or take a bus marked 'Ouro Prêto' from the plaza to the Bank Itau stop, then walk about 100m further north.

POST

Main post office Near Praça do Carmo, it offers a poste restante service.

TELEPHONE

Telmar telephone office (Praça do Carmo)

TOURIST INFORMATION

Tourist information post (☎ 3305 1048; Praça do Carmo 100; 8am-noon & 2-5:30pm Mon-Fri) The city's tourist information post, inside the library, has English-speaking preteens offering church tour maps, basic information and their services as a free guide.

TRAVEL AGENCIES

Olinda is thin on travel agencies and in certain situations it is best to go to Recife or directly to the airport to arrange your travel needs.

S&B Turismo (☎ 3429 0892; Praça do Carmo; 9am-6pm) Can help with most bus tickets, plane fares, tourism packages and will deliver tickets to your pousada (guest-house).

Dangers & Annoyances

Olinda is not particularly dangerous, but crime (mostly petty) exists, especially during Carnaval. The city recommends that you only use its free yellow-shirted guides to avoid being fed false information or being put in sticky situations involving payment discrepancies.

Sights

Olinda's sights are all within walking distance and can be visited as part of a walking tour.

At Praça do Carmo, visit the restored **Igreja NS do Carmo** (1580). The 1585 **Convento São Francisco** (7-11:30am Mon-Fri, 7am-noon & 2-5pm Sat) is a large structure containing three parts: the convent, the **Capela de São Roque** (chapel) and the **Igreja de NS das Neves** (church).

From Rua Frei Afonso Maria you'll see the 1549 **Seminário de Olinda & Igreja NS da Graça** (8-11:30am & 3-5pm) on the hill above.

Climb up to **Alto da Sé** (Cathedral Heights), crowned by the imposing 1537 **Igreja da Sé** (8am-noon & 2-5pm). It's a good spot to enjoy the superb views of Olinda and Recife. There are food and drink street stalls here and a small craft market with woodcarvings, figurines and jewelry.

The **Museu de Arte Sacra de Pernambuco** (MASPE; 8am-12:45pm Mon-Fri) is housed in a building constructed in 1696 that once functioned as Olinda's Episcopal Palace and Câmara (Government Council). The museum contains a good collection of sacred art and a photographic homage to the city.

Visit the **Igreja NS da Conceição** (1585). **Igreja da Misericórdia** (🕒 8am-noon & 2-5pm), built in 1540, has fine *azulejos* (Portuguese ceramic tiles) and gilded carvings inside.

On Rua Saldanha Marinho, see the restored 1613 **Igreja NS do Amparo** (🕒 8-11:30am). Further along this street is the **Casa dos Bonecos** (🕒 8am-noon), which houses the Bonecos

Gigantes de Olinda, giant papier-mâché puppets used in Carnaval. If it is closed but the doors are open, you can usually pop in for a look.

The **Museu de Arte Contemporânea** (MAC, Museum of Contemporary Art; 🕒 9am-noon & 2-5pm Tue-Fri, 2-5pm Sat & Sun) is recommended for both its permanent and temporary exhibits. The

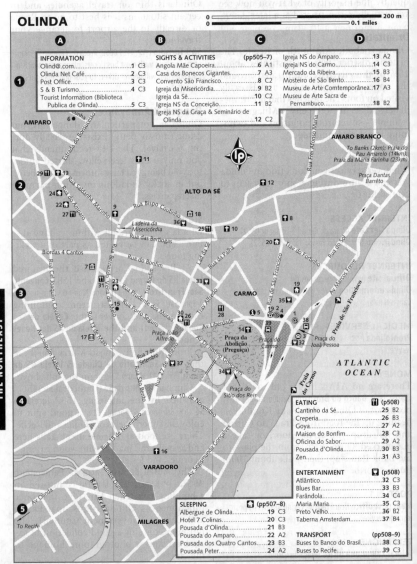

OLINDA

| | | 0 ___ 200 m |
| | | 0 ___ 0.1 miles |

INFORMATION
Olind@.com..............................1 C3
Olinda Net Café........................2 C3
Post Office................................3 C3
S & B Turismo...........................4 C3
Tourist Information (Biblioteca
Publica de Olinda).................5 C3

SIGHTS & ACTIVITIES (pp505–7)
Angola Mãe Capoeira..............6 A1
Casa dos Bonecos Gigantes....7 A3
Convento São Francisco...........8 C2
Igreja da Misericórdia..............9 B2
Igreja da Sé............................10 C2
Igreja NS da Conceição..........11 B2
Igreja NS da Graça & Seminário de
Olinda..................................12 C2

Igreja NS do Amparo...............13 A2
Igreja NS do Carmo.................14 C3
Mercado da Ribeira.................15 B3
Mosteiro de São Bento............16 B4
Museu de Arte Comtemporânea..17 A3
Museu de Arte Sacra de
Pernambuco.........................18 B2

EATING (p508)
Cantinho da Sé........................25 B2
Creperia...................................26 B3
Goya.......................................27 A2
Maison d'Olinda......................28 C3
Oficina do Sabor.....................29 A2
Pousada d'Olinda....................30 B3
Zen..31 A3

ENTERTAINMENT (p508)
Atlântico.................................32 C3
Blues Bar.................................33 B3
Farândola................................34 C4
Maria Maria.............................35 C3
Preto Velho..............................36 B2
Taberna Amsterdam................37 B4

SLEEPING (pp507–8)
Albergue de Olinda.................19 C3
Hotel 7 Colinas.......................20 C3
Pousada d'Olinda....................21 B3
Pousada do Amparo................22 A2
Pousada dos Quatro Cantos....23 B3
Pousada Peter..........................24 A2

TRANSPORT (pp508–9)
Buses to Banco do Brasil..........38 C3
Buses to Recife........................39 C3

AMPARO

AMARO BRANCO

To Banks (2km); Praia do
Pau Amarelo (14km);
Praia da Maria Farinha (23km)

Praça Dantas
Barrêto

ALTO DA SÉ

Biordas 4 Cantos

Ladeira da
Misericórdia
Rua das Bertiogas

CARMO

Praça João
Alfredo

Praça da
Abolição
(Preguiça)

Praça do
Carmo

Praça do
João Pessoa

ATLANTIC
OCEAN

Praça do
Sítio dos Reis

Praia do Carmo

VARADORO

To Recife

MILAGRES

museum is housed in an 18th-century *ajube* (a jail used by the Catholic Church during the Inquisition).

Mercado da Ribeira is an 18th-century structure that is now home to art galleries and souvenir shops. The huge **Mosteiro de São Bento** (☼ 8-11am & 2-5pm), built in 1582, has some exceptional woodcarving in the chapel. Brazil's first law school was housed here for 24 years. The monastery celebrates mass on Sunday morning at 10:30am, complete with Gregorian chants. Delicious homemade liqueurs are sold here too.

The city beaches are polluted, busy and not recommended for swimming. See p510 for nearby options.

Activities

If you'd like to check out a capoeira school, **Angola Mãe** (Rua Ilma Cunha 243) teaches the slower and more traditional *angola* style. To get there, turn up the dirt alley and knock on the metal gate painted in zebra stripes. The school welcomes visitors to take classes or watch an open *roda* (circle) at 6pm on Sunday. Come with a respectful attitude and unaccompanied by a guide.

Tours

Throughout Olinda you'll no doubt hear the offer *'Guia!'* ('Guide!'). If you're carrying this book, a guide will be of little use. Yellow-shirted young *guias mirins* (apprentice guides) are available free from the tourist office. Freelance guides who cluster near the bus stop on Praça do Carmo charge between US$5 and US$10 for a three-hour tour (fix the price before starting) and are a bit more informative.

Festivals & Events

Carnaval in Olinda lasts a full 11 days. There are organized Carnaval events, including balls, a night of samba and a night of *afoxé*, but everything else happens in impromptu fashion on the streets. The official opening events – with all the pomp and ceremony of the Olympic Games – commence with a *bloco* of more than 400 'virgins' (men in drag), and awards for the most beautiful, the most risqué and the biggest prude.

The Carnaval groups of thousands dance the *frevo* through the narrow streets. It's playful and very lewd. Five separate areas have orchestras (as the bands call themselves) playing nonstop from 8pm to 6am every night.

Olinda's Carnaval has an intimacy that you don't get in big-city Carnavals. Costumed *blocos* and spectators dance through the streets in this highly inclusive, colorful and traditional festival. The Carnavals of Recife and Olinda combined draw the second-largest crowd in the Northeast after Salvador.

As well as Carnaval, the festival known as **Folclore Nordestino**, held at the end of August, features dance, music and folklore from many parts of the Northeast. It's highly recommended.

Sleeping

Book several months ahead for accommodations during Carnaval and be prepared for massive price hikes. Some of the quasi-official pousadas that crop up for Carnaval are among the best deals.

Pousada d'Olinda (☎ 3494 2559; www.pousada dolinda.com.br; Praça João Alfredo 178; dm/s US$6/12, d US$17-30; 🕄 🐾) A central dining area, pool and lawn make this pretty pousada a good place to socialize with other travelers. The double rooms range from budget to nicer mid-range suites.

Albergue de Olinda (☎ 3429 1592; www.alber guedeolinda.com.br; Rua do Sol 233; dm/d US$7/16; 🐾) This hostel has modern rooms and a pretty garden, but the traffic noise is constant. It offers HI member discount.

Pousada do Amparo (☎ 3439 1749; www.pousada doamparo.com; Rua do Amparo 191; d US$40-95; 🕄 🐾) Amparo is a charming place with a lovely garden and views back toward Recife. This quaint pousada, tucked along the attractive Rua do Amparo, will give you the quintessential Olinda experience. Some of the tasteful suites also have a view at this highly recommended, comfortable spot. English, German and Spanish are spoken here.

Pousada dos Quatro Cantos (☎ 3429 0220; www .pousada4cantos.com.br; Rua Prudente dos Morais 441; s/d US$20/24, s/d ste US$75/85; 🕄 🐾) High ceilings, tall windows and doors, and bright rooms with hardwood floors overlooking a shaded courtyard, make this former colonial weekend home a delightful place to stay. The splurge option is the suite (with two rooms plus a veranda). English is spoken.

Pousada Peter (☎ /fax 3439 2171; www.pousada peter.com.br; Rua do Amparo 215; d US$18-50; 🕄 🐾)

Another tasteful place on scenic Rua do Amparo, this pousada is clean, quaint and highly regarded, with a relaxing pool area.

Hotel 7 Colinas (☎ /fax 3439 6055; www.hotel7 colinas.com.br; Ladeira de São Francisco 307; d US$67, tr US$70-115; P ☒ ☐ ☒) Set in spacious, leafy grounds in the heart of Olinda, this sprawling hotel is a nice escape from the tight colonial streets and alleyways. The rooms are comfortable and the quality restaurant is open to the public. At least stop in and have a coffee or drink by the pool.

Eating

The old city has a variety of restaurants tucked away among its cobblestone streets.

Oficina do Sabor (☎ 3429 3331; Rua do Amparo 335; mains US$8-12; ☯ noon-4pm & 6pm-midnight Tue-Sat, noon-5pm Sun) This well-known restaurant with a nice view is worth the prices. The most famous dishes on the menu are the baked pumpkins stuffed with delicacies such as shrimp or fish cooked in coconut sauce (US$10).

Goya (☎ 3439 4875; Rua do Amparo 157; mains US$3-8; ☯ noon-5pm & 6pm-midnight Mon & Wed-Sat, noon-10pm Sun) The owners here are artists who display their work in the restaurant. The food is creative too, with fish and delicious shrimp dishes served inside a coconut.

Maison do Bonfim (☎ 3429 1674; Rua do Bonfim 115; mains US$3-10; ☯ noon-4pm & 6pm-1am Wed-Sat, noon-6pm Sun, noon-4pm Tue) A smart French place that has been around for almost a decade, with nice décor and even better dishes.

Cantinho da Sé (☎ 3439 8815; Ladeira da Sé 305; mains US$5) Decently priced Brazilian food served on a patio overlooking Recife, but the view is unfortunately obstructed by power lines. The carne do sol (a tasty, salted meat, grilled and served with beans, rice and vegetables) and sucos are a good choice.

Pousada d'Olinda (☎ 3494 2559; Praça João Alfredo 178; per kg US$4; ☯ 1pm-4pm) Reasonably priced self-service lunch open to the public.

Zen (Rua Bernardo Veira de Melo 157; set menu US$3; ☯ 1-8:30pm Mon-Sat) The vegetarian set menu is always tasty at this restaurant, which doesn't even have a sign.

Creperia (☎ 3429 2935; Rua Prudente dos Morais 168; crepe US$2; ☯ 4-11pm Tue-Sun) The spinach-and-ricotta crepe makes for a nice break from rice and beans and the mixed veggie salad comes with a true vinaigrette dressing.

Entertainment

Olinda is justly famous for its nightlife. Alto da Sé can get busy in the evening as locals and visitors buy drinks from the numerous street vendors, watch capoeira and savor the view. Later in the evening the action moves to a relatively unattractive area around Rua do Sol for more street partying, and eventually on to one of Olinda's clubs. Music varies from forró and afoxé to rock and reggae.

Preto Velho (Alto da Sé; admission US$1-2; ☯ 9pm-late) Although it doesn't look like much from the front, this club is worth the small cover charge as it has a good variety of Brazilian music, fills up with local partygoers and has a spectacular view.

Farândola (Praça Sitio dos Reis; admission free; ☯ 5:30pm-late Tue-Sat) This lounge-lizard-like bar with a red interior is a great place to sit at a table with friends, have a drink and check out live MPB and bossa nova.

Atlântico (Praça do Carmo; admission US$1-2) One of the town's more popular clubs, Atlântico gets packed late at night and plays any variety of danceable music until the sun comes up.

Taberna Amsterdam (Rua 27 de Janeiro 65; admission free) This trendy combination bar/restaurant facing Praça João Alfredo has a large dance area out the back.

Maria Maria (Rua do Sol 225) This spot has a good dance floor and a gay-friendly reputation.

Blues Bar (☎ 9156 6415; Rua do Bonfim 66; admission free) This smallish, cool joint has good music and a chill ambience.

Shopping

Olinda is full of small shops selling a plethora of art and artisan work. It is best to walk around Rua do Amparo and the back streets to get a feel for what is being offered before buying anything. Some of the best purchases can be made directly from the artists and craftspeople at unnamed stores, stalls and tiny galleries, and from people's houses.

Getting There & Away

The main bus stop in Olinda is on Praça do Carmo. Buses marked 'Rio Doce/Conde da Boa Vista' and 'Casa Caiada' go to the center of Recife. The Rio Doce/Princesa Isabel bus stops outside the central metro station in

Recife. From Recife, take any Rio Doce, Casa Caiada or Jardim Atlântico bus to Olinda. Taxis between Recife and Olinda cost about US$6 and take about 20 minutes.

Buses marked 'Rio Doce/Piedade' and 'Barra de Jangada/Casa Caiada' run between Olinda and Boa Viagem (US$0.80). A taxi to or from the airport is US$9 to US$10.

BEACHES SOUTH OF RECIFE

South of the capital, the sea is calm, the waters are clear and the beaches are lined with coconut palms and white sand dunes. The coastal Hwy PE-060 doesn't hug the ocean like the road in northern Alagoas, so you have to drive a dozen or so kilometers on an access road to see what each beach is like. There is frequent bus service to all the beach towns from Recife. Many of the towns have just one or two simple hotels.

Gaibu & Calhetas

Although Gaibu is the larger, livelier and more popular beach town, Calhetas is the nicest beach in the initial stretch south of Recife. It is a small bay surrounded by rocks and is a decent spot for snorkeling.

Suape & Ilha do Paiva

Ilha do Paiva, nicknamed the island of lovers, is popular for its nude beaches. Take a boat from Barra de Jangada (US$3, 15 minutes) – it's worth a visit. You'll see boats along the beach.

The mainland beaches here – **Candeias**, **Venda Grande** and **Piedade** – are semi-urban, with many beach bars, hotels and crowds on weekends. But they are still good beaches, with clean water and sometimes strong surf. Suape has been developed as an industrial port and is worth avoiding.

Porto de Galinhas

☎ 0xx81 / pop 10,000

Sixty kilometers south of Recife, Porto de Galinhas (Port of Chickens) is one of Pernambuco's most famous beaches. The name is derived from the fact that after abolition in 1888, the port continued to receive slaves, referred to by the code word '*galinhas*', illegally.

Porto de Galinhas sits along a pretty bay lined with coconut palms, mangroves and cashew trees. The water is warm and clear,

but the beach gets very crowded with Recifenses on weekends and is being rapidly developed as a mass tourism destination.

Many travelers prefer the more tranquil **Praia de Maracaípe**, just 3km away, which also has accommodations, some excellent waves for surfing and easy access to Porto de Galinhas.

SLEEPING

Pousada dos Coqueiros (☎ 3552 1294; www.pousada doscoqueiros.com.br; Rua Projetada 7, Praia de Maracaípe; d US$21-55; P ✗ ✷) A recommended, relaxing pousada in Maracaípe, dos Coqueiros is good value for its clean rooms.

Pousada Beira Mar (☎ /fax 3552 1052; beiramar@ elogica.com.br; Av Beira Mar 12, Porto de Galinhas; s/d US$28/42; ✗ ✷) In a great location on the beachfront, this comfortable hotel has excellent discounts in the low season.

Nannai Beach Resort (☎ 3552 0100; www.nannai .com.br; Praia de Muro Alto; d US$275-330, bungalows US$392-556; P ✗ ✷) For an upscale choice, Nannai's French-Polynesian–style bungalows with private pools in gorgeous Atlantic rain-forest surroundings are the height of luxury. The restaurant at this romantic hotel is also recommended.

EATING

Famed for its seafood, Porto de Galinhas has several good eateries. The beach bars are a good choice for inexpensive, fresh crabs, and the locally made liqueurs are worth a try.

Beijupirá (☎ 3552 2354; Rua Beijupirá; mains US$6-10; ☽ noon-11pm) The most renowned of the local seafood restaurants, it is a pleasant location with a number of succulent dishes. Don't miss the *camarulu* – shrimp in sugarcane syrup with passion fruit sauce (US$7).

Peixe na Telha (☎ 3552 1323; Av Beira-Mar; mains US$6-10; ☽ 11am-10pm) Though not as well known as Beijupirá, Peixe na Telha has quality seafood dishes and a nice view.

Picanha Tio Dadá (☎ 3552 1319; Rua da Esperança 167; churrasco US$4; ☽ 11am-2pm) This is the place to go in Porto de Galinhas for an affordable barbeque lunch. Come prepared to eat, as you will be stuffed with steak.

GETTING THERE & AROUND

Eighteen buses a day travel to Porto de Galinhas (US$3, 1½ hours) from the intersection of Av Dantas Barreto and Rua do Peixoto (on the right-hand side of Dantas Barreto facing north) in Recife. Kombi vans and minibuses make the trip for US$6.

Minibuses and Kombi vans serve local destinations. A beach buggy to Praia de Maracaípe should cost around US$4.

Tamandaré

☎ 0xx81 / pop 2000

South of Porto de Galinhas, the best place to turn into the coast again before Maceió is Tamandaré, 10km from the main highway on a good road. It's a growing tourist destination, with calm waters and clear tide pools. **Pousada Recanto dos Corais** (☎ 3676 1444; Rua Hermes Samico; d US$20; ☒) is a good option near the main beach. It's busy on weekends, but during the week the beach is idyllic and you can see the 17th-century **Forte Santo Inácio**.

São José da Coroa Grande

The last beach town you reach before leaving Pernambuco and crossing into Alagoas is São José da Coroa Grande. It's 120km from Recife on coastal Hwy PE-060. This former fishing town now has many weekend homes and a bit of high-rise hotel development. Avoid it and continue your journey.

BEACHES NORTH OF OLINDA

You've got to get out of town for a fine, clean beach. Head north at least as far as **Rio Doce** (6km), past that to **Janga** beach (8km) or beyond to **Praia do Ó** (12km), **Praia do Pau Amarelo** (14km), **Praia da Conceição** (17km) and **Praia da Maria Farinha** (23km). The road goes along close to the beach, but don't be deterred by the ugly development beside it; the beaches are generally undisturbed except for beach bars and crowds on weekends. Enjoy crab dishes at the beach bars. There are local buses to these beaches from Praça do Carmo in Olinda about every 30 minutes during the day.

Itamaracá

☎ 0xx81 / pop 16,000

Only a little over 40km north of Olinda, the island of Itamaracá (separated from the mainland by a canal) is a pleasant and popular weekend beach scene. During the week it's considerably more calm. There is a regular bus service to the island, but getting to its many beaches takes time if you don't have a car.

SIGHTS

Itamaracá is really about one thing: beaches. The better beaches are north and south of **Pilar** and **Jaguaribe**, the most built-up and urbanized part of Itamaracá's coastline. For more-isolated beaches, hike 5km north along the coast to **Praia Lance dos Cações** and **Fortinho**. Immediately south of town is **Praia Baixa Verde**, and every 3km south are more beaches: **Praia Rio Ambo**, **Praia Forno de Cal**, **Praia de São Paulo** and finally **Praia de Vila Velha**.

Forte Orange (☎ 3544 1666; Estrada do Forte; ☒ 9am-4:30pm) was built on the south end of the island by the Dutch in 1631 and was reconstructed by the Portuguese in 1654. It served as a base in a series of battles against the Portuguese colonies in Recife and Olinda. It's an impressive citadel, with a nice view, right on the water.

Close to the fort, the IBAMA-run **Ecoparque Peixe-Boi** (☎ 3544 1056; Estrada do Forte Orange; ☒ 10am-4pm Tue-Sun) was established for studying the endangered *peixe-boi* (manatee or sea cow). There is a tank containing some live specimens, but keep your voice down or they'll dive down to the bottom where they're hard to see. They also customarily nap after lunch, and you're asked not to wake them.

Straight across from the fort is the small, pleasant island of **Coroa do Avião**, with natural reef pools and a few bars and *barracas*. Boat tours to the island (US$2) depart from the beach in front of Forte Orange.

Further south from town is **Vila Velha** (1526), the first port in the Northeast, and its church, **NS da Conceição** (1526), the second-oldest in Brazil. Take a Kombi van to get to these and other distant points from the town of Itamaracá.

SLEEPING & EATING

Casa da Praia (☎ 3544 1225; Estrada do Forte Orange 3525, Praia Forno da Cal; d US$13-24; ☒ ☒) A good budget option near the beach. Rooms are tidy but nondescript.

Orange Praia (☎ 3544 1885; Estrada do Forte Orange Km 5, Praia do Forte Orange; d US$50-65; ☒ ☒) A quality mid-range place with a beautiful view. Orange Praia comes recommended There's a tasty restaurant with a variety of dishes.

Peixada Forte Orange (☎ 3544 1220; Estrada do Forte Orange 3400; mains US$4-8) Not far from Casa da Praia, this is one of a number of good seafood restaurants in the area.

GETTING THERE & AWAY

There are 12 buses a day (US$4, one hour, 7am till midnight) from Itamaracá town to the center of Recife.

FERNANDO DE NORONHA

☎ 0xx81 / pop 2500

With its crystal-clear water, rich marine life and tropical landscapes, the Fernando de Noronha archipelago (Noronha) is one of the most stunning places in Brazil, if not the entire world. Brazilians consider Baía do Sancho, Baía dos Porcos and Praia do Leão to be three of the best beaches in the country. The main island, much of which is national park land, is sparsely populated and tourism has become the main source of income for locals.

Although Noronha used to be the domain of regulated package tours, it's now easier for independent travelers to visit. Except during the middle of summer, it is not even necessary to make hotel reservations. There are supposedly limits for the number of visitors on the islands, but if you are willing to pay, no one is going to shut you out. The rainy season is from February to July and the time zone in the islands is one hour ahead of Brazilian Standard Time. Bring everything you'll need for your stay (eg sunscreen, insect repellent, magazines) as prices are high due to the cost of transporting goods from the mainland.

As a guaranteed highlight of any trip to Brazil, Fernando de Noronha is worth the expense.

History

The archipelago was discovered by the Spanish adventurer and cartographer Juan de la Cosa, who had been Columbus' pilot in 1492. It first appeared on maps with the name Quaresma (Lent). A Portuguese aristocrat, Fernão de Noronha, was awarded the islands by his friend King Dom Manoel in 1504. He never set foot on the islands and forgot about them. They were taken back by the Crown years later.

The islands, with their strategic position between Europe and the New World, were occupied by the French and the Dutch, but in 1737 the Portuguese managed to reclaim Fernando de Noronha. They built 10 forts: all that remains today are the ruins of the fortresses of NS dos Remédios and São Pedro do Boldró, along with a few sunken shipwrecks.

Over the years, the islands have been used as a military base by the US (during WWII), a prison, a weather station, an air base and, in their present incarnation, a tourist destination.

There has been some misguided tampering with the island ecology. The teju, a black-and-white lizard, was introduced to eat the island rats that had come ashore with the Europeans in colonial days. Unfortunately, the teju prefers small birds and crabs to rats.

A struggle between developers and environmentalists over the future of the islands was resolved in 1988 when 70% of the archipelago was declared a national marine park in order to protect its natural treasures. Animal life includes 24 different species of marine bird, two species of endangered marine tortoise, sharks, stingrays, dolphins, whales and a vast number of fish species.

Orientation

The archipelago of Fernando de Noronha is located 145km from Atol das Rocas, 525km from Recife and 350km from Natal. There are 21 islands and these cover a total area of only 26 sq km. On the largest and only inhabited island, Ilha de Fernando de Noronha, the population is concentrated in the small villages of Vila dos Remédios, Vila do Trinta and the Floresta Velha and Floresta Nova neighborhoods. Morro do Pico, an extinct volcanic cone and the highest point on the island, is 321m above sea level – and more than 4300m above the ocean floor.

Information

INTERNET ACCESS

Cia. da Lua (☎ 3619 1631; Aeroporto e Bosque Flamboyant, Vila dos Remédios; per hr US$6; ⏱ 10am-10pm) This small gift shop has two high-speed connections. It's not cheap, but you're not going to do much better.

INTERNET RESOURCES

Official site (www.noronha.pe.gov.br/eng) Has every detail imaginable, in English, and is essential for planning an independent trip to the islands.

Tourism site (www.noronha.com.br/english) Has most of the basics, plus webcams, surf reports and good photos.

MEDICAL SERVICES

Hospital São Lucas (☎ 3619 1377; Bosque Flamboyant, Vila dos Remédios)

MONEY

The ATM at the airport accepts international cards, but it is a good idea to withdraw a fair amount of cash in the Natal or Recife airport prior to your trip (there is no need to worry about anyone stealing it on Noronha). Some of the fancier shops will exchange euros and dollars at a rate they could only get away with on an island.

Banco Real (Vila dos Remédios) The island's only bank; it does not change cash or traveler's checks.

POST

Post office (Vila dos Remédios) At the end of the park close to Terminal do Cachorro.

TELEPHONE

Telmar office (BR-363) Near the school.

TOURIST INFORMATION

Divisão de Turismo (☎ 3619 1352; Palácio São Miguel, Vila dos Remédios; ☼ 9am-noon & 2-6pm Mon-Fri) This is the official spot to get island information and also happens to have a really nice view.

Tamar Project (☎ 3619 1171; Alameda do Boldró) The visitor center at the Tamar office is also a good source of information, especially on wildlife issues.

TRAVEL AGENCIES

Your Way (☎ 3619 1796; www.yourway.com.br; Noronha Divers office, Vila dos Remédios) An indispensable contact on the island, this small agency is perfect for independent travelers of all budget levels who don't want to simply go to Noronha on a package tour. Adriana and Patricia will help you choose the accommodations and activities that suit you best (at no additional cost). As well as speaking flawless English, Adriana seems to have every phone number on the island memorized.

VISITORS TAX

The state government imposes a daily environment preservation tax on visitors to the

FERNANDO DE NORONHA

island. The first day costs US$10, four days US$38, a week US$60, two weeks US$115 and a month US$775. You can pay your tax by cash or credit card on arrival at the airport or ahead of time at www.noronha. pe.gov.br/eng. If you decide to stay longer than originally planned, you can pay the difference at the airport when you depart.

Sights

All of the 26 beaches are clean, beautiful and almost deserted. **Baía do Sancho**, **Baía dos Porcos** (named after the infamous Cuban Bay of Pigs) and **Praia do Leão** are all impossibly gorgeous. However, there is a lot of competition. The sandy beaches facing the mainland – **Cachorro** (at Vila dos Remédios), **Conceição**, **Boldró**, **Americano**, **Quixaba** and **Cacimba do Padre** are also good for surfing. **Baía do Sueste**, on the far side of the island, is the site of the Tamar station, where it's possible to swim with the turtles.

Inside the park boundaries, IBAMA allows bathing at certain beaches, but restricts access to others in the interest of protecting marine life. **Atalaia**, for example, only permits snorkelers with a guide and does not allow the use of sunscreen, which pollutes the shallow tide pools.

Baía dos Golfinhos (Dolphin Bay) is strictly off-limits to swimmers, but access is permitted to **Mirante dos Golfinhos**, a viewpoint where you can watch hundreds of dolphins cavorting in the water at approximately 5:30am every morning.

Activities

With 30m to 40m of underwater visibility and abundant marine life, diving and other water activities are the island's major attraction. There are 230 fish species, 15 coral varieties and five types of (harmless) shark. There are good things to do on land too, including hiking, horseback riding and Land Rover/buggy tours. Most of the trails require a guide, so it is best to check with Your Way agency (p512) about the regulations.

BOAT TOURS

There are a number of boat tours of the island, which are worth the price (US$10 to US$20) as they are the easiest way to see the spinner dolphins up close. The dolphins like to swim and perform acrobatics near the bow of the ships.

Naonda (☎ 3619 1307; www.barcanaonda.com.br) is a recommended boat company.

KAYAKING

Remos da Ilha (☎ 3619 1914; www.remosdailha.com.br; per person US$16) leaves the harbor twice a day (8am and 3:30pm), allowing you to kayak with friendly and knowledgeable Mauricio along the coast to Dois Irmãos rocks. It is a considerably more quiet and intimate way to take a boat tour and is an opportunity to interact closely with the dolphins. A small motorboat tails the kayaks at a distance, providing support (and food and drinks) in case you get tired. The sunset is also spectacular from the kayak.

SCUBA DIVING

Some of the best places to scuba dive, including Ilha Rata, Ilha de Fora (Ilha da Viuvinha), Enseada da Rasureta and Ponta da Sapata, are only accessible by boat. The three dive operators are:

Águas Claras (☎ 3619 1225; www.aguasclaras-fn.com.br; Av Boldró) The largest operation on the island, located past Tamar, and considered to have the most experienced staff.

Atlantis Divers (☎ 3619 1371; www.atlantisnoronha.com.br; Vila dos Remédios) Considered to have the best equipment.

Noronha Divers (☎ 3619 1112; Vila dos Remédios; www.noronhadivers.com) The most affordable and the only locally owned operator.

All the operators offer *batismo* (baptism) dives for first-timers (US$65), as well as guided dives for those who are certified.

SNORKELING

There are simply hundreds of good places to snorkel on the islands, from the tranquil tide pool of Atalaia to Sueste, where you can swim with marine turtles. Masks and flippers can be rented for US$3 at numerous stores and pousadas, although it is nice to snorkel at least once with a guide to discover the best spots. A popular activity is 'planasub', which is a tow device that lets you snorkel behind a motorboat and cover greater distances; try **Santuário** (☎ 3619 1247; Porto).

SURFING

Cacimba do Padre is the most famous surfing beach in Noronha. It hosts surf championships during the December to March season.

THE NORTHEAST

Waves can reach 5m in height. Most people bring their own boards but you can rent at **Bar do Jacaré** (Vila dos Remédios; per day US$7-10), next to Banco Real.

Tours

Organized tours sold by travel agencies in Recife usually include your airfare to and from Fernando de Noronha, lodging (sometimes with full board) and guided tours of the island by land and sea. Higher prices apply during the high season. Good options include **Andratur** (☎ 0xx81-465 8588; andratur@hotmail.com; Recife; 4-day/3-night package US$420) and **Manary Ecotours** (☎ 0xx84-219 2900; www.manary.com.br; Natal; 4-day/3-night package around US$400). Flying in from Natal is slightly cheaper.

Independent travelers can buy airline tickets directly from Varig/Nordeste or Trip, and should have little difficulty negotiating lower prices for lodging and board on the island.

Sleeping

There are more than 120 pousadas and *pensões* (pensions), and many of the islanders rent out *quartos* (rooms with shared bathroom) in their private homes. Accommodations are classified by a one-, two- and three-dolphin system, with the one-dolphin as the most simple and three as the most upscale. Prices are inflated, so generally expect less for your money than you would get on the mainland.

BUDGET

There are a number of family homes in Vila dos Remédios that rent rooms in the US$12 to US$20 range. **Golfinhos** (☎ 3619 1738) and **Solymar** (☎ 3619 1965) are two that are more popular but about the same quality as the numerous other options.

Alamoa (☎ 3619 1839; www.pousadaalamoa.hpg .com.br; Floresta Nova; d US$35-60; ⊠) Close to Vila dos Remédios, this small, attractive pousada is good value, with attentive service.

Barcelar (☎ 3619 1249; Major Costa, Vila do Trinta; d US$30-40; ⊠) This is another clean and friendly option, in the sedate Vila do Trinta area.

MID-RANGE

Beco de Noronha (☎ 3619 1285; www.becodenoronha .com.br; Floresta Nova; d US$87-107; ⊠) A small,

newer place decorated with local art. It has nice wood paneling and good light. Although it is not cheap, you will be happy with your choice to stay here.

Solar de Loronha (☎ 3619 1105; Floresta Velha; d US$92-115; ⊠) Another smaller place, Solar has a good view out toward the beach, as well as friendly service and clean rooms.

Mabuya (☎ 3619 1205; www.mabuya.com.br; Major Costa, Vila do Trinta; d US$42-50; ⊠) With nice grounds, tasty breakfast and cozy *quartos*, Mabuya is good value and popular with Brazilians and international visitors.

Pousada Tia Zéte (☎ 3619 1242; fax 3619 1459; Rua Nice Cordeiro 8, Floresta Velha; d US$40; ⊠) About 500m from Vila dos Remédios, this mustard-colored favorite has 12 comfortable rooms, hammocks and partially uses solar power.

TOP END

Pousada Maravilha (☎ 3619 0028; www.pousada maravilha.com.br; Sueste; d US$335-500; ⊠ ⊠) Although it doesn't exactly look exquisite from the front, Maravilha is the most luxurious place to stay on the island. The well-appointed bungalows will round out the perfect trip to Fernando de Noronha and are a good option for a honeymoon. The entire hotel, including the reception and restaurant (open to the public), has a spectacular view of Bahia do Sueste.

Pousada Zé Maria (☎ 3619 1258; www.pousadaze maria.com.br; Floresta Velha; US$140-200; ⊠ ⊠) With a close-up view of Morro do Pico, an attractive pool, good restaurant and spacious rooms, Zé Maria is good value for a top-end hotel on the island. The pousada also hosts Noronha's best New Year's Eve party.

Eating

Flamboyant (☎ 3619 1510; Bosque de Flamboyant, Vila dos Remédios; per kg US$6; ⊙ 11:30am-4pm & 6:30-11pm) This mid-range buffet (the only per-kilogram place in Noronha) is very popular with visitors and locals. It has well-prepared food and even the raw vegetables are safe to eat for gringos. It might not be considered to be all that special if it were on the mainland, but you'll really appreciate it here.

Trattoria di Morena (☎ 3619 1142; morena@ noronha.com.br; Floresta Velha; mains US$6-8; ⊙ noon-3pm & 7-10:30pm) Fine Italian dishes are served at the restaurant in the attractive Pousada da Morena. Have a glass of wine and try one of the seafood pastas.

Visual do Porto (☎ 3619 1129; BR-363, Vila do Porto; ⏱ noon-10pm Mon-Sat) As the name suggests, this place has a great view of the harbor; it also has a good wine selection and fish dishes.

Ekologicus (☎ 3619 1404; Estrada do Sueste; mains US$7; ⏱ noon-3pm & 7-10pm) A consistently good seafood restaurant near the airport, it has some delicious large fish platters for groups.

Restaurante do Biu (☎ 3619 1235; buffet US$3; ⏱ 11am-3pm & 6-10pm) This inexpensive self-service place has a huge variety of food and is a good place to stuff yourself after a long day of snorkeling. It is suggested that you get here close to when it opens or before 7pm – the buffet is rarely refreshed.

Café com Arte (☎ 3619 1200; Terminal do Cachorro; coffee US$1, sandwiches US$2; ⏱ 9:30am-8:30pm) Ultra-relaxing café, across from Palacio, with some small art pieces for sale, some made from recycled items used by the café.

Açaí Noronha (☎ 3619 1901; BR-363, Floresta Nova; açaís & sucos US$2-4) This café, across from the school, serves good *açaí* with close view of Morro do Pico; the store inside has artisan work with a Jamaican vibe and tables with checkerboards out front.

Entertainment

Most of the beaches outside of the park area have one bar/café. The bar on Praia da Conceicão is especially recommended for a drink at sunset.

Bar do Cachorro (Vila dos Remédios; ⏱ 5pm-late) The *forró* epicenter of Noronha, the famous Bar do Cachorro (Dog Bar), near Praia do Cachorro, has something almost every night of the week, but really gets packed Thursday through Sunday. If you don't know how to dance *forró* this is as good a place as any to learn. It is also a relaxing place to watch the sunset.

Pizza da Ilha (Vila dos Remédios; ⏱ 5pm-late) Starting at about 9pm, this bar/pizzeria, next to a church, showcases local and Pernambucano singer-songwriters and then plays everything from good reggae to bad techno. At a certain point in the evening, most people move on to Bar do Cachorro.

Sushi Bar (Vila do Porto; ⏱ 5pm-late) A more sophisticated nightspot, Sushi Bar has live music, with good food and cocktails.

Getting There & Away

Going to Fernando de Noronha, the view is considerably better on the left side of the plane; returning to the mainland it's better on the right, so make sure to reserve your seat. If you decide to stay longer in Noronha, as many people do, it is easiest to just go to the airport and deal with the change in person. To get to the airport, take the Sueste bus or taxi, which will cost less than US$5 from anywhere on the island.

Nordeste (☎ 3619 1144; airport) flies twice a day between Recife and Fernando de Noronha. The flight takes an hour and a round-trip ticket costs around US$280.

Trip (☎ 3619 1530; airport) flies once a day between Recife and Fernando de Noronha. It's cheaper, but it's a propeller plane. The flight takes 50 minutes and a round-trip ticket costs around US$265. Trip also flies twice a day to and from Natal for around US$230 round-trip.

Getting Around

BUS

The easiest way to get around town is by bus. There are two buses running through Vila dos Remédios: one to Porto (the harbor) and one to Baía do Sueste (which also stops at the airport). They make their circuit every 15 to 30 minutes and both cost US$1. You will see small bus-stop signs along the road and can usually flag them down en route.

TAXI

The taxi point is near the post office in Vila dos Remédios. All taxis on the island are buggies and they can also be found along the roads and at some of the major beaches.

LOCAL TRANSPORTATION

Buggies, cars, small motorcycles and bicycles are available from several operators, including the recommended **Mulungu** (☎ 3619 1755), where staff speak English and deliver the vehicle. The average cost of buggies and cars is US$70 per day with a driver. Motorcycles are US$30 a day and are a good idea if you want to see the dolphins arriving at Baía dos Golfinhos at 5:30am. Bicycles are US$3 to US$5 a day. Boats are available at Vila Porto de Santo Antônio, near the point. Hitching is possible.

THE NORTHEAST

INLAND

CARUARU

☎ 0xx81 / pop 300,000

Modern and without architectural appeal, this inland city, about 138km southwest of Recife, contains unexpected cultural riches. Known as the capital of *forró*, Caruaru hosts the largest *forró* festival in the country – 30 straight days of couples swaying to the accordion and triangle. It is a huge market town and is also South America's center for ceramic-figurine art, famous for brightly painted little people captured in activities such as dancing and chasing chickens.

Sights

MARKETS

Caruaru's open market, **Feira Livre** (Open Market; ☯ 9am-5pm Wed & Sat), is the largest in the Northeast and has become a popular tourist attraction. Alongside pots, leather bags and straw baskets are representations of strange beasts and mythical monsters, and the colorful figurines. To see the artists at work, visit Alto de Moura (p516). If you want to buy some figurines, wait until you see what is offered in Alto de Moura before buying at the fair. Leather goods are sold here, at some of the best prices in Brazil.

In addition, you can hear singers and poets perform *literatura de cordel* (string literature), poetry by and for the people, sold in little brochures that hang from the market stands by string.

In a separate section of the main market, there's the *feira do troca-troca* (barter fair), where junk and treasure are traded.

Feira de Artesanato (Parque 18 de Maio; ☯ 9am-5pm Mon-Sun) is the handicraft fair, but has a bit of everything.

Feira da Sulanca (Parque 18 de Maio; ☯ 9am-5pm Mon) is the textile market that also boasts the title of largest in the Northeast.

MUSEUMS

Museu do Forró (☎ 3721 0012; Praça José de Vasconcelos; ☯ 8am-5pm Tue-Sat, 9am-1pm Sun) holds every bit of memorabilia on Luis Gonzaga, the father of *forró* music, that it could get its hands on. There is a bonus side room on the singer Elba Ramalho, which includes her *Playboy* shots.

Museu do Barro (☎ 3721 0012; Praça José de Vasconcelos; ☯ 8am-5pm Tue-Sat, 9am-1pm Sun), upstairs from Museu do Forró, displaying nearly 70 original pieces by Mestre Vitalino, and numerous works of other accomplished local potters. This is a better option than visiting Vitalino's house in Alto de Moura.

Museu Casa do Mestre Vitalino (Alto de Moura; ☯ 8am-noon & 2-6pm Mon-Fri, 8am-noon Sun), 6km west of Caruaru, is housed in the simple home of the master, and contains his tools and personal effects.

FORRÓ

During WWII, the officers' clubs at the American military bases in Pernambuco would have balls open to the general public under the title 'For All'. The music was provided by local bands that played the accordion, triangle and a hand-held African drum, the *zabumba*. The rhythm was a fast-paced, two-by-four dance beat originally called *baião*. Couples danced to songs with simple lyrics speaking of the hard life of the countryside, the trials and tribulations of love and the beauty of dance. 'For All' became *forró* (fo-hoh) in Portuguese and the name became synonymous not only with the events, but with the spirit, the dance and the music.

The first icon of *forró* was the late Luiz Gonzaga (1912–89). Gonzaga was responsible for taking the sound of Pernambuco to the rest of the country, later becoming the musical influence of some internationally renowned Brazilian musicians. Despite Gonzaga's personal popularity, *forró* continued to be looked down upon by São Paulo, Rio de Janeiro and other southern cities as a backwoods Northeastern music.

During the 1990s, after the international success of lambada and inspired by the country bands of São Paulo, *forró* musicians modernized their sound. They added electric guitars, keyboards and drum sets. The music and the dance became a national craze, with *forró* events throughout Brazil. It filled a void for an upbeat music that is easily danced with a partner – it's a simple two steps to the left and two steps to the right. The music is now spreading across the world, with CDs for sale in Tokyo and live *forró* bands in New York City.

ALTO DE MOURA

The home town of Mestre Vitalino is a small **community of potters** that still specializes in producing *figurinhas* (figurines). Many of the potters are descendants of Mestre Vitalino himself. Other noted artists are Zé Caboclo, Manuel Eudocio and Cunhado de Zé Caboclo.

Catch a taxi (US$2 to US$3) or bus (which leave from Praça Porto, in the center of town) to here, then wander the streets and browse through the dozens of workshops and galleries. If you want to purchase figurines, you're better off buying them here than in Caruaru.

Sleeping & Eating

Caruaru is a long day trip from Recife, but there's no real need to stay here overnight. There are a lot of places serving regional food at good prices.

Vila Rica (☎ 3722 9666; Rua Dalvino Pedrosa 160; d US$20-30) If you do decide to stay, this is a good budget place, with clean and basic *apartamentos* (rooms with private bathroom) and a restaurant.

Do Korôca (☎ 3722 8207; Rua Floriano Peixoto 160) For excellent regional cuisine in a tasteful setting, Do Korôca is a favorite.

Getting There & Around

Caruaru is linked by shuttle buses from the TIP in Recife every 30 minutes (US$5, two hours). There is a daily bus service (US$2, one hour) from Caruaru to Fazenda Nova. The **bus station** (☎ 3721 3869; Km 68 Hwy BR-104) is 3km from the center, from which it's very easy to get a taxi, Kombi van or local bus into town.

FAZENDA NOVA & NOVA JERUSALÉM

☎ 0xx81 / pop 4000

The small town of Fazenda Nova, 50km northwest of Caruaru, is famous for its theater-city reconstruction of Jerusalem, known as Nova Jerusalém. Surrounded by a 3m-high wall with seven gateways, 70 towers and 12 granite stages, the reconstruction occupies an area equivalent to one-third of the walled city of Jerusalem as it stood in the time of Jesus.

The time to visit is during Semana Santa (Holy Week, which is the week before Easter), when several hundred of the inhabitants of Fazenda Nova and imported *novela* (soap opera) stars from Rio perform the Paixão de Cristo (Passion of Christ play).

Sleeping & Eating

Pousada da Paixão (☎ 3732 1602; www.pousadadapaixao.com.br; Teatro de Nova Jerusalém; d US$25; 🔀 💷) If you do make it out here, you may as well stay at this Passion Play–themed pousada and soak it all in. This is where the cast stays during Semana Santa. The restaurant is open to the public, so at least stop in.

Grande Hotel (☎ 3732 1137; Av Poeta Carlos Pena Filho; d US$15) Your local budget choice. During Semana Santa you'll have to defer to the actors and stay here.

Getting There & Away

During Semana Santa, there are frequent bus services direct from Recife, and travel agencies (see p499) sell package tours to see the spectacle. During the rest of the year, there are daily bus connections between Fazenda Nova and Caruaru.

GARANHUNS

☎ 0xx81 / pop 110,000

Garanhuns, situated 109km southwest of Caruaru and 229km southwest of Recife, is popular as a holiday resort because of its relatively high altitude (842m). It's not exactly the 'Suiça Pernambucana' (Switzerland of Pernambuco) that it is touted as in the tourist brochures, but it does have pleasant parks and gardens and cool air – all of which are a respite from the oppressive heat present in the interior of the state.

Sleeping & Eating

Fazenda Sambaíba (☎ 9988 1233; PE-218, Brejão; d US$20-40) Stay in one of the basic double *chalés* (chalets) at this former ranch and enjoy the Pernambucano countryside. You can also hike and arrange horseback riding from here.

Hotel Permanente (☎ /fax 3762 9080; Av Santo Antônio 179; s/d US$18/22) An affordable, clean option for those on a tighter budget.

Chez Pascal (☎ 3761 2643; Av Rui Barbosa 891; mains US$6-12; ☺ 6-11:30pm) Fondue lovers prepared to pay a bit extra should visit this French restaurant, which has a variety of dishes.

THE NORTHEAST

Buchada do Gago (☎ 3761 3894; Rua Mariano 1, Vila do Quartel; mains US$3-6; ⏱ 11am-7pm) The local food specialty is called *buchada de bode* (goat stomach). It's a classic Northeastern dish and not for the faint of heart, but if you want to delve into this aspect of local culture, Gago is the place to do it.

Getting There & Away

The **bus station** (☎ 3761 1554; Av Caruaru, Heliópolis) is 3km from town. There are taxis and local buses from there. There are several bus departures a day to Recife (US$6, 3½ hours) and eight buses daily from Recife to Garanhuns (US$6, 3½ hours, 7am till 9pm).

Paraíba & Rio Grande do Norte

HIGHLIGHTS

- Cruising down the enormous mountains of sand at **Genipabu** (p535) in a dune buggy
- Letting it all hang out at Tambaba's famous **nudist beach** (p526)
- Walking among **dino-saur footprints** (p527) at Sousa
- Taking to the streets for **Carnatal** (p531), Natal's lively out-of-season Carnaval
- Chasing bliss on **Praia da Pipa** (p533) and other idyllic beaches around Tibaú do Sul

Genipabu ★
★ Natal
Praia da Pipa ★
★ Sousa
Tambaba ★

THE NORTHEAST

- POPULATION: 6.4 MILLION
- AREA: 109,892 SQ KM

Outside of Carnatal, Natal's famous out-of-season Carnaval, and the adrenaline-pumping dune-buggy rides offered up and down the coast, you will probably never raise your heart rate in Paraíba or Rio Grande do Norte. One thing that these two states have in common is that they are consummately chill. If you have come to Brazil to unwind, this is the place for you.

This northeastern tip of Brazil is made up of sand, more sand, palm trees, some beach towns and a few relaxed, small cities. Natal, the capital of Rio Grande do Norte, and João Pessoa, the capital of Paraíba, are worth visiting for some decent urban beaches and for dealing with travel logistics, but these states are best experienced out along the coast. It is a good place to explore villages and uninhabited beaches and lose contact with the modern world for a few days, weeks or longer.

Rio Grande do Norte receives many more visitors than Paraíba, and Natal has swelled into a bit of a transportation hub. The large sand dunes and cliff-backed shoreline of Rio Grande do Norte make it particularly attractive. There are well-known beaches south of Natal, around Tibaú do Sul. The most popular is Praia da Pipa, the once bohemian beach utopia that is now becoming a chic destination. North of Natal are smaller and less famous beaches that are also staggeringly beautiful. There are excellent dunes within the city limits of Natal, but it is Genipabu to the north that is known for having some of the largest and best dunes in the country.

Paraíba has its attractions, too. João Pessoa provides the opportunity to experience a Northeastern state capital that has not been transformed by tourism. Crime, prostitution and tourism hustlers are almost nonexistent here and the city beaches are remarkably clean. Outside of the capital there are some fantastically relaxed spots, including the famous nudist beach Praia de Tambaba.

History

This area of Brazil was a hotly contested colonial property, with both the French and Dutch vying for control of the region against the Portuguese. The French had a decent foothold in Rio Grande do Norte until the Portuguese sent an armada from Paraíba to kick them out in 1597. Natal was lost again to the Dutch in 1633, but quickly retaken by the Portuguese, who were firmly established in neighboring Paraíba.

The states of Paraíba and Rio Grande do Norte languished in obscurity until the early 20th century. Paraíba made a name for itself as the home state of João Pessoa, who allied himself with Getúlio Vargas in 1929 in a bid for the vice-presidency. Judging by the sheer number of João Pessoa tributes in the state, it seems that not much has happened since.

In 1935 rioting in Natal led to the declaration of a short-lived communist government in Rio Grande do Norte. The communist movement was suppressed and Rio Grande do Norte gained in importance due to its strategic location facing Nazi-occupied Africa. The US established Allied military bases to attack Africa and protect the Americas. The injection of military money spurred significant development in the region. Today, Paraíba and Rio Grande do Norte only war for tourist dollars.

Climate

Although this area is not any hotter than neighboring states, Rio Grande do Norte in particular is really dry and the sun can be very strong in the almost-always clear skies. Temperatures in both states can top 40°C (104°F) at the height of summer. Although the weather is nice year-round, some find it the most pleasant in the slightly cooler months of June though August.

Getting There & Away
AIR
Natal has direct and indirect flights from every major Brazilian city, an increasing number of European charter flights and, once in a while, an American charter flight. João Pessoa's airport receives stopover flights on their way to Natal and Recife, as well as a few direct flights.

BUS
Natal has buses from João Pessoa, Recife, Fortaleza and other Northeastern cities, while João Pessoa has a large bus station with frequent buses to Recife and many connections to southern destinations in Brazil.

Getting Around
The bus network is good for travel between larger towns and more popular beach spots. For anything more remote you should either get a group together to hire a 4WD with a driver or hire a buggy and stick to the coastline.

PARAÍBA

Sandwiched between Pernambuco and Rio Grande do Norte, the small, sunny state of Paraíba contains the easternmost point of the continent, Ponta do Seixas, where you are considerably closer to Senegal than you are to southern Brazil. The coast is this small state's most important economic region, fueled by the farming of sugarcane and pineapples, and also aided by a bit of tourism. The interior is severely affected by drought, and many of those Paraíbanos who haven't already left it live in poverty. You would never know this along the coast, which is tranquil and reasonably well developed.

PARAÍBA & RIO GRANDE DO NORTE

JOÃO PESSOA

☎ 0xx83 / pop 600,000

The coastal city of João Pessoa is the capital of Paraíba and is the third-oldest city in Brazil. It claims to have more trees than any other capital city, including an Atlantic rain forest preserve, and has a reputation for being friendly and safe (some would say boring). Tourism has been slow to develop here, but the city is not without its attractions and is an increasingly popular destination for Brazilian families. The city center has a few interesting churches and Praia de Tambaú is particularly clean and relaxed for an urban beach.

History

Founded in 1585, the city was originally known as Vila de Felipéia de NS das Neves. It was later renamed for João Pessoa, the governor of Paraíba who formed an alliance with Getúlio Vargas to run for the presidency of Brazil in 1929. When courted by opposing political parties, João Pessoa uttered a pithy 'nego' ('I refuse'), which is now given prominence in all Brazilian history books and is emblazoned in bold letters on the state flag of Paraíba.

João Pessoa's aspirations to the vice-presidency were short-lived. In July 1930 he was assassinated, an event that sparked a revolutionary backlash that swept Getúlio Vargas to power (along with plenty of help from the military) later that year.

Orientation

The bus station is on the western edge of the city. The main urban district, known as Praça, is further east, and close by is Parque Solon de Lucena, a park containing a large lake, which locals simply call Lagoa, circled by trees. Praia de Tambaú, 7km from the center, is the heart of João Pessoa's tourism industry and contains the majority of its hotels and pousadas (guesthouses).

Information

INTERNET ACCESS

Gameleira Internet (Map p524; ☎ 247 8642; Av João Maurício 157, Tambaú; per hr US$2; ⏱ 8am-9pm) Owner David, from San Diego, is also a good source of unofficial tourist information.

JOÃO PESSOA

0 — 400 m
0 — 0.2 miles

INFORMATION	
Banco do Brasil	1 B3
Bradesco ATM	2 B2
Câmbio Turismo	3 B2
Post Office	4 A2
Telpa (Main Telephone Office)	5 B2

SIGHTS & ACTIVITIES	(p523)
Igreja São Francisco	6 C1

SLEEPING	(p524)
Hotel Aurora	7 B3

EATING	(pp524–5)
Cassino da Lagoa	8 C3

SHOPPING	(p525)
Casa do Artesão Paraibano	9 A2

TRANSPORT	(p525)
Buses to Tambaú	10 C2

INTERNET RESOURCES
City tourism board (www.joaopessoa.pb.gov.br)
State tourism board (www.pbtur.pb.gov.br)

MEDICAL SERVICES
Samaritano (☎ 218 2100) Private medical facility.

MONEY
Banco do Brasil Praça (Map p522; Praça João Pessoa; 🕑 10am-4pm Mon-Fri); Tambaú (Map p524; Centro Turístico, Av Almirante Tamandaré 100; 🕑 10am-4pm Mon-Fri)
Bradesco (Map p524; Rua Duque de Caxias, Praça) ATM.
Câmbio Turismo Praça (Map p522; Rua Visconde de Pelotas 54, Praça); Tambaú (Shopping Tambaú, Tambaú) Also changes cash and traveler's checks.

POST
Main post office (Map p522; Av Guedes Pereira)

TELEPHONE
Telpa (main telephone office; Map p522; Rua Visconde de Pelotas 259)

TOURIST INFORMATION
PBTUR (Map p524; ☎ 226 7078; Centro Turístico, Av Almirante Tamandaré 100, Tambaú; 🕑 8am-7pm) This state tourism office is a good source of maps and leaflets. English is spoken here. PBTUR also operates the English-speaking tourist telephone hotline **Disque Turismo** (☎ 1516).
Tourist information stands airport (🕑 10am-4pm); bus station (🕑 8am-6pm)

TRAVEL AGENCIES
Cliotur (Map p524; ☎ /fax 247 4460; www.cliotur .com.br; shop 4, Av Almirante Tamandaré 310, Tambaú; 🕑 8am-6pm) This very organized agency, with a comprehensive website, also offers a range of tours in and around the city, from sedate city tours to hiking and adventure trips.
Orlando Berton (☎ 9984 8010; orlandopessoa@ hotmail.com) Known as the pousada's public relations officer, Orlando speaks English and is the most professional and knowledgeable guide you will encounter in João Pessoa.
Pousada do Caju (Map p524; ☎ 247 8231; www .pousadadocaju.com.br; Rua Helena Meira Lima 269, Tambaú) Well-advertised and also runs a number of local and regional excursions.

Sights & Activities
IGREJA SÃO FRANCISCO
The **Igreja São Francisco** (Map p522; ☎ 218 4505; Praça São Francisco; 🕑 9am-noon & 2-5pm), the prin-

cipal tourist attraction in the center, is considered to be one of Brazil's finest churches. Construction was interrupted by successive battles with the Dutch and French, resulting in a beautiful but architecturally confused complex that was built over three centuries. The facade, church towers and monastery (of Santo Antônio) display a hodgepodge of styles. Portuguese-tile walls lead up to the church's carved jacaranda doors. The complex also contains a cultural center and an exhibition hall with temporary art exhibits.

PRAIA DE TAMBAÚ
Praia de Tambaú (Map p524), 7km directly east of the center of Natal, is rather built-up, but remains pleasant. There are bars, restaurants, coconut palms and fig trees along Av João Maurício (north) and Av Almirante Tamandaré (south). Immediately north of Tambaú there are good urban beaches: **Manaíra**, **Praia do Bessa**, **Praia do Macaco** (a surfing beach) and **Praia do Poço**.

Twenty five kilometers north of Tambaú, **Praia Cabedelo** has a couple of pousadas, restaurants and bars.

PONTA DO SEIXAS
Ponta do Seixas, the easternmost tip of the Americas, has a restaurant, camping ground and lighthouse at the point. Clear water and coral make this a good spot for diving.

Connecting Tambaú to Ponta do Seixas, **Praia Cabo Branco** and **Praia da Penha** are beautiful stretches of sand, surf, palm groves and creeks.

ILHA DE AREIA VERMELHA
Ilha de Areia Vermelha is an island of red sand that emerges off the coast of João Pessoa at low tide. In summer dozens of boats park around the island and the party lasts until the tide comes in. You can catch a boat out there from Praia da Camboinhas (13km north of Tambaú) for around US$3.

Festivals & Events
Micaroa, João Pessoa's out-of-season Carnaval, takes place in January, but preparations for it begin as early as September. It features Bahia-style *trios elétricos* (an 18-wheel sound truck that plays Carnaval music) and is a chance for this tame town to cut loose.

THE NORTHEAST

TAMBAÚ

0	200 m
0	0.1 miles

Praia do Bessa 3km;
Praia do Macaco 9km;
Praia do Pocó 10.5km;
Praia Cabedelo (25km)

Praia de Manaíra

Praia de Tambaú

Ponta do Seixas 7km;

SLEEPING	(p524)
Aruanda Praia	4 A2
Pousada do Caju	5 A2
Rhema	6 A2
Tropical Hotel Tambaú	7 B1

EATING	(pp524–5)
Peixada do Duda	8 A1
Toca do Caju	(see 5)

DRINKING	(p525)
Bahamas Chopp	9 A1
Choperia Biergarten	10 A1
Miralha	11 A3

INFORMATION	
Cliotur	1 A2
Gameleira Internet	2 A1
PBTUR	3 A1

SHOPPING	(p525)
Craft Market	12 A1

João Pessoa's **Paixão do Cristo** (Passion of Christ play) is second in size and fame only to the spectacle at Nova Jerusalém (p517). It is held outdoors on the Praça Pedro Américo and recruits some well-known actors.

Sleeping

João Pessoa's main attraction is Praia de Tambaú, and that's where many of the hotels are. Although there are cheaper hotels in the center, it's worth spending a bit extra to stay near the beach.

BUDGET

CCB-PB-01 (☎ 251 1371; Praia da Ponta do Seixas; per person US$7) If you fancy camping at the easternmost tip of continental Brazil, the Camping Club of Brazil runs an excellent campground on the beach. To get here, take one of the infrequent (about every hour) Penha buses from the local bus station or catch a cab for US$5. The grounds fill up in summer, so it's advisable to book in advance.

Hotel Aurora (Map p522; ☎ 2401 3238; Praça João Pessoa 51; s/d US$6/12) The Aurora has adequate

quartos (rooms with shared bathroom) and is a good place to crash for the night if you have a long layover between interstate buses, or if you are some sort of masochist who'd rather stay in the city center than the considerably more pleasant beach neighborhoods.

Rhema (Map p524; ☎ 247 1900; Av Antônio Lira 127, Tambaú; s/d US$15/22; ☒) This clean, modern beach option is quiet and reasonably priced.

MID-RANGE

Lagoa Park Hotel (☎ 241 1414; Parque Solon de Lucena 19; d without/with views US$40/45; ☒ ☒) Near the lake, this hotel has modern, well-appointed rooms. It has a good self-service restaurant and gives discounts during the low season.

Pousada do Caju (Map p524; ☎ 247 8231; www .pousadadocaju.com.br; Rua Helena Meira Lima 269, Tambaú; dm/s/d/tr US$12/17/25/30; ☒ ☐ ☒) This sprawling guesthouse is two blocks from the beach and contains two swimming pools, a large games area and numerous giant *caju* (cashew) and dolphin sculptures (among other random accoutrements). It has a good restaurant, complete breakfast and a full range of services to make sure that you enjoy João Pessoa.

Aruanda Praia (Map p524; ☎ 226 1864; aruanda@ hotmail.com; Av Almirante Tamandaré 440, Tambaú; s/d US$25/35; ☒) Aruanda is a small, comfortable place, which is perfect if you are looking for something sedate.

Pousada dos Estrangeiros (☎ 226 4667; Rua Alberto Falcão 67, Miramar; s/d US$20/25; ☒) This recommended pousada is close to the beach but also gives you access to the city. It is clean, friendly and relaxing.

TOP END

Tropical Hotel Tambaú (Map p524; ☎ 218 1919; www.tropicalhotel.com.br; Av Almirante Tamandaré 229, Tambaú; d US$60-96; ☒ ☒ ☒ ☐ ☒) Although the exterior is a touch shabby these days, the Tropical must have looked very space age when it was built in 1971. It is still a landmark, with a fantastic view and is quite affordable for an upmarket hotel.

Eating

Rua Coração de Jesus, one block from the beach and close to Tropical Hotel Tambaú, is a compact restaurant strip with a variety of choices.

Museu Villa-Lobos (p127), Botafogo, Rio de Janeiro

Bruno Giorgi's *Os Candangos*, Praça dos Trés Poderes (p357), Brasília

Museu do Arte Contemporânea (p141), Niterói, Rio de Janeiro

GUY MOBERLY

Colonial architecture, Salvador (p412), Bahia

JOHN MAIER JR

Ilha Fiscal (p141), Baía de Guanabara, Rio de Janeiro

Olinda (p504), Pernambuco
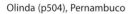

PAUL B

Cassino da Lagoa (Map p522; ☎ 221 4275; Parque Solon de Lucena s/n; buffet per kg US$6.50; ☒ 11am-9pm Mon-Fri, 11am-6pm Sun) Positioned beside the lake, this restaurant has an open patio and a tranquil atmosphere. The food isn't extra-ordinary, but it's good and the view is great. Seafood and chicken dishes are recommended.

Mangai (Map p524; ☎ 226 1615; Av General Édson Ramalho 696, Tambaú; set-price buffet US$5; ☒ 6am-10pm Tue-Sun) The buffet at this favorite restaurant gives you the chance to sample a variety of regional food. It doesn't serve alcohol.

Peixada do Duda (Map p524; ☎ 247 8212; Rua Coração de Jesus 147, Tambaú; mains US$6-8; ☒ 11am-midnight Mon-Sat, 11am-5pm Sun) This basic place has superb fish dishes. Try the excellent *peixe frita al molho de camarão* (fried fish in shrimp sauce) for US$7.

Toca do Caju (Map p524; ☎ 247 3002; Av NS dos Navegantes 750, Tambaú; mains US$4-6; ☒ 11am-9pm) Part of the Pousada do Caju empire, this restaurant has a daily *rodízio* (smorgasbord) and a good *feijoada* (bean-and-meat stew) on Saturday. Closed Monday during the low season.

Entertainment

Nightlife in Tambaú centers on the beachfront along Av João Maurício and Av Olinda, which run off the beachfront near the Tropical Hotel Tambaú. For details of current events, ask at the tourist office or check Caderna 2 in the daily newspaper *Correio da Paraíba*.

Choperia Biergarten (Map p524; ☎ 226 9200; Rua Coração de Jesus 138, Tambaú; ☒ 6pm-late Tue-Sat) Just off the beach, this is the closest thing you'll find to a real beer garden in these parts. Serving light and dark beers, the Biergarten is a good place to get your evening going.

Bahamas Chopp (Map p524; ☎ 226 3767; Av João Maurício, Tambaú; ☒ 11am-late) Next to the pier, this is another popular meeting and beer-drinking place, which has live music on weekends.

Miralha (Map p524; ☎ 226 1299; Av Pres Epitácio Pessoa 4468, Tambaú; ☒ 8pm-late) Miralha is a restaurant during the day, but on Monday night it has authentic *pé de serra* (foot of the hills) *forró* (popular music of the Northeast). It is quite a spectacle and worth joining in if you are feeling brave.

Shopping

Tambaú's **craft market** (Rua Carneiro) has ceramic, wicker, straw and leather goods for sale. On weekends, craft stalls set up in front of Tropical Hotel Tambaú. In the city center, **Casa do Artesanato Paraibano** (Rua Maciel Pinheiro 670) also has crafts for sale.

Getting There & Away

AIR

Presidente Castro Pinto Airport (☎ 232 1200) is 11km west of the city center. Flights operate to Rio, São Paulo and the major cities of the Northeast and the Amazon.

Contact details for Brazilian airlines:
TAM (☎ 232 2002; airport)
Varig (☎ 232 1515; Av Pres Epitácio Pessoa 1251)
VASP (☎ 232 1757; Rua Corálio Soares de Oliveira 497)

BUS

The **bus station** (Map p522; ☎ 221 9611; Av Francisco Londres) is located west of the city center. There are frequent bus services to Fortaleza (US$23, 10 hours, 699km, two daily), Natal (US$7, 2½ hours, 180km, every hour from 5:30am to 7:30pm), Recife (US$4, two hours, 125km, every 30 minutes from 5am to 7pm), Salvador (US$24, nine hours, 956km, 7:30pm) and Sousa (US$19, six hours, 436km, 11 daily).

Getting Around

The local buses stop directly in front of the main bus station. Walk straight ahead as you leave the bus station and pass through the many stalls. You'll find three parallel platforms. Buses to Tambaú leave from the first platform you reach, and buses to Jacumã leave from the third platform. Bus Nos 510 and 511 run frequently to Tambaú (US$0.50, 25 minutes). If you catch them from the lake they will loop back through the city, pass the bus station and continue to Tambaú. Bus No 507 runs to Cabo Branco. Most local buses pass the lake.

A taxi to the airport from Tambaú costs around US$10; from the bus station to Tambaú costs around US$7.

SOUTH OF JOÃO PESSOA
Jacumã

☎ 0xx83 / pop 2000

Jacumã has a long, thin beach featuring colored sandbars, natural pools and mineral springs by day, and *forró* bars by night.

There are beautiful beaches nearby, such as **Praia do Amor** to the north, and **Praia dos Coqueirinhos**, the increasingly popular **Praia da Tabatinga** and **Praia de Tambaba** (right) to the south. If you are looking for a simple, unpolished fishing village with a relatively mellow tourism scene, this is it. There are no banks here.

SLEEPING & EATING

Pousada das Conchas (☎ 290 1303; Tabatinga; s/d US$25/32; ❑ ❑) On the beach at Tabatinga, 5km south of Jacumã, this is a newer place built in a rustic style, and all *apartamentos* (rooms with private bathroom) have verandas and hammocks. There's also a pool, craft shop and ice-creamery.

Pousada do Inglês (☎ 290 1168; pousadadoingles@uol.com.br; s/d US$20/28; ❑ ❑) Right next to the beach, in the center of Jacumã, Pousada do Inglês has well-appointed rooms, mini-golf and a nice pool area.

Pousada das Flores (☎ 9309 0414; r per person US$10) South of Jacumã, on Praia de Carapibus, Pousada das Flores has a lot of character. Round bungalows are scattered through a gorgeous garden and guests can use the kitchen. It is a long, hot, 2km walk out of town, so catch the Jacumã PB008 bus from João Pessoa and ask to be let off at Carapibus.

Hotel Viking (☎ 290 1015; www.hotelviking.com.br; Rua Niterói, Jacumã; s/d US$25/35; ❑ ❑) This Swedish-owned hotel is perched on a hill overlooking town, easily identifiable by the Viking ship on its water tower. The rooms are comfortable and decorated, and the pool area has theme-park touches. The adjoining restaurant has live music in summer. It's a quick walk from the final bus stop.

Peixada de Jacumã (☎ 290 1397; Av Beira Mar, Jacumã; mains US$3-6; ◷ 11am-10pm) In the center of town, this is always a good choice for fish and other seafood dishes.

Zeka's (☎ 290 1185; Praia de Carapibus; mains US$3-6; ◷ 11am-10pm) Pousada Zeka's has a quality restaurant with a great view. The traditional meat and bean soups are very tasty.

GETTING THERE & AWAY

Traveling north from Pernambuco on Hwy BR-101, ask to be dropped off at the Conde/Jacumã turnoff and catch a local bus from there. In João Pessoa, 'Jacumã' buses (US$1, one hour and 10 minutes, hourly until 9:10pm) leave from the third platform in front of the long-distance bus station. The last bus back to João Pessoa leaves at 10:20pm from the main road in Jacumã's center.

Praia de Tambaba
☎ 0xx83
About 10km south of Jacumã is Praia de Tambaba, the only official nudist beach in the Northeast. The beach, considered to be among the top 10 in Brazil, is divided into two parts: one section is reserved exclusively for nudists, and the other is clothing-optional. To prevent problems, the nude section has public relations officers who explain the rules to bathers. Men are not allowed in the nude section unless accompanied by a woman. Interestingly, lesbian couples are permitted but gay male couples are not (unless accompanied by women).

Dom Quinzote (☎ 290 1185; Tambaba; d US$30), a rustic, wooden pousada, is the only lodging in the nudist zone. It may well be Brazil's only nudist hotel, although the staff wear clothes.

The easiest way to get to Tambaba is by taxi or Kombi van from Jacumã, although it is possible to walk.

Praia Pitimbu
Praia Pitimbu, 75km south of João Pessoa, has a long, broad beach, a coconut grove, some thatched-roof houses and a couple of bars frequented by sugarcane farmers, fishermen and sailmakers for *jangadas* (the beautiful, traditional sailing boats of the Northeast). There are no hotels, but if you look friendly and bring a hammock, someone will put you up for a nominal fee. You can also arrange some quality snorkeling trips with local boats.

Traveling north on Hwy BR-101 from Pernambuco state into Paraíba state, there's a turnoff just after the border that leads 35km down to Praia Pitimbu.

BAÍA DA TRAIÇÃO
☎ 0xx83 / pop 3500
Despite its peaceful, reef-sheltered waters, coconut palms and gentle breezes, Baía da Traição has a bloody past. In 1501 the first Portuguese exploratory expedition was

slaughtered here by the Tabajara Indians. In 1625 the Portuguese had it out with the Dutch. They claimed victory and left some rusty cannons and the ruins of a fortress in their wake.

This fishing village, 85km north of João Pessoa, is more pleasant than the built-up beaches at Cabedelo and Lucena further south. It is also a place where you can visit the nearby Potiguara indigenous reservation (ask for details at one of the pousadas).

Pousada Ponto do Sol Nascente (☎ 296 1050; Rua Dom Pedro 537; d US$18) is a friendly, comfortable place. Ask for a room upstairs to catch the sea breeze. It also serves local dishes.

Hotel Pousada Tropical (☎ 296 1223; Rua Osvaldo Trigueiro; d US$35) is a more upmarket choice, with clean *apartamentos*. It also has a decent self-serve restaurant and convenience store.

There's a turnoff to the beach from Hwy BR-101 at Mamanguape. There are eight buses daily from João Pessoa's bus station (US$2.50, two hours, 7am till 9pm).

SOUSA

☎ 0xx83 / pop 46,000

Sousa, 436km west of João Pessoa, is known for an offbeat tourist attraction: **dinosaur footprints**. The tracks were discovered in 1920 by a geologist who was researching drought – a major preoccupation in the *sertão* (the drought-stricken interior of the Northeast). Later discoveries of tracks at over 13 different sites along the Rio do Peixe showed that the whole region had once been a *vale dos dinossauros* (valley of dinosaurs). There are at least three sites in the vicinity of Sousa. The best is 4km from town, at **Sítio Ilha**, on the banks of the Rio do Peixe, where more than 50 prints have been left by dinosaurs that, judging by the depth and size of the imprints, weighed between three and four tons each.

This site is subject to flooding during the rainy season and is best visited with a guide. Transportation options are limited to either hiring a taxi at the bus station in Sousa (around US$10) or asking the staff at the Hotel Gadelha Palace (below) to arrange for transportation and a guide.

Travelers who are interested in handicrafts should make a side trip to the town of **Aparecida**, 14km east of Sousa, which is famed as a center for the production of superb hammocks, textiles and leather and straw goods.

Sleeping & Eating

Hotel Gadelha Palace (☎ 521 1880; Rua Presidente João Pessoa 2; s/d US$20/25; ✗) A decent place that will arrange tours of the dinosaur site and has a restaurant with a variety of dishes.

Tropical (☎ 521 2500; Rua José Vicente 2) If you need to have pizza, this is the place to go. In the pedestrian mall.

Getting There & Away

From the **bus station** (☎ 521 1458; Rua José Facundo de Lira) there are 11 departures a day that run via Patos and Campina Grande to and from

---

CARNE DO SOL

Carne do sol (meat of the sun) is a lightly salted and partially dehydrated meat that is the dish most commonly associated with Rio Grande do Norte. Typically made from beef (although sometimes from goat meat), *carne do sol* has a somewhat salty taste and looks like a thin steak with a brownish tinge. It was developed generations ago due to a lack of proper food storage and has a shelf life comparable to refrigerated fresh meat.

The name *carne do sol* belies the fact that the meat is rarely exposed to the sun during dehydration. Its original name, *carne de vento* (meat of the wind), is closer to the truth, as it is dried in covered, ventilated areas allowing for greater control of the process (and a better way to keep the insects out).

Before drying, the flattened meat is dusted with ground sea salt and stacked on a salted floor. The pile is remade and inverted after four to six hours. It is then covered with a heavy layer of salt for another four to six hours. The meat is washed and moved to a covered area where it's hung over rails with the fatty side up for eight to14 hours.

Refrigerators or no refrigerators, *carne do sol* is the favorite dish of Rio Grande do Norte and it can be found everywhere from kitchens in the smallest towns to the fanciest city restaurants.

João Pessoa (US$19, seven hours). Buses also depart four times a day to and from Juazeiro do Norte.

RIO GRANDE DO NORTE

Pure air, sun, fine beaches and sand dunes symbolize this small state in the extreme northeast of Brazil. This is where the coast changes direction from north/south to northwest/southeast, and the strong, dry ocean winds pile sand in huge dunes – the most famous being the 50m-tall dunes at Genipabu. The locals, known as Potiguenses, are friendly and welcoming. As is the case in Paraíba, the interior of the state is drought-stricken, and many former inhabitants have already migrated to other parts of Brazil.

NATAL

☎ 0xx84 / pop 800,000

Natal, the capital of Rio Grande do Norte, is a clean, bright and rather bland city that has swelled as the entry point for package resort tourism on the nearby coast. Surrounded by impressively large sand dunes, Natal's main attractions are beaches, buggy rides and nightlife – don't come here if you seek museums and theater.

The urban beaches of Praia do Meio and Praia dos Artistas are no longer the attraction they once were. These days, most visitors stay in the southern beach neighborhood of Ponta Negra, which is a little over 10km from the center. Although Ponta Negra's reputation has also been sullied due to a spike in sex tourism, it is a striking location, with fantastic dunes, steady surf and some great nightlife in the Alto de Ponta Negra area.

Natal's Carnatal (out-of-season Carnaval), in the first week of December, draws huge crowds from all over Brazil. It's basically an excuse to party, and if you can't make it to Carnaval, this is the next best thing (many locals argue that it's actually better).

History

In 1535 a Portuguese armada left Recife for the mouth of the Rio Ceará-Mirim (12km north of present-day Natal) to drive out

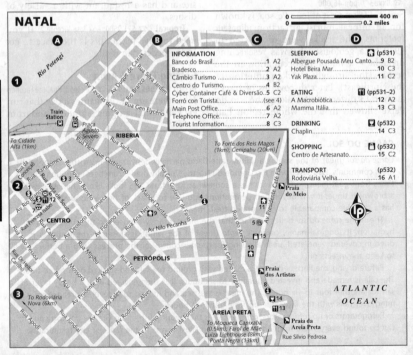

NATAL

INFORMATION	
Banco do Brasil	1 A2
Bradesco	2 A2
Câmbio Turismo	3 A2
Centro do Turismo	4 B2
Cyber Container Café & Diversão	5 C2
Forró con Turista	(see 4)
Main Post Office	6 A2
Telephone Office	7 A2
Tourist Information	8 C3

SLEEPING	(p531)
Albergue Pousada Meu Canto	9 B2
Hotel Beira Mar	10 C3
Yak Plaza	11 C2

EATING	(pp531–2)
A Macrobiótica	12 A2
Mamma Itália	13 C3

DRINKING	(p532)
Chaplin	14 C3

SHOPPING	(p532)
Centro de Artesanato	15 C2

TRANSPORT	(p532)
Rodoviária Velha	16 A1

To Cidade Alta (1km)

RIBERIA

To Forte dos Reis Magos (1km); Genipabu (20km)

Praia do Meio

CENTRO

Praia dos Artistas

PETRÓPOLIS

To Rodoviária Nova (6km)

AREIA PRETA

To Moqueca Capixaba (0.5km); Farol de Mãe Luiza Lighthouse (8km); Ponta Negra (13km)

Praia da Areia Preta

Rue Silvio Pedrosa

ATLANTIC OCEAN

THE NORTHEAST

the French, who had set up trading posts in the area. Although the territory had been proclaimed by King João III of Portugal in 1534 as one of the 15 coastal captaincies, the Portuguese then abandoned the area for 60 years, until the French again began to use it as a base for attacks on the south. The Portuguese organized a huge flotilla from Paraíba and Pernambuco that met at the mouth of the Rio Potengi on Christmas Day 1597 to battle the French.

On January 6, 1598, the day of Os Reis Magos (Three Wise Men), the Portuguese began to work on the fortress, the Forte dos Reis Magos, which they used as their base in the victory against the French. The Brazilian coastline was hotly contested, and in 1633 the fortress was taken by the Dutch, who rebuilt it in stone but retained the five-point-star shape. Under Dutch and thereafter Portuguese occupation, Natal grew from the Forte dos Reis Magos.

With the construction of a railway and a port, Natal continued to develop as a small and relatively unimportant city until WWII. Recognizing Natal's strategic location on the eastern bulge of Brazil, Getúlio Vargas and Franklin D Roosevelt decided to turn the sleepy city into the Allied military base for operations in North Africa. The city became known as the 'Trampoline to Victory.' These days, it's known as the Cidade do Sol (Sun City), for good reason.

Orientation

Natal is on a peninsula flanked to the northwest by the Rio Potengi and the east by Atlantic reefs and beaches. The peninsula tapers, ending at the Forte dos Reis Magos, the oldest part of the city. The city center, Cidade Alta, was developed around the river port, which was built in 1892. The city's southern point is the beach neighborhood of Ponta Negra, which is crowned by the huge Morro da Careca sand dune.

Information

BOOKSTORES

Sodiler (☎ 643 3807; airport; ⏰ 9am-9pm) Books in a variety of languages. Bookstores are hard to find in town.

EMERGENCY

Ambulance (☎ 192)
Police (Map p530; ☎ 232 7404; Central do Cidadão, Av Engenheiro Roberto Freire 8790)

INTERNET ACCESS

Café.com (Map p530; ☎ 236 4658; Rua Bezerra s/n, Alto de Ponta Negra; per hr US$2; ⏰ 1-10pm Mon-Sat)
Cyber Container Café & Diversão (Map p528; ☎ 202 7932; Av Presidente Café Filho 680 B, Praia do Meio; per hr US$2; ⏰ 8am-9pm Mon-Fri, 9am-9pm Sat & Sun)

INTERNET RESOURCES

Carnatal site (www.carnatal.com.br)
General Natal information (www.uol.com.br/natal online)
Official tourism site (www.natal.rn.gov.br)

MEDICAL SERVICES

Casa de Saude São Lucas (☎ 220 5433)
Walfredo Gurgel (☎ 201 9727)

MONEY

Banco do Brasil (Map p528; Av Rio Branco 510, Centro; ⏰ 10am-4pm Mon-Fri) Also in Praia Shopping, near Ponta Negra.
Bradesco (Map p530; Av Rio Branco) ATM opposite Banco do Brasil. Also on Praia Ponta Negra and in Praia Shopping.
Norte Câmbio & Turismo (shop 2, Rua Trairi 433; ⏰ 8am-8pm) Changes cash and traveler's checks.

POST

Main post office (Map p528; Av Rio Branco 538)

TELEPHONE

Telephone office (Map p528; Rua Princesa Isabel 687)

TOURIST INFORMATION

Centro de Tourismo (Setur; ☎ 232 2516/2500; Centro Convenções, Mossoró 359, Petrópolis) The tourism office is a bit out of the way. More convenient and useful are the information booths at Praia dos Artistas (Map p528) and the airport. They have maps and tour pamphlets.

TRAVEL AGENCIES

Alfatur (Map p530; ☎ 219 3933; alfatur@zipmail.com .br; Av Erivan França 153, Ponta Negra; ⏰ 9am-6pm) This agency, located by the beach, can help with most basic travel needs.
Manary Ecotours (Map p530; ☎ 219 2900; www .manary.com.br/ecotours/ingles; Rua Francisco Gurgel 9067, Ponta Negra; ⏰ 9am-6pm) This very organized agency offers a wide range of services and provides tours ranging from ecotourism to adventure to relaxation.

Dangers & Annoyances

The dramatic increase in visitors has attracted a few petty thieves and a pretty serious prostitution scene, especially along the beaches at night.

Sights & Activities

FORTE DOS REIS MAGOS

Enjoy a tapioca ice cream where the Portuguese struggled to repel the French invasion in the late 16th century at the **Forte dos Reis Magos** (Map p528; admission US$0.65; ☼ 8am-4:30pm). The views of the city and the dunes across the Rio Potengi are fantastic from this prime location at the tip of the peninsula north of town.

BEACHES

Natal's city beaches stretch over 9km south from the fort to Farol de Mãe Luiza lighthouse. Ponta Negra, in the south of town, is the nicest beach in Natal. If you want to visit the truly beautiful beaches of Rio Grande do Norte, you must travel outside of Natal.

As the name suggests, **Praia do Forte** is at the Forte dos Reis Magos. It has natural pools, but is nothing too special. **Praia do Meio** is an urban beach with reefs and a lot of people getting drunk. The water is calm and good for inexperienced swimmers. **Praia dos Artistas** is another urban spot, which has become a bit more sketchy at night.

The beach at **Ponta Negra** is nearly 3km long and full of hotels, pousadas, restaurants, beach bars, surfers and sailing boats – on weekends the place gets pretty packed. At the far end of the beach is **Morro da Careca**, a monstrous sand dune with a steep face that drops straight into the sea.

BUGGY RIDES

Dune-buggy excursions are offered by a host of would-be Ayrton Senna *bugeiros* (buggy drivers), mostly in Brazilian-built vehicles with brand names such as Bird, Baby, Praya or Malibuggy. To the north are the dunes of **Genipabu**, which are the biggest around. You'll be asked if you want the trip *com emoção* (with emotion), and if you agree you'll be treated to thrills such as Wall of Death and Vertical Descent. It is possible to go all the way to Fortaleza by dune buggy – 760km of gorgeous coastline.

There are pirate *bugeiros* and accredited *bugeiros*; the latter are represented by the **Associação de Bugeiros** (☎ 225 2077). An eight-hour trip costs around US$13 per person and can be arranged through most pousadas, agencies or, if you speak Portuguese and want to get a better deal, directly with the drivers.

SURFING

Ponta Negra is the place to go for some of the most consistent (yet small) waves in the region. Boards can be rented (US$3 per day) from a number of stands on the beach.

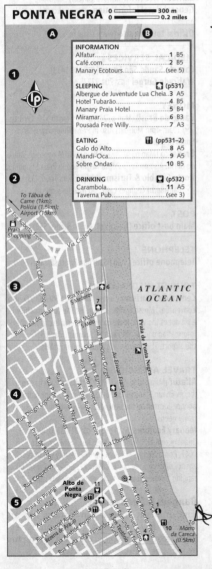

PONTA NEGRA

0 — 300 m
0 — 0.2 miles

INFORMATION	
Alfatur	**1** B5
Café.com	**2** B5
Manary Ecotours	(see 5)

SLEEPING	(p531)
Albergue de Juventude Lua Cheia	**3** A5
Hotel Tubarão	**4** B5
Manary Praia Hotel	**5** B4
Miramar	**6** B3
Pousada Free Willy	**7** A3

EATING	(pp531–2)
Galo do Alto	**8** A5
Mandi-Oca	**9** A5
Sobre Ondas	**10** B5

DRINKING	(p532)
Carambola	**11** A5
Taverna Pub	(see 3)

To Tábua de Carne (1km); Polícia (1.5km); Airport (15km)

Praia Shopping

Av Roberto Freire

Via Costeira

Rua Cipó de S Roque

Rua Manoel S Medeiros

ATLANTIC OCEAN

Rua Praia de Tibau

Rua Maior S Meio

Rua Francisco Cunzei

Rua Skal

Rua Erivan Franca

Praia de Ponta Negra

Rua Pedro Fonseca

Rua P de Camboinhas

Rua Diogo Lopes de Souza

Av Eng Roberto Freire

Av Praia de Jacumã

Rua Liberdade

Rua Coqueiros

Rua do Pirangi

Praia do Pirangi

Alto de Ponta Negra

Av das Algas

Av das Conchas

Rua Dr Manoel Augusto Bezerra de Araújo

Rua Ver Manoel Sátiro

Rua Dr Damião Fonseca Filho

Av Erivan Franca

Rua Praia Josefa Gonzaga Fernandes

Av Prof Teodorico Bezerra

Av Erivan Franca

To Morro da Careca (0.5km)

Festivals & Events

Natal's out-of-season Carnaval, **Carnatal**, takes to the streets at the beginning of December with *blocos* (drumming and dancing processions) named *Jerimum* (Pumpkin) and *Burro Elétrico* (Electric Donkey). It is the most highly acclaimed out-of-season Carnaval in the country and is a decent substitute for anyone who couldn't make it to the real deal.

Sleeping

Natal has hotel districts around Cidade Alta (in the city center) and along the city beaches. However, most visitors stay in the more scenic and tranquil beach neighborhood of Ponta Negra.

BUDGET

Albergue Pousada Meu Canto (Map p528; ☎ 212 2811; Rua Ana Neri, Petrópolis; dm US$5) Within minutes, Tia Helena will add you to her international family at this simple pousada with pretty greenery. Take bus No 21 and get off at the first stop on Rua Manoel Dantas.

Hotel Beira Mar (Map p528; ☎ 202 1470; Av Presidente Café Filho 886, Praia dos Artistas; s/d US$8/10; ☒) Basic rooms are rounded out by the TV, mini-fridge and hammock at this breezy, oceanfront hotel.

Albergue de Juventude Lua Cheia (Map p530; ☎ 236 3696; luacheia@digi.com.br; Rua Dr Manoel Augusto Bezerra de Araújo 500, Ponta Negra; dm US$14, with HI membership US$11) This famous castle-like structure (drawbridge, turrets and all) has a bizarre Halloween theme that you may as well go along with. Facilities are good, staff are helpful and it is located in the heart of Alto de Ponta Negra. Don't expect to go to bed early on weekend nights and don't expect to sleep in too late, as the music comes back on after breakfast. But if you are looking for fun in Natal, you should stay here.

MID-RANGE

Yak Plaza (Map p528; ☎ 202 4224; www.yakplaza.com.br; Rua Mascarenhas Homem 25, Praia do Meio; s/d US$28/36; ☒ ☒) This modern hotel, with its glassy lobby and tidy rooms, is a bit out of place on the decaying Praia do Meio.

Pousada Free Willy (Map p530; ☎ 236 2825; www.freewilly.com.br; Rua Francisco Gurgel 9292, Ponta Negra; d without/with ocean views US$33/36; ☒ ☒) Free Willy – try to excuse the name – is recom-

mended for its friendly owners, excellent location on the beach and clean rooms. This is your best mid-range choice in Natal.

Hotel Tubarão (Map p530; ☎ 641 1029; Rua Manoel Coringa Lemos 259, Ponta Negra; s/d US$32/40; ☒ ☒) An attractive hotel set on the hill above Ponta Negra, Tubarão has a beautiful sea view, good common areas and relaxing *apartamentos*. The manager speaks fluent English and is very helpful.

Miramar (Map p530; ☎ 219 2131; Rua da Praia 3398, Ponta Negra; d US$60; ☒ ☒ ☒) Close to the beach, with two pools, great views and comfortable rooms, this larger hotel is still good value.

TOP END

Manary Praia Hotel (Map p530; ☎ 219 2900; www.manary.com.br; Rua Francisco Gurgel 9067, Ponta Negra; d US$120-150; ☒ ☒ ☒) All rooms have a sea view at this good-value upmarket hotel. The pool and patio are idyllic and the hotel runs a highly professional travel agency (see p529). If you can afford it, stay here.

Eating

Galo do Alto (Map p530; ☎ 236 2330; Rua Dr Manoel Augusto Bezerra de Araújo 142, Ponta Negra; mains US$7; ☾ 6pm-late) Sit on the patio at this restaurant and enjoy drinks, pastas and seafood while observing all the action on the street.

Moqueca Capixaba (☎ 202 9673; Av Sílvio Pedrosa, Praia de Areia Preta; mains US$5; ☾ 11am-11pm Tue-Sat, 11am-6pm Sun) Among other delicious seafood dishes, this highly regarded spot serves, yes you guessed it, a fantastic *moqueca* (Bahian fish stew cooked in a clay pot).

Tábua de Carne (Map p530; ☎ 642 1236; Av Eng Roberto Freire 8353, Capim Macio; mains US$5; ☾ 11:30am-11pm) This is one of the best places in town to get the favorite regional dish, *carne do sol*.

Sobre Ondas (Map p530; ☎ 219 4222; Av Erivan França s/n; mains US$4-8; ☾ 8-1am) Sobre Ondas has a large, two-tiered beachfront veranda, which is a perfect escape from the noon sun. It has a full menu and good *sucos* (fruit juices).

A Macrobiótica (Map p528; ☎ 222 6765; Rua Princesa Isabel 528, Centro; per kg US$4; ☾ 11:30am-2pm & 3:30-6pm Mon-Sat) The food may not be exquisite, but veggies and soy abound at this rare vegetarian spot.

Mamma Itália (Map p528; ☎ 202 1622; Rua Silvio Pedrosa 43, Praia dos Artistas; dishes US$5; ☾ 11am-2pm

& 3-8pm) The spinach-and-ricotta ravioli is divine at this fine Italian restaurant.

Mandi-Oca (Map p530; ☎ 3091 3294; Rua Sen Teotônio Vilela 1111, Alto de Ponta Negra; açaí US$2; ⏰ 9am-6pm Mon-Sat) This sand-floored, faux-Amazonian café has excellent *açaís* (berry-like fruit), drinks made from *guarana* (type of berry) and about everything that you can imagine made from *macaxeira* (manioc). It is one of the few places in Alto de Ponta Negra that is open straight through the day.

Entertainment

The Alto de Ponta Negra neighborhood along Rua Dr Manoel Augusto Bezerra de Araújo and its side street has good nightlife with a variety of fun bars and restaurants. Away from the beach prostitution scene, it is full of locals and more-savvy travelers. If you are arriving by bus, ask to be let off at the Ilha da Fantasia stop on the corner and walk up the street a couple of blocks.

Taverna Pub (Map p530; ☎ 236 3696; www.tavernapub.com; Rua Dr Manoel Augusto Bezerra de Araújo 500; ⏰ 10:30-late Mon-Sat) Attached to the Lua Cheia youth hostel and advertised as a 'medieval bar,' this tavern has rock and a variety of other live music (sometimes with a US$1 to US$2 cover charge).

Carambola (Map p530; ☎ 236 4778; Rua Dr Manoel Augusto Bezerra de Araújo 175; ⏰ 8pm-late Mon-Sat) Across the street from Taverna Pub, this bar specializes in *caipifrutas* (fruit juice and *cachaça* cocktails) and other fresh-fruit-based cocktails. It also has food and snacks.

Forró com Turista (☎ 211 6218; www.forrocomturista.com.br; Centro do Turismo, Rua Aderbal Figueiredo 980; ⏰ 10pm-late Thu) The name of this local staple may sound corny, but don't miss the chance to dance live *forró* in an open courtyard.

Chaplin (Map p528; ☎ 211 7457; Av Presidente Café Filho 27, Praia dos Artistas; cover US$6) Thursday and Saturday are the happening nights at this huge club with various bars, including Hooters and Mexicano. People from all over Natal descend on Chaplin for late-night partying.

Shopping

The **Centro do Turismo** (Rua Aderbal Figueiredo 980) has lots of stalls selling bottles of colored sand, ceramics and other local handicrafts. The **Centro de Artesanato** (Praia dos Artistas) is a good spot to look for that perfect (and inexpensive) gift.

Getting There & Away

AIR

Natal's **Augusto Severo Airport** (Map p528; ☎ 643 1811) is served by all of the major Brazilian airlines. International flights leaving from Natal are more expensive than those leaving from Recife or Fortaleza. The airport code is NAT.

TAM (☎ 202 3385; Rua Seridó 746)

Trip (☎ 234 1717; Rua Prudente Morais 4283)

VASP (☎ 221 4453; Rua João Pessoa 429)

Varig/Nordeste (☎ 221 4453; Rua Mossoró 598)

BUS

The long-distance buses leave from the **Rodoviária Nova** (New Bus Station; Map p528; ☎ 205 4377; Av Capitão Mor Gouveia 1237), located 6km south of the center, heading to Aracati (to Canoa Quebrada, US$13, five to six hours, 385km, six daily), Fortaleza (US$18, eight hours, 552km, 10 daily), Goianinha (to Praia da Pipa, US$2, 1½ hours, every hour), João Pessoa (US$6, 2½ hours, 180km, eight daily), Praia da Pipa (US$2.50, two hours, 85km, seven daily), Recife (US$14, 4½ hours, 288km, nine daily), Rio (US$95, 44 hours, 2680km, two daily) and Salvador (US$50, 18 hours, 1111km, one daily at noon).

Getting Around

TO/FROM THE AIRPORT

Natal's airport is 15km south of town on Hwy BR-101. Bus A-Aeroporto runs between the airport and the Rodoviária Velha (Old Bus Station) in the city center. The taxi fare to the city center is about US$15 and US$5 to Ponta Negra.

BUS

Bus Nos 38 and 20 connect the Rodoviária Nova with the **Rodoviária Velha** (Praça Augusto Severo) in the city center.

The Rodoviária Velha is the hub for bus services to the airport (Bus A), the Rodoviária Nova, city beaches such as Praia dos Artistas (Nos 21 and 38), beaches further south such as Ponta Negra (Nos 46 and 54) and Pirangi, and beaches as far north as Genipabu.

If you're arriving by bus from the south and you are trying to get to Ponta Negra, ask the driver to let you off at Shopping Cidade Jardim and catch a Ponta Negra Bus or minivan at the bus stop in front of the shopping center (US$0.50).

THE NORTHEAST

TAXI

The taxi fare to the center from the Rodoviária Nova is US$5. A taxi from the center to Praia dos Artistas costs around US$3, while to Ponta Negra it's US$8.

SOUTH OF NATAL
Pirangi do Sul & Pirangi do Norte
☎ 0xx84

The pretty twin beach towns of Pirangi do Sul and Pirangi do Norte, 10km south of Ponta Negra, are split by a river that weaves through palm-crested dunes on its way to the ocean. It's a quiet area where wealthy folk from Natal have their weekend homes and people come to snorkel in the clear tide pools. There are a few pousadas in the palm grove where the road crosses the river. The town is home to the **world's largest cashew tree**: its sprawl of branches is over 500m in circumference, and it's still growing!

Pousada Esquina do Sol (☎ 238 2078; www .esquinadosol.com.br; Av Marcío Marinho 2210; s/d US$20/25; ❄) is a friendly place right on the main street, with tidy rooms and a good breakfast. There are less-expensive rooms without air-con.

Búzios to Senador Georgino Avelino
☎ 0xx84

Like the rest of Rio Grande do Norte, this stretch has some fantastic beaches – it's difficult to find one that's not worth raving about.

Búzios is a beach town 40km south of Natal. The beach is nice, but the area is a bit dry and barren, so continue down the road. After Búzios, the road crosses a stream and follows the coast – there's nothing here but small waves crashing against the beach, white dunes, coconut palms, uncut jungle and little farms.

From Natal, take one of the frequent Tabatinga buses to Búzios (US$2, one hour) along the winding, cobblestone coastal road or there are five buses a day directly to Senador Georgino Avelino.

Tibaú do Sul

The small, rocky beaches just south of Tibaú do Sul – **Praia da Madeira**, **Praia da Cancela** and **Praia da Pipa** are gorgeous and backed by steep cliffs. From Goaininha, 75km south of Natal on Hwy BR-101, there's a 20km paved road to the coast.

Praia da Pipa
☎ 0xx84 / pop 3000

Pipa rivals Jericoacoara as the Northeast's hippest beach town. However, it is more developed than the others, with its share of upscale boutiques and nicer restaurants. It also boasts good nightlife, decent surfing, dolphin-filled waters and pristine beaches

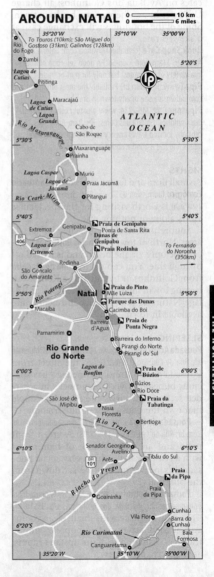

AROUND NATAL

backed by tall cliffs. Pipa has some of the highest prices in the region, but don't let the scene along the main drag fool you; a laid-back vibe still dominates Pipa, which is considered by locals to be the 'global village.'

INFORMATION
There are a number of overpriced Internet cafés on Av Baía dos Golfinhos; all charge US$5 per hour. There are no banks in town. Some of the boutiques will exchange cash at a skewed rate.

Book Shop Café (cintiabook@yahoo.com; Galeria de Arte; ☒ 11am-8pm Mon-Sat) A good selection of books in a variety of languages, but only for rent or trade.

Pipa (www.pipa.com.br) Probably the most organized and comprehensive site of any town in Brazil.

Pipatour (☎ 246 2234; www.pipatour.com.br; Av Baía dos Golfinhos, Galeria das Cores; ☒ 9am-6pm) This centrally located travel agency can arrange most travel needs and has a good website.

SIGHTS
A small flora and fauna reserve, the **Santuário Ecológico** (admission US$1; ☒ 8am-5pm Mon-Sat, 8am-1pm Sun) is worth visiting for the spectacular views alone, if nothing else.

Southernmost of the beaches is **Praia do Amor**. North of town, **Praia dos Golfinhos** is accessible only via the beach and is closed off by high tide. You can get to **Praia do Madeiro** from Golfinhos or by catching a Kombi van leaving town, then descend the stairs at Village Natureza. Surf lessons and boards are available in town.

SLEEPING
Pousada Aconchego (☎ 246 2439; aconchego@bluemail.ch; Rua do Céu; s/d US$16/23) Up the street from Pousada do Golfinho, Aconchego has spacious bungalows with hammocks in a garden setting. The Swiss and Brazilian couple that own the pousada are quite friendly.

Pousada da Pipa (☎ 246 2271; pousadadapipa@uol.com.br; Rua do Cruzeiro; s/d US$8/13) A green front patio and an entire porch of hammocks with a sea view make this a very social pousada. It's located on a cul-de-sac down from the pharmacy.

Pousada do Golfinho (☎ 246 2393; www.pousadagolfinhopipa.com.br; Av Baía dos Golfinhos; s/d US$10/14) This colorful place with small, clean rooms and a good restaurant is popular among travelers. Ask for one of the upstairs rooms, as they have a sea view.

Pousada da Mata (☎ 502 2304; www.pousadadamata.com.br; Estrada Tibau do Sol; d/chalet US$60/75; ☒) Set in the forest about 2km north of the center of Pipa, Pousada da Mata has luxurious *quartos* and private chalets surrounded by idyllic greenery. A perfect choice for total relaxation.

Toca da Coruja (☎ 246 2225; www.tocadacoruja.br; d/chalet US$100/225 ☒ ☒ ☒) One of the best-value luxury pousadas in the Northeast, Toca da Coruja is wrapped in an oasis of sprawling tropical gardens with monkeys and birds. The exquisite deluxe chalets, which are a great honeymoon option, are nicely detailed and have private spas on the verandas. Some of the *apartamentos* are wheelchair-accessible.

EATING
It is more difficult to find an affordable restaurant in Pipa than it is to find a quality restaurant. Many of the places are closed for lunch during the low season.

Jack's on the Beach (☎ 246 2337; mains US$5-9; ☒ 10am-sunset) Jack's sits on the side of a cliff along the beach toward Praia do Amor and offers delicious seafood and pastas – paella on Sunday. The restaurant is worth visiting simply for its character, let alone the good food and splendid sunset view.

Cruziero do Pescador (☎ 246 2262; Rua da Gameleira; mains US$8-20; ☒ 6pm-midnight Tue-Sun) As the name would suggest, Cruziero do Pescador is seafood restaurant with good fish dishes, but correspondingly high prices.

Colher de Pau (☎ 246 2521; Rua do Céu s/n; buffet per kg US$4, mains US$2-4; ☒ 11am-10pm Mon-Sat) An affordable self-service option just off the main drag, this is popular with locals and serves seafood and other dishes in the evenings.

Caligula Restaurant (☎ 246 2383; Av Baía dos Golfinhos; pizzas US$3-7; ☒ 4-10pm Tue-Sun) With its pseudo-Ionic columns, this pizza restaurant tries to be a level above your average Brazilian pizzeria – and it is successful, with arguably the best pizza in town.

ENTERTAINMENT
Nightlife tends to start off in front of **Blue Bar** (Av Baía dos Golfinhos). People then move on to one of the clubs: Lampião and Calangos have *forró*, while the more sedate Garagem has MPB and reggae.

Sometimes one of the pousadas will host a party with a DJ. Ask around to find out

THE NORTHEAST

where it is, and don't expect to come home before sunrise.

GETTING THERE & AWAY

From the Rodoviária Nova in Natal, there are eight buses a day to Pipa and back (US$3, two hours, from 7:15am to 6:45pm). There are only four buses on Sunday. If you are arriving from the south, get out at Goaininha (1½ hours from João Pessoa). Taxi drivers will take you to Pipa for around US$8.

NORTH OF NATAL

The beaches immediately north of Natal, where sand dunes plunge into the surf, are beautiful, but not quite as spectacular as the southern beaches.

Praia Redinha

Praia Redinha, 25km north of Natal by road, features 40m-high dunes, a good view of Natal, lots of bars and *capongas* (freshwater lagoons). Catch a ferry (US$1.50) from the waterfront close to the Rodoviária Velha in Natal for the 20-minute trip to Redinha. It's more relaxing than the bus.

Genipabu

☎ 0xx84 / pop 5000

About 5km further north you'll find Genipabu, where palm trees, dune buggies and enormous golden sand dunes converge on a beach lined with bars, pousadas and restaurants. It's a popular, crowded place,

where you can take adrenalized buggy rides, swim, surf, toboggan down the dunes, or take camel and boat trips. The beach has lots of buggy traffic, so it's not a good place to lie around.

Pousada Soleil (☎ 225 2064; www.pousadasoleil .com.br; Praia de Genipabu; d US$25-50; P 🏊 🍴) is a very clean and organized pousada, with 10 rooms set around a small pool.

Pousada Villa do Sol (☎ 225 2132; www.viladosol.com .br; Enseada de Genipabu; d US$33-53; P 🏊 🍴) is 3km northwest of town next to the river. It's a more upmarket place with a beautiful grounds and even better views. Lon, the American owner, has lived here for many years and is a good source of local knowledge.

Restaurante 21 (☎ 224 2484; Praia de Genipabu; mains US$6-12; 🕙 11am-10pm) has great seafood. Try Italian chef Lúcio's *peixada* (fish cooked in broth with vegetables and tomatoes; US$12). It will feed two easily.

Buses to Genipabu and Redinha leave Natal regularly from the Rodoviária Velha. If you haven't come here via dune buggy from Natal, you can rent one with a driver from numerous places for around US$35 a day.

Touros

☎ 0xx84

Touros is the Rio Grande do Norte's most developed town north of Natal. This fishing village has several beaches, bars and a couple of pousadas. It's also a convenient base from which to explore the isolated, yet

---

NATAL TO FORTALEZA BY BUGGY

Adventurous travelers who have time on their hands and don't mind sand in their faces or wind in their hair can choose to travel the 760km along the shore from Natal to Fortaleza by buggy. You can travel in either direction. The trip takes five days and you'll pass approximately 92 beaches.

Beach buggies average 40 km/h, and it takes a skilled driver to negotiate the uneven tracks, soft sand and small rivers that empty into the sea. You also have to drive certain parts only at low tide. Locals will ferry you on rafts over the wide river mouths.

This stretch of coastline is one of the most beautiful and underdeveloped in Brazil. There are cliffs of colored sands, rolling dunes, salt flats, reefs, palm-lined beaches and beaches with freshwater lagoons. It's fascinating to pass through or stay the night in the small fishing villages where the pace of life is slow.

Anyone can hire a buggy in Fortaleza or Natal and drive on the beaches, but a trip of this kind requires an experienced driver, such as **Cládio Chueiri** (☎ 0xx84-641 2019) or **Marcelo Cossi** (☎ 0xx84-236 4217), both from Natal. **Top Buggy** (☎ 0xx84-219 2820) in Natal and **HM** (☎ 0xx85-242 7799) in Fortaleza are both recommended agencies that can organize this trip. Average cost is US$80 to US$100 a day, including the drivers.

increasingly popular, beaches to the north, such as **Galinhos**, **São Miguel do Gostoso** and **Praia do Cajueiro**.

Pousada do Atlântico (☎ 263 2218; Av Atlântica 4; d US$18; ✖), on the beach, is a good-value pousada with friendly management and tidy rooms.

Pousada Sinos do Vento (☎ 263 2353; www.sinos dovento.com.br; Praia das Garças; d US$85; ✖ ✿) is

the local upscale option, with clean, comfortable rooms, well-maintained grounds and a beautiful pool.

O Castelo (☎ 263 2325; Av Atlântica 427; mains US$3-7; ✿ 11am-10pm Mon-Sat) serves locally caught fish in a variety of tasty recipes.

Seven buses a day leave the Rodoviária Nova in Natal for Touros (US$3, 1½ hours, 6:15am to 6:15pm).

Ceará, Piauí & Maranhão

THE NORTHEAST

HIGHLIGHTS

- Letting loose in lively beach towns such as **Canoa Quebrada** (p549) and **Jericoacoara** (p551)
- Listening to reggae in the colorful colonial center of **São Luís** (p562)
- Hiking through the magnificent dunes in the **Parque Nacional dos Lençóis Maranhenses** (p570)
- Exploring the verdant **Parnaíba delta** (p559) by boat
- Traveling by 4WD from Jericoacoara (p570) across pristine, sandy beaches and through the endless dunes to the entrance of Parque Nacional dos Lençóis Maranhenses (p570)

- POPULATION: 16.6 MILLION
- AREA: 732,092 SQ KM

Nestled between the top of the northeastern peninsula and the mouth of the Amazon are the states of Ceará, Piauí and Maranhão. Together, they constitute the northern coast of Brazil, which transitions from the dry, windswept beaches of Ceará to the lush vegetation of western Maranhão. Beyond the variety of landscapes, there is a range of towns, from modern Fortaleza to colonial São Luís and from provincial Teresina to hip Jericoacoara. You will encounter many types of people in the region, including traditional fishermen, subsistence farmers, nomadic windsurfers and even the odd tie-wearing businessman.

Most travelers just go to the beaches of Ceará, but there is much more to experience in these parts, such as Parque Nacional dos Lençóis Maranhenses – a giant sand-dune preserve in Maranhão – and the Parnaíba delta, the only river delta facing the open sea in the Americas. One of the most beautiful sights is the coast from points in Ceará and Piauí and from the towns around Parque Nacional dos Lençóis Maranhenses. You must travel by 4WD to cross the endless, unpopulated beaches and undulating dunes. Because of the direction of the coast in this part of the country, at some beaches it is actually possible to watch the golden sun set over the Atlantic.

These states are poor and underdeveloped – hapless Piauí holds the title of the most impoverished state in Brazil. The interior lands are drought-stricken and rural life is fraught with hardship, but there is no reputation for violence, especially against foreigners. You will generally find the region to have an easy-going attitude, with provincial charm and hospitality.

A trip to Ceará, Piauí and Maranhão offers infinite possibilities and will allow you to explore both your inner adventurer and your inner beach bum.

History

Ceará was originally settled in the early 17th century by Portuguese colonists from the Azores. It was a hard-fought battle to colonize the land and it was taken by the Dutch in 1635, subsequently lost to the Tabajara Indians and then taken back by the Dutch. The Portuguese seized control in 1654, but continued to battle the indigenous population well into the 18th century. Once the wars ended, colonists were faced with serious droughts, which killed many more people than the fighting. As many as two million people died in droughts in the 1870s, and this problem still affects the interior of the state. People flooded into Fortaleza in search of work in shipping, fishing or whatever they could find. The development of the city powered most of the economic strength in the state.

Neighboring Piauí was settled by poor cattle herders moving westwards from Ceará in the late 18th century and also has a violent and harsh history. After years of territorial skirmishes, the indigenous population was slowly assimilated with the colonists in the interior. Massive droughts and famine drove the settlers toward the coast and eventually a land swap was made with Ceará so that Piauí could have a small amount of coastline. It is still the poorest state in the country and has the lowest population density.

Maranhão grew along a different, yet equally violent, trajectory. São Luís was founded and forcibly settled by the French in 1612. The Portuguese, in turn, stepped in a couple of years later, but the Dutch took the land and held on to it from 1641 to 1644, when they were again ejected by the Portuguese. The state's agriculture production boomed for a short while and then went into a long decline. Maranhão straddles the Amazon and the Northeast and here you can see the culture and landscape transition from Piauí and Ceará to Amazonas and Pará.

Climate

These states are warm year-round and experience a slightly cooler rainy season from December through March. Temperatures are higher in the interior as the coast receives steady wind off the ocean. Nowhere in this region does it ever get particularly cold or rainy and the interior of Piauí claims to be the hottest part of the country.

National Parks

Lençóis Maranhenses (p570) is a massive expanse of rippling sand dunes only interrupted by clear pools of water. Barreirinhas is the major entrance point, but you must travel by 4WD or boat for some distance (usually with a tour group) before you can enter the park. Atins is the best entrance point for independent or more intrepid travelers who really want to see the best parts of the park. It can also be entered from numerous smaller towns along its perimeter. There is very little infrastructure, so unless you are experienced and prepared, hire a guide or go in a tour.

In deep southern Piauí, **Serra da Capivara** (p561) holds 260 prehistoric rock-painting

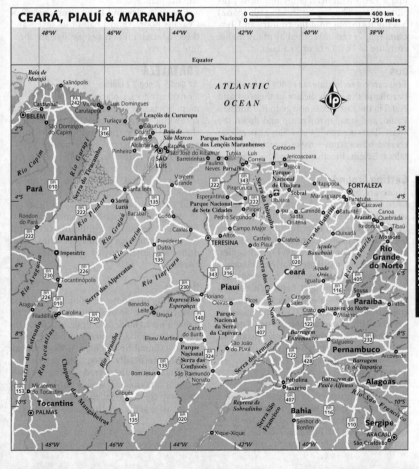

CEARÁ, PIAUÍ & MARANHÃO

THE NORTHEAST

sites (with 30,000 actual paintings). It is a Unesco World Heritage site and is worth the trip if you have time.

Considered one of the most important archeological sites in South America, **Sete Cidades** (p560) contains bizarre rock formations that resemble seven cities, and marks of an unknown, undated prehistoric civilization.

The small **Ubajara** (p555) is famous for its vast caves, which can be accessed on foot or by cable car. During the rainy season, there are also some impressive waterfalls.

Getting There & Away

AIR

Fortaleza (p540) has an international airport that receives flights from Europe, other major Latin American cities and most Brazilian cities. The airport in São Luís (p562) has flights throughout the country and Teresina (p557) can be reached by many flights en route to Fortaleza or São Luís.

BUS

You can get to Fortaleza (p540) by bus from Brasilia in the south, Belém in the west and Natal in the east. Buses also go to Rio and São Paulo, and smaller towns up and down the coast. Teresina (p557) and São Luís (p562) receive buses from smaller towns and Fortaleza, Belém, Brasilia, Rio and São Paulo.

Getting Around

There are buses linking pretty much every town in this region. The major impediment to bus travel is road quality, but pavement is being laid daily to improve the connection between the major destinations. It is possible to rent cars (always get a 4WD) or buggies, although lesser roads are poorly marked and you should never count on there being a gas station around the next bend. Unless you are going between larger cities, it is easiest to travel by minivan or 4WDs with professional drivers. Almost every travel agency listed in this chapter can help to organize groups in order to lessen the price of a ride.

CEARÁ

The pride of Ceará is its coastline – nearly 600km of glorious beaches. From the busy urban beaches of Fortaleza to the trendy communities of Jericoacoara and Canoa Quebrada to the smallest of isolated fishing villages, Ceará has it all. It is a short trip from Fortaleza's international airport to coastal towns where people continue to fish on *jangadas* (distinctive single-sailed boats of the Northeast), sleep in hammocks and live in thatch-roofed homes.

Should you stray inland into the *sertão* (backlands of the Northeast), you will see a rugged land of dust and *caatinga* (semi-arid land with little vegetation), peopled by *vaqueiros* (cowboys) who still rely on their cattle for almost everything. If you've been on the road for a while and desire a cooler climate, visit the Serra de Baturité. This small chain of hills southwest of Fortaleza features agreeable weather and coffee and banana plantations.

For all its size and rich culture, much of Ceará is poor. Almost half of its seven-and three-quarter million people live in absolute poverty.

FORTALEZA

☎ 0xx85 / pop 2.2 million

Considering its isolation on the Brazilian map, Fortaleza is a surprisingly large and sprawling city. In fact, it rivals Recife as the Northeast's most important fishing port and commercial center above Salvador. Its attractions are packed along the beaches and the rest of the city is endlessly residential. The beaches are not as attractive as you might hope, yet with its wild party atmosphere Fortaleza deserves at least a short visit. For many travelers, Fortaleza serves as a jumping-off point for some truly spectacular beaches, sand dunes and idyllic towns up and down the coast.

History

According to some revisionist Cearense historians, the Spanish navigator Vicente Yañez Pinzón landed on Praia Mucuripe on February 2, 1500, two months before Pedro Álvares Cabral first sighted Monte Pascoal, in Bahia (officially recognized as the first Brazilian land discovered by Europeans). Despite this claim, it wasn't until 1612 that the first colonists sailed from the Azores to actually settle on the banks of the Rio Ceará.

This settlement at present-day Fortaleza was hotly contested: it was taken over by the Dutch in 1635, then, in turn, lost to the Tabajara Indians. In 1639 the Dutch, this time under the command of Matias Beck, landed once again, fought off the Indians and constructed a fortress. In 1654 the Portuguese captured the fortress and reclaimed the site. A town grew around the fortress, which was given the name of Fortaleza de Nossa Senhora da Assunção (Fortress of Our Lady of Assumption). Fierce battles with the local Indian people continued to delay colonization until the 18th century.

Orientation

The city is laid out in a convenient grid pattern. The center lies above the historic section and includes the new Mercado Central (Central Market), the Catedral da Sé and major shopping streets and government buildings.

East of the center are the beaches of Praia de Iracema and Praia do Ideal. Further east, Avenida Beira Mar (also known as Avenida Presidente Kennedy) links Praia do Diário and Praia do Meireles (their center is known as Nautico), which are lined with high-rise hotels and restaurants. Beyond here are Porto do Mucuripe (the port) and the Farol Velha (Old Lighthouse). The town's best beach, Praia do Futuro, begins at the industrial zone near the lighthouse and extends 5km south along Avenida Dioguinho to the Clube Caça e Pesca (Hunting & Fishing Club). The tourism agency Setur (p541) has good maps of Fortaleza and Ceará.

Information

BOOKSTORES

Fortaleza is principally a beach town and bookstores are hard to come by.

Livraria Alaor (☎ 221 3000; Rua Floriano Peixoto 621, Centro; ⏰ 8am-7pm Mon-Fri, to 1pm Sat)

CULTURAL CENTERS

US Consulate (☎ 252 1539; Av Júlio Abreu 250)

EMERGENCY

Fire Department (Bombeiros; ☎ 193)
Federal Police (Policia Federal; ☎ 277 4900, 277 4927 for passport issues; Av Borges de Melo 820, Fatima)
Police (Policia; ☎ 190)
Tourist Police (Delegacia do Turista; ☎ 261 3769; Rua Silva Paulet 505, Aldeota)

INTERNET ACCESS

Beira-Mar Internet Café (☎ 248 8324; Av Beira Mar 2120A, Aldeota; per hr US$2.50; ⏰ 8-2am)
Cearápontocom (☎ 219 4920; Av Beira Mar 720, Iracema; per hr US$1.50; ⏰ 24hr Mon-Sat, from 8am Sun)

INTERNET RESOURCES

Official state site (www.fortaleza.ce.gov.br)
Official tourism site (www.turismo.ce.gov.br)

LAUNDRY

There are laundries all over town and most will pick up and deliver. Many hotels and pousadas (guesthouses) also offer services.
Lav & Lev (☎ 242 3345; Av Abolição 2685, Meireles; per kg US$2; ⏰ 8am-7pm Mon-Fri, to 6pm Sat)
Lavamatic (☎ 248 1120; cnr Av Monsenhor Tabosa & Rua Monsenhor Bruno; per kg US$2; ⏰ 8am-7pm Mon-Fri, to 6pm Sat)

MEDICAL SERVICES

SAT Emergency Medical (☎ 261 2220) This private medical service has English-speaking doctors and accepts most travel insurance and credit cards.
Unimed Hospital (☎ 277 7000; Av Visconde Rio Branco 4000, Fatima)

MONEY

There are ATMs in front of the Mercado Central and along the Nautico section of Meireles. There are also casas de câmbio (exchange offices) in Meireles, and large hotels there will change cash at a decent rate.
Banco do Brasil (Rua Floriano Peixoto 941; ⏰ 10am-4pm Mon-Fri)
Itaú (Rua Floriano Peixoto 397; ⏰ 10am-4pm Mon-Fri)

POST

Central post office (Rua Senador Alencar 38; ⏰ 8am-5:30pm Mon-Fri)

TELEPHONE

Pôsto Telefônico Beira Mar (☎ 242 2946; Nautico; ⏰ 9am-8pm)
Telemar airport (⏰ 24hr); bus station (⏰ 24hr)

TOURIST INFORMATION

Setur (☎ 231 3566; www.turismo.ce.gov.br; Rua Senador Pompeu 350; ⏰ 7am-6pm Mon-Sat, to noon Sun) The state tourism organization has a convenient branch office in the Centro de Turismo, inside a renovated prison. It has English-speaking attendants and stacks of information and can help with booking accommodations, tours to the beaches and details on bus transportation. Offices at the airport and bus station are open 24 hours.

CEARÁ COAST

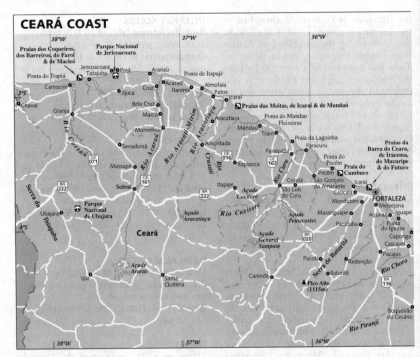

Funcet Praça da Ferreira (☎ 455 8515; Praça da Ferreira; ⏰ 9am-5pm); Meireles (Nautico; ⏰ 8am-10pm); Mercado Central (⏰ 9am-5pm) The municipal tourism organization has numerous information booths.

Disque Turismo (☎ 1516) This is a tourist-information telephone service; English operators are available.

TRAVEL AGENCIES

In Out Intercâmbio & Turismo (☎ 242 4347; www .inoutturismo.com.br; Av Abolição 2687, Meireles; ⏰ 9am-6:30pm) This small agency is friendly, helpful, and the owner, Jonas, speaks excellent English. It can help design your travels around Ceará or further afield.

Libratur (☎ 248 3355; Av Antonio Justa 2194; ⏰ 9am-8pm) This recommended agency has friendly, bilingual staff and competitive prices for national and international ticketing. It also runs a money-exchange service.

Transflying Operadora & Turismo (☎ 242 5290; www.transflying.com.br; cnr Av Desembargador Moreira & Rua Silva Jatahy; ⏰ 9am-6pm Mon-Sat) This is a good, one-stop location to deal with national and international flight arrangements.

Bioboard Travel (☎ 219 3851; www.bioboard.com.br; Av Beira Mar 914; ⏰ 9am-6pm Mon-Sat, to 2pm Sun) This surf shop runs a tourism agency and can coordinate special-ity surfing, windsurfing and other adventure-travel trips.

Dangers & Annoyances

Travelers have reported pickpocketing in the city center and petty theft on the beaches. There is an increasing amount of prostitution in the city, particularly in Iracema, and it has come with all the usual problems. If you leave your valuables in your hotel room and steer clear of the sex trade, you'll be fine.

Sights

CENTRO DRAGÃO DO MAR DE ARTE E CULTURA

This **cultural center** includes a planetarium, cinemas, theaters and art galleries in a modern complex that blends well with the old surrounding buildings, many of which have been restored and now house bars and restaurants. It's a popular place with locals and a good alternative to the Iracema bar/restaurant scene, especially on weekends.

TEATRO JOSÉ DE ALENCAR

Dating from 1910, the **Teatro José de Alencar** (☎ 252 2324; Praça José de Alencar) is an impres-sive building – a pastel-colored hybrid

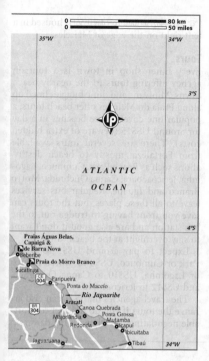

de Iracema to Rio in 1941 to bring their life of 'misery and suffering' to the attention of the federal government.

CENTRO DE TURISMO

The **Centro de Turismo** (Rua Senador Pompeu 350; 7am-6pm Mon-Sat, to noon Sun) contains a folk museum and the **Museu de Arte e Cultura Popular** (admission US$0.35), which houses a variety of interesting displays of local handicrafts, art and sculpture, from wood-block prints to incredibly intricate colored sand bottles.

BEACHES

Far and away the greatest attractions in Fortaleza are the beaches. The coast is divided up by the beaches and each neighborhood is named after the corresponding beach.

Praia do Futuro is a clean length of sand that stretches 5km toward the south along Avenida Dioguinho to the Clube Caça e Pesca. It is easily the best city beach, although it is far from most accommodations. *Barracas* (kiosks) line the beach, serving crab and beer, and it is packed on weekends. It doesn't start getting really nice until you are about 1km to 2km down the beach and away from the industrial port.

Praia do Meireles fronts Avenida Beira Mar and contains most of the mid-range and upmarket hotels and restaurants. The frantic pace of high-rise hotel construction seems to ensure that the beach will someday look like Copacabana. Its numerous beach bars, shaded among the leafy trees, are popular places to hang out during the day and sip a drink well into the evening. The walkway behind the beach is a good spot to people-watch or catch a capoeira performance. **Nautico**, the center of Meireles and the best spot to visit, is named after the nautical club across the street.

Near the Ponte Metálica, the city's old port, **Praia de Iracema** was a source of inspiration to Luís Assunção and Milton Dias, Ceará's bohemian poets of the 1950s, and some of this atmosphere lives on in a few bars and restaurants around Rua dos Tabajaras. Otherwise, it has been taken over by larger restaurants, brothels and theme bars that cater to visiting partygoers. It is your best bet for wild nightlife and it is nice enough walking along the promenade watching local surfers, but the beach itself is not worth your time.

of classical and art-nouveau architecture, which was constructed with cast-iron sections imported from Scotland. It is now used for cultural events and is worth a visit in the evenings, especially Friday and Saturday nights.

PARQUE ECOLÓGICO DO CÔCO

This **park**, opposite Shopping Center Iguatemi, is the city's main recreational park. It was set up in 1991 after local ecological groups pressed for protection of the mangrove swamps from encroaching highways and the industrial zone. Entrances to the park, which is 7km southeast of the center, are on Avenida Engenheiro Santana and Rua Vicente Leite. From the center, take the bus marked 'Edison Quieroz' to Shopping Center Iguatemi.

MUSEU DO CEARÁ

There are good exhibits on the state's history and anthropology at the **Museu do Ceará** (Rua São Paulo 51; admission US$0.65; 8:30am-5pm Tue-Sat, noon-5pm Sun), including a display on the four fishermen who sailed from Praia

The beaches immediately northwest of Fortaleza, **Cumbuco** and **Icaraí**, are both pleasantly tranquil and much cleaner than the city beaches. They are an easy, short day trip. You can catch a minivan from Nautico for less than US$2.

Activities

Relaxing is the main activity in Fortaleza, although locals surf in Iracema's cloudy waters and other beach sports are popular on Meireles and Futuro.

SWIMMING

Praia do Futuro is the best place to swim, but unless you are a strong swimmer beware of the rough waves. The water at Praia do Meireles is not as clean as Praia do Futuro, but it is right in town.

SURFING, WINDSURFING & KITE SURFING

Meireles and Iracema are decent for surfing. Kite and windsurfing are best at Praia do Futuro. You can rent surfboards and windsurfing equipment in Iracema at **Bioboard surf shop** (☎ 219 3851). **Chandler board rental**

(☎ 8803 4487; surfboard per day US$6) is housed in a tent right on the edge of Meireles.

Tours

Every other shop in town is a tourism agency offering tours to the nearby beach towns. Minivans and dune buggies lined up along Praia do Meireles offer beach tours; a popular one covers three beaches in a day for around US$15 (beware of extra hidden costs). There are several tours available from Fortaleza, mostly to beach destinations such as Beach Park, Cumbuco, Lagoinha, Jericoacoara, Canoa Quebrada, Morro Branco and Iguape. Regular bus services leave to all these places, but the tours can save you from having to trudge out to the bus station and are also good if don't want to stay overnight at the beach towns.

Expect to pay around US$5 to Beach Park or Cumbuco, US$8 to Morro Branco or Lagoinha, US$10 to Canoa Quebrada, and US$12 to Jericoacoara.

The travel agencies on p541 can also arrange the tours if you do not feel comfortable negotiating directly with the drivers.

FORTALEZA

INFORMATION		
ATM.................................1 G3	Funcet..............................8 H3	Setur................................16 A2
ATM.................................2 G3	Funcet...........................(see 47)	Tourist Police....................17 F3
ATM.............................(see 47)	In Out Intercâmbio & Turismo....9 G3	Transflying Operadora &
Banco do Brasil...................3 B3	Itaú.................................10 B3	Turismo............................18 G3
Banco do Brasil...................4 G3	Lav & Lev Laundry................11 G3	
Beira-Mar Internet Café 5 F3	Lavamatic.........................12 E3	
Bioboard Travel................(see 19)	Libratur.............................13 D2	
Cearápontocom...................6 D2	Livraria Alaor.....................14 B3	
Funcet.............................7 A3	Post Office.........................15 B3	
	Pôsto Telefônico Beira Mar...(see 8)	

Festivals & Events

Fortal, Fortaleza's lively out-of-season Carnaval, is held during the last week of July. The **Iemanjá festival**, which celebrates the sea goddess, is held on August 15 at Praia do Futuro. **Regata de Jangadas**, a sailing regatta with traditional Northeastern *jangadas*, takes place between Praia do Meireles and Praia Mucuripe, during the second half of July. **Semana do Folclore**, the city's folklore week, runs from the 22nd to the 29th of August.

Sleeping

There are endless accommodations available in Fortaleza, from dingy, inexpensive rooms in the Centro to Meireles' five-star high-rise hotels. If you are in Fortaleza strictly for nightlife, stay in Iracema; for the beaches and relaxation, stay in Meireles (or nearby); and if you are on a really tight budget or want to experience the city outside of the tourist zone, you can try the Centro.

Note that in addresses, 's/n' means *sem número* – without number.

BUDGET

Albergue da Juventude Atalaia (☎ 219 0755; pousada @pousadaatalaia.com.br; Av Beira Mar 814, Iracema; dm/ s/d US$8/15/18; ✖) The rooms are bright and modern at this hostel, which is the nicest in Iracema. Good kitchen, common areas and location. Better than many of the pousadas. Lockers in dorm room.

Alamo Praia Hotel (☎ 219 7979; alamohotel@ baydenet.com.br; Av Almirante Barroso 885, Iracema; s/d US$17/23; ✖ 🖵) Well put together by Iracema standards, this hotel is a block back from the action. Lots of competition in the surrounding blocks, but this place is friendlier and cleaner than most.

Hotel Passeio (☎ 226 9640; Rua Dr João Moreira 221, Centro; s/d US$10/13; ✖) The rooms here are nicer than the average city-center accommodations. Most of the rooms could use a paint job, but it's friendly enough and located just across the street from the Mercado Central.

Backpackers, CE (☎ 3091 8997; backpackers@hot mail.com; Rua Monsenhor Bruno 742, Meireles; r per person US$5) The vibe is super informal at this hostel in the home of two young women.

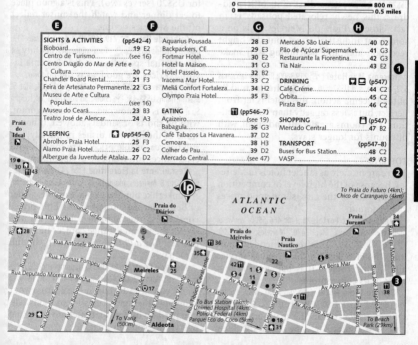

SIGHTS & ACTIVITIES	(pp542–4)
Bioboard	19 E2
Centro de Turismo	(see 16)
Centro Dragão do Mar de Arte e Cultura	20 C2
Chandler Board Rental	21 F3
Feira de Artesanato Permanente	22 G3
Museu de Arte e Cultura Popular	(see 16)
Museu do Ceará	23 B3
Teatro José de Alencar	24 A3

SLEEPING	(pp545–6)
Abrolhos Praia Hotel	25 F3
Alamo Praia Hotel	26 C2
Albergue da Juventude Atalaia	27 D2

Aquarius Pousada	28 E3
Backpackers, CE	29 E3
Fortmar Hotel	30 E2
Hotel la Maison	31 G3
Hotel Passeio	32 B2
Iracema Mar Hotel	33 C2
Meliá Confort Fortaleza	34 H2
Olympo Praia Hotel	35 F3

EATING	(pp546–7)
Açaizeiro	(see 19)
Babagula	36 G3
Café Tabacos La Havanera	37 D2
Cemoara	38 H3
Colher de Pau	39 D2
Mercado Central	(see 47)

Mercado São Luiz	40 D2
Pão de Açúcar Supermarket	41 G3
Restaurante la Fiorentina	42 G3
Tia Nair	43 E2

DRINKING	(p547)
Café Créme	44 C2
Órbita	45 C2
Pirata Bar	46 C2

SHOPPING	(p547)
Mercado Central	47 D2

TRANSPORT	(pp547–8)
Buses for Bus Station	48 C2
VASP	49 A3

THE NORTHEAST

Guests have use of the kitchen and washing machine. Can fit up to 12 people.

MID-RANGE

Hotel la Maison (☎ 242 6836; Av Desembargador Moreira, Meireles; d/tr US$33/38; ✕) Not luxurious but the best-value mid-range place in Meireles, La Maison is just a couple of blocks from the beach. It has bright, clean rooms and a good breakfast in a nice dining room. The French owner knows the city very well and can point you in the right direction, no matter what your interest.

Abrolhos Praia Hotel (☎ 248 1217; Av Abolição 2030, Ideal; d US$40; ✕ ▯) This sunny place, a couple of blocks back from the beach, is on a busy part of Avenida Abolição. It is friendly and clean, with a large eating area.

Fortmar Hotel (☎ 219 5363; www.fortmar.com.br; Av Beira Mar 1160, Iracema; d/tr US$30/37; ✕ ▣) A recently built small hotel on the corner between Praia do Iracema and Praia do Ideal. It is clean and sunny and the location makes for easy access to nightlife and is still within view of Meireles.

Aquarius Pousada (☎ 219 4888; aquarius@aquariuspousada.com.br; Av Monsenhor Tabosa 1078, Iracema; s/d US$20/23; ✕ ▣) Regardless of its official address, this newly relocated pousada is, in fact, close to Praia do Meireles. It is on a somewhat industrial street, but the bright reception area and welcoming staff make up for it.

Iracema Mar Hotel (☎ 219 3600; Rua dos Tabajaras 532, Iracema; s/d US$20/30; ✕ ▣) In the middle of the Iracema action, this hotel is far from perfect, but is less raggedy than its competition. The rooms are decent and small, with discounts for longer stays.

TOP END

There are numerous fancier hotels in Meireles. Because of the high level of competition and the size of the city, some good prices can be found.

Meliá Confort Fortaleza (☎ 466 5500; www.solmelia.com; Av Beira Mar 3470, Meireles; d US$90; ⓟ ✕ ✕ ▯ ▣) This recommended landmark hotel is known for its good service and quality rooms. It is better value that most of its competitors.

Olympo Praia Hotel (☎ 266 7200; www.olympo.com.br; Av Beira Mar 2380, Meireles; d US$75; ⓟ ✕ ▣) Olympo is located in the main beach area and is a tranquil escape from the busy beachfront. With all the modern amenities, it is well worth the price.

Eating

There are several local dishes worth tasting in Fortaleza. *Peixe a delícia* (fish with melted cheese and assorted herbs and spices) is a highly recommended favorite. Try *paçoca*, a typical Cearense dish made of sun-dried meat ground with a mortar and pestle, mixed with manioc and then roasted.

RESTAURANTS

Babagula (☎ 266 7222; Av Beira Mar 2361, Meireles; per kg US$3; ✕ 5pm-midnight) Babagula is a pleasant outdoor buffet on the beach-walk. It caters to couples, Brazilian tourists and has a family area that is good for kids. The food quality is particularly good for the price, especially in Meireles.

Tia Nair (☎ 219 1461; Rua Ildefonso Albano 68, Iracema; mains US$8-20; ✕ 11am-11pm) Tia Nair is an open-air seafood place, with an attentive staff and multilingual menu. The excellent house speciality is *barriga cheia* (full belly), a whole fish stuffed with lobster and shrimp for US$20 (serves two). This is a good place to eat dinner and watch the sunset reflect off the Meireles skyline.

Colher de Pau (☎ 219 3605; Rua dos Tabajaras 412, Iracema; mains US$3-6; ✕ 6pm-midnight) Try any of the regional specialities at this Iracema favorite. Prices are good, as is the *paçoca*.

Cemoara (☎ 263 5001; Av Abolição 3340A, Flat St Martin; mains US$8-15; ✕ noon-midnight Mon-Sat, to 5pm Sun) This is a renowned seafood restaurant, with no shorts or sandals allowed. It boasts some of the best fish dishes in the city, but still has reasonable prices. Try the fish with clam sauce; you won't be disappointed.

Restaurante la Fiorentina (☎ 242 2064; Rua Osvaldo Cruz 8, Meireles; mains US$5-8; ✕ 11am-midnight) A bunkerlike but breezy place on the corner of Beira Mar, La Fiorentina is a little pricey considering the ambience. However, it is one of the few mid-range choices in Meireles. The *filet à la Francês* will keep you full for a day.

Mercado Central (Av Alberto Nepomuceno 199, Centro; ✕ 7:30am-6:30pm Mon-Fri, 8am-4pm Sat, to noon Sun) If you need to take a break from your shopping, the market has lot of food stalls and per-kilo buffets that offer anything and everything you can imagine.

CAFÉS & QUICK EATS

Café Tabacos La Havanera (☎ 219 2259; Rua dos Arariús 2; coffee US$1; ❤ 9am-8pm) If you are in search of a real coffee shop, La Havanera has the most character of any spot in town. Not only does it have a good variety of speciality coffees, tobaccos and juices, it has a cool, airy ambience with wicker furniture watched over by framed photos of Fidel, Ché and Camilo.

Açaizeiro (☎ 219 3851; Av Beira Mar 914, Iracema; açaí US$3) Above Bio Board surf shop, this café has a variety of açaís (vitamin-rich berries). They are healthy and individually prepared.

GROCERIES

There are small grocery stores throughout the Centro. **Mercado São Luiz** (Av Beira Mar 693) is the best option in Iracema, while there is a **Pão de Açúcar supermarket** (Av Aboliçao 2900; ❤ 24hr) in Meireles.

Entertainment

Fortaleza is well known for its nightlife. Iracema is packed with bars and clubs playing everything from *forró* (music and dance style of the Northeast) to techno, and the *barracas* on Meireles serve icy beer from morning through the night. Centro Dragão do Mar caters to locals and is regarded as one of the best places to go out in the city. Ceará is also known for its comedy, and there are usually signs posted in front of bars in Iracema that have upcoming shows. The Setur website (www.turismo.ce.gov.br) keeps an updated list of weekly highlights.

Pirata Bar (☎ 219 8030; Rua dos Tabajaras 325; ❤ 8pm-late Mon) At Praia de Iracema, the long-standing Pirata is famous for its *'segunda-feira mais louca do planeta'* (craziest Monday on the planet). The pirate ship–themed spot includes live music for avid fans of *forró* or lambada, who dance until sunrise. Admission is up to US$10, depending on the season. The surrounding bars also get very lively.

Café Crème (☎ Rua Dragão do Mar 322; ❤ 6pm-late) Crème is one of the main spots in Dragão do Mar. You can start here and see what live music and other action start in the surrounding plaza.

Órbita (☎ 219 1233; Rua Dragão do Mar 207) This Dragão do Mar bar is recommended as a relaxed spot to have drinks and meet locals.

Chico de Caranguejo (☎ 234 6808; Av Zezé Diogo 4930; ❤ 9pm-late Thu) Out on Praia do Futuro, Chico de Caranguejo hosts a Thursday music night with plenty of *forró, pagode* (popular samba music) and *axé* (contemporary Afro-Brazilian pop). There is a couple of comedy acts as well.

Clube de Vaqueiro (Anel Contôrno) For more of a *sertão* experience, try this huge, cowboy-themed *forró* club on Saturday nights. It's a long way from the center, between Hwys BR-116 and CE-04, and is best reached by taxi.

Shopping

Fortaleza is one of the most important centers in the Northeast for crafts. Artisans work with *carnaúba* palm fronds, bamboo, vines, leather and lace. Much of the production is geared to the tourist, but there are also goods for urban and *sertanejo* (residents of the *sertão*) customers. Setur has a complete list of the ever-changing daily markets and fairs.

Feira de Artesanato Permanente (Praia Meireles) There is a craft market every afternoon (and well into the evening), where you can purchase any variety of local goods, watch the artists work and have them customize your design.

Mercado Central (Av Alberto Nepomuceno 199, Centro; ❤ 7:30am-6:30pm Mon-Fri, 8am-4pm Sat, to noon Sun) The market has cheaper prices for everything from hammocks to excellent local cashews and *cachaça* (white spirit made from sugarcane).

Central de Artesanato (☎ 3131 6551; Av Santos Dumont 1589, Aldeota; ❤ 9am-8pm Mon-Sat) This official art center has lace work, embroidery, leather goods, ceramics and articles made of straw.

There are also tourist boutiques along Avenida Monsenhor Tabosa for clothing, jewelry and fashion (generally open from 8am till 3pm).

Getting There & Away

AIR

Pinto Martins airport (☎ 477 1200) is 6km south of the city center. There are daily flights to international cites and every major Brazilian destination. The airport code is FOR.

Gol (☎ 477 1945; airport)
TAM (☎ 477 1881; airport)
Varig/Nordeste (☎ 477 1710; Av Santos Dumont 2727, Aldeota)
VASP (☎ 477 5001; Rua Barão do Rio Branco 959)

BUS

The **bus station** (☎ 256 4080, for information 186) is also approximately 6km south of the center. To get to the bus station from Praia de Iracema, catch the Aguanabi 1 or Siqueira /Mucuripe bus across Av Tamancaré from Centro Dragão do Mar.

Buses run daily to Aracati (US$4, three hours, 156km, 15 a day), Baturité (US$3, 2½ hours, 10 a day), Belém (US$44, 22 hours, 1610km, departs 4:30pm), Camocim (US$12, 7½ hours, 369km, four a day) via Sobral, Canoa Quebrada (US$6, 3½ hours, 167km, four a day), Jericoacoara (US$12, six hours, 305km, departs 9am, 10:30am and 6:30pm), Natal (US$16, eight hours, 552km, eight a day), Juaziero do Norte (US$13, nine hours, 600km, four a day), Recife (US$20, 12 hours, 799km, four a day), Rio de Janeiro (US$112, 42 hours, 2808km, departs 9am), Salvador (US$55, 23 hours, 1386km, departs 11pm), Teresina (US$27, 10 hours, 634km, seven a day), São Luís (US$25, 18 hours, 1070km, seven a day) and Ubajara (US$8, six hours, 324km, six a day).

The Jericoacoara bus also stops at Nautico, Praia do Meireles, 30 minutes before arriving at the bus station.

Getting Around

Pinto Martins airport is just a couple of kilometers from the bus station. The air-conditioned Guanabara Top Bus (US$1.50, every 30 minutes from 7am to 10:15pm) passes the local bus stop outside the bus station and runs to all major beaches and destinations. To reach the city center, you can also take any bus marked '13 de Maio' or 'Aguanambi' (passes the Centro de Turismo). A taxi to the center costs around US$9.

From Rua Dr João Moreira, outside the Centro de Turismo, take the bus marked 'Circular' along the beachfront to Praia de Iracema and Praia do Meireles. A taxi from the center to Praia de Iracema costs US$3 and about US$5 to Meireles.

From Rua Castro E Silva (close to the Centro de Turismo), Praia do Futuro and Serviluz buses run to Praia do Futuro. A taxi from Meireles is about US$10 to the center of the Futuro beach.

For beaches west of the city, such as Icaraí and Cumbuco, you can take a Cumbuco bus from Praça Capistrano Abreu, on Avenida Tristão Gonçalves. You can also get to Cumbuco if you pick up the Vitória minibus that runs frequently along Avenida Beira Mar for a little over US$1.

Cooperttur (☎ 485 3145) is the official taxi cooperative.

BEACHES SOUTHEAST OF FORTALEZA

The coastal road from Fortaleza southeast to Aracati, Hwy CE-040, runs about 10km inland. It's mostly a flat, dry landscape of shrubs, stunted trees and some lakes. The towns are small, with good beaches, *jangadas* and dunes.

Beach Park

This full-blown **water park** (admission US$25), 22km from Fortaleza, is one of the most modern in Brazil, complete with surfboards, dune buggies and ultralight planes. It also features a huge swimming-pool complex with the highest water slide in Brazil – the adrenaline-inducing Insano (Insane), 41m high, with speeds up to 110km/h. The park is quite expensive and would probably appeal most to tourists in search of structured fun. Children under 1m tall get in free. From Praça Tristão Gonçalves in Fortaleza, take a 'Beach Park' bus. This bus also runs along Avenida Beira Mar. Tours to Beach Park cost US$8.

Iguape

☎ 0xx85

Iguape, 54km southeast of Fortaleza, has a long stretch of white-sand beach with *jangadas*, a few lonely palm trees and sand dunes along the horizon. Parts of the town are still traditional and it's an interesting place to watch local women dexterously weave their lacework. Save your buying for the **Centro das Rendeiras**, 6km inland, where the lace is just as fine and cheaper. Also on sale are sweet cakes made from raw sugarcane broth, which is boiled into a thick mass, pressed and reboiled in vats.

Down the beach is the attractive and relaxing **Jangadeiro Praia Hotel** (☎ 361 6039; www.hoteljangadeiro.com.br; Praia do Presídio; d US$36; ❄ ❧). All of the 30 *apartamentos* (rooms with bathroom) have splendid sea views. It also serves food.

Sitting along the sandy street, **João do Camarão** (☎ 370 1031; Rua Luis Eduardo Studart 8; mains US$3-6) has delicious and reasonably priced seafood.

São Benedito buses to Iguape (hourly until 8pm) leave from Fortaleza's Terminal Domingos Olympio, on the corner of Av Domingos Olympio and Av Aguanambi.

ARACATI
☎ 0xx88 / pop 45,000

Aracati is a relatively large town by the Rio Jaguaribe, which in the 18th century was a transport center for cattle. The town is industrial and most of its visitors only pass through on their way to Canoa Quebrada. Aracati does have a good selection of handicrafts on display at the daily open-air market on Rua Pompeu and it is known to have a good street Carnaval.

The only reason to stay overnight in Aracati is if you are arriving late from Natal and don't have the energy to continue on to Canoa Quebrada. If you decide to sleep before making the short trip, there are a few options close to the bus station, including the affordable **Pousada Litorânea** (☎ 421 1001; Rua Cel Alexandrino 1251; s/d US$8/12; 🔀), which has a restaurant downstairs.

Getting There & Away
From the Fortaleza bus station, take one of 15 daily buses to Aracati (three hours, US$4). There are also six buses a day from Natal.

There are sharks waiting at Aracati's bus station to whisk you off to Canoa Quebrada in taxis for US$10 – ignore them and walk 800m to Rua Dragão do Mar and take a bus, passenger truck, minibus, motorcycle taxi or VW Kombi from the stop across from the Igreja Matriz. The fare is US$0.50 to US$2. There are also regular buses from Aracati to the nearby resort of Majorlândia.

CANOA QUEBRADA
☎ 0xx88 / pop 2800

Once a tiny village cut off from the world by its huge, pink sand dunes, Canoa Quebrada (13km southeast of Aracati) is now one of the most popular beach destinations in Ceará. In a matter of a few years the road from Aracati was paved, electricity was hooked up and even the town's sandy streets were cobbled. Canoa claims a variety of pousadas, restaurants and the best nightlife outside of Fortaleza. The craggy, eroding sand cliffs that back the narrow beach lend the otherworldly, mystical feel

for which Canoa is famous. Other than the beach, the main attractions are exploring the endless stretches of dunes by buggy, kite surfing (the season is from July to December), horseback riding, sailing in *jangadas*, simply relaxing or dancing *forró* and reggae until the sun comes up. It is a social town, particularly on weekends, and is a good place to meet locals and other travelers.

Information
INTERNET ACCESS
Canoa.Net (☎ 421 6173; Praça Canoa, Rua Principal; per hr US$1.50; 🕙 noon-1am) Next to Sushi Bar.

INTERNET RESOURCES
General Canoa website (www.canoa-quebrada.com)

MONEY
There are no banks in town. You'll need to go to Aracati or change cash with one of the boutiques on the main street.

Tours
There are lots of dunes and secluded beaches to the north and south of Canoa and it is a shame if you don't get out of town and see them. Hire a buggy and driver from Rua Dragão do Mar (per person US$10 to US$15, depending on type and length of trip). Some of the dunes even have zip lines that you can race down and drop off into the pools below. You can also visit the fish and shrimp farms and eat a delicious, freshly caught meal.

Sleeping
There are lots of foreign-owned pousadas in Canoa Quebrada, and the standards are relatively high. In summer, it's best to make a reservation.

Pousada do Toby (☎ 421 7094; www.pousada -do-toby.com; Rua Nascer do Sol; US$17-70; 🔀 🔊) This ever-evolving pousada is a Canoa landmark, with rooms ranging from modest to upscale. The rooftop pools and deck have the best view in town and the restaurant serves breakfast at any time of day (for those who have truly enjoyed the nightlife). It's a good place to unwind and meet other guests from all over the world. If you don't meet Toby himself, you haven't experienced Canoa Quebrada.

Pousada Califórnia (☎ 421 7039; californiacanoa@ yahoo.co.uk; Rua Nascer do Sol 136; d US$20, less without

THE NORTHEAST

& breakfast;) This large pousada has a variety of clean rooms and an attractive inner courtyard with a bar and pool. It also has a decent library for guests.

La Dolce Vita (☎ 9964 3834; dolcevita@pronto.it; d US$25;) La Dolce Vita is a relaxed spot with friendly staff. The cabins have more character than your average pousada, with each room named after a Fellini film and decorated with movie memorabilia. There is also a good Italian restaurant on site.

Tranquilândia Village (☎ 421 7012; www.tranquil andia.it; d US$40;) These comfortable cabins are set among a rare grassy courtyard with a good ocean view from the pool area. The Italian owner is an avid kite surfer and can help facilitate outings for everyone from beginners to pros.

Pousada Holandes (☎ 964 3504; Rua Nascer do Sol 128; s/d US$6/12;) The first pousada in town, after all these years the Holandes is still a friendly place and is still good value.

Quebramar Pousada (☎ 421 7421; d/tr US$13) Set on the beach, Quebramar doesn't have some of the frills of the other pousadas, but the seven large thatched-roof rooms with balcony views over the water are excellent value. Besides, who needs a pool when you are 25m from a gorgeous beach?

Eating

The main street of Canoa Quebrada, officially known as Rua Principal but locally called Broadway, is the restaurant and bar strip.

Feitiço da Lua (☎ 9181 5554; Rua Principal; mains US$4-8; 5pm-midnight) This small restaurant has been around for a few years now and is always a good dinner choice. It has a variety of creative seafood and other dishes.

Sushi Restaurante (☎ 421 6173; Praça Canoa, Rua Principal; sashimi plate US$6; 5pm-midnight) You wouldn't necessarily expect good sushi in a place as remote as Canoa, but this chill restaurant is a pleasant surprise. There are other nonsushi Japanese and Brazilian dishes and the table service is friendly.

Restaurant Dali (☎ 9951 1087; Rua Principal; pizza US$4-6; 11am-2pm & 5-11pm) This pizza and pasta restaurant is considered to have the best pizza in town.

Bistrô Natural (☎ 421 7162; Rua Dragão do Mar; mains US$5-10; 5pm-midnight) Natural has a selection of quality seafood and meat dishes.

Entertainment

Broadway also hosts some lively bars. There is no need to structure your evening, just walk down the street and you will find what's going on. Before sunset, and sometimes after dark, the beach *barracas* can also host some good parties. A large dance club was under construction in the middle of Broadway at the time of writing.

Todo Mundo (Rua Principal; 4pm-late) This internationally themed bar is a good place to people-watch and start your evening. It can get pretty rowdy, so if you stay a while, it can end your evening too.

Bar Meia (Rua Principal; 8pm-late) Across the street from Todo Mundo, Bar Meia pumps out music and is the main place to dance in Canoa.

Coração de Canoa (Rua Principal) Although it's not much more than a little open space and a large refrigerator stocked with beer, it lives up to its name as 'the heart of Canoa.' This bar is frequently the epicenter of the late night/early morning street party.

Barraca do Paulinho and Antonio Côco are two recommended bars on the beach.

Getting There & Away
BUS

There are four buses to Fortaleza (US$6, 3½ hours) daily. It is a US$0.50 Kombi van ride to Aracati.

SOUTHEAST TO RIO GRANDE DO NORTE

Access by road to this stretch of coast is limited, so there are some great deserted beaches and small fishing villages. Buggies zoom along, but the rest of the time it's pretty quiet. The first town after Canoa Quebrada is **Majorlândia**, 7km southeast, a popular resort that gets crowded on weekends. There are places to stay, but they're not as nice as others you can find, so it's best to keep moving. Another 4km southeast on a sandy track are the distinctive, chalky-white sandstone bluffs of **Quixaba**. From the bluffs, cut by gullies between cacti and palms, you can see the pink hills of Canoa Quebrada. You can rent a *jangada* and visit the neighboring beaches.

The 60km of coast southeast from Quixaba to the border with Rio Grande do Norte is a series of relatively underdeveloped little beaches and towns: **Lagoa do Mato**, **Fontainha**,

Retirinho, **Retiro Grande Mutamba**, **Ponta Grossa**, **Redonda**, **Retiro** (a waterfall), **Peroba**, **Picos**, **Barreiras**, **Barrinha** and, finally, **Icapuí**.

A dirt road from Icapuí continues to **Ibicuitaba** and **Barra do Ceará** beach. It's possible to drive from there to Tibaú, in Rio Grande do Norte.

BEACHES NORTHWEST OF FORTALEZA
Paracuru
☎ 0xx85 / pop 20,000

Paracuru, 100km northwest of Fortaleza, is a popular weekend retreat from Fortaleza and a fairly affluent beach town in its own right. It's a relaxed spot with palms, natural freshwater springs, good surfing and rustic fishing boats. Although it can get crowded on weekends, it's quiet during the rest of the week. Paracuru also has a good Carnaval for a town of its size.

Set in lovely gardens with huge, shady trees, **Pousada Villa Verde** (☎ 344 1181; Rua Professora Maria Luísa Sabóia; s/d US$12/17; 🕸) has nice, basic rooms and is close to the beach.

Close to the beach, the recommended **Tropical Hotel** (☎ 344 2400; Rua Ormezinda Sampaio; s/d US$13/22; 🕸 🖭) has nice rooms, some with decks.

The well-known **Formula 1** (☎ 344 2048; Praia da Munguba; mains US$6; 🕑 10am-midnight) has a variety of dishes and is a good place to hang out and have a drink.

Paiol (☎ 344 1216; Rua Ormezinda Sampaio 811; mains US$6; 🕑 5pm-2am Fri-Sun) has a wide range of pastas and seafood dishes.

Twelve buses a day run to Paracuru from Fortaleza (US$2, 2½ hours), the first at 5:45am, the last at 7pm.

Praia da Lagoinha
☎ 0xx85

A short distance up the coast from Paracuru, Praia da Lagoinha has coconut palms and a small, deep lagoon near the sand dunes. The beach is considered to be one of the best in the state (and it has some good competition). It is still not heavily developed and is a good choice for a short visit from Fortaleza.

Right on the beachfront, **Pousada Milton** (☎ 363 5078; Praia da Lagoinha; s/d US$17/24; 🕸 🖭) is in a scenic location and has a popular restaurant – try the delicious fish stew. You should ask for one of the remodeled rooms.

On top of the cliff is **Pousada Mar à Vista** (☎ 362 5034; www.pousadamaravista.cjb.net; Av Azevedo;

s/d US$23/27; 🕸 🖭), with small, well-equipped rooms and a great view.

Five buses a day run to Lagoinha from Fortaleza (US$4, three hours), the first at 7:15am and the last at 3:30pm.

Mundaú, Guajira & Fleixeiras
The beaches of Mundaú, Guajira and Fleixeiras, just over 150km from Fortaleza along Hwys BR-222 and CE-163, are traditional fishing areas with wide stretches of beautiful sand. They are becoming increasingly popular destinations from Fortaleza.

Buses run from the Fortaleza bus station to Mundaú and Fleixeiras (US$6, around four hours, depart 6:15am and 4pm) daily.

JERICOACOARA
☎ 0xx88 / pop 2000

Jericoacoara (jher-ee-kwah-kwah-rah), more simply know as 'Jeri,' is Ceará's trendy beach town, boasting a perfect combination of scenery, relaxing activities and nightlife. The village, which consists of five sandy streets, is wedged between the broad gray beach, a series of grassy hills and the majestic Pôr do Sol (Sunset) dune. It is an easy place to make new friends – both travelers and locals – and almost everyone ends up staying longer than they planned. The high season runs from July to January and it is advised to make a hotel reservation during those months, as the town can get full.

Information
INTERNET ACCESS
There are a few places around town and all have the same rate.

Cyber Cangaçu (Rua Principal; per hr US$3; 🕑 9am-midnight)

INTERNET RESOURCES
Jericoacoara tourism site (www.jericoacoara.tur.br)
'Official' site (www.jericoacoara.com) English site with a variety of information.

MONEY
Sabor de Terra (Rua do Forró) This restaurant usually changes dollars or euros for reis. You won't get a fair rate, but you won't do any better. Knock if it isn't open.

TRAVEL AGENCIES
Dadinho Off-Road (☎ 669 2068; dadinhojeri@ig.com .br; Rua do Forró) Dadinho (aka Ronaldo) is the man to talk to if you want to head up the coast in a 4WD. He will take

you up to Tatajuba, Camocim and Lençóis Maranhenses (approximately US$30 to US$40 per person, one way). He knows everything about the region and can also be contacted through Koala Passeios.

Koala Passeios (☎ 669 2175; koalapasseios@bol.com .br; Rua do Forró; ☻ 9am-8pm Mon-Sat, to 2pm Sun) Professional, organized and a little expensive, but no messing around.

Activities

The steady winds between August and December make Jericoacoara a top destination for windsurfing and kite surfing, and the gigantic dunes make it one of the best spots for sandboarding. There are also nightly capoeira classes on the beach and decent waves for surfing. If you are of a calmer demeanor, you can visit the dunes outside of town by buggy and take a dip in the freshwater pools between them, sail on a *jangada*, take yoga classes at one of the pousadas or stroll to **Pedra Furada**, an arched rock 3km from town.

BUGGY RIDES

It is a memorable trip to Lagoa Azul, Coração and Paraíso in a buggy. Get a group together. The price for a day is US$50.

CAPOEIRA

Classes are held in the afternoon on the beach followed by a *roda* (open capoeira performance) at sunset. There are also night classes at the Solar da Malhada pousada (for more advanced capoeiristas). Prices vary and it is best to negotiate for multiple classes. Either way you should at least watch the *roda*.

KITE SURFING

Zê Antônio is regarded as the best kite-surfing teacher. He can be found at **Pousada Recanto Sonho** (Rua Principal; per lesson US$25).

SURFING & SANDBOARDING

Jeri Aqua Sport (Rua do Forró; surfboard/sandboard per hr US$3/2; ☻ 8am-7pm) This surf and sandboard shop rents them out. Other places around town offer similar prices.

WINDSURFING

You can windsurf any time of the year in Jeri, but July to January is the best. There is a number of international competitions held each year.

Clube dos Ventos (☎ 669 2288; www.clubedos ventos.com) This is your best choice for gear and instruction as it is the most professional and has the best resources. Classes run from a basic one-hour class (US$50) to a three-hour package (US$150). Located on the beach.

Sleeping

There are dozens of pousadas and smaller hotels in Jericoacoara. During the high season, it is best to reserve ahead. The pousadas listed below are standouts, but if they are full, ask them to refer you to one of the many other fine places in town.

Pousada Calanda (☎ 669 2285; www.jericoacoara .tur.br/calanda; Rua das Dunas; s/d US$15/30; ☒) Close to the dune, this romantic and nicely detailed pousada has a relaxing charm, similar to the town itself. It has a famous breakfast and uses solar power. English, German and Spanish spoken.

Pousada Papagaio (☎ 669 2142; www.jericoacoara .tur.br/pousadapapagaio; s/d US$15/25; ☒ ☒) Set on one of the side streets between Ruas Principal and Forró, this pousada is on private, landscaped grounds with comfortable outdoor furniture. It's immaculately clean, has a kind owner and a decent bar.

Hotel Mosquito Blue (☎ 669 2203; www.mosquito blue.com.br; s/d US$60/80, r with sea view US$110) Also between Principal and Forró, Mosquito Blue is the town's new luxury addition. Some complain that it's lacking in character, but it's definitely an attractive, clean, comfortable place with international hotel standards. The grounds lead out to the beach.

Pousada Casa do Turismo (☎ 669 2000; www .casadoturismo.com; s/d US$20/25) This reasonably priced, professional pousada also serves as the agent for the Fortaleza bus, which leaves from in front. It is a reliable choice for a comfortable stay.

Solar da Malhada (☎ 669 2094; www.jericoacoara .tur.br/solardamalhada; Rua da Igreja; camping US$3-4, r per person US$12) With group rooms, yoga, music classes, capoeira class and massage, this pousada is a world unto itself. Although the plaza out front is unattractive, there is a gorgeous view out back to the sea. It is good value.

Eating

The town offers an unusual variety of food for such a small place and has a number of restaurants that serve healthy and vegetarian dishes (one pizza restaurant even has 'diet pizza').

Padaria do Sr Antônio (Rua do Forró; ☽ 2-6am) It's a late-night tradition to eat at this simple, yet delicious bakery. It only has three or so items on the menu, so try one of each (or a few of each, depending on how many drinks you've had).

Chocolate (☎ 9611 2344; chocolatejeri@hotmail .com; Rua do Forró; ☽ noon-midnight, closed Mon; mains $7-12) This relaxed and romantic restaurant has flavorsome food prepared with the highest standards of cleanliness. It is set on an attractive terrace and has arguably the best chocolate desserts in Ceará. It serves *ceviche* (marinated raw seafood) and a variety of risottos, try the *camarão com funghi* (shrimp and mushroom risotto, US$7).

Café Brasil (sandwiches US$2-3; ☽ 9am-5pm, closed Sun) In an alley between Rua Principal and Rua São Francisco, Café Brasil offers quality coffee, *sucos* (juices), *açaí* and even cappuccino. The tasty sandwiches are on wholegrain bread.

Gord'Ana (Rua Nova Jeri; soups US$2-4; ☽ 7pm-2am, closed Sun) Across from Pousada Calandra, this new soup bar has more than 20 types of healthy and delicious soups. For a little place, it has a lot of character and a nice view of the night sky.

Pizza Nômade (☎ 669 2134; www.pizzanomade .com.br; pizzas US$5; ☽ 6pm-late) Jeri has a glut of wood-oven pizza places, most of similar quality, but this venerated spot, between Rua Principal and Rua do Forró, wins for its chill ambience and good music.

Entertainment

Everything starts – and frequently ends – at **Planeta Jeri** (Rua Principal) and at the drink carts parked on the street in front. Things don't get going until at least 10pm, and the music runs the gamut from hip-hop to samba to drum 'n' bass.

In the high season, the late-night crowd moves on to dance at **Bar do Forró** (Rua do Forró) or **Mama Africa** (Rua Nova Jeri).

Getting There & Away

Three buses a day leave Fortaleza's bus station for Jericoacoara (US$12, about six hours, depart 9am, 10:30am and 6:30pm). The 10:30am bus drops you off in Preá and you take an off-road bus for the last stretch. The other buses go to Jijoca, where you are transferred to a passenger truck (included in the ticket price) for the 24km rodeo ride to Jericoacoara. The night bus is quicker and cooler, but you arrive in Jericoacoara after midnight. Someone from one of the pousadas will meet the bus, and you can always move to another pousada the next day.

Transportation leaves Jericoacoara for Fortaleza at 7:30am, 2pm and 10:30pm daily from in front of the Pousada Casa do Turismo.

To get to Jeri from Sobral, you must catch a bus at 11:15am over an abysmal road to Jijoca (US$5, three hours), which will connect (hopefully) with the Fortaleza bus.

If you have come by car, leave it parked in Jijoca, where some of the pousada owners can keep an eye on it. The ride to Jericoacoara – over and around sweeping dunes, lagoons, bogs and flat scrub terrain – is beautiful, but very hard on people and machines.

Unless you are going straight back to Fortaleza, and especially if you are heading on to Camocim or further up to Parnaíba or Lençóis Maranhenses, you should go in a 4WD to save time and your sanity.

If you are a masochist or have demolished your budget by going out every night to Planeta Jeri, you can travel by bus to Sobral and head north from there. You will have to catch a minibus leaving Jijoca at 2am – take the 10:30pm truck out of Jericoacoara and think up new and interesting ways to entertain yourself in Jijoca for three hours.

TATAJUBA
☎ 0xx88

Tatajuba, about 30km west of Jericoacoara, is a tiny, isolated fishing village at the mouth of a tidal river. The beach is broad and lonely, and there's a lagoon surrounded by extensive dunes on the edge of town. One of the dunes actually overtook the old Tatajuba, which had to be moved out of the way – brick by brick. You can still see evidence of where the church used to be.

Tatajuba is a good place to completely unwind, read the book you've been meaning to tackle or spend solitary time on beach.

The windblown **Pousada Brisa do Mar** (☎ 9961 5439; s/d US$13) offers basic, but reasonably comfortable rooms. The restaurant at the pousada serves locally caught fish.

There is no regular transportation, but you can ride in one of the buggies heading north from Jericoacoara or find out about boats going either way.

CAMOCIM
☎ 0xx88 / pop 41,000

Camocim is a fishing port and market town at the mouth of the Rio Coreaú, in northwestern Ceará, near the Piauí border. The town's economy revolves around the saltworks, lobster fishing and a busy daily market. After Jericoacoara's blissed-out traveler vibe, Camocim is a reintroduction into the rest of Brazil.

Just a short distance from town, you can sip coconut milk while tanning at **Praia dos Barreiros**, **Praia do Farol**, **Praia dos Coqueiros** or **Praia de Maceió**. However, for the great majority of travelers, Camocim is just a stop on the road.

Information

MONEY
Banco do Brasil (Rua José de Alencar) Here's the ATM that you've been missing in Jericoacoara.

TRAVEL AGENCIES
Sol Nascente (☎ 621 6251; solnascente@sobral.org; Shop 7, Rua Alcindo Rocha 49; ◐ 9am-5pm, closed Sun) This helpful agency can help you to maneuver through a region with little public transportation.

Sleeping & Eating
Hotel Marilha (☎ 621 1570; Av Beira Mar 2081; s/d US$15/17; [P] [X] [R]) The dated interior may need a bit of renovation, but, hey, you're in Camocim. Marilha is spacious, with comfortable rooms set around a pool. It is good value and there's a tourist-info post with Internet access right across the street.

Fortim (Av Beira Mar; mains US$3-6; ◐ 11am-9pm, closed Sun) This basic restaurant on the waterfront has excellent and affordable fresh seafood dishes.

Getting There & Away
Four buses a day run to Camocim's **bus station** (☎ 621 0028; Praça Sinhá Trévia) via Sobral from Fortaleza (US$12, 7½ hours), the first at 7:30am and the last at 6:30pm.

A jeep leaves the central market in Camocim for Jijoca at around 10:30am daily, and if there are enough people it will carry on to Jericoacoara. An alternative is to hire a

beach buggy in Camocim for the ride to Jericoacoara. Prices are very negotiable.

During the high season there are boats sailing from Camocim to Jericoacoara (price negotiable, four hours).

SOBRAL
☎ 0xx88 / pop 135,000

Although Sobral is an industrial center of some economic importance, this hot, characterless place is perhaps the most widely reviled town in the region. The only reason to stay overnight here is if you are stuck in transit.

There are six buses a day to Camocim (US$5, 2½ hours) from Sobral. The earliest bus leaves at 5:30am, the last at 7pm. One bus leaves Sobral daily at 11:15am for Jijoca, where you can connect with a truck that will take you to Jericoacoara.

SERRA DE BATURITÉ

The interior of Ceará is not limited to the harsh landscapes of the *sertão*. There are also ranges of hills, which break up the monotony of the sun-scorched land. The Serra de Baturité is the range closest to Fortaleza. A natural watershed, it is an oasis of green, with coffee and bananas cultivated around the cliffs and jagged spines of the hills. The climate is tempered by rain, the evenings are cool and morning fog obscures Pico Alto (1115m), the highest point in the state.

Baturité
☎ 0xx85 / pop 25,000

Founded in 1745, the town of Baturité (95km west of Fortaleza) was once at the forefront of the fight against slavery, and is now the economic and commercial center of the region. Most of its points of interest are grouped around the Praça Matriz and include the **pelourinho** (whipping post), the baroque **church of Matriz NS de Palma** (1764), the **Palácio Entre-Rios** mansion, and the **Museu Comendador Ananias Arruda**, which contains exhibits from the town's past (though surprisingly little on the struggle to abolish slavery). There are also a few *termas* (resorts with mineral pools) clustered around the town. Local handicrafts on sale in Baturité include embroidery, tapestry and straw goods.

Most visitors get out of town and stay in the nearby villages of Guaramiranga and Pacoti (below). Baturité has a few of its own accommodations, including **Hotel Canuto** (☎ 347 0100; Praça Santa Luiza 703; d US$20), a mid-sized, quiet hotel where you will get a good night of sleep.

Ten buses leave Fortaleza's bus station daily for Baturité (US$3, 2½ hours).

Guaramiranga & Pacoti
☎ 0xx85

The two prettiest villages on the heights of Serra de Baturité are Guaramiranga and Pacoti, 19km and 26km respectively from Baturité. Everywhere you turn seems to have a fantastic view. As the hills are a popular weekend retreat from Fortaleza, prices can go up on Saturday and Sunday. Most of the hotels also offer breakfast, lunch and dinner (some included in the room price).

Hotel Escola de Guaramiranga (☎ /fax 321 1106; Sítio Guaramiranga; d US$33; P ⊠ ⊠) doubles as a training center for hotel staff in Guaramiranga. It has well-worn but spotless *apartamentos*, a bar and ping-pong tables. The hotel is a little tricky to find (no sign), but it's a good deal.

Close to Pacoti, the attractive **Estância Vale das Flores** (☎ 325 1233; www.valedasflores.com.br; Sítio São Francisco; d/chalet US$25/30; P ⊠ ⊠) has a swimming pool, sports facilities, horse rental and minizoo. Breakfast and lunch are included.

Hofbräuhaus (☎ 328 0004; www.hofbrauhaus-brasil .com; Estrada de Aratuba, Mulungu; d US$18-35; P ⊠), a group of newly opened mountain chalets, is your little bit of Deutschland in Brazil. Each of the 20 chalets was designed by a different architect and artist from Ceará. Beyond dozens of activities and good prices, this place has hearty food and plentiful beers. A stay at Hofbräuhaus makes for a fun change of pace.

The Empresa Redentora bus company runs daily buses direct to Guaramiranga (US$3.50, three hours, 7:30am and 3pm) from Fortaleza's bus station. From Baturité, there's a bus at 10am to Guaramiranga and Pacoti, and another at 5:30pm to Guaramiranga only.

PARQUE NACIONAL DE UBAJARA
☎ 0xx88

The **Parque Nacional de Ubajara** (admission US$1; ☼ 9am-5pm, closed Mon) is just a few kilometers from the small town of Ubajara, 325km

west of Fortaleza by Hwy BR-222. The main attractions are giant caves and the cable-car rides down into them.

The park, with its beautiful vistas, forest, waterfalls and walking trail out to the caves, is worth a visit in its own right. At 850m above sea level, temperatures in the surrounding area are cool and provide a welcome respite from the searing heat of the *sertão*.

Caves
Nine chambers with strange limestone formations extend more than 500m into the side of a mountain. The main formations seen inside the caves are **Pedra do Sino** (Bell Stone), **Salas da Rosa** (Rose Rooms), **Sala do Cavalo** (Horse Room) and **Sala dos Retratos** (Portrait Room). You can arrive by cable car or by foot.

The **cable car** (per person US$4; ☼ 10am-3:30pm) makes the trip a lot easier and faster, but if you fancy a strenuous hike take the 3km trail down to the caves. Allow at least half a day for the round-trip. Start in the cool of the early morning, wear sturdy footwear and take enough to drink. Alternatively, you can walk down to the caves and take the cable car back up.

IBAMA (☎ 634 1388; www.ibama.gov.br; tours US$0.50; ☼ 8am-5pm), the government environmental agency at the entrance to the park, 5km from Ubajara, provides guides for cave tours daily.

Sleeping & Eating
As hotels and restaurants are pretty widely spread, it is a good idea to just eat at your hotel.

Sítio do Alemão (☎ 9961 4645; Sítio Santana 4km; chalets US$10; ⊠) Run by a German-Brazilian couple who can provide walking maps for the park and loads of information about local attractions. There are wonderful vistas over the *sertão* from the property, 1.5km from the park entrance. Day trips to Parque Nacional de Sete Cidades (140km away on a good road) can also be arranged. The chalets are immaculate and include a huge breakfast.

Pousada da Neblina (☎ /fax 634 1270; Estrada do Teleférico; s/d US$13/23; ⊠ ⊠) Right at the park is this affordable option with decent rooms. It is nice to get into the pool after a day of hiking.

THE NORTHEAST

Getting There & Around

There are six buses a day from Fortaleza to Ubajara (US$8, six hours). The first bus leaves at 6:30am, the last at 9pm. There are also bus connections to Teresina (US$8, six hours), the capital of Piauí state.

To reach the park entrance from Ubajara, either walk the 3km or take a taxi (US$4).

JUAZEIRO DO NORTE

☎ 0xx88 / pop 200,000

Juazeiro do Norte, 528km south of Fortaleza, is a magnet for followers of Padre Cícero, who lived in this town in the early 20th century and became a controversial figure of the *sertão*. Not only was he a curate with several miracles to his credit, he also exercised a strong political influence. His astonishing rise to fame started when an elderly woman received the host from him at Mass and claimed that it had miraculously turned to blood. Soon he was being credited with all kinds of miracles, and was later drawn into a leading role in the social and political upheavals in the Northeast. Padre Cícero died in 1934 and, despite the Catholic Church's unwillingness to beatify him, the claims and adoration of his followers seem to be as strong as ever.

Sights

COLINA DO HORTO

On the hill above town, the **Colina do Horto**, accessible either by road or along a path laid out like a cross, is the colossal **statue of Padre Cícero** (25m), which was built in 1969 and ranks as the fourth-tallest statue in the world – only beaten by Cristo Rey (Cochabamba, Bolivia), Cristo Redentor on Corcovado (Rio) and the Statue of Liberty (New York). Nearby are a small chapel and a building filled with wooden or wax replicas of every conceivable body part – offerings to the chapel that represent the area of the body supposedly cured.

Padre Cícero's tomb (Praça do Socorro) is beside the Capela NS do Perpétua Socorro.

GRÁFICA DE LITERATURA DE CORDEL

If you are interested in *literatura de cordel* (string literature), the cheaply produced pamphlets for the masses with topics such as biographies of famous figures, love stories, opinions and views, visit the **Gráfica de Literatura de Cordel** (Rua Santa Luzia; ☼ 7-11am &

1-5pm Mon-Fri, 8am-noon Sat), a workshop where you can see the pamphlets being produced for sale.

Festivals & Events

The best time to witness Padre Cícero's magnetic attraction and the devotion he inspires is during the festivals and pilgrimages. On March 24, the **Aniversário do Padre Cícero** celebrates Padre Cícero in legend and song. The commemoration of his death takes place on July 20. The *romaria* (pilgrimage) to Juazeiro do Norte in honor of Padre Cícero takes place on November 1 and 2 and is known as the **Dia do Romeiro e Festa do Padre Cícero**.

Sleeping & Eating

Since this town is a pilgrimage center, there is no lack of accommodations, except during the main festivals.

San Felipe (☎ /fax 511 7904; Rua Dr Floro 285; d US$10-22; ✖) This is one of the more affordable options for a decent hotel.

Panorama (☎ /fax 512 -3100; Rua Santo Agostinho 58; d US$25-35; ✖ ⊠) Panorama is a bit older, but much nicer and offers comfortable *apartamentos*. It also has a good restaurant and bar.

Mão de Vaca (☎ 512 2543; Rua Rui Barbosa 25; mains US$3-6; ☼ 11am-3pm & 6pm-midnight Tue-Fri, 6pm-midnight Mon & Sat) Mão de Vaca is recommended for regional food at a decent price.

Getting There & Away

From the **bus station** (☎ 571 2868; Rua Delmiro Gouvéia) there are four daily departures for Fortaleza (US$13, nine hours), and regular buses to all the major cities in the Northeast.

PIAUÍ

Piauí, one of the largest states in the Northeast, is the poorest in Brazil. It was originally populated in the arid *sertão* in the south and gradually moved toward the coast, creating an oddly shaped territory with underdeveloped infrastructure. The interior still suffers oppressive heat and regular debilitating droughts.

The climate on the coast is kept cool(er) by sea breezes. If you're heading into the interior, the best time for festivals and bearable temperatures is July and August. The

TOM COCKREM

Porto de Galinhas (p509), Pernambuco

Waterfall, Parque Nacional de Itatiaia
(p193), Rio de Janeiro state

LEE FOSTER

ANDREW DRAFFEN

Parque Nacional da Chapada dos Guimarães
(p384), Mato Grosso

JANE SWEENEY

The Pantanal (p388), Mato Grosso

JUDY BELLAH

Hang gliding (p145) over São Conrado with a view of Ipanema, Rio de Janeiro

JOHN MAIER JR

Surfers, Arpoador beach (p123), Rio de Janeiro

Capoeira performer (p432), Terreiro de Jesus, Salvador, Bahia

BRUCE YUAN

PAUL BERNHARDT

Schooner tour, Costa Verde (p180), Rio de Janeiro state

worst time, unless you want to cook yourself, is between September and December.

Although Piauí is usually bypassed by travelers, it has several fantastic natural attractions, including the Delta do Parnaíba, the Parque Nacional de Sete Cidades and the Parque Nacional da Serra da Capivara (one of the top prehistoric sites found in South America).

TERESINA

☎ 0xx86 / pop 700,000

Teresina, the flat and sun-baked capital of Piauí, is famed as the hottest city in Brazil. It has a lot of hospitals and, as a regional medical center, receives patients from neighboring states. However, most people who have a choice in the matter don't make it to Teresina or, if they do, are simply there in transit.

Locals seem to be interested in meeting foreigners and, like the British, they instantly warm to discussion of the weather, especially of their favorite topic: *o calor* (the heat). If you are keen to see a provincial Brazilian city that is unadulterated by tourism, this is your chance; otherwise, keep moving.

Information

Piemtur (☎ 221 7100; www.piemtur.pi.gov.br)
Centro do Convenções (☼ 8am-6pm Mon-Fri, 9am-1pm Sat) Centro de Artesanato (Praça Dom Pedro II; ☼ 8am-6pm Mon-Fri, 9am-1pm Sat) The helpful staff at the state tourism agency happily dole out literature, maps and advice.

Centro de Artesanato

Centro de Artesanato (☎ 221 3368; Praça Dom Pedro II; ☼ 8am-6pm Mon-Fri, 9am-1pm Sat & Sun) This center has crafts from all over Piauí. It is pleasant to browse among the shops that sell small sculptures, leather articles, furniture, extremely intricate lacework, colorful hammocks, opals and soapstone (from Pedro Segundo) and liqueurs and confectionery made from such native plants as *genipapo* (local fruit), *caju* (cashew), *buriti* (a palm-tree fruit) and *maracujá* (passion fruit).

Festivals & Events

Salão Internacional de Humor do Piauí (Piauí International Festival of Humor) is held during October or November depending on the year (check with Piemtur, left) and features comedy shows, exhibitions of cartoons, comedy routines and lots of live music.

Micarina is Teresina's out-of-season Carnaval, which takes place in early July, when it is cool enough for crazed *blocos* (large groups of singing and dancing Carnaval revelers) to take to the streets.

Sleeping

Hotel São Raimundo (☎ 221 3397; Rua Senador Teodoro Pachêco 1199; s/d US$8/12; ☒) The best budget option is this friendly, laid-back place with decent rooms and adequate *apartamentos*.

Hotel Real Palace (☎ 221 2768; www.realpalacehotel.com.br; Rua Areolino de Abreu 1217; d US$35-45; ☒ ☒) This is a smooth mid-range option

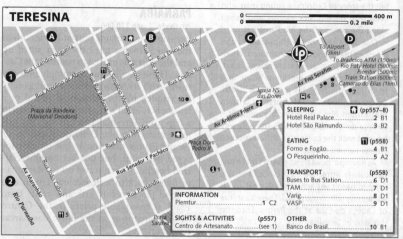

TERESINA

SLEEPING (pp557–8)
Hotel Real Palace................2 B1
Hotel São Raimundo..............3 B2

EATING (p558)
Forno e Fogão....................4 B1
O Pesqueirinho...................5 A2

TRANSPORT (p558)
Buses to Bus Station.............6 D1
TAM.............................7 D1
Varig...........................8 D1
VASP............................9 D1

INFORMATION
Piemtur.........................1 C2

SIGHTS & ACTIVITIES (p557)
Centro de Artesanato.........(see 1)

OTHER
Banco do Brasil.................10 B1

THE NORTHEAST

that guarantees a comfortable stay in Teresina and has a good restaurant.

Rio Poty Hotel (☎ 223 1500; www.riopoty.com .br; Av Marechal Castelo Branco 555; s/d/tr US$67/75/97; (P 🗙 🗶 🖳 🗩) Shaped like a pyramid, this 'five-star' is the poshest place in town. The deluxe apartments get rather inexpensive during the low season and are really a steal.

Eating

There are lots of inexpensive places around town with *prato feitos* (plates of the day) and basic meals.

Camarão do Elias (☎ 232 5025; Av Pedro Almeida 457; mains US$5-9; 🕒 5:30pm-late Mon-Sat, 11am-5pm Sun) If you feel like seafood, try the house speciality *moqueca á moda do Elías*, a delicious fish stew with lemon sauce, garlic and vegetables.

O Pesqueirinho (☎ 225 2268; Av Jorge Velho 6889) This is a popular spot, several kilometers outside town on the river side. It is well-known for its fish and also serves crab and shrimp stew.

Forno e Fogão (☎ 221 3306; Luxor do Piauí Hotel, Praça Deodoro 310; buffet US$6; 🕒 1-3pm) The gigantic buffet lunch here is worth the splurge and is particularly nice if you need to refuel while on a long layover between bus trips.

BE NICE TO YOUR MOTHER

If you happen to be a virgin named Maria (or Mary for that matter), you should be very careful when traveling in Teresina. Locals tell the story of Crispim, a young man who lived with his old, sick mother and fished along the banks of the Rio Parnaíba.

One day, after fishing without success, he returned home angry and frustrated. When he asked his mother what there was to eat, she could only offer him bone soup. In a fit of rage, he beat his mother to death. Before she died, she laid a curse on Crispim that turned him into a terrible monster – Cabeça-de-Cuia (Bowl-Head). The only way he can break the curse is to deflower seven virgins named Maria.

As having a 'bowl head' doesn't make one particularly attractive to the opposite sex, Crispim hasn't yet achieved his goal and is apparently still on the prowl. There's a statue of Cabeça-de-Cuia at the Parque Encontro dos Rios in Teresina.

Getting There & Away

AIR

The airport is on Avenida Centenário, 6km north of the center. There are flights between Teresina and Brasília, Rio, São Paulo and the major cities in the Northeast and the Amazon.

TAM (☎ 221 1912; Rua Félix Pacheco 2008)

Varig (☎ 223 4940; Rua Frei Serafim 1932)

VASP (☎ 223 3222; Rua Frei Serafim 1826)

BUS

Teresina's main bus station is 6km from the center on BR-343. From the center, you can catch a local bus to the station from the bus stop on Avenida Frei Serafim.

Teresina has regular bus connections with Belém (US$20, 15 hours, 984km, five a day), Fortaleza (US$17 to US$30, 10 hours, 634km, seven a day) via Sobral, Parnaíba (US$9 to US$12, six hours, 354km, eight a day), Pedro Segundo (US$8, four hours, hourly), Piripiri (US$4, three hours, 183km, 14 a day), São Luís (US$15, seven hours, 445km, six a day) and São Raimundo Nonato (US$18, nine hours, 456km, two a day).

Getting Around

The cheapest option from the bus station is to take the bus from the stop across the road – this is OK if you arrive at night, when it's cooler, but during the day it can be unbearably hot. Taxis into the center will cost around US$4.

PARNAÍBA

☎ 0xx86 / pop 170,000

Parnaíba was a major port at the mouth of the Rio Parnaíba until the river silted up and the port was moved to nearby Luís Correia. These days it is a charmingly peaceful town, with its warm, sedate evenings only interrupted by the occasional sound of a truck or children's fireworks. It's well worth a trip from Teresina. You can visit the primary attraction, the Delta do Parnaíba, or escape Piauí's notoriously hot interior for some beautiful, but not yet commercialized beaches – then travel on to Maranhão or buggy back to Jericoacoara. This is also a good place to buy arts and crafts from Piauí at reasonable prices in the Centro de Artesanatos or in the Porto das Barcas neighborhood.

Information
INTERNET ACCESS
You can use the Internet facilities at **Casa do Turismo** or at most of the travel and tour agencies in Porto das Barcas for US$2 to US$3 an hour.

MONEY
There's an ATM at Bradesco, opposite the telephone office on Avenida Presidente Vargas.
Banco do Brasil (Praça da Graça) Also changes money.

POST
Main post office (Praça da Graça) Next to the Banco do Brasil.

TELEPHONE
Telephone office (Av Presidente Vargas 390)

TOURIST INFORMATION
Piemtur (☎ 321 1532; Rua Dr Oscar Clark 575; ☼ 8am-1pm & 2:30-6pm Mon-Fri) The staff at the state tourism agency can provide limited information about boat trips around the Delta do Parnaíba and buses to local destinations. Private agencies are more efficient and can arrange excursions for you directly.

TRAVEL AGENCIES
Casa do Turismo (☎ 323 9937; casadoturism@bol.com.br; Shop 17, Porto das Barcas; ☼ 7am-10pm Mon-Sat) The helpful owner of this agency, Antônio, can arrange tours or passage to the delta, Sete Cidades, Jericoacoara and Lençóis Maranhenses. He will also try to set lone travelers up with groups, if so desired.
Igaratur (☎ 322 2141; Porto das Barcas)
Morais Brito (☎ 321 1969; Porto das Barcas)

Sights
DELTA DO PARNAÍBA
The **Delta do Parnaíba**, the only delta in the Americas facing the open sea, is a 2700-sq-km expanse of islands, beaches, lagoons, sand dunes and mangrove forest straddling the Piauí/Maranhão state border. The delta teems with wildlife. Around 65 percent of its area is in Maranhão, but the easiest access is from Parnaíba. Day trips by boat around the delta run from Porto das Barcas, with a stop on Ilha do Caju; the cost is around US$20 (depending on how many people there are). Ilha do Caju has been owned for several generations by an English family that has established an ecological reserve there.

PORTO DAS BARCAS
The restored warehouse section along the riverfront, **Porto das Barcas**, contains a maritime museum, an art center, galleries, bars, travel agencies and restaurants.

Sleeping
Refúgio Ecológica Ilha do Caju (☎ /fax 321 1308; www.ilhadocaju.com.br; reservation office Av Vargas 235; d/chalet US$66/75) This famous pousada, on the Ilha do Caju, is three hours by boat from Parnaíba into the delta. If you are going all this way, you may as well opt for the more comfortable chalet. Staying on the island and participating in the various activities is one of the best ways to experience this region. Boat trip included in price.

Residencial Pousada (☎ 322 2931; Av Almirante Sampaio 375; s/d US$6/7; P ✖) This budget spot doesn't look like much from the outside, but the rooms are large, clean and have high ceilings.

Hotel Cívico (☎ 322 2470; fax 322 2028; Av Governor Chagas Rodrigues 474; s/d/tr US$21/30/37; P ✖ ✖) In the town center, with pleasantly campy 1970s décor, this place has a huge buffet breakfast, wide hallways and an attractive pool area. Rooms have small balconies.

Eating
Caranguejo Express (Rua Quentinha Peres 64; mains US$3-5; ☼ 11am-11pm) Locally famous for its enormous and delicious torta de caranguejo crab cake (US$5), don't expect express service but do expect it to be worth the wait.

Sabor e Arte (☎ 323 1974; Av Vargas 37; ☼ 11am-11pm Mon-Sat, 6-11pm Sun) This Porto das Barcas favorite is a relaxed place with interesting original art on the walls. The dishes themselves are works of art – beautifully presented, delicious fruit and meat combinations. Try any of the *frutos do mar* (seafood) dishes. The owner is enthusiastic and friendly.

Zé Grosso (☎ 983 1530; Ilha Grande; mains US$2-5; ☼ 11am-11pm Mon-Fri, 5-11pm Sat) 'Fat Joe's' is a very friendly place with great, cheap regional dishes. It's 3km from town, over the bridge, but well worth the effort it takes to get there. Consider taking a cab as it gets dark early and the road, although not dangerous, is not well lit.

Getting There & Away
There are frequent bus services between Teresina and Parnaíba (six hours, US$9 to

THE NORTHEAST

US$12), with other daily buses running to Fortaleza, São Luís, Camocim, Sobral and Ubajara.

For the short trip to Luís Correia, buses leave every hour from the local bus station next to Praça Santo Antônio. Agencia Empresa São Francisco runs two buses daily from Praça Santa Cruz (Farmacia Cruz Vermelha) to Tutóia (2½ hours, depart noon and 5pm). Schedule and times are flexible. From Tutóia there are trucks running via Rio Novo to Barreirinhas, for access to the Parque Nacional dos Lençóis Maranhenses.

A small wooden boat plies daily through the Delta do Parnaíba to Tutóia (US$10, about six hours). This is a good way to check out some of the delta – ask for a hammock so that you can sling it on the deck and enjoy the scenery in repose. The boat leaves from Porto Salgado, on the riverfront close to Porto das Barcas, between 10am and noon – check at the port in the morning for exact departure time. On Monday, Thursday and Saturday the boat leaves at 11am. Take some food and water along. Call **Lanch Cidade Tutóia** (☎ 321 2850) for more information.

AROUND PARNAÍBA

Piauí's 66km coastline is the result of a land swap with Ceará in the late 1800s. There are some fine beaches, many of which are fast being developed. **Praia Pedra do Sal**, 15km northeast of Parnaíba, on Ilha Grande Santa Isabel, is a good beach, divided by rocks into a calm section suitable for swimming and a rough section preferred by surfers. **Lagoa do Portinho** is a lagoon surrounded by dunes about 14km east of Parnaíba on the road to Luís Correia. It's a popular spot for swimming, boating, sailing and fishing.

The prime beaches east of Luís Correia are **Praia do Coqueiro** and **Praia de Atalaia**. The latter is very popular on weekends and has plenty of bars selling drinks and seafood. The nearby lagoon, **Lagoa do Sobradinho**, is renowned for its shifting sands that bury surrounding trees. **Macapá**, 43km east of Luís Correia, has a few pousadas and is a good base for exploring the deserted beaches further east – **Barra Grande** (considered by many to be the pick of the bunch), **Barrinha**, **Sardi**, **Morro Branco** and **Cajueiro da Praia**. Adventurous travelers should bring their hammocks if they want to stay at these beaches.

Aimberê Eco Resort (☎ 366 1144; www.aimbere resorthotel.cjb.net; Rua Projetada s/n, Praia do Coqueiro; d US$33; P 🏊 🌀) is a former beach mansion that's been transformed into a resort. It is the best higher-end choice in the area and is a stylish way to experience the coastline of Piauí. It also has a good view.

PARQUE NACIONAL DE SETE CIDADES
☎ 0xx86

Sete Cidades is a small national park with interesting rock formations that resemble *sete cidades* (seven cities). Some researchers who have analyzed nearby rock inscriptions have deduced that the formations are indeed ancient ruined cities of a mysterious culture. There is a lot of speculation over who lived here: from aliens to Vikings. Either way it is an intriguing spectacle.

The **park** (admission US$1, mandatory guide US$7; 🕐 8am-5pm) has an **IBAMA office** (☎ 343 1342; Centro de Visitantes), 6km from the park entrance, which can supply a useful map and is where you can arrange for a guide. The basic hike around the park is a loop requiring a couple of hours of leisurely walking – you'll need more time if you go to the **swimming pool** at Primeira Cidade. It's best to start your hike early in the morning. Bring drinking water because it gets hot, and watch out for the *cascavelas* – black-and-yellow rattlesnakes. **Sexta Cidade** (Sixth City) and **Pedra do Elefante** (Elephant Rock), the first sites on the hike, are lumps of rock with strange scaly surfaces. The **Pedra do Inscrição** (Rock of Inscription) at Quinta Cidade (Fifth City) has red markings, which some say are cryptic Indian runes. The highlight of Quarta Cidade (Fourth City) is the **Mapa do Brasil** (Map of Brazil), a natural hole in the rock shaped almost exactly like a backward-facing Brazil. The **Biblioteca** (Library), **Arco de Triunfo** (Triumphal Arch) and **Cabeça do Cachorro** (Dog's Head) are promontories with good views.

Sleeping & Eating

Parque Hotel Sete Cidades (☎ 343 1342; camping US$3, d US$15; 🌀) This good-value hotel near the IBAMA office has *apartamentos* with fans. It is a great place to crash after a long day in the park. There's a restaurant attached.

Hotel Fazenda Sete Cidades (☎ /fax 276 2222; s/d US$23/26; P 🏊 🌀) This hotel, just outside the park entrance, has attractive poolside *apartamentos*. Even if you don't stay overnight, it's good for lunch and a quick dip in the pool.

Getting There & Around
The park is 26km from Piripiri, 180km from Teresina and 141km from Ubajara (Ceará state). Buses leave Teresina hourly between 5:45am and 6pm for Piripiri (US$4, three hours). There are several daily buses from Piripiri to Fortaleza (US$11, nine hours) and Parnaíba (US$3, three hours).

The small IBAMA courtesy bus for the 26km trip to the park leaves daily at 7am from Praça da Bandeira, in the center of Piripiri. There is usually some transportation returning from the IBAMA office to Piripiri between 9am and 10am, and the bus returns at 5pm. A taxi from Piripiri costs around US$12. A mototaxi (motorcycle) is US$4. Hitchhiking is also safe and relatively easy. In the park itself, you can drive on the roads or follow the trails on foot – they're well marked.

PEDRO SEGUNDO
☎ 0xx86 / pop 23,000
The town of Pedro Segundo (also written Pedro II) lies in the hills of the Serra dos Matos, around 50km southeast of Piripiri. Close to the town are several mines that are the only source of opals in South America.

One of just a couple of places to stay in town, the **Hotel Rimo Pedro Segundo** (☎ 271 1543; Av Itamaraty; d US$10-15; 🔀) is a fine place to sleep between visits to the opal mines.

Buses run hourly from Teresina to Pedro Segundo (US$8, four hours).

PARQUE NACIONAL DA SERRA DA CAPIVARA
In the south of the state, near São Raimundo Nonato, **Parque Nacional da Serra da Capivara** (3-day entrance US$2) was established in 1979 to protect the many prehistoric sites and examples of rock paintings in the region. It is the only national park set entirely in *caatinga* country.

The park was declared a Unesco World Heritage site in 1991. Archaeological research in the park has dated the human presence here as far back as 50,000 years – much earlier than used to be believed for anywhere in the Americas.

There are more than 300 excavated sites that are open to the public depending on the research schedule. If the staff have time, you may be lucky enough to be given a lift and be shown around. For details about guides, access and archaeological sites, contact the **Fundação Museu do Homem Americano** (FUMDHAM; ☎ 582 1612; Rua Abdias Neves 551, São Raimundo Nonato). Paved roads have been made to some of the 260 rock-painting sites (with 30,000 paintings), and 30 sites are open to visitors.

Serra da Capivara (☎ /fax 582 1389; Santa Luzia; US$20-25; P 🔀 🔀), the closest hotel to the park, is rustic but comfortable and can arrange guides and provide park information. It's 2km north of São Raimundo Nonato on Hwy PI-140.

There are two daily buses from Teresina to São Raimundo Nonato (US$18, nine hours).

MARANHÃO
Maranhão, little known outside of Brazil, is one of the most exciting destinations in the country and is guaranteed to become an established spot on the tourist map in years to come. It is full of natural and cultural treasures from the exciting colonial town of São Luís to the gorgeous Parque Nacional dos Lençóis Maranhenses. If you have the time to travel to Maranhão, you will not be disappointed.

For many years after they first came to Brazil, the Portuguese showed little interest in the area that now forms the state of Maranhão. It was the French, who arrived in 1612 to construct a fort at São Luís, who really started to develop the region. Once the French had some success, the Portuguese became a lot more interested in reclaiming the land.

Although the southern and eastern areas of Maranhão are characterized by vast expanses of *babaçu* palms and typical *sertão* landscapes, the western and northwestern regions of the state merge into humid Amazon rain forests.

The rural economy of Maranhão is dependent on the *babaçu*, a plant that serves an amazing multitude of purposes, from food to use in construction and the creation of charcoal.

THE NORTHEAST

SÃO LUÍS

☎ 0xx98 / pop 950,000

The historic center of São Luís is an enchanting neighborhood of steamy cobbled streets and pastel-colored colonial buildings. However, São Luís is more than just a Unesco World Heritage site with attractive architecture. It is also the reggae capital of Brazil with unique festivals, relaxed local culture and some decent beaches just 10 to 15 minutes from the center.

The city has recently captured the romantic imagination of Brazilians as the site of the wildly popular novella *Da Cor do Pecado* and can rightfully claim to be one of the most charming state capitals in the country. Many visitors end up staying longer than they planned and then continue to the majestic Lençóis Maranhenses national park or make the trip across Baía de São Marcos to visit Alcântara, an impressive historic town slipping regally into decay.

History

São Luís is the only city in Brazil that was founded and settled by the French. In 1612 three French ships sailed for Maranhão to try to commandeer a piece of the country. They allied themselves with the local Indian population, the Tupinambá, who were eager to embrace any fellow enemy of the Portuguese. Once settled in São Luís, the French used the Tupinambá to attack other tribes around the mouth of the Rio Amazonas and try to expand their precarious foothold in the region.

French imperial support for the new colony was not strong enough to hold off the imminent Portuguese attack, which came in 1614. Within a year, the French fled and the Tupinambá were 'pacified.'

Except for a brief Dutch occupation between 1641 and 1644, when the economy boomed, São Luís slowly developed as a port for the export of sugar, and later cotton. Despite relatively poor land, the plantation system was established with slaves, Indian labor and a lot of misplaced optimism. When demand for São Luís' crops slackened in the 19th century, the city went into a long decline.

In recent years, São Luís' economy has been stimulated by several megaprojects. A modern port complex was constructed to export the mineral riches of the Serra dos Carajás, a range of hills in the southeast of neighboring Pará state with the world's largest deposits of iron ore. In the 1980s, Alcoa built an enormous factory for aluminum processing – you'll see it along the highway south of the city. A missile station was established in Alcântara, and oil was discovered in the bay. Domestic and international tourism are of growing importance for the city's economy.

Orientation

São Luís is divided in two by the Rio Anil. On the southern side, the city center sits on a hill above the historic center, called Projeto Revivir by locals. On the northern peninsula lie the more modern and

---

BUMBA MEU BOI

São Luís is famous for its Bumba Meu Boi – a fascinating, wild, folkloric festival. Derived from African, Indian and Portuguese influences, it's a rich mixture of music, dance and theater. There's a Carnavalesque atmosphere in which participants dance, sing and tell the story of the death and resurrection of the bull – with plenty of room for improvisation. More than 75 parade groups spend the year in preparation, so you can catch some aspect of the event no matter when you visit town. Costumes are lavish and new songs and poetry are created every year.

The story and its portrayal differ throughout the Northeast, but the general plot is as follows: Catrina, goddaughter of the local farm owner, is pregnant and feels a craving to eat the tongue of the best *boi* (bull) on the farm. She cajoles her husband, Chico, into killing the beast. When the dead bull is discovered, several characters (caricatures drawn from all levels of society) do some detective work and finally track down the perpetrator of the crime. Chico is brought to trial, but the bull is resuscitated by various magic incantations and tunes. A pardon is granted, and the story reaches its happy ending when Chico is reunited with Catrina.

The festival starts in the second half of June and continues into the second week of August. Give the São Luís **Fumtur tourist office** (☎ 231 9086) a call to get the exact dates of all events.

wealthy suburbs, such as São Francisco, as well as the city's beaches. Many city streets in the center have multiple names, but this shouldn't prevent you from navigating easily by foot as the area is not very large.

The following is a short list of streets, with their official names in parentheses:

- Rua do Giz (Rua 28 de Julho)
- Rua da Estrêla (Rua Candido Mendes)
- Rua Formosa (Rua Afonso Pena)
- Rua do Sol (Rua Nina Rodrigues)
- Rua do Egito (Rua Tarquinho Lopes)
- Rua do Veado (Rua Celso Magalhães)
- Rua dos Afogados (Rua José Bonifácio)
- Rua de Nazaré (Rua de Nazaré e Odilo)
- Rua das Barrocas (Beco dos Barracas; Rua Isaacs Martins)
- Rua da Cascata (Rua Jacinto Maia)
- Rua Portugal (Rua Trapiche)
- Rua da Alfândega (Rua Marcelino de Almeida)
- Praça Dom Pedro II (Av Dom Pedro II)
- Rua da Cruz (Rua 7 de Setembro)

Information

BOOKSTORES

Livraria Poem-se (☎ 232 4068; poemesse@elo.com.br; Humberto de Campos s/n; 🕒 8am-7pm Mon-Fri, to 1pm Sat) This smart secondhand bookstore has many books in English, French and German. It also has a large collection of CDs, postcards and magazines with a large Internet café upstairs.

EMERGENCY

Ambulance (Pronto Socorro; ☎ 192)
Fire department (Corpo de Bombeiros; ☎ 193)
Police (Policía Militar; ☎ 190)
Tourist Police (Delegacia Especial do Turista; ☎ 232 4324)

INTERNET ACCESS

A number of pousadas and hotels in the historic center with Internet access usually allow nonguests to use the machines for around US$1.50 per hour.

Livraria Poem-se (☎ 232 4068; poemesse@elo.com.br; Humberto de Campos s/n; per hr US$1.50; 🕒 8am-7pm Mon-Fri, to 1pm Sat) Many machines and fast connections in an excellent upstairs Internet café.

INTERNET RESOURCES

There are unfortunately no good up-to-date English websites on São Luís.

São Luís/Maranhão Tourism Site (www.guiasaoluis.com.br) This website is full of good information on every aspect of the city and much of the state, but is only in Portuguese.

Photos of São Luís (www.ddbstock.com/largeimage/saoluis)

LAUNDRY

Most pousadas, hostels and hotels will do laundry for their guests at a reasonable price. **Lavamatic** (☎ 235 4306) will also pick up and drop off laundry for US$3 per kg.

MEDICAL SERVICES

Santa Casa (☎ 232 0144) Public hospital.
São Domingos (☎ 216 8100) Private medical facility.

MONEY

There is a number of banks and ATMs in town and there are also moneychangers hanging about outside Fumtur (below), who change cash and traveler's checks at good rates. Bradesco has an ATM at the Mercado Central.

Banco da Amazônia (Av Pedro Segundo II 140; 🕒 10am-4pm Mon-Fri) Also changes money.

Banco do Brasil (Travessa Boa Ventura; 🕒 9am-4pm Mon-Sat, ATMs 6am-10pm Mon-Sun) Just off Rua da Estrêla.

POST

Main post office (Praça João Lisboa 292; 🕒 9am-5pm Mon-Fri, to 1pm Sat)

TELEPHONE

Telemar telephone office (cnr Ruas da Palma & de Nazaré)

TOURIST INFORMATION

São Luís operates well-developed tourist-information facilities.

Airport tourist booth (🕒 8-2:30am)
Bus station tourist booth (🕒 8am-10pm)
Fumtur (☎ 231 9086, 222 5881; Praça Benedito Leite; 🕒 8am-7pm Mon-Fri, 9am-5pm Sat) This is the most useful office, providing brochures and maps in English and French, as well as having helpful English-speaking attendants.

TRAVEL AGENCIES

Giltur (☎ 231 7065, 221 5630; giltur@terra.com.br; Rua Montanha Russa 22; 🕒 8am-6pm Mon-Fri, to 2pm Sat) This helpful and trustworthy agency offers organized tours of the historic center, Alcântara, Parque Nacional dos Lençóis Maranhenses and other destinations at reasonable prices.

Taguatur (☎ 232 0906; Rua do Sol 141, shop 15; 🕒 9am-6pm Mon-Fri, to 3pm Sat) Recommended out of a number of agencies in this shopping gallery. Most of the agencies offer package tours and sell bus tickets, which will save you a rather expensive cab ride or long bus trip out to the station.

Sights

The historic center is one of the best-preserved colonial neighborhoods in the Northeast. Beyond simply walking around the area, it is also worth visiting some of the specific buildings for their history and architecture.

PROJETO REVIVER

During the late 1980s, state authorities finally agreed to restore the historic district,

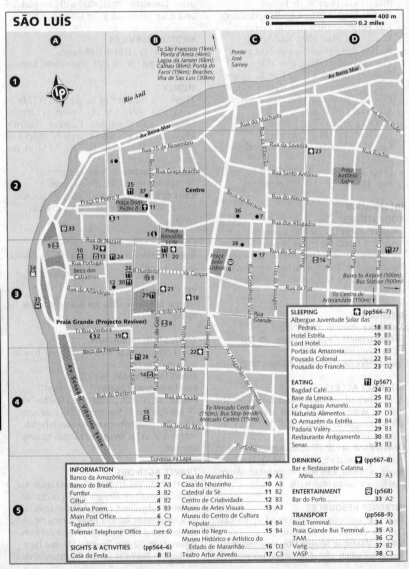

SÃO LUÍS

0 — 400 m
0 — 0.2 miles

INFORMATION
Banco da Amazônia.................1 B2
Banco do Brasil.......................2 A3
Fumtur..................................3 B2
Giltur....................................4 B2
Livraria Poem.........................5 B3
Main Post Office......................6 C3
Taguatur................................7 C2
Telemar Telephone Office........(see 6)

SIGHTS & ACTIVITIES   (pp564–6)
Casa da Festa.........................8 B3
Casa do Maranhão....................9 A3
Casa do Nhozinho...................10 A3
Catedral da Sé.......................11 B2
Centro de Criatividade............12 B3
Museu de Artes Visuais...........13 A3
Museu do Centro de Cultura
   Popular..............................14 B4
Museu do Negro.....................15 B4
Museu Histórico e Artístico do
   Estado de Maranhão............16 D3
Teatro Artur Azvedo...............17 C3

SLEEPING   (pp566–7)
Albergue Juventude Solar das
   Pedras..............................18 B3
Hotel Estrêla.........................19 B3
Lord Hotel.............................20 B3
Portas da Amazonia.................21 B3
Pousada Colonial....................22 B4
Pousada do Francês.................23 D2

EATING   (p567)
Bagdad Café..........................24 B3
Base da Lenoca.......................25 B2
Le Papagaio Amarelo................26 B3
Naturista Alimentos.................27 D3
O Armazém da Estrêla..............28 B4
Padaria Valéry........................29 B3
Restaurante Antigamente.........30 B3
Senac...................................31 B3

DRINKING   (pp567–8)
Bar e Restaurante Catarina
   Mina..................................32 A3

ENTERTAINMENT   (p568)
Bar do Porto...........................33 A2

TRANSPORT   (pp568–9)
Boat Terminal.........................34 A3
Praia Grande Bus Terminal.........35 A3
TAM.....................................36 C2
Varig....................................37 B2
VASP....................................38 C3

which had been neglected and decaying for many decades. The initial restoration project was completed in 1990, and the city's 1997 Unesco World Heritage designation has kept the work going.

More than 200 buildings have already been restored. To appreciate the superb colonial mansions and the many designs and colors of their tiled facades, just wander around the district. *Azulejos* (decorative ceramic tiles, often blue or blue-and-white) were first produced in Portugal and later became a popular product in France, Belgium and Germany. Since tiles provided a durable means of protecting outside walls from the humidity and heat in São Luís, their use became standard practice during colonial times.

CATEDRAL DA SÉ

Constructed by the Jesuits in 1629, the **Catedral da Sé** (Praça Dom Pedro II; ☺ variable) became the official cathedral in 1762. Inside are ceiling frescoes decorated with *babaçu* motifs and a fine baroque altar.

TEATRO ARTUR AZVEDO

Dating from 1815, **Teatro Artur Azvedo** (Rua do Sol 180; tours US$1; ☺ 3-5pm Mon-Fri) is a neoclassical structure and is one of the oldest and most beautiful theaters in Brazil. If you can, see a show here, or at least take the tour.

MUSEU DO CENTRO DE CULTURA POPULAR

The **Centro de Cultura Popular** (Rua 28 de Julio 221; ☺ 9am-6pm Tue-Sat) has a trio of excellent Candomblé houses that should not be missed – Casa Fanti-Ashanti, Casa das Minas and Casa Nagô.

CASA DA FESTA

The **Casa da Festa** (Party House; Rua do Giz 221; admission free; ☺ 9am-7pm, closed Mon) has four floors of colorful costumes and props from local festivals and religious practices.

CASA DO MARANHÃO

Inside a gigantic converted warehouse, the 1st floor of **Casa do Maranhão** (Rua do Trapiche; admission free; ☺ 9am-7pm, closed Mon) is basically a multimedia state-tourism brochure. The 2nd floor is dedicated entirely to the different regional flavors of Bumba Meu Boi (p562) costumes.

CASA DO NHOZINHO

At the **Casa do Nhozinho** (Rua Portugal 185; admission free; ☺ 9am-7pm, closed Mon) you can see items from quotidian Maranhanense life, including delicate wooden fish traps and improvisational children's toys made from garbage.

MUSEU DE ARTES VISUAIS

There's a fine collection of old *azulejos*, engravings and paintings at the **Museu de Artes Visuais** (Rua Portugal 273; ☺ 9am-7pm Tue-Sat). Opposite the museum is the **old round market**, selling dried salted shrimp (eaten shell and all), *cachaça*, dried goods and basketwork; lunch counters here offer inexpensive local cooking.

MUSEU DO NEGRO

In Cafua das Mercês, the building that held the old slave market, you'll find the **Museu do Negro** (Rua Jacinto Maia 43; ☺ 9am-6pm Tue-Sat). This is where slaves were kept after their arrival from Africa until they were sold – notice the absence of windows. A small and striking series of exhibits documents the history of slavery in Maranhão.

MUSEU HISTÓRICO E ARTÍSTICO DO ESTADO DE MARANHÃO

Housed in a restored mansion built in 1836, the **Museu Histórico e Artístico** (Rua do Sol 302; ☺ 9am-6pm Tue-Fri, 2-6pm Sat & Sun) provides an insight into daily life in the 18th century, with an attractive display of artifacts from wealthy Maranhão families. You will see furnishings, family photographs, religious articles, coins, sacred art – even President José Sarney's bassinet.

CENTRO DO CRIATIVIDADE

The **Centro do Criatividade** (Rua da Alfândega 200; ☺ 8am-10pm Tue-Fri) is an exhibition and performance space for those interested in the local art scene. There's a theater for local plays and dance productions, an art gallery and a cinema showing art-house films.

BEACHES

The beaches are beyond the São Francisco district. From the Reviver (p564 you must take a bus (running frequently along the waterfront) or taxi (US$3 to US$7). The beaches can be busy and fun, but are far from Brazil's finest. Beware of rough surf, tides and pollution in the area.

THE NORTHEAST

Ponta D'Areia is the closest beach to the city, only 4km away, and gets a lot of visitors, but can be polluted. It's a popular beach for those who want to make a quick exit from the city and visit the bars and restaurants for beach food.

São Marcos (Marcela), leading up to Calhau, is frequented by younger groups from São Luís and is also popular with surfers.

The best local beach, **Calhau**, is broad and attractive, with hard-packed sand that is perfect for soccer games. It is only 8km from the city and is popular on weekends. The large circular *barracas* along the beach on Avenida Litorânea cater to late-night partiers throughout the week. The calm far end of the beach is known as Caolho.

Olho d'Água, 12km from São Luís, has plenty of houses and kiosks backed by cliffs and dunes.

Another 7km further is spacious and enjoyable **Praia do Araçagi**, with a lighthouse, bars and restaurants.

Tours

The travel agencies described on p563 offer city tours of São Luís and day trips to São José do Ribamar and Alcântara. Prices average US$20 per person and include transport and guide services only – you pay for admission fees and food.

Festivals & Events

São Luís has one of Brazil's richest folkloric traditions, evident in its many festivals. There are active samba clubs and distinctive local dances and music. During Carnaval, most activity is out on the streets and the tourist influence is minimal. **Marafolia**, the out-of-season Carnaval, is held in mid-October, and can be livelier than the main one. For four days in mid-November, local, national and, of course, Jamaican reggae talent descends on São Luís for the **Festival Maranhense do Reggae**. This is a newish event and is increasing in popularity.

The **Tambor de Mina** festivals, held in July, are important events for followers of the Afro-Brazilian religions in São Luís. The city's famous **Bumba Meu Boi** (p562) festival commences in the second half of June, and its special events continue until the second week of August. The **Festa do Divino**, celebrated 40 days after Lent, is spectacular in Alcântara.

Sleeping

BUDGET

Albergue Juventude Solar das Pedras (☎ 232 6694; aj.solardaspedras@bol.com.br; Rua da Palma 127; dm/d US$5/10; 🖳) Backpackers gravitate toward this hostel in a restored colonial home for its charm and social atmosphere. All rooms have shared bathrooms, and discounts are offered for HI members. It's a good place to meet Brazilian and international travelers.

Lord Hotel (☎ 221 4655; Rua Joaquim Tavora 258; s/d/tr US$10/13/20; 🔀) This well-worn but well-kept hotel is comfortable and more spacious than its budget brethren. Rooms without air-con and television are slightly cheaper.

Hotel Estrêla (☎ /fax 232 7172; Rua da Estrêla 370; s/d US$8/13) Although the rooms are small and a bit dark, this popular cheapie has a great location in the heart of the historic center. Make sure to leave valuables in the safe at reception.

MID-RANGE

Pousada Colonial (☎ 232 2834; Rua Afonso Pena 112; s/d US$17/22; 🔀) Pousada Colonial offers comfortable rooms and luxurious suites in a restored colonial mansion with fantastic views over the old city. The building is covered inside and out with unique raised *azulejos*, which the tourism authority has adopted as its mascot for brochure covers. A 20% discount is offered for payment in cash.

Pousada do Francês (☎ 231 4844; fax 232 0879; Rua 7 de Setembro 160; s/d US$30/38; 🔀) Housed in a beautifully restored colonial building, *apartamentos* with fridge and TV are great value (and the higher floors have a view). There's a nice restaurant and bar in the hotel.

Pousada Portas da Amazônia (☎ 222 9937; portasdaamazonia@terra.com.br; Rua do Giz 129; s/d/tr US$23/28/43; 🔀 🖳) Also in a renovated colonial home, but with a sunny garden and wooden floors, this pousada is centrally located and serves a good breakfast.

Chalé da Lagoa (☎ 226 4916; Rua da Lagoa, Araçagi; d US$35; 🔀) This mid-priced hotel is a tranquil place surrounded by gardens and is a good choice for those who want to stay out on the more relaxing beaches.

Pousada Tia Maria (☎ 227 1534; Quadra 1, lot 12, Ponta D'Areia; s/d US$25/32; 🔀) Pousada Tia Maria is a smart option for those who want to enjoy the beach bars, but be relatively close to the historic center of town. The restaurant is recommended and open to the public.

TOP END

Sofitel (☎ 216 4545; www.accorhotels.com.br; Av Avicênia, Calhau; s/d US$110/130; ✴ ▣ ▨) This five-star hotel is surrounded by attractive gardens and is considered the nicest place to stay in town. Beyond having all the amenities of a fancy hotel, it is close to the beach and much of the better nightlife.

Hotel Brisamar (☎ 212 1212; www.brisamar.com.br; Av São Marcos 12, Ponta D'Areia; d US$60-75; ✴ ▨) Closer in toward the historic center, the Brisamar is a good-value, high-end beach option, with particularly clean rooms and sea views.

Eating

The best Maranhense food comes from the sea. In São Luís you'll find many of the familiar dishes of the Northeast, and regional specialities such as *torta de sururu* (mussel pie), *casquinha de caranguejo* (stuffed crab), *caldeirada de camarão* (shrimp stew) and the city's special rice dish, *arroz de cuxá* (rice with vinegar, local vegetables and shrimp).

RESTAURANTS

Maracangalha (☎ 233 6769; Av Litorânea 45, Calhau; mains US$5-10; ✆ 11am-midnight) Nicely decorated and located in the middle of Praia do Calhau, Maracangalha is a popular, if slightly pricey, restaurant serving quality seafood to those who want to have a nice meal along the beach.

Senac (☎ 232 6377; Rua de Nazaré 242; buffet US$6; ✆ 11am-3pm Mon-Thu, to midnight Fri) This cooking school offers a high-class, all-you-can-eat buffet lunch featuring regional dishes. Consider wearing long pants as Senac is not as casual as the average São Luís restaurant, yet it is still good value.

Base da Lenoca (☎ 227 5545; Rua Montanha Russa 181; mains US$5-6; ✆ noon-11pm) Base da Lenoca is a popular seafood restaurant in a great location overlooking the Rio Anil – order a beer and a crab dish and enjoy the breeze.

Bagdad Café (☎ 211 0603; bagdadcafesiz@yahoo.com.br; Rua Portugal 243; mains US$4-8; ✆ 11am-11pm) This prominent corner restaurant is newly renovated with a stage and art displays. The food is high quality, and the *filet recheado* (steak stuffed with sun-dried toma-

toes, US$5) is recommended. However, the breakfast is nothing special.

Restaurante Antigamente (☎ 232 3904; Rua da Estrêla 220; ✆ 11am-late) Although it is a bit of a tourist trap, it's worth dining at this sidewalk restaurant just to soak in the feeling of the historic center. The *picanha* (Brazil's favorite rump-cut of beef, eaten pinkish, salty and fresh from the grill) can be overcooked, but some of the pastas and pizza are good. There's live music here on weekend evenings. Also recommended is the similar, but smaller and slightly less expensive **Le Papagaio Amarelo** next door.

Naturista Alimentos (☎ 222 4526; Rua do Sol 517; buffet per kg US$4; ✆ 11:30am-3pm Mon-Fri) Naturista is a legitimate vegetarian buffet and a real treat for vegetarians who have been surviving on cheese sandwiches.

CAFÉS

Although São Luís has many restaurants, there aren't a lot of places for snacks and sandwiches. Fruit and *sucos* can be hard to come by.

Padaria Valéry (☎ 221 3677; Rua do Giz s/n; quiche US$1, pastries US$0.50) Good coffee, French breads and pastries. Try the *quiche provençale* at this relaxing bakery.

O Armazém da Estrêla (☎ 232 5082; Rua da Estrêla 401; mains US$5-12) A new and sophisticated place, O Armazém has magazines, CDs and an Internet café along with cappuccino, wine, antipasti and whiskey. The upstairs Italian restaurant serves some pricey, high-quality dishes, including a good lasagna.

Drinking

Most people drink at the restaurants around town or head out to the beach *barracas* that line Avenida Litorânea, then to music clubs. Well-to-do Brazilians go to Lagoa da Jansen to listen to relaxing music and sip drinks at the numerous lakeside bars.

Bar e Restaurante Catarina Mina (☎ 232 9594; Beco Catarina Mina 121; ✆ 10am-late, closed Sun) The tables from this bar/restaurant spill out onto the quaint, staired Beco Catarina Mina. It is a good place to sit and drink beer, listen to live music and possibly start dancing on the stairs.

Restaurante Antigamente (☎ 232 3904; Rua da Estrêla 220; ✆ 11am-late) The tables in the street are a great place to have drinks and start off the evening.

O Armazém da Estrela (☎ 232 5082; Rua da Estrêla 401) Good cocktails, draught beers and relaxing music make O Armazém ideal for a romantic or more sedate evening.

Entertainment

São Luís is the reggae center of Brazil, and many bars and clubs here have regular reggae nights. To find the happening spots, it's worth asking locals or taxi drivers for recommendations or checking the daily newspaper *Estado do Maranhão* for its entertainment listing. Many of the radio stations, including 94.3 FM, play reggae on weekdays from 8am to 10pm.

Bar do Porto (Rua do Trapiche 49; US$1 cover) This vast club hosts live reggae shows (and sometimes other types of music). It's particularly good on Wednesday night when the street out front becomes a party, and reggae fans pack the inside.

Bar do Nelson (Avenida Litorânea, Calhau; US$2 cover; ⊙ 9pm-late Thu-Sat) Although it is smaller than the other reggae bars and has a shanty clubhouse feel, Bar do Nelson is the most famous reggae spot in town and is good for live music and dancing.

Creôle Bar (Av dos Holandeses, Ponta D'Areia) Another of the popular reggae spots, this is closer to the more upscale Lagoa da Jansen. It's near the Number One Flat.

Flamingo (Rio Poty Hotel, Ponta D'Areia), **Studio 7** (Av dos Holandeses, Calhau) and **Fabrica** (Av dos Holandeses, Calhau) are popular clubs that play music other than reggae, locally described as 'techno-pop.' Large crowds on weekends.

Shopping

São Luís is the place for the traditional handicrafts of Maranhão such as woodcarving, basketry, lacework, ceramics, leather work and woven goods made from linen. Also on sale are featherwork and items made from straw or plant fibers (from baskets to bracelets) by the Urubus-Caapor and Guajajara Indians, both from the interior of Maranhão state.

The **Centro de Artesanato** (Rua de São Pantaleão 1232; ⊙ 9am-7pm Mon-Sat, to 1pm Sun) is housed in a renovated factory and functions as an exhibition hall and sales outlet for handicrafts. Also worth visiting are the **Mercado Central** (Praça do Mercado) and the many craft stores and small art galleries in the surrounding streets.

Getting There & Away

São Luís is a transportation hub and is connected to most major Brazilian cities by both bus and air.

AIR

All major Brazilian airlines have offices at the airport. The following offices are in town:

TAM (☎ 227 0816; Rua das Afogados 16; ⊙ 8am-6pm Mon-Fri, to noon Sat)

Varig (☎ 231 5066; Av Dom Pedro Segundo 221; ⊙ 8am-6pm Mon-Fri, to noon Sat)

VASP (☎ 231 4433; Rua do Sol 43; ⊙ 8am-6pm Mon-Fri, to noon Sat)

BOAT

The boat terminal is just beyond the western end of Rua Portugal. From here, it's possible to sail on boats along the coast. Schedules are approximate and depend on the tides. For details on the regular daily service to Alcântara, see p570.

There are also departures on Tuesday and Friday to Guimarães, a major center for boatbuilding and fishing, and infrequent departures from there to destinations further along the west coast, including Turiaçu, Luís Domingues and Carutapera (on the Pará border).

BUS

The **bus station** (☎ 243 2320) is 8km southeast of the city center on Avenida dos Franceses and is a US$5 cab ride from Reviver. You can also take the city bus marked 'Rodoviária' for US$0.50 from Praça Deodoro. Long-distance bus tickets can be purchased in the city center at travel agencies (563).

Buses run to Belém (US$30, 12 hours, 803km, departs 8pm), Barreirinhas (US$7, 3½ hours, 272km, seven daily), Brasília (US$65, 26 hours, 2254km, one daily), Imperatriz (US$25, 12 hours, 637km, four daily), Fortaleza (US$25, 18 hours, 1070km, seven daily), and Teresina (US$12, seven hours, 445km, seven daily). The Fortaleza bus connects to Natal and Recife, and stops in Piripiri.

Getting Around

Aeroporto Marechal Cunha Machado (☎ 217 6101) is 15km southeast of the city. The bus marked 'São Cristóvão' or 'Aeroporto' runs from the bus stop opposite Banco do Brasil on Praça Deodoro to the airport in 35 minutes. There's a ticket booth for taxis at the airport – a taxi to the center costs around US$10.

Several buses go to the bus station from Praça Deodoro, and you can also pick one up at the Praia Grande bus terminal on Avenida Beira Mar. From the bus station to the city center, a taxi should cost you about US$5.

Buses run to Ponta d'Areia and Calhau from the Praia Grande bus terminal – take buses marked 'Ponta d'Areia', 'Calhau' or 'Cal Litorâneo.' For buses to Araçagi, Raposa and São José do Ribamar, there's a bus stop beside the Mercado Central. To get to Olho d'Água, take a bus marked 'Olho d'Água' from Praça Deodoro.

ILHA DE SÃO LUÍS
Raposa

Out at the tip of the Ilha de São Luís, 30km from the city, is the interesting and very dirty fishing center of Raposa, which is chiefly worth visiting for its well-known lacework. It's a poor town, built on stilts above mangrove swamps, which gives it an unusual appearance. The bulk of the population is descended from Cearense immigrants. There are no tourist facilities, but the ocean here is pretty and very shallow. There are lots of small fishing boats and it's not too hard to negotiate a ride. Bathing at the beach is dangerous due to extreme tidal variations: the water recedes by as much as 1km at low tide.

There are frequent buses from São Luís (45 minutes) – there is a convenient bus stop beside the Mercado Central.

São José do Ribamar

This fishing town is on the east coast of the island, 30km from the city. There's a busy little waterfront where you can catch one of the boats leaving for small towns along the coast – a good way to explore some of the more out-of-the-way villages on the island. On Sunday, buses go from São José to nearby Ponta de Panaquatira, a popular weekend beach.

Frequent buses and minibuses leave from the bus stop beside the Mercado Central in São Luís (45 minutes). The last bus back to São Luís leaves at 10:30pm.

ALCÂNTARA
☎ 0xx98 / pop 6000

Across the Baía de São Marcos from São Luís is the colonial town of Alcântara. Built in the early 1600s with extensive slave labor, the town was the hub of the region's sugar and cotton economy. The people who benefited from this wealth, Maranhão's rich landowners, preferred living in Alcântara to São Luís.

While the town has been in decline since the latter half of the 19th century, it is still considered an architectural treasure, and some experts claim that it is the most homogeneous group of colonial buildings and ruins from the 17th and 18th centuries in Brazil.

In the early 1990s, the Centro do Lançamento de Alcântara (CLA), the rocket-launching facility for the Brazilian space program (below), was constructed here. It is an odd juxtaposition: rockets alongside a slumbering colonial town.

Keep an eye out for red ibis (guará in Portuguese), beautiful red birds that are plentiful here but threatened with extinction in other parts of Brazil.

THE BRAZILIAN SPACE PROGRAM

The Brazilian space program is pulling itself back together after an accident on August 22, 2003, in which a US$6 million, 20m-tall VLS-1 VO3 rocket exploded on the launch pad in Alcântara. Sadly, 21 engineers and technicians were killed. The fire was so intense that it melted the enormous steel foundation, causing the entire structure to collapse. It was later determined that a booster with solid rocket fuel had ignited.

The rocket was three days from liftoff and was to carry two research satellites into orbit, which would have been the first satellites launched by a Latin American country. The accident was unfortunately not the first failure of the Brazilian space program. In 1997, a rocket crashed into the ocean shortly after liftoff and in 1999, officials destroyed a rocket after it veered off course three minutes into flight.

Now Brazil and the Ukraine are planning a joint project that will launch a medium-class Ukrainian rocket from the Alcântara launch site for commercial missions. Liftoff is planned for 2006.

THE NORTHEAST

Information

Fumtur, the tourist office in São Luís, has brochures and information on Alcântara – as do most travel agencies.

Sights

HISTORIC BUILDINGS

The town is very poor and decaying, but don't miss the beautiful row of two-story houses on **Rua Grande**, the **Igreja de NS do Carmo** (1665) on Largo do Carmo and the best-preserved **pelourinho** (whipping post) in Brazil.

MUSEU HISTÓRICO

Displaying a collection of sacred art, festival regalia and colonial furniture, each room in the **Museu Histórico** (Praça da Matriz; 9am-5pm, closed Mon) has its own guardian – a source of employment for the locals.

Festivals & Events

The **Festa do Divino** is held on the first Sunday after Ascension Day. Check the date for the festival (usually held in May) with Fumtur in São Luís. This is considered one of the most colorful annual festivals in Maranhão. It represents a fusion of African and Catholic elements and features two children dressed as the emperor and empress, who are paraded through the town accompanied by musicians.

Sleeping & Eating

For many travelers, Alcântara is simply a day trip from São Luís. If you decide to stay, there are simple campsites close to Praça da Matriz and near the lighthouse. There are a few inexpensive pousadas around town.

Pousada dos Guarás (337 1339; Praia da Baronesa; d US$7-18) Right on the beach, this is a quiet, relaxing place to stay with a good restaurant/bar.

Restaurante da Josefa (337 1109; Rua Direita; mains US$3-6; noon-10pm) This is a basic and decent seafood restaurant where you can eat some locally caught fish.

Getting There & Away

Boats from São Luís depart from the boat terminal on the quayside, just beyond the western end of Rua Portugal. It's a good idea to book your ticket the day before departure, and check the departure times, which vary according to the tide.

A large motorboat, the *Diamantina*, leaves twice a day (US$3, one hour, departs 7am and 9:30am). If you have more time on your hands and are more adventurous, you can arrange to ride on one of the sailboats or catamarans that cross the bay.

PARQUE NACIONAL DOS LENÇÓIS MARANHENSES

The name of this 1550-sq-km national park refers to its immense dunes, which look like *lençóis* (bed sheets) strewn across the landscape. Halfway between São Luís and the Piauí border, the park also includes beaches, mangroves, lagoons and some interesting fauna, especially turtles and migratory birds. The area's designation as a national park in 1981 staved off potentially ruinous land and oil speculation. It is a spectacular place, especially from March to September, when rain that has filtered through the sand forms crystal-clear pools between the dunes.

The park has minimal tourist infrastructure, but it's possible to arrange a visit from the town of Barreirinhas (p571), two hours by boat from the dunes. You can get a ride on a boat going downriver to the beginning of the park for a few dollars. You can also stay closer to the park in Caburé or Atins and hire a private guide. There is no admission fee.

While traveling from Caburé to Atins, you can visit the fishing village of Mandacaru. It is worth seeing the view from the top of the **Mandacaru lighthouse** (US$.50) and there are a couple of restaurants on the river.

Organized Tours

Motor vehicles are not allowed in the park, so you can arrange tours that will drive you to the park near Barreirinhas or take you by boat to the entrance near Atins.

Ecotrilha (349 0372; Av Joaquim Soeiro de Cavalho 682, Barreirinhas; tour US$13; 9am-6pm Mon-Sat, to 3pm Sun) Ecotrilha is one of the best-equipped and most professional tour operators in Barreirinhas. It offers motorized tours of the park.

Giltur (231 7065, 221 5630; giltur@terra.com.br; Rua Montanha Russa 22, São Luís; 8am-6pm Mon-Fri, to 2pm Sat) A three-day tour costs around US$190, including accommodations in Barreirinhas, bus and boat transportation. A three-day package, where you fly instead of taking a bus, costs US$315 per person. The aerial view of the park is fantastic.

Sleeping & Eating
CABURÉ

As you go downriver from Barreirinhas, the boat passes the sandy little town of Caburé. This is where you will arrive if you come overland from Jericoacoara, Tutóia and Paulino Neves.

Pousada do Paulo (Beira Rio, Caburé; per person US$10) This is an almost absurdly relaxing spot, right on the river, with basic rooms and plenty of hammocks.

ATINS

Further downriver, close to the park, is the small village of Atins. It is the only place you can stay and enter the park on foot. There are a few pousadas in Atins.

Filhos do Vento (☎ 9966 7100; filhosdovento@yahoo .com.br; d US$10) This pousada is a group of attractive circular *rancho* cabins with mosquito nets, comfortable beds and nice bathrooms. Guides can be arranged through the pousada.

Rancho dos Lençóis Pousada (☎ 349 0669; rancho doslencois@packpacker.com.br; d US$12; 🏊) Set around a large central *rancho*, this pousada has cabins, a good common area and well-prepared food. It's a little way from Atin's main strip, but you're not missing much. The owner, Buna, can arrange guides and a boat to Barreirinhas.

Barreirinhas
☎ 0xx98 / pop 13,000

Barreirinhas, the main jumping-off point for the national park, has an attractive waterfront on the Rio Preguiça. There is a river beach with sand dunes near the center of town, and some decent pousadas and restaurants. There is also a **Banco do Brasil** (Av Joaquim Soeiro de Cavalho), but beware of endless lines to use the ATMs.

The well-known **Pousada Lins** (☎ 349 1203; Av Joaquim Soeiro de Cavalho 550; s/d US$12/24; 🏊) is a nice place to stay, with friendly staff and comfortable rooms. It has a restaurant serving good seafood and chicken dishes.

The bathrooms are so big they rival the size of the rooms, in the tidy **Pousada D'Areia** (☎ 349 0550; Av Joaquim Soeiro de Cavalho s/n; s/d US$10/20; 🏊). There isn't a lot of character, but the place is functional and orderly.

Restaurante Barlavento (☎ 349 0627; Av Beira Rio s/n; mains US$6-8) has great seafood and other well-prepared dishes on the riverfront. Try the *filet de peixe al molho de maracujá* (fish fillet in passion-fruit sauce).

There are numerous buses every day to São Luís (US$7, 3½ hours), although you can catch a group taxi that is faster for the same amount of money.

To get to Tutóia, there are a couple of ruts through the sand passable only by 4WD vehicles. You'll need to go via Rio Novo, about halfway to Tutóia. The 'road' passes by (and over) some superb dunescapes and very isolated, traditional fishing communities of straw huts. From Rio Novo, there are regular (more frequent on weekends) jeeps to Tutóia.

Paulino Neves/Rio Novo
☎ 0xx98

Due to political redistricting, this town has ended up with two names that are used interchangeably (although Paulino Neves is the official name). A small fishing and farming community between Barreirinhas and Tutóia, Rio Novo is a tranquil place with one main attraction: its coastal dunes are almost an extension of those in the park to the west, and they're much more accessible – a short walk from the village itself.

The venerated **Pousada Oásis dos Lençóis** (☎ 9966 1351; per person US$8-10) is very comfortable and has the river running past the back gate. Dona Mazé oozes tranquility and cooks a fabulous *moqueca*.

The relaxing **Canto da Areia** (☎ 487 1044; cantodaareia@hotmail.com; per person US$10) is a good place to stay and the friendly owner, Ricardo, can help you to explore the surrounding areas.

There is a couple of riverside bars in town with small pool tables (which seem to be obligatory in this part of Maranhão).

There are 4WDs leaving for Tutóia (US$4, 1½ hours) and Barreirinhas (US$5, two hours) each morning. For the rest of the day, there's usually someone coming or going, but there's no set timetable.

Tutóia
☎ 0xx98 / pop 45,000

Tutóia is a relatively large yet somewhat underdeveloped town on the eastern edge of the Delta do Parnaíba – the 2700-sq-km expanse of rivers, dunes, beaches and mangrove forest that straddles the border of Maranhão and Piauí. People from all over the countryside descend on Tutóia to do their shopping and visit the Banco do Brasil (the ATMs get some pretty impressive lines). The main plaza is lined with 4WD trucks that wait until they are filled with people, sacks of rice, rolls of toilet paper and plastic broom handles before departing.

Pousada Tremembes (☎ 479 1819; Praça Tremembes 49; s/d US$6/13; [icon]) is the best budget option in town. The owner, Cacau, may look intimidating but is a friendly and helpful character of some local renown. He can arrange for the 4WD to Rio Novo to pick you up in the morning. The restaurant in the pousada serves a good, cheap plate of the day and an evening buffet. The last stop of the bus from Parnaíba is directly in front of the pousada.

Tutóia Palace Hotel (☎ 479 1115; fax 479 1247; Av Paulino Neves 1100; s/d US$13/25; [icon]) is a more upmarket option near the waterfront, close to where you get off the boat when arriving from Parnaíba.

Two buses a day run over a decent road to Parnaíba (US$3, 2½ hours); the schedule and frequency are flexible so check ahead of time. A small motorboat cruises to Parnaíba (check in your pousada as times and prices are ever-changing). To Rio Novo, there are a number of 4WD trucks leaving daily and a pick-up can be arranged through your accommodations. You can hopefully link up with another truck or jeep there to Barreirinhas, but you should be prepared to stay overnight.

THE NORTH COAST

The town of Guimarães is a center for boatbuilding and fishing. Further north is Cururupu, a small town that is the gateway to the **Lençóis de Cururupu** – a huge expanse of coastal dunes similar to, but not to be confused with, those in the Parque Nacional dos Lençóis Maranhenses.

Offshore is **Parcel de Manoel Luís**, a coral reef named after the Manoel Luís, the first ship to be lost there. The reef, extending over 288 sq km, is the largest in South America. It is a state park and with crystalline waters (up to 40m of visibility), abundant sealife

and a few shipwrecks, it is fast becoming an internationally known dive spot.

IMPERATRIZ

☎ 0xx98 / pop 300,000

A rapidly expanding city 636km southwest of São Luís, Imperatriz is on the border with Pará. The growth is due to the rabid logging and mining of the surrounding region. The only possible reason to visit would be to change buses – otherwise, just keep going.

There are four daily buses to Imperatiz from São Luís (US$25, 12 hours).

CAROLINA

☎ 0xx98 / pop 14,500

The town of Carolina, 242km south of Imperatriz, lies beside the Rio Tocantins and is a handy base for visiting nearby natural attractions. It is impossible to find a piece of Carolina tourism literature that does not feature a waterfall – and for good reason. **Pedra Caída**, 35km north of town (toward Estreito), is a dramatic combination of canyons and waterfalls. Some of the other spectacular waterfalls in the region are **Cachoeira do Itapecuruzinho**, 27km from town on the BR-230; **Cachoeira de São Simão**, at Fazenda São Jorge, about 10km from Carolina; and **Cachoeira da Barra da Cabeceira**. There are rock paintings and inscriptions at **Morro das Figuras**. Bat enthusiasts will want to visit the colony of bats in **Passagem Funda**, a large cave 70km from Carolina.

Sleeping & Eating

Pousada do Lajes (☎ 731 1499; d US$7-17; [icon]) This pousada, 3km toward Riachão, is a basic and affordable choice.

Recanto Pedra Caída (☎ 731 1318; Pedra Caída; d US$20; [icon]) At the famous Pedra Caida waterfall is this tourist complex, with chalets and sports facilities. If you make it to Carolina, you may as well stay near the falls. You can also eat here.

Getting There & Around

There are four buses daily from Imperatriz (US$3, four hour). A frequent ferry service (15 minutes) operates across the Rio Tocantins to the town of Filadélfia in the state of Tocantins.

The Amazon

There are some places that reside as near-mythical destinations in the imaginations of most travelers, like India, Tibet, the Serengeti, and, of course, the Amazon. The world's largest river system evokes images of dense rain forest (and its rampant destruction); of indigenous tribes who have not had contact with the outside world; of giant trees and abundant wildlife, including jaguars, anacondas and piranha.

The numbers are certainly mind-boggling: the Amazon basin contains 6 million sq km of river and jungle and spans eight countries. Just over half – 3.6 million sq km – is in Brazil, spread over seven states. The basin contains 17% of the world's fresh water and main river-flow at its mouth is 12 billion liters a minute – 12 times that of the Mississippi! There are 80,000 kilometers of navigable rivers, and oceangoing vessels can sail 3500km inland up the Amazon mainstream to Iquitos, Peru.

It was from the west that the Amazon was first fully explored by Europeans. In 1541 a Spanish expedition from Quito, led by Gonzalo Pizarro, ran short of supplies while exploring east of the Andes in what is today Peru. Pizarro's cousin Francisco de Orellana offered to take 60 men along with the boats from the expedition and forage for supplies. De Orellana floated down the Rio Napo to its confluence with the Amazon, near Iquitos (Peru), and then to the mouth of the Amazon. Along the way his expedition suffered numerous attacks by Indians; some of the Indian warriors, they reported, were female, like the Amazons of Greek mythology, and thus the world's greatest river got its name.

No one made a serious effort to claim this sweaty territory, however, until the Portuguese built a fort near the mouth of the river at Belém in 1616, and sent Pedro Teixeira up the river to Quito and back between 1637 and 1639.

Today travelers enter the Amazon by bus, boat and air. Good roads connect Venezuela to Manaus, and Belém and Palmas to the rest of Brazil; more challenging land routes are possible from Bolivia, Guyana and French Guiana. Many travelers come down the Amazon itself from Iquitos, Peru. Most larger Amazon cities have airports. Within the Amazon, boats are definitely the transport of choice, but flying can save a lot of time and is sometimes quite affordable.

Does the real Amazon live up to the imaginary one in the minds of travelers? Jungle trips from Manaus or elsewhere are necessarily limited, and Discovery Channel–like expeditions are beyond most travelers' budgets. But it's only in the halogen glare of unreasonable expectations (or too short a visit) that a trip to the Amazon can seem disappointing. The river and the rain forest are massive, unrelenting and incredible. Wildlife is hard to see, but that much more special when you do; the flora is everywhere and awesome. Indigenous tribes are extremely reclusive, but the Caboclo (mixed Indian and European) communities that populate the riverbanks are vital and compelling. Give it some time, forget your expectations, and the Amazon cannot fail to impress.

THE AMAZON

THE AMAZON

0 ____ 600 km
0 ____ 400 mi

ATLANTIC OCEAN

Equator

COLOMBIA

VENEZUELA

GUYANA

SURINAME

FRENCH GUIANA (France)

PERU

BOLIVIA

BOGOTÁ

CAYENNE

Puerto Ayacucho

Icana

Cucuí

São Gabriel da Cachoeira

Pico da Neblina (3014m)
Parque Nacional do Pico da Neblina

Monte Roraima (2875m)
Santa Elena de Uairén

BOA VISTA

Terra Indígena Yanomami

Reserva Xixuaú-Xiparina

Barcelos

Rio Negro

Rio Branco

Bonfim

Caracaraí

Terra Indígena Waimiri-Atroari

Presidente Figueiredo

Encontro das Águas

MANAUS

Manacapuru

Reserva de Desenvolvimento Sustentável Mamirauá

Parque Nacional do Jaú

Reserva de Desenvolvimento Sustentável Amanã

Tefé

Fonte Boa

Coari

Tabatinga
Benjamin Constant
Leticia

Terra Indígena Vale do Javari

Rio Javari

Rio Amazonas

Cruzeiro do Sul

Parque Nacional da Serra do Divisor

Serra do Divisor

Acre

Rio Juruá

Rio Purus

Amazonas

Silves
Itacoatiara

Manicoré

Humaitá

Lábrea

Boca do Acre

Porto Acre
RIO BRANCO
Xapuri

Brasiléia
Assis Brasil
Cobija

Senna Madureira

Reserva Extrativista Chico Mendes

Rondônia

PORTO VELHO

Ariquemes

Jaru
Cacaulândia

Cacoal

Ji-Paraná

Reserva Extrativista Pedras Negras

Parque Nacional de Pacás Novos

Guajará-Mirim
Guayaramerín
Riberalta

Forte Príncipe da Beira
Costa Marques

Ramonedo

Rolim de Moura

Mato Grosso

Alta Floresta

Vilhena

Rio Madeira

Rio Juruena

Rio Teles Pires

Serra dos Cachimbo

Rio Tapajós

Novo Aripuanã
Maués

Parintins

Óbidos

Monte Alegre

Alenquer

Santarém
Alter do Chão

Belterra

Rurópolis

Itaituba

Altamira

Transamazônica

Caracol

Pará

Rio Xingu

Uruará

Rio Amazonas

Porto Grande
Serra do Navio
Calçoene
Amapá
MACAPÁ

Amapá

Parque Nacional das Montanhas do Tumucumaque

St Georges
Oiapoque

Parque Nacional do Cabo Orange

Ilha Caviana
Ilha de Marajó

Soure
Salvaterra
Joanes

Souré
BELÉM
Abaetetuba

Camará

Tucuruí

Marabá

Serra Pelada
Projeto Grande Carajás
Serra dos Carajás

Floresta Nacional de Caxiuanã

Maranhão

Imperatriz

Carolina

Santa Inês

Pinheiro
Santa Helena

Algodoal
Salinópolis

Turiaçu

Bahia

Barreiras

Gilbués

Tocantins

PALMAS

Porto Nacional

Paranã

Natividade

Gurupi

Lagoa da Confusão

Araguaína

Conceição do Araguaia

Santa Terezinha

São Félix do Araguaia

Parque Indígena do Araguaia

Parque Nacional do Araguaia

Rio Araguaia

Tocantinópolis

Tucumã

Rio Iriri
Rio Paru
Rio Jari

Rio Trombetas

Rio Solimões
Rio Japurá
Rio Putumayo
Rio Javarí
Rio Purus

Claimed by Suriname & French Guiana

Claimed by Suriname & Guyana

Roraima

BR 174
BR 210
BR 347
BR 319
BR 174
BR 230
BR 163
BR 364
BR 230
BR 364
BR 158
BR 080
BR 163
BR 158
BR 153
BR 010
BR 222
BR 226
BR 230
BR 316
BR 135
BR 155
BR 316

Pará, Amapá & Tocantins

CONTENTS

HIGHLIGHTS

- Getting to know the rubber boomtown of **Belém** (p577), with the vibrant Ver-o-Peso market, late-night riverfront promenade and excellent museums

- Relaxing on white-sand beaches in **Alter do Chão** (p601), almost 500 miles from the ocean

- Roughing it with rubber tappers in **Floresta Nacional do Tapajós** (p598) outside Santarém

- Plying the windy Atlantic beaches at **Ilha de Marajó** (p592)

- Exploring the oft-forgotten state of Tocantins, with sand dunes and rock formations in **Jalapão** (p614) and great bird-watching on **Ilha Bananal** (p615)

- POPULATION: 8.8 MILLION
- AREA: 1,669,500 SQ KM

Pará, Tocantíns and Amapá are all transition states, where the dry Brazilian lowlands (or Atlantic seashore, in the case of Amapá) give way to the lush Amazonian rain forest. Many travelers pass right over this area, anxious to get 'deeper in.' If time is short, that may make sense, but the eastern Amazon is a fascinating and unique place in itself.

Pará, by far the largest of the three states, covers 1.25 million sq km and includes a major stretch of the Rio Amazonas and all or part of such huge tributaries as the Rio Tocantins, Rio Xingu, Rio Tapajós and Rio Trombetas. Its attractions include the cities of Belém and Santarém, the beach village of Alter do Chão, and some fine Atlantic beaches on Ilha de Marajó and the northern coast.

Tocantins, south of Pará, has attractive natural destinations such as the Rio Araguaia, the Ilha do Bananal and the unique Jalapão region. Here you can see caves, waterfalls, and sand dunes on excursions out of the state capital Palmas – an intriguing planned city.

Amapá occupies an isolated, unforgiving region and more than half of the state is under environmental protection, including the world's largest rain-forest park.

History

The Portuguese, having expelled the French from Maranhão in 1615, landed at Belém in 1616, building a fort to deter French, English, Spanish and Dutch ships from sailing up the Rio Amazonas and claiming territory. Until 1774 the area encompassing present-day Pará and Maranhão was governed as a colony separate from the rest of Brazil, with its capital in São Luís, Maranhão.

Creating a separate administration for this territory made sense: the prevailing winds and currents made the voyage from Belém to Salvador much longer and more arduous than the six-week trip from Belém to Lisbon, and the inland route was long and perilous.

In more recent times, Pará suffered some of the most devastating rain-forest destruction in the Amazon, a fact easily visible when you fly over the state. Worse, much of the cleared land became useless for agriculture after just a few years. Recently Brazilian farmers, with help from agriscientists, have had success growing soy beans in Pará, and the state is now an important soy producer. Amapá and Tocantins have stronger environmental records, thanks partly to more enlightened administration and partly to their relative isolation.

Climate

Temperature and humidity here vary greatly by location and season. Belém is one of the rainiest cities in the world, with no true dry season. Downpours can be expected almost daily from December to June, tapering off somewhat in October, the driest month. This isn't as bad as it sounds: the rain is often a brief, welcome relief from the early afternoon heat. The equator runs through Macapá, the capital of Amapá, so the climate there is, well, equatorial, with heavy rains January to June and hot, humid conditions year-round. Tocantins is a transition zone between the dry interior and the wetlands of the Amazon and Pantanal. Palmas is in a low river valley where the sun can be intense, while the nearby hilly areas can be cool, even chilly. The rainy season lasts from October to April.

National Parks

Amapá is home to Brazil's largest national park – **Parque Nacional das Montanhas do Tumucumaque** – as well as **Parque Nacional do Cabo Orange** and various reserves. None are open to visitors, however. To visit a park, head to **Floresta Nacional do Tapajós** near Santarém or the less-visited **Parque Nacional da Amazônia** near Itaituba, both in Pará. Tocantins has **Parque Nacional do Araguaia** on Ilha do

Bananal, arguably the largest river island in the world.

Getting There & Away

Belém is the major transportation hub in this region, and most travelers arrive there by bus or plane from northeastern or southern Brazil. Some travelers enter via the state of Tocantins, most commonly by bus or plane from Brasília or the Pantanal. Or you can make Belém your last stop on the Amazon, after floating or flying downriver from Manaus or even Iquitos, Peru. The state of Amapá is accessible by boat or plane from Belém, or overland from French Guiana.

Getting Around

Once you are in this region, there are only a few bus routes – the rest is by boat or by plane. From Belém, you can take a bus south to Palmas or north to the towns on the Atlantic. In Amapá there is a mostly-unpaved highway north to the French Guiana border. There, as elsewhere, bus travel during the rainy season can be treacherous, with mud, potholes and major delays. Passenger boats leave Belém three times a week upriver to Manaus and beyond, with stops in Santarém and other points along the way. (See 'Buses of the Waterways', p582, for tips on riverboat travel.) There are daily flights from Belém to most spots in the Amazon; flying allows you more time for jungle trips – ordinary riverboats are very slow and don't afford much sightseeing – and may be worth the extra expense.

PARÁ

The Tupi tribe who lived beside the Rio Amazonas estuary prior to colonization used the term *pa'ra* (vast ocean) to describe its awesome size. In 1500 the Spanish navigator Vicente Yáñez Pinzón sailed past the Amazon delta and noticed huge quantities of freshwater issuing into the ocean. He returned to Spain without investigating, though, having determined that navigation to the source of such a gigantic 'ocean river' would be too risky.

Pará, especially the eastern part, has borne the brunt of Amazonian deforestation. The region to the south of the state capital, Belém, contains the world's biggest hydro-electric installation, at Tucuruí, and one of its biggest mining projects, the Provincia Mineral de Carajás. This is a Wild West–like zone, infamous for human and ecological problems and for highway robberies and murdered land-rights campaigners.

Pará is divided into two time zones. East of the Rio Xingu, the state uses Brasília time; west of the Xingu, the time is one hour behind that.

BELÉM

☎ 0xx91 / pop 1.4 million

Belém is the economic center of the Amazon and the state capital of Pará. It's a lively and absorbing city, with a unique culture derived from its people and the ways of the forest and river. It is animated by the biggest port on the Amazon, where more than half of all cargo carried is timber. From here you can set sail for any navigable port of the river or its tributaries. The city's central area is pleasant, with streets and parks shaded by mango trees, and some fascinating monuments and architecture.

History

Between 1637 and 1639 Pedro Teixeira journeyed from Belém to Quito (Ecuador) and back, claiming lands as far as the Rio Napo (Peru) for Portugal. As elsewhere in Brazil, Jesuits came to Amazonia to 'save' the Indians and install them in *aldeias* (mission villages). It was through these missionaries and a scattering of forts that Portugal began to take control of the region.

The Portuguese settlers (predominantly poor farmers from the Azores islands) were dependent on the labor of indigenous peoples (known as *filhos do mato*, or sons of the forest) who knew the ways of the Amazon and who could find cacao, vanilla, indigo, cinnamon, animal skins and turtle shells for export to Europe. These riches, and the enslavement of the Indians, made Belém a relatively prosperous settlement. It survived by striking further and further into Amazonia, destroying tribes of Indians in one slaving expedition after another. Epidemics killed many Indians, while Catholicism killed much of their culture. Some Indians escaped this fate by fleeing deeper along small tributaries into Amazonia.

With the depletion of the Indian labor force, Belém's economy began to decline, and the 1820s and 1830s saw a period of intense civil war (see The Cabanagem Rebellion, p582).

Decades later, the regional economy was revitalized by the rubber boom. Vast numbers of poor peasants fled the drought-plagued Northeast, particularly Ceará, to tap Amazonia's rubber trees. Most of these

seringuieros (rubber gatherers) arrived and then died in debt, thanks to harsh living conditions and widespread exploitation at the hands of large plantation owners.

The population of Belém grew from 40,000 in 1875 to more than 100,000 in 1900. The city had electricity, telephones, streetcars and a distinctly European feel.

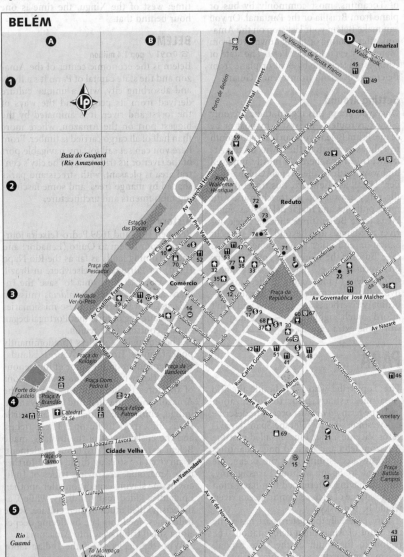

BELÉM

Officials erected a few grand monuments such as the Teatro da Paz, earning the city the nickname 'the tropical Paris.' The docks and warehouses that still line the riverfront were built during this period.

By 1910 rubber constituted 39% of Brazil's total exports and new ports and wharfs were commissioned and built in Belém to handle the flow. A second rubber boom during WWII was followed by a timber boom in the 1970s when the US and others scrambled to develop an alternative to Asian and African sources, which appeared to be nearing their limits. Today some 800,000 tons of cargo pass through Belém, mostly timber, but also soy, fish, shrimp, Brazil

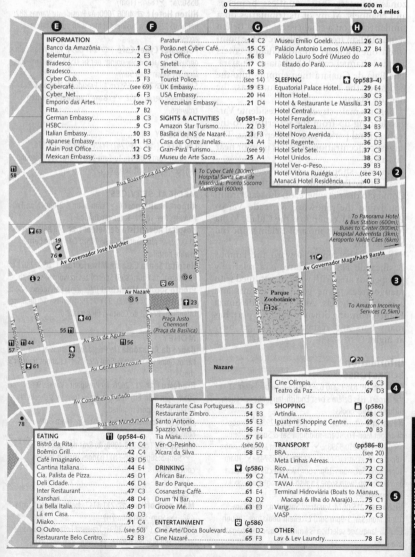

0 —————— 600 m
0 —————— 0.4 miles

INFORMATION
Banco da Amazônia.................................1 C3
Belemtur...2 E3
Bradesco...3 C4
Bradesco...4 B3
Cyber Club...5 F3
Cybercafé...(see 69)
Cyber_Net..6 F3
Emporio das Artes..............................(see 7)
Fitta...7 B2
German Embassy......................................8 C3
HSBC...9 C3
Italian Embassy......................................10 B3
Japanese Embassy..................................11 H3
Main Post Office....................................12 C3
Mexican Embassy...................................13 D5

Paratur..14 C2
Porão.net Cyber Café.............................15 C5
Post Office..16 B3
Sinetel...17 C3
Telemar...18 B3
Tourist Police...................................(see 14)
UK Embassy..19 E3
USA Embassy..20 H4
Venezuelan Embassy..............................21 D4

SIGHTS & ACTIVITIES (pp581–3)
Amazon Star Turismo..............................22 D3
Basílica de NS de Nazaré........................23 F3
Casa das Onze Janelas............................24 A4
Gran-Pará Turismo.............................(see 9)
Museu de Arte Sacra..............................25 A4

Museu Emílio Goeldi...............................26 G3
Palácio Antonio Lemos (MABE)..27 B4
Palácio Lauro Sodré (Museo do
   Estado do Pará).................................28 A4

SLEEPING (pp583–4)
Equatorial Palace Hotel..........................29 E4
Hilton Hotel..30 C3
Hotel & Restaurante Le Massilia.31 D3
Hotel Central...32 C3
Hotel Ferrador..33 C3
Hotel Fortaleza.......................................34 B3
Hotel Novo Avenida...............................35 C3
Hotel Regente...36 D3
Hotel Sete Sete.......................................37 C3
Hotel Unidos...38 C3
Hotel Ver-o-Peso.....................................39 B3
Hotel Vitória Ruaégia........................(see 34)
Manacá Hotel Residência........................40 E3

To Cyber Café (300m);
Hospital Santa Casa de
Miscórdia; Pronto Socorro
Municipal (600m)

Rua Boaventura da Silva

To Panorama Hotel
& Bus Station (600m);
Buses to Center (800m);
Hospital Adventista (3km);
Aeroporto Valde Cães (6km)

Av Governador José Malcher

Av Governador Magalhães Barata

Av Nazaré

Parque
Zoobotânico

To Amazon Incoming
Services (2.5km)

Praça Justo
Chermont
(Praça da Basílica)

Av Brás de Aguiar

Av Gentil Bittencourt

Nazaré

Av Conselheiro Furtado

Cine Olímpia...66 C3
Teatro da Paz...67 D3

Rua dos Mundurucus

Restaurante Casa Portuguesa.....53 C3
Restaurante Zimbro................................54 B3
Santo Antonio..55 E3
Spazzio Verdi..56 F4
Tia Maria...57 E4
Ver-O-Pesinho...................................(see 50)
Xícara da Silva..58 E2

SHOPPING (p586)
Artíndia...68 C3
Iguatemi Shopping Centre......................69 C4
Natural Ervas...70 B3

EATING (pp584–6)
Bistrô da Rita..41 C4
Boêmio Grill..42 C4
Café Imaginario......................................43 D5
Cantina Italiana.......................................44 E4
Cia. Palista de Pizza...............................45 D1
Deli Cidade..46 D4
Inter Restaurant.....................................47 C3
Kanshari..48 D4
La Bella Italia..49 D1
Lá em Casa..50 D5
Miako..51 C4
O Outro..(see 50)
Restaurante Belo Centro........................52 B3

DRINKING (p586)
African Bar..59 C2
Bar do Parque...60 C3
Cosanastra Caffé....................................61 E4
Drum 'N Bar..62 D2
Groove Me..63 E3

ENTERTAINMENT (p586)
Cine Arte/Doca Boulevard......................64 D2
Cine Nazaré..65 F3

TRANSPORT (pp586–8)
BRA..(see 20)
Meta Linhas Aéreas................................71 C3
Rico...72 C3
TAM..73 C2
TAVAJ...74 C2
Terminal Hidroviária (Boats to Manaus,
   Macapá & Ilha do Marajó)......75 C1
Varig..76 E3
VASP..77 C3

OTHER
Lav & Lev Laundry...................................78 E4

THE AMAZON

nuts and palm hearts. From 2000 to 2002, Belém made major renovations to its waterfront, turning disused warehouses and wharves into an excellent riverside esplanade, with restaurants, shops, museums, galleries and more.

Orientation

As it approaches the Atlantic, the Rio Amazonas splinters into countless branches and channels. Many of its tributaries do a similar thing on a smaller scale, and Belém stands 120km from the Atlantic at the point where one tributary, the Rio Guamá, enters a wider channel called the Baía de Guajará. The Baía de Guajará then empties into the widest of the estuaries of Amazonas, the Baía de Marajó.

Belém's main street is Av Presidente Vargas, leading up from the waterfront to the leafy central park, Praça da República. The largest concentration of hotels is on or near this axis.

Narrow shopping streets lead southwest off Av Presidente Vargas through the Comércio district where, on the waterfront, you'll find the renowned Mercado Ver-o-Peso. Beyond Comércio is the Cidade Velha (Old Town), with most of Belém's fine old architecture.

East of the center, toward the famous Basílica de NS de Nazaré, is a relatively prosperous area with wide streets lined with mango trees, some good restaurants and a few more hotels. Av Visconde de Souza Franco, running down toward the port, has many bars and restaurants that get busy at night.

Information

BOOKSTORES

Clio (☎ 210 6369, 210 6368) A 24-hour bookstore at the airport. Has Belém's best English-language selection, including guidebooks.

Newstime Estação das Docas (☎ 212 3298; ◷ noon-midnight Mon-Fri, 10am-midnight Sat & Sun); Iguatemi Shopping (☎ 250 5398; ◷ 10am-10pm Mon-Sat, noon-10pm Sun); Iguatemi Shopping (☎ 250 5574; ◷ 10am-10pm Mon-Sat, noon-10pm Sun) An eclectic newsstand and bookshop, with some English-language guidebooks and magazines.

Visão (☎ 215 0674; Iguatemi Shopping; ◷ 10am-10pm Mon-Sat, 3-9pm Sun) Excellent bookstore, though English-language selection is limited. Music and magazines available.

EMERGENCY

CIPTUR Estação das Docas (☎ 212 5307); bus station (☎ 246 7442); Paratur (☎ 212 0948 tourist police)
Police (☎ 190)

INTERNET ACCESS

Cyber Café (☎ 223 6361; Rua Antonio Barreto 945 at Travessa 14 de Março; per hr US$1; ◷ 24hr)
Cyber Club (☎ 212 6121; Av Nazaré 1054; per hr US$0.75; ◷ 8am-11pm)
Hilton Hotel (☎ 4006 7000; Av Presidente Vargas 882; per hr US$2) Has a business center with public Internet access.
Porão.net Cyber Café (☎ 241 0094; Rua Veiga Cabral opposite Iguatemi Shopping; per hr US$1; ◷ 9am-10pm Mon-Fri, noon-9pm Sun)
Sinetel (☎ 241 4965; crn Av Presidente Vargas & Rua Riachuelo; per hr US$2; ◷ 8am-7pm Mon-Fri) Often crowded.

LAUNDRY

Lav & Lev (☎ 223 7247; Travessa Dr Moraes 576; ◷ 8am-8pm Mon-Fri, to 4pm Sat) A large load (around 6kg) costs US$4 self-service, US$6 drop-off.

MEDICAL SERVICES

Airport health post (◷ 8am-noon & 2-6pm Mon-Fri) Provides free yellow-fever vaccinations.
Hospital Adventista de Belém (☎ 246 8686, 0800 91 0022; Av Almirante Barroso 1758) One of the better private hospitals.
Hospital Santa Casa de Misericórdia (☎ 212 0787; Rua Bernal do Couto 866) Specializes in women's health.
Pronto Socorro Municipal (Municipal Emergency Room; ☎ 241 0928, 241 6400, 241 7135; Travessa 14 de Março btwn Ruas Bernal do Couto & Oliveira Belo)

MONEY

Banco da Amazônia (Av Presidente Vargas at Rua Carlos Gomes; ◷ 10am-5pm Mon-Sat) Changes traveler's checks.
Bradesco (☎ 217 2626; Av Presidente Vargas 988; 10am-1pm Mon-Fri) Changes Amex traveler's checks on 4th floor; passport required.
HSBC (Av Presidente Vargas 670; ◷ 10am-5pm Mon-Sat)
Monopolio (☎ 242 4099; Av Brás de Aguiar 202A; ◷ 9am-5:30pm Mon-Fri) Changes various foreign currencies.

POST

Main post office (☎ 211 3147; Av Presidente Vargas 498; ◷ 9am-5pm Mon-Fri)
Post office (☎ 212 7093; Travessa Frutuoso Guimarães at Rua Sen Manoel Barata; ◷ 9am-5pm Mon-Fri)

TELEPHONE

Sinetel (☎ 241 4965; Av Presidente Vargas & Rua Riachuelo; ⏰ 8am-7pm Mon-Fri)

Telemar (Rua João Alfredo at Travessa Frutuoso Guimarães; ⏰ 8:30am-6:30 Mon-Fri, to3pm Sat) Cabins for national and international calls.

TOURIST INFORMATION

Both tourist departments also have desks at the airport.

Belemtur (☎ 242 0900; Av Governador José Malcher 592; ⏰ 8am-6pm Mon-Fri) The city tourism department is less helpful than Paratur.

Paratur (☎ 212 0669; Praça Waldemar Henrique s/n; ⏰ 8am-6pm Mon-Fri) The state tourism agency; is both friendly and helpful.

TRAVEL AGENCIES

Amazon Incoming Services (☎ 274 4904; amazon@amazonservice.com.br; Rua Dr Américo Sta Rosa 983) Offers a variety of tours, from half-day river and city tours to all-day trips to Ilha do Mosquiero.

Amazon Star Turismo (☎ 241 8624; fax 212 6244; www.amazonstar.com.br; Rua Henrique Gurjão 236) Also offers a variety of half- and full-day tours, including city tours, bird-watching tours and trips to Isla Marajó.

Gran-Pará Turismo (☎ 212 3233; fax 224 1687; Av Presidente Vargas 676) Flights only.

Lusotur (☎ 241 1011; fax 242 5010; Av Brás de Aguiar 471) Flights and tours.

Dangers & Annoyances

The Mercado Ver-o-Peso is notorious for harboring thieves and pickpockets – this shouldn't prevent you from going, but do take care. As always, consider taking cabs at night.

Sights

CENTRAL AREA
Estação das Docas

Beginning in 2000, an ambitious renovation project converted three down-at-heel riverfront warehouses into an attractive commercial center. Estação das Docas now houses restaurants, artsy shops, a small theatre, plus a post office and plenty of ATMs. The waterfront promenade is lined with attractive yellow cranes, reminders of Belém's port-town roots. Come here for great river views during the day and live music at night.

Teatro da Paz

One of Belém's finest buildings, the **Teatro da Paz** (☎ 224 7355, 212 7915; Praça da República) was built between 1869 and 1874 overlooking Praça da República. Built in neoclassical style, the architecture has all the sumptuous trappings of the rubber-boom era: columns, busts, crystal mirrors and an interior decorated in Italian theatrical style. The theater has hosted Brazilian and international stars ranging from Anna Pavlova to the Vienna Boys' Choir to the Cossacks. Half-hour guided tours (US$1.50) are offered hourly from 9am to 5pm weekdays, 9am to 1pm weekends.

Mercado Ver-o-Peso

A symbol of the city, this waterfront market's name comes from colonial times, when the Portuguese would *ver o peso* (check the weight) of merchandise in order to impose taxes. The four-turreted iron structure inside the market (and visible from well outside of it) is known as the Mercado do Ferro. It was brought over in parts from Britain, and assembled and inaugurated in 1901. A profile of the turrets is commonly used as a symbol of Belém.

The display of fruits and animals, not to mention the people, is fascinating. It's best to get there early, when the fishing boats are unloading at the southwest end of the market. Other shops sell medicinal plants, shoes, clothes, food and more, all at cut-rate prices.

At and around the Ver-o-Peso, be very alert for thieves and pickpockets, who may operate alone or in gangs. Avoid hanging around there after 5pm or on Sunday afternoon.

CIDADE VELHA

The oldest part of Belém, south of the Mercado Ver-o-Peso, is fairly run-down. You should avoid walking around here after dark, but the area does contain some fine buildings and museums, including the Palacio Lauro Sodré, Catedral da Sé and the recently refurbished Casa das Onze Janelas.

Forte do Castelo

Founded in 1616 and refurbished in 2001, **Forte do Castelo** (Praça Fr. Brandão; admission US$0.65; ⏰ 10am-6pm Tue-Fri, to 8pm Sat & Sun) has fine river views and a small but informative museum (Portuguese only) of pre- and post-colonial artifacts found here and nearby Ilha de Marajó (see Prehistoric Amazonia, p600).

Palácio Antonio Lemos & MABE

This rubber-boom **palace** on Praça Dom Pedro II was built to serve as the city hall between 1860 and 1883. By the early 1990s the palace was virtually abandoned, with animals roaming around inside, but it underwent renovation and once again houses the municipal government headquarters as well as the **Museo de Arte de Belém** (MABE; ☎ 219 8242; admission US$0.50, Tue free; ☾ 10am-6pm Tue-Fri, to 1pm Sat & Sun).

Constructed in the Brazilian imperial style, the building has a grand central staircase of Portuguese marble. The museum, upstairs, has gorgeous wood floors – cloth slippers are provided at the entrance – and a fine collection of Brazilian 20th-century paintings, including Cândido Portinari's 1957 oil *Seringal*.

Palácio Lauro Sodré & Museo do Estado do Pará

This former residence of Portugal's representatives in Belém, and later of various governors of Pará state, **Palácio Lauro Sodré** is also on Praça Dom Pedro II and now houses the **Museo do Estado do Pará** (Pará State Museum; ☎ 219 1130, 225 2414; admission US$0.50; ☾ 1-6pm Tue-Fri; 9am-1pm Sat & Sun). It was built between 1762 and 1772 by architect Antônio Landi, and is an attractive Portuguese version of the neo-Palladian style. In 1835 the Cabanagem invaded the palace, killing the governor, Ernesto Lobo, on the staircase (see the boxed text, below).

Casa das Onze Janelas

Part of a major restoration effort to Belém's waterfront area was the opening, in 2003, of the **Casa das Onze Janelas** (House of 11 Windows; ☎ 219 1165; Rua Siquiera Mendes s/n). Once the home of a sugar baron, then a military hospital, this sturdy riverfront structure now houses an excellent **art gallery** (admission US$0.50, Wed free; ☾ 10am-6pm Tue-Fri, to 8pm Sat & Sun) and one of Belém's finest restaurants, Boteco das Onze (see p585). The medium-sized gallery contains a mix of classical and modern artwork, plus a good photography exhibit upstairs.

Museu de Arte Sacra

The excellent **Museu de Arte Sacra** (Museum of Sacred Art; ☎ 219 8217; admission US$0.50, Tue free; ☾ 10am-6pm Tue-Fri, 9am-1pm Sat & Sun), on Praça Frei Brandão, consists of the Igreja do Santo Alexandre and the adjoining Palácio Episcopal (Bishop's Palace), both recently restored. Santo Alexandre, the first church in Belém when founded by Jesuits in the early 17th century, was rebuilt in baroque style in the 18th century. It contains some brilliant sculpture, done by Indians in plaster and red cedar from that era.

Catedral da Sé

Belém's **cathedral** (Praça Frei Brandão; ☾ 7am-noon & 2-7:30pm) is a 1750s colonial baroque-cum-neoclassical construction by Antônio Landi. The twin-towered main facade is handsome; the interior is unremarkable.

EAST OF THE CENTER

Basílica de NS de Nazaré

Built in 1909, the **basilica** (Rua da Basílica & Av Nazaré; admission free; ☾ 7am-noon & 3-7pm Tue-Sun, 6-7:30am & 3-7pm Mon) is visited by more than a

---

THE CABANAGEM REBELLION

In the 1820s a split between the white ruling classes of Belém led to civil war, which soon spread to the dominated Indians, *mestiços*, blacks and mulattos. After years of fighting, the war developed into a popular revolutionary movement that swept through Pará like wildfire.

In 1835 the guerrilla fighters marched on Belém, taking the city after nine days of bloody fighting. They installed a popular government, which expropriated the wealth of the merchants, distributed food to all the people and declared Belém's independence. But the revolutionary experiment was immediately strangled by a British naval blockade, Britain being the principal beneficiary of trade with Brazil at the time.

A year later a large Brazilian government force recaptured Belém. The vast majority of the city's population fled to the interior to resist again. Over the next four years, the military hunted down and slaughtered anyone they thought could be hostile. The Cabanagem massacre was one of the most savage of Brazil's many military campaigns against its own people. Altogether some 30,000 people out of Pará's population of 150,000 died in the conflict.

million people during the annual Círio de Nazaré (see p583). The artisans, as well as much of the material, were imported from Europe, and the colorful interior is lined with fine marble. Downstairs is a museum of sacred art.

Museu Emílio Goeldi & Parque Zoobotánico

The best **museum and zoo** (☎ 249 1233; Av Governador Magalhães Barata 376; park, aquarium & permanent exhibit each US$0.50; ☯ 9am-5pm Tue-Sun) in Belém contains many Amazonian animal species, from manatees and anacondas to jaguars and giant otters, plus an aviary, aquarium and excellent permanent exhibit of artifacts from ancient Amazonian peoples. The complex is divided into the outdoor park area, aquarium area and permanent exhibit area – tickets to each are sold separately at the gate. It's definitely worth visiting all three.

All this is part of a research institution for the study of the flora, fauna and peoples of Amazonia, founded in 1866 and reorganized in the 1890s by Dr Emílio Augusto Goeldi.

The park also contains a café and a good gift/crafts shop. Sundays are popular with families.

River Tours

The travel agencies mentioned earlier (see p580) offer various tours. Prices start around US$25 per person for a standard river tour (six to seven hours), which is not particularly exciting. You'll cruise the river, get out on an island, and walk down a path where many have walked before to see rubber trees, açaí palms and other local fauna. This voyage into the known is recommended only if you have no time to really see the jungle and rivers. Amazon Star is recommended.

Trips to Ilha dos Papagaios (Parrot Island) usually start before dawn so you can see parrots and other birds leaving the island to search for food. Amazon Star's 'Early Bird' version costs US$25 per person (US$35 each for two people).

For a quick trip on the river, the easiest option is an outing on the boat *Tribo dos Kayapós* from the Terminal Fluvial at Estação das Docas. Sunset and after-dark cruises of 1½ hours run daily Tuesday to Sunday for US$7.

Festivals & Events

Every year on the morning of the second Sunday of October, Belém explodes with the sounds of hymns, bells and fireworks. Started in 1793, the **Círio de Nazaré** is Brazil's biggest religious festival. People from all over the country flock to Belém, and even camp in the streets, to participate in the grand event.

The image of NS de Nazaré is believed by the faithful to have been sculpted in Nazareth (Galilee) and to have performed miracles in medieval Portugal before getting lost in Brazil. After its disappearance, it was rediscovered in 1700 by a humble cattleman, Placido de Souza, on the site of the basilica, to which it later returned of its own accord after being moved away several times.

The day before the main annual event, the little statue, having previously been taken 23km north to Icoaraci, is carried in a river procession back to the cathedral in Belém. On the Sunday itself, around a million people fill the streets to accompany the image from the Catedral da Sé to the Basílica de NS de Nazaré. The image is placed on a flower-bedecked carriage, and thousands squirm and grope in an emotional frenzy to get a hand on the 300m rope pulling the carriage. Five hours and just 3.5km from the cathedral, the Virgin reaches the basilica, where she remains for the duration of the festivities.

After the parade, the multitudes head to the fairgrounds for mayhem of the more secular kind: food, drink, music and dancing. *Pato no tucupí* (duck cooked in manioc extract with garlic and the *jambú* herb) is the traditional meal, and the party continues unabated for two weeks. On the Monday 15 days after the first procession, the crowd reassembles for the Recírio parade, in which the Virgin is returned to her niche in the basilica and the festivities are concluded.

Sleeping

Note that in addresses, the abbreviation 's/n' stands for *sem número* (without number).

BUDGET

Hotel Fortaleza (☎ 212 1055; Travessa Frutuoso Guimarães 276; s/d without bathroom US$4/6, incl breakfast US$4.50/8) A backpackers' favorite. In an old house with a central TV area, one drawback can be the close quarters and sometimes uneasy mix of travelers, family members and hangers-on. The rooms are basic, with fan and reasonably clean shared bathrooms. Guests can use the kitchen and laundry area for US$0.50 each.

Hotel Vitória Régia (☎ /fax 212 3301, 212 3628; Travessa Frutuoso Guimarães 260; s/d with breakfast & bathroom US$10/11.50, with [icon] US$13.50/15) Next door to hotel Fortaleza, there's less of a traveler's atmosphere here but rooms are more private and have private bathrooms, TV and minibar. Triple and quad rooms are available.

Hotel Central (☎ 242 4800, 241 8267; Av Presidente Vargas 290; incl breakfast s/d US$8.50/11.50, with bathroom US$13/17) This is a large art-deco hotel popular with foreign travelers. Rooms are bare and pretty rundown, but high ceilings give a spacious feel; some have basic patios. Rooms facing Av Presidente Vargas can be noisy.

Panorama Hotel (☎ 226 9724; Travessa Primeira de Queluz 81; s/d with bathroom & breakfast US$10.65/12.50) Behind the bus terminal, this place offers simple, clean, fan-cooled rooms – good if you are just passing through.

MID-RANGE
Many mid-range options are only slightly more expensive than budget listings, so even if you're on a tight budget you might consider a minor splurge.

Hotel Unidos (☎ 224 0660; fax 252 1880; Rua Ó de Almeida 545; s/d with bathroom & breakfast US$18.50/22; [icons]) A half-block off Av Presidente Vargas, this is the best of the mid-range options. Rooms, some of them quite large, are modern and spotless, and come with a large breakfast. A 10% discount is available if you pay with cash.

Hotel Ferrador (☎ 241 5999; ferrador@amazon.com .br; Rua Aristides Lobo 485; s/d with breakfast US$18.50/25; [icons]) Rooms are clean and decent-sized, if a bit plain, and come with TV and an ample breakfast. A discount of 10% is usually available if you ask.

Hotel Novo Avenida (☎ 242 9953; fax 223 8893; Av Presidente Vargas 404; s/d with bathroom US$11.50/13, incl [icon] $16.50/19.65) Also convenient for the center, this aging hotel is better than it looks from the outside. Small, clean rooms are reasonably pleasant and have TV; those facing the street have windows but can be noisy.

Hotel Ver-o-Peso (☎ /fax 241 2022; Av Castilho França 208; s/d with bathroom US$11/14.50, with view US$14.50/17; [icon]) Come here if you like the bustle of the market area. Rooms are large and fairly clean; triple and quads available. Breakfast is served on a pleasant rooftop terrace, overlooking the stall-filled street and waterfront.

Hotel Le Massilia (☎ /fax 224 7147; le_massilia@ yahoo.com; Rua Henrique Gurjão 236; incl breakfast s/d US$25/30; ste US$28/33; [icons]) Fairly close to the center, this French-run hotel has a guesthouse atmosphere, small swimming pool and a pleasant French **restaurant** ([icon] noon-2pm, 7-11pm Mon-Sat) at the front. Clean, attractive and homey, all rooms have TV and minibar; split-level suites sleep up to four.

Manacá Hotel Residência (☎ /fax 222 6227, 223 3335; manaca@amazon.com.br; Travessa Quintino Bocaiúva 1645; s/d/tr with [icon] & breakfast US$22/27/32.65) Very good value, with ultra-clean rooms in a stylishly renovated old house. Located in a hip upscale neighborhood, rooms here have thick beds and tasteful decor, though they are a wee bit dark. Curiously, there are single beds only.

TOP END
Its glory days long gone, Belém has only a few high-end accommodations.

Hilton Hotel (☎ 4006 7000; belemhil@amazon.com .br; Av Presidente Vargas 882; s/d incl breakfast US$133/140 plus 5% tax; [icons]) Overlooking Praça da República, this is Belém's top hotel with all the amenities you could hope for (except a swimming pool). Reserve in advance for discounts of up to 40%.

Hotel Regente (☎ 3181 5000; fax 3181 5001; Av Governador José Malcher 485; s/d US$45/50 plus 10% tax; [icons]) Catering to business people, a sleek lobby gives way to clean, no-nonsense rooms. Standard units are rather small, but larger ones available; 25% discount is available for longer stays.

Eating
CENTER
Estaçao das Docas is one of the best places in Belém to get a meal, no matter what you're in the mood for. The complex has almost a dozen restaurants, most with indoor and outdoor seating and serving perkilo lunches and à la carte dinners. Many stay open well past midnight on Friday and Saturday. A few are listed below, followed

by restaurants elsewhere in city, also worth checking out.

Restaurante Hatobá (☎ 3088 2900; Estação das Docas, Rua Castilho Franca; dishes US$7-15) Serves quality Asian food including sushi.

Capone (☎ 212 5566; Estação das Docas, Rua Castilho Franca; dishes US$7-15) Has a large selection of pasta and pizza.

Cairu (Estação das Docas, Rua Castilho Franca; ice cream US$1-2) This popular national chain serves excellent ice cream. Look for special Amazonian fruit flavors, such as the berry-like *açaí* or the acidic, slightly pearlike *cupuaçu*.

Miako (☎ 242 4485; Travessa Primeiro de Março 766; dishes US$6-10; ☺ lunch & dinner Mon-Sat, lunch Sun) This spacious second-floor restaurant behind the Hilton Hotel serves tasty Japanese and Chinese dishes.

Inter Restaurant (Rua 28 de Setembro 304; per kg US$5.25; ☺ lunch) The ample self-service spread here includes fresh-grilled meat. Or order the *quentinha* plate: fish, meat or chicken with rice, *farofa* (garnish of manioc flour sautéed with butter) and beans for US$5. Come early for the best and freshest choices.

Boêmio Grill (☎ 222 2592; Rua Carlos Gomes at Travessa Padre Prudêncio; per kg US$5.50; ☺ lunch Mon-Fri) With a fairly large spread including grilled meats, and air-con on full blast, this is another good option for self-service.

Restaurante Zimbro (Rua 15 de Novembro 314; per kg US$4; ☺ lunch Mon-Sat) This cheap, no-nonsense self-serve place in the heart of Comercio is popular with working folks.

Restaurante Belo Centro (☎ 241 8677; 2nd fl, Rua Santo Antônio 264; per kg US$4; ☺ lunch Mon-Fri) This friendly, airy restaurant cooks up tasty self-serve, with plenty of options for vegetarians and carnivores. It can be hard to find – look for a sandwich-board sign and narrow stairway between two shops.

Restaurant Açaí (☎ 4006 7000; Hotel Hilton, Av Presidente Vargas 882; dishes $6-12; ☺ 24hr) Huge fresh lunch and dinner buffet spreads are US$10; dishes of all prices on the menu. Though lacking in character, this is a decent option late or on weekends, when many other places are closed.

AROUND THE CENTER

Closer than they look on the map, these restaurants are a good excuse to get out of the center.

Boteco das Onze (☎ 212 4629; Rua Siqueira Mendes s/n; dishes US$7-14; ☺ lunch & dinner Tue-Sun) Part of the Casa das Onze Janelas art gallery (see p582), you can sit in either the low-stone-walled dining room with modern art on the walls, or on the breezy back patio overlooking the river and nearby fort. Meals include *muqueca de filhote*, a tasty stew prepared with catfish, shrimp and lobster. There is occasional live music (cover US$1.50).

Santo Antonio (☎ 212 0262; Travessa Quintino Bocaiúva at Av Brás de Aguiar; dishes US$2-7; ☺ breakfast, lunch & dinner) Classy but unassuming, this grocery-and-deli serves terrific sandwiches on fresh-baked bread. A French-Italian restaurant was due to open on the same site.

Spazzio Verdi (☎ 241 1515; Av Brás de Aguiar 824; per kg US$8 Mon-Fri, US$8.50 Sat & Sun; ☺ lunch & dinner) The main branch of this popular upscale chain has perhaps the most complete self-serve spread in the city.

Kanshari (Rua Gama Abreu 83; per kg US$7; ☺ lunch Mon-Sat) Come here for an all-vegetarian lunch buffet and a variety of fresh squeezed fruit and vegetable juices.

Lá em Casa (☎ 223 4222; Av Governador José Malcher 247; ☺ dinner) Jointly owned and operated with Ver-O-Pesinho and O Outro, all three restaurants share the same location northeast of the center. This place has outdoor seating and a string of awards for its classic Brazilian cuisine.

Ver-O-Pesinho (☎ 223 4222; Av Governador José Malcher 247; ☺ lunch Sun-Fri) Offers much of the same food as Lá em Casa, but self-serve.

O Outro (☎ 223 4222; Av Governador José Malcher 247; ☺ dinner Thu-Sat) This formal glass-walled restaurant has contemporary, international fare.

Restaurante Le Massilia (☎ /fax 224 7147; Hotel le Massilia, Rua Henrique Gurjão 236; dishes US$8-12; ☺ lunch & dinner Mon-Sat) In the same area as Lá em Casa, Ver-O-Pesinho and O Outro, this place serves quality French cuisine served in a small attractive dining area.

La Bella Italia (☎ 241 0102; Av Visconde de Souza Franco 567; dishes US$5-10; ☺ dinner) is one several good Italian restaurants in this area. Main dishes include good gnocchi and fettuccini, and there's a small-but-good self-serve antipasto spread.

Cia Paulista de Pizza (☎ 212 2200; Av Visconde de Souza Franca 559; ☺ noon-5pm & 6pm-1:30am; dishes US$7-10) Next door to La Bella Italia, you wouldn't know from looking that this is a national chain – wineglasses, tablecloths, attentive waiters and recorded jazz create a classy ambiance. Prices are quite affordable, however, and the pizza and pasta excellent.

Drinking

Cervejaria Amazonas (Estação das Docas, Rua Castilho Franca; ☺ 5pm-1am or 2am) This boutique brewery in Estação das Docas has five different beers brewed on the premises and good German-inspired food.

Bar do Parque (Praça da República s/n; ☺ 24hr) This outdoor bar is a popular meeting place. Prostitutes may approach male travelers here, but the area isn't intolerably seedy thanks to plenty of foot traffic.

Cosanostra Caffé (☎ 241 1068; Travessa Benjamim Constant 1499; ☺ noon-1am) This wood-beamed bar is popular among intellectuals and professionals, with varied live instrumental music starting at 11pm nightly (8pm on Sunday).

Entertainment

Av Visconde de Souza Franco has the busiest after-dark scene in Belém, where you can simply follow the music to find the latest hotspot.

Mormaço (☎ 9983 4320; Praço do Arsenal; ☺ Sat & Sun) At the end of the pier overlooking the river, this open-air club is hard to find but worth the effort, offering some of the best dancing in the city.

African Bar (☎ 241 1085; crn Av Marechal Hermes & Travessa da Piedade) Across from the tourist office, this longtime club often stages samba groups on Saturday nights. Check the posters by the door for upcoming events.

Drum 'N Bar (Travessa Quintina Bocaiúva 582) DJs play a variety of music at this stylish café and bar. Wednesday nights are Cuban; any night is good for kiwi *caipiroscas* (vodka cocktails) and other tropical drinks.

Groove Me (Rua Boaventura da Silva; cover US$2-4) A small unpretentious club dance club with good disco and techno music.

Cine Nazaré (☎ 242 5259; Av Nazaré 1187) This movie theater shows mostly recent Hollywood fare.

Cine Olimpia (☎ 223 1882; Av Presidente Vargas & Rua Silva Santos) Jointly operated with Cine Nazaré, this movie theater shows similar movies.

Cine Arte (☎ 241 1905; Doca Boulevard shopping center, Av Visconde de Souza Franco btwn Rua Ó de Almeida & Rua Aristides Lobo) Has somewhat better movies than either Cine Nazaré or Cine Olimpia.

Shopping

Feira de Artesanato (Praça da República; Fri-Sun) A large crafts fair that has the city's biggest range of attractive artwork, and a lot of it is homemade.

Natural Ervas (☎ 230 4667; Rua Gaspar Viana 228; ☺ 7am-6pm Mon-Sat, to noon Sun) One of a handful of shops on Rua Gaspar Viana that specialize in natural Amazonian medicines, good for everything from dandruff to cancer.

Mercado Ver-o-Peso and the surrounding area is probably the most interesting place to shop, whether for pants or piranha or anything in between. There are no set hours, but there is something interesting to see from 5:30am to 8:30pm every day. However, you should be especially wary of pickpockets and assailants in the early and late hours.

Artíndia (☎ 223 6248; end of arcade, Av Presidente Vargas 762; ☺ 9am-5pm Mon-Fri) Sells authentic and inexpensive Indian crafts at its main shop in the center and a **kiosk** (☺ noon-midnight) in Estação das Docas.

Iguatemi Shopping (Trav Padre Eutíquio btwn Rua Viega Cabral & Rua Gama Abreu) A modern shopping center with designer clothes, bookshops and music stores. Most shops are open from 10am to 10pm Monday to Saturday, and somewhat shorter hours on Sunday.

Getting There & Away

AIR

There are numerous international, domestic and Amazon-region flights from Belém's **Aeroporto Val de Cães** (☎ 257 0522). It is easier and no more expensive to buy plane tickets at travel agencies, rather than with the airline directly.

BRA airport (☎ 210 6260); Belém (☎ 259 7333; Av Conselheiro Furtado 2865)

Gol (☎ 210 6312; airport)

Meta Linhas Aéras airport (☎ 210 6298); Belém (☎ 225 6687; Av Assis de Vasconcelos 457)

Nordeste (☎ 3084 8484; Av Governador José Malcher 815)

Penta (☎ 210 6245; airport)

Puma Air (☎ reservations 246 2527, ☎ 210 6292; www.pumaair.com.br)

Rico airport (210 6456); Belém (☎ 241 4433; Av Assis de Vasconceles 207)

Rio Sul (☎ 3084 8484; Av Governador José Malcher 815)
Surinam Airways (☎ 210 6436; airport)
TAM (☎ 212 2166; Av Assis de Vasconcelos 265)
TAVAJ airport (☎ 212 1201); Belém (☎ 241 3670; Av
Assis de Vasconcelos 396)
Varig (☎ 3084 8484; Av Governador José Malcher 815)
VASP airport (210 6345); Belém (☎ 224 5588, Av Presidente Vargas 345)

BOAT
All long-distance boats leave Belém from
the **Terminal Hidroviária** (Av Marechal Hermes).

Purchase tickets from the booths just inside the entrance, preferably a day or two
in advance. See Buses of the Waterways
(below) for tips on riverboat travel.

Marques Pinto Navigação (☎ 269 8189, 9961
8189), **N/M Amazon Star** (☎ 224 1225, 224 6885)
and **Rodrigues Alves Navigação** (ticket booth at
Terminal Hidroviária) all have services to/from
Manaus. Boats to Manaus (per person hammock/cabin US$73/117, five days) leave at
6pm on Tuesday, Wednesday and Friday.
Most boats make several stops on the way,

BUSES OF THE WATERWAYS

Rivers are roads in Amazonia, and riverboat trips are a uniquely Amazonian experience. The boats
are slow and scenery quickly palls – these are not sightseeing excursions – but the people and
activity onboard, from card games to dancing, are certainly memorable.

Passenger-carrying public boats average about 20m long, have two or three decks. Conditions
are crowded, toilets are few and you have to watch your gear very carefully. Here are some tips
to make your trip more pleasant:

- You'll need a hammock (a basic fabric one costs between US$8 and US$20) and some rope to
  hang it. A sheet or light blanket is nice if the temperature dips.

- Your gear shouldn't get wet, but play it safe by keeping it in a large plastic bag. This also
  helps keep prying fingers out of any side-pockets.

- You can usually check the boat out before buying your ticket. Boats may differ somewhat in
  quality, but rarely in price.

- Get to your boat four to six hours early to secure a good hammock spot. By departure time,
  the hammock areas may be crowded with occupants and baggage. You might even end up
  with other passengers swinging above you or underneath you!

- Most boats have three decks. The top deck is for hanging out, while the middle and lower
  ones are for hammocks; some boats have air-conditioned or women-only hammock areas.
  The middle deck is much nicer than the lower one, where the engine is. On either level, the
  middle-front is best, away from foot traffic at the ends, and the bathroom smell and engine
  noise in the back.

- Theft can be a problem. Ask the captain if he will stow your bag in a secure area; it's not common, but worth a shot. Locks on your zippers are recommended; some people use rope or
  chain (corrente) to lash bags to a post or rail. Be especially alert when the boat stops in port.

- Most boats have a few cabins (camarotes) for two or four people or 'suites' with private
  bathrooms. Sometimes you can just book one place in a cabin and share with whoever else
  turns up. Cabins tend to be bare, basic, and can get hot and stuffy – ask if yours has a fan or
  air-conditioning. They do afford more privacy and security against theft; then again, given the
  extra price, you may as well fly.

- Three simple meals a day – mainly rice, beans and meat – and water or juice are usually
  included in the fare. Some people always get sick, and the bathrooms can become quite
  unpleasant. Scrutinize your meal before eating it. Dinners are especially suspect, as they are
  usually made from the leftovers from lunch. Bring supplies in case the food is really bad – one
  trick is to pack ripe bananas for the first couple of days and unripe ones for the last. Bring
  several liters of water, extra toilet paper and diarrhea pills as well.

- Downstream travel is considerably faster than up, but boats heading upriver go closer to the
  shore, which makes for a somewhat more scenic trip.

including Monte Alegre (US$40/67, two days), Santarém (US$47/83, three days) and Parantins (US$63/93, four days). Some of the newer boats have air-con hammock areas (US$80 to Manaus) or 'suites' with bathroom (US$133 to Manaus). There are two departures on Wednesday, but note with Rodriques Alves you change to a less comfortable boat between Santarém and Manaus. All rates include meals.

Navegaçao Bom Jesus (☎ 224 4121) has boats to Macapá (US$23 to US$25, 22 to 24 hours, departure 10am Tuesday and Friday). **N/M São Francisco de Paula** (☎ 242 2070) has somewhat less comfortable services on Wednesday and Saturday (same time and price).

Arapari Navigação (☎ 241 4977) serves Ilha de Marajó, including ordinary service to Camará (US$4, three hours, departures 6:30am and 2:30pm Monday to Saturday and 10am Sunday) and fast boats to Soure (US$7, 2½ hours, 7:30am Thursday and Saturday).

BUS
Belém's **long-distance bus station** (☎ 246 7442) is on Praça do Operário. Major destinations may be served by several lines; *leito* and *semileito* (luxury and semiluxury) seats available on some longer routes.
Beira-Dão (☎ 226 1162) Runs buses to Vila Mosqueiro (US$1, 1½ hours, departures every 30 minutes 6am to 11pm).
Boa Esperança (☎ 228 3107 or 266 0033) Serves São Luís (US$31, 12 hours, four daily), Recife (US$70, 34 hours, daily), Fortaleza (US$44.50, 25 hours, four to five daily), and Salinópolis (US$5; four hours; five daily) and others.
Guanabara (☎ 226 1083) Serves Teresinha (US$27, 16 hours, four daily) and Sobral (US$38, 22 hours, two daily) with connection to Fortaleza.
Itaperim (☎ 226 3382) Serves Salvador (US$77, 36 hours, daily) and has *semileito* buses to Fortaleza (US$53).
Rápido Excelsior (☎ 249 6365) Has service to Marudá (US$4, 6am, 9am, 12:30pm, 4:30pm, plus 2:30pm daily except Sunday and 7pm Friday) and Curuça (US$3.50, three hours, 7am, 10am, noon, 5pm, plus 3pm daily except Sunday).
Transbrasilia (☎ 226 1243) Serves dozens of cities, near and far, including Rio de Janeiro (US$110, 45 hours, daily), São Paulo (US$108, 45 hours, daily); Belo Horizonte (US$96, 48 hours, daily) and Brasília (US$62, 36 hours, daily).

Getting Around
Aeroporto Val de Cães is 8km north of the center on Av Júlio César. The 'Pratinha-P Vargas' bus runs between the airport and

Av Presidente Vargas (US$0.50, 40 minutes); the 'E Marex' bus also goes there, but you may have to change buses at the depot (no extra charge). At the airport, buses stop at the traffic circle about 50m from the end of the airport terminal building. A taxi between the airport and center is US$8.

The **bus station** (☎ 228 0500) is on the corner of Av Almirante Barroso and Av Ceará, 3km east of the city center. Going into town, catch almost any westward bus on Av Governador José Malcher or cross to the far side of Av Almirante Barroso and catch any bus saying 'Aero Club' or 'P Vargas' – both can drop you at Praça de República. Going out to the bus station, take an 'Aeroclube,' 'Cid Nova 6/8' or 'Pratinha-P Vargas' bus from Av Presidente Vargas.

AROUND BELÉM
Icoaraci
The small town of Icoaraci, 23km north of Belém, is the source of nearly all the imitations of prehistoric Marajoara pottery that you see in Belém and elsewhere. The talented potters of Icoaraci's Paracuri district also produce some beautiful original designs. Head along Travessa Soledade, the first main street to the right as you enter Icoaraci from the south, and you'll come upon a dozen workshops with products on display. You can observe the pottery-making process and, if you buy the products, you know your money is going directly to the craftspeople.

Frequent city buses marked 'Icoaraci' leave from Av Presidente Vargas in central Belém.

Ilha do Mosqueiro
☎ 0xx91 / pop 25,000
Thousands of Belenenses (Belém residents) beat the heat by flocking to Mosqueiro's 18 freshwater beaches. The area gets particularly crowded on weekends between July and October. The beaches on Ilha de Marajó and the Atlantic coast are nicer overall, but if you just want to get out of Belém for a day or so, Mosqueiro on a weekday is a decent option.

ORIENTATION
The island's main town, Vila Mosqueiro, is on the southwest tip of the island. Av Beira Mar, the main drag, starts in town

at Praia Farol (below) and runs northward along the shore past Praia Chapéu, Praia do Murubira, Praia Marahú and Praia Paraíso, in that order. The other main road in Vila Mosqueiro is Av 16 de Novembro, which intersects with Av Beira Mar between Praia Farol and Praia Chapéu, at a small plaza and church.

SIGHTS & ACTIVITIES

The best beaches are **Praia do Farol** (in town) and **Praia do Paraíso** and the more remote **Baía do Sol** in the north. Stingrays may be present – shuffle your feet when entering the water to scare them off.

Mosqueiro's traditional **folklore festival**, in June, features the dance and music of *carimbó* (music of the Amazon region) and *bois-bumbás*. The Círio de NS do Ó is celebrated on the second Sunday of December. Like Belém's Círio, this is a beautiful and joyous event, well worth seeing if you're in the area.

SLEEPING & EATING

Hotel Farol (☎ 3771 1219, 3771 2095; Praia do Farol; incl breakfast r without bathroom US$13.50, with bathroom & fan/ US$20/23.50) In a converted lighthouse overlooking the south end of Farol (Lighthouse) beach, this unique hotel is a good value and easy to get to even if you don't have a car. The building's circular shape makes for interestingly-shaped rooms; definitely ask for one with a view.

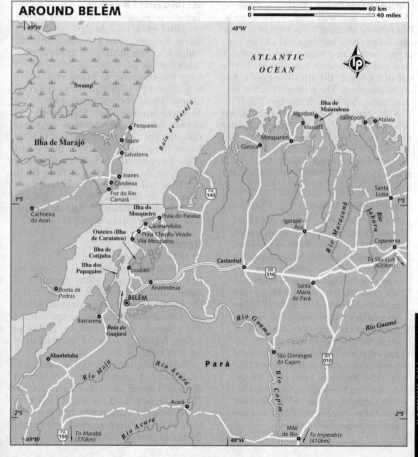

AROUND BELÉM

Ilha Bela (☎ 3771 3120; Av 16 de Novembro 463; r incl breakfast & bathroom US$13.50; ⚡) About 400m from the beach, rooms here are basic and clean, if a bit dark and sterile, and include TV and minibar.

Apart Hotel Murubira (☎ 772 1256; Av Beira Mar s/n, Praia do Murubira; d incl breakfast US$27/32.50; P ⚡) Primarily condos, this high-rise has a few units for rent. Plain, smallish rooms are made comfortable with modern furnishings and large, clean bathrooms; some rooms have carpet. Sauna included.

Hotel Furacão (☎ 3772 2354; Praia do Murubira; s/d US$3.50/7.50) Three doors down from Apart Hotel Murubira and a world apart, this hotel-restaurant offers extremely basic, wood-construction rooms with marginally clean shared bathrooms.

Hotel Fazenda Paraíso (☎ 228 3950 reservations, ✆ 3618 2008 hotel; www.hotelfazendaparaiso.com.br; Praia do Paraíso; d/tr US$40/50, 4-person chalet US$63-66; ⚡) Rooms here are large and chalets even larger, both with pleasant wood construction and comfortable furnishings. If you tire of the beach, the attractive pool is just across the street. The restaurant serves seafood meals big enough for two (US$7 to US$10). Praia do Paraíso is one of the best beaches on the island, but gets quite busy during the weekends. Discounts of around 10% to 20% are available on weekdays.

Pousada Beach House (Praia do Paraíso; r with bathroom & fan/ ⚡ US$13.50/17) Just down the

road from Hotel Fazenda Paraíso, this is a more economical way to stay on this end of the island. Rooms are a bit dark, but large enough for four people and come with TV, minibar and clean bathrooms.

Food can be a bit hard to find, especially late at night and on weekdays. The restaurant at Hotel Farol serves good, standard dishes for US$4 to US$7. There are lots of *barracas* (food stalls) serving inexpensive local fare on Praça Matriz, the main square in Vila Mosqueiro, and also along Praia do Farol and Praia Chapéu Virado (try *tapioca com recheio de queijo* – a spongy white pancake made from tapioca, served warm, either folded or rolled up, with cheese in the middle).

GETTING THERE & AROUND

Ilha do Mosqueiro is connected to the mainland by a road bridge, 55km from Belém by good, paved roads. From the bridge it is 25km further to Vila Mosqueiro. Buses from Belém (US$1, 1½ hours, depart every half-hour 6am to 11pm, return 5am to 8pm) first past Praia Murubira and Praia Chapéu Virado before turning up Av 16 de Novembro (just before Praia Farol); you can ask the driver to let you off anywhere along the line. The bus terminal is another 4.5km from the beach. Local buses start at the bus terminal, turn at the plaza and church on the north edge of Praia Farol, and pass Praia Chapéu Virado and Praia Marubira on their way to either (but not both!) Praia do Paraíso or Baía do Sol Via. A taxi to Praia Farol costs US$5.

Algodoal
☎ 0xx91 / pop 1000

The small fishing village of Algodoal on Ilha de Maiandeua, 180km northeast of Belém, attracts younger Belenenses and a few foreign travelers. It's an attractive natural retreat with hard, windswept beaches and a sometimes turbulent sea. Unlike in Belém, it rains little in the second half of the year here.

The island's name comes from an Indian word meaning 'uncountable riches beneath the sea.' Legend has it that an enchanted city is submerged off the island's northern tip; it emerges occasionally and is visible from Praia da Princesa, which was named for the city's royal daughter.

SURF THE POROROCA!

The small town of São Domingos do Capim, at the confluence of the Rio Guamá and Rio Capim, 120km east of Belém, is the venue of the national *pororoca* (tidal bore) surfing championships, held annually since 1999 during the full moon nearest the March equinox. This is when the waves of the *pororoca* on the Guamá are likely to be at their highest (they can reach a few meters). The event attracts surfers and curious onlookers from far afield. The town has a couple of hotels and pousadas (guesthouses), and during the surf event locals rent out beds for around US$7 to US$14. No regular buses go to São Domingos from Belém, but you might get one from Castanhal, on Hwy BR-316 some 70km from Belém. Amazon Star (p581) organizes *pororoca* packages from Belém.

ORIENTATION & INFORMATION

Algodoal village is on the island's west coast. All of the hotels and restaurants, save one, are there. Across a small canal north of the village, and stretching to the island's northern tip, is attractive **Praia do Farol**. Beyond that is **Praia da Princesa**, the island's best beach, with rough waves and backed by dunes and palms. **Lagoa da Princesa** is a freshwater lake about an hour's walk inland from Algodoal village; orchids can be seen in some seasons. Ocelots, coatis and numerous bird species are among the wildlife found in the island's interior.

Ilha Maiandeua has no motor traffic and no public electrical supply, an unfortunate consequence of which is that the dozens of gas generators can create quite a din at night. Be sure your hotel room is not next to the generator!

There is no bank or ATM on the island, and no businesses accepted credit cards at the time of research. Internet is available at Pousada Kakurí (right).

SLEEPING

It can be hard to find a room during high season, especially Carnaval, Semana Santa, the month of July and all holiday weekends. Prices listed here are high-season rates; ask for a discount the rest of the year.

Hotel Bela Mar (☎ 3854 1128, in Belém ☎ 222 7582; d/tr without bathroom US$16.50/20; d/tr with bathroom US$23/27) The first hotel you reach from the boat pier has a nice garden area, but the rooms are rather stuffy and plain. The restaurant serves decent, basic meals.

Pousada do Boiador (☎ 279 0060 in Belém; r with breakfast & without/with bathroom US$13.50/16.50-20) At the northern edge of the village, rooms here are small but clean, with newish wood construction, fans and mosquito nets. Some have nice views of the sea. The hotel bar can get loud.

Pousada Chalés do Atlântico (☎ 3854 1114; r incl breakfast & bathroom US$16.50) Directly across from the Pousada do Boiador, the seven 'chalets' here have a double bed on the ground level and another in a hot stuffy loft above – with a hammock you could fit five people but it would be a tussle for the fan. The units are run-down, but have good mosquito screens, large-ish bathrooms and face a reasonably pleasant courtyard, complete with pet monkey.

Pousada Paraíso do Norte (☎ 9628 4186, in Belém ☎ 241 6122; r incl breakfast US$10) This tall wooden building is like a Nebraska hay loft with a sea-view. Smallish, cleanish rooms sleep up to three people (two in saggy beds, one in hammock) but do not have fans and could get hot. Shared bathrooms are clean. It's at the north end of town on the shore.

Pousada Kakurí (☎ 3854 1138; dm US$7, r without/with bathroom US$10/12-16.50) The second little pig evidently oversaw the construction of this hotel, the largest stick house you may ever see. Accommodations are very basic – you can peek through the walls – but the laid-back atmosphere keeps it popular with backpackers and young Brazilians.

Algodoal Camping Club (☎ 229 0848 in Belém; site & 2 people/with tent & sleeping bag rental US$3.50/5, extra person US$2; r US$13.50) Camp in grassy-sandy yard with large trees. The shared bathrooms are fairly clean. A wood cabin in the middle of the grounds has two very basic units, each with fan, bathroom and two beds.

Jardim do Eden (☎ 9967 9010, 9623 9690; jardim doeden@hotmail.com; camping US$15, d/bungalow US$25/50, extra person US$7) Easily the best place on the island, not only for the quality of its lodging and restaurant (both excellent) but its location just out of town on pretty Praia do Farol. Run by an English-speaking, Brazilian-and-French couple, accommodations are in three bungalows (one tiny, the others large enough for three or more, with small kitchens). A good breakfast is included, and a variety of walking, canoeing, sailing, horse-cart and fishing trips can be arranged (per person US$10 to US$50). You can pay in any currency or traveler's checks.

The mainland village of Marudá has several inexpensive hotels and an OK beach, so it's no problem if you're stuck there overnight.

Pousada Santa Barbara (☎ 466 1401; 50m north of bus station; d US$16.50; 🖳 🖳) Has clean, pleasant rooms and the pool is small.

Pousada do Seu Ed (☎ 466 1307; 3 blocks southwest from bus station; d US$10; 🖳) More basic than Pousada Santa Barbara.

EATING

The Pousada Kakurí and Jardim do Eden have recommended restaurants. Hotel guests are always welcome, but there may not be service for nonguests during busy periods.

THE AMAZON

Pousada Kakurí (☎ 3854 1138; dishes US$5-10) There's not much of a dining area, unless the owners set up tables in the street in front, but the food here is tasty and reliable: mostly fried or grilled fish.

Jardim do Eden (☎ 9967 9010, 9623 9690; dishes US$5-10) Serves only seafood and vegetarian dishes, all excellent.

Marhesias (☎ 9601 4004; dishes for 3 US$4.50-5.50; ✺ lunch & dinner, bar till late) Down the street from the Pousada do Boiador, serving creative pizzas plus grilled fish and meats. Regular live and DJ music.

GETTING THERE & AROUND

Access to Algodoal is via the mainland village of Marudá.

Cars must be left at Marudá – there are guarded parking areas near the pier (per day US$1) where boats leave several times a day for Algodoal (US$2, 40 minutes). Leave Belém by 12:30pm to be sure to catch a boat to Algodoal (see p587 for fare and schedules); the bus can drop you right at the pier.

Arriving at Algodoal, catch a donkey cart (US$2 to US$3.50) or else lug your gear across the beach into town. Boats return to the mainland at 5:30am, 10:30am and 1:30pm, in time to catch Belém-bound buses at 7am, noon and 3pm.

Ilha de Marajó

☎ 0xx91 / pop 250,000

The 50,000-sq-km Ilha de Marajó, slightly larger than Switzerland, lies at the mouths of the Amazonas and Tocantins Rivers. It was the ancient home of the Marajoaras indigenous culture, notable for their large ceramic burial urns. Today, Marajó's friendly residents live in a few towns and villages and on the many *fazendas* (ranches) spread across the island. This is a world apart, where bicycles outnumber cars and water buffalo graze around town. Legend is the buffalo are descended from animals that swam ashore from a French ship that sank while en route from India to French Guiana. The island is well-known for its buffalo cheese and buffalo-mounted police force.

Marajó is very wet from January to June, with almost daily rain. The island's lowlands (nearly half the island) become submerged under a meter or more of water, and many roads become impassable. The island has many snakes, and you should be careful of stingrays at the beach. There are hordes of birds, especially during the dry season, including the graceful scarlet ibis (*guará* in Portuguese), with its long, curved beak. Note that *bichos de pé* (unpleasant bugs that burrow into human feet) are found in and around the towns, and the island has other nasty parasites. Keep your shoes on!

There are four main towns on the island: Foz do Rio Camará, known simply as Camará, where the boat arrives; Joanes, a sleepy town about 5km off the main road; Salvaterra, larger and another 18 km north; and Soure, the island's unofficial capital located on the other side of a large inlet/river. Joanes and Salvaterra have the best beaches and most interesting accommodations, while Soure has better restaurants and all the services.

It is a good idea to bring extra cash from Belém, as credit cards are rarely accepted and the one ATM in Soure does not recognize all foreign cards. Bring plenty of insect repellent, too.

GETTING THERE & AWAY

For boats from Belém to Ilha de Marajó, see p587. To return, boats leave Camará at 9am and 3pm Monday to Friday, 9am Saturday and 3pm Sunday. You can also fly – ask about air-taxis at the airport in Belém.

GETTING AROUND

Buses and minivans (US$1 to US$2 depending on your destination) meet boats arriving at Camará to carry passengers to Joanes, Salvaterra or at the ferry landing across from Soure. Small motorboats carry passengers across the river for US$0.50, or you can go free on the vehicle ferry (*balsa*), almost hourly from 6am to 6pm.

Ask at your hotel about getting back to the port at Camará. Some minivans pick up passengers in time for the ferries, and the hotel owner can call in advance. A taxi costs US$15.

Local fishing boats sail the high seas, and it's possible to use them to get all the way around the island and to some of the *fazendas*. Ask around in Soure or Salvaterra.

JOANES

It is thought that Spanish navigator Vicente Yáñez Pinzón landed on Joanes beach on

February 26, 1500 – a couple of months before Pedro Cabral's 'discovery' of Brazil for Portugal. Sleepy Joanes is good for total isolation, with a decent sandy beach and the scanty ruins of a 17th-century Jesuit church. Salvaterra and Soure have more movement.

There are no services in Joanes, save a **post office** (⊙ 8am-noon Mon-Fri) on the main road.

Sleeping & Eating

Pousada Ventania do Rio-Mar (☎ 3646 2067, 9992 5716; ventaniapousada@hotmail.com; s/d/tr US$13.50/23/26.50) On a small, very breezy headland with direct access to the beach, this pleasant hotel is as good a reason as any to stop in Joanes. Run by a Brazilian-Belgian couple, rooms are individually decorated with nicely tiled bathrooms. There is a book exchange, and inexpensive guided walks, fishing trips and horse, bike and canoe rental are all available. Room rates drop if you stay a few days; breakfast is included.

Pousada Paraíso de Joanes (☎ 3646 2146; incl breakfast s/d with fan US$8/13.50, with ❄ US$12/20) A few meters up the same grassy street, rooms here are shabby and a distant second to the Ventania. Some rooms are cleaner than others.

Lanches Fino Gusto (behind post office; large pizza US$4; ⊙ 6:30pm-9:30pm) With no menus and only one table, you are literally eating in the driveway of a private home. Pizzas are made with whatever ingredients are on hand; a large feeds two.

Several beach restaurants serve straightforward meals, mostly seafood, for US$3 to US$7.

SALVATERRA

About 18km north from Joanes, Salvaterra (population 5800) is larger than Joanes, but still much slower than Soure, especially at night. Accommodations are better here, though, and it's easy enough to go into Soure if need be. A long ocean beach, Praia Grande, is one of the best on the island. Salvaterra can get crowded on weekends and holidays.

Orientation & Information

The main streets in town are Av Victor Engelhard and Rua Learense; the school, bus stop, market and main taxi stand are all at or near this intersection. Praia Grande

is about 500m south of town. Bikes can be rented at **Pousada Bosque dos Aruãs** (☎ 3765 1115; per hr/half-/full-day US$0.50/3/4). The pier to get to Soure is 8km from Salvaterra; a taxi there costs US$1.50.

Sleeping & Eating

All hotels listed here include breakfast. Ask about discounts.

Pousada Bosque dos Aruãs (☎ 3765 1115; juran dir@supridados.com.br; s/d US$13.50/16.50; P ❄) A few blocks from the center, the wooden cabins are clean with comfy beds and are set on an oceanfront lot shaded by mango trees. The patio restaurant is quite good.

Pousada dos Guarás (☎ 3765 1149, in Belém ☎ 4005 5658; s/d/tr/q US$33/35/42/47; P ❄ ❄) Right on Praia Grande, this upscale resort is another good value. Suites here are spacious and attractively decorated, with solar-heated water and surrounded by large grassy grounds. There's a mid-sized swimming pool if you tire of the ocean.

Hotel Beira Mar (☎ 3765 1400, 3765 1251; hotelbeira mar@hotmail.com; incl breakfast s/d with fan US$7/10, with ❄ US$13.50/16.50) Large, clean, plain rooms have tile floors, TV and minibar. Fake flowers add a little character.

Pousada Bosque dos Aruãs restaurant (☎ 3765 1115; ⊙ lunch & dinner) This low-key restaurant serves well-prepared meat, chicken and fish dishes, even salmon.

Pousada dos Guarás (☎ 3765 1149; dishes US$4-12) This hotel also has a decent restaurant. Meals are served in a large, open-air dining area in the center of the resort's grassy grounds. The menu is large and standard, offering beef, chicken and seafood (grilled, baked or fried), most served with rice, beans and veggies.

There are several beach restaurants on Praia Grande, where you can fill up for around US$5.

SOURE

The principal town in Marajó, Soure (population 18,800) is on the north bank of the mouth of the Rio Paracauari. It is the only place with services and any sort of after-dark activity. Tides here can oscillate a remarkable 3m.

Orientation & Information

The streets running parallel to the river are Ruas (with Rua 1 closest to the river). The perpendicular streets are Travessas, with Travessa 1 closest to the seashore. Getting off the ferry, you will be nearest the corner of Rua 1 and Travessa 15.

Banco do Brasil (Rua 3, btwn Travessa 17 & 18; 10am-3pm Mon-Fri) has an ATM that supposedly accepts Visa and MC; if not, see if the teller will run your card (Visa only).

A guy named **Bimba** (9161 9850; per hr US$50) rents bicycles at his shop on Rua 4 between Travessa 18 and 19.

There's a **tourist information kiosk** (8am-5pm Mon-Fri, to noon Sat & Sun) on Rua 2 at Travessa 17.

Beaches

The bay beaches near Soure, fronting on water that is a mixture of salt and fresh, are often covered with fantastic seeds washed down from the Amazonian forests. You can easily bicycle or walk the 3km to **Praia Barra Velho**. Follow Travessa 14 out of town till you see a path diverging to the right. If you continue past the Barra Velho turnoff you'll reach a river where you will see the ruins of a footbridge. If a boat is on hand to take you over, you can reach **Praia de Araruna**, the most beautiful beach, just beyond the river. At low tide you can walk about 5km in either direction along the beach, which is practically deserted most of the time. **Praia do Pesqueiro**, 9km from town (reached by heading inland along Rua 4), is another very nice beach, popular on weekends. Ask about buses at Soure. Barracas here serve great crab.

Festivals & Events

On the second Sunday in November, Soure has its own Círio de Nazaré (see p583) with a beautiful procession. Hotels can be booked up.

Sleeping & Eating

Hotels listed here include breakfast.

Soure Hotel (3741 1202; Rua 3 No 1347; s/d with fan US$7/9, with US$10/13.50) In the center of town, rooms here are livable, if rather dark and basic.

Hotel Araruna (Travessa 14 btwn Rua 7 & 8; r US$13.50) Next to the tall Cosampa water towers, this is better option, with clean simple rooms opening on a breezy corridor.

Hotel Ilha do Marajó (3741 1315; ocean end of Rua 8; s/d US$30/35;) Soure's best hotel,

with spotless rooms, good pool and several buildings linked by raised walkways.

Restaurante Patú Anú (3741 1359; Rua 2 at Travessa 14; meals about US$2.50; 7:30am-9pm) There's no real menu here, but large servings of chicken, beef or shrimp, plus rice and beans.

SANTARÉM

 0xx93 / pop 200,000

Santarém is a pleasant city, blessed with river breezes and a relatively mild climate (22°C to 36°C). The Amazon's third-largest city, it is strategically placed at the confluence of the creamy-brown Rio Amazonas and the reddish-black Rio Tapajós. The two rivers flow side by side for a few kilometers before their waters mingle; seen from the city's waterfront, their bands of different-colored water are clearly distinguishable.

Santarém is growing in popularity, with modern services and easy access to the interesting Floresta Nacional do Tapajós (FLONA Tapajós). A stop here is a good way to break up the five-day boat trip between Belém and Manaus, especially with nearby **Alter do Chão**, an outstanding river-beach town just 35km away and an emerging mecca for foreign and Brazilian travelers alike.

History

The Santarém region has been a center of human settlement for many thousands of years (see 'Prehistoric Amazonia', p600). In 1661, more than 20 years after Pedro Teixeira's expedition first contacted the local Tupaiu Indians, a Jesuit mission was established at the meeting of the Tapajós and Amazonas, and officially named Santarém in 1758.

The later history of Santarém was marked by the rubber boom and bust, and a series of gold rushes that started in the 1950s. The economy today is based on rubber, soy and hardwoods, plus Brazil nuts, black pepper, mangoes, jute and fish. The discovery of gold and bauxite and the construction of the Curuá-Una hydroelectric dam, 60km southeast of Santarém, have brought some development in the last 25 years, but it is still largely isolated. A movement to form a new state of Tapajós has some popular support here, but little traction outside the region.

Orientation

The Docas do Pará, where most of the long-distance riverboats dock, are 2.5km west of the city center. See p597 for information on transport to the city center.

Information

BOOKSTORES

BMT (☎ 523 6013; Av São Sebastião 396; ☺ 7:30am-8pm Mon-Fri, to 3pm Sat)

EMERGENCY

24 hour police kiosk (☎ 512 1014, 190) Catercorner from the post office.
Ambulance (☎ 192)

INTERNET ACCESS

Cyber Café Orla (☎ 523 0023; Av Tapajos 13; per hr US$1; ☺ 8am-11pm)
Explorer Internet (☎ 522 2270; Av São Sebastião at Travessa Barão do Rio Branco; per hr US$1; ☺ 7am-midnight Mon-Sat, 2pm-midnight Sun)
Net House (☎ 3062 0817; Travessa Barão do Rio Branco 896; per hr US$1; ☺ 8am-10:30pm Mon-Fri, noon-11pm Sat)

LAUNDRY

Lavandería Storil (☎ 523 1329; Travessa Turiano Meira 167; ☺ 7am-noon, 2-6pm Mon-Sat)

MEDICAL SERVICES

Hospital Municipal (Av Presidente Vargas & Travessa Barão do Rio Branco) Has an emergency room.

MONEY

Bradesco (Av Rui Barbosa at Travessa 15 de Agosto) Reliable ATMs.
HSBC (Av Rui Barbosa at Travessa Francisco Correa) Reliable ATMs.
Ourominas (☎ 522 7655; Travessa dos Mártires 198; ☺ 7:30am-5:30pm Mon-Fri, 8am-noon Sat) Good rates for Euros and US dollars.
Exchange Office (☎ 522 2281, 3064 0258; Av Rui Barbosa 641; ☺ 8am-noon & 2-6pm) A man named Sr. Edézio changes traveler's checks at this nameless, signless shop. His exchange rates are pretty low, though.

POST

Main post office (Rua Siqueira Campos, facing Praça da Matriz; ☺ 8am-4pm Mon-Fri)

TELEPHONE

Posto TeleTrin (☎ 523 2615; Rua Siqueira Campos 511; ☺ 7:30am-6pm Mon-Fri, to 2pm Sat) Has a bank of pay phones and can place international telephone calls.

TRAVEL AGENCIES

Santarém Tur (☎ 522 4847, 523 1836; www.santarem tur.com.br; Rua Adriano Pimentel 44; ☺ 7:30am-6pm Mon-Fri, 8am-noon Sat) Plane tickets and tour packages. Has friendly and helpful staff.
Alter do Chão Turismo (☎ 527 6609, 522 6167; Rua Barão do Rio Branco 404-C; ☺ 8am-6pm Mon-Fri, to noon Sat) Plane tickets.
Amazon Tours (☎ 522 1928, 9122 0299; Travessa Turiano Meira 1084; www.amazonriver.com) Organizes trips to Bosque Santa Lucia and area sites. Can also offer tourist information.

Sights

MUSEU DE SANTARÉM

Housed in a large yellow waterfront mansion, the **Museu de Santarém** (Rua do Imperador, Praça Barão de Santarém; admission by donation; ☺ 8am-5pm Mon-Fri) is also known as the Centro Cultural João Fona, after the Pará artist who painted the frescoes on its interior walls. The building dates from 1867 and has been a jail, city hall and courthouse. In addition to several paintings and documents related to the city's founding, the museum features an interesting collection of stone pieces and pottery, including burial urns and ceremonial figurines, from the Tapajoara culture that flourished locally more than 6000 years ago.

MUSEU DICA FRAZÃO

Octogenarian Dona Dica Frazão (b 1920) is the creator, namesake, tour guide and No 1 advocate of the **Museu Dica Frazão** (☎ 522 1026; Rua Floriano Peixoto 281; admission free; ☺ daytime). Slight and cheerful, Dona Dica has spent more than 50 years making women's clothing and fabrics from natural fibers, including grasses and wood pulp. Pieces on display include reproductions of a dress made for a Belgian queen, a tablecloth for Pope John Paul II and costumes for the Boi-Bumbá festival at Parintins.

IGREJA MATRIZ

Facing Praça da Matriz, the city's pretty blue-painted church dates from 1761. Its predecessor church, made of palm fronds in 1661, was Santarém's first building.

WATERFRONT PROMENADE

The Nova Orla Fluvial promenade follows Av Tapajós over a mile from the Museu de Santarém almost as far as the Docas do Para. A nice stroll starts from Praça Matriz

THE AMAZON

heading west, passing colorful boats before ending in the shadow of the massive Cargill facility, a symbol of Brazil's burgeoning soy trade. There is little shade, so bring a hat.

Festivals

The patron saint of fishermen, São Pedro, is honored on June 29, when boats decorated with flags and flowers sail in procession before the city.

Sleeping

All hotels listed have free breakfast.

BUDGET

Hotel Brasil (☎ 523 5177; Travessa dos Mártires 30; s/d US$5/10) In a large old building in the commercial area, this hotel doesn't look like much from outside, but has an airy sitting room and clean rooms, some with large exterior windows. Often full, so call ahead.

Hotel Alvorada (☎ 522-5340; Rua Senador Lameira Bittencourt 179; s/d with fan US$6/$10, with ✖ US$12/$20) A block from the water, the airy front rooms at this nondescript hotel have river views and are not too bad.

Hotel Beira Rio (☎ 522 2519; Rua Adriano Pimentel 90; s/d US$5/8.50, with bathroom, ✖ & TV US$11.50/13.50) Simple wood-construction *quartos* and *apartamentos* (rooms without and with bathrooms) are relatively clean; some have walls have mosquito screens at the top, reducing privacy.

Brisa Hotel (☎ 522 1018; Av Senador Lameira Bittencourt 5; s/d with TV & ✖ US$11.50/15) *Apartamentos* in this newish hotel are very clean, though somewhat sterile, and have high ceilings.

Hotel Amazon Park (☎ 523 2800, fax 522 2631; amazon@netsan.com.br; Av Mendonça Furtado 4120; s/d/tr US$32.50/$35.50/$46.50; ☎) Four and a half kilometers out of town, this once run-down hotel has been nicely renovated by its current owners. It's a decent value, with comfortable rooms, large well-kept grounds, and an air-conditioned bar and **restaurant** (✆ noon-3pm & 7-10pm).

New City Hotel (☎ 522 4719; Travessa Francisco Correa 200; s/d with fan US$10/13.50, with ✖ US$15/20) Friendly staff and decent *apartamentos* with TV and minibar. It's a rambling, multilevel hotel so rooms vary in size and quality – look at a few before deciding.

SANTARÉM

0 ——— 300 m
0 ——— 0.2 miles

To Praça Tirandentes (1km); IBAMÁ (2km); Docas do Pará (2.5km)

Rio Tapajós

Av Tapajós

Praça da Matriz

Rua Senador Lameira Bittencourt

Praça do Pescador

Rua Adriano Pimentel

Market

Park

Cathedral

Rua Siqueira Campos

Rua Floriano Peixoto

Rua Barão do Rio Branco

Rua 24 de Outubro

Rua dos Mártires

Av Barão do Rio Branco

Av 15 de Agosto

Av 15 de Novembro

Tv 15 de Novembro

Tv F Correa

Rua do Imperador

Rio Amazonas

Rua Galdino Veloso

Tv João Olavino

Tv S Sirotheau Corrêa

Tv Padre João

Tv Augusto Montenegro

Rua dos Artistas

Av Rui Barbosa

Tv Tuliano Neta

Park

Tv Silvino Pinto

Av São Sebastião

To Hospital Municipal (350m)

To TAM (50m); Amazon Tours (1km)

MID-RANGE
Hotel Rio Dourado (☎ 522 0320; Rua Floriano Peixoto 799; s/d US$15/20; ☒) A modern hotel near the market; comfy *apartamentos* have polished wood floors, TV and minibar. Prices listed are with discount, which is apparently always available.

Brasil Grande Hotel (☎ 522 5660; Travessa 15 de Agosto 213; s/d US$18.50/21.50) Large, bright, aircon *apartamentos* – a good deal for the price. A discount of 10% is often available. There's also a **restaurant** (☒ lunch till 2:30pm & dinner till 8:30pm).

Santarém Palace Hotel (☎ 523 2820; Av Rui Barbosa 726; s/d US$23.50/27) Large, clean *apartamentos* have spare, eclectic decor and large windows. Ask for a side room – they have slightly smaller windows, but less street noise. An airport shuttle is available (US$8.50).

Eating
Restaurante O Mascote (☎ 523 2844; Praça do Pescador 10; all-you-can-eat lunch buffet US$4, dinner US$5-10; ☒ 10am-2:30pm & 5pm-midnight) The lunch buffet is tasty and a good deal. Fish dinners feed two – try the *tucunaré ao molho de camarão* (peacock bass in shrimp sauce) for US$9. Indoor and outdoor seating has views of the plaza and river. Also good for a late-night beer.

Sacy Caseiro (☎ 522 5111; Rua Floriano Peixoto 521; self-service per kg US$14.90; ☒ 10:30am-2:30pm) Well-prepared self-service spread, including fresh-grilled meats, and a clean, air-conditioned dining area.

Delícias Caseiras (☎ 523 5525; Travessa 15 de Agosto 121; buffet US$1.50/plate; ☒ 11am-3pm Mon-Sat) Hone your piling skills here, where you're charged by the plate, not the kilo. Dining area is a bit rundown, but the food is okay.

Restaurante O Mascotinho (Av Adriana Pimentel; dishes US$5-8; ☒ 5.30pm-midnight) A large open-air restaurant on a terrace overlooking the river, this is a great place to enjoy a beer, burger, pizza or sandwich.

Shopping
Loja Regional Muiraquitã (Rua Senador Lameira Bittencourt 131; ☒ 8am-noon & 2-6pm Mon-Fri, 8am-6pm Sat) A large selection of indigenous, local and imitation handicrafts.

Casa do Artesanato (☎ 529 1011; Rua Senador Lameira Bittencourt 69-A; ☒ 8:30am-12:30pm & 2:30-6:30pm Mon-Fri, 8:30am-6:30pm Sat) Just down the street from Loja Regional Muiraquitã, and with a similar selection.

Getting There & Away
AIR
Most flights go through Manaus (around US$110 to US$125) or Belém (US$125 to US$155).

Meta airport (☎ 523 0391); Santarém (☎ 523 0391, Av Rui Barbosa at Travessa Turiano Meira; ☒ 8am-noon & 4-8pm Mon-Sat)

Penta airport (☎ 523 1021); Santarém (☎ 523 2220, 512 5000, Travessa 15 de Novembro 183; ☒ 7am-noon & 1-5:30pm Mon-Fri)

Puma (☎ 522 6714; Rua Galdino Veloso 197)

Rico (☎ 523 3997, 3064 0192; Rua Floriano Peixoto 556) Part of the office of Belo Turismo.

TAM (☎ 523 9450; Av Mendoça Furtado 913, at Travessa Turiano Meira; ☒ 8am-6pm Mon-Fri, to noon Sat)

TAVAJ (☎ 522 7666; Travessa João Otaviano at Rua Floriano Peixoto; ☒ 8am-noon & 2-6pm Mon-Fri, 8am-noon Sat)

Varig (☎ 523 2488, 523 5156; Av Rui Barbosa 790; ☒ 8:30am-noon & 2:30-5:30pm)

BOAT
There are two ports for passenger boats. For tips on boat travel see Buses of the Waterways, p587.

From **Docas do Pará** (2.5km west of the center) you can catch slow boats to Belém (hammock US$33 to US$40, 34 hours, noon Wednesday, 4pm Thursday, 10am Friday, 6pm Saturday, 10am Sunday) and to Manaus (US$23 to US$40 hammock, 48 hours, 2pm Monday to Saturday). **AJATO** (☎ 9121 7134, 8111 3205) offers speedboat service Manaus (US$50, 14 hours, 6am Wednesday and Saturday) with comfortable, airplane-style seating, including two meals. This service continues to Tefé (see p629).

Praça Tiradentes (1km east of center on Av Tapajós) has a port that serves nearer destinations, which include Itaituba (hammock US$13.50, 15 hours, once daily at 6pm, check for speedboat service), Macapá (hammock US$23, 36 hours, once daily at 6pm), Parantins (hammock US$6.50, nine hours, departures 3pm) and Monte Alegre (US$12.50, six to seven hours; 1:30pm Monday to Friday, noon Saturday). Note that most boats going to Manaus and Belém also stop at Parantins and Monte Alegre, respectively.

THE AMAZON

BUS

The **bus station** (☎ 523 4940) is 2.5km west of town.

Buses run to Rurópolis (US$10, about six hours, one or two daily), Itaituba (US$16, nine hours, daily at 8pm) and Cuiabá (US$71, about three days, daily at 6pm). Roads here can be extremely rough, especially in the rainy season. During the drier part of the year there may also be buses (which are not recommended) along the Transamazônica to Marabá (1177km) in southeast Pará, a rough frontier town in an area noted for highway robberies.

Getting Around

The airport is 14km west of the city center; buses (US$0.50) run to the city every hour or so between 6:15am and 6:15pm. Going to the airport, buses marked 'Aeroporto' leave a stop on Av Rui Barbosa, west of Travessa Barão do Rio Branco, between 5:30am and 5:30pm. Avoid buses marked 'Aeroporto V...'; these go elsewhere.

The New City and Rio Dourado hotels offer clients free transportation from the airport in their shared van, and charge US$7 (open to anyone) to go back to the airport. Santarém Palace Hotel has a similar service. Taxi fare to or from the airport is about US$12.

Arriving by boat, 'Orla Fluvial' minibuses (US$0.50) shuttle between the city center and Docas do Pará, passing the Praça Tiradentes port, every 20 to 30 min-

utes until 7pm. The 'Circular Esperança' bus (US$0.50) runs from the center to the Docas and then the bus station; avoid it returning from the Docas, however, as it does not go directly to the center. A taxi costs US$3.50.

Moto-taxis are the best way, beyond walking, to get around town. Most trips cost US$0.75.

AROUND SANTARÉM
Floresta Nacional (FLONA) do Tapajós

This 6500-sq-km reserve on the east side of the Rio Tapajós is the only accessible large primary forest near Santarém. It is notable for its giant trees, including behemoth *sumaúná* trees (a type of ceiba tree). You can also take canoe rides in *igarapés* (small rivers) and, in the rainy season, *igapós* (flooded forests). Rubber harvesting is an important source of income for people living inside the park; you can visit two different latex-production facilities. While FLONA lacks the deep-jungle feel of areas deeper in the Amazon basin, it is still a very interesting and beautiful place to visit. There are many tours here, from Santarém and, increasingly, boat trips from Alter do Chão. It is easy to visit on your own, as well.

Two very rustic communities – Maguary, with around 50 families, and Jamaracuá, with around 20 families – are prepared to receive visitors. On arrival, you will be placed with a family, where you sleep and eat (typically rice and fish). Neither community had electricity, running water or indoor bathrooms at the time of research. Be sure to bring a hammock, bottled water, toilet paper, flashlight, and any additional food you may want. There are no stores, restaurants or pousadas.

You need authorization from IBAMA before visiting the park or villages. Organized tours from Santarém or Alter do Chão should arrange this for you. To go yourself, swing by the **IBAMA office** (☎ 523 2964; Av Tapajós 2267; ⏱ 7am-noon & 2-7pm Mon-Fri) where authorizations are usually issued in a few minutes. The cost is US$0.50 per day per person; you will need to specify the exact dates you will be visiting.

Guides are obligatory in the park. Hikes in the forest (three to seven hours) are US$10 per group, plus US$3.50 per person,

---

FAR FROM THE BEATEN TRACK

The **Tataquara Lodge**, which opened in 2000, is a low-impact ecolodge on an island in the Rio Xingu, 3½ hours by boat from the town of Altamira, which is on the Transamazônica highway, about 300km southeast of Santarém. It has been set up as part of an economic self-sufficiency program by eight Indian tribes in the Xingu region. Indian guides take visitors canoeing, fishing, walking, and animal- and birdwatching. Four- and five-day programs are available for US$180 per person per day, including transfers from/to Altamira (which you can fly into) and one night in a hotel in the town. For information visit the website www.amazoncoop.org.

which goes to the community. In Jamaracuá, canoe rides through the *igarapés* and *igapós* are US$5 per boat, plus US$1.35 per person for the community.

Buses heading for Maguary (US$1.65, three to four hours, 11am Monday to Saturday) leave from a stop on Av São Sebastião near the Telemar building. Ask the driver to drop you at the house of Sr Adalberto or Sr Almiro, brothers-in-law who oversee park visitation and will arrange a guide for you. You may well stay at the home of Sr Almiro and his friendly wife, Iréne. The return bus leaves at 3am (ouch!) Monday through Saturday.

There are a few other park entrances, but they have fewer services; ask at IBAMA.

Bosque Santa Lúcia

An easy, pleasant excursion from Santarém is to Bosque Santa Lúcia (Santa Lucia Woods), a private protected forest located 18km south of town. There are around 4km of trails, on which you can observe some 400 different species of native plants, from ironwood and Brazil-nut trees to famously medicinal plants like *andiroba* (decongestant, insect repellant, heals minor cuts) and *guaraná* (said to cure just about everything; see box on p628), and much more. There is also a new **Museum of Wood**, free for those on tours. The museum includes samples, cuttings and descriptions of the many types of Amazonian trees and their wood.

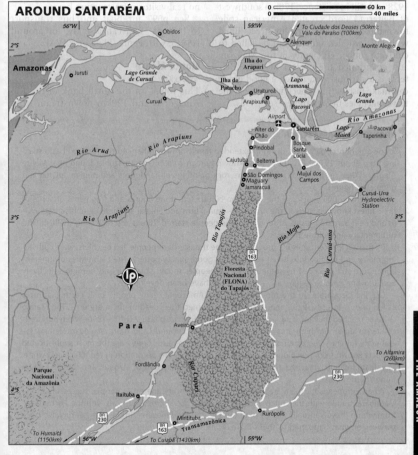

AROUND SANTARÉM

The forest is owned by American Steve Alexander, who offers tours through his agency **Amazon Tours** (☎ 522 1928, 9122 0299; Travessa Turiano Meira 1084; www.amazonriver.com). Interesting three- to four-hour guided trips, including lots of explanation of the farming and deforestation around the forest, cost US$55 per person; less for larger groups. Tours are available most days – call ahead.

Belterra
☎ 0xx93 / pop 5100

A 50km trip southwest of Santarém, Belterra, founded in 1933, was the heart of the larger of two Amazonian rubber plantations established by Henry Ford in an effort to break the British monopoly of the rubber business. (The other was Fordlândia, founded in 1928 and still in existence, 170km southwest of Belterra.) Ford created American-style townships, with wide, straight streets lined with little wooden houses. But he failed to cultivate rubber efficiently in the Amazon, and abandoned the project in 1946. Belterra is a curious spot, which a good guide can make fascinating (check with one of the travel agencies in Santarém – see p595).

Buses to Belterra (US$1.50, several daily) are run by Trans-Azevedo (leaving from Travessa Silvino Pinto in Santarém) and by Cidade de Belterra (from Av São Sebastião). Buy tickets for the latter at the Sucos Lanches *lanchonete* (snack bar) opposite.

Parque Nacional da Amazônia

This large (9940 sq km) Amazonian rainforest national park lies west of the town of Itaituba (population: 65,000), which is 250km southwest of Santarém. To visit, you must obtain prior permission from the **IBAMA office** (☎ 0xx93-518 1530; Av Marechal Rondon s/n), Itaituba, and an IBAMA staff member must accompany you on your visit. It is possible to stay at rudimentary facilities at an IBAMA post inside the park, but there's no real visitor infrastructure here.

See p597 for boat and bus transport to Itaituba. You can also fly, for around US$45, with Penta, Meta or TAVAJ.

Monte Alegre
☎ 0xx93 / pop 23,300

This town, on the north bank of the Rio Amazonas and 120km downstream from

---

PREHISTORIC AMAZONIA

Stone-age hunter-gatherers, living in extended family groups, inhabited the Amazon basin starting from about 10,000 BC. The earliest known human creations in Amazonia, found near Monte Alegre, 100km northeast of Santarém, are rock paintings of handprints and human, animal and geometric figures.

More than 6000 years ago the Tapajoara culture left stone figures and fragments of some of the earliest known pottery in the Americas – burial urns and animal and human representations – in and near Santarém itself. Around this time people started fishing and collecting shellfish, and rudimentary agriculture began.

By the last few centuries BC, groups of maybe thousands of people, led by chiefs, were cultivating maize and manioc intensively and making good-quality pottery. The techniques of itinerant agriculture still practiced by some rain forest peoples today – planting and burning selectively and allowing soils to regenerate – may already have been developed.

On Ilha de Marajó, in the mouth of the Rio Amazonas, early people built earth platforms called *aterros* to escape the annual floods, and buried their dead in elaborate urns. The Marajó cultures reached their most advanced stage in the Marajoara phase (AD 400–1350), when hundreds of *aterros* up to 6m high and 250m long were built around Lago Arari. Marajoara ceramics – elaborate funerary and ceremonial vases and simpler domestic ones – are the most sophisticated artifacts known from precolonial Brazil, exhibiting exuberant decoration in red, black and white. Marajoara influence reached as far as Lago de Silves, 200km east of Manaus, and the Rio Cunani in northern Amapá.

When Europeans hit the Marajó area in the 17th century, the Aruãs people, successors to the Marajoara, traded with the Dutch and consequently got at cross-purposes with the Portuguese, from whom they eventually fled by migrating up the Rio Amazonas in the 18th century. No trace survives of what happened to them there.

Santarém, is the base from which to visit the oldest known human creations in Amazonia: the rock paintings of the Serra Paytuna and Serra Ererê, estimated to be 12,000 years old. To arrange a visit to these sites, about 30km from town, contact the local teacher and engineer who bears much of the credit for the paintings' conservation, **Nelsí Sadeck** (☎ 533 1430; nelsi@netsan.com.br; Rua do Jaquara 320). In a 4WD trip of five to seven hours (US$80 for up to 10 people), Nelsí will take you not only to the paintings of human handprints and animal, human and geometric figures, but also to lookout points, strange rock formations and caves. Other outings, including visits to area waterfalls, can be arranged.

Monte Alegre Palace (☎ 533 1222; Av Presidente Vargas s/n; per person incl breakfast US$6), in the Cidade Baixa (the lower part of town) has basic rooms with shared bathroom and fan.

Pousada Panorámica (☎ 533 1282; per person incl breakfast US$8; 🔀), on Praça da Matriz in the Cidade Alta (Upper Town). One of the better places in town, with comfortable rooms.

Restaurante Panorama (Travessa Oriental 100; dishes US$3-7) is a reasonable fish restaurant.

See p597 for details of boats from Santarém. Most boats from Belém to Santarém also make a stop at Monte Alegre.

Alenquer
☎ 0xx93 / pop 27,300
Across the Amazon from Santarém, the village of Alenquer was founded in the 18th century by missionaries attempting to convert the local Abaré Indians. Alenquer has several impressive waterfalls relatively nearby, including **Cachoeira Açu das Pedras**. The town is also the gateway to **Ciudade dos Deuses** (City of the Gods), a field of bizarre rock formations 50km north of the town. Another 50km further is the **Vale do Paraíso** (Valley of Paradise), which has a fine pousada and additional waterfalls.

The easiest way to visit is on a tour with **Amazon Planet** (☎ 527 1172, 9654 4123; www.amazon planetadventur.com.br; Travessa Copacabana 150) in Alter do Chão (p602). Four-day all-inclusive tours to Ciudade dos Deuses and Vale do Paraíso, including visits to several waterfalls cost US$50 per day per person.

Adventurous travelers can try making it on their own. Motorcycles can be rented

in Alenquer (US$10 per day, plus gas and insurance), but the road is unpaved and can be quite rutted – only experienced motorcyclists should attempt it. Otherwise, a taxi to visit Ciudade dos Deuses and continue to Vale do Paraíso is US$70 to US$85 each way.

Pousada Vale do Paraíso (per person US$12.65) in Vale do Paraíso has quaint, comfortable bungalows sleeping four to seven people.

Boats from Santarém to Alenquer (9am and 3pm Monday to Friday, 3pm only Saturday and Sunday, three to four hours) depart east of the center, near the Restaurante O Mascotinho.

Return boats depart Alenquer at 6am daily plus noon Monday to Friday.

Alter do Chão
☎ 0xx93 / pop 7000
Alter do Chão, 33km west of Santarém by good paved roads, is justly the subject of a thousand postcards. A sandbar directly in front of the town forms a picturesque white-sand island, known as Ilha do Amor (Island of Love). The island is largest and most attractive when the water is low, roughly June to December. In the wet season it's greatly reduced, though still pretty.

Besides its famous beach, Alter do Chão also stands at the entrance to a picturesque lagoon, Lago Verde, which you can explore

---

THE TRANSAMAZÔNICA

The idea of the Transamazônica was born in 1970, during the military dictatorship, when President Garrastazu Médici decided that drought-stricken Northeasterners should colonize Amazonia. To that end, a 5600km 'Highway of National Integration' was to be cut across the caatinga (savanna) and rain forests from João Pessoa on the Atlantic coast to Boquerão da Esperança on the Peruvian border.

Only 2500km of highway was actually constructed, and only a few short stretches of this were paved. The Transamazônica today is full of potholes large enough to tip a bus and is all but impassable in the wet season. Even in dry weather, buses struggle for 34 hours to cover the 1000km from Marabá to Itaituba, and the road beyond there has been closed since 1999.

in rented canoes. FLONA do Tapajós and other spots on the Rio Tapajós make for good boat tours. Also accessible is the lesser-known Rio Arapiunes, whose nickname, 'the Caribbean of the Amazon,' is a forgivable exaggeration: the dry season reveals white-sand beaches and, on sunny days, transparent, even turquoise water. And don't miss Arariba, one of the best indigenous art stores in the Amazon region.

ORIENTATION

Alter do Chão is framed by the Rio Tapajós on its west side, Lago Verde to the east and a small channel connecting the two – where Ilha do Amor forms – on the north side. The center of town is Praça 7 de Septembro, facing the beach.

The highway from Santarém, known in town as Travessa Copacabana, runs north along the village's eastern edge before deadending at the beach. Rua Dom Macêdo Costa is a paved road running east–west about two blocks below the beach. Travessa Antônio A Lobato is the street running straight south from Praça 7 de Septembro; the bus stops at the intersection of Travessa Antônio A Lobato and Rua Dom Macêdo Costa. Most other roads in town are unpaved.

INFORMATION

At the time of research, there were no banks, ATMs or exchange offices, and most hotels and tour operators only accepted cash.

There is no government tourist office, but Gabriele Paduano of **Amazon Planet** (☎ 527 1172, 9654 4123; www.amazonplanetadventur.com.br; Travessa Copacabana 150) speaks several languages and is very helpful (see right).

There is a **post office** (Rua Lauro Sobre) and **public phones** (Praça 7 de Septembro), but no telephone office. There is no Internet service but rumor was that it was coming soon.

DANGERS & ANNOYANCES

Stingrays are a concern in some areas. When entering the water, shuffle your feet to scare them off, or else use a long reed or stick to poke the sand in front of you.

SIGHTS & ACTIVITIES
Beaches

Ilha do Amor has several stilted shacks that serve food and drinks year-round. When the water is low, you can wade across. Other-wise, rowboats take up to four people across from the village for US$0.75. Another good sandy beach, **Praia do Cajuiero**, faces the Rio Tapajós on the west side of the village. Other beaches further from town are best reached in a car. These include **Pindobal** (8km), **Cajutuba** (16km), **Aramanai** (26km) and **Ponta de Pedras** (28 km) – ask at Amazon Planet for directions and car rentals.

Lago Verde

There are tours through Lago Verde, but you can also do it yourself in a kayak or canoe – rent one on either beach for around US$1 an hour. Be careful not to get lost, though, especially when the water is high and the surrounding forest is flooded.

Boat Tours

As anywhere in the Amazon, there is no guarantee you will see wildlife on a boat or jungle tour. Birds and river dolphins do appear frequently, and monkeys are relatively common (but not always easy to spot) in Jamaracuá and Ilha Patacho.

Amazon Planet (☎ 527 1172, 9654 4123; www.amazon planetadventur.com.br; Travessa Copacabana 150) The friendly and multilingual owner-operator, Italian Gabriele Paduano, offers two- to three-day trips that include hiking and canoeing in Jamaracuá (a town within the FLONA do Tapajós), a boat tour of Ilha Patacho in the Amazon, and swimming and snorkeling at white-sand beaches on the Rio Arapiunes. (US$40 to US$50 per day). Tours include quality meals and service, and a clean, comfortable riverboat for sleeping (when not camping in the jungle or on a deserted beach). Amazon Planet also offers sport-fishing tours, mostly for the hard-fighting tucanaré (peacock bass). One/two day trips start at US$50/100 per person per day, all included. The best months for fishing are August to November. Other trips can be arranged, from day trips to Lago Verde to two-week, custom-designed expeditions. Portuguese-speaking guides only; two- to three-person minimum for most trips.

Mãe Natureza (☎ 527 1264, 9651 5819; maenatureza@hotmail.com; Praça 7 de Septembro 236) Operated by Argentinean transplants Claudio Chena and Jorge Bassi, this agency offers similar tours as Amazon Planet, including multi-day trips on a river boat to FLONA, the Amazon (though without the island tour) and Rio Arapiunes. Prices are slightly lower, but do not always include IBAMA and other fees – check before signing up. Some English-speaking guides available.

Vento do Popa (☎ 527 1379, 9654 4245; itaketami@ bol.com.br; Praça 7 de Septembro) Next door to Mãe Natureza, this operator specializes in half- and one-day tours.

FESTIVALS
The Festa do Çairé in the second week of September is the major folkloric event in western Pará. The Çairé is a standard held aloft to lead a flower-bedecked procession; its origins may go back to symbols used by early missionaries to help convert Indians.

SLEEPING
There are many more pousadas than those listed here and even more under construction. All those listed here include breakfast.

Albergue da Floresta (☎ 9651 7193; albergueda floresta@hotmail.com; Travessa Antonio Pedrosa s/n; hammock or camping per person US$3.50, 2-/4-person cabin US$10/18.50) Super laid-back and set in thick garden surroundings, hammock space is in an open-air *palapa* (thatched-roof hut) and cabins are simple but comfortable. Use of the kitchen is $1.50 extra. Run by friendly young Brazilian-Uruguayan couple.

Pousada Alter-do-Chão (☎ 527 1215; Rua Lauro Sodré 74; r with fan/ US$10/13.50) Facing the river and beach, rooms here are simple and somewhat run-down, but not unpleasantly so. Those at the front are best. Discounts are available for solo travelers and groups. It's friendly, with a good restaurant on-site.

Pousada Vila da Praia (☎ 527 1130; Rua Copacabana s/n; s/d US$8.50/11.50, chalets US$16.50;) Dumpy-looking from the outside, the double rooms and two-room 'chalets' here are actually pretty nice inside, with attractive wood construction; chalets have TV, too. Chalets sleep five but come with breakfast for two; extra breakfasts are US$1.50 each.

Pousada Tia Marilda (☎ 527 1144; Travessa Antônio A Lobato 559; s/d without bathroom US$6.50/10, with bathroom US$10/11.50;) Literally steps from the Santarém bus stop, rooms here are decent sized with TV, although a bit stuffy. *Quartos* upstairs are breezier. The service is very friendly; laundry done.

Pousada Tupaiulândia (☎ 527 1157, 9975 4928; Rua Pedro Teixeira 300; r US$20;) Suites are comfortable and quite spacious, enough so you may not notice their somewhat bare decor. Arranged in two circular blocks, all rooms have TV and fridge.

Pousada do Mingote (☎ 527 1158; Travessa Antônio A Lobato s/n; s/d/tw with US$13.50/16.50/20) Clean, modern rooms are smallish, but still comfortable, and face a small shady courtyard. Well located, just 50m from both the bus stop and the plaza.

Beloalter Hotel (☎ 527 1230, 527 1247; www.beloalter.com.br; end of Rua Pedro Teixeira; s/d US$60-80, suites US$80-150;) Alter do Chão's most upscale hotel is near Lago Verde, about 500m east of the highway down a shady dirt road. Rooms are modern and comfortable, with TV and prompt service.

EATING & DRINKING
Tribal (☎ 527 1226; Travessa Antônio A Lobato s/n; dishes US$5-10; 11am-3pm & 6-11pm) Huge, well-prepared fish dishes serve two easily, with potato salad to spare at this popular open-air restaurant. Good grilled beef and chicken also served. Single portions available.

Farol da Vila (Rua Jo Caisi de Arrimo s/n; dishes US$6-10; 11am-9pm Fri-Sun) With good views of the river and Ilha do Amor, this recommended restaurant serves an excellent *moqueca* – a sort of seafood stew that serves two easily. Other fish, beef and chicken dishes available; ask about single portions.

D'Italia (☎ 527 1371; east side of Praça 7 de Setembro; self-service lunch per kg US$4.50, dishes US$5-10; 8am-midnight) This 'Italian' restaurant serves a little of everything, from pizza and pasta to standard meat-rice-beans meals for two.

Pousada Alter do Chão (☎ 527 1215; Rua Lauro Sodré 74; dishes US$6-10; 7am-10pm) The *prato feito* (plate of the day) here includes meat, rice and beans for $1.50; many of the menu items serve two.

Alter Nativo and **Mãe Natureza** (Praça 7 de Septembro 236), a supermarket and tour operator side by side on Praça 7 de Septembro, both operate nightly bar service, and are a good place to meet other travelers.

SHOPPING
Arariba (☎ 527 1251; cnr Travessa Antônio A Lobato & Rua Dom Macêdo Costa; 8am-noon & 3-7pm Tue-Sun) One of the best indigenous art stores in the Amazon, with items ranging from inexpensive necklaces to museum-quality masks and ceremonial figures. Credit cards accepted.

GETTING THERE & AWAY
Buses run between Alter do Chão almost every hour. In Santarém, the official bus stop is Praça Tiradentes, but the bus stops (and often fills up) at a stop on Av São Sebastião east of Travessa Silvino Pinto. Note that the following schedule is for Praça Tiradentes –

buses leave the Av São Sebastião stop as much as 15 minutes before these times!

Monday to Saturday departures are at 5am, 6am, 7:20am, 9:20am, 10:30am, noon, 1pm, 3pm, 4:45pm and 6pm; there is a 10:30pm bus on school days. Sunday and holiday departures are at 7am, 8am, 9am, 10am, 11am, noon, 3pm, 4pm and 5pm.

In Alter do Chão, buses stop at the corner Travessa Antônio A Lobato and Rua Dom Macêdo Costa. Buses leave Monday to Saturday at 6am, 7am, 8:20am, 10:30am, 11:45am, 1:20pm, 2:20pm, 4:30pm, 5:45pm and 7:20pm. Sunday departures are at 8am, 9am, 10am, 11am and 3pm, 4pm, 5pm and 6pm.

The trip takes about an hour and costs US$0.50.

A taxi to or from Santarém, including the ports or airport, costs around US$18.

AMAPÁ

Stretching from the Amazon delta to the borders of French Guiana and Suriname, Amapá has just over a half-million inhabitants, most of whom live in the capital, Macapá. The climate is equatorial and superhumid, though drier from September to November. Owing to the proximity of French Guiana, many Amapaenses speak some French.

The English, Dutch and French all tried to establish themselves on the north side of the Amazon before Portugal settled colonists at Macapá in 1738, building an imposing fort later. The Treaty of Vienna (1815) fixed the French–Portuguese border at the Rio Oiapoque. But most of Amapá remained a no-man's-land (and refuge for escaped slaves from Brazil) until the 1893 Rio Calçoene gold rush. This prompted French invasion attempts, but international arbitration definitively awarded Amapá to Brazil, upon which it was promptly annexed by Pará. This annexation greatly displeased the Amapaenses, who relentlessly pursued autonomy until it was finally granted in 1943. The left-wing environmentalist João Alberto Capiberibe, elected state governor in 1995, set Amapá firmly on a path of environmentally sustainable development.

In 2002, Capiberibe stood for (and won) a federal senate seat; his vice-governor was defeated in the state gubernatorial election by the Democratic Workers Party (PDT) candidate Waldez Góes da Silva. The new governor is more closely tied to business interests than his predecessor, promising to expand jobs and economic growth. But it does not appear conservation will be forgotten – one of the governor's key projects is to interlink, physically and administratively, the state's many different protected areas. Still underway at the time of research, this would create the first 'biodiversity corridor' and greatly aid in preservation in the region, especially of wildlife.

MACAPÁ
☎ 0xx96 / pop 336,800

The state capital lies on the equator, in a strategic position on the north side of the Rio Amazonas estuary. Though not really worth a trip on its own, anyone headed to French Guiana must pass though Macapá and won't regret spending a day or two here, with its delectable sea breezes and a couple of nice sights. If you have extra time, visiting the San Antônio waterfall or forging a path to the national parks can be rewarding (though tough) before you head up to the border.

Information
BOOKSTORES
Livraría Nobel (☎ 223 9841; Av Presidente Vargas at Rua São José; ☾ 8am-8pm Mon-Fri, to 6pm Sat) A few guidebooks and other tourism-related books in French and English.

EMERGENCY
Ambulance (☎ 192)
Police (☎ 190)

INTERNET ACCESS
TV Som (Av Mendonça Furtado 253; per hr US$0.50; ☾ 8am-10pm)

LEFT LUGGAGE
The airport has left-luggage lockers (US$1.50 per day).

MEDICAL SERVICES
Hospital de Emergência (☎ 212 6179; crn Av Padre Júlio M Lombaerd & Rua Hamilton Silva)
Hospital de Especialidades (☎ 212 6127; Rua Odilardo Silva at Av Coiolano Jucá)

MONEY

Banco do Brasil (Rua Independência at Av Mendonça Junior; ☺ 9am-5pm Mon-Fri) Will exchange euros and US cash or traveler's checks between 11am and 2pm Monday to Friday; go upstairs to Window No 8.

Bradesco (Rua Cândido Mendes 1316) Reliable ATMs.

FITTA (☎ 223 2788; airport; ☺ 9am-5pm Mon-Fri) Changes euros, US dollars and traveler's checks.

HSBC (Av Padre Júlio M Lombaerd at Rua São José) Reliable ATMs.

POST

Post office (☎ 223 3803; Av Coriolano Jucá at Rua São José; ☺ 9am-4pm Mon-Fri)

TELEPHONE

Telemar (Rua São José at Av General Gurjão; ☺ 8am-5pm Mon-Fri) International phone calls from indoor and outdoor pay phones; cards sold at the window inside.

TOURIST INFORMATION

Detur (☎ 212 5335; www.detur.ap.gov.br in Portuguese; Rua Independência 29; ☺ 8am-noon & 2-6pm Mon-Fri) Genuinely helpful staff.

IBAMA (☎ 214 1122, 214 1116; Rua Hamilton Silva at Av Antônio Coelho de Carvalho; ☺ 8am-noon & 2-6pm Mon-Fri) For info on national parks.

TRAVEL AGENCIES

For plane tickets, there is a slew of agencies at and around the corner of Rua Independencia and Av Mendonça Junior.

Agencia Solnave (☎ 223 9090; Rua Padre Júlio M Lombaerd 48; ☺ 8am-6pm Mon-Fri, to noon Sat) Friendly office sells all plane and boat tickets.

Navios Bom Jesus (☎ 223 2342, 223 0021; Av Mendonça Junior 12; ☺ 8am-noon & 2-6pm Mon-Fri, 8am-noon Sat) Boat tickets sold here.

Eco Travel (☎ 243 0001, 9114 1013; Rua Beira Rio s/n, in the Complejo Arajá; ☺ 8am-noon & 2-6pm Mon-Fri, 8am-noon Sat) Arranges tours, including to see the *pororoca* phenomenon ('tidal bore'; massive waves caused by the collision of river and ocean waters that can roll for over an hour) on the Rio Araguari during full moons January to May.

Sights

FORTALEZA DE SÃO JOSÉ DE MACAPÁ

The Portuguese built the large stone **Fortaleza de São Jose de Macapá** (entrance Av Henrique Galúcio; admission free; ☺ 9am-6pm) between 1764 and 1782 to defend the north side of the Amazon against French incursions from the Guianas. More than 800 laborers were involved in the construction, mostly Indians, blacks and Caboclos (people of mixed Indian and Portuguese parentage). Many died from accidents, many others from violent and repressive overseers. Portuguese- and French-speaking guides are available.

The long pier just north of the Fortaleza, the **Trapiche Eliezer Levy**, dates from the 1930s. Reconstructed in 1998, it makes a pleasant stroll, and has a restaurant at the end (see p607).

MUSEU SACACA

About 2km from the city center is the unique **Sacaca Sustainable Development Museum** (☎ 212 5361; Av Feliciano Coelho 1509 at Rua Manoel Cudoxo Perreira; admission free; ☺ 9am-6pm Tue-Sun). The primary exhibits, arranged in a large outdoor plot, are reconstructions of various rural homes, from the thatched huts of *castanheiros* (Brazil-nut harvesters) to riverboats used by traveling merchants. Slightly corny, yes, but Portuguese-speaking guides give interesting explanations.

There are no convenient buses here, and it's a long, hot walk. Moto-taxis (motorcycle taxis) are a good option (US$0.50; you are required to wear a helmet).

MONUMENTO DO MARCO ZERO

The **Zero Line Monument** (Av Equatorial at Rodovía Juscelino Kubitscheck), a large obelisk-cum-sundial, stands on the equator, about 6km southwest of the city center. A hemisphere-straddling sports stadium and a sambadrome (a stadium built for the express purpose of holding huge samba concerts and dances) are part of the same complex.

To get there, take a southbound 'Fortaleza' or orange 'Universidad' buses on Rua Tiradentes at Av Mendonça Furtado, behind Igreja de São José. The same bus returns to the centro. The Zeráo bus also works, but takes a more roundabout route.

Festivals & Events

O Marabaixo is an Afro-Brazilian celebration, with music and dance, held 40 days after Semana Santa (Holy Week).

Sleeping

All the hotels listed following include free breakfast.

Hotel Santo Antonio (☎ 222 0226, 222 0244; Av Coriolano Jucá 485; dm US$4.10, with fan s without bathroom US$4.50, s/d with bathroom US$6/9.50, with ❄ s/d with bathroom US$8.50/11.50) Cheapest around and for a reason – bare clapboard rooms have seriously saggy beds and questionable cleanliness. Come here only if your cash supply demands it.

Hotel Amazonas (☎ 222 7011; Rua Tiradentes 785; s/d with fan US$8.50/11.50, with TV & ☒ US$11.50/15) A better budget option. Seems small and dark from the outside, but rooms are clean and decent-sized. Those facing the street have good light, but may be noisy.

Mercurio Hotel (☎ 223 5622; Rua Cândido Mendes 1300; s/d US$11.50/15) A good, centrally-located option, especially for those traveling with an entourage. Huge rooms have five beds and several hammock hooks, plus TV and air-con. There are no windows and it's a bit worn-down, but the size helps a lot.

Frota Palace Hotel (☎ 223 3999; fax 223 7011; Rua Tiradentes 1104; s/d US$22.50/28; ☒) On a somewhat noisy street, rooms are nevertheless clean and spacious, if a bit bare, and have TV and minibar. Friendly service includes transportation to/from Varig, TAM and VASP flights (US$1.50; see the hotel's airport desk on arrival).

Hotel Macapá (☎ 217 1350, 217 1352; Rua Azarias Neto 17; s/d US$31.50/38.50, with terrace & view US$36.50/43.50; ☒) For an upscale hotel, rooms here are surprisingly plain. Interior rooms aren't worth the price, exterior ones are a bit better, with large terraces and table and decent view. The pool helps.

Pousada Ékinox (☎ 223 0086; www.ekinox.com .br; Rua Jovino Dinoá 1693; s/d US$43/50; ☒) Run by a

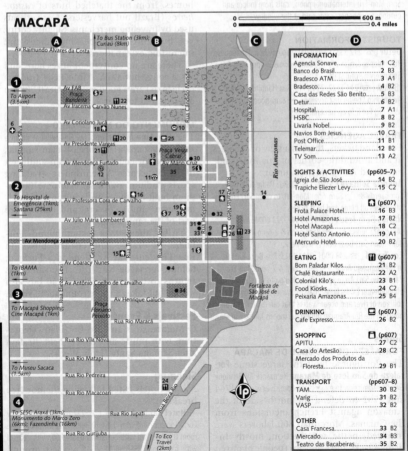

MACAPÁ

0 —————— 600 m
0 —————— 0.4 miles

hospitable French honorary consul and his Brazilian wife, these are Macapás choicest accommodations. Pleasant rooms have hot shower, TV, VCR and minibar, and guests can use the hotel's fitness area, video and book library, courtyard and excellent restaurant. Advance booking recommended.

Eating & Drinking

Peixaria Amazonas (☎ 225 2008; Rua Beira Rio at Rua Macacoari; dishes for 2 US$8-10; ☷ 11am-3pm & 7pm-midnight Mon-Sat, 11am-4pm Sun) The 2nd-floor open-air dining area has fine river views and breezes. The chef's special is an ample fillet of *tucanaré* stuffed with shrimp, tomato and cheese, served with rice, beans and *farofa*.

Chalé Restaurante (☎ 222 1970; Av Presidente Getúlio Vargas 499; dishes for 2 US$6-$11; ☷ 11am-10pm Tue-Thu, to midnight Fri-Sat; to 4pm Sun) Upscale ambiance, with tablecloths and a good selection of wines. Large menu includes seafood, chicken and pasta dishes for two people; some individual portions available.

Bom Paladar Kilos (☎ 223 0555; Av Presidente Getúlio Vargas 456; per kg US$6.50; ☷ 11:30am-3:15pm) Go across the street from Chalé Restaurante for excellent self-service that includes daily vegetarian dishes, creative seafood and fresh-grilled meats. Clean air-con dining area and good service.

Trapiche Restaurante (☎ 225 2665; dishes US$5-10; ☷ 10am-midnight Tue-Sun, dinner Mon) This would be just another typical restaurant if it weren't on the end of a long pier sticking into the Amazon river. Dishes are decent and large enough for two (mostly fish with a few meat and chicken options) but the best reason to come here is to have an afternoon beer and take in the view – during the rainy season you can watch storm clouds march up and down the river.

Colonial Kilo's (☎ 223 3156; Av Iracema Carvão Nunes 282; per kg US$5.50; ☷ 11am-4pm) Cheaper but still decent self-service, near Praça Bandeira.

Cafe Expresso (☎ 223 8585; Av Presidente Getúlio Vargas 184; ☷ 7:30am-6pm Mon-Fri, to noon Sat) A shot of coffee or a sturdy jug of freshly squeezed juice here both go for under a dollar.

Food kiosks lining the waterfront, north of the fort, are popular for evening snacks.

Entertainment

Cine Macapá (☎ 217 1499; Av Henrique Galúcio at Rua Leopoldo Machado; tickets US$2.50, Wed & before 7pm US$1.50) On the 2nd floor of Macapá Shopping, with two screens showing relatively recent Hollywood fare.

SESC Araxá (☎ 214 1314; Rua Jovino Dinoá 4311) About 3km south of the city center, SESC Araxá stages musical performances on Tuesday night. Performances vary, but generally include a mix of regional and popular music and usually start at around 8pm. Call ahead or ask at the tourist office for current schedules.

Shopping

APITU (☎ 222 4329; Av Mendonça Jr at Rua Independencia; ☷ 8am-noon & 2-6pm Mon-Sat) A small but authentic selection of art of the Tumucumaque indigenous people who come from the mountainous borders of Amapá, Pará and Surinam. The collection includes seed and bead necklaces, large woven baskets and ceremonial costumes.

Casa do Artesão (☎ 223 5444; Av Mendonça Junior at Rua Independencia; ☷ 8am-4pm Mon-Sat) Next door to APITU, this shop has a larger but mostly nonindigenous selection of *artesanía*. You may see artisans on site.

Mercado dos Produtos da Floresta (☎ 225 3433, 9972 5410; Rua São José 1500; ☷ 8am-6pm Mon-Fri) Excellent shop sells all-natural medicines, oils, shampoos and more.

Getting There & Away
TO/FROM THE AIRPORT
Taxis make the most sense, costing around US$3.50 to most hotels. There are buses into town, but the nearest stop is about a kilometer away on Av Fab. A cab from the airport to the bus stop costs $1.50.

TO/FROM THE BUS STATION
To get to the *rodoviária*, take bus 'Jardim' or 'Pedrinhas Novo Horizonte' bus on Rua São José, in front of Igreja de São José (US$0.50, 20 minutes). The same buses return.

AIR
Most flights from Macapá go through Belém, a 45-minute flight away. Airlines with offices in the airport keep irregular hours – call ahead.

Gol (☎ 222 4857; airport)

Meta (☎ 223 4146; airport) Regional routes including flights to Paramaribo (Surinam) and Georgetown (Guyana).

Penta (☎ 223 1970; airport) Destinations throughout Amazon, plus Cayenne (French Guiana).

Puma airport(9971 7442); Macapá (☎ 9971 2553) Flies to Oiapoque and other areas in eastern Amazon.

TAM airport (223 2688; Macapá(☎ 223 8100, at Av Júlio Maria Lombaerd 520; ☺ 8am-noon, 2-6pm Mon-Fri, 8am-noon Sat) Flies to most major Brazilian cities.

Varig airport ☎ 223 5880); Macapá(☎ 222 7733, Rua Cândido Mendes 1039; ☺ 8am-noon & 2-6pm Mon-Fri, 8am-noon Sat)

VASP (☎ 223 2411; Av Júlio Maria Lombaerd & Rua Independencia; ☺ 8am-noon & 2-6pm Mon-Fri, 8am-noon Sat) Has frequent promotions to Belém and throughout Amazon.

BOAT

Passenger boats to Belém and Manaus (via Santarém) leave from the large port town of Santana, 25km southwest of Macapá. To get there, take a southbound 'Santana' bus from the stop on Rua Tiradentes at Av Mendonça Furtado, behind Igreja de São José (30 minutes; $0.75) You can buy advance tickets in Macapá at **Agencia Solnave** (☎ 223 9090; Rua Padre Júlio M Lombaerd 48; ☺ 8am-6pm Mon-Fri, to noon Sat) and **Navios Bom Jesus** (☎ 223 2342, 223 0021; Av Mendonça Junior 12; ☺ 8am-noon & 2-6pm Mon-Fri, 8am-noon Sat). See 'Buses of the Waterways' (p587) for tips on riverboat travel.

Boats leave for Belém (US$23.50, 22 to 24 hours, departures 10am Monday, Thursday and Friday, noon Saturday) and for Santarém (US$30, three days, departures 6pm Monday to Saturday) continuing to Manaus (US$67, five days). Prices are for hammock-class; cabins usually available.

BUS

Macapá's **bus station** (☎ 251 5045) is on the BR-156 in Bairro São Lázaro, about 3km north of the center. Rain and mud make long-distance bus travel in Amapá very rough, especially January to June.

Buses to Oiapoque and the French Guiana border (US$16, 595km, 16 to 24 hours, daily at 1pm, 5pm, 6pm and 8pm) take Hwy BR-156, which is paved for the first 140km only. For Cachoeira Santo Antonio, take a bus to Laranjal do Jarí (US$7, seven to 12 hours, daily at 8am and 4pm); dirt road the entire way. Cancellations are common on both lines, so call ahead to confirm departures.

TRAIN

An infrequent train service links Santana, 25km south of Macapá where the docks

are located, and Serra do Navio, near the Parque Nacional Montanhas do Tumucumaque. Departures are on Monday, Wednesday and Friday. It's not significantly faster than the bus, but it's nice to get off the road and see the countryside in another way.

AROUND MACAPÁ
Curiaú

This African village 8km northeast of Macapá was founded by escaped African slaves. They chose this area for its natural pastures, perfect for raising buffalo. You can hire a local to take you for a canoe trip on the lakes and rivers in the area, which teem with bird life. The surrounding area is an Área de Protecão Ambiental (Environmental Protection Area; see p80 for more on such areas).

The Festa de São Joaquim in Curiaú, running from about 11–18 August, is an Afro-Brazilian party with *ladainha* (praying), *folia* (dancing in colorful costumes) and most notably *batuque* (drumming).

To get to Curiarú, catch a local bus from Macapá to Curiaú.

Praia da Fazendinha

Buses run to Praia da Fazendinha, in the town of Fazendinha, 16km southwest of Macapá. It is a decent beach, and beachside restaurants Julião and Naira are recommended for seafood.

Take a 'Fortaleza' or 'Santana – Vila Fazendinha' bus southbound from the stop on Rua Tiradentes at Av Mendonça Furtado, behind Igreja de São José (US$0.50, 20 minutes).

Oiapoque
☎ 0xx96 / pop 13,000

This is the remote town at the end of Hwy BR-156, 595km north of Macapá on the Brazil side of the Rio Oiapoque. On the other side of the river (a US$4, 20-minute motorboat ride) is the town of St Georges, French Guiana, about four hours (200km) southeast of Cayenne, the French Guiana capital. Oiapoque is thus a key point on the overland route between the Guianas and northeastern Brazil.

Oiapoque was long thought to mark the northernmost point of Brazil. The saying *Do Oiapoque ao Chuí* (From Oiapoque to

Chuí) is still a familiar catchall phrase. The town itself has a monument – **Marco Inicial do Brazil** – and a motto – *Aqui começa o Brazil* (Brazil starts here) – to mark the distinction. The only problem is that it is *not* the northernmost point: Monte Caburaí, on the Venezuelan border in Roraima, beats it by a good hundred kilometers! Oiapoque took the 'news' in stride, tweaking its claim to say the town has the northernmost coastline, which is true.

If tourism is ever allowed in the Parque Nacional do Cabo Orange, Oiapoque will surely be a main base for trips there. For now, local tour operators offer trips around the edges of the park. Try **Marripá Tour** (☎ 521 2520) or ask at your hotel.

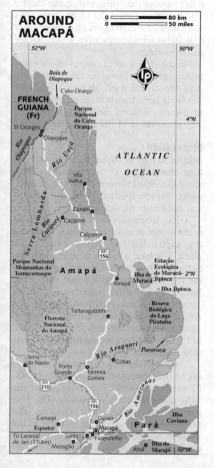

AROUND MACAPÁ

0 — 80 km
0 — 50 miles

ORIENTATION & INFORMATION
The Rio Oiapoque forms the curving northern edge of town. Av Barão do Rio Branco is the principal avenue in town, running from the Marco Inicial do Brasil on the riverfront south past Igreja NS das Graças and through the residential part of town.

The pier is a block west of Av Barão do Rio Branco. The **Hospital Geral** (☎ 521 1280; Rua Presidente Vargas & Av Veiga Cabral) is four blocks south of the pier.

The Brazilian **Polícia Federal post** (☎ 521 1380; ☺ Mon-Sat) here, where you must get your passport stamped and obtain or surrender your entry/exit card if crossing the border, is open daily except Sunday.

Oiapoque has branches of Banco do Brasil and Bradesco.

SLEEPING & EATING
Breakfast is included in the room rate of all of the following hotels.

Hotel de Oiapoque (☎ 521 1809, 521 1681; Rua Joaquim C da Silva; ☒) At the waterfront, rooms here have TV.

Arizona Hotel (☎ 521 2185; Av Coaracy Nunes 551; r with fan/ ☒ US$11.50/15) A few blocks inland, rooms are basic but clean with TV and minibar.

Restaurante Beija Flor (☎ 521 1368; Rua Joaquim C da Silva near the pier; dishes US$5-12) Recommended for Brazilian and French food.

Hotels in St Georges are more expensive, at around US$25 for a double room.

GETTING THERE & AWAY
The bus station is on BR-156, a few hundred meters southeast of the center. The airport is further east, also off BR-156.

See Getting There & Away in the Macapá section (p607) for information on bus and air transportation.

NATIONAL PARKS & RESERVES
To look at the map, Amapá seems an outdoor adventurer's paradise. Half the state is protected land, including the massive **Parque Nacional Montanhas de Tumucumaque**, Brazil's largest national park and the largest block of protected tropical rain forest in the world (3.8 million hectares). The park also overlaps part of the similarly immense Parque Indígena do Tumucumaque (mostly in the state of Pará) and French Guiana is considering forming an adjacent preserve

THE AMAZON

of its own. Other protected areas in Amapá include **Ilha de Maracá**, the **Floresta Nacional do Amapá** and **Parque Nacional do Cabo Orange**, where even the park rangers use local guides to avoid getting lost in the dense and unforgiving wetlands.

And now the bad news: none of Amapá's protected areas are open for visitation. Under federal law, the government must complete a lengthy environmental study before opening any protected area for visitation; Amapá's studies are years from completion.

You can still visit – sort of. Tour operators in Oiapoque offer boat trips along the fringe of Cabo Orange, which is not all that different from the park itself; see the Oiapoque section, above. Likewise, there are guided trips around the small town of Serra do Navio; it's not within the actual park boundaries, but it's close enough that IBAMA plans to put its park base station there. Contact 'Gilson' at the **Pousada Cupuaçu** (☎ 321 1374; r with bathroom & breakfast US$15) for lodging and guides.

TOCANTINS

The state of Tocantins was created in 1989 by hiving off what was previously the northern half of Goiás. Southern Goiás had mostly been colonized by people from southern Brazil, who mixed little with the local Indians or Black slaves. Northern Goiás had mostly been colonized by people from Northeastern Brazil, with mixing between Indians, Blacks and those of European descent creating a distinctive culture. Separatist campaigns in what's now Tocantins began in the early 19th century.

Palmas is the state's only large city (and even so, it's relatively small); the rest is *fazendas* and small towns. The climate is humid, with average temperatures between 25°C and 36°C. Most rain falls between October and April. Ecologically Tocantins is a transition zone between the Amazon rain forest that makes up its northern part and the cerrado (scrubland) in the southeast. This variety means there are considerable natural attractions for those with time and budget on their side. Most notable is the Rio Araguaia/Ilha do Bananal zone in the west, where Pantanal-like wetlands meet rain forest and cerrado.

PALMAS
☎ 0xx63 / pop 151,000

Less than 20 years ago, the broad valley bisected by the Rio Tocantins held just a scattering of rural *fazendas*. Starting in 1989, a new state capital was built from scratch, and construction, state government and economic incentives brought thousands of Brazilians to this unlikely landscape, 1000km north of Brasília and 1600km south of Belém.

The excitement and bustle of Palmas' early years has waned somewhat – now that it's built, there is virtually no industry here, and efforts to cast Palmas as Brazil's 'ecological capital' or 'nature's heart' (two slogans proffered by the local municipal tourist agency) are progressing, but slowly. The fact that Palmas is 14 hours by bus from Brasília and 20 hours from Belém, and that flights remain expensive, is perhaps the main problem.

For travelers who do come, there is a surprising number of good outdoor excursions. And the capital itself, though admittedly sterile, is nevertheless strangely intriguing in the way Brasília, Brazil's first planned city, once was (and still is to some).

Orientation

Palmas' layout is confusing to most first-time visitors. The current system is actually a simplified version of the original one, which was scrapped partly because the mail was constantly misdelivered.

A few landmarks help: Praça Girossóis is the center of town and Palacio Araguaia (the capital building) is the center of the plaza. The lake is to the west; the hills are to the east. Palmas' two main thoroughfares are the only streets with actual names: Av Juscelino Kubitschek (known as Av JK, or 'Jota-Kah'), which runs north–south, and Av Teotônio Segurado, running east–west. They do not cut through Praça Girossóis, but if they did they would intersect at Palacio Araguaia.

The rest of the streets are named according to their direction and location. Av NS-01 runs north–south (*norte-sul*, hence the 'NS') along the plaza's west side. The next avenue west is NS-03, then NS-05 etc. The north–south avenue on the east side of the plaza is NS-02, followed by NS-04, NS-06 etc. East–west avenues follow the same pattern, but have the prefix 'LO': *leste–oeste* or east–west. The odd-numbered LOs are to the south of the plaza, the even-numbered ones to the north.

Most hotels and restaurants listed here are clustered around Galería Bela Palma, a small commercial center on NS-01 near Av JK, facing the Praça Girossóis. Buses to and from the airport, the bus station and Taquarussú (p613) stop right in front. Palmas Shopping, a large red-painted mall with movies and restaurants, is nearby at the intersection of LO-01 and NS-01, at the southwest corner of the plaza. All other listings are on the other (east) side of the plaza, on Av JK and NS-02. The plaza is lit up all night.

Note that to really enjoy Palmas' outdoors areas, you will need to rent a car. Public transport is either nonexistent or too infrequent to be useful.

Information

Pontonet Internet Café (☎ 215 1613; Galleria JK Center, Av Juscelino Kubitschek at Av NS-02; per hr US$1; ☽ 9am-7pm Mon-Fri, to 2pm Sat) has friendly owners and a fast connection. It often stays open past closing time.

Hospital Regional de Palmas (☎ 214 1424; ARNE 51, Av NS-02 & Av LO-11) has an emergency room. Dial ☎ 192 for an ambulance or ☎ 190 for the police. There are several pharmacies in Galería Bela Palma; one or more is usually open late.

Bradesco (cnr Av Juscelino Kubitschek at Av NS-02) and HSBC (across the street) have reliable ATMs. There's a **post office** (Av Juscelino Kubitschek at Av NS-04; ☽ 8am-5pm Mon-Fri, to noon Sat) one block east of Praça Girossóis.

You may get useful tourist info at **Embratur** (☎ 218 2357; Secretaria da Industria, Comércio e Turismo; east side of Praça Girossóis; ☽ 8am-6pm Mon-Fri) or the **Centro de Atendimento ao Turista** (CATUR; ☎ 218 5339; Parque Cesamar, Quarda 506 Sul; ☽ 8am-noon & 2-6pm), a branch of Amatur, Palmas' municipal tourist agency, which arranges guided visits to Serra do Lajeado (see right).

Bananal Ecotour (☎ 215 4333, 215 7624; www .bananalecotour.com.br; Quadra 103-S, Rua SO-11, Loja 28; ☽ 8am-6pm Mon-Fri, 9am-noon Sat) operates two well-recommended ecolodges outside Palmas, one outside Tuquarassú (p614) and another at Ilha do Bananal (p615). The folks here are generally more helpful than

those at CATUR. **Viagem & Cia** (☎ 215 2040; Quada 104-N; Av NS-02, 1 block north of Av JK; ☽ 8am-6pm Mon-Fri) is a friendly and professional place to purchase airline tickets.

Sights & Activities

The best reason to come here is for the outdoor activities around the city, but Palmas itself is definitely worth looking around for a day or two. Most of the sights of interest are in **Praça Girossóis**, purportedly Brazil's largest municipal plaza and the second-largest in the world (after Moscow's Red Square).

PALACIO ARAGUAIA

Built on perhaps the only hill in town, the **Palacio Araguaia** (☎ 218 1000; admission free; ☽ 8am-10pm Mon-Fri, to 6pm Sat & Sun), the state capital, looks over the plaza and Palmas itself. Inside the building there's a small **museum** (admission free; ☽ 8am-noon & 4-6pm Mon-Fri) with displays about Tocantins and Palmas. The lobby is adorned with huge mosaics and has a large scale model of Praça Girossóis, which you can then compare to the real thing from windows on the second floor. At the foot of the stairs is a small brass mark – it is the geographic center of Brazil.

Note that you may not enter the palace with shorts or tank tops, and the second floor is closed on weekends.

MEMORIAL COLUNA PRESTES

In the early 20th century, urban activists and sectors of the Brazilian military led opposition to Brazil's semiautocratic rule of the time. Seeking to integrate rural Brazilians into the reformation movement (and the nation), an army captain named Luis Carlos Prestes led 1500 rebel soldiers on a 25,000km journey through Brazil's vast interior, including parts of Tocantins. The march lasted from 1924 to 1927 during which the Coluna Prestes (Prestes Column) defeated a succession of larger, better-equipped federal divisions in intense trench battles. Housed in a curious white, tubular structure near Palacio Araguaia, the **Memorial Coluna Prestes** (admission free; ☽ 8am-noon & 2-6pm Tue-Sun) tells the life story of Prestes, who is credited with bringing democracy to the Brazilian hinterland.

SERRA DO LEJEADO

In the hills east of town, **Serra do Lejeado** is one of three ecological 'poles' being developed by the state and city tourist authorities (the others are Palmas proper, and Taquarassú). Around a hundred waterfalls, caves and vista points have been identified, and about a dozen can be easily visited if you have a car. You must first go to the Palmas office of **CATUR** (☎ 218 5339; Parque Cesamar, Quarda 506 Sul; ☽ 8am-noon & 2-6pm) to pick up a guide, who will direct you to the various sites. (It's a good idea to call the day before, to be sure a guide will be available.) While there, look through the office's photo album to see which sites you want to visit – the most popular are Cachoeira do Minindiba, Cachoeira do Macaco, Cachoiera Aqua Verde and Cachoiera Brejo do Chiquiero. The cost is US$5 per site; expect to be able to visit three or four in a day, accounting for time spent driving and visiting the sites. Bring water and lunch.

Sleeping

All of the hotels listed here come with free breakfast.

Hotel São Paulo (☎ 215 1630; Rua NO-03 at NS-01; without bathroom s/d US$5/9.50, with bathroom & fan US$6.50/11.50, ⛶ US$11.50/15) North side of Galeria Bela Palma. The cheapest option has decent-sized and fairly clean rooms, but the atmosphere is somewhat surly.

Hotel Serra Azul (☎ 215 1505; Rua NO-03 at NS-01; s/d US$11.50/15; P ⛶) Next door to the São Paulo, but much more pleasant. Clean smallish rooms has TV and minibar; very friendly service. Parking in front.

Turim Palace Hotel (☎ 215 1484, 215 2876; south side of Galería Bela Palma; s/d US$20/26.50; P ⛶ ⛴) Large hotel with long corridors and a interior courtyard with pool and tables. Clean rooms have curiously old-fashioned decor. Ten percent discount is usually available.

Eduardu's Palace Hotel (☎ 215 8114; half-block west of Turim Palace Hotel; s/d standard-larger US$25-33/33-41; ⛶ ⛴) Too bad the rooms here aren't a little better value – they're somewhat dim and plain – because the rooftop pool has about the best view in the city. You may be able to bargain a better price.

Pousada dos Girassós (☎ 215 1187; fax 215 2321; NS-01 at LO-01; s/d standard-larger US$34-41/40-49; P ⛶ ⛴) A good upscale option, with smallish but very clean, modern, comfortable rooms, some with terrace. Small courtyard with pool, plus bar and restaurant.

Eating

Trattoria Toscana (☎ 3028 2795; Av LO-04 at Av LO-04; dishes US$4.50-$10; ☽ 6pm-midnight Mon-Fri, 11am-4pm & 6pm-midnight Sat, 9am-4pm Sun) Fine Italian fare in an understated bistrolike eatery. Pasta dishes, like salmon linguine, are served piping hot; chicken and beef options available. For dessert, splurge on the divine *petit gateau di cioccolato* (US$3).

Pizzaria Oasis (☎ 215 1219; south side of Galería Bela Palma; dishes US$3.50-7; ☽ noon-2pm & 6-midnight Mon-Fri; 6pm-midnight Sat & Sun) Across from the Turim Palace Hotel, the Oasis is not only convenient but one of Palmas' more popular restaurants. A range of well-made pizzas is served in a bright, breezy streetside dining area.

Restaurante Finezza (☎ 212 1717; Av NS-02 at Av JK; per kg US$3.50; ☽ 11am-2:30pm Mon-Sat) Directly across from the Miniterio Público building, this popular low-key lunch-spot has good self-service with covered outdoor seating. At night, come here for beer and bar food.

Getting There & Around

AIR

Airlines serving Palmas include **GOL** (☎ 218 3738; airport only), **TAM** (☎ 215 7722; Av NS-01 & Av LO-1) and **Varig** (☎ 215 7722; Av JK at NS-03). At the time of research, all flights from Palmas went via Brasília.

The **airport** (☎ 219 3700) is located 28km south of the city. A taxi to/from the airport costs US$15. Or take any bus from the airport to the nearest stop for the 'Jardim Areny' bus, which goes to the center. Buses to the airport are infrequent and do not go all the way there. A new bridge was being built in 2004, which should reduce the taxi fare and may change the bus connection – ask at the airport info booth.

BUS

The **bus station** (☎ 228 5688, 216 1793; at LO-27 at NS-06) is at the far southeast corner of town. Taxi fare to/from the station is US$8. Coming into town, cross the main road in front of the *rodaviária* – almost every bus goes to the center and stops in front of Galería Bela Palma, where you can also pick up the return bus.

Regional routes include Natividade (US$5.50, three hours; 6:30pm), Paraíso de

Tocantins (US$1.50, 1½ hours, every 30 to 40 minutes from 6am to 8:30pm). For Taquarussú, take Bus No 90 from Praça Girossóis in front of Galería Bela Palma.

Longer-range service from Palmas includes Goiâna (US$20, nine hours, eight daily), Brasília (US$21, 12 hours, one or two daily); Salvador (US$28, 19 hours, one or two daily); Recife (US$54, 36 hours, one or two daily); Belo Horizonte (US$37, 24 hours, daily except Saturday); Rio de Janeiro (US$54, 36 hours, one or two daily) and Imperatriz (US$18, 10 hours) with connections from there to São Luis (US$43, 13 hours), Terezinha (US$36, 14 hours) and Belém (US$18, 10 hours).

CAR
Driving around Palmas is a blast, with huge roundabouts instead of traffic lights.

Hertz (☎ 215 1900; Av Teotônio Segurado at LO-04) is convenient to the center and is the only agency that offers full coverage insurance. Others include **Autos Rent-a-Car** (☎ 215 2550), **Locadora Araguaía** (☎ 214 3207) and **Verde** (☎ 215 1707). All should bring the car to your hotel if you ask.

AROUND PALMAS
Taquarussú
The green Serra do Carmo around this pleasant small valley town, 30km southeast of Palmas, is studded with beautiful waterfalls. Once a sleepy little town, it is now the focus of a major ecotourism effort by Palmas tourist authority (who rewrote the town's name as 'Taquaruçu'). Decent hotels, ecolodges and a well-organized guide service make this a nice place to spend a few days.

ORIENTATION & INFORMATION
Street signs are rare in Taquaussú, and few people seem inclined to even remember the street names. Fortunately it's a small town, and locals and the folks at CATUR are happy to give directions.

You really need a car to visit the waterfalls and caves here – see above for rentals in Palmas. There are no banks or money-changers in Taquarussú, so bring extra cash from Palmas. Weekends and holidays can be quite busy.

Centro de Atendimento ao Turista (CATUR; ☎ 554 1515; Rua 24 near plaza; ⏰ 8am-noon & 2-6pm Mon-Fri) A block from the plaza, this is where

you hire guides to visit the falls. Rates are US$1.25 per person per site (minimum four people; otherwise US$5 per waterfall). Note that some falls are on private land, and charge a small entrance fee (US$1 or less). You can also rent mountain bikes here.

ACTIVITIES
There are 80 identified waterfalls, caves and pools in the area and about 15 are open to the public. You should be able to visit three to five in a day, depending on your fitness, which ones you choose and how long you stay at each one. Trails to the falls range from a few hundred meters to 8km; some are near town and others are 15km or more away. Some are tall, others good for swimming, and some are a series of tumbling rapids. Before setting out, discuss with your guide what type of falls you'd like to see, how much hiking and driving you want etc.

Popular sites include the **Cachoeria de Roncadeira**, wispy 72m falls; **Vale do Vai-Quem-Quer**, with a series of falls and good swimming spots; and the **Cachoeria do Rapel**, where you can rappel down the falls (per person US$5).

SLEEPING & EATING
You can stay in town or at one of several nearby ecolodges.

Lokau (☎ 554 1238; 3a Av 12; r per person incl breakfast US$8) Clean, comfortable rooms are nicely decorated and open onto a pleasant garden. Very friendly owners also operate

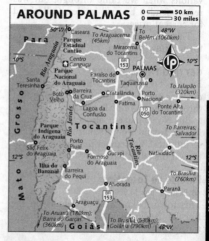

AROUND PALMAS

0 ___ 50 km
0 ___ 30 miles

an art gallery here. To get here, take road to the Fazenda Ecológica, veer right at the blue church and turn right again at the top. Also ask here about camping.

Pousada Catarse (☎ 554 1237; 2 blocks from CATUR; s/d US$5/10) Really a private home with extra space, rooms here vary in size, privacy and bathroom facilities (either private or shared). From CATUR, go downhill, turn left, then first right – it's the yellow two-story house on the corner.

Fazenda Ecológica (☎ 9994 8530, in Palmas ☎ 215 4333; 9km from Taquarussú; d/tr/q incl breakfast US$20/25/33) Reached by graded dirt road, this excellent ecolodge has large comfortable rooms, good food and breezy patios for reading, games or just enjoying the views. Easy trails, all less than a kilometer long, lead to waterfalls and swimming holes, even a long rope-swing; trips to other waterfalls can be arranged. Run by Palmas-based **Bananal Ecotour** (☎ 215 4333, 215 7624; www.bananal ecotour.com.br; ⏰ 8am-6pm Mon-Fri, 9am-noon Sat), this is good for those interested in a painless, low-key visit, even with kids. Lunch costs US$4 and dinner US$5. Reservations are recommended. If you don't have a car, Bananal Ecotour can arrange transfers to/from Palmas (US$20).

Hotel Fazenda Encantada (☎ 214 2102, 9977 4457; 2km from Fazenda Ecológicar; US$45-50; 🛏️) This is a more upscale ecolodge, with modern rooms and bungalows, an attractive pool and six different waterfalls accessed by a network of paths. It was closed for renovations when we came through, but was recommended by area guides. Call ahead for current prices.

There are several simple restaurants in town facing the plaza.

GETTING THERE & AWAY
By car, take Hwy TO-010 past the *rodoviária* and follow the signs, passing first through the town of Taquaralto.

Bus No 90 passes Galería Bela Palma on its way to and from Taquarussú (US$1.50; 45 minutes). Remember that you need a car to visit the falls there.

Paraíso do Tocantins
☎ 0xx63 / pop 34,000
This town, 60km west of Palmas on the Brasília–Belém Hwy BR-153, is primarily a transportation hub.

SLEEPING
Hotel Triángulo (☎ 602 2330; Rua Alfredo Nascer 941; with fan r without bathroom US$3.50, s/d with bathroom US$5/8:30, with 🕹️ US$8.50/10). Directly opposite the bus station, rooms here are small and clean.

Mirante Plaza Hotel (☎ 602 2099; Av Transbrasiliana s/n; s/d US$11.50/20) About a kilometer from the *rodoviária*, on the main highway near the intersection with Rua Alfredo Nascer, this spiffy hotel has spotless modern rooms and fine views from its patio.

GETTING THERE & AWAY
From the station in **Paraíso** (☎ 6026644), mid-size buses zip to Palmas (US$1.50, 1½ hours, every 30 to 45 minutes between 6am and 8:30pm) while **Transbrasiliana** (☎ 602 6644) has a long-range service to Brasília (US$29, 14 hours, six daily 7am to 9pm); Goiâna (US$21.50, 12 hours, five daily 7am to 11:30pm); Belém (US$35, 22 hours, four daily 6pm to 2am) and other cities.

Jalapão
Jalapão is a unique 34,000-sq-km area in far eastern Tocantins, combining cerrado vegetation, hills, caves, crystalline rivers and springs, 40m-high sand dunes, waterfalls, freshwater bathing spots, odd rock formations, quite a range of wildlife – including anteaters, armadillos, macaws and rheas – and very few people indeed. The season to explore Jalapão is the dry season from June to September.

Andrey Luciano (☎ 8111 1208; curupiraradical@bol .com.br) is an experienced guide and all-around friendly guy who leads recommended tours of Jalapão. A four-day/three-night trip including transportation, meals and plenty of hiking costs US$300 to US$350 per person for a group of four. You can sleep in tents or modest pensions; Luciano has all the necessary gear except sleeping bags and pads. You can also contact **Bananal Ecotour** (☎ 215 4333; 215 7624; www.bananalecotour.com.br) in Palmas.

Jalapão Adventure (☎ 244 1595, 9977 2233; jalapaoa dventure@hotmail.com) is run by an amiable English-speaking Brazilian who takes guests to Jalapão in a converted Mack truck with windows and benches – those prone to carsickness should see the truck first. A three-day/two-night trip costs US$167 per person, with visits to the major sights and overnighting in three-person tents.

RIO ARAGUAIA & ILHA DO BANANAL

The Rio Araguaia rises in the southwest of Goiás state and flows 1600km northward along the western boundaries of Goiás and Tocantins before joining the Rio Tocantins near Marabá. About 650km from its source the Araguaia bifurcates, the lesser (eastern) branch being known as the Rio Javaés. The Javaés rejoins the main river some 350km north, and the 19,000-sq-km island thus formed, the Ilha do Bananal, is arguably the world's biggest river island. (Ilha Marajó in Pará is the other candidate.) You can also access the river further south via Barra do Garças in Mato Grosso state.

The Araguaia around Ilha do Bananal and upstream to Aruanã offers some of the best freshwater fishing in the world. During the May to October fishing season, fish such as *tucunaré, pintado* (catfish), *pirarucu* and *pacu* are there for the taking. There are several agencies in Barra do Garças, Goiânia and Brasília that do all-inclusive, multiday trips here. Alternatively, take a bus from Barra do Garças to São Felix do Araguaia, which is opposite the Ilha do Bananal itself, and hire a boat there.

Peter Fleming, in his excellent and hilarious book *Brazilian Adventure*, describes an excursion in this region undertaken in an attempt to discover what had happened to the disappeared explorer Colonel Fawcett.

Ilha do Bananal

This island in the middle of a river is so big that it has its own 250km-long rivers within it! Three ecosystems – rain forest, cerrado and wetland – converge here, and it's a very good area indeed for bird-watching, with plenty of other wildlife too. About 82% of the island is cerrado, 18% rain forest, and 75% is flooded during the high-water season (which peaks about March).

Some 3500 indigenous people inhabit the island – chiefly the Karajás and Javaés tribes – some of whom produce skillfully painted pottery figurines and neatly carved wooden animals. Most of the island is Terras Indígenas (Indigenous Lands). An area of 5623 sq km in the north and northeast forms the Parque Nacional do Araguaia, but the Indians occupied this too in 2000 after falling out with IBAMA, the government environmental agency.

CENTRO CANGUÇU (BIRC)

The Centro de Pesquisas Canguçu (Canguçu Research Center), also known as Bananal Island Research Center (BIRC), is both a beautiful and comfortable ecolodge and a research center for the Palmas-based Ecológica institute, which works to preserve rain-forest areas on and around the island.

Centro Canguçu, a marvelous, rambling, stilt-built wooden lodge, stands on the east bank of the Rio Javaés facing the northeastern Ilha do Bananal. The rooms are comfortable and spacious, with private bathroom.

A standard three-day, two-night visit (US$85 per person per day, including meals) includes forest walks, nighttime alligator spotting, boat trips, and visits to a freshwater turtle rescue program. The birding is great, and mammals inhabiting the lodge area – many are nocturnal – include tapirs, brocket deer, crab-eating raccoons, crab-eating fox, pumas, margays, even jaguars. Most commonly seen are pink and gray dolphins, black caimans and giant river turtles.

Bananal Ecotour (☎ 215 4333, 215 7624; www .bananalecotour.com.br) operates the lodge as part of Ecológica, a research institute active in carbon sequestration research (related to global warming), reforestation, environmental education and more; researchers are often on-site. Transfer is not included in the price, but an Ecológica vehicle goes from Palmas about three times a week and can normally carry a few visitors for US$10 to US$15 each.

Note the park is only open July through October, due to flooding the rest of the year; reservations are strongly recommended. The park is 220km from Palmas; only about half of the road is paved.

LAGOA DA CONFUSÃO

Set beside a 15-sq-km lake in a rural area east of the Ilha do Bananal, this small, somewhat dumpy town (population 3400) is a popular getaway for Palmas families, with a sandy beach year-round. It is unlikely to make the itinerary of most travelers, but those who have a car and/or determination to see every corner of the country may find it a relaxing stop with a few decent daytrips.

The main intersection is Rua Firmino Lacerdes and Rua João Maximino de Alenquer, though there were no street signs at

THE AMAZON

the time of research. You can withdraw money on your ATM card at the post office, which cooperates with Bradesco.

Sights & Activities

There are a few lakes worth visiting in this area (most on private *fazendas*, or ranches), where birds and alligators are especially prevalent.

Raimunda Rodriguez de Souza (☎ 364 1718) is the friendly, unofficial guide here; you can usually find her working at **Bar Meu Cantinho & Restaurante** (Rua Vicente Peirera Desá 190). Popular trips include Fazenda Praia Alto, where you can see a river-turtle nursery, and Fazenda Emperador, with decent hiking. Other spots include Lago dos Pássaros (Bird Lake) and Lagoa do Coco, both good for birding. Rodriguez charges US$12 per group (up to 6 people); if you don't have a car, it is an extra US$33 for her to arrange one. Definitely call ahead.

You might ask about visiting the Indian villages of Boto Velho or Macauba, both on Ilha Bananal. In the past, Boto Velho villagers provided tours of the island, but new leadership has halted that and has even led to a split with IBAMA over the protection of the island. Note the village is very 'acculturated' – some travelers reported being disillusioned by the western clothes and satellite dishes – and you must be careful of snakes. Partly because of these problems, Rodriguez was trying to set up trips to Macauba instead, although still just an idea when we passed through.

Sleeping & Eating

Pousada Gaivota (☎ 364 1238; s/d with fan US$6.50/11, with ⚏ US$8.50/12.50) Across from the post office, this may be the first hotel you see coming into town. Rooms are clean and simple.

Pousada Raiza (☎ 364 1118; s/d with ⚏ US$8.50/11.50) Around the corner from Pousada Gaivota and facing the lake, rooms were freshly painted when we came through, but oddly crowded with hefty bunk-beds. Look for the huge white fence.

Hotel e Club Lagoa da Ilha Praia (☎ 364 1110; Rua Neuza Ribeiro s/n; s/d US$23.50/36.50; ⚏) On the west edge of town, this large complex is crowded on holidays but virtually empty otherwise. A pool and huge waterslide are fun; rooms are clean though a bit sterile for

the price. It has its own private beach and soccer field. Ask for a discount.

There are several restaurants on the waterfront, serving basic per-kilo and à la carte meals.

Getting There & Away

Buses to Lagoa da Confusão leave Palmas at 9am and 4pm (direct/via Paraíso do Tocantins US$5/US$3.50, four to five hours). As a last resort, there is also a van (☎ 923 3788) that, if you call ahead, may pick you up at your hotel; however, it seems to be a service that is unofficially restricted to locals. Buses and vans return daily to Palmas, departing from the main intersection (US$3.50 to US$5, four to five hours, departing 5:30am, 7:30am, 4:30pm, 6:30pm and 5pm). The 7:30am and 5pm departures go through Paraíso do Tocantins.

NATIVIDADE

☎ 0xx63 / pop 6200

The pleasant little town of Natividade is 230km from Palmas in southeast Tocantins, in a valley beneath the green and wooded Serra Geral. Natividade is Tocantins' oldest town, founded in 1734. The Portuguese and their African slaves had come to the Serra Geral in a minor gold rush in the 1720s. When the gold gave out they moved down the hill and turned to cattle herding. Some travelers find Natividade quaint and cozy, but a stop here really only makes sense only if you have a car and/or plenty of time.

Sights & Activities

The cobbled streets and prettily painted, tile-roofed, 18th- and 19th-century houses of Natividade's historic center are protected as part of the national historic heritage.

Igreja NS do Rosário dos Pretos known as the Igreja dos Escravos (Slaves' Church), was built in 1828 by slaves, who were not allowed to use the Whites' Church. Construction was reportedly never completed, and it remains roofless.

Museu Municipal (Praça Leopoldo de Bulhões; ⏰ 8am-1pm Mon-Fri) occupies the old prison, evident by the thick walls and heavy doors. Simple exhibits tell the story of Natividade; among the artifacts is a tree trunk to which slaves were tied for whipping.

Half a kilometer down a side street from Praça Leopoldo de Bulhões – and reputedly connected to it by a tunnel – are the **Poções**, a series of small waterfalls and refreshing natural bathing pools. From the Poções a trail leads up the Serra Geral to the remains of **São Luiz**, the original settlement of the 1720s gold prospectors. Children from the town will lead you up there for a dollar or two; you should allow a few hours for the outing.

A famous local spiritual medium, **Dona Romana**, awaits the end of the world amid a garden of her own fantastic sculpture, 1.5km north along Hwy TO-280 toward Dianópolis from the Trevo Norte junction at the north end of town. Dona Romana will cleanse your spirit if you take along some '*pinga*' (*cachaça*, or sugarcane spirit) – she mixes it with herbal potions and prays for bad spirits to be released as you drink. Or take candles and she'll place them around you and pray for the evil to depart. Or you can just talk with her and she'll walk you through the garden and tell you about the *ligações* (connections) she has experienced and about what's going to happen when the Earth's axis tilts.

About 4km from town in the same direction are the **Cachoeiras do Paraíso**, another series of natural bathing pools (dry from July to September).

You may be able to arrange a guide at the **Hotel Serra Geral** (☎ 372 1160). Daily rates are around US$20 to US$35 per group. The owner was anxious to point out that she can't guarantee anything – a day or two advance notice helps – but until a proper tourist office opens in town, it's worth a shot.

Sleeping

All the hotels below include breakfast. The first two are convenient to the center, but the last is definitely preferable if you can afford it.

Hotel Brazão (☎ 372 1916; Rua Deocleciano Nunes; r US$2.50) Small, very basic rooms with shared bathroom have saggy beds but high sloping ceilings.

Hotel July (☎ 372 1448; Rua 7 de Setembro, s/d US$3.50/6) A wee step up, rooms here are larger and have bathrooms but are still very plain.

Hotel Serra Geral (☎ 372 1160; 1.7km north of the center, 300m before the Trevo Norte; s/d with fan US$9.50/13.50, with ❄ US$15.50/23.50). Has clean, modern rooms which open onto breezy corridors.

Getting There & Away

Natividade is on the best road between Palmas and Brasília (it is longer but in much better condition than Hwy BR-153).

Between one and three buses run daily to Natividade from Palmas (US$5, three to four hours) and two from Gurupi (US$5, three hours). From Natividade, buses or vans go daily to Palmas (US$5, three hours, departing 7am, 9am, 10am, 11am, 2pm and 3pm; ensure that you arrive 30 minutes early); Gurupi (7am, 9:40am, 4pm, 7pm); Barreiras (US$9, six hours, 8:30am) and Brasília (US$17, eight hours, two departures 9pm to 10pm), with connections to Lençóis, Salvador and Goiânia.

Amazonas & Roraima

HIGHLIGHTS

- Gliding through a flooded forest in **Mamirauá Reserve** (p638), in search of the elusive uakari monkey
- Exploring the **Rio Javari** (p644) on the Peru–Colombia border
- Hiking and camping around **Boa Vista** (p648)
- Dozing in a hammock on a **riverboat** (p630) headed up the Amazon
- Enjoying night sounds and sunrises at **jungle lodges** (p634) outside Manaus

- POPULATION: 3.8 MILLION
- AREA: 1,802,900 SQ KM

The state of Amazonas, with an area of 1.58 million sq km, covers most of the western Amazon Basin and is Brazil's largest state. Here, life is lashed inextricably to the river: transportation, food, water, waste removal and, of course, tourism are all dependent on the massive river system. The river enters the state at the 'triple frontier,' where Brazil, Peru and Colombia all come together. Called the Amazon in those countries, the river is actually known as the Rio Solimões by Brazilians in this area. It flows eastward across the middle of the state, meeting one of its major tributaries, the Rio Negro, a few kilometers from the state's largest city, Manaus. East of Manaus, the river is called the Rio Amazonas (Amazon River).

Roraima, a small state north of Manaus, is mostly a land route into Venezuela or Guyana, but it also offers some interesting excursions. It is the transition zone between the tropical rain forest and the dry highlands of Venezuela, and is known for its waterfalls, rivers and strange rock and hill formations.

History

In 1842 the American Charles Goodyear developed the vulcanization process that made natural rubber durable, and in 1890 Ireland's John Dunlop patented pneumatic rubber tires. Soon there was an unquenchable demand for rubber in the recently industrialized USA and Europe, and the price of rubber on international markets soared.

In the 1880s, even as slavery was abolished a feudal production system was established, locking the *seringueiros* (rubber tappers) into serfdom. Driven from the *sertão* (backlands) by drought, and lured into the Amazon by the promise of prosperity, they signed away their freedom to *seringalistas* (owners of rubber-bearing forests).

The *seringalistas* sold goods – fishing line, knives, manioc flour, hammocks – to the *seringueiros* on credit and purchased the *seringueiros'* balls of latex. The illiteracy of the *seringueiros*, the brutality of the *pistoleiros* (hired guns), deliberately rigged scales, and the monopoly of sales and purchases all combined to perpetuate the *seringueiros'* debt and misery. The *seringueiros* also had to contend with loneliness, jungle fevers, Indian attacks and all manner of deprivation.

Despite Brazilian efforts to protect the country's world rubber monopoly, Henry Wickham managed to smuggle rubber seeds from the Amazon to London. Botanists in Kew Gardens, London, grew rubber-tree seedlings and exported them to the British colonies of Ceylon and Malay,

where they were planted in neat and efficient groves. Brazil's rubber monopoly was punctured, and as more Asian rubber was produced, the price of latex on the world market plummeted. By the 1920s the rubber boom was over.

During WWII, when Malay was occupied by Japan, Allied demand created a second brief rubber boom. The *seringueiros* became known as the 'rubber soldiers,' and 150,000 Nordestinos were recruited once again to gather rubber. Rubber prices sank again after WWII, however, and have never again reached anything like boom levels.

Brazil has always feared foreign domination of the Amazon region. One of the official slogans of the military government of the 1970s was *'Integrar para não entregar'* (essentially, 'Use it or lose it'). Governments have made a determined attempt to consolidate Brazilian control of Amazonia by cutting roads through the jungle and colonizing the interior. But anyone who braves those roads will see that nature had other plans; see the boxed texts on p601 and p660 for more information. The Amazon, while unlikely to be invaded by foreign armies, remains isolated from the rest of its country.

Climate

The Amazon has only two seasons, rainy and dry. The rainy season runs from December to June, with temperatures ranging from 23°C (73°F) to 30°C (86°F). The dry season lasts from July to November, with temperatures from 26°C (78°F) to 40°C (104°F). It is humid most of the year. That said, the rain-forest floor can be chilly, especially at night or when there's rain. Long sleeves and long pants are good to have, for cold spells and to ward off mosquitoes.

National Parks

Amazonas state has two national parks, both of which are difficult to access. Parque Nacional do Jaú (Jaú National Park) takes several days to reach by boat west of Manaus, while Parque Nacional do Pico Neblina, home of 'Foggy Peak' – at 3014m the highest point in Brazil – is almost a thousand kilometers up the Rio Negro in the northwest corner of the state.

Jaú National Park adjoins two important sustainable development reserves: Reserva de Desenvolvimento Sustenável Amanã and Reserva de Desenvolvimento Sustenável Mamirauá. The latter has an excellent ecotourism program; together, Jaú, Amanã and Mamirauá form the second-largest block of protected tropical rain forest in the world.

Roraima is home to a small national park named Parque Nacional da Serra da Mocidade, and to the famous Terra Indígena Yanomami (Yanomani Indian Reserve). Another reserve, the Reserva Indígena Waimiri Atroari, straddles Roraima and Amazonas states.

Dangers & Annoyances

Malaria exists in the Amazon and antimalarials are recommended by most tropical medicine experts. The exception is the Brazilian medical establishment, which still questions whether the effectiveness of the pills (not 100%) justifies their side effects (severe in some cases). The result is that antimalarials are hard to find in Brazil, so you should bring a full supply.

You should also get a yellow-fever vaccine, offered for free at almost any Brazilian airport, bus station or health center. The shots are effective for 10 years and may be required when entering bordering countries or to re-entering Brazil. Note that the vaccine is not effective until 10 days after its administration, and border officials may not let you pass sooner than that.

For more information about malaria, yellow fever and other health matters, see p708.

Getting There & Away

Manaus is without question the transportation hub of the Amazon. Flights arrive from all over Brazil and abroad, including Miami and Buenos Aires, and the majority of people arrive here by plane. You can also get to Amazonas state by boat, either downstream from Colombia or Peru, upstream from Belém and Santarém, or on the Rio Madeira starting in Porto Velho, in the state of Rondônia near the Bolivian border. The only land crossings are between Roraima and Venezuela or Guyana, passing through Boa Vista, the state capital.

Getting Around

Amazonas has fewer kilometers of paved road than almost any other Brazilian state. With the exception of buses to Venezuela or Guyana, boat and plane are the only means of long-distance transportation. Choosing between flying and boating is really a matter of time, money and your own preference, as virtually every town has both a port and an airstrip. Boat travel is certainly an experience, and most travelers cover at least one or two legs by water. But the distances are enormous and the boats very slow, especially going upstream. If you plan to travel much beyond Manaus, flying gives you more time to do the fun stuff (hiking, canoeing etc) and frequent promotions can make air-travel viable for all but the tightest budgets.

AMAZONAS

Half of the three million inhabitants of Amazonas live in the metropolis of Manaus. The rest are scattered in small and medium-sized villages and towns along the state's myriad rivers. Remote and far from fully explored, this state harbors more of the great Amazon rain forest and more indigenous people than any other in Brazil. With a few exceptions – chiefly the Manaus area and the areas close to the Solimões, Amazonas and Madeira Rivers – the forests are relatively intact, and opportunities for jungle experiences and wildlife spotting are at their most abundant here.

Most of Amazonas state is one hour behind Brasília time. The area west of a line drawn southeast from Tabatinga on the Colombian border to Porto Acre in eastern Acre is two hours behind Brasília time.

MANAUS

☎ 0xx92 / pop 1.67 million

Manaus stands on the north bank of the Rio Negro, 10km upstream from the Negro's confluence with the Solimões, beyond which the mighty combined river is called the Rio Amazonas. The city is an international port some 1500km from the mouth of the Amazonas – and only 40m to 80m above sea level. Upstream, it's 1500km to Leticia, Colombia, and 1900km to Iquitos, Peru.

The city itself is humid and not very clean, and has limited appeal – and the

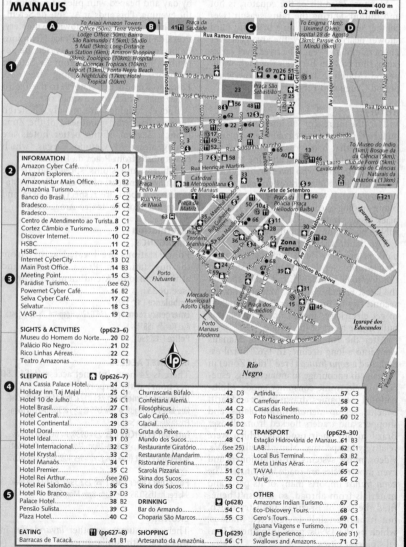

MANAUS

0 — 400 m
0 — 0.2 miles

INFORMATION

Amazon Cyber Café	1 D1
Amazon Explorers	2 C3
Amazonastur Main Office	3 B2
Amazônia Turismo	4 C3
Banco do Brasil	5 C2
Bradesco	6 C2
Bradesco	7 C1
Centro de Atendimento ao Turista	8 C1
Cortez Câmbio e Turismo	9 D2
Discover Internet	10 C2
HSBC	11 C2
HSBC	12 C1
Internet CyberCity	13 D2
Main Post Office	14 B3
Meeting Point	15 C3
Paradise Turismo	(see 62)
Powernet Cyber Café	16 B2
Selva Cyber Café	17 C3
Selvatur	18 C3
VASP	19 C2

SIGHTS & ACTIVITIES (pp623–6)

Museu do Homem do Norte	20 D2
Palácio Rio Negro	21 D2
Rico Linhas Aéreas	22 C2
Teatro Amazonas	23 C1

SLEEPING (pp626–7)

Ana Cassia Palace Hotel	24 C3
Holiday Inn Taj Majal	25 C1
Hotel 10 de Julho	26 C1
Hotel Brasil	27 C1
Hotel Central	28 C3
Hotel Continental	29 C3
Hotel Doral	30 D3
Hotel Ideal	31 D3
Hotel Internacional	32 C3
Hotel Krystal	33 C2
Hotel Manaòs	34 C1
Hotel Premier	35 C2
Hotel Rei Arthur	(see 26)
Hotel Rei Salomão	36 C3
Hotel Rio Branco	37 D3
Palace Hotel	38 D3
Pensão Sulista	39 C3
Plaza Hotel	40 C3

EATING (pp627–8)

Barracas de Tacacà	41 B1
Churrascaria Búfalo	42 D3
Confeitaria Alemã	43 C2
Filosóphicus	44 C2
Galo Carijó	45 D3
Glacial	46 D2
Gruta do Peixe	47 C2
Mundo dos Sucos	48 C1
Restaurante Giratório	(see 25)
Restaurante Mandarim	49 C2
Ristorante Fiorentina	50 C2
Scarola Pizzaria	51 C1
Skina dos Sucos	52 C2
Skina dos Sucos	53 C2

DRINKING (p628)

Bar do Armando	54 C1
Choparia São Marcos	55 C1

SHOPPING (p629)

Artesanato da Amazônia	56 C1
Artíndia	57 C3
Carrefour	58 C2
Casas das Redes	59 C3
Foto Nascimento	60 D2

TRANSPORT (pp629–30)

Estação Hidroviária de Manaus	61 B3
LAB	62 C1
Local Bus Terminal	63 B2
Meta Linhas Aéras	64 C2
TAVAJ	65 C2
Varig	66 C2

OTHER

Amazonas Indian Turismo	67 C3
Eco-Discovery Tours	68 C3
Gero's Tours	69 C1
Iguana Viagens e Turismo	70 C1
Jungle Experience	(see 31)
Swallows and Amazons	71 C2

THE AMAZON

flora and fauna have been despoiled for some distance around it. Many travelers use Manaus as a brief stopover before making excursions far beyond it, where it is still possible to experience the rain forest wonders that Manaus cannot deliver.

See p631 for information on jungle trips that you can make from here, and places to stay in the surrounding area.

Manaus, 3° south of the equator, is hot and humid. During the rainy season (December to May), count on a brief but hard shower nearly every day; the area gets over 2m of rainfall per year. The river level varies from 10m to 14m between the high-water period (March to July) and the low-water period (August to February).

History

In 1669 the fortress of São José da Barra was built here by Portuguese colonizers. In 1856 the village that had grown up around the fort was renamed Manaus, after the Manaos, a tribe of Indians who lived in the Ponta Negra area (on the northwestern edge of the modern city). It remained little more than a minor trading outpost populated by traders, black slaves, Indians and soldiers until the rubber boom pumped up the town.

The landowners, rubber traders and bankers prospered and built palaces with their wealth. Gentlemen sent their shirts to London to be laundered, and ladies sported the latest French fashions. Manaus was the second city in Brazil (after Rio de Janeiro) to get electricity, and an opera house was built in the heart of the jungle.

After the rubber boom faded, Manaus went into a long decline. In 1967 Brazil established a *zona franca* (Free Trade Zone) in Manaus to encourage manufacturing, especially of electronic consumer goods. Multinational companies, drawn by tax and tariff benefits, set up manufacturing plants, and shoppers and traders flocked from all over Brazil to buy their products, which were relatively inexpensive. Many Brazilian TVs, videos, music systems, air-conditioners and even motorcycles are made in Manaus. The *zona franca* imports many of its parts and materials from abroad, so it hasn't benefited the rest of Brazilian industry much, but it has certainly invigorated Manaus, which by the 1990s, grew into one of Brazil's biggest cities.

Orientation

Downtown Manaus stretches from the Rio Negro to the Teatro Amazonas area, about 1km back from the waterfront. The streets nearest the main passenger port, the Porto Flutuante (Floating Dock), are crowded and fairly grungy. A little inland is an area of shopping streets known as the Zona Franca (Free Trade Zone), lined with street vendors by day and heaped with piles of garbage in the evening. This ends at Av Sete de Setembro, the main east–west downtown artery. Praça da Polícia (officially Praça Heliodoro Balbi), on the south side of Av Sete de Setembro, is a focal point. From Av Sete de Setembro, a fancier shopping street, Av Eduardo Ribeiro, heads north to the Teatro Amazonas, which tops a small rise.

Budget lodgings are mostly clustered across a few streets southeast of the Zona Franca. Several of the better hotels are strung along Av Getúlio Vargas, which heads north from Praça da Polícia.

Suburbs and slums spread far to the north, west and east of the city. The bus station and airport are respectively 6km and 13km north of the Teatro Amazonas.

Information
EMERGENCY

Police stations are located across from the bus station on Praça da Matriz and at the Centro de Atendimento ao Turista (see p623).

Ambulance (☎ 192)

Emergency room (☎ 236 0326; Hospital 28 de Agosto, Rua Recife 1581)

Police (☎ 190)

INTERNET ACCESS

There is 24-hour Internet access (US$3.50 per hour) at the airport.

Discover Internet (☎ 233 0121; Rua Marcílio Dias at Rua José Paranaguá; per hr US$1; ⊗ 8:30am-7pm Mon-Fri, 8:30am-5pm Sat)

Internet CyberCity (☎ 234 8930; Av Getúlio Vargas 188; per hr US$1; ⊗ 8am-10pm Mon-Fri, 9am-9pm Sat)

Meeting Point (Rua dos Andrades 408; per hr US$0.85; ⊗ 9am-11pm)

Powernet Cyber Café (☎ 232 3927; Rua 24 de Maio 94; per hr US$0.85; ⊗ 8am-8pm Mon-Sat)

LAUNDRY

There are numerous other *lavandarías* in this area, with similar prices.

Meeting Point (Rua dos Andrades 408; per small/large item US$0.15/0.25; ⏲ 9am-11pm) Same-day laundry service.

LEFT LUGGAGE
The airport and bus station both have left-luggage service.

MEDICAL SERVICES
Hospital 28 de Agosto (☎ 236 8896, 236 0326; Rua Recife 1581) Nearest emergency room, 3km north of center.
Hospital de Doenças Tropicais (Hospital of Tropical Illnesses; ☎ 238 1767, 238 1146; Av Pedro Teixeira 25) Specializes in tropical diseases.
Unimed (☎ 633 4431; Av Japurá 241) One of the best private hospitals in the city.
Yellow fever vaccines airport (⏲ 24hr); bus station (⏲ 8am-noon & 2-5pm Mon-Fri) Given for free at the Hospital de Doenças Tropicais, and at *postos de saude* (health clinics) at the airport and bus station.

MONEY
The airport has Banco 24 Horas ATMs just outside the terminal building.
Amazônia Turismo (☎ 622 7206; Rua Dr Moreira 88; ⏲ 9am-5pm Mon-Fri, 9am-noon Sat) Good exchange rates for US dollars and euros, plus Amex and Visa traveler's checks.
Banco do Brasil (Rua Guilherme Moreira 315; exchange office ⏲ 9am-3pm Mon-Fri) Exchange foreign cash and traveler's checks at the exchange office on the 3rd floor.
Bradesco Av Sete de Setembro (Av Sete de Setembro at Rua Barroso); Av Eduardo Ribeiro (Av Eduardo Ribeiro at Rua Saldanha Marinho) Both branches have reliable ATMs.
Cortez Câmbio e Turismo (☎ 621 4444; Av Sete de Setembro 1199; ⏲ 9am-5pm Mon-Sat) Good rates for US, Canadian, Australian, Japanese and European cash, plus Amex and Visa traveler's checks.
HSBC Rua Dr Moreira 226 (Rua Dr Moreira 226; ⏲ 9am-3pm Mon-Fri); Rua 24 de Maio (Rua 24 de Maio at Rua Azevedo; ⏲ 9am-3pm Mon-Fri) Reliable ATMS for both banks are available from 8am-5pm daily.
Selvatur (☎ 622 2577; Praça Tenreiro Aranha 17; ⏲ 8am-6pm Mon-Fri, 8am-noon Sat, 8-9am Sun) The local Amex representative.

POST
Airport post office (lower level; ⏲ 9:30am-12:30pm & 1:30-5pm)
Branch post office (Rua Marcílio Dias 160; ⏲ 9am-5pm Mon-Fri, 8am-noon Sat)
Main post office (Rua Marechal Deodoro 117; ⏲ 9am-5pm Mon-Fri, 8am-noon Sat)

Selvatur (☎ 622 2577; Praça Tenreiro Aranha 17; ⏲ 8am-6pm Mon-Fri, 8am-noon Sat, 8-9am Sun) Will hold packages sent to Amex cardholders for up to 30 days. The mailing address is: Praça Adalberto Vale 17; Centro, CEP. 69005-290; Manaus, Amazonas, Brasil.

TELEPHONE
Embratel cards, available at the post office, are best for making international calls from payphones (US$0.50 per minute).
Discover Internet (☎ 233 0121; Rua Marcílio Dias at Rua José Paranaguá; ⏲ 8:30am-7pm Mon-Fri, 8:30am-5pm Sat) Has Web-based international phone service to most countries for US$0.35 to land lines and US$0.65 to overseas mobile phones.

TOURIST INFORMATION
Amazonastur (Amazonas state tourism secretariat; www.visitamazonas.com.br); main office (☎ 233 1095; Rua H de Figueiredo 321; ⏲ 8am-5pm Mon-Fri); Centro de Atendimento ao Turista (Tourist Assistance Center; ☎ 622 0767, 231 1998; Av Eduardo Ribeiro at Rua José Clemente; ⏲ 9am-5pm Mon-Fri, 9am-1pm Sat) Possibly open Sun by 2005; airport (☎ 652 1120; ⏲ 7am-11pm); Amazon Shopping (☎ 648 1396; ⏲ 9am-10pm Mon-Sat, 3-9pm Sun) The airport and main offices, which have multilingual attendants, are the most helpful. All should have information on jungle lodges and tour operators – although they cannot give specific recommendations – plus maps and brochures about Manaus itself.

TRAVEL AGENCIES
There is no shortage of travel agencies in Manaus. A few well-established companies include:
Amazon Explorers (☎ 232 3052; Praça Tenreiro Aranha; ⏲ 7:30am-noon & 2-5pm Mon-Fri, 7:30-11:30am Sat, 7:30-9am Sun)
Paradise Turismo (☎ 633 8301; Av Eduardo Ribeiro 656; ⏲ 8am-6pm Mon-Fri, 8:30am-noon Sat)
Selvatur (☎ 622 2577; Praça Tenreiro Aranha; ⏲ 8am-6pm Mon-Fri, 8am-noon Sat, 8-9am Sun)

Dangers & Annoyances
The area around the boat docks and northeast of Praça da Matriz can get quite seedy at night – it's best to avoid them. The city has plans to install more lights and police at Praça da Matriz and Praça da Polícia, which will help.

Sights
TEATRO AMAZONAS
Manaus' famous opera house, the **Teatro Amazonas** (☎ 622 2420, tickets ☎ 232 1768; Rua

Jose Clemente at Av Eduardo Ribeiro; 🕙 9am-5pm), was designed in eclectic neoclassical style by engineers from Lisbon and a team of interior designers at the height of the rubber boom. Opened in 1896, this beautiful theater symbolizes the opulence that once was Manaus. The artists and most of the materials (Italian marble and glass, Scottish cast iron) were imported from Europe. The wood is Brazilian but even some of that was sent to Europe to be carved. One truly homespun feature was the roadway outside the entrance; it is made of rubber, so that late-arriving carriages wouldn't create too much noise. The theater has been restored four times (most recently in 1990).

Interesting guided tours (US$1.75, 30 minutes, 9am to 4pm) are offered every day except Sunday, often in English. Concerts (classical and popular), opera, theater and dance events are held all year, with tickets rarely costing more than US$6.50. There's an excellent opera festival held here every April and May (see opposite).

PORTO FLUTUANTE & ALFÂNDEGA

Officially called the Estação Hidroviária de Manaus, the **Porto Flutuante** (Floating Dock) is where you'll disembark if you come to Manaus by boat. Inaugurated in 1902 and designed by the British, it was considered a technical marvel because it rises and falls with seasonal water levels, which can vary as much as 14m (annual high-water points are marked on the wall beside the bridge leading to the dock). It's quite a scene, with cargo and passengers being loaded and unloaded. You used to be able to just wander around, but it is now restricted to passengers only. A bridge just to the right of the port entrance leads to a very pleasant shopping and eating area with good views of the docks.

The **Alfândega** (Customhouse; admission free; 🕙 9am-noon & 2-5pm Mon-Fri), beside the Porto Flutuante's entrance, dates from 1906. It was imported from the UK in prefabricated blocks.

MERCADO MUNICIPAL ADOLFO LISBOA

This imposing cast-iron city market building opened in 1882, a copy in miniature of Paris' famed Les Halles market. Although the Art Nouveau ironwork was imported from Europe, the place has acquired Amazonian character. In and around the mar-

ket, you can purchase just about anything, from leather hats and Indian crafts to bizarre fruits and traditional medicines.

PALÁCIO RIO NEGRO

Built in the early 20th century as a home for an eccentric German rubber baron, Waldemar Scholz, the **Palácio Rio Negro** (☎ 232 4450; Av Sete de Setembro 1546; admission free; 🕙 10am-5pm Tue-Fri, 4-9pm Sun) later served the state capital before being converted into a cultural center in the 1990s. Worth visiting, the main house hosts concerts, temporary art exhibits and has a good coffee shop, while outlying buildings contain the **Pinacoteca de Amazonas** (the state art gallery), a coin museum, a sound-and-image library and a tourist office. Free guided tours (sometimes available in English) are given to some parts of the center.

MUSEU DO HOMEM DO NORTE

Renovated in 2001 the **Museu do Homem do Norte** (Museum of Northern Man; ☎ 232 5373l; Av Sete de Setembro 1385; admission US$1; 🕙 8am-noon, 1-5pm Mon-Fri) is an ethnology and anthropology museum dedicated to the lifestyle of the people of northern Brazil, especially the riverbank-dwelling Caboclos (literally 'copper-colored;' the mixed descendents of indigenous peoples and Portuguese). The collection includes an interesting array of Indian weapons, including the vicious *furador de olhos* (eye piercer).

MUSEU DO ÍNDIO

Sandwiched between two churches and run by Salesian nuns, the **Museu do Índio** (Rua Duque de Caxias 296; admission US$1.50; 🕙 8:30-noon & 2-5pm Mon-Fri, 8am-noon Sat) displays artwork, musical instruments, fishing and hunting tools and ritual objects of the Indian tribes of the northwest Pará, where the nuns operate as missionaries. Explanations are in Portuguese, English and German.

The museum is a long kilometer walk down busy Av Sete de Setembro, but the Museo do Homem do Norte and Palácio Rio Negro, plus the full range of Manaus architecture, from rubber-boom mansions to modern shops and stilted houses on the riverfront, are on the way. Alternatively, bus No 606 (US$0.50) from Av Floriano Peixoto, opposite Praça da Polícia, stops nearby.

BOSQUE DA CIÊNCIA

Occupying a 130,000-sq-m plot of rain forest within the city, the **Bosque da Ciência** (Forest of Science; ☎ 643 3135, 643 3192; admission US$2; ☉ 9am-4pm Tue-Sun, ticket office closed 11am-2pm weekdays) has several somewhat dreary animal enclosures, including giant otters, caimans and turtles. A highlight is the manatee pool, with underwater glass windows. These reclusive creatures, *peixe boi,* known in Portuguese as 'cow fish,' and virtually impossible to see in the wild, are best viewed after their pool is cleaned (usually Wednesday and Friday mornings). Sloths, anteaters, several bird species and monkeys that have apparently escaped from the monkey enclosures roam free and can sometimes be spotted. Also within the park is the Casa da Ciência, with exhibits ranging from medicinal plants to the harmful effects of gold prospecting.

The park is part of the **Instituto Nacional de Pesquisas da Amazônia** (INPA – National Institute of Amazonia Research; ☎ 643 3377; www.inpa.gov.br), which has a staff of around 700 and conducts both basic research and sustainable development projects.

Bosque da Ciência is located in the Petrópolis district, 5km northeast of central Manaus. Bus No 519 from Praça da Matriz or from Av Floriano Peixoto, opposite Praça da Polícia, takes about 20 minutes and stops just outside. Consider combining this with a visit to the (relatively) nearby Museu de Ciências Naturais da Amazônia.

MUSEU DE CIÊNCIAS NATURAIS DA AMAZÔNIA

Known by many locals as the Museu Japonesa (Japanese Museum), because it is run by Japanese-Brazilians and located in a predominately Japanese-Brazilian area, the **Museu de Ciências Naturais da Amazônia** (Amazon Natural Sciences Museum; ☎ 644 2799; Estrada Belém s/n; adult/student US$3.50/1.25; ☉ 9am-5pm Mon-Sat) has an extensive exhibit of stuffed fish, preserved butterflies and some unnervingly large beetles and spiders from the region, with descriptions in English, Portuguese and Japanese. A modest aquarium contains live Amazon fish, including the impressive 2m-long *pirarucu.*

You can get close by bus No 519, the same bus that goes to the Bosque da Ciência. Tell the conductor you're going to the

museum and ask for directions from there (a somewhat complicated, 20-minute walk through a semiresidential area). An easier option is to take the bus to the Bosque da Ciência and then cab it from there (US$4); to get back, ask the taxi driver to return (an hour ought to be enough) or ask in the museum gift shop for directions – it has free maps on hand for car-less visitors.

PARQUE DO MINDÚ

Six kilometers from the center and occupying some 330,000 sq m of forest within the city, **Parque do Mindú** (Av Perimetral s/n; admission free; ☉ 8am-5pm Tue-Sun) is one of the last refuges of the pied bareface tamarin, a small primate threatened with extinction. The park has trails, elevated walkways and an orchid house. The entrance is in the Parque Dez district. Take bus No 423 or 433 from Praça da Matriz (US$0.50, 30 minutes).

ZOOLÓGICO

Operated by CIGS, a jungle survival unit of the Brazilian army, the **zoo** (☎ 625 2044; admission US$0.75; ☉ 9am-4:30pm Tue-Sat, 9am-6:30pm Sun) contains hundreds of animals that have reportedly been 'rescued' by soldiers training in the rain forest. The exhibit most people seem to remember is the large pit accessed by a small walkway and filled with anacondas. Take bus No 120 from Praça da Matriz (US$0.50, 20 minutes).

PRAIA DE PONTA NEGRA

A strip of river beach on the edge of Manaus 13km northwest of the center, **Praia de Ponta Negra** (Ponta Negra Beach) is a popular weekend hangout. It has many restaurants and bars and a riverbank amphitheater. The beach is largest from September to December, but it's worth a visit year-round. While here you can pop into the luxury Hotel Tropical (see p627). From Praça da Matriz or the corner of Av Floriano Peixoto and Rua Quintino Bocaiúva, take the No 120 'Ponta Negra Centro' bus (30 minutes). On the way you will see the contrast between the *favelas* (slums) with fenced residential compounds, and the beginnings of high-rise, beachfront development.

Festivals & Events

The June **Festival Folclórico do Amazonas** features a wide variety of regional folklore performances, including rehearsals of the Parintins Boi-Bumbá teams (see p636). The festival culminates on June 29 with the Procissão Fluvial de São Pedro (St Peter River Procession), when hundreds of riverboats parade on the Rio Negro before Manaus to honor the patron saint of fishers.

Inaugurated in 1997, the annual **Manaus Opera Festival** brings high-quality opera deep into the rain forest at the Teatro Amazonas. The three-week gala takes place in April and May, and regularly features world-renowned soloists, and both classical operas and a selection of Brazilian compositions. The city does an admirable job of making events accessible to all – unsold tickets are often given away free to children and audience apparel ranges from tuxedos to jeans and T-shirts that have obviously done duty out on a recent jungle trek. Tickets and schedules are available at the Teatro Amazonas (p623) several weeks before the festival opens.

Sleeping

All hotels listed here include free breakfast unless otherwise indicated. For information on jungle lodge accommodations outside the city, see p634.

BUDGET

The area east of the center and south of Av Sete de Setembro has been a budget area for many years – and still is – but has grown somewhat seedy, with many hotels charging by the hour.

Pensão Sulista (☎ 234 5814; Av Joaquim Nabuco 347; s/d/tr with shared bathroom & fan US$5/8.25/12.50, with private bathroom & air-con US$8.25/11.75/16.75) On a somewhat nicer block than some in this area, this pleasant, wood-constructed building has small *quartos* (rooms with shared bathroom) with clean bathrooms. Private rooms have good bathrooms as well, and are slightly larger. Good value and, not surprisingly, often full – call ahead.

Hotel Ideal (☎ 622 0038; Rua dos Andradas 491; s/d/tr with fan US$5.50/8.75/10.75, with air-con US$8.75/11.75/14, with TV US$11.75/14.75/16.75; ✿) The basic, relatively clean rooms are okay but dim; those with windows or even a small balcony are much more pleasant. Jungle Experience, an experienced tour operator, is based here.

Hotel Rio Branco (☎ 233 4019; Rua dos Andradas 484; s/d with shared bathroom US$5.75/6.25, with private bathroom & fan US$6.75/10, with air-con US$9.25/12.75; ✿) Across the street from the Hotel Ideal, the rooms here are about the same quality.

Hotel Doral (☎ 232 4102; Av Joaquim Nabuco 687; s/d with fan US$5/6.75, with air-con $6.75/8.25; ✿) Another of the same standard, although closer to the center and across from an excellent restaurant. There are other cheapies nearby, but most of them double as short-stay hotels.

Hotel Continental (☎ 233 3342; Rua Coronel Sergio Pessoa 189; s/d/tr US$11/$14.75/16.75; ✿) A step up from most of the other hotels, all rooms here have air-con and TV and are reasonably sized, if a bit rundown. Ask to see a few before choosing. This place is near the city market and the port for speedboats to Tefé and Santarém. Discounts are often available.

Hotel 10 de Julho (☎ 232 6280; www.hoteldezde julho.com; Rua 10 de Julho 679; s/d US$11.75/13.25, with minibar US$15/16.75; ✿) Large and rambling with friendly staff, this hotel has basic, clean, comfortable rooms, all with air-con and TV. A bit far from the center, but in a safer area, not far from the Teatro Amazonas. A good choice, overall. Gero's Tours and Iguana Tours operate in and around here.

Hotel Rei Arthur (☎ 622 5525; Rua 10 de Julho 681; r US$10, with breakfast US$11.50; ✿) Next door to the Hotel 10 de Julho, the rooms here are large and boxy, and a bit stuffy but with high ceilings. All have TV, air-con, minibar and private bathroom.

MID-RANGE

Hotel Brasil (☎ 233 6575; Av Getúlio Vargas 657; s/d/tr US$26.25/33/38.25; ✿ ✿) On a busy, safe street, the rooms at Brasil have air-con, TV, sofas and large beds; a few have patios. They're a bit dated, but decent value. There's a small swimming pool. Discounts are available for two nights or more, or if you stay less than 12 hours.

Hotel Rei Salomão (☎ 234 7374; Rua Dr Moreira 119; s/d/tr US$16/21/26.75) One of several hotels in the city's commercial district, the service is good and rooms are sizable, although a bit sterile – hospital rooms c 1971 comes to mind. Prices here are for cash payment – a full 50% off the listed rate.

Hotel Central (☎ 622 2600; fax 622 2609; Rua Dr Moreira 202; s/d/tr US$24/29.25/37.25) Also in the commercial district, rooms here are somewhat aged but comfortable, with nice details, such as tiled bathrooms. Upstairs rooms are better. Prices seem negotiable, on top of the 10% discount for longer stays.

Plaza Hotel (☎ 232 7766; plazahot@internext.com.br; Av Getúlio Vargas 215; s/d US$25.25/29.25; ✵) Comfortable and modern, if unspectacular, all rooms here have air-con and TV. There's a decent restaurant, as well.

Hotel Internacional (☎ 633 7034; fax 231 2070; Rua Dr Moreira 168; s/d/tr US$32.75/40/46.75; ✵) A few doors down from the Central, this hotel has clean, sizable rooms in good condition, all with air-con, TV and fridge. It's the best of the hotels in this area.

Hotel Krystal (☎ 233 7535; krystalhotel@internext .com.br; Rua Barroso 54; s/d/tr US$27/33/45; ✵) A clean, comfortable, modern hotel. Rooms have air-con, TV, fridge and spotless bathrooms with glass shower stalls. A great breakfast is served and discounts are available for staying two or more nights.

Ana Cassia Palace Hotel (☎ 622 3637; fax 234 4163; hacassia@internext.com.br; Rua dos Andradas 14; s/d/tr US$36/46.25/55; ✵ ✵) Near the port, the rooms here are modern and large, with TV and air-con; the higher south-facing ones have spectacular views of the river, as do the top-floor restaurant and pool. In fact, ask for a discount if you *don't* get a view, or if you stay two days or more.

TOP END

Hotel Manaós (☎ 633 5744; manaos@horizon.com.br; Av Eduardo Ribeiro 881; s/d US$36/45) Well located across from the Teatro Amazonas, this is the place to come for a bit of old-fashioned solidity and comfort, with excellent rooms sporting thick wood furnishings and comfy beds.

Holiday Inn Taj Mahal (☎ /fax 627 3737; tajmahal@ internext.com.br; Av Getúlio Vargas 741; s/d US$58/67; ✵) Upscale, high-rise rooms with all the fixings. Some have great views of the opera house, as does the rotating rooftop restaurant. There is a small pool on the roof, and a travel agency and jewelry shop in the lobby.

Hotel Tropical (☎ 658 5000; fax 658 5026; Av Coronel Teixeira 1320, Ponta Negra; www.tropicalhotel .com.br; d/tr/ste from US$121/182/242; ✵) Manaus' premier luxury hotel is a self-contained resort, 16km northwest of the center at Ponta Negra. Add 12% for taxes to room prices (although you might get a cheaper

deal through a travel agency). This huge complex boasts lush gardens, its own little shopping center, a mini-zoo, travel agencies, an orchidarium, a superb giant pool and numerous sports facilities.

Eating

Filosóphicus (☎ 234 2224; 3rd fl, Av Sete de Setembro 752; self-service per kg US$4.75; ✵ 11am-2:30pm Mon-Fri) Vegetarians should head to this small upstairs restaurant, serving a creative lunch buffet – the only truly no-meat place we could find in town.

Churrascaria Búfalo (☎ 633 3773; Av Joaquim Nabuco 628; buffet US$10; ✵ lunch & dinner) Decidedly nonvegetarian, this Manaus institution serves an excellent buffet, including fresh salads and endless meats, sliced right onto your plate from huge sizzling skewers.

Restaurante Mandarim (Rua Joaquim Sarmento 224; self-service per kg US$5.50, dishes US$5-10; ✵ lunch & dinner Mon-Sat) Serving decent Chinese dishes, in typically huge portions, this is one of few places in this area that is open late.

Scarola Pizzaria (☎ 234 8542; Rua 10 de Julho 739; dishes US$5-10) Offers an unbeatable combination of good pizzas, good service and good *chope* (draft beer). One of the few places open late, and it delivers as well.

Restaurante Giratório (Holiday Inn Taj Mahal; ☎ /fax 627 3737; tajmahal@internext.com.br; Av Getúlio Vargas 741; dishes US$7-10; ✵ lunch & dinner) A revolving restaurant overlooking the Teatro Amazonas, with an international menu, including salmon, shrimp and filet mignon.

Ristorante Fiorentina (☎ 215 2231; Rua José Paranaguá 44; dishes US$6-10; ✵ lunch & dinner) Facing Praça da Polícia, this old-standby serves a good per-kilo buffet lunch and equally good à la carte fare in the evening, with pasta, pizza, fish and meats.

Confeitaria Alemá (Rua José Paranaguá 126; self-service per kg US$6.25, dishes US$3-5) A few doors down from Ristorante Fiorentina, this spot offers more low-key dining, with a large per-kilo lunch buffet and a range of sandwiches and *refeições* (main dishes, served with rice and beans) served all day.

Galo Carijó (cnr Rua dos Andradas & Rua Pedro Botelho; dishes US$2-7; ✵ lunch Mon-Sat) Good, cheap fish dishes. As much a bar as a restaurant, join the locals on hot days for *uma cerveja estupidamente gelada* (an idiotically cold beer).

Barracas de tacacá (Praça da Saudade; ✵ 4pm-midnight) These are street stalls serving *tacacá*, a gummy soup made from dried shrimp, manioc root (a major staple of Amazon river dwellers; packed with cyanide, it is deadly if not prepared properly) and *jambú* (Amazonian herb) leaves, which can create a tingly, jumpy feeling in your lips. Still game? Try *tacacá sem goma* (*tacacá* without the gooey stuff) – it is less off-putting.

Glacial (Av Getúlio Vargas 161 & 188) The most popular ice-cream chain in town. There are two branches on this one corner – No 161 sells per kilo, a good way to sample flavors.

Skina dos Sucos (Juice Corner; ☎ 233 1970; ices US$0.75, snacks US$1-4; ☉ 7am-7:45pm Mon-Fri, 7am-7pm Sat)); Av Eduardo Ribeiro (cnr Av Eduardo Ribeiro & Rua 24 de Maio); Rua Joaquim Sarmento (cnr Rua Joaquim Sarmento & Rua Saldanha Marinho) Great juices of more than a dozen Amazonian fruits – our favorites are guaraná (a type of berry), *acerola* (acidic, cherry-flavored fruit), *cupuaçú* (acidic, slightly pear-like fruit) and *graviola* (custard apple). You can also order sandwiches and other simple snacks here.

Entertainment

There are a few quiet bars in town, but for more of a party scene, head to Ponta Negra.

Bar do Armando (Rua 10 de Julho 593; ☉ noon-midnight Mon-Sat) Near the opera house, this is a traditional rendezvous place for Manaus' intellectual types and it is known for its ice-cold beer.

Choparia São Marcos (Rua Quintino Bocaiúva 369; ☉ 8am-8pm Mon-Sat) On the noisy corner of Av Floriano Peixoto, this is another traditional bar recommended for *chope* and *bolinhos de bacahau* (fish balls; US$0.50).

Scarola Pizzaria (☎ 234 8542; Rua 10 de Julho 739) Yet another decent spot to take in a few beers.

Laranjinha Bar (admission free; ☉ from 9pm Mon-Sat) On the waterfront, Laranjinha is the heart of the action at Ponta Negra and a good place to start out your night. Live music and shows are held on weekends and many weekdays.

Purão do Alemão (admission free; ☉ from 11pm Fri & Sat), **Coração Blue** (☎ 658 4057; admission US$3.50; ☉ from 9pm Mon-Sat) and **Hollywood Beer** (admission US$3.50; ☉ from 11pm Fri & Sat) are located in that order on Estrada de Ponta Negra. All are lively, safe places frequented by tourists and locals alike. Coração Blue is good for dancing, with a different theme every night, including *forró* (the music and dance style of the Northeast) on Monday and 'Tourist Night' on Tuesday. Hollywood Beer has a DJ on Friday and live rock on Saturday.

Club de Forró (Estrada do Aleixo s/n, near Bosque de Ciência; ☉ from 11pm Thu only) A good *forró* spot, also known as the Club dos Sargentos da Aeronautica (Sargents Aeronautical Club).

Jack and Blue (Estrada de Ponta Negra s/n; ☉ daily) Right on the beach, this club plays mostly reggae music.

Fellice (Studio 5 mall; ☉ 11am-late) This bar and restaurant brews its own beer and features live music of various genres.

Enigma (☎ 234 7985; Rua Silva Ramos 1054; ☉ 11pm-late Thu-Sat) A mixed gay/lesbian/straight *boate*

GUARANÁ: FOUNTAIN OF ETERNAL YOUTH

Indigenous Amazonians have drunk guaraná for hundreds of years. The Sateré-Maûé Indians believe themselves to be descended from a guaraná tree, and *çapo* of guaraná, prepared from the tree's berries, is a ritual drink for them. The berries, which resemble eyeballs, are collected before the fruit opens, then dried, washed and cooked in earth ovens. Water is added, and the guaraná is molded into black sticks, which are then dried in a smokehouse. The Maûé shave guaraná flakes from the sticks, using either the raspy tongue of the *pirarucu* fish or a rough stone. The flakes are then mixed into water to make the *çapo*.

The Maûé drink *çapo* of guaraná on important occasions – to affirm the life force, to cure all illness, to bring strength in times of war and to enhance fertility in times of peace. In late November or early December the Festa do Guaraná is celebrated in the town of Maûés (about 200km east of Manaus), in the main guaraná-cultivating area.

Guaraná, which has a higher caffeine content than coffee, is drunk by other Brazilians both in carbonated 'champagne' form and in cocktails with other liquids such as milk, syrups and even quail eggs. Among dozens of beneficial effects, believers say guaraná improves blood circulation, reduces 'menstrual colic,' treats hemorrhoids and diarrhea, regulates the uterus and ovaries and even cures hangovers.

(nightclub) about 1km north of the center, with beat music and dancing.

Shopping

Artíndia (Praça Tenreiro Aranha s/n; 8:30am-noon & 2-5pm Mon-Fri) Housed in a prefabricated English-built cast-iron building from the rubber-boom days, this shop has perhaps the city's largest selection of Indian crafts, ranging from junky to spectacular.

Artesanato da Amazônia (232 3979; Rua José Clemente 500; 8am-5pm Mon-Fri, 8am-noon Sat) Another shop with a large and varied selection of Indian and Brazilian art and crafts. It is one of several shops in a row, facing the Teatro Amazonas.

Museu do Índio (Rua Duque de Caxias 296; 8:30-noon & 2-5pm Mon-Fri, 8am-noon Sat) The museum has a gift shop with a decent selection of *artesanato* (handicrafts), including some good baskets and palm-fiber hammocks.

Street market (Av Eduardo Ribeiro, north of Av Sete de Setembro; 6am-2pm Sun) A chance to browse some unusual homemade crafts, soak up a relaxed atmosphere and eat inexpensive home-cooked food. Often there's an entertainment stage, too.

Zona Franca (Av Sete de Setembro, btwn Praça da Matriz & Praça da Polícia, & surrounding streets) A tax-free zone with tons of shops, especially shoes, clothes and electronics.

Foto Nascimento (215 8900; Av Sete de Setembro 1194; 8am-6pm Mon-Sat) A good place for photographic supplies, even 400 ISO slide film and digital accessories.

Carrefour (Av Eduardo Ribeiro) The biggest and best downtown supermarket.

For hammocks, head to any of numerous *casa das redes* (house of hammocks) on Rua Rocha dos Santos and the side streets, or the street vendors around Praça Tenreiro Aranha. For riverboat trips, suitable cloth hammocks start at US$5 to US$7 and go up to US$12 to US$20 for larger, prettier, or more durable ones.

Mercado Municipal (p624) is good for inexpensive crafts and T-shirts, cheap stuffed piranhas (US$3 to US$6) and natural medicines.

Getting There & Away

AIR

The **Aeroporto Internacional Eduardo Gomes** (652 1212; Av Santos Dumont 1350) is 13km north of the city center. Smaller regional airlines, including TAVAJ and Meta, use a smaller airport (called Eduardinho), about 600m east of the main one.

For international flights, LAB (Lloyd Aéreo Boliviano) and Varig have the most options. At the time of research, sample one-way fares from Manaus included Buenos Aires US$364, Caracas US$364, La Paz US$217, Miami US$527 and Santa Cruz, Bolivia US$217. Note that you must have a confirmed ticket out of South America (ie your ticket home) to be able to buy one-way international tickets within the continent.

For domestic flights outside of the Amazon try Varig, TAM, Gol and VASP. One-way fares include to Brasília US$165 to US$200, Fortaleza US$225, Rio de Janeiro US$250 to US$286, Salvador US$295 and São Paulo US$210 to US$264.

Within the Amazon, Varig and Rico have the only jet service; VASP, Meta, and TAVAJ are often cheaper, but use propeller planes and typically make one or more *escalas* (stops) along the way. One-way fares from Manaus include Belém (US$178), Boa Vista (US$60 to US$100), Porto Velho (US$100), Rio Branco (US$133), Santarém (US$95 to US$110), Tabatinga (US$150) and Tefé (US$83).

Fares fluctuate greatly – ask travel agents about promotions, especially when flying within the Amazon region. The following is a list of airlines:

Gol (652 1634 airport only; www.voegol.com.br)

LAB (Lloyd Aéreo Boliviano; 633 4511, 0800-118111, airport 652 1513; www.labairlines.com.br; 2nd fl, Av Eduardo Ribeiro 650; 8:30am-5:30pm Mon-Fri)

Meta Linhas Aéreas (232 9353, airport 652 1645; Rua Barroso 316; 8am-6pm Mon-Fri, 8am-noon Sat)

Rico Linhas Aéreas (633 5166, airport 652 1652; www.voerico.com.br; Rua 24 de Maio 60; 7am-6pm Mon-Fri, 7am-noon Sat)

TAM (232 8833, airport 652 1300; www.tam.com.br; Av João Valaria 123; 8am-6pm Mon-Fri, 8am-noon Sat) This location is quite a way from the center of town – use the office at the airport instead.

TAVAJ (622 6699, airport 652 1214; www.tavaj.com.br; Rua Rui Barbosa 200; 8am-6pm Mon-Fri)

Varig (3083 4521, 3083 4525, airport 652 1598; www.varig.com.br; Rua Marcílio Dias 284; 8:30am-6pm Mon-Fri, 8:30am-noon Sat)

VASP (622 3470, airport 652 1355; www.vasp.com.br; Av Sete de Setembro 993; 8am-6pm Mon-Fri, 8am-noon Sat)

THE AMAZON

BOAT

Large passenger boats arrive and depart at the Estação Hidroviária de Manaus (aka Porto Flutuante). Speedboats to Tefé and Santarém use the Porto Manaus Moderna, near the municipal market. See the boxed text on p587 for tips on riverboat travel.

Agencia Rio Amazônas (☎ 621 4359, 621 4319) sells passenger-boat tickets from booths just inside the boat terminal. Boats going downstream to Belém usually make stops in Itacoatiara, Parintins, Santarém and Monte Alegre. Up the Rio Solimões, boats call at Tefé, Benjamin Constant and Tabatinga. Boats to Porto Velho, along the Rio Madeira, make stops at Manicoré and Humaitá.

If you don't speak any Portuguese, there is a **ponto de atendimento** (assistance desk; 🕑 8am-5pm Mon-Fri) inside the terminal. You can buy tickets at slightly discounted prices from the men hanging around the entrance, but you may be bumped if the boat is full. A small bus will shuttle you from the terminal to your boat.

AJATO (☎ 9984 9091, 622 6047) operates comfortable speedboats from Manaus upstream to Tefé (US$43, 14 hours, departing at 7am Wednesday and Saturday; return US$43, 12 hours, departing at 7am Thursday and Sunday) and to Santarém (US$47, 13 hours, departing at 7am Tuesday and Friday; return US$50, 14 hours, departing at 6am Wednesday and Saturday). The trip includes two meals and is a quick, affordable way to get out of Manaus.

Boats going up the Rio Negro leave from Porto São Raimundo, in the Bairro São Raimundo, an unsavory district 1.5km northwest of the Porto Flutuante. A few boats a week go as far as São Gabriel da Cachoeira (around US$50, five to six days).

BUS

The **long-distance bus station** (☎ 642 5805; Rua Recife 2784) is 6km north of the city center. Road travel south to Porto Velho on Hwy BR-319 has been suspended for more than a decade because of poor conditions.

Eucatur (☎ 648 1493, 648 1524) has bus services to Boa Vista (US$22.25, 12 hours, 805km, departing at 10am, 7pm, 8:30pm; *semi leito* at 9pm and midnight) and to Itacoatiara (US$8, four hours, 235km, four times daily). To Venezuela, one bus departs daily at 8pm, stopping in Santa Elena (16 hours), Puerto Ordaz (20 hours), Puerto La Cruz (32 hours) and Caracas (36 hours). Oddly, the price is the same for all four stops: US$46.75. If you are only going to Santa Elena, take the 8:30pm bus to Boa Vista, where you can hop off and buy a US$6.75 ticket (on the same bus!) the rest of the way.

Aruanã (☎ 236 8305) has a bus service to Presidente Figueiredo (US$1.50, 1½ hours, 107km, eight daily) and to Silves (US$8, seven hours, departing at 7am).

Getting Around

City buses and downtown streets get super busy around 1pm to 2pm and 5pm to 7pm; avoid trying to move too far across the city at these times. Bus fare is US$0.50 on most routes. Taxis are plentiful and moderately cheap.

TO/FROM THE AIRPORT

Bus No 306 'Aeroporto Centro' runs about every half-hour between a stop on the main road opposite the airport and the local bus terminal in the center of town on Praça da Matriz (US$0.50, 30 minutes). Buses go to the airport from Praça da Matriz until

RIVERBOAT SCHEDULE

Riverboats from Manaus (Estação Hidroviária)

Destination	Days	Time	Upper Deck	Lower Deck	Cabin
Belém	Wed & Fri; noon	3½ days	US$87	US$72	US$200-267
Porto Velho	Tue & Fri	4 days	US$67	US$65	US$167-183
Santarém	Mon-Sat; noon	30-36 hr	US$38	US$33	US$116-133
Tabatinga	Wed & Sat; 6pm	5-6 days	US$89	n/a	US$233-267
Tefé	Wed, Fri, Sat; noon	30 hr	US$38	US$33	US$87-100

11pm or midnight, with stops at the corner of Av Floriano Peixoto and Rua Quintino Bocaiúva, and on Av Getúlio Vargas opposite the Plaza Hotel.

Taxis at the airport charge US$14 into town; the other way costs about the same by meter.

TO/FROM THE BUS STATION

Bus No 306 'Aeroporto Centro' (the same one you take to the airport) stops on Av Constantino Nery, a one-minute walk from the long-distance bus station; pick it up at Praça da Matriz and tell the conductor you're going to the *rodoviária* – it's the second stop after the stadium on the left.

Catch the same bus back into town. Cross Rua Recife by the pedestrian bridge and turn left along the busy street on the far side of the gas station there. The bus stop is 100m further along, on the far side of the street.

A taxi from the bus station to the center costs around US$8.

AROUND MANAUS
Encontro das Águas & Parque Ecológico Janauary

Just down river from Manaus, the 'black' (actually reddish-brown) water of the Rio Negro meets the 'white' (light brown) water of the Rio Solimões. Owing to differences in speed, density and temperature, the waters don't immediately mix, instead flowing side by side for several kilometers. The **Encontro das Águas** (Meeting of the Waters) is easily visible from a boat – dip your hand in to feel the difference in temperature. The phenomenon (which occurs in several places along the river) was the inspiration for the wavy black-and-white tilework in front of the Teatro Amazonas (Opera House); the design here pre-dates the more famous but nearly identical work on Rio de Janeiro's beachfront. **Parque Ecológico Janauary** is on Lago Janauary (on the point of land between the Negro and Solimões) and is famous for its huge Vitória-Régia water lilies.

Amazon Explorers (p623) is the main operator for Meeting of the Waters and Parque Ecológico Janauary tours, with a large boat and daily departures (US$25 per person, 8:30am to 3pm). There's a seriously packaged feel to these tours: everyone bangs on the flying buttresses of the same samba-iaba tree, cuts the same rubber tree for latex sap, looks at the same monkey, sloth, snake and alligator tied up to amuse visitors and browses the same make-believe Indian craft stalls. Still, it's one way to spend a day.

Alternatively, you can visit these sites by motorized canoe (US$45, minimum four people). Any tour agency can arrange this, but be sure they aren't just selling tickets to the Amazon Explorers trip. Private boatmen belonging to the Associação dos Canoeiros (Boatmen's Association) can be hired at the Estação Hidroviária. A private trip allows you to get further up the Lago Janauary waterways and may include meals.

Also note that virtually any longer trip from Manaus will include a stop at the Meeting of the Waters.

Amazon Ecopark & Amazon Monkey Jungle

These neighboring establishments up the Igarapé Tarumã Açu, a tributary of the Rio Negro, are half an hour by boat from Manaus and make for an interesting day trip. **Amazon Ecopark** (☎ 9146 0594, 9146 0595; www.amazonecopark.com.br) is a private nature reserve and jungle lodge. The park operates the **Amazon Monkey Jungle**, which was founded by the Fundação Floresta Viva (Living Rain forest Foundation) for rehabilitating and returning to the wild monkeys that have been illegally captured or are from areas scheduled to be flooded for dams. The best time to see the monkeys is during feeding time – 11am and 4pm every day. A one-day visit (US$45) normally includes transportation there and back, a jungle walk, visits to an orchid garden, bird sanctuary and the monkey jungle, lunch, a canoe trip and a visit to a rubber-tapper's home. A half-day trip costs US$25. Rain-forest survival classes, taught by retired army officers, are offered on request. You can also stay overnight here; two-day/one-night packages start at US$220.

Jungle Tour Operators

Most agencies can set up almost anything you might want to do, but some have certain experience and expertise in particular kinds of trip.

Amazonas Indian Turismo (Map p621; ☎ 633 5578; www.amazonindian.tk; 2nd fl, Rua dos Andradas 311; per person per day US$45) This long-time budget agency uses English-speaking Indian guides and a rustic camp on the Rio Urubú, a black-water river 200km northeast of Manaus. Hammocks and latrines only. Pre-programmed trips can include all-day hikes and overnights in the forest.

Eco-Discovery Tours (Map p621; ☎ 3082 4732, 9977 9175; www.ecodiscovery.hpg.com.br; Rua L Coelho 301; per person per day US$60; ☯ 8am-6pm) Also offers trips to the Lago Mamorí area, based at a river lodge with options to stay a night

---

JUNGLE TRIPPING

The top priority for most foreign visitors to Manaus is a jungle trip. While anything's possible, the most common trip is two to four days, including hiking in the jungle, fishing for piranha, spotting alligators at night and visiting a local village. Best of all, you'll canoe through *igarapés* (channels cutting through the jungle) and *igapós* (flooded forests), which are beautiful themselves and have more wildlife and plantlife than the larger channels. This is one reason the high-water period (roughly March to July) is the best time to come.

Different agencies offer different things; deciding what kind of trip you want will help narrow down your choices. First and foremost, how much do you want to rough it? Do you want a bed or a hammock? What about sleeping on board a boat? Private bathroom, shared, or pit toilet? Do you want to spend a night or two in the forest or do day trips from the lodge? How much do mosquitoes bother you? Do you prefer hiking or canoeing? There is no shame in choosing more or less comfort – you are there to enjoy yourself after all.

There are also a few questions to ask the tour operator: does the guide speak English (or a language you understand)? How long will you spend getting there? What is the trip itinerary? How much hiking and/or canoeing will you do? Ask to see recent pictures of the accommodations and activities, and a guest comment book. When discussing the trip, be sure you feel comfortable with the outfit. If not, go elsewhere.

And talk to other travelers! (Breakfast at the hotel is a good time.) Virtually every foreigner you see in Manaus is planning a trip or returning from one, and they are the best source of honest, up-to-date info.

A word about what you'll see: many travelers come to the Amazon expecting to see jaguars in every tree and spear-toting Indians in every village. This just doesn't exist, not in Manaus and not anywhere in the Amazon. The vegetation is too thick, the animals are too shy and the cultural gap too great. (To penetrate deep into the forest or visit 'unacculturated' communities, you'll need an expedition of a week or more.) On a typical trip, you are likely to see dolphins and plenty of birds. Alligators, sloths and monkeys are relatively common, but no sure thing. Manatees, anacondas and jaguars are extremely hard to spot. 'White' rivers, like the Lago Mamorí region, do tend to have a higher density of animals than 'black' ones, like the Rio Negro. But they also have many more mosquitoes and somewhat thicker vegetation, which can inhibit even the keenest observer. No matter what trip you take, the single biggest factor in seeing animals is luck.

It should be obvious, but don't book jungle trips off the street. Sellers will undoubtedly approach you: at the airport, on the street, even at your hotel, where the receptionist earns a commission for providing names and room numbers. Trips like these are usually overcrowded or woefully uninspired – hiking through pastures, viewing captured animals etc. It's not worth the US$50 (at most) that you might save.

That said, if you feel you were ripped off – typically unsatisfactory lodging and/or not doing promised activities – you should first complain directly to the tour operator. If you cannot reach an agreement, file a complaint at the main office of **Amazonastur** (☎ 233 1095; www.visitamazonas .com.br; Rua H de Figueiredo 321; ☯ 8am-5pm Mon-Fri), the state tourism agency. Results are not guaranteed, but the office has gotten refunds for disgruntled tourists in the past.

Finally: you'll need sturdy shoes or boots, a raincoat, flashlight and a water bottle. High-power binoculars are heavy, but great for observing birds and animals. If there will be mosquitoes (white-water areas), bring a long-sleeve shirt, long pants and plenty of insect repellent. For photos, high-speed film and/or flash are usually necessary. And ask the tour operator if you should bring along you passport (not just a copy) – at the time of research federal police turned back some foreigners for not having them.

AROUND MANAUS

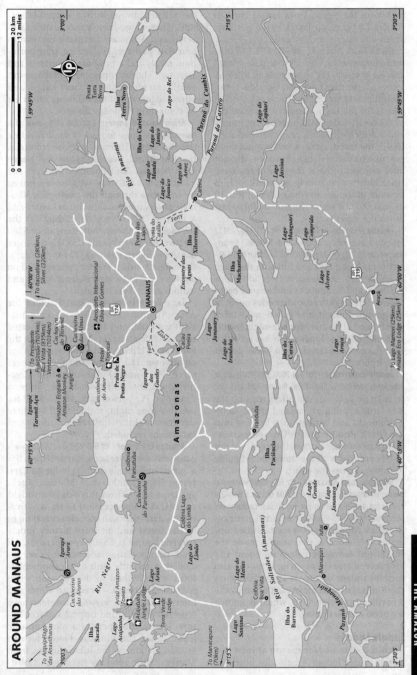

or two in the forest. Does longer trips to Parque Nacional do Jaú (US$100 per day; seven-day minimum), as well.

Gero's Tours (Map p621; ☎ 9983 6273, 8125 0630; www.amazongerotours.com; geromesquita@hotmail.com; Rua 10 de Julho 632; per person per day US$50) A semi-independent operator, Geraldo 'Gero' Mesquita arranges budget tours at Lago Tucunaré, in the Lago Mamorí area. Stay in a new woodsy lodge with beds or hammocks and indoor bathrooms, or in thatched shelters in the forest. Gero, an all-around good guy who has helped many travelers, did not have a proper office at the time of research; reach him by email or phone, or ask for him by name at the laundry/hair salon at Rua 10 de Julho 637 or at the Hotel 10 de Julho just down the street.

Iguana Viagens e Turismo (☎ 633 6507, 9132 9367; www.amazonbrasil.com; Rua 10 de Julho 667; per person per day US$60; ☼ 7am-6pm, ring bell after hrs) Offers tours based on Lago Juma, in the Lago Mamori area. A pleasant riverside lodge has beds and hammocks and shared bathrooms. The English co-owner does much of the guiding himself, and occasionally takes guests (and his guitar) for late-night swim-and-sing-a-longs. Iguana also has an office next door in the Hotel 10 de Julho, and at the airport.

Jungle Experience (☎ 233 2000, 645 4101; jungle experience@bol.com.br; Hotel Ideal, Rua dos Andradas 491; per person per day US$60) Also offers trips up the Rio Urubú, using an isolated rustic camp (hammocks and latrines only; bathing is in the river). Run by British/Guyanese transplant Christopher Gomes, this agency is not to be confused with the independent guide 'Cristian,' across the street.

Swallows and Amazons (☎ 622 1246; www.swallowsandamazonstours.com; 2nd fl, Rua Quintino Bocaiúva 189; lodge only per person per day US$65, riverboat per person per day US$75-95) Run by an American/Brazilian couple, this long-established operator specializes in riverboat tours on the Rio Negro, where you sleep on board and visit several areas in one trip. Trips can also include a night or two at a river lodge on the Rio Negro, and may reach as far as the Anavilhanes Archipelago, which is known for good bird-watching.

Jungle Lodges

Within 250km of Manaus are at least two dozen jungle lodges – basically hotels in the jungle, always with a waterside setting. They range from super luxurious to very basic. Visits are normally by two- to four-day packages, including transportation, meals and a program of outings and activities. The tour operators listed here can usually arrange visits to these lodges and other lodges, and at the same price you get by contacting the lodge directly.

Ariaú Amazon Towers (☎ 234 7308; www.ariautowers.com) is on a tongue of land dividing the Rio Negro from a narrow tributary, the Rio Ariaú, two hours up the Negro from Manaus. This complex for over 300 guests stands on stilts, with towers linked by walkways through the treetops, a 50m-high observatory, a convention center and a helipad. Rates vary depending on the package you choose, but start at US$280 for two days/one night, US$312 for three days/two nights, and US$375 for four days/three nights; prices are per person based on double occupancy, with transfer, meals and various excursions included.

Terra Verde Lodge (☎ 622 7305), near the Ariaú Amazon Towers, is more economical. It's a small and friendly place located off Lago Acajatuba on the south side of the Rio Negro. Hiking and other activities are on its own 110-sq-km private jungle reserve. The owner, Polish-born film director Zygmunt Sulistrowski, is quite a character. Per person rates are US$170 for two days/one night, and US$220 for three days/two nights, with transfer, meals and excursions included.

Amazon Eco-Lodge (☎ 656 6033, fax 656 6101; www.naturesafaris.com; Nature Safaris, Rua Flavio Espiritu 1) is a quaint small-scale floating lodge on Lago Juma, 60km southeast of Manaus. Package trips range from three-day/two-night trips (US$495 per person) to six-day/five-night safaris that also include several night in the forest and an introductory jungle survival course (US$1040 per person). All food, transportation and activities are included. A recently built 65m canopy platform – the highest in the Amazon when we passed through – is easy to climb and offers spectacular views. Travelers have reported friendly and helpful service. Nature Safaris also operates a more upscale lodge called the Pinanha Flotel, located around 150km up the Río Solimões from Manaus, with good fly-fishing and bird-watching. Cabins there have private bath and air-conditioning and start at US$490 per person for a four-day, three-night trip including transfer – a better deal, but there are only two departures weekly.

Hotel Aldeia dos Lagos (bookings Viverde Turismo ☎ 248 9988; www.viverde.com) is on Silves island in the Rio Urubú, amid a lake-strewn area some 240km east of Manaus (4½ hours by road and river). The hotel is an ecotourism venture by a local community group intended to provide income to help the local subsistence fishing community protect its fish stocks. Viverde Turismo will send a taxi to bring you to its office, for photos and more info. A four-day package runs at US$378 per person.

PRESIDENTE FIGUEIREDO
☎ 0xx92 / pop 30,000

Self-named the 'Terra de cachoeiras' (Land of waterfalls), this dusty little town is surrounded by dozens of waterfalls and caves, many of which are quite pretty. Just 100km north of Manaus by good highway, this is the only leisure spot easily accessible by road from the capital, and it gets obscenely packed on weekends year-round. A visit during the week, however, can be a nice way to while away any extra days you have in Manaus.

Sights & Activities

You need a vehicle to visit the waterfalls here. Renting one in Manaus is an option; otherwise you can hire a taxi (US$27, up to four people) or a mototaxi (US$16.50) for the day to take you to four or five different sites. Perhaps the best option, though, is to stay at Pousada das Pedras (see p636) and arrange a trip there, which can include a combination of driving and hiking. Most falls have pools that are great for swimming.

The best and easiest falls to visit are Iracema (12km from town), Santuario (16km), Portera (19km) and Suframa (11km); further away is Pedra Furada (60km). About 12km from town is the town of Balbina, where the **Water Mammals Preservation Center** (☎ 312 1202; admission free; ☽ 8am-noon & 2-4pm Mon-Sat, 8am-noon Sun) shelters manatees and other animals. You can combine a visit here with a stop at **Caverna Maruaga** – an attractive cave with a waterfall at its entrance and a clear shallow river running over its floor – but you need to obtain special permission from the tourist office and there was also talk of closing the cave for preservation; ask about the current situation before visiting.

The **tourist office** (☎ 324 1158; ☽ 7:30am-noon & 2-6pm) has an office in the bus station and across the street, above the grocery store.

BLACK & WHITE

The stingrays found up and down the Amazon are most closely related to their saltwater cousins found not in the Caribbean or Brazilian coastal waters, but on the other side of the continent, in the Pacific Ocean. That and other evidence suggests that the Amazon once flowed west to the Pacific, not east into the Atlantic. Then, maybe 15 million years ago, up rose the Andes. With nowhere for the water to go, the western Amazon Basin turned into huge wetland before the river finally broke through the slightly raised terrain in the Manaus-Santarém area and flowed out to the Atlantic.

Today the multitudes of rivers snaking their way across the Amazon Basin are classified into three types: black, white and clear. Although these terms are really euphemisms for different shades of brown, they point out some interesting differences.

The 'white-water' (actually more of a creamy brown) rivers, such as the Rio Solimões and Rio Madeira, are laden with nutrient-rich sediments carried down from the geologically young and still-being-eroded Andes. White water supports a much heavier organic load, and lands seasonally flooded with white water are among the richest in the Amazon. The concentration of animals and plants (and the people who live off them) tends to be higher.

The 'black-water' Rio Negro and others flowing from the north originate in lowland forests with sandy soils in northern Amazonia. They're slower and warmer than the Solimões. The rotting vegetation that gives them their color (actually a translucent reddish-brown) also makes them more acidic. The acidity kills many insect larvae; some black-water areas have amazingly few mosquitoes and insect-borne diseases such as malaria are rarer.

'Clear-water' rivers, such as the Rio Tapajós flowing down from the Brazilian shield to the south, come from an older geological formation now lacking in sediment and organic materials.

Sleeping & Eating

All hotels listed here include breakfast.

Pousada das Pedras (☎ 324 1296, 9141 4523; s/d US$7/14, d/q ste US$20/27) Operated by friendly Francisco 'Pimenta' de Mazi, this is easily the best and most convenient place to base your visit. Rooms are small but attractive with private bathroom; suites are quite spacious. Meals are served in a nice garden patio. De Mazi arranges guided trips in the area, including long hikes to beautiful Neblina and Natal falls (guide US$10; guide and vehicle for up to four people US$33, for five or more people US$40). A taxi from the bus station is US$1, but de Mazi will pick you up if you call ahead.

Hotel Marauga (☎ 324 1110; across from bus station; d/tr US$12/16.50; ✖) Large but plain rooms have air-con, TV and minibar. The hotel owner can arrange tours.

Delícias no Esteto (✪ 8am-10pm) Basic self-serve and menu restaurant, across from the bus station, with soups, fish and more.

Getting There & Away

Eight daily buses go to Presidente Figueiredo from the Manaus bus station (US$1.50, 1½ hours). The last return bus is at 4:30pm Monday to Thursday, 6:30pm on Friday and 6pm on Sunday; a Manaus-bound bus from Boa Vista passes later (around 7pm; US$3.50), but it is sometimes full. Buses to Boa Vista (US$19, 10 hours) leave at 11:30am, 8:30pm, 10:30pm and 1:30pm.

PARINTINS

☎ 0xx92 / pop 67,800

The Boi-Bumbá festival held here on June 28, 29 and 30 is the biggest annual shindig in Amazonas. It's an Amazonian version of Bumba Meu Boi, a traditional festival of mixed African and European origins that uses music, theater and dancing to enact the kidnapping, death and resurrection of an ox – a metaphor for agricultural cycles. In Parintins the event is turned into a competition between two Boi teams, each with several thousand members – Caprichoso, in blue, and Garantido, in red. The rivalry between the teams apparently grew out of a 'friendly' feud between two families.

Tens of thousands of people descend on Parintins to watch the dazzling Boi parades in the *bumbódromo*, a purpose-built, 35,000-capacity stadium. The teams are judged on their music, dance performance and costumes. The competition is intense, every citizen supports either red or blue, and the over-the-top spectacle rivals Rio's Carnaval.

Parintins hotels are booked out during the festival, and many people take package tours that include nightly accommodations aboard a boat. A five-night boat trip from Manaus (transportation, hammock space and meals) costs around US$250. Any of the travel agencies listed in Manaus can arrange a trip.

The **Hotel Avenida** (☎ 533 1158; Av Amazonas 2416; ✖) and **Pousada Ilha Bela** (☎ 533 2737; Rua Agostinho Cunha 2052; ✖) both have rooms with air-conditioning, TV and minibar for around US$20 at normal times, and sell four- to five-day festival packages for US$500. Other options are the Hotel Uyrapurú, Hotel Palace, Hotel Cabocla, Hospedaria Siridó and the Hotel Torres de Melo. Private houses also rent rooms during the festival. There is no tourist office in Parantins, but the travel agencies in Manaus (p623) may be able to help you book a room in a private house. A better, if less convenient, approach is to go to Parantins well before the festival and ask at local travel agencies or look for rental signs.

Rico, Penta and TAVAJ fly to Parintins from Manaus and Santarém.

Most passenger boats between Manaus and Belèm stop at Parantins (including the AJATO speedboats), and there is service from Santarém as well.

NORTHWEST OF MANAUS

The remote regions northwest of Manaus offer outstanding opportunities for jungle, river and nature lovers with a bit of cash.

Parque Nacional do Jaú

This 22,720-sq-km park in the Rio Negro basin is Brazil's biggest national park and one of the world's largest pieces of protected tropical rain forest. Rich in biodiversity, the park received Unesco World Heritage listing in 2000. This remote area has only 1000 inhabitants and is far from fully explored. Several agencies in Manaus, including Eco-Discovery Tours, do tours here.

Reserva Xixuaú-Xiparaná

This 1720-sq-km ecological reserve, run by a joint Brazilian and international NGO, the **Associação Amazônia** (in Manaus ☎ 232 1757; xixuauxiparina@hotmail.com; www.amazonia.org) is on the west side of the Rio Jauaperí in southern Roraima. It is reached by a boat trip of 450km (35 to 40 hours, depending on river conditions) northwest from Manaus. The Associação Amazônia is involved in nature conservation and research and in health, employment and education projects with the sparse local population.

The reserve is a virtually untouched area of primary rain forest, with good opportunities to view Amazonian fauna, including the rare giant otter. In the heart of the reserve is a group of palms where hundreds of macaws nest. Accommodations are in *malocas*, Indian-style dwellings. A standard two-week trip, including transportation to and from Manaus, with all lodging, meals and excursions included, costs around US$1000 per person. The association no longer has an office in Manaus; contact Cris Clark by email for reservations and up-to-date fares and schedules.

TEFÉ

☎ 0xx97 / pop 50,500

Tefé is the largest town on the Rio Solimões between Manaus and the Colombian/Peruvian border. The main reason to come here is as a stepping stone to the Mamirauá reserve. Tefé's economy is based on fishing, logging and drugs. Tributaries entering the Solimões not far upstream from Tefé include the Rio Japurá, which flows down from one of Colombia's supposed coca- and cocaine-producing areas, and the Rio Juruá, which comes from Peru's coca-producing area.

Information

EMERGENCY
Ambulance (☎ 192)
Hospital São Miguel (☎ 343 2469, 343 2446; Rua Marachal Deodoro 66)
Police (☎ 190)

INTERNET ACCESS
Plataforma (☎ 343 3864; Ruas Getúlio Vargas & Daniel Servalho; per hr US$1.50; ☾ 8am-noon & 2-6pm Mon-Sat) Has a decent Internet connection and often stays open beyond 6pm.

LAUNDRY
Lavandaría do Paulo (Rua Daniel Servalho 345; per item US$0.25-50)

MONEY
Banco do Brasil (☎ 343 2561; Rua Olavo Bilac at Praça Tulio Azevêdo; ☾ 9am-2pm Mon-Fri) Exchanges traveler's checks, euros and US cash.
Bradesco (Ruas Getúlio Vargas & Daniel Servalho) ATMS at here accept most foreign cards.

POST
Post office (Estrada Aeroporto; ☾ 8am-4pm Mon-Fri) Next to the Rico and IBAMA offices.

TOURIST OFFICES
Mamirauá Institute (☎ 343 4160; www.mamiraua .org.br; Rua Brasil 197; ☾ 8am-6pm Mon-Sat) Oversees the Mamirauá reserve; come here for info and reservations.

Sleeping & Eating

All hotels listed here include breakfast.

Hotel Raydiene (☎ 9612 4711, 9613 7266; Rua Olavo Bilac 342; s with shared bathroom US$3.30; s/d with private bathroom & fan US$4/5, with air-con US$5/6.60; ☒) The run-down but clean rooms here are the cheapest in town. Beds are saggy, but the rooms in back have partial views of the river.

Panoramic Hotel (☎ 343 2483, 343 2517; Rua Olavo Bilac at Rua Floriano Peixote; s/d with fan US$6.60/13.30, with air-con US$11.60/15; ☒) Larger rooms and better beds than the Raydiene, although still a bit run-down. Big windows help, but may let in street noise. Some rooms have curiously huge stereo systems.

Monte Carlo Hotel (☎ 343 3472; Travessa Santa Teresa 85; s/d with shared bathroom US$8.30/10, with private bathroom US$11.60/20; ☒) Around the corner from the Raydiene, a half-block from the church, this has large, clean air-con rooms with satellite TV; some also have big windows.

Hotel Anilçe (☎ 343 2416; Praça Santa Tereza 294; s/d US$13.30/16.60) Tefé's best hotel faces the church plaza. Rooms are good-sized and very clean, with satellite TV. There is also a nice rooftop breakfast area.

Stylos (☎ 343 3227; Rua Floriano Peixoto 190; dishes for 2 US$4-6; ☾ lunch & dinner Mon-Sat) Standard fish, meat and chicken dishes are well made and served indoors or outdoors. Single portions are available.

Petisco (Praça Santa Tereza 286; dishes US$2.50-5) Home-style beef kebabs with rice, or large, cheap *prato feito* (plate of the day). Petisco is a popular hang-out at night.

Gato Branco (Rua Olavo Bilac at Rua Floriano Peixote, near waterfront; ☾ evenings & weekends) Across from the Panoramic Hotel, Gato Branco has the best juices in town. Try the camu-camu–juice: tasty and a Vitamin C depth charge.

Getting There & Away

AIR

Rico (☎ 343 3636, 343 3201; Estrada Aeroporto 376, next to post office; ☯ 8am-5pm Mon-Fri, 8am-noon Sat) has daily flights to Manaus (US$81) and Tabatinga (US$99). Flights to Manaus on Tuesday, Thursday and Saturday go via Tabatinga (US$81, 3½ hours, 9am). There are direct flights on Monday, Wednesday and Friday (US$81, one hour, 12:05pm and 7:50pm) and on Sunday (12:05pm and 2:45pm). The direct flights are code-shared with Varig.

To Tabatinga, flights Monday, Wednesday and Friday make one stop (2½ hours, 4pm); direct flights are on Tuesday, Thursday and Saturday (one hour; 9am) and on Sunday.

BOAT

Slow boats to Manaus depart at around 6pm or 6:30pm every day except Wednesday (US$25 to US$30, two days). Prices vary according to the boat, and the very cheapest ones may not include meals – ask ahead. Alternatively, AJATO has comfortable speedboats to Manaus (see p630).

To Tabatinga, most passenger boats do not enter Tefé proper, but stop in the town of Alvarães, on the river's main channel. To get there, take a lancha (small motor boat) from the small boat port to the village of Nogueira (US$1.50, 15 minutes) and then a truck or mototaxi to Alvarães (US$1.50, 15 minutes). Boats typically pass Monday and Friday – frustratingly, there is no fixed hour and even the day can change. There is basic food and accommodations in Alvarães. Small boat operators in Tefé may know when the next boat will pass; they can also ferry you to the channel to intercept the boat (US$10 to US$20, depending on how long you have to wait there.)

MAMIRAUÁ RESERVE

The Reserva de Desenvolvimento Sustentável Mamirauá (Mamirauá Sustainable Development Reserve) covers 1.24 million hectares of forest northwest of Tefé between the Rio Solimões and Rio Japurá. The park is Brazil's last large area of várzea – forests seasonally flooded with sediment-rich 'white water,' as opposed to igapós, which are forests flooded with 'black water.' Mamirauá is adjoined to the east by the even bigger Reserva de Desenvolvimento Sustentável Amanã and the Parque Nacional do Jaú, together forming the second-largest (57,000 sq km) continuous block of protected tropical rain forest in the world. Ably run by the Mamirauá Institute (see p637), this pristine environment of jungles, rivers and lakes offers some of the best wildlife-viewing in Amazonia.

Mamirauá was Brazil's first 'sustainable development reserve' (there are now five) to combine nature conservation and scientific research with improved opportunities for the local population. Many locals work as guides and are responsible for patrolling protected areas, while traditional activities, such as fishing, planting, hunting and harvesting timber, continue under a sustainable-use plan. Visitors here can be reasonably assured of seeing three or four different types of monkey – a fifth species, the white uakari with its crimson face and shaggy white coat, is more elusive – plus sloths, alligators, dolphins and dozens of bird species, including macaws and toucans.

High water here is in May/June, when the forest is completely flooded and you glide through the water in canoes. In low water, roughly October/November, hiking is possible and aquatic animals, especially fish and alligators, are more concentrated. Animals are visible year-round, although most people will enjoy high-water season the best; not surprisingly, it is also the busiest time, and reservations are recommended.

Accommodations are in comfortable floating bungalows with private bathrooms. Prices are US$380 per person (double occupancy) for a four-day/four-night package, currently offered Tuesday to Saturday. Three-day/three-night packages are US$320, from Saturday to Tuesday. Solo travelers who want their own room pay US$8.30 per night extra. Both packages include food, lodging, guides, and boat transfer to and from Tefé. English-speaking staff, night-time presentations and a village visit are standard; ask about visiting with some of the biologists working in the reserve – it can be fascinating.

Contact **Mamirauá Reserve** (☎ 343-4160; www .mamiraua.org.br) for information; online reservations are preferred. Visa, MC, traveler's checks, euros and US dollars are all accepted.

THE TRIPLE FRONTIER

The Brazilian town of Tabatinga and the Colombian town of Leticia, both on the eastern bank of the Amazon about 1100km west of Manaus, are separated by nothing except an international border line. The opposite bank of the river here, and the islands in the middle of it, are Peru. This 'triple frontier' provides travel routes linking all three countries and is also a good area for taking jungle trips. From this area there is relatively easy access to somewhat remote areas up the Rio Javari, which forms the Brazil–Peru border to the west, and up the Rio Amazonas in Colombia. The highwater period here is April to June, and the least rainy months are July to September.

Leticia is a more prosperous place than Tabatinga and overall a more pleasant place to hang out. The Peruvian border settlement here, Santa Rosa, is just a small village on an island.

Tabatinga
☎ 0xx97 / pop 30,500

Tabatinga is a nondescript border town, mostly notable as the point the at which Amazon River enters Brazil. Tabatinga's two ports are the departure points for boats to Manaus and Iquitos, Peru, and its airport serves Brazilian and Peruvian destinations. If you plan to stay any length of time, Leticia, just across the border in Colombia, is nicer and more convenient.

ORIENTATION

Tabatinga's main drag is Av da Amizade (also called Av Principal), running 3km from Tabatinga's airport, at the far southern end, to the international border and the Colombian town of Leticia. Av da Amizade parallels the river, about 500m to the east; the most important cross streets include (in north–south order): Rua Marechal Rondon (250m from the border), Rua Rui Barbosa (650m), Av Marechal Mallet (900m), Rua Santos Dumont (1.2km) and Rua Duarte Coelho (1.7km). Rua Santos Dumont leads directly to the Porto da Feira, Tabatinga's

small-boat port; you can also get there by going down Av Marechal Mallet, turning left at the end and passing the market. The Porto Fluvial, where boats for Manaus dock, is at the end of Rua Duarte Coelho.

INFORMATION
Emergency
Ambulance (☎ 192)
Hospital Militar (☎ 192, 412 2403, 412 2117; Rua Duarte Coelho at Av da Amizade)
Police (☎ 190)

Immigration
Federal Police (Polícia Federal; ☎ 412 2180; Av da Amizade 650; ⏰ 8am-6pm) Handles immigration matters at the station 100m south of Rua Duarte Coelho.

Internet Access
Digital Net (☎ 412 3505; Rua Pedro Teixeira 397; per hr US$0.80; ⏰ 8am-9pm Mon-Sat, 9am-6pm Sun) Relatively fast Internet connection; Rua Pedro Teixeira parallels Av Marechal Mallet one block south.

Money
See also Pousada Rio Mar (p640).

THE TRIPLE FRONTIER

0 —————— 20 km
0 —————— 12 miles

Parque Nacional Natural Amacayacu
Rio Amacayacu
Quebrada Matamatá
Puerto Nariño
San Martin
PNN Amacayacu Lodge
Isla El Cacao
Isla Mocagua
Zaragoza
Isla Cerra
Santa Sofia
Isla Corea
Arara
Isla de los Micos
Bellavista
Nazareth
Puerto Alegria
Isla Ronda
Leticia
Santa Tabatinga
Rosa
Zacambu
Palmari
Rio Javari
Rio Amazonas

COLOMBIA

PERU

BRAZIL

3°45'S
4°00'S
4°15'S

70°15'W
70°00'W

Islandia
Ilha do Cleto
Ilha do Aramaça
Atalaia do Norte
Benjamin Constant
Rio Solimões
Rio Quixito
Rio Itaquaí

To Manaus (1400km by air; 1900km by boat)

THE AMAZON

Banco do Brasil (across from Bradesco; ⏰ 8am-1pm Mon-Thu) Gives advances on some Visa cards.

Bradesco (Av da Amizade at Av Marechal Mallet) Has reliable ATMs.

CNM Cambio e Turismo (☎ 412 3281; Av da Amizade 2017) Changes cash and traveler's checks but usually pays less per dollar than you can get in Leticia.

Post

Post office (Av da Amizade s/n; ⏰ 8am-5pm Mon-Fri) Is 300m north of the federal police station.

Travel Agencies

Blue Moon Turismo (☎ 412 2227; Rua Marechal Rondon 55; ⏰ 8am-noon & 2-4pm Mon-Sat, knock on Sun) Has air tickets to Peru, including Iquitos, Lima and Cuzco. From Av da Amizade, take Rua Rui Barbosa or Rua Marechal Mallet toward the river. If you do purchase a ticket, be sure to confirm which airport (Tabatinga or Leticia) your flight departs from, and plan your immigration procedures accordingly.

Turamazon (☎ 412 2244, 412 2026; Av da Amizade 2271, 200m south of border; ⏰ 8am-noon & 2-5pm Mon-Fri, 8am-noon Sat) Has air tickets on Rico and Varig.

SLEEPING & EATING

Unlike those in the rest of Brazil, these hotels do not include free breakfast.

Hotel Cristina (☎ 412 2558; Av Marechal Mallet 248, next to River Fox; s/d with fan US$5/6.60, with air-con US$8.30/10; ❄) Clean, basic rooms, most with TV. Friendly owner.

Hotel Brasil (☎ 412 3186, 412 2648; Av Marechal Mallet 306, at Transtur; s/d US$10/13.30; ❄) Slightly better than Hotel Cristina, all rooms here have air-con, TV and telephone.

Pousada Rio Mar (☎ 412 4996; in front of Porto da Feria; s/d US$7.30/10) Right in the gritty port and market area, the fan-cooled rooms here are actually pretty decent. Convenient for Peru-bound boats; accepts and exchanges euros, US dollars, pesos and soles.

Hotel Restaurant Te Contei? (☎ 412 4548; Av da Amizade 1813; s/d US$10/15, with breakfast US$11.60/16.60) This place has large rooms off a breezy upstairs patio and corridor. The back rooms have less street noise. The **restaurant** (dishes US$2-7; ⏰ lunch & dinner) downstairs is a popular self-service lunch spot and has bar and dinner service at night.

Restaurante Tres Fronteiras (Rua Rui Barbosa, 200m west of Av da Amizade, south side of road; dishes US$3.50-8) This pleasant palm-roofed restaurant has excellent lunch and dinner options – try the *peixe tres fronteiras*, a fish fillet with

spices from Peru, Brazil and Colombia, served on a large banana leaf.

GETTING THERE & AWAY

Air

Rico (☎ 412 2244, 412 4000) has flights from the **Tabatinga airport** (☎ 412 2211) to Manaus (US$152, daily) co-operated by **Varig** (☎ 412 2356), and to Tefé (US$97; Monday, Wednesday, Friday and Sunday).

TANS (☎ 412 2045; Rua Pedro Teixeira 100) has service to/from Iquitos, Peru (sometimes in a seaplane) Wednesday and Saturday at 3pm (US$60, 55 minutes). From Iquitos, there are flights daily to Lima (US$135), Cuzco (US$74) and elsewhere. Get tickets and information at **Blue Moon Turismo** (see left).

Boat

Boats to Manaus (US$50 hammock, three to four days, Wednesday and Saturday, twice-monthly on Tuesday) depart at 3pm from the Porto Fluvial. You should arrive four to six hours in advance, to reserve a spot.

To Iquitos, Peru (US$50, nine to 12 hours), there are two companies offering similar speedboat service: **Transtur** (☎ 412 3186, 412 2648; Av Marechal Mallet 306; ⏰ 8am-noon & 2-6pm Mon-Sat) has departures on Tuesday, Wednesday, Friday and Saturday at 4:30am. **River Fox** (☎ 412 2945; Av Marechal Mallet 248; ⏰ 8am-noon & 2-6pm Mon-Sat) has departures on Tuesday, Thursday and Sunday at 4:30am. The return trip is slightly faster, but costs the same. Transtur returns to Tabatinga on Tuesday, Thursday, Saturday and Sunday at 6am; River Fox on Wednesday, Friday and Sunday at 5am. Usually, two meals are served; depart from the Porto da Feria.

Deslizadores (which are small, fast, passenger launches) go whenever they have a boatload, from the Porto da Feira across to Santa Rosa, Peru (US$0.60, five minutes) and to Benjamin Constant, the Brazilian town at the mouth of the Rio Javari (US$5, 30 minutes) daily from around 6am to 6pm.

To/from Colombia

The international border is marked by nothing more than a few moneychangers on the Brazilian side and a Colombian police officer directing traffic on the other side. You are free to move between Tabatinga and Leticia as much as you like, but if you plan to travel onward, even to Amacayacu national park, you should clear immigration for both countries before leaving town.

To/from Peru

Small boats to Santa Rosa, Peru, depart from the Porto da Feria (US$0.60, five minutes) daily from around 6am to 6pm.

For Iquitos, Peru, fast passenger boats go to and return from the Porto da Feria every day except Monday (US$50 one way, nine to 12 hours), passing immigration in Santa Rosa. See opposite page for details.

GETTING AROUND

For a *colectivo* (minibus) from the airport to town (US$0.30), walk to the left out-

side the airport terminal and down the approach road to the corner of the main road. Some vehicles continue into Leticia from Tabatinga.

A taxi from the airport costs US$3.30 to Tabatinga and US$5 to Leticia. Mototaxis cost US$0.30 within Tabatinga and US$0.60 to Leticia.

Leticia (Colombia)

☎ 098 / pop 30,000

This far-southern corner of Colombia remained mercifully free from the troubles afflicting much of the country at the time of research, and hopefully it will stay that way. The small agreeable town of Leticia is the starting point for trips to the Parque

LETICIA

0 —————— 300 m
0 —————— 0.2 miles

INFORMATION	
BBVA Banco Ganadero	1 B4
Brazilian Consulate	2 B1
DAS Office	3 B3
Exchange Offices	4 A3
Hospital San Rafael	5 A2
Indio Net	6 C3
Orange Net	7 A4
Peruvian Consulate	8 A2
Police Station	9 A2
Post Office	10 B3
Telecabinas-Telecom	11 B3
Tourist Office	12 B3

SIGHTS & ACTIVITIES	(p642)
Amaturs	13 A3
Iglesia de NS de la Paz	14 B3
Museo Alfonso Galindo	(see 32)
Museo del Hombre Amazónico	15 A3

SLEEPING	⌂ (pp642–3)
Hospedaje Los Delfines	16 A2
Hotel Amazonas	17 A3
Hotel Anaconda	18 A4
Hotel Yurupany	19 B3
Residencias Colombia	20 B3
Residencias Fernando	21 B3
Residencias Marina	22 B3

EATING	⌂ (p643)
El Sabor	23 B3
La Casa del Pan	24 A2
La Casona Tolimense	25 B3
Restaurante Carola	(see 23)
Restaurante El Viejo Tolima	26 B3
Restaurante Hotel Colonial	27 B4
Tierras Amazónicas	28 B3

DRINKING	⌂ (p643)
Tío Tom	29 A4

SHOPPING	⌂ (p643)
Almacén El Remate	30 A3
Distribuidora Guevara	31 A3
Galería Uirapuru	32 A3

TRANSPORT	(p643)
Colectivos to Leticia Airport	33 A4
Minibuses to Tabatinga	34 B3
Taxi Stand	35 B3
Ticket Office for Boats to PNN Amacayacu	36 A4

OTHER	
Agencia Operadora Río Yavarí	37 A2
Amazon Jungle Trips	38 C4
Librería Juan Pablo Montoya	39 A4
Manoa Tours	40 A3
Parque Nacional Natural Amacayacu Office	41 A2
Selvaventura	42 C3
Siempre Columbia	(see 19)

To Jardín Botánico Zoológico (800m); Airport (1km)

Cemetery

Calle 14
Av Vásquez Cobo
Calle 13
Calle 12
Av Victoria Regia
Parque Santander
Calle 10
Carr 9
Carr 6
Carr 10
Calle 9
Av Internacional
Carr 7
Carr 8
Carr 5
Calle 8
Calle 8A
Market
Parque Orellana
Calle 7
Calle 6
Calle 5
Calle 4

Río Amazonas

To Muelle Fluvial (1km)

To Tabatinga Airport (3km)

COLOMBIA
BRAZIL

THE AMAZON

Nacional Natural Amacayacu and up the Rio Javari into Peru. When telephoning to Leticia from outside Colombia, use the Colombia country code 57 and drop the 09 part of the area code.

ORIENTATION

Leticia has two parks, but the real center of town can be found at the intersection of Calle 8 and Carrera 10. Calle 8 runs west to Leticia's main port (Porto Civil) and Carrera 10 runs 2km north to the airport, turning into Av Vásquez Cobo along the way. The international border is located southeast of the center, at Calle 3 and Av International, the extension of Tabatinga's Av da Amizade.

INFORMATION

Emergency

Ambulance (☎ 137)

Hospital San Rafael (☎ 592 7075; Calle 13 btwn Carreras 9 & 10) Has a 24-hour emergency room and pharmacy;

Police (☎ 112)

Immigration

DAS (Departamento Administrativo de Seguridad; ☎ 592 7189); Calle 9 (Calle 9 btwn Carreras 9 & 10; ☼ 8am-noon & 2:30-6pm); airport (☼ 8am-noon & 2-6pm) Handles immigration matters at the airport post only.

Internet Access

Indio.net (Centro Comercial Acuarios, Calle 8 at Carrera 7; per hr US$1; ☼ 9am-10pm Mon-Sat, 10am-10pm Sun)

Orange Net (Carrera 11 next to Hotel Anaconda; per hr US$1; ☼ 7am-11pm Mon-Sat, 3-11pm Sun) Has Internet access and international phone calls for slightly cheaper rates than Telecom.

Money

BBVA Banco Ganadero (cnr Calle 7 & Carrera 10; ☼ 8-11:30am & 2-4:30pm) Has reliable ATMs and will change Amex traveler's checks if you have a current Colombia entry stamp in your passport.

Casas de cambio (several at cnr Calle 8 & Carrera 11) Exchanges Colombian, Brazilian, Peruvian, US or European currency. Some stay open late.

Post & Telephone

The post office is near the Telecom office.

Telecabinas-Telecom (☎ 592 6725; Calle 8 & Carrera 10; ☼ 7am-11pm; calls to USA/Europe & Australia per min US$0.70/0.85) One of several places to make long-distance calls.

Tourist Offices

Tourist office (Departamento Administrativo de Fomento Ecoturístico; ☎ 592 7569; Carrera 10, next to post office; ☼ 7am to noon & 2-5:45pm Mon-Fri) This is not very helpful.

Travel Agencies

Manoa Tours (☎ 592 5150, 592 6951; Canoa commercial center, No 6, Carrera 11 at Calle 8; ☼ 8am-noon & 2-6pm) Sells plane tickets and arranges visits to Amazon Heliconia Lodge on Rio Javari.

DANGERS & ANNOYANCES

At the time of research, there was no reported security risk for foreigners visiting Leticia or Parque Nacional Natural Amacayacu – indeed, this is one part of Colombia travelers have long and safely visited. Still, it is a good idea to ask if any problems have arisen recently. Travel agents, police officers or the gun-toting folks at the DAS office are a good start.

SIGHTS

Museo del Hombre Amazónico (☎ 592 7729; inside Banco de la República, Carrera 11 at Calle 10; ☼ 9am-noon & 2:30-5pm Mon-Fri, 9am-1pm Sat) has a small collection of Indian artifacts and implements.

Museo Alfonso Galindo (Calle 8 No 10-35) Inside the Galería Uirapuru, this is less a museum than the personal collection of shop owner Gustavo Navia. Nevertheless it's an interesting and extensive display of indigenous artifacts, dried plants and woods, and preserved animals (mostly reptiles).

Jardín Botánico Zoológico (Av Vasquez Cobo, 150m south of airport; admission US$1; ☼ 8am-noon & 2-6pm) has an average sample of the local flora and fauna, including monkeys, crocodiles, anteaters, anacondas and manatees.

SLEEPING

Unlike those in Brazil, hotels here do not include free breakfast.

Residencias Colombia (Carrera 10 No 8-56; r with shared bathroom US$5.75) The fan-cooled rooms here are very basic and the bathrooms only marginally clean, but the owner is friendly. Enter up a narrow wooden stairway.

Hospedaje San Francisco (☎ 592 5005; Carrera 10 No 8-32; s/d US$5.75/7.70) A few doors down from Residencias Colombia, the rooms here are slightly better, with private bathrooms and fans. Walls are mostly screens – cooler perhaps, but less private.

Residencias Fernando (☎ 592 7362; Carrera 9 No 8-80; s/d with fan US$9.60/13.40, with air-con US$13.45/19.25; ✷) Clean rooms line a narrow pleasant garden. Air-con rooms are a bit bigger and more modern. There's friendly service.

Hospedaje Los Delfines (☎ 592 7488; Carrera 11 No 12-83; s/d US$9.60/15.35) Large, clean rooms, with fan, hammock and private bathroom, line a tree-filled patio. It's often full, so call ahead.

Hotel Amazonas (☎ 592 8026; Calle 8 No 10-32; s/d with fan US$8.50/10, with air-con US$11.50/13.50; ✷ ☻) Good value, with clean, relatively modern rooms, TV and laundry service. There's also friendly staff and a nice private outdoor pool.

Hotel Yurupary (☎ 592 4743; Calle 8 No 7-26; s/d/tw US$20/26.50/31; ✷) More upmarket, the rooms here are spacious and clean, if a bit eclectic in decor – they've all got air-con and TV. There's a tourist agency and pleasant restaurant inside the hotel. Ask about discounts for longer stays.

Hotel Anaconda (☎ 592 7119; Carrera 11 No 7-36; s/d US$34.40/57.70; ✷) Leticia's top hotel is no Hilton, but the rooms are comfortable, modern and quite big. Those on the top floor are better value, with less street noise and nice views over the Amazon. There's a welcoming cocktail bar and large outdoor pool, too.

EATING
Leticia doesn't have much fine dining, but cheap, decent fish, chicken and meat dishes are easy to find.

El Sabor (☎ 592 4774; Calle 8; dishes US$2.50-5; ☾ 24hr) Good menú del día (set meal) of fish, meat or chicken with soup and a jug of juice. The banana pancakes are a treat.

Restaurante Carola (☎ 592 4148; Calle 8; dishes US$2.50-5; ☾ 24hr) Next door and virtually identical to El Sabor, from the fish painted on the walls, to the juice jugs.

La Casa del Pan (☎ 562 7660; Calle 11 No 10-20; ☾ 7am-noon & 2-11pm Mon-Sat) Facing Parque Santander, this is an excellent spot for breakfast (eggs, French bread, coffee and juice for US$2) or for a coffee while watching the park's hordes of screeching parrots return to their nests at dusk. Av Vicoria Regia is the official name of this street, but most locals use Calle 11.

Tierras Amazónicas (☎ 592 4748; Calle 8, next to Hotel Yurupary; dishes US$5-10; ☾ lunch & dinner Tue-Sun) Comfortable dark-wood tables and a nice cantina atmosphere.

ENTERTAINMENT
Tierras Amazónicas (Calle 8, next to Hotel Yurupary) This good lunch and dinner spot turns into a mellow bar scene as the night wears on. Popular with a 20s and 30s crowd.

Tío Tom (☎ 592 4540; Carrera 11 & Calle 7; ☾ 7-2am) This popular, somewhat gritty downtown bar has dim booths inside and folding tables outside.

SHOPPING
Galería Uirapuru (☎ 592 7056; Calle 8 No 10-35; ☾ 9am-noon & 3-7pm Mon-Sat, 9am-noon Sun) Large selection of crafts for sale, from cheap knick-knacks to quality indigenous artesanía. The museum in the back is worth visiting.

Almacén El Remate (Calle 8A) and **Distribuidora Guevara** (Calle 8A), both near Porto Civil, are good shops to pick up a hammock if a long boat ride or jungle trip is in your future.

GETTING THERE & AWAY
AeroRepública flies from Leticia's **airport** (☎ 592 7771) to Bogotá several times weekly (US$90 to US$110), with onward connections from there. Aviaselva has flights to Iquitos, Peru (US$60, Saturday only). Buy tickets at Manoa Tours (opposite) or most travel agencies.

Boat tickets up the Amazonas to the Parque Nacional Natural Amacayacu visitor center (US$7, 1½ hours, 10am and 2pm Monday to Friday, 10am and 1pm Saturday to Sunday; return boats pass the park around 8:30am and 4:30pm) are sold at a small office at the west end of Calle 8. Most boats continue to Puerto Nariño (Colombia) and/or Caballococche (Peru).

Small boats will carry you across to Santa Rosa, Peru, for US$1 per person from Leticia's Muelle Fluvial at the end of Calle 3 (250m west from the south end of Carrera 11, or 1km west from the international border).

GETTING AROUND
Colectivos (minibuses) to Leticia airport go from Parque Orellana (US$0.50). A moto-taxi costs US$0.50 in town or US$0.75 to Tabatinga.

Colectivos to Tabatinga wait at the corner of Carrera 10 and Calle 8 (US$0.50) – in Tabatinga, they pass Porto da Feria, the turnoff for Porto Fluvial, the Polícia Federal post and the airport, before turning back. A taxi from central Leticia to Tabatinga airport costs US$5.

Parque Nacional Natural Amacayacu

Amacayacu national park covers 2935 sq km of jungle on the north side of the Amazonas, 75km upstream from Leticia. Here you can take a variety of interesting guided canoe and hiking trips, most half-day or full-day and usually including a visit to a local village. This was once a major cocaine-producing area, and much of the original forest, especially along the river, was cut down to make room for coca plantations. Some say the park was created to allow the government to seize the land. The forest is growing back well, but an overnight trip into the jungle – which you should arrange at the park center in Leticia – is the only way to get into truly primary forest. Mosquitoes can be intense, so bring plenty of repellent. Ask about talking with some of the researchers who live and work at the park center; many speak English and their work can be fascinating.

The park has a spacious visitor center beside the river, where accommodations in a hammock/bunk cost US$5/7 per person and three meals a day cost US$7; add US$6.50 for the park entry fee. Trips for up to five people vary in cost from US$8 to US$30. Be sure to bring enough Colombian pesos to pay the entry fee, lodging and guides – it's cash only. You can pay for your food and the boat trip in Brazilian reais, if necessary.

Reservations are recommended; visit the **park office** (☎ 592 7124; www.parquesnacionales.gov .co; Carrera 11 next to Hospedaje Los Delfines; ☻ 8am-5pm Mon-Fri), where you can get additional info on current trips and costs. The park can be extremely crowded during Semana Santa (Holy Week).

Siempre Colombia (☎ 592 6621; siempre_col ombia@yahoo.com; Hotel Yurupary; ☻ 9am-noon & 2-7pm Mon-Sat, some Sun) offers package trips to Amacayacu. Prices start at around US$60 per person per day, but vary considerably depending on the size of your group – ask at the office for current rates and schedules.

Rio Javari

The Rio Javari forms the Brazil–Peru border for about 500km upstream from its conflu-

ence with the Rio Solimões at the town of Benjamin Constant (named for the 19th-century Brazilian positivist thinker and politician), 20km southwest of Tabatinga. The jungle region it runs through is very remote, and the hinterlands even more so. The area known as the Vale do Javari (Javari Valley), south and east of the river on the Brazilian side, is little populated except for 3000 or 4000 Indians. Most of it is in the process of registration as the Terra Indígena Vale do Javari, an 85,000-sq-km area that forms one of the largest Indian lands in Brazil.

There are believed to be several uncontacted Indian groups in the forests here; some of the known tribes have a reputation for aggressiveness to outsiders. You'll probably hear tales of the isolated Korubo tribe, which lives somewhere up the Rio Ituí. Its members have assassinated dozens of intruders such as loggers and rubber tappers (and at the same time have themselves been assassinated in even greater numbers). Anyone interested in this region should try to get hold of Petru Popescu's book *Amazon Beaming*, which relates photographer Loren McIntyre's extraordinary experiences among the Mayoruna (Matses) people.

JUNGLE LODGES

Three good jungle lodges provide you with the chance to get close to nature and offer typical jungle lodge activities such as forest walks, fishing, nighttime alligator spotting, bird-watching, dolphin-watching, village visits and the chance to camp out in the jungle.

Zacambu Lodge (operated by Amazon Jungle Trips; ☎ 592 7377; amazonjungletrips@yahoo.com; Av Internacional 6-25, Leticia), about a 70km boat trip from Tabatinga (three hours by motorized canoe), is in an area of lakes on the Peruvian side of the Javari and is reportedly a good area for wildlife-spotting. Rooms are simple but comfortable and there is plenty of hammock space. Rates are US$50 per person per day for groups of four or more, including transportation, meals and guides. Price may be negotiable depending on the season. Owner Antonio Cruz Pérez is friendly and experienced.

Reserva Natural Rio Yavarí (operated by Agencia Operadora Río Yavarí; ☎ 592 7457; Carrea 10 11-27, or ask at Hotel los Delfines), about 20km upstream, is on the Brazilian side of the river overlooking a small lake. Simple, comfortable rooms have private bathroom; hammock space is also available. Rates, including transportation, food, lodging and guided excursions, start at US$50 per day per person.

Reserva Natural Palmari (www.palmari.org) is another 20km upstream on the south bank of the river, overlooking a bend where pink and gray dolphins are often seen. **Selvaventura** (☎ 592 5104; selvaventura@latinmail.com; Av Internacional 9-01; ⏰ 8am-noon & 2-6pm Mon-Sat), a

---

THE YANOMAMI

The Yanomami, who inhabit a remote area straddling the borders of Brazil's Roraima and Amazonas states and Venezuela, are one of the most numerous and also one of the most recently contacted indigenous peoples of Amazonia. Literally a Stone Age people, living a seminomadic life with stone implements, pottery, animal hides and plants, they were dragged abruptly into the late 20th century.

The Yanomami probably had first contact with outsiders in the 1950s, but such contact remained slight until the mid-1970s when Hwy BR-210 was cut westward across Roraima and into their lands. Yanomami mixed with the construction workers and died from measles, influenza and venereal diseases. Several villages were wiped out.

In the mid-1980s a gold rush sent prospectors swarming into Yanomami territory, polluting rivers and destroying forest. By 1989 the miners' numbers had reached an estimated 40,000. As a result, in the period 1986–93 – nearly 20% of the Yanomami population died, chiefly from malaria and other introduced diseases. In 1988 an absurd plan to create 19 separate pockets of land for the Yanomami, depriving them of 70% of their territory, was initiated by the Sarney government and Funai. Two years later, growing international and national criticism of the genocide being perpetrated on the Yanomami forced the authorities to designate only a handful of zones open for mining.

In 1991 the Venezuelan government officially recognized the Yanomami territory in Venezuela as a special Indian reserve; a few months later President Collor defied opposition and followed suit on the Brazilian side, creating the 96,650-sq-km Terra Indígena Yanomami, Brazil's largest single Indian territory.

The Yanomami are a slight people, with typical Amerindian features. The center of each community is the *yano*, a large round timber-and-thatch structure where each family has its own section facing onto an open central area used for communal dance and ceremony. Each family arranges its own area by slinging hammocks around a constantly burning fire that forms the center of family life.

Intertribal visits are an opportunity to eat well – if the hunt has been successful everyone gets to eat monkey, which is a delicacy. Otherwise, tapir, wild pig and a variety of insects provide protein, which is balanced with garden fruits, yams, bananas and manioc. Once the garden soils and hunting grounds are exhausted, the village is dismantled and moves on to a new site.

The Yanomami hold elaborate ceremonies and rituals and place great emphasis on intertribal alliances. The latter are intended to minimize feuds or violence.

Disease is cured with shaman dances, healing hands and various herbs. Sometimes the village shaman will enlist good spirits to fight evil spirits by using *yakoana* (a hallucinogenic herbal powder). When a tribe member dies, the body is hung from a tree until dry, then burned to ashes. The ashes are mixed with bananas, which are then eaten by friends and family of the deceased to incorporate and preserve the spirit. Mourning rituals are elaborate.

There has long been a widespread notion that the Yanomami are an aggressive people who live in a state of chronic warfare. This view stems largely from the influential work of US anthropologist Napoleon Chagnon, who first encountered the Yanomami in the 1960s and whose book *The Fierce People* became an academic bestseller. Chagnon's theories were strongly challenged in 2001 in the book *Darkness in El Dorado* by Patrick Tierney, and are also challenged by Survival, the respected international organization that campaigns for tribal peoples. Survival characterized the Yanomami as 'a generally peaceable people who have suffered enormous violence at the hands of outsiders.'

youthful adventure agency, uses the lodge as a base for hikes, river trips and canopy tours. Rates average US$50 per person per day, including all meals, transportation and guides. You can also visit the lodge independently (hammocks US$6, beds US$8, meals US$3 to US$5) and make use of the canoes and guides as they are available. Getting there is a bit complicated, though – catch a boat from Leticia to Benjamin Constant by 9am to catch an Atalaia do Norte-bound boat (US$4, three hours). There, hire a local boat to Palmari (US$8 to US$10, 30 minutes to two hours depending on the boat).

Selvaventura also conducts longer jungle expeditions, usually to visit remote indigenous and *coboclo* (people of mixed Indian and European descent) communities. The trips are not cheap – US$1500 to US$2500 – but visits to 'unacculturated' Indian communities rarely are any more. You must reserve a month in advance, to allow for processing the necessary permits. Another guide is **Tony 'Mowgly' Vargas** (in Tabatinga ☎ 412 5060; amazondiscover@yahoo.com; Rua Marechal Rondon 86, 200m north of Blue Moon Turismo).

RORAIMA

The remote and beautiful mountain region straddling Roraima's frontier with Venezuela is perhaps the ultimate Amazon frontier. With around 400,000 inhabitants, Roraima is the least populated state in Brazil. Still, it has quite a lot more than the 19,700 people that were counted here in 1943. The equator passes through southern Roraima, and much of the state is still tropical rain forest, but the northeast is chiefly savanna. Roraima includes most of the Brazilian territories of the Yanomami, one of the country's largest surviving indigenous peoples, and several other sizable Indian territories. Roraima state governments are not renowned, however, for favoring indigenous or nature reserves that hamper such activities as mining or logging.

Access to most places off the main north–south Hwy BR-174 is not easy, and although the capital, Boa Vista, has a few places of interest, for many travelers Roraima is just somewhere to pass through between Venezuela and Manaus.

BOA VISTA
☎ 0xx95 / pop 197,000

The state capital, a planned city on the banks of the Rio Branco, is home to more than half of Roraima's population. Many are public servants who were lured to the frontier by government incentives. Although still relatively isolated from Manaus and the rest of Brazil, Boa Vista is growing as a result of increased tourist interest in Venezuela's beautiful high plains, just three hours north. Boa Vista is already the center of an active market for small-time businessmen buying cheap gasoline in Venezuela and re-selling it in Brazil.

Orientation

The city is laid out in an arch shape, with the base on the Rio Branco and the arch itself formed by Av Major Williams along with Av Terencio Lima. The state government building at the center of the arch, and the simple Monumento ao Garimpeiro (Monument to the Gold Prospector) in the park in front of it, mark the center of the street plan. Broad avenues radiate from the arch, dividing the outskirts into wedges. The city planners were clearly a race of giants: the scale of the place is ill-suited to pedestrians, who could quite easily spend a whole day trying to do a couple of errands.

Boa Vista's commercial district stretches between the central park, Praça do Centro Cívico, and the river.

Information
BOOKSTORES
Nobel (☎ 621 3422; Av Glaycon de Paiva 789-A; ⊙ 9am-7pm Mon-Sat) This national chain has a decent selection of travel guides, including some in English.

CONSULATES
Guyana (Av Benjamin Constant 1020; ⊙ 9am-noon)
Venezuela (☎ 623 9285; Av Benjamin Constant at Rua Barão do Rio Branco; ⊙ 8am-noon Mon-Fri)

EMERGENCY
Ambulance (free call ☎ 192)
Emergency room (☎ 623 1155; Hospital Geral, Rua Recife 1581)
Police (free call ☎ 190)

INTERNET ACCESS
G-Tech Informática (☎ 623 3927; Rua José Magalhães 151-A; per hr US$1; ⊙ 8am-6pm Mon-Fri, 8-noon Sat)

The Internet area is up the narrow white stairs to left of the store's main doors.

Nobel (Av Glaycon de Paiva 789-A; per hr US$1; 9am-7pm Mon-Sat) Connection ranges from reasonably fast to excruciatingly slow. Charges by the hour only – no fractions.

MEDICAL SERVICES

Hospital Geral (236 0326; Rua Recife 1581) Located two kilometers from the center of town toward the airport, this is the area's nearest *pronto de socorro* (emergency room).

MONEY

Banco do Brasil (Av Glaycon de Paiva 56; 8am-2pm Mon-Fri) Changes euros and US dollars and traveler's checks.

Bradesco (Av Sebastão Diniz & Rua Inácio Magalhães) Reliable ATMs.

Edson Ouro Safira Joyas (Av Benjamin Constant 64 W; 8am-5pm Mon-Fri) Changes US, Venezuelan and Guyanese currencies, and US-dollar traveler's checks.

POST

Main post office (621 3535; Praça do Centro Cívico; 8am-5pm Mon-Fri, 8am-noon Sat)

TELEPHONE

Telemar (Av Capitan Ene Garcez 100) Has a bank of payphones in front of its office here.

TOURIST INFORMATION

The following state agencies are supposedly working to get information into the hands of tourists; they're both located in the same building. DITUR has offices at the airport and bus station but rarely any personnel there. You may have some luck going to the offices directly, but don't count on it.

DITUR (Divisão de Difusão Turística; 623 1238; 8am-noon & 2-5pm Mon-Fri, 8am-noon Sat)

Proecotur (Programa do Ecoturismo; 624 4115; 8am-noon & 2-5pm Mon-Fri, 8am-noon Sat)

TRAVEL AGENCIES

Below are agencies that sell travel tickets. See p648 for a list of tour operators serving the region.

Águia Tours (624 1516; Av Benjamin Constant 1683; 8am-noon & 2-6pm Mon-Fri, 8am-noon Sat)

BV Tours (224 9000; Rua Araújo Filho 287; 8am-noon & 2-6pm Mon-Fri, 8am-noon Sat) Also sells bus tickets.

BOA VISTA

INFORMATION		
Águia Tours	1	B2
Banco do Brasil	2	B1
Bradesco	3	C2
BV Tours	4	B2
Edson Ouro Safira Joyas	5	B2
G-Tech Informática	6	C2
Guyana Embassy	7	C1
Hospital Coronel Mota	8	B1
Nobel	9	B2
Post Office	10	C1
Telemar	11	B1
Tourist Office	12	B1
Venezuelan Consulate	13	C1

SIGHTS & ACTIVITIES	(pp648-9)	
Igreja NS do Carmo	14	C2
Iguana Tours	15	D2
Monumento ao Garimpeiro	16	B2

SLEEPING	(p649)	
Hotel Aipana Plaza	17	B2
Hotel Barrudada	18	B2
Hotel Euzébio's	19	A1
Hotel Ideal	20	B2
Hotel Monte Líbano	21	B2
Uiramutam Palace	22	A1

EATING	(pp649-50)	
Bistro Gourmet	23	B2
Crepe & Cia	24	B2
La Gondola	25	B2
Mister Quilo	26	C2
Peixada Tropical	27	A1
Pigalle	28	A1
Restaurant Ver O Rio	29	C3
Sorveteria Pik Nik	(see 26)	

SHOPPING	(p650)	
Centro de Artesanato	30	C2

TRANSPORT	(p650)	
Buses to Airport	31	B1
Meta	32	B2
Mini-Terminal Urbano	33	B1
Municipal Bus Terminal	34	C2
Porto de Babazinho	35	D1
Varig	36	C2

THE AMAZON

Dangers & Annoyances

The area at the bottom of Av Dr Silvio Botelho, toward the river, can get fairly seedy with drunks, so it's best to steer clear of this area.

If you go to Praia Grande, be careful of stingrays, especially in low-water season. When entering or exiting the water, scare off the rays by shuffling your feet or poking the sand in front of you with a stick or reed.

Sights & Activities

PARQUE ANAUÁ & MUSEU INTEGRADO DE RORAIMA

About 2.5km northwest of the center, the vast grounds of **Parque Anauá** (Av Brigadeiro Eduardo Gomes) contain gardens, a lake, a museum, an amphitheater and various sporting facilities. The **Museu Integrado de Roraima** (admission free; ☺ 8am-6pm) is limited but has a range of displays on the state's archaeology, indigenous peoples, wildlife and history. Free guided tours (available in English most mornings) make this an interesting visit. The museum is 300m into the park from the entrance opposite the end of Rua General Penha Brasil.

PRAIA GRANDE

During low water (usually from December to April) a sandbar emerges opposite Boa Vista on the Rio Branco. Known as **Praia Grande**, it is indeed big and beachy. The best way to visit it is from so-called Porto do Babazinho at the end of Av Major Williams. Babazinho (real name: Sebastião de Souza e Silva) will ferry you there and back (US$1 per person round-trip) or you can rent a kayak from him (US$1 per hour)

and explore up and down the river yourself. Babazinho usually has a tent with food and drink for sale on Praia Grande, but if not, he can also put together a little lunch cooler for you for a small price. He also does tours in the area; see below. Also ask about windsurfing classes.

HIKING & CAMPING

Boa Vista has a number of interesting hiking and camping possibilities nearby, served mostly by independent tour operators.

Jean-Luc Felix (☎ 624 3015), a Belgian transplant, and his Brazilian business partner **Lula** (☎ 9965 2222) lead camping trips to Serra Grande (two to three days) and Serra de Tepequém (four days plus) – a *tepuis*, or steep-sided, flat-topped mountains, typical of northern Roraima and southeast Venezuela. Good hiking, orchids and bird-watching are highlights (US$15 to US$30 per person per day, including meals and transport). The pair is also building a forest lodge along the Rio Branco about 75km from Boa Vista, where small groups will be able to hike, sport fish and bird-watch for around US$17 per day per person. Felix can often also be reached at the Bistro Gourmet restaurant (see opposite).

Eliezer Rufino de Souza (☎ 9971 0787, 623 0787; Rua Floriano Peixoto 505) is run by a local artist and tour operator who speaks English. He offers two-hour riverboat tours (US$8 per person, minimum two people) and half-day boat excursions (US$55 for up to six people) up the Rio Branco to the Fazenda São Marcos (a historic cattle ranch founded in 1799) and the site of the Forte São Joaquim, a fort built by the Portuguese in 1775.

THE ROAD THROUGH A RESERVE

The Manaus–Boa Vista highway (BR-174) has a violent history. A 125km stretch of this road cuts across the 25,000-sq-km Terra Indígena Waimiri Atroari.

The Waimiri fiercely defended their land against the construction of the road, combating the forces of the Brazilian army in the 1970s. During the confrontations more than 200 soldiers were killed by poison arrows. Casualties on the Indian side, however, were a lot higher. From a population of 1500 in 1974, their numbers were reduced to a mere 374 in 1986, when finally they agreed to negotiate with the government.

Today the population is increasing, with around 800 people living in 14 *aldeias* (villages). On the part of the road that crosses Indian land, drivers are not allowed to get out of their vehicles, and (with a few exceptions such as the Manaus–Boa Vista bus service) the road through the reserve is closed between 6pm and 6am.

Sebastião 'Babazinho' de Souza e Silva (☎ 9111 3511, 624 8382; Major William 1) is a registered and long-time guide offering customized camping trips to Serra de Tepequém and Fazenda Bacabal, northwest of Boa Vista, and other destinations.

Sleeping

All hotels listed following include free breakfast.

Hotel Monte Líbano (☎ 224 7232; Av Benjamin Constant 319 W; s/d with shared bathroom US$4.60/6, with private bathroom & air-con US$9.30/11; 🟦) The least worst of the cheap hotels has drab *quartos*, with fan and shared bathroom, and somewhat better air-con rooms, with private bath, TV and minibar.

Hotel Ideal (☎ 224 6342; Rua Araújo Filho 533; s/d with fan US$8.30/10, with air-con US$10/13.30; 🟦) Popular with travelers, rooms at this large, rambling hotel are small and bare, but definitely a step up from the Monte Líbano. You can rent a TV for another US$2. Friendly service.

Hotel Tres Nações (☎ 224 3439; Av Ville Roy 8534; s/d US$10/12; 🟦) Basic, clean air-con rooms, convenient to the bus station.

Hotel Barrudada (☎ 623 9335; Rua Araújo Filho 228; s/d US$20/27; 🟦) One of the newer hotels in town, rooms here are spotless with air-con, TV, fridge, phone and excellent breakfast. Discounts up to 30% are usually available, making this a pretty good deal.

Hotel Euzébio's (☎ 623 0300; Rua Cecília Brasil 1107; standard s/d US$14/17, superior US$22.60/28.30; 🟦) Standard rooms are clean but small; superiors are bigger, more cheerful and come with hot water, minibar and telephone. All rooms have air-con and TV. The hotel has a free airport shuttle for guests to (but not from) the airport, and a reception desk in the airport lobby.

Uiramutam Palace (☎ 624 4700; Av Capitan Ene Garcez 427; s/d simple $20/27, completo US$27/36.60; 🟦 🈴) The cheaper of the two hotels with swimming pools, the rooms here are awfully plain for the price. All have TV, air-con and minibar – the *completos* are larger, and have hot water and the all-important TV remote control.

Hotel Aipana Plaza (☎ 224 4800; fax 224 4116; Praça do Centro Cívico 53; s/d/tr US$45/50/58; 🈴) Boa Vista's most upscale hotel has classy, muted decor, including sculptures in the hallway, slate floors, glass showers and good beds. The pool area makes a nice escape from the heat, which can sometimes become intense.

Eating

Pigalle (dishes US$2-6; Av Capitan Ene Garcez 153; 🌙 dinner) Serves up cheap pizza and *churrasco* (grilled meat) starting at US$2 and US$3 respectively.

La Gondola (Av Benjamin Constant 35 W; self-service per kg US$4.15, dishes US$3-7; 🌙 lunch & dinner Sun-Fri, lunch Sat) Facing the plaza, come here for good per-kilo lunch and standard à la carte dinner.

Mister Quilo (Rua Inácio Magalhães 346; 🌙 lunch) Another decent per-kilo spot.

Restaurant Ver O Rio (Praça Barreto Leite; ☎ 624 1683; dishes US$5-10; 🌙 lunch & dinner Tue-Sun, dinner Mon) This restaurant is perched in a fine spot just above the river (there's even a breeze sometimes). The fish dishes here are good – many are large enough for two people. A good place to relax over a beer, too.

Peixada Tropical (cnr Rua Ajuricaba & Rua Pedro Rodrigues; dishes for 2 US$8-12) A popular lunch spot, with airy outdoor seating. Come here for fish prepared every way thinkable, from a Portuguese fish stew to fried-up spicy, Baihian style.

ENTERING VENEZUELA & GUYANA

At the time of research, travelers of many nationalities, including US and British passport-holders, needed to obtain a Venezuelan tourist card in advance in order to enter Venezuela by land. (That said, enforcement at the border seemed somewhat lax.) At the consulate in Boa Vista, you need to present a photocopy of your passport data page, one passport photo (available at booths in the main plaza), a photocopy of your yellow-fever vaccination certificate and a photocopy of your Brazilian entry/exit slip. Note that this office is only open until noon and processing takes around 30 minutes. At the time of research, Israeli citizens were not allowed to enter Venezuela unless they had a confirmed international plane ticket out of the country, and even then were permitted to stay for 72 hours only.

Entering Guyana, citizens of USA, Canada, Australia and EU countries do not normally need a Visa. Israelis do, however.

Crepe & Cia (☎ 623 9869; Av Benjamin Constant 1765; dishes US$4-6; ☽ dinner) The crepes here aren't exactly light and fluffy, but are still a nice alternative to another dinner of beans, rice and *farofa* (garnish of manioc flour sautéed with butter). Chocolate or banana crepes make a nice dessert.

Bistro Gourmet (☎ 624 2200; cnr Rua Araújo Filho & Av NS da Consolata; dishes for 2 US$5-12; ☽ dinner) Run by an expat Belgian, this is one of Boa Vista's finer restaurants, and it's not too pricey. Dishes are mostly French-influenced, with saucy fish, meat, chicken and pasta all available. Indoor and outdoor seating, often with live music. Also ask here about area tours (see p648).

Sorveteria Pik Nik (☎ 624 4622; Rua Inácio Magalhães 340; ☽ 8am-6pm Mon-Fri, 2-6pm Sun) Just down from Mister Quilo, this is a good spot for ice cream.

Hotel Barrudada (☎ 623 9335; Rua Araújo Filho 228) and **Hotel Aipana Plaza** (☎ 224 4800; fax 224 4116; Praça do Centro Cívico 53) also have good restaurants that are open for breakfast, lunch and dinner.

Shopping

Centro de Artesanato (☎ 623 1615; Rua Floriano Peixoto 158; ☽ 8am-6pm Mon-Sat) A large selection of crafts, much of it distinctly knick-knacks, but with some genuine Indian work as well.

Getting There & Away

AIR

All domestic flights from Boa Vista go through Manaus. At the time of research only Meta had international flights, to Georgetown (Guyana) and Paramaribo (Suriname), but no flights to Venezuela. Meta often has great fares, but is also known to cancel its flights somewhat regularly – plan accordingly. Note that schedules and fares change often.

Varig (☎ 224 2226; Rua Araújo Filho 91; ☽ 8am-6pm Mon-Fri, 8am-noon Sat) has daily flights to Manaus, with onward connections from there.

Rico (in Manaus ☎ 633 5166, 652 1652) flies to Manaus three times a week for the same price as Varig.

Meta (☎ 224 7677, 224 7438; cnr Av Benjamin Constant & Rua Antonio Bittencourt; ☽ 8am-6pm Mon-Fri, 8am-noon Sat) flies to Manaus four times weekly for about US$15 less than Rico and

Varig, and three times weekly to Georgetown (US$70) and Paramaribo (US$185).

BUS

Eucatur (☎ 623 2233, 624 1322) has four standard buses to Manaus (US$22, 12 hours, 10am, 6pm, 7:30pm and 8pm) and one *semi leito/leito* bus (US$25/US$33, 10 hours, 8:30pm). Buses to Venezuela originate in Manaus and pass Boa Vista once a day at 7am, stopping in Santa Elena Uairén (US$7, 3½ hours) and continuing to Puerto Ordaz, Puerto La Cruz and Caracas (US$27). Buses to Pacaraima, on the Venezuelan border, leave at 7am, 1:30pm and 5pm (US$5, three hours).

Amatur (☎ 224 0004, 224 0009) operates daily buses to/from Bonfim on the Guyana border (one way/round-trip US$3.75/4.50, 1½ hours, 7am, 10am, 2pm and 4:30pm). From Lethem, just across the border, there is service to Georgetown (US$30, 10 hours, 1am Monday, Wednesday and Friday).

Getting Around

The **airport** (☎ 224 4143) is 3.5km northwest of the city center. To get there, you can take an 'Aeroporto' bus (US$0.70) from the *terminal urbano* (municipal bus terminal) on Av Dr Silvio Botelho or the *mini-terminal urbano* at the top of Praça do Centro Cívico; buses depart roughly every 30 to 40 minutes from 6am till 7pm, then hourly until 11pm). Taxis to/from the airport and center charge a fixed rate of US$6.60.

The **bus station** (☎ 623 2233; Av das Guianas, in Bairro São Vicente) is 2.5km southwest of the center. Several buses go there to/from the *terminal urbano* via the *mini-terminal urbano*, including 'Jockei Clube,' 'Raiar do Sol,' and 'Nova Ciudad' (all US$0.50). Catch any of the same buses back to the center. A taxi from the center to the bus station costs about US$3.

Getting around town, taxis marked 'Lotação' go along fixed routes for US$1 per passenger. Just ask if they're going where you want, or nearby.

AROUND BOA VISTA
Bonfim & Lethem (Guyana)

Bonfim ☎ 0xx95 / pop 3000
Lethem (Guyana) ☎ 072 / pop 900

The small town of Bonfim, 125km northeast of Boa Vista, is the stepping stone to

AROUND BOA VISTA

Guyana. The Guyanese town of Lethem is about 5km west across the Rio Tacutu. Whichever direction you're crossing the border in, start early to get to your destination before nightfall.

The Polícia Federal (for Brazilian immigration procedures) is between Bonfim bus station and the river, so you have to walk or get taxi (about US$1) to the police and onward from there. A canoe across the river costs US$0.75. You should check in with the police at Lethem (about 1.5km from the river) immediately, as officials are wary about smuggling on this border.

The Kanuku mountains near Lethem are full of wildlife and there are several expensive ecotourism ranches in the area; for information, try Don & Shirley's shop at the Lethem airstrip.

The Guyana telephone country code is ☎ 592.

Neither Lethem nor Bonfim are exactly pleasant, but Lethem is the better of the two; both have hotels in case you get stuck.

Takatu Guest House (☎ 2040; r US$7), in Lethem, has clean, basic rooms and cheap meals.

Pousada Fronteira (☎ 552 1294; Rua Aluísio de Menezes 26, Bonfim; r US$6) is one of various not-so-good options in Bonfim, with basic rooms and okay bathrooms.

See opposite for buses between Bonfim and Boa Vista, and air and ground transportation onward to Georgetown, Guyana.

SANTA ELENA DE UAIRÉN (VENEZUELA)

☎ 0289 / pop 12,000

Santa Elena is a few kilometers north of the only land-border crossing between Brazil and Venezuela. It's a pleasant and relaxed border town, higher and cooler than Boa Vista, and it provides access to southeast Venezuela's vast, beautiful and silent Gran Sábana and to Mt Roraima, the spectacular mountain rising where Brazil, Venezuela and Guyana meet.

Brazilian and Venezuelan immigration procedures are all dealt with at the border, from posts situated about 1km apart from each other. Entering Venezuela, travelers of most nationalities are supposed to have a tourist card (see the boxed text on p649); however, officials at the border will probably let you through without it. Entering Brazil, a yellow-fever vaccination certificate is required. There is a Brazilian health-ministry vaccination post at the border, but you have to have had the vaccine at least 10 days prior to entering (it is not considered effective until then). Definitely plan ahead for this. The Brazilian border office is open daily from 8am till noon and 2pm till 6pm.

Orientation

The bus from Boa Vista passes the entrance to the town on its way to the new bus station, about 2km further east. If you don't want to go all the way to the station, get off at the large faux-Indian lodge at the busy intersection – not only a useful landmark, it is the office of Ruta Salvaje, one of the main tour operators in town.

From Ruta Salvaje, Av Mariscal Sucre extends westward, with many hotels. After 250m, the road bends sharply left (south) at a military barracks and turns into Calle Bolivar. This is the main drag, with banks, hotels, Internet access and restaurants. The next large cross street is Calle Urdaneta – to

THE AMAZON

the right is Plaza Bolívar with a bank and restaurant, among other things; to the left are more restaurants, hotels and Internet places. Further down, Calle Urdaneta turns to dirt before hitting Av Perimetral – turn left again and you've completed a square, with Ruta Salvaje another 250 meters ahead. If you turn right on Av Perimetral, you head to the airport, passing the hospital on the way.

Information

INTERNET
Cafe Iruk (☎ 416 0588; Calle Bolívar across from Hotel Panazarelli; per hr US$0.50 until 3pm, US$0.75 thereafter; ☺ 9am-midnight) Has the fastest Internet connection in town.
Global Internet (☎ 995 1655; Calle Urdaneta; per hr US$0.75; ☺ 8am-10pm) Located just before La Casa de Gladys.
Mobiltepuy (☎ 995 1563; per hr US$0.50; ☺ 8am-8pm Mon-Fri, 8am-1pm Sat) Across the street from Cafe Iruk, you can also place long-distance phone calls here.

LAUNDRY
Lavandaría Rocío (☎ 414 5263; Av Mariscal Sucre, near barracks; per kg US$0.75; ☺ 8:30am-7pm Mon-Fri)

MEDICAL SERVICES
Hospital (☎ 171, 995 1155) Has basic medical services.

MONEY
Moneychangers hang out at the corner of Calle Bolívar and Calle Urdaneta; until the Venezuelan government relaxes exchange restrictions, moneychangers have significantly better rates than the banks are able to offer.
Banco Guyana (Plaza Bolívar; ☺ 8:30am-3:30pm Mon-Fri) Has an ATM.
Banco Industrial de Venezuela (Calle Bolívar, 50m north of Hotel Augusta; ☺ 8:30am-3:30pm Mon-Fri) Has an ATM; Visa cardholders can withdraw from the teller inside.

TRAVEL AGENCIES
The following are among several tour operators offering trips in the region; see Mt Roraima and Gran Sabana, p653 for more information on these operators.
Adrenalin Expeditions (☎ 0414/385 2846, 0414/854 2940; af14scorpion@hotmail.com; 2nd fl, Hotel Panazarelli, Calle Bolívar)
Ruta Salvaje Tours (☎ 995 1134; www.rutasalvaje .com; Av Mariscal Sucre; ☺ 8am-noon & 2-5pm Mon-Sat)

Sleeping & Eating

There are many more hotels than those listed here. Other than during holidays, you should not have any trouble finding a room.

Hotel Augusta (Calle Bolívar; r US$4, tr/q US$6/7) Spick-and-span rooms in jolly colors with fan, hot shower and fridge. Owners are installing air-con, so expect prices to go up US$2 to US$3, but it's still an excellent value.

Hotel Panzarelli (☎ 995 1196; Calle Bolívar; r US$5) Affordable and centrally located. Rooms are small but sleep two and are pretty clean, and they open onto a long wide corridor with chairs for relaxing. A good value.

Hotel Panayma (☎ 414 5288; Av Mariscal Sucre; r with fan/air-con US$4/8; ☒) One of many similar hotels on Mariscal Sucre, with no-frills cement rooms facing either the street or a large parking lot.

Hotel Los Castaños (☎ 995 1450; Av Mariscal Sucre; r with fan/air-con US$6.50/10; ☒) Probably the nicest option on Mariscal Sucre. Small but clean and attractively painted rooms have TV and hot water. Rooms sleep up to three – larger units (US$15) are available.

La Casa de Gladys (☎ 995 1530; Calle Urdaneta 187; dm US$2.50, s/d/tr/q US$3/4/6/8) About 200m from Calle Bolívar, this long-running budget place, with a charmingly cantankerous owner, has dim, basic rooms with fan and private bathroom. The small dormitory has a shared bathroom. You can do your own cooking.

Cafe Colonial (Calle Urdaneta 25; ☺ most mornings) The Cafe Colonial does bargain breakfasts of eggs, ham, bread, butter, jam, coffee and juice for US$2.

Nova Opção II (☎ 995 1702; Calle Urdaneta next to Cafe Colonial; dishes US$2-3; ☺ 7am-11pm Mon-Sat) This bright, clean eatery is popular with locals, serving decent fish, chicken and meat dishes, both Brazilian and Venezuelan style. The same owners have a per-kilo place called **Nova Opção Servi-Kilo** (Calle Bolívar; meat/veg per kg US$3.75/3; ☺ 11am-5pm).

Restaurante Toquín (☎ 416 0610; Av Mariscal Sucre, near barracks; dishes US$2-5; ☺ 11:30am-9pm) This small, airy restaurant has friendly owners, fake flowers on the tables and specializes in Colombian food. We can highly recommend it.

Pizzeria Alfredo (Av Perimetral) Recommended for more upscale food and atmosphere.

Getting There & Away

AIR

Rutaca (in Ciudad Bolivar ☎ 0285-632 6290; ☒ at airport 7am-4pm Mon-Sat) flies most days to Ciudad Bolivar (US$90), usually mid-morning, but it is not a regularly scheduled flight. You must go to the airport, about 7km south of town, for ticketing. There is no public transport there; taxis cost about US$5.

BUS

Eucatur has once-daily service to Caracas (US$20, 19 hours, departing at noon) with stops in Puerto Ordaz (US$10, 8½ hours) and Puerto La Cruz (US$17, 15 hours). Another bus departs at 7pm, stopping in San Felix (10 hours), Puerto Ordaz (10½ hours), and Ciudad Bolivar (11½ hours); the cost is $10 regardless of destination. To Manaus, a bus leaves daily at 8am (US$33, 12½ hours).

To Boa Vista, a bus usually leaves the Santa Elena terminal at 8am and noon daily (US$5, three hours). A comfy bus from Caracas passes the border at around 9am, and ordinary buses leave from there at 7am, 1pm and 5pm. Alternatively, collective taxis leave from the border every day from 6am to 6pm. The taxis make the trip in two hours (US$6.50), but wait for four passengers before leaving – morning and afternoon are the best times. The **Hotel Pacaraima** (☎ 592 1515; r US$10) is nearby, in case you get stuck. To get to *la linea* (the border), taxis charge US$3.50 to US$4, including stops at the Venezuelan and Brazilian immigration posts.

MT RORAIMA & THE GRAN SABANA

Santa Elena is at the southern tip of the massive (3 million hectares/30,000 sq km) Parque Nacional Canaima. At its heart is the **Gran Sabana**, a high savanna dotted with *tepuis*, stark flat-topped mesas, and crisscrossed by rivers. Trips here include great vista points, swimming in natural pools and visiting spectacular waterfalls, including the 100m Salto Aponwao.

At 2810m, **Mt Roraima**, straddling Brazil, Venezuela and Guyana on the park's edge, is one of the largest and highest of the *tepuis*. The top is a 60-sq-km moonscape, more than half of which is Venezuelan, including the only nonvertical route to the top. The popular ascent (typically six days/

five nights) involves no technical climbing and can be done by anyone who's fit.

River rafting is also possible in the Gran Sabana; one-day and overnight trips offered by Ruta Salvaje can include some Class IV rapids and portages around (and exploring *under*) sizable falls. Just outside the park, **El Pauji** can be visited in a day, offering excellent vistas of the region and the Amazon rain forest to the south.

Ruta Salvaje Tours (☎ 995 1134; www.rutasalvaje .com; Av Mariscal Sucre; ☒ 8am-noon & 2-5pm Mon-Sat) offers tours of Mt Roraima (six days/five nights, including two nights on top) and the Gran Sabana (one to three days; lodging in tents or simple *pousadas* (guesthouses). All-inclusive trips (US$40 to US$50 per person per day) include all food, equipment, transportation and guides. At the time of research, this was also the only agency to offer river rafting; one-day trips are US$35, all-inclusive three-day trips are US$150. Owner Iván Artal has some 20 years experience here.

Adrenalin Expeditions (☎ 0414/385 2846, 0414/854 2940; af14scorpion@hotmail.com; 2nd fl, Hotel Panzarelli, Calle Bolivar) is a Ciudad Bolivar–based operator that recently opened an office in Santa Elena, after offering tours here for many years. Its enthusiastic co-owner Franciso Alvarez quoted prices of US$25 to US$35 per day for similar Gran Sabana, Mt Roraima and Pauji tours, for a minimum four-person group.

Both agencies may reduce prices if you have your own equipment. It is always a good idea to call or email ahead for reservations.

If you want to go independently, particularly to Mt Roraima, Ruta Salvaje rents most gear – tents and camp stoves both run at US$15 to US$20 for six days, sleeping bags US$10, pads US$3. The trail starts at an Indian village called Paraitepui, about 91km from Santa Elena – transportation there for up to six people costs US$80 each way. Or you can bus it to San Francisco de Yuruaní, another indigenous village, and try hopping a ride there (US$4.50 for the bus, US$40 to Paratepui). Be sure to arrange your return trip.

Park regulations require you to have an indigenous guide who can be hired in Santa Elena, San Francisco de Yuruaní or Paraitepui for US$15 per day. Ruta Salvaje

THE AMAZON

can also arrange a specialized guide (who should speak English, be able to explain the area's geology and flora and fauna, and have first-aid training and a radio) for US$50 per day. Guides will bring their own food and gear. Good water can be found in streams every 4km or 5km along the walk.

There is no true dry season here, and clouds frequently cover Mt Roraima. The park can be visited year-round, but the best time is November to February, when the rain is somewhat diminished but the rivers and falls still full. Independent travelers should definitely avoid traveling here during Semana Santa (late April) and the first 10 to 12 days of January – these are major Venezuelan and Brazilian holidays, when Santa Elena is mobbed by as many as 15,000 tourists.

Rondônia & Acre

HIGHLIGHTS

- Hiking and canoeing in the **Reserva Extrativista Pedras Negras** (p667) in the remote Guaporé Valley

- Visiting **Xapuri** (p672), home town of Chico Mendes, Acre's environmental martyr

- Exploring **Rio Branco** (p668), with its surprisingly good museums, restaurants and cafés

- Perusing train-memorabilia galore in the cavernous **Museu da Estrada de Ferro Madeira-Mamoré** (p658) in Porto Velho

- Relaxing at the river-front swimming pool at **Pakaas Palafitas Lodge** (p663) in Guajará-Mirim

★ Rio Branco
★ Xapuri
★ Guajará-Mirim
★ Reserva Extrativista Pedras Negras

■ POPULATION: 2.2 MILLION   ■ AREA: 391,660 SQ KM

THE AMAZON

The states of Rondônia and Acre, previously undeveloped frontier regions, underwent rapid development and severe deforestation in the 1970s and 1980s, as a result of government colonization programs and the construction of Hwy BR-364 from Cuiabá in Mato Grosso. Vast tracts of land were left looking like the aftermath of a holocaust, and the hopes of many colonists were quickly dashed as their plots of cleared jungle soon turned infertile. Both states have also served as major conduits for cocaine trafficking from Peru and Bolivia.

Deforestation has slowed considerably and the Brazilian police and army have made several high-profile drug busts in recent years. Porto Velho remains a somewhat edgy town (though tourists are generally left alone), while Rio Branco has transformed itself into a surprisingly pleasant place to visit, with good restaurants and well-organized museums. In both cities, federal police may ask to see your passport (even on the street) as foreigners are often a part of the ongoing drug trade.

History

During the 17th and 18th centuries, Portuguese *bandeirantes* (a group of roaming adventurers), in pursuit of gold and Indian slaves, crossed the line drawn by the Treaty of Tordesillas (signed between Spain and Portugal in 1494) and entered what is now Rondônia to roam the Guaporé and Madeira river valleys. Portugal secured its new possessions by building the Forte Príncipe da Beira, an imposing fortress on the Guaporé, between 1776 and 1783.

By the 1903 Treaty of Petrópolis, Bolivia ceded Acre to Brazil in return for UK£2 million and a promise to build a railway bypassing the waterfalls and rapids on the Rio Mamoré and upper Rio Madeira. This would give landlocked Bolivia access to world rubber markets via the Amazon. Since the railway never reached its ultimate intended goal (the Bolivian town of Riberalta, on the Rio Beni), and the price of rubber soon plummeted on the world market, the project turned out to be effectively useless. The towns of Porto Velho and Guajará-Mirim, however, were founded at either end of the completed section in Brazil (see the boxed text on p660).

In 1981 the Polonoroeste program opened Rondônia to agricultural colonization by land-hungry settlers from all over the country. Rondônia's population leapt from 111,000 in 1970 to 1.13 million in 1991, while about one-fifth of the virgin jungle that covered almost the whole state was felled. The rate of deforestation in the 1980s was equivalent to more than a football field a minute, for a whole decade.

A major impetus of all this was the paving of Hwy BR-364 from Mato Grosso in 1983–84, with World Bank funding. This project was described by George Monbiot in *Amazon Watershed* (1991) as 'perhaps the single most destructive piece of engineering in the world.' Indians suffered severely from new diseases and deliberate killings.

Ironically, the highway has been all but eclipsed by the Rio Madeira as the region's artery to the outside world. Soy beans grown in Mato Grosso state are trucked to Porto Velho, where they are loaded onto Brazil's largest river convoy – 16 connected barges, measuring 275m, carrying 34,000 tons of soy beans per trip. The convoy chugs nearly 1200km north to Itacoatiara on the Amazon (about 300km east of Manaus), where the beans are loaded onto oceangoing ships for export worldwide. The Maggi Group, the world's largest single soy producer, created and operates the barge and now exports 90% of its Brazilian crop (and that of hundreds of smaller operations) this way. Company officials say it would take a thousand trucks to carry the same load.

National Parks

Neither of this region's two national parks – Parque Nacional da Serra do Divisor in western Acre or Parque Nacional de Pacaás Novos in central Rondônia – is easily accessible. Instead, go to the **Reserva Extrativista Pedras Negras** (p667) in the long, unspoiled Guaporé Valley in southern Rondônia, where three- to four-day package trips (organized in Porto Velho) include canoeing, wildlife-spotting and visiting local villages.

Getting There & Away

Rondônia and Acre are sandwiched between the virtually impenetrable Amazon rain forest to the north and the greatly under-developed Bolivian countryside to the south. By far the easiest way to get to both states is to fly – there are frequent flights from Manaus, Belém and Brasília. From Bolivia, you can fly into the border towns of Guayaramerín or Cobija and cross into Brazil there. The next best way here is by boat – passenger boats from Manaus go south on the Rio Madeira to Porto Velho, a trip of about five days. There are also buses to Porto Velho from Brasília, which take about 40 hours. Bus travel from the interior of Bolivia is tough in the dry season and very much *not* recommended in the rainy.

Getting Around

Both states' highway systems are slowly improving, and there are now good roads between Porto Velho, Rio Branco and Bolivian and Peruvian border towns. In fact, the best way to get from Guayaramerín and Cobija (both in Bolivia) is to cross into Brazil and take a bus there. You can also fly quite cheaply between the capitals (US$30 at the time of research). Beyond the main corridors, there are plenty of bus services, but ask ahead about conditions.

RONDÔNIA

In 1943 President Getúlio Vargas created the Territory of Guaporé from chunks of Amazonas and Mato Grosso. In 1981 it became the state of Rondônia, named for Marechal Cândido Rondon, the enlightened and humane soldier who 'tamed' this region in the 1920s when he constructed a telegraph line linking it to the rest of Brazil. Rondon also founded the Serviço de Proteção ao Índio (SPI), predecessor of Funai (Fundação Nacional do Indio; government

Indian agency). He exhorted SPI agents to '*Morrer, se preciso for, matar nunca !*' ('Die, if necessary, but never kill!').

Rondônia is a transition zone between dense Amazonian forests and cerrado (savanna), and despite its sad environmental past, it still has some of the richest fauna and flora in Amazonia.

PORTO VELHO

☎ 0xx69 / pop 311,500

Porto Velho's new economic importance is helping improve and modernize the city. Glossy shops and some fine public buildings help counter the capital's reputation as an edgy frontier town. Change is slow, however – Porto Velho remains a major conduit for cocaine smuggling and the town still feels a bit rough around the edges, especially at night.

Orientation

Porto Velho's main street is Av Sete de Setembro, starting just inland from the riverfront and Madeira–Mamoré train station. Av Carlos Gomes, parallel to Av Sete de Septembro and three blocks north, is another major street, housing many shops and the small mall Rio Shopping. About 2.5km east, both streets intersect with Av Jorge Teixeira, which runs north to the bus station, past the Ibama (Instituto Brasileiro do Meio Ambiente e dos Recursos Naturais Renováveis; Brazilian Institute of the Environment and Renewable Natural Resources) office and eventually to the airport.

Information

BOOKSTORES

Bons Livros (☎ 221 2000; 2nd fl, Rio Shopping, Av Carlos Gomes; 🕑 10am-10pm Mon-Sat, 5am-9pm Sun) Has some simple but nice photography books of Brazilian destinations.

EMERGENCY

Ambulance (☎ 192)
Emergency room (☎ 224 5225; Hospital Central, Rua Julio de Castiho 149)
Police (☎ 190)

INTERNET ACCESS

Games & Videos (☎ 224 2724; Av Sete de Setembro 1925; per hr US$1.75; 🕑 9am-10pm)
Net Games (☎ 224 5478; 2nd fl, Rio Shopping, Av Carlos Gomes; per hr US$1.25; 🕑 10am-10pm)

LAUNDRY

Many hotels offer laundry service.

Lavanderia Mamoré (☎ 221 3266; Av Pinheiro Machado 1455; per piece US$0.50-75; ☯ 7:30am-6:30pm Mon-Fri, 7:30am-2pm Sat) Quick and professional.

MEDICAL SERVICES

Hospital Central (☎ 224 5225; Rua Julio de Castiho 149)

MONEY

Banco do Brasil (Rua Dom Pedro II 607; ☯ 10am-2pm Mon-Fri) Changes traveler's checks.

Bradesco (Av Carlos Gomes) Across from the cathedral. Reliable ATMs.

Casa de Câmbio Marco Aurélio (☎ 223 2551; Rua José de Alencar 3353; ☯ 8:30am-3pm Mon-Fri) Changes several foreign currencies.

HSBC Av Jorge Teixeira **(Av Jorge Teixeira** 1350); Rua Prudente de Morais **(cnr Rua Prudente de Morais & Av Sete de Setembro)** Reliable ATMs. The branch on Av Jorge Teixeira is next to the bus station.

POST

Post office (☎ 217 3667; cnr Av Presidente Dutra & Av Sete de Setembro; ☯ 8am-5pm Mon-Fri, 9am-noon Sat)

TELEPHONE

Telemania (Av Carlos Gomes 728)

TOURIST INFORMATION

Embratur (Av Presidente Dutra 3004; ☯ 8am-5pm Mon-Fri) Has limited information.

Ibama (☎ 223 2023; esecunia.ro@ibama.gov.br; Av Jorge Teixeira 3559) Check here on progress toward opening nearby protected areas, including Lago do Cuniã (p661), for ecotourism. The office is a couple of kilometers north of the center – bus No 201 signed 'Hospital de Base via Aeroporto' passes here.

TRAVEL AGENCIES

HHC (☎ 221 9403; www.pedrasnegras.com; Rua Salgado Filho 2954-A at Rua Abunã) Arrange trips to Pedras Negras Lodge (p667) here.

Nossa Viagens e Turismo (☎ 224 4777; Rua Tenreiro Aranha 2125; ☯ 8am-6pm Mon-Fri, 8am-noon Sat) Buy bus tickets here to save yourself a trip to the bus station.

Vip'Stur (☎ 224 2144, 224 7389; Av Carlos Gomes 1700; ☯ 8am-7pm Mon-Fri, 8am-noon Sat) For air tickets.

Sights & Activities

MUSEU DA ESTRADA DE FERRO MADEIRA-MAMORÉ & SANTO ANTÔNIO

The city's only real sight of interest, the **Museu da Estrada de Ferro Madeira-Mamoré** (Madeira-Mamoré Railway Museum; admission free; ☯ 8am-6pm)

is housed in one of several huge sheds that made up the original train station, and displays train relics, memorabilia, and photographs charting the railway's story. The locomotive 'Colonel Church,' built by the Baldwin Locomotive Works of Philadelphia, became the first locomotive to run in Amazonia when it inaugurated the Madeira–Mamoré Railway in 1878 (see the boxed text on p660). A variety of other old US- and German-made locomotives and rolling stock can be seen standing around nearby.

You used to be able to take a ride on the steam engine 'Maria Fumaça' (Smoking Mary) to and from **Santo Antônio**, about 7km southwest of Porto Velho. The trips weren't being offered at the time of research, but it's worth asking when you visit. Santo Antônio was the original northern terminus of the Madeira–Mamoré Railway. All that remains there today is a chapel, built in 1913, but it's a popular dry-season swimming spot and near the Cachoeira de Santo Antônio waterfalls.

RIVER TRIPS

The broad Rio Madeira forms the western boundary of Porto Velho. Measurements of the length of the mud-brown river usually include its main tributary, the Rio Mamoré, and *its* tributaries, which originate in the Bolivian Andes, making the Madeira 3200km long. With an average flow of 1.4 billion liters a minute, the Madeira has the sixth-greatest volume of all the world's rivers. It enters the Rio Amazonas 150km downstream from Manaus.

From about 9am to 7pm daily, riverboats make 45-minute cruises along the Rio Madeira from the dock in front of the Madeira–Mamoré train station (US$1.25 per person). While not exactly thrilling, this is a reasonable way to idle away an hour or so. With luck you'll see a few pink dolphins. You can buy snacks and drinks on board, and a full (but rather gross) lunch is served on weekends.

Sleeping

Hotel Messianico (☎ 221 9600; Av Sete de Setembro 1180; s/d with shared bathroom US$3.50/5, with private bathroom US$7, with air-con US$10; ❄) Small rooms open onto a courtyard and are kept reasonably clean. Breakfast isn't included.

Hotel Tia Carmen (☎ 221 7910; Av Campos Sales 2895; s/d with shared bathroom & fan US$5/8, with private bathroom, TV & air-con US$9/13; ❄) In a quiet location, rooms are clean but a bit musty until you get some air circulating. Prices include a simple breakfast (except on Sunday).

Vitória Palace Hotel (☎ 221 9232; Rua Duque de Caxias 745; s/d with fan US$10/13.50, with air-con & TV US$13/16.50; ❄) Some rooms are a bit mustier than others, but are in general good value, and are in a safe, quiet location.

Hotel Amazonas (☎ 221 7735; Av Carlos Gomes 2838; r with shared bathroom US$3.50, s/d with private bathroom & fan US$5/7, with air-con US$10; ❄) Near the bus station, this very basic cheapie is OK for late arrivals and early departures, but not too pleasant for much longer.

Novo Hotel (☎ 224 6555; Av Carlos Gomes 2776) Also near the bus station, this is a much better option than Hotel Amazonas, with clean, new-ish rooms and friendly service.

Hotel Yara (☎ 221 2127; Rua General Osório 255; s/d US$10/16.50, with minibar US$13.50/18.50) Ordinary, somewhat stuffy rooms but still the best option in this part of town.

Hotel Regina (☎ 224 3411; Rua Almirante Barroso 1127; s/d/tr with air-con & TV US$16/26/33; ❄) A bit removed from the center, but still good value in this price range, with comfortable rooms and friendly service. Ask for a discount.

Hotel Central (☎ 224 2099; fax 223 5114; Rua Tenreiro Aranha 2472; s/d US$28/37) Modern, comfortable rooms come with an excellent breakfast.

PORTO VELHO

0 500 m
0 0.3 miles

INFORMATION	
Banco do Brasil ATM	1 B3
Bons Livros	(see 12)
Bradesco	2 B3
Casa de Câmbio Marco Aurélio	3 A3
Embratur	4 A3
Games & Videos	5 D3
HHC	6 C1
Hospital Central	7 B3
HSBC	8 B4
Lavandería Mamoré	9 C2
Net Games	(see 12)
Nossa Viagens e Turismo	10 B4
Post Office	11 A4
Rio Shopping	12 C3
Telemania	13 B3
VIP'STUR	14 C3

SIGHTS & ACTIVITIES	(p658)
Museu da Estrada de Ferro Madeira-Mamoré	15 A4

SLEEPING 🛏	(pp658–60)
Hotel Central	16 B3
Hotel Messianico	17 C3
Hotel Regina	18 C4
Hotel Tereza Raquel	19 B3
Hotel Tia Carmem	20 B3
Hotel Vila Rica	21 C3
Hotel Yara	22 B4
Vitória Palace Hotel	23 B3

EATING 🍴	(p660)
Caffé Restaurante	24 B3
Fiorella	25 B3
Food & Drink Stands	26 A4
Mirante II	27 A3
Pizzaria Agua na Boca	28 B2
Remanso do Tucunaré	29 C4
Restaurante Maná	30 B3
Richard Grill	31 A3
Sanduba's	32 B3

ENTERTAINMENT	(p660)
Cinema	(see 12)

SHOPPING	
Casa do Artesenato Madeira Mamoré	33 A4

TRANSPORT	(p661)
Bus No 201 to Bus Station & Airport	34 C3
Bus No 201 to Bus Station & Airport	35 B4
Porto Cai n'Água	36 A4
Rico	37 B3
Varig	38 B3
VASP	39 B3

THE AMAZON

Hotel Vila Rica (☎ 224 3433; Av Carlos Gomes 1616; s/d US$60/70; ✗ ⚏) Porto Velho's finest hotel has nice views from the top floors, plus an impressive foyer, bar, swimming pool and small business center. Ask for a discount, which can be as much as 40%.

Eating

Remanso do Tucunaré (☎ 221 2353; Av Brasília 1506; dishes US$7-11; ☽ 7am-3:30pm & 6pm-midnight) Good fish dishes serve two easily; try a delicious *caldeirada de tucunaré* (river-fish stew) or *tambaquí* – big fish chunks boiled with onion and tomatoes in a souplike sauce, accompanied by rice.

Caffé Restaurante (☎ 224 3176; Av Carlos Gomes 1079; per kg US$4.50; ☽ lunch Mon-Sat) This place does a good daily lunch buffet in air-con cool, including six or eight types of salad and succulent desserts.

Pizzaria Agua na Boca (☎ 221 6488; Rua Tenreiro Aranha 201; ☽ dinner Tue-Sun) Porto Velho's best pizza, with excellent service. It's a large, loud but pleasant place with outdoor tables.

Richard Grill (☎ 221 3003; Rua Major Amarante 263; per kg US$6, per kg US$7 on Sun; ☽ lunch) An upscale *por-kilo* (restaurant selling food by weight) with great river views.

Fiorella (☎ 224 7650; Av Pinheiro Machado 1133) Here you can get good, sizable meat or fish dishes for US$10 or so; pasta or pizza start at around US$5 or US$6.

Mirante II (end of Rua Dom Pedro II; ☽ lunch & dinner) Serves fish dishes for US$4 to US$10 and sandwiches for around a buck.

Sanduba's (☎ 221 3413; Av Campos Sales 2913; ☽ 5pm-3am) This late-night watering hole serves cheap, basic pizzas and big multi-ingredient burgers with all the trimmings.

Entertainment

The riverbank by the Madeira–Mamoré train station holds a dozen food and drink stands with tables, and a couple of floating docks that double as bars, which feature live music on Saturday and Sunday nights. If you're looking for beer and sweaty dancing, this is the place to head for. It can get a bit

---

DEATH RAILWAY

An American, Colonel George Earl Church, was the first to try to build a railway bypassing the 23 waterfalls and rapids that make navigation impossible on the Madeira and Mamoré Rivers, between Porto Velho and Guajará-Mirim. The idea was to carry rubber from the Mamoré and Guaporé Valleys down to the navigable section of the Madeira and thus also to the Rio Amazonas, North America and Europe. In 1871 Church contracted Britain's Public Works Construction Company to build the line. The first construction materials reached Santo Antônio do Madeira, 7km southwest of Porto Velho, in 1872 by ship from the US. But the project was abandoned a year later in the face of rampant disease among workers, attacks by Indians and mounting costs. The US firm of P & T Collins tried again for Church in 1878, managing to build 11km of embankments and nine bridges before it gave up in 1879 for the same reasons.

Following Brazil's commitment to build the railway in the 1903 Treaty of Petrópolis (p656) another American, Percival Farquhar, contracted the US firm of May, Jeckyll & Randolph to build the line. Work started in 1907, and a 364km line to Guajará-Mirim was completed in five years by old Panama Canal hands and other workers from Brazil and elsewhere. The northern terminus was moved from Santo Antônio to a healthier spot 7km downstream, around which the town of Porto Velho grew up.

The line rapidly became known as the Railway of Death, and with good reason. Building it is believed to have cost the lives of at least 5000 workers – some say 25,000 – from tropical diseases, Indian and animal attacks, accidents, gunfights, disappearances in the jungle and so on. 'One death for every railway sleeper' was the expression of the day.

And their sacrifice was tragically wasted, because just as the railway was being completed, the new British rubber plantations in Malaya killed demand for the more expensive Amazonian rubber. Percival Farquhar's Madeira Mamoré Railway Company had a 60-year contract to operate the line, but it ceased operations in 1931. Brazil's government took over the railway, finally closing it in 1972 when the Porto Velho–Guajará-Mirim road opened. The road largely follows the course of the railway, and still uses some of the line's ancient bridges on the stretch north of Guajará-Mirim.

seedy late at night – check to see if police security is around.

Getting There & Away

AIR

Porto Velho airport (☎ 225 1675, 225 1755) is 6km north of town. There are daily flights to Manaus (US$350 to US$365), Brasília (US$250 to US$300), Rio (US$325 to US$375), São Paulo (US$300 to US$370) and Rio Branco (US$35). VASP and Tavaj usually have the lowest fares, but check for promotions on all lines.

Rico (☎ 224 2105, airport check-in desk ☎ 222 0879; Av Pinheiro Machado 744; ☯ 7:30am-5:30pm Mon-Fri, 8am-noon Sat)

TAM (☎ 222 6666, airport check-in desk ☎ 225 2777; Porto Velho airport; ☯ 8am-noon & 2-6pm Mon-Fri, 8am-noon Sat)

TAVAJ (☎ 222 0859, airport check-in desk ☎ 225 2999; Porto Velho airport; ☯ 8am-noon & 2-5pm Mon-Fri, 8am-noon Sat)

Varig (☎ 224 4224, airport check-in desk ☎ 224 2262; Av Campos Sales 2666; ☯ 8am-noon & 2-6pm Mon-Fri, 8am-noon Sat)

VASP (☎ 224 5388, airport check-in desk ☎ 224 2944; cnr Rua Gonçalves Dias & Av Carlos Gomes; ☯ 8am-noon & 2-6pm Mon-Fri, 8am-noon Sat)

BOAT

Boats to Manaus via the Rio Madeira and Rio Amazonas leave at 6pm on Tuesday and Friday (hammock US$33 to US$40, three days, meals included) from Porto Cai n'Água, the dock at the end of Rua 13 de Maio. Small cabins are usually available (doubles with fan US$85 to US$100, with air-con US$100 to US$115). Boats also leave to Manicoré (about halfway) leave on Tuesday, Wednesday, Friday and Saturday (US$20); you may be able to catch a Manaus-bound boat from there. There are ticket offices on Rua 13 de Maio: you may need to bargain a bit to get the above prices. Check out the boat and fellow passengers for unsavory characters before committing yourself.

BUS

The **bus station** (cnr Av Jorge Teixeira & Av Carlos Gomes) is 2km east of the center.

Viação Rondônia (☎ 225 2891) runs four daily buses to Rio Branco (US$14 to US$17, seven to eight hours, departing at 7am, noon, 10pm and 11pm; noon and 11pm departures are direct) and six to Guajará-Mirim

(US$8 to US$10, five hours, at 1am, 6am, 9:30am, 2pm, 9pm and 11:30pm; 1am and 2pm departures are direct, with air-con). For Guajará-Mirim, you can also try catching a collective taxi (per person US$13.25, four hours). Price is based on four passengers; ask taxi drivers at the bus station.

Eucatur (☎ 222 2233) offers long-distance services with departures to Cuiabá (US$43, 22 hours, seven daily), to São Paulo (US$80, 48 hours, twice daily) and also to Brasília (US$60, 40 hours, once daily).

Andorinha (☎ 225 3025) has services to Campo Grande (US$70, 36 hours, at 7am daily) and Brasília (US$73, 42 hours, at 10am and 7pm daily).

Acailândia (☎ 225 2448) runs buses to Imperitriz (US$102, three days, Monday, Wednesday and Friday only), where you can connect to Belém and São Luís.

Since 1991 Hwy BR-319 to Manaus has been impassable from not far beyond Humaitá, 205km north of Porto Velho.

Getting Around

Bus No 201 (US$0.50), signed 'Hospital de Base via Aeroporto,' runs between the city center and airport via the bus station; buses pass hourly and are supposedly co-ordinated with arriving flights. Going to the airport, the same bus runs along Av Sete de Setembro, with stops near the corners of Av Presidente Dutra and Rua Marechal Deodoro. A taxi between the airport and center costs US$8.25.

From the bus station, buses to the center stop opposite the north side of the terminal; other routes stop here as well, so ask the driver if he's headed to the center before getting on.

AROUND PORTO VELHO
Reserva Extrativista do Lago do Cuniã

This 558-sq-km reserve, created in 1999, lies 150km down the Rio Madeira from Porto Velho and is accessible only by river. It's Rondônia's largest fish-spawning ground (pirarucu and *aruanã* are among the species breeding here) and is renowned for its abundant bird life. The reserve was due to be opened for ecotourism by 2001, but as of 2004 Ibama, the Brazilian environmental agency, had still not completed the required environmental studies. At the time of research, officials said the plan was still on; travelers can contact **Ibama** (☎ 223 2023; eseccunia.ro@ibama.gov.br; Av Jorge Teixeira 3559) in Porto Velho to check the progress.

GUAJARÁ-MIRIM
☎ 0xx69 / pop 35,500
This low-key town on the Rio Mamoré came into existence as the southern terminus of the Madeira–Mamoré Railway. Both Guajará-Mirim and Bolivian Guayaramerín across the river are free-trade zones with a steady stream of shopping tourists.

Information
EMERGENCY
Emergency room (☎ 192; Hospital Regional, cnr Rua Marechal Deodoro & Av Costa Marques)
Police (☎ 190)

INTERNET ACCESS
Informática (☎ 541 4270; Av Presidente Dutra 331; per min US$1.75; ☻ 8am-noon & 2pm-6pm Mon-Fri, 8am-noon Sat)
NR Técnica (☎ 521 1613; Av Leopoldo de Mateo; per min US$1.25; ☻ 8am-9pm Sun-Fri, 8am-1pm Sat) Across from the cathedral.

MEDICAL SERVICES
Hospital Regional (☎ 541 7129, 541 2641, emergency room ☎ 192; cnr Rua Marechal Deodoro & Av Costa Marques)
Vaccinations (cnr Av Beira Rio & Travessa do Navigante; ☻ 7am-7pm Mon-Sat, 7am-noon Sun) Available at a health post near the port. Yellow fever shots are free; other vaccines, including hepatitis, are sometimes available.

MONEY
A signless **exchange house** (Av Mendonça Lima 145; ☻ 8am-noon Mon-Fri) exchanges US and Bolivian currencies. The door is immediately east of Drogaria Fialho. There are also money changers in Guayaramerín (p664), on the Bolivian side.
Banco do Brasil (Av Mendonça Lima 388; ☻ 9am-2pm Mon-Fri) Exchanges cash in US dollars but not traveler's checks.
Bradesco (cnr Av Costa Marques & Av Leopoldo de Mateos) Reliable ATMs.

POST & TELEPHONE
Post office (☎ 541 2777; cnr Av Presidente Dutras & Rua Marechal Deodoro; ☻ 8am-noon & 2-6pm Mon-Fri, 8am-noon Sat)

GUAJARÁ-MIRIM

Approximate Scale

INFORMATION	
Alfatur	1 B2
Banco do Brasil	2 B2
Bolivian Consulate	3 B1
Bradesco	4 B1
Exchange House	5 B2
Hospital Regional	6 B2

Informática	7 B2
NR Técnica	8 C1
Polícia Federal	9 A1
Post Office	10 B2
Telephone Office	11 C2
Vaccinations Post	12 A3
Varig	13 B1

SIGHTS & ACTIVITIES	(p663)
Cathedral	14 C1
Museu Histórico Municipal	15 B2

SLEEPING	(p663)
Alfa Hotel	16 B1
Hotel Jamaica	17 C1
Hotel Mini-Estrela Palace	18 C2

EATING	(p663)
Lanchonete & Pizzaria Pit Stop	19 C2
Restaurante Oásis	20 C2

TRANSPORT	(pp663–4)
Boats to Forte Príncipe da Beira	21 A3
Guayaramerín Passenger Boat Ticket Office	22 A3
Passenger Boats to Guayaramerín	23 A3
Vehicle Ferry to Guayaramerín	24 A2

OTHER	
OCA Turismo	25 C2

To Bus Station (2km)

To Pakaas Palafitas Lodge (8km by river)

THE AMAZON

Posto Telefónico (☎ 541 3991; Av 15 de Novembro 620; ✆ 8am-9pm)

TOURIST INFORMATION
There is no official tourist office in town, but the folks at the travel agency Alfatur (below) are friendly and can answer most questions.

TRAVEL AGENCIES
Alfatur (☎ 541 1073, 541 1811; alfaturvt@ig.com.br; Av 15 de Novembro 149-A; ✆ 8am-noon & 2-6pm Mon-Fri, 8am-noon Sat) Friendly helpful office for air travel from Porto Velho.
Varig (☎ 541 3914; cnr Av Presidente Dutra & Av Quintino Bocaiúva; ✆ 8am-noon & 2-6pm Mon-Fri, 8am-noon Sat)

Sights & Activities
MUSEU HISTÓRICO MUNICIPAL
Housed in the old Madeira–Mamoré train station, the **Museu Histórico Municipal** (cnr Av Constituição & Av 15 de Novembro; admission free; ✆ 8:30-11:30am & 2:30-5:30pm Mon-Fri, 8:30-11:30am Sat) is a mildly interesting museum that has exhibits on natural history and two old steam locomotives parked outside. Examples of Rondônian fauna include a stuffed anaconda stretched the length of the main salon and a pair of conjoined-twin piglets preserved in formaldehyde.

PAKAAS PALAFITAS LODGE
A visit to the relatively new eco-hotel **Pakaas Palafitas Lodge** (☎ 541 3058; www.pakaas.com.br; all-day entry incl buffet US$12.75) also makes a nice day trip. Walk along mellow scenic trails or take canoe rides through nearby channels and flooded forest. Or just relax beside the beautiful semicircular pool, with comfortable chairs and a fine buffet lunch. Call about arranging transport, or hire a boat at the port.

Sleeping & Eating
Hotels listed here include free breakfast.
Pakaas Palafitas Lodge (☎ 541 3058; www.pakaas .com.br; s/d with all meals & transfer from Guajará-Mirim US$53/94), a superior jungle hotel, 20 minutes by boat up the Rio Mamoré, offers 28 pleasant chalets, 2.5km of walkways, a restaurant, bar and a gorgeous swimming pool and patio overlooking the river. Jungle walks, boat trips and alligator-spotting expeditions can also be arranged.

Near the cathedral, **Hotel Jamaica** (☎ 541 3721/2; Av Leopoldo de Mateos 755; s/d US$13.25/16.75; ✖) is the best place in town. It has comfortable, modern air-con rooms; larger rooms cost US$20.
Hotel Mini-Estrela Palace (☎ 541 1140; Av 15 de Novembro 460; s/d US$5/7; ✖) is close to restaurants and convenient for catching cabs to and from the bus terminal. Basic but large rooms have air-con; you can pay more to get a TV.
A bit run-down outside, the inside of the **Alfa Hotel** (☎ 541 3121; Av Leopoldo de Mateos 239; s/d US$10/16.75; ✖) is better. Rooms here are decent-sized and come with air-con, TV and minibar. The service is friendly.
Restaurante Oásis (☎ 541 1621; Av 15 de Novembro 460; self-service per kg US$5; ✆ 11am-3pm), Guajará-Mirim's best restaurant, is open for lunch only, unfortunately. A good buffet, including fresh grilled meats, is served in a pleasant, airy dining area.
Lanchonete e Pizzaria Pit Stop (☎ 541 4213; Av 15 de Novembro 620; dishes US$4-6; ✆ 6pm-2am) is a popular if somewhat sterile eatery serving pretty good pizzas. It even has a small disco upstairs that's open most weekends.

Getting There & Around
The **bus station** (☎ 541 2448; Av 15 de Novembro) is about 2km east of the center. There is no public transportation to the bus station; a taxi from the station to the centre of town costs US$2, and slightly less from town to the station. There may be a taxi or two at the park at Av 15 de Novembro and Av Costa Marques, or by the passenger-boat ticket office on Av Beira Rio. Otherwise, you may have to wait a while for an empty one to cruise by – Av 15 de Novembro is the best place to flag one down. Plan accordingly, especially if you are catching a bus out.
Viação Rondônia (☎ 541 2302) runs four daily buses to Porto Velho (US$8 to US$10, five hours, departing at 7am, 2pm, 4pm and midnight), and one to Rio Branco (US$13, seven to eight hours, at 11:30am).
Passenger boats cross the Rio Mamoré to/from Guayaramerín, Bolivia, all day, every day – see p664 for information.
Passenger boats sail up the Mamoré and Guaporé Rivers from Guajará-Mirim to the Forte Príncipe da Beira (hammock including meals US$13.50, 40 hours) about

every eight to 10 days. Return trips are the same frequency, but take about half as long. Ask at the moorings at the end of Av Dr Antônio da Costa. Fast launches known as *voladores* can do the trip in about eight hours for about US$50 a person, but they need eight passengers.

Occasional boats go up the Guaporé as far as Vila Bela da Santíssima Trindade in Mato Grosso.

TO/FROM BOLIVIA

Medium-sized boats ferry passengers the short distance from Guajará-Mirim to Guayaramerín, Bolivia (US$1, 10 minutes). A minimum of 10 passengers is usually required, so plan to wait for up to 30 minutes on either side. Mornings and afternoons are the busiest. Entering Bolivia, 30-day tourist visas are issued at the immigration office in Guayaramerín. Entering Brazil, you will probably be required to show a yellow fever vaccine certificate. The port and **ticket office** (☎ 541 7221; ✆ 24hr) in Guajará-Mirim are on Av Beira Rio, near the east end of 15 de Novembro. Ask here about the vehicle ferry, as well. Money changers on the Bolivian side change reais and bolivianos.

Bolivian consulate (Av B Menezes 377; ✆ 8am-3pm Mon-Fri)

Polícia Federal (☎ 541 2437; cnr Av Presidente Dutra & Av Quintino Bocaiúva; ✆ 24hr, but best btwn 6am-10pm) Ring bell for exit/entry stamps if you are leaving/entering Brazil.

GUAYARAMERÍN (BOLIVIA)

☎ 0xx855 / pop 35,000

Guayaramerín, on the Rio Mamoré opposite Guajará-Mirim, is a frontier town, river port, trading center and the start of a road to La Paz, the Bolivian capital, via Riberalta (90km away) and Rurrenabaque. Accommodations here are cheaper than those in Guajará-Mirim.

Information

Emergency (hospital ☎ 112; police ☎ 110)

Helen's Tour (☎ 885 3731; cnr Av Federico Román & Calle Mamoré; ✆ 8:30am-12:30pm & 2:30-6:30pm Mon-Fri, 8:30am-12:30pm Sat & Sun) Best in town for air tickets, area tours and general information.

Hospital Guayaramerín (☎ 112, 885 3007, 885 3008; Calle Mamoré s/n) Basic medical services.

Hotel San Carlos (☎ 855 3555; Calle 6 de Agosto 347) Changes foreign cash and traveler's checks.

Milán Cambio y Turismo (☎ 885 3400, 885 3544; Plaza Principal; ✆ 8am-noon & 2-6pm Mon-Fri) Changes US, Bolivian and Brazilian cash.

Money changers (Guayaramerín port) Change US, Bolivian and Brazilian cash.

Post office (Av Mariscal Santa Cruz s/n; ✆ 8am-noon & 2-5pm Mon-Fri, 8am-noon Sat)

Punto Entel (☎ 885 3603; Plaza Principal; calls to US & Europe per min US$0.50; ✆ 7:30am-11pm)

Activities

Helen's Tour (☎ 885 3731; cnr Av Federico Román & Calle Mamoré; ✆ 8:30am-12:30pm & 2:30-6:30pm Mon-Fri, 8:30am-12:30pm Sat & Sun), one block from the ferry building, offers **boat trips** up the Rio Mamoré to Laguna La Merced. This area of virgin jungle offers many opportunities

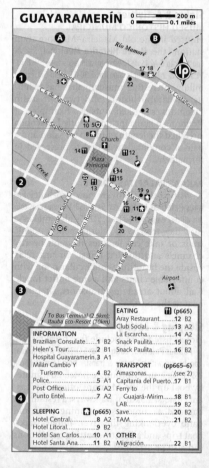

GUAYARAMERÍN

INFORMATION
Brazilian Consulate......1 B2
Helen's Tour.................2 B1
Hospital Guayaramerín.3 A1
Milán Cambio Y
  Turismo...................4 B2
Police...........................5 A1
Post Office...................6 A2
Punto Entel.................7 A2

SLEEPING
Hotel Central...............8 A2
Hotel Litoral................9 B2
Hotel San Carlos........10 A1
Hotel Santa Ana.........11 B2

EATING (p665)
Aray Restaurant.........12 B2
Club Social.................13 A2
La Escarcha...............14 A2
Snack Paulita............15 B2
Snack Paulita............16 B2

TRANSPORT (pp665–6)
Amazonas.............(see 2)
Capitanía del Puerto..17 B1
Ferry to
  Guajará-Mirim......18 B1
LAB...........................19 B2
Save.........................20 B2
TAM.........................21 B2

OTHER
Migración.................22 B1

To Bus Terminal (2.5km);
Itauba Eco-Resort (10km)

to spot wildlife. A three-day trip, with the two nights spent in the home of a villager, costs US$300 per person for four people or more.

Sleeping & Eating

Hotel Litoral (☎ 855 3895; cnr Calle 25 de Mayo & Av 16 de Julio; s/d with shared bathroom US$2.50/5, with private bathroom US$3.50/6.50), near the airport, has clean, basic rooms facing a large interior courtyard.

Hotel Santa Ana (☎ 855 3900; Calle 25 de Mayo 611; s/d with shared bathroom US$2.50/5, with private bathroom US$3.50/6.50, with TV US$4.50/8.50) is across the street from the Hotel Litoral. It's a quiet place with a shady, plant-filled courtyard and basic, clean rooms.

Hotel Central (☎ 855 3911; Calle Mariscal Santa Cruz 235; per person US$2.50) is operated by a friendly family and offers spartan but clean rooms with shared bathrooms. Flowers spruce up the courtyard somewhat, but this is still the most low-key hotel on the list.

Hotel San Carlos (☎ 855 3555; Calle 6 de Agosto 347; s/d US$13/26, ste US$26/31) is the upmarket place in town and they know it. Guests can make use of a pool, restaurant and billiards table; all rooms are modern and comfortable and include TV and air-con, while suites have an additional small sitting area. Breakfast is included.

About 3km out of town, **Itauba Eco-Resort** (Av Federico Román s/n; s/d US$15/30) offers comfy chalets. You can go canoeing or horseback riding here, or just relax. Prices include breakfast; book at Helen's Tour.

Aray Restaurant (cnr Av Federico Román & Av 24 de Septiembre; dishes US$2-5; ☽ 11am-2pm) used to be called the Karla Greta Restaurant and the name is about the only thing that's changed. It still serves standard meat, chicken and fish dishes (lunch only) in a large, open-ended dining room facing the street.

Small and friendly, **La Escarcha** (cnr Calle Mariscal Santa Cruz & Av 24 de Septiembre; dishes US$1-4; ☽ 8am-11pm, closed Tue) opened the same day we passed through. Simple lunches and fruit drinks are served on pleasant little tables set up facing the plaza.

Snack Paulita Av Beni (cnr Av Beni & Calle Sucre; ☽ 7am-12:30pm); Av Federico Román (☎ 885 3338; Av Federico Román, facing the plaza; ☽ 7am-7pm Mon-Sat) specializes in *salteñas* – little fried or baked pastries, usually with a simple cheese or meat filling, that sell for US$0.50. Made

fresh, they make for a nice snack in the leafy town plaza.

Club Social (☎ 885 3918; Calle 25 de Mayo, facing the plaza; dishes US$3-5; ☽ noon-2pm Mon-Sat, 6-8pm daily) is good for a sandwich or light meal, served in an old, airy building and courtyard.

Getting There & Away

AIR

Guayaramerín's simple airport is on the eastern edge of town. Buy tickets at **Helen's Tour** (☎ 885 3731; cnr Av Federico Román & Calle Mamoré; ☽ 8:30am-12:30pm & 2:30-6:30pm Mon-Fri, 8:30am-12:30pm Sat & Sun) to compare prices and departures more easily. TAM, a passenger airline run by the Bolivian military, has the most flights and lowest prices.

TAM (☎ 885 3924, 885 3925; cnr Av 16 de Julio & Calle Sucre) has services to La Paz (US$87, Wednesday and Friday at noon), Trinidad (US$56, Tuesday, Wednesday and Friday at noon, Saturday at 7am), Santa Cruz (US$92, Saturday only, at noon), Cobija (US$53, Monday, Wednesday and Friday at noon) and Cochabamba (US$83, Monday and Tuesday at noon). **Amaszonas** (see Helen's Tour, above) has services to La Paz (US$125, Monday, Thursday, Saturday and Sunday at 4pm), with a stop in Trinidad (US$70). **Save** (☎ 885 3882, at airport ☎ 885 4171; Calle Sucre 409) has services to Trinidad (US$72, daily except Friday, at 1pm), continuing to Santa Cruz (US$130). **Aeroeste** (airport only ☎ 885 3991) has services to Trinidad (US$70, Friday only, at 2pm). **LAB** (☎ 885 3540, at airport ☎ 885 3541; cnr Calle 25 de Mayo & Av 16 de Julio) was not offering flights here at the time of research, but may start up again soon.

BOAT

There was no regular passenger-boat travel at the time of research, but in the past it has been possible to catch boats up the Rio Mamoré to Trinidad (hammock including meals US$25 to US$35, five to seven days) and beyond. Ask at the office of the Capitanía del Puerto for current information.

BUS & TAXI

Think twice about getting onto any long-distance buses here, especially in the rainy season (roughly from November to April). Flooded roads and bridges can triple the estimated travel time, and two-, three- and even five-day epics are not uncommon.

Most locals either fly or wait for the roads to clear. Depending on where you're headed, consider crossing into Brazil, where the roads are much better, and reentering Bolivia closer to your destination.

Guayaramerín (☎ 885 3528) has services to Riberalta (US$2.50, two hours, six daily from 6:45am to 5pm), to Trinidad (US$19, 24 to 36 hours, at 8am on Monday, Thursday and Sunday), La Paz (US$19, 60 to 72 hours, at 8am on Tuesday, Thursday and Saturday) and Cobija (US$12.50, 16 to 24 hours, at 6am on Tuesday, Saturday and Sunday). **Flota Yungueña** (☎ 885 4514) has services for the same prices to La Paz (8am, daily) and Trinidad (8am Monday and Wednesday). **Vaca Diez** (☎ 885 4896) and **1a de Maio** (☎ 885 4903) are smaller companies with services to Trinidad on Wednesday and Friday at 7:30am, and Tuesday and Saturday at 8am, respectively.

The bus terminal is 2.5km from the river along Av Federico Román; a taxi there costs US$1. You may also be able to reach Riberalta by shared taxi (US$3.75 per person, US$15 for the whole vehicle; ask at the bus terminal).

TO/FROM BRAZIL
See p664 for information about boats between Bolivia and Brazil. Thirty-day visas are standard on both sides, though you may be able to get up to 60 days from the Bolivians and 90 days from the Brazilians. Officials on both sides usually look for the other's exit stamp, so get one before crossing the river.

Bolivian immigration (☎ 855 4413; cnr Av Costañera & Calle Mariscal Santa Cruz; ☸ 8am-6pm Mon-Fri, 8am-3pm Sat, 8am-noon Sun)

Brazilian consulate (cnr Av 24 de Septiembre & Av Beni)

Getting Around
The town is so small you can walk just about anywhere, except to the bus terminal. *Motokares* (motorcycle rickshaws) charge US$0.50 between the bus terminal and the center or ferry port. There are also motorcycle taxis, which cost US$0.30 anywhere around town.

GUAPORÉ VALLEY
The Rio Guaporé consititutes the Brazil–Bolivia border for a stretch of 600km or more from its confluence with the Rio Mamoré (approximately 150km upstream of Guajará-Mirim).

Forte Príncipe da Beira & Costa Marques
Remote **Forte Príncipe da Beira**, beside the Rio Guaporé, 210km south of Guajará-Mirim, was constructed by the Portuguese between 1776 and 1783 to consolidate their hold on the lands east of the Guaporé and Mamoré against the Spanish. The star-shaped fort, one of only two ever constructed by Portugal in the Brazilian interior, has 10m-high walls and four corner bastions, each of which held 14 cannons. Today just one cannon remains. The walls, nearly 1km around, are surrounded by a moat and enclose the ruins of a chapel, armory, officers quarters and prison cells in which bored convicts scrawled poetic graffiti. Underground passageways lead from the fortress to the river. The fort was abandoned as a military post in 1889. Today Brazil maintains a garrison of around 70 soldiers beside the fort. There's also a village, Vila Príncipe da Beira, here.

The town of **Costa Marques** (population 7000), about 25km from the fort, is home to an attractive church, orchid park and a turtle nursery.

SLEEPING & EATING
In Costa Marques, air-con *apartamentos* (rooms with private bathroom) at **Hotel Girassol Palácio** (☎ 651 2215; Av Demétrio Melas 1796; s/d US$9/15.50; ☒) have TV and come with free breakfast.

At **Peixaria do Reis** (Av Demétrio Melas 1918; dishes US$4-7) the speciality is fish, served in a variety of styles and flavors.

GETTING THERE & AWAY
Ordinary air service to Costa Marques has been suspended for several years – some say it will start up again, but don't count on it.

Charter flights can be arranged through **HHC** (☎ 221 9403; www.pedrasnegras.com; Rua Salgado Filho 2954-A at Rua Abunã) in Porto Velho; the cost is US$440 round-trip for a group of five.

Real Norte (in Porto Velho ☎ 225 2891) has connecting bus services to Costa Marques (US$27, 18 to 24 hours with a change in Presidente Medici, at 7am, noon and 10pm). The Presidente Medici–Costa Marques road is impassable from about November to April, but the reserve is closed then anyway.

Two daily buses run from Costa Marques to the fort and back.

For information on boats to Forte Príncipe de Beira, see p663.

Reserva Extrativista Pedras Negras

Two hundred and forty kilometers upstream from Costa Marques is the **Reserva Extrativista Pedras Negras**, the main ecotourism site in this area and in the state. The Pedras Negras Lodge (www.pedrasnegras .com) has two simple but comfortable cabins with hot water, mosquito screens, 24-hour electricity and beds or hammocks for up to 12 people. Activities include hiking, canoe rides and visiting area villages, which are dedicated mostly to rubber harvesting. The best months to go are August to November, when river beaches are exposed. From September, turtle nesting sites can be observed. Throughout the summer, you stand varying chances of seeing rare orchids, macaws, toucans, alligators, deer, river dolphins and jaguars (extremely rare).

HHC (☎ 221 9403; www.pedrasnegras.com; Rua Salgado Filho 2954-A at Rua Abunã), a travel agency in Porto Velho, arranges visits to the lodge. Prices for the all-inclusive three-day/four-night packages vary according to the number of people on the trip, from US$404 per person for two people to US$304 per person for four people. Transport to/from Costa Marques is not included. The reserve is open from June 15 to November 15 only, due to heavy rainfall the rest of the year.

CENTRAL RONDÔNIA

The center of the state has, in general, suffered the severest deforestation, but it does contain a successful jungle-cum-ranch hotel and Rondônia's only national park.

Hotel Fazenda Rancho Grande

The German-run **Hotel Fazenda Rancho Grande** (☎ 535 4301; www.ariquemes.com.br/pou sada; Linha C 20, lote 23 - TB 65, Cacaulândia; s/d/tr apartamento US$65/90/120) is set amid a tropical forest rich in wildlife, especially butterflies. Forest walks, swimming, horseback riding and meals are all included in the prices. The Schmitzes, the host family, speak English and German. Rancho Grande is 162km southeast of Porto Velho

on Hwy BR-364, then 26km south of the highway between Ariquemes and Jaru, near Cacaulândia. You can book on the multilingual website.

Parque Nacional de Pacaás Novos

This rugged, 7648-sq-km national park includes Rondônia's highest peak, Pico do Tracoá (1230m) and some spectacular waterfalls. Fauna includes jaguars, tapirs, giant anteaters, howler monkeys and rare blue macaws. The park lies inside an Indian reserve, Terra Indígena Uru-Eu-Wau-Wau. Ibama has plans to open the park to visitors, including constructing a research and visitor center, but as with other reserves in the state, the necessary studies have not been completed. Officials had originally said the park would be open by 2002; now they have no estimate.

ACRE

Present-day Acre was originally a remote part of Bolivia, but by the end of the 19th century it was mostly populated by Brazilian *seringueiros* (rubber tappers), spreading south from the Amazonas. In August 1902, Bolivia sent its army to assert control and was met by fierce resistance from the *seringueiros* in what is known here, not a little disingenuously, as the 'Acrean Revolution.' After fighting for six months, Bolivia ceded the territory to Brazil in the Treaty of Petrópolis in exchange for UK£2 million and a promise to build an international railroad. (The railroad was never completed and some in Bolivia say the money was never paid.) The Brazilian government, however, had never really supported the upstart Acreans and refused to name Acre a state, designating it the nation's first 'federal territory' instead. Thus the 'autonomist' movement was born, a sometimes-armed conflict that took 60 years to be resolved.

The remote jungle state of Acre has seen not only some wanton environmental destruction and rampant high-level crime and corruption, but also some of the most hope-generating movements against such horrors. As loggers and ranchers moved into Acre in the 1970s, Acre's rubber tappers, whose ancestors had started arriving in the 1870s, began to resist the destruction of the forests on which their livelihood depended. They formed human blockades against the chainsaws and opposed the paving of Hwy BR-364 into Acre. Their struggle received massive international attention in 1988 when their charismatic leader, Chico Mendes, was assassinated in his home town of Xapuri (see the boxed text on p672).

Partly thanks to the struggles of Mendes and others, today one-third of Acre's 153,000 sq km is under environmental protection or designated as indigenous lands. This has not stopped deforestation, but the proportion of deforested land in Acre (9%) is below average for Brazilian Amazonia, and environmentalists have scored some political successes. In 1995 Marina Silva, a young unionist and former colleague of Mendes, was elected as a federal senator for Acre as a member of the left-wing Partido dos Trabalhadores (PT; Workers' Party) and on a campaign focused on sustainable use of the forests. In 1998 Jorge Viana, another environmentalist and PT member, was elected state governor at the head of an anticorruption electoral coalition.

Viana's predecessor, Orleir Cameli, meanwhile, was under investigation for smuggling, enslaving Indians, encroaching on their land and logging illegally. Further revelations of the kinds of things that had gone on in Acre came in 2000 when Hildebrando Pascoal, formerly a deputy for Acre in Brazil's federal congress, was jailed for six years for corruption. Reportedly the head of a huge cocaine-smuggling operation from Bolivia, Pascoal was said to have run death squads responsible for dozens of murders and, according to a witness in a congressional drug inquiry, had personally cut off one live victim's arms and legs with a chainsaw. The same inquiry heard that Pascoal's gang of cocaine traffickers had allegedly included two Acre state governors, three state justices, half of Acre's top businessmen and hundreds of police officers.

In 2002, Viana's political opponents allegedly bribed officials to keep him off the ballot; a public uproar got his name reinstated and he went on to win a second term. Since then, Viana has turned his attention to continuing Acre's progressive environmental policies. A vocal proponent of sustainable development (he has a degree in forest management), Viana has supported establishing an official certification process for products derived from the Amazon forest – certified as forest friendly, these products would then enjoy lower tariffs and taxes to be more competitive on international markets.

RIO BRANCO
☎ 0xx68 / pop 255,000

Rio Branco, the capital of Acre, was founded in 1882 by rubber tappers on the banks of the Rio Acre. Once a brash, uneasy town, Rio Branco has transformed itself into a genuinely pleasant place – too bad it's not really on the way to or from anywhere!

Rio Branco (and the rest of Acre) is two hours behind Brazilian Standard Time.

Information
EMERGENCY
Emergency room (☎ 192, 223 3080; Hospital Geral, cnr Av Nações Unidos & Rua Hugo Carneiro)
Police (☎ 190)

INTERNET ACCESS
ChipHouse.com (☎ 223 4127; cnr Rua Quintino Bocaiúva & Rua Benjamin Constant; per hr US$0.65; ⏰ 7am-10pm)
Kombat Internet & Lan House (☎ 223 0683; 1st fl, Mira Shopping; per hr US$1; ⏰ 9am-9pm Mon-Sat)
Razec Informática (☎ 223 2955; Rua Benjamin Constant 331; per hr US$1; ⏰ 8am-noon & 2-5pm Mon-Fri, 8am-noon Sat)

MEDICAL SERVICES
Hospital Geral (☎ 192, 223 3080; cnr Av Nações Unidos & Rua Hugo Carneiro)

MONEY
Banco do Brasil (Rua Porto Leal 85; ⏰ 9am-2pm Mon-Fri) Exchanges cash in US dollars, and traveler's checks if you're lucky. It's also worth trying for Visa-card cash advances.
Bradesco (Rua Porto Leal 83) Next to Banco do Brasil, with reliable ATMs.
HSBC (cnr Rua Rui Barbosa & Rua Marechal Deodoro) ATMs here accept most foreign cards.

POST
Post office (Rua Epaminondas Jácome 447)

TELEPHONE
Brasil Telecom (Av Brasil 378; ⏰ 7am-9pm) Open-air telephone center.

TOURIST INFORMATION

There used to be a state tourism office in Rio Branco, but it was closed the last time we came through. The staff members at the main tourist sites – Palacio Rio Branco, Memorial dos Autonomistas and Museu da Borracha – can be good resources; most are friendly, knowledgeable and accustomed to dealing with travelers.

TRAVEL AGENCIES

Inácio's Tur (☎ 224 9626, 223 7191; Pinheiro Palace Hotel, Rua Rui Barbosa 450; 🕑 8am-noon & 2-6pm Mon-Fri, 8-11am Sat) Plane tickets and hire cars.

Sights

PALACIO RIO BRANCO

Acre's first capital building, the imposing **Palacio Rio Branco** (Av Getúlio Vargas s/n; admission free; 🕑 8am-6pm Tue-Fri, 2-9pm Sat & Sun) is now mostly a tourist attraction. An interesting guided tour (Portuguese only) weaves through the palace rooms, with well-done displays on prehistoric artifacts, indigenous communities, Chico Mendes and the Acrean Revolution.

MEMORIAL DOS AUTONOMISTAS

Occupying a spiffy new cultural complex, just uphill from the Palacio Rio Branco, the **Memorial dos Autonomistas** (Autonomists Memorial; ☎ 224 2133; Av Getúlio Vargas s/n; admission free; 🕑 8am-6pm Tue-Fri, 2-9pm Sat & Sun) uses poster displays to tell the story of Acre's battle for statehood, and docents can give detailed explanations (Portuguese only). José Guiomard dos Santos and his wife are buried here as well. Highly revered, Guiomard dos Santos served as federal administrator of Acre in the early 1940s and was later (by then a senator) the chief sponsor of the bill that eventually gave Acre its statehood. But blood runs thicker than water, especially in Acre – Guiomard, born in Minas Gerais, lost to Acre native José Augusto in the state's first gubernatorial election.

MUSEU DA BORRACHA

Housed in an attractive mansion and well worth visiting, the **Museu da Borracha** (Rubber Museum; ☎ 223 1202; Av Ceará 1441; admission free; 🕑 8am-6pm Mon-Fri) is divided into sections relating to archaeology, Indian artifacts, the

RIO BRANCO
Approximate Scale
0 300 m
0 0.2 miles
To Hospital Geral (700m); Colônia Cinco Mil (12km)
To VASP (1km)
Capoeira
Stadium
Ipase
To Rico (2km); TAVAJ (2.5km); Alto Santo (7km); Airport (22km)
Av Ceará
Av Getúlio Vargas
Rua Rui Barbosa
Rua Marechal Deodoro
Rua Quintino Bocaiúva
Rua Rio Grande do Sul
Praça Plácido de Castro
Rua F Ribeiro
Av Brasil
To Razec Informática (100m)
Papouco
Centro
Cathedral
Rua Benjamin Constant
Travessa da Catedral
Praça Eurico Dutra
Rua Epaminondas Jácome
Rua Porta Leal
Rua Floriano Peixoto
Base
Praça Povos da Floresta
Av Beira Rio
Rua Diamantina
Av Uirapuru
Rua Barbosa Lima
To Parque Ambiental Chico Mendes (10km); Xapuri (241km); Brasiléia (290km)
Rua Nova Andirá
Rio Acre
Rua 17 de Novembro
SIGHTS & ACTIVITIES (p669)
Memorial dos Autonomistas......7 B2
Museu da Borracha......8 B1
Palacio Rio Branco......9 B2
SLEEPING (p670)
Albemar Hotel......10 B1
Hotel Chalé......11 A3
Hotel Guapindaia......12 B2
Hotel Triângulo......13 A1
Inácio Palace Hotel......14 B1
Pinheiro Palace Hotel......15 B1
Rio Branco Hotel......16 B1
EATING (p670)
Anexo Espaço Gastronômico......17 B2
Café do Theatro......18 B2
Churrascaria Triângulo......(see 13)
Mira Shopping......19 B1
Pizzaria Tutti Frutti......20 B1
Restaurante Flutuante......21 B3
DRINKING (p670)
Outdoor Bars......22 C1
SHOPPING (p670)
Casa d'Arte Rivasplata......(see 16)
TRANSPORT (p670–1)
'Norte-Sul' & 'Vila Acre' Bus Stop......23 B2
Bus Station......24 A3
City-Bus Terminal......25 C1
Varig......26 C2
OTHER
Viage Turismo......27 C1
INFORMATION
Banco do Brasil......1 B2
Basil Teleacre......2 B2
Bradesco......3 B2
ChipHouse.com......4 C2
HSBC......5 B1
Inácio's Tur......(see 15)
Post Office......6 B2

THE AMAZON

Acrean Revolution, rubber and the cult of Santo Daime. The free tours (occasionally in English) are recommended.

Sleeping

True budget options are hard to find in Rio Branco. Prices listed here are discount prices, which you may have to ask for to get. All hotels listed here include free breakfast.

Rio Branco Hotel (☎ 224 2681; www.rbhotel .hpg.com.br; Rua Rui Barbosa 354; s/d/tr US$10/14/20) A long-established hotel with cheerful staff, this is probably the best deal in town, for its location and overall quality. Air-con rooms are clean and comfortable, if a bit dated in their décor; the single and matrimonial rooms have nice little balconies.

Hotel Chalé (☎ 221 2293; Rua Palmeiral 334; s/d with fan US$5/6.60, with air-con US$8.30/11.60; 🔀) Just outside the bus station, this is a good option for those just passing through. Decent-sized rooms are clean, if a bit run-down. Upstairs rooms have small porches. The service is friendly.

Albemar Hotel (☎ 224 1938; fax 3026 2975; Rua Franco Ribeiro 99; s/d/tr US$10/14/20) The entryway and halls aren't too encouraging, but rooms here are actually pretty clean and comfy. There is somewhat less street noise than at nearby hotels.

Hotel Guapindaia (☎ 223 5747; Rua Floriano Peixoto 550; s/d US$16.30/21.30) Recently renovated, the clean, cozy *apartamentos* here have wood furniture, muted colors and spotless modern bathrooms. A good deal for the price; reservations are recommended.

Pinheiro Palace Hotel (☎ 223 7191; www.irmaos pinheiro.com.br; Rua Rui Barbosa 450; s/d US$30/43.30; 🔀 🖳) Large, fairly modern rooms have balconies, air-con and cable TV. Breakfast is served in a modern dining area beside a clean medium-sized pool. This hotel is older but still more pleasant than the Inácio, across the street, under the same management. The airport shuttle (US$10) is conveniently coordinated with Varig and VASP flights.

Hotel Triângulo (☎ 224 9206; Rua Floriano Peixoto 727; standard s/d US$9/14.30, luxo US$13.30/17.60; 🔀) Rooms are fairly large but starting to look worn down – the Rio Branco and Albemar are better options in this price range. All rooms here have TV and air-con; *luxo* (luxury) rooms are identical to the standard ones, save for the minibar and telephone.

Eating & Drinking

Anexo Espaço Gastronômico (☎ 224 1396; Rua Franco Ribeiro 99; self-service per kg US$5.30, dishes US$6-10; ✪ 11:30am-2pm daily, 7:30-10:30pm Mon-Sat) This is one of the best *por-kilo* lunch spots in the north of Brazil, and not terribly expensive. The city's professional classes pack in for fresh and original salad combinations, tender meat and fish dishes, and irresistible desserts. At night there's à la carte fare.

Café do Theatro (☎ 223 5862; cnr Av Brasil & Av Getúlio Vargas; dishes US$3-6; ✪ 7am-9pm Tue-Sat, 4-9pm Sun) Part of the new Memorial dos Autonomistas (see p669), this classy café serves great coffee, pastries, juice and light meals, including sandwiches and pasta. Indoor and outdoor tables are comfortable, with views of the park. Plus, you can get 15 free minutes of Internet time with your purchase. It often stays open past the advertised closing time.

Restaurante Flutuante (☎ 224 7248; end of Rua Floriano Peixoto; dishes US$6-14; ✪ 10:30am-10pm) A pleasant floating restaurant on the Rio Acre that serves fine fish dishes, plus meat and chicken options. During the wet season, the water level raises the restaurant by a whopping 10m.

Churrascaria Triângulo (☎ 224 9206; Hotel Triângulo, Rua Floriano Peixoto 727; dishes US$5-10; ✪ 11am-3pm & 6-10:30pm) A carnivore's paradise, the *rodízio* (a kind of meat buffet; US$5) includes as much self-serve salad as you like, and hot meats that keep arriving at your table until you just have to say '*Não mais*' ('No more').

Pizzaria Tutti Frutti (Av Ceará 1132; dishes US$3-7; ✪ 11am-3pm & 6-10pm Mon-Sat) Come here for four sizes of good pizza for US$4 to US$10, and decent and sizable chicken, meat and fish dishes. Lunch is self-service.

Several outdoor bars crammed into the small triangle sandwiched between Av Ceará and Rua Rui Barbosa are OK for whiling away the night. Mira Shopping is a popular place for a beer or three in the evening.

Getting There & Away

The paved Hwy BR-364 runs to Rio Branco from Porto Velho. Beyond Rio Branco Hwy BR-364 is paved as far as Sena Madureira, 170km northwest. The road from Rio Branco to Brasiléia (235km southwest) and Assis Brasil on the Peruvian border are also paved, but Acre has few other paved roads. Except in the driest months (June/July to September), the unpaved roads are difficult and often impassable, leaving plane or boat as the only viable transportation options.

AIR

It is easier and no more expensive to buy plane tickets through an agency than directly from the airline.

Varig airport (☎ 211 1066, 211 1063; ☺ 8am-6pm Mon-Fri, 8am-noon Sat); Rua Marechal Deodoro (☎ 224 2226; Rua Marechal Deodoro 115; ☺ 8am-6pm Mon-Fri, 8am-noon Sat) has services to Manaus (US$159, once daily except Sunday) with a stop in Porto Velho (US$36), and service to Brasília (US$218, once daily except Sunday).

Rico (☎ 223 5902; Galería João Paulo, Av Ceará; ☺ 8am-6pm Mon-Fri, 8am-noon Sat) code-shares with Varig on the Rio Branco–Porto Velho–Manaus flight. Prices are the same, but if one is fully booked, try the other.

VASP (☎ 224 6535; Rua Quintino Bocaiúva 1276; ☺ 8am-6pm Mon-Fri, 8am-noon Sat), just a little bit cheaper, also has flights to Manaus (US$135, daily) stopping in Porto Velho (US$33).

Tavaj (☎ 221 1666, at airport ☎ 211 1008; No 6, Av Ceará 2395; ☺ 8am-6pm Mon-Fri, 8am-noon Sat) costs the same as VASP, with Rio Branco–Porto Velho–Manaus flights on Monday, Wednesday and Friday. It also flies to Boca do Acre (US$31) and Cruzeiro do Sol (US$69) on the same days.

BOAT

The Rio Acre is navigable all the way to the Peruvian border at Assis Brasil but there's little river traffic. Alternatively, take a bus to Boca do Acre in Amazonas state (US$8, five hours), where boats ply the Rio Purus, some going as far as Manaus.

BUS

Acreana (☎ 221 1182), which operates jointly with **Viação Rondônia** (☎ 221 1182) has service to/from Xapuri (US$2.60, 3½ hours, departing at 7am and 1:45pm daily plus 6am Friday to Sunday), Brasília (US$6.30, 4½ hours, at 6am, 9am, noon, 3pm and 6pm), Guajará-Mirim (US$13, seven to eight hours, at 11am); Assis Brasil (US$8.50, six hours, at 6am and noon, returning at 6am and 4pm) and Porto Velho (US$14.50 to US$17.50; seven to eight hours; 7am, noon, 10pm and 11pm).

Eucatur (☎ 221 4180, 221 1660) and **Andorinha** (☎ 221 6757) each have nightly services to Rio de Janeiro (US$108, 70 to 75 hours, at 10pm), São Paulo (US$84, 54 to 56 hours, at 10pm); Brasília (US$66, 51 hours, at 10pm), Cuiabá (US$52, 36 hours), and Goiâna (US$67, 46 hours, at 7am and 4pm). Somewhat cheaper service is available on some routes on **Rotas** (☎ 221 1382) and other lines.

Getting Around

The **airport** (☎ 211 1000) is about 20km west of town, on Hwy BR-364. A taxi costs US$15 to US$20 in either direction. City bus No 304 (US$0.80), signed as 'Custódio Freire,' runs between the airport and the **city-bus terminal** (Rua Benjamin Constant) about once an hour (last departure at 10:30pm). **Inácio's Tur** (☎ 224 9626, 223 7191; Pinheiro Palace Hotel, Rua Rui Barbosa 450; ☺ 8am-noon & 2-6pm Mon-Fri, 8-11am Sat) runs a more commodious bus (per person US$10; departs from the Pinheiro Palace Hotel) to (but not from) the airport, coordinated with VASP and Varig flights. The bus is open to anyone; reservations are not necessary but arrive 20 to 30 minutes early.

The **bus station** (☎ 221 1177) is on Av Uirapuru, 1.25km southwest of the center, across the Rio Acre. At least four different buses go to and from the bus station and the city-bus terminal on Rua Benjamin Constant, including 'Norte-Sul', Amapá, Taquarí and 'Domoacir' (all US$0.80). Catch them outside the bus station, or, to get to the bus station from town, at the city-bus terminal or the stop on Av Getúlio Vargas. A taxi to/from the city center costs US$3.30.

AROUND RIO BRANCO
Parque Ambiental Chico Mendes

Only 52 hectares in size, of which roughly half is native forest, **Parque Ambiental Chico Mendes** (admission free) is nevertheless the most interesting park easily accessible to Rio Branco.

A memorial to Chico Mendes stands near the entrance. The park also has a picnic area, a funny cast-iron treetop lookout, bike paths and a small zoo. Along the paths are theme huts representing different aspects of life in the region, including rubber tapping, a *maloca* (Indian dwelling) and myths and legends. Some wildlife can be seen.

The park is located at Km 3 on Hwy AC-040, about 10km south of Rio Branco.

THE AMAZON

To get here take a 'Vila Acre' bus from Av Getúlio Vargas in the city center.

Santo Daime Centers

There are several centers of the **Santo Daime religious cult** in and around Rio Branco, where it was founded in 1930 by Raimundo Irineu Serra (1892–1971), also known as Mestre Irineu. The cult's practices revolve around a sacred hallucinogenic drink called ayahuasca (see p53).

The ceremonial center at the cult's birthplace, called **Alto Santo**, is 7km from Rio Branco in Colônia Custódio Freire. You can reach it on an 'Irineu Serra' bus from the city-bus terminal. To get to the ceremonial center, ask anyone for directions once you arrive.

Colônia Cinco Mil (Colony of the 5000), a community of Santo Daime followers, is 12km north of the city. If you wish to visit, it's ideal to try to find somebody from the community to organize your visit, especially if you're thinking about participating in ceremonies. Try asking at the Museu da Borracha (p669) in Rio Branco. You can reach the community by taxi (about US$7) or by catching a 'Porto Acre' bus along Hwy AC-010, which will drop you at the turnoff for Colônia Cinco Mil, from which it's a 2.5km walk.

Thursday is the cult's 'holy day,' and important ceremonies happen on the 15th and 30th of every month at Alto Santo and Colônia Cinco Mil.

XAPURI

☎ 0xx68 / pop 6200

This tidy little town of neat wooden houses along broad streets was home to environmental hero Chico Mendes. It lies about 12km northwest of Hwy BR-317, the main road between Rio Branco (241km away) and Brasiléia (74km away).

Sights

FUNDAÇÃO CHICO MENDES

Facing the plaza, one block southeast of the bus station along Rua Dr Batista de Moraes, the **Fundação Chico Mendes** (Chico Mendes Foundation; admission free; ☒ 7-11am & 1-5pm Mon-Fri & sometimes Sat) contains the martyred

---

CHICO MENDES & HIS LEGACY

Chico Mendes was born in 1944 into a rubber-tapping family at Seringal Cachoeira, in the forests 35km from Xapuri. At an early age he became interested in improving the lot of the uneducated rubber tappers of the area.

In the 1970s the Plano de Integração Nacional, an ambitious military government plan to tame the Amazon, attracted developers, ranchers, logging companies and settlers into Acre. In 1977 Chico Mendes organized the Sindicato dos Trabalhadores Rurais de Xapuri (Xapuri Rural Workers' Union) to defy the violent intimidation and dispossession practiced by the newcomers, who were destroying the jungle, substituting cattle for people and robbing the forest workers of their livelihood. In the 8400 sq km of the Xapuri municipality between 1970 and 1976, Mendes later wrote, the ranchers destroyed by fire and power saw 180,000 rubber trees, 80,000 giant Brazil nut trees, and over a million other valuable trees.

Mendes organized large groups of rural workers to form nonviolent human blockades around forest areas threatened with clearance, and these actions soon attracted the wrath of developers – used to getting their way either through buying corrupt officials, or by hiring *pistoleiros* (gun-toting thugs) to clear human impediments. These *empates* (confrontational standoffs) proved effective in saving thousands of hectares of forest. Mendes also founded the Conselho Nacional de Seringueiros (National Council of Rubber Tappers) and launched the movement to set up extractive reserves – areas subject only to sustainable exploitation by their traditional 'extractive' populations (rubber tappers, nut collectors, fishers and so on).

International interest focused on Mendes as a defender of the forests. Among numerous honors, he was elected to the UN Environment Organization's Global 500 Honor Roll in 1987. But his role as a leader also made him a target for infuriated opponents at home, and he received numerous death threats. In December 1988 he moved to establish his birthplace, Seringal Cachoeira, as an extractive reserve, defying a local rancher and strongman, Darly Alves da Silva, who claimed

environmentalist's tomb, as well as photos and some personal effects (including the clothes he was wearing the night he was killed).

CASA CHICO MENDES

Just across the street from the Fundação, **Chico Mendes' house** can also be visited. This is the simple house where Mendes, his wife and two children lived, and it is maintained as it was then. The caretaker can show you around, and will likely describe to you in graphic detail the fatal shooting at the kitchen door, where bloodstains remain on the wall.

CASA BRANCA

A large white wooden building overlooking the Rio Acre at the north end of town, **Casa Branca** (8am-noon & 2-6pm Tue-Sat) was built in the 19th century as the Intendencia Boliviana, a Bolivian government post. It was here that the 'Acrean Revolution' of 1902 (a euphemism for Brazil's armed takeover of what had been part of Bolivia) started, when Xapuri townspeople joined Plácido de Castro's Brazilian force to capture this building. The Casa Branca houses a museum of historical memorabilia.

Sleeping & Eating

Pousada das Chapurys (☎ 542 2253; Rua Sadala Koury 1385; s US$7.50-11, d US$13.50/20;), half a block off the central plaza, has decent air-con *apartamentos* with TV and minibar.

Restaurant Açai, next door to Pousada das Chapurys and operating under the same management, offers a decent lunch for US$6.50.

Getting There & Away

Acreana has services from Rio Branco to Xapuri (US$2.60, 3½ hours, departing at 7am and 1:45pm daily plus 6am Friday to Sunday) and back (6am and 1pm). There is also service from Brasiléia (US$3, two hours, departing at 10am and 4:30pm) and back (1:30pm).

Alternatively, any Rio Branco–Brasiléia bus can drop you at the turnoff stop for Xapuri; a taxi into town (if one passes!) costs around US$6. You can also pick up buses here.

---

the land. Mendes had already denounced Silva to the police for threatening his life and for the murder of a union representative earlier that year.

On December 22, Mendes left the bodyguards in his house in Xapuri for just a moment and stepped onto the back porch. He was hit at close range by shots fired from the bushes and died shortly afterward.

His murderers gave themselves up to police, but they were considered beyond justice because of their connections with the influential landowners and corrupt officials – common in Brazil's frontier lands. Intense national and international pressure finally brought the case to trial. In December 1990 Darly Alves da Silva received a 19-year prison term for ordering the assassination; his son, Darci Pereira da Silva, was given an identical sentence for pulling the trigger.

Of the many hundreds of murders of union leaders and land-rights campaigners in Brazil since the late 1970s, this was the first to be thoroughly investigated and prosecuted. Even this success looked to have been short-lived when both Silvas escaped from jail in Rio Branco in 1993, apparently just walking free with the complicity of corrupt police. After another outcry, both were recaptured in 1996, but in 2000 they were granted day release, being required to spend only the nights in their prison in Brasília. We'd be surprised if they were still there by the time you read this.

The violent death of Chico Mendes – an environmentalist martyrdom – served to focus yet more attention on the fate of the Amazon rain forests. Ilzamar Mendes, his wife, was courted by numerous Hollywood producers to sell the film rights to the story of her husband's life. – *The Burning Season: The Chico Mendes Story*, directed by John Frankenheimer and staring Raul Julia as Chico, was released in 1994.

One lasting aspect of Chico Mendes' legacy is that there are now more than a dozen extractive reserves around Brazil, including the 9705-sq-km Reserva Extrativista Chico Mendes in southeast Acre, and a similar number are in the process of being created. But defending these and other protected areas against predatory loggers and ranchers remains a challenge.

THE AMAZON

BRASILÉIA

☎ 0xx68 / pop 10,500

The border town of Brasiléia is separated from Cobija, Bolivia, by the meandering Rio Acre and Igarapé Bahia. Lodging prices are cheaper in Brasiléia than in Cobija, and the atmosphere is decidedly more mellow. On the other hand, Cobija has more and better services, including Internet access and travel agencies.

Orientation

Hwy BR-317 from Rio Branco approaches Brasiléia from the southeast, through the adjacent but newly independent municipality of Epitáciolândia. The **Polícia Federal station** (☼ 24hr), where you need to obtain an exit/entry stamp if you're leaving/entering Brazil, is in Epitáciolândia. Ask buses coming from Rio Branco to drop you there.

A bridge over the Igarapé Bahia connects Epitáciolândia to Cobija, Bolivia; to get there, veer left (west) off Epitáciolândia's main street, Av Santos Dumont, at a gas station about 500m from the Polícia Federal station. It's another 1km to the bridge.

A new bridge was completed in 2004 across the Rio Acre, connecting downtown Brasiléia to Cobija. This will certainly do away with the old system of ferrying people back and forth in rickety little rowboats. At the time of research, there was no Polícia Federal post at this crossing, but it would be a logical (and very convenient) addition – definitely ask ahead.

Information

Banco das Amazonas (☎ 546 3362; Av Prefeito R Moreira s/n; ☼ 8am-1pm Mon-Fri) Changes foreign cash and Amex traveler's checks.

Casa Net (☎ 9986 7268; Av José Ruilino 150; per hr US$1; ☼ 8:30am-midnight) Has Internet access.

Police (☎ 190)

Post office (Av Prefeito R Moreira; ☼ 8am-noon & 2-6pm Mon-Fri) Twenty-five meters short of the new bridge.

Tourist kiosk (Av Prefeito R Moreira; ☼ 8am-noon & 3-5pm) Rather unhelpful. Near the bank, overlooking the river.

Sleeping & Eating

All the hotels listed here include free breakfast, which you should take advantage of since eating options in town are amazingly slim.

Pousada Las Palmeras (☎ 546 3284; Av Geny Assis 425; s/d/tr US$10/16.50/20), near the church, is Brasiléia's best lodging option. Clean air-con rooms have TV and minibar and breakfast is excellent. Newer rooms are spotless; older ones have a bit more character – or at least less faux-tile. A pleasant sitting area in front looks onto the street.

Modern but rather plain *apartamentos* at **Hotel Vitória Régia** (☎ 546 4743; Av Geny Assis 345; s/d US$10/16.50) have TV, air-con and minibar. This is a decent option if the Palmeras is full. Discounts are often available.

The **Hotel Fronteira** (☎ 546 4405; Av Geny Assis 347; s/d US$6.50/11.50) is an acceptable option if your budget is tight, but expect reluctant service and dull, marginally clean rooms. Air-con and TV are included.

Several no-name eateries line Av Prefeito R Moreira, serving self-service lunch and /or standard à la carte dinners.

In Epitáciolândia, **Hotel Kador** (☎ 546 3752; Av Santos Dumont 887; s/d US$9/13), about 400m from the Polícia Federal station, has rooms that are basic but clean. Pizzaria Ribeira, across the street, serves adequate pizzas.

Getting There & Away

BUS

The bus station is 500m north of the center. **Acreana** (☎ 546 3257) has daily services to Rio Branco (US$5 to US$6, four hours, departing at 6am, 8am, 11am, 3pm and 6pm), Xapuri (US$2, two hours, at 10am and 4:30pm) and Assis Brasil (US$3.50, two hours, at 7am, 10am and 4pm, return 6am, 1pm and 4pm). You can also usually catch a collective taxi to Rio Branco (US$8.50, three hours); ask taxi drivers at the bus terminal. As well as these being quicker, the driver will usually drop you at your hotel door.

TO/FROM COBIJA

A taxi from the Polícia Federal station to Bolivian immigration on the international bridge then on to one of Cobija's hotels or bus terminals costs around US$5.

The new bridge was opened after we had already completed research, but a taxi ride across should cost around US$2 to US$3. It is not necessary to go through immigration if you are staying in Cobija for just a day or two. But if you plan to go beyond Cobija, or stay much longer, do get your passport stamped on both sides of the border.

COBIJA (BOLIVIA)

☎ 03 / pop 15,000

The capital of Bolivia's Pando department is the wettest spot in Bolivia, with 1770mm of precipitation annually. It is a hilly town on the banks of the Rio Acre, with a pleasant enough plaza but a somewhat gritty atmosphere.

Orientation

From the international bridge over Igarapé Bahia (Arroyo Bahía to Bolivians), Av Internacional heads 600m uphill to a junction marked by a Christ statue. Turn right onto Av 9 de Febrero – it is 1.5km to the town center, passing Cobija's bus terminals, Internet cafés and one hotel. To reach the main plaza, turn right at the intersection of Calle Teniente Coronel Cornejo, where there are traffic lights and police directing traffic. Or as a shortcut, veer right onto Calle Beni at the Hotel Nanijo, passing by or near the other listed hotels, restaurant and airline offices.

Bolivian immigration is on the international bridge. It's open 24 hours daily. The **Brazilian consulate** (🕙 8am-1pm Mon-Fri) is on Av General Rene Barrientos.

Information

12 Cotas (☎ 842 3751; Av 9 de Febrero 161; Internet per hr US$0.50, calls to US & Europe per min; US$0.50 🕙 7am-11pm) Phone and Internet.
Casa de Cambio Cachito (☎ 842 3277; Calle Teniente Coronel Cornejo 88; 🕙 8am-noon & 3-6pm Mon-Fri, 8am-noon Sat) A block west of the central plaza. Exchanges Bolivian, Brazilian and US currencies.
Internet Jandy (☎ 842 2921; Av 9 de Febrero 156; per hr US$0.75; 🕙 8:30am-midnight)
Police (☎ 110).

Sleeping & Eating

Except for the Hotel Avenida, the places below are all within two blocks south of the central plaza. It is not custom in Bolivia to include free breakfast.

Residencial Cocodrilo (☎ 842 2215; Av Fernández Molina 48; s/d with shared bathroom US$4/5, r with private bathroom & TV US$8), the cheapest place in town, is run by a nice lady, offering small, clean (but far from opulent) rooms, some facing a little garden.

Fan-cooled rooms at **Residencial Frontera** (☎ 842 2740; Calle Beni s/n; s/d with shared bathroom US$6.50/7.50, r with private bathroom & TV US$10) are clean and decent-sized, though rather plain. This is a step up from the Cocodrilo, but a bit pricey for what you get.

One of Cobija's more upscale hotels, **Hotel Nanijo's** (☎ 842 2230; Av 9 de Febrero 147; s/d estimated US$15/22) was closed for renovations when we came through. Rooms (and prices) are being completely redone, but will probably maintain the original breezy style, with private bathrooms, TV and complimentary breakfast. Reservations are recommended.

A five-minute walk from the center, rooms at the **Hotel Avenida** (Av 9 de Febrero s/n; s/d with fan US$10/15, with air-con US$16.50/23) are large and clean, with wood floors, cable TV and complimentary breakfast. A smidge overpriced, but still a good mid-range option.

Across from the Residencial Cocodrilo, the friendly **Esquina de la Abuela** (☎ 842 2364; cnr Av Fernández Molina & Calle Sucre; dishes US$2.50-3.50; 🕙 8-11am, noon-3pm & 7pm-midnight) has pleasant indoor and outdoor seating and standard meat and chicken fare. Breakfast consists of *salteñas* (salty breakfast pastries) only.

Getting There & Away
AIR

The **airport** (☎ 842 2260) is 3km southeast of town on the Porvenir road. A taxi to/from the town center is US$1.50. Microbuses (US$0.25) stop on the airport approach road, 100m from the terminal. Flights in June, July, August, December and January get heavily booked, and advertised schedules are not entirely reliable. TAM, the

Bolivian military airline, is probably the most dependable, and you can sometimes get additional discounts just by asking.

TAM (☎ 842 2692; Av 9 de Febrero 59) has flights to La Paz (US$71, Monday, Tuesday, Wednesday and Friday at 10am), Riberalta (US$63, Monday, Wednesday and Friday at 10am) and Trinidad (US$50 to US$60, Friday at 10am) continuing to Santa Cruz (US$78).

AeroSur (☎ 842 3132; Calle Teniente Coronel Cornejo), facing the central plaza, was altering its routes and fares at the time of research; call ahead for current information. Services go to Trinidad (US$120, Thursday only) and to La Paz (US$122, Monday, Thursday and Saturday afternoons), continuing to Cochabamba and Santa Cruz, for the same price.

Save (☎ 842 2418; Av Fernández Molina 53) had recently suspended service from Cobija at the time of research, but was expected to resume soon.

BUS

Bus companies are dotted along Av 9 de Febrero, between the town center and Av Internacional. Note that bus travel during the rainy season (roughly November to April) can be extremely arduous. The roads are unpaved and there are four river crossings in the Cobija–Riberalta stretch alone – travel times can easily double or triple due to mud and flooding.

Guayaramerín (☎ 842 2703) buses to all destinations leave Monday, Tuesday, Thursday and Sunday at 6am, including to Riberalta (US$12.50, nine to 15 hours) and Guayaramerín (US$14, 12 to 18 hours) on Tuesday, Thursday, Saturday and Sunday. At Riberalta you can connect to Trinidad.

Transpando (☎ 7111 4142) goes to Riberalta (US$12.50, nine to 15 hours, Sunday, Monday, Wednesday and Friday at 6:30am) and Trinidad (US$26.50, 36 hours, Thursday at 8am).

Flota Yugeña has service to La Paz (US$25, 48 to 62 hours, Tuesday, Thursday and Saturday at 8am).

TO/FROM BRASILÉIA

A taxi from one of Cobija's bus terminals to the Bolivian immigration office then to the Brazilian Polícia Federal (with waiting time at each), and finally on to Brasiléia's bus station or town center, usually costs between US$2.50 and US$3. The completion of the new bridge should shave a few cents off this price, especially if and when both countries put immigration posts at the bridge.

BORDER CROSSINGS
Bolivia

Brazilian immigration procedures are handled at the Polícia Federal station in Epitáciolândia – see Orientation, p674. Bolivian border officials are posted at the old bridge, and will also likely crew the new bridge now that it is completed. Expect Brazilian officials to request your yellow fever vaccine certificate when entering.

Peru

Access to Peru is through the village of Assis Brasil, 110km west of Brasiléia. Once an adventure route, the road is now paved and has daily bus services. Complete Brazilian immigration procedures in Brasiléia, and Peruvian immigration at the border town of Iñapari.

Acreana has bus services to Assis Brasil to/from Rio Branco and Brasiléia; see those sections for schedules, fares and contact info. From Iñapari, buses head south on an unpaved road to Iberia (about US$9, five hours) and onward by a better road to Puerto Maldonado (about US$22, 10 hours); travel time can lengthen a great deal in the wet season. Puerto Maldonado has transportation to Cuzco and Lima and is a center for exploring part of Peruvian Amazonia. Alternatively, ask about flights from the Iñapari airstrip (7km from the village) to Iberia, Puerto Maldonado and possibly Cuzco.

Assis Brasil, Iñapari and Iberia all have some basic hotels.

Directory

ACCOMMODATIONS

Brazilian accommodations range from battered, windowless cells to sumptuous guesthouses overlooking the sea, with a range of options in between. Nearly every pousada (guesthouse), hostel and hotel serves *café da manhã* (breakfast) – though it may be nothing more than instant coffee and a dry roll. Private rooms with communal bathrooms down the hall are called *quartos*. Rooms with a private bathroom are *apartamentos*.

For our listings, all double rooms that cost less than US$25 are placed in the budget category. At the bottom end of the scale, you can find cheap hotel rooms that cost as little as US$5/US$7 for single/double

quartos. At that price expect a bare, shabby room with nothing but a bed and maybe a fan. The walls *may* reach up to the ceiling, you *may* have a window and it's *possible* that the sheets have been changed since the previous occupancy. The door will probably be lockable and the room will probably be swept daily. A step up (US$12 to US$20) will give you simple rooms, most commonly with fans, and dormitories in hostels (usually air-conditioned).

Mid-range listings run from US$25 to US$75 and are usually comfortable – though not terribly stylish – affairs. Decent beds, air-conditioning, hot-water bathrooms and cable TV are the norm. The top end runs from US$76 and up. Here you'll find spacious digs, well furnished with swimming pools, verandas and other amenities (workout and business centers if you're in Rio or Sampa). Both medium-priced and top-end hotels have safes at the front desk that you can use with confidence as long as you get a receipt.

PRACTICALITIES

- **Newspapers & Magazines** Biggest daily newspapers are *Jornal do Brasil* (www.jbonline.com.br) and *O Globo* (www.globo.com.br), both out of Rio, and *O Estado de São Paulo* and *Folha de São Paulo*, out of Sampa. The weekly *Veja* is an excellent current-affairs magazine, and in Rio and São Paulo it comes with a good pullout guide to what's happening locally.

- **TV** Programming revolves around sports, comedy shows and the nightly *telenovelas* (soap operas). *O Globo* is the largest nationwide TV network.

- **Video** PAL.

- **Electricity** Electrical current is not standardized in Brazil and can be almost anywhere between 110V and 220V. Carry a converter and use a surge protector with electrical equipment.

- **Weights & Measures** Metric.

In tourist centers, especially Rio, reservations are a good idea during July and from Christmas to Carnaval. This is true for mid-range and top-end hotels, and for the most popular budget ones as well. The same goes for any vacation mecca (eg Búzios) on weekends, and anywhere during major festivals. For prime peak times (eg Carnaval in Rio or Salvador), try to make contact at least a few weeks ahead. Many places now allow you to book online. Check the website www.cade.com.br (in Portuguese) to access Brazilian hotels that allow you to book online. For Rio, visit www.ipanema.com to get good rates on many hotels.

Booking ahead can also save you 30% or more. If your language skills aren't up to it, get a travel agent to do it for you.

Accommodations in Remote Areas

Where there are no hotels – as in parts of Amazonia and the Northeast – a hammock and mosquito net are essential. With these basics (inexpensively bought in almost any town) and friendly locals, you can get a good night's rest anywhere. Most fishing villages along the coast have seen an outsider or two and will put you up for the night. If they've seen a few more outsiders, they'll probably charge you a couple of dollars.

Another type of remote-area accommodation is the jungle lodge – a hotel catering to tourists in or on the edge of the forest. These usually have all the amenities of a mid-range or even top-end hotel, with a considerably more exotic setting and architecture (they're usually made of wood and often stand on stilts).

Camping

Camping is popular in Brazil and is a viable alternative in many parts of the country for travelers on limited budgets or for those who want to explore some of the national or state parks – as long as you're prepared to carry a tent and the other necessary gear. The biggest concern is safety. Many campsites are near urban areas, and it's unwise to camp in these spots, unless locals have assured you it's safe.

The **Camping Clube do Brasil** (Map pp136-7; ☎ 0xx21-2210 3171; www.campingclube.com.br; 29th fl, Rua Senador Dantas 75, Centro, Rio de Janeiro) has 48 sites as far apart as Fortaleza and Porto Alegre. Check its website for info.

MINIMUM-IMPACT CAMPING

The following guidelines are recommended for those camping in wilderness or other fragile areas of Brazil:

- Select a well-drained campsite and, especially if it's raining, use some type of waterproof groundsheet to prevent having to dig trenches.
- Along popular routes, camp in established sites.
- Carry as little packaging in as possible, and carry out all your rubbish.
- Use established toilet facilities if available. Otherwise, select a site at least 100m from water sources and bury wastes in a small hole about 15cm deep. If possible, burn used toilet paper or bury it well.
- Use only biodegradable soap products (you'll probably have to bring them from home). Disperse wastewater at least 50m from watercourses.
- Try to select an established site for fires and keep them as small as possible. Use only fallen dead wood and make sure the fire is fully extinguished before leaving.

Hostels

Youth hostels in Brazil are called *albergues da juventude*. The Federação Brasileira de Albergues da Juventude (FBAJ) has more than 50 hostels in 14 states, including many in state capitals and popular travel destinations. Quality varies but many hostels are excellent, and the cost is very reasonable. They're great places to meet young Brazilians.

A dormitory bed in an FBAJ hostel costs between US$7.50 and US$16 per person. Non-Hostelling International (HI) members usually pay 50% extra, but you can buy an HI guest card for US$15 at many hostels and at youth hostel association offices in Brazil.

The headquarters of the **FBAJ** (Map pp132-3; ☎ 0xx21-2286-0303; www.hostel.org.br; Rua General Dionísio 63, Botafogo, Rio) is at the Albergue da Juventude Chave do Rio de Janeiro. The FBAJ's English-and-Portuguese website lists all FBAJ hostels, often with links to the hostels' own sites. Booklets listing the hostels and describing how to reach them (in Portuguese) are available free at hostels, hostel offices and travel agents.

There are also a few dozen non-FBAJ hostels around the country, many of which are also fine.

Hotels

Brazil has good, modern, luxury hotels, old, shabby, moldy hotels, and everything in between. At more expensive places, taxes of 10% or more are often added to the basic price. The price you're initially quoted normally includes all taxes, but it does no harm to check. Prices are, in fact, often flexible. Many mid-range and top-end hotels will give you a discount of up to 30%, occasionally even 40%, from their posted prices, just for the asking (*Ha algum desconto?*), especially if business is slow. Sometimes the discount is available only if you pay cash, or if you stay a few days; sometimes it's available to anyone who asks for it. Hotels in tourist areas often raise prices during the high seasons. Hotels in business-oriented cities such as Goiânia, Curitiba, Porto Alegre and Brasília readily give discounts on weekends.

Pousadas

Many travelers stay at pousadas where a room without a bathroom can go for as little as US$10 per person. They range in quality and price and, at the upper end of the scale, they're more like European B&Bs, costing anywhere from US$40 to US$100. The small scale of pousadas, and the personal touch this often brings, can make them some of the most pleasant places to stay in Brazil. Breakfast is almost always included in the price.

Rental Accommodations

It's possible to rent vacation, short- or long-term apartments through a number of sources. Real-estate agencies in most large cities will be able to provide information on rentals for foreigners. The best bet is to speak to other foreigners in Brazil to get an idea of current prices, which vary from city to city. In the classified real-estate sections of newspapers, apartments are usually listed under *temporada* or *apartamentos para aluguel*. If you just want a room in someone else's house or apartment, look under *vaga* or *quarto*. Generally, an apartment that costs US$200 per week in Belo Horizonte will cost you two to three times that in Rio or São Paulo.

ACTIVITIES

Mountains, coast and sea all provide some great opportunities for fresh-air adventure.

Websites 360 Graus (www.360graus.com .br) and Guia Verde (www.guiaverde.com .br) cover a host of activities: canyoning, paragliding, kitesurfing or wakeboarding to rafting, surfing, trekking, diving or mountain climbing. They're in Portuguese, but need little translation.

Climbing

Climbing in Brazil is best from April to October. The best thing about rock climbing in Brazil is that in one hour you can be on the beach, and the next on a world-class climb, 300m above a city. Brazil has lots of fantastic climbs, ranging from beginner level to routes yet to be conquered. Within 40 minutes of central Rio de Janeiro, the hub of Brazilian climbing, are some 350 documented climbs. The national parks of Serra dos Órgãos (p199) and Itatiaia (p193) and Caparaó (p262) have some particularly good climbs. For climbing clubs in Rio, see p146.

CLIMBING VOCABULARY

Although most Brazilians in the clubs know a little English, it helps to know a little Portuguese to smooth the way.

baudrie – harness
corda – rope
dar segurança – to belay
equipamento – equipment
estar preso – to be secured
fenda – crack
fita – webbing
grampo – bolt
mochila – backpack
mosquetão – carabiner
pó de magnésio – chalk powder
queda – a fall
rocha – rock
tomar uma vaca – to make a stupid mistake and fall
topo – summit; also cume
uma agarra – a hold
via – route; also rota

Hang Gliding & Paragliding

It's easy – and fantastic – to hang glide *duplo* (double) in Rio (p146). Paragliding (*parapente*) can be set up, too. Another place you can double hang glide is Rio da Barra (p461), near Trancoso, Bahia.

Hiking

Hiking in Brazil is highly popular. It's best done during the cooler months of April to October. During the summer, the tropical sun heats the rock to oven temperatures and turns the jungles into steamy saunas.

There are lots of great places to hike in Brazil, both in the national and state parks and along the coastline, and especially in the Southeast and South. Plenty of good hikes are mentioned in the regional chapters. Outstanding areas include the national parks of Chapada Diamantina (p471), Serra dos Órgãos (p199) and Itatiaia (p193), Chapada dos Veadeiros (p347) and Caparaó (p262), as well as the Parque Estadual Marumbi (p302), the Serra de São José (p251), near Tiradentes, and the Canela area (p342).

Contact some of the local hiking and rock-climbing clubs (see p146), which have details of trekking options.

Horseback Riding

In Minas Gerais you can ride stretches of the old gold road, the Estrada Real, or take a five-day horse trek from the state capital, Belo Horizonte (p224), to its most famous historic town, Ouro Prêto (p231). The Pantanal (p388) is another attractive riding area.

Surfing

Surfing is very popular, and several Brazilian professionals are usually to be found in the top 20 of the world rankings.

SURFING VOCABULARY

Despite their reputation for aggressiveness in the water, once on land Brazilian surfers become very interested in foreign surfers and their travels. They are also reasonably willing to lend you their boards if you ask politely.

body board – boogie board

onda – wave

Pode me emprestar sua prancha por favor? – Could I borrow your board please?

prancha – surfboard

quebrar – to break

surfista – surfer

Tem ondas? – Are there any waves?

Vamos pegar ondas. – Let's go surfing.

vento – wind

There's surf virtually all along the coast, with particularly good waves in the South. The best surf beaches are in Santa Catarina state and the Brazilian championships are held at Praia Joaquina (p330), on Ilha de Santa Catarina. São Francisco do Sul (p321), Ilha do Mel (p305), Ubatuba (p283), Ilhabela (p285), Maresias (p286) and the Boiçucanga area (p286) all serve up good waves.

The best surf is in Rio state, Saquarema (p201). Búzios (p206) and Itacoatiara (see the boxed text on p141) beach in Niterói are also popular breaks. There's plenty of surf close to the city of Rio and there are places to rent boards and take classes (p147). Prainha (p144) is the best surfing beach near the city. The waves are best in the Brazilian winter (from June to August).

On other surf beaches surfing is still a way of life – even in Espírito Santo state with its breaks of only 1m to 3m – boogie boarding is popular too. Renting boogie boards and surfboards is easy to do right on the beach wherever you go.

Further north, Itacaré (p448) and Sítio (p443) and Porto de Galinhas (p509) and Fernando de Noronha (p513) are among the better spots.

A curious event is the national *pororoca* (tidal bore) surf championship held at São Domingos do Capim (p590) at the time of the full moon nearest the March equinox. The waves here are formed by the tidal bore on a tributary of the Rio Amazonas, a long way from the ocean. Waves can reach a few meters in height.

Windsurfing

Windsurfing has caught on in Brazil. In Rio you can rent equipment at Barra da Tijuca, but there are better conditions, and again equipment to rent, at Búzios (p206) in eastern Rio state. In São Paulo state there's good windsurfing at Ilhabela (p285) and around Boiçucanga (p286). But Brazil's hardcore windsurfing mecca is much further north, along the Ceará coast, northwest of Fortaleza, where constant, regular, strong trade winds blow from July to December. Jericoacoara (p551) is one of the best spots in the country for windsurfing. Near Fortaleza, the beaches of Praia do Futuro (p543) and Praia de Iracema (p543) are also popular spots.

Other Water Sports

Sailing is big at Búzios in Rio state and the larger resorts along the coast.

Mergulho (diving) doesn't match the Caribbean, but is worthwhile if you're keen. You can arrange diving excursions or rent equipment in Rio (p145). Good dive spots are Arraial do Cabo (p203); the Reserva Biológica do Avoredo (p322), near Porto Belo in Santa Catarina state; Boipeba (p447); Ponta do Seixas (p523), near João Pessoa in Paraíba; and Fernando de Noronha (p511), perhaps the country's finest diving spot.

Fishing in the interior of Brazil is fantastic. The Rio Araguaia in Goiás and Tocantins is known as a fishing paradise with a large variety of fish, including the pintado, dourado and *tucunaré* (peacock bass). The legendary fighting qualities of the *tucunaré* attract sport fishers from far and wide to the Araguaia and other Amazonian rivers. Fishing for piranha is not undertaken by serious anglers, though it's good fun. Fishing is brilliant in the Pantanal (p390) too, and is allowed from February to October.

You can also ride an inner tube down the Rio Nhundiaquara (p302).

BUSINESS HOURS

Most shops and government services (including post offices) are open from 9am to 6pm Monday to Friday and 9am to 1pm Saturday. Shopping malls usually stay open till 10pm Monday to Saturday, and some even open on Sunday (usually late, from 3pm to 9pm). Because many Brazilians have little free time during the week, Saturday morning is often spent shopping.

Restaurants tend to be open from 8am to 10.30am, from noon till 3pm and from 6pm till 10pm.

Banks, always in their own little world, are generally open from 9am or 10am to 2pm or 3pm.

CHILDREN

Brazilians generally love children, who are welcome at nearly all hotels, cafés and restaurants. Many hotels let children stay free, although the age limit varies. Babysitters are readily available, and most restaurants have high chairs. The common bond shared by all parents of all nationalities will often bring you that welcome extra personal contact and attention from Brazilians.

Apart from the obvious attractions for children of beaches, coasts and swimming pools in Brazil, you can also find excellent special attractions in many areas, such as amusement parks, zoos, aquariums, and train and boat rides.

Diapers are widely available in Brazil, but you may not easily find creams, baby foods or familiar medicines outside larger cities.

See Visas & Documents (p695) for information on special bureaucratic requirements for unaccompanied travelers under the age of 18.

Children under two years old generally fly for 10% of the adult fare. Those between two and 12 usually pay 50% on international flights and 67% on Brazilian domestic flights. Lonely Planet's *Travel with Children* contains lots of practical advice on this subject, as well as firsthand stories from many parents who have traveled with kids.

CLIMATE CHARTS

For information about weather and seasonal patterns, see When to Go (p13). For climate charts see (p682).

COURSES

Language

There are lots of ways to learn Portuguese in Brazil. It's easy to arrange classes through branches of the Instituto Brazil-Estados Unidos (IBEU), where Brazilians learn English. Rio de Janeiro offers the most opportunities for classes (see p150), but there'll be a language institute in each large city. Website www.onestoplanguage.net has a small database of Portuguese-language schools in Brazil. In the US **National Registration Center for Study Abroad** (☎ 414-278-0631; www.nrcsa.com) has information on Portuguese language schools in some Brazilian cities. You can also check out www.languageschools.com, which lists several dozen Brazilian language programs, all sponsored by US affiliates.

CUSTOMS

Travelers entering Brazil are allowed to bring in one radio, tape player, typewriter, notebook computer and video and still camera each. Plants and seeds must be declared on arrival. Apart from clothes, books, periodicals and other personal articles for domestic or professional use, or consumption, goods that have cost more

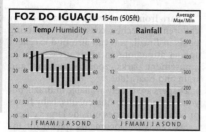

FOZ DO IGUAÇU 154m (505ft)

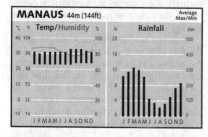

MANAUS 44m (144ft)

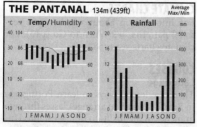

THE PANTANAL 134m (439ft)

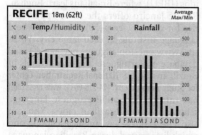

RECIFE 18m (62ft)

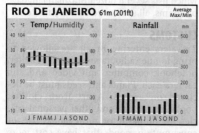

RIO DE JANEIRO 61m (201ft)

than US$500 (US$150 if you are arriving by land, river or lake) are subject to 50% import duty.

DANGERS & ANNOYANCES

Brazil receives a lot of bad press about its violence and high crime rate. We feel that the dangers to travelers, while they do exist, get exaggerated. By using common sense, there is much you can do to reduce the risks of getting robbed. Don't start your trip by wandering around touristy areas in a jet-lagged state soon after arrival: you'll be an obvious target. Accept the fact that you might be mugged, pickpocketed or have your bag snatched while you're in the country. If you carry only the minimum needed for the day, and don't try to resist thieves, you're unlikely to come to any real harm. Other tips:

- Dress down in casual clothes that blend in. Clothes bought in Brazil are a good choice.
- Keep small change handy so you don't have to flash a wallet to pay bus fare.
- Don't wander around with a camera in view – keep it out of sight. Consider carrying it in a plastic bag from a local store. Disposable cameras are much less worry.
- Before arriving in a new place, get a map or at least have a rough idea of the area's orientation. Use taxis to avoid walking through high-risk areas.
- Be alert and walk purposefully. Criminals will home in on dopey, hesitant, disoriented-looking individuals.
- Use ATMs inside buildings. When using any ATM or exchanging money, be aware of those around you. Robbers sometimes watch these places looking for targets.
- Check windows and doors of your room for security, and don't leave anything valuable lying around. If you consider your hotel to be reliable, place your valuables in its safe and get a receipt.
- If you're suspicious or uneasy about a situation, don't hesitate to make excuses and leave, change your route, or whatever else is needed to extricate yourself.
- Don't take anything to city beaches except your bathing suit, a towel and just enough money for food and drinks. No camera, no bag, no jewelry.
- After dark, don't walk along empty or nearly-empty streets or into deserted parks.

■ Don't wander into the *favelas* (shanty-towns) unless you're with a trustworthy guide who really knows the area.

■ Never carry any more money than you need for the specific outing you're on, and keep it discreetly stashed away in a money belt, sock, secret pocket or shoe. But always have enough cash on hand to appease a mugger (US$5 to US$10).

■ If something is stolen from you, you can report it to the police, but it can be an enormous hassle just to get a police report for your insurance company. The tourist police are the best equipped to deal with foreigners, but are rare outside of Rio.

Scams & Robbery Techniques

Distraction is a common tactic employed by street thieves in Brazil and elsewhere around the world. The aim is to throw potential victims off guard so that they're easier prey. It may be something as simple as asking you for a cigarette or a light so that you slow down and take your attention off other people around you.

Techniques are continually being developed, and imported or exported across national borders, to relieve the unwary of their belongings. Keep abreast of new scams by talking to other travelers. Theft and security are sources of endless fascination and stories.

A classic, revolting distraction method is the 'cream technique,' common the world over, including in Brazil. You're walking down the street or standing in some public place, when someone surreptitiously sprays a substance on your shoulder, your daypack or anything else connected with you. The substance can be anything from mustard to chocolate or even excrement. An assistant (young or old, male or female) then taps you on the shoulder and amicably offers to clean off the mess…if you'll just put down your bag for a second. The moment you do this, someone makes off with it in a flash. The golden rule is to ignore any such attempt or offer, and simply endure your mucky state until you can find a safe place, such as your hotel, where you can wash.

There have also been reports of druggings, including spiked drinks. While you're temporarily unconscious or semiconscious as a result of some noxious substance being slipped into your beverage, you're powerless to resist thieves. There have even been reported cases of rape in such circumstances. If you start to feel unaccountably dizzy, disoriented, fatigued, or just mentally vacant not long after imbibing, your drink may have been spiked.

Exercise *extreme* caution when someone you don't know and trust offers you a drink of *any* kind or even cigarettes, sweets etc. If the circumstances make you suspicious, the offer can be tactfully refused by claiming stomach or other medical problems.

DISABLED TRAVELERS

Travelers in wheelchairs don't have the easiest of times in Brazil, but in the large cities there is a concerted effort to keep people mobile. Problems you'll encounter include immensely crowded public buses and restaurants with entrance steps. It pays to plan your trip through contact with some of the organizations listed here.

Rio is probably the most accessible city in Brazil for disabled travelers to get around, but that doesn't mean it's always easy. The metro system has electronic wheelchair lifts, but these aren't always operational. The streets and sidewalks along the main beaches have curb cuts and are wheelchair accessible but most other areas do not have cuts. Many restaurants also have entrance steps.

Most of the newer hotels have wheelchair-accessible rooms, and some cable TV is closed-captioned.

Useful Organizations

The **Centro de Vida Independente** (Map pp124–5; ☎ 0xx21-2512 1088; fax 2239 6547; Rua Marquês de São Vincente 225, Gávea) can provide advice for the disabled about travel in Brazil.

Those in the US may like to contact the **Society for Accessible Travel & Hospitality** (SATH; ☎ 212-447 7284; www.sath.org). SATH's website is a good resource for disabled travelers. Another excellent website to check out is www.access-able.com.

Other useful organizations in the US include the following:

International Association for Medical Assistance to Travelers (IAMAT; ☎ 716-754 4883; www.iamat.org; 417 Center St, NY 14092)

Mobility International USA (☎ 541-343-1284; www.miusa.org) Advises disabled travelers on mobility issues, runs an exchange program and publishes the quarterly *Over the Rainbow* newsletter.

Moss Rehabilitation Hospital (☎ 215-456-5995; www.mossresourcenet.org) Offers an online travel information service with a disability fact sheet.

In Australia, try **ACROD** (☎ 02-6282 4333; www.acrod.org.au; ACROD House, 33 Thesiger Ct, Deakin, ACT). Its website has excellent links, among them the highly useful www.independentliving.org.

In the UK, **RADAR** (☎ 020-7250 3222; www.radar.org.uk) is run by and for disabled people. Its website is very organized, and, although travel is not a feature, there are travel-specific links to excellent sites such as www.holidaycare.org.uk.

EMBASSIES & CONSULATES
Brazilian Embassies & Consulates

The following listings are for embassies unless noted:

Argentina Consulate in Buenos Aires (☎ 011-4394-5255; www.brasil.org.ar; Carlos Pellegrini 1363, 5¼ Piso, 1011 Buenos Aires); consulate in Puerto Iguazú (☎ 03757-21348; Av Guaraní 70, Puerto Iguazú; ☒ 8am-2pm Mon-Fri)

Australia ACT (☎ 02-6273 4837; www.brazil.org.au; 19 Forster Cres, Yarralumla, ACT 2600)

Bolivia consulate in Cobija (Av General Rene Barrientos, Cobija; ☒ 8am-1pm Mon-Fri); consulate in Guayaramerín (☎ 0855-3766; Av 24 de Septiembre, Guayaramerín; ☒ 9am-1pm & 3-5pm Mon-Fri); La Paz (☎ 02-440202; www.brasil.org.bo; Calle Capitán Ravelo 2334, Edificio Metrobol, La Paz); consulate in Santa Cruz (☎ 03-344400; Av German Busch 330, Santa Cruz)

Canada consulate in Montreal (☎ 514-499 0968); Ottawa (☎ 613-237 1090; 450 Wilbrod St, Ottawa, Ontario K1N 6M8); consulate in Toronto (☎ 416-922 2503; www.consbrastoronto.org; 77 Bloor St West, Suite 1109 & 1105, Toronto, Ontario M5S1M2)

Colombia Bogotá (☎ 571-218-0800; www.geocities.com/secombra in Portuguese; Calle 93 No 14-20, Piso 8, Bogotá); consulate in Leticia (☎ 578-592-7530; Carrera 9 No 13-84, Leticia; ☒ 8am-2pm Mon-Fri)

France Paris (☎ 01 45 61 63 00; www.bresil.org; 34 Cours Albert, 1er, 75008 Paris)

French Guiana consulate in Cayenne (☎ 29-6010; www.nplus.gf/~cbrascay); 444 chemin Saint-Antoine, 97337 Cayenne)

Germany Berlin-Mitte (☎ 030-726280; www.brasilianische-botschaft.de; Wallstrasse 57, 10179 Berlin-Mitte)

Guyana Georgetown (☎ 02-57970; 308 Church St, Queenstown, Georgetown)

Ireland Dublin (☎ 01-475 6000; Harcourt Centre, Europa House, 5th fl, Harcourt St, Dublin 2)

Netherlands The Hague (☎ 070-302 39 59; Mauritskade 19, 2514 HD, The Hague)

New Zealand Wellington (☎ 04-473 3516; 10 Brandon St, Level 9, Wellington 1)

Paraguay consulate in Asunción (☎ 021-448084; www.embajadabrasil.org.py; General Díaz 523 at 14 de Mayo, 3¼ Piso, Asunción) consulate in Ciudad del Este (☎ 061-500984; Calle Pampliega 205, Ciudad del Este; ☒ 7am-noon Mon-Fri)

Peru Lima (☎ 01-421-2759; Av José Pardo 850, Miraflores, Lima 100)

Spain Madrid (☎ 91 700 4650; Calle Fernando El Santo 6, 28010 Madrid)

UK consulate in London (☎ 020-7930 9055; www.brazil.org.uk; 6 St Alban's St, London SW1Y 4SQ); embassy in London (☎ 020-7399 9000; 32 Green St, London W1K, 7AT)

Uruguay consulate in Montevideo (☎ 02-900-6282; www.brasmont.org.uy; Convencion 1343, 6¼ Piso, Montevideo)

USA consulate in Boston (☎ 617-542-4000; www.consulatebrazil.org; 20 Park Plaza, Suite 810, Boston MA 02116; ☒ 9am-3pm Mon-Fri); consulate in Chicago (☎ 312-464-0244; 401 North Michigan Av, Suite 3050, Chicago, IL 60611); consulate in Houston (☎ 713-961-3063; www.brazilhouston.org; 1233 West Loop South, Park Tower North, Suite 1150, Houston, TX 77027); consulate in Los Angeles (☎ 323-651-2664; 8484 Wilshire Blvd, Suites 730-711, Beverly Hills, CA 90211); consulate in Miami (☎ 305-285-6200; www.brazilmiami.org; 80 SW 8th St, 26th fl, Miami, FL 33130); consulate in New York (☎ 917-777-7777; www.brazilny.org; 1185 Av of the Americas, 21st fl, New York, NY 10036); consulate in San Francisco (☎ 415-981-8170; www.brazilsf.org; 300 Montgomery St, Suite 900, San Francisco, CA 94104); Washington DC (☎ 202-745-2837; www.brasilemb.org; 3006 Massachusetts Ave NW, Washington, DC 20008)

Venezuela Caracas (☎ 02-261-7553; Calle Los Chaguaramos at Av Mohedano, Centro Gerencial Mohedano, Piso 6, La Castellana 1060, Caracas); consulate in Santa Elena de Uairén (☎ 088-951262; Av Gran Mariscal, Santa Elena de Uairén; ☒ 8am-noon Mon-Fri)

Embassies & Consulates in Brazil

Embassies are all in Brasília, but many countries have consulates in Rio and São Paulo, and often other cities too. For addresses in Brasília, SES stands for Setor de Embaixadas Sul.

Argentina Brasília (☎ 0xx61-365 3000; www.embarg.org.br; SHIS, Q L-2, conj 01, casa 19, Lago Sul, Brasília); consulate in Foz do Iguaçu (Map p309; ☎ 0xx45-574 2969;Rua Dom Pedro II 28, Foz do Iguaçu; ☒ 10am-2:30pm Mon-Fri); consulate in Porto Alegre (☎ 0xx51-321 1360; Rua Coronel Bordini 1033, Porto Alegre); consulate in Rio (Map pp132-3; ☎ 0xx21-2553 1646; Praia de Botafogo 228, Sobreloja 201, Botafogo, Rio de Janeiro);

consulate in São Paulo (☎ 0xx11-284 1355; Av Paulista 1106, 9¼ andar, São Paulo)

Australia Brasília (☎ 0xx61-248 5569; SHIS, Q I-9, conj 16, casa 1, Brasília); consulate in Rio (Map pp136-7; ☎ 0xx21-3824 4624; 23rd fl, Av Presidente Wilson 231, Centro, Rio de Janeiro)

Bolivia consulate in Brasiléia (☎ 0xx68-546-3595; Rua Major Salinas 205, Brasiléia; ☺ 8am-noon Mon-Fri); Brasília (☎ 0xx61-364-3362; SHIS, Q L-10, conj 01, casa 06, Lago Sul, Brasília); consulate in Corumbá (Map p399; ☎ 0xx67-231-5605; Rua Antônio Maria Coelho 881, Corumbá; ☺ 8:30am-1:30pm Mon-Fri); consulate in Guajará-Mirim (☎ 0xx69-541 5876; Av Beira Rio 505, 1¼ andar, Guajará-Mirim; ☺ 8am-1:30pm Mon-Fri); consulate in Rio (☎ 0xx21-2551 1796; Av Rui Barbosa 664, Apt 101, Botafogo, Rio de Janeiro)

Canada Brasília (☎ 0xx61-321 2171; www.dfait-maeci .gc.ca/brazil; SES, Av das Nações, Q 803, lote 16, Brasília); consulate in Rio (Map pp128-9; ☎ 0xx21-2543 3004; 5th fl, Av Atlântica 1130, Copacabana, Rio de Janeiro); consulate in São Paulo (☎ 0xx11-5509 4321; Av Nações Unidas 12901, 16¼ andar, São Paulo)

Colombia Brasília (☎ 0xx61-226 8902; SES, Av das Nações, Q 803, lote 10, Brasília); consulate in Rio (☎ 0xx21-2552 6248; Praia do Flamengo 284, No 101, Rio de Janeiro); consulate in Tabatinga (☎ 0xx92-412 2597; Av da Amizade 2205, Tabatinga)

France honorary consulate in Belém (☎ 0xx91-224 6818; Rua Aristides Lobo 651); Brasília (☎ 0xx61-312 9100; www.ambafrance-br.org.br; SES, Av das Nações, Q 801, lote 04, Brasília); honorary consulate Macapá (☎ 0xx96-223 7554; Rua Jovino Dinoa 1693, Macapá; ☺ 9am-noon Mon & Tue, Thu & Fri); consulate in Rio (Map pp136-7; ☎ 0xx21-2210 1272; Av Presidente Antônio Carlos 58, 6¼ andar, Rio de Janeiro) Note: French honorary consulates do not issue visas for French Guiana or France.

Germany Brasília (☎ 0xx61-443 7330; www.embaixada -alemanha.org.br; SES, Av das Nações, Q 807, lote 25, Brasília); consulate in Rio (☎ 0xx21-2553 6777; Rua Presidente Carlos de Campos 417, Laranjeiras, Rio de Janeiro)

Guyana Brasília (☎ 0xx61-326 9269; SBN, Q 02, Edifício Paulo Mauricio, 13¼ andar, sala 1310, Brasília)

Ireland honorary consulate in Rio (☎ 0xx21-2501 8455; Rua 24 de Maio 347, Riachuelo, Rio de Janeiro)

Netherlands Brasília (☎ 0xx61-321 4769; SES, Av das Nações, Q 801, lote 05, Brasília); Rio (☎ 0xx21-2552 9028; Praia de Botafogo 242, 10¼ andar, Rio de Janeiro)

New Zealand consulate in São Paulo (☎ 0xx11-288 0307; Alameda Campinas 579, 15¼ andar, São Paulo)

Paraguay Brasília (☎ 0xx61-244 9449; SES, Av das Nações, Q 811, lote 42, Brasília); consulate in Foz do Iguaçu (Map p309; ☎ 0xx45-523-2898; Rua Marechal Deodoro da Fonseca 901, Foz do Iguaçu; ☺ 8:30am-4:30pm Mon-Fri); consulate in Rio (☎ 0xx21-2553-2294; Praia de Botafogo 242, 2¼ andar, Rio de Janeiro);

Peru Brasília (☎ 0xx61-242 9435; SES, Av das Nações, Q 811, lote 43, Brasília); consulate in Rio (☎ 0xx21-2551-9596; Av Rui Barbosa 314, 2¼ andar, Flamengo, Rio de Janeiro)

Spain Brasília (☎ 0xx61-244 2121; SES, Av das Nações, Q 811, lote 44, Brasília); consulate in Rio (☎ 0xx21-2543 3200; Rua Lauro Müller 116, salas 1601/12, Torre Rio Sul, Botafogo, Rio de Janeiro)

UK Brasília (☎ 0xx61-225 2710; www.reinounido.org.br; SES, Av das Nações, Q 801, lote 08, Brasília); consulate in Rio (Map pp132-3; ☎ 0xx21-2555 9600; Praia do Flamengo 284, 2¼ andar, Flamengo, Rio de Janeiro); consulate in Salvador (☎ 0xx71-243 7399; Av Estados Unidos 18B, 8¼ andar, Comércio, Salvador); consulate in São Paulo (☎ 0xx11-816 2303; Rua Fereira de Araujo 741, Pinheiros, São Paulo)

Uruguay Brasília (☎ 0xx61-322 1200; www.emburuguai .org.br; SES, Av das Nações, Q 803, lote 14, Brasília); consulate in Porto Alegre (☎ 0xx51-224 3499; Rua Siqueira Campos 1171, Porto Alegre); consulate in Rio (☎ 0xx21-2553 6030; Praia de Botafogo 242, 6¼ andar, Rio de Janeiro)

USA Brasília (☎ 0xx61-321 7272; www.embaixada-ameri cana.org.br; SES, Av das Nações, Q 801, lote 3, Brasília); consulate in Rio (☎ 0xx21-2292-7117; www.consulado -americano-rio.org.br/rio5.htm; Av Presidente Wilson 147, Rio de Janeiro); consular agency in Salvador (☎ 0xx71-345 1545; Rua Pernambuco 51, Pituba, Salvador); consulate in São Paulo (☎ 0xx11-3081 6511; www.consuladoamerica nosp.org.br; Rua Padre João Manoel 933, Cerqueira César, São Paulo)

Venezuela consulate in Boa Vista (☎ 0xx95-623 9285; Av Benjamin Constant 525E; ☺ 8am-noon Mon-Fri); Brasília (☎ 0xx61-322 1011; SES, Av das Nações, Q 803, lote 13, Brasília); consulate in Manaus (☎ 0xx92-233-6004; Rua Ferreira Pena 179, Centro, Manaus); consulate in Rio (☎ 0xx21-552 6699; Praia de Botafogo 242, 5¼ andar, Botafogo, Rio de Janeiro)

FESTIVALS & EVENTS

Highlights of Brazil's many festivals are listed below. See the regional chapters for details of these and many other events.

January

Bom Jesus dos Navegantes (p491) Four-day festival starting on the second Sunday in January, Penedo, Alagoas.

Festa de Santo Amaro (Lavagem da Purifição; p440) January 23 to February 2, Santo Amaro, Bahia.

Lavagem do Bonfim (p425) Second Thursday in January, Salvador, Bahia.

Processão do Senhor Bom Jesus dos Navegantes (p425) January 1, Salvador, Bahia.

February

Festa de Iemanjá (p425) February 2; Salvador, Bahia.

Shrove Tuesday and Carnaval (p106) February or

March depending on the Easter date; the famous Fat Tuesday celebration and the days preceding it. Nationwide.

March

Semana Santa The week before Easter, in March or April; celebrations in Congonhas (p241), Ouro Prêto (p237), Goiás Velho (p369).

April/May

Cavalhada (see the boxed text on p372) Held 50 days after Easter, Pirenópolis, Goiás.

Festa do Divino (p570) The first Sunday after Ascension Day, Alcântara, Maranhão.

Festa do Divino Espírito Santo (p187) In May or June, 40 days after Easter, Paraty, Rio de Janeiro state.

Micareta (p466) In April or early May, Feira de Santana, Bahia.

June

Boi-Bumbá (p636) Three days in late June, Parintins, Amazonas.

Bumba Meu Boi (see the boxed text on p562) From late June to the second week of August, São Luís, Maranhão.

Festa de São João (p439) Held June 22 to 24, Cachoeira, Bahia.

Festas Juninas Celebrated throughout June in Rio state and much of the rest of the country.

Festival Folclórico do Amazonas (p625) Throughout June, Manaus, Amazonas.

July

Fortal (p545) Last week of July, Fortaleza, Ceará.

Festival de Dança (p319) Second half of July, Joinville, Santa Catarina.

Regata de Jangadas (p545) Second half of July, Fortaleza, Ceará.

August

Festa da NS de Boa Morte (p439) Held in mid-August, Cachoeira, Bahia.

Festa de Iemanjá (p545) Held August 15, Fortaleza, Ceará.

Folclore Nordestino (p507) In late August, Olinda, Pernambuco.

September

Festa de NS de Nazaré (p201) On September 7 and 8, Saquarema, Rio de Janeiro state.

Festa de NS dos Remédios (p187) On September 8, Paraty, Rio de Janeiro state.

Festa do Çairé (p603) Second week of September, Alter do Chão, Pará.

Jubileu do Senhor Bom Jesus do Matosinhos (p241) Takes place from September 7 to 14, Congonhas, Minas Gerais.

October

Círio de Nazaré (p583) Starts the second Sunday in October, Belém, Pará.

NS do Rosário Second half of October in Cachoeira (p439), Bahia and October 23 to 25 in Ouro Prêto (p237), Minas Gerais.

Oktoberfest (p323) The middle two weeks in October, Blumenau, Santa Catarina.

Rio Jazz Festival (p152) Varying dates in October, Rio de Janeiro.

November

Dia do Romeiro e Festa do Padre Cícero (p556) Held November 1 and 2, Juazeiro do Norte, Ceará

Maceió Fest (p486) Held in the 3rd week of November, Maceió, Alagoas.

December

Carnatal (p531) First week of December, Natal, Rio Grande do Norte.

Festa Santa Barbara (p424) Celebrated December 4 to 6, Salvador, Bahia.

Reveillon and Festa de Iemanjá (p152) December 31, Rio de Janeiro.

FOOD

Check out the Food & Drink chapter (p97) for complete details on Brazil's culinary breadth. Where we have divided our restaurant reviews into different price ranges, you can expect a main course to cost under US$5 in a budget eatery, US$5 to US$10 in a mid-range one and over US$10 in a top-end restaurant.

GAY & LESBIAN TRAVELERS

Brazilians are pretty laid-back when it comes to most sexual issues, and homosexuality is more accepted here than in any other part of Latin America. That said, the degree to which you can be out in Brazil varies greatly by region, and in some smaller towns discrimination is prevalent.

Rio is the gay capital of Latin America, though Salvador and São Paulo also have a lively scene. Gay bars in Brazil are all-welcome affairs attended by GLS (Gays, Lesbians e Simpatizantes), crowds full of heterosexuals, homosexuals and who-gives-a-sexuals – who are far more concerned with dancing and having a good time than determining your sexual preference.

There is no law against homosexuality in Brazil, and the age of consent is 18, the same as for heterosexuals. Rio's **Arco Iris Association**

(☎ 0xx21-2552 5995; www.acro-iris.org.br; Rua Mundo Novo 62, Botafogo, Rio de Janeiro) is a gay lobbying group that assists and informs the local gay and lesbian community. In Salvador you can contact the **Grupo Gay da Bahia** (Map pp418-9; ☎ 0xx71-322 2552; Rua Frei Vicente 24, Pelourinho).

The Rio Gay Guide at www.riogayguide .com is an excellent resource for gay and lesbian travelers in Rio. Another informative site that has lots of good links is www .pridelinks.com/Regional/Brazil.

HOLIDAYS

April 19, the **Dia do Índio** (Indian Day), is not a national holiday, but it's marked by festivities in indigenous villages around the country.

The official national holidays consist of the following:

New Year's Day January 1 – officially the Day of Universal Confraternization

Carnaval February/March – the two days before Ash Wednesday, which fall 46 days before Easter Sunday

Good Friday & Easter Sunday March/April

Tiradentes Day April 21 – in honor of Tiradentes, an 18th-century Brazilian nationalist martyr

May Day/Labor Day May 1

Corpus Christi Late May/June – 60 days after Easter Sunday

Independence Day September 7

Day of NS de Aparecida October 12 – holiday of Brazil's religious patron

All Souls' Day November 2

Proclamation of the Republic Day November 15

Christmas Day December 25

INSURANCE

A travel insurance policy to cover theft, loss and medical problems is a good idea. The policies handled by STA Travel and other student travel organizations are usually good value. Some policies offer lower and higher medical expense options; the higher ones are chiefly for countries, such as the US, that have extremely high medical costs. There is a wide variety of policies available, so check the fine print.

Some policies specifically exclude 'dangerous activities,' which can include scuba diving, motorcycling and even hiking. Note that a locally acquired motorcycle license is not valid under some policies.

You may prefer a policy that pays doctors or hospitals directly rather than you having to pay on the spot and claim later. If you have to claim later, make sure you keep all documentation.

Some policies ask you to call back (reverse charges) to a center in your home country for immediate assessment of your problem.

Check that the policy covers ambulances or an emergency flight home.

INTERNET ACCESS

Most top-end hotels and a few mid-range ones in São Paulo and Rio have the technology to allow you to plug in your laptop and access the Internet from your room. Download the details of your ISP's access numbers before you leave home. The major Internet providers in Brazil are **Universo Online** (www.uol.com.br in Portuguese) and **Brazil Online** (www.bol.com.br in Portuguese).

Internet cafés are prevalent throughout the country. Most places charge between US$1.50 and US$3 an hour.

LEGAL MATTERS

If something is stolen from you, you can report it to the police. No big investigation is going to occur, but you will get a police report to give to your insurance company. The police, however, aren't always to be trusted. Brazilian police have upon occasion planted drugs and stung gringos for bribes.

Speaking of drugs, the former military regime had a pathological aversion to drugs and enacted stiff penalties, which are still in force. Drugs provide a perfect excuse for the police to extract a fair amount of money from you, and Brazilian prisons are brutal places.

Police checkpoints along the highways stop cars and buses at random. Police along the coastal drive from Rio to São Paulo are notorious for hassling young people and foreigners. Border areas are also dangerous, particularly around the Bolivian border.

A large amount of cocaine is smuggled out of Bolivia and Peru through Brazil. Be very careful with drugs. If you're going to buy, don't buy from strangers and don't carry anything around with you.

Marijuana is plentiful in Brazil and very illegal. Nevertheless, it's widely used, and, like many other things in Brazil, everyone except the military and the police has a rather tolerant attitude towards it. Bahia seems to have the most open climate. But because of the laws against possession, you won't bump into much unless you know someone or go to an 'in' vacation spot with the young and hip, such as Arraial d'Ajuda, Morro de São Paulo or Jericoacoara, or at quasi hippie hangouts such as São Tome das Letras.

If you're coming from one of the Andean countries and have been chewing coca leaves, be especially careful to clean out your pack before arriving in Brazil. Sentences are stiff even for possession of coca leaves.

Because of the stiff penalties involved with possession or apparent possession, we advise you to stay away from it in any form.

MAPS

Given the size of Brazil, it's essential to be armed with reasonable maps that give a clear idea of scale. It's easy to underestimate distances and the time required for travel, particularly if you plan to visit several regions using roads rather than airports.

Decent maps for general planning include Bartholomew's *Brazil & Bolivia World Travel Map* (1996), GeoCenter's *Brazil, Bolivia, Paraguay, Uruguay*, and the South America sectional maps published by International Travel Map Productions (ITM). Coverage of Brazil is provided in ITM's *South America Southern* (1993), *South America North East* (1994), *South America North West* (1993) and *The Amazon Basin* (1992). At least some of these can be obtained from online bookstores.

In the US, **Omni Resources** (☎ 336-227 8300; www.omnimap.com) is a good source of Brazil maps. It ships worldwide and you can order online.

Brazilian-published maps are harder to get outside Brazil, but once you get here it's easy to obtain the very useful publications in the Quatro Rodas series from newsstands and some bookstores. These include *Guia Rodoviário,* a compact book of maps covering individual states, the *Atlas Rodoviário* road atlas (larger but it fits into a backpack), and excellent street atlases for Rio de Janeiro, São Paulo, Belo Horizonte and Fortaleza. Each costs between US$10 and US$16.

Good topographical maps at various scales are published by the Instituto Brasileiro de Geografia Estatísticas (IBGE), the government geographical service, and the Diretoria de Serviço Geográfico (DSG), the army geographical service. They cost around US$6 and US$15, respectively, per sheet. Availability is erratic, but IBGE offices in most state capitals sell IBGE maps. Office locations can be found on the IBGE website (www.ibge.gov.br) – look for the IBGE addresses under 'Locais de Atendimento.' One of the country's best sources of DSG and IBGE maps is **Editora Geográfica J Paulini** (Map pp136-7; ☎ 0xx21-2220 0181; Shop K, Rua Senador Dantas 75, Centro) in Rio de Janeiro.

Searchable street maps of 128 Brazilian cities are online at www.terra.com.br/turismo (in Portuguese). Street maps from tourist offices are a matter of potluck. But telephone directories in many states include excellent city maps as well as phone numbers.

MONEY

Brazil's currency is the real (hay-*ow*; often written R$); the plural is reais (hay-*ice*). One real is made up of 100 centavos. The real was introduced on a one-for-one parity with the US dollar in 1994 but had declined bit by bit to a value of around US$0.33 by 2004.

Banknotes are easy to distinguish from each other, as they come in different colors. There's a green one-real note, a blue/purple five, a red 10, a brown 50 and a blue 100.

ATMs

ATMs are the easiest way of getting cash in big cities and are widely found. In many smaller towns, ATMs exist but rarely work for non-Brazilian cards. Make sure you have a four-digit PIN (longer PINs may not work). In general HSBC, Banco do Brasil and Bradesco are the best ATMs to try. Look for the stickers on the machines that say Cirrus, Visa, or whatever system your card uses – though this may not mean the machine will necessarily work.

Bargaining

A little bargaining for hotel rooms should become second nature. Before you agree to take a room, ask for a better price. *'Tem desconto?'* (Is there a discount?) and *'Pode fazer um melhor preço?'* (Can you give a better price?) are the phrases to use. It's also possible to reduce the price if you state that you don't want a TV, private bathroom, or air-conditioning.

There's often a discount for paying *á vista* (cash) or for staying during the low season *(baixa estação* or *época baixa)*. If you're staying longer than a couple of days, ask for a discount. Once a discount has been quoted, make sure it is noted on your bill at the same time – this avoids 'misunderstandings' at a later date. You should also bargain when shopping in markets and riding in unmetered taxis (and don't forget to arrange the price before departing).

Cash & Traveler's Checks

Even if you are relying mainly on credit or debit cards as your source of funds, it's a good idea to take a little cash and a few traveler's checks too. You can change these in banks or in *casas de câmbio* (exchange offices). Banks have slower, more bureaucratic procedures but on the whole give better exchange rates (an exception being Banco do Brasil which charges US$20 commission for every traveler's check transaction). You'll usually get a 1% or 2% better exchange rate for cash than for traveler's checks. Checks, of course, have the advantage of being replaceable if lost or stolen.

Both cash and traveler's checks should be in US dollars, and Amex is easily the most recognized traveler's check. Thomas Cook, Barclays and Citibank traveler's checks are less widely accepted, but you should be able to cash them in large cities.

Credit Cards

You can use credit cards for many purchases and to make cash withdrawals from ATMs and banks. Visa is the most widely accepted card, followed by MasterCard. Amex and Diners Club cards are also useful. Visa cash advances are widely available, even in small towns with no other currency exchange facilities; you'll need your passport, and the process can be time-consuming, especially at the ubiquitous but superbureaucratic Banco do Brasil. In Brazilian banks generally, it's preferable to deal with machines than to try to make contact with human beings. Credit-card fraud is extremely common in Brazil. Keep your card in sight at all times, especially in restaurants.

Tipping

Workers in most services get tipped 10%, and as they make the minimum wage –

which is not enough to live on – you can be sure they need the money. In restaurants the service charge will usually be included in the bill and is mandatory. If a waitperson is friendly and helpful you can give more. When the service charge is not included, a 10% tip is customary.

There are many places where tipping is not customary but is a welcome gesture. The local juice stands, bars, coffee corners, street and beach vendors are all tipped on occasion. Parking assistants receive no wages and are dependent on tips, usually the equivalent of US$1. Gas-station attendants, shoe shiners and barbers are also frequently tipped. Most people round taxi fares up to the nearest real, but tipping is not expected.

PHOTOGRAPHY & VIDEO

Cameras will suffer on the road and they may get broken, lost or stolen. But there are so many good shots in Brazil that you'll kick yourself if you don't bring a camera along on your travels. If you're nervous about losing an expensive camera, disposable ones are readily available in most large cities.

Kodak and Fuji print film are sold and processed almost everywhere, but for high-quality results you should use a large lab in Rio city or São Paulo. If you're shooting professional-quality print film or slides it's best to bring film with you. Slide film is expensive in Brazil (around US$15 a roll) and high-ISO slide film is only obtainable in a few cities. For camera repairs and professional needs in Rio, **Unimagem** (☎ 0xx21-2507 7745; Rua dos Andradas 29, Centro; ☽ 9am-6pm Mon-Fri, to noon Sat) is recommended.

Heat and humidity can ruin film, so remember to keep it in the coolest, driest place available. Use a lead film bag to protect film from airport X-ray machines. This is especially important for the sensitive high-ISO films. Useful accessories include a cable release, polarizing filter, lens-cleaning kit, plenty of silica-gel packs, and a bean bag or clamp or monopod. Don't carry a flashy camera bag – it may attract the attention of thieves – and make sure your equipment is insured.

Video cameras are no longer a big deal in Brazil so you won't get any weird stares as you shoot.

Technical Tips & Restrictions

Photography in the rain forest requires attention to the dimness of the light. You'll have to experiment with a combination of fast film (400 ISO and upward), a tripod, flash unit and cable release. When exposed to the forest's humid conditions for an extended period, your cameras and lenses may have their functioning impaired by fungus growth. The standard preventative measure is to keep your gear sealed in plastic bags together with silica-gel packs.

When shooting on beaches, remember to adjust for the glare from water or sand. Don't take a camera to a beach unless it will be closely guarded – see Dangers & Annoyances (p682).

Some Candomblé temples do not permit photography. Avoid taking photographs or video in banks or near military bases or other sensitive areas.

Be respectful of the locals and don't photograph anyone without asking their permission.

POST

A postcard or letter weighing up to 20g costs US$0.50 to the US, US$0.75 to Europe and US$0.90 to Australia.

There are mailboxes on the street, but it's safer to go to a *correios* (ku-*hey*-oosh; post office). Most post offices are open from 9am to 6pm Monday to Friday, and Saturday morning. Airmail letters to the US and Europe arrive in a week or so. For Australia, allow about two weeks.

Brazilian postal codes are five numbers followed by three; the first five are the code for the city, the others specify the location.

For receiving mail, the *posta restante* (poste restante) system seems to function reasonably well. Post offices hold mail for 30 days. A reliable alternative for Amex customers is to have mail sent to one of its offices.

SHOPPING

Smart souvenir hunters can do well in Brazil, provided they know a little about Brazilian culture. Many people find the best souvenirs to be recorded music, musical instruments, local crafts (Indian and otherwise) and artwork.

Glitzy, air-conditioned shopping malls – imaginatively called *shoppings* – are in every self-respecting medium-sized city, and São Paulo has hundreds of them. Browsing the many markets and small streetside stores yields, for better or worse, less predictable results.

Art & Crafts

Although nearly everything can be found in Rio and São Paulo, there is a premium for moving craft and art pieces from the hinterland into the fancy stores of the big cities. The inexpensive exceptions include the Hippie Fair (p173), the wild Feira Nordestina (p173) and the popular Babilônia Feira Hype (p173). Among Rio's handicrafts shops, O Sol in Jardim Botânico (p173) and Trilhas Urbanos (p173) and La Vareda (p173), both in Santa Teresa, offer some of the best selections.

Most of the Indian crafts in Funai stores are inexpensive, but quality generally matches price. Museum gift shops, on the other hand, stock some very worthwhile souvenirs. They're good for items made by artisans and prints of local art. The Carmen Miranda museum in Rio sells T-shirts of the great lady herself, complete with her famous fruit headdress.

Outside the two big cities, your best bets for craftwork are artisan fairs – held on Saturday and Sunday in many cities – cooperative stores, and government-run shops. The Northeast has a rich assortment of artistic items. Salvador and nearby Cachoeira are notable for their rough-hewn wood sculpture. Artisans in Fortaleza and the southeastern coast of Ceará specialize in fine lace. The interior of Pernambuco, in particular Caruaru, is famous for its wildly imaginative ceramic figurines.

Some Amazonian Indian peoples now make artifacts such as bows, arrows, baskets, feather headdresses, carvings, pottery and beads specifically as commodities to sell. Some are very attractive even if not quite the genuine article.

Gemstones

Gemstones are the most famous souvenir/luxury items from Minas Gerais. But if you're in the market for fine jewelry and precious stones, wait until you return to the big cities to make your purchases. Buy from a large and reputable dealer such as Amsterdam Sauer (p123) or H Stern (p123) in Rio. Stern is an international dealership based in Ipanema, and its reputation for quality and honesty is beyond reproach. It isn't a discount store – in fact it has a check-in desk where you have to get an identity tag before you can enter – but its jewelry is less expensive in Brazil than at its outlets in other parts of the world.

Leather

Brazilian leather goods are moderately priced, but the leather isn't particularly supple. The better Brazilian shoes, belts, wallets, purses and luggage are sold in the upmarket shops of Ipanema and Copacabana. Shoes are extremely good value, but many of the best are reserved for export, and larger sizes are difficult to find. Good-quality, cheap, durable, leather soccer balls with hand-stitched panels are sold all over Brazil in sporting-goods stores. (Inflated soccer balls should not be put in the cargo hold of a plane.)

In interior Pernambuco, the Sertanejos' curious traditional leather hats appeal to some travelers.

Music

Don't leave the country without buying some music. Rio (p172) has the best stores in the country, with plenty of used and new shops, places for DJs, and open-air music markets. In other cities, your best bet may be the big malls. New-release CDs cost anywhere from US$7 to US$20 in stores, but compilation albums of a star's best songs, such as those in the *Pérolas* and *XXI Vinteum* series, are about half that price and can be good value. Street stalls sell bootleg CDs for around US$2.

Brazil's many varieties of percussion, wind and string instruments make fun souvenirs and presents. You can often find inexpensive ones at craft markets as well as in music stores.

Other Purchases

Functional and decorative hammocks are available in cities throughout Amazonia. These string, mesh or cloth slings are fixtures in most Brazilian homes. They're indispensable for travelers and make fine, portable gifts. A typical one-person hammock costs around US$8 to US$10; a large *casal* (double) hammock might run to US$20.

Coffee-table picture books on Brazil, videotapes of Carnaval and of highlights of the national football team and Pelé in various World Cup matches are hawked in the streets of Copacabana and are available in stores too. *Guaraná* powder, a stimulant (said to be an aphrodisiac) derived from an Amazonian fruit, is sold by health stores and pharmacies around the country. Especially in the Amazon region itself, there are plenty of shops and market stalls devoted to herbal and other natural medicinal preparations – oils, powders, infusions – just name your ailment.

A Brazilian *fio dental* (dental floss bikini) is fun to have. If nothing else, you can prove to people back home just how little Brazilians really do wear on the beach. Plenty of stores sell very brief beachwear.

Candomblé stores are a good source of curios. They range from magical incense guaranteed to bring good fortune and increase sexual allure, wisdom and health to amulets and ceramic figurines of Afro-Brazilian gods.

If you're in Brazil during Carnaval, make sure you pick up a copy of the Carnaval edition of *Manchete* magazine.

SOLO TRAVELERS

On your own, you need to be alert about what's going on around you, and be particularly prudent about where you go. These are cardinal rules for solo female travelers.

Brazil is an excellent place to meet other travelers. There's a growing network of hostels, and many towns that are particularly suited for meeting travel companions (Rio, Salvador and Jericoacoara topping the list). Language schools, group tours and volunteer work provide fine opportunities for mingling with travelers and locals.

Since double rooms don't cost much more than single ones, solo travelers face higher accommodation costs than others. If you're on a tight budget – or simply want to meet other travelers – the hostels are your best bet.

TELEPHONE
Domestic Calls

You can make domestic calls – intercity or local – from normal card pay phones on the street and in telephone offices. The telephone cards you need are sold for US$1.40

per 30 units at telephone offices and for around US$2 by vendors, newsstands and anywhere else where you see advertising *cartãos telefônicos*. The most common denomination is 30 units, but 20-, 60- and 90-unit cards are sometimes available.

For calls within the city you're in, just slide the card into the phone, then check the readout to see if it's given you proper credit, and dial the number (either seven or eight digits). Local calls cost only one or two units. For directory information, call ☎ 102.

For calls to other cities, you need to precede the number with 0, then the code of your selected carrier (see the boxed text below), then the two or three digits representing the city. City codes are therefore

---

BRAZILIAN CITY CODES & CARRIERS

Brazil has several rival long-distance telephone carriers. When making an international or inter-city call, you have to select a carrier and include its two-digit *código de prestadora* (code) in the number you dial. Brazilian city codes are commonly quoted with an xx representing the carrier code – eg ☎ 0xx21 for Rio de Janeiro or ☎ 0xx71 for Salvador. You'll find city codes listed in this way beneath each city and town heading in this book.

Different carriers cover different areas of the country, and you have to use one that covers both the place you are calling from and the place you're calling to. The carriers are as follow:

Carrier	Code	Area of Coverage
Brasil Telecom	☎ 14	Distrito Federal, states of Mato Grosso, Mato Grosso do Sul, Acre, Goiás, Tocantins, Rondônia, Santa Catarina, Paraná (except Sercontel area), Pelotas, Capão do Leão, Morro Redondo & Turuçu (Rio Grande do Sul)
Canbrá	☎ 85	states of Rio de Janeiro, Minas Gerais (except CTBC Telecom areas), Espírito Santo, Bahia, Sergipe, Alagoas, Pernambuco, Rio Grande do Norte, Ceará, Piauí, Maranhão, Pará, Amapá, Roraima & Amazonas
Ceterp	☎ 16	Guataparrá & Ribeirão Preto (São Paulo state)
CRT	☎ 51	Rio Grande do Sul (except Brasil Telecom area)
CTBC Telecom	☎ 12	Some areas of São Paulo, Minas Gerais, Mato Grosso do Sul & Goiás states
Embratel	☎ 21	All of Brazil & international calls
Intelig	☎ 23	All of Brazil & international calls
Sercontel	☎ 43	Londrina & Tamarana (Paraná state)
Telefônica	☎ 15	São Paulo state (except CTBC Telecom & Ceterp areas)
Telemar	☎ 31	Same as Canbrá
Vésper	☎ 89	São Paulo state (except CTBC Telecom & Ceterp areas)

This may look complicated, but in practice it's straightforward. For one thing, you can use **Embratel** (☎ 21) or **Intelig** (☎ 23) for any call; for another, other major carriers usually have their names and codes widely displayed in their localities, so you absorb them unconsciously.

For example, to call from Rio de Janeiro to Fortaleza (city code ☎ 0xx85), in the state of Ceará, you dial 0 followed by 21 or 23 or 31 or 85 (the codes of the four carriers that cover both Rio and Ceará), followed by 85 for Fortaleza, followed by the number.

For an international call, dial 00 followed by 21 or 23 (the international carriers), followed by the country code, city code and number.

There appears to be little appreciable difference between the carriers, but at least the system gives you alternatives if the lines on your initial choice always seem to be busy.

usually given in the format 0 x x digit digit, with the 'x x' representing the carrier code. A long-distance call usually eats up between five and 10 phone card units per minute.

You need to include the city code (0xx digit digit) when calling to another city even if that city has the same city code as the one you're calling from.

To make a *chamada a cobrar* (intercity collect) call, stick a 9 in front of the 0xx. To make a local collect call, dial 9090 and then the number. A recorded message in Portuguese will ask you to say your name and the name of the state where you're calling from, after the beep.

International Calls

To phone Brazil from abroad, dial your international access code, then 55 (Brazil's country code), then the city code (omitting the initial 0xx), then the number.

The cost of international calls from Brazil depends on where you call from, but expect it to be about US$0.75 a minute to the US or Canada, and US$1.25 a minute to Europe or Australia. Prices are about 20% lower during *hora reduzida* (off-peak hours), which is typically from 8pm to 6am daily and all day Sunday.

To make an international call at your own expense, ordinary card pay phones – nicknamed *orelhões* (big ears; you'll soon understand why when you get to see one) – are of little use unless you have an international calling card. For one thing, most pay phones are restricted to domestic calls only. For another, even if they are enabled for international calls, 30-unit Brazilian phone cards (often the only denomination available) may last less than a minute on an international call, and there's no facility for switching cards mid-call.

If you have an international calling card, or if you only have to talk for less than a minute, you need to find a phone that will make international calls. Every town has a *posto telefônico* (telephone office) and international calls should be possible on at least some of its phones. Some phones in airports and on the streets of the bigger cities will also make international calls. They may be marked '*Este aparelho faz ligações internacionais*' (This apparatus makes international calls) – or they may not be identified in any way at all.

If you don't have an international calling card, you can buy Embratel phonecards from newsstands and pharmacies (sold in denominations of US$10, US$15, and US$35). These have a bar on the back that you scratch off to reveal a code to enter along with the number you are calling. (Instructions are printed on the cards in English and Portuguese.) You can make calls from any phone. Rates are generally about US$0.50 a minute for calls to the US, US$0.75 to Europe and about twice that to Asia and Australia.

Another option – and probably the easiest one – is to find an Internet or phone café, where you pay in cash after you finish talking (don't forget to establish the cost per minute before you call). Normally you'll be directed to a booth and will dial the call yourself. Country codes include the following: Argentina ☎ 54, Australia ☎ 61, Bolivia ☎ 591, Colombia ☎ 57, France ☎ 33, Germany ☎ 49, New Zealand ☎ 64, Paraguay ☎ 595, Peru ☎ 51, UK ☎ 44, US and Canada ☎ 1, and Venezuela ☎ 58.

You can also make calls from your hotel or a private phone, but in hotels it's essential to attempt to establish beforehand what it will cost you. Hotels often add a markup.

For *a cobrar* (international collect) calls, try dialing ☎ 000107 from any phone, although this only works to some countries. Or try dialing the local operator (☎ 100) and asking to be transferred to a *telefonista internacional* (international operator). Failing that, you need to locate a phone that can do international calls. Home Country Direct services get you through to an operator in the country you're calling (or at

---

USEFUL TELEPHONE PHRASES

I would like to make an international call to...
 Quero fazer uma ligação internacional para...
I would like to reverse the charges.
 Quero fazê-la a cobrar.
I am calling from a public (private) telephone in Rio de Janeiro.
 Estou falando dum telefone público (particular) no Rio de Janeiro.

My name is...	*Meu nôme é...*
The area code is...	*O código é...*
The number is...	*O número é...*

least an interactive recorded message there) which will connect the collect call for you. For most Home Country Direct services, dial ☎ 00080 followed by the country code (for North America, instead of the country code use ☎ 10 for AT&T, ☎ 12 for MCI and ☎ 16 for Sprint; for Australia, dial ☎ 0008006112). Alternatively, you can get a Brazilian international operator by dialing ☎ 000111 or ☎ 000333. They usually speak English, but if not, you could experiment with some of the phrases in the boxed text on p693.

If you're having telephone troubles, staff at reception desks at larger hotels can be helpful.

Be careful with services advertised by stickers on some phones announcing free calls to multilingual operators who can get you collect calls to the US or international credit-card calls. Make sure you establish the costs of any call before making it.

Mobile Phones

Cell phones in Brazil are known as *celular* (cellular phones; often shortened to *cel*). They have eight-digit numbers starting with a 9, and calls to them run through your phonecard units much faster than calls to regular numbers. Mobiles have city codes just like normal phone numbers (0 x x digit digit), and if you're calling from another city you have to use them.

Mobile telephones are very common in big cities. In Rio and São Paulo, you can rent one for around US$7 a day plus call charges. The following are in Rio:

ConnectCom (☎ 0xx21-2275 8461; www.connectcomrj .com.br; No 712, Av NS de Copacabana) Offers pick-up and drop-off service to your hotel.

Fast Cell (☎ 0xx21-2548 1008; www.fastcell.com.br; No 919, Rua Santa Clara 50, Copacabana) Provides excellent service. English-speaking staff will pick up and deliver to your hotel. You can also email the company before your trip and it can set you up with a number before you arrive.

TIME

Brazil has four time zones. Brasília time, which is GMT/UTC minus three hours, covers the whole of the Southeast, South and Northeast regions, plus, in the Central West section, Distrito Federal (including Brasília) and the state of Goiás, and, in the Amazon, the states of Tocantins, Amapá and the eastern half of Pará.

The remainder of the Central West (Mato Grosso and Mato Grosso do Sul states) and the rest of the Amazon (except Acre and far southwest Amazonas state) are one hour behind Brasília time (GMT/UTC minus four hours). Acre and southwest Amazonas (southwest of a line drawn between Tabatinga and Porto Acre, which is on the Amazonas–Acre border, just north of Rio Branco) are two hours behind Brasília time (GMT/UTC minus five hours). The Fernando de Noronha archipelago, out in the Atlantic Ocean, 350km off Natal, is one hour *ahead* of Brasília time (GMT/UTC minus two hours).

Thus when it's noon in London and 7am in New York, it should be 9am in most of Brazil, but 10am in Fernando de Noronha, 8am in Mato Grosso and most of the Amazon, and 7am in Acre. We say 'should be' because daylight saving means that it usually isn't. Brazilian daylight-saving time runs from mid-October to mid-February, during which period clocks are advanced one hour – but only in the Southeast, South and Central West and the states of Bahia and Tocantins! And of course Northern Hemisphere daylight saving happens in the other half of the year, so in reality the time difference between Rio and New York is three hours in December and one hour in July. And the time difference between Rio and Manaus is three hours from October to February but two hours otherwise. Got that clear then?

Not surprisingly, Brazilians, as well as foreign travelers, sometimes don't know what time of day it is, and a lot of travelers have a few tales to tell about connections missed due to temporal ignorance.

Even when they do know the time, Brazilians are not noted for respecting it. Don't be surprised, or angry, if they arrive a couple of hours later than expected. To them it is acceptable, and they always have the most inventive reasons for it.

TOILETS

Public toilets are not common but they exist at every bus station and airport and somewhere else in most cities and towns; there's usually an entrance fee of around US$0.40. Brazilians are quite nice about letting you use toilets in restaurants and bars. As in other Latin American countries, toilet paper isn't flushed. There's usually a nice smelly basket next to the toilet to put it in.

TOURIST INFORMATION

Most tourist offices in Brazil are sponsored by individual states and municipalities. In many places, they have shoestring budgets that are chopped or maintained according to the whims (or feuds!) of regional and local politicians. Some tourist offices clearly function only as a sinecure for politicians' relatives; others have a dedicated, knowledgeable staff who cares about tourism in their locality is are interested in providing information. Some offices are conveniently placed in the center of town; others are so far out of range that you'll spend an entire day getting there. Keep your sense of humor, prepare for potluck and don't expect too much!

Embratur (☎ 0xx61-429 7777; www.embratur.gov .br; Setor Comercial Norte, Quadra 2, Bloco G, 70712-907 Brasília, DF), the Brazilian tourism institute, has its headquarters in Brasília, but maintains an **office** (☎ 0xx21-2509 6017; 8th fl, Rua Uruguaiana 174, Centro) in Rio de Janeiro.

Outside of the country, Brazilian consulates and embassies are able to provide limited tourist information, although the embassy in the UK actually has a dedicated tourist information section (see Embassies & Consulates, p684). Several Brazilian embassies and consulates provide useful tourist information on their websites.

VISAS & DOCUMENTS

Brazil has a reciprocal visa system, so if your home country requires Brazilian nationals to secure a visa, then you will need one to enter Brazil. At the time of writing, American, Canadian, Australian and New Zealand citizens need visas, but citizens of the UK, Ireland, France, Germany, the Netherlands, South Africa, Portugal, Spain and Scandinavian countries do not. Check with the Brazilian embassy or consulate in your home country.

Tourist visas are issued by Brazilian diplomatic offices. They are valid from the date you arrive in Brazil for a 90-day stay. They are renewable in Brazil for an additional 90 days. In most embassies and consulates visas can be processed within 24 hours.

In many Brazilian embassies and consulates it takes only a couple of hours to issue a visa if you go in person (it's instant in some places), but the processing can take a couple of weeks or more if you do it by mail. You will normally need to present a passport valid for at least six months, a passport photograph, and a round-trip or onward ticket or a photocopy of it or a statement from a travel agent that you have it. If you don't have the ticketing requirements, proof of means of support – such as credit cards or bank statements – may be acceptable.

If you decide to return to Brazil, your visa is valid for five years.

The fee for visas is also reciprocal. It's usually between US$40 and US$60, though for US citizens visas cost US$100 (those who find this excessive should write to their local congressional representative and ask why the US charges Brazilians so much to enter the US).

Applicants under 18 years of age who are traveling alone must also submit a notarized letter of authorization from a parent or legal guardian.

Business travelers may need a business visa. It's also valid for 90 days and has the same requirements as a tourist visa. You'll also need a letter on your company letterhead addressed to the Brazilian embassy or consulate, stating your business in Brazil, your arrival and departure dates and your contacts. The letter from your employer must also assume full financial and moral (!) responsibility for you during your stay.

Depending on where you are coming from when you arrive in Brazil, you may need a yellow-fever vaccination certificate. On your arrival in Brazil, immigration officials sometimes ask to see your onward or return ticket and/or proof of means of support such as credit cards or traveler's checks.

Visa regulations change from time to time, and you should always get the latest information from your local Brazilian embassy or consulate (see p684).

Passport

By law you must carry a passport with you at all times, but many travelers opt to carry a photocopy (preferably certified) when traveling about town and leave their passport securely locked up at their hotel. It's convenient to have extra passport photos for any documents or visas you may need to acquire in Brazil.

Entry/Exit Card

On entering Brazil, all tourists must fill out a *cartão de entrada/saida* (entry/exit card); immigration officials will keep half, you keep the other. They will also stamp your passport, and, if for some reason they are not granting you the usual 90-day stay in Brazil, the number of days will be written beneath the word *Prazo* on the stamp in your passport.

When you leave Brazil, the second half of the entry/exit card will be taken by immigration officials. Make sure you don't lose your card while traveling around Brazil, or your departure could be delayed until officials have checked your story.

EXTENSIONS TO ENTRY/EXIT CARDS & VISAS

These are handled by Brazil's Polícia Federal (Federal Police), which has offices in the state capitals and border towns. You must apply before your entry/exit card or visa lapses, and don't leave it until the last minute. Tourist offices can tell you where the nearest Polícia Federal office is. When you go, dress nicely! Some Fed stations don't take kindly to people in shorts.

In most cases an extension seems to be pretty automatic, but sometimes you may not be given the full 90 days. The police may well require that you have a ticket out of the country and proof of sufficient funds, though this seems to be at the discretion of the officer. You may be told to complete a Documento de Arrecadeção de Receitas Federais (DARF; Federal Revenue Collection Document) form (US$1), which you have to buy from vendors outside the police station or from a *papelaria* (stationery shop). After filling it out, you must go to a bank and pay a fee of about US$40. You then return to the Polícia Federal with the DARF form stamped by the bank. The extension should then be routinely issued.

If you opt for the maximum 90-day extension and then leave the country before the end of that period, you cannot return until the full 90 days have elapsed.

WOMEN TRAVELERS
Attitudes Toward Women

Depending on where they travel in Brazil, women traveling alone will experience a range of responses. In São Paulo, for exam-

ple, where there are many people of European ancestry, foreign women without traveling companions will scarcely be given a sideways glance. In the more traditional rural areas of the Northeast, where a large percentage of the population is of ethnically mixed origin, blonde-haired and light-skinned women, especially those without male escorts, will certainly arouse curiosity.

Although machismo is an undeniable element in the Brazilian social structure, it is less overt than in Spanish-speaking Latin America. Perhaps because attitudes towards sex and pornography are quite liberal in Brazil, males feel little need to assert their masculinity or prove their prowess in the eyes of peers.

Flirtation – often exaggerated – is a prominent element in Brazilian male/female relations. It goes both ways and is nearly always regarded as amusingly innocent banter; no sense of insult, exploitation or serious intent should be assumed.

Safety Precautions

If you encounter unwelcome attention, you should be able to stop it by merely expressing displeasure.

Although most of Brazil is nearly as safe for women as for men, it's a good idea to keep a low profile in the cities at night and to avoid going alone to bars and nightclubs if you'd rather not chance your behavior being misinterpreted.

Similarly, women should not hitchhike alone or even in groups (even men or couples should exercise caution when hitching). Most importantly, the roughest areas of the north and west, where there are lots of men but few local women, should be considered off-limits by lone female travelers.

In the event of unwanted pregnancy or the risk thereof, most pharmacies in Brazil stock the 'morning-after' pill, which costs about US$7.

What to Wear

Once you've spent an hour or two in Copacabana or Ipanema, where some women run their errands wearing *fio dental* (dental floss – the famous skimpy bikini) you'll be aware that in some parts of Brazil, the dress restrictions aren't quite as strict as in others. What works in Rio will probably not be appropriate in a Northeastern city or in a Piauí backwater. Dress standards seem largely a matter of personal taste, but it's still best to blend your clothing in to meet local standards.

WORK

Brazil has high unemployment, and visitors who enter the country as tourists are not legally allowed to take jobs. It's not unusual for foreigners to find English-teaching work in language schools. The pay isn't great (if you hustle you can make around US$700 a month), but you can still live on it. For this kind of work it's always helpful to speak some Portuguese, although some schools insist that only English be spoken in class. Private language tutoring may pay a little more, but you'll have to do some legwork to get students.

To find this type of work, log on to a Brazilian web server such as **Terra** (www .terra.com.br), **UOL** (www.radaruol.com.br) or **Radix** (www.radix.com.br), and search for English academies. Also, look for 'Professor de Ingles' (English Teacher) in newspaper classified ads, and ask around at the language schools.

Volunteer Work

RíoVoluntário (☎ 0xx21-2262 1110; www.riovoluntario .org.br), headquartered in Rio de Janeiro, supports several hundred volunteer organizations, from those involved in social work and the environment to health care. It's an excellent resource for finding volunteer work.

In the UK **Task Brasil** (☎ 020-7394 1177; www .taskbrasil.org.uk) accepts volunteers both in Brazil and abroad for work with homeless children.

In the US **Action Without Borders** (☎ 212-843-3973; www.idealist.org; 350 Fifth Ave, Suite 6614, New York City) lists Brazilian volunteer openings on its website. Also check website of the **Learning Abroad Center** (☎ 612-626-4782; www.istc.umn.edu).

Earthwatch (☎ toll-free 800-776 0188; www.earth watch.org) runs environmental and archaeological projects in Brazil that you pay to take part in (usually US$1500 to US$2000 for 10 to 15 days).

A little door knocking can help you find volunteer work with welfare organizations in Brazil. One traveler reported walking up to the front door of a Catholic home for abandoned children in Recife and asking if there was anything he could do. The priests gave him a bed and he spent two months helping with the cooking, getting the children out of jail, telling them stories and breaking up knife fights. He said it was the highlight of his trip.

International NGOs (Non-Governmental Organizations) work in all sorts of fields in Brazil, including environmental, medical and social welfare projects. If you have some particular interest or skill, try contacting relevant organizations to volunteer your services.

Transportation

GETTING THERE & AWAY

ENTERING THE COUNTRY

Most travelers start their Brazilian odyssey by flying down to Rio, but this is only one of many ways to arrive. The country has several other gateway airports and land borders with every other country in South America except Chile and Ecuador. So while some travelers are in the air en route to Rio, others will be busing in from Uruguay in the south or Venezuela in the north, and yet others may be arriving by the *trem da morte* (death train) from Bolivia or coming in by boat along the Amazon from Peru or Colombia.

AIR
Airports & Airlines

The most popular international gateways are Aeroporto Galeão (GIG) in Rio de Janeiro and São Paulo's Aeroporto Guarulhos (GRU). From both these airports, connecting flights to airports throughout the country leave regularly. Further north, Salvador (SSA) and Recife (REC) receive a few direct scheduled flights from Europe. Recife, Fortaleza (FOR), Belém (BEL), Manaus (MAO) and Belo Horizonte (CNF) receive some direct scheduled flights from the US.

Varig, Brazil's international airline, flies in to the country from Miami, New York, Los Angeles, Mexico City and nine European and 11 South American cities. The US Federal Aviation Administration has assessed Varig as Category 1, which means they are in compliance with international aviation standards.

Airlines flying to/from Brazil are listed below. All numbers that begin with 0xx21 numbers are based in Rio de Janeiro. All 0xx11 numbers are in São Paulo. For Brazil's regional carriers, see p703.

Aerolineas Argentinas (AR; ☎ 0800-707 3313; www .aerolineas.com.ar; Buenos Aires)

Aeroméxico (AM; ☎ 0xx11-3253 3888; www .aeromexico.com; Mexico City)

Aerosur (5L; ☎ 0xx11-3231 5808; Santa Cruz, Bolivia)

Air Canada (AC; ☎ 0800-127 590; www.aircanada.ca; Toronto)

Air France (AF; ☎ 0800-127 590; www.airfrance.com; Paris)

Alitalia (AZ; ☎ 0800-704 0206; www.alitalia.com; Rome)

American Airlines (AA; ☎ 0300-789 7778; www .aa.com; Dallas & Miami)

Avianca (AV; ☎ 0xx21-2240 4413; www.avianca.com; Bogotá)

British Airways (BA; ☎ 0300-789 6140; www .britishairways.com; London)

Continental Airlines (CO; ☎ 0800-554 777; www .continental.com; Houston & Newark)

COPA (CM; ☎ 0xx11-3138 6200; www.copaair.com; Panama City)

Delta Airlines (DL; ☎ 0800-221 1121; www.delta.com; Atlanta)

Iberia (IB; ☎ 0800-770 7900; www.Iberia.com; Madrid)

THINGS CHANGE...

The information in this chapter is particularly vulnerable to change. Check directly with the airline or a travel agent to make sure you understand how a fare (and ticket you may buy) works and be aware of the security requirements for international travel. Shop carefully. The details given in this chapter should be regarded as pointers and are not a substitute for your own careful, up-to-date research.

Japan Airlines (JL; ☎ 0xx21-2220 6414; www.jal.com;
Tokyo)
KLM (KL; ☎ 0xx21-2524 1453; www.klm.com;
Amsterdam)
LAB Airlines (LB; ☎ 0800-118 111; www.labairlines
.com; La Paz, Bolivia)
Lan Chile (LA; ☎ 0xx21-2220 9722; www.lanchile.com;
Santiago)
Lufthansa (LH; ☎ 0xx21-3687 5000; http://cms
.lufthansa.com; Frankfurt)
Penta (5P; ☎ 0300-789 2029; Belém, Brazil)
South African (SA; ☎ 0800-118 383; www.flysaa.com;
Johannesburg)
Spanair (JK; ☎ 0xx21-2544 6779; www.spanair.com;
Madrid)
Suriname Airways (PY; ☎ 0xx91-210 6284;
Paramaribo)
Swissair (LX; ☎ 0xx21-2223 6400; www.swiss.com;
Zurich)
TAP Air Portugal (TP; ☎ 0xx21-2541 9072; www
.tap-airportugal.pt; Lisbon)
United Airlines (UA; ☎ 0800-162 323; www.united
.com; Los Angeles)
Varig (RG; ☎ 0300-788 7000; www.varig.com.br; São
Paulo)

Tickets
For high-season travel, which basically means
flying to Brazil between mid-December
and the end of February, tickets cost
about US$200 more than they do during
the rest of the year. There's also more travel
between mid-June and mid-August –
you should book as far ahead as possible as
the less-expensive seats fill up early.

AIR PASSES
If you're combining travel in Brazil with
other countries in southern South America,
the Mercosur Airpass is valid for flights
within Argentina, Brazil, Chile (except
Easter Island), Uruguay and Paraguay. The
pass has to be bought before you travel to
South America and is available to holders
of an international round-trip ticket from
outside South America to Argentina, Brazil,
Chile, Uruguay or Paraguay. The pass gives
you up to two stopovers in each country
(plus your starting and finishing points) in
one month, and its price (from US$280 to
US$870) depends on how many miles you
will fly. Ask your travel agent for details.

For information on air passes for flights
solely within Brazil, see p703 in the Getting
Around section.

COURIER FLIGHTS
Courier flights are a great bargain if you're
lucky enough to find one. A New York–Rio
round-trip ticket, for example, could be
yours for US$200.

They are occasionally advertised in the
press, or you could contact air-freight companies listed in the phone book. You should
also visit www.courier.org or www.aircour
ier.co.uk for info on being an air-courier.
You'll have to pay an annual US$45 mem-
bership fee, but you'll likely save substantially more than that on your first flight.

IN BRAZIL
Rio de Janeiro is Brazil's most popular international gateway, and there are many travel
agents here. For student fares try the **Student Travel Bureau** (STB; ☎ 0xx21-2512 8577; www
.stb.com.br; Rua Visconde de Pirajá 550, Ipanema), with
some 30 branches around the country. Discount agencies in São Paulo include **US Tour**
(☎ 0xx11-3813 1308; www.ustour.com.br). Websites
with cheap flights include www.passagem
barata.com.br and www.viajo.com.br.

Australia & New Zealand
Qantas flies twice a week from Sydney,
via Auckland, to Buenos Aires, where you
can connect with an Aerolineas Argentinas
flight to Rio de Janeiro. Round-trip fares
start at around A$2150. If you're planning
a longer trip through Latin America, an
open-jaw (into one city, out of another)
or even an around-the-world ticket will be
your best bet.

For online booking, try www.lastminute
.com.au, www.travel.co.nz, and www.travel
.com.au websites.

DEPARTURE TAX

The airport tax for international departures
from Brazil is a hefty US$36. This may be in-
cluded in the price you pay for your ticket.
If it's not, you have to pay cash, in US dollars or in reais, at the airport before or at
check-in, so remember to keep that amount
of cash in reserve. If your ticket price included the tax, it may be shown in the taxes
section at the bottom of your ticket by the
letters BR following the amount – but to be
certain, you should ask the agent when you
buy the ticket.

Well-known agents for cheap fares with branches throughout Australia and New Zealand include the following:

Flight Centre Australia (☎ 133 133; www.flightcentre .com.au); New Zealand (☎ 0800-243 544; www.flight centre.co.nz)

STA Travel Australia (☎ 1300 733 035; www.statravel .com.au); New Zealand (☎ 0508-782 872; www.statravel .co.nz)

Canada

The *Globe & Mail, Toronto Star, Montreal Gazette* and *Vancouver Sun* carry travel agents' ads and are good places to look for cheap fares. Airlines flying between Canada and Brazil include Canadian Airlines and Air Canada, but many routings are with US airlines, involving a change of planes in the US.

Travel Cuts (☎ 800-667 2887; www.travelcuts.com) is Canada's national student-travel agency and has offices in all major cities.

Continental Europe

A variety of European and Brazilian airlines flies direct to Rio and São Paulo. There are also less-frequent flights connecting Salvador with Frankfurt (Varig), Madrid (Varig, Spanair) and Lisbon (Varig, TAP Air Portugal). From Lisbon you can also fly to Recife (Varig, TAP Air Portugal) and Fortaleza (TAP Air Portugal).

Fares are pretty similar from starting points across Western Europe. You're looking at discounted fares to Rio or São Paulo for between US$550 and US$850, and usually several hundred dollars more for most other destinations.

The following are recommended websites for fares from Europe:

- www.airstop.be (Belgium)
- www.cts.it (Rome)
- www.degriftour.com (France, Belgium, or Switzerland)
- www.nouvelles-frontieres.com (Paris)
- www.otu.fr (Paris)
- www.ssr.ch (Switzerland)
- www.wasteels.fr (Paris)

South America

In addition to flights between South American capitals and the major Brazilian cities, shortish cross-border flights provide alternatives to some overland routes into or out of Brazil.

Surinam Airways flies between Belém and Cayenne (French Guiana), Paramaribo (Suriname) and Georgetown (Guyana). Penta, a Brazilian regional airline, flies between Belém, Macapá and Cayenne.

From Bolivia you can fly between Santa Cruz and Manaus (LAB). From Iquitos, Peru, there's a flying-boat service to Tabatinga on the Rio Amazonas on the Brazil/ Peru/Colombia Triple Frontier. From Bogotá (Colombia) you can fly to Leticia, the Colombian town at the triple frontier, then take a Kombi van or taxi or walk across the border into Brazil.

The Bolivian towns Cobija, Guayaramerín and Puerto Suárez, across the border from the Brazilian towns of Brasiléia, Guajará-Mirim and Corumbá, respectively, can all be reached by domestic flights from several cities inside Bolivia.

Further south, you can fly from Asunción (Paraguay) to Ciudad del Este (across the border from Foz do Iguaçu, Brazil) and from Buenos Aires to Puerto Iguazú (also opposite Foz do Iguaçu), Porto Alegre, Curitiba or Florianópolis.

For more information on flights to other South American destinations, see the relevant sections of the towns and cities listed above.

Check www.viajo.com for online airfares and reservations from Argentina, Brazil, Chile, Mexico, Uruguay or Venezuela.

UK & Ireland

Varig and British Airways offer direct flights from London. Prices start at UK£500/800 in low/high season. You can often find cheaper fares on flights from Europe. At the time of writing, there were no direct flights from Ireland. The cheapest fares from Dublin are currently with Lufthansa, via Frankfurt.

For online bookings, try www.dialaflight .com and www.lastminute.com.

Recommended UK ticket agencies include the following:

Journey Latin America (☎ 020-87473108;www.journey latinamerica.co.uk)

STA Travel (☎ 0870-160 0599; www.statravel.co.uk)

Trailfinders (☎ 020-7937 1234; www.trailfinders.co.uk)

USA

Nonstop flights to Brazil arrive from New York, Miami and Los Angeles. Prices can range from US$450, in the low season, to US$800, in the high season. If you don't want to arrive in Rio or São Paulo, there are direct flights connecting Miami with Manaus (Varig and LAB) and Belém (Varig). You can also fly to Fortaleza and Recife, though you'll have to connect through São Paulo or Rio.

The following are recommended for on-line bookings:

- www.brol.com
- www.cheaptickets.com
- www.expedia.com
- www.hotwire.com
- www.itn.net
- www.lowestfare.com
- www.onetravel.com
- www.orbitz.com
- www.sta.com
- www.wonderlink.com

LAND

There's direct land access to Brazil from nine countries. Several border towns can also be reached by air or river – see the Air (p700) and River (p703) sections for details.

Bus

International buses travel between Brazil and Argentina, Paraguay, and Uruguay, along decent roads. Prices of bus tickets between countries are substantially more than you'd pay if you took a bus to the border, crossed on foot and caught another on the other side, but you'll lose a lot of time that way. If arriving by bus, make sure your papers in order. See Visas & Documents on p695 for more information.

Car & Motorcycle

If you plan to take a vehicle into Brazil, see the p706 for information on the documents you need, and p706 for the road rules, as well as more information about fuel and spare parts. At the border you will be asked to sign a bond (*termo de responsabilidade*) containing the owner's identification details and home address, destination, and description of the vehicle (make, model, year, serial number, color and tag number). You will also be asked to pay a bank guarantee (to be determined by customs) and sign a statement agreeing that if you stay for more than 90 days, you will contact customs in

the area where the entry was registered to apply for an extension for the permit. This must be presented to customs at the time of departure. If your vehicle overstays its permitted time in Brazil, it is liable to be seized and the bank guarantee forfeited. It's illegal to sell the vehicle in Brazil.

Argentina

The main border point used by travelers is Puerto Iguazú/Foz do Iguaçu, a 20-hour bus ride from Buenos Aires (see p314 for more information). Further south, you can cross from Paso de los Libres (Argentina) to Uruguaiana (Brazil), which is also served by buses from Buenos Aires in Argentina.

Direct buses run between Buenos Aires and Porto Alegre (US$32, 20 hours), Florianópolis, Curitiba, São Paulo and Rio de Janeiro (US$88, 44 hours).

Bolivia

Brazil's border with Bolivia is its longest. Most of it runs through remote wetlands and lowland forests, and it's much used by smugglers. The main crossings are at Corumbá, Cáceres, Guajará-Mirim and Brasiléia.

Corumbá, opposite the Bolivian town of Quijarro, is the busiest crossing point. Corumbá is a good access point for the Pantanal and has bus connections with São Paulo, Rio de Janeiro, Campo Grande and southern Brazil. The Bolivian train service between Quijarro and Santa Cruz is known as the Death Train (because of what happens to some of those who attempt to ride free on the roof), but it's a beautiful ride.

For more information, see p402 .

The Bolivian border town of San Matías is 115km southwest of Cáceres in Mato Grosso, Brazil. Cáceres has several daily bus connections with Cuiabá, 215km east. A daily bus runs between Cáceres and Santa Cruz in Bolivia (US$24, 24 hours, departs at 6am). The Cáceres–San Matías trip takes 4½ hours (US$10).

Guajará-Mirim, in Rondônia (Brazil), is a short boat ride across the Rio Mamoré from Guayaramerín, Bolivia. Guajará-Mirim has daily bus service to Porto Velho (5½ hours), and buses run between Guayaramerín and the Bolivian towns of Riberalta, Cobija, Trinidad, Santa Rosa, Reyes, Rurrenabaque and La Paz. From late December to late

February, rains can make the roads very difficult. See p665 for more information on bus and car travel in this area.

Brasiléia, a 4½-hour bus ride from Rio Branco, in Brazil's Acre state, stands opposite Cobija, Bolivia, which has bus connections to Riberalta, Guayaramerín and La Paz (see p676 for details). This route is less direct than the Guayaramerín–Guajará-Mirim route between Bolivia and Brazil, and buses face the same wet-season difficulties.

Chile

Chile does not share a border with Brazil, but direct buses run between Santiago and Brazilian cities such as Curitiba (US$120, 52 hours), Porto Alegre (US$116, 36 hours), São Paulo (US$120, 56 hours) and Rio de Janeiro (US$130, 62 hours).

Colombia

Leticia, on the Rio Amazonas in far southeast Colombia, is contiguous with Tabatinga, Brazil. You can cross the border by foot, Kombi van or taxi. From within Colombia, Leticia is only really accessible by air. Tabatinga is a quick flight (or a several-day Amazon boat ride) from Manaus or Tefé. See p640 for details.

French Guiana

The Brazilian town of Oiapoque, a rugged 560km bus ride north of Macapá (US$30, 12 to 24 hours depending on weather conditions), stands across the Rio Oiapoque from St Georges in French Guiana. An unpaved road from St Georges to Régina, about halfway to the French Guiana capital of Cayenne, was recently cut through the jungle, though you'll find that travel along it is still arduous. Taxi-buses between Régina and Cayenne cost around US$10. Flights from St Georges to Cayenne cost around US$53.

DOMESTIC DEPARTURE TAX

Embarkation tax on domestic flights ranges from US$2.50 to US$6, depending on the airport (the bigger the airport, the bigger the tax). If it isn't already included in the price of your ticket, you have to pay it in cash reais at check-in.

Guyana

Lethem, in southwest Guyana and Bonfim, in Brazil's Roraima state, are a short boat ride apart. You can travel between Lethem and the Guyanese capital of Georgetown by plane or truck. The latter takes between two days and two weeks depending on weather conditions. Bonfim is a two-hour bus ride from Boa Vista, the Roraima state capital. See p650 for details.

Paraguay

The two major border crossings are Foz do Iguaçu/Ciudad del Este (p314) and Ponta Porã/Pedro Juan Caballero (p406). Use the latter if you're going to/from the Pantanal. Direct buses run between Asunción and such Brazilian cities as Curitiba (US$30, 14 hours), São Paulo (US$30, 20 hours) and Rio de Janeiro (US$45, 24 hours).

Peru

Peru and Brazil share a long border in the Amazon basin, but the only land route across it is a fairly adventurous one at its far southeastern end. Iñapari (Peru) is a 10-hour minibus or truck ride north of Puerto Maldonado, Peru. You have to wade across the Rio Acre between Iñapari and the small Brazilian town of Assis Brasil, which is a three- to four-hour bus or 4WD trip from Brasiléia.

Suriname

It isn't possible to travel overland between Suriname and Brazil without first passing through either French Guiana or Guyana.

Uruguay

The crossing most used by travelers is at Chuy/Chuí. This is actually one town, with the international border running down the middle of its main street. See p346 for details.

Heading west along the border, there are other crossings at Río Branco/Jaguarão, Isidoro Noblia/Aceguá, Rivera/Santana do Livramento, Artigas/Quaraí and Bella Unión/Barra do Quaraí. Buses link Jaguarão with Pelotas (p346) and Santana do Livramento with Porto Alegre (p335).

Buses run between Montevideo and Brazilian cities such as Porto Alegre (US$58, 12 hours), Florianópolis (US$53, 19 hours) and Curitiba (US$61, 24 hours).

VASP

Venezuela

Roads from northern Venezuela go southeast to Ciudad Bolívar, Ciudad Guayana and Santa Elena de Uairén (p651), on the border near Pacaraíma, Brazil. From here a paved road heads south to Boa Vista (215km) and Manaus (990km). Buses run to Manaus and Boa Vista from as far north as Venezuela's Puerto La Cruz. Santa Elena has buses to and from Caracas. See p653 for more.

RIVER
Bolivia

From Trinidad in Bolivia you can reach Brazil by a boat trip of about five days down the Río Mamoré to Guayaramerín, opposite the Brazilian town of Guajará-Mirim (p664). You can even start from Puerto Villarroel on the Río Ichilo, a tributary of the Mamoré. See p665 for details.

Paraguay

The passenger-boat service on the Rio Paraguai between Corumbá (Mato Grosso do Sul) and Asunción (Paraguay) has been discontinued. You might be able to travel this route using a sequence of cargo and/or naval boats, but it would necessitate asking around and taking potluck.

Peru

Fast passenger boats make the 400km trip (US$40 to US$50, eight to 10 hours) along the Rio Amazonas between Iquitos (Peru) and Tabatinga (Brazil). From Tabatinga you can continue 3000km down the river to its mouth. See p640 for more information.

GETTING AROUND

AIR

Because of the great distances in Brazil, the occasional flight can be a necessity. If you intend to take more than just a couple of flights, a Brazil Airpass (p703) will probably save you a lot of money. Book ahead for busy travel times – from Christmas to Carnaval, Easter, July and August. Always reconfirm your flights, as schedules frequently change. See p704 for flight paths.

Airlines

Brazil has three major national carriers and many smaller regional airlines. The biggest airlines are Varig, TAM and VASP. At least one of these flies to every major city. Varig, Brazil's biggest airline, has two affiliates, Nordeste and Rio Sul, which offer flights all over the Northeast and in the South. Of the big three, VASP is usually the cheapest, though Varig tends to have better service.

Gol is the biggest of the budget airlines, with a decent number of routes and usually the lowest prices of any carrier. Fly and Trip are also budget airlines.

Usually tickets can be booked online. The following are recommended:

Fly (☎ 0300-313 1323)
Gol (☎ 0300-789 2121; www.voegol.com.br)
TAM (☎ 0300-123 1000; www.tam.com.br)
Trip (☎ 0800-701 8747; www.airtrip.com.br)
Varig (☎ 0300-788 7000; www.varig.com.br)
VASP (☎ 0300-789 1010; www.vasp.com.br)

Air Passes

A Brazil Airpass is a good investment, if you're planning on covering a lot of ground in a short amount of time. Each of the three major Brazilian airlines (Varig, TAM and VASP) offers a version of the Brazil Airpass, giving you five flights on its domestic routes, within a 21-day period, for around US$500. Up to four additional flights can usually be added for US$100 each. Varig has the most extensive network, but it can only be purchased if you fly into Brazil on Varig or one of their alliance carriers (United, Continental and British Airways among others).

You have to buy the pass before you go to Brazil, and to do so you must also have an international round-trip ticket to Brazil. The agent who sells you your international ticket will normally be able to sell you the air pass too. You have to book your air pass itinerary at the time you buy it, and sometimes there are penalties for changing reservations.

If for any reason you do not fly on an airpass flight you have reserved, you should reconfirm all your other flights. Travelers have sometimes found that all their airpass reservations had been scrubbed from the computer after they missed, or were bumped from, one flight.

Air Taxis

Many areas, especially Amazonia, feature air-taxi companies that will fly you anywhere

TRANSPORTATION

their small planes can reach. Unfortunately, these planes and the runways they land on aren't always maintained. You might think twice before booking one of these flights.

BICYCLE

You don't see many long-distance cyclists in Brazil. Crazy drivers who only respect vehicles larger than themselves, lots of trucks on the main roads spewing out unfiltered exhaust fumes, roads without shoulder room and the threat of theft are just some of the reasons for this. Long-distance cycling in Brazil is not recommended; it's a dangerous thing to do.

If you're still determined to tackle Brazil by bike, go over your bike with a fine-tooth comb before you leave home and fill your repair kit with every imaginable spare part. There are a few decent bike shops in Rio for buying equipment and gear – as well as renting bikes (which average US$10 per day). See p145 for details.

BOAT

The Amazon region is probably the last great bastion of passenger river travel in the world. Rivers still perform the function of highways throughout much of Amazonia, with passenger-carrying vessels of many shapes and sizes putt-putting up and down every river and creek that has anyone living near it. For information on river travel in the Amazon region, see the boxed text on p587.

DOMESTIC AIR ROUTES

River travel in the rest of Brazil has decreased rapidly due to the construction of a comprehensive road network, but it's still possible to travel by boat along the lower reaches of the Rio São Francisco (see p482).

Boat is also the only – or at least, the most interesting – way of getting around many parts of the Pantanal and to the many islands and beaches along the Atlantic coast.

BUS

Except in the Amazon Basin, buses are the primary form of long-distance transportation for the majority of Brazilians and many foreign travelers. Bus services are generally excellent. Departure times are usually strictly adhered to, and most of the buses are clean, comfortable and well-serviced Mercedes, Volvos and Scanias. The drivers are good, and a mechanical governor limits their wilder urges to 80km/h.

All major cities are linked by frequent buses – one leaves every 15 minutes from Rio to São Paulo during peak hours – and there are a surprising number of long-distance buses. It is rare that you will have to change buses between two major cities, no matter what the distance. Every big city, and most small ones, has at least one main long-distance bus station (*rodoviária*; ho-do-vi-*ah*-ri-ya).

Bus service and road conditions vary by region. The South has the most and the best roads. Coastal highways are usually good; while the roads of Amazonia and the *sertão* (backlands of the Northeast) are quite bad. The Quatro Rodas *Atlas Rodoviário*, a very useful road atlas for any traveler, helpfully marks the worst stretches of road with lines of large Xs and classifies them as *estradas precárias*.

Brazil has numerous bus companies and the larger cities have several dozen rival agencies. Before buying a bus ticket from São Paulo or Rio de Janeiro to other destinations, be sure to shop around.

Classes

There are three main classes of long-distance bus. The ordinary *comum* or *convencional* is the most common. It's fairly comfortable and usually has a toilet on board. An *executivo* is more comfortable (often with reclining seats), costs about 25% more and stops less often. A *leito* can cost twice as much as a *comum* and is exceptionally comfortable. It has spacious, fully reclining seats with blankets and pillows, air-conditioning, and more often than not, an attendant serving sandwiches, coffee, soda and *água mineral*. If you don't mind missing the scenery, a *leito* can get you there in comfort and save you the additional cost of a hotel room.

With or without toilets, buses generally make pit stops every three or four hours. These stops are great places to meet other passengers, buy bizarre memorabilia, and load up on greasy plates of food.

Air-conditioning on buses is quite strong; carry a light sweater or jacket to keep warm.

Costs

Bus travel throughout Brazil is very affordable; *comum* fares average around US$2 per hour. For example, the six-hour trip from Rio to São Paulo costs US$12.50 *comum* or US$25 *leito*, and the 20-hour trip from Rio to Florianópolis is US$32 *comum* or US$55 *leito*. The 42-hour Rio–Recife ride costs US$64 *comum*, and for US$85 you could even take a 55-hour ride from Rio to Belém.

Reservations

Usually you can go down to the bus station and buy a ticket for the next bus out. If this is not the case (eg in Ouro Prêto), it will be mentioned in the relevant destination chapter. In general, though, it's a good idea to buy a ticket at least a few hours in advance or, if it's convenient, the day before departure. On weekends, holidays and from December to February, advance purchase is always a good idea.

Aside from getting you on the bus, buying a ticket early has a few other advantages. First, it gets you an assigned seat – many common buses fill the aisles with standing passengers. Second, you can ask for a front-row seat, with extra leg space, or a window seat with a view and the side of the bus to lean on (ask for a *janela*), and you can steer clear of the rear seats near the toilet, which can get smelly.

You don't always have to go to the bus station to buy your bus ticket. Selected travel agents in the major cities sell tickets for long-distance buses.

TRANSPORTATION

CAR & MOTORCYCLE

Especially in Rio, the anarchic side of the Brazilian personality emerges from behind the driver's wheel as lane dividers, one-way streets and sidewalks are disregarded. The police take little interest in road safety.

Bringing Your Own Vehicle

All vehicles in Brazil must carry the registration document and proof of insurance. To take a vehicle in or out of Brazil, you might be asked for a *carnet de passage en douane,* which is kind of a vehicle passport, or a *libreta de pasos por aduana,* which is a booklet of customs passes; in practice these are not often required. Contact your local automobile association for details about all documentation.

Driver's License

Your home-country driver's license is valid in Brazil, but because local authorities probably won't be familiar with it, it's a good idea to carry an International Driver's Permit (IDP) as well. This gives police less scope for claiming that you are not driving with a legal license. IDPs are issued by your national motoring association and usually cost the equivalent of about US$10.

Fuel & Spare Parts

Ordinary gasoline *(combustível* or *gasolina)* costs around US$1 per liter. Travelers planning to take their own vehicles need to check in advance what spare parts and gasoline are likely to be available. Unleaded gas is not on sale across Brazil, and neither is every little part for your car (Brazil does have plenty of Volkswagen parts).

Hire

A small four-seat car costs around US$40 a day with unlimited kilometers. If you take a car for five days, you will often get a sixth and seventh day for no extra cost.

To rent a car you must be 25 years old (21 with some rental firms, including Avis), have a credit card in your name and a valid driver's license from your home country (not just an IDP).

There is little price variation among the major rental companies, except for the occasional promotional deals. Some agencies have been known to charge your credit card long after you've returned the car. This is

less likely to happen with more-established agencies.

Insurance

You will probably be offered a variety of insurance options, and it's wise to take as much insurance as you can get (about US$20 a day).

Road Rules & Hazards

The number of fatalities caused by motor vehicles in Brazil is estimated at 80,000 per year. The roads can be very dangerous, especially busy highways such as the Rio–São Paulo corridor. This cult of speed is insatiable. Many drivers are racing fans and tend to imagine that they are Ayrton Senna, finding it impossible to slow down to anyone else's pace.

At night, many motorists don't stop at red lights – they merely slow down. This is because of the danger of robbery at stoplights, and it's particularly common in São Paulo. In big cities, keep your windows closed and doors locked when stopped.

Drivers use their horns without restraint, and buses, which have no horns, rev their engines instead. One of the craziest habits is driving at night without headlights. Driving at night is particularly hazardous; other drivers are more likely to be drunk and, at least in the Northeast and the interior, the roads are often poor and unreliable. Poorly banked turns are the norm.

Brazilian speed bumps are quite prevalent. Always slow down as you enter a town.

Further headaches for drivers in Brazil are posed by poor signposting; impossible one-way systems; tropical rainstorms; drivers overtaking on blind corners; flat tires (common, but fortunately there are *borracheiros* – tire repairers – stationed at frequent intervals along the roads); and, of course, the police pulling you over for bogus moving violations.

For security, choose hotels with off-street parking; most in the mid-range and above offer this option.

HITCHING

Hitchhiking is never entirely safe in any country in the world, and is not recommended. Travelers who decide to hitchhike should understand that they are taking a small but potentially serious risk. People who do choose to hitchhike will be safer if they travel in pairs and let someone know where they are planning to go.

Hitchhiking in Brazil, with the possible exception of the Pantanal and a few other areas where it's commonplace among local folk, is difficult. The Portuguese word for 'lift' is *carona*, so ask *'Pode dar carona?'* (Can you give us a lift?). The best way to hitch – practically the only way if you want rides – is to ask drivers when they're not in their vehicles, for example by waiting at a gas station or a truck stop. But even this can be difficult.

LOCAL TRANSPORTATION
Bus
Local bus services tend to be pretty good in Brazil. Since most Brazilians take the bus to work every day, municipal buses are usually frequent and their network of routes is comprehensive. They are always inexpensive.

In most city buses, you get on at the back and exit from the front, though occasionally the reverse is true. Usually there's a money collector sitting at a turnstile just inside the entrance.

Crime can be a problem on buses. Rather than remain behind the turnstile, it's safer to pay the fare and go through. Don't take valuables on the buses. See Dangers & Annoyances (p682) in the Directory chapter for more information.

Jumping on a local bus is one of the best ways to get to know a city. With a map and a few dollars you can tour the town and maybe meet some of the locals.

Metro
Both Rio and São Paulo have excellent metro systems. These are a safe, cheap and efficient way of exploring the city. Fares cost around US$0.80, one-way.

Taxi
Taxi rides are reasonably priced, and are the best option for getting around cities at night, and zipping across town in a hurry. Taxis in the cities usually have meters that start at US$1 and rise by something like US$0.75 per km. Occasionally, the taxi driver will refer to a chart *(tabela)* and re-

vise slightly upwards. This reflects recent official hikes in taxi rates and the meter has not yet been adjusted.

In small towns, taxis often don't have meters, and you'll have to arrange a price beforehand.

Some airports and bus stations now have a system for you to purchase a fixed-price taxi ticket from a *bilheteria* (ticket office). At a few such places it's much cheaper to go onto the street outside and find a cab that will take you for the meter fare or sometimes even less. In this book we've indicated places where this is the case. If you are carrying valuables, however, the special airport taxi, or a radio taxi, can be a worthwhile investment. These are probably the safest taxis on the road.

If possible, orient yourself before taking a taxi, and keep a map handy in case you find yourself being taken on a wild detour. The worst place to get a cab is where the tourists are. Don't get a cab near one of the expensive hotels. In Rio, for example, walk a block away from the beach at Copacabana to flag down a cab.

TRAIN
Brazil's passenger-train services have been scaled down to almost nothing in recent years, as the railways became more and more debt-ridden. There are still over 30,000km of track, but most trains carry only cargo. Rail enthusiasts should not quite despair, however, as there are still a couple of great rides. The outstanding one is the trip from Curitiba to Paranaguá (see the boxed text on p301), descending the coastal mountain range with some unforgettable views. The Belo Horizonte–Vitória run (p230), via Santa Bárbara and Sabará, is a cheaper and far more pleasant than the bus ride.

Steam trains in Brazil are affectionately known as *Marias Fumaça* (Smoking Mary), and a couple of them still run as leisure attractions. One is the 13km ride from São João del Rei to Tiradentes in Minas Gerais (see the boxed text on p247). Another pleasant short trip, this time by electric train, is the ride through the Serra da Mantiqueira of São Paulo state from Campos do Jordão to Santo Antônio do Pinhal, the highest stretch of track in the country (p291).

Health
Dr David Goldberg

CONTENTS

Prevention is the key to staying healthy while abroad. Travelers who receive the recommended vaccines and follow commonsense precautions usually come away with nothing more dangerous than a little diarrhea.

Medically speaking, Brazil is part of tropical South America, which includes most of the continent except for the southernmost portion. The diseases found in this area are comparable to those found in tropical areas in Africa and Asia. Particularly important are mosquito borne infections, including malaria, yellow fever and dengue fever, which are not a significant concern in temperate regions.

BEFORE YOU GO

INSURANCE

If your health insurer doesn't cover you for medical expenses incurred abroad, you'll need to get some extra travel insurance – see the links under www.lonelyplanet.com/subwwway for more information. Find out in advance if your travel insurer will make payments directly to providers or reimburse you later for overseas health expenditures.

RECOMMENDED VACCINATIONS

Since most vaccines don't produce immunity until at least two weeks after they're given, visit a physician four to eight weeks before departure. Ask your doctor for an International Certificate of Vaccination (otherwise known as the yellow booklet), which will list all the vaccinations you've received. This is mandatory for countries that require proof of yellow fever vaccination upon entry, but it's a good idea to carry it wherever you travel.

MEDICAL CHECKLIST

Bring medications in their original containers, clearly labeled. A signed, dated letter from your doctor describing your medical conditions and medications (including their generic names) is a good idea. If carrying syringes or needles, carry a physician's letter documenting their medical necessity.

INTERNET RESOURCES

There is a wealth of travel-health advice on the Internet. For further information, the Lonely Planet website at www.lonelyplanet.com is a good place to start. The World Health Organization (WHO) publishes a superb book called *International Travel and Health*, which is revised annually and is available online at no cost (www.who.int/ith/). Another website of general interest is the MD Travel Health website at www.mdtravelhealth.com, which provides free, complete travel health recommendations for every country and is updated daily.

It's usually a good idea to consult your government's travel-health website before departure, if one is available:
Australia www.dfat.gov.au/travel/
Canada www.hc-sc.gc.ca/pphb-dgspsp/tmp-pmv/pub_e.html
United Kingdom www.doh.gov.uk/traveladvice/index.htm
United States www.cdc.gov/travel/

FURTHER READING

For more detailed information on health matters, see *Healthy Travel Central & South America*, published by Lonely Planet. If you are traveling with children, Lonely Planet's

Travel with Children provides useful advice. The *ABC of Healthy Travel* by E Walker et al is another valuable resource.

IN TRANSIT

DEEP VEIN THROMBOSIS (DVT)

Blood clots may form in the legs (deep vein thrombosis: DVT) during plane flights, chiefly because of prolonged immobility. The longer the flight, the greater the risk. Though most blood clots are reabsorbed uneventfully, some may break off and travel through the blood vessels to the lungs, where they could cause life-threatening complications.

The chief symptom of DVT is swelling or pain of the foot, ankle or calf, usually but not always on just one side. When a blood clot travels to the lungs, it may cause chest pain and difficulty breathing. Travelers with any of these symptoms should seek medical attention immediately.

To prevent the development of DVT on long flights you should walk about the cabin, perform isometric compressions of the leg muscles (ie contract the leg muscles while sitting), drink plenty of fluids and avoid alcohol and tobacco.

JET LAG & MOTION SICKNESS

Jet lag is common when crossing more than five time zones and can result in insomnia, fatigue, malaise or nausea. To avoid jet lag try drinking plenty of (nonalcoholic) fluids and eating light meals. Upon arrival, get exposure to natural sunlight and readjust your schedule (for meals, sleep etc) as soon as possible.

Antihistamines such as dimenhydrin-ate (Dramamine) and meclizine (Antivert,

HEALTH

REQUIRED & RECOMMENDED VACCINATIONS

The only required vaccine is yellow fever, and that's only if you're arriving in Brazil from a yellow fever–infected country in Africa or the Americas. However, a number of vaccines are recommended:

Vaccine	Recommended for	Dosage	Side Effects
hepatitis A	all travelers	1 dose before trip; booster 6-12 months later	soreness at injection site; headaches; body aches
typhoid	all travelers	4 capsules by mouth, 1 taken every other day	abdominal pain; nausea; rash
yellow fever	all travelers, except those visiting only Rio de Janeiro, São Paulo, the central eastern area to the coast, & the coastal areas south of São Luís	1 dose lasts 10 years	headaches; body aches; severe reactions are rare
hepatitis B	long-term travelers in close contact with the local population	3 doses over 6-month period	soreness at injection site; low-grade fever
rabies	travelers who may have contact with animals & may not have access to medical care	3 doses over 3-4 week period	soreness at injection site; headaches; body aches
tetanus-diphtheria	all travelers who haven't had booster within 10 years	1 dose lasts 10 years	soreness at injection site
measles	travelers born after 1956 who have had only one measles vaccination	1 dose	fever; rash; joint pains; allergic reactions
chickenpox	travelers who've never had chickenpox	2 doses 1 month apart	fever; mild case of chickenpox

Bonine) are usually the first choice for treating motion sickness. Their main side effect is drowsiness. An herbal alternative is ginger, which works like a charm for some people.

IN BRAZIL

AVAILABILITY & COST OF HEALTH CARE

For an ambulance in Brazil, call ☎ 192, or an emergency number (listed following).

Good medical care is available in the larger cities, but may be difficult to find in rural areas. Medical care in Brazil may be extremely expensive. Most doctors and hospitals expect payment in cash, regardless of whether you have travel-health insurance.

The US embassy website at www.embaixada-americana.org.br has an extensive list of physicians, dentists, pharmacists, laboratories and emergency services. If you're pregnant, be sure to check this site before departure to find the name of one or two obstetricians in the area you'll be visiting, just in case.

The **Einstein Hospital** (for emergencies ☎ 55-11-3747 0200, for ambulance & air ambulance ☎ 0xx11-3747 1000/1100; Av Albert Einstein 627, Morumbi) in São Paulo is used by expatriates throughout Brazil, including US government personnel. English is also spoken at **Hospital Sírio-Libânes** (Map p268; for information ☎ 0xx11-3344 8877, for ambulance ☎ 0xx11-826 0111 or 926 0400; Rua da Adma Jafet 91, Bela Vista) in São Paulo.

If you develop a medical emergency while in Rio, you can call **Hospital Samaritano** (☎ 0xx21-2537 9722; Rua Bambina 98, Botafogo), **Clínica São Vicente** (☎ 0xx21-2529 4422; Rua João Borges 204, Gávea), **Hospital Ipanema** (Map pp124-5; ☎ 0xx21-3111 2300; Rua Antônio Parreiras 67, Ipanema), **Miguel Couto Hospital** (Map pp124-5; ☎ 0xx21-2274 2121; Av Bartolomeu Mitre 1108, Gávea), **Pró-Cardíaco** (for information ☎ 0xx21-2537 4242, for ambulance ☎ 0xx21-2527 6060; Rua General Polidoro 192, Botafogo), or **Galdino Campos Cárdio Copa** (Map pp128-9; ☎ 0xx21-2255 9966; 2nd fl, Av NS de Copacabana 492, Copacabana; ☒ 24hr) – the latter two specialize in cardiac emergencies.

If you develop a life-threatening medical problem, you'll probably want to be evacuated to a country with state-of-the-art medical care. Since this may cost tens of thousands of dollars, be sure you have insurance to cover this before you depart.

MEDICAL CHECKLIST

- Antibiotics
- Antidiarrheal drugs (eg loperamide)
- Acetaminophen (Tylenol) or aspirin
- Anti-inflammatory drugs (eg ibuprofen)
- Antihistamines (for hay fever and allergic reactions)
- Antibacterial ointment (eg Bactroban) for cuts and abrasions
- Steroid cream or cortisone (for poison ivy and other allergic rashes)
- Bandages, gauze, gauze rolls
- Adhesive or paper tape
- Scissors, safety pins, tweezers
- Thermometer
- Pocket knife
- DEET-containing insect repellent for the skin
- Permethrin-containing insect spray for clothing, tents and bed nets
- Sun block
- Oral rehydration salts
- Iodine tablets (for water purification)
- Syringes and sterile needles
- Malaria tablets (if going into an infected region)

You can find a list of medical evacuation and travel insurance companies on the US State Department website at www.travel.state.gov/medical.html.

Each Brazilian pharmacy has a licensed pharmacist. Most are well supplied. Many medications that require a prescription in the US and Canada are available over the counter in Brazil. If you're taking any medication on a regular basis, be sure you know its generic (scientific) name, since many pharmaceuticals go under different names in Brazil. Droga Raia is a large pharmacy chain; many stores are open 24 hours.

INFECTIOUS DISEASES
Cholera

Cholera is an intestinal infection acquired through ingestion of contaminated food or water. The main symptom is profuse, watery diarrhea, which may be so severe that it causes life-threatening dehydration. The key treatment is drinking oral rehydration solution. Antibiotics are also given, usually tetracycline or doxycycline, though quinolone antibiotics such as ciprofloxacin and levofloxacin are also effective.

Cholera sometimes occurs in Brazil, but it's rare among travelers. Cholera vaccine is no longer required, and is in fact no longer available in some countries, including the US, because the old vaccine was relatively ineffective and caused side effects. There are new vaccines that are safer and more effective, but they're not available in many countries and are only recommended for those at particularly high risk.

Dengue

Dengue fever is a viral infection found throughout South America. A large outbreak of dengue was reported from the Rio area in early 2002, ultimately affecting almost 800,000 people. Dengue is transmitted by aedes mosquitoes, which bite preferentially during the daytime and are usually found close to human habitations, often indoors. They breed primarily in artificial water containers, such as jars, barrels, cans, cisterns, metal drums, plastic containers and discarded tires. As a result, dengue is especially common in densely populated, urban environments.

Dengue usually causes flulike symptoms, including fever, muscle aches, joint pains, headaches, nausea and vomiting, often followed by a rash. The body aches may be quite uncomfortable, but most cases resolve uneventfully in a few days. Severe cases usually occur in children under the age of 15 who are experiencing their second dengue infection.

There is no treatment for dengue fever except to take analgesics such as acetaminophen/paracetamol (Tylenol) and drink plenty of fluids. Severe cases may require hospitalization for intravenous fluids and supportive care. There is no vaccine. The cornerstone of prevention is protection against insect bites (see p715).

Hepatitis A

Hepatitis A is the second most common travel-related infection (after traveler's diarrhea). It's a viral infection of the liver that is usually acquired by ingestion of contaminated water, food or ice, though it may also be acquired by direct contact with infected persons. The illness occurs throughout the world, but the incidence is higher in developing nations. Symptoms may include fever, malaise, jaundice, nausea, vomiting and abdominal pain. Most cases resolve without complications, though hepatitis A occasionally causes severe liver damage. There is no treatment.

The vaccine for hepatitis A is extremely safe and highly effective. If you get a booster six to 12 months later, it lasts for at least 10 years. You really should get it before you go to Brazil or any other developing nation. Because the safety of hepatitis A vaccine has not been established for pregnant women or children under the age of two, they should instead be given a gamma globulin injection.

Hepatitis B

Like hepatitis A, hepatitis B is a liver infection that occurs worldwide but is more common in developing nations. Unlike hepatitis A, the disease is usually acquired by sexual contact or by exposure to infected blood, generally through blood transfusions or contaminated needles. The vaccine is recommended only for long-term travelers (on the road more than six months) who expect to live in rural areas or have close physical contact with the local population. Additionally, the vaccine is recommended for anyone who anticipates sexual contact with the local inhabitants or a possible need for medical, dental or other treatments while abroad, especially if a need for transfusions or injections is expected.

Hepatitis B vaccine is safe and highly effective. A total of three injections, however, are necessary to establish full immunity. Several countries added hepatitis B vaccine to the list of routine childhood immunizations in the 1980s, so many young adults are already protected.

Malaria

Malaria occurs in every South American country except Chile, Uruguay and the Falkland Islands. It's transmitted by mosquito bites, usually between dusk and dawn. The main symptoms are high spiking fevers, which may be accompanied by chills, sweats, headache, body aches, weakness, vomiting or diarrhea. Severe cases may involve the central nervous system and lead to seizures, confusion, coma and death.

Taking malaria pills is strongly recommended for forested areas within the nine states of the 'Legal Amazonia' region, including Acre, Amapá, Amazonas, Maranhão (western part), Mato Grosso (northern part), Pará (except Belém city), Rondônia, Roraima and Tocantins, and for urban areas within this region, including the cities of Porto Velho, Boa Vista, Macapá, Manaus, Santarém and Maraba. Transmission is greatest in remote jungle areas where mining, lumbering and agriculture occur and which have been settled for less than five years. Malaria risk is negligible outside the states of 'Legal Amazonia.' Travelers visiting only the coastal states from the horn to the Uruguay border and Iguaçu Falls do not need prophylaxis.

There is a choice of three malaria pills, all of which work about equally well. Mefloquine (Lariam) is taken once weekly in a dosage of 250mg, starting one to two weeks before arrival and continuing through the trip and for four weeks after return. The problem is that a certain percentage of people (the number is debatable) develop neuro-psychiatric side effects, which may range from mild to severe. Atovaquone/proguanil (Malarone) is a newly approved combin-ation pill taken once daily with food starting two days before arrival and continuing through the trip and for seven days after departure. Side effects are typically mild. Doxycycline is a third alternative, but it may cause an exaggerated sunburn reaction.

In general, Malarone seems to cause fewer side effects than Lariam and is becoming more popular. The chief disadvantage is that it has to be taken daily. For longer trips, it's probably worth trying Lariam; for shorter trips, Malarone will be the drug of choice for most people.

Protecting yourself against mosquito bites is just as important as taking malaria pills (see p715), since none of the pills is 100% effective.

If you may not have access to medical care while traveling, you should bring along additional pills for emergency self-treatment, which you should take if you can't reach a doctor and you develop symptoms that suggest malaria, such as high spiking fevers. One option is to take four tablets of Malarone once daily for three days. Mala-rone should not be used for treatment, however, if you're already taking it for prevention. An alternative is to take 650mg of quinine three times daily and 100mg of doxycycline twice daily for one week. If you start self-medication, see a doctor at the earliest possible opportunity.

If you develop a fever after returning home, see a physician, as malaria symptoms may not occur for months.

Plague

The plague continues to occur among animals in the drier northern and eastern states, from Ceará south to Minas Gerais, but human cases are uncommon. Most occur in Bahia state. The infection is usually transmitted to humans by the bite of rodent fleas, typically when rodents die off. Symptoms include fever, chills, muscle aches and malaise, associated with the development of an acutely swollen, exquisitely painful lymph node, known as a bubo, most often in the groin. Most travelers are at extremely low risk of the plague. But if you may have contact with rodents or their fleas, especially in the above areas, you should bring along a bottle of doxycycline, to be taken prophylactically during periods of exposure. Those less than eight years old or allergic to doxycycline should take trimethoprim-sulfamethoxazole instead. In addition, you should avoid areas containing rodent burrows or nests, never handle sick or dead animals, and follow the guidelines in this chapter for protecting yourself from insect bites (see p715).

Rabies

Rabies is a viral infection of the brain and spinal cord that is almost always fatal. The rabies virus is carried in the saliva of infected animals and is typically transmitted through an animal bite, though contamination of any break in the skin with infected saliva may result in rabies. Rabies occurs in all South American countries. In Brazil, most cases are reported from the extreme western Minas Gerais state and northeastern areas. Dog bites are the most common cause, but bites from other animals can also lead to rabies. In 2004 several dozen people in the Amazon died from rabies after being bitten by vampire bats.

Rabies vaccine is safe, but a full series requires three injections and is quite expensive. Those at high risk of rabies, such as animal handlers and spelunkers (cave explorers), should certainly get the vaccine. In addition, those at lower risk of animal bites should consider asking for the vaccine if they may be traveling to remote areas and may not have access to appropriate medical care if needed. The treatment for a possibly rabid bite consists of rabies vaccine with rabies immune globulin. It's effective, but must be given promptly. Most travelers don't need rabies vaccine.

All animal bites and scratches must be promptly and thoroughly cleansed with large amounts of soap and water and local health authorities contacted to determine whether or not further treatment is necessary (see p715).

Typhoid

Typhoid fever is caused by ingestion of food or water contaminated by a species of salmonella known as *Salmonella typhi*. Fever occurs in virtually all cases. Other symptoms may include headache, malaise, muscle aches, dizziness, loss of appetite, nausea and abdominal pain. Either diarrhea or constipation may occur. Possible complications include intestinal perforation, intestinal bleeding, confusion, delirium or (rarely) coma.

Unless you expect to take all your meals in major hotels and restaurants, typhoid vaccine is a good idea. It's usually given orally, but is also available as an injection. Neither vaccine is approved for use in children under the age of two.

The drug of choice for typhoid fever is usually a quinolone antibiotic such as ciprofloxacin (Cipro) or levofloxacin (Levaquin), which many travelers carry for treatment of traveler's diarrhea. However, if you self-treat for typhoid fever, you may also need to self-treat for malaria, since the symptoms of the two diseases may be indistinguishable.

Yellow Fever

Yellow fever is a life-threatening viral infection transmitted by mosquitoes in forested areas. The illness begins with flulike symptoms, which may include fever, chills, headache, muscle aches, backache, loss of appetite, nausea and vomiting. These symptoms usually subside in a few days, but one person in six enters a second, toxic phase characterized by recurrent fever, vomiting, listlessness, jaundice, kidney failure, and hemorrhage, leading to death in up to half of the cases. There is no treatment except for supportive care.

Yellow fever vaccine is strongly recommended for all travelers to Brazil, except those visiting only Rio de Janeiro, São Paulo, the central eastern area to the coast, and the coastal areas south of São Luís. Major outbreaks have recently been reported from Minas Gerais state and additional cases occur elsewhere. Fatal cases of yellow fever among travelers who failed to get vaccinated are periodically reported. For an up-to-date map showing the distribution of yellow fever in Brazil, go to the Centre for Disease Control (CDC) website at www.cdc.gov/travel/diseases/maps/yellowfever_map2.htm.

Proof of vaccination is required from all travelers arriving from a yellow fever–infected country in Africa or the Americas.

Yellow fever vaccine is given only in approved yellow fever vaccination centers, which provide validated International Certificates of Vaccination. The vaccine should be given at least 10 days before any potential exposure to yellow fever and remains effective for approximately 10 years. Reactions to the vaccine are generally mild and may include headaches, muscle aches, low-grade fevers or discomfort at the injection site. Severe, life-threatening reactions have been described but are extremely rare. In general, the risk of becoming ill from the vaccine is far less than the risk of becoming ill from yellow fever, and you're strongly encouraged to get the vaccine.

Taking measures to protect yourself from mosquito bites (see p715) is an essential part of preventing yellow fever.

Other Infectious Diseases

Schistosomiasis, which is a parasitic infection acquired by skin exposure to contaminated fresh water, occurs in almost all states of the Northeast and two states (Minas Gerais and Espírito Santo) in the Southeast. When traveling in these areas, you should avoid swimming, wading, bathing or washing in bodies of fresh water, including lakes, ponds, streams and rivers. Salt water and chlorinated pools carry no risk of schistosomiasis.

Toxoplasmosis has been reported from various areas, including northwestern Paraná state and northern Rio de Janeiro state. Most cases have been related to contaminated water supplies. Pregnant women should be particularly careful to avoid drinking unfiltered water, since toxoplasmosis may cause severe fetal illness. In nonpregnant people with normal immune systems, most cases of toxoplasmosis clear uneventfully.

Chagas' disease is a parasitic infection that is transmitted by triatomine insects (reduviid bugs), which inhabit crevices in the walls and roofs of substandard housing in South and Central America. In Brazil, the disease has been eliminated in every state except Bahia and Tocantins through an aggressive program of insecticide spraying. The triatomine insect lays its feces on human skin as it bites, usually at night. A person becomes infected when they unknowingly rub the feces into the bite wound or any other open sore. Chagas' disease is extremely rare in travelers. If you sleep in a poorly constructed house, especially one made of mud, adobe or thatch, however, you should be sure to protect yourself with a bed net and a good insecticide.

Leishmaniasis occurs in the mountains and jungles of all South American countries except for Chile, Uruguay and the Falkland Islands. The infection is transmitted by sand flies, which are about one-third the size of mosquitoes. In Brazil, leishmaniasis has been reported from suburban areas in Rio de Janeiro and São Paulo. Most cases are limited to the skin, causing slowly growing ulcers over exposed parts of the body. The more severe type of leishmaniasis, which disseminates to the bone marrow, liver and spleen, occurs mainly in the Northeast. Leishmaniasis may be particularly severe in those with HIV. There is no vaccine. To protect yourself from sand flies, follow the same precautions as for mosquitoes (see p715), except that netting must be made of a finer mesh (at least 18 holes per 2.54cm or to the linear inch).

Hantavirus pulmonary syndrome is a rapidly progressive, life-threatening infection that is acquired through exposure to the excretions of wild rodents. Most cases occur in those people who live in rodent-infested dwellings in rural areas. In Brazil, hantavirus infections are reported from the states of Minas Gerais, Santa Catarina and São Paulo.

Echinococcus is a parasite that infects the liver, usually in people who work with sheep. Echinococcus infections occur chiefly in the southernmost part of the country.

Brucellosis is an infection of domestic and wild animals that may be transmitted to humans through direct animal contact or by consumption of unpasteurized dairy products from infected animals. In Brazil, most human cases are related to infected cattle. Symptoms may include fever, malaise, depression, loss of appetite, headache, muscle aches and back pain. Complications may include arthritis, hepatitis, meningitis and endocarditis (heart-valve infection).

Fascioliasis is a parasitic infection that is typically acquired by eating contaminated watercress grown in sheep-raising areas. Early symptoms may include fever, nausea, vomiting and painful enlargement of the liver.

Onchocerciasis (river blindness) is caused by a roundworm that may invade the eye, leading to blindness. The infection is transmitted by black flies, which breed along the banks of rapidly flowing rivers and streams. In Brazil, onchocerciasis is reported among the indigenous Yanomami population living along the Venezuelan border, as well as in nearby tribes and non-Indians visiting the area. Most cases occur near swift-flowing streams in densely forested highlands.

Venezuelan equine encephalitis which is transmitted by mosquitoes and causes brain inflammation, occurs sporadically.

Cases of **'caterpillar plague'** were reported from the Amazon delta region between 1983 and 1985 and from southern Brazil in 1995. The disease is caused by contact with the larvae (caterpillars) of the butterfly *Lamonia achelous*, which secrete venom through their skins. The illness is characterized by high fever, bleeding from the nose and ears, kidney failure and death. The caterpillar is found from December through March. The adult and pupal forms are harmless.

HIV/AIDS is a big problem in Brazil. An estimated 600,000 Brazilians carry the virus. Be sure to use condoms for all sexual encounters.

TRAVELER'S DIARRHEA

To prevent diarrhea, avoid tap water unless it has been boiled, filtered or chemically disinfected (iodine tablets); only eat fresh fruits and vegetables if they are cooked or peeled; be wary of dairy products that may contain unpasteurized milk; and be highly selective when eating food from street vendors.

If you develop diarrhea, be sure to drink plenty of fluids, preferably an oral rehydration solution containing lots of salt and sugar. A few loose stools don't require treatment, but if you start having more than four or five stools a day you should start taking an antibiotic (usually a quinolone drug) and an antidiarrheal agent (such as loperamide).

If diarrhea is bloody, persists for more than 72 hours or is accompanied by fever, shaking chills or severe abdominal pain, you should seek medical attention.

ENVIRONMENTAL HAZARDS
Animal Bites

Do not attempt to pet, handle or feed any animal, with the exception of domestic animals known to be free of any infectious disease. Most animal injuries are directly related to a person's attempt to touch or feed the animal.

Any bite or scratch from a mammal, including bats, should be promptly and thoroughly cleansed with large amounts of soap and water, followed by application of an antiseptic such as iodine or alcohol. The local health authorities should be contacted immediately for possible post-exposure rabies treatment, whether or not you've been immunized against rabies. It may also be advisable to start an antibiotic, since wounds caused by animal bites and scratches frequently become infected. One of the newer quinolones, such as levofloxacin (Levaquin), which many travelers carry in case of diarrhea, would be an appropriate choice.

Insect Bites & Stings

To prevent mosquito bites, wear long sleeves, long pants, hats and shoes (rather than sandals). Bring along a good insect repellent, preferably one containing DEET, which should be applied to exposed skin and clothing, but not to eyes, mouth, cuts, wounds or irritated skin. Products containing lower concentrations of DEET are as effective, but for shorter periods of time. In general, adults and children over the age of 12 should use preparations containing 25% to 35% DEET, which usually last about six hours. Children between two and 12 years of age should use preparations containing no more than 10% DEET, applied sparingly, which will usually last about three hours. Neurologic toxicity has been reported from DEET, especially in children, but appears to be extremely uncommon and generally related to overuse. DEET-containing compounds should not be used on children under the age of two.

Insect repellents containing certain botanical products, including oil of eucalyptus and soybean oil, are effective but last only 1½ to two hours. DEET-containing repellents are preferable for areas where there is a high risk of malaria or yellow fever. Products based on citronella are not effective.

For additional protection, you can apply permethrin to clothing, shoes, tents and bed nets. Permethrin treatments are safe and remain effective for at least two weeks, even when items are laundered. Permethrin should not be applied directly to skin.

Don't sleep with the window open unless there is a screen in the windowframe. If sleeping outdoors or in accommodations that allow entry of mosquitoes, use a bed net, preferably treated with permethrin, with edges tucked in under the mattress. The mesh size should be smaller than 1.5mm. If the sleeping area is not otherwise protected, use a mosquito coil, which will fill the room with insecticide throughout the night. Repellent-impregnated wristbands are not effective.

TRADITIONAL REMEDIES	
problem	**treatment**
altitude sickness	gingko
jet lag	melatonin
mosquito-bite prevention	oil of eucalyptus; soybean oil
motion sickness	ginger

Snake Bites

Snakes and leeches are a hazard in some areas of South America. In the event of a venomous snake bite, place the victim at rest, keep the bitten area immobilized and move the victim immediately to the nearest medical facility. Avoid tourniquets, which are no longer recommended.

Sun

To protect yourself from excessive sun exposure, you should stay out of the midday sun, wear sunglasses and a wide-brimmed sun hat, and apply sunscreen with SPF15 or higher, with both UVA and UVB protection. Sunscreen should be generously applied to all exposed parts of the body approximately 30 minutes before sun exposure and should be reapplied after swimming or vigorous activity. Travelers should also drink plenty of fluids and avoid strenuous exercise when the temperature is high.

Water

Tap water in Brazil is not safe to drink. Vigorous boiling for one minute is the most effective means of water purification. At altitudes greater than 2000m (6500ft), boil for three minutes.

Another option is to disinfect water with iodine pills. Instructions are usually enclosed and should be carefully followed. Or you can add 2% tincture of iodine to one quart or liter of water (five drops to clear water, 10 drops to cloudy water) and let stand for 30 minutes. If the water is cold, longer times may be required. The taste of iodinated water may be improved by adding vitamin C (ascorbic acid). Iodinated water should not be consumed for more than a few weeks. Pregnant women, those with a history of thyroid disease, and those allergic to iodine should not drink iodinated water.

A number of water filters are on the market. Those with smaller pores (reverse osmosis filters) provide the broadest protection, but they are relatively large and are readily plugged by debris. Those with somewhat larger pores (microstrainer filters) are ineffective against viruses, although they remove other organisms. Manufacturers' instructions must be carefully followed.

TRAVELING WITH CHILDREN

In general, children under the age of nine months should not be brought to areas where yellow fever occurs, since the vaccine is not safe in this age group.

When traveling with young children, be particularly careful about what you allow them to eat and drink, because diarrhea can be especially dangerous in this age group and because the vaccines for hepatitis A and typhoid fever are not approved for use in children who are under the age of two years.

The two main malaria medications, Lariam and Malarone, may be given to children, but insect repellents must be applied in lower concentrations.

TRAVELING WHILE PREGNANT

You can find an English-speaking obstetrician near your location in Brazil by going to the US embassy website at www.emb ixada-americana.org.br. However, medical facilities will probably not be comparable to those in your home country. It's safer to avoid travel to Brazil late in pregnancy, so that you don't have to risk delivering there.

If pregnant, it's preferable to avoid areas where yellow fever occurs, since the vaccine is not safe during pregnancy.

For malaria prevention, mefloquine (Lariam) is the safest during pregnancy.

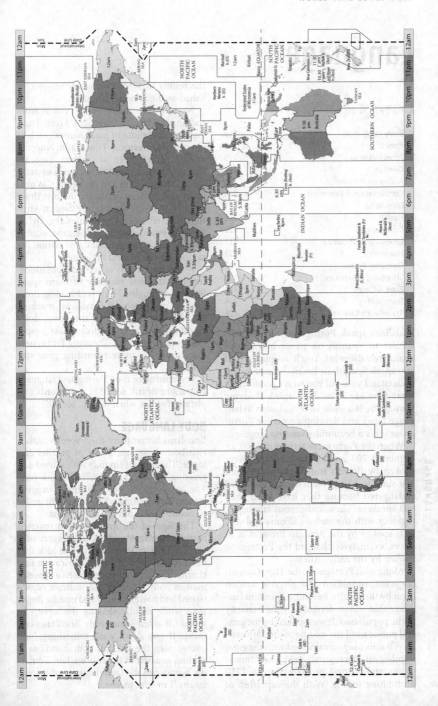

Language

CONTENTS

Brazilians speak Portuguese, which looks similar to Spanish on paper but sounds completely different. You'll do quite well if you speak Spanish in Brazil. Brazilians will understand you, but you won't get much of what they say – so don't think studying Portuguese is a waste of time. Listen to language tapes and develop an ear for Portuguese – it's a beautiful-sounding language.

When the Portuguese arrived in 1500, an estimated 700 indigenous languages were spoken by Brazil's Indian peoples. About 180 survive, 130 of them being considered endangered because they have fewer than 600 speakers. These indigenous languages, together with the various idioms and dialects spoken by the Africans brought in as slaves, extensively changed the Portuguese spoken by the early settlers.

Along with Portuguese, the Tupi-Guaraní language, simplified and given a written form by the Jesuits, became a common language that was understood by the majority of the population. It was spoken by the general public until the middle of the 18th century, but its usage diminished with the great number of Portuguese gold rush immigrants and a royal proclamation in 1757 prohibiting its use. With the expulsion of the Jesuits in 1759, Portuguese was established as the national language.

Nevertheless, many words remain from Indian and African languages. From Tupi-Guaraní come lots of place names (such as Guanabara, Carioca, Tijuca and Niterói), animal names (such as piranha, capivara and urubu) and plant names (such as mandioca, abacaxí, caju and jacarandá). Words from the African dialects, mainly those from Nigeria and Angola, are used in Afro-Brazilian religious ceremonies (eg Orixá, Exú and Iansã), cooking (eg vatapá, acarajé and abará) and in general conversation (eg samba, mocambo and moleque).

Brazilians are easy to befriend, but unfortunately the vast majority of them speak little or no English. This is changing, however, as practically all Brazilians in school are learning English. All the same, don't count on finding an English speaker, especially out of the cities. The more Portuguese you speak, the more rewarding your stay will be.

For information on Portuguese language courses in Brazil, see p681. For words and phrases for use when dining, see p97.

BODY LANGUAGE

Brazilians accompany their speech with a rich body language, a sort of parallel dialogue. The thumbs up *tudo bem* is used as a greeting, or to signify 'OK' or 'Thank you.' The authoritative *não-não* finger-wagging is most intimidating when done right under someone's nose, but it's not a threat.

The sign of the *figa*, a thumb inserted between the first and second fingers of a clenched fist, is a symbol of good luck that has been derived from an African sexual charm. It's more commonly used as jewelry than in body language. To indicate *rápido* (speed and haste), thumb and middle finger snap while rapidly shaking the wrist – a gesture it often seems only Brazilians can make. If you don't want something (*não quero*), slap the back of your hands as if ridding yourself of the entire affair. Touching a finger to the lateral corner of the eye means 'I'm wise to you.'

BOOKS

An excellent pocket phrasebook is Lonely Planet's *Brazilian Portuguese Phrasebook*. In addition to covering most travel situations, the book will also provide much help in social situations. It includes an easy-to-follow grammar guide, a comprehensive section on food and dining, plus a two-way dictionary.

Although Spanish and French take up far more shelf space at most bookstores, there's a growing selection of Portuguese language learning material. One of the best short-term introductions is *Portuguese Complete Course: Basic-Intermediate* by Living Language. In addition to an English-Portuguese dictionary, the kit includes a course book with 40 lessons and three audio CDs. The lessons are easy to follow and designed to get you speaking quickly.

For grammar, pick up a copy of *Essential Portuguese Grammar* by Alexander da Prista. Although it's old (published in 1966), this slim volume is still a gem, with clear and concise explanations of grammatical structures and the language in practice.

If you'd like to delve deeper into the language, and have the time to dedicate to a challenging self-study course, try the US Foreign Service Institute (FSI) series, which comes in two volumes. The first volume, *Mastering Portuguese*, includes twelve 90-minute cassettes and a textbook that covers pronunciation, verb tenses and essential nouns and adjectives. Volume 2 is harder to find, but polishes your skills even more with 22 tapes and an additional textbook.

Combine these with a few old bossa nova albums, recent Brazilian cinema (seek out any Walter Salles or Fernando Meirelles film) and some Jorge Amado novels, and you're ready for the next level of instruction – on the streets and beaches of Brazil.

PRONUNCIATION

Brazilian Portuguese pronunciation can be tricky for the uninitiated. The big shocker is that generally, an **r** is pronounced like an 'h': 'Rio' becomes 'hee-oh,' the currency is pronounced 'hay-ow' etc. In the same spirit of fun, a **t** (or **d**) followed by a vowel is pronounced 'ch' as in 'church' or 'j' as in 'judge', so the word *restaurante* is pronounced approximately 'hess-to-roch.'

The letter **ç** is pronounced like an English 's'; the letter **x** as the 'sh' as in 'ship.' So 'Iguaçu' is 'ig-wa-soo' and 'Caxambu' 'ka-sham-boo.'

You'll know you've mastered Brazilian Portuguese pronunciation when you've successfully ordered one of the country's more popular beers, *Antarctica* (that's right, you say 'ant-okt-chee-kah'!).

Within Brazil, accents, dialects and slang (*gíria*) vary regionally. The Carioca inserts the 'sh' sound in place of **s**. The gaúcho speaks a Spanish-sounding Portuguese, the Baiano (from Bahia) speaks slowly, and the accents of the Cearense (from Ceará) are often incomprehensible to outsiders.

Vowels

a	as the 'u' in run
a	as the 'a' in father
ai	as in 'aisle'
aw	as in 'saw'
ay	as in 'day'
e	as in 'bet'
ee	as in 'bee'
o	as in 'go'
oo	as in 'moon'
ow	as in 'how'
oy	as in 'boy'

Nasal Vowels

A characteristic feature of Brazilian Portuguese is the use of nasal vowels. Nasal vowels are pronounced as if you're trying to produce the sound through your nose rather than your mouth. English also has nasal vowels to some extent – when you say 'sing' in English, the 'i' is nasalized by the 'ng.' In Brazilian Portuguese, written vowels that have a nasal consonant after them (**m** or **n**), or a tilde over them (eg **ã**), will be nasal. In our pronunciation guide, we've used 'ng' after nasal vowels to indicate a nasal sound.

Consonants

The following lists a few of the letters used in our pronunciation guide that represent the trickier Portuguese consonant sounds.

ly	as the 'lli' in 'million'
ny	as in 'canyon'
r	as in 'run'
rr	as in 'run' but stronger and rolled
zh	as the 's' in 'pleasure'

LANGUAGE

Word Stress

Word stress generally occurs on the second last syllable of a word, though there are exceptions. When a word ends in **-r** or is pronounced with a nasalized vowel, the stress falls on the last syllable. Another exception is that if a written vowel has an accent marked over it, the stress falls on the syllable containing that vowel.

In our transliteration system, we have indicated the stressed syllable with italics.

GENDER

Portuguese has masculine and feminine forms of nouns and adjectives. Alternative endings appear separated by a slash, the masculine form first. Generally, 'o' indicates masculine and 'a' indicates feminine.

ACCOMMODATIONS

I'm looking for a ...
Estou procurando por ...   es·*to* pro·koo·*rang*·do porr ...
Where is a ...?
Onde tem ...?   *on*·de teng ...
  room
  um quarto   oom *kwarr*·to
  bed and breakfast
  uma pensão   oo·ma pen·*sowng*
  camping ground
  um local para   oom lo·*kow pa*·ra
    acampamento   a·kam·pa·*meng*·to
  guesthouse
  uma hospedaria   oo·ma os·pe·da·*ree*·a
  hotel
  um hotel   oom o·*tel*
  youth hostel
  um albergue   oom ow·*berr*·ge
  da juventude   da zhoo·veng·*too*·de
I'd like a ... room.
Eu gostaria um   e·oo gos·ta·*ree*·a oom
quarto de ...   *kwarr*·to de ...
  double
  casal   ka·*zow*
  single
  solteiro   sol·*tay*·ro
  twin
  duplo   *doo*·plo
What's the address?
Qual é o endereço?   kwow e o en·de·*re*·so
Do you have a ... room?
Tem um quarto de ...?   teng oom *kwarr*·to de ...
For (three) nights.
Para (três) noites.   *pa*·ra (tres) *noy*·tes

MAKING A RESERVATION
(for phone or written requests)

To ...	Para ...
From ...	De ...
Date	Data
I'd like to book ...	Eu gostaria de fazer uma reserva ... (see the list under 'Accommodations' for bed/room options)
in the name of ...	no nome de ...
for the nights of ...	para os dias ...
from ... to ...	de ... até ...
credit card ...	cartão de credito ...
number	número
expiry date	data de vencimento
Please confirm ...	Por favor confirme ...
availability	a disponibilidade
price	o preço

Does it include breakfast?
Inclui café da manhã?   eeng·kloo·ee ka·fe da ma·*nyang*
May I see it?
Posso ver?   po·so verr
I'll take it.
Eu fico com ele.   e·oo *fee*·ko kom e·lee
I don't like it.
Não gosto.   nowng *gos*·to
I'm leaving now.
Estou indo embora   es·*to* een·do em·*bo*·ra
agora.   a·*go*·ra

How much is it per ...?
Quanto custa por ...?   *kwan*·to *koos*·ta porr ...
  night
  noite   *noy*·te
  person
  pessoa   pe·*so*·a
  week
  semana   se·*ma*·na

Can I pay ...?
Posso pagar com ...?   po·so pa·*garr* kom ...
  by credit card
  cartão de crédito   karr·*towng* de kre·*dee*·to
  by traveler's cheque
  traveler cheque   *tra*·ve·ler *she*·kee

CONVERSATION & ESSENTIALS

Hello.
Olá.   o·*la*
Hi.
Oi.   oy

Good day.
Bom dia.   bong *dee*·a
Good evening.
Boa noite.   *bo*·a *noy*·te
See you later.
Até mais tarde.   a·*te* mais *tarr*·de
Goodbye.
Tchau.   chau
How are you?
Como vai?   *ko*·mo vai
Fine, and you?
Bem, e você?   beng e vo·*se*
I'm pleased to meet you.
Prazer em conhecê-lo.   pra·*zerr* eng ko·nye·*se*·lo (m)
Prazer em conhecê-la.   pra·*zerr* eng ko·nye·*se*·la (f)
Yes.
Sim.   seem
No.
Não.   nowng
Please.
Por favor.   por fa·*vorr*
Thank you (very much).
(Muito) obrigado/   (*mween*·to) o·bree·*ga*·do/
obrigada. (m/f)   o·bree·*ga*·da
You're welcome.
De nada.   de *na*·da
Excuse me.
Com licença.   kom lee·*seng*·sa
Sorry.
Desculpa.   des·*kool*·pa
What's your name?
Qual é o seu nome?   kwow e o se·oo *no*·me
My name is ...
Meu nome é ...   me·oo *no*·me e ...
Where are you from?
De onde você é?   de *ong*·de vo·*se* e
I'm from ...
Eu sou (da/do/de) ...   e·oo so (da/do/de)
May I take a photo (of you)?
Posso tirar uma foto   po so tee *rarr* oo ma *fo* to
(de você)?   (de vo *se*)

DIRECTIONS

Where is ...?
Onde fica ...?   *on*·de *fee*·ka ...
Can you show me (on the map)?
Você poderia me   o·*se* po·de·*ree*·a me
mostrar (no mapa)?   mos·*trarr* (no *ma*·pa)
What's the address?
Qual é o endereço?   kwow e o en·de·*re*·so
How far is it?
Qual a distância   kwow a dees·*tan*·see·a
daqui?   da·*kee*
How do I get there?
Como é que eu chego lá?   *ko*·mo e ke e·oo *she*·go la

Turn ...	Vire ...	*vee*·re ...
at the corner	à esquina	a es·*kee*·na
at the traffic lights	no sinal de trânsito	no see·*now* de *tran*·zee·to
left	à esquerda	a es·*kerr*·da
right	à direita	a dee·*ray*·ta

here	aqui	a·*kee*
there	lá	la
near ...	perto ...	*perr*·to ...
straight ahead	em frente	eng *freng*·te

LANGUAGE

north	norte	norr·te
south	sul	sool
east	leste	les·te
west	oeste	o·es·te

HEALTH

I'm ill.
Estou doente.　es·to do·eng·te
I need a doctor (who speaks English).
Eu preciso de um médico　e·oo pre·see·zo de oom me·dee·ko
(que fale inglês).　(ke fa·le een·gles)
It hurts here.
Aqui dói.　a·kee doy
I've been vomiting.
Estive vomitando.　e·steev vo·mee·tan·do
(I think) I'm pregnant.
(Acho que) estou grávida.　(a·sho ke) es·to gra·vee·da

Where's the nearest ...?
Onde fica ...is perto?　on·de fee·ka ... mais perr·to
　(night) chemist
　a farmácia (noturna)　a farr·ma·see·a (no·toor·na)
　dentist
　o dentista　o deng·tees·ta
　doctor
　o médico　o me·dee·ko
　hospital
　o hospital　o os·pee·tow
　medical centre
　a clínica médica　a klee·nee·ka me·dee·ka

I feel ...
Estou me sentindo ...　es·to me seng·teeng·do ...
　dizzy
　tonto/tonta (m/f)　tong·to/tong·ta
　nauseous
　enjoado/enjoada (m/f)　eng·zho·a·do/en·zho·a·da

asthma	asma	as·ma
diarrhea	diarréia	dee·a·he·ee·a
fever	febre	fe·bre
nausea	náusea	now·ze·a
pain	dor	dorr

I'm allergic to ...
Tenho alergia à ...　te·nyo a·lerr·zhee·a a ...
　antibiotics
　antibióticos　an·tee·bee·o·tee·kos
　aspirin
　aspirina　as·pee·ree·na
　bees
　abelhas　a·be·lyas
　peanuts
　amendoims　a·meng·do·eengs
　penicillin
　penicilina　pe·nee·see·lee·na

EMERGENCIES

Help!
Socorro!　so·ko·ho
It's an emergency.
É uma emergência.　e oo·ma e·merr·zheng·see·a
I'm lost.
Estou perdido/a. (m/f)　es·to perr·dee·do/a
Where are the toilets?
Onde tem um banheiro?　on·de teng oom ba·nyay·ro
Go away!
Vai embora!　vai eng·bo·ra

Call ...!
　a doctor
　um médico!　oom me·dee·ko
　an ambulance
　uma ambulância　oo·ma am·boo·lan·see·a
　the police
　a polícia　a po·lee·see·a

antiseptic
anti-séptico　an·tee·sep·tee·ko
contraceptives
anticoncepcionais　an·tee·kon·sep·see·o·now
painkillers
analgésicos　a·now·zhe·zee·ko

LANGUAGE DIFFICULTIES

Do you speak English?
Você fala inglês?　vo·se fa·la een·gles
Does anyone here speak English?
Alguém aqui fala inglês?　ow·geng fa·la een·gles
Do you understand?
Você entende?　vo·se en·teng·de
I (don't) understand.
Eu (não) entendo.　e·oo (nowng) en·teng·do
What does ... mean?
O que quer dizer ...?　o ke kerr dee·zerr ...

Could you please ...?
Você poderia por favor ...?　vo·se po·de·ree·a porr fa·vorr ...
　repeat that
　repetir isto　he·pe·teerr ees·to
　speak more slowly
　falar mais devagar　fa·larr mais de·va·garr
　write it down
　escrever num papel　es·kre·verr noom pa·pel

NUMBERS

0	zero	ze·ro
1	um	oom
2	dois	doys
3	três	tres

4	quatro	kwa·tro
5	cinco	seen·ko
6	seis	says
7	sete	se·te
8	oito	oy·to
9	nove	naw·ve
10	dez	dez
11	onze	ong·ze
12	doze	do·ze
13	treze	tre·ze
14	quatorze	ka·torr·ze
15	quinze	keen·ze
16	dezesseis	de·ze·says
17	dezesete	de·ze·se·te
18	dezoito	de·zoy·to
19	dezenove	de·ze·naw·ve
20	vinte	veen·te
21	vinte e um	veen·te e oom
22	vinte e dois	veen·te e doys
30	trinta	treen·ta
40	quarenta	kwa·ren·ta
50	cinquenta	seen·kwen·ta
60	sessenta	se·seng·ta
70	setenta	se·teng·ta
80	oitenta	oy·teng·ta
90	noventa	no·veng·ta
100	cem	seng
200	duzentos	doo·zeng·tos
1000	mil	mee·oo

QUESTION WORDS

Who?
Quem? — keng

What?
(O) Que? — (o) ke

When?
Quando? — kwang·do

Where?
Onde? — ong·de

Why?
Por que? — porr ke

Which/What?
Qual/Quais? (sg/pl) — kwow/kais

SHOPPING & SERVICES

I'd like to buy ...
Gostaria de comprar ... — gos·ta·ree·a de kom·prarr ...

I'm just looking.
Estou só olhando. — es·to so o·lyan·do

May I look at it?
Posso ver? — po·so verr

How much?
Quanto? — kwan·to

That's too expensive.
Está muito caro. — es·ta mweeng·to ka·ro

ON THE BEACH

I can't swim.	Eu não sei nadar.
Can I swim here?	Posso nadar aqui?
Is it safe to swim here?	É seguro nadar aqui?
What time is high/ low tide?	A que horas será a maré alta/baixa?
How's the surf?	Como estão as ondas?
Where's a good place to surf?	Onde tem um bom lugar para surfar?
beach	praia
beach towel	toalha de praia
coast	costa
lifeguard	salva-vidas
rock	pedra
sand	areia
sea	mar
sunblock	protetor solar
wave	onda

Can you lower the price?
Pode baixar o preço? — po·de ba·sharr o pre·so

Do you have something cheaper?
Tem uma coisa mais barata? — teng oo·ma koy·za mais ba·ra·ta

I'll give you (five reals).
Dou (cinco reais). — do (seen·ko he·ais)

I don't like it.
Não gosto. — nowng gos·to

I'll take it.
Vou levar isso. — vo le·var ee·so

Where is ...?
Onde fica ...? — on·de fee·ka ...

an ATM
um caixa automático — oom kai·sha ow·to·ma·tee·ko

a bank
o banco — o ban·ko

a bookstore
uma livraria — oo ma lee vra ree a

the ... embassy
a embaixada do/da ... — a eng bai sha da do/da

a foreign-exchange office
uma loja de câmbio — oo·ma lo·zha de kam·bee·o

a market
o mercado — o merr·ka·do

the police station
a delegacia de polícia — a de·le·ga·see·a de po·lee·see·a

a pharmacy/chemist
uma farmácia — oo·ma far·ma·sya

the post office
o correio — o co·hay·o

a supermarket
o supermercado   o soo·perr·merr·*ka*·do
the tourist office
a secretaria de turismo   a se·kre·ta·*ree*·a de too·*rees*·mo
a laundrette
uma lavanderia   oo·ma la·vang·de·*ree*·a

less	*menos*	*me*·nos
more	*mais*	mais
large	*grande*	*grang*·de
small	*pequeno/a*	pe·*ke*·no/a

What time does ... open?
A que horas abre ...?   a ke *aw*·ras *a*·bre ...
Do you have any others?
Você tem outros?   vo·se teng o·tros
How many?
Quantos/Quantas? (m/f)   kwan·tos/kwan·tas

Do you accept ...?
Vocês aceitam ...?   vo·ses a·*say*·tam ...
  credit cards
  cartão de crédito   karr·*towng* de kre·dee·to
  traveler's cheques
  traveler cheques   tra·ve·ler *she*·kes

letter
uma carta   oo·ma *karr*·ta
parcel
uma encomenda   oo·ma eng·ko·*meng*·da

I want to buy ...
Quero comprar ...   *ke*·ro kom·*prarr* ...
  an aerogram
  um aerograma   oom a·e·ro·*gra*·ma
  an envelope
  um envelope   oom eng·ve·*lo*·pe
  a phone card
  um cartão telefônico   oom kar·*towng* te·le·*fo*·nee·ko
  a postcard
  um cartão-postal   oom karr·*towng* pos·*tow*
  stamps
  selos   se·los

Where can I ...?
Onde posso ...?   on·de *po*·so ...
  change a traveler's cheque
  trocar traveler cheques   tro·*karr* tra·ve·*ler* she·kes
  change money
  trocar dinheiro   tro·*kar* dee·*nyay*·ro
  check my email
  checar meu e-mail   she·*karr* me·oo e·mail
  get Internet access
  ter acesso à internet   terr a·*se*·so a een·terr·*ne*·tee

TIME & DATES
What time is it?
Que horas são?   ke *aw*·ras sowng
It's (ten) o'clock.
São (dez) horas.   sowng (des) *aw*·ras

now	*agora*	a·*go*·ra
this morning	*esta manhã*	es·ta ma·*nyang*
this afternoon	*esta tarde*	es·ta *tarr*·de
today	*hoje*	*o*·zhe
tonight	*hoje à noite*	*o*·zhe a *noy*·te
tomorrow	*amanhã*	a·ma·*nyang*
yesterday	*ontem*	*on*·teng

Monday	*segunda-feira*	se·*goon*·da·fay·ra
Tuesday	*terça-feira*	terr·sa·fay·ra
Wednesday	*quarta-feira*	kwarr·ta·fay·ra
Thursday	*quinta-feira*	keen·ta·fay·ra
Friday	*sexta-feira*	ses·ta·fay·ra
Saturday	*sábado*	*sa*·ba·doo
Sunday	*domingo*	do·*meen*·go

January	*janeiro*	zha·*nay*·ro
February	*fevereiro*	fe·ve·*ray*·ro
March	*março*	*marr*·so
April	*abril*	a·*bree*·oo
May	*maio*	*ma*·yo
June	*junho*	*zhoo*·nyo
July	*julho*	*zhoo*·lyo
August	*agosto*	a·*gos*·to
September	*setembro*	se·*teng*·bro
October	*outubro*	o·*too*·bro
November	*novembro*	no·*veng*·bro
December	*dezembro*	de·*zeng*·bro

TRANSPORT
Public Transport

Which ... goes	*Qual o ... que*	kwoo o ... ke
to ...?	*vai para ...?*	vai *pa*·ra ...
boat	*barco*	*barr*·ko
bus	*ônibus*	*o*·nee·boos
city/local bus	*ônibus local*	*o*·nee·boos lo·*kow*
ferry	*balsa*	*bal*·sa
inter-city bus	*ônibus inter-*	*o*·nee·boos een-
	urbano	terr oorr·*ba*·no
plane	*avião*	a·vee·*owng*
train	*trem*	treng

When's the ...	*Quando sai o ...*	kwang·do sai o ...
(bus)?	*(ônibus)?*	(*o*·nee·boos)
first	*primeiro*	pree·*may*·ro
last	*último*	*ool*·tee·mo
next	*próximo*	*pro*·see·mo

JUNGLE EXCURSIONS

Does the tour include ...?
A excursão inclui ...?
Will we sleep in hammocks?
Iremos dormir em redes?
What is the breakdown of costs?
Como é dividido o custo?
Is the water level high or low?
O nível das águas esta alto ou baixo?
Does the boat have lifejackets?
O barco tem coletes salva-vidas?
How long does it take to get there?
Quanto tempo leva para chegar lá?
Can we shop for food together?
Podemos ir comprar comida juntos?
Do you have fishing gear?
Você tem equipamento de pesca?
Is it safe to go there?
É seguro ir lá?
Will we see animals?
Iremos ver animais?

Are there ...?	*Existem lá ...?*
dangerous animals	*animais perigosos*
spiders	*aranhas*
lots of mosquitos	*muitos pernilongos*
accommodations	*alojamento*
canoe	*canoa*
food/drinks	*comida/bebida*
fuel	*combustível*
guides	*guias*
jungle	*selva; mata; floresta*
tree	*arvore*

What time does it leave?
Que horas sai?   ke *aw*·ras sai
What time does it get to (Paraty)?
Que horas chega   ke *aw*·ras *she*·ga
em (Paraty)?   eng (pa·*ra*·tee)

A ... ticket	*Uma passagem*	*oo*·ma pa·*sa*·zhem
to (...)	*de ... para (...)*	de ... *pa*·ra (...)
1st-class	*primeira classe*	pree·*may*·ra *kla*·se
2nd-class	*segunda classe*	se·*goon*·da *kla*·se
one-way	*ida*	*ee*·da
round-trip	*ida e volta*	*ee*·da e *vol*·ta

How much is it?
Quanto é?   *kwan*·to e
Is this the bus to ...?
Este ônibus vai para ...?   es·te *o*·nee·boos vai *pa*·ra ...?
Do I need to change?
Preciso trocar de trem?   pre·*see*·so tro·*karr* de treng

the luggage check room
o balcão de guarda   o bal·*kowng* de *gwarr*·da
volumes   vo·*loo*·me
a luggage locker
um guarda volume   oom *gwarr*·da vo·*loo*·me
Is this taxi free?
Este táxi está livre?   es·te *tak*·see es·ta *lee*·vre
Please put the meter on.
Por favor ligue o   porr fa·*vorr lee*·ge o
taxímetro.   tak·*see*·me·tro
How much is it to ...?
Quanto custa até ...?   *kwan*·to *koos*·ta a·te ...
Please take me to (this address).
Me leve para este   me *le*·ve *pa*·ra es·te en·de·*re*·so
endereço por favor.   porr fa·*vorr*

Private Transport

I'd like to hire	*Gostaria de*	gos·ta·*ree*·a de
a/an ...	*alugar ...*	a·loo·*garr* ...
4WD	*um quatro*	oom *kwa*·tro
	por quatro	por *kwa*·tro
bicycle	*uma bicicleta*	*oo*·ma bee·see·*kle*·ta
car	*um carro*	oom *ka*·ho
motorbike	*uma motocicleta*	*oo*·ma mo·to·see·*kle*·ta

Is this the road to ...?
Esta é a estrada para ...?   es·ta e a es·*tra*·da *pa*·ra
(How long) Can I park here?
(Quanto tempo) Posso   (*kwan*·to *teng*·po) *po*·so
estacionar aqui?   es·ta·see·o·*narr* a·*kee*
Where's a gas/petrol station?
Onde tem um posto   *on*·de teng oom *pos*·to
de gasolina?   de ga·zo·*lee*·na
Please fill it up.
Enche o tanque, por   *en*·she o *tan*·ke porr
favor.   fa·*vorr*
I'd like ... liters.
Coloque ... litros.   ko·*lo*·ke ... *lee*·tros

diesel	*diesel*	*dee*·sel
LPG	*gás*	gas
ethanol	*álcool*	*ow*·kol
unleaded	*gasolina comum*	ga·zo·*lee*·na ko·*moon*

The (car/motorbike) has broken down at ...
(O carro/A motocicleta) quebrou em ...
(o ka·ho/a mo·to·se·*kle*·ta) ke·*bro* eng ...
The car won't start.
O carro não está pegando.
o *ka*·ho nowng es·ta pe·*gang*·do
I need a mechanic.
Preciso de um mecânico.
pre·*see*·so de oom me·*ka*·nee·ko

ROAD SIGNS

Entrada	Entrance
Estrada dê Preferência	Give Way
Mão Única	One-way
Pare	Stop
Pedágio	Toll
Proibido Entrar	No Entry
Rua Sem Saída	Dead End
Saída	Freeway Exit

I've run out of gas/petrol.
Estou sem gasolina.
es·*to* seng ga·zo·*lee*·na

I've had an accident.
Sofri um acidente.
so·*free* oom a·see·*den*·te

TRAVEL WITH CHILDREN

I need (a/an) ...
Preciso de ...
pre·*see*·zo de ...

Do you have (a/an) ...?
Aqui tem ...?
a·*kee* teng

baby change room
uma sala para trocar   oo·ma *sa*·la *pa*·ra tro·*karr*
bebê   be·*be*

baby seat
um assento de criança   oom a·*seng*·to de kree·*an*·sa
booster seat
um assento de elevaçã   oom a·*seng*·to de e·le·va·*sowng*
child-minding service
um serviço de babá   oom serr·*vee*·so de ba·*ba*
children's menu
um cardápio para   oom kar·*da*·pee·o *pa*·ra
criança   kree·*an*·sa
(English-speaking) babysitter
uma babá   oo·ma ba·*ba*
(que fale ingles)   (ke *fa*·le een·*gles*)
formula (milk)
leite em pó (para bebê)   *lay*·te (pa·ra be·*be*)
highchair
uma cadeira de criança   oo·ma ka·*day*·ra de kree·*an*·sa
potty
um troninho   oom tro·*nee*·nyo
pusher/stroller
um carrinho de bebê   oom ka·*hee*·nyo de be·*be*
(disposable) nappies/diapers
fraldas (descartáveis)   *frow*·das (des·karr·*ta*·vays)

Do you mind if I breast-feed here?
Você se importa se eu amamentar aqui?
vo·*se* se eeng·*porr*·ta se e·oo a·ma·meng·*tarr* a·*kee*
Are children allowed?
É permitida a entrada de crianças?
e perr·mee·*tee*·da a eng·*tra*·da de kree·*an*·sas

lonely planet   phrasebooks

Brazilian
Portuguese

with 2000-word two-way dictionary

Also available from Lonely Planet:
Brazilian Portuguese Phrasebook

LANGUAGE

Glossary

For a glossary of food and drink items, see p103.

abandonados – abandoned children

afoxé – music of Bahia, which has strong African rhythms and close ties to *Candomblé*

albergue – lodging house or hostel

albergue da juventude – youth hostel

aldeia – originally a village built by Jesuits to convert Indians to Christianity; now the term for any small, usually Indian, village

andar – walk; also a floor of a multistory building

apartamento – hotel room with a private bathroom

apelido – nickname

arara – macaw

artesanato – handcrafted workmanship

ayahuasca – hallucinogenic drink

azulejos – Portuguese ceramic tiles with a distinctive blue glaze, often seen in churches

babaçu – versatile palm tree that is the basis of the rural economy in Maranhão

bairro – district

bandeirantes – bands of 17th- and 18th-century roaming adventurers who explored the vast Brazilian interior while searching for gold and Indians to enslave; typically born of an Indian mother and a Portuguese father

banzo – a slave's profound longing for the African homeland, which often resulted in a 'slow withering away' and death

barraca – any stall or hut, including food and drink stands common at beaches, parks etc

bateria – rhythm section of a band, including the enormous ones in samba parades

beija-flor – literally 'flower kisser'; hummingbird; also the name of Rio's most famous samba school

berimbau – musical instrument that accompanies *capoeira*

bilheteria – ticket office

bloco – large group, usually numbering in the hundreds, of singing or drumming Carnaval revelers in costume, organized around a neighborhood or theme

boate – nightclub with a dance floor, sometimes featuring strippers; also boîte

bogó – leather water pouch typical of the *sertão*

bonde – cable car, tram or trolley

bossa nova – music that mixes North American jazz with Brazilian influences

boteco – small, open-air bar

boto – freshwater dolphin of the Amazon

Bumba Meu Boi – the most important festival in Maranhão, a rich folkloric event that revolves around a Carnavalesque dance/procession

bunda – African word for buttocks

caatinga – scrub vegetation of the *sertão*

Caboclo – literally 'copper-colored'; person of mixed Caucasian and Indian ancestry

cachoeira – waterfall

camisa-de-Vênus – literally 'shirt of Venus'; condom; also *camisinha*

camisinha – condom

Candomblé – Afro-Brazilian religion of Bahia

cangaceiros – legendary bandits of the *sertão*

capitania hereditária – hereditary province or estate

capivara – capybara; the world's largest rodent, which looks like a large guinea pig and lives in the Pantanal

Capixaba – resident of Espírito Santo state

capoeira – martial art/dance developed by the slaves of Bahia

capongas – freshwater lagoon

Carioca – resident of Rio de Janeiro

cartão telefônico – phonecard

casa de câmbio – money-exchange office

casa grande – big house or plantation owner's mansion

casal – married couple; also a double bed

castanha – brazil nut

chapada – tableland or plateau that divides a river basin

churrascaria – restaurant featuring barbecued meat

cidades históricas – historic colonial towns

Círio de Nazaré – Brazil's largest religious festival, which takes place in Belém

cobra – any snake

comunidade – community

coronel – literally 'colonel'; rural landowner who typically controlled the local political, judicial and police systems; any powerful person

correio – post office

delegacia de polícia – police station

embolada – Brazilian rap in which singers trade off verbal jests, teasing and joking with the audience, most common at Northeastern fairs

Embratur – Brazilian Tourist Board

engenho – sugar mill or sugar plantation

escolas de samba – large samba clubs that compete in the annual Carnaval parade

estalagem – inn
estância hidromineral – spa, hot springs
estrangeiro – foreigner
Exú – spirit that serves as messenger between the gods and humans in Afro-Brazilian religions

fantasia – Carnavalesque costume
favela – slum, shantytown
favelado – resident of a *favela*
fazenda – ranch or farm, usually a large landholding; also cloth, fabric
fazendeiro – estate owner
feira – produce market
ferroviária – railway station
festa – party
ficha – token; machines that take tokens, rather than coins
fidalgos – gentry
figa – good-luck charm representing a clenched fist with the thumb between the index and middle fingers
Filhos de Gandhi – Bahia's most famous Carnaval *bloco*
fio dental – literally 'dental floss'; Brazil's famous skimpy bikini
Flamengo – Rio's most popular football team; also one of Rio's most populated areas
Fluminense – native of Rio state; also the football team that is *Flamengo's* main rival
forró – popular music of the Northeast, recently enjoying a wave of nationwide popularity
frevo – fast-paced, popular music from Pernambuco
frigobar – minibar
Funai – Fundação Nacional do Indio; government Indian agency
Fusca – Volkswagen Beetle, Brazil's most popular car
futebol – football
futevôlei – volleyball played without hands

gafieira – dance hall
garimpeiro – prospector or miner; originally an illegal diamond prospector
garimpo – mining camp
gaúcho – cowboy of southern Brazil
gíria – slang
gringo – foreigner or person with light hair and complexion; can even refer to light-skinned Brazilians
gruta – grotto or cavern
guaraná – Amazonian shrub whose berry is a stimulant; also a popular soft drink

hidrovia – aquatic freeway
hidroviária – boat terminal
hospedagem – cheap boardinghouse used by locals

lemanjá – Afro-Brazilian goddess of the sea
igapó – flooded Amazon forest
igarapé – creek or small river in Amazonia
igreja – church
ilha – island
INPA – Instituto Nacional de Pesquisas Amazonia; national agency for research on the Amazon

jaburú – jabiru; a giant white stork of the Pantanal with a black head and a red band on its neck
jacaré – alligator or caiman
jangada – beautiful sailboat of the Northeast
jangadeiros – crews who use *jangadas*
jeito or jeitinho – possibly the most Brazilian expression, both a feeling and a form of action; from dar um jeito, meaning 'to find a way to get something done,' no matter how seemingly impossible, even if the solution may not be completely orthodox or legal
jogo de bicho – a popular lottery in which each number is represented by an animal; technically illegal but played on every street corner by all Brazilians
Jogo dos Búzios – Casting of Shells; type of fortune-telling performed by a *pai* or *mãe de santo*

ladrão – thief
lavrador – peasant, small farmer or landless farmworker
leito – sleeping berth
literatura de cordel – literally 'string literature'; popular literature of the Northeast
litoral – coastal region

machista – male chauvinist
mãe de santo – female Afro-Brazilian spiritual leader
malandro do morro – vagabond; scoundrel from the hills; a popular figure in Rio's mythology
maloca – Indian dwelling
mameluco – offspring of a White father and Indian mother
Maracanã – Rio's soccer stadium
mercado – market
mestiço – a person of mixed Indian and European parentage
Mineiro – resident of Minas Gerais
miúdo – change
mocambo – community of runaway slaves; small version of a *quilombo*
moço/a – waiter or other service industry worker
morro – hill; also a person or culture of the *favelas*
mulato/a – person of mixed Black and European parentage

novela – soap opera; Brazil's most popular TV shows
NS – Nosso Senhor (Our Lord) or Nossa Senhora (Our Lady)

O Globo – Brazil's biggest media empire, with the prime national TV station and several newspapers and magazines

orixá – deity of the Afro-Brazilian religions

pagode – popular samba music

pai de santo – male spiritual leader in Afro-Brazilian religions

pajé – shaman, witch doctor

palácio – palace or large government building

palafita – stilt or a house built on stilts

pampas – grassy plains of the interior of southern Brazil

parque nacional – national park

pau brasil – now-scarce brazilwood tree; a red dye made from the tree that was the colony's first commodity

Paulista – resident of São Paulo state

Paulistano – resident of São Paulo city

PCB – Communist Party of Brazil

pensão – guesthouse

pistoleiro – gun-toting henchman

posseiro – squatter

posta restante – poste restante

posto – post; lifeguard posts along Rio de Janeiro's beaches, used as names for different sections of beach

posto de gasolina – a gas (petrol) station

posto telefônico – telephone office

pousada – guesthouse

praça – plaza or town square

praia – beach

prefeitura – city or town hall

PT – Partido dos Trabalhadores (Worker's Party); Brazil's newest and most radical political party

quarto – hotel room without a bathroom

quente – hot

quilombo – community of runaway slaves

Quimbanda – black magic

rápido – fast

real – Brazil's unit of currency since 1994; plural reais

rede – hammock

rio – river

rodoferroviária – bus and train station

rodoviária – bus station

s/n – abbreviation for sem número (without number) used in some street addresses

sambista – samba composer or dancer

sambódromo – street with tiers of seating built for samba parades

senzala – slave quarters

serra – mountain range

Sertanejo – resident of the *sertão*

sertão – the drought-prone backlands of the Northeast

shopping – shopping mall

telefonista internacional – international telephone operator

Terra da Vera Cruz – Land of the True Cross; the original Portuguese name for Brazil

terreiro – Afro-Brazilian house of worship

travessa – lane

travesti – transvestite; a popular figure throughout Brazil, considered by some to be the national symbol

trem – train

trio elétrico – three-pronged electrical outlet; electrically amplified bands that play atop trucks

troco – change

tropicalismo – important cultural movement centered in Bahia in the late 1960s

Tupi – Indian people and language that predominated along the coast at the time of the European invasion

Umbanda – white magic, a mixture of Candomblé and spiritism

vaqueiro – cowboy of the Northeast

várzea – Amazonian floodplain

violeiros – guitarists and guitar makers

zona da mata – bushland just inside the *litoral* in the Northeastern states

Behind the Scenes

THIS BOOK

This is the 6th edition of *Brazil*. Regis St. Louis served as coordinating author, writing the majority of the front and back chapters as well as the Rio de Janeiro city chapter. Ginger Adams Otis covered the remainder of the Southeast. Gary Prado Chandler covered the Amazon, and Andrew Draffen wrote the Central West section. Molly Green researched Bahia and Sergipe & Alagoas, while Thomas Kohnstamm covered the rest of the Northeast, plus the Environment chapter. Robert Landon wrote the South section and the Food & Drink chapter. Tom Phillips contributed the History chapter, and Dr David Goldberg MD wrote the Health chapter. The 5th edition was written by John Noble (coordinating author), Andrew Draffen, Robyn Jones, Chris McAsey and Leonardo Pinheiro.

THANKS from the Authors

Regis St. Louis At Lonely Planet I'd like to thank Wendy Smith. It was a pleasure working under such a distinguished editor, and I wish her all the best in future endeavors. I also thank Erin Corrigan, Kathleen Munnelly and the rest of the LP team for all their hard work. In Brazil, I owe a big thanks to Carina for her many introductions and showing me around the city, Alissa and Akemi for fashion tips and cunning insight into Rio's best restaurants, Beatriz for her extensive tips on all things Carioca, Damian for his cooking skills, Rodolfo and friends for showing off Ilha Grande, and Carmen and Fabio for introducing me to Lapa's best *gafieiras* (dance halls). Thanks also to Yolanda, Fernanda, João, Juliana, Claudio, Hans and Molly, all of whom helped

to elucidate the admirable Carioca philosophy. In the US, *abraços* (hugs) to Mom, France, Justine and Cassandra for their invaluable support throughout this project.

Gary Prado Chandler Thank you, first and foremost, to the hundreds of Brazilians whose expertise, patience and goodwill made researching the Amazon chapters possible (not to mention a lot of fun). I was equally well-received in the border towns of Colombia, Bolivia and Venezuela – thank you to the people I spoke with there. I am especially grateful to Gero Mesquita of Gero's Tours in Manaus for his invaluable and ever-friendly assistance, and to Wilson Castro of Iguana Tours in Manaus, Gabriel Paduano of Amazon Planet in Alter do Chão and Rodrigo Zomkowski Ozorio at the Instituto Mamirauá in Tefé. Thank you (and good luck) to Wendy Smith, who has helped me on this path in more ways than one. Love and thanks to my wonderful and happily expansive family: Mom, Ellen, Dad, Elyse, Joey, Sue, Katy and Kyle, and to Walter, Alma, Doñas Trini and Tina, David, Javier, Debbie and the little guys, who welcomed me home and put up with me while I was unshowered, unshorn and crashing on deadline (again!). And thank you, above all, to my brilliant and beautiful wife, Liza, the best thing that ever happened to me and the first and last person I think of every day.

Molly Green I'd like to warmly thank boat captain Alexandre (Caraíva), artist Vitor Machado (Trancoso), barman Charlie (Arraial d'Ajuda), wise

---

THE LONELY PLANET STORY

The story begins with a classic travel adventure: Tony and Maureen Wheeler's 1972 journey across Europe and Asia to Australia. There was no useful information about the overland trail then, so Tony and Maureen published the first Lonely Planet guidebook to meet a growing need.

From a kitchen table, Lonely Planet has grown to become the largest independent travel publisher in the world, with offices in Melbourne (Australia), Oakland (USA) and London (UK). Today Lonely Planet guidebooks cover the globe. There is an ever-growing list of books and information in a variety of media. Some things haven't changed. The main aim is still to make it possible for adventurous travelers to get out there – to explore and better understand the world.

At Lonely Planet we believe travelers can make a positive contribution to the countries they visit – if they respect their host communities and spend their money wisely. Every year 5% of company profit is donated to charities around the world.

woman Telma (Arraial d'Ajuda), taxi drivers Hestiveyrrevy Marino Guaster and his father Chico (Porto Seguro), guide Alexandre (Itacaré), church guide Eduardo (Salvador), hotel owners Jani (Lençóis) and Ada (Pontal de Coruripe), and desk man Enildo Paulo da Silva (Barra de São Miguel) for their help, tips, conversation and companionship. Thanks also to Gigi, Bruno and Manny (Praia do Francês) for retrieving my pack when I was too sick to do it myself, and Cacai and co (Maceió) for the birthday cake and living room samba. *Obrigadão* (big thank you) to Lêlê Alvares for opening up her apartment and the city of Salvador for me, to Guillermo for the insight, to Yoav for always making Rio 'the best', and to Guilherme, Claudine, Vinny, Freddy, Diogo, Marcelo, Moacir, Deivide and Marcinho for the hang time. Thanks to every unsuspecting traveler who divulged great tips, my family and others who thought what I was doing was cool, and to the previous authors. I couldn't have survived the write-up without the distraction and friendship of Mestre Railson, Buddha, Cisa and the rest of the Capoeira Sul da Bahia crew.

Thomas Kohnstamm At LP, I'd like to thank Erin Corrigan, Kathleen Munnelly, Danielle North, Helen Christinis, Wendy Smith, Cathy Lanigan and Regis St. Louis. I'd also like to thank all of the usual suspects: my family and friends for support and encouragement. And I must not forget Greg Norrell for Noronha advice and for hooking me up with a R$50 cab ride, Oded Shlezinger 'the world's biggest Israeli *forró* fan' for the impromptu beach party, Nicky Keyes for coffee, Mason Bragg and Oliver Hill for hospitality while I was writing, Jacob Maraya and David Simpson for tech assistance, Andrew Draffen for his work on the chapters over the years and Mindy Troutman.

Robert Landon Thanks to Paulo Bellot, who kept me well fed – including quantity, quality and variety – during the writing process. An *obrigadão* to Ann Williams for her Brazilian-style reception in São Paulo. Notice is also due to Manuel Beja, who patiently joined me for part of the research and invited me to housesit during much of the writing. For her recommendation, many thanks to Michele Posner, and for her trust in Michele's opinion, Wendy Smith. Other worthies include Anamaria Mendes de Assis, Leland Haskins, Pedro Rojas, Jorge Kuraiem, Norma Suely, Rodrigo Moraes, Valeria da Silva, and Valerio Antoniol. Thanks to my mother for joining me in Rio, and to my father for almost doing so. And finally there is Carlos Ponce, who fed the kitties during my long absence.

Ginger Adams Otis Thanks to all the Lonely Planet writers who blazed the trail before me. As always, their excellent work set the standard for me on this project. Thank you to the team at Lonely Planet, especially Erin Corrigan, Wendy Smith, Kathleen Munnelly and Regis St. Louis. I owe a huge debt of gratitude to Luis Nogueira, who has graciously hosted me many times in São Paulo. To the many, many Brazilians who helped me along the way, a big *obrigada*. And to Michael, Didem, Sinem and all my friends and family, a heartfelt thank you.

CREDITS

This title was commissioned and developed in Lonely Planet's Oakland office by Wendy Smith. Kathleen Munnelly assessed the book. Cartography for this guide was developed by Alison Lyall. Production was coordinated in Melbourne by Helen Christinis and Danielle North (editorial), Celia Wood and Jack Gavran (cartography), and John Shippick (color and layout). Overseeing production were Chris Love (project manager) and Alison Lyall (managing cartographer).

Andrew Bain, Jackey Coyle, Victoria Harrison, Kim Hutchins, Nancy Ianni, Thalia Kalkipsakis, Emma Koch, Suzannah Shwer, Gina Tsarouhas, Gabbi Wilson and Meg Worby provided editorial assistance. Cartographic assistance was provided by Louise Klep, Valentina Kremenchutskaya, Emma McNicol, Jacqui Saunders, Kelly Stanhope, Chris Thomas and Natasha Velleley, with map checking by Daniel Fennessy. Steven Cann, Laura Jane and Wibowo Rusli assisted with layout.

The language chapter was prepared by Quentin Frayne. The cover was designed by James Hardy, and Yukiyoshi Kamimura did the cover artwork.

THANKS from Lonely Planet

Many thanks to the following travelers who used the last edition and wrote to us with helpful hints, useful advice and interesting anecdotes.

A Theodore Abbond, Timon Abels, Áurea Abrantes, Murray & Lynda Adams, Sandi Addison, Tolani Adeboye, Daniel Adorno, Clare Agent, Joao Aguilera Junior, Imran Ahmed, Jochen Ahrens, Guilherme Albagli de Almeida, Fatima Albino, Ariel Albrecht, Marcelo Alexandre, Sebastian Alkofer, Arun Allen, Wayne Allen, Marcos Amatucci, Susan Amaya, Sara Amina Sultan, Clare Anderson, Marieke Anthonisse, Patrik Aqvist, Andrés Arango, Christina Arnet, John W Arnold, Alasdair Arthur, Liz Ashton, Jörg Ausfelt, Joe Avarne, Martin Aveling, Gloria Ayres **B** Roman Baba, Roman Baedorf, Serena Baehler, Borut Bajzelj, Jonathan Baker, Mark Baker, Joeri Baldinger, Davis Bales, Christian Balzer, Michael Baran, David Barriere, Andre Barth, Christian Bass, Barbara Bauer, Florian Bauer, Jenna Baum, Joachim Behrmann, Frank Belczyk, Gabrielle & Hilbert Belksma-Rutten, Samantha Bellamy, Luca Bellintani, Erin Bennion, David Berry, John Bessant, Johan Bexelius, Colin J Biggs, Erick Bijlsma, Christopher Blakeley, Pascal Blaser, Avram Blum, Michael T Bohndorf, Tor Even Bole, Michael Boller, Paul Bonavia, Stephane Bone, Erick Bonnard, Luci Bonner, Nick Borg, John Borgo, Dirk Borowski, Arnaud Bos, Nena Bourgaize, Monica Bouwer, Bernice Bovenkerk, L Bowers, Richard Bowers, Benjamin Boye, Nick Boyle, Renata Bradford, Kendal Bradley, Heath Bradshaw, Tom Brailsford, Michael Brandenburgsky, Rodrigo Brasil, Jeremy Bray, Benno Breitenmoser, T Brenan, John Breski, Karel Brevet, Martin Brewerton, She Rise Bright, Claire Brissenden, Christopher Brown, Heather Brown, K Brumwell, Dean Bubley, Quentin & Nicky Buckingham, Yasmin & Ricardo Buitinga, Karen Bullen, Jan Burgmans, Tony Burson, Joel Burstyner, Mike Buser, Andrea A Byck **C** Matteo Calabresi, Renee Callaghan, Suzanne Cameron, Daniel Cane, Adam Canter, Sally Cantrell, Luca & Ann-Christin Cardholm, Francine Cardinal, Gavin Carey, Nick Carney, Arnaud Caron, Henry Carson, Franco Caruso, Mauricio Carvalho, Nicola Cauchy, Larissa Cavalheiro, Moira Cayetano, Adriana Caznoch Kurten, Deborah Chaffe, Parth Chanda, Brandyn Chapman, Jim Chappell, Denton Chase, Rodrigo Chaves, Alexandra M Chciuk-Celt, Matthew Chell, Chris Childs, Claudia Cho, Frank Chou, Thomas Clement Christensen, Willi Christiansen, Helene Clappaz, Austin Clayton, Elisa Clemson, Jason Clemson, Karel Coenen, Galit Cohen, Niv Cohen, Ralph Colbert, Ruth Collinge, Stephen Collins, Elena Como, Paul & Lisa Conroy, Lucy Cooke, Ron Coolen, Edward & Cathy Cooper, Rob Cooper, Brandi Copher, Paula Cormack, Renae Cosgrove, Marianna Costa, Chris Courtheyn, Paul Cousins, Nicko Coxon, Mike Crisp, Tim Crockett, Heloisa Cunha, Frank Curzon-Hobson **D** Sandra da Conceicao Fontinha, Sergio Da Gatta, Ninna Dalgaard, Vincent D'Angelo, Ann Dannemann, Diane Darrach, Robert D'Avanzo, Phill Day, Tolga Dayibas, Walter de Boef, Laura de Carvalho, Barbara De Fruytier, Ignacio de la Vega, Gaspard de Laaf, Koen De Rijcke, Katrien de Ruyter, Johnathan Dean, Edo Dekel, Peter & Nicole Dekkers, Aaron De La Garza, Joseph Deleonardo, Philippe Delhaise, Christine Devane, Stephanie Dew, Jeffrey Dhont, Andrea Di Napoli, Ian C Dickinson, Andrea Dijkstra, William Dinwoodie, Corrine Dipple, Markus Doebele, Jeff Doolittle, Sandra Dos Santos, Luis Eduardo & Luciana Dosso, Naomi Douglas, Dan Dragonetti, Darcelle Dumas, Jacob Dutilh, Nicole Dyer **E** Andy Eagleton, Todd Edgar, Roger Paul Edmonds, Carolann Edwards, Sylvia Edwards, Gerd & Maria Egner, Roland Ehrat, Jimena Elias, Paula Elias, Katrin Eliasson, Sarina Rita Eliyakim, Ian Elliott, Carol Ellis, Rolf J Ellmers, Gerhard Enzenberger, Kit Erickson, Magnus Eriksson, Susan Erk, Steven Espindola, Niebla Estival, Ruth Ettl, Sheila Eustace, Don Evans, Sara & Yonatan Eyal **F** Fyaz Faisal, Paddy Farrell, Lisa Fawcett, Mary Feher, Angelo Fenili, Gabrielle Fennessy, B Fenton, Sara Fernandez, Charles Feros, Andreas Fertin, Knut Andre Fiddan, Ingrid Firmhofer, Peter Fiske, Jon Fitzgerald, Henrik Flamink, Christopher Flynn, Robert Fogelnest, Kennet & Pernille Föh, Daniel Fortier, Neil Foster, Damian Francabandiera, Jonathan France, Filipe Franco, Bart Franken, Marion Freijsen, Marcia Freire Cavalcante, Felix Freist, Bettina Freyland, Burghard Fritzsch, Rüdiger Fürll, Eugene Fytche **G** Nienke Gaastra, Linus Gabrielsson, Carlos Gagliardi, Markus Gajer, Katharina Gallauer, Margaret Gallery, Jason Gamble, Michelle Gansmann, Michelle Gansmann, Kier Garcia, Monique Gardien, Donovan Garnett, Loredana Gatt, Christiane Gaul, Bernd Genser, Pascal Gerber, Flavio Germano Petry, Will Gibson, Nathalie Gilgenkrantz, John Gillis, Nick Gilroy,

Merel Gilsing, Michael Gleeson, Marko Globocnik, Marko Gnann, Jutta Gnilsen, David Gochman, Alexandre Godard, Anna-Liisa Goggs, Ricardo Gomes, Emilio Gómez Membrillera, Vanessa Gorecki, Anthony Gorella, Leonardo Filipe Goulart, Roberta Graham, Doug Graiver, Yvonne Gramsch, Rachel Grant, Asger Grarup, Moses Graubard, John P Graven, Kristoffer Gravgaard, Giorgio Grazzini, Chris Green, Kate Green, Michael Griffey, Liz Grime, Ana Lidia Guerra, Humberto Guerrero, Paul Gurn, Diego Gutierrez **H** Joachim Haas, Moshe Haber, Katje Haeussler, Louise Hall, Jenni Hamara, Leon Hamui, Bas Hangmatten, Fred Hanson, Tim Harcourt, Rachel Hardisky, Aaron B Harnett, Eugenie Harper, Samantha Harrison, Michael Hartmann, Haavard Haugen, Markus Hauk, Michel Heemskerk, Pieter Heesterbeek, Peter & Rosemarie Heinig, Kris Hellebuyck, Petter Hellstrom, Susan Henderson, Jay Henning, Tom Henry, Carla Heyworth, Jesus Hidalgo, Alex Hijmans, Belinda Hill, Steve Hill, W Hill, Kay Hinchsliffe, Amir Hindie, Andre Hintermann, Tamara Hocherl, Kate Hoel, Merete Hoel, Christoph Hoffmann, Anders Hofset, Debby & Jim Hogan, Michele Holdener, Roos Hollenberg, Pierre Hollinger, Karen S Hollweg, Moriah Hoover, Ned Hopkins, Bjorn Horlin, Pat & Chris Horton, Steven Houben, Bryan Houck, Alex Howarth, Damien Huffer, Elaine & John Hughes, Janina Humke, Michaela Hümmer, David M Hunt, Kim Hunter, Cristian Huse, Eva Huthoefer, Francoise Hutton, Victor Hwang **I** Trebor Iksrazal, Hana Inai, Peter Ingerfeld, Rebecca Irani, Jeremy Ireland, Stephen Ireland, Annette Irvine, David Irwin, David Issokson, Kathrin Iten, Marijan Ivanua **J** John Jackman, Paul & Carole Jackman, Hellemans Jakke, Outi Jalassuo, Deborah James, Ariane Janér, M Jansen, Melanie Jay, Katja Jedliczka, Alden Jencks, Richard Jenkins, Nini Skovgaard Jensen, Tanja Jernss, Carina Johnson, Peter Johnson, Matt Jones, Oscar Juarez **K** Katrin Kaempgen, Anna Kåhre, Mari Rose Kalile Passos, Andre Kalvin, Katia Kamogawa, Jan Karlsvik, Andreas Katechakis, Yorgos Kechagioglou, Miriam Kelly, Shraga Kelson, John Kennedy, Kieran Kenny, Mary Kenny, William Kersten, Zia Asad Khan, Shaun Kiddell, Maciek Kiersztyn, Andrea Kinauer, Bob King, Dave King, Paula King, Lucie Kinkorova, April Klavins, Claudia Klein-Hitpass, Reiner Kloecker, Jean-Claude Knobbe, H Knoflach, Bjorn Koerselman, Rick Kolinsky, Kirstin Koller, Paul Kondratko, Efrat Konforty, Matthew Konsa, Joyce Kool, Freek Koopmans, Barbara Krantz, Joanna Kreckler, Guus Kruitwagen, Frauke Kubischta, Anita Kucharska, Iikka Kuosa, Kalle Kupski, Lydia Kuster **L** Susan King Lachance, Johannes Lahti, Gregor Laing, Paul Lambert, Fernanda Lamego, Jeff Lamppert, Evangeline Lane, John Lane, David Langbroek, Frank-Michael Lange, Christy Lanzi, Pierre Larose, Ron Leach, Brandon Lee, Richard Lee-Hart, Karin Leisibach, Sohm Lena, Norv Leong, Philippe Lesne, Ludovico Lesti, Milton Lever, Adeline Levine, Sam Levitt, John Lewis, Ralph Lewis, Steve Lidgey, Dan Littman, Simon Livingston, Paloma Llado, Elaine Lloyd, Ian Lochore, Jose M Lomas, Peter Louw, Donnchadh Lucey, Michael Luck, Hannie Luijpen, Sally Luscombe, Veronica Lushington **M** Marco Macchi, Euan MacLennan, Jerry Maggi, Denise Mainville, Volker Maiworm, Ignazio Majolino, Zukiso Makalima, Romain Mallard, George Malliaros, Megan Mann, Oliver Mann, Darryl Mar, Jacques Marcais, Ana Rosa Marcolini Pereira, Mauro Janine Margiotta, Felipe Mariani, Bob Marino, Roy Marques, David Marsden, Chip Martinson, Jeanine Mas, Georgina Mason, Dan Massey, Anna Matova, Valentino Mattei, Nick Matthews, Stacey Dee Maurer-Kramer, Michael T Maus, Nicholas May, Ben Mayers, Margaret McCabe, Michael McCarthy, Laura McDonald, Megan McGrath, Cathleen McGuire, Alexander McIntyre, John McLaverty, Barry McLean, Ronald Mcleod, Ciaran McPeake, Alberto L Mederos, Marieke Meijer, Hedde Meima, Laura Mello, Harald Mellwig, Flavio Melo, Erika Menamkat, Manuel Menezes de Oliveira Neto, Anja Menkhaus, Gerard Menkhorst, Asha Metharam-Jones, Justin Meunier, Neal Meyer, Suzanne Miau, Fred Midtgaard, Luiz Antonio Milani, Carlos Millan, JL Miranda, Giovanni Mirieri, Ian Mitchell, Konark Modi, Jesper E Mogensen, Paul Moir, Joachim Möller, Grégoire Monconduit, Peter Monk, Ann Moore, Geraldine & Bertrand Moret, Dan Morris, M Morton, Adee Moses, Phillip Müller, Michael Munchehofe, Tan Mutlu, Asger Muurholm, Emile Myburgh **N** Bregje Nabben, Inke Nabben, Antonella Namorado, Patricia Nascimento, Barbara Navarro, Augusto Negrillo, Danie Nel, Anne & John Nelson, Yannick Neron, Manoel Netto, David Neumann, Piers Newberry, Lynea Newcomer, Tommy Nguyen, Linda Nieminen, Travis Ning, Emanuel Nitsch, Linde Nobre, Nora Nordland, Daniel Norton, Renate Notter, Elisha Novak, Pedro Novak, Tamas Novak, Tom Novak, Adrian Nugent, Mats Nygaard **O** Michal Obrebski, John O'Duinn, Patricia Oey, Zeyn Oleary, Franco Olgiati, Jose Olimpio, Guilherme Oliveira, Aaron Olivo, Gary Olson, Caroline Oppl, Jeffrey L Orr, Oliver Orton, Caroline Osborne, Bernard O'Shea, Adriana Otero, Martin Oti, Miriam Otten, Aleksandra Oziemska **P** Edson Roberto Pacheco, Aristea Parissi, Dylan Passmore, Ebony Pattenaude, Sala Patterson, Jurgen Paudtke, Alexander Pavelka, Peter Pearson, Oscar Pedros, Jan Pejlare, Omer Pelman, Denise Pendexter, Richard Pendry, Rui

Pereira, Brad Petersen, Flavio Germano Petry, Christian Pfeiffer, Barbara Pfister, Kirsten Pilih, Christine Pintat, Gabriela Pinto, Elisabeth & Gerd Pircher, Agostinho Pissarreira, Mark Plattner, Anne Podt, Carol Poliak, Dominique Poncin, Adrian Pope, Robert Pospiech, Brigitte Poulsen, M H Pratley, Chris Preager, Laura Price, Dina Priess dos Santo Penha, Joop Proveniers, Leacy Pryor **Q** Joanna Querelle, Peter Quiros **R** Maggie Racklyeft, Scott Rains, Kjell Ramfjord, María Concepción Ramos Suárez, John Ranweiler, Eric Rawson, Sally Reader, Belinda Recinella, Richard Remsberg, Lukas & Ann Repa, Carlo Rettore, Marco Antonio Reyes, Jana Richter, Edda Riedel, Marion Rimmer, Brian Riordan, Alex Robert, Camillo Roberti, John Roberts, Carmen Robin, Nicola Robinson, Sheila Rodgers, Walace Rodrigues, Ramiro Rodriguez, Machiel M Roelofsen, Hubertine Roessingh, Wally Rogelstad, Britta Rohde, Anne-Sofie Rønningen, Carlos Roquette, Bill Rose, Marilynn Rose, Katherine Ross, Jeff Rothman, Erik Roupe, Michael Rowann, Karen Rowland, Aaron Rudner, Dan Ruff, Nathalie Rühmann, Ben Rule, Michael Rusch, David Rusek, Mark Ryser **S** Martin Sackett, Silvana Saibene, Hagai Salmor, Wesley Salter, Monica Silva Salter, Julianne Saltzer, Juan Cristobal Sanchez Gonzalez, Al Sandine, Peter Sapper, Alexandra Satori, Ross Savoy, Barry Sayer, Elena Scanferla, Dr Hanno Schaefer, Bettina Schaetzl, Hanno Schafer, Andrew Schell, Luregn Schlapbach, Beate Schmahl, Klaus-Dieter Schmatz, Matthias Schmutz, Jerad Schomer, Dieter Schoop, Ramses Schouman, Jaap & Maria Schouten, Peer Schouten, Eneas Schramm, Jim Schulte, Massimo Schutte, Bas Schuurman, Vitor Schwartz Coelho, Hanna Schwarz, Kay Schwarzer, Miguel Schweitzer, Terilyn Scott, Erich Seelye, Henk Segaert, Bill Seidel, Katja Seifert, Carlo Senna, Emmanuel Serruys, Ana Severo, Abby Sewell, Sharlene Shah, Jennifer Shin, Markus Shmidt, Tsipi Shmilorich, Helen Short, Miriam Frehe Siermann, Juha Sillanpää, Antonio Silva, Arielle Silverstein, Carolina Simon, Alastair Simpson, Wai Fung Sit, Jonathan Siverling, Juriaan Slee, Jenny Slepian, Jeroen Slikker, Jan-Mark Slootweg, Karen Smetana, Andrea Smith, Peter Smolka, Nickolaos Smylianis, Kuan Sng, Sandy Snively, Douglas Snyder, Vania Soares De Souza Gomes, Paul Sodemann, Vic Sofras, Maria Sol, Heidi Sola, Teresa Soop, Susan Sotelo, Cristiane Spaccasassi, Eduardo Spaccasassi, Emmanuelle Spadone, Tracy Sparkes, Maike Sparrius, J S Spijker, Ezra Spilke, Bronwyn Spiteri, Toby Sprunk, Menno Staarink, John Stahl, William K Stark, Andre Starobin, Lisa Starr, Pauline Staves, Max Steden, Paul Steele, Jørn Stegelmann,

Juerg Steiner, Sibylle Steiner, Marian Stephenson, Itshak Stern, Sarah Stewart, Nicolas Stockmann, HP & G Stoffel, Louis H Stone, Marika Stone, Julia Straetmans, Louie Strano, Sean Sullivan, Moon Sun Kim, Nicole Suwito, Judy & Ariana Svenson, Stefan Svensson, Charlotte Swing, Andrea Swintek, Eileen Synnott, Vesa Sytelä **T** Gary C Tagalog, L Tam, Benita Tapster, Tatiana Taranov, Claire & David Tarrant, Roman Tatarsky, Robert Taylor, Tania Taylor, Thomas Teltser, Patricia Testoni, Sonia Tevelow, Tim Tewsley, Siddhartha Thanawala, Frank Thianer, Sara Thofte, Adrian Thomas, Rachel Thomas, Niels Thommesen, Isobel Thompson, Mikko Tihverainen, Theo Tjes, Nicole Tobin, Isabel Toebelmann, Debra Townsend, Lani Trenouth, Robert Trevor, Giovanni Troianiello, John Tustin, Christine Tutt, Geoff Tutt, Mark Tyrrell **U** Peter Udell, Sine Uhd Ronberg, Nicolas Uldry, Wendy Underwood, Daniel Ungar, Craig Ungaro **V** Rogier van Anholt, Gerrie van Battum, Henk van Caan, Carina van den Barg, Charlotte van der Meer, Bert van der Woude, Gabriel van Diepen, Friso van Endt, Piet van Geelen, F van Gisteren, Marcel van Kampenhout, Jack van Messel, Kees van Oorschot, Gerhard van Wyngaardt, Jeroen Vanhee, María Varela, Zoe Veater, Andres Velasques, Edinildo Venturin, Carolien Verhagen, Mariska Verplanke, Hannah Viehoff, Jason Vigneron, Zeeger Vink, Rodolfo Viquez, Fernanda Vitalino, Bernard Vixseboxse, Connie Voeten, Yanna Vogiazou, Brandon Vogler, Thomas Vogt, Bernd von Richter, Rachel von Simson, Judith Vonwil **W** James Wade, Ute Waditschatka, Joo-Hee Waelzlein, Heike Wagner, Chenoa Walker, Colin Walker, Karin Wallestad, Garth Ward, Michael Ward, Peter Ward, Maciek Wasielewski, Josh Wasserman, Yumi Watanabe, Rachel Watkins, Dal Watts, Dora Webder, Claudia Weber, Katherine Weedon, Jonathan Weerts, Elisabeth Weingraber-Pircher, Peter Weis, Jeffrey Weiss, Rachael & Anthony Wellby, Sarah Wheeler, Schuyler Whelden, Heather White, Linda White, Jan Wielaard, Nills Alex Wilken, Eric Willemssens, Wayne & Pat Williams, Geoffrey Winfield, Christina Winter, Karen Winter, Orawan Wongcharoen, Robert Worthington, Rachel Worzencraft, Alister Wright, Christina Wu, Katharina Wulf **Y** Andrew Young **Z** Cathy Zacarovitz, Manuel Zeh, Ronja Zigler, Frank Zimmermann, John Zubatiuk, Magda Zupancic, Yotam Ben Zvi, Robert Zylstra

ACKNOWLEDGMENTS

Many thanks to the following for the use of their content: Globe on back cover © Mountain High Maps 1993 Digital Wisdom, Inc.

Index

000 Map pages
000 Location of color photographs

INDEX

INDEX

MAP LEGEND
ROUTES

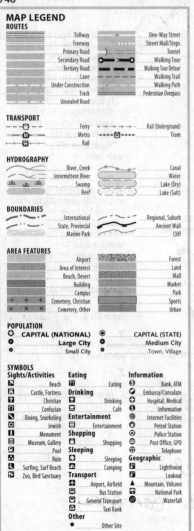

Tollway	One-Way Street
Freeway	Street Mall/Steps
Primary Road	Tunnel
Secondary Road	Walking Tour
Tertiary Road	Walking Tour Detour
Lane	Walking Trail
Under Construction	Walking Path
Track	Pedestrian Overpass
Unsealed Road	

TRANSPORT

Ferry	Rail (Underground)
Metro	Tram
Rail	

HYDROGRAPHY

River, Creek	Canal
Intermittent River	Water
Swamp	Lake (Dry)
Reef	Lake (Salt)

BOUNDARIES

International	Regional, Suburb
State, Provincial	Ancient Wall
Marine Park	Cliff

AREA FEATURES

Airport	Forest
Area of Interest	Land
Beach, Desert	Mall
Building	Market
Campus	Park
Cemetery, Christian	Sports
Cemetery, Other	Urban

POPULATION

CAPITAL (NATIONAL)	CAPITAL (STATE)
Large City	Medium City
Small City	Town, Village

SYMBOLS

Sights/Activities
- Beach
- Castle, Fortress
- Christian
- Confucian
- Diving, Snorkeling
- Jewish
- Monument
- Museum, Gallery
- Pool
- Ruin
- Surfing, Surf Beach
- Zoo, Bird Sanctuary

Eating
- Eating

Drinking
- Drinking
- Café

Entertainment
- Entertainment

Shopping
- Shopping

Sleeping
- Sleeping
- Camping

Transport
- Airport, Airfield
- Bus Station
- General Transport
- Taxi Rank

Other
- Other Site

Information
- Bank, ATM
- Embassy/Consulate
- Hospital, Medical
- Information
- Internet Facilities
- Petrol Station
- Police Station
- Post Office, GPO
- Telephone

Geographic
- Lighthouse
- Lookout
- Mountain, Volcano
- National Park
- Waterfall

LONELY PLANET OFFICES

Australia
Head Office
Locked Bag 1, Footscray, Victoria 3011
☎ 03 8379 8000, fax 03 8379 8111
talk2us@lonelyplanet.com.au

USA
150 Linden St, Oakland, CA 94607
☎ 510 893 8555, toll free 800 275 8555
fax 510 893 8572, info@lonelyplanet.com

UK
72–82 Rosebery Ave,
Clerkenwell, London EC1R 4RW
☎ 020 7841 9000, fax 020 7841 9001
go@lonelyplanet.co.uk

Published by Lonely Planet Publications Pty Ltd
ABN 36 005 607 983

© Lonely Planet 2005

© photographers as indicated 2005

Cover photographs by Lonely Planet Images: Carnaval mask for sale, Paul Bigland (front); Characteristic 'wavy tile' pavement, Copacabana Beach, John Pennock (back). Many of the images in this guide are available for licensing from Lonely Planet Images: www.lonelyplanetimages.com.